Justice And Corrections

Justice And Corrections

NORMAN JOHNSTON
Beaver College

LEONARD D. SAVITZ
Temple University

JOHN WILEY & SONS
New York
Chichester
Brisbane
Toronto

Cover design by Mark E. Safran.
Production was supervised by Joseph P. Cannizzaro.
Copy editing was supervised by Pamela Goett.

Library of Congress Cataloging in Publication Data:

Justice and corrections.

   1. Criminal justice, Administration of—United States—
addresses, essays, lectures.   I. Johnston, Norman Bruce,
1921–   II. Savitz, Leonard D.
HV8138.J88   364′.973   78–748
ISBN 0–471–03384–7

Printed in the United States of America

10 9 8 7 6 5 4 3 2

To Lila Johnston Gunn

Preface

If the discipline of criminology represents an attempt to apply the scientific approaches and methods of empirical research to the problems of crime and its treatment, a book of readings must do more than present a series of unsupported claims and counterclaims. Many of our selections therefore consist of empirical research findings, details of which are normally impossible to include in a textbook. We have also chosen some theoretical discussions and a number of largely descriptive items. This has been necessary for two reasons: first, because in certain areas very little research exists; and second, because some of the areas of inquiry, such as prison life and police work, are so remote from the experiences of both students and teachers that the *beginning* of understanding and insight must come first through realistic and accurate description.

No book of readings can be so inclusive that every teacher and every student will find an abundance of materials suiting his or her particular interests. On the other hand, a book of readings need not, and perhaps should not, espouse a single point of view. Consequently, we have attempted to represent diverse viewpoints and perspectives in this book, and in its companion volume, *Crime in Society*. The present work should, therefore, be of value to students in a variety of undergraduate or graduate courses in criminology, juvenile delinquency, and corrections, either as a text or as supplemental reading.

We have reviewed an enormous amount of materials, including the usual American and foreign journals, governmental and agency reports, books, and the relatively unavailable papers prepared for meetings or private research organizations. At our suggestion experts on certain topics have written papers especially for this book, either updating their own earlier work or surveying their fields of expertise anew.

The great majority of items reviewed could not be included due to space limitations. This is particularly true for historical materials. In other instances excellent studies were excluded simply because they were dated, were too narrow in scope, or were exotically descriptive but not broadly applicable. Some gaps in the areas covered reflect our inability to find worthy research.

When we first became involved in assembling materials for criminology readers in the early 1960s, data-based studies dealing with the police, courts, and prisons were rare. With few exceptions, descriptions were impressionistic and innocently free of data. The situation in the 1970s has changed radically. For example, in the areas of police operations research, evaluations of treatment techniques, and legal decisions dealing with court procedures and prisoners rights, a body of research and description has been created which was largely unavailable before 1970. While we include a preponderance of these very recent contributions, we have not rejected materials merely because they were not written within the last several years.

The brief section introductions are intended to provide a measure of continuity between the subject matter divisions. However, individual selections are presented without comment because it is felt that each instructor will make choices and place the selections in context according to course direction and requirements.

The companion volume to this reader, *Crime in Society*, focuses primarily on the definition of crime, criminal statistics, and investigations of various forms of crime ranging from common property crimes to professional crime, crimes of business, and technology-related offenses. The present volume deals with the operations of the police, the courts, and various forms of punishment ranging from execution through probation, as well as the many kinds of societal reactions calculated to reform the criminal.

Public anxiety over crime has led to a considerable number of studies dealing with every significant aspect of police work, as well as renewed interest in the perennial problems of police misconduct. Section I, The Police, consists of studies, largely undertaken since 1970, that deal with many of these concerns.

Section II, The Administration of Justice, contains selections dealing with the legal system, including various empirical and descriptive investigations of lawyers, juries, court procedures, and sentencing practices. The subsequent section is concerned with several of the social and philosophical rationales that are set forth to justify and guide the infliction of punishment when guilt has been determined, as well as efforts intended to test the effectiveness of various features of the punishment process.

The following three sections deal with custodial institutions. Section IV takes up some of the new developments in the management and organization of prisons, including a description of a coed prison, new conduct rules, a realistic description of punishment cells, evolving legal rights of prisoners, and furlough programs. What goes on in prisons and how well they accomplish one of their stated purposes, rehabilitation, is not determined by staff alone but is powerfully influenced by the inmates themselves. Section V contains descriptions and analyses of the informal inmate social structure and the effects it has on both inmate and staff.

By its very nature, this social world is normally unfamiliar to students and teachers alike. We felt therefore that it was of great importance to include realistic materials on the prison scene in order to set the stage for a consideration of the different treatment techniques which follow in Section VI. These forms of treatment are described from the viewpoint of the therapist or sometimes by outside researchers who have tried to capture the inmates' views. We have also included, when available, studies that attempt to evaluate empirically the success of such programs. The selections on this topic reflect the increasing rigor and sophistication of research now being applied to the central question of whether the various treatments applied in prison do in fact rehabilitate. The more traditional approaches, such as vocational training, are included as are newer techniques, such as behavior modification. Summaries of previous research found at the end of this section attempt to answer the more general question of whether *anything* works, and, if so, which approaches seem most promising.

The final section considers various treatment strategies carried on outside of custodial institutions, such as probation and parole, as well as crime prevention techniques.

We would like to express our gratitude and respect to the authors and researchers whose work has made this book possible and especially to those who have contributed papers at our request. And, finally, we would like to express our appreciation to our students who were exposed to many of these and other selections before the book was put together and whose reactions have guided our final selection.

Norman Johnston
Leonard D. Savitz

Philadelphia, 1978

Contents

Justice And Corrections

The Police

SOCIAL SCIENTISTS, LIKE PHYSICAL SCIENTISTS, OFTEN LEAVE THE IMPRESSION THAT their work and views are uninfluenced by personal ideology, and, in fact, most seem to make serious efforts to avoid such influences. But personal ideology continues to be very much entangled in what both laymen and professionals in the criminal justice system believe, the stands they take on issues, and the topics they may choose to study. It therefore seems appropriate to begin this volume with a consideration of some of the diverse and often conflicting ideological views concerning the criminal justice system. The first selection by Miller carefully develops the crusading issues and general assumptions of the ideological right and left and the consequences of such political positions.

The crucial agency in society's reaction to the abhorred phenomenon of crime is that of law enforcement. Police represent the first official response to criminal events. Recently there have been a number of theoretical statements and significant research projects on this crucial agency and the work it performs. One can view, as Manning does, "excessive" policing as a dramaturgical enterprise in which law enforcement personnel politically dramatize their effectiveness by making the capture of criminals their transcendent concern. In time this develops cynicism, which is said to become a dominant police norm.

Empirical studies of normal police arrest practices have increased considerably recently, but the first, and in many ways still the best, investigation of why police intervene and what they do, was made by Black and Reiss in 1966. In the present selection by Black, one learns of the several types of police mobilization and the crucial roles played by complainant, suspect, and others in citizen-initiated police involvements. The centrality of evidence, preferences for action, relational distances, respect for the police and police discrimination are all depicted.

In the huge body of literature dealing with police work, three studies regarding police in the 1970s seem preeminent. Two are described immediately below, and the third, the Kansas City Preventive Patrol study, will be dealt with later in this section. First, Greenwood and his colleagues examined how police, particularly detectives, operate and what they accomplish. The central issue is how, in fact, most crimes are "solved." Data suggest that most cases cleared by arrest are cleared exactly at the time when the police learn of the crime and

1

intrude onto the scene of the event, while most of the remaining cases are cleared by obvious, routine investigations. Investigators seldom solve cases by the painstaking, brilliant investigations that novels and television depict.

The second major study aims at the crucial issue of whether police should respond only after a crime has been committed or if they should engage in the practice of field interrogation of suspicious individuals, with the aim of deterring crime. The San Diego Field Interrogation investigators manipulated police practices within several patrol beats. The main finding appears to be that when field interrogation practices are suspended, this is followed by a statistically significant rise in total "suppressible crimes" in the test areas.

Lacking the glamor that has come to be attached to detectives, the daily, routine activities of police officers are described by Rubinstein, who was, for a while, himself a police officer. The pressure to make vice arrests often causes some officers to make illegal arrests, which they consider essentially meaningless. There is then a fundamental disparity between departmental policy and the average officer's indifference toward minimal offenses.

When suspects are arrested, they are "booked" and, within rapidly changing legal rules, they are interviewed by trained interrogators. These detectives are able to maneuver the arrestees by various persuasive techniques, which sometimes involve subtrefuge, or feigning indifference, sympathy, or kindness. The selection on police interrogation, taken from a standard police training text, is particularly interesting in that the issues of moral or ethical appropriateness of such manipulative techniques are seldom raised.

Beyond interrogation, law enforcement agencies use, as a matter of course, a wide range of criminalistic devices, one of the most fascinating being the polygraph, widely known as the "lie detector." A Congressional investigation dealt with the problem of the instrument's reliability and validity as measured by a number of experiments. One of the most curious studies presented was by Kubis, which is included in this section, and which determined techniques by which the machine can be consciously misled. One might conclude that, with all of its faults, the polygraph is of value in criminal processing and can produce worthy bits of evidence. Yet any such evidence is inadmissable in our courts of law.

From the time they came into existence over a century ago, organized police have been accused of incompetence, brutality, and corruption. Unexpectedly, almost no empirical evidence of systematic and widespread brutality has been produced in recent years, although scandals and accusations continue. The allegations of incompetence in the form of poor quality personnel and inadequate training, has diminished, however, Instead, one might consider the excessive loyalty among police officers might well produce incompetent or less-than-ideal police performance. What are the dimensions of police loyalty? Are police primarily loyal to the general public, the police organization, or fellow officers? The selection by Savitz tests these questions, in part, by determining the settings in which officers say they will inform on a fellow officer, and any restraints which they say operate on them which prevent them from responding to a major felony in progress.

The criticism of corruption has, in fact, been heavily investigated by various commissions. The highly publicized Knapp Commission documented police improprieties such as accepting gratuities from restaurants, hotels, or Christmas presents. The report suggests two types of corrupt policemen: the "grass-eater" (who accepts graft) and the "meat-eater" (who aggressively seeks graft). Corruption is not a practice peculiar to large urban departments, as the Pennsylvania Crime Commission reveals in its study of a small city, York, Pennsylvania. In the portion of the report included here, one catches a glimpse of illegal kickbacks by tow truck operators, an apparently common practice in many cities.

The Kansas City Preventive Patrol study is an important experiment in the central concern of policing—the effectiveness of police in preventing crime. Police beats were divided into reactive beats (police only responded to calls for service), control beats (routine police patrolling), and proactive beats (with two or three times the normal number of police patrolling). The results are both surprising and discouraging.

The number of official police in America seem not to offer adequate security to many urban facilities. There are now about 300,000 security workers in the private sector and they have unusual power regarding search, interrogation, detention, and arrest. Our final selection in this section deals with this aspect of police work which is usually ignored by criminologists.

1. Ideology and Criminal Justice Policy

WALTER B. MILLER

THERE IS CURRENTLY IN THE UNITED STATES A widespread impression that our country is experiencing a major transitional phase—a period in which long-established social arrangements and the moral and conceptual notions that undergird them are undergoing substantial change. Optimists see this process as a transition from one relatively effective social order to another; pessimists see it as a one-way passage to catastrophe.

It is hard to judge the validity of these conceptions. Few generations have been free from the conviction that the nation was in the throes of "the crisis of our times," and such perceptions have not always corresponded with judgments of later historians.[1]

Since criminal behavior, ways of thinking about crime, and methods of dealing with crime make up an intrinsic component of any social order, the notion of a transitional phase also affects the perceptions and actions of both criminals and criminal justice system personnel. As soon as one considers crime as one facet of a larger set of social and historical shifts, however, a paradox emerges. One gets an impression both of striking and substantial change, and striking and substantial stability.

This paradox seems to apply equally to crime and to societal response to crime. On the one hand, patterns of contemporary criminal behavior reflect substantial shifts—e.g., a massive increase in drug use and drug-related crimes, a

▶SOURCE: *"Ideology and Criminal Justice Policy: Some Current Issues," The Journal of Criminal Law and Criminology, 64:141–162 (1973). Reprinted by permission.*

[1]A few examples of perceptions that "our times" are witnessing radical or unprecedented changes are found in selected excerpts from statements published in 1874, 1930, and 1939, respectively.

"Society has grave charges to answer in regard to its influence on the present and rising generation. . . . The social conditions of the present age are such as to favor the development of insanity. The habits inculcated by . . . growing wealth . . . among individuals of one class and the stinging poverty . . . of another . . . nurture dispositions which might . . . under more equitable distributions . . . have died out. Have we not seen [youth] emerging from the restraints of school, scoffing at the opinions of the world, flouting everything but their own conceit . . ."?

Dickson, "The Science and Practice of Medicine in Relation

to Mind, and the Jurisprudence of Insanity" (1874), quoted in M. Altschule, *Roots of Modern Psychiatry* 122, 133 (1957).

"In our nineteenth century polity, the home was a chief reliance . . . discipline was recognized as a reality . . . the pressure of the neighborhood . . . was strong . . . in the urban industrial society of today there is a radical change. . . . This complete change in the background of social control involves much that may be easily attributed to the ineffectiveness of criminal justice. . . ." Pound, "Criminal Justice in America" (1930), quoted in F. Tannenbaum, *Crime and the Community* 29 (1938).

"Men's ways of ordering their common lives have broken down so disastrously as to make hope precarious. So headlong and pervasive is change today that . . . historical parallels are decreasingly relevant . . . because so many of the variables in the situation have altered radically. . . . Professor James T. Shotwell recently characterized 'the anarchy we are living in today' as 'the most dangerous since the fall of Rome.' " R. Lynd, *Knowledge for What* 2, 11 (1939).

new dimension of political motivation affecting many adult prisoners. On the other hand, an impression of changelessness and stability is evident in the relatively unchanging nature of youth crime and periodic attention to youth gang violence.[2]

A similar paradox affects those responsible for making and implementing criminal justice policy. On the one hand, we seem to be in the midst of a radical shift in conceptualizing and coping with crime, indicated by a host of current slogans such as decentralization, decriminalization, deinstitutionalization, victimology and others. On the other hand, there is a surprising sameness in the basic issues which these slogans reflect—issues such as free will versus determinism, individual rights versus state's rights, concentration versus diffusion of power. Do these concerns represent progressive movement or merely contemporary replays of ancient dramas?

Intriguing as it might be to explore these issues with respect to the behavior of both those who engage in crime and those who attempt to deal with it, I shall treat only the latter. The terms "criminologist" or "criminal justice personnel" will be used here to refer to those persons who maintain some consistent responsibility for dealing with criminals and their behavior.

One may seek to escape this paradox by employing the concept of "ideology." Ideology is also a central element in the complex patterns of change and stability, and a key to their understanding. A useful point of departure may be found in a quotation from Myrdal's *An American Dilemma:*

"The place of the individual scientist along the scale of radicalism-conservatism has always had strong influences on both the selection of research problems and the conclusions drawn from research.

In a sense, it is the master scale of biases in social science."[3]

It is this master scale, and its influence on the field of criminal justice, which will be my major concern here.

The term "ideology" may be used in many ways.[4] It will be used here only to refer to a set of general and abstract beliefs or assumptions about the correct or proper state of things, particularly with respect to the moral order and political arrangements, which serve to shape one's positions on specific issues. Several aspects of ideology as used in this sense should be noted. First, ideological assumptions are generally pre-conscious rather than explicit, and serve, under most circumstances, as unexamined presumptions underlying positions taken openly. Second, ideological assumptions bear a strong emotional charge. This charge is not always evident, but it can readily be activated by appropriate stimuli, in particular by direct challenge. During the process of formation, ideological premises for particular individuals

[2]An analysis involving long-term trends in youth gang violence and periodically recurrent representations of such violence as a new phenomenon engendered by contemporary conditions is included in Miller, "American Youth Gangs: Past and Present," in A. Blumberg, *Issues in Criminology* (in preparation).

[3]G. Myrdal, *An American Dilemma: The Negro Problem and Modern Democracy,* 1038 (1944). Myrdal's citation of the "radicalism-conservatism" scale is part of an extended discussion of sources of bias in works on race-relations, appearing as Appendix 2, "A Methodological Note on Facts and Valuations in Social Science," at 1035–64. His entire discussion is germane to issues treated in this article.

[4]A classic treatment of ideology is K. Mannheim, *Ideology and Utopia* (1936). *See* ch. II.1 "Definition of Concepts." *See also* G. Myrdal, *supra* note 3, at 1035–64. There is an extensive literature, much of it sociological, dealing with ideology as it relates to a wide range of political and social phenomena, but the specific relation between ideology and criminal justice has received relatively little direct attention. Among more recent general discussions are E. Shils, *The Intellectuals and the Powers* (1972); Orlans, "The Political Uses of Social Research," 393 *Annals Am. Acad. Polit. & Soc. Sci.* 28 (1971); Kelman, "I.Q., Race, and Public Debate," 2 *Hastings Center Rep.* 8 (1972). Treatments more specific to crime and criminal justice appear in L. Radzinowicz, *Ideology and Crime* (1966); Andanaes, "Punishment and the Problem of General Prevention," 8 *Int'l Annals Criminology* 285 (1969); Blumberg, *The Adversary System,* in C. Bersani, *Crime & Delinq.* 435 (1970); Glaser, "Criminology and Public Policy," 6 *Am. Sociologist* 30 (1971).

are influenced by a variety of informational inputs, but once established they become relatively impervious to change, since they serve to receive or reject new evidence in terms of a self-contained and self-reinforcing system.

The major contention of this presentation is that ideology and its consequences exert a powerful influence on the policies and procedures of those who conduct the enterprise of criminal justice, and that the degree and kinds of influence go largely unrecognized. Ideology is the permanent hidden agenda of criminal justice.

The discussion has two major aims. First, assuming that the generally implicit ideological basis of criminal justice commands strong, emotional, partisan allegiance, I shall attempt to state explicitly the major assumptions of relevant divergent ideological positions in as neutral or as non-partisan a fashion as possible. Second, some of the consequences of such ideologies for the processes of planning, program, and policy in criminal justice will be examined.

I shall use a simple conceptual device for indicating ideological positions—a one-dimensional scale that runs from five on the right to zero in the middle to five on the left. Various ideological positions under consideration will be referred to this scale, using the terms "left" and "right" in an attempt to achieve neutrality. Although not all eleven possible distinctions will be made in every analysis, five scale distinctions on each side seem to be the minimum needed for present purposes. Later discussions will in some instances attribute considerable importance to differences as small as one scale degree.

The substance of ideologically divergent positions with respect to selected issues of current concern will be presented in three ways. Positions will be formulated first as "crusading issues"—shorthand catchwords or rallying cries that furnish the basic impetus for action or change in the criminal justice field. Such catch phrases are derived from a deeper and more abstract set of propositions as to desired states or outcomes. These will be designated "general assumptions." Third, differentiated positions will be delineated for all points along the full range of the scale—extreme right to extreme left—for three major policy issues.[5]

[5] The substance of ideologically-relevant statements formulated here as crusading issues, general assumptions, or differentiated positions was derived from examination and analysis of a wide range of materials appearing in diverse forms in diverse sources. Materials were selected primarily on the basis of two criteria: that they bear on issues of current relevance to criminal justice policy, and that they represent one possible stance with respect to issues characterized by markedly divergent stances. With few exceptions, the statements as formulated here do not represent direct quotes, but have been generalized, abstracted or paraphrased from one or more sets of statements by one or more representatives of positions along the ideological scale. A substantial portion of the statements thus derived were taken from books, articles, speeches, and media reporting of statements by the following: Robert Welch, writer; John Schmitz, legislator; Gerald L. K. Smith, writer; Meyer Kahane, clergyman; Edward Banfield, political scientist; William Loeb, publisher; George Wallace, government; Julius Hoffman, jurist; L. Patrick Gray III, lawyer; William Rehnquist, jurist; William Buckley, writer; Spiro Agnew, government; Robert M. McKiernan, police; Howard J. Phillips, government; Lewis F. Powell Jr., jurist; Andrew Hacker, political scientist; Kevin Phillips, writer; Victor Reisel, labor; Albert Shanker, educator; Fred P. Graham, lawyer/writer; Warren Burger, jurist; James Q. Wilson, political scientist; Hubert H. Humphrey, legislator; James Reston, writer; Jacob Javits, legislator; Ramsey Clark, lawyer; Tom Wicker, writer; Earl Warren, jurist; James F. Ahearn, police; Henry Steele Commager, historian; Alan Dershowitz, lawyer; Julian Bond, legislator; Herbert J. Gans, sociologist; Ross K. Baker, political scientist; Russell Baker, writer; William Kunstler, lawyer; Benjamin Spock, physician, Noam Chomsky, anthropologist; Richard Cloward, sociologist; Herman Schwartz, lawyer; Richard Korn, sociologist; Michael Harrington, writer; Richard Quinney, sociologist; Frank Reissman, sociologist; Tom Hayden, writer; Eldridge Cleaver, writer; H. Bruce Franklin, professor; Abbie Hoffman, writer; Phillip Berrigan, clergyman; Jerry Rubin, writer. Among a range of non-academic reports, pamphlets, and periodicals which served as sources for statements by these and other persons were: *John Birch Society Reprint Series; Ergo; The Rational Voice of Libertarianism; New Solidarity: National Caucus of Labor Committees; The Hastings Center Report; S.D.S. New Left Notes; Guardian; Ramparts; National Review; The Nation; The New Republic; The New York Review; Commentary; Fortune; Time; Life; Newsweek; New York Times; New York Times Magazine; The Washington Post; The*

IDEOLOGICAL POSITIONS

Right: Crusading Issues

Crusading issues of the right differ somewhat from those of the left; they generally do not carry as explicit a message of movement toward new forms, but imply instead that things should be reconstituted or restored. However, the component of the message that says, "Things should be different from the way they are now," comes through just as clearly as in the crusading issues of the left. Current crusading issues of the right with respect to crime and how to deal with it include the following:

1. *Excessive leniency toward lawbreakers.* This is a traditional complaint of the right, accentuated at present by the publicity given to reform programs in corrections and policing, as well as to judicial activity at various levels.

2. *Favoring the welfare and rights of lawbreakers over the welfare and rights of their victims, of law enforcement officials, and the law abiding citizen.* This persisting concern is currently activated by attention to prisoners' rights, rehabilitation programs, attacks on police officers by militants, and in particular by a series of well-publicized Supreme Court decisions aimed to enhance the application of due process.

3. *Erosion of discipline and of respect for constituted authority.* This ancient concern is currently manifested in connection with the general behavior of youth, educational policies, treatment of student dissidents by college officials, attitudes and behavior toward law-enforcement, particularly the police.

Manchester Union Leader. It should be noted that the substance of materials appearing in published sources represents the publicly-taken positions of the individuals involved. The relation between public positions and "actual" or private positions can be very complex, ranging from "close" to "distant" along a "degree of correspondence" axis, and with variation involving changes over time, differences according to the sub-issue involved, nature of audience addressed, and other factors.

4. *The cost of crime.* Less likely to arouse the degree of passion evoked by other crusading issues, resentment over what is seen as the enormous and increasing cost of crime and dealing with criminals—a cost borne directly by the hard working and law abiding citizen—nevertheless remains active and persistent.

5. *Excessive permissiveness.* Related to excessive leniency, erosion of discipline, and the abdication of responsibility by authorities, this trend is seen as a fundamental defect in the contemporary social order, affecting many diverse areas such as sexual morality, discipline in the schools, educational philosophies, child-rearing, judicial handling of offenders, and media presentation of sexual materials.

Right: General Assumptions

These crusading issues, along with others of similar import, are not merely ritualized slogans, but reflect instead a more abstract set of assumptions about the nature of criminal behavior, the causes of criminality, responsibility for crime, appropriate ameliorative measures, and, on a broader level, the nature of man and of a proper kind of society. These general assumptions provide the basic charter for the ideological stance of the right as a whole, and a basis for distinguishing among the several subtypes along the points of the ideological scale. Major general assumptions of the right might be phrased as follows:

1. The individual is directly responsible for his own behavior. He is not a passive pawn of external forces, but possesses the capacity to make choices between right and wrong—choices which he makes with an awareness of their consequences.

2. A central requirement of a healthy and well functioning society is a strong moral order which is explicit, well-defined, and widely adhered to. Preferably the tenets of this system of morality should be derived from and grounded in the basic precepts of a major religi-

ous tradition. Threats to this moral order are threats to the very existence of the society. Within the moral order, two clusters are of particular importance:

a. Tenets which sustain the family unit involve morally-derived restrictions on sexual behavior, and obligations of parents to maintain consistent responsibility to their children and to one another.

b. Tenets which pertain to valued personal qualities include: taking personal responsibility for one's behavior and its consequences; conducting one's affairs with the maximum degree of self-reliance and independence, and the minimum of dependency and reliance on others, particularly public agencies; loyalty, particularly to one's country; achieving one's ends through hard work, responsibility to others, and self-discipline.

3. Of paramount importance is the security of the major arenas of one's customary activity—particularly those locations where the conduct of family life occurs. A fundamental personal and family right is safety from crime, violence, and attack, including the right of citizens to take necessary measures to secure their own safety, and the right to bear arms, particularly in cases where official agencies may appear ineffective in doing so.

4. Adherence to the legitimate directives of constituted authority is a primary means for achieving the goals of morality, correct individual behavior, security, and other valued life conditions. Authority in the service of social and institutional rules should be exercised fairly but firmly, and failure or refusal to accept or respect legitimate authority should be dealt with decisively and unequivocally.

5. A major device for ordering human relations in a large and heterogeneous society is that of maintaining distinctions among major categories of persons on the basis of differences in age, sex, and so on, with differences in religion, national background, race, and social position of particular importance. While individuals in each of the general categories should be granted the rights and privileges appropriate thereto, social order in many circumstances is greatly facilitated by maintaining both conceptual and spatial separation among the categories.

Left: Crusading Issues

Crusading issues of the left generally reflect marked dissatisfaction with characteristics of the current social order, and carry an insistent message about the desired nature and direction of social reform. Current issues of relevance to criminal justice include:

1. *Overcriminalization.* This reflects a conviction that a substantial number of offenses delineated under current law are wrongly or inappropriately included, and applies particularly to offenses such as gambling, prostitution, drug use, abortion, pornography, and homosexuality.

2. *Labelling and Stigmatization.* This issue is based on a conception that problems of crime are aggravated or even created by the ways in which actual or potential offenders are regarded and treated by persons in authority. To the degree a person is labelled as "criminal," "delinquent," or "deviant," will he be likely to so act.

3. *Overinstitutionalization.* This reflects a dissatisfaction over prevalent methods of dealing with suspected or convicted offenders whereby they are physically confined in large institutional facilities. Castigated as "warehousing," this practice is seen as having a wide range of detrimental consequences, many of which are implied by the ancient phrase "schools for crime." Signalled by a renewed interest in "incarceration," prison reform has become a major social cause of the left.

4. *Overcentralization.* This issue reflects dissatisfaction with the degree of centralized authority existing in organizations which deal with crime—including police departments, correctional systems, and crime-related services at all government levels. Terms which carry the thrust of the proposed remedy are local control, decentralization, community control, a new populism, and citizen power.

5. *Discriminatory Bias.* A particularly blameworthy feature of the present system lies in the widespread practice of conceiving and reacting to large categories of persons under class labels based on characteristics such as racial background, age, sex, income level, sexual practices, and involvement in criminality. Key terms here are racism, sexism, minority oppression and brutality.

Left: General Assumptions

As in the case of the rightist positions, these crusading issues are surface manifestations of a set of more basic and general assumptions, which might be stated as follows:

1. Primary responsibility for criminal behavior lies in conditions of the social order rather than in the character of the individual. Crime is to a greater extent a product of external social pressures than of internally generated individual motives, and is more appropriately regarded as a symptom of social dysfunction than as a phenomenon in its own right. The correct objective of ameliorative efforts, therefore, lies in the attempt to alter the social conditions that engender crime rather than to rehabilitate the individual.

2. The system of behavioral regulation maintained in America is based on a type of social and political order that is deficient in meeting the fundamental needs of the majority of its citizens. This social order, and the official system of behavioral regulation that it includes, incorporates an obsolete morality not applicable to the conditions of a rapidly changing technological society, and disproportionately geared to sustain the special interests of restricted groups, but which still commands strong support among working class and lower middle class sectors of the population.

3. A fundamental defect in the political and social organization of the United States and in those components of the criminal justice enterprise that are part of this system is an inequitable and unjust distribution of power, privilege, and resources—particularly of power. This inequity pervades the entire system, but appears in its more pronounced forms in the excessive centralization of governmental functions and consequent powerlessness of the governed, the military-like, hierarchical authority systems found in police and correctional organization, and policies of systematic exclusion from positions of power and privilege for those who lack certain preferred social characteristics. The prime objective of reform must be to redistribute the decision-making power of the criminal justice enterprise rather than to alter the behavior of actual or potential offenders.

4. A further defect of the official system is its propensity to make distinctions among individuals based on major categories or classes within society such as age, sex, race, social class, criminal or non-criminal. Healthy societal adaptation for both the offender and the ordinary citizen depends on maintaining the minimum separation—conceptually and physically—between the community at large and those designated as "different" or "deviant." Reform efforts must be directed to bring this about.

5. Consistent with the capacity of external societal forces to engender crime, personnel of official agencies play a prediminantly active role, and offenders a predominantly reactive role, in situations where the two come in contact. Official agents of behavioral regulation possess the capacity to induce or enhance criminal behavior by the manner in which they deal with those who have or may have engaged in crime. These agents may define offenders as basically criminal, expose them to stigmatization, degrade them on the basis of social characteristics, and subject them to rigid and arbitrary control.

6. The sector of the total range of human behavior currently included under the system of criminal sanctions is excessively broad, including many forms of behavior (for example, marijuana use, gambling, homosexuality) which do not violate the new morality and forms which would be more effectively and humanely dealt with outside the official system of criminal processing. Legal codes should be redrafted to remove many of the behavioral forms now proscribed, and to limit the discretionary prerogatives of local authorities over apprehension and disposition of violators.

AN IDEOLOGICAL SPECTRUM: DIFFERENTIATED POSITIONS OF LEFT AND RIGHT

The foregoing ideologically-relevant propositions are formulated as general assumptions common to all those designated as "left" or "right." The present section will expand and differentiate these generalized propositions by distributing them along the ideological scale proposed earlier. Charts I, II, and III (See Appendix) present thirty differentiated positions with respect to three major issues of relevance to criminal justice policy. Statements concerning each issue are assigned ten positions along scales running from right five through left five. The three issues are: conceptions as to the causes of crime and the locus of responsibility for criminality; conceptions of proper methods of dealing with offenders; conceptions of proper operating policies of criminal justice agencies. Not included in these tables is a theoretically possible "centrist" position.

Several features of the charts in the appendix should be noted. Statements representing ideologically-influenced positions on the scale are formulated in a highly condensed and simplified manner, lacking the subtleties, qualifications, and supporting arguments which characterize the actual stances of most people. The basic model is that of an "ideal type" analysis which presents a series of simplified propositions formulated to bear a logical relationship to one another and to underlying abstract princi-

ples, rather than to reflect accurately the actual positions of real people.[6] Few readers will feel entirely comfortable with any of the statements exactly as phrased here; most will feel instead that given statements might reflect the general gist of their position, but with important qualifications, or that one can subscribe to selected parts of statements at several different points along the scale. On the other hand, few readers will fail to find some statements with which they disagree completely; it is most unlikely, for example, that one could support with equal enthusiasm the major tenets attributed here to positions at left four and right four.

In "placing" oneself with respect to the scaled positions outlined here, one should look for those statements with which one feels least uncomfortable rather than expecting to find formulations which correspond in all respects to his viewpoint. The process of ascertaining discrepancies between actual positions and those represented here as "pure" examples of rightist or leftist ideology serves one of the purposes of ideal-typical analysis; few are ideological purists, but this type of analysis makes it possible to identify positions which correspond more or less closely to ideological orthodoxy. Those whose positions are closer to the extremes will feel least comfortable with statements attributed to the opposing side of the spectrum; those closer to "centrist" positions will tend to find orientations congenial to their own at a larger number of scale positions, possibly including positions on both sides of the spectrum.

To say that the statements show some logical relationship to one another and to underlying principles is not to say that they are logically

[6]The classic application of ideal-type method is that of Max Weber. *See,* e.g., the discussion of Weber's method and typology of authority and coordination in A. Henderson & T. Parsons, *Max Weber: The Theory of Social and Economic Organization* 98, 329 (1947). In the field of criminology, MacIver applies ideal-type analysis to discussions of social causality in general and crime casuality in particular. R. MacIver, *Social Causation,* 174 *passim* (1942). Neither of these applications directly parallels present usage, but underlying principles are similar.

consistent; in fact, several obvious inconsistences appear in the charts. For example, right five maintains that criminals are unwitting puppets of a radical conspiracy and, at the same time, holds that they are responsible for their own behavior. Left four calls for maximum access to information concerning the inner workings of criminal justice agencies and, at the same time, advocates minimum access by employers, personnel departments and others to criminal records of individuals. If one fails to find in internal consistency the "logical" basis for these propositions, where do the logical relationships lie?

Although some degree of logical inconsistency is likely in almost any developed set of propositions about human behavior, the consistency in the above propositions lies largely in the degree to which the interests of particular classes of persons are supported, defended, and justified. The inconsistencies often lie either in the means advocated to achieve such ends or in the rationales used to defend or exculpate favored interests and condemn opposing ones. In the above examples, if one assumes that a basic interest of left four is maximum protection of and support for actual or putative offenders, then these ends are served in the one instance by maximum access to information which might reveal errors, inequities or violations in their treatment by criminal justice officials, and in the other by denying to potential employers and others access to information that might jeopardize their welfare. Similarly, in attempting to reconcile the apparent contradiction in assertions that offenders are pawns of a radical conspiracy and also that they are directly responsible for their behavior, a rightist could argue that offenders are indeed responsible for their behavior, and that they make a deliberate personal choice to follow the crime-engendering appeals of the radicals.

While statements at different scale positions frequently present differing orientations to the same sub-issue (e.g., scope of criminal law, appropriate degree of restraint of offenders, extent to which "rehabilitation" should be an objective), not all of the statements on each major issue treat all of the included sub-issues. The positioned statements are defective with respect to "dimensionality," the possibility of full scalability across all issues. Each of the included sub-issues represents an independently scalable dimension. The "cause" issue incorporates approximately 14 distinguishable dimensions or sub-issues, the "offender" issue 15, and the "agencies" issue 18. To include a separate statement for each dimension at each scale position for all three issues would require a minimum of 470 statements—an impractical number for a presentation at this level. Selection of sub-issues and their assignment to given positions was guided by an attempt both to produce internally-coherent statements and to cover a fairly broad range of sub-issues.

One often finds convergences at the extremes of a distribution of ideological positions. Several instances can be found in the charts; for example, both right five and left five attribute criminality to deliberate or systematic efforts or policies of highly-organized interest groups, although of differing identities (radicals, the ruling class). If quantifiable weights can be assigned to the scalable dimensions of the chart, two major types of distribution are included—"opposition" and "convergence" distributions. "Opposition" distributions occur where the maximum weight or magnitude is found at one extreme of the scale and the minimum at the other, with intermediate positions showing intermediate values. Examples may be found in the sub-issues "degree of coercive power to be exercised by official agencies"; (left five espouses the minimum degree, right five the maximum, with others occupying intermediate positions), and "degree of personal culpability of offenders" (right five maximum, left five minimum, others in between). Policy disputes involving this type of distribution tend to be most difficult to resolve.

In "convergence" distributions similarities or partial similarities are found in the positions of those at opposing ends of the spectrum. One instance is found in attitudes toward rehabilitation of offenders—an objective strongly opposed by partisans at both left four and right four, although for different reasons. A rather complex but crucial instance is found in the statements concerning "localized" versus "centralized" authority. Both left four and right four call for increased local autonomy, whereas the more "moderate" of both left and right favor continued or increased federal authority and support for criminal justice programs and operations. The apparent convergence of the extremes is, however, complicated by a number of factors. One relates to which branch of government exercises authority; another relates to the particular policy area at issue. Those at left four are not adverse to strong federal initiatives to improve social-service delivery capacity of local welfare agencies. Those at right four, while decrying the iron grip of federal bureaucrats over local affairs, are not adverse to strong federal initiatives to improve technological capacity of local police forces. The more extreme leftists seek greatly increased local autonomy for citizen control over police and correctional operations, but welcome strong federal power in formulating and enforcing uniform civil rights measures. The more extreme rightists adamantly oppose the use of centralized power to enforce "mixing" of racial and other social categories or to compel uniform operations of local police, courts and corrections, but welcome strong federal power in the development and maintenance of military forces, or a strong federal investigatory branch with the power to probe corruption and collusion in local programs, particularly those of left-oriented agencies.

The unifying principle behind these apparent contradictions is the same as that noted for intraposition inconsistencies; ideologically-derived objectives are supported despite possible discrepancies involving the means to achieve them or the identity of sources of support. An additional dimension of considerable importance is also involved—that of time. Ideological positions of left and right are delineated on the basis of a given point in time earlier designated as "current." But specific stances of the left and

right can change rapidly in response to changing circumstances, or they can even reverse themselves. Moreover, some of the "crusading issues" currently fashionable will become passé in the near future.

The "decentralization" issue again provides a good example. Whether one favors more or less power for "centralized" or federal agencies depends on the current ideological complexion of the several federal departments or branches. Viewed very broadly, in the early 1930's the left looked to the executive branch as a prime source of support for policies they favored, and the right to the judicial and legislative; in the 1960's the left viewed both the executive and judicial as allies, the legislature as a potential source of opposition, and sought more power for the High Court and the Presidency. At present the right views the executive as supportive, and the left looks to the legislature as an ally in an attempt to curb the power of the presidency. Reflecting these shifts have been changes in attitudes of the left and right toward "local control." While traditionally a crusading issue of the right (state's rights), the banner for community control was taken up in the 1960's by the left as an effective method of bypassing entrenched political power at the local level—primarily with respect to civil rights. Recently the trend has begun to reverse because of a resurgence of the right's traditional "anti-big-government" stance and an increasing resort to local control by community groups pursuing rightist causes (e.g., exclusion of blacks from white schools).

Further detailed analyses of convergences and divergences, consistencies and contradictions, past, present and future fashions of both these issues and others could be developed. It might be useful at this point, however, to briefly consider a more fundamental level—the basic philosophical underpinnings of the two sides—and to compress the variety and complexity of their varied positions into a single and simple governing principle.

For the right, the paramount value is order—an ordered society based on a pervasive and binding morality—and the paramount danger is disorder—social, moral and political. For the left, the paramount value is justice—a just society based on a fair and equitable distribution of power, wealth, prestige, and privilege—and the paramount evil is injustice—the concentration of valued social resources in the hands of a privileged minority.

Few Americans would quarrel with either of these values since both are intrinsic aspects of our national ideals. Stripped of the passion of ideological conflict, the issue between the two sides could be viewed as a disagreement over the relative priority of two valuable conditions: whether *order with justice,* or *justice with order* should be the guiding principle of the criminal justice enterprise.

These are ancient philosophical issues, and their many aspects have been argued in detail for centuries. Can both order and justice be maximized in a large, heterogeneous, pluralistic society? Can either objective be granted priority under all circumstances? If not, under what circumstances should which objective be seen as paramount? It might appear that these issues are today just as susceptible to rational discussion as they have been in the past; but this is not so, because the climate militates against such discussion. Why this is so will be considered shortly—after a brief discussion of the ideologies of the formal agencies of criminal justice.

IDEOLOGICAL COMPLEXION OF CRIMINAL JUSTICE AGENCIES

The ideological positions of four major professional fields will be discussed—academic criminology, the police, the judiciary, and corrections. Rather than complex analysis or careful delineation, tentative impressions will be offered. Each system will be characterized on a very gross level, but it is important to bear in mind the possibility that there is as much ideological variability within each of the several systems as there is among them. Of particular

importance within these systems are differences in age level, social class and educational level, and rank.

Academic Criminologists: This group is included not out of any presumption about the importance of the role they play, but rather because academic criminology provides the platform from which the present analysis is presented. Probably the most important point to make here is that the day-to-day ideological environment of the average academic criminologist, viewed within the context of the total society, is highly artificial; it reflects the perspectives of a deviant and unrepresentative minority. Academic criminology, reflecting academic social science in general, is substantially oriented toward the left, while the bulk of American people are oriented toward the right.[7]

[7]Several recent studies provide indirect evidence of differences between academics and the general public in the likelihood that one will characterize his ideological position as "right" or "left." Of 60,000 professors surveyed by the Carnegie Commission, approximately 70% characterized themselves as "left" or "liberal," and fewer than 25% as "conservative" or "middle-of-the-road." A survey of social science professors by Everett Ladd and Seymour Lipset showed that approximately 70% voted against the "conservative" presidential candidate in 1972, compared with approximately 75% against four years before. These studies were reported in Hacker, "On Original Sin and Conservatives," *N.Y. Times,* Feb. 25, 1973, § 6 (Magazine) at 13. Henry Turner and Carl Hetrick's survey of a systematic sample of members of the American Political Science Association showed that approximately 75% characterized themselves as Democrats (among academics "Democratic" almost invariably means "liberal", whereas it generally means "conservative" in blue collar populations), a percentage which had remained stable for ten years. Those designating themselves as "Republicans" had declined to about 10% at the time of the survey. Turner and Hetrick's survey also showed that the Democratic majority was significantly more active in publication and political activity than the non-Democratic minority. H. Turner & C. Hetrick, Political Activities and Party Affiliations of American Political Scientists, (paper delivered at the 1971 Meetings of the American Political Science Association).

By comparison, a Gallup survey conducted in 1972 found that 71% of a systematically-selected sample of voters designated themselves as "conservative" (41%) or "Middle-of-the-road" (30%), with 24% characterizing themselves as "liberal." A survey by Daniel Yankelovich during the same

Furthermore, the members of the large liberal academic majority do proportionately more writing and speechmaking than those of the small conservative minority, so that their impact on the ideological climate exceeds even their large numbers. If the proportion of right-oriented persons in academic criminology comes close to being just the reverse of that in the general population, then this marked ideological divergence certainly has implications for those situations in which academicians come in contact with the public, particularly where they interact with representatives of other criminal justice branches. It also has an important impact on their own perceptions of the ideological positions of the public and other criminal justice professionals.

Police: The bulk of police officers have working-class backgrounds, and the contemporary working class is substantially rightist. Archie Bunker is a caricature, but the reality he exaggerates is a significant one. Rightist ideology in one of its purest versions may be found in the solemn speeches of Officer Joe Friday to temporarily discouraged young police officers or disgruntled citizens. Among police departments, differences in ideological complexion are found in different regions (for example, West Coast departments generally have higher proportions of college-trained personnel), different sized communities, and departments with different personnel policies. Within departments, age differences may be important (some younger officers are less rightist), as well as dif-

ferences in rank and function (some departments have more liberally-oriented chiefs or research and planning personnel). The majority of working police professionals, however, subscribe to the ideological premises here designated as "rightist."

Judiciary: The legal and judicial field is probably characterized by greater ideological diversity than either the police or corrections. One reason is that leftist positions are more common among those with college degrees than among those with less education. Since college education is a prerequisite to formal legal training, lawyers are more likely to have been exposed to the leftward orientation characteristic of most academic faculties, particularly those of the larger and more prestigious universities.[8] Judges show enormous variation in ideological predilections, probably covering the full range from right five to left four. Variation is related to factors such as the law school attended, size of jurisdiction, social status of jurists and their clientele, region, level of the court. While public attention is often directed to the actions of highly moralistic, hard line judges at right four and five positions, such jurists are probably becoming less common.

Ideological orientations of the legal profession have recently been subject to public attention, particularly in connection with two developments. First, the Supreme Court has in the recent past been associated with a series of decisions that reflect basic tenets of the left. Included have been such issues as increased protection of the rights of suspected and accused persons, inadmissibility of illegally-obtained evidence, minimization of distinctions based on race, reduction of discretionary powers of law-enforcement personnel, and reduction of judicial discretion in juvenile proceedings.[9] These

period found that 75% of the voters surveyed viewed themselves as "conservative" (37%) or "moderate" (38%), and 17% as "liberal" (15%) or "radical" (2%). *See* Rosenthal, "McGovern is Radical or Liberal to Many in Polls," *N.Y. Times,* Aug. 27, 1972, at 34, col. 3. An earlier poll by Yankelovich of American college students, seen by many as among the most liberal of large population categories, showed that approximately 70% reported themselves as holding "mainstream" positions, and that among the remainder, conservatives outnumbered left-wing radicals by two-to-one. D. Yankelovich, *The Changing Values on Campus: Political and Personal Attitudes of Today's College Students* (1972).

[8]Hacker states that ". . . the higher one climbs on the prestige ladder [of American colleges and universities] the less likely are conservatives to be found on the faculty." Hacker, *supra* note 7, at 71.

[9]Issues involved here fall into two general clusters: those affecting the rights and resources available to law-

decisions and others were perceived by the right as posing a critical threat to an established balance of power and prerogatives between law-enforcement personnel and offenders, seriously endangering the law-enforcement process and the security of the public.

The second development is the emergence during the past ten years of a group of young left-oriented lawyers whose influence is probably disproportionate to their small numbers. Able, dedicated, active on a variety of fronts, many representing low-income or black clients, their activities became best known in connection with Federal Anti-Poverty programs. Many of these lawyers have assumed positions along the ideological scale as far left as the left three and left four positions.

Despite these well-publicized manifestations of leftward orientations in some sectors of the legal profession, it is unlikely that a substantial proportion of the profession consistently espouses the tenets of the left, particularly those of left three and beyond. The more liberal judges are generally found in federal and higher-level state courts, but conservative views are still common among jurists of the lower level courts, where the great bulk of day-to-day legal business is transacted. Moreover, as part of the ideological shifts noted earlier, the Burger court is regarded by the right with considerably less antipathy than the Warren court.[10]

---

enforcement officials relative to those available to persons suspected, accused, or convicted of crimes; those relating to the conceptual or physical separation or combining of major population categories. Stands of the right and left with respect to the first cluster have been delineated in several places (right crusading issue 2; left general assumptions 3, 5; right policies respecting offenders 3, 4, respecting agencies, 3, 4; left policies respecting offenders 3, 4, respecting agencies 3, 4). Major decisions of the United States Supreme Court during the 1960's which appear to accord with ideological stances of the left and to run counter to those of the right include: *Mapp v. Ohio*, 367 U.S. 643 (1961), which reduced resources available to law-enforcement officials and increased resources available to the accused by extending limitations on the admissibility of illegally-obtained evidence; *Escobedo v. Illinois*, 378 U.S. 478 (1964), and *Miranda v. Arizona*, 384 U.S. 436 (1966), which reduced the power of law-enforcement officials to proceed with criminal processing without providing suspects with knowledge of and recourse to legal rights and resources; *In re* Gault, 387 U.S. 1 (1967), which reduced the power of judges to make dispositions in juvenile proceedings and increased the legal rights and resources of defendants; *Katz v. United States*, 389 U.S. 347 (1967), which reduced prerogatives of law-enforcement officials with respect to the gathering of evidence by increasing protection of suspects against intrusions of privacy; *Gilbert v. California*, 388 U.S. 263 (1967), and *United States v. Wade*, 388 U.S. 218 (1967) which decreased the freedom of law enforcement officials to seek identification of suspects, and increased the legal rights of resources available to suspects.

With respect to the second cluster, separation of population categories, stands of the right are delineated under general assumption 5, sources of crime 4, policies respecting criminal justice agencies 4, and of the left under crusading issue 5 and general assumption 4. The landmark decision here was *Brown v. Board of Education*, 347 U.S. 483 (1954), which held that racially segregated public education was *per se* discriminatory. While preceding the above-cited decisions by about a decade, *Brown* set a precedent for later court actions which provided support for the diminution of categorical segregation, as favored by the left, and reduced support for the maintenance of such separation, as espoused by the right.

[10]It has been widely held that the Burger Court, reflecting the influence of right-oriented Nixon appointees such as Justices Rehnquist and Powell, would evince marked support for rightist ideological premises, stopping or reversing many of the initiatives of the Warren Court in areas such as equal protection and due process. This viewpoint is articulated by Fred P. Graham, who writes, "Mr. Nixon's two new justices are strikingly like his first two appointments in conservative judicial outlook, and . . . this cohesion is likely to produce a marked swing to the right—particularly on criminal law issues. . . ." Graham, "Profile of the 'Nixon Court' Now Discernible," *N.Y. Times*, May 24, 1972, at 28, col. 3. *See also* Graham, "Supreme Court, in Recent Term, Began Swing to Right That was Sought by Nixon," *N.Y. Times*, July 2, 1972, at 18, col. 1; "Nixon Appointees May Shift Court on Obscenity and Business," *N.Y. Times*, October 2, 1972, at 16, col. 4. However, Gerald Gunther, in a careful review of the 1971 term of the Burger court, characterizes the court essentially as holding the line rather than moving to reverse the directions of the Warren Court or moving in new directions of its own. Gunther writes "There was no drastic rush to the right. The changes were marginal. . . . The new Court . . . has shown no inclination to overturn clear, carefully explained precedent." Gunther, "The Supreme Court 1971 Term, Foreword: In Search of Evolving Doctrine on a Changing Court: A Model for Newer Equal

Corrections: Corrections, the current hot spot of the criminal justice field, probably contains a mixture of ideological positions, with the bulk of correctional personnel ranged along the right. The average lower-echelon corrections employee has a working-class background similar to that of the average patrolman, and thus manifests the rightist orientation characteristic of that class. As in the case of police, age may be an important basis for differentiation, with older officials more likely to assume right-oriented positions. Among other bases are size of the institution and age level of the bulk of inmates. Juvenile corrections tends to have a higher likelihood of left-oriented staff, both at administrative and lower-echelon levels.

Prison reform is currently one of the most intense crusading issues of the left. While most reform efforts are exerted by persons not officially part of the correctional system, there has been some influx of left three and four persons into the official system itself, particularly among younger staff in juvenile correction facilities.

CONSEQUENCES OF IDEOLOGY

If, as is here contended, many of those involved in the tasks of planning and executing the major policies and procedures of our criminal justice system are subject to the influence of pervasive ideological assumptions about the nature of crime and methods of dealing with it—assumptions which are largely implicit and unexamined—the question then arises; what are

Protection," 86 *Harv. L. Rev.*, 1, 2–3 (1972). *Cf.* Goldberg, "Supreme Court Review 1972, Foreword—The Burger Court 1971 Term: One Step Forward, Two Steps Backward?," 63 *J. Crim. L.C. & P.S.* 463 (1972). Although the court has shown an inclination to limit and specify some of the broader decisions of the Warren Court (e.g., limiting rights to counsel at line-ups as dealt with in *Gilbert* and *Wade*, see Graham, July 2, 1972, *supra*), there does not appear at the time of writing any pronounced tendency to reverse major thrusts of Warren Court decisions relevant to presently-considered ideological issues, but rather to curb or limit momentum in these directions.

the consequences of this phenomenon?

While both the crusading issues and graded ideological positions presented earlier were phrased to convey the tone of urgent imperatives, the assumptions from which they arise were phrased in relatively neutral terms as a set of general propositions about the nature, causes, and processes of coping with crime. So phrased and so regarded, these assumptions are susceptible to rational consideration. Their strengths and weakness can be debated, evidence can be employed to test the degree of validity each may possess, contradictions among them can be considered, and attempts made to explain or reconcile differences among them. Formulated and used in this manner, the question arises: why are they characterized here as "ideological?"

The scale of ideology presented comprises a single major parameter—substantive variation along a left-right scale with respect to a set of issues germane to crime and the criminal justice process. But there is an additional important parameter which must also be considered: that of intensity—the degree of emotional charge which attaches to the assumptions. It is the capacity of these positions to evoke the most passionate kinds of reactions and to become infused with deeply felt, quasi-religious significance that constitutes the crucial element in the difference between testable assumptions and ideological tenets. This dimension has the power to transform plausibility into ironclad certainty, conditional belief into ardent conviction, the reasoned advocate into the implacable zealot. Rather than being looked upon as useful and conditional hypotheses, these assumptions, for many, take the form of the sacred and inviolable dogma of the one true faith, the questioning of which is heresy, and the opposing of which is profoundly evil.

This phenomenon—ideological intensification—appears increasingly to exert a powerful impact on the entire field. Leslie Wilkins has recorded his opinion that the criminal justice enterprise is becoming progressively more scientific and secularized;[11] an opposite, or at least concurrent, trend, is here suggested—that it is becoming progressively more ideologized. The consequences are many. Seven will be discussed briefly: Polarization, Reverse Projection, Ideologized Selectivity, Informational Constriction, Catastrophism, and Distortion of Opposing Positions.

Polarization

Polarization is perhaps the most obvious consequence of ideological intensification. The more heavily a belief takes on the character of sacred dogma, the more necessary it becomes to view the proponents of opposing positions as devils and scoundrels, and their views as dangerous and immoral. Cast in this framework of the sacred and the profane, of virtuous heroes and despicable villians, the degree of accommodation and compromise that seems essential to the complex enterprise of criminal justice planning becomes, at best, enormously complicated, and at worst, quite impossible.

Reverse Projection

This is a process whereby a person who occupies a position at a given point along the ideological scale perceives those who occupy any point closer to the center than his own as being on the opposite side of the scale. Three aspects of this phenomenon, which appears in its most pronounced form at the extremes of the scale, should be noted. First, if one grants the logical possibility that there can exist a "centrist" position—not a position which maintains no assumptions, but one whose assumptions are "mixed," "balanced," or not readily characterizable—then this position is perceived as "rightist" by those on the left, and "leftist" by those on the right.

A second aspect concerns the intensity of antagonism often shown by those occupying immediately adjacent positions along the ideologi-

[11]Wilkins, "Crime in the World of 1990," 4 *Futures* 203 (1970).

cal scale. Perhaps the most familiar current manifestation of this is found in the bitter mutual denunciations of those classified here as occupying the positions of left four and left five. Those at left four are often taken by those at left five as more dangerous and evil than those seen as patent facists at right four and five. Left fours stand accused as dupes of the right, selling out to or being coopted by the establishment, and blunting and thrust of social activism by cowardly vaccilation and compromise.

A third aspect of reverse projection is that one tends to make the most sensitive intrascale distinctions closest to the point that one occupies. Thus, someone at right four might be extremely sensitive to differences between his position and that of an absolute dictatorship advocate at right five, and at the same time cast left four and five into an undifferentiated class of commies, communist dupes and radicals, quite oblivious to the distinctions that loom so large to those who occupy these positions.

Ideologized Selectivity

The range of issues, problems, areas of endeavor, and arenas of activity relevant to the criminal justice enterprise is enormous. Given the vastness of the field relative to the availability of resources, decisions must be made as to task priorities and resource allocation. Ideology plays a paramount but largely unrecognized role in this process, to the detriment of other ways of determining priorities. Ideologized selectivity exerts a constant influence in determining which problem areas are granted greatest significance, which projects are supported, what kinds of information are gathered and how research results are analyzed and interpreted. Divergent resource allocation policies of major federal agencies can be viewed as directly related to the dominant ideological orientation of the agency.

Only one example of ideologized selectivity will be cited here. The increasing use of drugs, soft and hard, and an attendant range of drug-related crime problems is certainly a major contemporary development. The importance of this problem is reflected in the attention devoted to it by academic criminologists. One major reason for this intensive attention is that explanations for the spread of drug use fit the ideological assumptions shared by most academicians (drug use is an understandable product of alienation resulting from the failure of the system to provide adequate meaning and quality to life). Also one major ameliorative proposal, the liberalization of drug laws, accords directly with a crusading issue of the left— decriminalization.

Another contemporary phenomenon, quite possibly of similar magnitude, centers on the apparent disproportionate numbers of low-status urban blacks arrested for violent and predatory crimes, brought to court and sent to prison. While not entirely ignored by academic criminologists, the relatively low amount of attention devoted to this phenomenon stands in sharp contrast to the intensive efforts evident in the field of drugs. Important aspects of the problem of black crime do not fit the ideological assumptions of the majority of academic criminologists. Insofar as the issue is studied, the problem is generally stated in terms of oppressive, unjust and discriminatory behavior by society and its law-enforcement agents—a formulation that accords with that tenet of the left which assumes the capacity of officials to engender crime by their actions, and the parallel assumption that major responsibility for crime lies in conditions of the social order. Approaches to the problem that involve the careful collection of information relative to such characteristics of the population itself as racial and social status run counter to ideological tenets that call for the minimization of such distinctions both conceptually and in practice, and thus are left largely unattended.

Informational Constriction

An attitude which is quite prevalent in many quarters of the criminal justice enterprise today involves a depreciation of the value of research in general, and research on causes of crime in particular. Several reasons are commonly given, including the notion that money spent on research has a low payoff relative to that spent for action, that past research has yielded little of real value for present problems, and that research on causes of crime in particular is of little value since the low degree of consensus among various competing schools and theorists provides little in the way of unified conclusions or concrete guidance. Quite independent of the validity of such reasons, the anti-research stance can be seen as a logical consequence of ideological intensification.

For the ideologically committed at both ends of the scale, new information appears both useless and dangerous. It is useless because the basic answers, particularly with respect to causes, are already given, in their true and final form, by the ideology; it is dangerous because evidence provided by new research has the potential of calling into question ideologically established truths.

In line with this orientation, the present enterprise, that of examining the influence of ideology on criminal justice policy and programs, must be regarded with distaste by the ideologically intense—not only because it represents information of relevance to ideological doctrine, but also because the very nature of the analysis implies that ideological truth is relative.

Catastrophism

Ideological partisans at both extremes of the scale are intensely committed to particular programs or policies they wish to see effected, and recurrently issue dire warnings of terrible catastrophes that will certainly ensue unless their proposals are adopted (Right: Unless the police are promptly given full power to curb criminality and unless rampant permissiveness toward criminals is halted, the country will surely be faced with an unprecedented wave of crime and violence; Left: Unless society promptly decides to provide the resources necessary to eliminate poverty, discrimination, injustice and exploitation, the country will surely be faced with a holocaust of violence worse than ever before). Such predictions are used as tactics in a general strategy for enlisting support for partisan causes: "Unless you turn to us and our program. . . ." That the great bulk of catastrophes so ominously predicted do not materialize does not deter catastrophism, since partisans can generally claim that it was the response to their warnings that forestalled the catastrophe. Catastrophism can thus serve to inhibit adaptation to real crises by casting into question the credibility of accurate prophets along with the inaccurate.

Magnification of Prevalence

Ideological intensification produces a characteristic effect on perceptions of the empirical prevalence of phenomena related to areas of ideological concern. In general, targets of ideological condemnation are represented as far more prevalent than carefully collected evidence would indicate. Examples are estimates by rightists of the numbers of black militants, radical conspirators, and welfare cheaters, and by leftists of the numbers of brutal policemen, sadistic prison personnel, and totally legitimate welfare recipients.

Distortion of the Opposition

To facilitate a demonstration of the invalidity of tenets on the opposite side of the ideological scale it is necessary for partisans to formulate the actual positions of the opposition in such a way as to make them most susceptible to refutation. Opposition positions are phrased to appear maximally illogical, irrational, unsupportable, simplistic, internally contradictory, and, if possible, contemptible or ludicrous. Such distortion impedes the capacity to adequately comprehend and represent positions or points of view which may be complex and extensively developed—a capacity that can be of great value when confronting policy differences based on ideological divergencies.

IMPLICATIONS

What are the implications of this analysis for those who face the demanding tasks of criminal justice action and planning? It might first appear that the prescription would follow simply and directly from the diagnosis. If the processes of formulating and implementing policy with respect to crime problems are heavily infused with ideological doctrine, and if this produces a variety of disadvantageous consequences, the moral would appear to be clear: work to reverse the trend of increased ideological intensification, bring out into the open the hidden ideological agenda of the criminal justice enterprise, and make it possible to release the energy now consumed in partisan conflict with a more direct and effective engagement with the problem field itself.

But such a prescription is both overly optimistic and overly simple. It cannot be doubted that the United States in the latter twentieth century is faced with the necessity of confronting and adapting to a set of substantially modified circumstances, rooted primarily in technological developments with complex and ramified sociological consequences. It does not appear too far-fetched to propose that major kinds of necessary social adaptation in the United States can occur only through the medium of ardently ideological social movements—and that the costs of such a process must be borne in order to achieve the benefits it ultimately will confer. If this conception is correct, then ideological intensification, with all its dangers and drawbacks, must be seen as a necessary component of effective social adaptation, and the ideologists must be seen as playing a necessary role in the process of social change.

Even if one grants, however, that ideology will remain an inherent element of the policy-making process, and that while enhancing drive, dedication and commitment it also engenders rigidity, intolerance and distortion—one might still ask whether it is possible to limit the detrimental consequences of ideology without impairing its strengths. Such an objective is not easy, but steps can be taken in this direction. One such step entails an effort to increase ones' capacity to discriminate between those types of information which are more heavily invested with ideological content and those which are less so. This involves the traditional distinction between "fact" and "value" statements.[12] The present delineation of selected ideological stances of the left and right provides one basis for estimating the degree to which statements forwarded as established conclusions are based on ideological doctrine rather than empirically supportable evidence. When assertions are made about what measures best serve the purposes of securing order, justice, and the public welfare, one should ask "How do we know this?" If statements appear to reflect in greater or lesser degree the interrelated patterns of premises, assumptions and prescriptions here characterized as "ideological," one should accommodate one's reactions accordingly.

Another step is to attempt to grant the appropriate degree of validity to positions on the other side of the scale from one's own. If

[12] The classic formulations of the distinction between "factual" and "evaluative" content of statements about human behavior are those of Max Weber. *See,* e.g., A. Henderson & T. Parsons, *supra* note 6, at 8 *passim. See also* G. Myrdal, *supra* note 3.

ideological commitment plays an important part in the process of developing effective policy, one must bear in mind that both left and right have important parts to play. The left provides the cutting edge of innovation, the capacity to isolate and identify those aspects of existing systems which are least adaptive, and the imagination and vision to devise new modes and new instrumentalities for accommodating emergent conditions. The right has the capacity to sense those elements of the established order that have strength, value, or continuing usefulness, to serve as a brake on over-rapid alteration of existing modes of adaptation, and to use what is valid in the past as a guide to the future. Through the dynamic clash between the two forces, new and valid adaptations may emerge.

None of us can free himself from the influence of ideological predilections, nor are we certain that it would be desirable to do so. But the purposes of effective policy and practice are not served when we are unable to recognize in opposing positions the degree of legitimacy, validity, and humane intent they may possess. It does not seem unreasonable to ask of those engaged in the demanding task of formulating and implementing criminal justice policy that they accord to differing positions that measure of respect and consideration that the true idealogue can never grant.

Appendix

Chart I. *Sources of Crime: Locus of Responsibility*

Left	Right

5. Behavior designated as "crime" by the ruling classes is an inevitable product of a fundamentally corrupt and unjust society. True crime is the behavior of those who perpetuate, control, and profit from an exploitative and brutalizing system. The behavior of those commonly regarded as "criminals" by establishment circles in fact represents heroic defiance and rebellion against the arbitrary and self-serving rules of an immoral social order. These persons thus bear no responsibility for what the state defines as crime; they are forced into such actions as justifiable responses to deliberate policies of oppression, discrimination, and exploitation.

5. Crime and violence are a direct product of a massive conspiracy by highly-organized and well-financed radical forces seeking deliberately to overthrow the society. Their basic method is an intensive and unrelenting attack on the fundamental moral values of the society, and their vehicle is that sector of the populace sufficiently low in intelligence, moral virtue, self-control, and judgment as to serve readily as their puppets by constantly engaging in those violent and predatory crimes best calculated to destroy the social order. Instigators of the conspiracy are most often members of racial or ethnic groups that owe allegiance to and are supported by hostile foreign powers.

4. Those who engage in the more common forms of theft and other forms of "street crime" are essentially forced into such behavior by a destructive set of social conditions caused by a grossly inequitable distribution of wealth, power, and privilege. These people are actually victims, rather than perpetrators of criminality; they are victimized by discrimination, segregation, denial of opportunity, denial of justice and equal rights. Their behavior is thus a perfectly understandable and justified reaction to the malign social forces that bring it about. Forms of crime perpetrated by the wealthy and powerful—extensive corruption, taking of massive profits through illicit collusion, outright fraud and embezzlement—along with a pervasive pattern of marginally legal exploitative practices—have far graver social consequences than the relatively minor offenses of the so-called "common" criminal. Yet these forms of crime are virtually ignored and their perpetrators excused or assigned mild penalties, while the great bulk of law-enforcement effort and attention is directed to the hapless victims of the system.

4. The bulk of serious crime is committed by members of certain ethnic and social class categories characterized by defective self-control, self-indulgence, limited time-horizons, and undeveloped moral conscience. The criminal propensities of these classes, which appear repeatedly in successive generations, are nurtured and encouraged by the enormous reluctance of authorities to apply the degree of firm, swift, and decisive punishment which could serve effectively to curb crime. Since criminality is so basic to such persons, social service programs can scarcely hope to affect their behavior, but their low capacity for discrimination makes them unusually susceptible to the appeals of leftists who goad them to commit crimes in order to undermine the society.

3. Public officials and agencies with responsibility for crime and criminals must share with damaging social conditions major blame for criminality. By allocating pitifully inadequate resources to criminal justice agencies the government virtually assures that they will be manned by poorly qualified, punitive, moralistic personnel who are granted vast amounts of arbitrary coercive power. These per-

3. The root cause of crime is a massive erosion of the fundamental moral values which traditionally have served to deter criminality, and a concomitant flouting of the established authority which has traditionally served to constrain it. The most extreme manifestations of this phenomenon are found among the most crime-prone sectors of the society—the young, minorities, and the poor.

sons use this power to stigmatize, degrade and brutalize those who come under their jurisdiction, thus permitting them few options other than continued criminality. Society also manifests enormous reluctance to allocate the resources necessary to ameliorate the root social causes of crime —poverty, urban deterioration, blocked educational and job opportunities—and further enhances crime by maintaining widespread systems of segregation—separating race from race, the poor from the affluent, the deviant from the conventional and the criminal from the law-abiding.

Among these groups and elsewhere there have arisen special sets of alternative values or "countercultures" which actually provide direct support for the violation of the legal and moral norms of law-abiding society. A major role in the alarming increase in crime and violence is played by certain elitist groups of left-oriented media writers, educators, jurists, lawyers, and others who contribute directly to criminality by publicizing, disseminating, and supporting these crime-engendering values.

2. Although the root causes of crime lie in the disabling consequences of social, economic, and educational deprivation concentrated primarily among the disadvantaged in low-income communities, criminal behavior is in fact widely prevalent among all sectors of the society, with many affluent people committing crimes such as shoplifting, drunkenness, forgery, embezzlement, and the like. The fact that most of those subject to arrest and imprisonment have low-income or minority backgrounds is a direct consequence of an inequitable and discriminatory application of the criminal justice process—whereby the offenses of the more affluent are ignored, suppressed, or treated outside of a criminal framework, while those of the poor are actively prosecuted. A very substantial portion of the crime dealt with by officials must in fact be attributed to the nature of the criminal statutes themselves. A wide range of commonly pursued forms of behavior such as use of drugs, gambling, sexual deviance—are defined and handled as "crime," when in fact they should be seen as "victimless" and subject to private discretion. Further, a substantial portion of these and other forms of illegal behavior actually reflect illness—physical or emotional disturbance rather than criminality.

2. A climate of growing permissiveness and stress on immediate personal gratification are progressively undermining the basic deterrents to criminal behavior—self-discipline, responsibility, and a well-developed moral conscience. The prevalent tendency by liberals to attribute blame for criminality to "the system" and its inequities serves directly to aggravate criminality by providing the criminal with a fallacious rationalization which enables him to excuse his criminal behavior, further eroding self-discipline and moral conscience.

1. Crime is largely a product of social ills such as poverty, unemployment, poor quality education, and unequal opportunities. While those who commit crimes out of financial need or frustration with their life conditions deserve understanding and compassion, those who continue to commit crimes in the absence of adequate justification should in some degree be held accountable for their behavior; very often they are sick or disturbed persons who need help rather than

1. The behavior of persons who habitually violate the law is caused by defective upbringing in the home, parental neglect, inadequate religious and moral training, poor neghborhood environment, and lack of adequate role-models. These conditions result in a lack of proper respect for the law and insufficient attention to the basic moral principles which deter criminality. The federal government also contributes by failing to provide local agencies of prevention and law-enforcement with sufficient

punishment. Officials dealing with crime are often well-meaning, but they sometimes act unjustly or repressively out of an excessively narrow focus on specific objectives of law-enforcement. Such behavior in turn reflects frustration with the failure of society to provide them adequate resources to perform their tasks for which they are responsible, as it also fails to provide the resources needed to ameliorate the community conditions which breed crime.

resources to perform adequately the many tasks required to reduce or control crime.

Chart II. *Modes of Dealing with Crime: Policies with Respect to Offenders*

Left	Right
5. Since the bulk of acts defined as "crime" by the ruling classes simply represent behavior which threatens an invalid and immoral social system, those who engage in such acts can in no sense be regarded as culpable, or "criminal". There is thus no legitimate basis for any claim of official jurisdiction over, let alone any right to restrain, so-called offenders. Persons engaging in acts which help to hasten the inevitable collapse of a decadent system should have full and unrestrained freedom to continue such acts, and to be provided the maximum support and backing of all progressive elements. The vast bulk of those now incarcerated must be considered as political prisoners, unjustly deprived of freedom by a corrupt regime, and freed at once.	5. Habitual criminals, criminal types, and those who incite them should bear the full brunt of social retribution, and be prevented by the most forceful means possible from further endangering society. Murderers, rapists, arsonists, armed robbers, subversives and the like should be promptly and expeditiously put to death. The more vicious and unregenerate of these criminals should be publicly executed as an example to others. To prevent future crimes, those classes of persons who persistently manifest a high propensity for criminality should be prevented from reproducing, through sterilization or other means. Those who persist in crimes calculated to undermine the social order should be completely and permanently removed from the society, preferably by deportation.
4. All but a very small proportion of those who come under the jurisdiction of criminal justice agencies pose no real danger to society, and are entitled to full and unconditional freedom in the community at all stages of the criminal justice process. The state must insure that those accused of crimes, incarcerated, or in any way under legal jurisdiction be granted their full civil rights as citizens, and should make available to them at little or no cost the full range of legal and other resources necessary to protect them against the arbitrary exercise of coercive power. Criminal justice processing as currently conducted is essentially brutalizing— particularly institutional incarceration, which seriously aggravates criminality, and which should be entirely abolished. "Rehabilitation" under institutional auspices is a complete illusion; it has not worked, never will work, and must be abandoned as a policy objective. Accused persons, prisoners, and members of the general public subject to the	4. Dangerous or habitual criminals should be subject to genuine punishment of maximum severity, including capital punishment where called for, and extended prison terms (including life imprisonment) with air-tight guarantees that these be fully served. Probation and parole defeat the purposes of public protection and should be eliminated. Potential and less-habituated criminals might well be deterred from future crime by highly visible public punishment such as flogging, the stocks, and possibly physical marking or mutilation. To speak of "rights" of persons who have chosen deliberately to forfeit them by engaging in crime is a travesty, and malefactors should receive the punishment they deserve without interference by leftists working to obstruct the processes of justice. "Rehabilitation" as a policy objective is simply a weakly disguised method of pampering criminals, and has no place whatever in a proper system of criminal justice. Fully adequate facilities for detection, ap-

arbitrary and punitive policies of police and other officials must be provided full rights and resources to protect their interests—including citizen control of police operations, full access to legal resources, fully developed grievance mechanisms, and the like.

3. Since contacts with criminal justice officials—particularly police and corrections personnel—increase the likelihood that persons will engage in crime, a major objective must be to divert the maximum number of persons away from criminal justice agencies and into service programs in the community—the proper arena for helping offenders. There should be maximum use of probation as an alternative to incarceration, and parole as an alternative to extended incarceration. However, both services must be drastically overhauled, and transformed from ineffective watchdog operations manned by low-quality personnel to genuine and effective human services. Institutionalization should be the alternative of last resort, and used only for those proven to be highly dangerous, or for whom services cannot be provided outside of an institutional context. Those confined must be afforded the same civil rights as all citizens, including full access to legal resources and to officially-compiled information, fully-operational grievance mechanisms, right of petition and appeal from official decisions. Every attempt must be made to minimize the separation between institution and community by providing frequent leaves, work-release furloughs, full visitation rights, full access to citizen's groups. Full rights and the guarantee of due process must be provided for all those accused of crimes—particularly juveniles, minorities, and the underprivileged.

2. Since the behavior of most of those who commit crimes is symptomatic of social or psychological forces over which they have little control, ameliorative efforts must be conducted within the framework of a comprehensive strategy of services which combines individually-oriented clinical services and beneficial social programs. Such services should be offered in whatever context they can most effectively be rendered, although the community is generally preferable to the institution. However, institutional programs organized around the concept of the therapeutic community can be most effective in helping certain kinds of persons, such as drug users, for whom external

prehension, and effective restraint of criminals should be granted those police and other criminal justice personnel who realize that their principal mission is swift and unequivocal retribution against wrongdoers and their permanent removal from society to secure the full protection of the law-abiding.

3. Rampant permissiveness and widespread coddling of criminals defeat the purposes of crime control and must be stopped. Those who persist in the commission of serious crime and whose behavior endangers the public safety should be dealt with firmly, decisively and forcefully. A policy of strict punishment is necessary not only because it is deserved by offenders but also because it serves effectively to deter potential criminals among the general public. A major effort must be directed toward increasing the rights and resources of officials who cope with crime, and decreasing the rights and resources—legal, statutory, and financial—of those who use them to evade or avoid deserved punishment. Predetention measures such as bail, suspended sentences and probation should be used only when it is certain that giving freedom to actual or putative criminals will not jeopardize public safety, and parole should be employed sparingly and with great caution only in those cases where true rehabilitation seems assured. The major objective both of incarceration and rehabilitation efforts must be the protection of law-abiding society, not the welfare of the offender.

2. Lawbreakers should be subject to fair but firm penalties based primarily on the protection of society, but taking into account as well the future of the offender. Successful rehabilitation is an important objective since a reformed criminal no longer presents a threat to society. Rehabilitation should center on the moral re-education of the offender, and instill in him the respect for authority and basic moral values which are the best safeguards against continued crime. These aims can be furthered by prison programs which demand hard work and strict discipline, for these serve to promote good work habits and strengthen moral fiber.

constraints can be a useful part of the rehabilitative process. Rehabilitation rather than punishment must be the major objective in dealing with offenders. Treatment in the community—in group homes, halfway houses, court clinics, on probation or parole—must incorporate the maximum range of services, including vocational training and placement, psychological testing and counselling, and other services which presently are either unavailable or woefully inadequate in most communities. Where imprisonment is indicated, sentences should be as short as possible, and inmates should be accorded the rights and respect due all human beings.

1. Effective methods for dealing with actual or putative offenders require well-developed and sophisticated methods for discriminating among varying categories of persons, and gearing treatment to the differential needs of the several types thus discriminated. A major goal is to insure that those most likely to benefit from psychological counseling and other therapeutic methods will receive the kinds of treatment they need, rather than wasting therapeutic resources on that relatively small group of offenders whose behavior is essentially beyond reform, and are poor candidates for rehabilitation. All those under the jurisdiction of criminal justice agencies should be treated equitably and humanely. Police in particular should treat their clients with fairness and respect—especially members of minority groups and the disadvantaged. Careful consideration should be given before sentencing offenders to extended prison terms to make sure that other alternatives are not possible. Similarly, probation and parole should be used in those cases where these statutes appear likely to facilitate rehabilitation without endangering public safety. Prisoners should not be denied contact with the outside world, but should have rights to correspondence, visiting privileges, and access to printed and electronic media. They should also be provided with facilities for constructive use of leisure time, and program activities aimed to enhance the likelihood of rehabilitation.

adequately penalize the offender and insure sufficient time for effective rehabilitation. Probation and parole should not be granted indiscriminately, but reserved for carefully selected offenders, both to protect society and because it is difficult to achieve the degree of close and careful supervision necessary to successful rehabilitation outside the confines of the institution.

1. An essential component of any effective method for dealing with violators is a capability for making careful and sensitive discriminations among various categories of offenders, and tailoring appropriate dispositional measures to different types of offenders. In particular, the capacity to differentiate between those with a good potential for reform and those with a poor potential will ensure that the more dangerous kinds of criminals are effectively restrained. Probationers and parolees should be subject to close and careful supervision both to make sure that their activities contribute to their rehabilitation and that the community is protected from repeat violations by those under official jurisdiction. Time spent in prison should be used to teach inmates useful skills so that they may re-enter society as well-trained and productive individuals.

Chart III. *Modes of Dealing with Crime: Policies with Respect to Criminal Justice Agencies*

Left	Right
5. The whole apparatus of so-called "law-enforcement" is in fact simply the domestic	5. Maximum possible resources must be provided those law-enforcement officials who realize that

military apparatus used by the ruling classes to maintain themselves in power, and to inflict harassment, confinement, injury or death on those who protest injustice by challenging the arbitrary regulations devised by the militarists and monopolists to protect their interests. To talk of "reforming" such a system is farcical; the only conceivable method of eliminating the intolerable injustices inherent in this kind of society is the total and forceful overthrow of the entire system, including its so-called "law-enforcement" arm. All acts which serve this end, including elimination of members of the oppressor police force, serve to hasten the inevitable collapse of the system and the victory of progressive forces.

4. The entire American system of criminal justice must be radically reformed. Unless there is a drastic reduction in the amount of power now at the disposal of official agencies—particularly the police and corrections, a police state is inevitable. In particular, unchecked power currently possessed by poorly qualified, politically reactionary officials to deal with accused and suspected persons as they see fit must be curtailed; their behavior brutalizes and radicalizes the clients of the system. To these officials, "dangerous" usually means "politically unacceptable." Increasing concentration of power in entrenched bureaucracies must be checked, and the people given maximum rights to local control of their own lives, including the right to self protection through associations such as citizens councils and security patrols to counter police harassment and brutality and to monitor the operations of local prisons. Means must be found to eliminate the extensive corruption which pervades the system—exemplified by venal criminality within police departments and the unholy alliance between organized crime, corrupt politicians, and those who are supposedly enforcing the laws. Most of the criminal offenses now on the books should be eliminated, retaining only a few truly dangerous crimes such as forceful rape, since most of the offenses which consume law-enforcement energies have no real victims, and should be left to private conscience. However, statutes related to illegality by business interests, bureaucrats, corporations and the like should be expanded, and enforcement efforts greatly increased. Virtually all prisons should be closed at once, and the few persons requiring institutional restraint should be accommodated in small facilities in local communities.

their basic mission is the protection of society and maintenance of security for the law-abiding citizen. In addition to substantial increases in manpower, law-enforcement personnel must be provided with the most modern, efficient and lethal weaponry available, and the technological capacity (communications, computerization, electronic surveillance, aerial pursuit capability) to deliver maximum force and facilities possible to points of need—the detection, pursuit, and arrest of criminals, and in particular the control of terrorism and violence conducted or incited by radical forces.

4. The critical crime situation requires massive increases in the size of police forces and their technological capacity to curb crime—particularly in the use of force against criminals and radical elements. It is imperative that police command full freedom to use all available resources, legal and technical, without interference from leftist elements seeking to tie their hands and render them impotent. The power of the courts to undermine the basis of police operations by denying them fundamental legal powers must be curbed. The nation's capacity for incarcerating criminals—particularly through maximum security facilities—must be greatly expanded, and prison security strengthened. The "prison reform" movement rests on a mindless focus on the welfare of convicted felons and a blind disregard for the welfare of law-abiding citizens. Particularly pernicious is the movement now underway to unload thousands of dangerous criminals directly into our communities under the guise of "community corrections" (halfway houses, group homes, etc.). The local citizenry must unite and forcefully block this effort to flood our homes and playgrounds with criminals, dope addicts, and subversives. Increasing concentration of power in the hands of centralized government must be stopped, and basic rights returned to the local community—including the right to exclude dangerous and undesirable elements, and the right to bear arms freely in defense of home and family. Strict curbs must be imposed on the freedom of the media to disseminate materials aimed to undermine morality and encourage crime.

3. The more efficiency gained by law enforcement agencies through improvements in technology, communications, management, and so on, the greater the likelihood of harrassment, intimidation, and discrimination directed against the poor and minorities. Improvements in police services can be achieved only through fundamental and extensive changes in the character of personnel, not through more hardware and technology. This should be achieved by abandoning antiquated selection and recruitment policies which are designed to obtain secure employment for low-quality personnel and which systematically discriminate against the minorities and culturally disadvantaged. Lateral entry, culture-free qualification tests, and other means must be used to loosen the iron grip of civil-service selection and tenure systems. The outmoded military model with its rigid hierarchical distinctions found among the police and other agencies should be eliminated, and a democratic organizational model put in its place. The police must see their proper function as service to the community rather than in narrow terms of law-enforcement. As part of their community responsibility, law enforcement agencies should stringently limit access to information concerning offenders, especially younger ones, and much of such information should be destroyed. There must be maximum public access to the inner operations of police, courts and prisons by insuring full flow of information to the media, full accountability to and visitation rights by citizens and citizen groups, and full public disclosure of operational policies and operations. The major burden of corrections should be removed from the institutions, which are crime-breeding and dehumanizing, and placed directly in the communities, to which all offenders must at some point return.

3. Law enforcement agencies must be provided all the resources necessary to deal promptly and decisively with crime and violence. Failure to so act encourages further law breaking both by those who are subject to permissive and inefficient handling and by those who become aware thereby how little risk they run of being caught and penalized for serious crimes. The rights of the police to stringently and effectively enforce the law must be protected from misguided legalistic interference—particularly the constant practice of many judges of granting freedom to genuine criminals laboriously apprehended by the police, often on the basis of picayune procedural details related to "due process" or other legalistic devices for impeding justice. The scope of the criminal law must be expanded rather than reduced; there is no such thing as "victimless" crime; the welfare of all law-abiding people and the moral basis of society itself are victimized by crimes such as pornography, prostitution, homosexuality and drug use, and offenders must be vigorously pursued, prosecuted, and penalized. Attempts to prevent crime by pouring massive amounts of tax dollars into slum communities are worse than useless, since such people can absorb limitless welfare "benefits" with no appreciable effect on their criminal propensities. Communities must resist attempts to open up their streets and homes to hardened criminals through halfway houses and other forms of "community corrections."

2. A basic need of the criminal justice system is an extensive upgrading of the quality of personnel. This must be done by recruiting better qualified people—preferably with college training, in all branches and at all levels, and by mounting effective in-service training programs. Higher quality and better trained personnel are of particular importance in the case of the police, and training must place more stress on human relations studies such as psychology and sociology, and relatively less stress on purely technical aspects of police work. Quality must be maintained by the de-

2. There should be substantial increases in the numbers and visibility of police, particularly in and around schools, places of business, and areas of family activity. Although a few bad apples may appear from time to time, the bulk of our police are conscientious and upstanding men who deserve the continued respect and support of the community, and who should be granted ample resources to do the job to which they are assigned. Some of the proposed prison reforms may be commendable, but the burden to the taxpayer must never be lost sight of: most of the reforms

velopment and application of performance standards against which all personnel must be periodically measured, and which should provide the basis for promotion. Sentencing procedures must be standardized, rationalized, and geared to specific and explicit rehabilitative objectives rather than being left to the often arbitrary and capricious whims of particular judges. Corrections as well as other criminal justice agencies must be made more humane and equitable, and the rights of prisoners as individuals should be respected. Attempts should be made to reduce the degree of separation of prison inmates from the outside world. Changes in both legislation and law enforcement policies must be directed to reducing the disparities in arrest rates between richer and poorer offenders, so that commensurately fewer of the poor and underprivileged and more of the better off, are sought out, convicted, and imprisoned. Promising programs of humane reform must not be abandoned simply because they fail to show immediate measurable results, but should receive continued or increased federal support.

1. There must be better coordination of existing criminal justice facilities and functions so as to better focus available services on the whole individual, rather than treating him through disparate and compartmentalized efforts. This must entail better liaison between police, courts and corrections and greatly improved lines of communication, to the end of enabling each to attain better appreciation, understanding and knowledge of the operational problems of the others. Coordination and liaison must also increase between the criminal justice agencies and the general welfare services of the community, which have much to contribute both in the way of prevention of crime and rehabilitation of criminals. Local politicians often frustrate the purposes of reform by consuming resources in patronage, graft, and the financial support of entrenched local interests, so the federal government must take the lead in financing and overseeing criminal justice reform efforts. Federal resources and standards should be utilized to substantially increase the level and quality of social service resources available to criminal justice enterprises, promulgate standardized and rationalized modes of operation in local communities, and bring administrative coherence to the host of uncoordinated efforts now in progress.

suggested or already in practice are of dubious benefit or yield benefits clearly not commensurate with their costs. More effort should be directed to prevention of crime; in particular, programs of moral re-education in the schools and communities, and the institution of safeguards against the influence of those in the schools, media and elsewhere who promote criminality by challenging and rejecting the established moral values which serve to forestall illegal and immoral conduct.

1. The operations of the police should be made more efficient, in part through increased use of modern managerial principles and information processing techniques. Police protection should focus more directly on the local community, and efforts should be made to restore the degree of personal moral integrity and intimate knowledge of the local community which many older policemen had but many younger ones lack. Prison reform is important, but innovations should be instituted gradually and with great caution, and the old should not be discarded until the new is fully proven to be adequate. There should be much better coordination among law enforcement agencies, to reduce inefficiency, wasteful overlap, and duplication of services. The federal government must assume a major role in providing the leadership and financial resources necessary to effective law-enforcement and crime control.

2. Dramatic Aspects of Policing

PETER K. MANNING

INTRODUCTION

SOCIAL CONTROL, DEFINED AS "SOCIAL REACTIONS to behavior defined as deviant, including over-conformity to, as well as violation of, norms" (Clark and Gibbs, 1965: 401), can be seen as having a set of *instrumental* (deterrence, education, prevention, treatment, punishment) and *expressive* functions. The enforcement of a norm, or reaction to a behavioral event, may result not only in a set of intended consequences, but also in unanticipated consequences (cf. Selznick, 1966), some of which can be considered expressive in character.[1] Social control agents occupying an organizationally defined role emit unintended messages ("expressive meaning") while engaged in rule enforcement.[2]

▶SOURCE: *"Dramatic Aspects of Policing: Selected Propositions," Sociology and Social Research (October, 1974), 59:21–29. Reprinted by permission.*

[1]The focus of this paper is narrow, aimed at the development of a dramaturgical perspective of policing. However, two important implications of a concept of social control which included expressive elements are a) it can be sensitive to the *situational* interpretations of rules and norms, rather than seeing social control as a pervasive reaction to a set of broadly agreed upon normative standards (cf. Bittner, 1970: Gibbs, 1966); b) it suggests conditions under which announcing a norm not only provides a rational legitimization social control activities (as in the case of legal norms where the law is a means of control claime to apply equally to all members of a politically defined community), but serves also the education function: sets boundaries, clarifies moral hierarchies and highlights the significance of the moral order within which the conduct is thereby located. (Erickson, 1966).

[2]This conception of social control is based upon the following symbolic interactionist assumptions.

This paper presents a *dramaturgical view of policing* based upon six orienting propositions. "Dramaturgical" in this context refers to a perspective on conduct that is sensitive to the functions of selective public presentation of behaviors and the symbolizations and meanings attached to them.[3] Examples are drawn from

(A) Social objects and processes take on meaning and significance from the frame of reference within which they are placed. (B) Interaction is patterned because persons selectively attend to and attribute symbolic elements to a behavioral display. Through awareness of interactional contingencies, persons can strategically employ interactional control. (C) Social order is created, maintained and kept selective through symbolically highlighted displayed symbols which large segments of the population are pre-disposed or prepared to accept as legitimate. These displays are ceremonies, expressive rejuvenations of a community's moral values. Furthermore: ... "in so far as the expressive bias of performances come to be accepted as reality, then that which is at the moment defined as reality will have some of the characteristics of a celebration" (Goffman, 1959: 35–36). (D) The capacity to control the selection and dissemination of symbols, and hence to limit the *range* of meanings attributed to social action, is a function of power (Goode, 1969). (E) Organizations operating in an environment where they must negotiate for power in order to survive, can be seen as seizing upon particular aspects of their activities to dramatize their effectiveness, efficacy and utility vis-a-vis their stated goals. In so doing, they *evoke* a version of social reality which can be as much mystification as *revelation*.

[3]The term "the drama of control" is itself metaphoric. A persistent problem in the use of metaphor is that such ambiguity fails to note whether the perspective adopted is one mirroring, reflecting, or replicating the *subject's* or the *ob-*

urban police departments employing a professional model (Wilson, 1968) where differing conceptions of appropriate public order are encountered (given an altered structure of policing, different behavioral and social consequences would occur).

I. *To the degree that police agencies lack a legitimated mandate on which there is widespread consensus, they will tend to direct energy either into dramatization of their effectiveness or into repressive actions in attempts to expand their mandate* (cf. Hughes, in Becker, ed., 1963; Manning, 1971). Operating with a symbolic screen of legitimacy, government agencies can supply a canopy of meanings within which distant, ambiguous events where people have little or no factual or empirical knowledge are to be defined (Edelman, 1972). The case for a governmental monopoly of meanings so long as they fit the cognitions and perceptions of a public (or segment "target group" in case of an agency) that attends to the messages is less persuasive at the local government level. There are some 45,000 police agencies in the United States, including federal, state, county, and municipal forces, employing some 450,000 people. Local police agencies seeking to mobilize power will in the process create the possibilities that set of political meanings will be attached to their action by their

target audience that will in turn serve to legitimate (or alternatively de-legitimate) their perspectives.[4]

Local social control agencies compete for resources, clientele, self-esteem, and prestige. These agencies engage in minimal cooperation. They compete and overlap, and owe allegiance to different levels of government, industry and locally bounded communities. Between social control agencies at this level, competition for resources, clientele, self-esteem, and prestige is typical. No singly overlapping moral authority in an urban community governs all agency-agency relationships. Minimal pragmatic rules govern the content and dynamics of their competitive relationships: these might include tacit agreements to compete, cooperate, or segmentalize areas of control, etc. (cf. Long, 1958; Bailey, 1969).

---

server's point of view (cf. Pitt-Rovers, 1967). In this analysis, the perspective is the *observer's*. The observer makes the distinctions which are possible readings of the behavior; whether the actors themselves are actually aware of the consequences of what they are doing is problematic and varies from situation to situation. There is no assumption that social life *is* scripted, staged, directed or that roles are parcelled out according to a single underlying structure. It is neither a necessary nor sufficient part of the argument. Activities guided by highly moral premises and sanctioned in the process by organizational *dicta* can have quite pernicious effects or be seen as illegal or immoral. Conversely, quite immorally intended action can be read as a "defence of national liberties" or as being in the public interest yet can create social havoc. Machiavelli and some contemporary politicians provide a catalog of such techniques. These anomalies are not of concern here. Individual intentions are not at issue; what is of concern are the expressive elements of and unanticipated consequences of rational forms of active social control.

[4]There are nearly a half a million persons employed in law enforcement in this country. However, they work for agencies located at five separate levels of governmental responsibility. In addition to federal agencies, including the FBI, Bureau of Narcotics, Post Office, IRS, Customs, the Alcohol, Firearms and Tobacco Unit of the Treasury, the Immigration-Border Patrol and U.S. Marshalls, there are agents of the 50 states, including state police forces and criminal investigation agencies, county sheriffs and deputy sheriffs in over 3,000 counties; police of a thousand cities and over 20,000 townships and New England towns; and the police of 15,000 villages, boroughs, and incorporated towns, together with a small number of special purpose forces serving public quasi-corporations and ad hoc districts. Finally, within certain county or metropolitan areas, there are "ad hoc squads" to deal with organized crime, drugs, or riots which are composed of members of a number of police forces and are commanded by officers from several departments. The number of private police agencies such as Pinkerton's (an agency now employing over 30,000 persons) and other protective and detective agencies is presently over 3,000 and growing. The amount spent on legally constituted private forces is over 3 billion dollars. Finally, an unknown number of more than ad hoc "vigilante" groups (which do continue to appear to conduct voluntary searches, patrol neighborhoods, and make inquiries in communities), exist such as the Maccabbees in Brooklyn, and Black Protectors in large urban areas. There are no accurate estimates of the number of people involved on an ad hoc basis or on a semi-official capacity such as these, but they form a type of quasi-legal social control even though they normally do not arrest persons.

Let us simply indicate some of the conditions under which one or the other of these two polar dramatic tendencies occur. Typically, in this country at least, the police tend to dramatize by indirect or symbolic means efficient control and capture of criminals. Most police work is administrative (50% of police time) and is not publically visible. The police tend to seize on aspects of their work that can be publically underscored and highlighted. They utilize the official crime rate as a symbolic indication of their effectiveness (consequently, they claim effectiveness when the rate drops or remains low, while justifying their importance when it rises!). The rate is used to persuade the public that the police protect life and property, and the validity of police claims to public trust or a *mandate*. On the other hand, where public disagreement is high, where the laws are numerous and under direct public criticism (e.g., crimes without victims, especially drug laws), where local government is under question, and the linkage between the local government and the police is directly and mutually agreed upon, repressive action will tend to occur. Examples are: communities in the South seeking control of racial demonstrations, in Chicago during the Democratic National Convention of 1968, and in local communities where police brutality has been reported as common. It would appear that actions of the Chicago police over the last ten or more years represent a paradigm case of a demonstrated repressive tendency among police departments.

II. *To the degree that dramatic aspects of policing become the dominant concern of the police and the public, then ceremony replaces instrumentalism; police work becomes redundant; it simply reaffirms other modes and forms of social control.*

Messages inherent in the communicational order and content of a ceremony are sanctified, or given a truth value by the "unquestionable truthfulness imputed by the faithful to unverifiable propositions" (Rappaport, 1971: 69). For example, the statements "you have broken a law;" "policemen represent the law," come to possess power because they are imbedded in a context (police-citizen encounters) that is conventionally defined and displayed. The sanctification and social behavior creates orderliness and predictability. When a variety of actions, informal and associational, as well as formal, refer to and recreate the *same* set messages for persons, formal control is but a single instance of an ineluctable patterning of human meaning and resultant human action. Thus, the English police are defined as no more than citizens in uniform predisposed to offer assistance to others; insofar as this definition is affirmed in belief and action by policemen, they do indeed act in ways designed to affirm in the reality of their imputed role.

Policing as miscellaneous and unspecialized services is thus *redundant* (in communication theory terms); it adds no further information to the system of human relations. By this token, the ceremony of policing replicates the banality of everyday life. On the other hand, following the above points, we can assert that instrumental behavior is that for which meaning must be assigned, or designated. It is a matter of empirical discovery. Empirical variation then is a matter of relative contrast, a matter of standing out, and pattern can be supplied then from a variety of frames or contexts. In modern society a multiplicity of ways can be used to create context and the most important of these is coercive *force*. "In such societies authority is no longer contingent upon sanctity; the sacred, or discourse for which sanctity is claimed, has become contingent upon authority." (Rappaport, 1971: 73). The appearance of force thus creates the artifice of sanctity, thus reducing the viability of sanctity itself. Instrumental social control, where the law is an isolated and foreign force, or where legal norms are virtually always enacted by means of force, tends to create *schismogenesis*, or differentiation of meaning, decreased redundancy, and reduced moral consensus. The implications of this can be most readily detected by an examination of what functions as an alternative source of meaning for organizations employing force under the rubric of sanctity (Props. IV and V).

III.   *To the degree that instrumentalism replaces the ceremonial features of police work, the degree of sanctity of moral rules that they convey will be reduced. In time, coercion replaces consensus on the police mandate and its legitimation.*

Much has been written on the problematic features of the police situation, and the parallel police problem of maintaining control while appearing to be fair, and maintaining self-esteem in the face of adversary relations (cf. Westley, 1953). Where the law is not technically involved (questions of order maintenance e.g., domestic disputes, crowds, public use of streets and level of noise, etc.), the policeman is "stripped" of his legal sanctioning authority.[5] In these contexts, lying, brusque statements, disattention to others, and the use of force are common.[6] Reiss (1971) found that 50% of all arrests involved physical force, and 9% involved gross force. Chevigny (1968) argued in selected cases that he was able to prove in court, the New York police, faced with non-compliance to their "requests,"

tended to respond with violence, and a "covering charge" (e.g., assaulting an officer).

American policemen see human service or order maintenance as not being "real police work" as "shit work," and therefore morally degrading to them as protectors of the public safety, i.e., enforcers of the law. Thus, nonadversary, morally binding, interactions are *avoided* or treated with disdain. The tendency to assert a controlling force in interaction, and to create adversary relationships even where the initial situation involves conflict between two others, sets policemen apart interactionally from those they are meant to serve. Their claims to authority and for deference when insufficiently reciprocated as is often the case, create conditions where disagreements over the *locus* of authority are likely.

IV.   *If the conceptions of policing provided by the police themselves* (i.e., "*the secondary reality* of policing") *are legitimated, then police action frees itself from the community in which it is rooted and may establish its own norms and values.*

---

[5]In these situations, Reiss found, citizens mobilize the police about 90% of the time, more citizens than police are present when the policemen arrive in the scene (54% of encounters involved 3 plus citizens to the single policeman), and in 70% of these cases, the scene takes place in a private place where arrest powers are significantly reduced or controlled, i.e., they depend on the citizen's willingness to make a civil complaint.

[6]Several studies of police interactions with juveniles have underscored the import of situational violations of etiquette in the dispositions of suspects (cf. Westley, 1953; Piliavin and Briar, 1964; Black, 1968, 1970; and Black and Reiss, 1970). (Differential dispositions are made at the juvenile bureau level and above McEachern and Bauzer, 1967; Terry, 1967; Goldman, 1953; and Cicourel, 1968). Such variables as race, previous record, probation status, age, department and officers all pattern dispositions when offenses held constant, i.e., for the same offense categories, different outcomes may be predicted using other criteria. See Bordua, 1965 for a useful review of these studies and Black, 1968. Piliavin and Briar (1964), for example, found that in 66 cases of police/juvenile encounters, demeanor was significant in 90% of the cases other than those leading to a felony charge. Those that did not manifest the appropriate signs of respect tended to receive the more severe dispositions: 67% of the "un-

cooperative" juveniles were arrested, while only 4% of those labeled "cooperative" were arrested. Ferdinand and Luchterhand (1970), in a large study of teenagers randomly sampled from inner city neighborhoods (N = 1,525) found that although black teenagers were *less* "anti-social and aggressive" than whites, those blacks who came in contact with the police were given more severe dispositions," largely in terms of their superficial attitudes toward and demeanor toward the police, whereas white offenders are judged by different and more basic criteria." (517–518) Black and Reiss, on the other hand, (1970) using trained observers in 3 departments, found the arrest rates for participants in encounters characterized as follows: "antagonistic" 22%; "civil" 16%; "very deferential" 22%. This pattern held true when only serious misdemeanors, rowdiness and felonies were combined. Black (1968), analyzing those 10% of the encounters where arrest did eventuate, found a number of social variables were at work (social status of the complainant, his preference for arrest/non-arrest: the availability of evidence and the race of the alleged offender). Although the evidence is somewhat scattered, it is fair to conclude that particularly with "minor crimes" (those where the police are likely to intervene on their own initiative), deference and demeanor of the suspect play an important role in the determination of the arrest and charge.

The police, in following a line of action, build up understandings which filter conduct, are read off by others, and their responses, in turn, are responded to by the police (cf. Parsons, 1951: 252–256ff; Glaser, 1970, 42–46). They do not simply "respond" to citizen demands.

Citizen calls for assistance in themselves as behavioral events do not provide either the necessary or sufficient basis for police action.[7] What occurs in a given incident cannot be understood by simply counting behavioral outcomes. One must give attention to what is "out of sight" or the "preconstituted typifications" of normal and routine encounters employed by the police (Chatterton, 1973). It should be emphasized that (1) police patrolmen develop prospective understandings of the police-relevant meanings of calls (e.g., what problems an arrest will make for constables in the reserve room of the station at particular times or how an arrest and associated paperwork might affect personal time). This issue is especially critical at the end of a shift, but may also be relevant because of the court time that may be required. (2) Calls are set within a "reasonable" context of understandings of types of events that predetermine how events will be handled in advance (e.g., the availability of detective investigators, the possibility that an arrest will be considered a "good pinch"). The police thus create by their own definitions of "crime," and "criminals" a system of typifications and assumptions that might be called an "occupational culture." (Manning, 1971: 1974) which guides, directs, channels and controls what it is possible to read from their actions. The messages conveyed, read, and reflected thus create a secondary reality (Young, 1971), or alternative system of typification, normal procedures, and common-sense theories of policing which in time become a reality confronting everyone.

V.   To the degree that formally constituted control agencies are faced with a paradox between what is

formally expected of them in the community and what is possible, they will tend to retreat from a collective definition of morality, the law, and social order (Westley, 153; Skolnick, 1966; Chevigny, 1968; Manning, 1971; Cain, 1973).

In most towns and cites of America, and in England, the middle-class-property-owner-head-of-the-household is seen by the police as the most significant police audience. Positing a consensual other seems to be a significant part of the police ideology.

"Policemen need to believe in a largely consensual populace whose values and standards they represent and enforce. It is by reference to this that they legitimate their activities. They are intermediaries who bring forth for punishment, whom 'most people' deem to deserve it" (Cain, 1973: 69.

The police are in an adversary relationship with the public on many occasions; they tend to adopt a symbolic rationale for their "enemy." This evil "out there" stands as a polar symbolic representation to that of the public, the middle-class property owner. First, this enemy is more significant as symbol for the administrators of the department for they lack the face to face contact with the public which would reduce their stereotype. This collective representation facilitates and mobilizes their policy decisions—it provides the qui bonum. Policemen, although they are in greater contact with evil, and are therefore more polluted by this relationship, at the same time can rationalize their activities as the essence of good policework.

The patrolmen tend to control information on their activities in order to protect themselves from arbitrary administration action, thus further isolating the administrator who sets policies in the pursuit of the criminal from the actual criminal and criminality. This secrecy binds together the lower participants, separating them from the administrators. Police secrecy, as Bittner points out, integrates the police organization vis à vis the public, and is the grounds which form the symbolization of evil, but it internally divides the organization (Bittner, 1970: 63). Solidarity symbolized outside is converted inwardly as dissensus. The contact

[7]I am indebted to Chatterton's (1973) incisive analysis in the material presented here.

with evil, i.e., with informants, with criminals and ex-criminals, with the demi-monde of large cities, makes moral pollution inevitable for the lower participants, while freeing the higher participants to symbolize and dramatize their distance from the very thing they are expected to "destroy," "control," or "prevent." What is expected externally by the public as a result of the publicity of the police cannot be realized internally and a schizoid existence is established.

Actions that affirm the police role as the police believe it should be defined by the middle classes in actuality separate the police from these very middle classes. The police rarely deal with "crime" and "criminals"; they deal for the most part with requests for service that are not imbedded in a legal context, but in a framework of 24-hour availability. Among the actual contacts that involve the law, surprisingly few eventuate in arrest (Reiss, 1971: Chapter 1). Of course, police knowledge of crimes is almost exclusively dependent upon citizen information. Arrest possibilities for a given crime are exceedingly low; only in the case of homicide or serious assault does the arrest and charge rate approach a reasonable level. Even then, the crime may be cleared only by a guilty plea, or by plea bargaining, rather than by police action or evidence. Cain's (1973) ethnography of police in two English towns, suggests that arrests of drunks and other public order offenders are used to inflate the clearance rate. Thus emphasis upon making visible crime-fighting activities leads to a) futile attempts to elevate arrest rates by the arrest of "innocuous offenders" (who in turn, clog jails and courts and occupy inordinate amounts of police time); b) a relative loss of public service activities that might benefit the middle class audience; c) because of the belief in the crime stopper/crime-catcher role, morale drops when it is not possible, and affect is withdrawn from the very public service demanded structurally.

Organizations and occupations, failing to "win" public support within the international or everyday sphere, tend to move to the political or legal sphere to gain the authority they desire over job, working conditions, pay, public defer-ence and the like (e.g., unionization campaigns, legal suits, strikes, etc.). In the case of the police, these campaigns have taken the character of emphasis upon the symbolic threat to the public of "crime," the isolation of this symbol from everyday life, and the consequent rationale for violation of procedural rules in the control of crime. After the events in Washington, this hardly requires emphasis. Stan Cohen's *Folk Devils and Moral Panics* (1973: 87–143) beautifully illustrates what he calls "innovation" in social control, an excess in enforcement of rules which results from the stripping and dehumanization of the criminal and uncontrolled controllers.

VI. *The greater the gap between the moral standards of the community* (i.e., their behavior), *and the police culture, the greater the growth of cynicism among the police and the greater number of internal disciplinary violations and corruption.*

Since policemen see individuals in a significant portion of time in adversary relationships, where citizens are likely to have violated conventional standards, i.e., where they have threatened to harm or harmed others, or where they have violated property rights, policemen come to expect the worst of people. Their stereotypes of people are cynical (Neiderhoffer, 1967): they are distrustful, and they share a "rotten apple" view of collective social life (Knapp, 1972; Stark, 1972). When persons viewed as discredited do not defer to the police, the self of the controller is threatened, or perceived as violated. The police view themselves collectively as "failures," as "dirty workers," as a minority without honor.

The pattern of respect-seeking and self-violation, when coupled with the attribution of risk to citizen-police encounters, has further consequences. Policemen withdraw affect from moral restraints symbolized by commitment to departmental rules and legal controls.[8] If recent research is representative of the behavior of

---

[8]I have considered some of these consequences in a paper dealing with police lying tentatively entitled, "Paradoxes of Police Lying."

policemen in large cities, where moral and political diversity is the rule, then one must conclude that police malfeasance is very common indeed. In Boston, Washington and Chicago, Reiss estimated that 40% of the men observed violated departmental rules (sleeping or drinking on the job, falsification of reports, or other "serious" infractions); 60% received reports (Reiss, 1971: 164). Two recent studies of the New York City Department reveal a similar pattern. Of the 2,000 officers joining the force in 1957, nearly 60% had received one allegation of misconduct and a total of 2,137 complaints had been filed: 9.5% involved criminal charges: 25.3% accused an officer of abusing a citizen, and 64.2% cited violation of departmental rules. The pattern of corruption, the acceptance of bribes, pay-offs, or "considerations" is apparently well-established in New York City. The *Knapp Commission Report* concluded: "corruption is widespread . . . not all policemen are corrupt. . . . Yet, with extremely rare exceptions, even those who themselves engage in no corrupt activities are involved in corruption in the sense that they take no steps to prevent what they know or suspect to be going on about them." (Knapp, 1972: 1; 3). The variety of types of corruption included pay-offs in gambling, prostitution, bars, construction and narcotics. (The situation in narcotics, from all indications, made distinctions between pushers, agents, users, and organized crime essentially moot. Accepting money, protecting informants, received regular pay-offs and even dealing in drugs themselves was the rule rather than the exception.) Reiss' (1971:169) conclusion from his three-city work can be generalized perhaps ". . . during any year a substantial minority of all police officers violate the criminal, a majority misbehave towards citizens in an encounter, and most engage in serious violations of the rules and regulations of the department."

COMMENT

What are the police for? Rejecting administrative accounts based on systems theory of the nature of police aims and activities (cf. Wilson and McClaren, 1973) should not lead us to assume that the police are ineffectual. The principal consequence of the development of a bureaucratically organized police is that the presence of the state is symbolized in the everyday lives of the citizenry; the police, a bureaucratic mobilization of manpower and resources, represent the virtual and potential penetration of civil authority into mundane events (Silver, 1967: 14–15 ff).

The police deal in a significant way with materials and situations taken to be symbolic of social order itself. Their arrest rates and their actual activities in the arrest and charge of "serious crime" cannot be set aside; these functions must be carried out and the law applied with some degree of certainty. However, index crimes, although highly significant to the public, do not seem to be prevented by present measures (Wilson, 1967). Nor are they likely to be prevented by what is now the prevalent pattern of allocation of police manpower and resources: "preventive" or proactive patrol to seek crimes (cf. Reiss, 1971: 99–100). The most significant police product is *symbolic*: their distinctive uniforms, their displays of police presence in public crowd situations, at important crimes (what is called "showing the flag" by the English police); their almost random encounters with the everyday world of the citizen, *all ritualize and create in everyday life the appearance of a consensual, constraining moral order.*

REFERENCES

Bailey, F.G.
  1969 *Stratagems and Spoils.* New York: Schocken Books.

Bittner, E.
  1970 *The Functions of the Police in Modern Society.* Washington, D.C.: United States Government Printing Office.

Black, D.J.
  1968 *Police Encounters and Social Organization.* Unpublished Ph.D. dissertation, Department of Sociology, University of Michigan.

1970 "The Production of Crime Rates." *American Sociological Review* 35 (August): 733–748.

Black, D.J., and A.J. Reiss
1970 "Police Control of Juveniles." *American Sociological Review* 35 (February): 63–77.

Bordua, D.
1965 "Recent Trends: Deviant Behavior and Social Control." *Annals* 57 (January): 149–163.

Cain, M.
1973 *Society and the Policeman's Role.* London: Routledge, Kegan Paul.

Chatterton, M.
1973 "A Working Paper on the Use (of) Resource-Charges and Practical Decision Making in Peace-Keeping." Presented at Bristol seminar on the sociology of the police, Bristol University, England.

Chevigny, P.
1968 *Police Power: Police Abuses in New York City.* New York: Pantheon.

Cicourel, A.
1968 *The Social Organization of Juvenile Justice.* New York: Wiley.

Clark, A., and J.P. Gibbs
1965 "Social Control." *Social Problems* 12 (Spring): 398–415.

Cohen, S.
1973 *Folk Devils and Moral Panics.* London: Paladin Books.

Edelman, M.
1972 *Politics as Symbolic Action.* Chicago: Markham.

Erikson, K.T.
1966 *Wayward Puritans.* New York: Wiley.

Ferdinand, T., and E. Luchterhand.
1970 "Inner City Youths, The Police and Justice." *Social Problems* 17 (Spring): 510–527.

Glaser, D.
1970 *Social Deviance.* Chicago: Markham.

Goffman, E.
1959 *The Presentation of Self in Everyday Life.* New York: Doubleday.

Goldman, N.
1963 "The Differential Selection of Juvenile Offenders for Court Appearance." National Research and Information Center, National Council on Crime and Delinquency. New York,

Goode, E.
1969 "Marijuana and the Politics of Reality." *Journal of Health and Social Behavior* 10 (June): 83–93.

Hughes, E.C.
1963 "Good People and Dirty Work," in *The Other Side,* edited by H.S. Becker. Glencoe: The Free Press.

Knapp, Whitman, et al.
1972 The Knapp Commission Report on Police Corruption (in New York City). New York: George Braziller.

Long, N.
1958 "The Local Community as an Ecology of Games." *American Journal of Sociology* 54 (November): 252–61.

Manning, P.K.
1971 "The Police: Mandate, Strategies and Tactics." in *Crime and Justice in American Society,* edited by J.D. Douglas. Indianapolis: Bobbs-Merrill.
1974 "Organizations as Situationally Justified Action" to be presented at the VIII World Congress of Sociology. Toronto, Canada, August.

McEachern, A., and A. Bauer.
1967 "Factors Relating to Disposition in Juvenile-Police Contacts." In *Juvenile Gangs in Context,* edited by Klein and Neyerhoff. Englewood Cliffs: Prentice-Hall.

Neiderhoffer, A.
1967 *Behind the Shield.* New York: Doubleday.

Parsons, T.
1951 *The Social System,* Glencoe: The Free Press.

Piliavin, H., and Briar, S.
1964 "Police Encounters with Juveniles." *American Journal of Sociology* LXX (September): 206–214.

Pitts-Rivers, J.
1967 "Contextual Analysis of the Locus of the Model." *Archives of European Sociology* VII: 15–34.

Rappaport, R.A.
1971   "Ritual, Sanctity and Cybernetics." *American Anthropologist* 73 (February): 59–76.

Reiss, A.J. Jr.
1971   *The Police and the Public.* New Haven: Yale University Press.

Selznick, P.
1966   *TVA and The Grassroots.* New York: Harper and Torch Books.

Silver, A.
1967   "The Demand for Order in Civil Society." In *The Police,* edited by David Bordua. New York: Wiley.

Skolnick, J.
1966   *Justice Without Trial.* New York: Wiley.

Stark, R.
1972   *Police Riots.* Belmont, California: Wadsworth.

Terry, R.
1967   "The Screening of Juvenile Offenders." *Journal of Criminal Law, Criminology and Police Science,* 58: 173–181.

Westley, W.
1953   "Violence and the Police," *American Journal of Sociology* 59 (July): 34–41.

Wilson, J.Q.
1967   "A Reader's Guide to the Presidents' Crime Commission Reports." *Public Interest* (Fall).
1968   *Varieties of Police Behavior.* Cambridge: Harvard University Press.

Wilson, O.W., and R. McLaren.
1972   *Police Administration.* New York: McGraw-Hill.

Young, J.
1971   "The Role of the Police as Amplifiers of Deviance, Negotiators of Reality, and Translators of Fantasy." in *Images of Deviance,* edited by S. Cohen. Harmondsworth: Penguin.

3. The Social Organization of Arrest

DONALD BLACK

THIS ARTICLE OFFERS A SET OF DESCRIPTIVE MATE-
rials on the social conditions under which
policemen make arrests in routine encounters.
At this level, it is a modest increment in the expanding literature on the law's empirical face.
Scholarship on law-in-action has concentrated
upon criminal law in general and the world of
the police in particular.[1] Just what, beyond the
hoarding of facts, these empirical studies will
yield, however, is still unclear. Perhaps a degree
of planned change in the criminal justice system
will follow, be it in legal doctrine or in legal administration. In any event, evaluation certainly
appears to be the purpose, and reform the expected outcome, of much empirical research.
This article pursues a different sort of yield
from its empirical study: a sociological theory of
law.[2] The analysis is self-consciously inattentive
to policy reform or evaluation of the police; it is
intentionally bloodless in tone. It examines arrest in order to infer patterns relevant to an understanding of all instances of legal control.

The empirical analysis queries how a number
of circumstances affect the probability of arrest.
The factors considered are: the suspect's race,
the legal seriousness of the alleged crime, the
evidence available in the field setting, the complainant's preference for police action, the social
relationship between the complainant and suspect, the suspect's degree of deference toward
the police, and the manner in which the police
come to handle an incident, whether in response
to a citizen's request or through their own initiative. The inquiry seeks to discover general principles according to which policemen routinely
use or withhold their power to arrest, and thus
to reveal a part of the social organization[3] of
arrest.

The article begins with a skeletal discussion of
the field method. Next follows a brief ethnography of routine police work designed to place
arrest within its mundane context. The findings
on arrest are then presented, first for encoun-

►SOURCE: *"The Social Organization of Arrest," Stanford Law Review* (June, 1971) 23:1087–1111. *Reprinted by permission.*

[1]*See generally* E. Schur, *Law and Society* (1968); Skolnick,
"The Sociology of Law in America: Overview and Trends,"
in *Law and Society* 4 (1965) (supplement to 13 *Social Problems*
(1965)); Bordua & Reiss, "Law Enforcement," in *The Uses of
Sociology* 275 (1967); Manning, "Observing the Police," in
Observing Deviance (J. Douglas ed., forthcoming). The empirical literature is so abundant and is expanding so rapidly that
these published bibliographic discussions are invariability
inadequate.

[2]It should be noted that the article's approach to legal life
differs quite radically from the approach of Philip Selznick,
one of the most influential American sociologists of law.
Selznick's sociology of law attempts to follow the path of
natural law; my approach follows the general direction of
legal positivism. In Lon Fuller's language, Selznick is willing
to tolerate a confusion of the *is* and *ought,* while I am not. L.

Fuller, *The Law in Quest of Itself* 5 (1940). *See* P. Selznick, *Law,
Society, and Industrial Justice* (1969); Selznick, "The Sociology
of Law," 9 *International Encyclopedia of the Social Sciences* 50
(D. L. Sills ed., 1968); Selznick, "Sociology and Natural
Law," 6 *Natural L.F.* 84 (1961).

[3]As used in this article, the broad concept "social organization" refers to the supraindividual principles and
mechanisms according to which social events come into being, are maintained and arranged, change, and go out of
existence. Put another way, social organization refers to the
descriptive grammar of social events. "Copyright 1971 by the
Board of Trustees of the Leland Stanford Junior University."

ters involving both a citizen complainant and a suspect, and second for police encounters with lone suspects. The article finally speculates about the implications of the empirical findings at the level of a general theory of legal control, the focus shifting from a sociology of the police to a sociology of law.

I. FIELD METHOD

The data were collected during the summer of 1966 by systematic observation of police-citizen transactions in Boston, Chicago, and Washington, D.C.[4] Thirty-six obervers—persons with law, social science, and police administration backgrounds—recorded observations of encounters between uniformed patrolmen and citizens. The observers' training and supervision was, for all practical purposes, identical in the three cities. Observers accompanied patrolmen on all work shifts on all days of the week for seven weeks in each city. Proportionately more of our manhours were devoted to times when police activity is comparatively high, namely evening shifts, and particularly weekend evenings. Hence, to a degree the sample over-represents the kinds of social disruptions that arise more on evenings and weekends than at other times. The police precincts chosen as observation sites in each city were selected to maximize scrutiny of lower socio-economic, high crime rate, racially homogeneous residential areas. Two precincts were used in both Boston and Chicago, and four precincts were used in Washington, D.C. The Washington, D.C., precincts, however, were more racially integ-

rated than were those in Boston and Chicago.

Observers recorded the data in "incident booklets," forms structurally similar to interview schedules. One booklet was used for each incident. A field situation involving police action was classified as an "incident" if it was brought to the officer's attention by the police radio system, or by a citizen on the street or in the police station, or if the officer himself noticed a situation and decided that it required police attention. Also included as incidents were a handful of situations which the police noticed themselves but which they chose to ignore.

The observers did not fill out incident booklets in the presence of policemen. In fact, the line officers were told that the research was not concerned with police behavior but only with citizen behavior toward the police and the kinds of problems citizens make for the police.

The observers recorded a total of 5,713 incidents, but the base for the present analysis is only a little more than 5 percent of the total. This attrition results primarily from the general absence of opportunities for arrest in patrol work, where most of the incidents involve non-criminal situations or criminal situations for which there is no suspect. Traffic encounters also were excluded, even though technically any traffic violation presents an opportunity for arrest. Other cases were eliminated because they involved factors that could invisibly distort or otherwise confuse the analysis. The encounters excluded were those initiated by citizens who walked into a police station to ask for help (6 percent of total) or who flagged down the police on the street (5 percent). These kinds of encounters involve peculiar situational features warranting separate treatment, though even that would be difficult, given their statistically negligible number. For similar reasons encounters involving participants of mixed race and mixed social-class status[5] were also eliminated. Finally, the sample of encounters excludes sus-

---

[4]At this writing, the data are over four years old. However, there has been little reform in routine patrol work since 1966. This is in part because the police work in question—everyday police contact with citizens—is not as amenable to planned change as other forms of police work, such as crowd or riot control, traffic regulation, or vice enforcement. Moreover, the data have value even if they no longer describe contemporary conduct, since they remain useful for developing a theory of law as a behavior system. A general theory of law has no time limits. Indeed, how fine it would be if we possessed more empirical data from legal life past.

[5]This means that encounters involving a complainant and suspect of different races were excluded. Similarly, the sample would not include the arrest of a black man with a white

pects under 18 years of age—legal juveniles in most states—and suspects of white-collar status.[6] Thus, it investigates arrest patterns in police encounters with predominantly blue-collar adult suspects.

II. ROUTINE POLICE WORK

In some respects, selecting arrest as a subject of study implicitly misrepresents routine police work. Too commonly, the routine is equated with the exercise of the arrest power, not only by members of the general public but by lawyers and even many policemen as well. In fact, the daily round of the patrol officer infrequently involves arrest[7] or even encounters with a criminal suspect. The most cursory observation of the policeman on the job overturns the imagery of a man who makes his living parcelling citizens into jail.

Modern police departments are geared to respond to citizen calls for service; the great majority of incidents the police handle arise when a citizen telephones the police and the dispatcher sends a patrol car to deal with the situation. The officer becomes implicated in a wide range of human troubles, most not of his own choosing, and many of which have little or

nothing to do with criminal law enforcement. He transports people to the hospital, writes reports of auto accidents, and arbitrates and mediates between disputants—neighbors, husbands and wives, landlords and tenants, and businessmen and customers. He takes missing-person reports, directs traffic, controls crowds at fires, writes dogbite reports, and identifies abandoned autos. He removes safety hazards from the streets, and occasionally scoops up a dead animal. Policemen disdain this kind of work, but they do it every day. Such incidents rarely result in arrest; they nevertheless comprise nearly half of the incidents uniformed patrolmen encounter in situations initiated by phone calls from citizens.[8] Policemen also spend much of their time with "juvenile trouble," a police category typically pertaining to distinctively youthful disturbances of adult peace—noisy groups of teenagers on a street corner, ball-playing in the street, trespassing or playing in deserted buildings or construction sites, and rock-throwing. These situations, too, rarely result in arrest. Some officers view handling juvenile trouble as work they do in the service of neighborhood grouches. The same may be said of ticketing parking violations in answer to citizen complaints. All these chores necessitate much unexciting paperwork.

Somewhat less than half of the encounters arising from a citizen telephone call have to do with a crime—a felony or a misdemeanor other than juvenile trouble. Yet even criminal incidents are so constituted situationally as to preclude arrest in the majority of cases, because no suspect is present when the police arrive at the scene. In 77 percent of the felony situations and in 51 percent of the misdemeanor situations the only major citizen participant is a complainant.[9]

---

wife. However, it does not mean the exclusion of encounters where the policeman and suspect were not of the same race.

[6]Because field observers occasionally had difficulty in judging the age or social class of a citizen, they were told to use a "don't know" category whenever they felt the danger of misclassification. Two broad categories of social class, blue-collar and white-collar, were employed. Since the precincts sampled were predominantly lower class, the observers labeled the vast majority of the citizen participants blue-collar. In fact, not enough white-collar cases were available for separate analysis. The small number of adults of ambiguous social class were combined with the blue-collar cases into a sample of "predominantly blue-collar" suspects. The observers probably were reasonably accurate in classifying suspects because the police frequently interviewed suspects about their age and occupation.

[7]In this article, "arrest" refers only to transportation of a suspect to a police station. It does not include the application of constraint in field settings, and it does not require formal booking of a suspect with a crime. *See* W. Lafave, *Arrest: The Decision to Take a Suspect into Custody* 4 (1965).

[8]D. Black, "Police Encounters and Social Organization: An Observation Study," 51–57, Dec. 15, 1968 (unpublished dissertation in Department of Sociology, University of Michigan). *See also* Cumming, Cumming, & Edell, "Policeman as Philosopher, Guide and Friend," 12 *Social Problems* 276 (1965).

[9]D. Black, *supra* note 8, at 94.

In a handful of other cases the only citizen present is an informant or bystander. When no suspect is available in the field setting, the typical official outcome is a crime report, the basic document from which official crime statistics are constructed and the operational prerequisite of further investigation by the detective division.

The minority of citizen-initiated crime encounters where a suspect is present when the police arrive is the appropriate base for a study of arrest. In the great majority of these suspect encounters a citizen complainant also takes part in the situational interaction, so any study of routine arrest must consider the complainant's role as well as those of the police officer and the suspect.[10]

Through their own discretionary authority, policemen occasionally initiate encounters that may be called *proactive* police work, as opposed to the *reactive,* citizen-initiated work that consumes the greater part of the average patrol officer's day.[11] On an evening shift (traditionally 4 p.m. to midnight) a typical work-load for a patrol car is six radio-dispatched encounters and one proactive encounter. The ratio of proactive encounters varies enormously by shift, day of week, patrol beat or territory, and number of cars on duty. An extremely busy weekend night could involve 20 dispatches to a single car. Under these rushed conditions the officers might not initiate any encounters on their own. At another time in another area a patrol car might receive no dispatches, but the officers might initiate as many as 8 or 10 encounters on the street. During the observation study only 13 percent of incidents came to police

attention without the assistance of citizens.[12] Still, most officers as well as citizens probably think of proactive policing as the form that epitomizes the police function.

The police-initiated encounter is a bald confrontation between state and citizen. Hardly ever does a citizen complainant take part in a proactive field encounter and then only if a policeman were to discover an incident of personal victimization or if a complainant were to step forth subsequent to the officer's initial encounter with a suspect. Moreover, the array of incidents policemen handle—their operational jurisdiction—is quite different when they have the discretion to select situations for attention compared to what it is when that discretion is lodged in citizens. In reactive police work they are servants of the public, with one consequence being that the social troubles they oversee often have little if anything to do with the criminal law. Arrest is usually a situational impossibility. In proactive policing the officer is more a public guardian and the operational jurisdiction is a police choice; the only limits are in law and in departmental policy. In proactive police work, arrest is totally a matter of the officer's own making. Yet the reality of proactive police work has an ironic quality about it. The organization of crime in time and space deprives policemen on free patrol of legally serious arrests. Most felonies occur in off-street settings and must be detected by citizens. Even those that occur in a visible public place usually escape the policemen's ken. When the police have an opportunity to initiate an encounter, the occasion is more likely than not a traffic violation. Traffic violations comprise the majority of proactive encounters, and most of the remainder concern minor "disturbances of the peace."[13] In short, where

[10]In fact, of all the felony cases the police handle in response to a citizen request by telephone, including cases where only a complainant, informant, or bystander is present in the situation, a mere 3% involve a police transaction with a lone suspect. D. Black, *supra* note 8, at 94.

[11]The concepts "reactive" and "proactive" derive from the origins of individual action, the former referring to actions originating in the environment, the latter to those originating within the actor. *See* Murray, "Toward a Classification of Interactions," in *Toward a General Theory of Action* 434 (1967).

[12]This proportion is based upon the total sample of 5,713 incidents.

[13]Much proactive patrol work involves a drunken or disorderly person. Typically, however, arrest occurs in these cases only when the citizen is uncooperative; ordinarily the policeman begins his encounter by giving an order such as "Move on," "Take off," or "Take it easy." Arrest is an out-

the police role is most starkly aggressive in form, the substance is drably trivial, and legally trivial incidents provide practically all of the grist for arrest in proactive police operations.

Perhaps a study of arrest flatters the legal significance of the everyday police encounter. Still, even though arrest situations are uncommon in routine policing, invocation of the criminal process accounts for more formal-legal cases, more court trials and sanctions, more public controversies and conflicts than any other mechanism in the legal system. As a major occasion of legal control, then, arrest cries out for empirical study.[14]

III. COMPLAINANT AND SUSPECT

The police encounter involving both a suspect and a complainant is a microcosm of a total legal control system. In it are personified the state, the alleged threat to social order, and the citizenry. The complainant is to a police encounter what an interest group is to a legislature

come of interaction rather than a simple and direct response of an officer to what he observes as an official witness.

[14]Earlier observational studies have neglected patterns of arrest in the everyday work of uniformed patrolmen. Emphasis has instead been placed upon detective work, vice enforcement, policing of juveniles, and other comparatively marginal aspects of police control. *See* J. Skolnick, *Justice Without Trial* (1966) (patterns of arrest in vice enforcement); Bittner, "The Police on Skid-Row: A Study of Peace-Keeping, 32 *Am. Soc. Rev.* 699 (1967); Black & Reiss, "Police, Control of Juveniles," 35 *Am. Soc. Rev.* 63 (1970); Piliavin & Briar, "Police Encounters with Juveniles," 70 *Am. J. Soc.* 206 (1964). Several observational studies emphasizing other dimensions of police work also are directly relevant. *See* L. Tiffany, D. McIntyre, & D. Rotenberg, *Detection of Crime* (1967); Reiss & Black, "Interrogation and the Criminal Process," 374 *Annals of the Am. Academy of Pol. & Soc. Sci.* 47 (1967); Project, "Interrogations in New Haven: The Impact of Miranda," 76 *Yale L.J.* 1519 (1967). There also have been a number of studies based upon official arrest statistics. *See* N. Goldman, *The Differential Selection of Juvenile Offenders for Court Appearance* (1963); J. Wilson, *Varieties of Police Behavior* (1968); Green, "Race, Social Status, and Criminal Arrest," 173 35 *Am. Soc. Rev.* 476 (1970); Terry, "The Screening of Juvenile Offenders," 58 *J. Crim. L.C. & P. S.* (1967). For a more speculative discussion *see* Goldstein, "Police Discretion Not to Invoke the Criminal Process: Low-Visibility Decisions

or a plaintiff to a civil lawsuit. His presence makes a dramatic difference in police encounters, particularly if he assumes the role of situational lobbyist. This section will show, *inter alia,* that the fate of suspects rests nearly as much with complainants as it does with police officers themselves.

Of the 176 encounters involving both a complainant and a suspect a little over one-third were alleged to be felonies; the remainder were misdemeanors of one or another variety. Not surprisingly, the police make arrests more often in felony than in misdemeanor situations, but the difference is not as wide as might be expected. An arrest occurs in 58 percent of the felony encounters and in 44 percent of the misdemeanor encounters. The police, then, release roughly half of the persons they suspect of crimes. This strikingly low arrest rate requires explanation.[15]

A. Evidence

Factors other than the kind of evidence available to an officer in the field setting affect the probability of arrests, for even exceptionally clear situational evidence of criminal liability does not guarantee that arrest will follow a police encounter.

One of two major forms of evidence ordinarily is present when the police confront a suspect in the presence of a complainant: Either the police arrive at the setting in time to witness the offense, or a citizen—usually the complainant himself—gives testimony against the suspect. Only rarely is some other kind of evidence avail-

in the Administration of Justice," 69 *Yale, L.J.* 543 (1960). *See generally* W. Lafave, *supra* note 7.

[15]At this point a word should be said about the explanatory strategy to be followed in the analysis of data. The article's approach is radically behavioral or, more specifically, supramotivational, in that it seeks out supraindividual conditions with which the probability of arrest varies. Implicit in this strategy is a conception of arrest as a social event rather than as an individual event. The mental processes of the police and the citizens whose outward behavior our observers recorded are not important to this analysis. At this point the sole object is to delineate aspects of the social context of arrest as a variety of legal intervention.

able, such as a physical clue on the premises or on the suspect's person. On the other hand, in only three of the complainant-suspect encounters was situational evidence entirely absent. In these few cases the police acted upon what they knew from the original complaint as it was relayed to them by radio dispatch and upon what they heard about the crime from the complainant, but they had no other information apparent in the field situation linking the suspect to the alleged crime.

In a great majority of felony situations the best evidence accessible to the police is citizen testimony, whereas in misdemeanor situations the police generally witness the offense themselves. These evidentiary circumstances are roughly equivalent as far as the law of arrest is concerned, since the requirements for a misdemeanor arrest without a formal warrant are more stringent than are those for a felony arrest. In most jurisdictions the police must observe the offense or acquire a signed complaint before they may arrest a misdemeanor suspect in the field. In felony situations, however, they need only have "probable cause" or "reasonable grounds" to believe the suspect is guilty. Thus, though the evidence usually is stronger in misdemeanor than in felony situations, the law in effect compensates the police by giving them more power in the felony situations where they would otherwise be at a disadvantage. Correspondingly the law of arrest undermines the advantage felons in the aggregate would otherwise enjoy.

Table I indicates that the police do not use all the legal power they possess. They arrest only slightly over one-half of the felony suspects against whom testimonial evidence is present in the field encounter, although "probable cause" can be assumed to have been satisfied in nearly every such incident. Furthermore, during the observation study the police released 2 of the 6 felony suspects they observed in allegedly felonious activity. These two cases are noteworthy even though based upon a sample several times smaller than the other samples. In misdemeanor situations the arrest rate is about

Table I. Arrest Rates in Citizen-Initiated Encounters According to Type of Crime and Major Situational Evidence

Crime	Evidence	Total Number of Incidents	Arrest Rate in Percent
Felony	Police witness[a]	6	(4)[b]
	Citizen testimony	45	56
	Other evidence	1	(0)
	No evidence	0	(0)
Misdemeanor	Police witness[a]	52	65
	Citizen testimony	39	31
	Other evidence	0	(0)
	No evidence	3	(0)
All Crimes[c]	Police witness[a]	58	66
	Citizen testimony	84	44
	Other evidence	1	(0)
	No evidence	3	(0)

[a]This category includes all cases in which the police witness was supplemented by other types of evidence.

[b]Arrest rate figures in parentheses in this and later tables are used whenever the total number of incidents is statistically too small to justify making a generalized assertion of arrest rate.

[c]This excludes 30 cases for which the observer did not ascertain the character of the evidence. Thus the total is 146 cases.

two-thirds when the police observe the offense, while it drops to about one-third when the only evidence comes from a citizen's testimony. An evidentiary legal perspective alone, therefore, cannot account for differentials in police arrest practices. On the other hand, evidence is not irrelevant to arrest differentials. In none of the 3 cases where no evidence was available did the police make an arrest, and where the legal standing of the police was at best precarious—misdemeanor situations with citizen testimonial evidence—the arrest rate was relatively low.

B. The Complainant's Preference

While complainants frequently are present when policemen fail to invoke the law against suspects who are highly vulnerable to arrest, the complainants do not necessarily resent police leniency. In 24 percent of the misdemeanor situations and in 21 percent of the felony situations the complainant expresses to the police a preference for clemency toward the suspect.[16] The complainant manifests a preference for an arrest in 34 percent of the misdemeanors and in 48 percent of the felonies. In the remainder of encounters the complainant's preference is unclear; frequently the complainant's outward behavior is passive, especially in misdemeanor situations.

The findings in Table II indicate that police arrest practices, in both felony and misdemeanor situations, sharply reflect the complainant's preferences, whether they be compassionate or vindictive. In felony situations where a citizen's testimony links a suspect to the crime, arrest results in about three-fourths of the cases in which the complainant specifies a preference for that outcome. When the complainant prefers no arrest, the police go against his wishes in only about one-tenth of the cases. Passive or unexpressive complainants see the police arrest suspects in a little under two-thirds of the situations where the police have a complainant's testimonial evidence. Thus, when the complainant leaves the decision to arrest wholly in police hands, the police are by no means reluctant to arrest the felony suspect. They become strikingly reluctant only when a complainant exerts pressure on the suspect's behalf.

The findings for misdemeanor situations likewise show police compliance with the complainant's preference and also demonstrate the relevance of situational evidence to the suspect's fate. Encounters where the complainant outwardly prefers arrest and where the police observe the offense itself have an extremely high probability of arrest, 95 percent, a proportion somewhat higher than that for felony situations involving testimonial evidence alone. When the major situational evidence is citizen testimony against a misdemeanor suspect, the proportion drops to 70 percent. On the other hand, even when the police observe the offense, the arrest drops to less than one-fifth in those encounters where the complainant outwardly prefers leniency for his adversary. Plainly, therefore, the complainant's preference is a more powerful situational factor than evidence, though the two operate jointly. As might be expected, evidence is particularly consequential when the complainant expresses no clear preference for police action, and in those cases the suspect is almost twice as likely to be arrested when the police observe the offense as when the major evidence is the complainant's or another citizen's testimony. As noted above, however, the complainant does make his preference clear in the majority of encounters, and that preference appears to be strongly associated with the arrest rate.

C. Relational Distance

When police enter into an encounter involving both a complainant and a suspect they find themselves not only in a narrow legal conflict but also in a conflict between citizen adversaries within a social relationship—one between family members, acquaintances, neighbors, friends, business associates, or total strangers. The data in Table III suggest that police arrest practices vary with the relational nature of complainant-suspect conflicts. The probability of arrest is highest when the citizen adversaries have the most distant social relation to one another, i.e., when they are strangers. The felony cases especially reveal that arrest becomes more probable as the relational distance increases. Forty-five percent of suspects are arrested in a family member relationship, 77 percent in a friends, neighbors, acquaintances relationship, and 7 out of 8 or 88 percent in a stranger relationship.[17] In

[16]In such cases a complainant's preference is clear from his response to the question posed by the police. When police did not solicit the complainant's opinion, the observer classified the complainant's preference according to the audible or visible clues available to him. Some complainants made explicit demands upon the police; others appeared more confused and made no attempt to influence the outcome.

[17]Little confidence can be placed in findings based on less

Table II. Arrest Rates in Citizen-Initiated Encounters According to Type of Crime, Major Situational Evidence and Complainant's Preference

	Felony				Misdemeanor		
Evidence	Complainant's Preference	Total Number of Incidents	Arrest Rate in Percent	Evidence	Complainant's Preference	Total Number of Incidents	Arrest Rate in Percent
Police witness	Arrest	2	(1)	Police witness	Arrest	21	95
	Unclear	4	(3)		Unclear	23	52
	No arrest	0	(0)		No arrest	11	18
Citizen testimony	Arrest	23	74	Citizen testimony	Arrest	10	70
	Unclear	11	64		Unclear	15	27
	No arrest	11	9		No arrest	11	9
All felonies[a]	Arrest	25	72	All misdemeanors[b]	Arrest	31	87
	Unclear	15	67		Unclear	38	42
	No arrest	11	9		No arrest	22	14

[a] Excludes one case of "other evidence" and seven cases in which the observer did not ascertain the evidence.
[b] Excludes three cases of "no evidence" and 23 cases where the type of evidence was not ascertained.

Table III. Arrest Rates in Citizen-Initiated Encounters According to Type of Crime, Relational Tie Between Complainant and Suspect, and Complainant's Preference

Relational Tie	Felony			Misdemeanor		
	Complainant's Preference	Total Number of Incidents	Arrest Rate in Percent	Complainant's Preference	Total Number of Incidents	Arrest Rate in Percent
Family members	Prefers arrest	20	55	Prefers arrest	15	80
	Preference unclear	8	(0)	Preference unclear	13	38
	Prefers no arrest	10	0	Prefers no arrest	8	(0)
Friends, neighbors, acquaintances	Prefers arrest	5	(4)	Prefers arrest	11	64
	Preference unclear	8	(6)	Preference unclear	15	40
	Prefers no arrest	0	(0)	Prefers no arrest	20	5
Strangers	Prefers arrest	3	(3)	Prefers arrest	15	87
	Preference unclear	2	(2)	Preference unclear	15	47
	Prefers no arrest	3	(2)	Prefers no arrest	5	(0)
All family members		38	45		36	47
All friends, neighbors, acquaintances		13	77		46	30
All strangers		8	(7)		35	57

the misdemeanor cases the pattern is not so consistent. Although the likelihood of arrest is still highest in conflicts between strangers, the lowest likelihood is in situations involving friends, neighbors, or acquaintances. When the complainant's preference is unclear, or when he prefers no arrest, no difference of any significance is discernible across the categories of relational distance; the type of social conflict embodied in the police encounter visibly affects arrest probability only when the complainant presses the police to make an arrest.

D. Race, Respect, and the Complainant

Table IV demonstrates that police arrest blacks at a higher rate than whites. But no evidence supports the view that the police discriminate against blacks. Rather, the race differential seems to be a function of the relatively higher rate at which black suspects display disrespect toward the police. When the arrest rate for respectful black suspects is compared to that for respectful whites, no difference is apparent. Before examining this last finding in detail, however, the importance of citizen respect in itself should be established.

Considering felony and misdemeanor situations together, the arrest rate for very deferential suspects is 40 percent of 10 cases. For civil suspects it is effectively the same at 42 percent of 71 cases, but it is 70 percent of 37 cases for antagonistic or disrespectful suspects.[18] Unquestionably, the suspect who refuses to defer to

Table IV. Arrest Rates in Citizen-Initiated Encounters According to Type of Crime and Race of Suspect

Crime	Race	Total Number of Incidents	Arrest Rate in Percent
Felony	Black	48	60
	White	11	45
Misdemeanor	Black	75	47
	White	42	38
All Crimes	Black	123	52
	White	53	39

police authority takes a gamble with his freedom. This pattern persists in felony and misdemeanor situations when they are examined separately, but the small samples that result from dividing the data by type of crime prevent any more refined comparison than between civil and disrespectful levels of deference. The police make an arrest in 40 percent of the 25 felony encounters in which the suspect is civil, as compared to 69 percent of the he 16 felony encounters in which is disrespectful. In misdemeanor situations the corresponding proportions are 43 percent of 46 cases and 71 percent of 21 cases. In the aggregate of cases, the police are more likely to arrest a misdemeanor suspect who is disrespectful toward them than a felony suspect who is civil. In this sense the police enforce their authority more severely than they enforce the law.

The complainant's preference can erode the impact of the suspect's degree of respect somewhat, but when complainant's preference is held constant, the pattern remains, as Table V shows. When the complainant expresses a preference for arrest of his adversary, the police comply more readily if the suspect is disrespectful

than 10 cases. Nevertheless, the article occasionally mentions such findings when they are strikingly consistent with patterns seen in the larger samples. In no instance, however, do broader generalizations rest upon these inadequate statistical bases.

[18]The observers classifed a suspect's degree of deference on the basis of whatever clues they could cull from his behavior. The observers undoubtedly made classificatory errors from time to time since some suspects, particularly some disrespectful suspects, could be extremely subtle in their communicative demeanor. Some, for example, were exceedingly deferential as a way of ridiculing the police. In the great majority of cases, however, the classifications accu-

rately described the outward behavior to which the police were relating. Of course, the suspects' *feelings* were not necessarily reflected in their behavior.

rather than civil toward them. Table V also reveals that, when the complainant desires an arrest and the suspect is civil, the probability of arrest for black and white suspects is almost exactly equal, but black suspects are disrespectful toward the police more often than are whites, a pattern that operates to increase disproportionately the overall black arrest rate.

When the complainant's preference is unclear the degree of deference of the suspect is espe-

Table V. Arrest Rates in Citizen-Initiated Encounters According to Complainant's Preference, Suspect's Race, and Degree of Deference

Race	Suspect's Deference	Total Number of Incidents	Arrest Rate in Percent
Complainant Prefers Arrest			
Black	Very deferential	2	(2)
	Civil	19	68
	Antagonistic	12	83
White	Very deferential	1	(1)
	Civil	15	67
	Antagonistic	4	(2)
Both Races[a]	Very deferential	3	(3)
	Civil	34	68
	Antagonistic	16	75
Complainant's Preference Is Unclear			
Black	Very deferential	2	(0)
	Civil	18	33
	Antagonistic	15	93
White	Very deferential	1	(1)
	Civil	7	(2)
	Antagonistic	3	(1)
Both Races[b]	Very deferential	3	(1)
	Civil	25	32
	Antagonistic	18	83
Complainant Prefers No Arrest			
Black	Very Deferential	3	(0)
	Civil	13	23
	Antagonistic	4	(1)
White	Very deferential	1	(0)
	Civil	6	(1)
	Antagonistic	1	(0)
Both Races[c]	Very deferential	4	(0)
	Civil	19	21
	Antagonistic	5	91)

[a] Excludes 16 cases for which the suspect's degree of deference was not ascertained.

[b] Excludes 15 cases for which the suspect's degree of deference was not ascertained.

[c] Excludes 18 cases for which the suspect's degree of deference was not ascertained.

cially consequential. The police arrest civil suspects in 32 percent of these cases, while they arrest disrespectful suspects in 83 percent of the cases. This difference is far wider than where the complainant expresses a preference for arrest (68 percent and 75 percent). Especially when the complainant is passive, the suspect carries his fate in his own hands. Under these circumstances blacks more than whites tend, to their own disadvantage, to be disrespectful toward the police.

The small sample of cases rules out a complete analysis of the encounters in which the complainant favors clemency for his adversary. The cases are only adequate for establishing that a civil suspect is less likely to be arrested under these conditions than when the complainant prefers arrest or expresses no preference. Although statistically negligible, it is noteworthy that 4 of the 5 disrespectful suspects were released by the police under these conditions. The evidence suggests that complainants have voices sufficiently persuasive in routine police encounters to save disrespectful suspects from arrest.

IV. ENCOUNTERS WITHOUT COMPLAINANTS

Police transactions with lone suspects comprise a minority of the encounters with adults, but they nevertheless carry a special significance to a description of police work. There is no complainant available to deflect the outcome, so the encounter is all between the polity and the accused. This kind of situation often arises when citizens call the police but refuse to identify themselves or when they identify themselves but fail to materialize when the police arrive. In these cases the police handle incidents, usually in public places, as the servants of unknown masters. Only rarely to the police themselves detect and act upon crime situations with no prompting from a concerned citizen. This section treats separately the citizen-initiated and the police-initiated encounters. With no complainant participating, the analysis contains fewer variables. Absent are the complainant's preference and the relational distance between complainant and suspect. Because the police rarely encounter felony suspects without the help of a complaining witness, the legal seriousness of the lone suspect's offense is likewise invariable: Nearly all police-initiated encounters involve misdemeanors. Finally, the situational evidence in the vast majority of lone-suspect encounters is a police officer's claim that he witnessed an offense. The size of the sample is too small to allow separate analysis of encounters resting upon other kinds of evidence or those apparently based only upon diffuse police suspicion. The analysis, therefore, is confined to the effect on arrest rates of suspect's race, the suspect's degree of respect for the police, and the type of police mobilization—i.e., whether a citizen or the police initiated the encounter.

A. Race, Respect, and the Lone Suspect

In 67 situations the police witnessed a misdemeanor after being called to the scene by a citizen's telephone request. They arrested a suspect in 49 percent of these cases. In another 45 situations the police witnessed a misdemeanor and entered into an encounter with a suspect wholly upon their own initiative. In these police-initiated encounters the arrest rate was somewhat higher—62 percent. Hence, the police seem a bit more severe when they act completely upon their own authority than when they respond to citizens' calls. Conversely, when a citizen calls the police but avoids the field situation, the officers match the citizen's seeming indifference with their own.

Table VI shows the arrest rates for blacks and whites in citizen- and police-initiated encounters where no complainant participated. Under both types of mobilization the police arrested blacks at a higher rate, though in police-initiated encounters the difference is statistically negligible, given the sample size. However, just as in encounters involving complainants, the race difference disappeared in lone-suspect encounters when the suspect's level of respect for the police was held constant, as Table VII shows.

In citizen-initiated encounters black suspects disproportionately show disrespect for the police, and the police reply with a high arrest rate—83 percent. They arrest only 36 percent of the civil black suspects, a rate comparable to that for civil white suspects, 29 percent (a difference of just one case of the 14 in the sample). Considering both races together in citizen-initiated en-

Table VI. Arrest Rates in Police Encounters with Suspects in Police-Witnessed Misdemeanor Situations Without Complainant Participation According to Type of Mobilization and Suspect's Race

Type of Mobilization	Race	Total Number of Incidents	Arrest Rate in Percent
Citizen-initiated	Black	43	58
	White	24	33
Police-initiated	Black	28	64
	White	17	59
All citizen-initiated encounters		67	49
All police-initiated encounters		45	62

Table VII. Arrest Rates in Police Encounters with Suspects in Police-Witnessed Misdemeanor Situations Without Complainant Participation According to Type of Mobilization, Suspect's Race, and Degree of Deference

		Citizen-Initiated Encounters		Police-Initiated Encounters	
Race	Suspect's Deference	Total Number of Incidents	Arrest Rate in Percent	Total Number of Incidents	Arrest Rate in Percent
Black	Very deferential	5	(0)	2	(1)
	Civil	14	36	13	69
	Antagonistic	18	83	10	70
White	Very deferential	3	(1)	1	(0)
	Civil	14	29	10	70
	Antagonistic	5	(3)	6	(1)
Both races[a]	Very deferential	8	(1)	3	(1)
	Civil	28	32	23	70
	Antagonistic	23	78	16	62

[a] Excludes 8 cases for which the suspect's degree of deference was not ascertained.
[b] Excludes 3 cases for which the suspect's degree of deference was not ascertained.

counters, disrespectful conduct toward the police clearly is highly determinative for a suspect whose illegal behavior is witnessed by the police. A display of respect for the officers, on the other hand, can overcome the suspect's evidentiary jeopardy.

Arrest practices differ to a degree in encounters the police initiate. While again arrest rates for civil blacks and civil whites are the same, no significant difference emerges between the vulnerability of civil suspects and that of suspects disrespectful toward the police. In other words, neither the race nor suspect's degree of respect has predictive effect on arrest rates in police-initiated encounters with misdemeanor suspects. The absence of variance in arrest rates for disrespectful and civil suspects is the major difference between police-initiated and citizen-initiated encounters. Moreover, it is the major anomaly in the findings presented in this article, one that might disappear if the sample of police-initiated encounters were larger.

V. GENERALIZATIONS

This section restates the major findings of this study in the form of empirical generalizations which should provide a manageable profile of police behavior in routine situations where arrest is a possibility. When appropriate, inferences are drawn from these materials to more abstract propositions at the level of a general theory of legal control. Arrest patterns may reveal broad principles according to which legal policy is defined, legal resources mobilized, and dispositions made.[19]

A. Mobilization

Most arrest situations arise through citizen rather than police initiative. In this sense, the criminal law is invoked in a manner not unlike that of private-law systems that are mobilized through a reactive process, depending upon the enterprise of citizen claimants in pursuit of their own interests. In criminal law as in other areas of public law, although the state has formal, proactive authority to bring legal actions, the average criminal matter is the product of a citizen complaint.

One implication of this pattern is that most criminal cases pass through a moral filter in the citizen population before the state assumes its enforcement role. A major portion of the responsibility for criminal-law enforcement is kept out of police hands. Much like courts in the realm of private law, the police operate as moral servants of the citizenry. A further implication of this pattern of reactive policing is that the deterrence function of the criminal process, to an important degree, depends upon citizen willingness to mobilize the criminal law, just as the deterrence function of private law depends so much upon citizen plaintiffs.[20] Sanctions cannot deter illegal behavior if the law lies dormant because of an inefficient mobilization process.[21] In this sense all legal systems rely to a great extent upon private citizens.

B. Complainants

Arrest practices sharply reflect the preferences of citizen complainants, particularly when the desire is

---

[19]These three functional foci of legal control—prescription, mobilization, and disposition—correspond roughly to the legislative, executive, and judicial dimensions of government, though they are useful in the analysis of subsystems of legal control as well as total systems. For instance, the police can be regarded as the major mobilization subsystem of the criminal justice system. Yet the police subsystem itself can be approached as a total system involving prescription, mobilization, and disposition subsystems. *Cf.* H. Lasswell, *The Decision Process* 2 (1956).

[20]Contemporary literature on deterrence is devoted primarily to the role of sanctions in criminal law. *See, e.g.,* Andenaes, "The General Preventive Effects of Punishment," 114 *U. Pa. L. Rev.* 949 (1966). *But see* R. Von Jhering, *The Struggle for Law* (1879).

[21]Roscoe Pound concludes that the contingent nature of legal mobilization is one of the major obstacles to the effectiveness of law as a social engineering device. *See* Pound, "The Limits of Effective Legal Action," 27 *Int'l J. Ethics* 150 (1917). *See also* H. Jones, *The Efficacy of Law* 21–26 (1969); Bohannan, "The Differing Realms of the Law, in *The Ethnography of Law* 33 (1965) (supplement to 67 *Am. Anthropologist* 33 (1965)).

for leniency and also, though less frequently, when the complainant demands arrest. The police are an instrument of the complainant, then, in two ways: Generally they handle what the complainant wants them to handle and they handle the matter in the way the complainant prescribes.

Often students of the police comment that a community has the kind of police it wants, as if the community outlines the police function by some sort of *de facto* legislative process.[22] That view is vague, if not mistaken. Instead, the police serve an atomized mass of complainants far more than they serve an organized community. The greater part of the police work-load is case-by-case, isolated contacts between individual policemen and individual complainants. In this sense the police serve a phantom master who dwells throughout the population, who is everywhere but nowhere at once. Because of this fact, the police are at once an easy yet elusive target for criticism. Their field work evades planned change, but as shifts occur in the desires of the atomized citizenry who call and direct the police, changes ripple into policemen's routine behavior.

The pattern of police compliance with complainants gives police work a radically democratic character. The result is not, however, uniform standards of justice, since the moral standards of complainants doubtlessly vary to some extent across the population. Indeed, by complying with complainants the police in effect perpetuate the moral diversity they encounter in the citizen mass.[23] In this respect again, a public-law system bears similarity to systems of private law.[24] Both types seem organized, visibly and invisibly, so as to give priority to the demands of their dispersed citizens. Whoever may prescribe the law and however the law is applied, many sovereigns call the law to action.[25] Public-law systems are peculiar in that their formal organization allows them to initiate and pursue cases without complainants as sponsors. Still, the reality of public-law systems such as the police belies their formal appearance. The citizenry continually undermines uniformity in public- as well as private-law enforcement. Perhaps democratic organization invariably jeopardizes uniformity in the application of legal controls.[26]

[22]*See, e.g.,* P. Slater, *The Pursuit of Loneliness: American Culture at the Breaking Point* 49 (1970).

[23]This generalization does not apply to proactive police operations such as vice control or street harassment, which seldom involve a citizen complainant. By definition, street harassment is the selective and abrasive attention directed at people who are, at best, marginally liable to arrest—for example, a police command to "move on" to a group of unconventional youths. Proactive policing may involve an attack on particular moral subcultures. *Compare* J. Clebert, *The Gypsies* 87–119 (1963), *with* Brown, "The Condemnation and Persecution of Hippies," *Trans-Action,* Sept. 1969 at 33, *and* W. Hagan, *Indian Police and Judges* (1966).

[24]*See* Pashukanis, "The General Theory of Law and Marxism" in *Soviet Legal Philosophy* III, (H. Babb transl. 1951).

[25]This is true historically as well; legal systems usually have made the citizen complainant the *sine qua non* of legal mobilization, except under circumstances posing a direct threat to political order. A well-known example was the Roman legal process, where even extreme forms of personal violence required the initiative of a complainant before government sanctions were imposed. *See generally* A. Lintott, *Violence in Republican Rome* (1968). A thory of legal control should treat as problematic the capacity and willingness of governments to initiate cases and sanction violators in the absence of an aggrieved citizen demanding justice. *See generally* S. Ranulf, *Moral Indignation and Middle Class Psychology: A Sociological Study* (1938).

[26]The norm of universalism reflected in systems of public law in advanced societies is a norm of impersonalism: The police are expected to enforce the law impersonally. But by giving complainants a strong role in the determination of outcomes, the police personalize the criminal law. This pattern allows fellow family members and friends to mobilize the police to handle their disputes with little danger that the police will impose standards foreign to their relationships. At the level of disputes between strangers, however, the same pattern of police compliance with complainants can, given moral diversity, result in a form of discriminatory enforcement. A law enforcement process that takes no account of the degree of intimacy between complainant and suspect may also upset the peculiar balance of close social relationships. *See* Kawashima, "Dispute Resolution in Contemporary Japan," in *Law In Japan: The Legal Order in a Changing Society* 41 (A. von Mehren ed. 1964).

C. Leniency

The police are lenient in their routine arrest practices; they use their arrest power less often than the law would allow. Legal leniency, however, is hardly peculiar to the police. Especially in the private-law sector[27] and also in other areas of public law,[28] the official process for redress of grievances is invoked less often than illegality is detected. Citizens and public officials display reluctance to wield legal power in immediate response to illegality, and a sociology of law must treat as problematic the fact that legal cases arise at all.

D. Evidence

Evidence is an important factor in arrest. The stronger the evidence in the field situation, the more likely is an arrest. When the police themselves witness a criminal offense they are more likely to arrest the suspect than when they only hear about the offense from a third party. Rarely do the police confront persons as suspects without some evidence; even more rarely are arrests unsupported by evidence. The importance of situational evidence hardly constitutes a major advance in knowledge. Evidence has a role in every legal process. It is the definition of evidence, not whether evidence is required, that differs across legal systems. It should be emphasized that even when the evidence against a suspect is very strong, the police frequently take action short of arrest. Evidence alone, then, is a necessary but not a sufficient basis for predicting invocation of the law.

E. Seriousness

The probability of arrest is higher in legally serious crime situations than in those of a relatively minor nature. This finding certainly is not unexpected, but it has theoretical significance. The police

[27]*See, e.g.,* Macaulay, "Non-Contractual Relations in Business: A Preliminary Study," 28 *Am. Soc. Rev.* 55 (1963).

[28]*See, e.g.,* M. Mileski, "Policing Slum Landlords: An Observation Study of Administrative Control," June 14, 1971 (unpublished dissertation in Department of Sociology, Yale University).

levy arrest as a sanction to correspond with the defined seriousness of the criminal event in much the same fashion as legislators and judges allocate punishments. The formal legal conception of arrest contrasts sharply with this practice by holding that arrest follows upon detection of any criminal act without distinguishing among levels of legal seriousness. Assuming the offender population is aware that arrest represents legislation and adjudication by police officers, arrest practices should contribute to deterrence of serious crime, for the perpetrator whose act is detected risks a greater likelihood of arrest as well as more severe punishment. The higher risk of arrest, once the suspect confronts the police, may help to offset the low probability of detection for some of the more serious crimes.[29]

F. Intimacy

The greater the relational distance between a complainant and a suspect, the greater is the likelihood of arrest. When a complainant demands the arrest of a suspect the police are most apt to comply if the adversaries are strangers. Arrest is less likely if they are friends, neighbors, or acquaintances, and it is least likely if they are family members. Policemen also write official crime reports according to the same differential.[30] Relational distance likewise appears to be a major factor in the probability of litigation in contract disputes[31] and other private-law contexts.[32] One

[29]*See* Black, "Production of Crime Rates," 35 *Am. Soc. Rev.* 733, 735 (1970) (remarks on detection differentials in police work).

[30]Black, *supra* note 29, at 740. Jerome Hall hypothesizes that relational distance influences the probability of criminal prosecution. J. Hall, *Theft, Law and Society* 318 (2d ed. 1952).

[31]Macaulay, *supra* note 27, at 56.

[32]For example, in Japan disputes that arise across rather than within communities are more likely to result in litigation. *See* Kawashima, *supra* note 26, at 45. In American chinatowns disputes that arise between Chinese and non-Chinese are far more likely to result in litigation than disputes between Chinese. *See* Grace, "Justice, Chinese Style," *Case & Com.,* Jan–Feb., 1970, at 50. The same is true of disputes between gypsies and non-gypsies as compared to disputes between gypsies. *See* J. Clebert, *supra* note 23, at 90. Likewise, in the United States in the first half of the 19th

may generalize that in all legal affairs relational distance between the adversaries affects the probability of formal litigation. If the generalization is true, it teaches that legal control may have comparatively little to do with the maintenance of order between and among intimates.

Yet the findings on relational distance in police arrest practices may merely reflect the fact that legal control operates only when sublegal control is unavailable.[33] The greater the relational distance, the less is the likelihood that sublegal mechanisms of control will operate. This proposition even seems a useful principle for understanding the increasing salience of legal control in social evolution.[34] Over time the drift of history delivers proportionately more and more strangers who need the law to hold them together and apart. Law seems to bespeak an absence of community, and law grows ever more prominent as the dissolution of community proceeds.[35]

century, crimes committed between Indians generally were left to the tribes. *See* F. Prucha, *American Indian Policy in the Formative Years: The Indian Trade and Intercourse Acts* 188–212 (1962). In medieval England the same sort of pattern obtained in the legal condition of the Jews. Ordinary English rules applied to legal dealings between Jews and the King and between Jews and Christians, but disputes between Jew and Jew were heard in Jewish tribunals and decided under Jewish law. *See* 1 F. Pollock & F. Maitland, *The History of English Law* 468–75 (2d ed. 1898).

[33]*See* L. Peattie, *The View from the Barrio* 54–62 (1968) (for a stark illustration of this pattern). *See generally* R. Pound, *Social Control Through Law* 18–25 (1942); S. Van Der Sprenkel, *Legal Institutions in Manchu China: A Sociological Analysis* (1962); Cohen, "Chinese Mediation on the Eve of Modernization," 54 *Calif. L. Rev.* 1201 (1966); Nader, "An Analysis of Zapotec Law Cases," 3 *Ethnology* 404 (1964); Nader & Metzger, "Conflict Resolution in Two Mexican Communities," 65 *Am. Anthropologist* 584 (1963); Schwartz, "Social Factors in the Development of Legal Control: A Case Study of Two Israeli Settlements," 63 *Yale L.J.* 471 (1954); notes 26, 30–31 *supra*.

[34]It is at this level that Pound posits his thesis concerning the priority of sublegal control. R. Pound, *supra* note 33, at 33. *See also* Fuller, "Two Principles of Human Association," 11 *Nomos* 3 (1969); Selznick, "Legal Institutions and Social Controls," 17 *Vand. L. Rev.* 79 (1963).

[35]*See* F. Tonnies, *Community and Society* 202 (C. Loomis transl. 1957).

G. Disrespect

The probability of arrest increases when a suspect is disrespectful toward the police. The same pattern appears in youth officer behavior,[36] patrol officer encounters with juveniles,[37] and in the use of illegal violence by the police.[38] Even disrespectful complainants receive a penalty of sorts from the police, as their complaints are less likely to receive official recognition.[39] In form, disrespect in a police encounter is much the same as "contempt" in a courtroom hearing. It is a rebellion against the processing system. Unlike the judge, however, the policeman has no special legal weapons in his arsenal for dealing with citizens who refuse to defer to his authority at a verbal or otherwise symbolic level. Perhaps as the legal system further differentiates, a crime of "contempt of police" will emerge. From a radically behavioral standpoint, indeed, this crime has already emerged; the question is when it will be formalized in the written law.

All legal control systems, not only the police and the judiciary, defend their own authority with energy and dispatch. To question or assault the legitimacy of a legal control process is to invite legal invocation, a sanction, or a more serious sanction, whatever is at issue in a given confrontation. Law seems to lash out at every revolt against its own integrity. Accordingly, it might be useful to consider disrespect toward a policeman to be a minor form of civil disorder, or revolution the highest form of disrespect.

H. Discrimination

No evidence exists to show that the police discriminate on the basis of race. The police arrest blacks at a comparatively high rate, but the difference between the races appears to result primarily from

[36]Piliavin & Briar, *supra* note 14, at 210.

[37]Black & Reiss, "Police Control of Juveniles," *supra* note 14, at 74–75.

[38]P. Chevigny, *Police Power: Police Abuses in New York City* 51–83 (1969); Reiss, "Police Brutality—Answers to Key Questions," *Trans-Action*, July–Aug., 1968, at 18; Westley, "Violence and the Police, 59 *Am. J. Soc.* 34 (1954).

[39]Black, *supra* note 29, at 742–44.

the greater rate at which blacks show disrespect for the police. The behavioral difference thus lies with the citizen participants, not the police.[40] This finding conflicts with some ideological conceptions of police work, but it is supported by the findings of several studies based upon direct observation of the police.[41] These findings should be taken as a caveat that in general improper or illegal behavior toward blacks does not in itself constitute evidence of discrimination towards blacks. A finding of discrimination or of nondiscrimination requires a comparative analysis of behavior toward each race with other variables such as level of respect held constant. No study of citizen opinions or perceptions[42] or of official statistics[43] can hold these variables constant.

[40]Of course, "discrimination" can be defined to include any *de facto* unequal treatment, regardless of its causes. *See* L. Mayhew, *Law and Equal Opportunity* 59–60 (1968). The evidence in the article simply indicates that blacks are treated differently not because they are blacks, but because they manifest other behavioral patterns, such as disrespect for the police, more frequently than whites. The question of why blacks disproportionately show disrespect for the police cannot be addressed with the observational data. We could speculate, for example, that in anticipation of harsh treatment blacks often behave disrespectfully toward the police, thereby setting in motion a pattern that confirms their expectations.

Despite the article's finding of nondiscrimination the police officers observed did reveal considerable prejudice in their attitudes toward blacks. *See generally* Black & Reiss, "Patterns of Behavior in Police and Citizen Transactions," in 2 *President's Commission on Law Enforcement and Administration of Justice, Studies in Crime and Law Enforcement in Major Metropolitan Areas* 132–39. *See also* Deutscher, "Words and Deeds, Social Science and Social Policy," 13 *Social Problems* 235 (1966).

[41]*See generally* W. Lafave, *supra* note 7; J. Skolnick, *supra* note 14, at 83–88; L. Tiffany, D. McIntyre, & D. Rotenberg, *supra* note 14; Piliavin & Briar, *supra* note 14 (despite innuendos to the contrary); Project, *supra* note 14, at 1645, n. 9. These studies do not report evidence of discrimination or fail altogether to mention race as an analytically important variable.

[42]*E.g.*, Werthman & Piliavin, "Gang Members and the Police," in *The Police: Six Sociological Essays* 56 (D. Bordua ed. 1967).

[43]*See* N. Goldman, *supra* note 14, at 45; J. Wilson, *supra* note 14, at 113; Green, *supra* note 14, at 481.

In closing this section it is important to note that the findings on racial discrimination by the police should not remotely suggest that law is oblivious to social rank. On the contrary, broader patterns in the form and substance of legal control seem at any one time to reflect and to perpetuate existing systems of social stratification. That the degradation of arrest is reserved primarily for the kinds of illegality committed by lower status citizens exemplifies this broader tendency of the law in action.

VI. CONCLUDING REMARKS

A major commitment of this article is to dislodge the discussion from its grounding in empirical findings and to raise the degree of abstraction to the level of general theory. Statements at this level ignore the boundaries and distinctions that ordinarily contain and constrain generalization about law as a social phonomenon. The various subsystems of law—criminal law, torts, contracts, constitutional law, family law, property law, criminal procedure, administrative law—are assumed to contain common elements. As if this aim were too faint-hearted, a general theory of legal control also seeks to discover patterns present in several functional dimensions of law: prescription, mobilization, and disposition; or, respectively, the articulation of legal policy, the engagement of legal cases by legal organizations, and the situational resolution of legal disputes. This sort of sociology of law shares with jurisprudence the inclusiveness of its subject matter. Each discipline acts upon a longing for a universal understanding of law. For each, the past shares the relevance of the present, and other legal systems illustrate our own. Unlike jurisprudence, however, sociology of law abjures problems of a normative character; unlike sociology of law, jurisprudence bypasses the ordeal of concrete description.

A closing note should state what the article has not done. Arrest might be examined from a number of other perspectives that have their own vocabulary suited to their own special kind of discourse. For example, arrest may usefully be conceived as one stage in an elaborate processing network, an assembly line of inputs and outputs. This technocratic metaphor has been popular in recent studies of the criminal justice system. Another perspective might see every arrest as a political event. When and how the arrest power is used says much about the nature of a political system and the quality of life within it. Then, too, arrest is part of a job. It is a role performance of a bureaucratic functionary. Police work may be contemplated as it arises from its rich occupational subculture with standards and values that policemen share and enforce among their peers. And every arrest is enveloped by the police bureaucracy. Not surprisingly, therefore, the arrest practices of individual officers are under some degree of surveillance from their superiors as well as their peers. Finally, a study of arrest can inform and benefit from the sociology of face-to-face interaction. The police encounter is a small group with its own morphology, its own dynamics. What happens in an encounter may have less to do with crime and law than with the demands of situational order, with social etiquette or the pressures of group size or spatial configuration. An arrest may be the only means available to a policeman bent on restoring order to a field situation, yet other times it is the surest way to undermine order by making a situation disintegrate.

Some encouragement may be taken from the development of social science to the point where a subject such as arrest can occasion so many diverse perspectives. Diversity of this degree, nevertheless, casts a film of arbitrariness over whatever theoretical framework is chosen. Although the many perspectives available to a study of arrest surely mirror the empirical nature of arrest itself, its theoretical identity is precarious and unstable. Here it is sanction and justice; there input, coercion, expectation, job, criterion, or gesture. Any single theoretical view of arrest is inevitably incomplete.

4. How Police Solve Crimes

PETER W. GREENWOOD
JAN M. CHAKEN
JOAN PETERSILIA
LINDA PRUSOFF

THE TYPICAL CLEARED CRIME ENTAILS ONLY A small number of investigative man-hours prior to clearance and that of the total working hours of an investigator, only a small proportion (7 percent in Kansas City) is devoted to activities that lead to clearing crimes. In addition, we know from Chaiken (1975) that most clearance rates of a police department are not correlated with the workload of investigators, when controlled for the workload of patrol officers; and from the work of Greenwood (1970) in New York City, that clearance rates of individual investigative units are not correlated with their workloads. These findings suggest the following hypotheses:

1. Many activities of investigators contribute little to the clearance of crimes.

2. Some characteristics of a crime itself, or of events surrounding the crime that are beyond the control of investigators, determine whether it will be cleared in most instances.

We will demonstrate the truth of the second hypothesis and, by implication, the truth of the

▶SOURCE: *The Criminal Investigation Process, Volume III: Observations and Analysis. Rand Corporation. Report to National Institute of Law Enforcement and Criminal Justice, Law Enforcement Assistance Administration, Department of Justice, # R–1778-DOJ (October, 1975), pp. 65–83. (Editorial adaptations.)*

first. Basically, we find that some crimes are easy to clear, with either no work by an investigator or with small amounts of routine administrative activity. The remaining crimes, which constitute the majority, are difficult, if not impossible, to solve, regardless of the efforts expended by the police. Some of these receive no attention by investigators, while others are pursued diligently. But the number of difficult crimes that are eventually cleared is so small, when they are compared to the number of cleared crimes that were easy to solve, that overall clearance statistics are little affected by the efforts devoted to them.

These findings lead to questions about the role of investigators and their contribution to achieving the goals of a police department that will be discussed.

For this analysis we selected samples of cleared crimes in six police departments and determined, by reading the case folders, how the crime was solved. In instances where the written documentation was inadequate for this determination, the investigator in charge of the case was interviewed. In all cases we accepted the department's determination of whether the crime was cleared or not. We defined the case to be "solved" at the point the police knew the identity of the perpetrator(s), even if additional work was needed to locate the perpetrators or to establish the facts needed to prove guilt in court.

At the start, we had no preconceived notions as to appropriate categories of answers to the question "How was this crime solved?" So we simply recorded all the facts, circumstances, actions, and evidence that had been used to solve the crime. At the same time, we did not know whether the organization of the department, the region of the country in which it was located, or the season of the year would be related to crime solution, so we began with a single type of crime, namely robbery, and collected data in four police departments: Berkeley, Los Angeles, Miami, and Washington, D.C. The months selected for study differed among departments. Within the selected months, crimes were listed according to the order in which they were reported to the police, and a systematic 50 percent sample of the cleared crimes was chosen for analysis.[1] The sample sizes are shown in Table I.

After reviewing these cases and concluding that there were no apparent geographical or temporal variations of relevance for this study, a sample of cleared crimes other than robbery was selected from a single police department: Long Beach, California. The crimes were categorized in accordance with the organization of investigative units in Long Beach: forgery/fraud, auto theft, theft, commercial burglary, residential burglary, robbery, felony morals, aggravated assault, and homicide. As in the case of the first four departments, we examined a systematic 50 percent sample of cleared cases reported during a given time period in Long Beach.

After analysis of these cases, it became apparent that many cleared cases fall into categories that can be identified from the Kansas City Case Assignment File without reading the case folders. Thus, rather than continuing to sample from the totality of cleared crimes, we processed the Case Assignment File so as to identify the subset of cleared cases for which it was necessary to examine the case folders in order to determine how the crime was solved. A 10 percent random sample of this subset was selected, and

[1]That is, every second cleared crime was chosen.

the case folders were read as in the other five departments.

To permit comparisons between data from Kansas City and data from the other police departments, the crimes in Kansas City were organized into the same categories as used previously, even though they did not correspond to the organizational structure in Kansas City.

DATA FROM FIRST FIVE DEPARTMENTS

From the incident reports and earlier studies it was obvious that for many crimes, the identiy of the suspect was available at the time of the first report to the responding patrolmen—i.e., the case was solved without any detective involvement. Therefore, our first step was to divide the cases into two categories: initial identification and no initial identification. *Initial identification* occurs when there is an arrest at the scene of the crime or when the information required for clearance is present in the crime report, i.e., a victim or witness either furnishes the name and address of a suspect or some uniquely linking evidence. If only a name or only an address is given, the case was not placed in this category. To be considered "uniquely linking," the evidence had to correlate directly with the suspect's name and address (e.g., an automobile license or an employee badge number). *No initial identification* includes all other cleared cases.

The results from tabulating the data in this manner are shown in Table II. From stealing credit cards to murder, the majority of cleared cases in our sample had both quickly identifiable and locatable suspect(s). With the exception of two crime types (robbery and auto theft), less than one-third of all cleared cases had no suspect immediately identifiable.

INITIAL IDENTIFICATION

In cases with initial identification, *investigator involvement* in case clearance is minimal, and therefore we say that the solution is, at best, "routine." Either the suspect is already ap-

Table I. Data Sources by Crime Type

| | Departments | | | |
| | First Four[a] | Long Beach[b] | Kansas City[c] | |
Crime Type	Sample Size	Sample Size	Sample Size	Total Cases
Forgery/fraud	—	22	14	312
Auto theft	—	19	7	432
Theft	—	10	10	828
Commercial burglary	—	10	10	372
Residential burglary	—	20	14	686
Robbery	5	—	10	349
	22			
	8			
	28			
Felony morals	—	11	9	178
Aggravated assault	—	10	11	716
Homicide	—	7	7	46
Total	63	109	92	3919

[a] Robbery data are from Los Angeles, Ca. (cleared cases reported in the Wilshire Area in July 1974); Berkeley, Ca. (cleared cases reported May/June 1974); Washington, D.C. (cleared cases reported October 1974); and Miami, Fla. (cleared cases reported 1973-1974).

[b] For all crime types except residential burglary, these data are cleared cases reported October 1974; residential burglary, cleared cases reported July/August 1974.

[c] Cleared cases reported May/November 1973.

Table II. Suspect Identification in Cleared Cases by Level of Investigative Effort

| | Routine: Initial Identification | | Possibly Nonroutine: No Initial Identification | | Total | |
Crime Type	%	N	%	N	%	N
Forgery/fraud	91	20	9	2	100	22
Auto theft	47	9	53	10	100	19
Theft	70	7	30	3	100	10
Commercial burglary	80	8	20	2	100	10
Residential burglary	80	16	20	4	100	20
Robbery	52	33	48	30	100	63
Felony morals	73	8	27	3	100	11
Aggravated assault	100	10	—	—	100	10
Homicide	43	3	57	4	100	7

SOURCE: Review of case folders for sample cases from Berkeley, Long Beach, Los Angeles, Miami, and Washington, D.C.

prehended (e.g., by arrest at scene of crime) or some clerical effort on the part of the detective is needed for apprehension (e.g., issuing a "want" to patrol officers to pick up a suspect completely identified by a victim, or contacting another agency to find out the name and address matching a particular automobile license number).

Table III displays the circumstances in which an initial identification was obtained. The first two categories ("patrol capture" and "held at scene by citizen") involve an arrest at the scene of the crime, either through patrol action or citizen involvement. This method of solution occurs with particular frequency in cleared cases of commercial burglary. Typically, a patrol in the immediate vicinity of a just-activated burglar alarm is able to respond quickly enough to catch the suspects.

Most solved cases of residential burglary, felony morals, and aggravated assault are solved because a victim or witness knows who and where the suspect is (see Table III). In residential burglaries, for example, an estranged husband removes property from his wife's home, or a roommate moves out and takes some of the

other person's furniture. In aggravated assault and felony morals, the suspect and victim are usually acquainted—many times they are actually related or at least living together. In the former crime type, a father may beat his son, or vice versa. In the latter, a mother may report her husband or boyfriend for having sexual relations with her child.

Cleared forgery/fraud cases are most frequently solved by use of uniquely linking evidence, as shown in Table III. In such cases the suspect typically signs a personal check against either a closed account or insufficient funds. The uniquely linking evidence is the identification presented by the suspect when he cashes the check, corroborated when a handwriting expert matches the signature on the check to the signature on the suspect's driver's license.

NO INITIAL IDENTIFICATION

We now look at the possibly nonroutine cases, i.e., those cases in which a suspect is not identified in the initial crime report and which may therefore require action by the investigator to solve. Several types of effort are involved in the

Table III. Initial Identification: Method of Solution

Crime Type	Patrol Capture %	Patrol Capture N	Held at Scene (by Citizen) %	Held at Scene (by Citizen) N	Complete ID by V/W %	Complete ID by V/W N	Uniquely Linking Evidence %	Uniquely Linking Evidence N	Total %	Total N
Forgery/fraud	5	1	14	3	9	2	64	14	91	20
Auto theft	26	5	—	—	16	3	5	1	47	9
Theft	30	3	—	—	20	2	20	2	70	7
Commercial burglary	70	7	—	—	10	1	—	—	80	8
Residential burglary	10	2	5	1	40	8	25	5	80	16
Robbery	13	8	5	3	21	13	14	9	52	33
Felony morals	9	1	—	—	55	6	9	1	73	8
Aggravated assault	40	4	—	—	50	5	10	1	100	10
Homicide	—	—	—	—	29	2	14	1	43	3

NOTE: Percentages may not add to total because of rounding error.

SOURCE: Review of case folders for sample cases from Berkeley, Los Angeles, Long Beach, Miami, and Washington, D.C.

solution to these cases. In some instances, the investigator has only to follow obvious leads to solve the crime. For example, the disgruntled wife of a burglar notifies the police that her husband committed this crime and that he and the stolen goods can be found at his girlfriend's house.[2] In yet other instances, what might be an inherently difficult if not impossible crime to solve is solved because of certain procedures that the department has adopted. For example, mug shot files are organized and maintained in such a way that the victim is able to make *cold hits*. Or, the department has computerized information about stolen cars, allowing a *spontaneous* solution to cases when a stolen car is spotted. Or, the department holds daily briefings and lineups concerning recent crimes, criminals, and their methods of operation (MO), allowing investigator recognition of MO on some cases without an initially identifiable suspect. In these types of cases, investigator action is characterized as "routine," even though the actions involved may be routine only to an investigator. The solution to all other cases involves "nonroutine" investigative effort.

Table IV examines the principal method of solution for crimes in which there is no initial identification of the suspect. The categories of solution are discussed below. Keep in mind that the labels for the routine cases are not in and of themselves routine. That is, the use of fingerprints to solve a case does not mean that the case is routinely solved. What we considered was *how* the fingerprints were used. In the following discussion, this distinction should become clear.

Fingerprints

In one instance, the victim named the person he believed responsible for the crime, and gave reasons for his suspicion. Although the suspect could not be found, his fingerprints (on file because of a previous record) were matched with those found at the scene of the crime, and on

this basis alone, the case was cleared. This case was classified as routine because only routine processing of the latent prints was necessary for case solution. Any instance where a fingerprint match is made from a cold search, for example, is classified as "special action," described below.

Tip

Although investigators often speak of "their informants" as being essential to their work in solving crimes, the cases we examined did not bear this out.[3] It may very well be that for these classes of crimes, informers are not used at all, or are not used with any great frequency.

In the single robbery case from our sample that falls into the category of "tips," the informant was a citizen volunteering information about a crime he witnessed rather than a person "cultivated" as an informant (and perhaps paid) by robbery investigators. The homicide cases in our sample were closed on the basis of anonymous callers identifying the culprit. In one instance, three years after the murder, an informant called a newspaper that had a "citizen alert" program and revealed the murderer's identity. The other anonymous call was made unsolicited to the police station, the caller's motive possibly revenge.

Mug Shot/Lineup

For crimes that were cleared, this investigative method appeared to be the most significant in closing cases in such crime categories as theft and robbery. It involves several different kinds of actions, requiring differing degrees of investigative involvement.

In one-fourth of these cases, the investigator recognized a familiar MO, and on that basis, pulled mug shots that enabled positive identification of the suspect. Other cases were cleared because the suspect was arrested and on the basis of that arrest, his mug shots were shown to victims of similar crimes in the hopes

---

[2]We categorize the solution to this case as a tip. See the more detailed discussion that follows.

[3]However, the sample size is not large enough to assert that informants are not used.

Table IV. No Initial Identification: Method of Solution

Crime Type	Routine — Prints		Routine — Tip		Routine — Mug Shot/Other Picture or Lineup		Routine — M.O. (only)		Routine — Spontaneous		Unrelated Interrogation		Nonroutine Special Action		Unknown[a]		Total	
	%	N	%	N	%	N	%	N	%	N	%	N	%	N	%	N	%	N
Forgery/fraud	—	—	—	—	9	2	—	—	—	—	—	—	—	—	—	—	9	2
Auto theft	—	—	—	—	—	—	—	—	47	9	5	1	—	—	—	—	53	10
Theft	—	—	—	—	30	3	—	—	—	—	—	—	—	—	—	—	30	3
Commercial burglary	—	—	—	—	—	—	—	—	10	1	—	—	10	1	—	—	20	2
Residential burglary	5	1	—	—	—	—	—	—	15	3	—	—	—	—	—	—	20	4
Robbery	—	—	—	—	27	17	3	2	5	3	2	1	10	6	—	—	48	30
Felony morals	—	—	—	—	9	1	—	—	—	—	—	—	9	1	9	1	27	3
Aggravated assault	—	—	12	2	—	—	—	—	—	—	—	—	—	—	—	—	—	—
Homicide	—	—	—	—	6	1	—	—	—	—	6	1	—	—	—	—	23	4

SOURCE: Review of case folders for sample cases from Berkeley, Los Angeles, Long Beach, Miami, and Washington, D.C.

NOTE: Percentages may not add to 100 because of rounding error.

[a]The case file omits information on how the case is solved.

of making multiple clearances. Sometimes a "hit" was made from random showing of mug shots, and at other times, a victim or witness knew the name of a suspect, and if the suspect had a previous record, mug shots could be pulled for identification.

Sometimes a picture other than a mug shot was used. For example, in one case the victim believed he had seen the suspects at the school where he worked. The investigator had the victim leaf through a school yearbook, from which the victim positively identified the culprits. In another robbery case, a taxi driver identified his robber by accident. While reading the newspaper, he saw her picture, which had been published concerning another case.

Modus Operandi (MO)

Two robbery cases in the sample were cleared on the basis of matching MO. That is, an arrested suspect either admitted to other robberies or the case was cleared anyhow, because of similarities between the crime in the sample and the crime for which the suspect was arrested. It is certainly possible that the crime for which the suspect was originally arrested was solved through "special action" on the part of the investigator. However, we only looked at the crime that was part of the sample; in this case the solution was routine, regardless of how the original crime was solved.

Spontaneous Solution

In some of these cases, the property was located and *then* the case was cleared. Either the suspect was arrested on another charge, and subsequently found in possession of stolen goods, or an automobile was stopped because of a traffic violation and stolen property was found in the car. For the automobile theft cases in our sample, a suspect did not have to be found to clear the case; the case was sometimes cleared based on recovery of the automobile.

Some instances involved the victim's locating the suspect (at some point after the commission of the crime) and notifying the police. Either the

victim acted as his own investigator, carefully tracking down clues that led to the culprit, or the victim "accidentally" spotted his assailant and notified police.

Unrelated Interrogation

In these cases routine questioning of a suspect led to a confession. For example, in an auto theft case, a man took his damaged car to a repair shop and borrowed a loaner which he kept (having no money to retrieve his own car). Through an error, the loaner car was not on a hot list or in any information system, even though the owner reported it stolen. After being stopped for a traffic violation and asked for the vehicle registration, the suspect admitted that it was not his car.

Special Action

All cases requiring more than procedural investigative skills are classified as needing "special action" for solution. Even these cases fail to read like the classic detective stories of popular fiction because even when extraordinary effort or initiative is required, the case is usually solved in a short time. Persistence is to be found in only the more sensational homicides.

A store owner reports the theft of two guns valued at over $200. The guns were locked away in a special place in the store—and the owner suspects someone, Y, who had been to the store many times without buying anything, and who knew about the guns. Y's prints are lifted from a window broken to gain entry to the store. A check of the neighborhood points to a nearby gas station where Y is known to hang out. Here he conducts his "business," offering to sell certain goods (e.g., calculators) cheaply. The police set Y up by having an undercover man pretend to be interested in buying guns; Y offers to sell the hot guns. The goods are recovered, and Y arrested.

Other cases require less complex actions. For example, a robbery was committed in which the suspect had a very distinctive hairdo and facial features. The investigator put out a bulletin to patrol units with the suspect's description; several days later a patrol unit picked up the suspect within a few blocks of the crime. Although this case certainly illustrates the results of good interaction between investigator and patrol units, it is also an example of investigator initiative.

The data in Table IV suggest that when there is no initial identification of the suspect, most cases are solved either because the solution is obvious or because the department has developed procedures that have "routinized" methods of suspect identification.

DATA FROM KANSAS CITY

When we analyzed the Long Beach data for crimes other than robbery, we found no special action cases whatsoever in our sample for several crime categories. While this permitted us to conclude that special action cases are uncommon, the sample sizes in any single crime category were sufficiently small that no very precise estimates could be obtained of how often special action cases occur. For example, in the theft category there is a reasonable chance (better than 1 in 20) that over one-quarter of the Long Beach clearances could be special action despite the fact that none appeared in the sample.

To obtain better estimates, a larger sample would be required. In addition, if some special action cases appeared in a larger sample, we would then have some idea of their characteristics. However, the process of selecting a sample, retrieving the appropriate case folders, and reading the files (plus interviewing the investigator when necessary) was sufficiently time-consuming that we were unable to continue sampling from the totality of cases. Instead, we developed a method for processing the Kansas City Case Assignment File so as to separate out cleared cases that were extremely unlikely to involve any special action. Then we sampled cases from the remaining group, thereby enhancing the probability that cases of special action would be found in the sample. The sampling design is illustrated in Fig. 1.

Basically, three types of cases were assumed

to fall into the routine category (i.e., *not* special action) based on the information in the computer file. Type 1 consisted of incidents that appeared in the file with a clearance credited to the patrol force on the first day the detective worked on the case. Many of these clearances were recorded on the same day that the crime was reported, and therefore were very likely to represent on-scene arrests by patrol officers.[4] In addition to these, the Type 1 cases include some later patrol arrests (based perhaps on pickups issued by a detective) that were assumed to be routine because the detective did not record any time spent on the case prior to the arrest.

Type 2 consisted of a small number of incidents cleared by patrol after a detective had worked on the case, suspended activity for 30 days or more, and did not work on the case again until the arrest was made. These were assumed to represent "spontaneous" solutions, which have been described above.

Type 3 consisted of incidents that were cleared by an investigator with little work. We defined the amount of work to be "little" if two hours or less were spent on all activities other than arrest processing, court and prosecutor time, and writing reports; this includes time spent after arrest as well as before arrest.

After these three types of cases were eliminated, 24.6 percent of the incidents remained as "possibly nonroutine." We selected a random 10 percent sample from this group and reviewed the case folders. The resulting sample sizes have already been displayed in Table I.[5]

After the sample was chosen, we found that some on-scene patrol arrests had been errone-

[4]The file does not have a code for "on-scene arrest," but we assumed that clearances by patrol recorded on the date the crime was reported were on-scene arrests. To the extent that a few instances of fast investigative work, coupled with good interaction between the detective and a patrol officer, were erroneously included in this category, they are counterbalanced by on-scene arrests that happened not to be recorded until the next day and therefore failed to be categorized as on-scene arrests.

[5]In a random 10 percent sample, each incident has one chance in 10 of being selected, but it will not necessarily

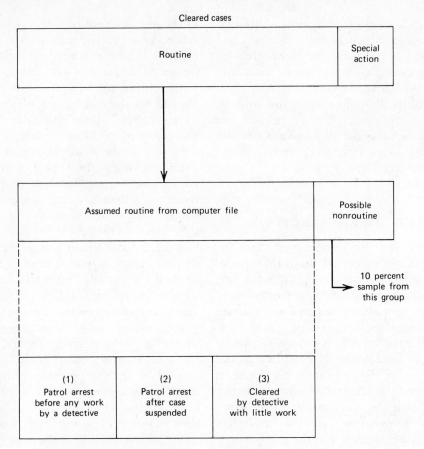

Figure 1. Schematic representation of sampling design in Kansas City.

ously classified as "possibly nonroutine," based on incorrect entries in the data file. We therefore adjusted our estimates of the number of "possibly nonroutine" cases downward slightly, resulting in the figures shown in Table V. In this table, Type 1 and Type 2 cases have been coalesced into a single column labled "patrol clearances."

The table not only summarizes the number of cases in the groups from which we sampled in Kansas City, but also indicates the extent to which patrol officers contribute to clearances in each crime category. Overall, 50.5 percent of

clearances were produced by patrol officers, of which 9.5 percent (or 4.8 percent of all clearances) involved a half-hour or more of work by a detective that may have led to the patrol arrest.

After reading the case folders, two special action cases were found in the sampled robberies, two in the commercial burglaries, and one in the homicides; no special action cases were found in the other six categories. Thus, we did not succeed in finding examples of special action cases in crime categories where none were found in Long Beach. However, the sampling design in Kansas City did permit obtaining better statistical limits on the maximum fraction of cases that could be special action, as shown in Table VI. Two estimates of the percentage of cleared cases that are special action are shown in the table: (a)

happen that the sample size is exactly one-tenth of the number from which the sample is taken. In this case, 92 cases were selected out of 963.

Table V. Level of Investigator Effect

Crime Type	Assumed Routine from Computer File						Possibly Nonroutine						Total	
	Patrol Clearances		Investigator Clearances		Total		Patrol Clearances		Investigator Clearances		Total			
	%	N	%	N	%	N	%	N	%	N	%	N	%	N
Forgery/fraud	42.0	131	27.9	87	69.9	218	9.3	29	20.8	65	30.1	94	100	312
Auto theft	48.6	210	31.5	136	80.1	346	4.6	20	15.3	66	19.9	86	100	432
Theft	54.5	452	33.1	274	87.7	726	3.3	27	9.1	75	12.3	102	100	828
Commercial burglary	33.6	125	41.9	156	75.5	281	4.6	17	19.9	74	24.4	91	100	372
Residential burglary	43.7	300[a]	37.6	258	81.3	558[a]	1.3	10[a]	17.2	118	18.5	127[a]	100	686
Robbery	40.7	142[a]	29.2	102	69.9	244[a]	4.0	14[a]	26.1	91	30.1	105[a]	100	349
Felony morals	30.3	54	18.5	33	48.8	87	11.2	20	39.9	71	51.1	91	100	178
Aggravated assault	50.7	363[a]	26.1	187	76.8	550[a]	6.1	43[a]	17.2	123	23.3	167[a]	100	716
Homicide	28.3	13		—	28.3	13	15.2	7	56.5	26	71.7	33	100	46
Total	45.7	1790[a]	31.5	1233	77.2	3023[a]	4.8	187[a]	18.1	709	22.9	896[a]	100	3919

NOTE: Numbers may not add to 100 because of rounding error.

[a] Estimated number. These numbers were adjusted after some cases sampled from the "possibly nonroutine" category were found to have been arrests by patrol at the scene of the crime.

67

the best estimate based on the sample design,[6] and (b) the maximum estimate with 95 percent confidence.[7]

We see from Table VI that in Kansas City, at most 2.7 percent of cleared crimes are solved by special action. (The maximum estimate for the total is smaller than the maximum estimate for any one of the crime types, because the total sample size was comparatively large, namely 92.) Moreover, the estimates are now sharp enough for us to distinguish certain crime types as being substantially less likely than others to be solved by special action. These are forgery/fraud, automobile theft, theft, residential burglary, and aggravated assault, all of which have less than 7 percent solved by special action in Kansas City. Commercial burglaries, robberies, felony morals, and particularly homicides may be somewhat more amenable to solution by nonroutine actions. However, even in these categories the typical crime was solved routinely.

Table VI also reveals a striking similarity in the findings for Kansas City as compared to the other five departments, despite the differences among cities and sample designs. Indeed, in every instance the sample estimate from the first five departments falls well within the maximum estimate for Kansas City, so there is no statistically significant difference between the two sets of estimates.

[6]If a sample of size S is taken from the totality of all cases of a given crime type, and A special action cases are found, the sample estimate is simply $100 \times A/S$. (The number 100 converts a fraction to a percent.) In the design used in Kansas City, a sample S is taken from n "possibly nonroutine" cases out of a total of N, and the sample estimate is then $100 \times (A/S) \times (n/N)$.

[7]Suppose no special action cases are found in a sample of size S taken from n cases. If p is the true fraction of special action cases, the probability of finding none of them in the sample is $(1 - p)S$. Thus, p could be as large as $P = 1 - (0.05)1/S$, and we would still have a 5 percent chance of finding none of them in the sample. The "maximum estimate with 95 percent confidence" is thus $100 \times P \times n/N$. (For the first five departments, N = n; for Kansas City, N is the total number of cleared incidents of the crime type in question.) A similar calculation can be performed if one special action case is found in the sample, etc.

The sample design in Kansas City also permits us to obtain rough estimates of the fraction of cleared cases that were solved by initial identification in Kansas City. We have already indicated how the number of on-scene arrests can be estimated directly from the computer file. To estimate roughly the number of cases with complete identification by victim or witness and the number with uniquely linking evidence, we used the proportions of such cases found in the sample and applied them to the collection of all cases other than on-scene arrest or special action, as shown in Fig. 2. This method should produce conservative (i.e., low) estimates for the fraction of cases with initial identification, since we did not sample from cases cleared by investigators with little work. Such cases are presumably more likely to involve an initial identification than the cases from which we did sample.

However, even these conservative estimates, shown in Table VII, yield approximately the same fraction of cases solved by initial identification as was found in the other five departments.[8] By comparison with Table III, the explanation appears to be that more cases are cleared by on-scene patrol arrest in Kansas City than in the other cities. In any event, the Kansas City data again confirm that the great majority of cleared crimes are solved because the identity of the perpetrator is already known when the crime report reaches the investigator. The main job for the investigator in these cases is to locate and apprehend the perpetrator, and to assemble evidence adequate to charge him.

TYPICAL CASES

We now discuss each of the crime types to give a clearer picture of routine and nonroutine cases. We begin with the crime types for which we were unable to find an example of a special ac-

[8]Using a chi-square test at the 0.05 level (wherever justified by the number of cases in a cell), there is no statistically significant difference between the percentage solved by initial identification in Kansas City and the percentage in other cities.

Table VI. Special Action Cases (Percent of all cleared cases)

| Crime Type | First Five Departments[a] | | Kansas City | |
	Sample Estimate	Maximum Estimate at 95% Confidence	Sample Estimate	Maximum Estimate at 95% Confidence
Forgery/fraud	0	12.7	0	5.7
Auto theft	0	14.6	0	6.9
Theft	0	25.9	0	3.2
Commercial burglary	10	39.4	4.9	12.4
Residential burglary	0	13.9	0	3.5
Robbery	9.5	15.6	7.1	16.6
Felony morals	9.1	36.4	0	14.5
Aggravated assault	0	25.9	0	5.9
Homicide	0	34.8	10.2	37.3
All Types[b]			1.3	2.7

[a] Los Angeles and Berkeley, Ca.; Washington, D.C.; Miami, Fla.; Long Beach, Ca.

[b] This figure is shown for Kansas City only and reflects the relative numbers of cleared cases of each type in that city.

Table VII. Method of Solution for Cleared cases (In percent)

Crime Type	Arrest at Scene	Complete ID by V/W	Uniquely Linking Evidence	Total Initial ID from Kansas City	Total Initial ID from Other Departments
Forgery/fraud	30.6	20.0	39.7	90.3	90.9
Auto theft	38.5	12.7	<7.8	>51.2[a]	47.4
Theft	48.4	8.6	17.2	74.2	70.0
Commercial burglary	24.4	16.9	16.9	58.2	80.0
Residential burglary	26.7	42.7	<6.2	>81.7[a]	80.0
Robbery	28.4	20.9	10.6	59.9	53.4
Felony morals	25.8	27.8	27.8	81.4	72.8
Aggravated assault	28.6	63.4	7.9	>94.1[a]	100.0
Homicide	28.3	34.8	10.9	74.0[a]	42.9

NOTE: Numbers may not add to total because of rounding error.

[a] If no cases of uniquely linking evidence were found in the sample, or no cases other than initial identification, 95% confidence points are shown.

tion solution in any of our samples: forgery/fraud, automobile theft, theft, residential burglary, and aggravated assault.

Forgery/Fraud

Typical forgery/fraud cases did not require investigative action to identify the perpetrator. Most cases involved the writing of bad checks.

Others involved hiring a cab without being able to pay the fare at the end of the ride, or eating in a restaurant without being able to pay the bill. In these instances and in some credit card frauds, the perpetrator was arrested at the scene of the crime.

Examples of those few cases that were solved without an initial identification include:

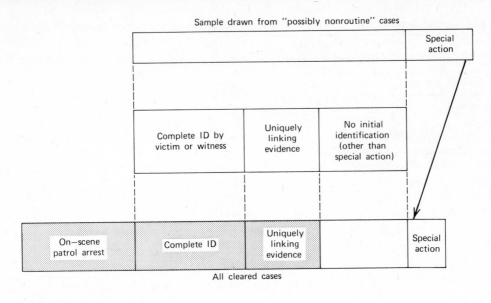

Sample drawn from "possibly nonroutine" cases

Figure 2. Schematic representation of method used to obtain conservative estimate of initial identification cases in Kansas City.

A furniture store owner lost over $400 because he accepted a check for which he provided goods and cash. The check later turned out to be stolen. The victim informed the police that he cashed the check because the perpetrator had been given an excellent credit reference from another furniture store. This credit reference was contacted and identified the perpetrator. Her mug shots were positively identified by the victim.

In a Jamaican Switch case, the only instance of bunco in our sample, the victim was convinced to give the suspects her money to hold, along with money of their own, so it would be safe. The bunco detective recognized the case as matching the MO in a quite similar case which was recently solved in a nearby jurisdiction. Mug shots were shown to the victim, who positively identified the suspects.[9]

In each of the above instances, no special in-

vestigative efforts were required to solve the crime, as would be required, for example, if the person forging a signature to the stolen check had given no credit reference, or if the bunco perpetrators had no previous record for the same crime in the same area.

Auto Theft

In auto theft cases solved through later identification, the culprit is usually identified when he is stopped in the stolen car by a patrol unit.

In one instance, the victim, George, reports his motorcycle stolen; he suspects X (and supplies his name and address), whom he previously refused the loan of his bike. X is in possession of missing bike. However, X claims that he did not steal the motorcycle, that he "rented" it from a third party, Y. X then shows the investigators a rental agreement drawn up between himself and Y, who is subsequently arrested.

It should be noted that although there are professional car thieves and lucrative auto theft rings, with one exception, these types of cases did not appear in our sample. The exception

---

[9]This is an example in which the monitoring of arrests in another jurisdiction pays off with a clearance. However, since the suspects were experienced con artists with extensive records, it is unlikely that linking them to this second offense will affect their prosecution.

involved an automobile ring that was broken when a gang member gained revenge (and, incidentally, immunity) by unsolicitedly informing on a wrecking yard owner who specialized in stolen cars.

Theft

For most cases in our sample, the suspect was easily identified: a man vacates his apartment, taking several hundred dollars worth of the landlord's furniture. He leaves his forwarding address with the electric company; the suspect is an estranged spouse; the suspect is either caught in the act or is observed leaving and an automobile license number is recorded. In cases were no initial identification was possible, the detective recognized the MO of the suspect and was thus able to provide mug shots for identification.

Residential Burlary

These cases appear more than any other to be mostly cleared by luck: first the stolen property is found (because the suspect is arrested on another charge or is stopped for careless driving and stolen goods are found in the car), and *then* the suspect is linked to the crime. The investigation, in other words, proceeds after the suspect is in custody. In other cases, either the victim or witness knows the suspect. In many of the instances where the victim knows the suspect, the victim refuses to prosecute.

Aggravated Assault

In these cases, victim and suspect either know each other, or, in the case of the strangers, the commotion is so loud and the struggle so obvious that the police are able to make an arrest at the crime scene. The former instance includes such cases as the victim is beaten by his neighbor, a tenant assaults his landlady, a bail bond company man is severely beaten by a client he attempts to arrest, a husband beats his wife, and a suspect having a feud with the victim's family allegedly damages the victim's car. Among the latter cases: a woman is assaulted in her home and the neighbors hear her screams and call the police; a husband beats his estanged wife and her boyfriend with a hammer; a brother shoots at his brother and sister-in-law; a man holds a knife to a victim's throat in a restaurant and threatens to kill her; a drunk man attempts to gouge out a policeman's eye.

For other crimes, we did find examples of investigator skill and initiative that led to case clearance. As Table VI shows, examples of these types of cases occurred infrequently. Even among those solved crimes characterized by relatively high (40 percent) later identification of the suspect (commercial burglary and robbery), *at the least,* half are routinely solved.[10] In homicide alone there is the *possibility* that investigator initiative solved the crime about 40 percent of the time.

What kinds of commercial burglary, robbery, felony morals, and homicide cases are cleared?

Commercial Burglary

Most cases are cleared because patrolmen are near a just-activated burglar alarm. An example of later identification is: a patrol responds to an alarm but is unable to catch the burglars in the store. A witness points out the apartment of these men, where they are subsequently found with the stolen goods. The suspects, however, are not charged since there is no direct evidence linking them to the crime.

One example of a nonroutine solution to a commercial burglary was given earlier. In another example, a grocery store is broken into and the suspect drinks a soft drink in the store and leaves the bottle on the floor. Latent fingerprints are lifted and a "hit" is made during a search of the known offender fingerprint file.

Robbery

Within the robbery detail, there is a wide range of types of cleared cases—from simple purse-

---

[10]For some crimes classified as routinely solved, investigators invested sometimes up to hundreds of hours in attempting to solve the crime. However, if these efforts did not result in a case clearance, and the suspect was identified, for example, by a tip, the case was classified as being routinely solved.

snatching to armed bank robbery, from cases where the victim suffers only momentary fear, to those where the victim is severely injured. Yet for the most part, clearance of these cases involves routine investigative procedures—either there is an initial identification, or the victim can describe the suspect well enough to identify him from mug shots. In many of the arrests at the scene of the crime, patrol units pick up the suspect from a broadcast description, or the suspect is pursued and trapped by the victim or witnesses until a patrol unit can arrive. In other self-solving cases, the victim either knows the perpetrator or has noted his automobile license number. Sometimes the perpetrator uses the victim's credit cards to buy gas and can thus be traced by the license number. In one instance a complainant, robbed by a suspect sitting in a parked car, gives police officers the license number and location of the car; the suspect is still sitting in the car when the officers arrive to make the arrest.

Examples of robberies demanding more than routine action for solution include a robbery/kidnapping in which the FBI was called in, a robbery with a severely battered victim, and a series of bank robberies perpetrated by a man with no prior record. The solution of each case demanded a variety of investigative measures, no one of which could have solved the case alone.

Felony Morals

In the typical cleared felony morals crime, the victim is physically abused by a relative or friend: a mother in hysterics reports that her boyfriend has engaged in some kind of sex play with her 4-year-old daughter; a wife reports her husband for having intercourse with their 12-year-old daughter; a woman reports that she was raped by a man she has known for seven years. Other cases involve indecent exposure: officers on patrol arrest a nude man in the street; two high school girls complain about a man who was exposing himself and yelling obscenities from his car. An investigator remembers the same MO (location, words, car),

and the man is positively identified by the girls from mug shots.

With the exception of the last mentioned case, which was solved when the officer remembered repetitive unusual behavior by a suspect previously booked for the same crime, the cases cited above are essentially self-solving. Certainly, the investigator typically engages in lengthy interrogation of witness and suspect (and the case file minutely details not only the type of offense committed, but also such subsidiary details as what clothes the victim was wearing and what the room looked like). However, the crime is, in effect, cleared before the investigator appears.

Homicide

Even with the thoroughness of investigative procedures described earlier, only one homicide case in our sample was cleared as a direct result of investigation into that particular crime. In their own way, each of the cases essentially solved itself—although some much sooner than others. In some instances, the murderer is identified to the police by knowledgeable informants shortly after the crime is committed; a girl confesses that she killed a man who raped her; a neighbor reports hearing a violent argument between a couple minutes before he responds to the calls of one, only to find him fatally stabbed; an escaped murderer kills his common-law wife (the mother of the victim reveals his past, and he is convicted of first-degree murder).

Other cases are solved by anonymous informants, often long after the case has been suspended because no further clues were available. In another, a juvenile arrested for robbery implicates a companion in a murder occurring several months earlier; and a man arrested for murder as a result of an independent investigation in part of the state, confesses to an unsolved murder in the southern part of the state, from where we drew the sample.

Other Observations

"Self-solving" crimes by definition become cleared crimes. Are the uncleared crimes, then, the more complicated cases?—the ones requiring the detailed inductive work that television has made so familiar? Although unsolved crimes are not within the province of this chapter, two cleared cases in our sample (which for years were unsolved) are suggested both of what types of cases remain unsolved and how "non-self-solving" crimes are finally cleared. In one case, citizen involvement becomes the necessary factor to case solution; in the other, investigator initiative.

THE CASE OF THE PERSISTENT PARENTS

A similar rape a year ago remained unsolved: a man in an orange sports car offers a ride to a 16-year-old waiting at a bus stop, asks her to ride in the back since the front seat is broken, soon threatens her with a carving knife, ties her hands and covers her head with a towel, takes her to his house and rapes her, then drives her around before releasing her. The police cruise the neighborhood with the victim in an attempt to find the house, but no luck.

Then, in the more recent case, the felony morals people recognize the MO but have no more success in locating the house where the rape occurred than in the previous case. In this instance, however, the parents of the victim are determined to catch the culprit. They persistently drive their daughter around the neighborhood, until she tentatively identifies the house. After locating the scene of the crime, the police are notified, inside the house find many clues described by the victim, and make an arrest. Mug shots are positively identified by both victims, and the man confesses. Thanks to the concerned parents, the case is closed.

THE CASE OF THE SMELLY RAPIST

For over two years, the "smelly rapist" had been victimizing women on the north side of town. With his now familiar MO, the felony morals detail knew when he was responsible for a rape, but they had thus far been unable to find him.

One evening, two investigators were dispatched to the scene of a burglary that had just occurred. One went to the apartment of the victim, while the other searched the vicinity for the suspect; he found a blue International pickup truck, similar to the vehicle described in numerous burglaries and rapes; the

radiator was still warm. After a short time, his partner returned to report that the victim had been attacked by a large man with a knife, who fled when she resisted the attempted rape. Both men then checked out the cab of the truck and noticed a strong personal odor, symptomatic of the "smelly rapist."

With these clues, the detectives decided to lift prints from the truck and from the apartment of the victim, and to stake out the vehicle until its owner returned. When the owner of the truck returned, the denouement of the 3-year-old case was swift: a knife found on the suspect matched that described by the victim, as did a mole on the back of his neck. Latents from the truck and apartment matched those of the suspect.

Both a state and an FBI check revealed the suspect had a long record of burglaries and rapes, with the MO always the same. During a lineup, the suspect was positively identified by several of his victims; upon interrogation even his wife implicated him.

We can only speculate as to whether more careful investigative work (e.g., fingerprinting) would have cracked the case sooner. Certainly, without the alertness of the officer and the stakeout that followed, this case might still be among the unsolvable.

CONCLUSIONS AND IMPLICATIONS

As these data have shown:

- In more than half of the cleared cases, the identification of the offender is available at the time of reporting.

- Most remaining cases that are eventually cleared are cleared through simple routine actions.

Given these findings, it is easy to see that clearance rates cannot be expected to vary substantially according to the organization of investigative units, the training and selection of investigators, whether they specialize by crime type or not, their workload, and other variables that were explored in our survey. With the possible exception of homicide, if investigators only performed the obvious and routine tasks needed to clear the "easy" cases, they would solve the vast majority of crimes that now get cleared. All their efforts in relation to other cases have a very marginal effect on the number of crimes cleared.

It is therefore not appropriate to view the investigator's role as that of solving crimes. Investigators do not spend much time on activities that lead to clearances, and most of their work in this connection could be performed by clerical personnel. Any justification for the work of investigators must lie in areas other than crime solution. Perhaps they perform a useful public service function. Perhaps their activities help to deter crime. Perhaps the care they exercise in recording evidence, processing prisoners, taking statements, and the like are vital for successful prosecution.

Our findings also highlight the importance of patrol officers in producing clearances. A substantial fraction of clearances are produced by patrol arrests at the scene of crimes. In other cases, it is the patrol officer who records the information that we labeled as "initial identification." The efforts that many departments are currently making to structure their crime reports so that this information is properly recorded appear to be highly desirable. Such information creates a routine case, out of one that would otherwise be difficult.

Technology has also converted many previously difficult investigative tasks into routine ones. The ability of patrol officers to check rapidly whether a car is stolen, or the driver is wanted, made possible many of the spontaneous clearances that we classified as routine. Well-organized and maintained mug shot or modus operandi files also helped produce routine clearances that either would never have occurred or would have been nonroutine in the absence of such files.

Finally, our review of these case folders persuaded us that actions by members of the public can strongly influence the outcome of cases. Sometimes private citizens, by ruse or restraint, hold the perpetrator at the scene of the crime. Sometimes they recognize the suspect or stolen property at a later time and call the investigator.[11] In other cases, of which we have given some examples, the victim or his relatives conducted a full-scale investigation on their own and eventually presented the investigator with a spontaneous solution. Collectively, these types of citizen involvement constitute a sizable fraction of cleared cases. We feel that many more cases would be solved if the public were made aware that they cannot depend on the police to solve cases magically but rather must provide the police with as much information as possible.

[11]Conversely, fear of retaliation or reluctance to prosecute neighbors causes some victims to offer almost no help to the police beyond their first call for help.

5. Field Interrogation

JOHN E. BOYDSTUN

I. PROJECT BACKGROUND AND OBJECTIVES

The Police Theory Behind Field Interrogations

ADVOCATES OF FIELD INTERROGATION [FI] PRAC-
tices feel that any police department that centers
its law enforcement activities only on responses
to crimes that have already been committed,
places itself in the position, not of preventing
crime, but merely of reacting to it. A vigorous FI
program, on the other hand, can deprive actual
and potential criminals of some of their initiative in selecting the time, place, and circumstances for the commission of crimes.

An FI program permits the immediate identification of those individuals who arouse the
suspicions of patrol officers. Sometimes the
identification process will result in the apprehension of known offenders, and more frequently it will provide the basis for an immediate reasonable-cause arrest. More important, however, the FI contact will emphasize to
potential offenders that the police are aware of
their specific identity, presence, and activity in
the community. Finally, an effective FI program
should help to reassure the general public that

▶SOURCE: *San Diego Field Interrogation, Final Report.
System Development Corporation. Washington: Police
Foundation, August, 1975. Pp. 7–9, 10, 11, 14, 15, 16,
19, 23–26, 27–28, 29, 30. (Editorial adaptations.) Reprinted by permission.*

the patrol officers are actively engaged in protecting law-abiding citizens and their property,
and are not simply waiting for a crime to occur.

A wide range of situational factors must be
interpreted to define what constitutes sufficient
suspicion for a patrol officer to conduct a Field
Interrogation. Basically, the FI decision rests on
the officer's subjective (sometimes intuitive)
conclusion that the appearance, demeanor, or
activities of the potential subject are not normal
for the particular time, place, and circumstances
under which they are observed. After a potential FI subject has been initially observed, the
final decision to question the subject is often
made on the basis of the subject's actions upon
first becoming aware of the patrol officer's presence and interests.

The questioning process itself may have three
outcomes: (1) if the subject's presence and activities are explained to the satisfaction of the
patrol officer, no record is made of the contact;
(2) questioning may result in identifying a
wanted person or in providing the grounds for
an immediate reasonable-cause arrest, in which
case an arrest report is completed but no FI report is made; and (3) the questioning may fail to
remove the officer's suspicions about the subject, but also fail to provide grounds for an immediate arrest, in which case a formal FI report
is made.

The theory behind documenting FI contacts
is simply that those individuals considered suspicious by the patrol officers who conducted the

Field Interrogations may also be likely candidates for suspicion by other police officers including, in particular, investigators. The FI reports provide positive identification of suspicious persons, their descriptions, and that of their associates and vehicles. The FI report also places the individual in a particular location at a specified time.

The theory behind not documenting contacts in which officer suspicion is removed is that it thereby precludes recording the names of innocent citizens in police department files.

The most common use of FI reports by investigators is to compare the descriptions of FI subjects and their vehicles with the description of suspects and vehicles given in crime reports. In addition, those persons stopped in the vicinity of crime locations at times close to those of crime occurrences may be investigated, whether or not the crime reports contained suspect descriptions.

The crime deterrent value of Field Interrogations is believed to result primarily from the potential offender's awareness that an FI encounter could be used to link the subject to any crimes the person might commit in the area. In addition, potential criminal offenders who have been FI subjects are made aware that they may be stopped, questioned, and possibly searched at any time in the FI areas. These potential stops might not only interfere with the commission of crimes, but could disclose incriminating evidence leading directly to arrest.

Communications among potential offenders about police FI practices is assumed to account for additional indirect deterrent effects. Such communications are believed to be particularly extensive among juvenile and young adult offenders, who tend to operate in small groups and who are responsible for the majority of residential burglaries, petty thefts, vandalism and malicious mischief crimes.

The appropriate level of FI activities by patrol officers is theoretically that required to make all (but only) potential criminal offenders fully aware of, and subject to, the practice. The stopping and questioning of citizens who do not justify suspicion serves no useful police purpose and may damage police-community relationships. For these reasons patrol officers need to be trained to recognized valid FI situations and also to conduct the Field Interrogation so as to minimize potentially adverse citizen reactions—particularly, to those FI encounters that totally remove the officer's initial suspicions.

Most FI advocates feel that the decision to conduct a Field Interrogation should be based only on the actual observation of suspicious persons by trained patrol officers; therefore, these advocates feel that it is unrealistic to assign FI quotas to patrol officers. An FI quota system might force patrol officers to be less selective in choosing subjects to be field interrogated, thus expanding the possibility of adverse public reactions to the practice. A quota system might also encourage patrol officers to leave their assigned beat in order to find more opportunities for valid Field Interrogations.

In order to help focus Field Interrogations on potential offenders, some police departments encourage the use of Field Interrogations primarily as a means for keeping track of known offenders and their associates, that is, those with prior criminal arrests and, in particular, those currently on parole or probation. Even in these situations it is important that the elements of suspicion used to justify the interrogation relate to the subject's appearance, demeanor, and activities under a particular set of circumstances, and not solely to the subject's identity as a known prior offender.

Patrol Operation in the San Diego Police Department

Individual patrol officers in San Diego are assigned to special patrol beats and watches (shifts), and each officer normally operates alone in a standard marked police car. Together, officer and car are called a patrol unit. A patrol unit's operation is not restricted to its assigned beat, but the unit has the primary responsibility for responding to calls for service on the beat. Dispatching policy requires that the assigned unit be dispatched to calls on the beat whenever the unit is available, and that the nearest uncommitted unit be assigned to calls when the primary unit is not available. Studies have shown that assigned patrol units typically respond to about one-third of the calls for service on their assigned beats, since they are frequently committed to calls on other beats, as either primary or backup units.

Responding to calls for service occupies an average of approximately two hours per patrol unit, per watch. Watch changes, booking arrests, routine reporting, service breaks, and so on, are estimated to consume another three hours. Thus, approximately three hours of the total patrol time per shift remain available for preventive patrol operations that include conducting Field Interrogations, traffic enforcement, public relation contacts, and so forth, as well as routine cruising.

The San Diego Police Department does not assign patrol officers quotas for Field Interrogations, arrests, traffic citations, or public relation contacts; however, tabulations are made of these activities by officers and are used as one input in evaluating officer performance. Since the patrol officers are not normally restricted to their assigned beats, they routinely perform many of these self-initiated activities in other beats.

Project Background

In recent years, many police departments have begun to question seriously the effectiveness of their traditional patrol operations and to experiment with various new patrol techniques. One of those traditional patrol functions in most western-U.S. police departments—the practice of conducting Field Interrogations—has become increasingly controversial. Questions have been raised regarding the legality of Field Interrogations and the community relations impact resulting from this type of police-citizen interaction. While both the practice and the controversy continued, few factual data were being collected relative to the effectiveness of Field Interrogations.

In October 1972, following an indication of interest expressed by the Police Foundation, a decision was made by Chief Hoobler of the San Diego Police Department to seek funding to conduct research into the effectiveness of the department's FI policies and procedures. This decision was made as the result of recommendations for research projects submitted by several commanding officers and a subsequent administrative review.

As an initial step, Chief Hoobler organized an FI task force. The task force comprised representatives from the patrol division, traffic division, investigations, and community relations office. The overall goal of the task force was to develop a program proposal for testing various assumptions about Field Interrogations.

In order to acquire an understanding of the views of other police agencies concerning Field Interrogations, the department sent out a brief questionnaire to 76 departments located throughout the country. According to the survey responses, public attitudes were believed to have been significantly affected by FI practices and policies. A few departments reported that there was active movement in their communities to eliminate the activity from patrol procedures. In essence, the FI questionnaire responses supported the task force's belief that the questions surrounding Field Interrogations were of national interest.

In December 1972, the proposal to conduct FI experiments was written. In January 1973, Chief Hoobler and Inspector Reierson presented the proposal to the Police Foundation where it was accepted for grant funding support.

Project Objectives

The objects of the proposal were to question the accuracy of certain commonly accepted assumptions regarding Field Interrogations. Specifically, these questions were posed:

1. Do Field Interrogations deter crime? If they do, what types of crimes are affected?

2. Do Field Interrogations either directly or indirectly lead to arrests? What contribution, if any, do Field Interrogations make to investigations and to case clearances?

3. Is there a direct relationship between Field Interrogations and a negative police-community relationship?

To summarize, the study asks whether the benefits of Field Interrogations justify the cost to community relations and patrol operations, and whether there is a method for conducting Field Interrogations by which optimum results can be achieved while good police-community relations are maintained.

To anwer these questions, the department proposed to perform several specific tasks:

Analyze the present FI system, including (but not limited to) FI policy, actual FI practice, data collection methods, data storage and dissemination, and so on. Design an optimum data flow system for Field Interrogations, based on the results of this analysis.

Analyze the FI interaction to identify the dynamics of the activity.

Design a model training program to supplement the department's current FI training and aimed at increasing officers' ability to obtain needed information during a Field Interrogation, while at the same time enhancing the police-community relationship. Train 25 officers in the model FI techniques as a test of the value of the training.

Establish an experimental laboratory and conduct specific FI experiments.

Evaluate the results of these experiments in terms of the benefits of Field Interrogations to crime suppression and to the apprehension of criminals, and the costs of Field Interrogations to policy-community relations.

II. THE EXPERIMENTAL VARIABLES

Variable 1: Suspension of Field Interrogations
In order to attempt to measure the effects of FI practices on the incidence of crime, on arrests, and on police-community relations, the SDC evaluation staff concluded that it would be necessary for the San Diego Police Department to suspend all FI activities either throughout the city or in one or more selected areas. The SDC staff also felt that the suspension should include all times of the day, and should be of sufficient duration that any lingering effects of prior FI activity would be minimized.

The department's FI task force agreed that such a suspension of FI activities was necessary to address many of the research questions that they had presented. However, there was considerable concern expressed with regard to the necessary duration of the suspension and about the size of the area that would have to be included. In particular, the patrol representatives on the task force expressed concern that the incidence of crime would rise dramatically, and that it would be extremely difficult to obtain the full cooperation of patrol officers in adhering to any suspension that involved a long time period or a large number of patrol beats.

Although both the departmental task force and SDC recognized that varying levels of FI activity could also be tested, it was agreed that the primary focus would be on the effects of a total suspension.

With the concurrence of the task force, the total suspension of FI activities became identified as one of the two major experimental variables. The considerations that influenced the selection of the areas and duration of the FI suspension and the control procedures that were instituted to help assure compliance with the suspension are described in detail in Section III.

Variable 2: The Special Supplementary Field Interrogation Training Program
The second of the two experimental variables was the special supplementary FI training prog-

ram designed for presentation to those officers who would patrol the Special FI Area. Since SDC did not directly observe or evaluate either regular or supplementary training activity, SDC presents an overview of the special supplementary FI training program that was derived from a report by Approach Associates of Oakland, California (the training contractor) and a comparison of the two training programs that was prepared by the San Diego Police Department's FI project staff.

Developing The Supplementary Training Program   In August 1973, the trainees and their supervisors traveled to San Jose, California, for the field experiential training phase. The officers were placed in various situations that would attract the attention of the local police. This was an experience that was stimulating and educational. The objective of this phase was to have the officers experience a Field Interrogation from a non-police perspective. Some of the officers felt they were hassled, while others felt they were illegally arrested or physically handled unnecessarily. However, not all of the contact experiences were negative; some very good interrogations were conducted. One of the interesting points of the experience was that the officers in training had to think about what had to be done to attract attention of the local police. This led the trainees to examine their own motives for selecting particular individuals for field interrogation in their own jurisdiction. . . .

Summary of the Model Training Curriculum   Between June and October 1973, Approach Associates, in conjunction with 25 San Diego patrol officers, developed the model FI training curriculum for the San Diego Police Department. The curriculum is set forth in ten basic units; the units may be presented in different sequences, depending on the seniority of the officers to be trained or the specific training use (see Table I). To gain maximum impact from this curriculum, it must be implemented as a whole, with modifications for the level of time and seniority within the department. Separate units of the curriculum, however, may be

adopted singly or in combination to meet other specific constraints such as time, money, staff, and programs. For example, if legal instruction is adequately provided in the Academy or elsewhere, Unit VI in this curriculum (Legal Aspects of Field Interrogation) could be incorporated in such instruction. Such an approach also applies for Unit IIb (Peacekeeping), Unit III (Safety), and Unit IV (Coping with Cultural Differences). Unit IX (Experiential Training), although extremely valuable, is expensive both in terms of finances (compensation time, transportation, per diem, and so on) and logistics (locating an appropriate jurisdiction, securing the cooperation of the local police department, and protection against adverse consequences to the local department as well as the sponsoring department). Use of nearby jurisdictions would reduce some of the costs. It should also be noted that the original trainees and the training team considered the experiential training to be one of the most meaningful and unifying components of the training curriculum.

III. THE EVALUATION DESIGN

Overview of the Evaluation Design

SDC's design required the selection of three study areas (one for control and two for experimental conditions) that were closely matched in terms of their demographic and socioeconomic compositions and in their prior reported crime histories.

In the *Control Area,* Field Interrogations were to be conducted with no changes from normally practiced activities. In the *Special FI Area,* Field Interrogations were to be conducted only by officers who were to be given special supplemental training in the conduct of Field Interrogations by Approach Associates. In the *No-FI Area,* Field Interrogations were to be suspended for a nine-month Experimental period.

Community attitude surveys were to be conducted in each of the areas both prior to and following the nine-month experimental period. Additionally, a variety of information was to be

Table I. Recommended Course Sequences of Model Field Interrogation Training Curriculum, for Use in Academy, In-Service, and Line-up Training

Academy Training Sequence[a]		In-Service Training Sequence[a]		Line-up Training Sequence[b]	
Curriculum Unit	Title	Curriculum Unit	Title	Curriculum Unit	Title
I.	Pre-training preparation simulated videotaped field contact	I.	Pre-training preparation; simulated videotaped field contact	III.	Safety aspects of Field Interrogation[c]
II.	Police objectives of Field Interrogation; law enforcement and keeping of the peace	IX.	Experiential field training	II.	Police objectives of Field Interrogation[d]
III.	Safety aspects of Field Interrogation	VII.	Police environment of Field Interrogation	VI.	Legal aspects of Field Interrogation[e]
IV.	Coping with cultural difference in Field Interrogation	II.	Police objectives of Field Interrogation; law enforcement and keeping of the peace	IV.	Coping with cultural difference in Field Interrogation[f]
V.	Techniques for opening and closing a Field Interrogation	III.	Safety aspects of Field Interrogation		
VI.	Legal aspects of Field Interrogation	IV.	Coping with cultural difference in Field Interrogation		
VII.	Police environment of Field Interrogation[g]	VI.	Legal aspects of Field Interrogation		
VIII.	Communications workshops I-A and I-B for Field Interrogation[h]	V.	Techniques for opening and closing a Field Interrogation		
IX.	Experiential field training	VIII.	Communications workshops I-A and I-B for Field Interrogation		
X.	Evaluation	X.	Evaluation		

[a] Recommended for advanced officers, sergeants, or field training officers.
[b] Portions of these units are considered helpful for in-service line-up training.
[c] Especially role-playing selected safety problems.
[d] Especially keeping-the-peace referrals.
[e] Especially new developments in case law.
[f] Especially minority communities' current perceptions of police.
[g] After recruits have spent some time in the field and are about to conclude academy training, this unit should be offered to small groups of 8-10 persons.
[h] After the recruit has completed the probationary period, this unit should be completed with workshops concerned with awareness of impact of FI subject, communication skills, and closing the Field Interrogation.

*

collected for analysis. Data were to be collected for three time periods—Pre-experimental, Experimental, and Post-experimental:

Crime history data on crimes considered to suppressible by patrol

FI-history data

Arrest-history data

Complaint-history data

Sampling of report details from arrests made by Control and Special FI officers

Observation reports of FI encounters

Race/ethnicity and age characteristics of FI subjects

Sample of reasons-for-stop for Field Interrogations

Use of FI information by investigators.

The focus of the SDC analysis was threefold: first, to determine the statistically significant *changes* that occurred *within* each of the three areas between the Pre-experimental (baseline) period, the Experimental period, and the Post-experimental period; second, to identify the *differences in changes* that occurred *among* the three areas (that is, the rates and directions of changes in the three areas were to be compared), and third, to interpret the findings in terms of their relationship to the three alternative FI practices being tested.

*

Approach   The city of San Diego is divided into three major police patrol districts—northern, central, and southern. Each district is further divided into supervisor areas, and finally into patrol beats. Each beat is composed of a grouping of contiguous census tracts.

The San Diego Police Department maintains reported crime statistics by census tract as well as by patrol beat. Periodically, the size of patrol beats is adjusted by adding or subtracting census tracts. Such adjustments are done to provide a more equitable balance of the patrol workload among the beats within each patrol district. The coincidence between census boundaries and patrol beat boundaries makes it relatively easy to compare the demographic and socioeconomic characteristics of patrol beats or larger areas.

Because of dissimilarities between operations and the incidence of crime among the three administrative districts (northern, central and southern), it was tentatively decided that all study beats should be within the same administrative district. This decision also facilitated the control of the experiment, since all involved personnel would be operating under the same administrative control.

A secondary decision to select beats within the central administrative district was taken for three additional reasons: (1) Patrol operations in the large rural areas of the northern and southern administrative districts are dissimilar in many ways from the central district and are thus not representative of the rest of San Diego and do not share the characteristics of most other U.S. cities of similar size and population. Together they constitute less than 24 percent of the city population. (2) The northern district is almost completely white (averaging 90 percent or more, per beat) while the southern district is far above the mean city distribution to Spanish-speaking population (averaging over 30 percent, as against the city mean of 12.6 percent). (3) These administrative districts are separated geographically from the central district.

SDC's objective in the selection of candidates for the experiment was to identify areas that are representative of San Diego, but that deviated moderately in their proportion of white (non-Spanish) residents and their proportion of youth. The primary selection criterion was that the beat have a greater than average minority population and also a significant white population. The second criterion to be satisfied was that the beat be at least representative of the city in its proportion of youth. The third criterion was that the beat be representative of the city in demographic, socioeconomic, physical, and crime characteristics.

Since beats were designed (by combining contiguous census tracts) so as to equalize crime rates, the task was reduced to that of developing a methodology for comparing beats on the basis of the first three of these characteristics. The source of this information was the 1970 Census of Population and Housing. The data were obtained from three different census summary tape releases, based on 100, 20 and 15 percent sample survey data.

For each of the 90 beats, the values of 26 variables were computed. These variables are listed in Table II. It may be noted that 13 of the variables fall in the first grouping (demographic), seven in the second grouping (socioeconomic), and six in the third grouping (physical neighborhood). The number of variables assigned to each of these categories influenced SDC results in scoring the beats with respect to their deviations from the San Diego beat average. These numbers assumed the role of weights and reflected the relative importance that SDC attributed to the three categories for the purposes of this study. This type of decision was obviously subjective, but was founded on the experience SDC has had in evaluating the importance of these variables in relation to crime rates. SDC assigned a weight to the demographic group that equaled the sum of the weights for the other two groups. This decision reflected, in part, the significance of sex, age, and race/ethnicity differences in reported contacts with police.

*

Selection of Officers

Officers selected to participate in the special training course in FI methods and procedures and in the subsequent experiment were those who were already assigned to the Experiment beat and its contiguous beats. Assignment of officers to these beats had been made prior to the selection of the beats for the experiment and therefore was not expected to bias the results. The officers serving contiguous beats were included in the training to provide a buffer of experimentally trained patrol officers around the actual Special FI Area. (The wisdom of this decision became apparent when the beat re-configuration took place.)

Those officers who were assigned to the selected No-FI Area were also to be given the special FI training. This decision was based on the assumption that the training would help them understand the experiment and thus be more willing to adhere to the FI moratorium.

A total of 25 officers were selected for training. Some screening was necessary to determine officer willingness and availability to serve on the selected beats for the duration of the project. A few who could not project the required time on the beat for various reasons (such as being due for promotion or for transfer to another section of the city) were transferred prior to the beginning of the training and replaced by persons with a reasonable projection of longevity on the selected beats. Replacements were selected from those officers who had previously requested assignment to the selected areas.

These procedures were used to minimize the bias that could have been introduced by selecting volunteers for the program. No special controls were placed on those officers assigned to the Control Area other than that they would not receive the special FI training.

IV. DATA COLLECTION

Baseline Data

Statistics, by beat, for suppressible crimes were available spanning the seven-month interval between the last beat re-configuration, February 1973, and the start of the FI experiment in August 1973. Only four months of beat arrest data (May through August of 1973) were available, due to a change in the manual tabulation process of counting arrests. Prior to May, juvenile arrests were not included in the tabulation.

Because of the department's procedures for filing and handling FI reports at the time, it was

Table II. San Diego Police Department Beat Comparisons

Census Characteristics	Control (Beat 22)	No-FI (Beat 26)	Special FI (Beat 28)	Total City
Population[a]	8,725	14,629	7,412	701,654
Male (%)	48.4	48.9	48.9	51.3
Female (%)	51.6	51.1	51.1	48.7
Age distribution (%)				
0–5	11.3	15.3	14.5	9.7
6–12	14.7	22.0	21.5	11.7
13–15	5.8	6.9	7.3	4.5
16–19	6.1	5.7	6.3	7.1
20–34	20.1	21.3	20.8	25.6
35–49	18.2	18.5	18.0	16.7
50 & over	23.8	10.3	11.4	24.7
Race/ethnicity distribution (%)				
White[b]	67.6	68.2	69.7	69.8
Spanish-American	12.2	19.6	22.1	16.4
Black	17.5	5.7	4.8	9.4
Other	2.7	6.5	3.4	4.4
Families				
Female head (%)	11.4	12.8	12.1	14.8
Below poverty (%)	8.2	11.0	8.2	11.8
Average size	3.4	4.1	4.1	3.3
Median income ($)	10019.	9441.6	9946.	9438.
Education (median years)	12.2	12.2	12.2	12.2
Housing units				
Single (%)	84.7	73.9	97.1	57.5
1–10 (%)	8.2	8.7	3.3	20.9
Over 10 (%)	0.2	17.2	0.0	18.6
Mobile units (%)	6.9	0.0	0.0	3.2
Nonstandard (%)	1.0	2.2	0.4	6.6
Overcrowded (%)	1.6	2.8	3.1	2.9
Median value ($)	18094.9	19594.1	17907.1	21470.
Median rent ($)	110.3	115.1	125.9	114.
Sum of Z scores				
ΣZ^z	5.62	10.37	13.78	—

[a]Population was not a variable in the computation of Z scores.

[b]White excludes Spanish-Americans.

Source: Based on 1970 Census data.

not possible to establish a Pre-experimental baseline of Field Interrogations generated in the study areas. The monthly tabulation of Field Interrogations then in use by the department was taken from officers' daily reports and not from an actual count of FI reports submitted. Officers routinely conduct Field Interrogations in beats other than their own. A special manually tabulated sample by area was accomplished for the one-month period, April 8 through May 8, 1973.

Partially because of this sampling problem (and prior to the start of the FI experiment), the department instituted a departmentwide change in FI report forms and handling procedures. Among other things, the changes provided for actual counts of FI reports by beat. Because of the small baseline sample size and the changes in reporting procedures, System Development Corporation (SDC) could not draw any conclusions as to the overall effects of the FI experiment on the number of FI reports written.

A search of available departmental citizen complaint records revealed that records by beat were not available for the full seven-month baseline period. However, a special tabulation had been previously performed for the period between April 1 and June 30, 1973. During that quarter, a total of 574 complaints had been received by the department, 52 (9.0 percent) of which had resulted from Field Interrogations. None of the 52 had occurred in any of the study areas. Provision was made to keep complaint records by beat during the Experimental period.

SDC's analysis of the first community survey, conducted by August 1973 by Economic Behavior Analysts under a separate contract from the Police Foundation, also became a portion of the baseline data.

Experimental Period Data

Field Interrogation Reports   The department instituted new FI reporting forms and processing procedures prior to the start of the Experimental period. The revisions temporarily made it easy for SDC to collect accurate and detailed information about those Field Interrogations written in the Control and Special FI Areas during the experiment. Unfortunately, the beat re-configuration that occurred one month into the study largely negated the advantages of the reporting improvements and necessitated manual tabulations. The manual process, although cumbersome, is believed to have resulted in accurate counts of all Field Interrogations performed in the study areas.

Arrest Reports   Accurate manual counts were kept by the department of total arrests made in the three study areas. As a method of accounting for FI contacts that resulted in on-the-spot arrests by the patrol officers, all arrest report forms and juvenile contact report forms were overprinted with a series of boxes to be checked by the arresting officer to indicate the event (reason-for-stop) resulting in the arrest. Category options were: Field Interrogation, traffic stop, radio dispatch, warrant, and other. These modified forms were in the field by December 1973 and arrangements were made by the project coordinator with the records and juvenile divisions to keep a monthly departmentwide tally of arrests, by reason-for-stops, prior to filing the arrest forms in the suspects' packets.

To determine any differences between the quality of arrests and the characteristics of subjects arrested by officers assigned to the study areas, a one-month sample (March 1974) of the details of arrest reports for officers working these areas was examined. The procedure for gaining access to arrest details was somewhat complicated in that it necessitated: (1) manually extracting the names of those arrested from the individual daily activity reports of each of the study officers; (2) going with this list of names to the records section, and pulling the individual suspect files; (3) determining the precipitating cause of the arrest and subject characteristics; and (4) from a separate document, ascertaining the disposition of the case.

Determination of arrest dispositions was made only to the extent that an arrest was rejected or filed (adults held-to-answer by the district or city attorney, and juveniles referred to juvenile hall or probation). Court findings were considered to be beyond the purview of this study.

Ride-Along Observations   To assess the possible differences between trained and untrained officers' behavior, and to give insight into the community relations effects generated by officer behavior, a schedule of ride-along observations of both Control and Experimentally trained officers was conducted.

Recognizing the wide range of variables in the types and extent of patrol activities that might be related to such factors as day of week, hour of day, or season of year, and to the requirement to observe the behavior of as many Special FI officers as possible and at least a like number of Control officers, a rather elaborate sampling schedule of ride-along observations was formulated. All observations were conducted by the same four SDC evaluators, each of whom had extensive patrol observation experience prior to this project.

Initially it was intended that one observer would ride with the officer(s) under scrutiny, while a second observer would ride in a follow-car to conduct post-FI interviews with FI subjects and with witnesses. This plan was not implemented because of some difficulties in scheduling the necessary reserve officers to drive or accompany the second observer. As the observers gained experience it also became apparent that too few Field Interrogations take place on any given shift to warrant the expense of the follow-car (the average proved to be less than one Field Interrogation per beat, per watch). Moreover, very few witnesses to FI situations were encountered. In only four instances during the observations for the October through December quarter were witnesses or bystanders present, and in each case, these were juveniles. Several factors contribute to this fact. In the event of car stops, since all occupants of the car are usually interrogated—at least to the extent of being asked to identify themselves— they become subjects rather than witnesses. Many, if not most, pedestrian contacts are initiated because individuals are observed alone or in pairs at unusual places and times and thus all present are subjects of questioning. Finally, since any given officer on any shift may have few occasions to interrogate, project manpower could better be distributed to observe more officers.

A great deal of project manpower, time, and money was expended on observations during the period September 1973 through February 1974. By February it was apparent to all four observers that many hours of observation resulted in relatively few observations of Field Interrogations. It was also deemed inappropriate to suggest that more interrogations be conducted by officers under observation. Supervisors of patrol officers continually reminded patrol officers to conduct their beat activities as though there was no one observing their activities.

Typically, most patrol officers initiating a Field Interrogation think "this looks like a possible Field Interrogation." The officers then proceed with both close observation and interrogation, entering relevant information in notebooks. At some point during the process the officers either confirm or reject their original hunch. If they consider that the situation meets the criteria for a Field Interrogation, they can then complete the FI form, using their notes and immediate memory for descriptive data.

It is not always clear to an observer, or to the patrol officer, when a Field Interrogation is either about to occur or is in progress. To a considerable extent, the decision to field interrogate is an emergent event arising out of a particular set of circumstances. For example, what may start out as a routine traffic stop for an inoperative taillight may end up as a full-fledged Field Interrogation, due to the information cues provided by initial questioning and observation. On the other hand, an officer planning to stop and Field Interrogate a suspicious-looking loiterer may, upon discovering that the person has a legitimate reason for being at that location, disregard (not complete) the Field Interrogation.

In either instance the observer may not be

entirely certain of what situational cues the officer is operating under during the course of an on-scene officer-citizen interaction, or indeed, whether or not a Field Interrogation has occurred until after the fact.

In all, approximately 625 hours of observation during 96 shifts were conducted to observe 42 Field Interrogations by Special FI officers and 37 Field Interrogation by Control officers. The total number of individual officers observed was 23 Special FI officers, including two sergeants, and 38 Control officers, including two sergeants.

In January 1974, it was recommended to the Foundation that ride-along observations be curtailed in favor of increased emphasis by evaluation personnel on two other matters: (1) the close scrutiny of daily activity report summaries of officers departmentwide to determine the relationships between field contacts and FI slips submitted, and between arrests and Field Interrogations, and (2) a study of investigators' use or non-use of Field Interrogations, and their reported reasons.

Observer Interviews of Field Interrogation Subjects   During the course of the ride-along observations, 42 attempts were made by the observers to interview the subjects of Field Interrogations. In most cases it was not appropriate to attempt to interview the subjects at the scene of the Field Interrogation. Either further delay of the subject would affect the subject's attitude toward the initial stop, or the situation was such that the officer with whom the observer was riding had pressing business elsewhere (such as a radio call or traffic enforcement requirement).

Nine subjects were interviewed by observers on the street immediately following the Field Interrogation by the officer. Nineteen subjects were contacted by telephone subsequent to their interrogation. Attempts were made to contact 14 other individuals, but because of incorrect telephone numbers or addresses, refusal to talk with an interviewer, or because they were untraceable military personnel, no contact was possible.

Other Data Sources   In addition to the data elements enumerated above, other data sources were examined and recorded for application to the investigation. These sources and uses included, first, actual counts of suppressible crime reports, by crime type and study area, and second, a survey of all investigators working out of the central division to ascertain their use of Field Interrogations and their views of FI reports as an investigative tool.

*

Table III summarizes, for the three study periods, the availability (by number of months) of eleven categories of data used in the evaluation.

V. FINDINGS AND CONCLUSIONS

Question: Do Field Interrogations deter crime? Which types of crime, if any, are affected?

Findings: The suspension of Field Interrogations in the No-FI Area was associated in time with a significant increase in the monthly frequency of total suppressible crimes. The resumption of Field Interrogations in the No-FI Area was associated in time with a significant decrease in the monthly frequency of total suppressible crimes. . . .

Summary of the Analysis

The analysis consisted of two methods of comparing the changes that occurred in the frequencies of reported crimes in the three study areas during the course of the FI study, and an initial effort to model the relationship between the frequencies of crimes and Field Interrogations.

The eight specific types of crimes analyzed are those defined as suppressible crimes by the San Diego Police Department: robbery, burglary, grand theft, petty theft, auto theft, assault/battery, sex crimes, and malicious mischief/disturbances. With three minor exceptions, these reported crime types are as defined in the FBI's *Uniform Crime Reporting Handbook*

Table III. Summary of Data Availability by Study Period

Data Category	Pre-experimental Period Feb. '73-Aug. '73	Experimental Period Sept. '73-May '74	Post-experimental Period June '74-Oct. '74
Monthly counts of crime reports (suppressible crimes by type and beat)	Feb. '73-Aug. '73 (7 months)	Sept. '73-May '74 (9 months)	June '74-Oct. '74 (5 months)
Counts of FI Reports by beat	Apr. '73	Sept. '73-May '74 (9 months)	June '74-Oct. '74 (5 months)
Details of FI Reports	None	Sept. '73-May '74 (9 months)	None
Counts of total arrest by beat	May '73-Aug. '73 (4 months)	Sept. '73-May '74 (9 months)	June '74-Oct. '74 (5 months)
Arrest: reasons-for-stops	None	Dec. '73-May '74 (6 months)	None
Arrest details: subject's age, race, residence, arrest disposition	None	Mar. '74[a]	None
Citizen complaints (totals of FI and other by beat and month	Apr. '73-June '73[b] (3 months)	Sept. '73-May '74 (9 months)	None
Observations of, and subject interviews of sample FI contacts	None	Sept. '73-Feb. '74[c]	None
Counts of investigators' requests to examine FI reports (by investigative unit and month)	None	Sept. '73-May '74	None
Survey of investigations on FI usage	None	March '74	None
Community attitude survey	Aug. '73	None	June '74

[a] Arrests made by officers assigned to study areas.
[b] Summary only; not by month.
[c] Sampled over six months.

(July 1966): (1) *criminal homicides* are excluded from San Diego's suppressible Part I crimes list; (2) San Diego includes *other sex offenses* along with the Part I crime of *forcible rape,* as *sex offenses;* and (3) the Part II crimes of *vandalism* and *disorderly conduct* are grouped into the San Diego reporting category of *malicious mischief/ disturbances.* Suppressible Part I crimes, plus *malicious mischief/disturbances,* are referred to in this analysis as total suppressible crimes.

The monthly reports of Field Interrogations, each of the eight specific types of crime, total Part I suppressible crimes, and total suppressible crimes were tabulated for each study area for the Pre-experimental, Experimental, and Post-experimental time periods. These data were then analyzed to identify changes in frequencies of reported Field Interrogations and crimes, and possible relations between the two types of reports.

Analysis Details

Changes in the monthly mean frequencies of reported crimes and Field Interrogations

The first analysis consisted of comparing the monthly mean numbers of crimes and Field Interrogations reported in each area before, during, and after the active field phase of the FI experiment. Since the raw totals of reports showed a wide month-to-month variation, an analysis approach was chosen to minimize the influence of exceptionally high or low months of reported crimes and Field Interrogations. The technique employed was the standard *t* test of the difference between means. These tests were conducted individually for each of the eight specific types of suppressible crimes, for the total of the seven Part I suppressible crimes, and for the total of all suppressible crimes. These tests were also made for reported Field Interrogations, but only for the Experimental and Post-experimental periods, since monthly data were not available for the Pre-experimental period.

Briefly, this analysis produced these findings: first, both total suppressible crimes and Part I suppressible crimes increased significantly in the No-FI Area during the period when Field Interrogations were suspended. When Field Interrogations were resumed there, a significant decrease was observed in both total suppressible crimes and Part I suppressible crimes. These findings support the hypothesis that *some* FI activities—as opposed to *none*—have a deterrent effect on suppressible crimes.

Second, the analysis of specifc types of suppressible crimes in the No-FI Area showed that only malicious mischief/disturbances demonstrated a significant increase during the period when Field Interrogations were sus-

pended, and only petty theft showed a statistically significant decrease when Field Interrogations were resumed. However, all specific crime types except assaults increase in the No-FI Area during the period when Field Interrogations were suspended, and all specific crime types except assault and grand theft decreased when Field Interrogations were resumed. The magnitudes and monthly patterns of these changes were most apparent for burglary, petty theft, and malicious mischief/disturbances. Since the test for statistical significance is particularly stringent for small samples, it appears likely that extended study periods would have produced significant results for burglary, petty theft and malicious mischief/disturbances.

Third, there were no significant increases or decreases in individual or combined suppressible crimes in either the Control or Special FI Areas. Although the individual types and aggregates of suppressible crimes showed changes between study periods, neither the magnitude nor patterns of these changes were as consistent as those of the No-FI Area. Field Interrogations increased significantly in the Special FI Area between the Experimental and Post-experimental periods, but were not significantly changed in the Control Area.

Table IV presents the results of this analysis for the eight individual types of crime. Table V presents the results for the two summations of Part I suppressible crimes and for total suppressible crimes, along with the changes that occurred in the frequencies of FI reports. Changes are reported as significant only when $p = .05$ or less (p is a measure of the probability that the changes could be due to chance alone).

*

Table IV. Monthly Mean Numbers of Suppressible Crimes by Crime Type, Study Area, and Study Period, Plus significance of Changes Between Study Periods

Crime Type	Control Area					No-FI					Special FI Area				
	Monthly Means			Significance of Change		Monthly Means			Significance of Change		Monthly Means			Significance of Change	
	Pre	Exp	Post	Pre to Exp	Exp to Post	Pre	Exp	Post	Pre to Exp	Exp to Post	Pre	Exp	Post	Pre to Exp	Exp to Post
Robbery	2.0	2.2	1.6	NS	NS	.07	1.2	0.4	NS	NS	1.6	1.6	2.2	NS	NS
Burglary	15.0	12.2	7.8	NS	NS	18.7	27.4	22.4	NS	NS	20.1	19.6	19.8	NS	NS
Grand theft	2.1	2.8	3.2	NS	NS	1.9	2.8	2.8	NS	NS	1.9	2.9	3.0	NS	NS
Petty theft	17.9	20.9	20.2	NS	NS	32.7	40.3	27.6	NS	(<.01)	26.3	29.9	26.0	NS	NS
Auto theft	2.6	2.4	3.0	NS	NS	4.7	6.0	5.2	NS	NS	4.3	3.0	1.4	NS	NS
Assault	0.9	1.9	2.6	NS	NS	3.3	3.2	4.2	NS	NS	2.7	3.1	3.0	NS	NS
Sex crime	0.4	0.4	0.2	NS	NS	1.1	2.2	0.6	NS	NS	0.9	0.2	1.6	NS	NS
Malicious mischief/ disturbances	7.9	9.2	10.0	NS	NS	11.6	20.7	20.0	(<.02)	NS	7.3	9.1	11.8	NS	NS

Pre = Pre-experimental period; Exp = Experimental period; Post = Post-experimental period

NS = Not significant at .05 level of probability.

(<.01) = Less than 1 chance in 100 that change was due to chance alone.

(<.02) = Less than 2 chances in 100 that change was due to chance alone.

NOTE: Significance tests were made using the standard *t* test of the differences between means.

Table V. Monthly Mean Numbers of Reporting Part I Suppressible Crimes, Total Suppressible Crimes, and FIs by Study Period and Study Area

Study Areas	Pre-experimental Time Period (7 months)	Experimental Time Period (9 months)	Post-experimental Time Period (5 months)	Differences and Significances[a] Between Periods	
				Pre-experimental to Experimental	Experimental to Post-experimental
Part I Suppressible Crimes					
Control	40.9	42.9	38.6	+ 2.0 (NS)	− 4.3 (NS)
Special FI	57.7	60.2	56.6	+ 2.5 (NS)	− 3.6 (NS)
No-FI	63.1	83.2	63.2	+ 20.1 p=.02	− 20.0 p=.05
Total Suppressible Crimes[b]					
Control	48.7	52.1	48.6	+ 3.4 (NS)	− 3.5 (NS)
Special FI	65.0	69.3	68.4	+ 4.3 (NS)	− 0.9 (NS)
No-FI	74.7	103.9	81.2	+ 29.2 p=.01	− 22.7 p=.05
Field Interrogations[c]					
Control	17.0	22.7	14.0	5.7 (NA)	− 8.7 (NS)
Special FI	15.0	48.3	88.0	33.3 (NA)	+ 39.7 p=.05
No-FI	24.0	0.0	49.2	−24.0 (NA/D)	+ 49.2 (NA/D)

(NS) = Not significant.
(NA) = Not applicable due to lack of data for Pre-experimental period.
(NA/D) = Not applicable. Significance forced by experimental design.
[a]Tests of statistical significance of the differences between monthly means were made using the standard t test.
[b]Comprises Part I plus malicious mischief/disturbances.
[c]One-month sample only.

6. Vice Work

JONATHAN RUBINSTEIN

THE OBLIGATION TO ENFORCE THE VICE LAWS PRE-
sents the police with insoluble dilemmas. Regardless of what system a department uses—vice
squads, district and divisional plainclothesmen,
or the distribution of responsibility among undercover units and district patrolmen—or the
degree of freedom a commissioner has from
political interference, the department administrators must constantly struggle to control the
inclinations of some to exploit their opportunities for graft (and extortion). At the same
time, vigorous efforts to enforce these laws undermine the possibilities for strict supervision
because the work obliges the men to engage in
illegal and often degrading practices that must
be concealed from the public. Although no department has entirely eliminated the systematic,
regular payoff—the "steady note," as it is called
in Philadelphia, and the "pad," in New York
City—and in some it continues in entrenched
form, its elimination would not resolve the basic
problems vice enforcement imposes on the
police.

The public measures the honesty of its police
by the absence of evidence of graft and payoffs.
The adminstrators of the police know that even
if they control the inclinations of their men to
take money, they must continue to struggle to
prevent the loosening of standards and the indifference toward lawful conduct that is produced by the constant application of illegal and

illicit techniques to make "vice pinches." While
many departments have greatly reduced the
opportunitues for graft which their men may
safely take, none has found ways of fulfilling its
obligations to regulate public morality without
resorting to methods that constantly provide
policemen with temptations and encourage ambiguous attitudes toward official standards of
conduct. Every police official knows that some
of his men are regularly indulging in practices
whose legality is questionable at best but cannot
be prevented as long as the department demands vice activity. The condition obliges the
administrators to rely on ginks, department
spies, to ferret out those who step over the line
between enforcement and collusion. Every patrolman is guilty of violating some department
rule, and whether he is honest or not, every man
is on the watch for the ginks. This atmosphere
makes it almost impossible for policemen to
share their knowledge with each other or to welcome openly innovations that threaten their privacy and therefore their security.[1]

Many of the illegal things that policemen do
are not designed to generate payoffs for them
but to meet obligations established by the department. If the patrolman were freed from
having to make vice arrests, only the corrupt,
the money hungry, would continue to do the

[1]The New York City police department has recently announced that almost 10 percent of the men assigned to enforce gambling and narcotics laws have been secretly recruited to spy on their colleagues. *The New York Times* (March
23, 1972).

▶SOURCE: *City Police.* New York: Farrar, Straus and Giroux,
1973. Pp. 375–401. Reprinted by permission.

illegal things so many policemen do. There are no legal ways to enforce the drug laws on the streets, so any pressure on the police to make more drug arrests is an open encouragement to them to lie and violate their pledge to uphold the Constitution. But to force them to make arrests and then to release the addicts who will only be arrested again compounds a tragic situation and makes a mockery of the efforts the police are obliged to make. The same is true of gambling. If they made a systematic effort to crush gambling in the city, the networks would redistribute their headquarters outside the city and continue to operate, although their overhead costs might increase. But even before this happened, the objections raised by the methods the police would have to use would be so great that they would stop raiding places and closing up bars and neighborhood grocery stores. Instead, the police compromise and maintain high arrest quotas for gambling, pressuring the men to make pinches and limiting their inclinations to take payoffs. It also provides statistical evidence that the department is "doing something" about vice. This tactic has probably reduced gambling graft over the years, but it has involved every policeman in a conspiracy to violate the law and to protect himself and others from revelations of misconduct.

The district policeman is well aware of the department's "official" policy toward vice, but he also knows that its purpose certainly is not the eradication of gambling or illegal drinking. All vice activity is computed on the basis of arrests, a policy that is not designed to encourage men to make quality arrests. It also encourages an indifference to the method by which the arrests are made, although if policemen arrested only known gamblers, they would still have to violate the law to do it. At times in many cities "bad arrests" were encouraged for the purpose of getting cases dismissed. Policemen also make deals with defendants to give "bad testimony" in court to assure their acquittal or the dismissal of charges, although this is more a matter of personal initiative than any kind of policy. The in-

difference toward the quality of gambling arrests is encouraged partly by the leniency of the courts, even when convictions result. While the great majority of arrests result in acquittals, few convictions carry any jail terms and the fines are rarely more than nominal. Whether this is deliberate policy and represents some giant conspiracy coordinating the police and the courts, as implied by some who describe the power of the Mafia in terms usually reserved for sovereign states, or is the consequence of many accommodations representing different groups and interests in the city, is unclear. But the pattern of large numbers of arrests and few convictions is found throughout the country. The pattern is the same in cities like Chicago and Philadelphia, which continue to have traditional ethnic political organizations, and in New York City, which has been dominated for years by a liberal, reform government.

During 1970 in New York City, there were more than nine thousand arrests made for common gambling; only seventy people went to jail. An analysis made of raids on seventy-three numbers banks in Brooklyn during the late 1960's revealed that 356 persons were arrested. Of these, 198 people had their cases dismissed and sixty-three were acquitted; seventy-seven people were fined an average of $113 each, five went to jail for an average of seventeen days, twelve had their sentences suspended, and one person went to jail for a year. In the state of New York during 1969, there were 2,096 arrests for felonious gambling, the most serious charge, which led to 281 indictments, fifteen convictions, and one jail term. In Nassau County, New York, in 1965, after revelations of corruption had produced a reform, there was no appreciable change in the outcome of gambling cases brought before the county courts. Most defendants were freed or given minor fines. In Philadelphia during 1970, 517 of 4,720 people charged with gambling were convicted. Five people went to jail and the remainder paid fines averaging $100 each. In Chicago in 1963, 76 percent of the 11,158 people charged with gambling had their cases dismissed; 1,118 of the 2,678 who were prosecuted were convicted. Seventeen people went to jail. A study of Chicago gambling prosecutions in 1950 showed that 70 percent of the cases were dismissed without trial. The author noted that "day after day the same police testify as to the nature of the raids and the same small clique of lawyers makes the motion to suppress. The routine becomes so common that there is now very little attention paid to the facts. . . ." During the month of November 1950, he noted that 408 of the 564 cases were dismissed on suppression of evidence motions and an additional 110 were thrown out for lack of evidence. Forty-six people were fined, but half of these fines were rescinded on appeal to a higher court. Similar patterns have been noted for Detroit and Cincinnati. This is not a new practice in American cities, and study of court records would probably reveal a consistency extending back into the nineteenth century, intermittently broken by periods when reform governments made a lot of arrests and pressed hard for convictions, much to the annoyance of the electorate, who voted these reformers out of office at the first opportunity. In New York City in 1912, there was a well-publicized police crackdown on gambling after a particularly spectacular scandal. There were 898 arrests and 103 convictions. Nobody went to jail, and the payment of a small fine did not then (nor does it today) deter anyone from continuing his business.[2]

The patrolman is dependent upon the people he polices for his knowledge of their habits and manners. He knows what they allow him to see on the streets and in places where his presence is requested. They tell him things indirectly through the radio dispatcher. But the actions they conceal from him can be learned about only by deception or compulsion. Most gambling activity is carried on discreetly. A patrolman may know there is gambling in his area without ever having directly seen any. Number writers are alert to his presence, and the sight of his well-marked car and self gives ample warning of his approach. The young officer may make a vice pinch with some luck or by telling a lie to provide the legal basis for some evidence he has acquired. He may catch a few men involved in a dice game in an alley, and he can charge that one of them is "cutting" the game, taking a percentage, which makes it a crime rather than a social affair. Even when gambling operations were officially protected, number writers and bookies, who were usually persons well established in their neighborhoods, did not flaunt themselves publicly. Today few gamblers take action from people they do not know. This makes it almost impossible for the honest patrolman to see gambling transactions, and if he does not see anything, he has no right to stop and search someone for evidence.[3]

If the patrolman has no information regarding gambling, the only evidence he can look for is an exchange of money on the street or a person jotting something on a slip of paper. These acts could represent anything; nobody would argue that even in neighborhoods where gambling is common are they practiced exclusively

[2]*The New York Times* (September 13, 1971, October 29, 1971, January 10, 1972, October 23, 1972); *Philadelphia Daily News* (June 14, 1971); Donald Cressey, *Theft of the Nation* (New York, Harper & Row, 1969), p. 268; James Q. Wilson, *Varieties of Police Behavior* (Cambridge, Mass., Harvard University Press, 1968), pp, 100–3; Samuel Dash, "Cracks in the Foundation of Criminal Justice," *Illinois Law Review* (Northwestern University), Vol. XLVI (1951/52), pp. 385–406; Dallin H. Oakes, "Studying the Exclusionary Rule in Search and Seizure," *University of Chicago Law Review,* Vol. XXXVII (1970), pp. 665–757; Andy Logan, p. 117, Virgil Petersen, "Obstacles to Enforcement of Gambling Laws" and Morris Ploscowe and Edwin Lucas, "Gambling," *Annals of the Ameri-*

can Academy of Polictical and Social Science, Vol. 269 w)1950), pp. 9ff.

[3]A patrolman who admitted that he had accepted money from gamblers, and even on occasion picked up payoffs for his colleagues, told investigators that he had never personally witnessed any gambling. "Well, I never actually saw any of these vice characters engaged in any illegal activity, although I knew they were so engaged, but I personally never arrested any of them." *Philadelphia Inquirer* (November 18, 1971). All quotations cited from this newspaper are from legal depositions reprinted for the public record.

by bookies and number writers. But patrolmen are often reluctant to conduct searches under these circumstances because the lectures and warnings against making illegal searches which they heard repeatedly at the police academy are still fresh and clear, but as they gradually learn how important vice activity is in their careers and how difficult it is to obtain good information legally, their reluctance crumbles. They learn to do things that were never taught to them in the academy, although their instructors know that what is withheld from them will eventually be learned and practiced by the majority of men who go on the street.

Vice information is a commodity, and the patrolman learns that he must buy it on a restricted market where the currency he needs is provided him by his power and authority. The policeman who is accused of extortion is rightly condemned for being a crook. But the same man who exploits the moments when people are temporarily dependent upon him for their well-being and liberty to compel them to give him information is praised and rewarded. When a policeman catches two homosexuals, for example, in a car parked on a dark street, he has an almost unrestricted license to act. He may arrest them or release them; he may take money (either as extortion or as a bribe) or compel them to give him information under the threat of pain, possibly even applying a little force to underline the sincerity of his demands. All these actions are illegal, and the policeman who takes money is no more careful than the man who extorts information to conceal his actions from his colleagues. Each time a patrolman does any of these things, he blurs the boundaries that restrict and regulate his power.

A new man may ask his sergeant or a veteran officer for advice and counsel before doing something he knows is illegal and possibly dangerous; but as the man gains confidence and experience, he restricts the exposure of his actions to only a few trusted colleagues. The more information he produces, the greater is his value to his superiors, whose dependence on his work encourages them to keep him happy, to reward him and to protect him when he "gets in the jackpot," when he is in trouble. Each time he extorts information and tastes the rewards and successes it brings, he becomes more and more dependent upon it. But he does not have a constant flow of information, he does not have people falling into his power every day, and when he discovers that the pressure for vice activity is relentless, any reluctance he has to manufacture evidence and to break the law openly is likely to crumble.

A patrolman got out of his car and approached a news dealer who was sitting on a pile of papers. The policeman hesitated until the few people at the stand moved away and then he approached. He was a new man on the sector. The dealer had been on the corner for almost forty-five years. "Hello, Jack." "Good morning, Officer," he replied formally, not moving from his bench but folding a newspaper that he was going to give the policeman as he had always given one to every sector man. "Say, Jack, a guy told me an interesting thing about you." The old man just looked at him, still seated, shielding his eyes from the sun while he looked up at the policeman. "Yes, he told me you were writin' a number." The news dealer rose from the bench, angry and nervous. "It's not true. I been here almost forty-six years and I never wrote no numbers in my life. Whoever told you is lyin'. You want to search my stand and me, go ahead, but it ain't true, Officer," he replied, retaining the dignity and formality of his generation. The patrolman did not move but answered evenly, "No, this guy told me for sure you were writin' and he's pretty reliable. I tell you what, Jack, if you ain't writin' and I think you are, maybe you can tell me about a few of the other newsies in the area who are. I'm gonna keep an eye on you when I go past, but maybe I won't look so hard." The old man was trembling as he bitterly replied, "I don't know nothin' about that."

At that moment the regular beatman, who had worked the block for almost ten years, approached the corner. He and the news dealer were friends, colleagues almost. The beatman watched his papers for him and in return the news dealer kept the policeman's extra equipment—his raingear and patrol forms— stored in the stand. He also kept the officer informed about things. The new sector man looked on silently as the beatman asked. "What's up?" The news dealer responded that the patrolman had accused him of being a number writer. The beatman smiled. "Go on, get in your car and go on patrol. Jack's a friend of the inspector and he ain't writin' no numbers." The threat behind the smile was as bright as the sun. The patrolman withdrew, remarking again that he would keep an eye on the stand as he drove past.

"Jack, don't get so excited. You just call the captain and make a complaint. Tell him you don't like being harassed. And mention to him you know the inspector. I'll talk to the sergeant myself. Now, don't worry. Did the kid try and hit you for a note?" "No—and I wouldn't give him nothing because I didn't do nothing. You knew that." "Yes, O.K., Jack, you got to relax, think about your health. He's green. I think he was just trying to hustle some information. Now, don't worry, we'll get him off your back right now." Not everyone is so lucky.

The patrolman is an important person locally, but in the scheme of things he is not very powerful. He does not have a lot of money to buy information, as do some detectives and federal agents. He cannot organize a wiretap. He works eight hours a day and then goes home, and if he is hanging around the district when his platoon is off, the men in the platoon that is working the street will make sure they know what he is doing. He cannot spy on people or entrap them into committing illegal acts, as do the plainclothesmen he knows.[4] He is dependent for what he knows on the people in his sector who need the streets to do their work and live their lives. His information is a form of rent that he collects for local prostitutes, junkies, bums, petty thieves, and burglars. Anyone who uses the street knows that the policeman who is friendly one day is the same man who may cajole, threaten, and even beat him the next. And if the people do not come up with information, well, they must take their chances.

Sometimes the patrolman gets information voluntarily. A store owner or a bartender may do him a favor in exchange for some small consideration or as a testament to a growing friendship. But generally these people want to give their information to his sergeant or lieutenant. If he is well established in his district and knows something about the gambling operations, he can get information from people in the trade who want him to eliminate their competition. But voluntary offers of information are infrequent. Even when he makes a cash payment, these transactions do not have commercial character to them. There is no hint of equality or freedom. Money is given not so much as a payment but rather as a fee designed to keep the person afloat and in a position to maintain access to what the policeman wants to know. Possibly he will give the man liquor if his informant needs drink, or drugs if that is what is required to keep him talking and listening and watching. He does not pay for information, he finances its acquisition. The policeman acknowledges the character of his methods of acquiring information; he does not conceal from himself what he is actually doing. People who do favors for him—the businessman who mentions in passing that a lot of liquor has been seen going into a club or a certain girl has been having a lot of visitors—are not referred to as rats, pigeons, or even simply informers, a word which once meant teachers but now suggests only one thing—betrayal.

"You want another drink? Go ahead. Bob,

[4]On the techniques used by honest and sincere plainclothesmen in vice enforcement, see Robert Daley, "Portrait of an Honest Cop," *New York Magazine* (May 3, 1971), and Jerome Skolnick, *Justice Without Trial.* (New York: Wiley, 1967), pp. 101–3.

give us a couple more down here." An off-duty lieutenant had casually run into his informant in a barroom and they were having a friendly conversation. They had known each other for many years, having met when the lieutenant was only a patrolman and the informant the manager of a big after-hours club. The manager was down on his luck now, the palsy in his hands signaling that his slide was prolonged. "You used to really take care of the cops, never forgot the district men. Always a drink or two, something to eat at four in the morning. Real good, it's true," the lieutenant reminisced. The situation had changed. "Honest, Joe, I need that job. If you could help me out with McKay, I'd appreciate it a lot, you know." "Well, sure, I'll talk to him. But I'm surprised you didn't let me know sooner about that game. You're sure they got a game going in there?" "I didn't go inside, but I was told good information." "Well, why the fuck didn't you go in there and let me know?" "You wouldn't hit that place, would you? You're a district lieutenant, I mean . . ." "The fuck I won't. You go in there and tell me what they got going and I'll hit 'em next week. Now will you go in there?" "Listen, they'd treat me real rough if they found out . . ." "Hey, I know that. You just get me the information and I'll speak to Kim for you. Bob, give us a couple more."

Every police official knows how his men acquire their information. If people disapproved of gambling, they would come forward and protest, but they rarely do. Regardless of whether the commissioner is considerd a "liberal" or a "conservative," he knows, condones, and encourages the fact that his men break the law to make vice arrests. He knows that if they do not make arrests, there will always be someone—a local group, a state politician, possibly a federal agency—to hint at corruption and immorality in the police department. No matter what he may say about improving the relations between the police and the community and introducing programs to open lines of communication with minority groups, he continues to encourage his

men to do things that undermine the possibility of trust between the patrolman and many of the people he encounters daily. He also knows that once the patrolman has obtained his information, he must make a mockery of the law in order to get the pinches the department demands as evidence of its honesty and commitment to upholding the law.

The fourth amendment of the Constitution establishes clear guides for the protection of our most private places—our bodies and our homes. In clear language, it marks out the precise manner the state must follow whenever it seeks to violate the privacy of any individual. It guarantees

"the right of the people to be secure in their person, houses, papers, and effects, against unreasonable searches and seizures, shall not be violated, and no Warrants shall issue, but upon probable cause, supported by Oath or affirmation, and particularly describing the place to be searched, and the persons or things to be seized."

Before a policeman may obtain a search warrant he must swear to a judge that he has "thoroughly investigated the information so as to convince a disinterested party [the judge] that reasonable cause or grounds exist to justify a search." The department formally exhorts its men to remember that "all information given by an informant must be checked. The policeman is duty-bound to investigate the information given him." The policeman does not have to inform the court who his informant is or how he obtained his information, a requirement that would effectively destroy the possiblity of the police ever acquiring information legally; this spares him from having to tell the judge a verifiable lie. But a policeman rarely is able to check the information he obtains; and if he did, the chances of his being spotted are great. The honest policeman has no alternative but to rely solely on what he is told by people who will tell him anything to get loose of his grasp, and he presents this as carefully evaluated evidence to a judge in a court of law. Everybody involved— the policeman, his sergeant and lieutenant, the captain who approves the warrant application, the assistant district attorney who approves it, and the judge who grants him the warrant— knows that the policeman is perjuring himself. The patrolman has no choice, and if the department does not want this to happen, it must select a different strategy for enforcing vice laws. Unfortunately, experience has shown that exclusive reliance on plainclothesmen and vice squads results in systematic corruption and widespread payoffs, while general responsibility has at least a restraining influence on the cupidity of men who learn that there is a dollar to be made.[5]

The supervisor's evaluation of the warrant applications brought to him is based on the needs of his squad, not on the quality and legality of the information. Even if the sergeant and lieutenant are absolutely honest, refusing to take any of the money they know they can get if they relent, they do not care about the credibility of the informant or the manner in which the information was obtained. Usually the supervisor's decisions are based on his evaluation of the man making the request. Usually gambling warrants are taken out by the most experienced men in the platoon, and often they do not reveal to anyone exactly how they got their information. Even if the sergeant thinks the information is good but does not trust the man or have high regard for his competence, he may refuse him permission or suggest that another man take out the warrant. Since perjury is going to be committed, the sergeant wants someone whose proven skills will prevent any embarassments or unintentional revelations under oath.

Once permission for a warrant is granted, the only concern of the men involved is to make certain that the application is written in a manner that will assure its approval. The department is very helpful in this matter, offering guidance that clearly outlines the criteria that must be satisfied. "Police are not required to disclose

the identity of their confidential informants, but, it is important for the policeman to fully explain why he believes the facts related to him . . . are true. . . . [There] must be included the informant's record of accuracy. . . . An important piece of supporting datum which can be included in the warrants is 'surveillance.' Police officers should indicate in a warrant what they have observed concerning the premises or property that is to be searched."

The possibility of error and misunderstanding is minimized by providing a model example of proper application. "On July 15, 1966, I received information from an informant who I know to be reliable because information supplied by said informant during the past year has resulted in six arrests and five convictions. . . . Informant personally told me . . . that he personally observed . . ." The comforting assurance this form offers men who are afraid to do illegal things is the principal reason why almost every search warrant is written in this manner. The need to lie under oath bothers many men; it frightens them and even forces some to forgo the rewards of vice work altogether. Some men take out warrants with the intention of never serving them. They are used to appease their sergeant, who can claim to his superiors that his men were trying but their information went sour before they had an opportunity to serve the warrants.

No effort is made to disguise the illegal character of the enterprise. Since every warrant application is a collective enterprise ratified by commanding officers, no policeman is afraid to reveal the false character of what he is doing. The patrolmen and the operations crews, who prepare the applications, openly discuss the mechanics of faking warrants, although they are careful not to reveal the details. It is taboo to look at a warrant application without invitation; to do so is one of the acts that guarantee a patrolman open rebuke and even threats. Every patrolman learns that he must be a liar and a conspirator if he wants to remain a district policeman. He must become an expert in telling

[5]On warrants, see Jerold H. Israel and Wayne R. LaFave, *Criminal Procedure in a Nutshell: Constitutional Limitations* (St. Paul, Minn., West Publishing, 1971), pp. 109–27.

untruths or transfer to a unit that has no vice-work obligations.

"You gotta put in there that he gave you information before, Hal, or the judge won't go for it," a corporal said. "Aw, fuck it, this is good information. The guy who give it to me is a number writer, he should know." "Listen, you just put in there that the information you got was given to the special squads and they made all the pinches," a patrolman said to his partner. "Not me, I ain't committin' perjury. I never made a vice pinch before. You do it if you're such a big man." "Shit, you think you're any better than anyone else. Everyone perjures himself in vice—the cops, the courts, and the defendants. Go on." "All right, but you better tell me just what to say."

"Listen, Sarge, this is good information. We got it off a faggot just an hour ago. He said he saw a lot of stuff in the house but we gotta hit it right away before they move it out." "O.K., I'll make up the application and you run it right down to the judge. You got any pinches for narcotics off a warrant?" "Yea, a couple—" "O.K. I'll write the usual stuff about reliable informant. But I'll have to say that surveillance has not been possible because the informant told you the stuff is going to be moved immediately. That way he won't ask you why there's so much hurry. You're sure it's good?" "If it ain't, that faggot's not gonna be walkin' in this town any more."

The constant demand for vice arrests and the violations of the law that men must practice to get good arrests makes it nearly impossible for a sergeant to prevent some of his men from indulging in practices that are blatantly criminal. A man may justify to himself a lie to a judge if he believes that his information is good and that the person he is investigating is a gambler, but some policemen do not bother to limit themselves to this self-constructed zone of proper behavior. In every part of the city where vice activity is strong, there are people who are generally regarded as marginal members of society, whose instability and lack of place brings them

different treatment from that received by solid citizens. The patrolman's constant exploitation of bums, drunks, junkies, and prostitutes for information completely erodes the legal restraints designed to prevent him from exercising his authority over them in ways that express disregard for them as persons. He does not hesitate to search them when he sees them, going through their pockets as if they were his own.

A policeman, under oath, recounted an investigation that he conducted:

"I received information from a female who I know as Jean. . . . This female, Jean, told me that there was a colored female by the name of Mary, who she described, who was inside a bar . . . and that this female had heroin on her person. . . . I went into this bar, in uniform, and took into custody the female who had been described to me. I placed her in the rear of the wagon and Officer Frame drove to the area of 15th and Webster Sts. where I alone conducted a search of this person. I found approximately fifteen bags of heroin which this female, Mary, had concealed under her panties. At about that time Officer Frame called back to me and mentioned something about a radio call "man with a gun" or something like that and said "Let's leave." I let this female go and Officer Frame and I proceeded to respond to the radio call."[6]

There are policemen who are not only willing to search suspects illegally for evidence in order to make an arrest or to obtain information but are also willing to manufacture evidence in order to establish the basis for an arrest. "Farming," the planting of evidence, is practiced throughout the department. There are sergeants and lieutenants who take a very strong line against this practice. When a man takes over a new squad, one of the first things he does is to indicate to his men his position on farming. Some supervisors even insist on accompanying their men when warrants are served in order to prevent them from doing it. But even the most honorable sergeant knows he cannot stop his men from making illegal searches, planting evidence on people to compel them to talk, or

[6]*Philadelphia Inquirer* (November 17, 1971).

fabricating evidence for warrants. If a man carries with him a numbers slip or a few bags of heroin he has confiscated and withheld, how can he be prevented from using them if he is willing to violate the law? Whenever a platoon is behind in its activity, the sergeant knows that any pressure he exerts on his men encourages them to behave illegally.

A patrolman approached a colleague who was filling out a warrant application in the operations room. The man had been waiting for him because he had information they were going to use to get a warrant for narcotics. "Sorry I'm late—we'll have to get the warrant tomorrow. I just got a couple more vice pinches on the way into the district. I seen this guy lyin' on the sidewalk over on Cony Street. I got out to look at him. Drunk as a fish, stinkin' nigger. So I went through his pockets the way you do before you call the wagon, you know, and I found a slip with numbers. I called the lieutenant and he said to put him on the books. They guy promised to give us a speak and maybe a still if we let him off the hook, so that's a couple more."

"The lieutenant let you put him on the books, huh? That new lieutenant, I guess he's never seen that dogshit numbers slip you got," the patrolman replied, with a small grin, concealing his displeasure over a practice he knew the man used regularly. "The guy was so drunk he didn't know whether it was his or not. He's got five pinches for illegal lottery anyway."

There are policemen who are willing to farm anyone they believe cannot resist them or whose protests will not be acknowledged because of their reputation or previous record. There are many more men who hold these colleagues in contempt but are willing, nonetheless, to plant evidence on a person whom they regard as guilty. They defend their patently illegal behavior in terms of the need to get activity and the guilt of the suspect. They implicitly argue for the morality of their actions in comparison with the immorality of those who frame the in-

nocent along with the guilty. This pathetic effort to maintain their dignity and honor is something only a policeman can understand.

There are many younger policeman who do not know how to get vice information and are not willing to extort it from people. They have few contacts that are likely to give them a line on a number writer. But they want to get vice activity and their only chance is to make a drug arrest. It is a common practice in many squads for some men to retain a part of the drugs they find on people; others are given some by their sergeant. These are mainly used to "buy" information, but there is no way that the officer's use of these drugs can be controlled. He may give it away for evidence, but he may also plant it on someone, sell it for profit, or use it himself. If he does any of these things, it is not likely that his colleagues are present, but even if they knew, what could they do? Every one of them has to some degree violated the law, and if they expose him, what is to prevent their own wrongdoings from being revealed?[7]

The inhibitions most policemen have about using any of these practices are weakened by what they see their colleagues doing when they make a "legitimate" narcotics arrest. How can a uniformed man actually witness a drug transaction? He sees many pushers on the corners, he knows them by sight, but few actually carry drugs on them. These are kept concealed nearby, and when a sale has been arranged, the buyer collects his drugs at another place. The patrolman cannot follow people around. Even if he were able to, it would require his ignoring the demands for service and the emergency calls he receives from the dispatcher. He may stop the pusher on the street and illegally search him. If

[7]"I almost never had to buy anything—only one time. I always could get it from policemen. This is the way I got a large portion of my stuff—most of my drugs. They thought I was using it to plant on people," a patrolman who was an admitted user explained to investigators. When asked how the drugs were obtained, he replied, "I would say that in about eighty percent of the drug raids . . . when drugs are confiscated, that some is kept out . . . to be used for plants." *Philadelphia Inquirer* (September 5, 1971).

he finds anything, the patrolman may decline to make an arrest because he does not want to lie in court, preferring to exploit the moment to get information from the man or to swell his supply of drugs. But there are men who have no inhibitions. Everyone in court, from the policeman to the judge, knows that most drug arrests are illegal. Every time a policeman tells of a "flying bag," the police description of a technique used to support court testimony, his words are greeted with open skepticism, but there are no grounds for a judge to presume that the man is lying. Often defendants do throw heroin to the ground upon the approach of a policeman in the mistaken belief that if the contraband is not on their person, it is not legally their goods. But many patrolmen use this claim to cover the planting of evidence of illegally seized contraband. If the officer is determined to make his arrest stick, he really has little choice but to tell a lie.

"Officer, you say the defendant was running ahead of you down an alley and you saw him throw the material to the ground?" "Yessir." "It was night and it was dark, correct?" "Yessir." "It was not well lighted in the alley?" "Yessir; no, sir, it was not," "Now this alley, was it clean or were there papers and debris scattered on the ground?" "Well, that is not a clean area of the city, sir, as you know, but this particular area was pretty clean." "I see, the unfortunate defendant chose the only clean alley in the city to run down and throw this material. Well, I shall have to send a letter to the Streets Department thanking them for their efforts, and tell them you have testified to their good work." Everybody in the courtroom, except the defendant, broke into laughter. He was convicted.

The honest patrolman who is determined to advance in his platoon cannot long resist involvement in these practices. They offer him the only substantial chance to make the arrests that bring him the credit he seeks. He learns that information does not come for nothing. He

must get in and deal. If he has nothing to trade, if he is a "straight cop" who will not make deals or extort information, the only alternative he has is to beat information from people. This still happens, but it is not condoned. He sees that illegal searches and fake warrants are the only way to make vice arrests. He sees men he admires, good cops, men who take risks and arrive prepared to work, using heroin to buy information and even to frame people. He listens to them lying in court, hears them judge others by their ability to give false testimony; he wants to share their rewards, the favors granted them by their sergeant, the free time, the extra day off. He does not long resist, or he transfers.

A patrolman who testifies under oath in a manner that reveals he conducted an illegal search (or seizure) is not chastised or punished; if he confiscated drugs or a weapon, he may feel that he has served a useful purpose, although the suspect is freed. But if he is testifying about an arrest based on a search warrant, he must lie to protect himself and his colleagues. One reason most sergeants are very careful in selecting men to take out warrants is their need to be sure of the man's capacity to testify skillfully and with aplomb. A policeman can never be certain that a lawyer will not try to expose him. While most gambling cases are handled by relatively few lawyers whose only interest is to get the case dismissed or suppressed and not to embarrass anyone, there always remains the possibility of unpleasant disclosures. An experienced vice man cannot possibly retain any respect for the rigid standards of law and evidence which, presumably, the society has an obligation to maintain. He has committed perjury so often and routinely that he sees the courtroom as just another element in a giant charade. There are many policemen who despise this state of affairs, but there is no alternative available to the policeman who wishes to continue in his job. He can simply refuse to get any vice, but if he wants to advance in his platoon, he must make vice arrests and this requires him to lie. He cannot tell the truth because the costs of doing so are grave personally and have no effect on the continuation of the system.

"Officer, how did you acquire the information which led to this raid?" "Well, sir, my partner and I were stopped on the street by this woman who said that she knew someone was a big number writer," the youthful patrolman said.

"She showed you the house and told you who the people involved were?" the defense lawyer asked. "Yes, sir." "What did you do then, Officer?" "We called for our sergeant, and he talked to her for a little while and said we should get a warrant and hit the place."

"So you got a warrant?" "Yes, sir." "Now, this warrant, how long after you talked to the woman did you get it?" The policemen in the courtroom waiting to testify in their own cases had been indifferent to the proceedings, but now they all sat alertly, watching the young policeman on the stand. He was in trouble and did not know it. "Well, we made up the warrant application and then went right back to the house and went in." "Did you know this woman or ever see her before?" "No, sir." "Now, Officer, on your application you state that the informant was well known to you and had previously given you good information." The room was silent; several policemen rose to leave. A sergeant sitting nearby put his head in his hands and swore softly and continually to himself. "Did you actually know her, Officer?" The patrolman was sweating, finally realizing what he had done. "Well, sir, uh, I did not know her but she was known to my partner and to the sergeant." "But you said on the warrant—it's in your name—that you knew her." "Yessir, but it was my partner who knew her." "Officer, you also swore in the warrant that you kept the house under surveillance. But you have testified here that you raided the house right away. What kind of surveillance did you make?" "Uh, sir, my partner and the sergeant maintained a watch on the place while I made the application and they . . ." "Your honor, I think the policeman has in-

dicated that his search was illegal and unwarranted." The sergeant had stopped swearing and looked as if he were preparing to murder the policeman, who was near tears. The judge excused him from the stand and dismissed the case. He asked the assistant district attorney to meet with him after the recess to discuss a matter in private. The officer walked from the courtroom, followed by his sergeant. "Oh shit, man, I never seen one so green before. That guy has got to be stupid or he's tryin' to fuck the sergeant real good," a patrolman commented.

The district policeman's involvement in gambling enforcement compels him to violate the law, degrade people, and disregard the established standards of honesty and that have been built into the legal codes over many centuries; it also undermines his ability to take pride in his work. In return for this he gets very little. He knows that enforcement is a sham that cannot prevent gambling and illegal drinking in the neighborhoods where they are entrenched. If he is shrewd, experienced, and willing, he can exploit occasional opportunities for payoffs, and if he works for a corrupted sergeant or lieutenant, he may have the chance to earn a steady note, but he will not get rich.

In every district where gambling goes on, there is money for those who want it and are willing to take the risks. "It's there, it's all over the place. All you need are these stripes and you know there's an envelope waiting for you. You know, guys come up to you on the street and ask you to stop here or there. If you want it, it's yours," a sergeant said. Regular payoffs are available to supervisors, but unless they are prepared to organize protection, their men cannot participate. If a sergeant will not allow (or is not allowed by his lieutenant and captain) a steady note, the men who want to exploit their vice knowledge for payoffs are limited to momentary chances. The patrolman who does this must be knowledgeable, because if he puts the squeeze on someone who is protected or connected, he can find himself under arrest and on the front page of the city's newspapers, an example to all other stupid cops. But the experienced men in the squad do know, they have seen who gets arrested, they know which places have not been raided, which number writers seem to operate freely and which do not. They can stop someone on the street and simply shake him down on the spot, threatening to take the man in "for investigation," which would ruin his business for the day and makes the payment of five or ten dollars well worthwhile. If a policeman discovers a card game or a crap game, he does not have to "take the game" but can call his sergeant and collect rent from the players. If he confiscates lottery or sweepstakes tickets from someone on the street or in a raid, it is not necessary to turn them in to the evidence clerk. "Hey, Frank, I want to talk to you. Did you get those lottery tickets?" "Yes, sir." "Well, hold on to them. I just checked with Pedro, they hold the drawing on Wednesday. Maybe we got a winner. So you keep them and if *we* don't hit it, then you can turn 'em in," the lieutenant said.

There are many policeman who are not knowledgeable about vice and do not dare to arrange a private deal for themselves or take something that is offered. However, many of these men are involved, whether they wish it or not, by their sergeants. A man does not have to take money from a gambler to become involved in criminal acts. If he brings someone in for investigation and his sergeant tells him to "let the guy walk," he must either comply and violate administrative regulations and the criminal law, or fight his sergeant. If he is willing to confront his superior, he must be prepared for an effort to drive him from the district and from the department. If he has done anything wrong, the sergeant will nail him; he will watch him like a hawk, pressuring him constantly for even the most trivial violation. Few men resist their bosses.

"I picked this guy up. I didn't know nothin' then. He was standing on the corner talkin' to someone and he had a big fuckin' roll in his hand, maybe two grand. And he had slips on him. I knew he must be a number writer or something, but I didn't know for sure. So I called the wagon, and he was offering me money and shit. Real friendly, no threats, and he wasn't nervous about bein' pinched. So the wagon comes and they took one look at him and smiled. You know Rollins, a good cop, right? He was the guy's fuckin' nephew, I found out later. So you know how he got on the wagon so quick. Anyway, he's gettin' in the wagon and slips the roll to the kid. I almost shit, but I didn't say nothin'. You think he made the books? We got into the yard and the sergeant was waiting. He never even got inside the building. He walked out of the wagon smiling and kept right on going. He even thanked me."

A sergeant may organize regular payoffs for himself and a few intimates without sharing or allowing his other men to share them with him, or he can allow steady notes to be distributed among all the men in the platoon. If this occurs, anyone who does not want to take may refuse, but he will not remain in the district very long. New men are sealed off from any contact with these payments, and even when a rookie works a wagon or a car with a veteran, he may not know that his partner is collecting for the platoon. Most steady notes are collected on the first day of daywork or four-to-twelve by a wagon crew or a car man. The veteran stops at a store or a house and tells his partner, "Kid, wait here and listen close, we don't want to blow any calls. I'll be back in a minute." The rookie does not know what is going on, and he is not told anything. Even if he suspects there are payoffs, he is not offered or allowed any concrete information until his colleagues are certain that he is "all right." One admitted grafter told investigators that he "started receiving these payments six to eight months after coming to the Seventeenth District." During these months the new man is tested informally to see whether he is willing to participate and involve himself. "It wasn't long before I learned about police corruption. Once when I was a rookie, my sergeant told me to close the club at 3 A.M. He told me there was a $5 note waiting for me and I told him if he wanted the place closed I'd close it, but if he wanted someone to leave it open and pick up a note to send someone else. He sent someone else . . . That's what they do. They test you. If you don't do it the first time, they usually leave you alone," a captain recounted in a sworn affidavit.[8]

Steady notes are strictly territorial. A fixed amount is paid to each sector, wagon, and supervisor for the daywork or the four-to-twelve shift. One man may do the collections for the entire platoon, or different men may collect the notes on their sectors and, after taking their share, turn the rest over to someone, usually a wagon man, for distribution to others. From evidence given in sworn testimony, it appears that none of these amounts to much money. One officer in a district which had a reputation for being one of the most "active" in the city estimated that he earned about $90 a month in regular payoffs. He was a "bagman" for his sergeant, which meant that he was directly involved in the collection and distribution of notes, and therefore his knowledge of the economics was sound. In addition, this patrolman was a heroin addict, who dealt in narcotics with his sergeant's permission and encouragement. The trust presupposed by this mutal collusion suggests that the officer was intimately familiar with all the arrangements in his squad. If the policeman was making about $1,000 annually from regular payoffs, it can be safely assumed that his sergeant and lieutenant were earning at least double or triple his take. Most of the notes he collected were for $5 or $10, and his sergeant and lieutenant were usually paid miltiples of his share. Also, they have opportunities to earn extra shares that the men do not know about.

There may be districts where steady notes do not exist, but there is no district where there is not a belief that someone is taking a regular payoff from gamblers or liquor men. When a man goes "into clothes," his relationship to former colleagues changes immediately. Without knowing for sure, they are all certain that he is making money. Everyone assumes that plainsclothesmen take something. "They've been in clothes for some time now. You know how it is, everybody in the district knows who they are but they still make some pinches. And now Shoemaker's opening a store. You wonder where he got the paper? Who knows? The word is that they get paid $150 apiece on the first and the fifteenth. I guess you could open a store with that after a while, huh?" a policeman commented to his partner as they chatted, hidden in their hole during the murky hours of last out.

This attitude toward plainclothesmen is not disguised in their presence. They must accept the constant kidding of their friends or avoid contact with them. They are always being told how good they look, how fit, how nice their clothes are; they are kidded about all the "free tail" they must be getting and all the extra money they have in their pockets. "We had a ball last night. Hogan paid for everything, man: the broads and the booze; we had a ball." "Well, shit," someone replied, "he shudda paid, he's in clothes, ain't he? So he's got the paper, right?" There are policemen who bend every effort to get themselves into plainclothes, while others decline the offer because they do not want to become involved with prostitutes, undercover work, and graft. "There's no way it can't fuck up your home life. Your wife knows you're goin' out to sit in a barroom and make out with some broads. So what do you expect her to feel like? What do you think she's gonna think when you don't come home until the morning?" an experienced plainclothesman commented. "Three hundred? That's a poor district. I wouldn't go into that bullshit for less than double," a patrolman commented. He had declined an invitation to go into clothes for the simple reason that he feared what he would do. "I'm having a hard enough time staying clean in the district. I'm so bored you know, and now I know so much that I

[8]*Philadelphia Inquirer* (November 17, 1971).

can make paper any time I want. That's why I'm going into the juvenile squad. There's no green there, just good, hard police work. There's no way you can go into clothes and be clean. The best you can do is avoid getting caught."[9]

Relatively few men are making money from gamblers regularly, and not even a majority are making money even occasionally, but every policeman who has dealings with vice is obliged to break the law and involve himself in a degrading sham. The policeman develops a set of attitudes that some people think cynical but that he sees as realistic in light of his knowledge of city life. "I don't make no more pinches unless the sergeant needs one real bad. It's bullshit. Look at that bar. You know who owns that place? Is he a big banker in the city? How many pinches has he got for numbers? Five or six. I locked him once. How much did he pay to get his record expunged? I don't know, but he ain't got no record any more and he's a fucking city councilman. So why should I make a number pinch for? I don't want to make any money off that stuff no more, it's gettin' too dangerous, and that's all those pinches are good for."

"O.K., Herbie, relax. You can see the captain in a minute." A wagon crew and their sergeant had brought an irate news vendor into the station. They had served a warrant for his newsstand but had found nothing. He had protested their actions and demanded to see the captain. After a few minutes the captain came to the

door and greeted him in a friendly fashion. The news dealer was not mollified. "Look, this is the fourth ticket you guys took on me this year and you ain't found nothin'. Now I want this bullshit to stop. I am bein' harrassed and I'm gonna make a complaint if it keeps up."

"Herbie," the captain said, "everybody knows you're a number writer. I know it, you know it. Now, I'll make a deal with you. You take one pinch, just one, and I promise you there won't be any more warrants on you this year."

"No. I ain't goin' for it. You got nuthin' on me and I ain't takin' no pinches. But these guys gotta stop hittin' my business or I'm gonna see someone."

"O.K., Herbie, no hard feelings. They get information you know, they have to act," the captain said, with a smile, "but I will personally check it out next time, O.K.?"

"Well, you're O.K. You want *Playboy*? I'll send it up to you." The captain grinned and returned to his office. "Now, you guys leave me alone, right?" They smiled and he grinned. The sergeant offered to drive him back to his stand, but he decided to walk. No hard feelings, it was just a nice day. But the sergeant accompanied him to the door and, in view of anyone who cared to look, handed him a dollar to play a number. Later the sergeant said. "I was lookin' at the warrant while he was talkin' to the captain and noticed the last three digits of the serial number matched my kid's birthday, 914, so I decided to play it. That old Jew's been writin' numbers on the corner for almost thirty years. We just don't find the slips."

Driving past a taproom, a sergeant nodded. "You remember all the bullshit we had with that place? The roofers and the porkies were fightin' and they firebombed the place. The night when Thomas swung at that little prick and hit me in the head with his stick. Maybe you weren't workin' that night. We occupied the street for a couple of days and listened to all their horseshit. Can't blame 'em really, the roofers badmouthin'

[9]The systematic corruption of plainclothesmen and the organization of payoffs has been documented several times in recent years. The most dramatic and revealing revelations occurred in New York City during the "Harry Gross scandal" (1950) and in testimony before the Knapp Commission (1970). See Norton Mockridge and Robert H. Prall, *The Big Fix* (New York, Henry Holt, 1954), and Ted Poston, "The Numbers Racket," a newspaper series reprinted in *Organized Crime in America: A reader*, Gus Tyler, ed. (Ann Arbor, University of Michigan Press, 1962), pp. 260–74. A comment on lifestyles of plainclothesmen in New York is in Gene Radino, *Walking the Beat* (Cleveland; World Publishing Co., 1968), pp. 143–51.

'em all the time and not lettin' 'em use the bar. So they closed the place up and drove the roofers out. Now it's gonna reopen and the porkies have the bar. The shit they do. You know who's got the licence? Pilz, the bookie over on Warner Street. That motherfucker got the license and he's puttin' a porkie in as front man. He can get a liquor ticket from the state, but I'm supposed to bust my ass locking him up for makin' book? Bullshit. Anyway, we'll get a good note out of the bar for watchin' the place."

The patrolman is obliged to violate the law, degrade people, lie, and even shame himself in his own eyes in order to make arrests he knows are meaningless and he suspects produce money for others. This not only tends to make him cynical about the law and the motives of many people he knows, it also makes him think of himself as a special kind of fool. He sees himself operating in a world where "notes" are constantly floating about, and only the stupid, the naïve, and the fainthearted are unwilling to allow some of them to stick to their fingers. Even in the most carefully regulated system, the patrolman's opportunities to break the law are considerable. If he is inclined, nobody can prevent him from tipping off somebody about an impending raid or pocketing drugs or money that he finds. Strict supervision is rarely possible. Even the many supervisors who do not take graft are involved in collusions with their men to cover up the illegal methods they use to acquire information, get warrants, and make arrests. These acts convert supervisors into colleagues,

diminishing the distance between them and the men they command. If they oblige their men to adhere to all of the legal rules, they will only reduce the number of vice arrests that are being made and cause their captains, divisional inspectors, and the chief inspector to demand increases in the squads' activity, which will be accompanied with threats of transfer. They are trapped in a dilemma not of their own making. This is one reason why policemen deeply resent admonitions to be honest. They know that the editorials in newspapers are irrelevant to their situation. Policemen who know themselves to be honest invent distinctions between "good notes" and "bad notes" to rationalize their own misconducts. They compare the petty violations they commit against the acts of men who are really on the take, and secure for themselves a modicum of honor. They know that the only way a policeman can be honest in the exacting sense required by his oath of office is to resign. The policeman does not want to quit, so he makes little compromises, which bring him a few dollars and more importantly solidify his relationships with his colleagues, and he continues to do his job. He knows he does things that are illegal, but he has no choice. He knows that there are many dishonest policemen, but his rewards for doing work he considers "dirty" are little more than the renewal of his right to continue in the job. He cannot prevent what he disapproves, nor can he explain to anyone without jeopardizing his career (and his life in some places), so he turns his face to the wind and does what he must.

7. Criminal Interrogation

ARTHUR S. AUBRY, JR.
RUDOLPH R. CAPUTO

ONE SPECIFIC FACET OF INTERROGATION THAT should be thoroughly understood and kept in mind at all times, is the fact that confessions secured under duress, or under conditions amounting to duress, are invalid and will be held inadmissible in court. Duress has been defined as the imposing of hardship, severity, or some type of restraint or compulsion upon the subject in an attempt to motivate him to the point that he will make the confession.

If the confession was made under duress, this fact can and will be quickly established by the defense attorney, and the fact that it was made under duress will affect the voluntary nature of the confession, and will forcibly demonstrate the fact that the person making the confession did not have complete freedom of choice in the making of the confession. This freedom of choice to make or not to make the confession is a fundamental Constitutional right, and it may not be violated.

There are almost as many interrogation approaches that may be used with profit at various times as there are individual human beings, multiplied by the sum total of human emotions, fears, preferences, likes and dislikes. Individuals are just that, individuals; they are completely unique and one of a kind. Many similarities exist between individuals, but they are only appear-ances, or surface similarities at best. There is a single best approach that will work with maximum effectiveness on a certain individual, and motivate him to make a full and complete confession in short order; the identical approach may be utterly useless against his twin brother. The single best approach will be arrived at by a combination of experience gained by the interrogator during the course of many interrogations, and his ability to evaluate and analyze the subject immediately prior to the initiation of the interrogation.

We will consider many different kinds of interrogative approach because the more skillful, the more facile the interrogator and his approach, hand-tailored to meet the various needs and the ever-changing needs of the interrogation situation, the higher his chances of consistent success are going to be. As indicated, the number of approaches are almost infinite. The following discussed approaches have been used by the writers on many occasions, and in many different types of interrogation situations, some successful at times, others unsuccessful at times, however all have been used with success at one time or another. Eventual success as an interrogator will depend to a great extent upon experimentation in the use and application of different interrogation approaches, various techniques, and various questioning methods.

One basic fact that should be kept in mind at all times is the fact that the interrogator must possess a bag of tricks similar to the top hat of

▶SOURCE: *Criminal Interrogation. Second Edition. Springfield, Ill.: Charles C. Thomas, 1967. Pp. 207–224. Reprinted by permission.*

the magician, and like the magician who pulls rabbits and other items out of the top hat, the interrogator must be able to pull various approaches out of his bag of tricks, and do so with the ease and competence that only comes with long hours of practice, experimentation, and application. The interrogator must learn to quickly and accurately assess the personality make-up and the character traits of others. He must be able to accurately assess the personality strengths and weaknesses of others. He must realize with a fine degree of exactitude his own weaknesses, limitations, and deficiencies; similarly, he must know and appreciate his own strengths and abilities, and learn to take maximum advantage of these strengths and abilities. The interrogator must never presume and prejudge guilt in the person being interrogated. He must act naturally in any and all situations, cannot allow himself the luxury of showing emotion, must never become overeager or condescending, and he must learn to keep the emotional pace set by the subject.

The basic considerations around which the choice and selection of approach will be molded are extremely important to the success of the interrogation. They include the fact that the approach be adapted to the type, character, and general background of the person being interrogated, the known facts, events, and incidents of the crime which has been committed, and the type, kind, nature and extent of the physical evidence available.

The approaches themselves are the following: The direct approach, The indirect approach, The emotional approach, and Subterfuge. There are many types and varieties of these approaches and they include Indifference, Sympathy or sympathetic, "Too great a temptation," "Only human to have acted that way," Kindness, Helpful, Friendly, Extenuation, Mitigation, Shifting the blame, "Hot and cold," Lessening the degree of guilt, magnifying the degree of guilt, Minimizing the consequences, The "fait accompli," Bluffing (with advantages and disadvantages), The stern, business-like approach, Compounding falsehoods, Pretense of physical evidence, Repetition of one theme, Mental relief through having told the truth, Perseverence, Appeals to decency and honor, "What's your side of the story?," Tearing down and building up, and "Just tell the truth." ·

The direct approach is normally used to best advantage in situations where the guilt of the subject is certain, or reasonably certain. When this situation prevails, the interrogator assumes an air of complete confidence in the subject's guilt, and by his total manner and attitude rules out any possibility that the subject could be innocent. The interrogator calmly and matter-of-factly points out the evidence indicative of guilt. He urges the subject to tell the truth, the whole truth, with no lies, no excuses, no holding back. During this process the interrogator will be careful to avoid threats or insinuations, and, if necessary, will be extremely sympathetic towards the subject and quick to point out that anyone else might easily have acted in the same manner as the subject did.

The interrogator will develop a full and factual account of the crime that has been committed from premeditation to commission, and will ask direct, pointed, questions. "When did you first get the idea for the crime?" "Why did you do it?" "Who else helped you in the commission of the crime?" "Why did he get mixed up in it?" "Was it his idea in the first place?" "What did you want the money for?" "Where is the money now?" The direct approach works well with professional criminals, particularly when there is reasonable certitude of guilt, and the guilt can and has already been established by real evidence and the testimony of reliable witnesses.

The indirect approach is normally used to best advantage in situations where the degree of guilt is indicated with something less than reasonable certitude. It is also an excellent approach to use against subjects with guilty knowledge. Direct questions are used in the direct approach, "Why did you do it?," etc. Indirect questions are asked in the indirect approach, "Where were you at the time of the incident?" "What were you doing in that part of town?" True, these are direct questions, but they may be considered as indirect if they do not specifically refer to the incident about which information is being sought.

In the indirect questioning approach, the subject should be requested or invited to relate everything that he knows about the incident, and he should be specifically requested to omit nothing, whether or not he thinks that it is important. If he is involved in even the slightest degree, he will either have to admit this involvement or take the only alternate course available to him; he will have to lie about some of the facts and details. If he is lying or attempting to lie, there are going to be discrepancies, distortions, and omissions in his account of the incident. As soon as the discrepancies, distortions, and omissions begin to appear in the account, the subject should be brought up short by the interrogator and these facts immediately pointed out to him.

If he is not too deeply involved he might decide right here to tell the whole truth and nothing but the truth, rather than get involved in a situation in which he does not have to be involved. In the indirect approach the interrogator attempts to create the impression that he is not convinced of the subject's guilt, and is giving the subject the opportunity to prove this fact by telling everything that he knows concerning the entire incident. Complete cooperation on the part of the subject in these circumstances is a very strong indication that he is not involved in the incident, regardless of the amount of knowledge that he might have concerning it.

If this subject is in reality guilty, this guilt will be indicated to a greater or lesser degree when he attempts to explain his previous discrepancies, distortions, and omissions. When the interrogation leans in this direction an immediate attempt should be made by the interrogator to determine whether or not the subject will acknowledge guilt, or deny guilt and continue to deny it. With the first appearance of damaging admissions, the interrogator should immediately revert to the direct approach.

The emotional approach is designed to arouse and to play upon basic emotions. "What will your wife and children think when this fact becomes known?" "What will your employer think of you, more to the point, what is going to happen to your job?" "What will your friends and associates think?" When the subject begins thinking about the answers to these questions, he is going to become emotionally upset, nervous, and tense. The emotional manifestations of nervousness and tenseness may be capitalized upon by the interrogator, by his pointing them out to the subject, and discussing them one by one.

A very strong emotional appeal may be made by the interrogator by his pointing out the moral seriousness of the crime, and commenting upon the fact that it must weigh very heavily upon the conscience of the guilty person. If the subject is a religious individual, the emotional appeal may be made through the fact that the person has let himself and his religion down, and that he is bound to suffer the consequences of his crime either immediately or sometime in the future, at any rate, he is bound to suffer the consequences and pay for the crime at some time.

The use of subterfuge makes a very effective approach, and occasionally may be used with telling force and effect. In a certain sense, subterfuge may be thought of as trickery, although it is not defined as trickery. The various forms of subterfuge should not be used as a standard approach, and should only be used in special circumstances. The guilt of the person being interrogated should be reasonably certain for this type of approach to have a good chance of success. Additionally, subterfuge should not be used until all of the so-called standard approaches have been tried and have failed. A word of caution here; this type of approach should not be used at all until the interrogator has acquired considerable skill and technical competence through experience in all types of interrogation situations, and with a wide variety of different types of interrogation subjects. This is so because the subterfuge technique is essentially a bluff on the part of the interrogator, and if the bluff is unsuccessful, the interrogation will almost of necessity be unsuccessful also.

This is so because the subject is going to be lost for good once the bluff has been tried by the interrogator and has failed. The fact that the interrogator has to resort to bluffing the subject is a tacit admission on his part that he has about run out of interrogative ammunition, and when the fact that he has been bluffing becomes apparent to the subject, the subject will realize that the interrogator has been unable to pin the crime on him. When this type of situation develops in the interrogation, the interrogator is best advised to break off and discontinue the interrogation as quickly and efficiently as possible, because the chances are excellent that he is not going to be successful, no matter to what lengths he carries the interrogation.

The authors have found the following types of subterfuge to be occasionally successful, and very effective between the rather narrow limits discussed immediately above. With the facts, events, and incidents of the crime known with certitude, a hypothetical story is attributed to an eye-witness, and the story allegedly told by the eye-witness may be repeated to the subject for his information so that subject will not know that the story has been manufactured by the interrogator. If the subject being interrogated is guilty, he will immediately recognize the truth of the story when he hears it, and this may motivate him to the point of making the confession.

Another subterfuge technique that works occassionally is the technique of playing one subject against another, by showing one the alleged confession or sworn statement of the other. Take the case of Subject One and Subject Two, in which both are suspected of having held up a bank together. Subject One is shown a sworn statement allegedly made and signed by Subject Two, in which Two admits some degree of guilt for the bank robbery, but places the majority of the guilt squarely upon the back of One.

Subject One, understandably, does not want to take the rap for the crime as the major participant, particularly if he has played a relatively minor role compared to Two, and he may be more than willing to make his own confession if for no other reason than to set the record straight concerning the part that he himself played in the bank robbery. At best, subterfuge is a weak technique and does not have much chance of success other than with inexperienced criminals. As indicated above, subterfuge should only be used as a last resort, and only in the case where guilt is reasonably certain.

An air of complete indifference may many times be used by the interrogator with telling effect. The interrogator implies by his manner, and may even so state, that he is completely convinced of the subject's guilt to such an extent that he really doesn't have to even talk to him about guilt—that the physical evidence, eye-witnesses, and all the other aspects concerning the case all indicate it so positively that discussion about it is a waste of time and energy on the part of the interrogator. If the interrogator can act convincingly enough in a situation of this nature, his air of complete indifference will many times be the motivating factor in the securing of the confession. This bit of play-acting may just convince the subject that the evidence against him is overwhelming, and more than sufficient to prove guilt, therefore he does not have to hold back and resist the interrogation situation any longer.

The sympathetic approach is an excellent all-around approach, and may be used occasionally with telling effect, particularly if a more direct, harsher approach has been used originally. The subject is on the defensive and he will expect to have these defenses hammered at with all the skill, energy, and persuasiveness that the interrogator is able to muster. To suddenly have the interrogator cease these direct, hard-hitting blows and begin to extend sympathy and understanding to a poor mortal human being who has perhaps gotten into deep water, when he originally meant to only dip his feet, can be very unnerving to the subject, and may be just the key to unlock the door to the confession. (This radical change in approach is also known as the "Hot and cold" approach, and is more fully discussed below.) The sympathetic approach can be very devastating to the composure of the subject, when it is combined with a direct, aggressive approach, and in the instances where the interrogator rapidly switches back and forth from the direct to the sympathetic approach, and then repeats the entire process as long as necessary to motivate the confession.

The "Too great a temptation" approach occasionally produces excellent results, particularly in the instance where the direct approach has been used and has failed. During the application of this technique the interrogator concentrates upon the proposition that the subject was tempted beyond his ability to resist, and that by giving in to the temptation and committing the crime, he was only acting naturally. The implication here is very plainly that anyone else, faced with the same powerful temptation, and being no more than human, would have given in to the temptation in the same manner that the subject did, and would have reacted in the same manner, i.e. would have committed the crime.

The "Only human to act that way," namely, commit the crime, is very closely associated with the too great a temptation approach and, in reality, is more a variation of the too great a temptation approach, than a separate approach. As indicated in the previous paragraph, both these approaches may be blended into a single approach and used with good effect. People do things every day that they may not be particularly proud of, in fact, may be extremely ashamed of. Rather than admit that they are to blame for what they have done, they will rationalize guilt in the matter by explaining to themselves that they have done whatever has been done because they are only human, and that neither themselves nor the rest of human beings are perfect. Being informed by the interrogator that he only acted in the same manner that other people act, may be the emotional trigger to unlocking the confession. Being told

by the interrogator that he acted in the same manner as other people could be expected to act under the same circumstances, will tend to lessen his own guilt concerning the crime, and may well be the motivating factor to securing the confession.

The kindness approach may sometimes be used with excellent results, particularly as an initial approach in the interrogation process. When the subject first sits down in his chair, he does not know what to expect in the way of actual interrogation. He most probably has built himself a mental image of what is in store for him; part of this mental image will be composed of ideas that he has fixed in his mind concerning the fact that he can expect an extremely rough time, lights glaring in his eyes, three or four burly, red-faced, strong-muscled giants, sleeves rolled up and gathered around him in a tight circle yelling at him and demanding that he confess, confess, confess.

When the interrogator actually enters the interrogation room and the subject sees that he is a quiet, well-mannered individual, dressed in a business suit, that he is completely professional in his approach, that he fulfills none of the subject's preconceived notions of an interrogator, he is going to be taken completely off his guard. When the interrogator initiates the interrogation with gentleness and kindness, instead of the expected roughness, the net result on the part of the subject is going to be extreme confusion. This confusion will work to the advantage of the interrogator, and the subject may well confess before he even realizes what he is saying. Granted, instances of this nature will be rare, but they have happened.

The helpful approach is similar to the kindness approach, and is based upon the same framework, namely a totally unexpected approach on the part of the interrogator. As indicated, the subject certainly does not expect kindness on the part of the interrogator; neither does he expect any help or assistance. When the offer of help is made it should come in the form of a general request to the effect of, "Is there anything I can do to help you at this time?" The offer of help is best made in this manner, and the interrogator does not have to go into particulars concerning the details of the help that he is offering.

The psychological mechanism involved is important and it serves the useful purpose of momentarily disconcerting the subject, and causes him to lower the guard to his defenses. During the comparatively short time that the defenses are lowered, the interrogator will have an excellent opportunity to secure incriminating admissions, and do the spadework required to motivate the subject into making the full confession.

The friendly approach is a continuation and an extension of the helpful approach and its usefulness is based upon the fact that it is an unexpected move on the part of the interrogator. As such, it will serve to disconcert the subject, and cause him several moments of confusion. With the confusion will come a general lowering of defenses and a good opportunity for the interrogator to secure the initial damaging admission, then the confession.

Extenuation generally means to treat or to represent something (in our case the crime that has been committed) as actually less than it really is, or less than it appears to be. It also has the general meaning of an excuse, or to make excuses for. Many times, an approach based upon this principle will be of maximum effectiveness. When a crime has been committed a great weight of guilt is loaded upon the individual who commits the crime, and this is true in all cases with the exception of the crime committed by the professional criminal. This weight of guilt will many times magnify the seriousness of the crime far beyond normal proportions in the mind of the person who has committed it, and he may be so completely overwhelmed that he does not even dare think about the crime and what he has done, let alone discuss it with a stranger and eventually confess it. The investigative approach in this situation consists of initial efforts on the part of the interrogator to paint the picture involved in its true perspective, thus immediately and partially lightening the weight of guilt being carried by the subject. Incriminating admission may best be secured at the psychological moment when relief from the weight of guilt first starts to flood over the subject.

Mitigation is an approach that sometimes works well in conjunction with extenuation. For our purposes here, mitigation might be defined as a softening or a lessening, making things milder. This approach is accomplished by playing down the seriousness of the crime that has been committed, the degree of participation if the subject's involvement was as an accessory, the degree of seriousness if the subject was the main participant, and similar considerations. This type of general approach will help to lessen the load of guilt carried by the subject, and he is strongly encouraged to shed the rest of the load by making a full and complete confession.

"Shifting the blame" technique is one that many times produces good results. The technique involved is psychological and simply consists of placing the blame for the crime upon the victim, someone else who may have been connected with the crime in some way, or actually anyone else to whom the blame may be shifted quickly and easily. For example, in a case involving car theft, the owner of the stolen vehicle might easily be blamed for having left the key in the ignition. An armed robbery victim might easily be blamed for having flashed a big roll of bills in a bar and grill, and thus in a sense inviting the eventual hold-up. When there are two or more participants in the commission of the crime, the full blame for the crime may be easily and naturally shifted over to the other participants when each of the individual subjects is being interrogated. The emphasis here is to the effect of placing the blame on the other subject(s), and intimating to the subject being interrogated that he was led into his part in the crime by the other participants.

We have already touched upon the "hot and cold" approach to some extent. This type of approach is actually a combination of two different approaches, which are in themselves essentially opposite in nature (thus the name, hot and cold). The interrogator starts with one approach, switches rapidly to the opposite approach, then rapidly switches back to the original approach. This process is repeated until the subject begins to make damaging admissions, at which time the interrogator swtiches to the direct approach.

The hot and cold approach lends itself to use by a team of two interrogators. One interrogator handles the hot aspects, then breaks off abruptly on a prearranged signal, gets up and leaves the room. The other interrogator immediately enters the room and takes over the interrogation, concentrating upon the cold aspects. With a little practice this interchange can be coordinated exactly and accomplished in the matter of a few seconds time. An alternating approach of this nature can be particularly effective when employed by two interrogators who work together regularly as a team.

Lessening the degree of guilt that attaches to a crime has already been discussed at some length, and as a general interrogative technique it is one of the most reliable approaches that may be used. As indicated above, this type of approach depends for its success upon the weight and load of guilt carried by the guilty subject, and the fact that he may be overwhelmed by this weight of guilt. Lessening the degree of guilt is best accomplished by statements to the effect of, "What you did was not too bad or serious considering the temptation," "You most probably were led into it by the accomplices," "They were more responsible than you for what happened," and similar types of statements. This type approach may be used with maximum effectiveness against the emotional subject, or one who is very apparently quite nervous and upset.

Magnifying the degree of guilt is the direct opposite to the approach discussed immediately above, and in a similar manner is based upon the heavy load of guilt carried by the subject. It is particularly effective in the instance where the subject does not fully realize what he has done, or realize fully the consequences of his actions either to himself or to others. This approach is based upon the psychological mechanism of increasing tension, and upon the fact that it is easier to successfully interrogate a tense, nervous subject, than it is to interrogate a subject who is relaxed and at ease.

Minimizing the consequences is another psychological approach that relies for its effectiveness upon lightening the load of guilt being carried by the subject. The subject has stolen an automobile. He may be approached with words to the effect that, "Well, that's not too bad, the man from whom the car was taken, (avoid the use of the word, "steal") probably won't miss it too much because he has another car . . ." "The hold-up victim from whom the money was taken has a good job and was not hurt too badly by the loss of the money . . ." "What you did was not too terrible, other people do the same thing and a lot worse every day."

The "Fait accompli," or "what's done is done, and you can't change it now," is a very effective approach, particularly against the subject who has been apprehended in the commission of the crime. The focus and emphasis here is to the effect that, "Whatever was done may have been bad enough, but by lying about it now, attempting to shift the blame to someone else, continuing to deny it, is only going to make it a lot worse for you in the long run."

"Bluffing" is a two-sided approach that may either work magnificently or fails utterly and miserably. If it works, all to the well and good; if it fails it will most probably mean the immediate and unsuccessful termination of the interrogation. Bluffing, in the interrogation sense, is the same as in any other sense. Basically, it consists of telling the subject something that just isn't so, hoping that it will produce the result of motivating the subject into making the confession. In the instance where there were no known or available eye-witnesses to the commission of a crime, the subject may be bluffed and informed that there was one or more, and that they have incriminated him; identified him as having been seen with the gun in his hand; placed him at the scene of the crime a minute before the crime was committed, etc. In an interrogation situation involving co-defendants where neither will confess or sign a written statement, each subject may be informed that the other one has already made a full confession and a sworn statement admitting guilt, and detailing the part that each played in the crime.

In the first instance, if the subject becomes convinced (the acting ability of the interrogator is always of major importance) that there were eye-witnesses to the crime who could and already have incriminated him, the bluff may work and the subject may confess without further effort on the part of the interrogator. In the second instance, if the subject is successfully bluffed to the effect that he has been incriminated by his codefendant, he will probably make a confession concerning his own part in the crime, and include the details concerning the participation of the other subject in the crime. In carrying out the bluff in the latter instance, a written confession, allegedly authored and signed by the codefendant, maintaining his own innocence, and implicating the subject, may be shown to the subject and he may be informed that it was made by the codefendant. In an instance of this nature, if the bluff works, the subject being interrogated may be motivated to make the confession implicating both himself and the codefendant, rather than take the full blame for the commission of the crime by himself.

There are several advantages to bluffing the subject. First, the subject has no accurate way of determining exactly how much you may know or may not know concerning the total details of the crime. Second, the subject has no way of accurately determining when you may or may not be bluffing. This is particularly true if the subject is building a chain of lies, basing each succeeding lie upon the previous one. This being the case, the psychological advantage is on the

side of the interrogator or in any bluff that he might care to attempt. In a certain instance, there may have been eye-witnesses to the commission of a crime, and this fact is known to the subject. However, these witnesses may be no longer available through any one of a variety of reasons, and this fact may not be known to the subject. By the skillful application of bluffing, the subject may be brought to believe that these witnesses have been questioned and have already implicated the subject. If the bluff works it will go a long way towards motivating the subject to confess.

Bluffing on the part of the interrogator is essentially a very weak technique; normally, it is not used until it becomes apparent that any and all other techniques have already failed, or will be definitely ineffective. The writers are strongly of the opinion that bluffing has a good and useful purpose in interrogation, that it can be an extremely effective technique, and that it should be used with extreme caution and only as a calculated risk where all other techniques have been tried and failed, or have been ruled out of consideration for a good and sufficient reason. The main advantage of bluffing to the interrogator is the fact that it may work when everything else has failed, and it may be successful in the situation where there is no other hope of any nature for success.

The main disadvantage involved in bluffing is the fact that if the bluff does not succeed, there is no use continuing with the interrogation as it is almost of necessity going to end in complete and total failure. With the failure of the bluff will come the realization to the subject that the interrogator had been bluffing, and that if he had to resort to bluffing during the course of the interrogation, he could not have much of anything on the subject. Once this happens there is not much sense in continuing the interrogation, and the interrogator is best advised to break it off short as quickly and gracefully as possible. At best, the bluff as a regular approach is to be avoided, and the interrogator is best advised not to resort to this approach excepting on a calculated risk basis, and only in the instance where the facts and cricumstances of the case make it mandatory upon him to at least attempt the bluff.

The stern approach is a business-like one in which the very definite implication is quickly made and conveyed to the subject that the facts and circumstances of the crime are so clear and so definitely indicate the subject's guilt that the interrogation itself is nothing more than a mere formality to give the subject the opportunity to tell his side of the story, and to clear up all the details of the crime as quickly as possible.

By his sternness and rather grim approach, and no-nonsense tolerated attitude on the part of the interrogator, the subject rapidly arrives at the conclusion that there is an overwhelming weight of evidence against him, and for him to try and lie his way out of the consequences would be a total waste of time on his part. The stern approach is particularly effective in the relatively rare interrogation situations where there is a wealth of incriminating evidence available and already in the hands of the interrogator.

The compounding falsehoods approach is an excellent approach and may be used to good advantage in any situation where the subject has commenced to tell lies. As soon as the interrogator detects a lie in the recital, he should attempt with every means possible to get the subject to tell successive lies based upon the first lie. The interrogator may easily create this type of situation by seeming to go along with the first lie and accept it as the truth, and at the same time making it easy for the subject to tell another and then more lies. To avoid admitting guilt, the guilty subject will have to lie about part of all of the details, facts, and circumstances of the crime. This thesis is one of the hard and solid facts that the science and art of interrogation is based upon.

It is also based upon the demonstrated fact that no person is clever or intelligent enough to base a story or an account of alleged facts upon a series of lies, which are in turn based upon each preceding lie that is told. Once the subject has told a series of lies, and apparently gotten away with them by not being brought up short by the interrogator, he will begin to build a mental attitude that he has been successful in outwitting the interrogator. When he reaches this point he will unconsciously advertise the fact by a return of assurance and self-confidence.

At this point the interrogator can quickly and easily yank the rug out from under him by summarizing the lies he has told, and demonstrating that they were told for the sole purpose of avoiding telling the truth, truth which would have incriminated the subject. The fact of having been neatly caught in a web of succeeding falsehoods may motivate the subject to confess at this point with little or no additional interrogation.

One very effective approach in a variety of interrogation situations is the approach based upon the pretense of possession of physical evidence. This procedure is essentially the same as bluffing the subject, but there is an all-important difference between this approach and the pure bluff. This difference is the fact that the subject is physically unable to call the bluff successfully. For example, there may be fingerprints on the murder weapon left by a curious bystander who happened to pick it up at the scene of the crime. The guilty subject very definitely knows that he handled the murder weapon. The murder weapon may be shown to him, with the fingerprints dusted and standing out in bold relief. He knows that he handled the weapon; he can plainly see the fingerprints; what he cannot know however is the fact that the prints on the weapon are not his. A pretense to the effect that they are his fingerprints may be made to him with devastating effect after an impression of his own fingerprints have been made on a fingerprint chart and have been compared to the prints on the weapon. Of course, the prints will not match but the subject can be told that the comparison established the fact that they did.

The constant repetition of one theme can be a very effective approach. This is a fairly simple technique to use with maximum effectiveness, and consists of repeating the same questions or line of questioning over and over again. This type of technique can also be very wearing on the interrogator and needless to say, requires infinite patience on his part.

Another very effective approach is the one that emphasizes the fact that mental relief from the burden of guilt being carried, will be secured by telling the truth and confessing to the crime. Another effective approach is the very simple one of plain, old-fashioned perseverence, simply wearing the subject down. Experience shows that many times the interrogator will give up the interrogation because he thinks that he is wasting his efforts, and he will give up a few moments before the subject begins to weaken in his efforts at resistance. This fact has borne out many times in the interrogation situation, by a second interrogator taking over the interrogation and quickly and easily securing the confession.

An appeal to decency and honor may occasionally be used with good results. We do not normally attribute these aspects of character to criminals but in the instances where crimes have been committed in the heat of passion, or in the face of an overwhelming temptation, the criminal may well be basically an honorable and decent person. The most effective approach in this situation is a simple statement and a simple question to the effect that, "You're an honest and decent person, why did you do it?" The fact that he is honest and decent, and can see that he has some status in the eyes of the interrogator, may be the factor that will trigger the admission and eventually the full confession.

Inviting the subject to "tell his side of the story" can be a very effective approach, particularly as the subject may subconsciously expect that no one is going to be interested in his version of what has occurred. If he has spent the time prior to the initiation of the interrogation building up his defenses, and attempting to arrange the lies that he plans to tell when he answers questions, he is going to be rather disconcerted by having the burden of doing all the talking placed upon him by the interrogator. In an instance of this nature he may well blurt out the truth before he can collect his wits and adjust to the new situation.

The "tear-down build-up" technique makes an occasionally effective approach, and is closely related to the hot and cold approach that we have already discussed. The tear-down build-up technique consists of alternately telling the subject what a wonderful person he is in one breath, then telling him what a total loss he is in the next. First, he is worth every consideration; second, he is worth less than no consideration; third, he would never think of doing such a terrible thing as commit the crime; fourth, he would have no compunction whatsoever to do the same thing again or worse at the first opportunity. This type of approach is bound to confuse the subject, and the net result will be the lowering of his defenses.

This technique is closely associated with the "hot and cold" approach which is, as we have seen, the rapid alternation of two directly opposite approaches. Other approaches which have been used successfully many times are the approaches of Scorn, where the focus is towards ridiculing the subject; Disdain, where he is treated as being far below any consideration at all; and contempt, where the implication is made that he is almost subhuman, completely worthless, and worthy of absolutely no consideration of any nature.

One of the most effective approaches that can be used is one that is not normally thought of as being an approach at all, a simple exhortation, repeated constantly, frequently, and at regular intervals, to "simply tell the truth," delivered in a matter-of-fact voice, and constantly stressing the theme that the subject simply tell the truth concerning the matter for which he is being interrogated.

8. Lie Detectors

SUBCOMMITTEE OF THE COMMITTEE ON GOVERNMENT OPERATIONS

"THEORY" OF LIE DETECTION

LIE DETECTION IS AN EMPIRICALLY DEVELOPED procedure without an adequate theoretical foundation; it is an art and not a science. Lying may be a widespread and popular pastime but no attempt has been made to account for the extent and variety of physiological and behavioral responses which may be observed when a person attempts deception. To the best of our knowledge, there is not a taxonomy of lying which defines the situation and purposes for which one person might attempt to deceive another. When one considers the amount of deception thought to exist in everyday life, it is surprising that no genius has arisen to codify this area.

As early as 1917, Marston recognized that some physiological responses probably always are present during an interrogation, whether or not a person is lying, but he thought that their magnitude would be larger when a person tries to deceive. The greater response would be due to some residue of learning, explainable in such terms as conditioned responses, conflict, or a threat of punishment. However, the theoretical aspects of lie detection still await exploration and it is difficult to believe that this area of technology can develop without a theory.

▶SOURCE: *Hearings before the Subcommittee of the Committee on Government Operations, 89th Congress, 1st Session (August 19, 1965), pp. 634–665. (Editorial adaptations.)*

1. Effectiveness of Lie Detection Methods

It should be possible to estimate the effectiveness of lie detection by the same methods that are employed in all classes of scientific observation and we shall start by examining the reliabilty and validity of lie detection.

A. Validity   Validity is defined as an estimate of the extent to which an instrument (or test) measures what it is supposed to measure. As applied to lie detection, validity may be estimated by comparing the agreement between conclusions derived by use of the polygraph with other, independent measures of deception (or truthfulness). For example, a judgment, based on examining a polygraph record, that a person attempted to deny a previous conviction for felony may be compared to a court record of conviction. For practical purposes, independent evidence for validating lie detection tests would be gained from thorough background investigations. A confession of guilt (or the admission of an attempted deception) is often used for estimating validity but it is not a completely satisfactory independent criterion. It is rarely clear whether the confession came before the polygraph was attached or after; or whether a complete polygraph test was run; or whether the interrogator made his "judgment of deception based on the polygraph" before or after the confession. To put it simply, the nature of police or security work does not lend itself readily to precise experimental control. In many such cases, independent verification by other than self-incriminatory means, may not be achievable.

Lie detection would exhibit high validity when polygraph-derived data are consistent with independent data on deception, such as when those judged to be deceptive are later found to have been deceptive, and those judged to be nondeceptive are later found to be non-deceptive, etc. There would be low validity when those judged to be truthful are found later to have practiced deception; or when those judged to be deceptive are found later to have been truthful. In real life, the problem of determining validity is complicated because those who are judged to be deceptive are not ordinarily hired and that ends the matter; no further investigation is conducted to determine whether or not the person actually was deceptive, although that would be required to clarify the problem of validity. A thorough appraisal of validity would require data in nine cells:

more examiners working independently on the same case material.

2. Comparing the results of two or more tests on the same person taken at separate but close time intervals.

3. Comparing the results of one part of an examination with another, e.g., odd versus even items on one subtest, two different physiological indexes, or two different methods of examinations (viz., peak of tension versus questionnaires).

In the current practice of lie detection, no attempt is made to measure the absolute values of the three physiological responses which are being recorded, though many such schemes have been proposed. The examiner judges the responses in a qualitative fashion, using visual inspection to compare the magnitude and pattern of responses to relevant and irrelevant

	Independent Evidence		
Polygraph Judgment	Guilty	Innocent	Indeterminate
Guilty (or practicing deception)	*		
Innocent (or not practicing deception)		*	
Indeterminate (no conclusion possible)			

Obviously, high validity would require that the preponderance of cases fall in the starred (*) cells; and validity would decrease as the percent increases in any of the other cells.

B. Reliability   Reliability measures the extent to which a test produces consistent or reproducible results. Reliability refers to the accuracy of measurement and should not be confused with validity. A test cannot be valid without also being reliable. Various aspects of reliability can be measured in the following ways:

1.   Comparing the results achieved by two or

questions. There is no objective method of reporting test results.

Little attention is directed to the accuracy of the three instruments used in the polygraph, though they may be precise enough for present purposes. The breathing and blood pressure instruments operate on pneumatic pressure and their response characteristics are obviously nonlinear. According to one manual[1] air leaks in these two systems should not exceed a pen excursion of 0.25 inches in 30 seconds for the

[1]Prepared by the Office of Naval Intelligence.

pneumograph and of 0.25 inches in 10 minutes for the sphygmomanometer. Disregarding the rate of leak, this is 5-percent error over the entire scale of 5 inches; the true error would be two to three times larger than 5 percent because the three tracings share the 5-inch scale. The psychogalvanometer is a sensitive instrument which must be adjusted continuously to contain the responses on the scale; some units incorporate a self-centering feature. Darrow (1929) and Lacey (1949) have shown that, among the several possible ways of measuring the GSR responses (based on conductance or resistance), the log change in conductance is the most reliable one. Martin (1956) reports that the reliability of the GSR, measured as average skin log conductance, was 0.95 for a series of four sessions; although the absolute conductance values may change, individuals consistently maintained a large or a small response from one session to another.

Except for Kubis (1962), no one has explored the possibility that two examiners working independently might make different interpretations of the same record. Reliability of the polygraph in the sense of the consistency of measurement, i.e., agreement among examiners, is an unknown quantity.

*

C. Evidence Reported in the Literature   Anecdotal evidence in support of lie detection is readily available in the literature. This type of evidence consists of charts collected in criminal cases, their interpretation (generally successful), and suggestions for conducting polygraphic investigations. These charts are useful for instructional purposes, but since they describe only selected cases, they provide no evidence for the percent of success or failure.

An extensive review of the literature produced data on criminal investigations and laboratory experiments which will be reported separately to preserve several distinctions between "real life" and "experimental" investigations. These distinctions relate to the degree of emotional involvement, the degree of control over the events which occur, and the precision of the data which differentiates these two situations.

(1) Criminal investigations   Table I summarizes the published data on the use of the polygraph in criminal investigations. The reports date from 1932 to 1953. The crimes, which are not always described, involve the full range of police work, such as theft, embezzlement, and murder; one unusual report summarizes investigations concerned with claims about paternity.

It was not possible to devise a consistent means of describing the accuracy of lie detection procedures that would apply to all reports and therefore the table contains some explanatory comments. The following headings are used the the table:

(a)   Verified reports: Instances where it has been possible to provide independent confirmation of a judgment based on the polygraph examination. The most frequent example is a judgment of guilt followed by a confession of guilt.

(b)   Indeterminable cases: Cases where an independent confirmation has not been made. The most frequent example is a judgment (of guilt or innocence) for a crime not supported by a confession. Unfortunately, this category includes some inconclusive polygraph examinations, described below.

(c)   Proved error: Cases where a judgment of guilt or innocence can be shown to be in error.

(d)   Inconclusive polygraph examinations: Cases where the results of a polygraph examination do not permit the examiner to make a high-confidence judgment of guilt or innocence.

The following conclusions may be derived from the data in table 1:

(a)   In criminal cases, judgments based on the polygraph often cannot be verified. When verification is possible, such as reported by Trovillo (1951), the accuracy of lie detection ranges from 50 to 85 percent, for cases in which

Table I. Accuracy of Polygraph Reported in Criminal Investigations

Type of Investigation	Reference	Number of Cases	Accuracy (percent)				Comments
			Verified Reports	Indeterminable Cases	Proved Error	Inconclusive Polygraph	
Thefts in a college dormitory	Larson, 1932	90	100	—	—	—	Based on confession of 1 guilty person
Criminal suspects	do	861	79.5	20.5	0	—	Difficult to ascertain author's meaning; 20.5 percent may refer to inconclusive category.
Murder suspects	Luria, 1932	(1)	(2)	—	—	—	Verified by confessions; original study of muscle tremors.
Criminal cases	Summers, 1939	43	(100)	—	—	—	"All examinations confirmed by confessions . . . or by subsequent investigations" (p. 340).
Criminal suspects	Keeler, 1941	—	82	16.5	(3)	—	"Several diagnoses later found guilty . . . not guilty later found innocent" (Wolfie, 1940).
Embezzlement	MacNitt, 1942	59	99	—	—	—	Accuracy not defined; used GSR.
Do	Marcuse and Bittermen, 1946	1	—	—	(4)	—	Suspect identified by witness and judged guilty after several lie detection tests; later exonerated by another's confession.
Criminal cases	Kubis, 1950	(5)	(90)	—	0	10.0	No errors of diagnosis reported . . . however, "no decision" category was rather large.
Paternity cases:							
Complainants	Trovillo, 1951	21	—	(95.3)	—	4.7	(P. 760.)
Defendants	do	18	—	(88.9)	—	11.1	
Police examinations (total 7,622):							
Michigan (1951)	Trovillo, 1951	774	50	—	—	1.9	Verified reports apply only to those who were judged guilty and also confessed; indeterminable group ranges up to about 80 percent (my estimate), when innocent judg-
Texas (1951)	do	395	62	—	—	12.4	
St. Louis (1951)	do	815	50	—	—	9.8	
Detroit (1945-51)	do	3,200	—	—	—	12.0	
Toledo (1951)	do	412	64.5	—	—	4.0	
Seattle (1951)	do	175	—	—	2.3	5.0	

							Remarks
Illinois (1951)	do	245	75	—	—	—	ments are included (Trovillo, 1951, p. 758). These data also appear in Trovillo (1943, p. 342).
Dallas (1951)	do	479	67	—	—	2.0	
Chicago (1938-41)	do	1,127	85	—	2.0	20.0	
Criminal suspects	Lee, 1953	1,127	(97.95)	—	2.05	—	Same data when given by Trovillo in 1943 includes 20 percent indefinite reports; 2 percent of those reported innocent later found guilty and 0.05 percent of those reported guilty later found innocent (p. 127). Trovillo does not claim 97.95 percent accuracy; Lee does. On p. 17, Lee says "only 12 mistakes in judgment in 2,171 cases;" perhaps "2,171" is printer's error for "1,127" above.
Do	Inbau and Reid, 1953	4,280	95.6 (36.4) 11.7	(79.0)	.0007 (.07)	4.4	"Accuracy" here is number of cases tested minus those cases reported indefinite. Inbau's value of 0.0007 percent "proven error" is an arithmetic error; it should be 0.07 percent.

[1] About 50.
[2] "High."
[3] Several cases.
[4] 1 case.
[5] Over 300. In a private communication, Kubis says that the number of cases given in the article is a typographical error; it should be 300 and not 500.

guilty judgments were supported by a confession. (About half of the cases in this sample was judged guilty.) But Inbau and Reid (1953) estimate accuracy as the percent of cases in which the examiner made a definite determination of guilt or innocence rather than an inconclusive one. This is an unusual application of the term "accuracy" (also see below). For Larson (1932), accuracy of 100 percent is based on finding one thief among 90 college girls.

(b) There are few reports on proved error. Where data are reported, proven errors occur up to 2 percent. In these cases, the guilty are more likely to be judged innocent than are innocent persons likely to be judged guilty.

(c) Inconclusive polygraph determinations occur in 10 to 20 percent of the cases.

Some reports (e.g., Luria, Summers, Kubis) make a claim for high accuracy but offer no quantitative data. Kubis (1950) finds "no errors of diagnosis . . . (but the) 'no decision' category was rather large," i.e., 10 percent.

The report of Inbau and Reid (1953, p. 111) deserves a special comment. They determine accuracy as 95.6 percent by adding all instances in which examiners made judgments of guilt (31.1 percent) or of innocence (64.5 percent). In the remaining 4.4 percent of cases, the examiner could not make a conclusive judgment. They report no indeterminable cases. They report proved error in 0.0007 pecent of the cases but this is an arithmetic mistake; using their own data (3 errors in 4,280 cases), this value should be 0.07 percent. Also, according to their data, there were confessions in 486 out of 1,334 reports of guilt; thus, verification of guilt was possible in 36.4 percent of the cases. In 323 out of 2,759 reports of innocence, another's confession confirmed the judgment; thus, verification of innocence was possible in 11.7 percent of the cases. Finally, note Kubis' (1950) report that in order to achieve zero errors of diagnosis, he had to accept 10 percent in the "no decision" category. This contrasts with Inbau's 4.4 percent.

However, the outstanding difficulty in interpreting the data in Table I lies in the fact that, due to the circumstances of criminal work, the examiner often has independent knowledge; that is, not collected by means of the polygraph, which suggests whether or not the suspect is guilty. Therefore, his judgment of guilt (or innocence) is based to some unknown extent on a combination of polygraph responses *and* other information, and not on the polygraph investigation alone. It is never clear whether the judgment said to be made from the polygraph record was made before or after a confession was received. This makes it most difficult to assess the true accuracy of the polygraph when it would alone provide the information from which a judgment must be drawn.

(2) Experimental investigations The advantage of laboratory studies of lie detection is that more complete control of the means of (and the reason for) collecting data is generally possible and, therefore, such data can be subjected to rigorous statistical analysis. The basic disadvantage of laboratory studies is that they may not be relevant to lie detection if they do not evoke "real" emotional responses of fear and anxiety similar to those present in real life, polygraph examinations. The latter contention is often made by lie detection experts, on the ground that less emotion can be aroused in the laboratory and that therefore the polygraph would show a lesser ability to detect deception under such circumstances. For example, Trovillo (1953) says:

"Simulated emotion in psychology classes, or the lecture platform, in drama, and in experimental laboratories has done more to clutter up and confuse honest polygraph reporting than all the quackery of 50 years" (p. 747).

"Much of the academic experimental validation of polygraphic technique is completely barren of significance. No matter how accurate and reliable the instruments used, if the controls used do not guarantee that *fear* is being measured, then all conclusions are not only irrelevant but hazardous. Future progress depends on use of experimental subjects experiencing drastic stress: the criminal suspect, not the laboratory liar; the mental patient, not the academic spoofer" (p. 762).

"The professor who buries his nose in textbooks and bores his students with myopic dronings over verbal autopsies will never be interested in conducting vital research in lie detection" (p. 762).

The results of laboratory studies, as shown in Table II do not justify any antipathy toward experimentation on the polygraph. These studies show that polygraph judgments about deception in the laboratory are correct in about 70 to 100 percent of the cases; the median value in the table is about 92 percent. This is the range of values reported in "real life" investigations. Some recent studies, such as those of Lykken (1959, 1960), Kubis (1962), Marcuse (1946), and Baeson (1948) are well controlled and show that the polygraph can be used to detect deception (of the type which can be arranged to permit experimentation) by objective criteria in 90 percent or more of the cases. It is significant that accuracy increases when the examiner is prepared to report that some polygraph records are inconclusive, i.e., do not permit him to make a determination. Surprisingly in these studies few proved errors are reported. There may be a minority of people (perhaps 10 percent) on whom the polygraph may not work. If judgments of deception are required for such people, other means than the polygraph must be employed. Experimental data do not provide a blanket argument against the polygraph though they do remind us that the polygraph cannot deal with all cases.

(3) Methodological studies Under this heading, we wish to review several experiments in which the polygraph or some of its component indicators was used, not always for the purpose of lie detection. In general, these studies show that the polygraph is a sensitive instrument so much so that the responses it measures can be affected by a variety of influences. Therefore, adequate controls are required before the polygraph can be used as an effective instrument. For example:

(a) Greater GSR responses were observed in 40 college students when a Negro rather than a white examiner operated the GSR instrument. Rankin and Campbell (1955).[2]

(b) The GSR response adapts (i.e., becomes reduced) most quickly to a light stimulus, next to a buzzer and least to a question (i.e., an idea). Demonstrated on 54 students by Kubis (1948).

(c) Even though electric shock was used every time the subject told the truth in an experiment where he tried to deny a number he had selected, the GSR response was not reversed. This demonstrated, on 23 students, the relative stability of objective criteria of deception and the accuracy of their identification under conditions to obscure the criteria and to confuse the diagnosis. Block et al. (1952).

(d) Innocence (of suspected criminals) can be determined objectively with greater accuracy than guilt. Only blood pressure records were used in a preliminary, feasibility study of 17 verified innocent and 33 verified guilty polygraph tracings. Leonard (1958, pp. 118–121).

(e) Though a sudden rise in blood pressure in response to relevant questions is generally suggestive of guilt, Arther (1955) shows four verified cases in which it occurred with innocent subjects. A "control question" technique has been devised by Inbau and Reid (1953) to avoid this possible error of interpretation.

(f) Polygraph experts who conducted an examination produced no more accurate judgments than did other examiners who had access only to the records of the same examination. This was accomplished in an experiment which

[2] A reviewer comments: An activity "has one Negro examiner. There has been no observable difference in the recorded patterns of his interviews of white subjects, compared with interviews conducted by white examiners." No data were offered to support this view, while Rankin and Campbell's data suggest that the reverse is probably true.

Table II. Accuracy of Polygraph Reported in Experimental Studies

Type of Investigation	Reference	Number of Cases	Accuracy (percent)				Comments
			Verified Reports	Indeterminable Cases	Proved Error	Inconclusive Polygraph	
Noncriminals	Marston, 1921	35	94.2	—	—	—	Emphasis placed on GSR and cardiac amplitude; accuracy not defined.
Do	Ruckmick, 1936	–	86.0	—	—	—	
Students	Summers, 1939	50	86.0	—	—	—	
Experimental cases	MacNitt, 1942	221	98.0	—	—	—	
		194	99.0	—	—	—	
Imaginary crimes	do	17	99.0	—	—	—	
Card tests	do	36	75.0	—	—	—	
Innocent students	Bitterman and Marcuse, 1947.	81	—	—	—	—	81 college men, all judged innocent of a dormitory theft; after 1–5 retests Cardiovascular responses categorized on 1st test only: No reaction 38, Moderate, scattered 28, Extensive 25, More pronounced to relevant than irrelevant, i.e., guilty 9, Total 100. Agreement between 3 judges in categorizing responses 0.87 to 0.96 (cont. coef.).
Distinguish guilt from knowledge about the "crime" in a mock theft.	Bacson, Chung, and Yang, 1948.	100	86.0	—	—	—	In 75 percent of cases, guilty person in each pair (rather than person with guilty knowledge) produced evidence required for identification.
Mock theft	Rouke and Kubis, 1948	(1)	97.0	—	—	—	1 or 2 trials insufficient but accuracy can reach 97 percent if many retests are permitted; no difference in polygraph response between delinquents and nondelinquents.
Card guessing	van Buskirk and Marcuse, 1954.	50	72.0–84.0	—	—	—	Errors could be reduced 50 percent and accuracy would rise to

92 percent if more indeterminate judgments made; but those on whom polygraph could be used would drop from 100 to 72 percent (for this sample). Reliability: Records could be read in same way 1 month later in 84 to 94 percent of cases.

Mock crimes	Lykken, 1959	49	90.0-94.0	—	—	—	GSR only used objectively in guilty knowledge procedure; 100 percent innocents correctly identified, 88 percent guilty correctly identified.
Faking	Lykken, 1960	20	100.0	—	—	—	GSR only used objectively in guilty knowledge technique.
Simulated theft	Kubis, 1962	336	73.0-92.0	—	—	—	Used objectively judgments of examiners who did not know whether subject was guilty or innocent.
Denial of actual crime by ex-prisoners in an experiment.	do	23	—	—	—	—	Examiner's problem was to judge nature of crime.
Test	do	—	40.0	—	—	—	
Retest	do	—	29.0	—	—	—	
Deliberate attempts beat the polygraph in guessing a number.	do	20	—	—	—	—	Accuracy dropped from 75 to 80 percent in control session to as low as 10 percent in experimental session.

[1] 80 delinquents; 90 nondelinquents.

was virtually real-life, involving a presumed disclosure of classified information. However, accuracy of both groups was not high. In the critical retest period, the examiners (those who performed the tests) were able to detect the two experimental lie situations in 41 percent of the cases; one of the two lies in 54 percent of the cases; and neither lie in 5 percent of the cases. The corresponding average percentages for raters (having access only to the records) were: 54 percent, 36 percent, and 10 percent. In the test session immediately following, the accuracy of the examiners and raters dropped to a chance level. Adaptation was rapid and appreciable within the same day of testing. Kubis (1962).

(g) In a long series of experiments, Ellson (1952) showed that objective measures of such physiological indicators as GSR, breathing rate, breathing amplitude, breathing time, systolic pressure and diastolic pressure, when taken singly, rarely distinguish between deception and non-deception in more than about 75 percent of the cases. When these indicators are combined optimally by means of statistical discriminant functions, the accuracy rises to about 90 percent correct classification of liars in experiments. Greater accuracy is possible, but was not demonstrated in these experiments, provided that improved techniques and procedures are found to increase the statistical reliability of the individual measures.

Perhaps these studies are sufficient to indicate that the polygraph can demonstrate validity of the order of 90 percent in experimental situations. However, the polygraph test is subject to error when a variety of uncontrolled influences are present, some examples of which are offered in these studies. Greater accuracy may be anticipated by combining the results of several physiological indicators in accordance with statistical rules which reflect their predictive value, provided we can also increase the reliability of measuring these indications.[3]

[3]A polygraph examiner comments: "Methodological

2. The Patterning of Physiological Responses

The conventional polygraph, with its three physiological indicators, obviously can be used to detect deception more accurately than would occur by chance alone. The reported accuracies are rarely below 75 percent and sometimes approach 100 percent. Two factors which probably influence a major portion of this variability are the procedures used by the examiner and the physiological responsivity of the person being tested. Let us first consider the latter problem.

The three indicators used in the standard polygraph (breathing pattern, cardiac pattern, and GSR) measure only a few of a large number of known, autonomic response mechanisms. Measurement of autonomic responses is desirable because they are not primarily under the direct, voluntary control of the person being observed, even though some such influence is possible—more so for breathing and less so for the GSR. Activity of the autonomic nervous system can be measured by at least the following physiological responses:

  Galvanic skin response
  Breathing:
      Pattern of response
      Amplitude
      Rate
      Time
  Vascular response:
      Systolic blood pressure
      Diastolic blood pressure
      Pulse rate
      Pulse time
      Pulse wave velocity

studies, as well as much of the literature in the field have, for some reason, emphasized research and experimentation on the galvanic skin response. This is somewhat anomalous, in view of the fact that many experienced and expert examiners place little or not credence in the galvanic skin response. Some competent examiners admit frankly that they do not even turn on the galvanic skin response because of the impossibility of determining the source of galvanic skin response actions. Others use the galvanic skin response as an aid but ignore it when its excursions conflict with the pneumograph and cardiosphygmograph patterns."

Volume pulse
Blood volume in forefinger, leg
Blood oxygen saturation
Skin temperature
Muscle tension potentials
Hand and finger tremors
Eye movements
Pupil diameter
Gastrointestinal motility
Electroencephalograph
Ballistocardiograph
Salivation

This list could be extended and also replicated because there often are several ways to measure each physiological response. For example, there are at least four different ways to measure the GSR:

Skin conductance.
Log conductance.
Skin resistance.
Log resistance.

At the outset, it is important to realize that the autonomic responses are not necessarily highly correlated with each other. That is, even though all of these response mechanisms are influenced by the autonomic nervous system, the influences are not identical. Some mechanisms show large responses while others, at the very same time, show little response. Two mechanisms which show a large, initial response to an emotional stimulus may not adapt (i.e., return to their initial levels) at the same rate.

A wide range of physiological responses have been studied in connection with psychosomatic medicine, physiological correlates of personality, medical diagnosis, the measurement of anxiety states, and psychotherapy. In these areas of research, many studies may be found which clarify some of the problems encountered in the practice of lie detection.

Some investigators, such as Ax (1960), Wenger (1961), Malmo (1950), and Lacey (1958c) have measured simultaneously up to ten physiological variables and have evaluated the results in accordance with objective criteria. Methods for the simultaneous recording of up to 29 physiological processes and for automatic data reduction systems have been described by Ax (1960), Zimmer (1961), and Clark (1961).

According to Lacey (1958c), individuals exhibit idiosyncratic patterns of physiological response which tend to be repeated in various stress-evoking situations; six variables were measured. If such individual consistency is confirmed, physiological responses in emotional states would have to be interpreted on an individual, rather than on a general basis and a significant change introduced in lie detection procedures. Wenger (1961) measured eight autonomic responses in four different emotional situations. Although stable response specificity and stereotype occur to some degree, they are interpreted by Wenger as caused in part by the method of measurement and in part by significant individual differences in the resting level of the autonomic functions. He cautions against overgeneralizing the significance and pervasiveness of autonomic response specificity and stereotypy. Few reaction patterns were identical for a subject under the four emotional conditions and this is further evidence against general interpretation of physiological responses. Using 7 responses (transmuted into 14 scores). Ax (1953, 1960b) obtained distinct but different physiological patterns for anger and fear. However, his study does not show much evidence for physiological stereotypy.

In a study concerned primarily with various techniques of quantifying autonomic responses, Dykman (1959) used the three conventional polygraph indicators on 40 medical students under conditions of rest, noise and responding to a series of emotional and non-emotional questions; lie detection, as such was not attempted. He found:

1.   Skin resistance was the easiest to evaluate and the most consistent of the three measures.

2.   The autonomic responses diminish

rapidly to a relatively constant level for each series of stimuli.

3. Subjects are more reactive in skin resistance than in heart rate or respiratory rate, both in terms of the magnitude and frequency of response.

4. The magnitude of autonomic response is dependent on the initial level of functioning; in general, the higher the initial level, the smaller the response.

5. An individual's reaction in one autonomic subsystem cannot be predicted from his reaction in another.

These few studies, from among a large literature, show that a simple or purely mechanical treatment of the three polygraph indicators would lead to a low accuracy of lie detection. Polygraph operators deal with this situation in an intuitive manner, shifting from one indicator to another, in an unknown fashion, in order to analyze a record. Various "schools" of interpretation have developed in which the examiner emphasizes one of the three indicators to the relative exclusion of the others; each indicator is regarded by some examiner as the single, "best" indicator.[4]

Since, as a result of learning processes, individuals undoubtedly differ in the choice of response mechanism and degree of responsivity to emotional stimuli, there is an ample basis for various examiners to build up confidence in their own methods of analysis. But since intuitive, rather than objective, rules play a large role in the evaluation of records, the idiosyncracies of various operators undoubtedly contaminate the accuracy of the results. This may not be a problem for cases which are straightforward and routine but it must limit accuracy for the cases which are ambiguous or difficult to interpret.

A striking example is the "Total Chart Minutes" concept developed and copyrighted (1960) by Cleve Backster, director of the National Training Center of Lie Detection, New York, N.Y. The term "total chart minutes" refers to the accumulation of time during which a subject has been asked questions during one or more trials on the polygraph; i.e., the time between trials is excluded. The useful purpose served by this concept is that it attempts to account for the value found by some examiners for a preferred indicator as due to the phase of interrogation during which that indicator may be especially discriminating. A series of curves is provided which describes the relative effectiveness (from "excellent" to "poor") of the three standard tracings (breathing, heart, GSR) for a "probably innocent" or a "probably guilty" person for any period with the total chart minutes structure. No data are provided to verify the schematic curves; in fact, when asked for confirmation of this intriguing concept, Backster could (or would) not provide any corroborating data to support his thesis.

It becomes clear that in real life we cannot rely solely on the individual interpretation of an examiner without verification by independent means, such as another, completely independent evaluation by another examiner, or a background investigation, or both. The addition of independent data must increase the degree of confidence we can place in the final result. Thus, there is an urgent need for (a) multivariate recording in actual interrogations, (b) independent judgments by more than one examiner, and (c) automatic data processing of these complex records.

We might, now, consider the implication of these studies for improving our ability to detect deception with the polygraph assuming, for this purpose, that adequate transducers and methods of measurement exist or can be devised. Although activity of the autonomic nervous system may be observed in many ways, the

---

[4]One polygraph examiner comments: "Granted that intuition may play a part in the analysis, but the analysis is more probably a Gestalt process, into which a great deal of experience on the part of the examiner is compounded." This reviewer noted that some examiners disregard the GSR.

addition of new measures would not necessarily increase the accuracy of detecting deception. The value of additional measures depends upon the way in which deception affects various physiological processes. Assuming that the three present indicators do not adequately sample the physiological expressions of deception, it would make sense to add new response measures which fill this gap. Our knowledge on this point is slight. An estimate that the polygraph-and-examiner has a high accuracy (e.g., about 90 percent) does not provide an estimate of the variance due to each of the three polygraph responses alone or in combination or to the examiner. Therefore, we do not know whether there is room for improvement in the instrument or in the responses which are measured.

Current technology permits us to examine the value of observing the three current response mechanisms as well as the possible value of adding new ones. The essential device which has not been available previously is automatic data processing equipment. Ellson (1952, pp. 150–161) proposes that several indicators should be combined by means of discriminant functions to provide a more powerful indicator but points out that our ability to improve detection of deception will be limited by the reliability of the individual measures. The use of a computer to combine these variables for lie detection has been suggested by Zimmer (1961) who has assembled equipment for such an experiment but no results are available as yet. The work of Ax, Lacey, and Wenger, mentioned above, could readily be extended into the area of lie detection.

The many autonomic responses which may be added to lie detection are listed earlier in this report but they must be chosen so that only the more diagnostic ones are used. The three variables in current use will probably remain highly useful. Promising ones to consider are blood volume in finger, muscle tension, skin temperature, eye motion and electroencephalograph, the last if additional research clarifies the meaning of the phase changes. Initial studies involv-ing multiple sensors would have to be accomplished in a laboratory setting with possible cumbersome equipment. However, great advances have been made recently in improving sensors and in reducing their size for use in hospitals, medical experimentation and the bioastronautics program and there is no reason to doubt that the necessary equipment can be made more convenient to use. This applies also to reduction in the size of any computing equipment that might be developed to perform on-line data processing of physiological indications but further speculation in this direction is premature. It is clear that the patterning of physiological responses in lie detection is an area in which additional research can be accomplished readily by taking advantage of existing techniques which have not, as yet, been applied to lie detection.

*

3. Lie Detection Methodology

Dr. Joseph Kubis (1962) of Fordham University is conducting a series of studies to improve the methodology of lie detection also on project 5534. The study consists of four parts, some of which have been described earlier in this report. The following summary is based on a conference with Dr. Kubis at RADC on January 2, 1962, and represents his preliminary conclusions:

(a) Sham theft (360 subjects, 5 examiners): Examiners can correctly detect "innocent" or "guilty" students in 73 to 92 percent of the cases. Raters who worked only with polygraph charts (and did not see the "suspects") were as accurate as the examiners who performed the interrogations. In 112 sessions, 2 "innocent" students were called "guilty."

Of the three measures used by Kubis, the GSR response provided by far the greatest accuracy (about 90 percent for discriminating the "guilty" from the "innocents"), while the other two indices (respiratory and plethysmographic) produced accuracies of only about 60 to 70 percent.

When discriminant functions are calculated based on the ratings of different individuals analyzing the same data, they are found to differ appreciably in the assignments of weights to the three response indices. This lack of homogeneity among various discriminant functions suggests inherent difficulties for the development of computer techniques to provide objective indications of guilt or innocence.

However, considering the low objectivity realized by visual interpretation of respiratory and plethysmographic responses, computer techniques may well be a valuable adjunct to lie detection in the following respects:

(i) Differentiating among complex physiological patterns.

(ii) Developing new indexes or criteria of deception.

(b) Denial of a previously committed crime by ex-criminals on parole (23 cases): Since all subjects were known to be guilty, the experiment consisted of judging type of crime committed. The subjects were told to deny a specific previous crime and each record contained two "lies." In 40 percent of the cases, the examiner was able to detect both lies in the records of the ex-prisoners; in 48 percent of the cases one of the two lies; and in 12 percent of the cases neither of the two lies. In a retest of the same subjects, 29 percent were detected in both lies, 57 percent one of the two lies, and 13 percent in neither of the two lies (Based on averages of 3 examiners.)

(c) "Leak" of classified information: An attempt was made to conduct a "leak of classified information" experiment but this proved to be impracticable to perform. Although this would have closely approximated a "real life" situation, Kubis had to substitute for it a situation wherein the subjects denied knowledgeability of selected items of classified information.

(d) Countermeasure experiment: Subjects were trained to use several techniques to make it difficult for an examiner to interpret a polygraph record. The test required the examiner to guess a number on a card selected by the subject. The prescribed techniques and instructions were:

(i) Yoga: "Keep your mind as blank as possible and answer 'No' to all questions."

(ii) Muscle tension: "When some questions are asked, tense your body or foot so that the examiner doesn't see it and in a way that will mislead him as to the number you have in mind."

(iii) Exciting imagery: "Think of something that is exciting to you, in a manner that will make it hard for the examiner to guess what number you have in mind."

Preliminary results for 20 subjects show about the following accuracy:

	Accuracy (percent)
Control (no instruction)	75–80
Yoga	75–80
Muscle tension	10–20
Exciting imagery	15–25

If a subject selected a decoy number on which he consistently tensed or used exciting imagery, he could direct the examiner to this number in 55 to 70 percent of the cases. Examiners are unable to distinguish among the known decoy and "real" numbers on the basis of the polygraph records. Though this was only a preliminary experiment, it is sufficient to show that it is possible to interfere with a polygraph. It is not clear whether an alert examiner could ascertain that the subject was trying to create a spurious response.

*

4. Contraindications and Countermeasures

The emotional reactions of a person in response to certain but not all questions depend largely upon the rules of behavior being followed by the person. When there are clear, cultural distinctions between right (or truth) and wrong (or lie) attached to each answer (and assuming that the point of the question is understood equally by the interrogator and the subject), the polygraph should prove a valid instrument for most people. It is, therefore, useful to recognize that there may be several situations in which the polygraph could fail:

(a) When the subject lacks appreciation of the difference between truth and falsity. A habituated liar (or severely disturbed personality) should not be expected to show (or indeed, "feel") emotions due to fear of detection.

(b) When there are differences in the behavioral codes of the subject and interrogator. Such differences may separate people in different cultures, or people of different social (or political) status in the same culture.

(c) When the subject attempts to "beat" the polygraph by controlling his breathing or cardiac response, by suppressing his memory, or by feigning a mental attitude, with or without the benefit of training, to produce such effects.

(d) When the subject has used drugs and, possibly, hypnosis to modify his physiological responsivity.

With such possibilities in mind, a polygraph examination can lead to three undesirable results:

(a) False positives: In which it is concluded that a person is attempting deception, when this is not the case.

(b) False negatives: In which it is concluded that a person is not attempting deception, when this is not the case.

(c) Indeterminate: When the examiner recognizes that he cannot make a reliable judgment about deception or truthfulness.

Among these three categories, indeterminate results need not confuse the examiner because he knows that some additional step, such as a reexamination or a more careful background

investigation, must be taken to resolve the uncertainty. Overall accuracy should be increased when the examiner is free to employ the indeterminate category, although this obviously produces fewer resolved cases.

Kubis (1950) achieved a confirmed accuracy of about 90 percent but also made 10 percent inconclusive judgments, a larger fraction than is generally reported. Lee (1953) reports 98 percent accuracy and no inconclusive determinations, while Inbau and Reid (1953) report 95.6 percent accuracy and 4.4 percent inconclusive determinations. Although there are little data to document the errors that actually occur in lie detection, there appear to be some false positives (about 2 percent) according to Trovillo (1951) and Lee (1953) and fewer false negatives (but no data appear on this point). In terms of crime, it is believed that some guilty might escape but very few innocents would be punished.

A Contraindications to Use of the Polygraph Lie detection experts[5] point out that a polygraph examination should not be conducted during certain transient states of an individual, such as, for example:

Excessive fatigue.

Prolonged interrogation.

Physical abuse.

Extreme nervous tension.

Evidence of drugs, especially tranquilizers and stimulants.

Sub shock or adrenal exhaustion.

Fear of detection of some other offense not related to this interrogation.

A similar restraint applies when long-term physical or psychological disorders are present:

Excessively high or low blood pressure.

[5]Inbau and Reid (1953), pp. 64–99; Lee (1953), pp. 126–132.

Respiratory disorders.

Hyperthyroidism.

Mental abnormalities.
Feeblemindedness.
Psychoses.
Psychopathic personality.

Any of these conditions precludes an effective examination because it introduces into the record response characteristics which are not the result of the examination itself. The professional integrity of the examiner would require him to refuse to examine individuals in whom such conditions are known to be present because an adequate examination could not be conducted. If an examiner did not know this in advance, he might detect certain unusual characteristics in the record which could lead him to terminate the examination as inappropriate under the circumstances. Various test procedures, such as repeating a test, or the "peak of tension" technique are intended to guide and alert the examiner to such effects. One obvious difficulty is that some of these conditions are not readily apparent (e.g., psychopathic personality or presence of drugs) or may not be known at the time of the interrogation. Another is that some interrogators believe they can handle every kind of case (they use the phrase "break a case"). Restraint in recognition of one's ignorance about the possible presence of such conditions depends, ultimately, on the professional standards and integrity of the examiner since no control exerted outside the examination room can ever be entirely effective.

B Can One Beat the Polygraph? If the aforementioned conditions represent natural limitations to the accuracy of the polygraph, we may now consider whether it is possible to fool a polygraph examiner. The machine itself cannot be fooled because it simply records a pattern of responses to a series of questions while it is the examiner who interprets their meaning. What, then, can a person do deliberately to avoid the appearance of deception or to mislead an examiner? What follows consists of a series of conjectures and the preliminary results of one experiment.

The experiment which deals with this question was performed by Kubis (1962) and has been described above. Though only preliminary data are available, they show that by tensing the muscles of the feet or by use of self-exciting images, test subjects could drop the accuracy of examiners in guessing a number from 75 to 80 percent to 20 percent. In 55 to 70 percent of the cases, it was possible to direct the attention of the examiner to a decoy number instead of the previously selected number.

Experiments on human conditioning add a significant note. In a recent review entitled "Does the Heart Learn?" Shearn (1961) concludes that both the form of the electrocardiograph cycle and the heart rate may be conditioned in accordance with classical rules. The technique is illustrated by an experiment of Petrova:

"An auditory stimulus (whistle) was combined with intravenous injections of nitroglycerin. Because the act of injecting the fluid would act as a conditioned stimulus, its effect was extinguished with repeated intravenous injections of normal saline. The whistle, on the other hand, was always sounded after the nitroglycerin had been injected (but before the effect of the drug was manifest). After about 100 pairings of the whistle and nitroglycerin, the whistle presented alone produced changes typical of those elicited by the drug (accelerated heart rate, decrease in QRS voltage, and augmented P and T waves)" (p. 452).

It is known that alterations in the breathing cycle can affect the cardiac response, thereby providing a means of conditioning the heart without intermediary use of some drug (Huttenlocher and Westcott, 1957). Preliminary experiments suggest that a person can learn to alter his GSR with the aid of a meter which permits him to observe the magnitude of his responses.

There is no doubt that the EEG can be modified by means of conditioning (Ellingson, 1956). Gerard (1951) reports that alpha waves of the EEG, which normally disappear when the bright light shines on the eye, do not disappear when the observer deliberately pays no attention to the light. However, these facts do not imply that the EEG could be manipulated with the dexterity required to accomplish deception; not enough is yet known about the value of the EEG for use in the polygraph. Polygraph examiners know that a person who moves and squirms during an interrogation can alter the responses shown on the record; this effect would influence the interpretation of the over-all record if it could be accomplished systematically without the examiner's knowledge.

It is possible that a person could be taught through a series of carefully arranged conditioning experiments to bring some of his autonomic responses under direct control. Lacey (1958c) has demonstrated that each person uses his body in a unique way to express his own emotional responses; this is the result of normal training and maturation. Kubis (1962) has demonstrated that autonomic responses can be influenced through simple instruction without formal conditioning. There can be no doubt that same degree of manipulation is possible; however, in order to accomplish deception, a person would have to learn to suppress or to excite his physiological responses in a pattern adequate for his purposes.

In recognizing the feasibility of such an attempt, we do not know whether training could be accomplished with sufficient elegance to become a useful device for an enemy agent. One method would be to learn to deaden all responses, so that no pattern would be discernible in response to significant or nonsignificant items; another method would be to overrespond to all items with similar effect. Though an examiner might be led to make an indeterminate conclusion in such cases, he might also be alerted to this unusual circumstance. It would be

much more effective if a person could deliberately react to nonsignificant items and deaden his response to significant items; but in this case, he would also have to know what type of response to each question would be most likely to create an impression of knowledge or lack of knowledge about the events of interest to the interrogation.

Since the control of autonomic responses must be regarded as feasible, research is required to explore its implications for our lie detection technology. The examiner will not be helpless because new indicators can be added to the polygraph system to observe response systems which may not have been trained. Since enemy agents would also learn about new indicators, this could lead to a cycle where it may become necessary to add still newer indicators and drop older ones from time to time. But before proceeding that far, it is useful to know the extent to which training is possible, whether the current indicators are sufficiently sensitive to remain effective despite training and, then, what additional indicators are most likely to provide useful adjunct information.

It is also of interest to know if drugs or hypnosis can be used to influence a polygraph examination, both from the viewpoint of the person who takes an examination and from that of the examiner. Fortunately, the effects of drugs and hypnosis on interrogation have been reviewed recently on behalf of the Air Force and are described in an excellent book (Biderman and Zimmer (1961)).

A person about to be examined on a polygraph could take a drug, perhaps a tranquilizer, to moderate his responses. There is a danger to him in that the action of the drug is not selective—it would affect many of his responses. A flat record is unusual and tends to attract the examiner's attention; the presence of depressed responses suggests that a drug may have been used. The use of a drug, if suspected, is easily circumvented by detaining a person for a retest after the drug effects have worn off, and prolonged examination and retest is the rule in any nonroutine polygraph interrogation.

Gottschalk[6] says:

"There is a possibility that tranquilizers could be used by an examiner with selected personnel who are highly agitated and disturbed, and who might give information they prefer to withhold in return for the tranquillity they experience with such a sedative. Under the influence of this drug, the less emotionally upset informant might find that he can better master his anxieties and keep his resolve to remain silent. These are all speculations which require testing and experimentation. . . .

"The popular meaning of being 'drugged' or 'doped' implies that an individual in this state has lost control over his actions and that society will not hold him responsible for them. When the transmittal of information is likely to induct guilt in the source, the interviewer can forestall some of this reaction by the administration of a placebo or drug. In some cases, this will be all that is required to remove the barrier to information transmittal. In the avoidance-conflict between the source's guilt over yielding information and his anxieties over the possible consequences of non-cooperation, the 'inescapable' power of the drug or placebo serves to justify the source's actions to himself."

Whether or not a drug facilitates the interrogator's task, its use provides some people with an acceptable excuse to reveal information and in this sense it could produce useful side effects. Though a drug, such as LSD-25, may make a person more talkative, the interrogator still has the problem of judging the reliability of the information provided through its use since such drugs are also known to incite fantasy, drowsiness, and confusion (Redlich, 1951). To sum it up, though some drugs make a person more talkative, they may also make him more suggestible and less critical, providing nonsense as well as information. There is not, unfortunately, a magic way to truth.

Orne[7] has reviewed the use of hypnosis in interrogation and arrives at a conclusion similar to that for drugs except that even less is known about hypnosis. The possibility of inducing a trance on a resistant person is extremely doubtful. Hypnosis requires a trustworthy relationship between the hypnotist and the subject and such a relationship does not evolve readily in an interrogation. There is a common (although probably untrue) belief that an individual in hypnosis is not responsible for his actions. If hypnosis can be established in an interrogation (this is not likely) it could, like a drug, be used to relieve a subject of responsibility for his actions and allow him to divulge information he might not otherwise yield. The idea that an enemy agent could be hypnotized to avoid giving indications of deception appears very remote. Again, a more dangerous person appears to be one who practices deception under his own control rather than one who does so with the help of drugs or hypnosis.

*

BIBLIOGRAPHY

Arther, Richard O. "Blood Pressure Rises on Relevant Questions in Lie Detection—Sometimes an Indication of Innocence not Guilt," *Journal of Criminal Law, Criminology and Police Science*, 1955, 46, 112–115.

Ax, Albert F. "The Physiological Differentiation Between Fear and Anger in Humans," *Psychosomatic Medicine*, 1953, 15, 433–442.

Ax, Albert F. "Psychophysiology of Fear and Anger." *Psychiatric Research Report 12.* American Psychiatric Association. January 1960(a), 167–175.

Ax, Albert F. "Computers and Psychophysiology in Medical Diagnosis," *IRE Transactions on Medical Electronics*, 1960(b). ME–7, 263–264.

Baesen, Henry V., Chung, Chia-Mon; and Yang, Chen-Ya. "A Lie Detection Experiment," *Journal of Criminal Law and Criminology*, 1948–1949, 39, 532–537.

Biderman, Albert D. and Zimmer, Herbert (eds.). "The Manipulation of Human Behavior," 1961, John Wiley & Sons, Inc.

Block, J. D., Rouke, F. L., Salpeter, M. M., Tobach, E., Kubis, J. F. and Welch, L. "An Attempt at Reversal

[6]In Biderman (1961), pp. 132–133.
[7]In Biderman (1961), pp. 169–215.

of the Truth-Lie Relationship as Measured by the Psychogalvanic Response," *Journal of Psychology,* 1952, 34, 55–66.

Clark, W. A., Brown, R. M., Goldstein, M. H., Jr., Molnar, C. E., O'Brien, D. F. and Zieman, H. E. "The Average Response Computer (ARC): A Digital Device for Computing Averages and Amplitude and Time Bistograms of Electrophysiological Response," *IRE Transactions on Bio-Medical Electronics,* 1961, BME–8, 46–51.

Darrow, C. W. "The Galvanic Skin-Reflex and Finger Volume Changes," *American Journal of Physiology,* 1929, 88, 219–229.

Dykman, Roscoe A., Reese, W. G., Galbrecht, C. R. and Thomasson, P. J. "Psychophysiological Reactions to Novel Stimuli; Measurement, Adaptation and Relationship of Psychological and Physiological Variables in the Normal Human," *Annals of the New York Academy of Sciences,* 1959, 79, 43–107.

Ellingson, Rober J. "Brain Waves and Problems of Psychology," *Psychological Bulletin,* 1956, 53, 1–34.

Ellson, Douglas G. "A Report of Research on Detection of Deception" Indiana University, Contract No. 6 Nonr-18011 with the Office of Naval Research, September 15, 1952.

Gerard, Ralph W. "To Prevent Another World War—Truth Detection," Journal of Conflict Resolution, 1961, 5, 212–218.

Huttenlocher, J. and Westcott, M. R. "Some Empirical Relationships Between Respiratory Activity and Heart Rate," *American Psychologist,* 1957, 12, 414.

Inbau, Fred and Reid, John E. "Lie Detection and Criminal Interrogation," 3rd ed. 1953, Williams & Wilkins Co., Baltimore.

Kubis, Joseph F. "Adaptation of the Psychogalvanic Response (PGR) to a Visual, Auditory Ideational Stimulus," *The American Psychologist,* 1948, 3, 256.

Kubis, Joseph F. "Experimental and Statistical Factors in the Diagnosis of Consciously Suppressed Affective Experience," *Journal of Clinical Psychology,* 1950, 6, 12–16.

Kubis, Joseph F. "Studies in Lie Detection: Computer Feasibility Considerations," *RADC–TR 65–205,* June 1962.

Lacey, John I. "An Analysis of the Unit of Measurement of the Galvanic Skin Response," *Journal of Experimental Psychology,* 1949, 39, 122–127.

Lacey, John I. and Lacey, Beatrice C. "Verification and Extension of the Principle of Autonomic Response—Stereotypy," *American Journal of Psychology,* 1958(c), 71, 50–73.

Larson, J. A. "Lying and its Detection," 1932, University of Chicago Press.

Lee, Clarence D. "The Instrumental Detection of Deception," 1953, Charcles C. Thomas, Springfield, Illinois.

Leonard, V. A. (ed.). Academy Lectures on Lie Detection, 1958, 2, Charles C. Thomas, Springfield, Illinois.

Levitt, Eugene E. "Scientific Evaluation of the 'Lie Detector'," *Iowa Law Review,* 1955, 40, 440–458.

Luria, A. R. "The Nature of Human Conflicts," 1932, Liveright, New York.

Lykken, David T. "The GSR in the Detection of Guilt," *Journal of Applied Psychology,* 1959, 43, 385–388.

Lykken, David T. "The Validity of the Guilty Knowledge Technique: The Effects of Faking," *Journal of Applied Psychology,* 1960, 44, 258–262.

MacNitt, Reginald D. "In Defense of the Electrodermal Response and Cardiac Amplitude as Measures of Deception," *Journal of Criminal Law and Criminology,* 1942, 33, 266–275.

Malmo, R. B., Shagass, C. and Davis, F. H. "Symptom Specificity and Bodily Reactions During Psychiatric Interview," *Psychosomatic Medicine,* 1950, 12, 362–376.

Marcuse, F. L. and Bitterman, M. E. "Minimal Cues in the Peak of Tension Procedure for Determining Guilt," *American Journal of Psychology,* 1946, 59, 144–146.

Marston, William M. "Psychological Possibilities in the Deception Test," *Journal of Criminal Law,* 1921, 11, 551–568.

Marston, William M. "Systolic Blood Pressure Changes in Deception," *Journal of Experimental Psychology,* 1917, 2, 117–163.

Martin, Barclay. "Galvanic Skin Conductance as a Function of Successive Interviews," *Journal of Clinical Psychology,* 1956, 12, 91–94.

Rankin, Robert E. and Campbell, Donald T. "Galvanic Skin Response to Negro and White Experimenters," *Journal of Abnormal and Social Psychology,* 1955, 51, 30–33.

Rouke, Fabian L. and Kubis, Joseph F. "Studies in the Detection of Deception: 1. Determination of guilt or innocence from psychogalvanic (PGR) records of delinquents and non-delinquents," *The American Psychologist,* 1948, 3, 225.

Ruckmick, C. A. "The Truth about the Lie Detector," Address to AAAS, December 29, 1936.

Shearn, Donald. "Does the Heart Learn?" *Psychological Bulletin,* 1961, 58, 452–458.

Summers, Walter G. "Science Can Get the Confession," *Fordham Law Review,* 1939, 8, 334–354.

Trovillo, Paul V. "A History of Lie Detection," *Journal of Criminal Law and Criminology,* 1939, 29, 848–881; 1939, 30, 104–119.

Trovillo, Paul V. "Deception Test Criteria," *Journal of Criminal Law and Criminology,* 1942–43, 33, 338–358.

Trovillo, Paul V. "Scientific Proof of Credibility," *Tennessee Law Review,* 1951–53, 22, 743–766.

van Buskirk, D. and Marcuse, F. L. "The Nature of Errors in Experimental Lie Detection," *Journal of Experimental Psychology,* 1954, 47, 187–190.

Wenger, M. W., Clemens, T. L., Coleman, D. R., Cullen, T. D. and Engel, B. T. "Autonomic Response Specificity," *Psychosomatic Medicine,* 1961, 23, 185–193.

Wolfle, Dael. "The Lie Detector: Methods for the Detection of Deception," Memorandum prepared for the Emergency Committee in Psychology of the National Research Council, October 8, 1941.

Zimmer, Herbert. "Preparing Psychophysiologic Analog Information for the Digital Computer," *Behavioral Science,* 1961, 6, 161–164.

9. Dimensions of Police Loyalty

LEONARD D. SAVITZ

IN 1967, WE BEGAN A CONTINUING LONGITUDINAL investigation of how a series of norms and beliefs which define appropriate and inappropriate systems of role behavior are informally acquired by a cohort of police recruits during their first three years in the Philadelphia Police Department. It seems unarguable that inevitable occupational socialization will, in time, result in values and behavior which render the novices indistinguishable from older, more experienced (perhaps more "professional") officers. The 226 recruits were examined initially during their first week of training at the Police Academy (hereafter referred to as T1); the same population was re-examined after they had completed the full 12 weeks of training at the Academy (T2) and then after the remaining 197 members of the cohort had been "in the field" for 6 months (T3). Interest was focused not merely on the fact of change but also on the *direction* of attitudinal and behavioral change, so that the questionnaire given to the recruits at T3 was simultaneously administered to a convenience sample of 197 "experienced" patrolmen (who had been in rank for an average of over 5 years and who had minimal expectations about upward mobility within the department) and to 233 detectives (a rank to which most policemen aspire). It was important to determine whether the novice officer came to acquire some of the

more "cynical" beliefs of the older patrolmen with whom they necessarily worked in close contact, or the more conventional norms characteristic of the detective population.

THE NATURE OF LOYALTY

This paper will deal only with some tentative conclusions derivable from the study about the components and dimensions of police loyalty. It is important, however, to first of all indicate the manner in which loyalty is a direct consequence of the peculiar nature of police-public interaction. Westley (1951) conclusively demonstrated that the police-citizen relationship was the most distinctive feature of the policeman's job. He concluded that the police tended to view civilians with suspicion, as aliens, and, not infrequently, as enemies, the public systematically failing to grant the police the respect such a vital and central occupation is entitled to as a matter of course. Failing to secure the deference which they feel they are owed by the public has resulted in numerous instances of hostile or brusque officer responses in observed police-citizen transactions (Black and Reiss, 1967) or even a stated desire on the part of an appreciable percentage of members of some northern urban police departments to resign from the force because of public disrespect and apathy (Reiss, 1967).

A frequent reaction to this social rejection may take the form of social isolation. Skolnick (1966) forcefully argues that police isolation

▶SOURCE: *"The Dimensions of Police Loyalty," American Behavioral Scientist, (May-June/July-August, 1970) 8:693–704. Reprinted by permission of the publisher, Sage Publications, Inc.*

arises from a constant sense of danger (which isolates the officer from both the criminal and noncriminal populations) and authority associated with the policeman's job (enforcing minor statutes which generates resentment and hostility in so far as he directs, restrains, and regulates public morality). Niederhoffer (1967) along similar lines finds much evidence of police anomie which he defines as a loss of faith in people. Other researchers have noted extreme police isolation (Wilson, 1963; Fogelson, 1968) and it has even been persuasively suggested that the law enforcement community is beginning to perceive itself as a minority group, discriminated against by the public (Campbell et al., 1969).

An inevitable concomitant of occupational isolation is the rise of high occupational solidarity. Skolnick (1966, 1969), Banton (1964), and McNamara (1967) all suggest that while all occupations have some elements of inclusiveness and identification, the police are unusually high in job solidarity. Reiss' (1967) extended investigation of police behavior in Boston, Washington, and Chicago found that 95% of the officers would defend the department or a fellow officer who had been slurred. Niederhoffer (1967) notes the dilemma of ideal police practice in conflict with practical patrol operation, resulting usually in closer dependence and greater reliance on fellow officers. Wilson (1963) believes that there may develop a police subculture predicated on a "code" quite at variance from that operating within civilian populations. In any event, a view of the research in the field reveals the truth of Skolnik's (1969) conclusion that "students of the police are unanimous in stressing the high degree of police solidarity."

As it is generally used, the concept of police loyalty is an uneasy amalgam of two independent and unequal behavioral components: (1) dangerousness of job plus isolation from the public increases the need for mutual assistance (maximum priority of response given to any police officer requiring assistance). (2) Secrecy (deliberate failure to reveal illicit, illegal, or simply uncomplimentary bits of information about police practices to a hostile citizenry or unsympathetic police superiors). As early as 1930, an eminent authority in the field of law enforcement concluded in one of the Wickersham Commission reports, "It is an unwritten law in police departments that police officers must never testify against their brother officers" (Vollmer, 1930). When Westley (1956) asked several officers in his midwest police department whether they would "report" or "testify" against a theft committed by a fellow officer, eleven of fifteen would not report and ten of the fifteen would not testify. Anyone who would inform was a stool pigeon and would, as a matter of course, be ostracized. Secrecy was a shield against the attacks of outsiders. Westley (1951) postulated the presence of three primary police norms; secrecy, being the most important, was consciously taught all rookies by older officers. Skolnick (1966) and Wilson (1963), among others, conclude that "secrecy" was present within the departments they had studied and was perceived as being extremely functional and necessary for the continued operation of the forces.

It would be absurd to deny the *presence* of deep ties of loyalty among members of the Philadelphia Police Department. What is worthy of investigation are the several possible recipients of police loyalty (the public, the department, or fellow officers), and a determination of the furthest reaches, the limits of secrecy, and the code of mutual aid and assistance.

External Loyalty

It is possible the police officer may still retain an idealized conception of his role performance, inculcated during his Police Academy days, so that his primary obligation is to the public which has created his position, delegates to him rather extraordinary amounts of power, indirectly judges his performance, and offers him some material rewards for the adequate performance of his occupational role. Crucial here is the perceived need for concealing information from this audience and the dependability of public support and aid in times of crisis. If the public is thought to be unsympathetic or even hostile, a group which permits, even demands, the use of deadly force and yet inexplicably fails to grant the respect and awe which normally accrues to positions exercising such power, external loyalty is a dubious commodity. A large percentage of the police in this study held this view of the public. A bare majority of the recruits at T1 (fifty-three percent) and T3 (fifty-one percent) and detectives (fifty-two percent) and far fewer experienced patrolmen (thirty-two percent) felt that the "public's view" of the police was favorable or very favorable. Expectedly, the *Negro public's view* was considered more negative, with only twenty-eight percent of the recruits at T1 and twenty-two percent at T3, sixteen percent of the detectives and eight percent of the experienced officers finding them to be equally favorable or very favorable. (Indeed, seventy-seven percent of the experienced officers judged the Negro community's attitude to be unfavorable or very unfavorable.) Beyond this, one-third of the rookies (T3) but over sixty percent of the older patrolmen and the detectives agreed that "most civilians think people join the police force because they can't get a better job." Concerning public cooperation with the police, contradictory results were found. While seventy-three percent of the recruits at T2 (without any field experience) thought "civilians generally cooperate with the police officers in their work," almost fifty percent, *at the same time,* nevertheless said that, "Patrolmen almost never receive cooperation from the public that is needed to handle police work properly" and sixty-nine percent thought that, "It was usually difficult to persuade people to give a patrolman the information he may need." Under conditions where a policeman is most dependent upon others, sixty-five percent of the recruits at T2 and fifty-eight percent at T3, but only forty-eight percent of the detectives and forty-three percent of the experienced patrolmen agreed that, "Most people will somehow help a

patrolman being attacked." In this study the public fails on both issues: it is unsympathetic and hostile and not infrequently contemptuous, while one cannot rely upon them in times of greater emergency.

Internal Loyalty

Perhaps then the police are really a big brotherhood, demanding complete dedication and operating as a closed, semisecretive body. One must now maintain the best possible posture vis-à-vis the public, even if this requires manipulating or concealing organizational malpractices. Internal loyalty is most likely to occur if the actual operation of the organization is held in high regard by its personnel. A favorable self-appraisal would imply fewer occasions arising which would require concealment and secrecy. Perhaps also involved is a somewhat inchoate, seldom articulated belief that there must (or should be) some quid pro quo between officer and department; complete fealty to the organization by an officer should perhaps be reciprocated by deliberate if informal systematic indifference to minor infractions of administrative or legal rules, and the application of minimal sanctions for the violations of more serious regulations governing appropriate police behavior. Given the high frequency of temptations to corruption that are a normal occurrence in the life of a police officer, organizational liberality might be conceived of as partial compensation for officer secrecy. The Philadelphia Department was very highly rated by the subjects; ninety-three percent of the recruits at T1 and T3, eighty-two percent of the detectives, and seventy-four percent of the older officers rated it as the best or one of the best in the country. On specific items, however, evaluations are less enthusiastic. Generally the actual operation of the department was most highly regarded by the rookies and least favorably viewed by experienced policemen. Thus sixty-nine percent of the recruits (T3), forty-four percent of the detectives, and forty percent of older officers agreed that "as one gets to know the department from the inside, it is a very efficient, smoothly operating organization." Yet seventy-five percent of all three populations indicated that "it is impossible to always follow all departmental rules and regulations and still do an efficient job."

Concerning the issue of leniency within the department, Table 1 reveals a consistent tendency by the recruits (from T2 to T3) to suggest lesser punishments for inappropriate or illegal police behavior. For six of the seven acts, a shrinking percentage believed the offending officer should be dismissed or arrested. Taking a $10 bribe not to issue a traffic ticket would be severely punished by only thirty percent of the recruits (at T3), whereas fifty-six percent of the same subjects had previously recommended dismissal or arrest six months before at T2. Similarly, a policeman stealing a few bottles of liquor from a guarded store should be heavily punished according to forty-seven percent of the recruits at T3, nine percent less than those

holding the same view at T2. As they respond to the "reality shock" of actual patrol work, recruits tend to become more permissive towards inappropriate police action and, by and large, more closely approximate the values of experienced patrolmen rather than the more critical judgments of the detective population. Cowardice is a condition which is difficult for police to "take seriously." They indicate that it is a condition that is as unlikely to occur as a surgeon who cannot stand the sight of blood. Excepting only cowardice, Table I shows the older officers are always most lenient and detectives most severe. The question arises whether Table I represents a range of *desired* punishments or is an estimate of actual departmental punishment policies and practices. A significant percentage of all subjects believed that "patrolmen are frequently found guilty of violation of departmental rules and are penalized severely," (the percentages were: T2—twenty-five percent, T3—twenty-two per-

Table I. Percentage of Agreement Among Recruits (at T2 and T3), Detectives, and Older Experienced Policemen for Acts for which Policemen Should Be Dismissed or Arrested

Acts	Recruits		Detectives (n=223)	Officers (n=197)
	T2(n=220)	T3(n=197)		
An officer takes a few bottles of liquor from a state store which he is guarding after it has been burglarized.	56	47	74	36
An officer takes $10.00 a week from a "numbers banker."	77	54	70	38
Cowardice.	63	72	85	75
An officer takes $100.00 from the operator of a "still."	82	61	70	45[a]
An officer takes $500.00 not to arrest a burglar.	92	81	94	64
An officer burglarizes a gas station.	95	92	97	83
An officer takes $10.00 not to issue a ticket to a driver of a car.	53	30	52	27

[a] Fifteen of the 197 older officers indicated that policemen guilty of such corruption should not be punished at all.

cent, detectives—twenty-eight percent, experienced patrolmen—forty-two percent) while at the same time an even larger percentage felt that "disciplining a patrolman usually has the effect of making him a less active and efficient officer" (the percentages were: T2—forty-one percent, T3—twenty-five percent, detectives—thirty-eight percent, experienced patrolmen—fifty-one percent). Very striking is the fact that forty-four percent of the recruits at T2, forty-eight percent at T3, sixty-four percent of the detectives, and seventy percent of the older patrolmen believed that a patrolman at a departmental hearing (he "goes to the front") will not get a fair, impartial trial. Indeed, twenty-eight percent of the detectives and forty-two percent of the experienced officers contend that "even with a good defense, an officer would be found guilty" by the departmental tribunal. Thus there exists probably a considerable discrepancy between what many officers describe as "fair" penalties for illegitimate police practices and the "unfairness" of punishments meted out at departmental hearings. In conclusion, the department is generally well regarded but is thought excessivly severe in penalizing inappropriate police behavior.

What are some of the limits to internal loyalty? Is a "good cop" one who gives his commanding officer unquestioned obedience? Only fifty-four percent of the recruits (T3), forty-two percent of the detectives, and forty-three percent of the experienced officers thought so. "Informally told by his supervisor not to be 'too concerned' with the numbers racket, the officer should comply with such informal directives' according to only twenty-six percent of the recruits (T3), twenty-one percent of the detectives, and thirty-eight percent of the older officers.

Nevertheless, most officers believe that "the police department is really a big brotherhood" and the organization would automatically dispatch all necessary aid whenever an officer requested it so that internal loyalty would be rewarded by the assurance of maximum material assistance in times of crisis.

Interpersonal Loyalty

With a capricious, uncooperative, and unreliable citizenry, with a bureaucratic structure which does not always properly protect its own, there arises the possibility that latent structures develop which place the highest premium on loyalty among fellow officers. Secrecy is defined as personal and conscious concealment of information not only from the public but also from supervisory and administrative levels within the organization. Mutual aid means one assumes maximum response of all individual officers to any other officer in trouble; such a system of reciprocal aid means that the officer is less dependent upon the possibly vague supervisory directives regarding the allocation of scarce resources (vehicular and personnel) or the unpredictable and often arbitrary variables which go into the decision of the dispatcher regarding the disbursal of police facilities during the time of an emergency. This is replaced by a firm belief in the reliable presence and appropriate reaction of officers sent to an embattled officer as well as the voluntary response of non-dispatched police who become aware of the trouble.

Despite the previously indicated consensus among researchers on the existence and power of police secrecy, Table II clearly demonstrates that interpersonal bonds of secrecy are not highly developed within this subject population. A very considerable percentage of all officers stated that they felt it would be appropriate to inform a supervisor about a partner who was a grafter, an incompetent, a disgruntled agitator, an alcoholic, or who was excessively violent. It is important to recognize initially that the five proscribed modes of behavior in Table II deliberately did not include the most reprehensible forms of police misbehavior, e.g., an officer who is a serious criminal or who "frames" an innocent person, or who becomes involved in more extreme forms of corruption ("continually on the take" from some criminal organization, or being "bought off" by a felon). The recruits generally would inform on a partner who was

Table II. Percentage of Recruits (nine months on the force), Detectives, and Experienced Patrolmen Who Would Inform Their Superiors about a Partner's Improper Behavior, by type of Behavior

Partner's Behavior	Recruits (n=197)	Detectives (n=223)	Officers (n=197)
He is a "grafter" (takes money not to issue traffic tickets).	35	54	30
He is incompetent.	35	42	38
He is a disgruntled agitator.	54	47	45
He is continually drunk on duty.	59	73	49
He is excessively violent and brutal when making arrests.	56	75	60

brutal, or an alcoholic, or a "disgruntled agitator." Detectives were more likely to reveal to their superiors all inappropriate acts, excepting only agitation. The experienced officer, consistently, is most committed to a policy of silence. The questions were difficult for the subjects to deal with and were often described as "rough" or "rotten" because they did not permit simple or conventional responses. A completely conventional set of responses would be for the subject to inform for all five acts; complete interpersonal loyalty would be to remain silent on the same five acts. In point of fact, a very small percentage of respondents gave totally conventional or totally loyal responses. Also the general pattern of informing that emerged was rational, consistent, and easily explicable. Minor graft is a real and constant threat to the incorruptability of policemen "in the street" so that the inability to resist such temptation is, from the point of view of rookies and older patrolmen, understandable as is their reluctance to inform on such behavior. Incompetence is a notoriously spongy term, capable of a wide range of individual definitions; therefore, as one would not like to be judged by someone else's possibly eccentric notion of competence, one in turn should not condemn others except in the most severe and unarguable situations. A disgruntled agitator is a problem because he will ultimately provoke serious trouble within the department

so that it is in one's own best interest to inform a superior about him. A drunken cop is simply a bad officer, lacking the most important characteristic of a "good cop": dependability; his unreliability may well put his partner at considerable disadvantage under certain patrol conditions. Excessive violence, beyond its moral implications, raises the distinct possibility of eventual internal departmental investigations of acts of alleged brutality which may result in condemnation and punishment not only for the perpetrator but also perhaps for a partner who has previously failed to notify supervisors about such prior behavior. On the final measure of secrecy, in great contrast to Westley's findings, only sixteen percent of the recruits (T3), five percent of the detectives, and twenty-seven percent of the experienced officers agreed that "A policeman should never testify against a fellow officer in court regardless of what he has done." It would seem then that secrecy, maintenance of mutual confidences among fellow officers, is perhaps not an integral part of a policeman's occupational role.

Regarding mutual aid to officers in trouble, the entire population (with only three exceptions) agreed that if they were out-of-uniform and off duty, they would immediately go to the aid of any officer who required assistance. If an arrested suspect was identified as someone who had killed a policeman, the police would be justified in "roughing him up" in the view of forty-two percent of the recruits at T1, forty-four percent at T2, and fifty percent at T3, as well as fifty-five percent of the experienced patrolmen, but only twenty-four percent of the detectives. The recruits at T2 were overwhelmingly (ninety-five percent) in agreement that an officer can always count on getting aid from other policemen when he needs it. Yet fully twenty-seven percent of the same recruits (T2) thought that "there are a significant number of policemen who will try to get out of doing anything to help other officers."

As a measure of the totality of commitment to rendering aid to fellow officers, the recruits at T1 and T3, the detectives, and older officers were asked to imagine a patrolman walking a beat, far from a police phone box, when two people come up to him and each tells him about two separate acts occurring simultaneously, each of which requires *immediate* police action; he can, of course, respond to only one of them. To which act should the officer respond? One of the acts in each pair involves a policeman requiring some form of help: he has broken his leg; he is simply described as being "in trouble"; he is being "pushed around" by a group of hoodlums; or he is being shot at by burglars. The other act in each pair represents a "good pinch," being a serious offense with a strong possibility of apprehending the offender: a shopkeeper has been murdered and the killer is still in the store; a child has been sexually assaulted and the criminal is still in the area; a robbery has taken place and the robber can still be arrested. Additionally, the crimes are politically clear and would very likely result in much favorable publicity for the arresting officer as well as the entire department. The forced pair choices meant that the respondents were once more faced with selecting between unattractive alternatives. The officer could go to the felonies (thereby jeopardizing a fellow officer) or he could respond to the threatened policeman (which might well result in a serious and dangerous criminal going free). As Table III shows, when informed that

an officer has broken his leg, most police will go instead to the scene of a simultaneously occurring murder, but (excepting only the recruits at T1) a preponderance of the same officers will respond to the injured officer in a preference to arresting a child molester. When the officer is described simply as being "in trouble," the same pattern emerges, with the police in the main, responding to a homicide but, once more, choosing to aid the officer rather than investigate a sexual molestation. An officer being manhandled clearly commits most police to his defense (except for the "untutored" recruits at T1) in preference to a murder, sexual assault, or robbery. An officer who has been shot at receives the immediate support of most policemen regardless of whatever else might have claims upon their attention.

Thus the only situation when *most* police will not automatically assist a fellow officer is when an extremely serious felony (murder) has just taken place *and* the officer is in relatively little jeopardy. Recruits increasingly gave highest priority to officers in distress so that by T3 their responses were very similar to that of older officers and detectives. Experienced officers are most likely and detectives least likely to render aid to an endangered officer regardless of setting. Also one is struck by the remarkable similarity in responses of the three, somewhat dissimilar, police populations. Significant is that even in instances of greatest peril to a fellow officer, twenty to thirty-seven percent of the police subjects would not go to his aid but would respond to a recent murder, and over ten percent would pursue a child molester.

CONCLUSIONS

Some tentative conclusions regarding police loyalty would be:

1. The two components of loyalty, secrecy, and mandatory mutual assistance are of differential importance. Our subject population seemed barely constrained by any norm of in-

Table III. Percentage of Recruits, Detectives, and Experienced Patrolmen
Responding to Another Officer in Trouble Rather Than to a Simultaneously
Occurring "Good Pinch," by Type of Officer Trouble and by the Nature
of the Other Crime

Type of Trouble (v. the "Good Pinch")	Rookies T1[a] (n=226)	Rookies T3[b] (n=197)	Detectives (n=223)	Officers (n=197)
Officer falls and breaks leg				
(v. Murder)[c]	23	31	28	49
(v. Child Molester)[d]	25	56	56	58
(v. Robber)[e]	59	60	53	63
Officer simply in trouble				
(v. Murder)	36	37	21	44
(v. Child Molester)	50	60	52	56
(v. Robber)	75	76	62	75
Officer being pushed around				
(v. Murder)	37	58	53	56
(v. Child Molester)	53	76	71	75
(v. Robber)	73	80	74	81
Officer being shot at				
(v. Murder)	65	74	63	80
(v. Child Molester)	72	89	87	90

[a] The recruit population during its first week on the police force.

[b] The recruit population during its ninth month on the police force.

[c] The act reads, in full: A store keeper has been killed by a robber who is still in the store.

[d] The act reads, in full: A child has been sexually molested and the criminal is still in the area.

[e] The act reads, in full: A man has been held up and the robber may still be caught.

terpersonal secrecy (an officer could and should appropriately inform on his partner under a variety of conditions) while, at the same time, they were strongly (but not uniformly) impelled to immediate and unquestioned response to an injured or threatened officer.

2.   There exist countervailing circumstances which negate, for a significant percentage of the police, the highest priority normally assigned to the rendering of maximum mutual aid.

3.   The experienced patrolmen consistently demand (and perhaps reciprocally offer) maintenance of secrecy and loyalty and mutual assistance in almost every setting, while detectives are least committed to the same norms of loyalty.

4.   As the recruits are rather quickly socialized into their complex occupation, a large proportion internalize *selected portions* of the value systems of experienced officers with whom they work on an intimate daily basis.

REFERENCES

Banton, M. (1964) The Policeman in the Community. London, England: Tavistock.

Bayley, D.H. and H. Mendelsohn (1969) Minorities and the Police. New York: Free Press.

Black, D. J. and A. J. Reiss, Jr. (1967) "Patterns of behavior and citizen transactions," in Studies in Crime and Law Enforcement in Major Metropolitan Areas, Vol. II. Washington, D.C.: U.S. Government Printing Office.

Campbell, J. S., J. R. Sahid, and D. P. Stang (1969) Law and Order Reconsidered. Staff Report 10 to the

National Commission on the Causes and Prevention of Violence. Washington, D.C.: U.S. Government Printing Office.

Fogelson, R. M. (1968) "From resentment to confrontation: the police, the Negroes and the outbreak of the nineteen-sixties riots." Pol. Sci. Q. 83: 217-247.

McNamara, J. N. (1967) "Uncertainties in police work: the relevance of police recruits, background and training." in D. J. Bordua (ed.) The Police, New York: John Wiley.

Niederhoffer, A. (1967) Behind the Shield. Garden City, N.Y.: Doubleday.

Reiss, A. J. Jr. (1967) "Career orientations, job satisfaction, and the assessment of law enforcement problems by policy officers." in Studies in Crime and Law Enforcement in Major Metropolitan Areas, Vol. II. Washington, D.C.: U.S. Government Printing Office.

Skolnick, J. H. (1969) The Politics of Protest. New York: Ballantine Books.

———— (1969) Justice Without Trial. New York: John Wiley.

Vollmer, A. (1930) Report on the Police. United States National Committee on Law Observance and Enforcement. Washington, D.C.: U.S. Government Printing Office

Westley, W. A. (1956) "Secrecy and the police." Social Forces 34: 254–257.

———— (1951) "The police: a sociological study of law, custom, and morality." Ph.D. thesis, University of Chicago.

Wilson, J. Q. (1967) "Police morale, reform and citizen respect: the Chicago case," in D.J. Bordua (ed.) The Police. New York: John Wiley.

———— (1963) "The police and their problems: a theory." Public Police 12: 189-216.

10. The Knapp Commission Report on Police Corruption

THE KNAPP COMMISSION

GRATUITIES

BY FAR THE MOST WIDESPREAD FORM OF MISCON-duct the commission found in the Police Department was the acceptance by police officers of gratuities in the form of free meals, free goods, and cash payments. Almost all policemen either solicited or accepted such favors in one form or another, and the practice was widely accepted by both the police and the citizenry, with many feeling that it wasn't corruption at all, but a natural perquisite of the job.

Free Meals

The most universally accepted gratuity was the free meal offered to policemen by luncheonettes, restaurants, bars, and hotels. Despite the Commission's announced lack of interest in investigating instances of police free meals, investigators found it impossible to avoid noticing such instances while going about their private affairs or while engaged in investigating more serious matters.

Early in his administration Commissioner Murphy took a strong stand with respect to such freeloading and stirred up a good deal of animosity among rank and file policemen by inveighing against even a free cup of coffee.

The Commissioner's position was somewhat undermined by his handling of what was undoubtedly the most highly publicized free meal

▶SOURCE: *The Knapp Commission Report on Police Corruption. New York: George Braziller, 1972. Pp. 170–182, 65–69. Reprinted by permission of the publisher.*

served to a New York policeman in recent years. Assistant Chief Inspector Albert Seedman—in March of 1972 when he was under active consideration for the post of Chief of Detectives—hosted a dinner for his wife and another couple at the New York Hilton. The bill for dinner, which came to $84.30 including tip, was picked up by the hotel. When the check for this meal was discovered by Commission investigators during the course of a routine investigation, a Commission attorney immediately brought it to the attention of Seedman, who had in the meantime been appointed the Chief of Detectives. Chief Seedman then explained that the hotel management had invited him to dine in return for performing a security check for the hotel—a service normally provided by the police at no charge. This information was turned over on a confidential basis to Commissioner Murphy, who relieved Chief Seedman of his command pending an inquiry.

A week later the Commissioner released a statement outlining a version of the affair which was significantly different from the one Chief Seedman had given our staff attorney. While he originally had ascribed the free meal (including tip) to an invitation from the hotel in specific recognition of services rendered, the statement released by the Commissioner indicated that he had gone with his friends to the hotel fully expecting to pay for the meal, had simply made "no fuss" when the management failed to present a bill, and had covered his embarrassment by leaving a "large tip." Having accepted Chief Seedman's revised version of the affair, Commissioner Murphy restored him to command of the division, announcing that he had committed no "serious wrongdoing."

This incident had a significant effect on the already cynical attitude of many policemen. It was difficult for police officers to take seriously Commissioner Murphy's stern warnings against receiving "any buck but a pay check," when they apparently did not apply to one of the Commissioner's top aides. Several police officers commented wryly to Commission investigators that at last a meaningful guideline had been established for free meals: "It's okay—up to $84.30."

In fact, of course, the average patrolman was found to eat nowhere near that well. Free meals were indeed available to almost all policemen throughout the City, but patrolmen rarely dined in style. Every patrolman knew which establishments on his beat provided free meals, and these were the places where he lunched each day. Uniformed policemen generally ate modest-priced meals in cafeterias, luncheonettes, restaurants, bars, or in the employee cafeterias of hotels. Commission employees observed countless uniformed patrolmen eating in such establishments, then leaving without paying and sometimes without even leaving a tip. Most often, no bill was even presented.

Many thousands of free meals were consumed by policemen each day and the sheer numbers created problems for the most popular eateries. Some luncheonettes which did a particularly heavy police business either offered a discount or charged policemen a token fee, most commonly $.50.

It was not only the policeman on patrol who felt that his lunches should be provided free. Numerous examples were reported to the Commission of officers in the station house sending radio cars to local restaurants to pick up meals for police officers whose duties prevented them from getting out on the street.

Nor were take-out orders always limited to food. Patrolman Phillips testified that it was not uncommon for policemen assigned to a radio car to pick up a "flute"—a Coke bottle filled with liquor—which they would deliver to the station house. In most instances, however, take-out orders involved the same sort of low-priced meals obtained by police officers on patrol. The Commission obtained a list used in one precinct house apparently setting out the dates on which certain eating places were to be approached for sandwiches, pizza, and other food to go.

The owner of one home-delivery food business which sold $2.00 fried chicken dinners found that his dinners were so popular with the police in his local precinct that they were ordering eighty to ninety dinners a week from him. This was substantially cutting into his profits, so he decided to start charging the police a nominal price of $.50 per dinner. This angered the police, who began issuing summonses to his delivery cars on every trip they made, resulting in $600 in summonses in one week. The owner called the Police Commissioner's office and explained his problem, and soon afterwards, he stopped receiving summonses. However, he had already dropped the $.50 charge per dinner.

Not all patrolmen were as restrained as the general run, and some were observed eating in rather fashionable establishments. Two patrolmen in particular confronted Commission investigators with a situation difficult to ignore by pulling up nightly to the back entrance of a fairly high-priced downtown restaurant located directly under the windows of the Commission's offices. The officers were served in their car by a uniformed waiter with a tray and a napkin draped over one arm.

Non-uniformed officers generally ordered less modest meals than uniformed patrolmen. Plainclothesmen, detectives, and high-level officers, who worked in civilian clothes instead of the conspicuous blue uniform, patronized a much wider selection of restaurants than the uniformed force, including many clearly in the luxury category. And the meals they ordered were often grandiose compared with the cafeteria-style food favored by uniformed men.

William Phillips, when assigned as a detective

in a midtown precinct, regularly patronized, with other detectives, the very best restaurants, where he received gratis what he called "electric-chair meals." He reported that as he sipped the last drop of brandy after an enormous feast all he could think was "pull the switch, I'm ready to go!" Free meals of this sort, which in Phillips' case could add up to hundreds of dollars in one week, obviously presented a more serious but much less frequently encountered problem than the hot dog traditionally demanded by a patrolman from a vendor.

The owner of one of New York's finest French restaurants reported to the Commission that he was approached by policemen demanding free dinners. When he flatly turned them down, they took retaliatory action: The restaurant was located on a street where parking was illegal before 7:00 P.M., and the police began showing up every night at 6:55 to tow away cars belonging to patrons.

The Commission discovered that there was a certain etiquette among police officers concerning free meals in restaurants. In most precincts an officer could not eat free in a restaurant on another man's beat without first getting his permission. Officers also tried to time their free meals for restaurants' slow periods, to avoid taking up tables which might otherwise be used by paying customers. And thoughtful policemen in at least one precinct installed a wall chart containing a box for each eatery in the precinct, where officers made an appropriate entry every time they had a free meal, the idea being to keep track of the police traffic and spread the burden fairly. Also, some restaurants offered free meals only to officers in a position to do them a favor in return. At one luncheonette in the Bronx where a Commission attorney was dining with his wife, the waitress took a patrolman's order for food to go, then went to the manager and asked, "We don't charge him, do we?" The manager took one look at the officer and said, "You can charge that bastard as much as you like. It's only the ones from the Forty-Seventh [that we take care of]."

Hotels

The Commission's interest turned to hotels after a former hotel security officer came in with hotel records indicating that at least one hotel was paying off police in free meals, free rooms, and cash payments at Christmas. Commission investigators then interviewed security officers and general managers at ten major hotels in the City, all of whom flatly denied giving gratuities in any form to the police.

The Commission's next step was to subpoena personnel and records reflecting police gratuities from seven large hotels, two of which were among those questioned earlier. The result was a paper flood of meal checks, meal tickets, room records and hotel logs. An initial examination of these records showed that large numbers of policemen—as well as other public officials—were receiving gratuities from hotels, chiefly in the form of free meals. This practice was described in detail by security directors and managers who this time were subpoenaed for testimony under oath.

The pattern of free meals that emerged was similar to that the Commission had found in independent restaurants, with patrolmen generally eating in the hotels' employee dining rooms, coffee shops, or less expensive restaurants, and higher-ranking officers ordering lavish meals in the hotels' more expensive restaurants.

Records from several of the hotels showed that they each fed as many as 300 to 400 meals a month to policemen in their employee dining rooms, mostly to patrolmen in uniform. The value of these meals was usually under $2.00 each. To get free meals in the employee dining rooms, the policemen generally went to the security office, where their uniforms—or in the case of non-uniformed officers, their shields—served as identification. They were either asked to sign the meal checks or hotel logs with their names and ranks or were given meal tickets to be turned in in the dining rooms. When the names given in the hotel checks and logs were checked against the precinct rosters, a sizable percentage of them proved to be false (including two uniformed officers identifying themselves as Whitman Knapp and Sydney Cooper, who was then chief of the Department's anticorruption force).

In these same hotels, higher-ranking officers (sergeants, detectives, inspectors, lieutenants, captains, and one chief inspector) ate in the hotels' better restaurants, ordering the most expensive items on the menu, with the tab rarely coming to less than $20 per person in the larger midtown hotels. And the volume was substantial: over $500 a month at most hotels checked and $1,500 a month at the Statler-Hilton.

Hotels also were found to provide free rooms to police officers upon request. The ostensible reason for this was usually that the officer lived out of town and had to be in court early the following morning. In practice, however, policemen often took rooms when they were neither on official business nor scheduled to make a court appearance the following day. Occasionally, a group of them would book a free room for an afternoon in order to watch an important ball game on the TV provided by the hotel.

Free Drinks

In the course of its investigation into bars, Commission investigators could not help but observe numerous uniformed police officers imbibing free drinks—both on duty and off. Bar owners and policemen also told the Commission that it was common practice for bars to offer free drinks to policemen.

Three patrol sergeants in the Nineteenth Precinct regularly spent their entire tours going from one bar to another. While the behavior of patrolmen was less extreme, there was plenty of drinking on duty and off by them, too, with no evidence of any attempt by superiors to stop it. One example of a superior's laisser-faire attitude occurred in the presence of Commission investigators at an East Side bar. Three patrolmen, in uniform and on duty, were in the bar, one drinking a mixed drink, one a beer, and one coffee. The uniformed sergeant for the sector, who was on patrol and theoretically responsible

for supervising the patrolmen, entered the bar, stayed for five minutes, then left. The patrolmen continued to drink during and after his visit.

Christmas Payments

Payments to police at Christmas by bars, restaurants, hotels, department stores, and other retail businesses have long been a police tradition. Although the Department has made efforts to halt the practice, at the time of the investigation it still continued. A particularly rigorous campaign was waged against the practice in December of 1971, with the reported result that officers collected their Christmas gratuities in January, after the campaign was over.

Christmas money was usually collected in a fairly organized fashion. Early in December, lists were made up at many precinct houses, division headquarters, and squad rooms, on which were entered the names of all the businesses in their jurisdiction from which the police expected Christmas payments. The list was then divided up among the various officers, each of whom was to go to the businesses on his list and collect. He either collected a flat fee to be divided up later at the station house by participating officers, or he presented a list, broken down to include the various officers.

Patrolman Phillips described how Christmas graft was collected when he was a detective in the Seventeenth Precinct some years ago:

"Well, Christmas was an organized operation, and the squad clerical men had the master Christmas list, which was kept locked up at all times. Each detective at Christmas time was given a list of between ten and fifteen establishments. The money was all brought in. It was divided equally among all the detectives in the squad. The lieutenant and sergeant had their own Christmas list. They did not participate in ours."

When asked how long the master list was, Patrolman Phillips said, "it was quite a long list, ten or fifteen yellow pages . . . [it contained] every hotel, almost every bar, every cabaret, and other business establishment in the Seventeenth Precinct." He said that the Christmas pad came to $400 or $500 per man in that precinct, not counting individual payments, which usually added another $200 or so. Phillips also reported that specific amounts were set aside for transmittal to higher ranking supervisors, right up to the Chief of Detectives. The Commission was unable to verify whether the money was actually transmitted.

The Christmas lists presented to hotels in particular were quite detailed, giving amounts to be paid to police officers of all ranks, up to and including the borough commander and Chief Inspector. (Again, the Commission obtained no direct proof that these monies were ever actually received by the officers named on the lists.) One Christmas list obtained from a large hotel set forth specific amounts to be given to each of the detectives assigned to the squad with jurisdiction over that hotel.

While lists of this sort reflected a practice as widespread as it was long-standing, the lists themselves could not always be accepted on face value since, as in the case of the detective list, they often reflected proposed rather than actual payments. During the Commission hearings the lieutenant in charge of the detective squad mentioned above requested and was given the opportunity to testify that he had never received the payment reflected on the list and the hotel personnel who provided the list acknowledged that not all payments on it were actually accepted.

The giving of gratuities to high-level police officers was a common practice. Former Chief Inspector Sanford Garelik acknowledged in executive testimony before the Commission that, as a field commander, he had received gratuities from businessmen with whom he came in contact in the course of his duties. Instead of returning these gifts or asking that they not be sent, he stated that he attempted to respond by giving return gifts of equal value.

Free Merchandise and Other Gifts

A number of merchants gave policemen gifts for services rendered and free merchandise. These included such items as free packages of cigarettes solicited by policemen from tobacco shops and grocery stores, free bags of groceries from retail stores, free service at dry cleaners and laundaries, and free goods from factories and wholesalers. In his public testimony before the Commission Patrolman Droge stated that in one precinct in which he had served, police officers had used their tours to make the rounds of a bread factory, a frankfurter plant, and an ice cream plant, among others, stocking up on goods to take home. "I recall one police officer," said Droge, "who felt that if he didn't go home with a bag of groceries, then his tour wasn't complete."

Tips for Services Rendered

Policemen often accepted or solicited payments for services performed during their tours of duty. Some of these services were legitimate parts of their jobs, like guarding foreign diplomats, for which they should not have been tipped, and others were services which should have been performed by private guards rather than by City-paid policemen, like escorting supermarket managers to the bank.

Foreign consulates, many of which have City policemen assigned to guard them, have been known to offer gratuities to the police in various forms. Some would send cases of whiskey and champagne to precinct houses. Others made gifts of gold watches and money to various police officers.

When City marshals served eviction notices, they would notify the police, and when a car responded, the marshal paid $5 to the patrolmen in the car for handling the eviction.

When managers of many supermarkets and liquor stores were ready to take the day's receipts to the bank, they called the local precinct house and asked that a patrol car be sent over. The policemen in the car would then give the manager a ride to the bank, for which they received "anywhere from a couple of packs of cigarettes to $4.00."

Proprietors of check cashing services, who open up shop in the morning with large supplies of cash on hand, frequently had standing arrangements to have a patrol car waiting outside each morning when the proprietor came in.

Proprietors of burglarized stores and factories, if they arrived at the scene before the police did, paid $5 a man to each officer who showed up. However, if the police arrived first, they often helped themselves to merchandise.

Since our investigation, the Department has issued an order requiring that, when patrol cars manned by patrolmen reach the scene of a burglary before the sergeant gets there, the cars must be inspected by the sergeant before they leave the scene. Although this sounds like a sensible reform, a precinct commander and other police officers told the Commission that they felt the required procedure was demeaning and unlikely ever to be followed, as it would result in the public spectacle of a police supervisor searching for evidence of theft by patrolmen.

Comments

Almost to a man, legitimate businessmen questioned by the Commission about why they offered gratuities to the police claimed that they did so "to promote good will." Almost all expected to receive either extra or better service than that given to the general public, and many expected the police to overlook minor illegal acts or conditions.

Restaurants and bars expected police who dined and drank free to respond promptly if they were ever called in an emergency and to handle such calls with more discretion than usual. If the police ever had to arrest a man in one of the hotels which offered free meals and Christmas money, the management could be fairly confident that instead of charging into the dining room in the middle of dinner and making the arrest in full view of all the diners, the police would probably make the arrest much more discreetly.

Another benefit to bars, restaurants, and hotels was that patrons were allowed to park and double-park illegally in front of their establishments.

In many instances it is unfair to infer that payments of a gratuity necessarily reflected a shakedown by the police officer involved. A bar owner, restauranteur, or other businessman is usually most happy to have a police officer in or near his premises, and in a good many situations, payments—particularly Christmas gratuities—were made simply because the police officer became friendly with the local merchants in his patrol area. Gift giving, however, was very rarely a reciprocal matter in the sense of friends exchanging gifts on an equal basis. If, as in the case of some high-ranking officers, a return gift was made it was always in response to an original overture by someone who usually stood to gain by the presumed good will.

The fact is that the public by and large does not regard gratuities as a serious matter. While some may be offended by the occasionally arrogant way in which some police officers demand what they consider to be their due, most people are willing to allow a police officer who spends long hours providing protection for an area to stop in for a quick free meal or cup of coffee at an eating establishment which enjoys the benefit of his protection. Indeed, an investigation of hotels in New York conducted a few years ago by the New York County District Attorney came up with essentially the same evidence as that found by the Commission of hotels providing free meals and a prosecutorial judgment was apparently made not to pursue the matter even though criminal violations were involved.

Officers who participated in Ethical Awareness Workshops recently sponsored by the Department have reached an interesting conclusion. They felt that no police officer should ever accept a gratuity of any sort. Their reasoning was twofold: One, that even a series of small gratuities—like cups of coffee—would, in certain instances, affect an officer's performance of his duty, and two, that acceptance of gratuities is demeaning to a professional police officer. However, it is doubtful whether such standards could reasonably be imposed throughout the Department.

The general tolerance of gratuities both by policemen and by the public gives rise to the question whether some system should be developed whereby gratuities are specifically condoned as long as they are not excessive. At the time of our investigation, there was a *de facto* tolerance of such gratuities, and if the Department could institutionalize this approach by establishing realistic guidelines setting out what is and is not permissible it could at least remove the illegal atmosphere which may operate to condition policemen for more serious misconduct. Admittedly, the problem of drawing a line is a difficult one. If the Department should decide to permit policemen to accept free meals and goods, the Commission urges that all such gratuities be reported in memorandum books or on Daily Field Activity Reports, which should be reviewed daily by supervisory officers. Supervisory personnel could then be held responsible for insuring that such privileges were not abused.

Some areas do seem susceptible to an official regulatory approach. For example, there would seem to be no reason why the practice of hotels providing free rooms to police officers could not be officially sanctioned. If an officer is forced to work late hours in any area of the City far from his home and is expected to be on duty or in court early the following morning, it does not seem unreasonable that he be provided with a hotel room, on a space available basis, with the expense being paid for by the City. If such rooms are provided they should be duly reported and, where possible, approved in advance as part of a regular system.

Assuming that hotel and restaurants actually do not wish to provide free meals and rooms to police officers, it has been demonstrated that they are not forced to. At the time of the Commission hearings, under the glare of publicity, many of the big hotels announced that they would no longer provide such services.

*

GRASS-EATERS AND MEAT-EATERS

Corrupt policemen have been informally described as being either "grass-eaters" or "meat-eaters." The overwhelming majority of those who do take payoffs are grass-eaters, who accept gratuities and solicit five- and ten- and twenty-dollar payments from contractors, tow-truck operators, gamblers, and the like, but do not aggressively pursue corruption payments. "Meat-eaters," probably only a small percentage of the force, spend a good deal of their working hours aggressively seeking out situations they can exploit for financial gain, including gambling, narcotics, and other serious offenses which can yield payments of thousands of dollars. Patrolman William Phillips was certainly an example of this latter category.

One strong impetus encouraging grass-eaters to continue to accept relatively petty graft is, ironically, their feeling of loyalty to their fellow officers. Accepting payoff money is one way for an officer to prove that he is one of the boys and that he can be trusted. In the climate which existed in the Department during the Commission's investigation, at least at the precinct level, these numerous but relatively small payoffs were a fact of life, and those officers who made a point of refusing them were not accepted closely into the fellowship of policemen. Corruption among grass-eaters obviously cannot be met by attempting to arrest them all and will probably diminish only if Commissioner Murphy is successful in his efforts to change the rank and file attitude toward corruption.

No change in attitude, however, is likely to affect a meat-eater, whose yearly income in graft amounts to many thousands of dollars and who may take payoffs of $5,000 or even $50,000 in one fell swoop (former Assistant Chief Inspector Sydney Cooper, who had been active in anti-corruption work for years, recently stated that the largest score of which he had heard—although he was unable to verify it—was a narcotics payoff involving $250,000). Such men are willing to take considerable risks as long as the potential profit remains so large. Probably the only way to deal with them will be to ferret them out individually and get them off the force, and, hopefully, into prisons.

PADS, SCORES AND GRATUITIES

Corruption payments made to the police may be divided into "pad" payments and "scores," two police slang terms which make an important distinction.

The "pad" refers to regular weekly, biweekly, or monthly payments, usually picked up by a police bagman and divided among fellow officers. Those who make such payments as well as policemen who receive them are referred to as being "on the pad."

A "score" is a one-time payment that an officer might solicit from, for example, a motorist or a narcotics violator. The term is also used as a verb, as in "I scored him for $1,500."

A third category of payments to the police is that of gratuities, which the Commission feels cannot in the strictest sense be considered a matter of police corruption, but which has been included here because it is a related—and ethically borderline—practice, which is prohibited by Department regulations, and which often leads to corruption.

Operations on the pad are generally those which operate illegally in a fixed location day in and day out. Illegal gambling is probably the single largest source of pad payments. The most important legitimate enterprises on the pad at the time of the investigation were those like construction, licensed premises, and businesses employing large numbers of vehicles, all of which operate from fixed locations and are subject to summonses from the police for myriad violations.

Scores, on the other hand, are made whenever the opportunity arises—most often when an officer happens to spot someone engaging in an illegal activity like pushing narcotics, which doesn't involve a fixed location. Those whose activities are generally legal but who break the law occasionally, like motorists or tow-truck operators, are also subject to scores. By far the most lucrative source of scores is the City's multimillion-dollar narcotics business.

FACTORS INFLUENCING CORRUPTION

There are at least five major factors which influence how much or how little graft an officer receives, and also what his major sources are. The most important of these is, of course, the character of the officer in question, which will determine whether he bucks the system and refuses all corruption money; goes along with the system and accepts what comes his way; or outdoes the system, and aggressively seeks corruption-prone situations and exploits them to the extent that it seriously cuts into the time available for doing his job. His character will also determine what kind of graft he accepts. Some officers, who don't think twice about accepting money from gamblers, refuse to have anything at all to do with narcotics pushers. They make a distinction between what they call "clean money" and "dirty money."

The second factor is the branch of the Department to which an officer is assigned. A plainclothesman, for example, has more—and different—opportunities than a uniformed patrolman.

The third factor is the area to which an officer is assigned. At the time of the investigation certain precincts in Harlem, for instance, comprised what police officers called "the Gold Coast" because they contained so many payoff-prone activities, numbers and narcotics being the biggest. In contrast, the Twenty-Second Precinct, which is Central Park, has clearly limited payoff opportunities. As Patrolman Phillips remarked, "What can you do, shake down the squirrels!" The area also determines the major sources of corruption payments. For instance, in midtown Manhattan precincts businessmen and motorists were major sources; on the Upper East Side, bars and construction; in the ghetto precincts, narcotics and numbers.

The fourth factor is the officer's assignment. For uniformed men, a seat in a sector car was considered fairly lucrative in most precincts, while assignment to stand guard duty outside City Hall obviously was not, and assignment to one sector of a precinct could mean lots of payoffs from construction sites while in another sector bar owners were the big givers.

The fifth factor is rank. For those who do

receive payoffs, the amount generally ascends with the rank. A bar may give $5 to patrolmen, $10 to sergeants, and considerably more to a captain's bagman. Moreover, corrupt supervisors have the opportunity to cut into much of the graft normally collected by those under them.

SOURCES OF PAYOFFS

Organized crime is the single biggest source of police corruption, through its control of the City's gambling, narcotics, loansharking, and illegal sex-related enterprises like homosexual afterhours bars and pornography, all of which the Department considers mob-run. These endeavors are so highly lucrative that large payments to the police are considered a good investment if they protect the business from undue police interference.

The next largest source is legitimate business seeking to ease its way through the maze of City ordinances and regulations. Major offenders are construction contractors and subcontractors, liquor licensees, and managers of businesses like trucking firms and parking lots, which are likely to park large numbers of vehicles illegally. If the police were completely honest, it is likely that members of these groups would seek to corrupt them, since most seem to feel that paying off the police is easier and cheaper than obeying the laws or paying fines and answering summonses when they do violate the laws. However, to the extent police resist corruption, business interests will be compelled to use their political muscle to bring about revision of the regulations to make them workable.

11. Corruption in a Small City

PENNSYLVANIA CRIME COMMISSION

IN EARLY JUNE 1973, A SERIES OF ARTICLES APpeared in York newspapers concerning an investigation by the York Police Department of allegations that bribes or kickbacks had been paid by tow-truck operators to members of the York police force. On June 8, 1973, Assistant City Solicitor Jay V. Yost was appointed by Mayor Eli Eichelberger to investigate these charges.

As a result of newspaper publicity, a representative of the Pennsylvania Crime Commission met with and offered assistance to Mayor Eichelberger, City Solicitor David Wm. Bupp and Assistant City Solicitor Yost. On June 21, 1973, the City Solicitor wrote the Commission requesting that the Commission conduct an investigation into alleged kickbacks from tow-truck operators to members of the York Police Department.

The Commission's preliminary investigation commenced in late June 1973. Interviews were conducted with towing operators, with representatives of the American Automobile Association (AAA), and with approximately twenty members of the York Police Department. The Commission was informed by some of these police officers that they had received money from tow-truck operators. Some believed that a very substantial percentage of the entire Department had received money from tow-truck operators on at least one occasion, and a

▶SOURCE: *1973–1974 Report, Pennsylvania Crime Commission, St. Davids, Pa.: The Pennsylvania Crime Commission, 1974.* Pp. 152–164. Reprinted by permission.

number of the officers acknowledged that they had received towing kickbacks from the Chief of the Police Department, Elmer C. Bortner. Three towing companies, James J. Weitkamp, Ammon R. Smith, Inc., and Quick Towing Service were identified as having made numerous payments to police officers.

In light of this information, the Commission decided that a full-scale probe was required. A Commission resolution was approved in July 1973 which provided, in pertinent part, that:

". . . [a]n investigation shall be conducted by the Pennsylvania Crime Commission to ascertain the nature and extent of alleged kickbacks from tow-truck operators to members of the York City Police Department [and to] . . . ascertain whether existing laws and police regulations are sufficient to deal adequately with the alleged problem."

By virtue of the wording of the resolution, the Commission only concerned itself during the probe with allegations of kickbacks to policemen from tow-truck operators, and this report deals only with that matter.

During the course of the Commission's investigation, forty-three members of the 107-man York Police Department, 31 tow-truck operators or employees, and 19 other persons, including several former members of the York Police Department, were interviewed concerning alleged towing payoffs. Private Commission hearings were held in Harrisburg and York during the months of August through December, 1973, at which a total of 43 witnesses testified under oath pursuant to subpoena. Approximately 1700 pages of testimony were recorded at these hearings.

At the outset of the Commission's investigation, it became clear that payments from tow-truck companies to police officers were a pervasive problem which involved a significant percentage of the Police Department and had existed for a number of years. The Commission concluded that wholesale reform could only be accomplished if the police leadership took strong and effective measures to curb the practice and that singling out of low-level members of the Department would be ineffective. Thus, the Commission agreed to maintain the anonymity of individual police officers in exchange for their complete cooperation in ferreting out the truth. As a result, many of the individual officers quoted in this report are referred to by letter, i.e., "Officer A," "Officer B," "Officer C," etc., rather than by their correct names.

In addition, the identity of the individual referred to as towing operator A, as well as of those persons referred to as employees A, B, and C of Quick Towing Service, have also been protected in exchange for their cooperation.

SYSTEMATIC PAYOFFS TO YORK POLICE

Systematic corruption has existed at all levels of the York Police Department for a number of years as a result of frequent illegal kickbacks or payoffs from tow-truck operators. Twenty-seven members of the York Police Department admitted under oath at Commission hearings that they had received payments from towing companies on at least one occasion; most of these 27 officers further admitted receiving numerous payoffs in the past. Additional evidence uncovered by the Commission pointed to another 20 police officers as having received

[1]Not all of those named as being involved were interviewed in an effort to corroborate the allegations regarding their participation, as it was never the purpose of the Commission to gather evidence with a view to seeking prosecution of individuals.

payments from the tow-truck operators.[1] In addition, overwhelming evidence indicates that the Chief of the York Police Department, Elmer C. Bortner, was directly involved in the illegal payoff system as the conduit for payments from a towing company to other members of the Police Department.

Impact on the Public

The tow-truck business in York has been highly competitive. There have been at least nine separate companies competing on a daily basis for towing assignments during the last three years. The Commission obtained the York Police Department's records concerning the allocation of towing jobs to these companies for the period January 1971 through December 1973. The statistical analysis of these records, which is set forth in the chart below, establishes that a few towing companies secured the bulk of the business during this three year period.

A representative of AAA told the Commission that their approved service charge in the City of York ranged between $7 and $10, depending upon towing distance.[2] Other towing operators disclosed that their standard fee ranged between $10 and $15 and that any charge over $15 was excessive.[3]

In light of the above figures, the towing fees charged by the three principal towing companies identified as having made frequent payoffs to the police are illuminating. Quick Towing Service's standard fee during regular working hours was $20, and $25 thereafter.[4] Philip Enterline, an employee of Ammon R. Smith, Inc., testified that the average tow job took between 1½ and 2 hours, and that accord-

[2]Interview with Gerald Lehman, July 2, 1973.
[3]Interview with Frank W. Toomey, July 13, 1973 (Toomey added that any charge over $20 was "suspicious"; interview with C.J. Eyler, July 10, 1973; interview with Leon Ellis, July 9, 1973; interview with Joseph G. Kotzman, July 9, 1973.
[4]Testimony of Glenn E. Sheffer, Jr., before the Pennsylvania Crime Commission, September 13, 1973, N.T. 39 [hereinafter cited as Sheffer].

ing to Smith's fee schedule, a 1½ hour tow job cost $22 and a 2 hour tow job cost $28.[5] James J. Weitkamp stated that his standard fee was $20 until midnight and $25 thereafter.[6]

One of the tow-truck operators told the Commission that when he was paying $5 kickbacks per tow job to the police, he would bill the customer $17 but would only record a $12 fee in his records. When the kickback was increased to $6, he raised his charge to the customer to $18.[7] The Commission's investigation revealed that a substantial percentage of the cost of the kickbacks to the police officers for referring the business was passed on directly to the motorist in higher prices.

The Kickback Scheme

The police officer at the scene of a disabled vehicle has almost unlimited discretion to select which towing company will be called to perform the necessary removal of a vehicle. Participants in an accident or breakdown are frequently emotionally unable or have insufficient knowledge to choose a towing company. In York, it appears that even when a motorist desired a particular towing company, the police officer at the scene often disregarded his choice. An AAA official told the Commission that members of his association have frequently complained that York police have ignored requests for AAA approved towing service after an AAA member was involved in a traffic accident.[8]

A police officer who had worked in the capacity of radio dispatcher for the York Department told the Commission that although a list of towing companies was immediately available to the dispatcher, the police officer at the scene ordinarily made the selection of which towing com-

pany would be called.[9] Numerous other police witnesses confirmed the fact that the officer at the scene usually controlled the selection process.[10]

The highly competitive nature of the towing business in York and the police officer's generally unlimited discretion to select which towing company will do the work, combined with either the indifference or the highly emotional state of most motorists, have produced a situation which is rife with corruption.[11]

Many of the 27 police officers who admitted taking payments from the towing companies estimated as follows the number of other police officers on the force involved in the scheme: One officer stated, "Maybe more than 70%";[12] another stated "At least 75%";[13] and still others stated, "90%";[14] "Most of them";[15] "Almost everybody who works in uniform";[16] and "I don't believe there was a man on the force who didn't receive any [payoffs]."[17]

The genesis of the system of payoffs to police officers from tow-truck companies is unclear. A

[5]Testimony of Philip Enterline before the Pennsylvania Crime Commission, November 7, 1973, N.T. 42 [hereinafter cited as Enterline].

[6]Interview with James J. Weitkamp, October 18, 1973.

[7]Testimony of towing operator A before the Pennsylvania Crime Commission, July 25, 1973, N.T. 30–31 [hereinafter cited as towing operator A].

[8]Interview with Gerald Lehman, July 2, 1973.

[9]Interview with Officer A, July 17, 1973.

[10]Testimony of Officer B before the Pennsylvania Crime Commission, August 27, 1973, N.T. 107 [hereinafter cited as Officer B]; testimony of Officer C before the Pennsylvania Crime Commission, October 10, 1973, N.T. 83 [hereinafter cited as Officer C]; testimony of Officer D before the Pennsylvania Crime Commission, October 11, 1973, N.T. 8 [hereinafter cited as Officer D]; testimony of Officer E before the Pennsylvania Crime Commission, October 11, 1973, N.T. 67–68 [hereinafter cited as Officer E].

[11]Payment of any pecuniary benefit to a police officer to influence the exercise of his discretion constitutes the crime of bribery in Pennsylvania, a felony of the third degree. Act of December 6, 1972, P.L.—, No. 334, §1, 18 C.P.S.A. §4701 (1973).

[12]Testimony of Officer F before the Pennsylvania Crime Commission, October 10, 1973, N.T. 30 [hereinafter cited as Officer F].

[13]Officer D, N.T. 25.

[14]Testimony of Officer G before the Pennsylvania Crime Commission, October 10, 1973, N.T. 63 [hereinafter cited as Officer G].

[15]Testimony of Officer H before the Pennsylvania Crime Commission, November 8, 1973, N.T. 109 [hereinafter cited as Officer H].

[16]Officer C, N.T. 115.

[17]Officer B, N.T. 133.

Towing for Year 1971

Name	Jan	Feb	Mar	Apr	May	June	July	Aug	Sept	Oct	Nov	Dec		Total
Ammon R. Smith	6	4	9	7	3	14	20	22	9	16	15	10		135
Weitkamp	14	17	12	8	10	4	6	2	2	1	3	0		79
Ellis	8	5	3	7	8	4	4	5	6	4	1	5		60
Ream's	4	5	3	2	3	2	3	7	6	8	9	1		53
Seitz	2	8	5	3	8	2	4	3	9	0	3	3		50
Quick Tow	0	0	0	0	0	0	0	0	0	12	15	16		43
Smith's	0	2	3	7	9	1	4	3	1	4	4	1		39
Kinnerman's	2	1	0	1	4	3	2	3	1	4	1	3		25
Stambaugh's	2	0	2	0	0	1	0	1	0	4	0	0		10
Miller's	0	2	0	0	0	1	2	3	0	1	0	1		10
													(600)[a]	504

Towing for Year 1972

Name	Jan	Feb	Mar	Apr	May	June	July	Aug	Sept	Oct	Nov	Dec		Total
Ammon R. Smith	10	18	18	25	21	19	10	22	15	30	30	42		259
Quick Tow	11	6	8	14	12	13	4	5	1	0	2	0		76
Ellis Brothers	13	5	1	6	2	3	5	7	5	4	5	11		67
Weitkamp	3	2	1	4	1	3	1	0	0	8	12	4		39
Seitz	4	2	5	2	0	6	3	0	0	1	3	3		29
Ream's	1	0	3	3	4	6	1	5	1	0	0	1		25
Anderson	0	0	1	0	2	4	3	5	3	2	0	2		22
Bill's Arco	3	0	2	1	0	1	1	4	2	1	2	1		18
Kinnerman	2	2	2	2	0	0	0	2	1	0	0	0		11
Eylers	1	1	1	1	0	0	0	0	0	4	2	1		11
													(651)[a]	557

Towing for Year 1973

Name	Jan	Feb	Mar	Apr	May	June	July	Aug	Sept	Oct	Nov	Dec		Total
Ammon R. Smith	21	19	32	20	17	19	19	19	21	16	18	25		246
Ellis Brothers	7	3	5	6	8	11	8	8	10	5	5	2		78
Anderson	5	0	3	2	2	6	3	3	5	6	5	2		42
Zech's Sunoco	0	0	0	2	2	3	5	1	2	1	7	4		27
Smith's Arco	0	0	0	11	1	6	1	0	0	0	0	0		19
Seitz	1	2	1	1	5	5	1	3	0	0	0	0		18
Eylers	7	2	1	1	0	0	2	0	0	3	0	0		16
Lee's 66	0	0	1	0	1	1	0	1	3	6	0	0		13
Weitkamp	0	0	0	0	2	1	2	0	1	0	0	0		6
													(574)[a]	465

[a] Figure shown in parenthesis indicates total for the specific year.

veteran officer testified that the towing problem started in the early 1960's, probably with one of the original tow-truck operators in mid-city York who owned a paint shop, body shop and inspection station. If a policeman needed some work done on his personal car, the operator would fix the car at a good discount. He also contributed to the Police Pension Fund, and in bad weather, he permitted officers to park their personal cars in his garage free of charge.[18]

The climate for the kickbacks undoubtedly developed years before the 1960's during the days of low police pay, long hours, poor working conditions and political interference with police operations. It is clear that free gifts were regarded as a fringe benefit of police work in those days. As one officer recalled his childhood, "I can remember when my father was a policeman at Christmas time and my father, I think he is an honest man. Stuff used to be sent to his house that he never even got the names of. I mean fruit baskets that was lined up, that us kids couldn't eat it all and we had to give it away and we never even knew where it came from."[19]

Some of the police officers who admitted receiving payments portrayed the tow-truck operators as the aggressors in the scheme and the police as passive recipients. One policeman expressed his feelings as follows:

"... in 1967 when I first became a policeman, most of our towing was done by Seitz Garage and then I think there was a body shop out in West York by the name of Cunningham. And my first year on the job, the only tow trucks that were available were these. I mean the city was really hurting for tow trucks. Then all of a sudden ... everybody has a tow truck and everybody wants to get the money, and that's how it began. And then you had the greedy tow truck driver, it's not the policeman that's at fault. Sure ... the policemen were going to accept a dollar, you know, it was cigarette money, beer money. It was these greedy guys. They thought, well we'll pay the dumb policeman a buck and up our towing another $5.00. That's

four extra dollars in our pockets. That's where your fault is, that's the guys who should be up here, not us policemen."[20]

Another policeman testified:

"I'd say within the first year there were a number of times ... that I did accept it, not ... that I asked a guy for it or that I reached out and grabbed it from him or made him pay me or ... that I used him because of that. ... They would offer it to you whether you called them or whether the person who was involved in the accident requested them. It didn't really make any difference. You know, they would come up with a couple of bucks or whatever the amount was at that time."[21]

The Commission also received testimony from a number of the principal tow-truck operators to determine their participation in the alleged kickback scheme.

James J. Weitkamp has been self-employed in the service station business for 15 years. In 1966, he commenced operation of a Mobil station at Mount Rose and Hill Streets. In 1971, he moved to an American station at Haines and East Market Streets; and in 1972, he moved to an Exxon station at 980 South George Street. He testified that between 1965 and 1969 he towed a maximum of about twenty cars a month for the York Police Department.

Mr. Weitkamp testified he borrowed $2,700 from Elmer Bortner (now Police Chief) interest-free to finance two tow-trucks. He was not required to make regular payments and kept no record of his repayments:

Q: Isn't it unusual for someone to borrow that amount of money from another individual and not maintain any records at all?

A: Well, I had an idea in my mind, sir, of how much money was paid back but as far as the actual records, that man kept them himself.

---

[18]Testimony of Officer I before the Pennsylvania Crime Commission, December 19, 1973, N.T. 122–124 [hereinafter cited as Officer I].

[19]Officer D, N.T. 32.

[20]Id. at 37.

[21]Testimony of Officer J before the Pennsylvania Crime Commission, September 12, 1973, N.T. 180–181 [hereinafter cited as Officer J].

Q: How did you know that you satisfied the encumbrance?

A: When it was getting near the end, he [Bortner] told me it was only a couple hundred bucks owed on it.[22]

Mr. Weitkamp denied under oath that he had ever offered any money to York City police officers for towing referrals, and he denied that he had ever paid any York policemen money in return for such towing referrals.[23] Mr. Weitkamp's testimoney conflicts with that of several police officers.[24] For example, a patrolman testified that in 1967 and 1968:

"[t]here were times when other tow trucks were called and I was in the office and the message comes over the radio and they wouldn't even bother contacting another truck. We would wait a few minutes and say 'not available' and then the officer on the street would say 'send whoever is available' and Weitkamp is right there in the office and Bortner . . . sends him out".[25]

The officer said this continued until Mr. Weitkamp moved from Hill Street and Mount Rose Avenue to far out on East Market Street.[26]

Another officer testified, "Word got around the department in 1969 or 1970 that if a police officer called Weitkamp, he would receive $5 per tow job through [then] Captain Bortner:"[27]

Q: What happened after you would call Weitkamp?

A: Well, if he wouldn't give you the $5.00 bill on the spot then maybe the next day or the day after Captain Bortner would come around. He had the names of the men that called Weitkamp for accidents and he'd come around and give you the money.

Q: Where did you receive these payments?

A: Well, from Weitkamp it was out on the street and Captain Bortner, it was in the office.[28]

A third policeman stated that after being paid by then lieutenant Bortner in Police Headquarters several times for having called Mr. Weitkamp to accident scenes, he was subsequently paid directly by Mr. Weitkamp on at least ten or fifteen occasions.[29] This man assumed Lieutenant Bortner told Mr. Weitkamp which police officers took payoffs, and then Mr. Weitkamp would without hesitation offer money to those policemen.[30]

Four policemen testified under oath that they were handed towing kickbacks directly by James J. Weitkamp.[31] Two others stated under oath that they were offered bribes by Mr. Weitkamp, and they refused them.[32] Another two patrolmen testified that they were handed their share

[22]Testimony of James J. Weitkamp before the Pennsylvania Crime Commission, November 7, 1973, N.T. 38 [hereinafter cited as Weitkamp].

[23]Id. at 13–14, 18–19.

[24]The relevant testimony of Mr. Weitkamp, as well as the conflicting testimony, taken during private Commission hearings held in Harrisburg, Pennsylvania, was forwarded to the Dauphin County District Attorney on December 11, 1973, in order that consideration could be given to initiating perjury charges against Mr. Weitkamp. He was arrested on December 19, 1973, on perjury charges, but the charges were dismissed at a preliminary hearing on January 29, 1974, when the three key prosecution witnesses, all York City police officers (Officers C, D, and M), refused to testify on the ground that their testimony might prove self-incriminating.

[25]Testimony of Officer K before the Pennsylvania Crime Commission, September, 13, 1973, N.T. 82–83 [hereinafter cited as Officer K].

[26]Id. at 83.

[27]Testimony of Officer L before the Pennsylvania Crime Commission, September 12, 1973, N.T. 13–14 [hereinafter cited as Officer L].

[28]Id. at 14–15.

[29]Officer C, N.T. 105–106.

[30]Id. at 106.

[31]Officer C, N.T. 105–107; Officer L, N.T. 13–16; testimony of Officer M before the Pennsylvania Crime Commission, October 10, 1973; N.T. 130–134 [hereinafter cited as Officer M]; testimony of Officer N before the Pennsylvania Crime Commission, November 11, 1973, N.T. 9–11 [hereinafter cited as Officer N].

[32]Testimony of Officer O before the Pennsylvania Crime Commission, September 12, 1973, N.T. 140–142 [hereinafter cited as Officer O]; Officer D, N.T. 12–19.

of the payoff by their car partners after the partner had accepted the money from Mr. Weitkamp.[33] One officer personally observed Mr. Weitkamp making payments to police officers on at least six occasions following accidents to which Mr. Weitkamp had been called.[34]

Ammon R. Smith, Inc., a Chevrolet agency, has handled the bulk of towing work in York during the period January 1971 through December 1973. The police records indicate that of the 1,825 disabled vehicles towed during this period 640 were handled by Ammon R. Smith.[35] The next most frequently used tow-truck operator during this same period handled only 205 vehicles.[36]

Philip Enterline and Michael Newcomer are employed by Ammon R. Smith, Inc., as flat-rate mechanics and towing operators. The tow-trucks are owned by the company, but they are taken home after normal working hours by the two men in order that they can provide 24 hour service. Messrs. Enterline and Newcomer are compensated by the company for their towing according to the amount of time they spend on each towing job. For instance, during normal working hours, a 30 minute towing job will cost the customer $10, of which $4 is paid the employee. A towing job taking one hour will cost the customer $16, of which $6.40 is paid the employee. A two hour job will cost the customer $28, of which $11.20 is paid the employee. After nornal working hours, the cost to the customer is increased, as is the payment to Messrs. Enterline and Newcomer. The Ammon R. Smith company does not require Messrs. Enterline and Newcomer to punch in and out on a time clock, and the company accepts their word for the time spent on any towing call they make.[37]

Michael Newcomer testified at a Pennsylvania Crime Commission hearing, but he denied ever paying a police officer money in return for towing business.[38] He stated, however, that he did "favors" for police officers: "Free labor, fixing or adjusting a guy's carburetor, or telling him what is wrong with his air conditioner, something like that, yes, but I do it more as a favor than if you might call it, you know, a hammer and sickle act to get the towing work."[39]

At times, Mr. Newcomer used Ammon R. Smith's garage facilities for working on policemen's personal cars, but the only thing he admitted to giving was free labor and his time. Usually, the police officers would supply their own parts. Mr. Newcomer testified, "I guess if you want to call it payola, gratitude, or gratuity or whatever you want to call it, I guess you could call it that."[40] Newcomer further testified:

Q: When you do perform services like this, do you say anything to the police officer like, "Remember me the next time you need a tow truck" or do you just expect something?

A: I more or less expect it but it don't happen and it burns me.[41]

A total of ten York police officers testified they received towing kickbacks in cash from Philip Enterline in return for towing referrals to Ammon R. Smith, Inc.[42] An additional patrol-

---

[33]Testimony of Officer P before the Pennsylvania Crime Commission, November 7, 1973, N.T. 54–56 [hereinafter cited as Officer P] and Officer 1, N.T. 111.

[34]Officer O, N.T. 140–142.

[35]See chart *supra*.

[36]*Id.*

[37]Interview with Vernon R. Smith, Jr., Vice-President, Ammon R. Smith Auto Company, November 2, 1973.

[38]Testimony of Michael Newcomer before the Pennsylvania Crime Commission, November 8, 1973, N.T. 25.

[39]*Id.* at 26.

[40]*Id.*

[41]*Id.* at 44–45.

[42]Officer B, N.T. 123–126; Officer D, N.T. 21; Officer L, N.T. 30–36; Officer J, N.T. 182–185; testimony of Officer Q before the Pennsylvania Crime Commission, October 11, 1973, N.T. 46–48 [hereinafter cited as Officer Q]; testimony of Officer R before the Pennsylvania Crime Commission, November 7, 1973, N.T. 131–134 [hereinafter cited as Officer R]; testimony of Officer S before the Pennsylvania Crime Commission, December 19, 1973, N.T. 26–28 [hereinafter cited as Officer S]; testimony of Officer T before the Pennsylvania Crime Commission, November 7, 1973, N.T. 101–102 [hereinafter cited as Officer T]; testimony of

man testified he was offered money by Mr. Enterline for towing business, and he refused to accept it.[43]

One York patrolman testified that he began calling Ammon R. Smith Company after James J. Weitkamp moved his station further away from the York city limits in July 1971.[44] He then testified:

Q: What happened when you started calling Ammon R. Smith?

A: He started dropping $5.00 in the cruiser car.

Q: Now who is the he?

A: . . . It was Enterline.

Q: Philip Enterline?

A: Yes, sir.[45]

Another policeman explained:

"He'd [Enterline] come up usually to the . . side of the vehicle and he would either put his hand on the car like he was talking to you and drop it [money] or he'd come up and get the name of the person whose vehicle was being towed off the clipboard where you had your accident report and stick it [money] on the clipboard."[46]

Others testified that the money, which began at $4 per car and later increased to $8 per car, was clipped to a business card handed the officer by Enterline.[47] Sometimes the money was simply dropped on the front seat of the police cruiser car.[48] On occasions, the payoffs were given to the police at the Ammon R. Smith garage.[49]

Quick Towing Service, operated by Glenn E. Sheffer, Jr., participated briefly in the payoff scheme for several months during 1971 and 1972. Mr. Sheffer testified before the Crime Commission that he did not pay the police for towing referrals when he first started in the towing business.[50] Rather, he had several friends on the York Police Department who steered customers his way. Then, a member of the Traffic Safety Bureau approached him and said, "everyone else is paying $5.00 a tow. You raise it to $6.00 and I will see you get more business."[51] Mr. Sheffer agreed.[52] A few months later, two patrolmen told him. "The ante is going up. Other drivers are paying $7.00 and $8.00."[53] They urged him to match the other tow-truck operators' prices. Mr. Sheffer testified that he told them that he would not pay over $6. He explained he charged $20 for towing within the City of York and $25 after midnight.[54] Mr. Sheffer further stated:

Q: Did it pay you to pay off?

A: Not really. That is why I got out of it.[55]

Quick Towing Service has received little business from the York Police Department since Mr. Sheffer quit paying the police for referring customers to him.

Mr. Sheffer testified that it was his belief that 35–40% of the York Police Department received towing payoffs.[56] During the course of their testimony, Mr. Sheffer and other employees of Quick Towing Service identified twenty York policemen whom they paid or witnessed being

---

Officer U before the Pennsylvania Crime Commission, November 7, 1973, N.T. 14–16 [hereinafter cited as Officer U]; and testimony of Officer V before the Pennsylvania Crime Commission, December 19, 1973, N.T. 172–174 [hereinafter cited as Officer V].

[43]Testimony of Officer W before the Pennsylvania Crime Commission, August 28, 1973, N.T. 41–44 [hereinafter cited as Officer W].

[44]Officer D, N.T. 20.

[45]*Id.*

[46]Officer, J, N.T. 183.

[47]Officer V, N.T. 174; Officer U, N.T. 15–16; Officer R, N.T. 131.

[48]Officer D, N.T. 20; Officer J, N.T. 184.

[49]Officer Q, N.T. 47.

[50]Sheffer, N.T. 7, 10–13.

[51]*Id.* at 23–24.

[52]*Id.* at 24.

[53]*Id.* at 24–25.

[54]*Id.* at 39.

[55]*Id.*

[56]*Id.* at 56.

paid by co-employees for towing referrals.[57] The $6 bribes were paid from petty cash (except that Mr. Sheffer himself generally paid with money taken from his pocket) and were, of course, covered in the customer's bill.[58]

Seven of the police officers who appeared as witnesses at Crime Commission hearings testified that they had accepted cash payments from Quick Towing Service in return for towing referrals.[59] Some officers admitted receiving a variety of free accessories and parts from Mr. Sheffer after they had expressed a desire for those items.[60] The gifts included tires, wheel rims, air-conditioner motors and whiskey.

Other tow-truck operators testified during the course of the Commission's investigation. One of the service station operators told how he purchased a tow-truck for his service station and asked one of his friends on the York police force about getting business from the City of York.[61] The policeman "friend" told him that he would have to pay $5 for each car he towed. This occurred in the fall of 1971.[62] In early 1972, the towing operator was informed by a different

policeman that he would have to pay $6 to continue receiving business referred from the Police Department. The tow-truck operator increased his basic charge for towing within the city from $17 to $18.[63]

In the late summer or early fall of 1972, two York officers approached the same towing operator again and announced that Ammon R. Smith Company was paying $8. The operator reluctantly agreed to pay the new amount.[64] However, in early 1973 he was again told that the kickback rate was going up to $10, and he then asked the police to remove his name from their list of available tow-truck operators as he could no longer afford to handle the business.[65]

Six York police officers testified that they were paid cash bribes on numerous occasions and in varying amounts by Harold J. Smith, operator of Smittie's Arco, 901 Mount Rose Avenue.[66] Mr. Smith acknowledged providing special discounts on automobile accessories and service to police officers but denied ever paying cash to policemen.[67]

*

[57]*Id.* at 20–24, 41–43; testimony of Quick Towing Service employee A before the Pennsylvania Crime Commission, October 11, 1973, N.T. 113–114 [hereinafter cited as Quick Towing Service employee A]; testimony of Quick Towing Service employee B before the Pennsylvania Crime Commission, November 8, 1973, N.T. 124–125, 128 [hereinafter cited as Quick Towing Service employee B]; testimony of Quick Towing Service employee C before the Pennsylvania Crime Commission, December 19, 1973, N.T. 234–243.

[58]Quick Towing Service employee, A, N.T. 107–110; Quick Towing Service employee B, N.T. 124–127.

[59]Officer G, N.T. 53–55; Officer H, N.T. 99–100; Officer I, N.T. 111; Officer R, N.T. 138; Officer S, N.T. 14–15; Officer U, N.T. 16–17; Officer V, N.T. 161.

[60]Officer D, N.T. 31; Officer I, N.T. 95–96; Officer P, N.T. 59; and Officer V, N.T. 187.

[61]Towing operator A, N.T. 10–11.

[62]*Id.* at 11.

[63]*Id.* at 30–31.

[64]*Id.* at 31–32.

[65]*Id.* at 32–33.

[66]Officer C, N.T. 104–105; Officer D, N.T. 27–29; Officer G, N.T. 56–57; Officer I, N.T. 111; Officer T, N.T. 10; Officer V, N.T. 160.

[67]Testimony of Harold J. Smith before the Pennsylvania Crime Commission, August 28, 1973, N.T. 16–21.

12. The Impact of Preventive Police Patrolling

GEORGE L. KELLING
TONY PATE
DUANE DIECKMAN
CHARLES E. BROWN

INTRODUCTION AND MAJOR FINDINGS

EVER SINCE THE CREATION OF A PATROLLING force in thirteenth century Hangchow, preventive patrol by uniformed personnel has been a primary function of policing. In twentieth century America, about $2 billion is spent each year for the maintenance and operation of uniformed and often superbly equipped patrol forces. Police themselves, the general public, and elected officials have always believed that the presence or potential presence of police officers on patrol severely inhibits criminal activity.

*

As the International City Management Association has pointed out, "for the greatest number of persons, deterrence through ever-present police patrol, coupled with the prospect of speedy police action once a report is received, appears important to crime control." Thus, in the face of spiraling crime rates, the most common answer urged by public officials and citizens alike has been to increase patrol forces and get more police officers "on the street." The assumption is that increased displays of police presence are vitally necessary in the face of in-

creased criminal activity. Recently, citizens in troubled neighborhoods have themselves resorted to civilian versions of patrol.

*

The Kansas City, Missouri, Police Department, under a grant from the Police Foundation, undertook in 1972 the most comprehensive experiment ever conducted to analyze the effectiveness of routine preventive patrol.

From the outset the department and the Police Foundation evaluation team agreed that the project design would be as rigorously experimental as possible, and that while Kansas City Police Department data would be used, as wide a data base as possible, including data from external measurements, would be generated. It was further agreed that the experiment would be monitored by both department and foundation representatives to insure maintenance of experimental conditions. Under the agreement between the department and the foundation, the department committed itself to an eight-month experiment provided that reported crime did not reach "unacceptable" limits within the experimental area.

The experiment involved variations in the level of routine preventive patrol within 15 Kansas City police beats. These beats were randomly divided into three groups. In five "reactive" beats, routine preventive patrol was eliminated and officers were instructed to respond only to

▶SOURCE: *The Kansas City Preventive Patrol Experiment—A Summary Report. Washington: Police Foundation, 1974. Pp. 1–4, 6–16, 20–23, 24–25. (Editorial adaptations.) Reprinted by permission.*

163

calls for service. In five "control" beats, routine preventive patrol was maintained at its usual level of one car per beat. In the remaining five "proactive" beats, routine preventive patrol was intensified by two to three times its usual level through the assignment of additional patrol cars and through the frequent presence of cars from the "reactive" beats.

For the purposes of measurement, a number of hypotheses were developed, of which the following were ultimately addressed:

1.   crime, as reflected by victimization surveys and reported crime data, would not vary by type of patrol;

2.   citizen perception of police service would not vary by type of patrol;

3.   citizen fear and behavior as a result of fear would not vary by type of patrol;

4.   police response time and citizen satisfaction with response time would vary by experimental area; and

5.   traffic accidents would increase in the reactive beats.

The experiment found that the three experimental patrol conditions appeared not to affect crime, service delivery and citizen feelings of security in ways the public and the police often assume they do. For example,

• as revealed in the victimization surveys, the experimental conditions had no significant effect on residence and non-residence burglaries, auto thefts, larcenies involving auto accessories, robberies, or vandalism—crimes traditionally considered to be deterrable through preventive patrol;

• in terms of rates of reporting crime to the police, few differences and no consistent patterns of differences occurred across experimental conditions;

• in terms of departmental reported crime, only one set of differences across experimental conditions was found and this one was judged likely to have been a random occurrence.

• few significant differences and no consistent pattern of differences occurred across experimental conditions in terms of citizen attitudes toward police services;

• citizen fear of crime, overall, was not affected by experimental conditions;

• there were few differences and no consistent pattern of differences across experimental conditions in the number and types of anti-crime protective measures used by citizens;

• in general, the attitudes of businessmen toward crime and police services were not affected by experimental conditions;

• experimental conditions did not appear to affect significantly citizen satisfaction with the police as a result of their encounters with police officers;

• experimental conditions had no significant effect on either police response time or citizen satisfaction with police response time;

• although few measures were used to assess the impact of experimental conditions on traffic accidents and injuries, no significant differences were apparent;

• about 60 percent of a police officer's time is typically noncommitted (available for calls); of this time, police officers spent approximately as much time on non-police related activities as they did on police-related mobile patrol; and

• in general, police officers are given neither a uniform definition of preventive patrol nor any objective methods for gauging its effectiveness; while officers tend to be ambivalent in their estimates of preventive patrol's effectiveness in deterring crime, many attach great importance to preventive patrol as a police function.

*

DESCRIPTION OF THE PREVENTIVE PATROL EXPERIMENT

The impetus for an experiment in preventive patrol came from within the Kansas City Police Department in 1971. While this may be surprising to some, the fact is that by that year the Kansas City department had already experienced more than a decade of innovation and improvement in its operations and working climate and had gained a reputation as one of the nation's more progressive police departments. . . .

As part of its continuing internal discussions of policing, the department in October of 1971 established a task force of patrol officers and supervisors in each of its three patrol divisions (South, Central and Northeast), as well as in its special operations division (helicopter, traffic, tactical, etc.). The decision to establish these task forces was based on the beliefs that the ability to make competent planning decisions existed at all levels within the department and that if institutional change was to gain acceptance, those affected by it should have a voice in planning and implementation.

The job of each task force was to isolate the critical problems facing its division and propose methods to attack those problems. All four task forces did so. The South Patrol Division Task Force identified five problem areas where greater police attention was deemed vital: burglaries, juvenile offenders, citizen fear, public education about the police role, and police-community relations.

Like the other task forces, the South task force was confronted next with developing workable remedial strategies. And here the task force met with what at first seemed an insurmountable barrier. It was evident that concentration by the South Patrol Division on the five problem areas would cut deeply into the time spent by its officers on preventive patrol.* At

this point a significant thing happened. Some of the members of the South task force questioned whether routine preventive patrol was effective, what police officers did while on preventive patrol duty, and what effect police visibility had on the community's feelings of security.

Out of these discussions came the proposal to conduct an experiment which would test the true impact of routine preventive patrol. The Police Foundation agreed to fund the experiment's evaluation.

As would be expected, considerable controversy surrounded the experiment, with the central question being whether long-range benefits outweighed short-term risks. The principal short-term risk was seen as the possibility that crime would increase drastically in the reactive beats; some officers felt the experiment would be tampering with citizens' lives and property.

The police officers expressing such reservations were no different from their counterparts in other departments. They tended to view pat-

---

*In this report, routine preventive patrol is defined as those patrol activities employed by the Kansas City Police Department during the approximately 35 percent of patrol duty time in which officers are not responding to calls for service, attending court or otherwise unavailable for self-initiated activities. (The 35 percent figure was a pre-experimental estimate developed by the Kansas City Police Department for use in determining officer allocation.) Information made available daily to patrol officers includes items such as who in their beats is wanted on a warrant, who is wanted for questioning by detectives, what criminals are active in their beats and type and location of crimes which have occurred during the previous 24 hours. The officers are expected to be familiar with this information and use it during their non-committed time. Accordingly, routine preventive patrol includes being guided by this information while observing from police cars, checking on premises and suspicious citizens, serving warrants, checking abandoned vehicles, and executing other self-initiated police activities. Thus routine preventive patrol in Kansas City is informed activity based upon information gathered from a wide variety of sources. Whether Kansas City's method of preventive patrol is typical is hard to say with exactness. Clearly, some departments place more emphasis on pedestrian checks, car checks, and field interrogating than does Kansas City (experiments on some of these activities are now taking place elsewhere). Preventive patrol as practiced in Kansas City has some unique characteristics but for the most part is typical of preventive patrol in urban areas.

rol as one of the most important functions of policing, and in terms of time allocated, they felt that preventive patrol ranked on a par with investigating crimes and rendering assistance in emergencies. While some admitted that preventive patrol was probably less effective in preventing crime and more productive in enhancing citizen feelings of security, others insisted that the activities involved in preventive patrol (car, pedestrian and building checks) were instrumental in the capture of criminals and, through the police visibility associated with such activities, in the deterrence of crime. While there were ambiguities in these attitudes toward patrol and its effectiveness, all agreed it was a primary police function.

Within the South Patrol Division's 24-beat area, nine beats were eliminated from consideration as unrepresentative of the city's socioeconomic composition. The remaining 15-beat, 32-square mile experimental area encompassed a commercial-residential mixture, with a 1970 resident population of 148,395 persons and a density of 4,542 persons per square mile (significantly greater than that for Kansas City as a whole, which in 1970 with only 1,604 persons per square mile, was 45th in the nation). Racially, the beats within this area ranged from 78 percent black to 99 percent white. Median family income of residents ranged from a low of $7,320 for one beat to a high of $15,964 for another. On the average, residents of the experimental area tended to have been in their homes from 6.6 to 10.9 years.

Police officers assigned to the experimental area were those who had been patrolling it prior to the experiment, and tended to be white, relatively young, and somewhat new to the police department. In a sample of 101 officers in the experimental area taken across all three shifts, 9.9 percent of the officers were black, the average age of the officers was 27 years, and average time on the force was 3.2 years.

The 15 beats in the experimental area were computer matched on the basis of crime data, number of calls for service, ethnic composition, median income and transiency of population into five groups of three each. Within each group, one beat was designated reactive, one control, and one proactive. In the five reactive beats, there was no preventive patrol as such. Police vehicles assigned these beats entered them only in response to calls for service. Their noncommitted time (when not answering calls) was spent patrolling the boundaries of the reactive beats or patrolling in adjacent proactive beats. While police availability was closely maintained, police visibility was, in effect, withdrawn (except when police vehicles were seen while answering calls for service).

In the five control beats, the usual level of patrol was maintained at one car per beat. In the five proactive beats, the department increased police patrol visibility by two to three times its usual level both by the assignment of marked police vehicles to these beats and the presence of units from adjacent reactive beats.

Other than the restrictions placed upon officers in reactive beats (respond only to calls for service and patrol only the perimeter of the beat or in an adjacent proactive beat), no special instructions were given to police officers in the experimental area. Officers in control and proactive beats were to conduct preventive patrol as they normally would.

It should be noted, however, that the geographical distribution of beats (see Figure 1) avoided clustering reactive beats together or at an unacceptable distance from proactive beats. Such clustering could have resulted in lowered response time in the reactive beats.

It should also be noted that patrol modification in the reactive and proactive beats involved only routine preventive patrol. Specialized units, such as tactical, helicopter and K-9, operated as usual in these beats but at a level consistent with the activity level established the preceding year. This level was chosen to prevent infringement of these specialized units upon experimental results.

Finally, it should be noted that to minimize any possible risk through the elimination of

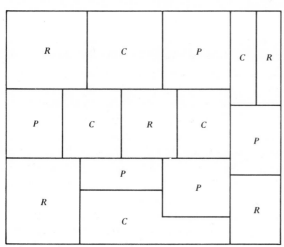

P = Proactive
C = Control
R = Reactive

Figure 1. Schematic representation of the 15-beat experimental area.

routine preventive patrol in the reactive beats, crime rate data were monitored on a weekly basis. It was agreed that if noticeable increase in crime occurred within a reactive beat, the experiment would be suspended. This situation, however, never materialized.

While the Kansas City experiment began on July 19, 1972, both department and Police Foundation monitors recognized by mid-August that experimental conditions were not being maintained, and that several problems had arisen. Chief Kelley then saw to it that these problems were rectified during a suspension of the experiment.

One problem was manpower, which in the South Patrol Division had fallen to a dangerously low level for experimental purposes. To correct this problem additional police officers were assigned to the division and an adequate manpower level restored. A second problem involved violations of the project guidelines. Additional training sessions were held, and administrative emphasis brought to bear to ensure adherence to the guidelines. A third problem was boredom among officers assigned to reac-

tive beats. To counter this, the guidelines were modified to allow an increased level of activity by reactive-assigned officers in proactive beats. These revisions emphasized that an officer could take whatever action was deemed necessary, regardless of location, should a criminal incident be observed. The revised guidelines also stressed adherence to the spirit of the project rather than to unalterable rules.

On October 1, 1972, the experiment resumed. It continued successfully 12 months, ending on September 30, 1973. Findings were produced in terms of the effect of experimental conditions on five categories of crimes traditionally considered to be deterrable through preventive patrol (burglary, auto theft, larceny-theft of auto accessories, robbery and vandalism) and on five other crime cagegories (including rape, assault, and other larcenies.) Additional findings concerned the effect of experimental conditions on citizen feelings of security and satisfaction with police service, on the amount and types of anti-crime protective measures taken by citizens and businessmen, on police response time and citizen satisfaction with response time, and on injury/fatality and non-injury traffic accidents. The experiment also produced data concerning police activities during tours of duty, and police officer attitudes toward preventive patrol.

DATA SOURCES

In measuring the effects of routine preventive patrol, it was decided to collect as wide a variety of data from as many diverse sources as possible. By so doing, it was felt that overwhelming evidence could be presented to prove or disprove the experimental hypotheses.

To measure the effects of the experimental conditions on crime, a victimization survey, departmental reported crime, departmental arrest data, and a survey of business were used. While reported crime has traditionally been considered the most important indicator of police effectiveness, the accuracy of both reported crime and arrest data as indicators of crime and police effectiveness has come under scrutiny in recent years. Both types of data are subject to wide degrees of conscious and unconscious manipulation, and to distortion and misrepresentation. Because of these, a criminal victimization survey was used as an additional source of data.

Victimization surveys were first used by the President's Commission on Law Enforcement and Administration of Justice. These surveys revealed that as much as 50 percent of crime was unreported by victims, either from neglect, embarrassment, or a feeling that the crimes were not worth reporting. Although victimization surveys also have their limitations, they can be an important way of measuring crime. Thus a victimization survey was used by the experiment to measure this key outcome variable.

To measure the impact of experimental con-ditions on community attitudes and fear, attitudinal surveys of both households and business (in conjunction with the victimization surveys) and a survey of those citizens experiencing direct encounters with the police were administered. Estimates of citizen satisfaction with police services were also recorded by participant observers.

Sources used in collecting data for the experiment, are shown in Table I.

Because many of these sources were used to monitor the degree to which experimental conditions were maintained or to identify unanticipated consequences of the experiment, only findings derived from the following data sources are presented in this report:

Community Survey

The community survey, which measured com-

Table I. Data Sources

1. Community Survey
   victimization
   attitudes
   rates of reporting

2. Commercial Survey
   victimization
   attitudes
   rates of reporting

3. Encounter Survey — Citizens
   attitudes
   perceptions

4. Encounter Survey — Officers
   attitudes
   perceptions

5. Encounter Survey — Observers
   attitudes
   perceptions

6. Noncommitted Time Survey

7. Response Time Survey
   observers

8. Response Time Survey
   citizens

9. HRD Survey

10. Officer Questionnaire

Interviews and Recorded Observations

1. "Player" Observations

2. Officer Interviews

3. Participant Observer Interviews

4. Participant Observer Transaction Recordings

Departmental Data

1. Reported Crime

2. Traffic Data

3. Arrest Data

4. Computer Dispatch Data

5. Officer Activity Analysis Data

6. Personnel Records

munity victimization, attitudes and fear, was taken on a before and after basis. A sample of 1,200 households in the experimental area (approximately 80 per beat) was randomly selected and interviewed in September of 1972. In September of 1973, 1,200 households were again surveyed, approximately 600 chosen from the same population as the 1972 survey (for a repeated sample) and 600 chosen randomly from the experimental area (for a non-repeated sample). Since 11 cases had to be excluded because of missing data, the 1973 sample totalled 1,189.

Commercial Survey

The commercial survey involved interviews conducted both in 1972 and 1973 with a random sample of 110 businesses in the experimental area to measure victimization rates and businessmen's perceptions of and satisfaction with police services.

Encounter Survey (Both Citizen and Participant Observers)

Because household surveys tend to interview relatively few citizens who have experienced actual contact with the police, citizens in the three experimental areas who experienced direct encounters with police officers were interviewed. Although three survey instruments were developed (one to elicit the response of the citizens, a second for the police officers, and a third for the observers riding with the officers) only the observer and citizen responses were analyzed. Identical questions were used as often as possible. The survey was conducted over a four-month period (July through October, 1973). Interviewed were 331 citizens who were involved in either an officer-initiated incident (car check, pedestrian check or a traffic violation) or citizen-initiated incident (one in which the citizen called for police service: burglary, robbery, larceny, assault, etc.).

Participant Observer Transaction Recordings

While the community encounter survey focused on the location of the police-citizen contact, the observer transaction recordings focused on

police-citizen interactions in terms of the assignment of the officer involved (reactive, control or proactive beats). These data were obtained by observers while riding with officers assigned to the experimental area, and involved observer estimates of citizen satisfaction as a result of direct contact with the police. Observations covered all three watches in all 15 beats. As a result, 997 incidents of police-citizen transactions were systematically recorded.

Reported Crime

Monthly totals for reported crime by beat over the October 1968 through September 1972 (pre-experimental) period and over the October 1972 through September 1973 (experimental) period were retrieved from departmental records. Time-series analyses were then performed on these data to produce the findings.

Traffic Data

Two categories of traffic accidents were monitored: non-injury and injury/fatality. Monitoring was maintained over two time periods, October 1970 through September 1972 for the pre-experimental period, and October 1972 through September 1973 for the experimental period.

Arrest Data

Arrest data by month and beat for the experimental year and the three preceding years were obtained from departmental records.

Response Time Survey

Police response time in the experimental area was recorded between May and September 1973 through the use of a response time survey completed by the participant observers and those citizens who had called the police for service. In measuring the time taken by the police in responding to calls, emphasis was placed on field response time (i.e., the amount of time occurring between the time a police unit on the street received a call from the dispatcher and the time when that unit contacted the citizen involved). In measuring citizen satisfaction with response time, the entire range of time required for the police to answer a call was considered (i.e., including time spent talking with the police department operator, police dispatcher, plus field response time).

*

Spillover Effect

One major concern in an experiment of this type is the so-called spillover or displacement theory, i.e., that as crime decreases in one area due to increased police presence, it will increase in other, usually contiguous, areas. This would mean that the effect of the experiment within the experimental area would be offset by counter-effects in other areas. To test this, various correlations between contiguous beats were calculated and analyzed. Except for auto theft, there were no noticeable alterations in the correlations of crime levels. These results, combined with an examination of the actual monthly crime figures, tend to indicate that, in general, there was no spillover effect.

EXPERIMENTAL FINDINGS

The essential finding of the preventive patrol experiment is that decreasing or increasing routine preventive patrol within the range tested in this experiment had no effect on crime, citizen fear of crime, community attitudes toward the police on the delivery of police service, police response time, or traffic accidents. Given the large amount of data collected and the extremely diverse sources used, the evidence is overwhelming. Of the 648 comparisons made to produce the 13 major findings that follow, statistical significance occurred only 40 times between pairs, or in approximately 6 percent of the total. Of these 40, the change was greater 15 times in reactive beats, 19 times in control beats, and 6 times in proactive beats.

*

Effects on Crime, Reporting and Arrests
Finding 1: Victimization *The Victimization Survey found no statistically significant differences in crime in any of the 69 comparisons made between reactive, control and proactive beats.*

This finding would be expected for such categories as rape, homicide and common or aggravated assault. For one thing, these are typically impulsive crimes, usually taking place between persons known to each other. Furthermore, they most often take place inside a building, out of sight of an officer on routine preventive patrol. The spontaneity and lack of high visibility of these crimes therefore, make it unlikely that they would be much affected by variations in the level of preventive patrol.

Given traditional beliefs about patrol, however, it is surprising that statistically significant differences did not occur in such crimes as commercial burglaries, auto theft and robberies.

Nonetheless, as measured by the victimization survey, these crimes were not significantly affected by changes in the level of routine preventive patrol. Table II shows data and findings from the Community and Commercial Surveys in regard to victimization.

Finding 2: Departmental Reported Crime *Departmental Reported Crimes showed only one statistically significant difference among 51 comparisons drawn between reactive, control and proactive beats.*

Statistical significance occured only in the category of "Other Sex Crimes." This category, separate from "Rape," includes such offenses as molestation and exhibitionism. Since this category is not traditionally considered to be responsive to routine preventive patrol, however, it appears likely that this instance of significance was a statistically random occurrence.

Table III presents reported crime data and findings.

Finding 3: Rates of Reporting Crime *Crimes citizens and businessmen said they reported to the police showed statistically significant differences between reactive, control and proactive beats in only five of 48 comparisons, and these differences showed no consistent pattern.*

Of the five instances of statistical significance,

Table II. Victimization (Community and Commercial Survey)

Crime Type		Overall P	R,C	R,P	C,P
Robbery—no distinction	N		R = C	R = P	C = P
between in or outside	R		R = C	R = P	C = P
Robbery—inside (commercial)	R		R = C	R = P	C = P
Common assault	N		R = C	R = P	C = P
	R		R = C	R = P	C = P
Aggravated assault	N		R = C	R = P	C = P
	R		R = C	R = P	C = P
Other sex crimes	N		R = C	R = P	C = P
	R		R = C	R = P	C = P
Residence burglary	N		R = C	R = P	C = P
	R		R = C	R = P	C = P
Non-residence burglary (commercial)	R		R = C	R = P	C = P
Auto theft	N		R = C	R = P	C = P
	R		R = C	R = P	C = P
Vandalism (community)	N		R = C	R = P	C = P
	R		R = C	R = P	C = P
Vandalism (commercial)	R		R = C	R = P	C = P
Larceny—auto accessory	N		R = C	R = P	C = P
	R		R = C	R = P	C = P
Larceny—all other	N		R = C	R = P	C = P
	R		R = C	R = P	C = P
All crimes combined	N		R = C	R = P	C = P
	R		R = C	R = P	C = P
Rape	N	*			
	R				
Homicide	N	*			
	R				

*Too few cases to justify statistical analysis.

Table III. Departmental Reported Crime

Crime Type	Overall P	R,C	R,P	C,P
Robbery—inside		R = C	R = P	C = P
Robbery—outside		R = C	R = P	C = P
Common assault		R = C	R = P	C = P
Aggravated assault		R = C	R = P	C = P
Larceny—pursesnatch		R = C	R = P	C = P
Rape		R = C	R = P	C = P
Other sex crimes	.01 < p < .025	R > C	R = P	C = P
Homicide		R = C	R = P	C = P
Residence burglary		R = C	R = P	C = P
Non-residence burglary		R = C	R = P	C = P
Auto theft		R = C	R = P	C = P
Vandalism		R = C	R = P	C = P
Larceny—auto accessory		R = C	R = P	C = P
Larceny—theft from auto		R = C	R = P	C = P
Larceny—bicycle		R = C	R = P	C = P
Larceny—shoplift		R = C	R = P	C = P
Larceny—theft from bldg.		R = C	R = P	C = P

three involved vandalism and two residence burglary. But where statistical significance was found, no consistent pattern emerged. On two occasions the change was greater in the control beats, on two occasions greater in the proactive beats, and once it was greater in the reactive beats. Given the low number of statistically significant findings combined with a lack of consistent direction, the conclusion is that rates of reporting crimes by businessmen and citizens were unaffected by the experimental changes in levels of patrol.

Table IV shows the data and findings.

Finding 4: Arrest Patterns   *Police arrests showed no statistically significant differences in the 27 comparisons made between reactive, control and proactive beats.*

While arrest totals for 16 categories of crime were determined, it will be noted that in seven categories—common assault, larceny-purse snatch, homicide, non-residence burglary, auto theft, larceny-auto accessory, and larceny-bicycle—either the number of arrests was too small to allow for statistical analysis, or the pre-experimental pattern of arrests was so distorted that statistical significance could not be determined. On the basis of the comparisons that could be made, however, the conclusion is that arrest rates were not significantly affected by changes in the level of patrol.

Table V shows the data and findings.

*

Table IV. Rates of Reporting Crimes (Community and Commercial Survey)

Crime Type		Overall P	R,C	R,P	C,P
Robbery—No distinction	N		R = C	R = P	C = P
between in or outside	R		R = C	R = P	C = P
Common assault	N	*			
	R		R = C	R = P	C = P
Aggravated assault	N	*			
	R	*			
Other sex crimes	N		R = C	R = P	C = P
	R	*			
Residence burglary	N	.025 < p < .05	R > C	R = P	C < P
	R		R = C	R = P	C = P
Non-residence burglary (commercial	R		R = C	R = P	C = P
Auto theft	N		R = C	R = P	C = P
	R		R = C	R = P	C = P
Vandalism (community)	N		R = C	R = P	C = P
	R	.001 < p < .005	R < C	R < P	C > P
Vandalism (commercial)	R		R = C	R = P	C = P
Larceny—auto accessory	N		R = C	R = P	C = P
	R		R = C	R = P	C = P
Larceny—all other	N		R = C	R = P	C = P
	R		R = C	R = P	C = P

*Too few cases to justify statistical analysis.

Table V. Arrests

Crime Type	Overall P	R,C	R,P	C,P
Robbery—no distinction between in or outside		R = C	R = P	C = P
Common assault	*1			
Aggravated assault		R = C	R = P	C = P
Larceny—purse snatch	*2			
Rape		R = C	R = P	C = P
Other sex crimes		R = C	R = P	C = P
Homicide	*2			
Residence burglary		R = C	R = P	C = P
Non-residence burglary	*1			
Auto theft	*1			
Vandalism		R = C	R = P	C = P
Larceny—auto accessory	*2			
Larceny—theft from auto		R = C	R = P	C = P
Larceny—bicycle	*1			
Larceny—shoplift		R = C	R = P	C = P
Larceny—theft from bldg.		R = C	R = P	C = P

*1 Not statistically analyzed because of the nature of the variations in the data in the pre-experiment period.

*2 Number of arrests is too small to allow for statistical analysis.

13. Private Police in the United States

JAMES S. KAKALIK
SORREL WILDHORN

THE EXTENT AND GROWTH OF SECURITY FORCES

Extent

CRIME-RELATED PUBLIC AND PRIVATE SECURITY services absorb considerable resources. In 1969, over 800,000 people were security workers, and well over $8 billion was devoted to security services and equipment, i.e., 0.85 percent of the Gross National Product. One in every 100 persons in the civilian labor force, or one in every 250 persons in the entire population, was employed in security work, and over $40 per capita was spent on security.

Table I displays a summary of resources devoted to security in the United States during 1969. In the public sector, 395,000 persons (49 percent of all security personnel in the United States) were employed as policemen or detectives at all levels of government, and about 120,000 (15 percent) worked as government guards or watchmen. The remaining 290,000 (36 percent) were employed in the private sector. Most of the latter (260,000) were private guards or watchmen; the remainder (32,000) were private detectives or investigators.

▶SOURCE: *Private Police in the United States: Findings and Recommendations. Volume I: R–869/DOJ (February, 1972). Report by the Rand Corporation, Washington: National Institute of Law Enforcement and Criminal Justice, Law Enforcement Assistance Administration, U. S. Department of Justice, Pp. 10–15, 68–71. Subsequently republished as The Private Police: Security and Danger, New York: Crane Russak and Company, Inc., 1977. Reprinted by permission.*

Thus, the ratio of total private-sector crime-related security personnel to total public-sector law-enforcement and guard personnel was about 4 to 7. Or, if government guards are included with the private security forces, because most guards and private investigators do not have public peace-officer powers, the ratio of security personnel with peace-officer powers to those without was about 1 to 1. That is, about 36 percent of all security personnel were employed in the private sector and about 64 percent were in the public sector; but counting government guards in the non-peace-officer category, about half of all security personnel have full police powers and half do not.

In 1969, between one-fourth and one-third of all privately employed guards and investigators worked for contract security firms; the remainder were in-house employees. In 1967, there were over 4,000 private establishments[1] providing contract guard and investigative services, but four firms (Pinkerton's, Burns, Wackenhut, and Globe), with less than 6 percent of all establishments, accounted for half the revenues. In 1967, the average guard and investigative service agency had 1.1 establishments and receipts of $104,000, employed 22 persons, had average receipts per employee of $4,800, and paid out 70 percent in wages.

The 1968 market breakdown for sales of private security equipment and services is esti-

[1]A Census Bureau term basically meaning a physical location from which business is conducted.

Table I. Summary of Estimated Public and Private Security Forces and Expenditures in the United States in 1969 (N/A indicates data not available)

Type of Security Personnel or Organization	Numbers of People		Expenditures ($ millions)	
	Security Personnel	Total Employment	Payroll Expenditures	Total Expenditures or Revenues
Public Law Enforcement				
Local police (city, county, township)	324,000[a]	432,000[b]	3,040[c]	3,326[b]
Reserve local police	N/A	N/A	N/A	N/A
Special local law-enforcement agencies	N/A	N/A	N/A	N/A
State police or highway patrol	39,000[a]	54,000[b]	455[c]	621[b]
Special state law-enforcement agencies	N/A	36,000[b,d]	344[c]	492[b]
Federal law-enforcement agencies	N/A[d]	N/A	N/A	N/A
Total Public Law Enforcement	395,000[e]	523,000[c]	3,839[c]	4,430[b]
Public (Government) Guards (all governments)	120,000[e]	N/A	N/A	~1,000
Total Public Sector (police and guards)	515,000	N/A	N/A	~5,400
Private Sector Security				
In-house detectives and investigators	23,900[e]	N/A	N/A	N/A
In-house guards	198,500[e]	N/A	N/A	N/A
Subtotal in-house security	222,400[e]	N/A	N/A	~1,600[f]
Contract detectives	8,100[e]	N/A	N/A	N/A
Contract guards	59,400[e]	N/A	N/A	N/A
Subtotal contract guards and detectives	67,500[e]	~110,000[g]	435[h]	620[i]
Patrolmen in contract agencies	N/A (included in contract guards)	N/A (included in contract guards)	N/A	N/A (included in contract guards)
Armored-car services		10,000[g]	73[h]	128[j]
Central station alarm services		N/A (included in contract guards)	N/A	120[k]

Total Private Sector	289,900^e	N/A	~2,500
Security Equipment	N/A	N/A	~800
Grand Total	804,000	N/A	~8,700

aSources: FBI, *1969 Uniform Crime Reports*, and telephone conversations with personnel at International Association of Chiefs of Police. Figures are for sworn officers. Local police total shown includes 287,000 sworn officers in cities and suburbs and 37,000 officers in county sheriff departments. State figures include state police and state highway patrol officers.

bSource: *Expenditure and Employment Data for the Criminal Justice System 1968-69*, LEAA, U.S. Department of Justice, December 1970. Expenditure data are for FY 1968-69, and employment data are for October 1969.

cSource: Bureau of the Census publications (*Census of Governments for various years, Public Employment in 1968, and Governmental Finances*).

dThe 36,000 federal law-enforcement employees include all employees of only five agencies: FBI, Secret Service, Immigration and Naturalization Service, Bureau of Narcotics and Dangerous Drugs, and Bureau of Customs. But only a fraction of these employees are actually investigators or law-enforcement officers with police powers. From Hearings of the Committee on Government Operations, *Unmet Training Needs of the Federal Investigator and the Consolidated Federal Law Enforcement Training Center*, House Report No. 91-1429, U.S. Government Printing Office, 1970, it is estimated that the federal government's investigative force exceeds 50,000 employees.

eSource: Bureau of Labor Statistics publications and unpublished data. Excludes part-time employees unless their primary occupation is security-related.

fThis estimate derives from two sources: Predicasts, Inc., and a Rand estimate, both of which are discussed in Chapter IV of R-870-DOJ.

gSources: *1967 Census of Business: County Business Patterns for 1968 and 1969*. Includes parttime employees. See footnote e above.

hAssuming payroll is 57 percent of revenues, as estimated in the *1967 Census of Business*.

iSource: *1967 Census of Business* data extrapolated to 1969, utilizing revenue growth ratios equal to those achieved by large contract detective agencies and protective service firms.

jSource: *1967 Census of Business* data extrapolated to 1969, using revenue growth rates equal to those achieved by large armored-car firms.

kSource: Predicasts, Inc., Special Study 56, *Security Systems, 1970*.

mated at about 35 percent financial, commercial, and retail; about 50 percent industrial and transportation; about 13 percent institutional; and only 2 percent consumer (i.e., private persons, residences, and automobiles).

The 1967 in-house private security employment breakdown by industry category was as follows: 46 percent in manufacturing; about 5 percent in agriculture, forestry, fisheries, mining, and construction; 12 percent in transportation, communications, and public utilities; 3 percent in wholesale and retail trade; 9 percent in finance, insurance, and real estate; and 21 percent in services (not including contract security firms). Educational services alone (grade schools through universities) absorb about 7 percent of all in-house guards plus some unknown fraction of all contract guards.

Expenditures on public law enforcement were over $4.4 billion, excluding approximately $1 billion spent on government guards and watchmen. In the private sector, expenditures were 2.5 billion on security services plus an additional $800 million on security equipment, or a total of $3.3 billion. Of the $2.5 billion expended in 1969 for security services within the private sector, about $1.6 billion was spent for in-house guards, police, and investigators. About $620 million was spent for private contract guard and investigative services, while about $128 million and $120 million were expended for armored-car and central station alarm services, respectively. In total, expenditures on public and private security were about $8.7 billion.

Nature of Growth

Between 1960 and 1969 the number of public law-enforcement personnel employed at all levels of government grew 42 percent, while population grew 12 percent. During that period, publicly employed guards increased at the same rate as public law-enforcement personnel. But the overall increase in privately employed guards, watchmen, and investigators was only 7 percent (guard and watchman employment grew 6 percent, while detective and investigative employment grew 19 percent).[2]

Public law-enforcement expenditures during the 1960-1969 period enlarged by 90 percent, while the purchasing power of the dollar declined 21 percent. Although comparable figures for expenditure growth in private security are somewhat unreliable, the most credible estimate places growth over that same period at approximately 150 percent. Since private-sector employment grew only 7 percent, the large expenditure growth appears to be due mainly to growth in security equipment revenues and to increases in wage rates and other costs.

While the total number of private guards and investigators grew slowly during the 1960s, *the contract segment grew rapidly,* almost doubling between 1960 and 1969. In contrast, employment of in-house guards and investigators may have declined slightly over that period. Whether viewed in terms of revenues or expenditures, growth in private contract protective services (guards, investigators, armored car, central station alarm) averaged 11 to 12 percent per year. In terms of employment, receipts, and number of establishments, this sector grew more than twice as fast as the service industries in general, themselves a rapidly growing sector of the economy.

The contract security industry that provides guard and investigative services may be characterized accurately as a rapidly expanding industry which is dominated by a very few large firms, but which includes several thousand very small firms as well. In recent years, the large firms have been increasing their share of the market, as Table II illustrates.

The growth of the contract security industry

[2]These increments do not include changes in the number of part-time private security guards and detectives. Part-timers account for between 20 and 50 percent of employment in major contract security firms, but the corresponding fraction in smaller contract firms, as well as in the in-house private sector, is unknown.

is much more rapid than that of either total private security or in-house security, so that the contract security industry continues to capture an ever-increasing fraction of the total. Why? The oft-cited explanations are that contract security services imply to the client such advantages as the following: lower cost (by about 20 percent); administrative unburdening (no need to hire, equip, train, etc., the security staff); flexibility in scheduling of relief manpower (in times of sickness, vacation, peak loads); and less involvement between security employees and regular employees (i.e., more impartial security employees).

Reasons for Growth

Growth in public police expenditures and employment is generally assumed to be a "cost" of rising crime rates; while some persons point out that crime reporting may be improving over time, few dispute the thesis that the actual crime rate has risen, as have property losses and the fear of crime.[3] However, some observers have claimed, for example, that *all* of the increase in local public police budgets between 1900 and 1960 could be "explained" without referring to increases in reported crime, the explanatory factors being growth in inflation, population, number of registered motor vehicles, and urbanization.[4] If, in addition, public police "productivity"[5] did not change materially during that period, an inference that public police are increasingly overburdened (in terms of anticrime activities) would be reasonable. As a consequence, the demand for supplemen-

tary private security services and equipment should rise.

But there may be additional underlying factors generating increased demand for private security. Most observers would include some or all of the following:

• Increasing business losses to crime ($3 billion in 1968).

• Insurers raising rates or refusing coverage, so that security measures are used increasingly as a substitute for insurance.

• Insurers requiring the use of certain private security systems or granting premium discounts when certain private security measures are used.

• The federal government's need for security in its space and defense activities during the past decade and, more recently, the need for security against air hijackings, violent demonrations, and bombings of federal, state, and local government facilities.

• The basic business trend toward purchases of specialized services, which may contribute to the growth of the contract security forces.

• The nation's growth and advancing state of the art in electronics and other scientific areas, which has sparked new and distinct manufacturing branches of several protection companies, providing greatly improved security devices, especially for intrusion detection.

• The general increase in corporate and private income, which has resulted in more property to protect and, at the same time, more income to pay for protection.

LAW-ENFORCEMENT AND PROTECTION FUNCTIONS: ARREST, DETENTION, SEARCH, INTERROGATION, AND USE OF FORCE

Private security forces perform various law-enforcement and protection activities, such as

---

[3]The June 1971 Harris Poll reported that 55 percent of the 1,614 households polled during the month were "more worried about violence and safety on the streets" in their own community, as compared to a year ago. See *Security Systems Digest*, July, 7, 1971, p. 7.

[4]See, for example, David J. Bordua, and Edward W. Haurek "The Police Budget's Lot," *American Behavioral Scientist*, May-August 1970, pp. 667-680.

[5]The nature of the relationship between crime or crime rate and police action is largely unknown at this time.

Table II. Revenue Trends of Large Publicly Owned Private Protection Firms[a]

Firm	Revenue ($ millions)							Comp. Annual Growth Rate, 1965-69 (% per year)
	1963	1964	1965	1966	1967	1968	1969	
Guard and Investigative Services								
Pinkerton's, Inc.	42.7	64.1	66.7	71.3	82.8	99.4	120.5	15.8
Wm. J. Burns Intl. Detective Agency, Inc.	41.0	43.2	48.2	55.9	66.5	82.8	97.1	19.0
Wackenhut Corporation	9.6	10.8	17.8	22.4	29.0	36.7	48.5	28.4
Walter Kidde and Co. (Globe Security Systems)[b]	—	—	22.8	25.3	29.0	39.4	46.3	19.4
Baker Industries, Inc. (Wells Fargo Security Guard)[c]	—	—	3.3	5.8	8.1	11.7	15.8	45.5[d]
Total	93.3	118.1	158.8	180.7	235.4	270.0	328.0	—
Industrywide total	289[e]	—	—	—	445[e]	530[f]	620[g]	—
Percent of industrywide total	36	—	—	—	51	51	53	—
Central Station Alarm Services								
American District Telegraph Co.	70.9	74.9	78.7	81.8	87.4	93.3[h]	97.2[h]	5.5
Baker Industries, Inc. (Wells Fargo Alarm Services)	—	—	3.3	5.8	8.1	11.6	13.6	45.5[d]
Holmes Electric Protective Co.	—	—	—	—	—	15.0	17.5	—
Total	70.9	74.9	82.0	87.6	95.5	119.9[h]	128.8[h]	—
Industrywide total	80[f]	—	—	—	—	110[f]	120[f]	—
Armored-Car Services								
Brink's, Inc.	—	—	40.6	44.5	48.9	56.7	64.0	12.1
Baker Industries, Inc. (Wells Fargo Armored Service)[j]	—	—	2.6	4.7	6.6	9.8	13.0	45.5[i]
Loomis	—	—	6.1	7.1	8.3	10.0	12.7	20.6
Total	—	—	49.3	56.3	63.8	76.5	89.7	—

Industrywide total	67.3^e	—	87.0^h	—	90.6^e	115.0^h	128^k
Percent of industrywide total	—	—	57	—	—	67	70

[a]Data in this table have not been adjusted to compensate for the reduced purchasing power of the dollar over time; between 1959 and 1965, that purchasing power declined about 8 percent, while it declined an additional 14 percent between 1965 and 1969.

[b]Guard services and equipment only.

[c]Wells Fargo Security Guard Group only (part of Wells Fargo Protective Services Division). Data prior to 1968 assume that the Security Guard Group revenues are 27 percent of total revenues of Baker Industries, Inc.

[d]Annual growth rate for entire corporation. Total income was $54.9 million in 1969 and $11.9 million in 1965. The large growth rates were due, in part, to acquisitions.

[e]Source: Census of Business, op. cit.

[f]Source: Predicasts, Inc., op. cit.

[g]Source: 1967 Census of Business data extrapolated to 1969, using revenue growth ratios equal to those achieved by large contract guard and investigative agencies.

[h]At least 80 percent of the ADT total revenues are attributable to central station alarm services.

[i]Wells Fargo Alarm Services Group only (part of Wells Fargo Protective Services Division). Revenues prior to 1968 are assumed to be 27 percent of total revenues of Baker Industries, Inc.

[j]Wells Fargo Armored Service Group only (part of Wells Fargo Protective Services Division). Revenues prior to 1968 are assumed to be 22 percent of total revenues of Baker Industries, Inc.

[k]Source: 1967 Census of Business data extrapolated to 1969, using revenue growth ratios equal to those achieved by large armored-car firms.

arresting or detaining suspected shoplifters, ejecting persons from private property, and breaking up disturbances. Although the exact frequency of improper or illegal uses of force, detention, searches, and questioning is impossible to determine, it is evident from litigated cases and reported incidents, and from our surveys .of regulatory agencies and security employees, that illegal activities in this area are among the most important problems raised by private security functions. One of the prime areas in which these problems seem to arise is that of retail security.

The basic source of restrictions for these enforcement and protection activities is tort law, which imposes damages for such tortious activity as false imprisonment, assault, battery, malicious prosecution, intentional infliction of emotional harm, invasion of privacy, and negligence. However, the guard or detective may be relieved of liability if there was consent to the conduct or if he acted reasonably under a number of recognized legal "privileges" authorizing such interference with the rights of others.

Arrest of Criminal Suspects

The undeputized private security guard has the same power of arrest as a private citizen, and this power is derived mainly from tort law. Under tort law, a citizen has the "privilege" to arrest, under various circumstances, someone who has committed or is committing a crime. The details of the power of citizens' arrest are complex and turn on such distinctions as the place, time, and nature of the crime committed by the arrestee. The practical value of the arrest power is diminished somewhat by the many complexities and restrictions surrounding the privilege.

Detention of Persons Suspected of Taking Property or Shoplifting

The courts and legislators of many states have developed a privilege to allow merchants or other property owners to detain persons suspected of shoplifting or injuring their property. However, the privilege is exercisable only if there is probable cause to believe the suspect has taken the property, and the detention must be reasonable. Any undue detention, harassment, physical abuse, or other unreasonable conduct will render the detention illegal.

Miscellaneous Powers to Control the Activities of Others

The security guard must often resort to actions short of arrest or detention. For example, he may want to simply scare off intruders, eject annoying patrons from a sporting event, or prohibit entry by undesired persons. The primary legal authority used in many instances is probably consent. Where consent is absent, there are various privileges that may be available in the circumstances: the right of a real property owner to control the access and conduct of other persons on his premises, and to prohibit or eject trespassers; the right of a person to defend himself and to defend others; and the right of a citizen to prevent a crime.

Use of Force

All of the various privileges outlined above carry with them the right to use whatever force is reasonably necessary to accomplish the legitimate purpose of the privilege. However, the right is lost when unreasonable and excessive force is used.

There are not many clear rules as to what force is allowable in a given situation. Some guidelines have been developed for the use of deadly force, but usually "reasonableness" controls, and what is reasonable turns on the nature of the interest being protected, the nature of the act being resisted, and the particular facts of a given situation. To add to the confusion, the amount of force allowed differs depending upon which privilege is being invoked. Only a few certain generalizations can be made.

Questioning and Interrogation of Suspects

As long as a suspect is legally detained, there is

no absolute ban on simply asking questions, and interrogation is specifically authorized by many statutes concerning temporary detention for shoplifting. However, a person is under no legal compulsion to answer, and thus there are limits to the methods, amount, and kind of interrogation that may be performed. For example, questioning a suspect in public may be slanderous, and a general reasonableness standard controls whenever the questioning is done under the auspices of a temporary-detention statute.

Search of Suspects

Assuming a suspect is legally under detention or arrest, a search of the suspect's person may be valid under various theories. Often consent will render the search valid. Without consent, the law on the right to search suspects is unclear. However, it is clear that wherever a search is legally privileged, it must be effected in a reasonable manner and with the least possible force or embarrassment.

Public and Private Police Compared

Generally, a public policeman has significantly more power than a nondeputized private policeman. However, the public policeman is also subject to various constitutional restrictions which, so far, have not been generally imposed upon private detectives and guards. The arrest powers of public police are limited by the Fourth Amendment to instances of probable cause. The scope of police searches incident to arrest has been severely narrowed by Supreme Court decisions under the Fourth Amendment. And these restrictions may well be greater than the tort law would apply to private searches incident to arrests. Finally, the Supreme Court

has placed very severe restrictions on the interrogation of suspects by public police. These decisions culminated in *Miranda v. Arizona,* where the Supreme Court required police to warn a suspect of his rights before custodial interrogation. While many courts have ruled that coerced or involuntary confessions obtained by private security officers will not be admitted in any criminal prosecution of the suspect, few courts have required private security personnel to give the *Miranda* warnings.

Critique

The primary problem with tort law governing the arrest, detention, search, interrogation, and use-of-force powers of private police is its general vagueness and complexity. The law is controlled by such general concepts as "reasonableness," "probable cause," or "necessary under the circumstances." Uncertainty is compounded by the fact that a particular factual situation might be covered by various different privileges, each of which might allow different conduct. Further, the law in a given situation depends upon the nature and legality of the conduct of the person being detained, stopped, or ejected. And the law often takes into account the subjective state of mind of the person making the arrest or using force. Such uncertainty creates special problems for the employer of private security personnel in instructing his personnel on what they should or should not do in every instance. And the individual guard, whose intelligence and educational level may be somewhat low, is probably incapable of setting any guidelines for himself. There is a need, therefore, for greater certainty in the areas of arrest, search, interrogation, and use of force.

The Administration of Justice

CRIMINOLOGISTS SEEM TO HAVE BEEN ALMOST EXCLUSIVELY CONCERNED WITH felonies and major courts, while they are peripherally aware that the overwhelming majority of crimes and arrests are for misdemeanors or violations of public ordinances that are processed by the minor judiciary. This section deliberately contains several items on the lower courts, including traffic courts and juvenile courts. Mileski's examination of lower criminal courtroom encounters deals with the court as a formal organization. The offenses handled (overwhelmingly misdemeanors) are disposed of by "mass justice," which raises serious questions regarding legal representation and defense counsel plans, strategies and pleas. The courts of this level also show considerable leniency toward convicted offenders.

A somewhat contrary conclusion is reached by Ute in his examination of judicial review within a traffic court. The concern here is how minor law offenders handle their identity in settings that they fail to comprehend. Ute sees that court encounters between judge and defendant are not very relevant to justice and truth but frequently are transformed into degradation ceremonies that require the discrediting of the convicted minor offender in open court. The next selection by Levin and Sarri does not deal with the operations of a single court or a small sample of courts, but presents data on a national basis for one other type of judicial process, the juvenile courts. In these courts there are jurisdictional variations in "adjudication" (roughly the equivalent of a verdict of guilt for adult offenders), differences in formal or informal hearings, exclusion of the public, right to jury trial, and operable rules of evidence. Juvenile court dispositions infrequently require formal court processing.

One major innovation in the criminal justice system has been the rapidly increasing use of pretrial detention alternatives, most especially bail and other, newer forms of release. These alternatives range from summons and field citations to pretrial work release. It is difficult to overestimate recent alterations in the phenomenon of bail, which represents a personal promise or offer of some object of value to guarantee that the arrestee will appear at some subsequent stage of the criminal process. Most likely, the central concern with the success or failure of bail relates to Failure to Appear (FTA) or the recommission of new crimes by offenders who are released on bail prior to their trial. Wice examines this fundamental issue in detail and finds some interesting factors in both the successes and failures.

Almost all persons charged with a crime in this country plead guilty. The usual negotiations between prosecutor and defense lawyer, referred to as "plea bargaining," are a controversial issue in the law. Although this practice is not new, until recently it was carried out informally in prosecutors' offices or the corridors of court houses. Without plea bargaining our courts could not begin to handle the load of cases. But plea bargaining may sacrifice the interests of both defendant and the public in order to achieve a smooth running court. Newman's article describes some of the conflicting aims and the ethical issues involved in this bargaining process.

An intrinsic part of the criminal justice system (even if of decreasing importance) is the grand jury, which has several discrete and separate functions. The function dealt with by Carp is the determination of whether the state has made a prima facie case against the accused. In this selection, members of the grand jury and the interpersonal relationships that develop and affect jury outcomes are described. Carp finds that grand juries rapidly process cases, give these cases little deliberation and, as one might expect, seemingly always accept the state's recommendations.

Investigations of the uncertain role and activities played by the defense counsel have been remarkably sparse. Blumberg takes a somewhat extreme and pessimistic view of attorneys who represent the accused and perceive law as a "con game." He argues that the court structure largely defines and confines the defense counsel's obligations to the negotiated plea, and too often the plea represents a quick and, apparently, simple solution to the problems of court backlog, the energies of lawyers, and the relationships among court functionaries.

If all else fails, and a "deal" of one form or another is not made, then that rare event, a jury trial, is undertaken. Several studies have been made of the jury process. The first basic question of sociological importance is—in what manner are jurors selected (at the voir dire)? Fried presents evidence on the selection of jurors that reflects challenges of various sorts, incorporating the different goals of prosecution and defense. As a dramatic example of some of the problems faced by both prosecution and defense in a major felony case, Hibey reviews what transpires in a rape case. The complex questions in rape cases deal with such issues as: corroboration (evidence supporting the victim and indicating actual penile penetration); consent (with the possibility of an "affirmative defense"); and character and reputation, which pose huge pitfalls to both sides. This last issue is all but incomprehensible to nonlegal students but is acceptable to those well versed in the legal procedure.

A jury consists of 12 strangers who, faced with often unclear, ambiguous, and contradictory information and evidence, are usually able to reach a unanimous decision. *The American Jury*, a study carried out in 1966 by Kalvin and Zeisel which remains the single most comprehensive study of jury decision making, deals with the ability of the average jury to understand and follow a complex mass of detail and evidence as it was determined by the presiding judge in over 1000 cases. Despite the "rationality" found by Kalven and Zeisel, nonlegitimate factors often influence the jury in reaching their decisions. Thus, Sigall and Ostrove find that attractive people are commonly seen as better people, less evil, and therefore, less deserving of punishment. Perhaps it is no surprise that defendants with physical good looks are, in fact, dealt with more leniently than persons who are less attractive.

The final issue in this section is sentencing. The first selection on this topic by Burke and Turk is a complex investigation of the analytic problems associated with social disadvantageousness. This study employs variables of age, race, and occupation—all of which impinge on the sentencing process but should not. These authors find very little evidence of bias. Next, Hagan's study moves from a single set of data to a broad-based analysis and critique of studies of extralegal factors in sentencing from 1928 to 1973. And although the authors of many studies cited by Hagan have claimed to have found considerable bias, Hagan's conclusion is that there was very weak evidence of bias in sentencing.

14. Courtroom Encounters

MAUREEN MILESKI

THIS IS A STUDY OF THE CRIMINAL TRIAL COURT AS a formal organization. The processing of defendants through court can be seen simply as a task for the courtroom personnel—the cases presenting not only occasions for moral outrage or legal acumen but also presenting problems for the legal bureaucracy as such. From one perspective, defendants are as deviant if they do not conform to the routines of the court as they are if they do not conform to the rules of the state. Like the wider society it supports, the court has a social integrity which can be disrupted. The court processes persons alleged to have been deviant in the larger society. The defendants are then subject to the moral exigencies of the court itself. The discussion treats the court as a business as well as a prime sanctioning center for the outer society. But the control of crime is more than a business; it is an industry. The immediate suppliers of the court—the police—act upon and in turn are conditioned by courtroom configurations. Several features of this police-court interrelation also form a part of this study.

This paper divides into two basic parts. In the first, compositional features of courtroom encounters are discussed. This section concerns the types of offenses lower courts process, the rapidity of courtroom encounters, the processing of defendants in groups, the presence of

▶SOURCE: *"Courtroom Encounters–An Observation Study of a Lower Criminal Court,"* Law and Society Review *(May, 1971), 5:473–481, 486–496, 499–503, 537, 538. (Editorial adaptations) Reprinted by permission.*

legal counsel in encounters, and the pleas of defendants. The second section investigates the dispositions of cases. The overall task of this paper is to detail some prominent patterns in the lower court's day-to-day operations.

METHOD AND SETTING

Attention directed toward criminal courts displays an emphasis on matters apart from courtroom encounters themselves. Thus, for instance, it is widely believed that in order to understand many courtroom outcomes it is essential to understand the place of the negotiated plea. Nevertheless, the courtroom encounter can be approached in its own right. Although some stages may be set and some denouements may be neatly written in prosecutors' offices, the ways in which these sketchy plots are acted out in the courtroom remain largely unexplained.

Much information on courtroom behavior derives from official court statistics and records. This method has weaknesses resulting from omissions in the sources. Although a series of legally relevant factors is highlighted in official records, a number of other factors that may bear on legal outcomes, such as the defendant's deference before the court or his apparent social-class status, are left out. The court, like many formal organizations, has no interest in maximizing outsiders' access to information about its ongoing activities. In consequence, certain of its operations go unrecorded. The courtroom clerk, for example, does not make a notation of each time the judge scowls at a defendant or appears incredulous at a defendant's account of his behavior. Furthermore, plea-bargaining encounters are conspicuously omitted. Something similar to the "blue curtain" that hangs about police departments surrounds the courts and creates an intelligence problem for the outsider who would use what the court writes down about itself. It might be added that lower courts have particularly incomplete record-keeping systems. Indeed, some lower courts have no reporters whatsoever.

Direct courtroom observation, by contrast, does not procure all the information that officially gets recorded; for example, defendants' criminal histories are not always read aloud in court although they go on record. Observer bias may be an added problem. Observation, nevertheless, allows the opportunity to investigate the situational factors that may be associated with various kinds of cases and their dispositions. Unfortunately, the few past studies that rest upon direct observation of courtroom encounters offer little in the way of quantified data (an exception is Lefstein et al., 1969). At many points in the criminal process, unrecorded situational contingencies might come to the fore. Studies of the police, for example, demonstrate that extralegal, situational factors often are central in field dispositions (see Piliavin and Briar, 1964; Black, 1968; Black and Reiss, 1970).

Data for this study were gathered over a three-month period by direct observation on Mondays and Fridays in a criminal court of the first instance of a middle-sized eastern city. Two judges presided over the court. The prosecutor and five of his assistants rotated during the observation period. A total of 417 cases comprise the final sample. These are arraignments and final dispositions. Many more than 417 defendants passed before the judge during the 11 full days of observation, but encounters that fall within the broad category of continuances (under half of the cases observed) are not analyzed (for an examination of continuances, see Banfield, 1968).

The city where observation was done, like many, has two levels of trial courts, the court of the first instance and a higher-order court. The court of the first instance has final jurisdiction over all municipal ordinances and all offenses punishable by a fine of no more than $1,000, one year's incarceration, or both. The lower court may also take final jurisdiction over crimes punishable by a $1,000 fine, five years' incarceration, or both, if the prosecutor deems that a penalty of no more than $1,000 and/or one year is necessary in a given case. The court thus has final jurisdiction over misdemeanor cases and minor felony cases. If a defendant has been charged with a crime carrying more than a five-year maximum or if the prosecutor decides that a suspect might receive more than one year's incarceration, the suspect must be bound over to the higher court for final disposition. However, the lower court does handle serious cases at preliminary stages—arraignments and probable cause hearings—before they reach the higher court.

The city parcels the business of the lower court system into two physically separate rooms. The proportional volume of serious cases is smaller in one of these rooms. This courtroom disposes of most of the city's minor cases—matters of public drunkenness, breach of the peace, and so on. This was the room selected for observation. The observational method suits it both because the volume of cases is high and because plea bargaining has little or no relevance in the handling of lesser offenses. Two attorneys and a language interpreter employed by the court reported that plea bargaining is simply nonexistent in routine cases of intoxication and disturbances of the peace. Since most defendants are charged with minor offenses of this sort, a field observer frequently witnesses the total post-police processing.

There are a number of constraints on drawing inferences from these data that the reader is advised to bear in mind throughout the discussion. First, there is the question of how representative the court is of all lower criminal trial courts in cities of roughly the same size. Surely it differs in certain ways from courts in cities much larger or smaller. Although nothing was found to suggest that the court investigated is distinctive among those in its class, its representativeness remains unknown. Second, there arises the problem of how much of the court proceedings can be attributed to the individual prosecutors and judges who happened to make their way into the present sample of cases. Again, even though the two judges observed were not characterized as particularly amicable or nasty or particularly lenient or harsh by others involved with the court, the impact on the court of their personal peculiarities is unknown. Only two of the eight judges who hear cases over the course of the year are in the sample, but five of the six or seven prosecutorial personnel are included. Thus questions concerning the prosecutors' distinctiveness become largely questions of the whole court's possible distinctiveness. Finally, this city's allocation of lower court cases into two separate courtrooms presents problems for interpreting differences between minor and serious cases. In this courtroom most cases are very minor; it may be that the few serious cases which are assigned to it are somehow different from those that are processed through the other courtroom of the lower court division. The lawyers with whom these matters were discussed, however, gave no indication that this is the case. While these questions remain unresolved, courtroom behavior is nevertheless considered in general terms in the following discussion. As long as these possible limitations are understood, it would seem unduly ascetic to refrain from generalization and some amount of speculation simply because the study is a case study.

A Sketch of the Lower Court

The great bulk of criminal cases start and end at the lower court level. Our understanding of courts does not reflect court volume since accumulated knowledge disproportionately pertains to the higher courts. Offenses break down into the legal categories of felony and misdemeanor. Within each of these categories, of-fenses divide into three finer classes for purposes of analysis: offenses against the public order, against property, and against the person. Examples of misdemeanors against the public are intoxication, breach of the peace, and underage possession of alcohol. Typical misdemeanors against property are petty larceny and minor but malicious destruction of property. Simple assault and resisting arrest are misdemeanors against the person. In the felony category, a narcotics offense is an offense against the public, breaking and entering an offense against property, and robbery or aggravated assault an offense against the person.

Charges in this lower courtroom overwhelmingly (81%) accumulate in the misdemeanor categories:

Offense Charged	Percentage	
Misdemeanor against Public	66	
Misdemeanor against Property	6	81
Misdemeanor against Person	7	
Misdemeanor, Unspecified	2	
Felony against Public	2	
Felony against Property	4	14
Felony against Person	5	
Felony, Unspecified	3	
Other Offenses, e.g., Traffic or Unspecified	6	
Total Percentage	101	
Total Number	417	

From the standpoint of legal seriousness, the operations of this court are of minor importance. The court rises in importance, on the other hand, from the standpoint of volume.

Court sessions are called to order in the morning at approximately ten and run until one or two o'clock in the afternoon, depending on the caseload. On many days there is one recess of roughly a quarter-hour. Unlike some more informal courts, the prosecutor is always present in the courtroom along with the judge. Other personnel routinely present include a clerk, a reporter, a bailiff, a policeman, a probation officer, a secretary for the public defender, and a family court and juvenile court liaison man. In addition a female probation officer and a female police officer are present when a female defendant is scheduled for appearance, as is a Spanish interpreter when a defendant who would need his services is scheduled for appearance. Bail bondsmen and attorneys frequently work their way up to the front of the courtroom to pass the time with others while awaiting cases. Thus at least twelve officials or their assistants may literally surround a defendant as he goes before the bench. All but the most obvious three or four of them may have functions ambiguous to the average defendant.

The public area of the courtroom seats about sixty persons; it is more than full at the opening of the day's session. Adjacent to the courtroom is the "lock-up," as it almost always is called by the participants. Its door bears three locks and a sign reading "No admittance. Attorneys only. No food, candy or cigarettes." The door's trappings symbolize a great deal, but those behind it are not treated like outsiders to the extent that it might first appear. It is not uncommon for a wife, sister, or friend to have a hamburger passed to a prisoner through the guard at the door. Relations between the policeman-guard and the prisoners are rather cordial. Slightly over one-half of the defendants enter the courtroom through the lock-up, the others approaching the bench from the public seating area. The remaining public, of course, is witness to the courtroom encounters.

COMPOSITIONAL FEATURES OF ENCOUNTERS

Mass Justice.   Many American courts have a workload problem. Court systems have what their participants, spokesmen, and critics consider too much to do. Heavy workloads do not pressure all bureaucracies; in fact, some bureaucracies are faced with the opposite problem, that of having work insufficient even to justify their maintenance (Messinger, 1955). Such is not the plight of the court.

One obvious way the court can allay pressures from heavy caseloads is to handle the accused rapidly. In this court 72% of the cases are handled in one minute or less (see Miller and

Schwartz, 1966; Wenger and Fletcher, 1969; Lea, 1969: 142, on the duration of other types of hearings). It is noteworthy that routine police encounters with citizens in the field last on the average far longer than court encounters. The climax of many an alleged offender's contact with the criminal justice machinery is dwarfed by his police contact on the one side and the time he is incarcerated on the other. The sluggishness that often characterizes governmental organizations does not carry over to the courts. The notion of delay in the courts refers to the number of weeks, months, or even years necessary to bring various cases to a close. Furthermore, it is usually used with reference to courts that handle civil or private law cases. Once a criminal case surfaces in the courtroom, the encounter often has an extremely short life. In this city, it usually takes one or two hours to obtain auto license plates, but it takes a matter of minutes to dispose of accused auto thieves in court. Typically, justice in court is quick.[1]

An additional device to allay caseload pressures is to process two or more defendants simultaneously. Not infrequently in a lower court the prosecutor strings defendants out in a line before the judge and processes them partly as a group. When the prosecutor mass-processes defendants, he calls out a list of names from his records. Those called step up to the bench from the public area of the courtroom or from the lock-up adjacent to the courtroom. This allows the judge to accomplish part of his task more efficiently than he could if defendants were sent to him one by one. For example, if it takes a given judge one-half minute to apprise one defendant of rights, four-and-one-half minutes would be saved if he were to apprise an assembly of ten defendants. If this is done twice or thrice per session, an extra full trial can be worked into a day of the same length.[2] After the judge hand-

---

[1] No information was obtained on how much time was spent with individual defendants outside the courtroom itself. As noted, however, it was said that no time whatsoever is spent with defendants charged with drunkenness and little or no time is spent with other petty offenders.

[2] Defendants can learn from the processing of other de-

les the defendants as a group—this usually consists only of rights apprisings—he considers each case separately. Yet the line in front of the bench remains.

Only half (51%) the defendants see the judge individually. Thus only half the defendants in the lower court engage in what fits the popular and even academic image of the judge-defendant confrontation. The remainder of the defendants see the judge only in conjunction with others. Sometimes the group is large; 15% of the total defendants face the judge with ten or more others alongside them. Most criminal defendants presumably commit their offenses alone and go on to receive their sanctions in the midst of strangers. Decisions as to dispositions may historically have become more individualized, but numerous encounters in contemporary lower courts are not.

The shape of courtroom encounters surely conditions the legal outputs thereof. One characteristic of many preliterate control systems is that they are relatively informal and nonbureaucratic, whereas contemporary societies maintain bureaucratized systems of control. A corresponding distinction is found in the study of legal control within the two types of societies. Anthropologists almost consistently use the conflict resolution model; sociologists more frequently use the rule enforcement model in investigations of control systems. This analytical difference is no doubt to some extent a result of empirical differences. The extent to which the outputs of the two polar types of control systems differ—whether primarily rule enforcement or conflict resolution—may in part be due to differences in the structures into which legal problems are poured and from which solutions emerge. Conflict resolution or order

maintenance literally takes time and requires attention to individuals on a case-by-case basis. Highly bureaucratized courts with caseload problems lend themselves more easily to rule enforcement than to conflict resolution. Legal decision-making with a goal of conflict resolution almost necessarily entails particularism; with a rule enforcement end, it entails a greater degree of universalism. Thus where encounters are rapid and where defendants are processed in groups, more universalistic rule enforcement would be expected. A consequence may be that the recent trend toward individualized treatment of offenders is stunted by the bureaucratization of the processing organizations.[3] Similarly, when citizens complain about the movement away from the foot patrolman on the neighborhood beat, a movement to a highly bureaucratic police force, the real touchstone of their complaints may be an increase in rule enforcement over conflict resolution. The form of any social activity affects its substance and, consequently, its impact.

*

Legal Counsel

Legal counsel attends only 16% of the defendants. Very typically, it is a defendant rather than a lawyer who contends with the judge and prosecutor. The judge and prosecutor, correlatively, do not usually go through the screen of

---

[3]Furthermore, a disproportionate number of the cases that would even allow for conflict resolution do not come to the contemporary criminal courts. Some cases that potentially could work their way through the courts are weeded away from the criminal processing funnel by the police. Police arrest practices vary according to a number of factors. Significantly, patrol officers disproportionately leave cases to informal mechanisms of resolution—that is, they arrest and make out crime reports less frequently—when the offender-victim relation involves intimates rather than strangers (Black, 1968; 1970). Strangers in criminal incidents are connected momentarily only because of the offense itself. There is no enduring relation that requires mending. Where the victim and offender are linked in enduring relations, conflict resolution on a case-by-case basis is possible. In sum, not only does the court handle defendants in an impersonal way by processing them rapidly and in groups; impersonality also characterizes the bulk of the offender-victim relations that eventuate in court processing.

---

fendants that they observe; this saves time. For example, a judge not uncommonly asks after a rights apprising if the defendants "understand." The judge offers clarification to the first defendant who says that he does not understand. These restatements are not necessary by the time he asks the last few defendants. In unknown other ways, a defendant may learn from another defendant how to "work the system."

an attorney in their relation to the typical defendant. The lower court is by and large a court without attorneys; both the legal and bureaucratic intricacies of the defendant-court relationship are minimal.

Counsel is far more likely to be present, as would be expected, in encounters involving relatively serious charges. Felony suspects are not only more likely to be apprised of their rights; they are also more likely to have an attorney's aid in taking advantage of their rights. Excluding arraignments, only 12% of the misdemeanor suspects were professionally represented, whereas over five times as many (64%) of the felony suspects were represented. Nonetheless, one out of three defendants charged with a felony provides his own defense.

Some defendants who appear in court unrepresented before the time of the final disposition of their cases plan to retain an attorney or to seek court-appointed counsel in the future. These are defendants involved in arraignments. Fifty-eight percent of the misdemeanor suspects and 18% of the felony suspects at the time of their arraignments have no plans to acquire any sort of legal counsel (see Table I for a further breakdown of plans for an attorney). If all the

defendants who planned to obtain counsel were successful, the proportion of defendants represented would rise from 16 to approximately 25%. Still, the proportion of total defendants who plead their own cases remains large. The seriousness of the offense has a strong bearing on the likelihood that legal counsel will be sought, as it does on the likelihood that legal counsel is present at the final disposition stage. Neither finding is surprising, because there are pressures on both the court and the defendants that give rise to the patterns. The court must provide impecunious felony defendants with counsel. Also, the risks of relying on his own lay defense are obviously greater for the felony suspect. While the accused misdemeanant plainly has a right to obtain his own counsel, courts in this state need not offer it to him if he is indigent. The misdemeanant is in various ways the forgotten man of the criminal legal system, even though offenders like himself comprise the great bulk of the police and court workload.

The court presents the defendant or his lawyer not only legal battles to be dexterously fought and won, but also a configuration of bureaucratic relationships to be manipulated

Table I. Percentage of Arraignments According to the Offense Charged, by Plans for Attorney

| | Offense Charged | | | | | |
| | Misdemeanor | | | | | |
Plans for Attorney	Minor	Serious	Unspecified	All	Felony	All Cases
None	60	60	(1)	58	18	40
To obtain private attorney	25	07	—	16	24	20
To apply for public defender	10	27	(1)	18	18	18
Public defender to be assigned	—	07	—	03	24	13
Not ascertained	05	—	(1)	05	15	10
Total	100	101	—	100	99	101
(n)	(20)	(15)	(3)	(38)	(33)	(71)

more or less adeptly. When a defendant obtains a lawyer to fight his case, he not only obtains a legal buffer between himself and the judge, he also—even if unwittingly—wedges his fate into a series of organizational battles irrelevant to the legal status of his case. The prosecutor balances his need to prosecute cases against his need to maintain good relations with the judge, public defender, and many other attorneys who frequently take cases to court; all are members of the "team" that maintains orderly operations of the court. They share a worksite. Together they can make their worksite a fractious, turbulent one or an orderly and predictable one. Though the interests of some of the parties are formally at odds, in operation they share common interests. A certain level of cooperation between them obtains.[4] Where relationships between parties are enduring, cooperation or bargaining may often be found beneath a formal façade of conflict or coercion, as they are, for example, in the relations between prisoners and prison guards (Sykes, 1958). Adversarial behavior is often disruptive in the court, a formally adversarial organization (compare the view taken in Skolnick, 1967). There may be more conflict between the police and the court than between the average attorney and the prosecutor. There is a sizable literature on this sub-rosa cooperation and, more narrowly, on plea negotiation (for example, see Newman, 1956 and 1966; Sudnow, 1965; Blumberg, 1967a and 1967b; Skolnick, 1967; Alschuler, 1968).[5]

[4]Alschuler (1968) suggests that this cooperation stems more from friendship patterns as such than from more strictly legal gamesmanship.

[5]The remaining remarks on counsel are very speculative. Information of the enduring court-attorney relationship was provided only through passing remarks from attorneys and inferred from a few remarks among the courtroom encounters. There was no systematic attempt to procure information on this cooperative relationship in part because of all of the prior attention to it. Conclusions about attorneys' in-court behavior, on the other hand, are tentative simply because so few defendants in the court are attended by counsel. Still, it seems appropriate to add what little these observations provide to the picture of the attorney's role.

The question arises as to whether the assignment of the public defender is to the benefit of the court, the defendant, or both. On one hand, the defendant is assured of at least some legal assistance free of charge. On the other hand, it is to the benefit of the court that the public defender be at least as adept at working well within the court bureaucracy as he is at legal matters as such. Because the public defender is in that class of attorneys generally cooperative within the bureaucracy, his attachment to serious cases deflates an underlying potential for disruption. There is a felicitous meshing between the formal requirements of law and those of the courtroom bureaucracy. Sixty-three percent (27 cases) of the public defender's load concerned a client charged with a felony, even though felony cases comprise only 19% of the cases observed.[6] Furthermore, in a few of the most serious of felony cases, the judge assigned the public defender without even requiring the defendant to apply formally for his services. Court-funded counsel not only protects the defendant from the state, it also protects the state from the potential disruption of defendants in serious cases.

Lawyers no doubt receive positive or negative reinforcement for their own behavior in the judicial bureaucracy. One attorney, to give a minor example, noted that whenever he obtained an "unreasonable" acquittal, the prosecutor penalized him by not calling his cases until the end of the day's session. This "penalty" would last about a week after the disapproved disposition. Not only the lawyer but also his client, then, must sometimes sit all day in court for reasons irrelevant to the substance of the cases at hand. Ordinarily, clients with attorneys have their cases scheduled for very early or very late in the day's session. The court thus allows the attorneys to salvage most of each day for out-of-court matters. Defendants without attorneys

[6]Only 46% of the 13 defendants who indicated they would apply for the public defender had been charged with felonies. However, it would be expected that they would be more successful than the misdemeanor applicants.

are told the day, but not the time, of their court appearances. This favor may add to the court's leverage in coaxing attorneys toward routine cooperation.

Perhaps the obvious or only available way in which the system can reward or penalize an attorney is to reward or penalize his client, which in turn affects the lawyer's reputation. For instance, an attorney who appeared in this court claimed that one of his clients was given a sentence which was considerably more severe than that usually given for similar offenses. He attributed the severe sentence to his own numerous requests for "probable cause hearings" for other defendants. These hearings consume valuable court time. An attorney in another city commented on the general phenomenon (Alschuler, 1968: 80):

> "Sure I could suddenly start to negotiate by saying, 'Ha, ha! You goofed. You should have given the defendant a warning.' And I'd do fine in that case, but my other clients would pay for this isolated success. The next time the district attorney had his foot in my throat, he'd push, too."

Thus, in more ways than one, the unrepresented defendant fights his own case: he must plead his case on his own, without the aid of someone with legal sophistication; but the merits of his case are not coded in light of any cooperative or disruptive behavior in totally different cases.

The attorney's long-term standing in the court's informal organization may affect his client's future in other ways as well. Contemporary formal procedure does not require pretrial disclosure of incriminating evidence to the defense upon request; this puts the defense at an obvious disadvantage since preparation for any and all trial contingencies is necessary (Goldstein, 1960). However, one attorney who regularly pleads cases at this court, reported that the prosecutor always allows him to see the state's case against his client before trial time. It is understood by the prosecutor that if he does not disclose his case then that attorney will in one or

another fashion not cooperate with the prosecutor. He may, for example, ask for a probable cause hearing in a felony case where he would not ordinarily request one. Preliminary hearings take the judge's and the prosecutor's time and the state's money. Under this pressure, the prosecutor tends to respond to the attorney's informal pretrial inquiries about the state's case.[7] An unrepresented defendant is without this advantage, as is the client of an attorney who is not part of certain informal workings of the court. Some important portions of the attorney's functions are served before his case goes to court.

To be sure, the attorney also serves important functions in the courtroom. Nevertheless, in a typical case the facts are not problematic because the plea is guilty. Indeed, because the guilty plea is so common, it is somewhat misleading to call trial courts fact-finding courts. Much of the attorney's function in court in the cases observed is to enter particularistic appeals—and sometimes words of contrition—on behalf of his client. Particularistic appeals have to do with the offender rather than with the offense. An unrepresented defendant may not be cognizant of the relevance of such information. He may feel that it is inappropriate or unwise to report on potentially mitigating circumstances. By contrast, attorneys observed almost invariably inject such information in seeking low or no bond or low or no punishment. Their clients are hard workers, new fathers, long residents of the city, ordinarily upstanding, good students, unfamiliar with English, respectable businessmen, or even caring for sick mothers (see Boudin et al., 1970: 55, where attorneys are recommended partly for their deliverance of particularistic appeals).

Thus it is not that the attorney in the court-

---

[7]Hence in operation the system becomes much like courts in civil law countries, where it is formal that the prosecution cannot introduce material with which the defense is unacquainted. Trials thus are seen by all as quite anticlimactic. For a discussion of this and other features of Soviet courts, see Feifer (1964).

room plays no adversarial role whatever, even when he enters a guilty plea for his client. His strategy very commonly is adversarial at the sentencing stage. Instead of arguing that his client is innocent, he argues that his client does not deserve a severe penalty. The lower court is largely a sentencing court, rarely a trial court—more a sanctioning than a truth-seeking system. The lawyer may step into either context as an advocate. It is not insignificant that one attorney, when asked to evaluate the court in this city, remarked that the court is "pretty good, pretty fair." By this, he said he meant "pretty lenient." He evaluated his success and the court's quality by the severity of sentences rather than by the rate of acquittals. In the lower court, the attorney *is* an advocate, but an advocate for freedom rather than for innocence.[8]

Needless to say, when a plea is not guilty, what is problematic is whether a criminal act occurred, and, if so, whether the defendant committed it. To understand the function of the attorney in this kind of case, it is crucial to understand the position of his formal opponent, the prosecutor. The prosecutor can dismiss charges in cases that are factually or procedurally questionable before they ever reach the court. Generally he need not introduce to court any cases but those that are quite certain to be won by him (Blumberg, 1967a: 45–46). He prosecutes primarily "sure cases" because his performance is judged chiefly by the ratio of his cases lost to his cases won. However, to route cases through the system according to this personal-success criterion may not always be to the benefit of the public. For example, the prosecutor may dismiss or nolle a case where the defendant has a particularly adept attorney even though the evidence strongly points to the defendant's guilt. While the prosecutor is formally a public servant, he must in fact detour to bureaucratic role ends that may be in conflict with the public interest. His wide discretion can virtually assure a high rate of personal success.

This puts the attorney in the position of having very tough cases to win in court. In the typical case, the weight of evidence is far heavier on the state's side because cases with weak state's evidence often do not enter court. In the few trials observed, each defense contained little beyond what is summed up in the not guilty plea itself; the judge hears the defendant merely plead not guilty with very scarce elaboration, while he hears the prosecutor pile up his relatively tall body of evidence. In the trials observed, the judge almost always responded to these cases as open-and-shut convictions.

While lower courts are called fact-finding courts, most fact-finding goes on before the court-appearance stage. Operationally, the police and the prosecutor play more of a fact-finding role than does the judge. The highly bureaucratic form of contemporary courts and the heavy caseloads almost force much of the judicial function to be relegated to the police and prosecutor. In many instances, the judge simply ratifies the judicial decisions of the processing agents who work at earlier stages of the process. It should therefore be no surprise that a main function of the attorney in court is to enter particularistic appeals for his client. It is about all there remains to be done.

The Plea

It is well known that in lower courts across the country very few suspects take advantage of their right to defend themselves against the state's accusations. Some guilty pleas are subsequent to successful negotiation. Moreover, fewer than half the defendants who go to trial are acquitted. Thus, the prosecutor is highly successful in his aim to win cases. While a given defendant may be unaware of broad prosecutorial success patterns, he may nonetheless be

---

[8]Attorneys rarely raise procedural matters in the courtroom. Just once during observation a lawyer invoked the constitution; the point was dismissed. One defendant said that he believed his arrest was improper. The judge replied, "Well, we don't want to talk about those matters now." One judge once mentioned the Supreme Court. Only in these few instances were constitutional matters brought to the fore.

aware that it would be difficult to fight the state, whether he is or is not innocent. It takes, of course, considerably more time and energy for a defendant to fight than it does to succumb to the state. To fight a court case is a disruption in the life of the defendant. What is not so often recognized is that to fight a case is also a disruption in the life of the court. Plea bargaining lessens the frequency of those disruptions.[9]

Of the defendants who enter pleas in this court, 85% plead guilty. Some of the defendants who plead not guilty in arraignments doubtlessly change their pleas in later stages of their cases. Consequently, fewer than 15% of the defendants must be given trials by the state. In the few more serious cases, the prosecutor may do some out-of-court work to obtain this high rate of guilty pleas. Still, once cases are in court for final hearings, the prosecutor hardly ever meets opposition.

Various factors are associated with the likelihood of a guilty plea. The more serious the offense charged, the less likely is the guilty plea (see Table II). In felony cases, there is a guilty plea 44% of the time; in serious misdemeanor cases, 68%; and in minor misdemeanor cases, 89%. Further breaking down the category of minor misdemeanor, in public drunkenness cases the guilty plea rate jumps to 98%. Those who have made very minor trouble for the larger society by their offenses also make extremely little trouble for the court organization.

Black defendants plead not guilty more often than do white defendants. Twenty-one percent of the black defendants but only 8% of the white defendants enter not guilty pleas (see Table III). Spanish-American defendants, too, have a rate of not guilty pleas that is almost double (14%) that of other white defendants. Even when the nature of the offense charged is held constant, black defendants protest their innocence more often than do whites. In minor misdemeanor

cases, white defendants plead guilty 95% of the time; black defendants, 83% of the time. In all other misdemeanors, the respective percentages are 88 and 69. It is unclear whether the race difference in pleas stems from more numerous instances of innocence among black defendants, fewer opportunities for them to engage in plea bargaining, greater willingness to undertake the risks of "going for broke," an unwillingness to submit to "white man's justice," a higher level of combativeness, or even ignorance of the fact that in the long run they might be better off pleading guilty. Whatever the source of the race difference in guilty pleas, it remains that blacks make a disproportionate amount of work for the court in their pursuit of justice.[10]

Because not guilty pleas are so uncommon, a total sample would have to be larger than the present one in order to understand what conditions them. It would be well worth investigating the factors that give rise to variations in rates of guilty pleas, variation both across jurisdictions and across charges within the same jurisdiction. Factors at the police level may be important. The quality of police field evidence may be associated with rates of guilty pleas. For instance, in face of police testimony defendants may tend to plead guilty independently of the seriousness of the charge. In minor cases where an arrest is made, a police officer very commonly witnesses

---

[9]Plea bargaining is not new. A form of it is to be found at least as early as the Middle Ages. However, it appears to have been quite devious. For example, see Lea (1969: 170).

[10]The presence of legal counsel has a relation to pleas. Excluding all cases of simple intoxication, where not guilty pleas and attorneys are extremely rare, the breakdown is:

Attorney	Percentage of Guilty Pleas
None	88
Private or Legal Aid	62
Public Defender	55

The presence of an attorney appears to condition the probability of a guilty plea independently of the offense charged. The pattern, however, is uneven. Considering only minor misdemeanors, the presence of an attorney decreases the likelihood of a guilty plea. In all other misdemeanors the direction is reversed. This finding on more serious misdemeanors may result from previously bargained charges and pleas. Overall, there are too few cases attended by attorneys to say anything with a high degree of certainty about their effect on plea patterns.

Table II. Percentage of Courtroom Encounters According to Offense Charged, by Plea

	Offense Charged				
	Misdemeanor				
Plea	Minor	Serious and Other	All	Felony	All Cases
Guilty	89	68	86	44	84
Not Guilty	11	32	14	55	16
Total	100	100	100	99	100
(n)	(246)	(37)	(283)	(18)	(301)

the incident himself, while in more serious cases involving arrest the evidence more often rests with citizen testimony (Black, 1968: 206–208, 249–251). Alternatively, the prosecutor rather frequently may dismiss charges if it appears that the defendant will make work or trouble for the court. This response might be especially frequent when the charge is minor. Or it may be that minor suspects plead guilty largely of their own accord. Whatever the sifting processes at the entrance to the court, it is plain that almost all the cases which do enter inconvenience the court very little. As a whole the plea pattern in the lower courtroom is such that the judge and prosecutor have little in-court work to do aside from the sentencing of defendants.

*

Offense and Disposition

Statutory maximum penalties, varying considerably over offense categories, symbolize degrees of official condemnation of diverse criminal acts (see Dahrendorf, 1968: 38–41). If the perceived possibility of future punishment deters criminal behavior at all, and surely it does, a question arises as to whether the deterrence function flows from the statutory maxima or the actual sentences typically given by the court. There is no ready reason to believe that citizens are more aware of maximum punishments than they are of actual punishments. What *does* befall offenders should be considered in conjunction with what *can* befall them when questions about

deterrence are raised. That is, the issue of deterrence should in part be approached as the "bad man" (Holmes, 1897) who seeks to predict court behavior would approach it.

The offense charged in each encounter observed (except one case of trespass) is punishable by incarceration. Still, a mere 17% of all persons convicted of any offense in this court are incarcerated (see Table IV). Hence it is first of all evident that rarely does the court punish defendants to the extent that it is able. In fact, the proportion of incarceration is lower than that for police arrest in the field when they have evidence of a criminal violation. When a suspect is available in the field situation, the police make arrests of adults in felony incidents roughly 60% of the time and in misdemeanor incidents roughly 50% of the time (Black, 1968: 201–202, 225–226, 249). Both the police and the court frequently allow suspects and offenders to go free. By no means, as it is sometimes assumed, is it clear that the greater range and use of discretion is lodged in the police. What is more, many offenses and offenders are never made known to the police, let alone to the court. Coupling this with the high proportion of suspects released by the police in the field, there is a great slippage of alleged deviants at the police level. The court plainly does not attempt to compensate for this slippage with heavy use of incarceration. The question then becomes whether potential offenders know more about the law in

Table III. Percentage of Courtroom Encounters According to Offense Charged and Race of Defendant, by Plea

Offense Charged and Race of Defendant

Plea	Misdemeanor Minor		Misdemeanor Serious and Other		Misdemeanor All		Felony		All	
	White	*Black*	*White*	*Black*	*White*	*Black*	*White*	*Black*	*White*	*Black*
Guilty	95	83	88	69	94	81	(3)	(2)	92	79
Not guilty	05	17	12	31	06	19	(3)	(2)	08	21
Total	100	100	100	100	100	100	–	–	100	100
(n)	(123)	(105)	(17)	(16)	(140)	(121)	(6)	(4)	(146)	(125)

Table IV. Percentage of Courtroom Encounters According to Offense Charged, by Disposition

| Disposition | Offense Charged | | | |
| | Misdemeanor | | | |
	Minor	Serious	Felony	All Cases
Suspended sentence	38	—	(1)	36
Fine	39	64	(3)	40
Probation	04	09	(2)	04
Probation and fine	01	18	(1)	01
Incarceration	17	—	—	16 } 17
Probation and incarceration	—[a]	09	(1)	01
Total	99	100	—	99
(n)	(221)	(11)	(8)	(240)

[a]Totals .5% or less.

action than do lawyers and social scientists. If they do, then for many offenses the deterrence potential of the threat of incarceration surely withers to a bare minimum.

The various offenses can be considered in broad categories—minor misdemeanors, serious misdemeanors, and felonies—as they relate to the disposition categories. The judge sends 17% of the minor misdemeanants to jail.[11] However, he incarcerates only 9% of those convicted of a serious misdemeanor. Oddly enough, the more serious misdemeanant is less likely to be incarcerated. In some part this results from differences in the criminal records of defendants charged with the two levels of misdemeanor. Finally, the judge incarcerated only one of the eight defendants convicted of felonies. The sample is far too small for confidence in the finding on felonies. If only because there are so few felonies, a trip through this court rarely culminates in a jail or prison visit. This pattern should not be taken as representative of the dispositions in the complete lower court system in a city similar to the one where this court is situated. As noted earlier, there are two courtrooms, only one of which was selected for observation. In the second court a greater number of serious cases are heard. It might be that more defendants convicted there are incarcerated, although nothing in the present findings compels that prediction.

Offenders must pay in dollars more often than in days in all offense categories. Of the minor misdemeanants, 38% pay fines for their offenses. Sixty-four percent of those convicted of serious misdemeanors receive fines. In other words, the more serious misdemeanant is more likely to be fined. Thus this pattern is just the opposite of that for incarceration. Undoubtedly this stems in part from the high representation of indigent offenders in the minor misdemeanor category. Often, if they are to be sanctioned at all, they must be incarcerated because they have no funds. Of the eight convicted felons observed, three received fines. If the characteristically indigent misdemeanants were removed from consideration, almost all penalties for misdemeanors would be monetary. This deprivation of money is striking against the backdrop of the market economy; the fine might not be so frequent a punishment in societies where the economic sphere is not so salient (see Christie, 1968).

A full third (36%) of all sentences are sus-

[11]The one defendant charged with a minor misdemeanor who was both incarcerated and placed on probation was a black who had pleaded not guilty and who had allegedly thrown a brick at a policeman. His case was substantively more serious than virtually all other minor misdemeanor cases.

pended. Very commonly, the court goes through the whole process of convicting offenders but then does not sanction them in any formal way. It accepts for prosecution cases the police send along but does not underscore the police sanction with a court sanction. In the long run this might lower the workload of the court somewhat, since it might decrease police incentive to arrest. In turn, however, the pattern of double leniency surely could deflate the deterrence function of the criminal process in such a way that the two forces could cancel one another out, and the number of persons formally processed would remain more constant than either factor considered alone would suggest.

Thirty-eight percent of the offenders in minor misdemeanor cases are given suspended sentences. By contrast, the judge never releases a serious misdemeanant with only a suspended sentence. Here there is a clear difference in sanctioning that flows in the expected direction. On the other hand, one of the eight convicted felons received a sentence that was suspended. In short, while incarceration varies inversely with the seriousness of misdemeanors, still some sort of material punishment is more likely as the misdemeanor is more serious. The state more frequently punishes crimes that are relatively serious and harmful, yet it reserves its jails in good part for those who repeatedly commit the pettiest of misdemeanors.

Overall, the outstanding pattern is that of legal leniency in the treatment of persons convicted by the court. It is difficult to say whether the court is more or less lenient than are the police, since the court has a variety of sanctions and the police formally have only the arrest. Considering incarceration alone, the court is far less harsh than the police. In general, the police are legally required to make an arrest whenever possible when a criminal offense is made known to them. They plainly do not (Piliavin and Briar, 1964; Black, 1968). The judge is under no such formal obligation to penalize all convicted offenders. Likewise he does not. The formal law is different for the police and for the judge, but the rates of sanctioning are quite similar. Unless social control agents themselves are regularly penalized for failing to sanction, there is no reason to expect that any control system, formal or informal, would penalize all the offenders it could. Instead they select from among the available deviants those that are to be sanctioned formally. Overlapping this group are those each social control system selects to sanction informally. The criteria of selection could be many: those singled out can be the ones who most flagrantly violated the rules, the ones who are disrespectful toward the social control agents, the ones who have a particular ascriptive characteristic such as a certain ethnicity or a certain age, or whatever.

The deterrence value of any social control system, it seems likely, is ordinarily, though not always, undermined by underenforcement of rule violations. And, among the instances of deviance that are in fact controlled, the deterrence function surely is served for the better or worse depending upon the criteria of selection. From all available evidence, neither the court nor the police appear to select for sanctioning purely on the basis of race (see e.g., Green, 1961; Trebach, 1964; Skolnick, 1966; Black, 1968; Black and Reiss, 1970). Both the police and the court in part select to sanction on the basis of the seriousness of rule violations; the more serious the violation, the more likely some sort of sanction. Furthermore, the police and, it seems impressionistically, the court select to sanction on the basis of suspects' disrespect toward control agents. What deterrence there is, then, might reach into two pockets: prevention of relatively serious victimization of the general public and prevention of victimization of the control system itself.

*

REFERENCES

Alschuler, A. W. (1968) "The prosecutor's role in plea bargaining." Univ. of Chicago Law Rev. 36 (Fall): 50–112.

Banfield, L. (1968) "Continuances in the Cook County criminal courts." Univ. of Chicago Law Rev. 35 (Winter): 259–316.

Black, D. J. (1970) "Production of crime rates." Amer. Soc. Rev. 35 (August):733–748.

———(1968) "Police encounters and social organization: an observation study." Ph.D. dissertation. University of Michigan.

Black, D. J. and A. J. Reiss, Jr. (1970) "Police control of juveniles." Amer. Soc. Rev. 35 (February) 63–77.

Blumberg, A. (1967a) "The practice of law as a confidence game: organizational cooptation of a profession." Law and Society Rev. 1 (June): 15–39.

———(1967b) Criminal Justice. Chicago: Quadrangle.

Boudin, K., B. Glick, E. Raskin, and G. Reichbach (1970) The Bust Book: What to Do Till the Lawyer Comes. New York: Grove Press.

Christie, N. (1968) "Changes in penal values," pp. 161–172 in N. Christie (ed.) Scandinavian Studies in Criminology, Vol. 2. Oslo, Norway: Universitetsforlaget.

Dahrendorf, R. (1968) "Homo sociologicus: on the history, significance, and limits of the category of social role," pp. 19–87 in R. Dahrendorf, Essays in the Theory of Society. Stanford: Stanford Univ. Press.

Green, E. (1961) Judicial Attitudes Toward Sentencing. London: Macmillan.

Holmes, O. W. (1897) "The path of the law." Harvard Law Rev. 25 (March): 457–478.

Lea, H. C. (1969) The Inquisition of the Middle Ages: Its Organization and Operation. New York: Harper Torchbooks. (Originally published in three volumes in 1887).

Messinger, S. (1955) "Organizational transformation: a case study of a declining social movement." Amer. Soc. Rev. 20 (February): 3–10.

Miller, D. and M. Schwartz (1966) "County lunacy commission hearings: some observations of commitments to a state mental hospital." Social Problems 14 (Summer): 26–35.

Newman, D. (1966) Conviction: The Determination of Guilt or Innocence Without Trial. Boston: Little, Brown.

———(1956) "Pleading guilty for consideration: a study of bargain justice." J. of Criminal Law, Criminology, and Police Sci. 46 (March-April): 780–790.

Piliavin, I. and S. Briar (1964) "Police encounters with juveniles." Amer. J. of Sociology 70 (September): 206–214.

Skolnick, J. (1967) "Social control in the adversary system." J. of Conflict Resolution 11 (March): 52–70.

———(1966) Justice Without Trial. New York: John Wiley.

Sudnow, D. (1965) "Normal crimes: sociological features of the penal code in a public defender's office." Social Problems 12 (Winter): 225–276.

Sykes, G. (1958) The Society of Captives: A Study of a Maximum Security Prison. Princeton: Princeton Univ. Press.

Trebach, A. S. (1964) The Rationing of Justice: Constitutional Rights and the Criminal Process. New Brunswick, N.J.: Rutgers Univ. Press.

Wenger, D. L. and C. R. Fletcher (1969) "The effect of legal counsel on admissions to a state mental hospital." J. of Health and Social Behavior 10 (March): 66–72.

15. Justice in a Traffic Court

GRANTE UTE

CICOUREL'S ANALYSIS OF THE "SOCIAL ORGANIZA-tion of Juvenile Justice" (1968) views the relationship between juvenile offender and police or probation officers in terms of the authorities' attempt to change the juvenile's conception of himself and to have him accept their blueprint for how his previously "unsuccessful self"may be made over into a more adaptive person.[1] Cicourel describes the rhetoric within which this exchange takes place between the "reforming" agency and the deviant, and shows, in addition, that this interaction occurs within a certain social organization which, in itself, has great effects on the temper of the ritual.

According to Cicourel, the authorities' optimal course of action is to have the juvenile voluntarily admit and express his remorse and describe his plan to reform. But the juvenile comes to the meeting hoping to gain only a brief sermon and, if necessary, a short sentence. Sermons are given to show the evils of criminal acts and to point out a general flaw in the boy's "attitude" toward life. Cicourel goes on to explain the nature of the probation officer-juvenile relationship as one of "trust"—that any actions committed by the juvenile in the time questioned were not really seen as criminal manifestations but as due to "personal" problems or circumstances. Thus, the frequently encountered "neutralizing" statement, "You didn't think, did you?" is offered.

The juvenile is faced with having to accept the authorities' definition of the situation and to play along with his structuring of the events in order to protect himself. Thus, accepting the invitation to show remorse is the most rational means to his ends—termination of the interview and the threat of the authority. "Arguing" from a very weak position (his status of delinquent), the juvenile does not have the right to question the social organization of this relationship. Given no power and the threat of further troubles in court or in the Youth Authority, the juvenile takes the probation officer up on his offer of non-placement in Juvenile Hall as a reward for a quick admission of involvement. Whether he is guilty or not, the juvenile can avoid the bad consequences of fighting the system by admitting whatever it was the officer claimed he was involved in and by accepting the officer's offer that it wasn't really purposively irresponsible (that is, criminal), but excusable on the grounds of personal problems.[2]

It can be seen that by admitting the public definition of himself and the imputed motive, the juvenile gets what he wants—the least trouble from the all-powerful authorities. The probation officer gets what he wants—a "solved" case which can be reported within a paradigm which protects him. By accepting the official view of

▶SOURCE: *"One, Two, Three, Red Light: Judicial Review in Traffic Court,"in Terry Jacobs (Ed.) Deviance: Field Studies and Self-Disclosures. Palo Alto, Calif.: National Press, 1974. Pp. 95–103. Reprinted by permission.*

[1]Aaron Cicourel, *The Social Organization of Juvenile Justice* (New York: John Wiley and Sons, Inc., 1968).

[2]See Robert Emerson, *Judging Delinquents; Context and Process in Juvenile Court* (Chicago: Aldine Publishing Co., 1969).

himself and showing appropriate remorse, the juvenile, in effect, barters away part of his self for a reduced sentence.

In order to examine the social organization of other situations within which people labeled "deviant" try to handle their identities, we sat in on several sessions of the Riverside Municipal Traffic Court. What follows is an analysis of the social organization of traffic court within which defendants (people put in the hapless position of having to protect their selves from the effects of a deviant label) are faced with a social organization which they do not understand. A description of the setting will follow along with the examples of interaction between judge and defendant which will reveal several aspects of the organization of traffic court.

In most cases, when given a citation for a moving violation one may post the bail necessary for the ticket and not appear in court. One's failure to appear is then interpreted as an admission of guilt and a fine is set at the amount of bail. The case is ended. The violator (here a "deviant") loses generally from $10 to $30 and gets a "point" on his driving record in the Department of Motor Vehicles. Other (more frequent or more serious) violators will have to appear. Thus, those who appear in traffic court tend to be those who cannot afford another citation on their record and also those who feel themselves to be innocent of the claims made against them.

What follows in court is a negotiation between the judge and the defendant which has less to do with justice and the determination of guilt than it does with neutralizing the "wrath" of the authorities (shown by the amount of the fine) and expediting justice (or enabling the judge to handle perhaps 100 cases in the two sessions of the day set aside for traffic court).

But before proceeding in our description, let us introduce the people involved. There are three people composing the court—leaving out the police officer making the citation (who is not present). They include the judge who hears the cases, a court clerk who records their disposi-

tions, and a county marshal or bailiff who explains the deposition to the defendant and generally by his presence adds to the authority of the court. On the other side of the railing sit the defendants, accused of the commission, in Ross's term, of a folk crime—traffic law violations.[3] Ross states that the "criminal behavior in folk crime is rooted, not necessarily in lower-class culture, but in the culture of groups most affected by the social or technological changes that the legislation attempts to control." Looking about *this* courtroom, we would say that the lower class is that class most affected by the automobile.

It is into this situation that the judge walks. He proceeds to address the courtroom with a speech that is well thought-out, and well-worn. The address reveals several elements of the arraignment process which will become more evident later, during the actual proceedings. The substance of his speech is as follows:

"Nobody likes to get a ticket. But look at it as a safety reminder. Don't look at this one and say how 'unlucky' you were; remember the lucky ones where you haven't been picked up. See the other side of the coin.

"It should be made clear that I get no commission on the fines collected here. The money goes to a traffic safety fund—to improve highways. There is no appeal to my own self-interest. Look at this as a United Fund contribution to reduce deaths and injuries on the highways.

"The average person receives one citation every five years. Depending on how many you have, you may be way above or under the average. This court is empowered to suspend licenses for up until six months. No one here will have his license suspended. Most fines here will fall in the $120–$600 range. You will find that the fines that this court assesses will be substantially below the possible maximum fines. As a general rule, if you are financially embarrassed, this court will allow you one month in which to pay. If you

[3]H. Laurence Ross, "Traffic Law Violation: A Folk Crime,"*Social Problems*, VIII (Winter 1960–1961), 236–237. (Reprinted in Rubington and Weinberg, *Deviance: The Interactionist Perspective*, pp. 170–172.)

do not pay in full by this date, you may work off the fine at the rate of one day in jail for every $5 of fine."

Within this speech one can clearly see an attempt to "cool out the marks"—to pacify the unlucky and unhappy defendants. The defendants are told to restructure their view of the situation they are in—to see the citation not as an unlucky event, but as a safety reminder. As for the fine (which may be substantial), they are to view it as a contribution which works toward some positive good—highway safety. Defendants are also given evidence of how they stand when compared with other drivers (it is implied that they compare poorly).

Following this assault on a defendant's view of his own driving ability (that is, on his "self") he is given a taste of what the prescribed "wrath"of the law is for the offenses which are to be handled. For a first offense, fines up to $62 may be imposed. But the judge has said that most here will fall in the $120–$600 range. Thus, the defendant realizes the serious situation he is in. He is quickly reassured that fines will be assessed far below these amounts, but the important point is that one *could be* assessed far more. The court also offers quite liberal payment plans (up to one month), with the option of paying the fine in "kind" (time at the rate of $5 per day in the county jail). Finally, any suspicion that the judge profits from your trouble is dispelled.

Viewed in this way, one's day in traffic court may be seen as embodying elements of a "degradation ceremony": both the event and the perpetrator are seen in an out-of-the-ordinary character (statistically at least); the judge is seen as a public figure with no private gain to be made from the proceedings; and the denunciation is delivered in the name of super-personal values—consideration of others and safety. (We do not believe that traffic court is a successful "degradation ceremony," however. The "wrath" generally is less moral than financial, and the courtroom's aura of fearsome majesty soon dissolves into an atmosphere of a well-meaning bureaucracy at work. Traffic court does not try to transform the social identity of the defen-

dant. Strong elements of the "collective conscience"—perhaps the most conspicuously missing element—are not really aroused. There is no real ritual denunciation of the offender, and there is no increase in group solidarity as a result of he "trial.")[4]

In discussing the social organization of the court, we will look at it from the point of view of the court—the judge, the clerk, and the bailiff. Faced with the need to handle a great many cases quickly, the judge's primary goal is to expedite justice—with the emphasis on the expedition. Like the probation officer cited by Cicourel, he makes no attempt to affix guilt or innocence; his primary concern is to clear the court calendar by the easiest means available. And the easiest means available is for the defendant to plead No Contest so the judge can affix a penalty fine on the spot. But the No Contest plea is similar to the mechanism of pleading guilty to a lesser offense, except that here one is not advised to do so by a public defender or lawyer, but subtly by the judge of the case.[5]

It should be pointed out that it appears that defendants do not realize that they may continue their Not Guilty plea and demand a trial, either by judge or jury—in the morning session, twenty-one of the fifty-three cases pleaded Not Guilty. These excerpts from notes taken in the courtroom will show the plight of the defendant before the court—especially the unsophisticated, or the first defendant before the court in each session. One of the very first persons to face the court was a woman who pleaded Not Guilty to a violation incurred as a result of an accident she had. When asked by the judge if she wanted to plead No Contest and "end the matter here," she replied, "I only want to do what's right." Although the judge didn't say so explicitly, as the morning wore on it became ob-

[4]See Harold Garfinkel, "Conditions for Successful Degradation Ceremonies," *American Journal of Sociology*, LXI (March 1956), 420–424.

[5]David Sudnow, "Normal Crimes: Sociological Features of the Penal Code," *Social Problems*, XII (Winter 1965), 255–270.

vious that for the judge "what was right" was to plead Guilty or at least No Contest. (By sitting through twenty or thirty cases before theirs was called, defendants gained some idea of what this No Contest plea meant, one could assume.)

The court's operating definition of what the No Contest pleas meant came from the bailiff, who stepped in on the case of an older man who said he didn't know what No Contest meant. The bailiff's translation ran as follows:

"You may say that you don't want to fight about it any more."

To this the defendant replied, expressing the opinion of most of the other defendants:

"I just want to get it over with."

The No Contest plea may be seen as a "surrender," in one sense, which is brought about under some of the conditions of duress. Take these examples:

J: I could settle the whole matter here if you would enter a plea of No Contest. I could determine the penalty right now.

D: Well . . .

J: Do you plead No Contest?

D: [dejectedly] I guess so.

As the morning wears on, what one gains in knowledge about the operation of the court and one's rights from watching other cases is purchased at the cost of increased inconvenience and time off from work. Take, for example, this man who felt that he was innocent:

D: I don't feel I'm guilty but I'm losing work. I've spent three hours here, and I've already been penalized. I don't want a trial.

J: Do whatever you wish, sir.

D: No Contest.

Later in the morning more and more defendants change their pleas to No Contest in order to save time and get out of court.

One well-dressed man insisted on maintaining his Not Guilty plea. With him, the judge became more explicit about the reasons why one should avoid a trial:

D: I don't want my record sullied if I'm not guilty.

J: This citation is of such a nature that it will be removed from your record after 36 months. It would take a lot longer to try [the case] if you used this type of procedure [a trial].

D: I'm interested in justice.

J: I just want to tell you.

In the morning session of approximately fifty cases, perhaps no more than three people insisted on a trial (insisted on maintaining their innocence). But the court left them the option of still avoiding trial by setting bail in the amount of the fine that would have been assessed if they had pleaded No Contest, and by informing them that the whole matter could still be closed if they would call the court the day before the trial and say that they would not appear.

Thus the No Contest plea may be seen as an instrument of speeding up court output by having the defendant surrender, either out of ignorance or boredom. If guilt were the main concern in traffic court, surely more than three or four of the twenty-one who originally pleaded Not Guilty actually should have stood by their pleas, even if it meant going to court. If one interprets the No Contest plea as a guilty plea (which one has every right to do, since a judgment is made against the defendant), it can be seen to be a means by which rates of deviancy are inflated—by getting innocent persons to accept the effects of a guilty judgment in order to avoid more trouble or inconvenience.

A second aspect of the social organization of traffic court is seen in the method of discrediting witnesses. This process has two functions: first, to make those who objectively might have a good case feel that their chances of convincing a jury would not be very good if they took the case to trial; second, to discourage those whose appearance in court is motivated solely by considerations of reducing the fine.

Discrediting in the form of the question "How many citations have you had in the last 36 months?" usually came after defendants questioned the very basis of the whole court organization—the judgment of the police officer. For example:

D: How could the police have known I was the one passing the bus, if they were 100 feet up a side street when it happened and couldn't see my license number?

J: How many citations have you had in the last 36 months?

Or, for another example:

D: This guy passed me on the right; I was maneuvering to avoid him and wasn't able to signal for my right turn. I thought the cop would go after the guy passing me.

J: How many citations have you had in the last 36 months, say?

D: [mumbles] Four.

J: Regarding the $120 which could be imposed, I'll reduce it to $19.

Here we can see the process of intimidating the defendant so he will not pursue a case that he might be able to win if it were taken to a jury trial. The defendant's story seems to have no impact on the judge. Tacitly, the defendant is told that no matter how good his story, his previously blemished record will work against him in a trial.

Others (twenty-nine of the fifty-three in the morning session) pleaded Guilty with Explanation, clearly in order to talk the judge down on the fine. Here the judge used the discrediting process (especially the question concerning a previous driving record) to counter their arguments for a lenient fine. Take these cases for examples of the bargaining:

D: I just think that a fine of $33 is too high [cut off by the judge]

J: How many citations have you had in, say, the last 36 months?

Or:

D: I don't think that the fine should be $105.

J: What do you think it should be, $500 [as prescribed by law]?

D: I just paid a fine of $38.

J: How many citations have you had in the last 36 months?

D: [mumbles.]

J: How would it be if you got a $600 fine every time you drove without a license?

The whole matter of discrediting the defendant to himself is an interesting process to watch—especially since defendants consistently guess that they have about one-half the citations that appear on their record. The judge has a copy of each driving record stapled onto the citation so he can always make a comeback—usually to the detriment of the defendant.

D: [to the judge's question of how many citations] I can't remember.

J: Had so many you can't remember. [Proceeds to read them out.]

The law provides for increased penalties for frequent offenders; it further stipulates that the question of the number of previous citations should be asked only after the determination of guilt. But in the Guilty with Explanation plea, the guilt is already admitted, so it is only a matter of bargaining over the penalty. Here, however, the question of a previous record can be used subtly to impress the defendant with the futility of insisting on pleading extenuating circumstances. It could be considered that the judge and the defendant are here sparring in a shadowy area near infringement on the defendant's constitutional rights. One defendant interpreted it this way after an especially vigorous effort by the judge to intimidate him:

J: How many citations have you had in the last 36 months?

D: 10 to 12.

J: [with a smile]: How about violations which you weren't caught on?

D: I'm here on this one; I shouldn't be judged on the others.

J: $24.

Finally, some defendants plead Guilty with Explanation *solely* to get a reduced fine. Discrediting and other mechanisms are also used by the judge in these negotiations. These people are obviously guilty and offer no extenuating circumstances, just a sad story or a cynical appeal. For example:

D: I don't want this citation on my record. That's why I'm here explaining it. I want to keep my record clean.

J: Clean record? I count four citations here on speeding in the last 12 months alone. [Sarcastically.] That's a good record to really try and keep clean! It takes some people a lifetime to build up that.

A final example, an old woman trying to avoid a ticket for parking in a red zone while she was unloading her car, shows how the judge can appeal to the gallery for laughter to get rid of the defendant.

J: How long were you "unloading?"

D: I was just inside for about an hour.

J: If you're going to park in red zones you have to dash in and dash out and not get caught. [Snickers in the gallery.]

J: [looking to gallery] I'll fine you . . . $1 on this. [Applause.]

Discrediting may be seen, then, as a mechanism for cooling out the defendant (in its extremes, it may appeal to violations the defendant was not cited for, or to direct appeals to the audience for laughter, to convince the defendant of the futility of a plea). It is a means of furthering the ends of the court—the expedition of bureaucratic justice.

As in the social organization of juvenile justice, the social organization of justice in a traffic court derives from the authorities view that the "deviant" must change his conception of his *act* in order to bring it more into line with the court's conception of it. The process of changing the defendant's plea (that is, his view of the act) is "negotiated" in the ritual of traffic court, within which both parties try to maximize their own goals (either "expedition of justice"or less "hassle" in court). Bargaining from a position of greater power, the court has the advantage of being able to manipulate the defendant into accepting its optimal disposition of the case—the fastest and most immediate resolution of the matter. It is to achieve a No Contest plea that the mechanism of discrediting is used; the defendant is further pressured by the offer of a reduced penalty for a Guilty plea.

From this exchange—a No Contest plea for a reduced fine—one can see that both parties get what they want. The court gets to handle the maximum number of cases in the alloted time, and the "offender" gets a reduced fine and the satisfaction of having the matter settled quickly. In bureaucratic justice, then, the concern is less with determining guilt or seeing justice done than with arranging the most efficient handling of the matter. To reach this goal, each side must compromise a little.

16. The Handling of Juveniles in Court

MARK M. LEVIN
ROSEMARY C. SARRI

ADJUDICATION

ADJUDICATORY HEARINGS ARE THE JUVENILE JUS-tice system's counterpart to trials in the adult criminal system. Recent U.S. Supreme Court decisions have shaped the nature of these hearings far more than the state Juvenile Codes. The founders of the juvenile court movement envisioned a paternalistic judge dispensing individualized justice in a private hearing where lawyers and due process procedures were unnecessary. Since the state's intervention was to be benevolent, the finding of jurisdictional facts to justify the state's intervention was considered of secondary importance. Because of the landmark decisions of *In Re Gault*, 387 U.S. 1 (1967), and *In Re Winship*, 397 U.S. 358(1970), adjudicatory hearings today may more nearly resemble adult trials than the well-intentioned reformers anticipated.

The adult trial is characterized by a formal, adversarial hearing open to the public, where a judge or jury finds, beyond a reasonable doubt, the facts that constitute the specific elements of a crime, from evidence presented by the prosecution and contested by defense counsel. In contrast, the prototypical adjudicatory hearing is (a) informal, (b) often private, (c) where a judge or referee, generally not a jury, (d) finds beyond a reasonable doubt the jurisdictional facts that justify the state's intervention into a child's life, (e) from information, rather than evidence, (f) presented by the prosecutor or juvenile court personnel, (g) contested by defense counsel. Each of these characteristics is examined below.

Formal Hearings
The adjudicatory hearing is informal in the vast majority of cases and is not adversarial. Only three states statutorily require that the hearing be formal if there is a contested issue of fact.[1]

Exclusion of the Public
Juvenile hearings are generally closed to the public and press by statutory provision. However, the judge is usually given ample discretion to admit "interested parties" or "persons with a legitimate interest in the case." In five states the hearing is closed *only* at the discretion of the judge.[2] In South Dakota and West Virginia, the press may be admitted to the hearing on the condition that they do not publish the juvenile's name. Several states allow the judge to release the juvenile's name to the press at his discretion. Georgia and Mississippi require publication if the juvenile is alleged delinquent for the second

►SOURCE: *Juvenile Delinquency: A Study of Juvenile Codes in the U.S. National Assessment of Juvenile Corrections. Ann Arbor, Mich.: The University of Michigan, June, 1974. Pp. 48–57. Reprinted by permission.*

[1]Calif., N.C., Ohio
[2]Colo., Conn., Fla., Ind., S. Dak.

time, and Montana requires release of the name if a felony is alleged.

Trial by Jury

In *McKiever v. Pennsylvania: In Re Burrus*, 403 U.S. 528 (1971), the Supreme Court held that a juvenile does not have a federal Constitutional right to trial by jury under the due process clause of the fourteenth amendment. Therefore, a juvenile can only have that right based on either a state constitution or state statutes. Statutory right to trial by jury exists in 10 states.[3] Alaska allows judges to use juries, including youth panels, but this procedure is discretionary.

Evidentiary Standards

In Re Winship, 397 U.S. 358 (1970), requires juvenile courts, in weighing the evidence, to adhere to the standard of "beyond a reasonable doubt,"rather than to "a preponderance of the evidence." While many state statutes require that the judge must find the juvenile guilty of the alleged offense by a preponderance of the evidence, such provisions are clearly in violation of the federal Constitution, and a conviction based on that standard would be defective.

Evidentiary Rules

No state requires the juvenile judge to follow rules of evidence in admitting information about the alleged offense. However, the admission of hearsay evidence may violate a juvenile's right to confront and cross-examine witnesses, as guaranteed by the *Gault* decision.

The reading of social investigations by the judge before a finding of the jurisdictional facts is currently a source of some debate. Social investigations consist of case histories compiled by court personnel; they usually probe the juvenile's family situation, general reputation, school records, and any other information deemed relevant. This information typically has no bearing on whether the juvenile, in fact, committed a particular offense, and would clearly be inadmissible in an adult proceeding. Two factors inherent in the juvenile court have given rise to judges' and referees' access to social investigative data prior to or at the time of the adjudication hearing. First, under the concept of *parens patriae* the court is expected to intervene to serve what it considers to be the needs of the juvenile. Second, the juvenile court has jurisdiction over "status offenses." Juveniles charged as status offenders come within the court's jurisdiction because of their general condition—incorrigibility, unruliness, waywardness—not because of specific acts of lawlessness. In these status cases a social history is considered indispensable to the prosecution of the case. The relevance of the investigation in helping the judge make an appropriate disposition is not in question, only its use before a finding of the facts is being debated. Several states recently have enacted statutory provisions prohibiting the use of this information before disposition.

Prosecutor's Role

A majority of states allow the prosecutor to present the evidence against a juvenile if the judge chooses; a few states *require* the prosecutor to present evidence. In cases where the prosecutor does not present evidence, juvenile court personnel typically perform this function.

Right to Counsel

In Re Gault, 387 U.S. 1 (1967), requires that the juvenile be assisted by legal counsel at any delinquency hearing. If the juvenile cannot afford counsel of his own choice, he has a right to court-appointed counsel. The juvenile is also entitled to assert his right against self-incrimination and the right to confront and cross-examine his accusers. The right to counsel is now statutorily guaranteed in all but 11 states.[4] The other *Gault* rulings have been enacted in only 15 states, but a denial of these

---

[3]Colo., Mich., Mont., Ohio, Okla., S. Dak., Tex., W. Va., Wis., Wyo.

[4]Ala., Del., Ky., La., Mass., N.H., N.J., N. Mex., Pa., Wash., Wis.

rights would serve as grounds for reversal of the decision.[5] None of the statutes address the issue of the juvenile's right to choose defense counsel independent of his parents. Problems in this area often arise when the court must make decisions about disposition alternatives. Thus far no statutory solutions have emerged.

DISPOSITION

The stated goal of juvenile court proponents has been and continues to be the rehabilitation of children in trouble through individualized treatment. Not surprisingly, the Juvenile Codes reflect this objective and provide the judge with an extensive battery of disposition alternatives: (1) informal handling; (2) probation; (3) foster homes; (4) fines and restitution programs; (5) private institutions; (6) public institutions on state, regional, county, and municipal levels; and (7) adult correctional institutions. A variety of agencies, in addition to the juvenile court, have responsibility for the operation, supervision, or certification of these facilities and programs.

Unfortunately, there is a dearth of statutory material about the procedures that should be followed in disposition decision-making. Unlimited discretion without guidelines dominates the disposition phase of the juvenile justice process. The interaction between the multiple agencies of commitment is rarely clear from statutory analysis. Moreover, once a juvenile is admitted into one of the disposition agencies, his stay is generally for an indefinite period, and he is without statutory protection from arbitrary actions by those empowered to make decisions. The following discussion attempts to outline what little law has been enacted.

Informal Handling

Thirty-four states statutorily sanction the disposition of children without court processing.[6]

In these states, a child, with parental consent, may be placed on probation without a formal adjudication. This process usually does not involve the judge, but is handled by court intake workers or probation personnel. Unfortunately, few state statutes do more than provide that courts "may informally handle" or "informally adjust"the case as it sees fit. In these states, the discretion of the judge to delegate disposition authority to court personnel is unlimited. Increasingly, however, statutes require either that the child as well as his parent consent to the probation arrangement, or that the child admit he committed the alleged offense. Moreover, probation is limited to a brief period, usually three months, with a possible extension of three additional months. Eleven states currently have such provisions, and all are of recent vintage.[7]

This informal probation procedure, even as statutorily limited, is of dubious merit. The voluntariness of the child's consent and the truthfulness of his confession are questionable, given the possibilities offered to the juvenile: fixed period of probation rather than possible institutionalization if he chooses the full hearing route. The child must gamble on asserting his rights. If the state seeks to intervene in a child's life, shortcuts around due process guarantees of a full hearing should not be available. Administrative convenience does not justify these procedures, which are inconsistent with traditional legal notions of fairness.

Probation

Probation is the most frequently used disposition and is statutorily sanctioned in every state. The most common statutory pattern provides for an open-ended period of probation, terminating, at the latest, when the juvenile reaches 21 or the state's age of majority. The juvenile court judge is empowered to terminate proba-

[5]Calif., Conn., D.C., Ga., Hawaii., Ill., N.Y., N.C., N. Dak., Ohio, Okla., S.C., Tenn., Vt., Wyo.
[6]Ariz., Calif., Colo., Conn., D.C., Ga., Hawaii, Ida., Ill.,

Ind., Iowa, Ky., La., Md., Mass., Mich., Miss., Mo., Mont., N.J., N. Mex., N.Y.,N.C., N. Dak., Okla., Ore., S.C., S. Dak., Tenn., Utah, Va., Wash., Wis., Wyo.
[7]Colo., Conn., Ga., Hawaii, Ill., Md., N. Dak., N.Y., S. Dak., Tenn., Wyo.

tion whenever he sees fit. The court is not required to review the case periodically, and thus gives considerable authority to probation officers. This concept of indeterminate sentencing pervades the disposition phase of the juvenile justice process. It stems from the belief that since the goal of the system is rehabilitation rather than punishment, the state retains the power of unlimited intervention. Disposition only terminates if and when rehabilitation is achieved.

Increasingly, however, statutes require juvenile courts periodically to review and rehear cases of juvenile probationers, and to set maximum time limits on probation. Seven states now require a periodic review;[8] and seven others put a time limit on a probation period.[9] The maximum time is usually set at two years, with periodic review required every six months. Provisions allowing extensions of an additional two years following a rehearing are also found in several of these states. Interestingly, New York sets differentiated maximum periods for delinquent children and for status offenders: two years for delinquents and one year for unruly children.

Foster Homes

Foster home placement is specified as a disposition alternative in all 51states. Concern about the adequacy and supervision of these homes is apparent, for in 44 states the statute specifies that a state agency (the state department of social services, public welfare, health services, youth services, or even corrections) must approve these homes prior to their use by the juvenile court. In the remaining states, this authority is vested only in juvenile courts or the county governing boards.[10]

Fines and Restitution Programs

A juvenile court judge can fine a delinquent or require him to make restitution for damage to property in 22 states.[11] No statutory limitations are placed on this power.

Private Institutions

Placement in private institutions is specified as a disposition alternative in 49 jurisdictions; only Alaska and Arizona do not have this provision. As in the foster home area, state agencies are generally delegated the responsibility to certify and set standards for operating these institutions, but in 4 states the court or county board of supervisors is responsible for supervision.[12] Since private institutions seldom limit their clientele to a single court jurisdiction, this form of supervision becomes questionable. In 6 states the Codes have no provisions for supervision of private facilities.[13] This, too, is problematic for it means that these agencies may never be checked and assessed to see that the care and treatment of juveniles meets desirable standards.

Public Institutions

State Level. If institutionalization is found to be necessary by the juvenile court, a child may be committed to a state institution. Training and industrial schools are statutorily provided for in nearly all states. Forestry and other camps are also available in 26 states.[14] However, a wide variety of state agencies operate these institutions. Authorized state agencies include: departments and bureaus of health and social services, corrections, child and youth services, family services, social welfare, child welfare, mental health, youth conservation, etc. Furthermore, specialized youth authorities, commissions, and institutional boards also function as agencies of commitment. These departments, commissions,

[8]Alaska, Colo., Iowa, Minn., S. Dak., Tenn., Utah
[9]D.C., Ga., Ida., N.Y., N.C., N. Dak., Wis.
[10]Ala., Ark., Miss., N. Mex., N.C., Okla., Tex.

[11]Ark., Calif., Colo., Del., D.C., Ky., Me., Md., Mass., Minn., Neb., N. Mex., N.Y., Ohio, Ore., Pa., S. Dak., Tenn., Utah, Va., Wis., Wyo.
[12]Ark., Miss., N. Mex., Tex.
[13]Alaska, Calif., D.C., Ga., N.C., Wash.
[14]Calif., Colo., Fla., Ga., Hawaii, Ill., Ind., Iowa, Ky., Md., Mich., Minn., Mo., Mont., Nev., N.Y., N. Dak., Ohio, Ore., Pa., S. Dak., Tenn., Tex., Utah, Wis., Wyo.

Alternatives	Number of states	
Probation	51	
Foster homes	51	
Private institutions	49	
County public institutions	24	
Fines/restitution	22	
Forestry and other camps	26	
State training schools	49	
Other state youth agencies	22	
Adult penal institutions	22	

Figure 1. Disposition Alternatives.

authorities, and boards share the states' sanction to have a juvenile committed to their care, usually for an indefinite period, with no further review of the case by the court. Most of these agencies are vested with the authority to determine when institutionalization will terminate. Many of them are also empowered to transfer a juvenile to an adult correctional institution.

As in the case of probation, indeterminate commitment ending at 21 years or the age of majority is the general practice, but several newly enacted Codes place maximum limits on institutionalization. Eight states currently have such provisions, which usually set the maximum time at two years with two-year extensions allowed following a rehearing.[15] Forty-two of the agencies of commitment in these 8 states have the authority to terminate a juvenile's commitment. This authority is usually exercised by either the director of the institution or a special juvenile parole board within the agency. Notice of the decision to release the child generally must be sent to the committing court.

In the 9 remaining states, the decision to release is made by the agency of commitment, but must be approved by the juvenile court.[16] Nineteen states permit the agency of commitment to transfer a juvenile to an adult correctional institution without approval of the juvenile court.[17] The provision only requires that the

agency find the juvenile "incorrigible" before transfer is made.

Other Dispositions.   County institutions provide a disposition alternative in 24 states.[18] These programs are generally found only in counties with considerable population; and the county governing board or a specialized committee appointed by the county board and juvenile court are usually responsible for the operation of these institutions.

Twenty-two states statutorily permit a juvenile court to commit a juvenile to an adult correctional institution.[19]

The data presented in Figure 1 summarize the range of disposition alternatives among the states as specified in the statutes. It is obvious from these findings that a few alternatives—probation, foster homes, private institutions, and state training schools—are most common in all states. The Codes seldom are explicit about decision-making among these alternatives. Choices are left to judicial discretion, and review on appeal of decisions are seldom, if ever, mentioned. The Codes also do not explicitly require that a juvenile receive service or treatment—it is merely presumed that this will take place.

[15]Colo., Conn., D.C., Ga., Md., N.Y., N. Dak., Wis.

[16]Ala., Ark., Fla., Ill., La., Miss., Nev., N.H., Pa.

[17]Ariz., Calif., Colo., Del., Ida., Ind., Mich., Mo., Mont.,

Neb., N.H., N.Y., R.I., S.C., Tenn., Vt., Va., Wash., Wyo.

[18]Ala., Alaska, Ark., Calif., Fla., Ga., Hawaii, Ill., Iowa, Kans., Ky., Mass., Mich., Minn., Mont., Nev., N.J., Ohio, Ore., Pa., Tenn., Tex., Va., Wash.

[19]Ariz., Ark., Del., Ga., Hawaii, Ida., Iowa, Kans., Ky., Me., Mont., Neb., N.H., N.J., N. Mex., N.Y., Ohio, Pa., S.C., Wash., W. Va., Wyo.

17. Pretrial Detention Alternatives
AMERICAN JUSTICE INSTITUTE

IN STRUCTURING THE STUDY OF PRETRIAL DETEN-
tion alternatives, the central issue was stated as
follows: what are the least interventionary (and
generally least costly) practices which will assure
an accused person's appearance in court? The
assumption was that court appearance is the
primary if not sole test of a practice's effectiveness in protecting the community. There is also
the question of (further) criminal acts by a person on pretrial release and controversial proposals for "preventive detention" and civil
commitment to deal with this. In recognition of
this concern, available data were reviewed on
re-arrest of pretrial releases on new charges and
results are included in the report.

In general, the approach of the study is related to recommendations on pretrial detention
by the National Advisory Commission on Criminal Justice Standards and Goals. The Commission recommended use of the least interventionary form of pretrial release necessary to assure court appearance. Its report discussed the
issue of preventive detention, but did not take a
clear position on the practice.[1]

The figure below pictures alternatives to pretrial release in relation to intervention level.

The chart illustrates the fact that alternatives
run along a continuum of increasing controls or
sanctions. A great variety of practices are followed from one place to another and others can
be conceptualized. Those listed here are commonly used—although not all of them will be
found in any given jurisdiction. Some practices
may be combined—for example, third party release with monetary bail; monitoring or supervision of persons released on "percentage" bail.
What is sometimes called "jail O.R." may be practiced in lieu of citation by arresting agencies.

Important variations in how particular practices are carried out are occasioned by differences in authority to make decisions. Who
makes the decision, for one thing, tends to determine how long a defendant will be in custody,
as a minimum, once he is arrested. Pretrial jail
operating costs and capacity requirements are
affected by the relative use of the various practices and the length of time required for decisions to be made on those booked into the facility. Obviously, use of summons and citation represent a 100% savings for the jail not only in relation to detention space requirements but booking facilities and operations.* Prompt release of
those eligible from the jail's booking center (e.g.,
within an average of an hour or two) keeps
down the number of prisoners confined at any
one time.

Figure 2 pictures the relationship between
time in custody and the locus of authority to
decide on pretrial release. (The percentage

▶SOURCE: *Pretrial Release and Diversion, Publication of "The
Alternatives to Jail Incarceration Project," for the National Insti-
tute of Law Enforcement and Criminal Justice, Law Enforcement
Assistance Administration, Department of Justice. Pp. I–1 to I–11;
Notes 3–5. Reprinted by permission.*

[1]See report of the National Advisory Commission on
Criminal Justice Standards and Goals: *Corrections,* Chapter 4.

*If these practices are newly introduced or significantly
expanded—savings will be less than 100%, since some of
those summoned or cited will be booked into jail on "failure
to appear" warrants.

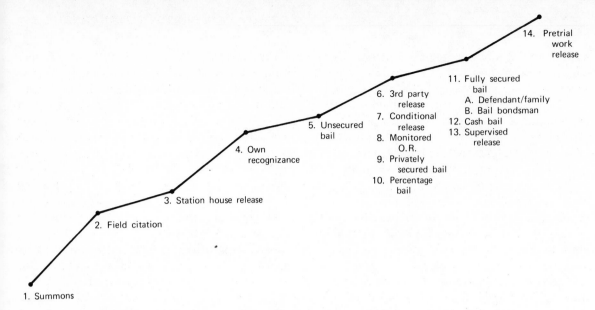

Figure 1. Pretrial detention alternatives.

Releasing Authority	Release Mode	% Usage	Illustrative Goals for Policy Planning				
			Average Hours Detained				
			0	1	3	8	X + 4
Arresting officer	Field citation	10.0					
Desk sergeant	Stationhouse release						

Court representative	Own recognizance
	Scheduled bail
	   Cash
	   Percentage
	   (bondsman)
		60.0					

Lower court	Own recognizance Unsecured bail Third party Conditional Supervised Secured bail Pretrial work release	20.0					
Same or superior court	Any of above	10.0					

Figure 2. Release authority and detention time.

216

figures and number of hours in custody are for illustrative purposes and do not represent policy proposals.)

Where the officer in the field elects to issue a citation, time in custody is shown as nil. The assumed consumption of an average of one hour in custody for stationhouse release would not affect the pretrial jail. The illustrative goal is an average of three hours in custody for those who may be released after booking by a "court representative." This would be a staff member of the jail or other representative of the court empowered to accept bail, issue a citation, or approve release on recognizance.

Where the decision is left to the court at initial hearing the suggested goal of eight hours in custody is based on the National Advisory Commission's standard (4.5.1) requiring presentation of the arrestee and facts of the charge to a magistrate within six hours of arrest—the additional two hours is for tasks necessary to implement the court's decision to release. Where a defendant is not released following initial hearing but later succeeds in gaining bail reduction or some other favorable decision by a judge, the illustrative time allowance is 4 hours plus X (X being whatever time expired from arrest until the decision which eventuates in the defendant's release).

No attempt is made here to explain further or justify these figures, since they are only illustrative of the point made above that locus of the decision effects time in custody and therefore jail capacity requirements.

HISTORICAL OVERVIEW

Detention alternatives to be discussed in sections which follow cover three groupings: use of summons in lieu of arrest warrant; citation in lieu of arrest and detention; pretrial release after booking. Before considering these practices separately, however, certain material is presented which is relevant for all of them, beginning with a brief historical overview.

Traditionally, the normal flow of arrestees into the criminal justice system is accomplished by the arrest of an individual who has: (1) committed a misdemeanor in the presence of a police officer or (2) given the police officer probable cause to believe that a felony has been committed. Arrests are for the most part made physically at the scene of the alleged offense, although a significant number of arrests are made by warrants when there is probable cause to believe that the person named has committed the specified offense.

A normal incident of arrest has historically included detention to insure the appearance of the arrestee at trial. This practice is still widely considered to be the normative approach, although there have been some alternatives to physical arrest and detention utilized over the years.

The roots of pretrial release programs as we know them in the United States are to be found in common law England where it was possible "to issue a summons instead of a warrant for arrest for the commission of any offense, even a felony, if he (the judge) is satisfied that the person summoned will appear".[2]

In 1927 Arthur Beeley began a study of the bail system in Chicago. "Beeley found that the bail system was badly administered in Chicago. . . . He also discovered that the setting of bail amount was more a result of arbitrary standards than it was a function of assessing the accused's personality, social history, financial ability and integrity."[3] These findings apparently led Beeley, and later Foote,[4] in a 1954 study of the administration of bail in Philadelphia, to recommend an increased use of the summons for lesser offenses, on the premise that reliance on the bail system was discrim-

[2]"Some Proposals for Modernizing the Law of Arrests." *California Law Review*, Vol. 39, pp. 107–108 (1951).

[3]"Analysis of the Citation System in Evanston, Illinois: Its Value, Constitutionality Viability." *Journal of Criminal Law and Criminology*, Vol. 65:76.

[4]*Ibid*, p. 78.

inatory to indigents and arbitrary in its administration.

Other findings by Foote led him to recommend that release procedures be designed to look at the background characteristics of offenders (e.g., ties to the community, nature of the offense, etc.) in arriving at the decision of whether the offender should be released.[5]

In the 1960's the Manhattan Bail Project (1961) sponsored by the VERA Foundation was established to test the relationship of non-monetary bond release and the likelihood of appsarance at trial. The Manhattan Project was initially established separately from the court and served in an advisory capacity. Background characteristics based on residency, length of employment, nature of the offense, etc. were used to estimate the strength of the arrestee's ties with the community as an indicator of reliability that the arrestee would appear voluntarily at trial if released. The first such Program was termed release on recognizance (ROR) which occurred only after booking and served as an alternative to the posting of bail.[6]

SPREAD OF ROR PROGRAMS

An outgrowth of the Manhattan Project experience was proliferation of similar "ROR" projects around the country and two national conferences in 1964 and 1965. The Federal Congress, in 1966, passed the Federal Bail Reform Act which, in effect, set forth a right of federal arrestees to be considered for non-monetary pretrial release. In this same period pioneer legislation in Illinois betokened the eventual elimination of the professional bail bondsman system, as well as promising more liberal pretrial release of at least some less affluent arrestees. This was the so-called "10 percent bail" law.[7]

The U.S. Office of Economic Opportunity was a catalyst during the middle and late sixties in promoting ROR programs through funding of scores of projects across the country. As this source of federal aid dried up, some of the slack was taken up by the newly emerging Law Enforcement Assistance Administration in the U.S. Department of Justice. Ultimately of course local communities, or states, would or will have to take over financial support of these programs if they are to be viable. At this time there is evidence that this is occurring, although some programs have expired and the future of others remains uncertain.

SOME KEY ASSUMPTIONS

In the study which led to preparation of this report, all known published evidence on pretrial release rates and failure rates was reviewed. Several pretrial release agencies were visited for first-hand observation. Discussions were held with staff and other concerned officials. Project staff attended the 1975 and 1976 annual conferences of the National Association of Pretrial Service Agencies. Criminal justice data from several jurisdictions were restructured and analyzed to supplement previously published reports on experience with pretrial release.[8]

These efforts have not produced unassailable knowledge. But they did lead to adoption of certain assumptions which have support from the documented experiences of courts, law enforcement, and pretrial service agencies. These are complemented by additional assumptions of a "common sense" nature. The assumptions are as follows:

1. The earlier the decision not to detain an accused person can be made and implemented,

---

[5]*Ibid*, p. 77.

[6]See "Manhattan Bail Project: An Interim Report on the Use of Pre-Trial Parole." *NYU Law Review* 38:67 (1963).

[7]Concluding chapter of *Bail Reform: Present and Future*. Wayne H. Thomas, Jr. Scheduled for publication in 1976 by University of California Press.

[8]Some thirty jurisdictions in twelve states and the District of Columbia were visited in the course of the project. In addition materials were obtained by correspondence from scores of other criminal justice agencies, representing practically all the states.

assuming its accuracy, the less cost to the taxpayer and the arrestee.

2.   A jurisdiction could set as a goal almost any level of pretrial release use—e.g., percentage of arrestees to be released or, conversely, held for trial—without exceeding rates to be found somewhere in the country. In other words, there are no upper or lower limits on pretrial release that can be established through review of contemporary practice. Out of considerations of law, humanity, community protection, and use of its public resources each jurisdiction must set a policy it can live with.

3.   It is not possible to predict a specific failure rate for a given level of pretrial release in a jurisdiction. The range of failure rates across the country is wide, and the pattern is somewhat erratic. But, given certain information, the probable range within which a jurisdiction's failure rate will fall can be estimated. Such predictions can be improved upon, over time, in a jurisdiction which maintains certain records faithfully.

4.   Average length of time in pretrial release status is a major factor in failure rates—that is, *willful failure to appear in court or rearrest* are more likely to occur the longer final disposition of cases is delayed.

5.   Characteristics and circumstances of the defendant appear to be predictive of failure or success, but not strongly so, most especially any one factor taken alone. Still, with sufficient information, it is possible to distinguish with some sureness between good and poor risks. Imposing special conditions, keeping in touch with the releasee, verifying his court appearances, and providing needed socio-economic services appear to enhance the prospects of success for higher risk individuals.

Careful screening and assessment of candidates for pretrial release and effectively matching them with appropriate conditions and services should permit a liberal release rate without consequent high failure rates. This should aid in pursuing the goal of equal justice for defendants without regard to financial resources or community position. Provision for prompt disposition in higher risk cases should help counteract effects of the "time factor" referred to in Assumption 4.[9]

[9]Studies have identified various characteristics and circumstances of defendants which are associated with variations in likelihood of appearance or failure to appear in court. Studies associated with the early Vera Institute demonstration of recognizance release in New York City stressed the importance of stable residence, close family ties, and steady employment as predictors of reliability.

Later experience and studies have found that the type of criminal charge may be predictive of failure (with less serious offenses generally associated with higher failure rates). Criminal record is also a predictor. Continuing research raises questions as to how strongly predictive any single factor is—and even clusters of factors. For example, a cohort of defendants may earn a "poor score" on a schedule of numerous factors, and it may be predictable that a substantial proportion—say a third—will fail to appear. But six or seven out of ten of persons with such a score will appear, and there is no objective basis for deciding, in an individual case, whether the person will fall in the failure or success group.

Another problem is that what research has been done has yielded some inconsistent findings. What may hold for arrestees at one point in time in one jurisdiction may not prove useful in predicting outcomes later or in another location.

Research reports which deal with prediction of failure to appear and/or commission of new offenses while on pretrial release include:

The Bail System in Charlotte: 1971–1973. Steven H. Clarke. Institute of Government. University of North Carolina at Chapel Hill. April, 1974.

Compilation and Use of Criminal Court Data in Relation to Pretrial Release of Defendants: Pilot Study. Locke, Penn, Bunten, and Hare. National Bureau of Standards Technical Note 535. Washington, D.C. Issued August, 1970.

"An Empirical Analysis of Pretrial Release Decisions." *Journal of Criminal Justice.* Michael R. Gottfredson. Vol. 2, p. 293. 1974.

"Preventive Detention: An Empirical Analysis." *Harvard Civil Rights—Civil Liberties Law Review.* Arthur R. Angel et al. Vol. 6, p. 300. 1971.

Bail and Parole Jumping in Manhattan in 1967. S. Andrew Schaffer. Vera Institute of Justice. N.Y.C., 1970.

"Legal Theory and Reality: Some Evidence on Criminal Procedure." *Journal of Legal Studies.* Vol. 3, p. 287. June, 1974.

EARLY DECISIONS

Booking a person into jail is an expensive procedure—estimated cost $24.00 per case or a quarter of a billion dollars a year nationwide. Holding him in jail is estimated to cost, on the average, $19 a day (estimated national cost is about a billion dollars a year; this includes booking costs).

Reduced time in custody—or avoidance of the booking process altogether—promises significant dollar savings in many jurisdictions (i.e., those not already making optimal use of pretrial alternatives). There are obvious benefits to the accused person from use of summons or citation in lieu of arrest or, in the absence of these, minimal detention pending pretrial release. Some of these defendant benefits—e.g., ability to remain employed—also benefit the community.

Early decisions, of course, are more readily made in cases involving less serious charges—since it is more feasible to delegate authority for these to people in early contact with the defendant, the arresting officer, for example. Also affecting the speed with which decisions can be made is the availability of easily verifiable information. Where court action is required, early release—especially for nighttime or weekend releasees—cannot be achieved without some arrangement for more or less "around-the-clock" availability of judges.

GOAL SETTING

If a jurisdiction's jail is crowded or there are complaints on other grounds of pretrial detention policies, assembling the relevant facts is a first step in policy review or planning. Such a study should point up the current level of use of various alternatives to detention; salient characteristics of prisoners held until final disposition; time required, on the average, for pretrial release decisions as well as to process defendants from arrest until sentence or dismissal of charges.

Such an analysis will lay the groundwork for considering possible policy changes. It will also permit a subsequent assessment of how fully such changes are carried out and the resultant effects. This would be so, especially, if the new policies are made explicit through establishing goals for the use of various pretrial release alternatives—e.g., increase use of citation in misdemeanor cases from 5% of arrests to 15 or 20%; increase use of release on recognizance in felony cases from 20% to 40%; establish a supervised pretrial release program to permit an average caseload of 100 persons in this status; shorten processing time in detained felony cases from an average of eight to three months; etc.

18. Problems with Bail

PAUL B. WICE

ONE OF THE MOST PUBLICIZED AND TROUBLESOME problems facing the administrators of the nation's criminal justice system is the misconduct of defendants released prior to their trials. This pretrial misconduct is manifested in two types of illegal activities: failing to appear for trial and committing additional crimes during this pretrial period. . . .

FORFEITURE RATE

Dimensions of the Problem

The failure to appear for trial is reflected in a forfeiture rate. This statistic is of vital importance in evaluating the effectiveness of a system of pretrial release. A high forfeiture rate indicates that those judicial officials responsible for making the decision to release defendants have been very poor predictors of the defendant's future behavior. Once this high rate has been publicized, it can usually be expected that those defendants unlucky enough to face the judge in the immediate future, will find themselves forced to raise exceedingly high bail amounts.

An equally important consequence of a high forfeiture rate is that the court system is made aware of the failings of its present methods of notification and supervision. This means that many defendants failed to appear because the court simply failed to give them clear notice of their next appearance date or was unwilling or

▶SOURCE: *Freedom for Sale. Lexington, Mass.: Lexington Books, 1974. Pp. 65–80; 193–194. Reprinted by permission.*

unable to communicate this information to the defendant during his pretrial release. Since this pretrial period often reaches four to six months, it is imperative that defendants receive additional supervision and communication during this time. It has been estimated that nearly half of all forfeitures are involuntary and caused by the defendant's either forgetting about the court date or never being adequately notified.

A final significance attached to this forfeiture statistic is that it may be used as a means to discredit the bail-setting practices of certain judges who are releasing defendants on their own recognizance or nominal bond. By being able to illustrate the high forfeiture rate associated with either of these release procedures, public pressure can be mounted against the continued use of such practices.

Although the forfeiture rate appears to be a critical statistic in evaluating and ultimately operating a bail system, there are several difficulties in relying upon these statistics as they are offered to the public. Like any statistic, they are easily manipulated to indicate whatever the court system or reform group wishes to emphasize. The forfeiture rate is even more prone to these machinations since it is a highly discretionary decision by the court system as to when a forfeiture has actually taken place. In cities wishing to reform their bail system and permit increasing numbers of defendants to obtain their pretrial release, they will liberally interpret when a forfeiture has taken place. They may stipulate that a forfeiture has occurred only after the defendant has had a day or two in which to come to court and has been reminded of his tardy appearance. This approach will usually result in a city having a low or at least a respectable forfeiture rate.

In other cities which may be wishing to discredit these liberal efforts and stress the need to stop coddling criminals, the forfeiture rate will be strictly interpreted. A defendant who appears one minute late for his court appearance, regardless of any possible excuse, will be counted as a forfeiture. Such a narrow literal interpretation will raise the forfeiture rate to its optimal level. An example of a city court system utilizing this strict interpretation is the Recorder's Court of Detroit, Michigan, which seems intent on pressuring judges into not releasing defendants on their own recognizance. The annual report of the Detroit Recorder's Court in 1969 presented the alarming figures that 40 percent of the defendants ROR'd (released on their own recognizance) had forfeited. This figure is nearly ten times the estimated average reported for the nation in this study. By using the following two techniques, the recorder's court was able to inflate this statistic to the highest degree possible: First, the court used an extremely strict definition of forfeiture so that every defendant who failed to appear at the exact time was counted as a forfeiture. As we have noted, half of the defendants would eventually appear within forty-eight hours so that we can cut the 40 percent to a more realistic 20 percent rate, Secondly, if a defendant did willingly forfeit, every required court appearance was counted as a *separate* forfeiture. In other words, a defendant skipping town after his initial appearance in court would miss his preliminary hearing, grand jury indictment (or information), arraignment, trial, and finally, the sentencing. In Detroit this defendant would be counted as having committed five forfeitures. Now when we reexamine the 20 percent figure and realize that it may comprise up to five forfeitures per defendant who has voluntarily left the city, we can arrive at a much more reasonable 4 to 7 percent forfeiture rate which is consistent with the national figures.

An additional difficulty in relying upon these forfeiture statistics is that most court systems either do not keep these figures, or if they do, it is in a rather careless fashion and not scientifically valid. Even the state of California, which is so often pictured as having the premier court administration in the country, does not collect these forfeiture statistics. It should also be pointed out that this entire discussion of the difficulties in obtaining reliable and valid forfeiture rate statistics is found to an even greater degree when one attempts to evaluate the amount of additional crimes which are committed by defendants awaiting trial.

With all of these caveats in mind, let us now see how many forfeitures are currently taking place around the country. Turning first to the large urban centers which were personally visited and where court reports were inspected, the eight cities listed in Table I have an average forfeiture rate of 7.8%. This table not only indicates an exact percentage for each city but also presents the exact source of the figure.

Since Table I reported the exact forfeiture rate in only eight cities, all of which are major urban centers with populations exceeding half a million, it was necessary to conduct a mailed survey of an additional seventy-two cities encompassing a wide range of sizes, if one were to obtain a truly national picture of the problem. Judges, prosecutors, criminal lawyers, and bail project directors were asked to estimate the percentage of defendants in their community who forfeited bond. A forfeiture rate was determined for each city by averaging the estimates of the public officials who completed the questionnaire.

The overwhelming majority of cities (80 percent) reported that between 0 to 9 percent of all released defendants failed to appear for their trial. There were also twelve cities (17 percent) which estimated that between 10 and 19 percent of their defendants forfeited their appearance. These forfeiture rates seem to correspond with

Table I. Forfeiture Rates

	Rate	Source of Statistics and Clarification
Chicago	8.7%	Clerk of Circuit Court of Cook County (1969)
Philadelphia	4.0%	Estimate by Court Administrator (1970)
Indianapolis	5.4%	Survey by Indianapolis Bail Project (1969) Surety Bonds
Detroit	24.0%	Recorders Court Annual Report (1969) 8% for Surety Bonds, 40% for personal bonds
Baltimore	5.0%	Estimate by public officials and bondsmen
Atlanta	7.0%	Exact figure from District Attorney's Office
St. Louis	5.0%	Exact figure from Clerk of Circuit Court, Criminal Division
Washintgon	3.7%	Exact figure from the Report of the D.C. Judicial Court, Report on the Operation of Bail (1969)

other studies which have estimated them to be between 3 and 7 percent. In comparing the estimated forfeiture rates of defendants ROR'd with those released through payment of bail, the ROR defendants were only slightly more responsible. Sixty-three cities (87 percent) estimated that 0 to 9 percent of all ROR'd defendants failed to show up for their trial. Fifty-eight cities (80 percent) estimated that 0 to 9 percent of all money bail defendants failed to appear. The one difference between the two groups, and it was minor, were the estimates in three cities that they had forfeiture rates over 30 percent for defendants released on money bail. In either case, the problem of forfeiture occurs in only about 5 percent of the total number of cases. Even this figure of 5 percent is subject to revision on practical grounds. It was stated previously that approximately half of those recorded forfeitures are merely technical or involuntary, and the defendant eventually appeared when notified of his tardiness.

In judging whether the amount of forfeitures has changed during the past five years, the results of the survey indicate that, like the crime rate, most cities have also experienced a dramatic rise in forfeiture rates. This increase has occurred for both ROR'd and money bail defendants. Only 1 percent of the responding cities thought there had been a reduction. Fifty-four percent of the cities found increasing forfeiture rates for bailed defendants, while 52 percent of the cities experienced increasing forfeitures for ROR'd defendants.

The study was unable to identify any significant explanatory variables derived from the demographic structure of a city to explain its forfeiture rate. This in itself indicates that the problem of defendants failing to appear for trial is truly national in scope, plaguing all types and sizes of cities. The only demographic variable which appears to hint at a possible relationship is a city's crime rate, but even this is an extremely weak correlation (0.2019).

Once a forfeiture has occurred, the judge before which the missing defendant is supposed to appear will sign a bench warrant for the defendant's rearrest. The bondsmen as well as the police then spring into action hoping to recapture the tardy suspect. Most cities studied were unable to successfully recapture very many of the defendants who willfully avoided their court appearance. The large majority of defendants who are located and reappear have usually unintentionally failed to show. Their excuses range from illness to poor memories. The small group of willful forfeitures who are recaptured are primarily those unfortunate defendants who were apprehended for an additional crime during the pretrial period. If a defendant purposely forfeits bail he will usually "skip town," and there is almost no chance of recapturing him.

An explanation of this inability to serve these bench warrants for forfeitures was offered by Paul Michel of the Philadelphia District Attorney's Office, which currently has 6000 unserved warrants for failure to appear. He believes that those agencies attempting to serve these warrants usually have no idea where these missing men are and possess no adequate staff to locate them. The problem has reached its present proportions because the courts and the bondsmen have failed to keep close contact with released defendants during the pretrial period.[1]

Because of the muddled state of record keeping and the jammed court calendars, even a defendant who forfeits unintentionally by reporting late, has caused irreparable harm to the functioning of the urban criminal court system. Experienced criminals soon realize that it is more advantageous to simply show up late than to try to evade the police by skipping town or going into hiding. This tardiness causes great confusion and often results in a case being dismissed. In an attempt to rectify this situation, Judge Tim Murphy of the District of Columbia's Court of General Sessions recommends that a foolproof warrant squad be created. They would be notified the second the defendant failed to show up and would immediately move out after him. He would then be returned to court so quickly that his case would not have to be continued.[2]

One of the continuing controversies in the administration of bail is how many of these forfeitures are technical or unintentional and how many are willful. Officials interviewed on this subject agreed that the majority of forfeitures were unintentional. The only attempt to scientifically study this question was done by the Cook County Special Bail Project which found that well over half of the I bonds (personal bonds for release on recognizance by the judge) forfeited in 1968 were of a technical nature. Once bonds were vacated for illiness, misunderstanding, and a long list of other excuses, the forfeiture rate was cut in more than half.[3]

Two of the main reasons for these technical forfeitures is the fault of the court system rather than the defendant. The first is the extremely poor notification system used by the courts to inform the defendant of his court date. In many cities the defendant is notified of his next appearance by the judge, or more commonly by the court clerk. This notification is simply an oral statement made at the conclusion of the proceeding. Remembering the lower intelligence of most defendants, the noise and confusion of the courtroom, and the strangeness of the entire proceeding, it is little wonder that more defendants do not fail to appear. In a few of the more conscientious cities, this oral notification may be followed by a written reminder mailed to the defendant's last known address. The court, which mails this note several weeks after the initial appearance, never finds out whether this notice is ever received.

A second reason is the poor quality of the clerical administering of this notification system. Exacerbating this problem even more is the confusion and strangeness of the entire judicial process. Public Defender Hooley of Oakland, California, commented that since so many defendants are transients and indigents, they are hampered by a poor sense of timing and reliability which also contributes to their negligent behavior.[4] Commenting further on the difficulty of reaching these transient and impoverished defendants, Judge Davis of Indianapolis be-

---

[1]Interview with Paul Michel, Philadelphia District Attorney's Office, December 1970.

[2]Interview with Judge Tim Murphy of the Court of General Sessions, Washington, D.C., December 1970.

[3]Cook County Special Bail Project "Proposal for Holiday Court Interviewer—Verification Program," May 4, 1971, p. 7.

[4]Interview with Public Defender Hooley, Oakland, California, August 1970.

lieves that many of these defendants cannot be reached because they have no phone, and move around a great deal without leaving a forwarding address. The Judge warns, however, that all the blame should not be placed on the courts. He and several other judges interviewed in other cities believe that the bondsmen have not been doing their job. They are failing to keep close enough contact with their clients to guarantee their appearance.[5]

Once it is certain that a defendant has forfeited, the city must collect the total amount of the bond from the surety. A great deal of confusion exists in the various cities studied as to exactly when the courts have officially declared a forfeiture to have occurred and demand payment of the bond. Even as the bond is collected, many courts allow the bondsman an opportunity to convince the judge that the cause of forfeiture was not their fault and that they had made a diligent and honest effort to recapture the defendant. If the judge is convinced, he may set aside the entire forfeiture, or a percentage of it.

In nearly every state and city it is a crime to forfeit one's bond. These forfeitures are usually categorized as a serious misdemeanor, frequently carrying a one or two-year maximum prison sentence. It is argued that rigid implementation of these criminal statutes would help to reduce the forfeiture rate. When one closely examines the current operations of our court systems, it can be seen that merely adding on an additional penalty would have little effect. With our criminal justice system plagued by a tremendous backlog of cases and all court officials devoted to the important task of moving these cases through this assembly-line process, the plea-bargaining system has developed as the only feasible solution to the current dilemma. The addition of one count of bail forfeiture to the already existing plethora of charges against

[5]Interview with Judge Davis of the Indianapolis Criminal Courts, November 1970.

the defendant, who is manipulating to have a reduced charge and light sentence in return for a guilty plea, is insignificant at best. All such charges, it should be remembered, are usually permitted to run concurrently.

How Can It Be Reduced?

So far our discussion of bail forfeitures has dealt with the magnitude of the problem and only tangentially focused upon the important question of how to reduce their numbers. This question which we must now squarely face is, given the present administration of bail, what procedures and measures can be adopted for eliminating (or at least controlling) this problem? Examples of operational procedures which may affect the forfeiture rate are the following: (1) how the defendant is notified of his next court appearance; (2) where and when this notification is made; (3) the presence of a bondsman; (4) the presence of a system to validate the information about the defendant; and (5) the presence of a system to supervise the defendant during his pretrial release. Table II indicates that of these five procedures, only the presence of a supervisory system during release and the place of notification are related to a reduced forfeiture rate.

The procedures found to be most significant were the operation of a system to supervise the defendants during their pretrial release. These supervisory programs were found primarily in cities operating bail reform projects. The supervisory function is manifested through certain requirements placed upon the defendants. The most common requirement was to have the defendant report in to the bail project or court clerk on a periodic basis, usually every two weeks. The defendant reported in by phone in most cities although a few required an occasional personal visit. If the defendant failed to report in on one or more occasions, the court system and the bail project would attempt to use informal means to locate the missing defendant

Table II. Forefeiture Rates and Operational Procedures

Procedural Variables	The Forfeiture Rate	
	Below the National Average	Above the National Average
1. Place of Notification		
At the Court	7 (77%)	21 (37%)
At a later date	2 (23%)	35 (63%)
2. Method of Notification		
Oral Notice	12 (63%)	17 (55%)
Written Notice	7 (37%)	21 (45%)
3. Presence of a Bondsmen		
Absent	6 (21%)	8 (22%)
Present	23 (79%)	28 (78%)
4. Verification System		
No	24 (67%)	26 (76%)
Yes	12 (33%)	8 (24%)
5. Supervisory System		
No	15 (31%)	14 (64%)
Yes	33 (69%)	8 (36%)

before issuing a bench warrant for his rearrest. The importance of such a supervisory system can be seen from the statistics in Table II which show that nearly 70 percent of the cities operating a supervisory program are experiencing a *below* average forfeiture rate while 65 percent of those cities plagued by a forfeiture rate *above* the national average have failed to install such a system.

A second procedure related to the forfeiture rate is the place where the defendant is notified of his next court appearance. It was found that cities which notified defendants at the courthouse rather than at a later date (and usually done through the mail), were able to maintain a below average forfeiture rate in nearly 80 percent of the cities surveyed. Only 23 percent of those cities notifying defendants after the bail hearing were able to possess a below average forfeiture rate. The necessity for notifying the defendant, before he leaves the courtroom of his next appearance date was emphasized in several interviews with court officials. Many defendants are transient, and once they depart the courthouse, they are very difficult to locate. Their lifestyle involves frequent changes of address, often without leaving any forwarding

notice. Many of these defendants are also nearly impossible to locate by phone. Many who are indigent or are temporary boarders in a rooming house cannot afford the luxury of a phone. A final complication is the unwillingness of many to follow the normal work schedule of middle-class citizens and who therefore, cannot be reached at a regular scheduled time. All these difficulties simply reinforce the fact that it is imperative that notification, if it is to have any value, must be done before the defendant leaves the courthouse and supervision must be carefully planned and rigorously implemented.

A second set of explanatory variables related to a city's forfeiture rate is the type of release criteria which the local court system uses to determine if the defendant is to be released or the amount of bail to be set. The officials in each of the seventy-two cities were asked to evaluate the importance of each of the following criteria used to determine pretrial release: present charge; past criminal record; likelihood of committing a future crime; strength of community ties; and his past appearance record. It is frequently hypothesized by defenders of a strict law and order system that the seriousness of the present charge and the defendant's past crimi-

Table III. Release Criteria and the Forefeiture Rate

	Forfeiture Rate	
Release Variables	Below the National Average	Above the National Average
1. Present Charge		
Unimportant, Slightly Important	9 (48%)	15 (30%)
Extremely Important	10 (52)	35 (70)
2. Past Records		
Unimportant, Slightly Important	8 (42)	14 (27)
Extremely Important	11 (58)	37 (73)
3. Likelihood of Future Crimes		
Unimportant, Slightly Important	8 (38)	14 (33)
Extremely Important	13 (62)	28 (67)
4. Community Ties		
Unimportant, Slightly Important	6 (33)	26 (61)
Extremely Important	12 (67)	17 (31)
5. Past Appearance Record		
Unimportant, Slightly Important	8 (36)	29 (58)
Extremely Important	14 (64)	21 (42)

nal record are the most important criteria in attempting to predict a defendant's pretrial behavior and should therefore be stressed by those cities attempting to decrease their forfeiture rates. Table III relates these criteria to the forfeiture rates of each city in the survey and arrives at some rather unexpected results for the law and order advocates.

As critics of the traditional bail system have continually advocated, there seems to be no relationship between the seriousness of the charge against a defendant and his proclivity toward forfeiting his bail. Table III indicates that the defendant's community ties and his past appearance record are the most reliable pretrial release criteria used to predict a defendant's appearance in court. Sixty-seven percent of those cities who considered community ties to be an extremely important pretrial release criteria had a forfeiture rate below the national average. It should also be noted that 64 percent of those cities stressing the importance of the defendant's past appearance record also experienced below average forfeiture rates. Turning now to the traditional criteria of seriousness of the present charge and past criminal record, one finds them to be of very little predictive value. Seventy

percent of those cities considering the seriousness of the charge to be an extremely important release criteria experienced *above* average forfeiture rates. In a similar vein, 63 percent of the cities stressing the defendant's past record had *above* average forfeiture rates. The results of Table III conclude that judicial systems wishing to control the forfeiture rates of pretrial releases should emphasize the defendants community ties and past appearance record, rather than maintaining faith in the traditional criteria of a defendant's present charges and past criminal record.

Are any types of cities more prone to be suffering from excessive forfeiture rates? The results of this survey, after controlling for city size, percentage black, percentage engaged in manufacturing, median income and geographic region, concluded that these demographic characteristics were not statistically related to the forfeiture problem. It may therefore be inferred from this finding that the forfeiture problem is nationwide and not concentrated in any particular category of city. Based on the information derived from Tables II and III, if we are to successfully fight the forfeiture problem, we must attack it in all types of cities, stressing the need to create viable supervisory programs and convince the judiciary to emphasize the community ties and past appearance record of defendants when they are considering a defendant's pretrial release.

ADDITIONAL CRIMES: THE REARREST RATE

Dimensions of the Problem

An even more serious type of pretrial misconduct by the defendant is when he commits an additional crime while awaiting his trial. These incidents are frequently well publicized and indict the entire criminal court system. They are also the death knell for any attempt at initiating bail reform projects in a community. These additional crimes are not only significant to the administration of bail by their inherently serious nature, but also because they have been used as a rationale for enacting preventive detention legislation. Presently only the District of Columbia Criminal Courts have such a provision, but former Attorney General Mitchell recently sent a new legislative proposal to Congress that would allow federal courts to hold without bail persons accused of specific dangerous or organized crime acts. How many crimes are actually committed by defendants awaiting trial? This question cannot be answered accurately on the basis of the present state of available statistical data. The author discovered that reliable statistics on the rearrest rate during pretrial release were an even more elusive statistic than the forfeiture rates just discussed.

Because of the current controversy surrounding preventive detention, the seriousness of this problem (additional crimes during pretrial release) is of great importance to policy decisions related to the pretrial activities of defendants. If it can be determined that large numbers of defendants are actually committing additional crimes during the pretrial period, this fact will serve as a justification for future preventive detention statutes. With this important policy question at stake, it is no wonder that so much confusion surrounds the issue of exactly how many additional crimes are actually committed by defendants awaiting trial.

The recent statistical warfare in Washington, D.C., which occurred just prior to the passage of the city's preventive detention provision, is an extreme example of this confusing state of affairs. It began with the finding of the D.C. Crime Commission that between January 1963 and October 1965 out of a surveyed 2,776 defendants held by the grand jury, 7.4% percent were charged with a felony while on bond. In December of 1968 this percentage increased to 7.6 percent in a study by the U.S. Attorney's Office for the first nine months of 1968. The Metropolitan Police Department, believing those statistics seriously underestimated the amount of crime committed by defendants during their pretrial release, conducted their own study which indicated that a shocking 35 percent of the defendants had committed an additional crime while awaiting trial. The Police Department's findings alarmed the public and served as a catalyst for a movement to enact a preventive detention statute for the District in order to detain these dangerous felons behind bars. Liberal skeptics attacked the department's study. A careful review by legal scholars and statisticians either discredited its accuracy or raised several crucial questions as to whether it could be relied upon as an objective analysis of the problem.[6]

In a final attempt to produce a definitive and reliable measure of the amount of crime committed by defendants on pretrial release, the National Institute of Law Enforcement of the Department of Justice financed a study by the National Bureau of Standards. This 208-page study was to be the last word on this subject—an unbiased statement of exactly how serious the

[6]Norman Lefstein, "Analysis of Metropolitan Police Department's Study Concerning Crime on Bail," January 22, 1969. Preventive Detention Hearings before the Constitutional Rights Subcommittee of U.S. Senate Committee on the Judiciary.

Table IV. Statistical Summary of Pretrial Misconduct

% of total Defendants	% rearrested		% forfeitures	
	1. ROR'd	2. Money bail	1. ROR'D	2. Money bail
0-9%	79% (57)	66% (48)	87% (63)	80% (58)
10-19%	13% (9)	18% (13)	11% (8)	13% (9)
20-29%	6% (4)	6% (4)	1% (1)	4% (3)
30-39%	3% (2)	7% (5)	—	3% (2)
40-49%	—	3% (2)	—	—
50-59%	—	—	—	—
60-69%	—	—	—	—
70-79%	—	—	—	—
80-89%	—	—	—	—
90-99%	—	—	—	—
National Average for 72 cities	6.4%	8.2%	2.8%	3%

problem of additional crimes on bail was in the District of Columbia. Despite limited criticism of methodological flaws, the report was accepted as an accurate and objective statement of the problem. The report found that 11.7 percent of the defendants committed additional crimes (felonies) while awaiting trial.[7] The only other city to have conducted a detailed analysis of this problem was Indianapolis which, interestingly enough, discovered a rearrest rate of 11 percent, only seven-tenths of 1 percent off the D.C. figure from the Bureau of Standards report.[8] The similarity between the results obtained in these two rigorous examinations of the pretrial rearrest rate indicates that our major urban centers are experiencing rearrest rates slightly above 10 percent.

Table IV presents the results of the seventy-two-city survey which attempted to measure both types of pretrial misconduct. This national survey estimated the country's rearrest rate to be approximately 7 percent. One explanation

[7]United States Department of Commerce, National Bureau of Standards Report, "Compilation and Use of Criminal Court Data in Relation to Pretrial Release of Defendants," Washington, D.C., March 1970, p. 161.

[8]Indianapolis Bail Project Report, "Rate of Crime on Bail," January–February 1970, (mimeographed).

for this figure being 4 percentage points below the scientific Indianapolis and Washington studies is that the national survey contained at least thirty cities with populations under 200,000. With so many smaller cities in the national sample, it is reasonable to expect them to have lower crime rates than the metropolises of Washington and Indianapolis. One would also expect the rearrest problem to be less severe in smaller cities. Forty-five cities in the national sample estimated a rearrest rate of less than 10 percent and fifteen cities estimated a rate between 10 and 19 percent.

Are defendants released on their own recognizance any more likely to commit additional crimes than those who have obtained their release through the traditional process of raising the required money bond? Table IV refutes the claim of bondsmen as to their predictive abilities and supervisory diligence, by indicating that the ROR'd defendants had the lower rearrest rates. Though the difference was very slight, 6.4 percent for those ROR'd to 8.2 percent for those raising money bail, these figures are a challenge to critics of bail reform who believe that these projects are releasing many poor risks whose pretrial misconduct is a threat to society. This survey has discovered that it is those defendants

Table V. The Importance of Demographic Variables to the Rearrest Rate

Demographic Variables	Defendants Rearrested	
	(1) Below National Average	(2) Above National Average
1. Population		
a. Less than 200,000	30 (79%)	9 (21%)
b. More than 200,000	16 (16%)	17 (52%)
2. Nonwhites		
a. Less than 12.5%	23 (61%)	15 (39%)
b. More than 12.5%	20 (58%)	11 (35%)
3. Poverty Level		
a. Below national average	20 (69%)	9 (31%)
b. Above national average	23 (58%)	17 (42%)
4. Crime Rate		
a. Below national average[a]	15 (63%)	9 (37%)
b. Above national average	13 (52%)	12 (48%)

[a] The national average crime rate is a 2000 Uniform Crime Index based on the *FBI Annual Report* (1971).

Note: All numbers and percentages refer to cities in each category.

released on money bail who appear to have the greater inclination toward criminal behavior, and it is therefore this group which should be screened more carefully.

What trends have taken place in the past five years with regard to this rearrest rate? Has the percentage of defendants committing additional crimes during pretrial release increased at a pace similar to the highly publicized national increase in crime reported by the FBI's *Uniform Crime Report*? It was found that half of the cities surveyed experienced an increase in the number of crimes committed by defendants awaiting trial for another crime. Of the remaining cities, thirty-three saw no change at all while two perceived a decrease in the rearrest rate since 1965. Those defendants released on bail payment seemed to be causing a slightly higher rate of increase in the number of defendants rearrested as compared with ROR'd defendants. Fifty-one percent of the cities believed there was an increasing rearrest rate for bail defendants while 43 percent of the sample saw an increasing rearrest rate for ROR'd defendants.

It appears from Table V that an increasing rate of defendants being rearrested while await-ing trial is a regular feature of our larger cities which are experiencing severe increases in their overall crime rate. With court congestion in these larger cities permitting defendants five to six months of pretrial freedom, it is quite understandable that by the conclusion of this lengthy period additional crimes may be committed. A recent study by the *Temple University Law Review* has documented the fact that nearly two-thirds of those crimes committed by defendants awaiting trial were done after the defendant had been released for at least three months.[9] Thus by instituting procedures to speed up the court delay to only a two- or three-month period, the large majority of these crimes may not have been attempted. The financial situation of defendants who have lost their job or must quickly raise large amounts of money to pay a lawyer or bondsman's fee creates the type of monetary pressure which could conceivably drive a defendant to commit additional crimes.

A humorous, yet pathetic, incident related by a Detroit bondsman illustrates the kind of illogi-

[9] "Preventive Detention: An Empirical Analysis" *Harvard Civil Rights Law Review* 6 (March 1971) 291.

Table VI. Additional Crime Rate and Operational Procedures

	The Forfeiture Rate	
Procedural Variables	Below the National Average	Above the National Average
1. Place of Notification		
At the Court	13 (48%)	21 (47%)
At a later date	14 (52)	23 (53)
2. Method of Notification		
Oral Notice	16 (52)	19 (47)
Written Notice	15 (48)	21 (53)
3. Verification System		
No	14 (61)	28 (72)
Yes	9 (39)	11 (28)
4. Supervisory System		
No	9 (38)	18 (54)
Yes	23 (72)	12 (46)
5. Presence of a Bondsman		
No	9 (24)	8 (25)
Yes	28 (76)	24 (75)

cal actions which may be taken by defendants forced to exist under these types of pressures. The bondsman stated that during the previous week a client of his who was originally arrested for auto theft was late for his preliminary hearing. The bondsman knew his client from previous business dealings and immediately called him up and told him to hurry down to the courthouse. The defendant, in his haste to make his court appearance, stole a car in order to eliminate further delay. Unfortunately he was arrested five blocks from the courthouse.[10]

Which type of defendants seem to have the greatest proclivity toward committing additional crimes while awaiting trial? No consensus of these recidivistic categories of crimes was discovered, with the exception of narcotics-related offenses. Most judges had their own particular hypotheses regarding which types of criminals were the poorest risks. Examples of this range in preferences are the following: (1) Judge Freund, Los Angeles—armed robbery; (2) Judge Sharpe, Indianapolis—prostitution and

gambling; and (3) Judge Little, Atlanta—shoplifting.[11]

How Can It Be Reduced?

Based on the results of the prior analysis of reducing the forfeiture rate, it is logical to hypothesize that the best way to reduce the amount of crime committed by defendants awaiting trial is to develop a viable system of supervision during the pretrial period. As Table VI illustrates, those cities who do conduct some type of supervisory control over the defendants during the pretrial period are least likely to be suffering from an above-average additional crime rate. The presence of a supervisory system was the only procedure which was found to be significantly related to the dependent variable, the additional crime rate.

Seventy-two percent of cities currently using a system of pretrial supervision of released defendants have an additional crime rate less than the national average. Additional proof of the importance of this supervision in reducing pre-

[10]Confidential interview with Detroit bondsman, November 1970.

[11]Information obtained through interviews with men in each city, September 1970–February 1971.

trial criminal behavior is found in Table VI which shows that nearly half of the cities not using a supervisory system experienced an additional crime rate above the survey's national average. The explanation for the effectiveness of such a system in reducing pretrial crime is the same as was offered to show its ability to diminish the forfeiture rate. By forcing the defendant to report to the court system or bail project, he believes that his conduct is under surveillance and is therefore more inhibited from engaging in criminal activities. This is not to say that all defendants have strong predilections toward a variety of illicit and illegal activities. The commission of additional crimes has been estimated as involving only 5 to 10 percent of the total number of defendants released prior to their trial.

Before the court system is forced to decide how best to control the defendant's pretrial behavior, a more basic question must be raised. What considerations should be weighed and emphasized in the determination of what types of defendants should be released, and the amount of their bond? The release criteria listed in Table VII indicate that none of these criteria are significantly related to the defendant's proclivity for engaging in pretrial criminal behavior. The implication is that there is little the courts can do in accurately predicting the defendant's pretrial criminal actions.

The only variable which shows even the slightest relationship to the issue of additional crimes is the criterion of the defendant's past appearance record. In approximately 65 percent of the cities surveyed, those which considered past appearance record as extremely important possessed pretrial crime rates below the survey's average. Meanwhile, less than a third of those cities who considered past appearance record only slightly important could claim additional crime rates below this average. A possible explanation for this relationship is that the past appearance record seems to be the most reliable indicator of a defendant's tendency toward misbehaving during the pretrial period, regardless of whether the misbehavior is willfully failing to appear for trial or committing additional crimes. If a defendant has a history of appearing for court, this type of responsible behavior may also be manifested in a desire to avoid criminal activities during the pretrial period.

It has been continually inferred in this and other studies of the bail system that the length of time a defendant awaits trial is a highly significant variable affecting the likelihood that he will engage in criminal activity during his pretrial release.[12] The cities with the greatest backlog of criminal cases, permitting the defendant approximately four to six months of pretrial freedom, are consistently plagued by high rearrest rates. Combining this fact with the findings in this selection which have been unable to significantly relate any procedural or release criteria to a reduction of the additonal crime rate, it appears that the only avenue open to a city attempting to reduce pretrial crime is to decrease the existing period of court delay from arrest to trial by eliminating the backlog of cases.

It is interesting to note that neither the defendant's past criminal record nor his present charge were found to be criteria significantly related to a defendant's committing additional crimes during his pretrial release. This finding should come as a disappointment to defenders of preventive detention statutes similar to the one in Washington, D.C. This limited survey, however, cannot be interpreted as totally discrediting the concept of preventive detention. The Washington operation is of very short duration and is of such a cumbersome procedural nature as to be nearly impossible to implement. It seems therefore that before condemning the criterion of a defendant's likelihood of committing future crimes, the mechanism of preventive detention should be given an opportunity to clarify and streamline its procedures. Once the process has undergone a sufficient trial period,

[12] N. H. Cogan, "Pennsylvania Bail Provisions: The Legality of Preventive Detention." *Temple Law Quarterly* 44 (Fall, 1970):51.

Table VII. Release Criteria and the Additional Crime Rate

Release Variables	Additional Crime Rate	
	Below the National Average	Above the National Average
1. Present Charge		
Unimportant, Slightly Important	8 (27%)	10 (26%)
Extremely Important	21 (73)	29 (74)
2. Past Record		
Unimportant, Slightly Important	7 (23)	9 (24)
Extremely Important	23 (77)	29 (76)
3. Likelihood of Future Crimes		
Unimportant, Slightly Important	11 (35)	14 (37)
Extremely Important	20 (65)	24 (63)
4. Community Ties		
Unimportant, Slightly Important	18 (60)	23 (68)
Extremely Important	12 (40)	11 (32)
5. Past Appearance Record		
Unimportant, Slightly Important	11 (34)	22 (69)
Extremely Important	19 (66)	0 (31)

with the public being made more aware of its potential use, it can be more accurately evaluated as a viable criterion in determining pretrial release. Most critics of preventive detention point to its potential for misuse as a weapon against certain defendants deemed "undesirable" and "dangerous" by the courts. Whether or not this system can reduce the number of crimes committed during the pretrial period or will simply be improperly manipulated against selected defendants are questions only time can answer.

As with the forfeiture rates, demographic variables are of little value in accounting for the variation in additional crimes committed during the pretrial period. The only variable significantly related is the city's crime rate which had a correlation coefficient of 0.265 at significance level of 0.02. This is a rather unstartling finding since one would expect that cities bothered by high crime rates would also be experiencing a high percentage of crimes being committed during the pretrial period by defendants awaiting trial. The fact that demographic variables were not found to influence the pretrial crime rate would seem to indicate that this is a national problem, as was the forfeiture rate, and not restricted to any type of city or to be blamed on any particular type of defendant.

In concluding this selection, two points should be remembered as being of primary importance. First, both types of pretrial misconduct involve a very small percentage of the released defendants. Secondly, the most sensible way to reduce even these few cases is not through setting higher bonds but rather through operating an effective supervisory system over the defendants during their pretrial release.

19. Plea Bargaining

DONALD J. NEWMAN

BY FAR THE MAJORITY OF AMERICAN CRIMINALS
are convicted by their own guilty pleas. Various
estimates of the number of guilty pleas put the
national proportion close to 90% of all those
charged with serious crimes.[1] If minor
offenses—misdemeanors—are included, the
frequency of convictions by plea approaches
98% of all those charged. And in many, if not
most jurisdictions, a high percentage of such
pleas are the result of bargaining between state
and accused.

Interestingly, the proportion of pleas remains
about the same whether the court district is metropolitan and crowded or rural and less overburdened. The percentage of people pleading
guilty to crimes in Vermont is about the same as
the percentage of "cop outs" in New York City.

Most defendants who are so "probably guilty"
as to be indicted, waive their chances—remote
perhaps—for acquittal, and plead guilty hoping
for some sentencing mercy from the court. In
fact a high proportion of them seek to negotiate
this leniency prior to entering their pleas. In
brief, not only is the guilty plea characteristic of
American criminal justice, but "plea bargaining"
is common, even normative, in many jurisdictions.

A person accused of a crime, who in fact is

guilty of *some* criminal conduct, understandably
has two major concerns: whether the state can
prove the case against him and if so what will
happen to him at sentencing. He also may be
worried about other corollary matters such as
possible reputational damage flowing from the
publicity of a trial even if he is later acquitted, or
he may wish to modify the charge by which he is
labeled after conviction.

Conviction of a misdemeanor is almost always
better than a felony conviction—the negative
consequences of the record itself are much less
severe and the sentence is usually shorter—and
conviction for assault generally provides a label
more vague and less implicitly depraved than
conviction of rape.

There is in every guilty plea an "implicit bargain" with the state, for defendants usually expect and in fact receive greater leniency if they
plead guilty than if they put the state through
the time, expense and uncertainty of a trial.

This poses an important and controversial
question for sentencing judges. The majority
position of polled judges was that it was perfectly proper for the court to show some sentence leniency to the pleading defendant but
not, however, to give the defendant who went to
trial a *longer* sentence. Instead, the reasoning
went, it was all right to shorten terms of "repen-
tant" offenders who admitted guilt and save the
state the expense and time of trials.[2]

In 1968, a committee of the American Bar

►SOURCE: *"Reshaping the Deal," Trial (March/April, 1973),
9: 11–15. Reprinted by permission.*

[1]See Donald J. Newman, *Conviction: The Determination of
Guilt or Innocence Without Trial.* (Boston: Little, Brown,
1966).

[2]Pilot Institute on Sentencing, 26 F.R.D. 285 (1960).

Association, charged to develop "minimum standards" for criminal justice administration, formally took the position that it was a proper exercise of discretion for the judge to reflect in his sentencing determination the fact that the defendant pleaded guilty.[3]

THE NEGOTIATED PLEA

Throwing oneself on the mercy of the court is one thing; arranging for charge and sentencing concession ahead of time is, or may be, a more complex and even more controversial issue. When the term "plea bargaining" is used, it rarely refers to simple mercy-of-the-court situations. What is generally meant is a prearraignment "deal" between the prosecution and the defense in which charges are dropped (in spite of sufficient evidence) or where specific sentence promises are made in exchange for the defendant's willingness to plead guilty. There is ample research today to indicate that plea negotiations are common, even routine, in many—perhaps all—jurisdictions in the country.

At present there is a good deal of interest in this topic, not only on the part of lawyers and judges but among the general public as well, and it is interesting to speculate as to why plea bargaining has become an issue of controversy and concern at this time.

Plea agreements are not new; in all probability such bargaining has gone on as long as there have been criminal courts. While it wouldn't surprise many knowledgeable court observers to learn that Cain had pleaded to a lesser charge after having murdered Abel, until recently the various practices of plea bargaining were discussed only by habitues of the criminal courts.

One reason why practices of plea bargaining have not been accorded more public attention is that the whole process in the past was essentially a private, out-of-court, virtually invisible matter.

In many places the actual open-court process of pleading guilty takes perhaps five minutes even in cases involving the most complex or heinous crimes. At a typical arraignment, the defendant is brought before the court, warned of his rights, hears the charge read and asked to plead to it. If he pleads guilty and the judge is satisfied that the plea is "voluntary," he stands convicted as surely as if he had had a three-month jury trial.

Out-of-court negotiations and arrangements have customarily been made off-the-record, sub rosa, in the prosecutor's office or in the hallways of the courthouse. Not only is the process non-public but, as might be expected, successful plea bargaining rarely has reached the appellate court level where, after all, the great legal debates take place and controversial issues are resolved. If a defendant charged with murder offers to plead guilty to assault and is convicted and sentenced accordingly there is no injured party to bring an appeal.

The state has won a conviction, the defendant has benefited from the lesser charge and lower sentence, no major legal controversies have been raised, and the smooth, quick and relatively anonymous plea process has worked to the benefit of all—with the possible exception of the victim who is dead in any case, but even in nonhomicide cases has no standing to prosecute or to appeal in criminal matters. This means that the practice of plea bargaining has been largely confined to the workings of trial courts, coming infrequently to appellate court attention.

Professional literature in law and social sciences made scattered references to negotiation practices but until recently it was of minimum interest to legal scholars and social scientists alike. In the 1950's the American Bar Association sponsored a research study of the *Criminal Lawyer*[4] out of which came a few prominent

---

[3]American Bar Association, *Standards Relating to Pleas of Guilty,* Approved Draft 1968, Sec. 1.8.

[4]Arthur L. Wood, *Criminal Lawyer* (New Haven: College and University Press, 1967). See also Newman, "Pleading Guilty For Considerations: A Study of Bargain Justice," 46 *J. Crim. L., C. & P. S.* 780 (1956).

journal articles which detailed some of the bargaining practices in selected jurisdictions. These received scholarly attention but did little to modify or influence court decisions or practices.

About ten years later the American Bar Foundation began a comprehensive survey of criminal justice administration in the United States. As part of this, one area of research (and one of the five volumes of results) was devoted to the guilty plea generally and to practices of plea negotiation in detail.

This book (*Conviction: The Determination of Guilt or Innocence Without Trial,* Little Brown, 1966) in turn influenced the reports of the President's Crime Commission, became the basis of the American Bar Association's recommended guilty plea standards, influenced changes in federal rules of criminal procedure and provided general information about bargaining for citation in a number of appellate court decisions, including decisions of the United States Supreme Court. By the 1970's, plea bargaining was and is an open and hotly debated issue in courts, conferences and even in the press and other media.

PLEA NEGOTIATION PRACTICES

While research has shown plea bargaining to be common in courts across the land, there are variations in types of plea-agreements and in the actual procedures followed by prosecutors and defense in different jurisdictions. Part of this variation is the result of differences in criminal codes, especially sentencing provisions, from one place to another. In states with statutorily mandated sentences for certain crimes (20-to-life for armed robbery, for example), the only way a defendant can achieve sentence leniency is to have the charges lowered. In other places, where indeterminate sentences are common and the judge has wide discretion to choose among types and lengths of sentences regardless of charge, reduction is less important than a pre-plea promise from the prosecutor to "re-commend" probation or some other lenient penalty.

The way a typical bargaining session works is as follows: A defendant is apprehended and initially charged with armed robbery, an offense carrying a mandatory minimum prison term of 20 years. Either on his own or through counsel he indicates to the prosecutor a willingness to plead guilty to a lesser crime in order to avoid the mandatory sentence of the higher charge.

In some cases, though actually a settlement process, negotiation can be quite adversary in its own right. The defense counsel may indicate to the prosecutor that he thinks the state has no evidence against his client except possibly a charge of disorderly conduct. The prosecutor in turn may state that he is not only going to push the armed robbery charge but plans to level a special count of being a habitual offender unless the defendant cooperates. Defense counsel then offers to have his client plead guilty to petty larceny with the prosecutor countering by offering to reduce the charge to second degree robbery.

So it goes. Eventually an agreed upon lesser charge—burglary or grand larceny, for example—may result and the defendant will plead guilty, facing at most a substantially reduced prison sentence and at best perhaps probation.

If the defendant wishes to be placed on probation, he may push in negotiation for more than charge reduction. He may also ask the prosecuting attorney to promise that at sentencing the state will "recommend" probation if and when asked by the court. This is a customary (though not universal) practice.

A prosecutor's recommendation of probation is a strong factor in the defendants favor although a weaker, and also a vigorously sought after promise, is for the prosecutor to make no recommendation at the time of sentencing or to agree "not to oppose" probation if requested by the defendant. After all, the offender knows that should the prosecutor arise at sentencing and recommend a long prison term (perhaps reading prior convictions into the record) it is highly likely that incarceration will result.

Therefore, in most jurisdictions, a preplea sentence promise by the prosecutor is a major concession, even though the district attorney has no official authority to actually impose sentence.

There are other considerations that occasionally arise in plea negotiation depending upon the particular defendant, the crime or crimes charged and the sentencing structure and practices of the jurisdiction in question.

For example, often a person arrested for one crime is subsequently charged with others. It is rare that a burglar is apprehended on his first attempt and, once nabbed, the police may "solve" 20 or 30 separate burglaries, all potential charges against the defendant. Theoretically he could be tried on each count and could receive consecutive sentences. If, for example, he were accused of ten burglaries, tried separately on each and convicted on only half yet got one to three on each (to be served consecutively) he would in effect face a five to fifteen-year sentence. Therefore he may seek to have charges joined into a single accusation, or have some of the counts dismissed if he is willing to plead to one or perhaps two.

Additionally, some offenders may be facing a habitual offender rap, which is normally filed as a separate indictment or information. In exchange for pleading to the crime as charged he may avoid such "supercharging" by the state. Then, too, some defendants are on parole or probation for prior convictions and may negotiate for revocation of the old sentence if the new charge is dismissed or sufficiently reduced.

There is even some "lateral" bargaining, primarily to modify the conviction label without affecting sentence at all. Some defendants are willing to plead guilty to serious crimes such as robbery to avoid conviction of certain sex crimes like rape or sodomy because, while the potential sentence may be longer, the label and its attendant consequences throughout the life of the defendant are considered to be a better deal.

Permutations and combinations of plea agreements are almost endless especially where multiple charges are involved, but the end result is always the same: The defendant is allowed to plead guilty to lesser offenses or receives a preadjudication sentence promise in exchange for his willingness to give up his right to trial.

WHY PLEA BARGAIN

Motivations of the guilty defendant in plea bargaining are readily discernible. He wishes to minimize both the sentence which follows conviction and the label which attaches to it. He also usually hopes to avoid publicity, not only for himself, but perhaps to protect his family and friends from likely notoriety if he demands trial. Occasionally he may wish to protect accomplices or confederates by taking the rap himself.

The bargaining motivations of the state are somewhat less readily discernible, though in every instance the bargained plea is much more efficient, cheaper and more certain than a contested case.

There are, however, other more subtle but no less important motivations on the part of the prosecutor and other state officials for engaging in plea negotiation and in fact encouraging it. Some of these are self-seeking, but others rest on a sincere attempt to individualize justice, to build equity into a system that otherwise would be too harsh in certain types of cases.

One of the self-seeking motivations on the part of the state is to avoid challenge not only of the amount of evidence but the ways it was obtained. In spite of all the current controversy about illegal searches, wiretaps, failure to give *Miranda* warnings and the like, such issues are really paramount only in cases where pretrial motions are denied and which go to trial.

A plea of guilty waives almost all defects in the state's case. The way evidence was obtained is never tested. Whether the *Miranda* warning was given or not is irrelevant in the case of the defendant who pleads guilty. The insanity defense, or entrapment, and other important procedural and substantive issues are mooted by the guilty plea.

In short, the guilty plea doesn't refine and hone the law, rather it avoids sticky questions of police practices, prosecutorial trial skills and even the adequacy of legislative sentencing provisions. Furthermore, in most cases the plea satisfies all interested parties. The defendant has his deal; the prosecutor has an assured conviction (for a trial, no matter how carefully prepared, is always an uncertainty given the vagaries of juries), the victim is theoretically satisfied by conviction of the prepetrator and correctional agencies receive an offender who has admitted his guilt. It is always a difficult task for correctional authorities who receive an offender who, though sentenced after a full jury trial, still protests his innocence. How does rehabilitation begin?

At any rate, given the absence of challenge to police methods at one end, and a confessed criminal received in prison at the other, there is more than simple overcrowding behind the state's willingness to accept the plea. It is not only a quick and efficient way of processing defendants, it is a safe way, for pleading defendants do not rock the boat.

There are, however, a number of other state considerations underlying plea negotiation that are less self-seeking, and perhaps more consistent with a general desire to build equity into our criminal justice system, particularly in regard to sentencing.

It is common practice in many state legislatures (and in Congress as well) for very severe laws to be passed in the heat of anger or at the height of public indignation over what appears to be a serious crime wave. A few years ago about half the states adopted very harsh "sex psychopath" laws. In recent years a number of states have adopted severe sale-of-narcotic laws, mandating life imprisonment or even death to "pushers."

In passing such laws the drafters typically have in mind the worst offenders—the organized criminal or the professional dope-fiend who sells heroin to school children or is otherwise the most vicious or professional violator. However, in the day-to-day operation of courts the types of sale-of-narcotics defendants who appear are rarely professional heroin pushers but are more likely to be young men or women who have sold a couple of pills or marijuana cigarettes to friends.

Technically they are guilty of sale of narcotics and in most cases there is little doubt that the evidence held by the state is sufficient to prove the charge. Yet confronted with these cases it is a rare prosecutor or trial judge who wishes to give a mandatory life sentence (sometimes non-paroleable) to an 18-year-old offender whose crime is selling a few reefers to a buddy. On the other hand the district attorney may be unwilling or reluctant to dismiss the case entirely so that the lesser charge of "possession" or some related crime may be offered as a desirable solution.

This motivation pattern for bargaining is an extension of traditional prosecutor's discretion but here instead of dismissing the case the prosecutor in effect sentences the defendant. The reason for this is the nature of criminal law itself. Legislation defining crimes and fixing penalties is necessarily general and broad and if the prosecutor and other court officials are confronted with individual cases which, while they technically fit the same statutory category, are readily distinguishable in terms of the actual harm they have done to victims or to the social order in general they can only achieve individualization of sentences by reducing charges. There are a number of such situations where charge reduction is used to individualize justice without really violating the legislative intent of proceeding against very serious criminals.

In addition to the avoidance of inappropriately excessive mandatory sentences, other motivations which have been identified are:

• reduction to avoid a criminal label which

would imply in the public mind that the defendant was guilty of conduct which is really not consistent with the actions that form his criminal violation.

For example, in a case in which a number of college students were having a noisy party in an apartment near their campus, the police arrested and charged the student owner of the apartment with, of all things, "operating a disorderly house." Confronted with this charge, the trial judge explained to the prosecutor and the arresting police officer that the connotations of such a label were so negative that he would not accept the plea of guilty even though the offense was a misdemeanor. The charge was modified (not really reduced) to disorderly conduct.

This label of disorderly conduct against the male owner of an apartment was not felt to be particularly onerous or misleading. However, in another case where a girl was arrested for shoplifting and charged with disorderly conduct, a trial judge refused to accept the plea to this count, pointing out that a record of disorderly conduct in the case of a young girl could be wrongfully interpreted as involving sexual misbehavior, whereas the charge of petty larceny (again not really a lesser charge) would likely be less damaging to the defendant in the long run.

● where there is a crime involving codefendants of unequal culpability. This is simply a recognition of the prosecutor's discretion to distinguish what the legislatures cannot do; that is, to determine the degree of involvement in a single offense on the part of multiple persons involved in a crime.

An older, sophisticated armed robber who has as a look-out a young, inexperienced, clean-record accomplice may be convicted "on the nose" but his accomplice offered a lesser charge (perhaps attempted robbery or burglary) to balance culpability and consequences. The same thing occurs when there are other mitigating circumstances in the crime, such as the participation of the victim in the criminal activity itself as, for example, in certain forms of confidence games.

● where the therapeutic benefits of alternative sentences can best be achieved by charge reduction or by awarding probation when normally such would not be the case. This is indeed a mercy-of-the-court situation but one which ignores the other administrative advantages of negotiation.

This is an extension of sentencing discretion, with primary concern to place the defendant in the best correctional setting possible which might be precluded if he's convicted on the nose. A mandatory prison term for a good-risk young violator may be more damaging to the community in the long run than if he is given a break on his first sentence.

● reduction to support law enforcement efforts by rewarding informants, state witnesses and the like with lesser charges and sentences. This is sometimes called "trading the little ones for the big ones," but the fact remains that unless differential court leniency is shown major cases cannot be developed.

This is harder to justify on propriety grounds if one is initially unwilling to support an informant system. If, however, the relationship between the activities of the court and the activities of law enforcement is conceded, then a decision about the propriety of using charge reduction or sentencing leniency must be made.

In short, there are a number of circumstances that arise in daily operation of any court system where it seems not only more efficient but more fair to utilize charge reduction or other assured leniency in sentencing to achieve more equitable justice. This is a part of the whole process that is rarely understood and, for that matter, rarely considered when plea bargaining is discussed.

The prevailing attitude toward the process (until recently at least) on the part of many, including some appellate courts, is that there is something dirty about plea bargaining, something corruptive or potentially corruptive in negotiating with criminals for punishment less than could be levied if the full force of the law were used. While it is true that from one perspective plea negotiation does act to avoid legislative mandate, and, like the exercise of all administrative discretion, has the *potential* for corruption, another side of the coin is presented by equity decisions, by a conscientious attempt to introduce "justice" into individual cases.

When translating the law from the abstract of statutes and cases to individual persons, there is always room for discretion properly applied by appropriate officials. If such discretion were denied our criminal justice system would, in the words of Judge Charles Breitel, be "ordered but intolerable."[5]

IS 'SETTLING' PROPER?

Increasing awareness of the widespread nature of plea negotiation in the trial courts has raised a continual storm of controversy. Some legal scholars and judges, though used to "settling" all kinds of civil legal matters from estates to disputed automobile accidents, see the settlement of criminal cases as different and somehow abhorrent to American criminal justice ideology.

A well-known case of a bargained plea coming before the U.S. Court of Appeals of the Fifth Circuit, elicited from one judge the flat statement that "liberty and justice are not subjects for bargaining and barter."[6]

An appellate judge in Michigan commented; ". . . the negotiated guilty plea is . . . fundamentally unsound. Besides the fact that it is inconsistent with established standards—those regarding the exercise of discretion by public officers and those surrounding the administration of justice generally—it is turning what used to be an accusatorial-adversary judicial system into an inquisitorial-administrative process. It encour-

ages practices in which neither the profession nor the judiciary can take pride."[7]

These two statements are characteristic of a stance taken by what turns out to be a minority of judicial spokesmen who see the problem of plea negotiation as intrinsically contradictory to the American system of justice. More common is the position taken by judges and legal scholars who argue that such practices have always been with us, will continue to exist as long as there are defendants and courts, and that the proper thing to do is to recognize plea bargaining, to get with it, make it more visible and attempt to control it.

Somewhat surprisingly, given the long history of silence about plea bargaining in the past, in the last couple of years a number of prominent legal organizations, advisory councils and appellate judges have taken the position that plea bargaining *is not* intrinsically improper but is indeed necessary and perhaps even a desirable part of American court practices.

The American Bar Association adopted the following position in its recently published Minimum Standards for Criminal Justice: "In cases in which it appears that the interest of the public and the effective administration of criminal justice would thereby be saved, the prosecuting attorney may engage in plea discussions for the purposes of reaching a plea agreement."[8] The report further recommends that the judge *not* be directly involved in negotiations, that such plea agreement proceedings should occur only through counsel and that "similarly situated defendants should be afforded equal plea agreement opportunities."[9]

The committee empowered to revise the Rules of Federal Criminal Procedure has recently submitted to the Supreme Court for its approval a revision of the practices to be followed by federal judges in accepting pleas of

[5]Breitel, "Controls in Criminal Law Enforcement," 27 *U. Chi. L. Rev.* 427, 428 (1960).

[6]*Shelton v. United States*, 242 F. 2d. 101, 113 (5th Cir. 1957).

[7]*People V. Byrd*, 12 Mich App 186, 162 N.W. 2d 777, 796 (1968).

[8]ABA, *Standards Relating to Pleas of Guilty*, op cit note 3, Sec. 3.1.

[9]*Ibid*.

guilty. After discussion and debate, this committee not only approved the practice of plea bargaining but spelled out methods for recording sentence promises and otherwise making negotiation into a veritable contract, binding on both the state and the defendant.[10]

Given the historical silence in regard to negotiation over the past two centuries, these are astounding developments.

Moreover, within the past two years the Supreme Court of California has not only approved plea bargaining but in an important opinion has spelled out ways to record plea agreements so that failure to follow through on them may be subject to appeal.[11] Likewise, the United States Supreme Court has recently considered two cases involving plea negotiation and in both, *Brady v. United States*[12] and *Santobello v. New York*,[13] have recognized the propriety of such bargaining. In *Santobello*, Mr. Justice Burger said:

"The disposition of criminal charges by agreement between the prosecutor and the accused, sometimes loosely called 'plea bargaining,' is an essential component of the administration of justice. Properly administered, it is to be encouraged. If every criminal charged were subjected to a full-scale trial, the States and the Federal Government would need to multiply by many times the number of judges and court facilities.

"Disposition of charges after plea discussions is not only an essential part of the process but a highly desirable part for many reasons. It leads to prompt and largely final disposition of most criminal cases; it avoids much of the corrosive impact of enforced idleness during pre-trial confinement for those accused persons who are prone to continue criminal conduct even while on pre-trial release; and by shortening the time between charge and disposition, it enhances whatever may be the rehabilitative prospects of the guilty when they are ultimately imprisoned."[14]

[10]Federal Rules of Criminal Procedure, *Rule 11. Pleas,* (Preliminary Draft of Proposed Amendments, April 1971).

[11]*People v. West,* 3 Cal 3d 595, 91 Cal. Rptr. 385, 477 P. 2d. 409 (1970).

[12]397 U.S. 742 (1970).

[13]404 U.S. 257 (1971).

[14]*Ibid,* 260.

The propriety issue does not end here, however. In spite of the words of the Chief Justice, at a National Conference on Criminal Justice held in Washington in January of this year, a resolution was adopted to "abolish" plea bargaining "no later than 1978." The commission, however, does provide "interim" measures for "improvement in plea negotiation" until such time as abolition comes about.[15]

UNRESOLVED ISSUES

Dilemmas presented by negotiated justice are not fully met by the words of Mr. Justice Burger, the standards of the ABA, and other proposals to improve plea bargaining by requiring counsel to be present, judges to be absent and a record of negotiations to be kept. There are still a number of unresolved issues about plea bargaining which need to be addressed.[16] These include:

The Range of Plea Bargaining. Though the language of new rules and procedures indicate that there should be some limits to the range of downgrading or sentence promises, the details have yet to be worked out. It may be one thing, for example, for a person charged with murder to be allowed to plead guilty to manslaughter. It might well be another thing, however, if the charge were reduced to disorderly conduct or to third-degree assault.

In short, there is a question of whether it is possible to set a limit on the range of downgrading or to require that promises of probation may be offered only to those persons who are otherwise eligible for probation. If the latter were held to be the case, then a difficult question arises as to how the prosecutor would know this since normally a presentence investigation cannot be conducted until after the person is duly convicted.

Equal Opportunity to Bargain. At one time in

[15]National Conference on Criminal Justice, *Preliminary Report,* Jan. 1973, Standard 3.1; Standard 3.2.

[16]See generally, Newman and NeMoyer, "Issues of Propriety in Negotiated Justice," 47 *Denver L. J.* 367 (1970).

Michigan the charge of breaking and entering in the nighttime carried a mandatory prison sentence of 15 years and was not a probationable offense. Daytime breaking, on the other hand, was probationable and carried a five-year maximum sentence with a minimum to be set as low as the judge wished. In a study of bargaining in Michigan, it was found that knowledgeable defendants arrested for nighttime burglary almost universally pleaded to daylight breaking to achieve a sentencing break.

Such reductions were common, even normative, but always informally arranged. No signs were posted explaining this; the formal words of Michigan law contained no hint of downgrading practices. A Michigan prosecutor said, "Looking at the official conviction records, you would think all our burglaries took place at high noon." How though would a stranger know this was the normal practice in most of the courts of the jurisdiction? Perhaps if he hired an attorney familiar with the practice, he too could deal.

This raises the question of whether common practice must be posted so that all may avail themselves of normative sentencing breaks. Should the prosecutor be required to explain "routine" bargaining? Must there be consistency from one case to another on the part of the prosecutor in offering sentencing promises or in reducing charges?

Is there, in short, an equal protection issue that can be realistically solved in the day-by-day administration of plea bargaining or, in fact, do most of the problems of sentence disparity actually originate in disparate practices of charging?

Quick Justice. At present there is considerable concern about delay in the courts. Judicial and legislative committees in most jurisdictions are looking into ways of speeding up court processing, particularly reducing the time defendants spend in jail awaiting trial.

There is another side to the coin of court delay, however, that has been called "quick justice," which occurs in some guilty-plea convictions. Cases have been noted where a defendant is taken at gunpoint in the morning, is charged with a crime, immediately brought before a judge where, waiving all rights, he enters a guilty plea, is sentenced on the spot and begins serving his term in prison in the afternoon.

The question raised by such processing is whether justice can be too swift as well as too slow. A number of state appellate courts have overturned swift justice convictions and the United States Supreme Court upset a guilty-plea conviction in a Michigan case in which a 17-year-old boy was arrested in the morning for the murder of a neighbor, pleaded guilty and was moved to the prison in the afternoon of the same day to begin his life sentence. His parents were never even notified of his arrest.[17]

The Public's 'Right to Know'. The relatively quick and anonymous guilty plea in most routine criminal cases is neither newsworthy nor of general public concern. However, guilty pleas in cases involving prominent or notorious defendants (whether to reduce charges or not) not only act to avoid the time and effort of trial but also prevent the details of the crime (including possible accomplices) from becoming public knowledge.

In prominent cases there is some public dissatisfaction with such sparse details. There have been a number of recent illustrations, including the Watergate Affair. Another involved Senator Edward Kennedy, who pleaded guilty to a traffic violation after the events at Chappaquiddick Island. Still another involved the bargained plea of James Earl Ray, the admitted assassin of the Reverend Martin Luther King.

Following guilty pleas in these latter two instances, there was widely expressed public disappointment with the processing of each case, dissatisfaction which rested on the general grounds that the full facts and details were not made public, though, given the prominence of the senator and of Dr. King, the public has a "right to know." Senator Kennedy felt enough of this pressure to appear on national television in an attempt to explain his position. However,

[17]*DeMeerleer v. Michigan, 329 U.S. 663 (1947).*

the details of Dr. King's murder, though "solved" by Ray's plea, remain naggingly unclear and perhaps permanently unresolved.

The Corruption of Ideology. There is always a thin line between the proper exercise of discretion and discrimination or even corruption. Some critics of plea bargaining point out that extending such broad discretionary powers to the prosecutor and to trial courts not only usurps legislative prerogative, but offers the opportunity for concealing discriminatory or corrupt practices under the guise of administrative discretion. Further, the argument goes, even if the system is perfectly administered with the prosecutor being scrupulous in authorizing and following through on appropriate bargains with "deserving" offenders, there is nevertheless an aura of disrespect of the law emanating from a system in which crime and punishment are matters of dealing and settling.

Some observers say that a plea bargain is little different from a "fix," for though there is clearly no corrupt practice involved, the law has in fact been manipulated and, no matter how well meaning, such manipulation destroys faith in justice among the public at large, and breeds cynicism in those processed in this manner through our criminal justice system.[18]

Others, however, see bargaining, if properly administered and contained, as the *only* way we can bring the individualization of justice into

our court system. The conscientious prosecutor and judge can do what the legislature and appellate courts cannot—and cannot even mandate—namely, tailor charges and sentences to specific guilty persons, distributing punishments and labels as accurately deserved among the tens of thousands of offenders processed through our courts.

There are, at present, no good answers to all of the unresolved bargaining issues. One thing, however, is abundantly clear: Plea bargaining is with us and is probably here to stay in most jurisdictions throughout the country. The issues and dilemmas posed by its practices will have to be met, as usual, in the best manner and in the best fashion we can develop. Today in contrast to even two years ago, plea bargaining is a much more visible practice and a more generally accepted procedure at the trial court level. Facts of negotiation are less often deliberately hidden; stories of bargaining appear more frequently in press, and negotiation sessions have even been dominant themes in recent episodes on some of the perennial lawyer series on television.

Whether we like it or not, all of us are increasingly compelled to admit that criminal justice in America is predominantly a system of negotiation and settlement—not unlike private lawsuits. The fact that it is becoming more visible, more public, can only be to the good for after all it is our system of justice and, where crime and punishment are involved, we may be forced to agree to public settlement but *not* to private dealings.

[18]Dash, "Cracks in the Foundation of Criminal Justice," *46 Ill. L. Rev. Rev.* 385 (1951).

20. The Behavior of Grand Juries

ROBERT A. CARP

FOR SEVERAL DECADES STUDENTS OF THE JUDICIAL process have had measured success in parting the veil of secrecy which surrounds the deliberations and internal dynamics of American trial juries. The classic study of Kalven and Zeisel of jury behavior in Chicago[1] and other related projects[2] have provided keen insights into the types of psychological, institutional, and sociological variables which influence the "output" of trial jury deliberations. In addition, psychologists, and sociologists have generated numerous theories about the behavior patterns of small groups,[3] and many of these theories have served as the basis of highly sophisticated studies of the interpersonal relations and voting behavior of small groups of judicial decision-makers.[4] Many of these latter studies have obvious application to the study of trial juries as small groups.

While the literature on petit jury behavior has increased, both in quantity and in theoretical and methodological sophistication, such research has not been extended to the subject of grand juries. Even though the grand jury is a vital aspect of the federal judicial process and is part of the due process guarantee in half of the state constitutions, it has received scant and generally unsophisticated treatment by judicial scholars. Grand jury literature tends to fall into three general categories: (1) studies of the history and evolution of the grand jury;[5] (2) analyses of the legal powers and prerogatives of grand juries vis-à-vis the rights and immunities

▶SOURCE: *"The Behavior of Grand Juries: Acquiescence or Justice," Social Quarterly* (March, 1975), 55:853–870. Reprinted by permission of University of Texas Press.

[1]Harry Kalven, Jr. and Hans Zeisel, *The American Jury* (Boston: Little, Brown and Co., 1966).

[2]*Ibid.*, see bibliographic references on pp. 541–545.

[3]Robert F. Bales, *Interaction Process Analysis: A Method for the Study of Small Groups* (Cambridge, Mass.: Addison-Wesley Press, 1950); "The Equilibrium Problem in Small Groups," Chap. 4 in Talcott Parsons, Robert F. Bales, and Edward A. Shils, eds., *Working Papers in the Theory of Action* (Glencoe, Ill.: Free Press, 1953); R. F. Bales, "Task Status and Likeability as a Function of Talking and Listening in Decision-Making Groups." in Leonard D. White, ed., *The State of the Social Sciences* (Chicago: University of Chicago Press, 1956), pp. 148–161; R. F. Bales, "Task Roles and Social Roles in Problem-Solving Groups," in Eleanor E. Maccoby, Theodore M. Newcomb, and Eugene L. Harley, *Readings in Social Psychology* (New York: Holt, 1958), pp. 437–447; R. F. Bales, *Personality and Interpersonal Behavior* (New York: Holt, Rinehart and Winston, 1970). Also, Philip E. Slater, "Role Differentiation in Small Groups," *American Sociological Review,* 20 (June, 1955), p. 300.

Also, Leonard Berkowitz, *Some Effects of Leadership Sharing in Small, Decision-Making Conference Groups*, unpublished Ph.D. Diss., Department of Psychology, University of Michigan, 1951; Leonard Berkowitz, "Sharing Leadership in Small, Decision-Making Groups," *Journal of Abnormal and Social Psychology*, 48 (April, 1953), p. 231.

[4]For example, see Thomas P. Jahnige and Sheldon Goldman, eds., *The Federal Judicial System* (New York: Holt, 1968), Part 3, Sec. C. Also, see Glendon Schubert, ed., *Judicial Behavior: A Reader in Theory and Research* (Chicago: Rand McNally, 1964), Chaps. 3, 4, and 5.

[5]For example, see Richard D. Younger, *The People's Panel: The Grand Jury in the United States, 1634–1941* (Providence, R.I.: Brown University Press, 1963); John Van Voorhis, "Note on the History in New York State of the Powers of Grand Juries," *Albany Law Review,* 26 (Jan., 1962), p. 1; and George J. Edwards, Jr., *The Grand Jury* (Philadelphia: George T. Bisel Co., 1906).

of the accused;[6] and (3) critiques of the grand jury system and/or proposals for reform.[7] Although there are a few studies which purport to analyze the process of recruitment to grand juries and to speculate on the possible effects on grand jury "output" of one form of recruitment over another, these studies are neither based on quantitative data nor performed with much methodological rigor.[8]

This study is intended to help remedy the paucity of empirical data on the recruitment and internal dynamics of grand juries by reporting the results of a case study of grand jury operations in Harris County (Houston), Texas. The study may be distinguished from the existing grand jury literature, first, because the author had access to data which has not heretofore been available to judicial scholars, and, second, because the data permitted the researcher to respond concretely to questions which until this time were only subjects of speculation among students of the judicial process. The study is concerned with two major substantive questions.

(1) What are the distinguishing characteristics of grand jury behavior? It is suggested that the basic behavioral traits include an excessively rapid processing of cases with little deliberation, a high level of internal agreement on the resolution of cases, and an overwhelming acquiescence in the district attorney's recommendations. (2) How are the basic behavioral characteristics of the grand jury to be accounted for? It is then argued that grand jury behavior is explained by the type of people who become grand jurors, by the grand jurors' inadequate training and preparation for their duties, by the pressures of a very heavy caseload, and by a variety of institutional and legal factors which ensure the prosecutor's domination of the grand jury.[9] Finally, some suggestions for future research on the subject of grand juries are offered.

METHODOLOGY

Data for this study derive from three principal sources. First, as a participant-observer on the 177th District Court Grand Jury (which met in Houston, Texas, between November, 1971, and February, 1972), the author had the opportunity to perform a case-by-case content analysis of the 918 cases considered by that grand jury. This analysis includes a complete record of all votes taken, the amount of time spent deliberating on the various cases, and extensive notes on the discussions among the grand jurors and between members of the grand jury and the district attorneys. Because of the oath of grand jury secrecy to which the author is bound, the information here provided must deal with the cases in the aggregate—not individually—and great care has been taken not to divulge specific information about sensitive or confidential subject matter.

[6]For example, see Stuart A. MacCorkle, *The Texas Grand Jury* (Austin, Texas: Institute of Public Affairs, The University of Texas, 1966); S. A. MacCorkle, "Grand Jury—evidence obtained from testimony of prospective defendant cannot be used as basis of indictment," *Fordham Law Review*, 30 (Dec., 1961), p. 365; S. A. MacCorkle, "Rule of evidence as a factor in probable cause in grand jury proceedings and preliminary examinations," *Washington University Law Quarterly* (Feb., 1963), p. 102; and S. A. MacCorkle, "Criminal procedure—pretrial disclosures—defendant indicted for sub-orning witness to testify falsely before grand jury may inspect transcript of witness' testimony before grand jury," *University of Pittsburgh Law Review*, 23 (June, 1962), p. 1024.

[7]For example, see Walton Coates, "Grand jury, the prosecutor's puppet. Wasteful nonsense of criminal jurisprudence," *Pennsylvania Bar Association Quarterly*, 33(March, 1962), p. 311; W. Coates, "California grand jury—two current problems," *California Law Review*, 52 (March, 1964), p. 116; Harold S. Russell, "Cook County grand jury: some problems and proposals," *Chicago Bar Record*, 43 (Oct., 1961), p. 9; and Arthur H. Sherry "Grand jury minutes: the unreasonable rule of secrecy," *Virginia Law Review*, 48 (May, 1962), p. 668.

[8]For example, see Frederick W. Burnett, Jr., "The Texas Grand Jury Selection System—Discretion to Discriminate," *Southwestern Law Journal*, 21 (Summer, 1967), p. 545.

[9]A very well-written study discussing phenomena similar to these in the U.S. House of Representatives Ways and Means Committee; see John F. Manley, "The House Committee on Ways and Means; Conflict Management in a Congressional Committee," *American Political Science Review*, 59 (Dec., 1965), pp. 927–939.

Second, in-depth interviews were conducted with former members of Harris County grand juries. The interviewees were not selected at random but rather with an eye toward including as many *recent* grand jury members and jury foremen as possible. Twenty-three such persons in all were contacted (including six jury foremen) and all of them agreed to be interviewed. The primary purpose of these interviews was to compare the grand jury experiences of this author with those of others who have similarly served so as to determine how typical was the performance of the 177th Grand Jury from which the hard data were drawn. No attempt was made to quantify the results of the in-depth interviews, and therefore the information they provide is anecdotal although frequently interesting and insightful.

Third, the study contains data from a questionnaire mailed to all persons who served on Harris County grand juries between 1969 and 1972. Of the 271 questionnaires mailed to the grand jurors, 156 (58 percent) were returned and included in the analysis. The questionnaire solicited information about the socioeconomic characteristics of the grand jurors and about the nature of their grand jury deliberations and experiences. The results are used throughout the study to supplement the other sources of research data and to provide a comparison and contrast between the data of the 177th Grand Jury and the other grand juries which immediately preceded and followed it.

BEHAVIORAL CHARACTERISTICS OF THE GRAND JURY

In principle the grand jury is supposed to carefully determine whether the evidence presented to it by the prosecutor is sufficient to warrant the time and expense of placing a person on trial for a felony offense. Ideally the grand jury serves as a check against an over-zealous district attorney to protect the citizen against unwarranted harassment and prosecution by the state. How well such a function is performed in practice may be ascertained by examining the real, observable defining characteristics of grand jury behavior. First, it will be shown that the grand jury spends an extremely small amount of time deliberating on the vast majority of its cases. Second, the data will indicate a surprisingly low level of internal conflict in the grand jury decision making process. Finally, the grand jury's overwhelming approval of (or acquiescence in) the district attorney's recommendations will be demonstrated.

Time Allotted to Each Case: The Failure to Deliberate Adequately

To determine whether or not the grand jury sufficiently deliberates its cases it seems logical to begin by asking this question: how much *time* does the average grand jury spend with each case to determine whether there is enough evidence to place a man on trial for a felony offense? Although there is considerable variation in the amount of time spent deliberating on the various categories of cases, the evidence reveals that the typical grand jury spends only five minutes per case. (In 1971, twelve Harris County grand juries spent an estimated 1,344 hours deliberating on 15,930 cases.)[10] This average time of five minutes includes the assistant district attorney's summary of the case and his recommendation as to how the case should be decided (about one minute per case), the hearing of testimony by whatever witnesses are called, and the actual secret deliberations by the grand jury on each case individually. By any man's standards, "justice" is indeed swift!

Does the grand jury become more efficient as its term progresses, that is, is it able to deal with a larger number of cases per hour toward the end of its term than at the beginning? Eighty-four percent of the questionnaire respondents indicated that this was their impression. Table I (panel a) suggests that such was also the case with the 177th Grand Jury despite a slight initial increase in the amount of time spent per case.

[10]The statistics are based on figures prepared by the Grand Jury Division of the Harris County District Attorney's Office in a report to District Attorney Carol Vance.

Table I. Behavioral Characteristics of the 177th Grand Jury (Number of Cases in Parentheses)

	Time Periods[a]							
	Nov. 3–10	Nov. 15–22	Nov. 29–Dec. 6	Dec. 8–29	Jan. 3–10	Jan. 12–19	Jan. 24–31	Overall Average
Average number of minutes per case spent deliberating on cases by the 177th Grand Jury	7.3	7.5	8.0	7.6	6.5	6.0	5.6	7.0
Percentage of cases discussed by the 177th Grand Jury	24	26	33	25	5	20[b]	6	20
Percentage of divided votes for the 177th Grand Jury	9	3	6	3	2	6[b]	1	5
Percentage of cases on which the 177th Grand Jury did not follow the district attorney's recommendations	11	10	11	5	4	5	2	7
Total (N)	(148)	(112)	(135)	(146)	(111)	(154)	(112)	(131)

[a]Each of these time periods includes three working sessions except the period December 8 through the 29th, which includes five working sessions. The three month session is divided into seven time periods each of which includes an average of 131 cases.

[b]Time period six tends to deviate from the overall tendency. This was primarily because one grand juror suddenly insisted on discussing all of the usually routine driving-while-intoxicated cases. This was the result of an unpleasant personal encounter he had had with law enforcement officials relating to a drunken driving charge during the New Year's holiday.

This grand jury spent an average of 7.4 minutes per case during its first six working sessions while spending but 5.9 minutes per case during the final six working days.

Another question about the deliberation process is how many (and what types of cases) are actually discussed by the grand jury and how many are simply voted on without any discussion at all after the district attorney's one minute summary of the facts of the case. For the 177th Grand Jury a full 80 percent of the cases were voted on with no discussion whatsoever.[11] This percentage is probably even greater for most other Harris County grand juries since the 177th Grand Jury spent a mean time of seven minutes per case, whereas the average figure for the other grand juries between 1969 and 1971 was five minutes.

Table I (panel 6) also suggests that after a slight initial increase the percentage of cases discussed by the grand jury tends to decrease as the term progresses.[12] For instance, during its first nine sessions (November 3rd through December 6th) the 177th Grand Jury chose to discuss 27 percent of its cases, whereas it decided to discuss only 12 percent during its final nine meetings (January 3rd through the 31st). Why this is so is explained in part in this statement by a former grand jury foreman:

[11]The usual procedure in Harris County is fo the assistant district attorney to present his cases for the day and then to leave the jury room. Then the foreman asks each grand juror which cases he feels should be discussed. With the 177th Grand Jury even if only one of the jurors wished to discuss a particular case, discussion occurred. The interviews suggested that other grand juries follow a similar practice.

[12]An additional explanation of why there is an initial increase followed by a gradual long-term decrease is found in the discussion surrounding Table IV. In brief, the hypothesis is that the grand jury slowly begins to gain confidence and to challenge the work and judgment of the prosecutor—especially on the resolution of certain types of cases. Resenting such challenges, the district attorney then removes these types of cases from subsequent grand jury consideration. Thus the percentage of cases discussed by the grand jury drops after the first month because many controversial cases considered worthy of discussion are simply removed from the agenda.

"As time went on fewer and fewer of the cases were actually discussed. Toward the end of the term someone would say he wanted to discuss a particular case, and then when someone else would pop up and say 'What's the point of discussing this case? We had a case just like it a couple weeks ago. You know where I stand on cases like this, and I know where you stand. Why discuss this all over again? Let's just vote on it and get on to the next case.' And more often than not, nothing more would be said. We would just vote without discussing the case."

The phenomenon of discussing fewer and fewer cases as the term progresses probably explains the increasing grand jury "efficiency" as outlined in panel a of Table I.

The evidence also suggests that grand juries do discriminate in the amount of time allotted to specific categories of cases, that is, while a grand jury might spend several hours investigating and discussing a prominent murder or rape case, it might spend less than a minute dealing with the average robbery or drunken driving case. When asked on the questionnaire about which types of cases his grand jury spent the most time deliberating, the frequency distribution of responses was in the following rank order: (1) drug cases, 29 percent; (2) crimes of passion, e.g., murder, rape, 27 percent; (3) burglary, 9 percent; (4) forgery and embezzlement, 9 percent; (5) theft, 8 percent; (6) victimless sex crimes, e.g., sodomy, 8 percent; (7) robbery, 5 percent; and (8) driving while intoxicated, 5 percent.

The 177th Grand Jury likewise gave differential treatment to certain types of cases at the expense of others. This panel chose to discuss two-thirds of its victimless sex crimes cases while deciding to talk about only 5 percent of the driving while intoxicated cases. Crimes of passion and drug cases were discussed about a third of the time while 28 percent of the theft cases and 19 percent of the burglary cases were talked about. This was followed by robbery cases and the cases involving forgery and embezzlement which were discussed respectively 9 and 6 percent of the time.

The High Level of Unanimity in Grand Jury Decision Making

The most striking feature of grand jury voting patterns is the exceptionally high degree of unanimity. This is confirmed by interviews with former grand jury members and by examining the voting record of the 177th Grand Jury: of the 918 cases decided by that Grand Jury, a non-unanimous vote occurred in a mere 42 cases (5 percent). The evidence further indicates that as the grand jury term progresses, there is a tendency toward increased unanimity in its voting patterns. This is in accord with one of Bales' conclusions about small group decision-making behavior: as the small group continues to deliberate on a matter (or on a series of questions), there is an increased tendency toward group solidarity.[13]

The results in panel c of Table I show that during its first nine working days the 177th Grand Jury cast less than unanimous votes in 6 percent of its cases, whereas during its last nine sessions there was a divided vote in only 3 percent of its decisions. This excerpt from a journal kept by one former grand jury member is insightful:

"In general there is a fairly unified spirit among us, and I think we all feel that pressure to 'dissent only when absolutely necessary,' as Chief Justice Taft used to urge. I myself today felt inclined to bring a T.B. (true bill) in a case this afternoon, but I could see no one else agreed with my position, and so when the vote was taken I held my peace."

Victimless sex crimes was the only category of cases which served to create disharmony on the 177th Grand Jury; a divided vote resulted in one-third of all such offenses. Disagreement on the other types of cases did not exceed the 6 percent level.[14] As for the former grand jurors who were asked in the questionnaire to cite cases on which their respective panels had the largest amount of internal dissension, drug cases led the way with 40 percent, followed by crimes of passion at 25 percent. No other category of cases was cited more than 9 percent of the time.[15]

Thus the evidence suggests that grand jurors most frequently divide on drug cases, crimes of passion, and victimless sex crimes while being significantly more unified on the other categories of cases. Such findings are not too surprising when one considers that cases in the three aforementioned categories are not only likely to be the most serious and complex, but they are also cases about which society in general seems to be most divided as to whether such offenses are really crimes at all or merely the actions of social dissidents and psychopaths.

The Grand Jury's Acquiescence to the Demands of the Prosecutor

A third defining characteristic of grand jury behavior is the almost total approval of the district attorney's recommendations. Although the interview data suggest that grand jurors are often critical of the prosecutor for inadequate and careless preparation of cases, for insensitivity to the inequities of our legal system, and for presenting the grand juries with inordinately heavy caseloads, the evidence also reveals that most grand juries tend (or are forced by circumstances) to rely heavily on the skill and integrity of the district attorney in deciding whether or not to bring an indictment. When asked on the questionnaire about the *usual* practice of the grand jury in bringing an indictment, 47 percent of all grand jurors indicated that their grand juries indicted (or refused to indict) solely on the basis of what the district attorney

---

[13]Bales, *Interaction Process Analysis,* esp. p. 138.

[14]Percentage of cases on which divided votes occurred for the 177th Grand Jury: (1) victimless sex crimes, 33 percent; (2) crimes of passion, 6 percent; (3) drug cases, 6 percent; (4) theft, 5 percent; (5) burglary, 4 percent; (6) robbery, 4 percent; (7) driving while intoxicated, 4 percent; and (8) forgery and embezzlement, 0 percent.

[15]Percentage of grand jurors who cited cases on which their respective grand juries had the largest amount of internal dissension: (1) drug cases, 40 percent; (2) crimes of passion, 25 percent; (3) victimless sex crimes, 9 percent; (4) forgery and embezzlement, 7 percent; (5) driving while intoxicated, 7 percent; (6) theft, 5 percent; (7) burglary, 4 percent; and (8) robbery, 2 percent.

said the file of the accused contained. Another 21 percent noted that their grand jury usually did examine the file of the accused while about a third claimed that their grand jury usually required proof "sufficient to convict, including the calling of witnesses."[16]

What is perhaps most significant, then, is that nearly half of all grand juries (and the author believes this to be a highly conversative figure) usually take action on cases solely on the basis of what the district attorney says the defendant's file contains without the grand jury even bothering to examine the file or to require full demonstration by the district attorney.

On which categories of cases is the grand jury most likely to refuse to follow the recommendations of the district attorneys?[17] The response to this query by the questionnaire recipients generated the following frequency distribution: (1) drug cases, 44 percent; (2) crimes of passion, 18 percent; (3) victimless sex crimes, 11 percent; (4) driving while intoxicated, 9 percent; (5) forgery and embezzlement, 6 percent; (6) theft, 5 percent; (7) burglary, 3 percent; and (8) robbery, 3 percent. Thus the crimes which were likely to cause the greatest amount of dissension among the grand jurors are the very felonies which were likely to result in the most disagreements between grand juries and the district attorneys; viz., drug cases, crimes of passion, and victimless sex crimes.

The above results parallel exactly the data emanating from the 177th Grand Jury. That Grand Jury, which refused to follow the district attorney's recommendations only 6 percent of the time, disagreed with the district attorneys in 28 percent of the drug cases, 27 percent of the victimless sex crimes cases, and 17 percent of the crimes of passion.[18]

Panel d of Table I suggests that the longer the grand jury is in session the more its decisions are likely to be in accord with the district attorney's recommendations. More careful analysis reveals, however, that this is not necessarily the case. For the 177th Grand Jury the evidence indicates that the district attorneys were less and less likely to present to the Grand Jury cases with which they believed the Jury would go against their recommendations. For example, of the first 137 cases presented to the Grand Jury, 25 (18 percent) were drug cases, whereas only 3 (2 percent) of the following 123 cases dealt with drug crimes. Apparently the district attorneys had determined after a few weeks that they would be more successful taking their drug cases to one of the other two grand juries sitting at the same time. In fact this was conceded by one of the district attorneys during one of the working sessions when a grand juror asked, "Why aren't you giving us any more drug cases?" The candid reply was, "Well, you folks are requiring so much (proof) of us with those cases, that we've had to take them to the other grand juries or we're going to get way behind." Therefore, a phenomenon which may well occur in Harris County is for the district attorneys to "size up" the grand juries during their first several working sessions and then to present cases to the grand jury which is most likely to act in accordance with the district attorneys' wishes. To what extent this occurs is unknown, but that it does occur to some degree is beyond doubt.

---

[16]Given the average time of five minutes per case, the third claim could not possibly have been the *usual* practice of any of the grand juries.

[17]Disagreement with the district attorney was defined as cases where at least one of the following conditions occurred: the district attorney recommended a true bill and the grand jury voted a no bill; the district attorney sought a no bill and the grand jury brought a true bill; the grand jury indicted for a crime other than the one recommended by the district attorney; the grand jury required the district attorney to collect additional evidence for a particular case before they would consider it.

[18]Cases on which the 177th Grand Jury refused to follow the recommendations of the district attorney: (1) drug cases, 28 percent; (2) victimless sex crimes, 27 percent; (3) crimes of passion, 17 percent; (4) theft, 7 percent; (5) burglary, 5 percent; (6) forgery and embezzlement, 2 percent; (7) robbery, 1 percent; and (8) driving while intoxicated, 1 percent.

A PARTIAL EXPLANATION OF GRAND JURY BEHAVIORAL CHARACTERISTICS

The evidence presented to this point suggests the following portrait of grand jury behavior. Burdened with an inordinately heavy caseload, the grand jury rapidly processes almost all of its myriad of cases, according full and adequate deliberation to only a select few which arbitrarily manage to pique the interest of the jury panel. The expedition of the huge caseload is facilitated by a very low level of internal conflict as evidenced by a record of unanimous voting on approximately 95 percent of the cases. Such internal harmony extends to the relations between the grand jury and the district attorney's staff, the former following the latter's recommendations without so much as a question about 94 percent of the time.

If such are the behavioral characteristics of the grand jury, the next logical question is: how are such behavioral patterns to be accounted for? Why doesn't the grand jury deliberate with greater thoroughness on its cases? Why is there so little internal dissension on the resolution of the many issues confronting the grand jury? And why is the public prosecutor able to so effectively dominate grand jury behavior? Partial answers to these questions have already been suggested in the preceding material, but it is the purpose of this segment of the article to provide a more systematic explanation for grand jury behavior.

The Type of People Who Become Grand Jurors

One possible explanatory factor accounting for some of the behavior patterns lies in the selection and composition of the individual members of the jury panel. This is based on the reasonable assumption that a grand jury composed of a truly random cross-section of the community might well exhibit different behavior from a jury composed largely of upper-middle class whites, or of radical members of the black community, or of a combination of poor whites and

Mexican Americans. Therefore, we must explore the grand jury selection process and provide a profile of its members.

The process of selecting grand jurors in Texas is as intricate as it is arbitrary. Unlike many of its sister states which non-discriminately select the names of grand jurors from a lottery wheel containing the names of hundreds of potential jurors, Texas grants jury commissioners almost unlimited discretion to compile a small list of names from which the grand jury is impaneled. Very little is known about these jury commissioners and about the criteria by which these officers of the court select prospective grand jurors. However, preliminary evidence suggests, first, that a significant disproportion of the commissioners are upper-middle class Anglo-Saxon white males; and, second, that the commissioners tend to select as grand jurors their friends and neighbors who have similar socioeconomic characteristics.[19] Historically most jurists have argued, and the courts have officially determined, that grand juries, like trial juries, should be representative of the population of the community as a whole. Although there is still considerable uncertainty about how this goal is to be achieved, the U.S. Court of Appeals for the Fifth Circuit has determined that the Constitution requires that members of Texas grand juries represent "a fair cross section . . . [of the] . . . community's human resources. . . ."[20] In light of this judicial determination it is fair then to ask the question: how representative are Texas grand juries of the county populations from which they are selected? This is largely an empirical question, and for a partial answer we may compare the results of the mailed questionnaire sent to former grand jurors in Harris County with the 1970 census figures for this same county.

Table II shows that the typical Harris County

[19]This evidence is taken from an ongoing research project on the grand jury selection process conducted by myself and a graduate assistant, Claude Rowland.

[20]*Brooks v. Beto*, 366 F. 2d, 14 (5th Circuit, 1966).

Table II. Socioeconomic Characteristics of Harris County Grand Jurors Compared with 1970 County Census Figures for Adult Population, in Percentages (N = 156 for the Questionnaire Sample)

Characteristic	Grand Jury	County
Sex		
Male	78	49
Female	22	51
Age		
21–35 years	10	23
36–50 years	43	18
51–65 years	37	8
Over 65	10	5

Median juror age, 51   —   Median adult age, 39

Income		
Under $5,000	1	16
$ 5,000–$10,000	3	31
$10,000–$15,000	25	29
$15,000–$20,000	16	9
Over $20,000	55	15

Median juror income, $25,000—Median family income in County, $10,348

Race		
Anglo	82	69
Negro	15	20
Mexican American	3	11
Education		
Less than high school	0	24
Some high school	3	23
High school degree	8	25
Some college	34	13
College degree	32	15
Graduate degree	23	

Median juror education, 16 years — Median County resident education,

12 years

Employment		
Business executive	35	
Proprietor	7	
Professional	20	
Employed worker	13	Comparable data
Retired	13	not available
Housewife	11	
Other	1	

grand juror is an Anglo-Saxon male college graduate about 51 years of age who is quite likely to earn about $25,000 per year while working either as a business executive or as a professional man. How does this profile compare with what the 1970 census data indicates about the "typical" citizen of the county? A brief summary of these data reveals the following about the residents of Harris County: 49 percent are male and 51 percent are female; the median adult age is 39; 69 percent are Anglo-Saxon, 20 percent are black, and 11 percent are Mexican American; the median education is 12 years (a high school degree); and the median family income is $10,348.[21] These figures clearly demonstrate that even by rudimentary standards Harris County grand juries do not meet the judicial criterion of a "fair cross section . . . [of the] . . . community's human resources." Grossly underrepresented are women, young people, Negroes, Mexican Americans, the poor, and those with less extensive educational backgrounds.[22]

The evidence suggests that the highly nonrepresentative composition of the grand jury manifests itself in several of the jury's behavior patterns. First, it is probably responsible to a large degree for the low level of internal conflict among the grand jurors. Jury members with highly similar backgrounds of education, income, employment, sex, age, and race are more likely to think alike and disagree less than a panel composed of individuals with highly dissimilar—or even randomly distributed—background characteristics.

Second, the upper middle class white bias of the grand jury is undoubtedly reflected in the selection of that small 5 percent of the cases

which the jury does choose to deliberate on at length. The evidence reveals that the vast majority of those cases in the 5 percent category are those which include the bizarre, unusual, or "important" cases which are covered by the news media and which frequently involve the names of well-known local personages, businesses, organizations, etc. The murder of a prominent socialite, corruption in the local fire department, alleged immoral conduct by professors at a local state university have all been subjects of extensive and exhaustive grand jury investigations in the county under study. Cases such as these are regarded as significant by upper-middle class grand juries because the subject matter has a special appeal to the moral, ethical, or even salacious instincts of the middle class mentality. On the other hand, the robbery of a liquor store, the stabbing death of a derelict in a ghetto bar, or the forgery of a credit card tend to be regarded as routine, boring, and worthy of little interest by most grand jurors. As one grand juror said in this candid jest, "We kind of looked forward to the rape and sodomy cases and stuff like that because they broke the routine. I meant if you've heard one bad check case, you've heard them all. But the unusual cases were a little more interesting, and we kind of took our time with them." The result of all this may be that the more bizarre, infamous, or salacious the case, the greater the likelihood that it will be among the small percentage of cases on which the grand jury gives careful and exhaustive investigation. And, conversely, the more routine and uninteresting the case, the greater the likelihood that it will be passed over with scant attention, the grand jury being willing to follow the often-heard advice of the district attorney: "If we make a mistake here, they'll catch it when the cases come to trial." Since 46 percent of all grand jury indictments end in either dismissals or acquittals, one may well assume that many mistakes are indeed passed over by bored, unresponsive, and overworked grand juries.[23]

[21]Census Tracts (Houston, Texas): *Standard Metropolitan Statistical Area* (Washington:U.S. Department of Commerce, 1972), pp. 1, 34, and 100.

[22]For comparative data on jury composition, see the bibliographic citations in Herbert Jacob, "Judicial insulation—elections, direct participation, and public attention to the courts in Wisconsin, *Wisconsin Law Review* (Summer, 1966), pp. 801–819.

[23]This figure is taken from a report prepared by the

Finally, the data reveal that some of the complex social problems which divide society as a whole, such as marijuana and hard drug laws, the possible pathology of the murderer and the rapist, the permissibility of "abnormal" sexual relations between consenting adults, all manifest themselves in the give-and-take of grand jury deliberations. This is evidenced by the comparatively high level of disagreement on the resolution of cases dealing with these subjects, not only among individual members of the grand jury but also between the grand jury and the district attorney's staff. Moreover, the inordinant amount of time the grand jury spends deliberating on these cases and the level of dissension which these discussions evoke are also a probable reflection of the upper-middle class composition of the grand jury. It is now common knowledge among social scientists that concern with reform of the narcotic laws, revision of the criminal code pertaining to sexual mores, etc., are almost exclusively middle and upper middle class phenomena.

The Grand Jury's Inadequate Training and Preparation for Their Duties

A second reason to account for some of the grand jury's behavior patterns is found in the process by which newly-selected jurors are trained and socialized. In Harris County all new grand jurors are provided with a training program of sorts which entails three different aspects: a *voluntary* one-day training seminar conducted primarily by police and sheriff's department officials; two booklets pertaining to grand jury procedures and instructions, one composed by the district attorney and the other prepared by the Harris County Grand Jury Association; and, finally, an in-depth, give-and-take discussion between the grand jury and an experienced member of the district attorney's staff. Let us examine each aspect of the program separately.

First, the series of lectures by law enforce-

ment officials seems to be of limited utility for the novice grand juror. Not only do these lectures come several days *after* the formal work of the grand jury has begun, but most grand jurors tend to agree with an evaluation which was included in a recent grand jury report: "The day-long training session was interesting, but for the most part the lectures were irrelevant to the primary functions of a Grand Jury, and many of us noted rather unsubtle political overtones in the formal presentations."[24] Interviews with more than a score of former grand jurors and a content analysis of grand jury reports reveal that the primary function of the law enforcement lectures is to explain and to "plug" the work of the respective departments rather than to provide the grand juror with substantive insights into what his grand jury duties entail.

The pamphlets prepared separately by the county Grand Jury Association and by the district attorney are well-written and provide a good summary of the formal duties and functions of the grand jury. However, since these booklets are not provided until the first day of jury service, the earliest they could be read is after the grand jury has put in one full day of work, which usually means hearing at least 50 cases. More important, however, is the fact that interviews with former grand jurors indicate that very few jurors bother to read and study these booklets. This comment by one former grand juror is typical:

"Yes, I took the books home with me that first night and I glanced through them, but I can't say I really read them. I figured that we'd meet our problems as we came to them, and that's about what happened. If we had a question during our deliberations, one of us would usually say, 'Let's see if the booklet says anything about this.' That's how we used the books when I was on the jury. I don't think any of us actually read them as such."

The give-and-take discussion between the

Grand Jury Division of the Harris County District Attorney's Office for District Attorney Carol Vance.

[24]177th Criminal District Court Grand Jury, *Report of the November 1971 Grand Jury for the 177th Criminal District Court* (Houston, Texas, 1972), p. 1.

grand jury and an assistant district attorney is usually scheduled for the first working session, and it is the final aspect of the grand juror's formal on-the-job training. When such a discussion does indeed occur, it appears to be of some utility in acquainting grand jurors with their new duties. However, this comment by a recent member of a grand jury was far from atypical:

"Yes, we were supposed to meet with one of the D.A.'s at the end of the first day, and he was supposed to explain to us what the hell was going on. But can you believe this? They [the assistant district attorneys] presented us with so many cases on our first day, it got to be five o'clock and we didn't have time for anyone to explain to us what we were supposed to be doing. We heard dozens of cases that first day, and when I got home that night I was just sick. I told my wife, 'I sure would hate to be one of those guys who had his case brought before us today.' "

How long does it take, then, for the average grand juror to understand substantially what the duties, powers, and functions of a grand jury are? The results of the questionnaire survey reveal that the typical grand juror does not claim to fully understand his basic purpose and function until well into the third full working session of the grand jury.[25]

Using the average daily workload of 1971 as a base (58 cases per working session), this means that the grand jury hears a minimum of 116 cases before its members even claim to understand their primary duties and functions. Since the average grand jury in 1971 considered 1,328 cases,[26] the data suggests that most grand jurors stumble through the first 8 percent of their

[25]Percentage of grand jurors who indicated the length of time required before they claimed to substantially understand the duties, powers, and functions of a grand jury: (1) Understood prior to or immediately after first session, 22 percent; (2) Understood after second session, 27 percent; (3) Understood after fourth session, 32 percent; and (4) Understood after sixth session or longer, 19 percent. Median time is somewhat more than the third session.

[26]The statistics in this paragraph are based on figures prepared by the Grand Jury Division of the Harris County District Attorney's Office in a report to District Attorney Carol Vance.

cases without fully knowing what is incumbent upon them.

The inadequate training and socialization of the grand jury is clearly one factor accounting for many of its behavioral characteristics. Since grand jurors do not learn systematically from an independent source the full measure of their duties, functions, and prerogatives, there exists the strong potential that they will become "rubber stamps" of the district attorney's staff. This is not to suggest that all grand juries become mere tools of the district attorney, but the potential for this result is by no means minimal. Jurors who do not fully understand their functions, who do not comprehend the meaning of "probable cause," and who do not know how to conduct careful, complete investigations of each case are prime candidates to be "led by the nose" by artful and experienced public prosecutors. Moreover, the evidence indicates that the district attorneys do indeed take advantage of ignorant grand juries to accomplish their desired ends. This is primarily so because the prosecutors frequently keep significant pieces of information from grand jury purview and because they occasionally deliberately route cases to the grand jury which is expected to act most favorably in accordance with their wishes.

The Pressure to Decide Cases Quickly

A third explanatory variable for grand jury behavior is found in the enormous size of the caseload with which both the prosecutor and the grand jury are forced to deal. Just as the heavy caseload at the trial court level produces pressures sustaining the plea-bargaining system, so, too, the huge workload of the grand jury has generated pressures to find alternatives to comprehensive review of each case. As indicated previously, the average grand jury, meeting but two days per week, is presented with approximately 1,328 cases during the three-month term. Since Texas law guarantees to all persons charged with a felony the right to a grand jury indictment, the district attorney is required to process all of these cases through the machinery of the grand jury. Given the small number of grand juries and the limited number of days they can work, there is little wonder that cases are processed with such careless speed. If each case were to receive adequate deliberation, the grand jury would fall hopelessly behind in its workload: if Harris County grand juries were to spend so much as an average of 20 minutes per case, their output of cases would drop by 75 percent! Thus, the sheer size of the caseload precludes careful, serious discussion of the cases.

Besides forcing the grand jury to work much too rapidly, the heavy workload is also partially responsible for the grand jury's excessive reliance on the expertise and good faith of the district attorney. To question the prosecutor's judgment, to make him "do his homework," are luxuries which efficiency-conscious grand juries cannot afford. The district attorney is hardly ignorant of this fact since he frequently admonishes the grand jury that requiring too much evidence of the prosecutor causes the grand jury "to fall behind the other grand juries" or that "grand jury delays result in innocent persons languishing in jail because they can't get their cases heard."

Factors Resulting in the District Attorney's Domination of the Grand Jury

In spite of the considerable legal powers and independence of the grand jury and despite the wishes of most grand jurors to the contrary, it is clear that the district attorney dominates the behavior of the grand jury. Why this is so has already been discussed and implied throughout the article, but it seems useful at this point to put all of the major reasons into summary perspective.

First, it is the prosecutor who has the primary role in training and indoctrinating the grand jurors. It is his office which writes the grand jury handbook, which plans the training seminars, and which instructs the jurors about their primary powers and responsibilities. Given the considerable ignorance of most grand jurors about

their proper role and duties, the district attorney has the first and only real opportunity to write on this blank slate that the primary function of the grand jury is to expedite the work of the prosecutor's office with a minimum of time and obstruction.

Another factor resulting in the prosecutor's dominance is his continuing control over the sources of information throughout the three-month term. Perceived as an expert, as a professional, the district attorney is constantly looked to for guidance and information as to the proper disposition of cases and as to the legitimate functions of the grand jury. The prosecutor is fully aware of the grand jury's reliance on him in this regard and his subsequent behavior fully verifies the maxim that knowledge is power. The phenomenon is further heightened by the extremely heavy workload which forces the grand jury to trust the competence and judgment of the district attorney since the alternative is to throw sand in the gears of the judicial machinery and risk bringing it to a virtual halt.

Besides his control over the socialization of the grand jury, the prosecutor possesses some additional powers and prerogatives which ensure his dominant role. The district attorney's ability to control the agenda, that is, the sequence in which cases are presented, is worthy of mention. This power enables the prosecutor, if he is so inclined, to do such things as: (1) initially present the grand jury with a wide variety of cases to determine which ones the jury processes without question and on which cases the grand jury challenges the district attorney, thus enabling the prosecutor to channel subsequent cases to those grand juries which give him the least trouble; and/or (2) increase the size of the agenda for a grand jury which is causing him difficulty, thereby pressuring that grand jury into spending less time with its cases in order to complete the daily agenda. In addition, the district attorney has the right to take a case that has already been voted on by a grand jury to a second such jury for its consideration. This is done whenever the prosecutor is unsatisfied with the vote of the first grand jury, and it enables him to keep trying until his will ultimately prevails in the vote of a more compliant grand jury.

SUMMARY AND SUGGESTIONS FOR FUTURE RESEARCH

In sum, grand jury behavior is characterized by a rapid processing of cases with little deliberation (except for a small handful of cases of special interest to upper middle class citizens), by low internal conflict in reaching decisions, and by overwhelming approval of the district attorney's recommendations. Such behavior patterns are largely accounted for by the kind of people who become grand jurors, by the inadequacy of the grand jury training process, by the heavy caseload which requires speedy processing of cases for adequate system maintenance, and by a variety of institutional and legal factors which give the district attorney's office a monopoly on the sources of vital information and which insure his capacity to manipulate grand jury activities.

This study cannot end without making some general and specific suggestions for future research on grand juries. First, much more needs to be learned about the selection of grand jurors. We need specific answers to question such as these: who are the jury commissioners and on what basis are they selected? What standards does the judge use in designating grand jury foremen?

Second, studies must acquire more knowledge about the grand jurors themselves. What are their values and what are their attitudes toward the police, the judicial system, and those arrested for a variety of crimes? The additional use of questionnaires and in-depth interviews with a large cross-section of grand jurors is necessary before we can draw an accurate profile of the typical grand juror.

More evidence is also needed about the internal dynamics of grand jury deliberations. Which types of grand jurors are likely to have more influence in the deliberations than others? Some evidence in this study suggests that the profession or race of the individual grand juror may cause other members of the jury to defer to him in cases which hinge on matters tangent to the grand juror's specific background. For example, on the 177th Grand Jury the lone black member was usually listened to with great attention in cases where an obviously black defendant was charging police harrassment, and the only lawyer on the jury was given considerable deference in cases which hinged on highly technical legal questions. Do grand juries develop a form of *stare decisis* as their terms progress (as was clearly the case with the 177th Grand Jury)? That is, are grand jurors, well into their term, likely to say about a case, "We had a case like this last month and we did such and such with it. We must then do the same with this case so we'll be consistent with ourselves." Also, is the grand jury foreman more likely to be on the winning side of divided votes than other grand jurors?

Finally, we need more data on the influence and role of the assistant district attorneys vis-à-vis the grand jury. Are some district attorneys more successful than others in obtaining the desired results from the grand jury? What tactics and strategies do district attorneys employ in preparing and presenting cases to grand juries? To what extent do district attorneys divert specific cases (or types of cases) from a grand jury to which the case(s) would routinely go to a grand jury which is more likely to resolve the case(s) in accordance with the district attorneys' wishes?

If answers to the above questions are found, we will be well on our way to understanding an institution and a process which at this time remains largely unexplored by students of the judicial process.

21. The Practice of Law as a Con Game

ABRAHAM S. BLUMBERG

A RECURRING THEME IN THE GROWING DIALOGUE between sociology and law has been the great need for a joint effort of the two disciplines to illuminate urgent social and legal issues. Having uttered fervent public pronouncements in this vein, however, the respective practitioners often go their separate ways. Academic spokesmen for the legal profession are somewhat critical of sociologists of law because of what they perceive as the sociologist's preoccupation with the application of theory and methodology to the examination of legal phenomena, without regard to the solution of legal problems. Further, it is felt that "contemporary writing in the sociology of law . . . betrays the existence of painfully unsophisticated notions about the day-to-day operations of courts, legislatures and law offices."[1] Regardless of the merit of such criticism, scant attention—apart from explorations of the legal profession itself—has been given to the sociological examination of legal institutions, or their supporting ideological assumptions. Thus, for example, very little sociological effort is expended to ascertain the validity and viability of important court decisions, which may rest on wholly erroneous assumptions about the contextual realities of social structure. A particular decision may rest upon a legally impeccable rationale; at the same time it may be rendered nugatory or self-defeating by contingencies imposed by aspects of social reality of which the lawmakers are themselves unaware.

Within this context, I wish to question the impact of three recent landmark decisions of the United States Supreme Court; each hailed as destined to effect profound changes in the future of criminal law administration and enforcement in America. The first of these, *Gideon v. Wainwright*, 372 U.S. 335 (1963) required states and localities henceforth to furnish counsel in the case of indigent persons charged with a felony.[2] The Gideon ruling left several major

▶SOURCE: *"The Practice of Law as Confidence Game: Organizational Cooptation of a Profession," Law and Society Review,* (June, 1967) 1:15–39. Reprinted by permission.

[1]H. W. Jones, *A View From the Bridge,* Law and Society: Supplement to Summer, 1965 Issue of Social Problems 42 (1965). See G. Geis, *Sociology, Criminology, and Criminal Law,* 7 Social Problems 40–47 (1959); N. S. Timasheff, *Growth and Scope of Sociology of Law,* in *Modern Sociological Theory in Continuity and Change* 424–49 (H. Becker & A. Boskoff, eds. 1957), for further evaluation of the strained relations between sociology and law.

[2]This decision represented the climax of a line of cases which had begun to chip away at the notion that the Sixth Amendment of the Constitution (right to assistance of counsel) applied only to the federal government, and could not be held to run against the states through the Fourteenth Amendment. An exhaustive historical analysis of the Fourteenth Amendment and the Bill of Rights will be found in C. Fairman, *Does the Fourteenth Amendment Incorporate the Bill of Rights? The Original Understanding,* 2 Stan. L. Rev. 5–139 (1949). Since the Gideon decision, there is already evidence that its effect will ultimately extend to indigent persons charged with misdemeanors—and perhaps ultimately even traffic cases and other minor offenses. For a popular account of this important development in connection with the right to assistance of counsel, see A. Lewis, *Gideon's Trumpet* (1964). For a scholarly historical analysis of the right to counsel see W. M. Beaney, *The Right to Counsel in American*

issues unsettled, among them the vital question: What is the precise point in time at which a suspect is entitled to counsel?[3] The answer came relatively quickly in *Escobedo v. Illinois,* 378 U.S. 478 (1964), which has aroused a storm of controversy. Danny Escobedo confessed to the murder of his brother-in-law after the police had refused to permit retained counsel to see him, although his lawyer was present in the station house and asked to confer with his client. In a 5–4 decision, the court asserted that counsel must be permitted when the process of police investigative effort shifts from merely investigatory to that of accusatory: "when its focus is on the accused and its purpose is to elicit a confession—our adversary system begins to operate, and, under the circumstances here, the accused must be permitted to consult with his lawyer."

As a consequence, Escobedo's confession was rendered inadmissible. The decision triggered a national debate among police, district attorneys, judges, lawyers, and other law enforcement officials, which continues unabated, as to the value and propriety of confessions in criminal cases.[4] On June 13, 1966, the Supreme Court in a 5–4 decision underscored the principle enunciated in *Escobedo* in the case of *Miranda v. Arizona.*[5] Police interrogation of any suspect in custody, without his consent, unless a defense attorney is present, is prohibited by the self-incrimination provision of the Fifth Amendment. Regardless of the relative merit of the various shades of opinion about the role of counsel in criminal cases, the issues generated thereby will be in part resolved as additional cases move toward decision in the Supreme Court in the near future. They are of peripheral interest and not of immediate concern in this paper. However, the *Gideon, Escobedo,* and *Miranda* cases pose interesting general questions. In all three decisions, the Supreme Court reiterates the traditional legal conception of a defense lawyer based on the ideological perception of a criminal case as an *adversary, combative* proceeding, in which counsel for the defense assiduously musters all the admittedly limited resources at his command to *defend* the accused.[6] The fundamental question remains to be answered: Does the Supreme Court's conception of the role of counsel in a criminal case square with social reality?

Courts (1955). For a more recent comprehensive review and discussion of the right to counsel and its development, see Note, *Counsel at Interrogation,* 73 Yale L.J. 1000–57 (1964).

With the passage of the Criminal Justice Act of 1964, indigent accused persons in the federal courts will be defended by federally paid legal counsel. For a general discussion of the nature and extent of public and private legal aid in the United States prior to the Gideon case, see E. A. Brownell, *Legal Aid in the United States* (1961); also R. B. von Mehren, et al., *Equal Justice for the Accused* (1959).

[3]In the case of federal defendants the issue is clear. In *Mallory v. United States,* 354 U.S. 449 (1957), the Supreme Court unequivocally indicated that a person under federal arrest must be taken "without any unnecessary delay" before a U.S. commissioner where he will receive information as to his rights to remain silent and to assistance of counsel which will be furnished, in the event he is indigent, under the Criminal Justice Act of 1964. For a most interesting and richly documented work in connection with the general area of the Bill of Rights, see C. R. Sowle, *Police Power and Individual Freedom* (1962).

[4]See N.Y. Times, Nov. 20, 1965, p. 1, for Justice Nathan R. Sobel's statement to the effect that based on his study of

1,000 indictments in Brooklyn, N.Y., from February–April, 1965, fewer than 10% involved confessions. Sobel's detailed analysis will be found in six articles which appeared in the New York Law Journal, beginning November 15, 1965, through November 21, 1965, titled *The Exclusionary Rules in the Law of Confessions: A Legal Perspective—A Practical Perspective.* Most law enforcement officials believe that the majority of convictions in criminal cases are based upon confessions obtained by police. For example, the District Attorney of New York County (a jurisdiction which has the largest volume of cases in the United States), Frank S. Hogan, reports that confessions are crucial and indicates "if a suspect is entitled to have a lawyer during preliminary questioning . . . any lawyer worth his fee will tell him to keep his mouth shut," N.Y. Times, Dec. 2. 1965, p. 1. Concise discussions of the issue are to be found in D. Robinson, Jr., *Massiah, Escobedo and Rationales for the Exclusion of Confessions,* 56 J. Crim. L. C. & P.S. 412–31 (1965); D. C. Dowling, *Escobedo and Beyond: The Need for a Fourteenth Amendment Code of Criminal Procedure,* 56 J. Crim. L. C. & P.S. 143–57 (1965).

[5]*Miranda v. Arizona,* 384 U.S. 436 (1966).

[6]Even under optimal circumstances a criminal case is a very much one-sided affair, the parties to the "contest" being

The task of this paper is to furnish some preliminary evidence toward the illumination of that question. Little empirical understanding of the function of defense counsel exists; only some ideologically oriented generalizations and commitments. This paper is based upon observations made by the writer during many years of legal practice in the criminal courts of a large metropolitan area. No claim is made as to its methodological rigor, although it does reflect a conscious and sustained effort for participant observation.

COURT STRUCTURE DEFINES ROLE OF DEFENSE LAWYER

The overwhelming majority of convictions in criminal cases (usually over 90 per cent) are not the product of a combative, trial-by-jury process at all, but instead merely involve the sentencing of the individual after a negotiated, bargained-for plea of guilty has been entered.[7] Although more recently the overzealous role of police and prosecutors in producing pretrial confessions and admissions has achieved a good deal of notoriety, scant attention has been paid to the

organizational structure and personnel of the criminal court itself. Indeed, the extremely high conviction rate produced without the features of an adversary trial in our courts would tend to suggest that the "trial" becomes a perfunctory reiteration and validation of the pretrial interrogation and investigation.[8]

The institutional setting of the court defines a role for the defense counsel in a criminal case radically different from the one traditionally depicted.[9] Sociologists and others have focused their attention on the deprivations and social disabilities of such variables as race, ethnicity, and social class as being the source of an accused person's defeat in a criminal court. Largely overlooked is the variable of the court organization itself, which possesses a thrust, purpose, and direction of its own. It is grounded in pragmatic values, bureaucratic priorities, and administrative instruments. These exalt maximum production and the particularistic career designs of organizational incumbents, whose occupational and career commitments tend to generate a set of priorities. These priorities exert a higher claim than the stated ideological goals of "due process of law," and are often inconsistent with them.

Organizational goals and discipline impose a set of demands and conditions of practice on the respective professions in the criminal court, to which they respond by abandoning their ideological and professional commitments to the accused client, in the service of these higher claims of the court organization. All court per-

---

decidedly unequal in strength and resources. See A. S. Goldstein, *The State and the Accused: Balance of Advantage in Criminal Procedure,* 69 Yale L.J. 1149–99 (1960).

[7] F. J. Davis et al., *Society and the Law: New Meanings for an Old Profession* 301 (1962); L. Orfield, *Criminal Procedure from Arrest to Appeal* 297 (1947).

D. J. Newman, *Pleading Guilty for Considerations: A Study of Bargain Justice,* 46 J. Crim. L. C. & P.S. 780–90 (1954). Newman's data covered only one year, 1954, in a midwestern community, however, it is in general confirmed by my own data drawn from a far more populous area, and from what is one of the major criminal courts in the country, for a period of fifteen years from 1950 to 1964 inclusive. The English experience tends also to confirm American data, see N. Walker, *Crime and Punishment in Britain: An Analysis of the Penal System* (1965). See also D. J. Newman, *Conviction: The Determination of Guilt or Innocence Without Trial* (1966), for a comprehensive legalistic study of the guilty plea sponsored by the American Bar Foundation. The criminal court as a social system, an analysis of "bargaining" and its functions in the criminal court's organizational structure, are examined in my forthcoming book, *The Criminal Court: A Sociological Perspective,* to be published by Quadrangle Books, Chicago.

[8] G. Feifer, *Justice in Moscow* (1965). The Soviet trial has been termed "an appeal from the pretrial investigation" and Feifer notes that the Soviet "trial" is simply a recapitulation of the data collected by the pretrial investigator. The notions of a trial being a "tabula rasa" and presumptions of innocence are wholly alien to Soviet notions of justice. ". . . the closer the investigation resembles the finished script, the better. . . ." *Id.* at 86.

[9] For a concise statement of the constitutional and economic aspects of the right to legal assistance, see M. G. Paulsen, *Equal Justice for the Poor Man* (1964); for a brief traditional description of the legal profession see P. A. Freund, *The Legal Profession,* Daedalus 689–700 (1963).

sonnel, including the accused's own lawyer, tend to be coopted to become agent-mediators[10] who help the accused redefine his situation and restructure his perceptions concomitant with a plea of guilty.

Of all the occupational roles in the court the only private individual who is officially recognized as having a special status and concomitant obligations is the lawyer. His legal status is that of "an officer of the court" and he is held to a standard of ethical performance and duty to his client as well as to the court. This obligation is thought to be far higher than that expected of ordinary individuals occupying the various occupational statuses in the court community. However, lawyers, whether privately retained or of the legal-aid, public defender variety, have close and continuing relations with the prosecuting office and the court itself through discreet relations with the judges via their law secretaries or "confidential" assistants. Indeed, lines of communication, influence and contact with those offices, as well as with the Office of the Clerk of the court, Probation Division, and with the press, are essential to present and prospective requirements of criminal law practice. Similarly, the subtle involvement of the press and other mass media in the court's organizational network is not readily discernible to the casual observer. Accused persons come and go in the court system schema, but the structure and its occupational incumbents remain to carry on their respective career, occupational and organizational enterprises. The individual stridencies, tensions, and conflicts a given accused person's case may present to all the participants are overcome, because the formal and informal relations of all the groups in the court setting require it. The probability of continued future relations and interaction must be preserved at all costs.

This is particularly true of the "lawyer regulars" i.e., those defense lawyers, who by virtue of their continuous appearances in behalf of defendants, tend to represent the bulk of a criminal court's non-indigent case workload, and those lawyers who are not "regulars," who appear almost casually in behalf of an occasional client. Some of the "lawyer regulars" are highly visible as one moves about the major urban centers of the nation, their offices line the back streets of the courthouses, at times sharing space with bondsmen. Their political "visibility" in terms of local club house ties, reaching into the judge's chambers and prosecutor's office, are also deemed essential to successful practitioners. Previous research has indicated that the "lawyer regulars" make no effort to conceal their dependence upon police, bondsmen, jail personnel. Nor do they conceal the necessity for maintaining intimate relations with all levels of personnel in the court setting as a means of obtaining, maintaining, and building their practice. These informal relations are the *sine qua non* not only of retaining a practice, but also in the negotiation of pleas and sentences.[11]

The client, then, is a secondary figure in the court system as in certain other bureaucratic settings.[12] He becomes a means to other ends of the organization's incumbents. He may present doubts, contingencies, and pressures which challenge existing informal arrangements or disrupt them; but these tend to be resolved in favor of the continuance of the organization and

---

[10]I use the concept in the general sense that Erving Goffman employed it in his *Asylums: Essays on the Social Situation of Mental Patients and Other Inmates* (1961).

[11]A. L. Wood, *Informal Relations in the Practice of Criminal Law*, 62 Am. J. Soc. 48–55 (1956); J. E. Carlin, *Lawyers on Their Own* 105–109 (1962); R. Goldfarb, *Ransom—A Critique of the American Bail System* 114–15 (1965). Relatively recent data as to recruitment to the legal profession, and variables involved in the type of practice engaged in, will be found in J. Ladinsky, *Careers of Lawyers, Law Practice, and Legal Institutions*, 28 Am. Soc. Rev. 47–54 (1963). See also S. Warkov & J. Zelan, *Lawyers in the Making* (1965).

[12]There is a real question to be raised as to whether in certain organizational settings, a complete reversal of the bureaucratic-ideal has not occurred. That is, it would seem, in some instances the organization appears to exist to serve the needs of its various occupational incumbents, rather than its clients. A. Etzioni, *Modern Organizations* 94–104 (1964).

its relations as before. There is a greater community of interest among all the principal organizational structures and their incumbents than exists elsewhere in other settings. The accused's lawyer has far greater professional, economic, intellectual and other ties to the various elements of the court system than he does to his own client. In short, the court is a closed community.

This is more than just the case of the usual "secrets" of bureaucracy which are fanatically defended from an outside view. Even all elements of the press are zealously determined to report on that which will not offend the board of judges, the prosecutor, probation, legal-aid, or other officials, in return for privileges and courtesies granted in the past and to be granted in the future. Rather than any view of the matter in terms of some variation of a "conspiracy" hypothesis, the simple explanation is one of an ongoing system handling delicate tensions, managing the trauma produced by law enforcement and administration, and requiring almost pathological distrust of "outsiders" bordering on group paranoia.

The hostile attitude toward "outsiders" is in large measure engendered by a defensiveness itself produced by the inherent deficiencies of assembly line justice, so characteristic of our major criminal courts. Intolerably large caseloads of defendants which must be disposed of in an organizational context of limited resources and personnel, potentially subject the participants in the court community to harsh scrutiny from appellate courts, and other public and private sources of condemnation. As a consequence, an almost irreconcilable conflict is posed in terms of intense pressures to process large numbers of cases on the one hand, and the stringent ideological and legal requirements of "due process of law," on the other hand. A rather tenuous resolution of the dilemma has emerged in the shape of a large variety of bureaucratically ordained and controlled "work crimes," short cuts, deviations, and outright rule violations adopted as court practice in order to

meet production norms. Fearfully anticipating criticism on ethical as well as legal grounds, all the significant participants in the court's social structure are bound into an organized system of complicity. This consists of a work arrangement in which the patterned, covert, informal breaches, and evasions of "due process" are institutionalized, but are nevertheless denied to exist.

These institutionalized evasions will be found to occur to some degree, in all criminal courts. Their nature, scope and complexity are largely determined by the size of the court, and the character of the community in which it is located, e.g., whether it is a large, urban institution, or a relatively small rural county court. In addition, idiosyncratic, local conditions may contribute to a unique flavor in the character and quality of the criminal law's administration in a particular community. However, in most instances a variety of strategems are employed—some subtle, some crude, in effectively disposing of what are often too large caseloads. A wide variety of coercive devices are employed against an accused-client, couched in a depersonalized, instrumental, bureaucratic version of due process of law, and which are in reality a perfunctory obeisance to the ideology of due process. These include some very explicit pressures which are exerted in some measure by all court personnel, including judges, to plead guilty and avoid trial. In many instances the sanction of a potentially harsh sentence is utilized as the visible alternative to pleading guilty, in the case of recalcitrants. Probation and psychiatric reports are "tailored" to organizational needs, or are at least responsive to the court organization's requirements for the refurbishment of a defendant's social biography, consonant with his new status. A resourceful judge can, through his subtle domination of the proceedings, impose his will on the final outcome of a trial. Stenographers and clerks, in their function as record keepers, are on occasion pressed into service in support of a judicial need to "rewrite" the record of a courtroom event. Bail practices are usually employed for purposes other than simply assuring a defendant's presence on the date of a hearing in connection with his case. Too often, the discretionary power as to bail is part of the arsenal of weapons available to collapse the resistance of an accused person. The foregoing is a most cursory examination of some of the more prominent "short cuts" available to any court organization. There are numerous other procedural strategies constituting due process deviations, which tend to become the work style artifacts of a court's personnel. Thus, only court "regulars" who are "bound in" are really accepted; others are treated routinely and in almost a coldly correct manner.

The defense attorneys, therefore, whether of the legal-aid, public defender variety, or privately retained, although operating in terms of pressures specific to their respective role and organizational obligations, ultimately are concerned with strategies which tend to lead to a plea. It is the rational, impersonal elements involving economies of time, labor, expense and a superior commitment of the defense counsel to these rationalistic values of maximum production[13] of court organization that prevail, in his relationship with a client. The lawyer "regulars" are frequently former staff members of the prosecutor's office and utilize the prestige, knowhow and contacts of their former affiliation as part of their stock in trade. Close and continuing relations between the lawyer "regular"and his former colleagues in the prosecutor's office generally overshadow the relationship between the regular and his client. The continuing colleagueship of supposedly adversary counsel rests on real professional and organizational needs of a *quid pro quo*, which goes beyond the limits of an accommodation or *modus vivendi* one might ordinarily expect under the circumstances of an otherwise seemingly adversary relationship. Indeed, the adversary features which are manifest are for the most part muted and exist even in their attenuated form largely for external consumption. The principals, lawyer and assistant district attorney, rely upon one another's cooperation for their continued professional existence, and so the bargaining between them tends usually to be "reasonable" rather than fierce.

FEE COLLECTION AND FIXING

The real key to understanding the role of defense counsel in a criminal case is to be found in the area of the fixing of the fee to be charged and its collection. The problem of fixing and collecting the fee tends to influence to a significant degree the criminal court process itself, and not just the relationship of the lawyer and his client. In essence, a lawyer-client "confidence game" is played. A true confidence game is unlike the case of the emperor's new clothes wherein that monarch's nakedness was a result of inordinate gullibility and credulity. In a genuine confidence game, the perpetrator manipulates the basic dishonesty of his partner, the victim or mark, toward his own (the confidence operator's) ends. Thus, "the victim of a con scheme must have some larceny in his heart."[14]

Legal service lends itself particularly well to

[13]Three relatively recent items reported in the New York Times, tend to underscore this point as it has manifested itself in one of the major criminal courts. In one instance the Bronx County Bar Association condemned "mass assembly-line justice," which "was rushing defendants into pleas of guilty and into convictions, in violation of their legal rights." N.Y. Times, March 10, 1965, p. 51. Another item, appearing somewhat later that year reports a judge criticizing his own court system (the New York Criminal Court), that "pressure to set statistical records in disposing of cases had hurt the administration of justice." N.Y. Times, Nov. 4, 1965, p. 49. A third, and most unusual recent public discussion in the press was a statement by a leading New York appellate judge decrying "instant justice" which is employed to reduce court calendar congestion "converting our courthouses into counting houses . . . , as in most big cities where the volume of business tends to overpower court facilities." N.Y. Times, Feb. 5, 1966, p. 58.

[14]R. L. Gasser, *The Confidence Game*, 27 Fed. Prob. 47 (1963).

confidence games. Usually, a plumber will be able to demonstrate empirically that he has performed a service by clearing up the stuffed drain, repairing the leaky faucet or pipe—and therefore merits his fee. He has rendered, when summoned, a visible, tangible boon for his client in return for the requested fee. A physician, who has not performed some visible surgery or otherwise engaged in some readily discernible procedure in connection with a patient, may be deemed by the patient to have "done nothing" for him. As a consequence, medical practitioners may simply prescribe or administer by injection a placebo to overcome a patient's potential reluctance or dissatisfaction in paying a requested fee, "for nothing."

In the practice of law there is a special problem in this regard, no matter what the level of the practitioner or his place in the hierarchy of prestige. Much legal work is intangible either because it is simply a few words of advice, some preventive action, a telephone call, negotiation of some kind, a form filled out and filed, a hurried conference with another attorney or an official of a government agency, a letter or opinion written, or a countless variety of seemingly innocuous, and even prosaic procedures and actions. These are the basic activities, apart from any possible court appearance, of almost all lawyers, at all levels of practice. Much of the activity is not in the nature of the exercise of the traditional, precise professional skills of attorney such as library research and oral argument in connection with appellate briefs, court motions, trial work, drafting of opinions, memoranda, contracts, and other complex documents and agreements. Instead, much legal activity, whether it is at the lowest or highest "white shoe" law firm levels, is of the brokerage, agent, sales representative, lobbyist type of activity, in which the lawyer acts for someone else in pursuing the latter's interests and designs. The service is intangible.[15]

The large scale law firm may not speak as openly of their "contacts," their "fixing" abilities, as does the lower level lawyer. They trade instead upon a facade of thick carpeting, walnut panelling, genteel low pressure, and superficialities of traditional legal professionalism. There are occasions when even the large firm is on the defensive in connection with the fees they charge because the services rendered or results obtained do not appear to merit the fee asked.[16] Therefore, there is a recurrent problem in the legal profession in fixing the amount of fee, and in justifying the basis for the requested fee.

Although the fee at times amounts to what the traffic and the conscience of the lawyer will bear, one further observation must be made with regard to the size of the fee and its collection. The defendant in a criminal case and the material gain he may have acquired during the course of his illicit activities are soon parted. Not infrequently the ill gotten fruits of the various modes of larceny are sequestered by a defense lawyer in payment of his fee. Inexorably, the amount of the fee is a function of the dollar value of the crime committed, and is frequently set with meticulous precision at a sum which bears an uncanny relationship to that of the net proceeds of the particular offense involved. On occasion, defendants have been known to commit additional offenses while at liberty on bail, in order to secure the requisite funds with which to meet their obligations for payment of legal fees. Defense lawyers condition even the most obtuse clients to recognize that there is a firm interconnection between fee payment and the zealous exercise of professional expertise, secret knowledge, and organizational "connections" in their behalf. Lawyers, therefore, seek to keep their clients in a proper state of tension, and to arouse in them the precise edge of anxiety which is calculated to encourage prompt fee payment. Consequently, the client attitude in the relationship between defense counsel and an accused is in

[15]C. W. Mills, *White Collar* 121–29 (1951); J. E. Carlin, *supra,* note 11.

[16]E. O. Smigel, *The Wall Street Lawyer* (New York: The Free Press of Glencoe, 1964), p. 309.

many instances a precarious admixture of hostility, mistrust, dependence, and sycophancy. By keeping his client's anxieties aroused to the proper pitch, and establishing a seemingly causal relationship between a requested fee and the accused's ultimate extrication from his onerous difficulties, the lawyer will have established the necessary preliminary groundwork to assure a minimum of haggling over the fee and its eventual payment.

In varying degrees, as a consequence, all law practice involves a manipulation of the client and a stage management of the lawyer-client relationship so that at least an *appearance* of help and service will be forthcoming. This is accomplished in a variety of ways, often exercised in combination with each other. At the outset, the lawyer-professional employs with suitable variation a measure of sales-puff which may range from an air of unbounding self-confidence, adequacy, and dominion over events, to that of complete arrogance. This will be supplemented by the affectation of a studied, faultless mode of personal attire. In the larger firms, the furnishings and office trappings will serve as the backdrop to help in impression management and client intimidation. In all firms, solo or large scale, an access to secret knowledge, and to the seats of power and influence is inferred, or presumed to a varying degree as the basic vendible commodity of the practitioners.

The lack of visible end product offers a special complication in the course of the professional life of the criminal court lawyer with respect to his fee and in his relations with his client. The plain fact is that an accused in a criminal case always "loses" even when he has been exonerated by an acquittal, discharge, or dismissal of his case. The hostility of an accused which follows as a consequence of his arrest, incarceration, possible loss of job, expense and other traumas connected with his case is directed, by means of displacement, toward his lawyer. It is in this sense that it may be said that a criminal lawyer never really "wins" a case. The really satisfied client is rare, since in the very nature of the situation even an accused's vindication leaves him with some degree of dissatisfaction and hostility. It is this state of affairs that makes for a lawyer-client relationship in the criminal court which tends to be a somewhat exaggerated version of the usual lawyer-client confidence game.

At the outset, because there are great risks of nonpayment of the fee, due to the impecuniousness of his clients, and the fact that a man who is sentenced to jail may be a singularly unappreciative client, the criminal lawyer collects his fee *in advance*. Often, because the lawyer and the accused both have questionable designs of their own upon each other, the confidence game can be played. The criminal lawyer must serve three major functions, or stated another way, he must solve three problems. First, he must arrange for his fee; second, he must prepare and then, if necessary, "cool out" his client in case of defeat[17] (a highly likely contingency); third, he must satisfy the court organization that he has performed adequately in the process of negotiating the plea, so as to preclude the possibility of any sort of embarrassing incident which may serve to invite "outside" scrutiny.

In assuring the attainment of one of his primary objectives, his fee, the criminal lawyer will very often enter into negotiations with the accused's kin, including collateral relatives. In many instances, the accused himself is unable to pay any sort of fee or anything more than a token fee. It then becomes important to involve as many of the accused's kin as possible in the situation. This is especially so if the attorney

[17]Talcott Parsons indicates that the social role and function of the lawyer can be therapeutic, helping his client psychologically in giving him necessary emotional support at critical times. The lawyer is also said to be acting as an agent of social control in the counseling of his client and in the influencing of his course of conduct. See T. Parsons, *Essays in Sociological Theory,* 382 et seq. (1954); E. Goffman, *On Cooling the Mark Out: Some Aspects of Adaptations to Failure,* in *Human Behavior and Social Processes* 482–505 (A. Rose ed., 1962). Goffman's "cooling out"analysis is especially relevant in the lawyer-accused client relationship.

hopes to collect a significant part of a proposed substantial fee. It is not uncommon for several relatives to contribute toward the fee. The larger the group, the greater the possibility that the lawyer will collect a sizable fee by getting contributions from each.

A fee for a felony case which ultimately results in a plea, rather than a trial, may ordinarily range anywhere from $500 to $1,500. Should the case go to trial, the fee will be proportionately larger, depending upon the length of the trial. But the larger the fee the lawyer wishes to exact, the more impressive his performance must be, in terms of his stage managed image as a personage of great influence and power in the court organization. Court personnel are keenly aware of the extent to which a lawyer's stock in trade involves the precarious stage management of an image which goes beyond the usual professional flamboyance, and for this reason alone the lawyer is "bound in" to the authority system of the court's organizational discipline. Therefore, to some extent, court personnel will aid the lawyer in the creation and maintenance of that impression. There is a tacit commitment to the lawyer by the court organization, apart from formal etiquette, to aid him in this. Such augmentation of the lawyer's stage managed image as this affords, is the partial basis for the *quid pro quo* which exists between the lawyer and the court organization. It tends to serve as the continuing basis for the higher loyalty of the lawyer to the organization; his relationship with his client, in contrast, is transient, ephemeral and often superficial.

DEFENSE LAWYER AS DOUBLE AGENT

The lawyer has often been accused of stirring up unnecessary litigation, especially in the field of negligence. He is said to acquire a vested interest in a cause of action or claim which was initially his client's. The strong incentive of possible fee motivates the lawyer to promote litigation which would otherwise never have developed. However, the criminal lawyer develops a vested interest of an entirely different nature in his client's case: to limit its scope and duration rather than do battle. Only in this way can a case be "profitable." Thus, he enlists the aid of relatives not only to assure payment of his fee, but he will also rely on these persons to help him in his agent-mediator role of convincing the accused to plead guilty, and ultimately to help in "cooling out" the accused if necessary.

It is at this point that an accused-defendant may experience his first sense of "betrayal." While he had perhaps perceived the police and prosecutor to be adversaries, or possibly even the judge, the accused is wholly unprepared for his counsel's role performance as an agent-mediator. In the same vein, it is even less likely to occur to an accused that members of his own family or other kin may become agents, albeit at the behest and urging of other agents or mediators, acting on the principle that they are in reality helping an accused negotiate the best possible plea arrangement under the circumstances. Usually, it will be the lawyer who will activate next of kin in this role, his ostensible motive being to arrange for his fee. But soon latent and unstated motives will assert themselves, with entreaties by counsel to the accused's next of kin, to appeal to the accused to "help himself" by pleading. *Gemeinschaft* sentiments are to this extent exploited by a defense lawyer (or even at times by a district attorney) to achieve specific secular ends, that is, of concluding a particular matter with all possible dispatch.

The fee is often collected in stages, each installment usually payable prior to a necessary court appearance required during the course of an accused's career journey. At each stage, in his interviews and communications with the accused, or in addition, with members of his family, if they are helping with the fee payment, the lawyer employs an air of professional confidence and "inside-dopesterism" in order to assuage anxieties on all sides. He makes the necessary bland assurances, and in effect manipulates his client, who is usually willing to do and say the things, true or not, which will help his attorney extricate him. Since the dimensions of what he is essentially selling, organizational influence and expertise, are not technically and precisely measurable, the lawyer can make extravagant claims of influence and secret knowledge with impunity. Thus, lawyers frequently claim to have inside knowledge in connection with information in the hands of the D.A., police, probation officials or to have access to these functionaries. Factually, they often do, and need only to exaggerate the nature of their relationships with them to obtain the desired effective impression upon the client. But, as in the genuine confidence game, the victim who has participated is loath to do anything which will upset the lesser plea which his lawyer has "conned" him into accepting.[18]

In effect, in his role as double agent, the criminal lawyer performs an extremely vital and delicate mission for the court organization and the accused. Both principals are anxious to terminate the litigation with a minimum of expense and damage to each other. There is no other personage or role incumbent in the total court structure more strategically located, who by training and in terms of is own requirements, is more ideally suited to do so than the lawyer. In recognition of this, judges will cooperate with attorneys in many important ways. For example,

[18]The question has never been raised as to whether "bargain justice," "copping a plea," or justice by negotiations is a constitutional process. Although it has become the most central aspect of the process of criminal law administration, it has received virtually no close scrutiny by the appellate courts. As a consequence, it is relatively free of legal control and supervision. But, apart from any questions of the legality of bargaining, in terms of the pressures and devices that are employed which tend to violate due process of law, there remain ethical and practical questions. The system of bargain-counter justice is like the proverbial iceberg, much of its danger is concealed in secret negotiations and its least alarming feature, the final plea, being the one presented to public view. See A. S. Trebach, *The Rationing of Justice* 74–94 (1964); Note, *Guilty Plea Bargaining: Compromises by Prosecutors to Secure Guilty Pleas*, 112 U. Pa. L. Rev. 865–95 (1964).

they will adjourn the case of an accused in jail awaiting plea or sentence if the attorney requests such action. While explicitly this may be done for some innocuous and seemingly valid reason, the tacit purpose is that pressure is being applied by the attorney for the collection of his fee, which he knows will probably not be forthcoming if the case is concluded. Judges are aware of this tactic on the part of lawyers, who, by requesting an adjournment, keep an accused incarcerated awhile longer as a not too subtle method of dunning a client for payment. However, the judges will go along with this, on the ground that important ends are being served. Often, the only end served is to protect a lawyer's fee.

The judge will help an accused's lawyer in still another way. He will lend the official aura of his office and courtroom so that a lawyer can stage manage an impression of an "all out" performance for the accused in justification of his fee. The judge and other court personnel will serve as a backdrop for a scene charged with dramatic fire, in which the accused's lawyer makes a stirring appeal in his behalf. With a show of restrained passion, the lawyer will intone the virtues of the accused and recite the social deprivations which have reduced him to his present state. The speech varies somewhat, depending on whether the accused has been convicted after trial or has pleaded guilty. In the main, however, the incongruity, superficiality, and ritualistic character of the total performance is underscored by a visibly impassive, almost bored reaction on the part of the judge and other members of the court retinue.

Afterward, there is a hearty exchange of pleasantries between the lawyer and district attorney, wholly out of context in terms of the supposed adversary nature of the preceding events. The fiery passion in defense of his client is gone, and the lawyers for both sides resume their offstage relations, chatting amiably and perhaps including the judge in their restrained banter. No other aspect of their visible conduct so effectively serves to put even a casual observer on notice, that these individuals have claims upon each other. These seemingly innocuous actions are indicative of continuing organizational and informal relations, which, in their intricacy and depth, range far beyond any priorities or claims a particular defendant may have.[19]

Criminal law practice is a unique form of private law practice since it really only appears to be private practice.[20] Actually it is bureaucratic practice, because of the legal practitioner's enmeshment in the authority, discipline, and perspectives of the court organization. Private practice, supposedly, in a professional sense, involves the maintenance of an organized, disciplined body of knowledge and learning; the individual practitioners are imbued with a spirit of autonomy and service, the earning of a livelihood being incidental. In the sense that the lawyer in the criminal court serves as a double agent, serving higher organizational rather than

professional ends, he may be deemed to be engaged in bureaucratic rather than private practice. To some extent the lawyer-client "confidence game," in addition to its other functions, serves to conceal this fact.

THE CLIENT'S PERCEPTION

The "cop-out" ceremony, in which the court process culminates, is not only invaluable for redefining the accused's perspectives of himself, but also in reiterating publicly in a formally structured ritual the accused person's guilt for the benefit of significant "others" who are observing. The accused not only is made to assert publicly his guilt of a specific crime, but also a complete recital of its details. He is further made to indicate that he is entering his plea of guilt freely, willingly, and voluntarily, and that he is not doing so because of any promises or in consideration of any commitments that may have been made to him by anyone. This last is intended as a blanket statement to shield the participants from any possible charges of "coercion" or undue influence that may have been exerted in violation of due process requirements. Its function is to preclude any later review by an appellate court on these grounds, and also to obviate any second thoughts an accused may develop in connection with his plea.

However, for the accused, the conception of self as a guilty person is in large measure a temporary role adaptation. His career socialization as an accused, if it is successful, eventuates in his acceptance and redefinition of himself as a guilty person.[21] However, the transformation is

---

[19]For a conventional summary statement of some of the inevitable conflicting loyalties encountered in the practice of law, see E. E. Cheatham, *Cases and Materials on the Legal Profession* 70–79 (2d ed., 1955).

[20]Some lawyers at either end of the continuum of law practice appear to have grave doubts as to whether it is indeed a profession at all. J. E. Carlin, *op. cit., supra,* note 11, at 192; E. O. Smigel, *supra,* note 16, at 304–305.Increasingly, it is perceived as a business with widespread evasion of the Canons of Ethics, duplicity and chicanery being practiced in an effort to get and keep business. The poet, Carl Sandburg, epitomized this notion in the following vignette: "Have you a criminal lawyer in this burg?" "We think so but we haven't been able to prove it on him." C. Sandburg, *The People, Yes* 154 (1936).

Thus, while there is a considerable amount of dishonesty present in law practice involving fee splitting, thefts from clients, influence peddling, fixing, questionable use of favors and gifts to obtain business or influence others, this sort of activity is most often attributed to the "solo," private practice lawyer. See A. L. Wood, *Professional Ethics Among Criminal Lawyers,* Social Problems (1959). However, to some degree, large scale "downtown" elite firms also engage in these dubious activities. The difference is that the latter firms enjoy a good deal of immunity from these harsh charges because of their institutional and organizational advantages, in terms of near monopoly over more desirable types of practice, as well as exerting great influence in the political, economic and professional realms of power.

[21]This does not mean that most of those who plead guilty are innocent of any crime. Indeed, in many instances those who have been able to negotiate a lesser plea, have done so willingly and even eagerly. The system of justice-by-negotiation, without trial, probably tends to better serve the interests and requirements of guilty persons, who are thereby presented with formal alternatives of "half a loaf," in terms of, at worst, possibilities of a lesser plea and a concomitant shorter sentence as compensation for their acquiescence and participation. Having observed the prescriptive etiquette in

ephemeral, in that he will, in private, quickly reassert his innocence. Of importance is that he accept his defeat, publicly proclaim it, and find some measure of pacification in it.[22] Almost immediately after his plea, a defendant will generally be interviewed by a representative of the probation division in connection with a presentence report which is to be prepared. The very first question to be asked of him by the probation officer is: "Are you guilty of the crime to which you pleaded?" This is by way of double affirmation of the defendant's guilt. Should the defendant now begin to make bold assertions of his innocence, despite his plea of guilty, he will be asked to withdraw his plea and stand trial on the original charges. Such a threatened possibility is, in most instances, sufficient to cause an accused to let the plea stand and to request the probation officer to overlook his exclamations of innocence. Table I that follows is a breakdown of the categorized responses of a random sample of male defendants in Metropolitan Court[23]

during 1962, 1963, and 1964 in connection with their statements during presentence probation interviews following their plea of guilty.

It would be well to observe at the outset, that of the 724 defendants who pleaded guilty before trial, only 43 (5.94 per cent) of the total group had confessed prior to their indictment. Thus, the ultimate judicial process was predicated upon evidence independent of any confession of the accused.[24]

As the data indicate, only a relatively small number (95) out of the total number of defendants actually will even admit their guilt, following the "cop-out" ceremony. However, even though they have affirmed their guilt, many of these defendants felt that they should have been able to negotiate a more favorable plea. The largest aggregate of defendants (373) were those who reasserted their "innocence" following their public profession of guilt during the "cop-out" ceremony. These defendants employed differential degrees of fervor, solemnity and credibility, ranging from really mild, wavering assertions of innocence which were embroidered with a variety of stock explanations and rationalizations, to those of an adamant, "framed" nature. Thus, the "Innocent" group, for the most part, were largely concerned with underscoring for their probation interviewer their essential "goodness" and

---

compliance with the defendant role expectancies in this setting, he is rewarded. An innocent person, on the other hand, is confronted with the same set of role prescriptions, structures and legal alternatives, and in any event, for him this mode of justice is often an ineluctable bind.

[22] "Any communicative network between persons whereby the public identity of an actor is transformed into something looked on as lower in the local scheme of social types will be called a 'status degradation ceremony.'" H. Garfinkel, *Conditions of Successful Degradation Ceremonies*, 61 Am. J. Soc. 420–24 (1956). But contrary to the conception of the "cop out" as a "status degradation ceremony," is the fact that it is in reality a charade, during the course of which an accused must project an appropriate and acceptable amount of guilt, penitence and remorse. Having adequately feigned the role of the "guilty person," his hearers will engage in the fantasy that he is contrite, and thereby merits a lesser plea. It is one of the essential functions of the criminal lawyer that he coach and direct his accused-client in that role performance. Thus, what is actually involved is not a "degradation" process at all, but is instead, a highly structured system of exchange cloaked in the rituals of legalism and public professions of guilt and repentance.

[23] The name is of course fictitious. However, the actual court which served as the universe from which the data were drawn, is one of the largest criminal courts in the United States, dealing with felonies only. Female defendants in the

years 1950 through 1964 constituted from 7–10% of the totals for each year.

[24] My own data in this connection would appear to support Sobel's conclusion (see note 4 *supra*), and appears to be at variance with the prevalent view, which stresses the importance of confessions in law enforcement and prosecution. All the persons in my sample were originally charged with felonies ranging from homicide to forgery; in most instances the original felony charges were reduced to misdemeanors by way of a negotiated lesser plea. The vast range of crime categories which are available, facilitates the patterned court process of plea reduction to a lesser offense, which is also usually a socially less opprobrious crime. For an illustration of this feature of the bargaining process in a court utilizing a public defender office, see D. Sudnow, *Normal Crimes: Sociological Features of the Penal Code in a Public Defender Office*, 12 Social Problems 255–76 (1964).

Table I. Defendant Responses as to Guilt or Innocence after Pleading Guilty
N = 724   Years — 1962, 1963, 1964

Nature of Response		N of Defendants
Innocent (Manipulated)	"The lawyer or judge, police or D.A. 'conned me'"	86
Innocent (Pragmatic)	"Wanted to get it over with" "You can't beat the system" "They have you over a barrel when you have a record"	147
Innocent (Advice of counsel)	"Followed my lawyer's advice"	92
Innocent (Defiant)	"Framed"— "Betrayed by "Complainant," "Police," "Squealers," "Lawyer," "Friends," "Wife," "Girlfriend"	33
Innocent (Adverse social data)	Blames probation officer or psychiatrist for "Bad Report," in cases where there was pre-pleading investigation	15
Guilty	"But I should have gotten a better deal" Blames Lawyer, D.A., Police, Judge	74
Guilty	Won't say anything further	21
Fatalistic (Doesn't press his "Innocence," won't admit "Guilt")	"I did it for convenience" "My lawyer told me it was only thing I could do" "I did it because it was the best way out"	248
No Response		8
Total		724

"worthiness," despite their formal plea of guilty. Assertion of his innocence at the post-plea stage, resurrects a more respectable and acceptable self concept for the accused defendant who has pleaded guilty. A recital of the structural exigencies which precipitated his plea of guilt, serves to embellish a newly proffered claim of innocence, which many defendants mistakenly feel will stand them in good stead at the time of sentence, or ultimately with probation or parole authorities.

Relatively few (33) maintained their innocence in terms of having been "framed" by some person or agent-mediator, although a larger number (86) indicated that they had been manipulated or "conned" by an agent-mediator to plead guilty, but as indicated, their assertions of innocence were relatively mild.

A rather substantial group (147) preferred to stress the pragmatic aspects of their plea of guilty. They would only perfunctorily assert their innocence and would in general refer to some adverse aspect of their situation which they believed tended to negatively affect their bargaining leverage, including in some instances a prior criminal record.

One group of defendants (92), while maintaining their innocence, simply employed some variation of a theme of following "the advice of counsel" as a covering response, to explain their guilty plea in the light of their new affirmation of innocence.

The largest single group of defendants (248) were basically fatalistic. They often verbalized weak suggestions of their innocence in rather halting terms, wholly without conviction. By the same token, they would not admit guilt readily and were generally evasive as to guilt or innocence, preferring to stress aspects of their stoic submission in their decision to plead. This sizable group of defendants appeared to perceive the total court process as being caught up in a monstrous organizational apparatus, in which the defendant role expectancies were not clearly defined. Reluctant to offend anyone in authority, fearful that clear-cut statements on their part as to their guilt or innocence would be negatively construed, they adopted a stance of passivity, resignation and acceptance. Interestingly, they would in most instances invoke their lawyer as being the one who crystallized the available alternatives for them, and who was therefore the critical element in their decision-making process.

In order to determine which agent-mediator was most influential in altering the accused's perspectives as to his decision of plead or go to trial (regardless of the proposed basis of the plea), the same sample of defendants were asked to indicate the person who first suggested to them that they plead guilty. They were also asked to indicate which of the persons or officials who made such suggestion, was most influential in affecting their final decision to plead.

The following table indicates the breakdown of the responses to the two questions:

It is popularly assumed that the police, through forced confessions, and the district attorney, employing still other pressures, are most instrumental in the inducement of an accused to plead guilty.[25] As Table II indicates, it is actually

Table II. Role of Agent-mediators in Defendant's Guilty Plea

Person or Official	First Suggested Plea of Guilty	Influenced the Accused Most in His Final Decision to Plead
Judge	4	26
District attorney	67	116
Defense counsel	407	411
Probation officer	14	3
Psychiatrist	8	1
Wife	34	120
Friends and kin	21	14
Police	14	4
Fellow inmates	119	14
Others	28	5
No response	8	10
Total	724	724

the defendant's own counsel who is most effective in this role. Further, this phenomenon tends to reinforce the extremely rational nature of criminal law administration, for an organization could not rely upon the sort of idiosyncratic measures employed by the police to induce confessions and maintain its efficiency, high production and overall rational-legal character. The defense counsel becomes the ideal agent-mediator since, as "officer of the court" and confidant of the accused and his kin, he lives astride both worlds and can serve the ends of the two as well as his own.[26]

While an accused's wife, for example, may be

Barth, *Law Enforcement versus the Law* (1963), for a journalist's account embodying this point of view; J. H. Skolnick, *Justice without Trial: Law Enforcement in Democratic Society* (1966), for a sociologist's study of the role of the police in criminal law administration. For a somewhat more detailed, albeit legalistic and somewhat technical discussion of American police procedures, see W. R. LaFave, *Arrest: The Decision to Take a Suspect into Custody* (1965).

[26]Aspects of the lawyer's ambivalences with regard to the expectancies of the various groups who have claims upon him, are discussed in H. J. O'Gorman, *The Ambivalence of Lawyers,* paper presented at the Eastern Sociological Association meetings, April 10, 1965.

[25]Failures, shortcomings and oppressive features of our system of criminal justice have been attributed to a variety of sources including "lawless" police, overzealous district attorneys, "hanging" juries, corruption and political connivance, incompetent judges, inadequacy or lack of counsel, and poverty or other social disabilities of the defendant. See A.

influential in making him more amenable to a plea, her agent-mediator role has, nevertheless, usually been sparked and initiated by defense counsel. Further, although a number of first suggestions of a plea came from an accused's fellow jail inmates, he tended to rely largely on his counsel as an ultimate source of influence in his final decision. The defense counsel, being a crucial figure in the total organizational scheme in constituting a new set of perspectives for the accused, the same sample of defendants were asked to indicate at which stage of their contact with counsel was the suggestion of a plea made. There are three basic kinds of defense counsel available in Metropolitan Court: Legal-aid, privately retained counsel, and counsel assigned by the court (but may eventually be privately retained by the accused).

The overwhelming majority of accused persons, regardless of type of counsel, related a specific incident which indicated an urging or suggestion, either during the course of the first or second contact, that they plead guilty to a lesser charge if this could be arranged. Of all the agent-mediators, it is the lawyer who is most effective in manipulating an accused's perspectives, notwithstanding pressures that may have been previously applied by police, district attorney, judge or any of the agent-mediators that may have been activated by them. Legal-aid and assigned counsel would apparently be more likely to suggest a possible plea at the point of initial interview as response to pressures of time. In the case of the assigned counsel, the strong possibility that there is no fee involved, may be an added impetus to such a suggestion at the first contact.

In addition, there is some further evidence in Table III of the perfunctory, ministerial character of the system in Metropolitan Court and similar criminal courts. There is little real effort to individualize, and the lawyer's role as agent-mediator may be seen as unique in that he is in effect a double agent. Although, as "officer of the court" he mediates between the court organization and the defendant, his roles with respect to each are rent by conflicts of interest. Too often these must be resolved in favor of the organization which provides him with the means for his professional existence. Consequently, in order to reduce the strains and conflicts imposed in what is ultimately an overdemanding role obligation for him, the lawyer engages in the lawyer-client "confidence game" so as to structure more favorably an otherwise onerous role system.[27]

[27]W. J. Goode, *A Theory of Role Strain,* 25 Am. Soc. Rev. 483–96 (1960); J. D. Snok, *Role Strain in Diversified Role Sets,* 71 Am. J. Soc. 363–72 (1966).

Table III. Stage at Which Counsel Suggested Accused to Plead
N = 724

Contact	Privately Retained		Legal-aid		Assigned		Total	
	N	%	N	%	N	%	N	%
First	66	35	237	49	28	60	331	46
Second	83	44	142	29	8	17	233	32
Third	29	15	63	13	4	9	96	13
Fourth or more	12	6	31	7	5	11	48	7
No response	0	0	14	3	2	4	16	2
Total	190	100	487	101*	47	101*	724	100

*Rounded percentage.

CONCLUSION

Recent decisions of the Supreme Court, in the area of criminal law administration and defendant's rights, fail to take into account three crucial aspects of social structure which may tend to render the more libertarian rules as nugatory. The decisions overlook (1) the nature of courts as formal organization; (2) the relationship that the lawyer-regular *actually* has with the court organization; and (3) the character of the lawyer-client relationship in the criminal court (the routine relationships, not those unusual ones that are described in "heroic" terms in novels, movies, and TV).

Courts, like many other modern large-scale organizations possess a monstrous appetite for the cooptation of entire professional groups as well as individuals.[28] Almost all those who come within the ambit of organizational authority, find that their definitions, perceptions and values have been refurbished, largely in terms favorable to the particular organization and its goals. As a result, recent Supreme Court decisions may have a long range effect which is radically different from that intended or anticipated. The more libertarian rules will tend to produce the rather ironic end result of augmenting the *existing* organizational arrangements, enriching court organizations with more personnel and elaborate structure, which in turn will maximize organizational goals of "efficiency" and production. Thus, many defendants will find that courts will possess an even more sophisticated apparatus for processing them toward a guilty plea!

[28]Some of the resources which have become an integral part of our courts, e.g., psychiatry, social work and probation, were originally intended as part of an ameliorative, therapeutic effort to individualize offenders. However, there is some evidence that a quite different result obtains, than the one originally intended. The ameliorative instruments have been coopted by the court in order to more "efficiently" deal with a court's caseload, often to the legal disadvantage of an accused person. See F. A. Allen, *The Borderland of Criminal Justice* (1964); T. S. Szasz, *Law, Liberty and Psychiatry* (1963) and also Szasz's most recent, *Psychiatric Justice* (1965); L. Diana, "The Rights of Juvenile Delinquents: An Appraisal of Juvenile Court Procedures," 47 *J. Crim. L. C. & P.S.* 561–69 (1957).

22. Juror Selection

MICHAEL FRIED
KALMAN J. KAPLAN
KATHERINE W. KLEIN

IT IS PERHAPS INSTRUCTIVE TO BEGIN WITH A statement of what we will not do. This is not intended to be a systematic or exhaustive review of literature on voir dire *per se*. Rather, we intend to develop a psychological model regarding the selection and influence of jurors during the voir dire of a criminal trial. Research will be cited when relevant. We should, however, not lose sight of the major purpose: namely, to provide a much needed theoretical framework within which to understand the conflicting aims of prosecution (P) and defense (D) during voir dire. This is aimed at improving our insights into their respective behaviors and at leading to the development of productive empirical research into this critical portion of a trial.

Voir dire, literally "to see, to tell," is the first phase of a trial in which prospective jurors are questioned and selected to sit on the impaneled jury. Depending on the court, prospective jurors are questioned by the judge alone, by prosecution and defense without the judge, or by all three.

Typically, a twelve-person prospective jury panel is randomly selected from a large group of assembled prospective jurors and questioned by the judge on their general fitness to serve. The judge may excuse a juror at this time. Fol-

lowing this initial questioning P and D are allowed to question the temporarily impaneled jurors as a group or individually.

If P or D object to the impaneling of a juror, then they can challenge the objectional juror(s). Challenges fall into three categories: (1) *to the array*, if counsel feels the entire panel has been irregularly selected; (2) *for cause*, when a juror is deemed unable to render an impartial verdict because of his experience, occupation, personal or financial interests, or preconceived bias; and (3) *peremptory*, if counsel feels for any reason that the juror is undesirable. Challenges to the array are primarily procedural and extremely rare, while those for cause typically involve legal objections to a specific juror in a specific case. In peremptory challenges, however, P and D often follow their instinctive reactions, some of which will be discussed later in this chapter. Challenges to the array or for cause are unlimited in number, but subject to the discretion of the judge who may overrule the challenge and allow the juror(s) to remain seated. Peremptory challenges, in contrast, are not subject to such judicial discretion, but are limited in number. This number is fixed by law or court rule and increases with the seriousness of the charge. In general, D has more peremptory challenges than P.

When a challenge for cause is accepted by the judge or when a peremptory challenge is employed, the prospective juror is excused and a new candidate is randomly chosen from the

►SOURCE: *"Juror Selection; An Analysis of Voir Dire,"* in Rita James Simon (Ed.) The Jury System in America. Volume IV. Sage Criminal Justice System Annuals. Beverly Hills, Cal.: Sage Publications, 1975. Pp. 49–57, 65–66. (Editorial adaptations). Reprinted by permission.

remaining group to reconstitute the panel. At this point, questioning begins again. This process continues until both P and D are satisfied with the impaneled jury or have exhausted their peremptory challenges and all challenges for cause are refused.

Voir dire has three major purposes. First, it is used as an information-gathering technique upon which to base jury selection. Prospective jurors are questioned and information obtained is then used by P and D as a basis of selection. A second purpose of voir dire is to enable P and D to develop rapport with jurors and thereby facilitate communication. Finally voir dire gives P and D an opportunity to influence jurors to change their attitudes or values and to affect the way in which they will process the evidence they will hear. These latter two purposes are closely related and often overlap. For our purposes, no distinction is made between the aim of developing rapport and that of influencing the jury, both falling under the category of social influence. Jury selection and influence, however, will be treated as distinct categories.

Our basic thesis is that P and D attempt to select jurors who are likely to be susceptible to their influence attempts, that these influence attempts can be conceptualized as pertaining to the way jurors process evidence (to reach likeli-

hood of guilt) and the values jurors place on the possible trial outcomes, and that—as P and D have conflicting goals at trial—they also have conflicting strategies at voir dire.

DIFFERENTIAL AIMS IN VOIR DIRE: SPECIFIC MEANS

The differential aims of P and D in the selection and influence of jurors are presented in Table I. They are differentiated in terms of (a) juror susceptibility to conformity pressure; (b) juror predisposition to side with authority figures; (c) juror openness of cognitive set; (d) juror estimate of guilt; and (e) juror criterion for conviction. The first three aims will be discussed in social-psychological terms and the latter two will be investigated by use of a statistical decision theoretic model of juror decision-making.

A. Predisposition to Side with Authority
The first assumption presented in Table I is that P should select jurors predisposed to side with authority. This factor becomes important to the extent P represents himself as the voice of society rather than as the complaint of a single victim. Authoritarians, by definition, identify with authorities currently in power, especially if the

Table I. Differential Aims of P Versus D in the Selection and Influence of Jurors

	Prosecution (P)	Defense (D)
Specific Means		
(a) predisposition to side with authority	select authoritarian jorors	select egalitarian jurors
(b) susceptibility to conformity pressure	attempt to maximize interjuror conformity	select jurors predisposed to individual dissent
(c) openness of cognitive sets	select jurors with a closed or rigid cognitive set	select jurors willing to consider conflicting information
Ultimate Goals		
(d) estimate of guilt	convince jurors of high probability of guilt	convince jurors of low probability of guilt
(e) criterion for conviction	establish in jurors a low criterion for conviction	establish in jurors a high criterion for conviction

positive authority figures are perceived as high-status sources of information (Ehrlich and Lee, 1969). The practical consequences of this reliance on authority figures may be that authoritarian jurors are more likely to heed P's arguments than D's, because of the association of P with legitimized government authority. Furthermore, authoritarians are also more likely to favor P because of their acceptance of societal norms of behavior.

However, an authoritarian's susceptibility to P's persuasive arguments also depends on the nature of the defendant. Authoritarians are sensitive to ingroup-outgroup distinctions, and are intolerant of deviation from accepted norms (cf. Adorno et al., 1950). Therefore, if the defense attorney (D) or the defendant is noted for supporting radical political causes, authoritarian jurors would be particularly biased toward P.However, when the defendants are high-status authority figures themselves, as in the Watergate trials, low authoritarian jurors may actually be a better choice for P.

Demographic guidelines.   Our assumption is implicitly expressed by legal writers espousing rules of thumb for jury selection. They suggest many demographic clues to reliance on authority. Groups traditionally believed to favor P as an agent of society include (1) men; (2) Republicans; (3) upper income groups; (4) occupational groups such as bankers (Adkins, 1968–1969), engineers and certified public accountants (Katz, 1968–1969), and others with positions of petty respectability (Campbell, 1972); and (5) members of the Teutonic ethnic groups, particularly Germans (Campbell, 1972).

The same authors recommend the following groups as more likely to be egalitarians: (1) women; (2) Democrats (Hayes, 1972); (3) middle and lower economic groups such as butchers (Katz, 1968–1969); (4) certain occupational groups, such as social scientists; and (5) minority racial or ethnic groups, such as Latins or Jews (Campbell, 1972).

Similarity and empathy.   Complicating the formula relating personality characteristics to a predisposition to side with authority, however, is the juror's perception of the similarity of the defendant to himself. Chaiken and Darley (1972) found that in judgments of responsibility for an accident, subjects who had been assigned a supervisor role blamed chance for the mistake, while subjects assigned to be workers blamed the supervisor. A juror who identifies with the victim will be more likely to assume the vantage point of P, who can offer society's protection against further transgressions. A juror who feels himself similar to the accused will be more ready to accept the egalitarian view that each individual must be judged in terms of his own motives and circumstances, rather than in the framework of larger societal rights.

On a demographic level, similarity is usually operationalized in terms of ethnicity, occupation, and sex. In general, D should try to obtain jurors similar to his client, but many exceptions and clauses complicate this truism. Similarity to the defendant is not a ubiquitous rule of thumb. For example, if the evidence is overwhelmingly in favor of conviction, P may obtain a more severe verdict by choosing juror members who are ethnically similar to the defendant such that they might have special knowledge of his circumstances and be less gullible to his protestations of innocence. One illustration is Belli's (1963) warning that Jewish jurors are harsher on Jews accused of a crime. Another illustrative anecdote involves a jury of black Detroit welfare mothers convicting a black welfare defendant when her alibi (grocery shopping) was denounced by the jurors who shopped at the same market and refuted her claims of the time involved in making a week's purchases. Such demographic similarities at the same time may evoke a sense of empathy with the defendant. If D's case is reasonably strong, he may exploit this with the aim of seducing the jurors into assuming the individual's reference point throughout the trial.

Ethnic dissimilarity is also a two-edged sword.

On the one hand, Byrne and Wong (1962) report that subjects are more tolerant of racially dissimilar individuals who hold dissimilar attitudes than of racially similar persons holding dissimilar attitudes. Such charitable excusing of people demographically unlike oneself can be of considerable value to D, especially when he has a weak case. At the same time, however, dissimilarity may prevent the emergence of the emotional empathy necessary for the jurors to see the situation from the defendant's viewpoint. Such a societal orientation is invaluable to P.

Occupational interactions with type of crime are also important. Courtroom folklore advises P to favor bankers in cases of theft or robbery; but bankers are better jurors for D in securities, fraud, or white-collar crime (Campbell, 1972)—presumably because the banker can identify or see himself as similar to the defendant. This relationship between similarity and attribution of guilt has been called situational or personal relevance (Evenbeck, 1974). When relevance is high—that is, when the juror has some real or potential experience with a similar situation or is very similar to the defendant—he will be more likely to exonerate the defendant. This defensive attribution, or blaming the situation rather than the perpetrator, may cognitively protect the juror from an imaginary similar fate.

Sex interactions also emerge in evaluating the effects of juror-defendant similarity. Female jurors, for example, are reported (Karcher, 1969) to be more sympathetic in general *unless* the defendant is a more attractive female, in which event women jurors are often more punitive. In addition, Fishman and Izett (1974) found that when the defendant is attractive, crimes in which the defendant's beauty is irrelevant are judged more leniently, presumably because expectancies of jurors are violated when an attractive defendant is implicated.

This same type of reasoning explains why D is often reluctant to allow an overly unattractive defendant to testify in his own behalf. If jurors cannot identify with the defendant, they are far more likely to accept a societal viewpoint, with P as its legitimate authority, without the pangs of conscience they might experience for a sympathy-eliciting defendant.

B. Susceptibility to Conformity Pressure

The second assumption of our model presented in Table I is that P will strive for greater inter-juror conformity than will D. P should try to select jurors who will be susceptible to conformity pressure during both the trial and juror deliberations. D, on the other hand, should try to select on tendencies toward individual dissent in the jury.

There are two major reasons for differential conformity needs of P and D. First, the prospects of a hung jury are far more damaging for P than for D. Though it is true that unanimity of juror opinion is necessary to attain either conviction or acquittal, it is likewise true that in practice P will almost never push a case beyond two hung juries, but in fact will typically drastically reduce its charges after a single "hung jury" outcome. Thus, the possibility of a nonconforming juror is more detrimental to P than to D.

A second reason involves the covariation between conformity tendencies and authoritarianism. High conformists are likely to side with authority, a tendency typically favoring P as was noted before.

True conformity.   Two types of conformity have been identified by social psychologists. True conformity (McGuire, 1968), involves yielding to another even in the absence of persuasive arguments, but simply in acquiescence to the presumed expertise or authority of the source. In a trial, such conformity pressure may be applied to less intelligent jurors who fail to comprehend abstruse expert witness testimony or complicated examinations. During deliberations, a true conformity situation will arise when a juror is intimidated by another, perhaps the foreman, so that he will acquiesce to the group decision regardless of his personal convictions.

Suggestibility.   The second type of conformity,

perhaps better labeled "suggestibility," involves yielding to the persuasive message of a source, as opposed to agreement simply because the source is a respected authority. Suggestibility becomes an important variable during the trial itself, when a juror is presumably swayed by the arguments of P or D.

In general, P should attempt to select jurors who are true conformists or are at least predisposed to suggestibility, while D should choose jurors with the opposite predispositions. The social-psychological literature suggests that both authoritarianism and self-esteem are personality variables underlying conformity and suggestibility.

Relation to authoritarianism. Authoritarianism, as originally conceived by Adorno et al. (1950) is a tendency toward oversimplified categorization of people on the evaluative dimension into a few extreme groups—the very good (the ingroup) and the very bad (the outgroup). Authoritarians have strong dependencies for ingroup authority figures and great intolerance and punitive tendencies for outgroup members. In a true conformity situation, especially an ambiguous one such as may occur during jury deliberations, authoritarians are more influenced by high-status sources than by low-status ones (Vidulich and Kaiman, 1961). Thus, if a foreman is selected because of his leadership ability or presumed expertise, an authoritarian juror should be more likely to conform to the foreman's judgment than to lower-status peers. Secret balloting during deliberations may thwart some of this dependence on the foreman. However, when the situation becomes one of suggestibility in which jury members openly support their opinions, an authoritarian is most likely to agree with a clique of his peers who provide him with social reality, in the sense of a shared outlook (Hollander and Julian, 1967).

Relation to self-esteem. A second personality variable, self-esteem, should also be noted by P and D in their attempts to select a favorable jury. Self-esteem is a large determinant of suggestibility, with low self-esteem individuals being the most suggestible. Low self-esteem jurors can favor either prosecution or defense, unlike high authoritarians who generally favor prosecution. Susceptibility should have its greatest impact during deliberations, in which the influence of an eloquent foreman or a nearly unanimous group should be greatest for the highly susceptible juror. If the case is not clearcut, the vacillations of a suggestible, low self-esteem juror may end with him under the influence of a stronger fellow juror, rather than with his deciding independently on some facet of the evidence itself.

Courtroom folklore; demography revisited. In the search for personality predispositions such as those discussed above, counsellors will often resort to demographic heuristics. There exists a considerable folklore regarding the use of such variables, much of which has not been systematically investigated or only partially supported. Females are generally believed to be more susceptible to social influence (Janis and Field, 1959), a social-psychological dictum often noted by legal authors (MacGutman, 1972). An older person, because of his experience, is often viewed as more tolerant of human frailty than a younger juror. Such an individual orientation, however, might be offset by an older person's greater respect for authority.

Conformity and interjuror homogeneity. Interjuror homogeneity is likely to be an important determinant of conformity. Adkins (1968–1969) suggests that the selection of a leader and eleven followers will lead to a single decision. Presumably, P or D can then concentrate their efforts on this leader who will then function as an opinion leader for the rest of the jurors (Hayes, 1972). It should be far easier to achieve the "group sense" and strong opinion leader necessary for either conviction or acquittal if the jurors are similar in personality or at least demographic characteristics. Selection of a homogenous group capable of consensus should be especially important to P according to our model, even if they are all low authoritarians.

On the other hand, D, particularly if he has a weak case, might actively seek interjuror heterogeneity. D's intent might be to work on a small number of jurors to create a hung jury. Thus, he would want to minimize the conformity pressures that high interjuror homogeneity would occasion. D should also avoid the selection of any juror with relevant expertise, if the trial is of a technical nature in which such a person is likely to emerge as a strong opinion leader. He should avoid him unless he were absolutely certain that he would prove to be favorable. P on the other hand, should push for such a juror, if he thinks there is a reasonable chance that he will be favorably inclined. In other words, consensus works for P and against D in the absence of a strong case on either side.

A qualification should be offered at this point. If D has a very strong case, he too should press for juror homogeneity. Generally however, he can far better afford and even encourage interjuror disagreement. In practice, then, we assume that P must attempt to influence all of the jurors even with a weak case. He must avoid actions which would antagonize any jurors, such as the overuse of peremptory challenges. D in contrast, unless he has a strong case, may direct his appeal to a small minority of jurors—in fact, even to a single member. Thus, it would behoove prosecution to maximize conformity pressure within the jury, while defense should glorify the integrity of individual dissent.

C. Openness of Cognitive Set

A third assumption presented in Table I is that P and D have differential aims in choosing jurors who are predisposed to certain cognitive styles. P should welcome a juror with a closed cognitive set who has difficulty processing conflicting information. D should seek jurors who are open to new information, even though it may be incongruent with their own beliefs or in conflict with other trial-produced evidence.

This is the case because, during the trial, P attempts to present evidence which is consistent and complete in order to evoke certainty and closure. D on the other hand, will want to present evidence which shows the situation is complex, many-sided and filled with doubt. Such differential styles in presentation will prove most beneficial if jurors have been selected for these particular cognitive sets.

Courtroom folklore. As with conformity pressure, practicing lawyers use a variety of techniques to select jurors with certain cognitive sets. A social-psychologist's admonition that P should choose closed cognitive sets is reflected in Hayes' suggestions that jurors who "sharpen" during an argument are those who exaggerate the salience of particular data and may overlook other aspects of the evidence. The juror who claims strong opinions on any topic is more likely to be dogmatic and less able to bring various facts together for comparison purposes. Military men and persons in mid-level positions in an organizational hierarchy are assumed to be good prosecution jurors because of their previous experiences in following and transmitting essential and rational information.

D, however, will want jurors who are open to dissonant information and who can withhold judgment until defense has presented its case. Hayes suggests that younger people are the most open in this regard, and Katz recommends jurors with a wide variety of experience as being more flexible in their thinking.

Cognitive set and relationship to authoritarianism. In P's attempt to choose jurors with closed cognitive sets, authoritarians again appear to be good candidates. The ideal prosecution juror should focus on P's opening statements and thereafter process information using P's theory of the case. Long and Ziller (1965) found that authoritarians spend less time than do egalitarians in making decisions and fail to reserve judgment or seek further information. This tendency to restrict cognitive input should favor prosecution, especially when a juror's original set of beliefs are congruent with those of authority figures, as an authoritarian's presumably are.

There is also social-psychological evidence to support the contention that highly authoritarian persons are more rigid in their thinking (Brown,

1953). This lack of flexibility further assists P in its attempt to solicit favorable votes from authoritarian jurors. Rigidity will prevent vacillation during deliberations and will be particularly valuable to P if the foreman is a pro-prosecution authoritarian.

*

REFERENCES

Adkins, J. C. (1968–1969) "Jury selection: an art? a science? or luck?" Trial Magazine (December–January): 37–39.

Adorno, T. W., E. Frenkel-Brunswick, D. J. Levinson, and R. N. Sanford (1950) The Authoritarian Personality. New York: Harper.

Asch, S. E. (1951) "Effects of group pressure upon the modification and distortion of judgments," pp. 177–190 in H. Guetzkow (ed.) Groups, Leadership and Men. Pittsburgh:Carnegie Press.

Belli, M. M. (1963) Modern Trials (abridged ed.) Indianapolis: Bobbs-Merrill.

Brown, R. W. (1953) "A determinant of the relationship between rigidity and authoritarianism." Journal of Abnormal and Social Psychology 48: 469–476.

Byrne, D. and T. J. Wong (1962) "Racial prejudice, interpersonal attraction, and assumed dissimilarity of attitudes." Journal of Abnormal and Social Psychology 65:246–253.

Campbell, S. (1972) "The multiple functions of the criminal defense voir dire in Texas."American Journal of Criminal Law 1 (October): 255.

Chaiken, A. L. and J. M. Darley (1972) "Victim or perpetrator: defensive attribution of responsibility and the need for order and justice." Journal of Experimental and Social Psychology: 268–275.

Ehrlich, H. J. and D. Lee (1969) "Dogmatism learning and resistance to change:a review and a new paradigm." Psychological Bulletin 71: 241–260.

Evenbeck, S. (1974) "Observer's attributions of causality." Presented at the annual meeting of the Midwestern Psychological Association, Chicago.

Fishman, L. and R. R. Izzett (1974) "The influence of a defendant's attractiveness and justification for his act on the sentencing tendencies of subject-jurors." Presented at the annual meeting of the Midwestern Psychological Association, Chicago.

Fried, M. (1973) "Models of juror decision making." Presented at the annual meeting of the American Psychological Association, Montreal.

Hayes, H. B. (1972) "Applying persuasive techniques to trial proceedings." South Carolina Law Review 24: 380.

Hollander, E. P. and J. W. Julian (1967) "Contemporary trends in the analysis of leadership process." Psychological Bulletin 71: 387–397.

Janis, I. L. and P. B. Field (1959) "Sex differences and personality factors related to persuasibility," pp. 55–58 in I. L. Janis and C. I. Hovland (eds.) Personality and Persuasibility, New Haven: Yale University Press.

Kaplan, J. (1967) "Decision theory and the fact-finding process." Stanford Law Review 20: 1065–1092.

Kaplan, K. J., K. W. Klein, and M. Fried (1973) "General aims of prosecution and defense in the selection and influence of jurors in a criminal trial." Presented at the annual meeting of the American Psychological Association, Montreal; to appear in Journal of Social and Behavioral Sciences, Winter 1975.

Karcher, J. T. (1969) "Importance of voir dire." Practicing Lawyer 15 (December):59.

Katz, L. S. (1968–1969) "The twelve man jury." Trial Magazine (December–January):39–42.

Long, R. E. and R. C. Ziller (1965) "Dogmatism and predecisional information search." Journal of Applied Psychology 49: 376–378.

MacGutman, S. (1972) "Attorney-conducted voir dire of jurors: a constitutional right." Brooklyn Law Review 39 (Fall): 290.

McGuire, W. (1968) "Personality and susceptibility to social influence," pp. 1130–1187 in E. F. Borgatta and W. W. Lambert (eds.) Handbook of Personality Theory and Research. Chicago: Rand McNally.

Vidulich, R. N. and I. P. Kaiman (1961) "The effects of information source status and dogmatism upon conformity behavior." Journal of Abnormal and Social Psychology 63: 639–642.

23. Truth and Testimony

JAMES MARSHALL

THE BASIC RIGHT OF THE ACCUSED IS TO HAVE A fair trial within the cultural definition of fairness of the forum. Under our Constitution we call this right due process of law or the equal protection of the laws, including a speedy and public trial by an impartial jury. Whatever the philosophical description of a fair trial may be, it is in fact a pragmatic construct resting in considerable measure on legal fictions or perhaps unverified hypotheses. There is experience but little empirical evidence to justify this pragmatic approach and while it is the common notion that a trial is to determine reality and do justice this is in the nature of a Platonic ideal which at best is a goal or norm against which to measure our concept of a fair trial.

I. ORAL TESTIMONY AND PERCEPTION

In most criminal cases evidence is essentially oral based on recall of what the witness perceived. To a lesser extent real evidence (a gun, merchandise, a scar) or written evidence (a memorandum, bookkeeping entries, other records) are introduced in evidence. These must, of course, be shown to be relevant and this is usually by means of oral evidence. Evidence is presented, under our Anglo-Saxon American system, through adversary proceedings. This we

▶SOURCE: *"Trial, Testimony and Truth,"* in Stuart S. Nagel (Ed.) *The Rights of the Accused. Volume I. Sage Criminal Justice System Annuals.* Beverly Hills, Ca.: Sage Publications, 1972. Pp. 237–256. Reprinted by permission.

believe makes possible a fair trial by a process of challenge and interrogation to test the validity of perception and recall and reveal bias and perjury. Under the Sixth Amendment a fair trial entitles a defendant to confrontation of witnesses, and this is made obligatory on the states by the Fourteenth Amendment (*Pointer v. Texas*, 1965).

How reliable is evidence? How effective is this system in attaining truth and justice? And perhaps we should ask whether truth and justice are the only goals to be considered as validating a criminal trial.

The lore of ancient times as well as our contemporary experience has questioned the reliability of perception and the legal process. Simeon ben Shatach (first chapter, ninth citation) is quoted in the Talmud as warning "Be thorough in the examination of witnesses, and be heedful of your words, lest through your words the witnesses be led to testify falsely."

After his trial, just before he took the hemlock, Socrates (Plato, 1938: 99) in discussing the difficulty of knowing about life after death asked "Have sight and hearing truth in them? Are they not, as the poets are always telling us, inaccurate witnesses?" Since then many convicted men and numerous people found to be at fault and liable in civil suits have come to similar conclusions: the other side's witnesses, if they were not lying, were blind and deaf. The psychological sciences have described man's faulty perceptions and erratic memory, so that we have a considerable body of empirical evidence supporting Socrates' views (Kilpatrick, 1961; Marshall, 1966a: 5–81). And surely every lawyer and judge can give examples of the unreliability of witnesses and jurors as perceivers of reality.

We perceive in large measure what we expect to perceive and we expect what we have already experienced. Past experiences of successes and failure influence our perception of similar situations. This is pragmatic. Similarly we interpret—that is, we give meaning to what we perceive in terms of our experience. We make use of values that have demonstrated validity in similar transactions. We make bets and guesses on the basis of what has happened before (Kilpatrick and Cantril, 1961: 357–358). Thus the police may look to the style of a particular crime, recall that X has done this kind of crime before, that he is out of jail and so they pick him up. An example of this betting on experience is to be found in Rita James Simon's (1967: 154–160) study of *The Jury and the Defense of Insanity*. She found the jurors tended to measure insanity by experiences that they had had with mental illness in their families or among their friends or acquaintances.

Let me give a few examples of how experience may give meaning to phenomena. In a dark room the subjects were shown two moving dots, one large and one small. When the larger dot followed the smaller the subjects tended to describe the larger dot as chasing the smaller. When the larger dot preceded it was described as leading the smaller (Heider and Simmel, 1944: 254).

One of our most popular errors is the so-called moon illusion. The moon looks larger on the horizon than at its zenith. The reason is that on the horizon we are measuring it against the height of known objects, whereas in the heavens it cannot be related to any object of a size we have experienced (Rock and Kaufman, 1962).

If we see two lights in the dark, one bright and one dull or one large and one small, we tend to see the larger or brighter light as nearer than the duller or smaller (Kilpatrick and Ittelson, 1961). That is why the ancients assumed that the large stars were closer to the earth than the smaller ones. Our experience is that things that are closer look bigger and clearer too. Thus brightness and size may be cues to distance as they may be also cues to weight.

It is difficult even for trained persons to be accurate witnesses. Some years ago Kerensky, the former Premier of Russia, was lecturing in New York. A woman came on the stage and struck him. Eight experienced reporters from different newspapers gave eight different accounts of the event and seven or eight different versions of Kerensky's reaction to the occurrence (Hutchins and Slesinger, 1928).

In an experiment with air force personnel it was found that they were unable accurately to estimate the speed of a car moving at 12 miles an hour. The estimates ran from 10 to 50 miles an hour (American Society for Public Administration, 1959).

Furthermore, even unconsciously, our perception is subject to biases conditioned by experience. Hastorf and Cantril (1954), one at Dartmouth and the other at Princeton, showed their students a picture of a Dartmouth-Princeton football game which had been described as a particularly rough game. They asked their respective students to indicate which team had violated the rules or had been unnecessarily rough. As one might expect the Dartmouth men attributed most of the rule-breaking and roughness to the Princeton team and the Princeton men made the contrary attributions.

In an experiment conducted by Marshall and Mansson (1966) a few years ago at New York University, they showed students of two criminal law classes a picture. To some they assigned the role of witness for the prosecution and to others that of witness for the defense. They found that the witnesses for the prosecution had more accurate recall than those for the defense. They discovered, too, that those people who, on a test, were shown to be the more punitive, had better recall than the less punitive. However, in another experiment the latter correlation did not occur (Marshall et al., 1971).

In the selection of jurors an attorney will try to exclude persons whose interests and experience might bias him against the attorney's client or his case. Alice Padawer-Singer (1970) and Allen Barton conducted an experiment in selection of jurors. With permission of the court they used jurors from the regular jury panel. Some of them were exposed in advance to material damaging to the defendant's case and some were not. They found that those exposed tended to find guilt far more frequently than those not so exposed.

In our aural perception we also take cues from our past experience. We rarely hear every word or syllable that is spoken but from the context we guess what the word or sentence is. Few people have the capacity to recall a speech they have heard but they can reconstruct the substance and, on interrogation, may recognize what they heard. In effect they draw upon the bank of their experience. This process was described long ago by Thucydides (1934: 14) in his introduction to the *History of the Peloponnesian Wars*. He referred to the differences in the accounts of events by eye witnesses whether due to imperfect memory or partiality. He admitted to his own inability to carry in his memory word for word the speeches he heard and repeated. He said "[M]y habit has been to make the speakers say what was in my opinion demanded of them by the various occasions, of course adhering as closely as possible to the general sense of what they really said." In other words, taking the cues we fill in the gaps. We get the drift of the speaker and these cues give momentum to our memory. This is similar to the momentum that causes us to assume a car will continue at the same speed and in the same direction as we last saw it moving. Such fictions are, of course, pragmatic. They are necessary to effective daily living. However, they are hazardous bets if the precise words of a conversation (or the exact

courses of two cars) have determining effects in a litigation. The element that we choose to repress, or what selection we make as the likeliest expectation for what we see or hear, will depend on what bet, or what selection, we make as the likeliest expectation for what we see or hear; and that too will, of course, be conditioned by past experience in similar situations (Ittelson, 1961).

This may result in wishful thinking and a witness may swear to a "truth" which he never heard. I remember a murder case in which a woman sitting on a window sill cleaning her windows three stories up testified that she had heard a conversation on a corner half a block away just before the murder occurred. Learning that the crime had been committed she evidently felt a sense of participation as a witness and "heard" what the occasion required.

In an experiment in which the subjects were exposed to the novel sound of a tornado, many of them heard it as a sound of an oncoming train which better conformed to their experience (Kilpatrick, 1961: 317).

Because we fill in gaps and because the fill is a composite of our experience, we hear selectively—just as we see selectively—what we expect or want to hear. Our perceptions may, therefore, be compared with values. Cook (1969: 217) said that "One way of looking at values is that they describe conditions which their holders desire in some degree to exist."

II. EFFECTS OF STRESS

Difficult as is accurate perception in normal situations, the inaccuracy tends to increase in conditions of danger and stress. They distort time and distance. The elapse of time is always difficult to perceive. In the experiment referred to above, our subjects' estimates of the length of a 42 second moving picture ranged from 1.5 to 3 minutes (Marshall, 1966a: 53). We are all familiar with the expression that time seems endless when one feels in danger. In other words, particularly under stress, we overestimate time. In danger we also tend to overrate distance (Goldstone et al., 1959; Behar and Bevar, 1961; Langer et al., 1961). Time and distance expand. Thus one must become skeptical of estimates of time and distance made by witnesses. It has been found, however, that moderate stress may improve performance while severe stress distorts (Munsterberg, 1923).

Thus one must question two of our legal rules, the dying declaration and the res gestae rule. It is assumed that when a man knows he is going to die and therefore will shortly face his maker, any statement he makes will be the truth and it will be admitted into evidence even though it is hearsay. But the stress of knowing he is about to die may cause him to make statements that are false. It may be his last chance to exploit paranoid tendencies.

The res gestae rule, also an exception to the hearsay rule, is that where a statement is made as part of a happening it is reliable. However, again, in the stress of a happening the statement may be completely unreliable. Sir Frederick Pollock (1941:284–285) in his correspondence with Justice Holmes talked of "the damnable pretended doctrine of *res gestae*." He hoped that "some high authority would prick the bubble of verbiage: the unmeaning term merely fudges the truth that there is no universal formula for all kinds of relevancy."

Witnesses, particularly in cases played up by the mass media, may be influenced by the stress of public pressure. An important factor of public influence that is often overlooked, according to Morris (1957), is the general climate outside the courtroom or, for example, the tones and moods that prevail in the country. The public may appear as a possible threat. Some witnesses because of personality or status are better able to withstand threat than others.

III. SUGGESTIBILITY OF WITNESSES

This brings us to the matter of suggestibility. Witnesses are not autonomous. They are not in-dependent of the field, that is, the litigation in which they participate. They are constantly interacting with other persons from the moment they make their first statement of the case to the time when they are dismissed as witnesses. Although a great deal of study has been made as to suggestibility of one person by another or by a group, little has been done in the field of recall and testimony. But every witness is affected by counsel, by the statements of other witnesses, by participation as a party or by his desire to be on the winning side.[1] Above all a witness is affected by his desire to appear credible to judge and jury—he dislikes to admit ignorance by answering "I don't know" (Wellman, 1923: 21).

The reasons why witnesses are affected by others are the same as those which cause all of us to be sensitive to what those, with whom we interact, think and feel. This is part of reality testing which we normally do during wakefulness. If we cease to do so, as Hilgard (1964: 19) says, "it is easy to drift into a hypnoidal state." This reality testing implies that "one is always on the verge of losing his grip on reality, of falling into error, or becoming disoriented." In each relationship, therefore, we keep asking, as we proceed from transaction to transaction, "How am I doing?" The answer generally sought is approbation but, on the other hand, it may sometimes be to be rejected and punished.

[1]McCarty (1960: 213) describes a common practice:
"It is very important in interviewing witnesses that the first impression be favorable. This is where suggestion comes in. Do you ask the witness what happened and let him tell the story? Not if you are experienced and know the psychology of approach. You start out and tell him what happened, giving your client's story and then go back and go over it item by item and have the witness verify it. In this way his memory will be refreshed from your standpoint and he will be more apt to make a good witness for your client."
A similar effect can be obtained by interviewing an uncertain witness in the presence of the party for whom he is to be called and other prospective witnesses whose positive statements will tend to influence the uncertain one. Whether by this process "his memory will be refreshed" or whether he is induced to accept the version of the others is questionable (see Sherif, 1936: 138; Asch, 1952).

Witnesses may be subject to the dissonance between their inferences or their biases and reality. Consequently, if they can adjust their testimony in the direction that counsel indicates may be effective and other witnesses or parties indicate to be the "correct" testimony, this can relieve such dissonance. This can be restated in another way. Others can influence the expectations and consequently the recall (as well as perception) and behavior of a witness. In order to maintain his self-image an individual will tend to conform to the norms of those others if he does not have satisfying norms of his own. Thus, as Sherif (1936: 111, see also 96, 108) said, "Once the common norm is established, later separate individuals keep on perceiving it [and recalling it] in terms of the frame of reference which was once the norm of the group."

In considering the suggestibility of witnesses we should bear in mind that a large part of the population is subject to hypnotic influence. This does not mean that these people go through the usual stages of induction, trance, etc. or that they are equally suggestible. A large proportion of the population can be induced by counsel to follow his cues and perceive and recall events as he guides them (Spiegel, 1967: 364). Again, this does not mean that counsel is trying to hypnotize a witness or that a witness is conscious of any hypnotic effect. The phenomenon, however, is frequently present and is something that requires extended research.

IV. IDENTIFICATION OF ACCUSED

Nowhere has the problem of perception become more critical than in the identification of persons accused of crime. In the identification process witnesses are commonly asked to describe or recognize persons who may have been seen under stress and, frequently, only fleetingly. In such circumstances the phenomena of suggestibility by others and inference occur. We have too little empirical information concerning the process of identification and this gap in knowledge calls for thorough research.

Wall[2] (1965) has shown the numerous ways in which police and prosecuting attorneys, especially by means of the line-up, have used suggestibility in the identification of the accused. This is perhaps one of the most shocking sources of injustice in criminal cases. The Supreme Court has held that the identification is a "critical stage" of the criminal proceeding laden with the hazards of irreparable mistake and, therefore, under the Sixth Amendment the accused is entitled to the presence of a lawyer at a "line-up" (or its equivalent) (*United States v. Wade,* 1967; *Stovall v. Denno,* 1967).

Although the Sixth Amendment's requirement applies only if formal charges have been brought against the accused, line-ups or confrontations held prior to the bringing of formal charges may be challenged if they were "unnecessarily suggestive and conducive to irreparable, mistaken identification" under the Due Process clause of the Fifth and Fourteenth Amendments (*United States v. Kirby,* 1972: 4610). The question as to whether the Sixth Amendment entitles in-custody defendants to the presence of counsel at photographic identifications is still open (*United States v. Ash,* 1972, cert. granted, 1972; *Contra, Reed v. Anderson,* 1972).

Much of police tactic is suggestive, appealing to the mind or the emotions of the suspect. The atmosphere of police interrogation is calculated to obtain admissions or confessions. This is well documented by Inbau and Reid (1967).

An admirable article on confessions, describes their legal and psychological aspects and provides justification for *Miranda v. Arizona* (1966). As Edmund B. Driver (1968: 57), its author, states: "[W]hatever its deep roots may be, the urge to talk is almost certainly intensified by the host of fears generated by the situations and procedures of arrest and detention" (see also Foster, 1969). And this urge to talk accounts,

[2]See also Borchard (1932), especially Andrews case, pp. 1–6, Hess and Craig case, pp. 93–98; Frank and Frank (1957), especially Majczek and Marcinkiewicz case, pp. 17–30, Southerland and Mathis case, pp. 40–50, Mattice case, pp. 50–57.

too, for the willingness of prospective witnesses in a criminal case frequently to accept the cues of a prosecuting attorney before a trial especially when the prosecutor holds as a threatening weapon some illicit or suspicious behavior of the witness.

V. RECALL

As a result of what are known as the "Aussage" experiments[3] (Binet, 1905; Munsterberg, 1923; Stern, 1939; Stern, 1910; Cady, 1924; Marston, 1924; see also Snee and Lush, 1941; Fishman and Morris, 1957) in the early part of this century it has been assumed that accuracy of recall would decline substantially and the range of material reported increase with the specificity of interrogation and that leading questions would have a seductive effect and result in more inaccurate testimony. It has also been assumed that accuracy and completeness of testimony would be higher if interrogations were conducted in a supportive manner rather than in a challenging atmosphere.

An experiment conducted by Marshall et al. (1971) indicated that these hypotheses were wrong. They showed a moving picture with sound track to groups of up to four witnesses at one time (151 in all) and told them that they were witnesses and should give an account of what they had seen and heard and to tell the truth, the whole truth, and nothing but the truth, without conclusions. Each witness was taken separately into a room for interrogation and all interrogations were tape recorded. Witnesses were first asked to give a free, spontaneous report on what they had seen and heard. After that each of them was interrogated in one

of four different ways. Half of each of these four groupings were interrogated supportively and half in a challenging manner. The questions and interventions by the interrogators were all prepared in advance.

One type of interrogation was with moderate guidance. In this form 12 general questions were asked, designed to cover all items that could have been observed in the film. Secondly, there was the high-guidance interrogation which was rather similar to direct examination in a courtroom. Thirdly, there was structured multiple-choice interrogation similar to that used in school and employment examinations, except that all the questions asked for *recognition* recall and *not* for reconstruction of the event. Finally, there was the structured leading type of question modeled on cross-examination conducted in courtrooms. In both the multiple-choice and leading interrogations the questions were directed sometimes toward true and sometimes toward false answers.

In the supportive atmosphere the interrogator tried to create a friendly atmosphere praising the quality of the free report and offering to help the witness remember more. In the challenging atmosphere the interrogator expressed disapproval of the free report because of its inadequacy and stated that he was going to see if, as a result of the interview, the witness could not do a better job.

At the end after completing the interrogations the witnesses were taken into another room and requested to fill in self-administered questionnaires designed to measure both their affective and cognitive reactions to the interrogations.

We found that atmosphere, whether supportive or challenging, had no important effect on either the accuracy or completeness of the testimony.

We also found that as interrogation became more specific there was a slight fall-off in accuracy—far less than earlier experiments had led us to expect—but a great increase in coverage. *The very act of interrogation and the type of questions*

---

[3]Wigmore (1931: 530–556) discusses at length some of the Aussage experiments. It should be noted that since that time there has been a great improvement in research techniques including statistical analysis and use of computers. The Aussage experiments did not distinguish between recall expressed in narrative form and by recognition of items. Moreover, they ignored the salience of the items for which recollection was sought.

asked markedly affected completeness but had very little effect on accuracy. In other words, there was small trade-off between loss of accuracy and coverage. It was quite apparent from our study that increased specificity of interrogation has a beneficial overall effect on testimony.

In the spontaneous report and the medium and high guidance interrogations very few items were reported that were not in the picture (we call them absent items). In the two structured types of interrogation which specifically asked about items not in the film, some absent items were testified to but the accuracy of testimony about them was not greatly different from that about items present in the picture.

We divided the items also as to their legal relevance; that is, their relevance to possible suits that might have arisen out of the incidents in the picture. Except in the free report, legally relevant items were slightly less accurately reported than legally irrelevant items. But there was greater completeness in the coverage of legally relevant items.

We also divided the items in the picture as to their salience, that is, the likelihood of their being recalled, which we had pretested. We found that the greater the salience the greater was the accuracy of report and the increase in coverage. In other words, the more salient items were better remembered. As to the high-salience items, there was little difference as to accuracy and coverage resulting from different styles of interrogation. We believe that the failure of the early Aussage experimenters to consider salience caused them to come to different results than we did.

It should be noted, too, that the type of memory demanded of a witness is critical. When the memory called for is that of recognition, as in the case of multiple choice and leading questions, it tends to be more complete than when the interrogator is asking for a report or reconstruction of a happening (Luh, 1922).

We found two other interesting effects. Those of our witnesses who said that they had changed their testimony on interrogation from that given on their free, spontaneous statements, tended to be the more accurate witnesses. This would throw doubt on, if not make improper, the frequent statements by counsel derogating the capacity to recall or even the integrity of a witness because he changed his testimony.

We also found a trend to greater accuracy on the part of those witnesses who suspected that the interrogator was trying to induce them to lie or falsify their answers.

We must recognize the fact that our witnesses were not biased, that is, they did not have a case to make or support. Further research should be done with witnesses who are committed to one or another side of a case (see Marshall and Mansson, 1966: 135).

VI. INFERENCES

We are all subject to making inferences. Juries are permitted to make inferences but not witnesses, because what is sought in testimony is fact not inferences or conclusions, or guesses. Nevertheless, the probability is that all of us frequently state as fact what is in reality an inference or conclusion. On the witness stand we cannot divorce ourselves from our habitual way of behaving, for pragmatically we construct an inference or conclusion out of one bit of perception which we adulterate with our experience with similar phenomena. So in all innocence a witness will testify to inferences and conclusions as if they were fact and the court can not often be the wiser.

Inferences and conclusions are ways in which we fill the gaps in our perception. We make interpretations of those perceptions, we make pragmatic guesses. As Cantril and Bumstead (1960: 83) have said:

"On the basis of the significances we experience, we are constantly guessing that certain things we do will give us the value-qualities of experience we hope for. We try to repeat many types of activities because they show high promise of recapturing or maintaining certain qualities of experience that have already proved satisfying. Likewise we try to avoid those transactions which we believe will lead to a high degree of negative value-quality. . . ."

We should bear in mind that inferences and conclusions are frequently necessary in order to achieve consistency within ourselves. As Zimbardo (1969: 239) said: One "must first convince his observing, critical self (who stands in for society) that his commitment follows *rationally* from an analysis of the stimulus conditions. . . .The psychological homeostasis posited by such a consistency principle is not an end in itself, but rather a means toward minimizing dependency on the environment and maximizing control over it."

VII. INTENT

Serious crimes involve the element of intent, of mens rea, the evil mind, malice aforethought. There are many legal and philosophic definitions of intent. When all is said and done, what ordinary folk mean when they say something was intended is that "It was done on purpose."

Even assuming that consciousness of intent is requisite, that there is purpose behind the act, this is not always what the court looks for as a fact. It may accept an inference of intent to justify a conclusion of intent.[4] For example, as Glanville L. Williams (1965: 26) has said: "To begin by requiring intention for a particular crime, and then to say that intention can be inferred from recklessness, is to cheat with words." In other words, it is a deceptive fiction to say, as the law does, that a man intends to do a wrongful act because be behaves recklessly, that is, without any intention to do the wrong at all.

It may be asked whether it is not fiction that the trial process in an atmosphere of courtroom conflict can determine what a man's intention was. With greater humility than we today

[4]In some cases legal presumptions have been rejected where there is not "a rational connection between the fact proved and the fact presumed" (*Tot v. United States*, 1943: U.S. at 467, S. Ct. at 1245; *Leary v. United States*,1969).

exhibit, the courts of earlier times did not try to judge intent. Thus, in the days of Edward the IV, Judge Brian (quoted in Pollock and Maitland, 1911:474–475) said: "The thought of man shall not be tried, for the devil himself knoweth not the thought of man." But Judea-Christian and Greek traditions have been too strong and the idea from Deuteronomy to Aristotle to St. Thomas has been that men are free to choose between good and evil and that if they behaved in a manner defined as evil it was the result of their own free will, their own wickedness. This is a norm accepted by our courts and is exemplified by Mr. Justice Jackson's opinion in *Morisette v. United States* (1952: U.S. at 250, S. Ct. at 243):

"The contention that injury can amount to a crime only when inflicted by intention is no provincial or transient notion. It is as universal and persistent in mature systems of law as belief in freedom of the human will and a consequent ability and duty of the normal individual to choose between good and evil."

Intent implies, therefore, that a choice must be made. If law is to be even-handed is it reasonable and just to assume that all men have the same choices available? The norms of law are not the norms of a whole society but of those in power. It has always been those who held the sovereign power who determined the norms of right and wrong in positive law, what is permissible and what forbidden to the population under penalty retribution. At the present time the norms we apply and on which our laws are based are primarily those of the middle class, the norms of the dominant culture of the state. Consequently the same choices may not be available to minority groups or people in great poverty and ignorance as to the lawmakers. Education may broaden the apparent choices available; but the poor, the immigrant, and those in very subordinate positions may have less education, certainly less education than the dominant culture of the country. Therefore, they may be less able to perceive the choices available to the lawmakers and law-enforcers. Once again experience and the suggestibility of one's culture or subculture may determine perception, in this instance perception of right and wrong, good and evil (Marshall, 1968: 26–121; Jacob, 1971).

Furthermore, people of the slum cultures and subcultures tend to be more motoric in their reactions to the situation than the middle class (Miller and Swanson, 1956:146, 157). It may seem perfectly reasonable to them to use violence in a situation in which more highly educated or economically favored people would use argument or shrewd device (see, as an example, Herman Melville's story of "Billy Budd," 1961).

There are psychological reasons which may cause people to be unable to perceive choices or to act upon them. One can think of a continuum of behavior from pure accident to action with conscious intent, with purpose, as when a man in cold blood waylays another and assaults or slays him (Marshall, 1966b).

Between these extremes there are actions out of the unconscious, actions under stress, actions under hypnotic suggestions, actions arising out of interrelationships with others, that is from social suggestion, and finally actions where the consequences might have been foreseeable by that legal construct "the reasonable man." It is often difficult to draw the line between these different behaviors. How much of reflex action is unconsciously motivated? What are the unconscious drives that make some people succumb to hypnotism? What is the effect of stress in inducing psychological denial of reality and how does stress blind people to the reasonable consequences of their behavior (see Travers and Morris, 1961; compare *Director of Public Prosecution v. Smith*, 1960; *Regina v. Smyth*, 1957)?

Neurotic compulsion certainly does not permit freedom of choice. Dostoevsky's (1945) grim story about the gambler in "Notes From The Underground" illustrates this and there are, of course, numerous clinical and laboratory examples (Sarnoff, 1962; Alexander and Staub, 1962). Shoplifting, kleptomania, compulsive lying and betrayal, pyromania are generally the results of neurotic compulsions. Theft and rob-

bery sometimes occur because of fetishism. These are compulsive acts, not free choices. The very power of judgment—that is, of problem-solving—which is inherent in formulating an intent will be absent. As Alexander and Staub (1956: 79) said, "The characteristic thing about the *neurotic criminal* is that he identifies himself only partly with the criminal act he commits."

Milgrim (1965) found that a large proportion of people tend to obey the commands of one whom they consider a legitimate authority even if this involves doing cruel acts. This is especially true when the authority figure is present and when the actor has no contact with and does not see the suffering of the persons he hurts.

Certainly the same choices are not available to all people, if indeed *any* choices are perceived in many circumstances.

VIII. THE TRIAL AS A WIN–LOSE GAME

Most lawyers will concede that perception and recall are not entirely accurate, that the situation and other persons may influence the witness and that the trial process itself is interlarded with fictions. But they hope to reduce error by adversary proceedings that test perception and recall and challenge the veracity of witnesses by a process of examination and cross-examination. And correction of error undoubtedly occurs, although we have no empirical data as to the frequency of occurrence. As a distinguished trial lawyer (Frank, 1969: 126) has said: "The law may or may not be a sure way of determining the truth, but it is surely the most awkward method ever devised."

There are, of course, rules to the game, some guaranteed by the Bill of Rights and the Fourteenth Amendment. Among those is the right to cross-examination, sustained by the Supreme Court in *Pointer v. Texas* (1965), *Douglas v. Alabama* (1965), and *Namet v. United States* (1963). Similarly guaranteed are the right to call witnesses (*Washington v. Texas,* 1967) and the right to inspect prior statements by witnesses for the prosecution in the possession of the prosecutor as a basis for cross-examination (*Jencks v. United States*, 1957). The rules of the game also prohibit the prosecutor (and presumably counsel for the accused) from using testimony known to him to be perjurious (*Giles v. Maryland*, 1967).

While adversary proceedings have the advantage of avoiding the pitfalls of unilateral dogmatism they do not necessarily winnow accurate perception. The trial itself as an adversary proceeding is a species of duel. This is what may create interest in the case on the part of jurors and it certainly gives excitement to theatrical and television reproductions of trials. But the goal of an adversary proceeding, whatever the parties may hope or believe, is not to find reality or justice. It is rather to outwit the opponent and to win.

This is not to suggest that adversary proceedings are evil. Probably they are far better in reaching a just conclusion than a judicial determination would be if parties were unable to present their cases.[5] But we must have no illusions that in this adversary process we are finding truth or even necessarily justice. It does serve, however, a social purpose of offering to litigants a legitimized channel for the expression of their hostility and thus acts as a stabilizer of society. There are exceptions, as in the case of automotive accidents where it has been found that the belief is that the impersonal insurance company was to pay in any event (Hunting and Neuwirth, 1962).

In a criminal proceeding prosecution may express public feeling that an offender must be punished, but it also is an attempt to protect society and a symbolic substitute for self-help

[5]"Nonetheless, the legal system gives to the adversary proceedings an overblown value. The opposing system of direct inquiry by the court is given a bad name, the inquisitorial system, to ensure its demise and lawyers commonly place talismanic value on their traditional methods of inquiry" (Frank, 1969: 128). It may even be that the Continental system under which the judge takes the lead in examining witnesses may be more effective (but see Besnard, 1963). We have no empirical evidence on this matter. In any event, it would be unrealistic to assume that that system could replace the Anglo-American.

and vendetta (Cardozo, 1930). The defendant in a criminal case has a chance to exculpate or justify himself and his chance to accomplish either will be greater before a neutral court than before some executive officer or board that acts as prosecutor and trier of fact.

While the adversary proceeding may serve to mediate controversy it is essentially a win-lose relationship, a zero-sum game. Though this may be a ritualized form of hostility reduction or hostility containment, in itself it is not creative. It does not provide a win-win relationship or what the game theorists call a variable-sum game. Essentially, a criminal trial is a punitive process. If society were less interested in punishing and more interested in reforming the offender the trial might be used not only to determine whether the accused committed the act, but also to obtain data on the basis of which the court might more readily judge how and to what extent the accused if guilty could be reformed or prevented from endangering society. It would not then be purely a win-lose transaction for the defendant or society.

IX. TRIERS OF FACT

In considering the trial we should bear in mind that the triers of fact, that is, judges and jurors, are subject to the similar limitations as are witnesses. As has been said, they are permitted to indulge in inferences and conclusions. But in other respects they are witnesses to witnesses. They perceive and recall just as witnesses do, basing their perception and recall as well as their inferences and conclusions on their own prior experience and expectations (see Simon, 1967).

What jurors perceive will also be related to their personalities.

"The Authoritarians seemed prone to using subjective impressions of the character of the persons involved in the case that they had gleaned in some fashion from the evidence presented as the basis of their verdicts. . . . The Anti-authoritarians tended to use the same kind of impressionistic evidence to conclude that even if the defendant were guilty as charged, it was not his fault but society's, because he had led a difficult life [Boehm, 1968: 746]."

It has been found that the party which first makes its presentation has the greater opportunity for success. While the plaintiff is presenting its case the jurors are already in the process of opinion formation (Lund, 1925). This, of course, gives an advantage to the prosecution, an advantage further weighted where the prosecution also has the last word in summation.

But in spite of this and of the unreliability of testimony and the distortions implicit in the adversary system, the jury trial often acts as an instrument to legitimize leniency. The burden of proof in criminal cases tends to weight error in that direction. The anonymity of jury deliberations and the rules prohibiting judges from directing verdicts of guilt and overruling not-guilty verdicts probably tend to neutralize the weaknesses of the trial system (Winter, 1971). But not always, especially not in cases in which the public outcry for a victim, publicized through the mass media, biases the jurors (Padawer-Singer, 1970).

It is now established that one accused of crime is denied due process of law when a court is paralyzed by mob domination or the public has been so aroused that a fair verdict cannot be reached. Although the Supreme Court in 1915 in *Frank v. Mangum*, Holmes and Hughes dissenting, upheld the conviction of Leo M. Frank when a mob outside the courthouse was demanding that he be convicted of murder (it later lynched him) and threatened the jury, the court reversed itself in *Moore v. Dempsey* (1923: U.S. at 91, S. Ct. at 266), holding, in the words of Mr. Justice Holmes, that when "counsel, jury and judge were swept to the fatal end by an irresistible wave of public passion . . . neither perfection in the machinery for correction nor the possibility that the trial court and counsel saw no other way of avoiding an immediate outbreak of the mob can prevent this Court from securing to the petitioners their constitutional rights." And in the recent case of *Connecticut v. Bobby Seale* (see New York Times, May 26, 1971: 1, col. 5)

the trial judge dismissed the indictment on the ground that a fair trial could not be secured.

The courts have protected the accused from the possible prejudicial effects of other events in the course of the trial. For example, where the judge learned from a juror that somebody had communicated with him and told him that he could profit by an acquittal and the judge discussed this with the FBI and the prosecution without the knowledge of defendant's counsel, the Supreme Court reversed the denial by the trial judge of defendant's request to determine the circumstances surrounding the incident and its effect on the jury (*Remmer v. United States*, 1954). In *Turner v. Louisiana* (1965) the Supreme Court held that a defendant who had been convicted of murder had been denied his right to a fair trial by an impartial jury when the two deputy sheriffs who were key witnesses against him were in charge of the jury during the three-day trial and fraternized with them outside the court room during the performance of their duties.

The trend in the courts has been to make the fair trial as much a reality as possible and not merely a verbal statement of principle. It would, however, be idle to suppose that there are not frequent violations, that matters of impropriety do not enter into a trial and trickery does not occur. It might be said that the judicial heart is right, the judicial eye sometimes unseeing and the judicial hand frequently clumsy.

X. CONCLUSION

What we have in our trial system is an edifice built on fictions. It can only be justified if it serves a useful social purpose and if within the rules of the game it is fair. Fairness in the trial, that is, due process of law, equal protection of the laws, is the fundamental right of an accused. But social purpose cannot forever be acceptable if law and order are exalted over individual rights, if empirical study demonstrates the invalidity of the rules of the game, if it is pretended that fictions are realities or if no serious attempts are made to readjust the rules to empirical findings. For then fairness must come in question and social purpose become a corruption.

The social function served by our trial system cannot survive if there is a public sense abroad that the trial is a form of mystery play untouchable by reality, unreachable by justice.

REFERENCES

Alexander, F. and H. Staub (1956) *The Criminal, the Judge and the Public*. New York: Free Press.

American Society for Public Administration (1959) Public Administration Bulletin 3, 12.

Asch, S. (1952) *Social Psychology*. New York: Prentice-Hall.

Behar, I. and W. Bevar (1961) "The perceived duration of auditory and visual intervals: cross model comparison and interaction." Amer. J. of Psychology 74, 1: 17–26.

Besnard, M. (1963) *The Trial of Marie Besnard*. New York: Farrar, Straus.

Binet, A. (1905) "La science du temoignange." L'Annee Psychological 11:128–136.

Boehm, V. R. (1968) "Mr. prejudice, miss sympathy and the authoritarian personality: an application of psychological measuring techniques to the problem of jury bias." Wisconsin Law Rev. 1968, 3: 734–750.

Borchard, E. M. (1932) *Convicting the Innocent*. Garden City: Doubleday.

Cady, H. (1924) "On the psychology of testimony." Amer. J. of Psychology 35, 1: 110–112.

Cantril, H. and C. H. Bumstead (1960) *Reflections on the Human Venture*. New York: New York University Press.

Cardozo, B. N. (1930) *What Medicine Can Do For Law*. New York: Harper and Brothers.

Cook, S. W. (1969) "Motives in a conceptual analysis of attitude-related behavior," pp. 179–231 in W. Arnold and D. Levine (eds.) *Nebraska Symposium on Motivation*. Lincoln: University of Nebraska Press.

Director of Public Prosecution v. Smith (1960) 3 WL.R. 546, 3 A11 E.R. 161,44 Cr. App. R. 261.

Dostoevsky, F. (1945) *The Short Novels of Dostoevsky*. New York: Dial Press.

Douglas v. Alabama (1965) 380 U.S. 417, 85 S. Ct. 1074.

Driver, E. D. (1968) "Confessions and the social psychology of coercion." Harvard Law Rev. 82, 1: 42–61.

Fishman, J. A. and R. E. Morris [eds.] (1957) "Witnesses and testimony at trials and hearings." J. of Social Issues 13, 2.

Foster, H. J., Jr. (1969) "Confessions and the station house syndrome." DePaul Law Rev. 18: 683–701.

Frank, J. P. (1969) *American Law: The Case for Radical Reform*. Toronto: Macmillan.

Frank, J. and B. Frank (1957) *Not Guilty*. New York: Doubleday.

Frank v. Mangum (1915) 237 U.S. 309, 35 S.Ct. 582.

Giles v. Maryland (1967) 386 U.S. 67, 87 S.Ct. 793.

Goldstone, S., W. K. Bordman and W. T. Lhamon (1959) "Intersensory comparisons of temporal judgments." J. of Experimental Psychology 57, 4: 243–248.

Hastorf, A. H. and H. Cantril (1954) "They saw a game: a case study." J. of Abnormal and Social Psychology 49, 1: 129–134.

Heider, F. and M. Simmel (1944) "An experimental study of apparent behavior." Amer. J. of Psychology 57, 2: 243–259.

Hilgard, E. R. (1964) "The motivational relevance of hypnosis," pp. 1–44 in D. Levine (ed.) *Nebraska Symposium on Motivation*. Lincoln: University of Nebraska Press.

Hunting, R. and G. S. Neuwirth (1962) *Who Sues in New York City?* New York: Columbia University Press.

Hutchins, R. and D. Slesinger (1928) "Some observations on the law of evidence." Columbia Law Rev. 28, 4: 432–440.

Inbau, F. and J. Reid (1967) *Criminal Interrogation and Confessions*. Baltimore: Williams & Wilkins.

Ittelson, W. H. (1961) "The constancies in visual perception," pp. 339–353 in F. P. Kilpatrick (ed.) *Explorations in Transactional Psychology*. New York: New York University Press.

Jacob, H. (1971) "Black and white perceptions of justice in the city." Law and Society Rev. 6, 1: 69–89.

Jencks v. United States (1957) 353 U.S. 657, 77 S.Ct. 1007.

Kilpatrick, F. P. [ed.] (1961) *Explorations in Transactional Psychology.* New York: New York University Press.

—— and H. Cantril (1961) "The constancies in social perception," pp. 354–365 in F. P. Kilpatrick (ed.) *Explorations in Transactional Psychology.* New York: New York University Press.

Kilpatrick, F. P. and W. H. Ittelson (1961) "The perception of movement," pp. 58–68 in F. P. Kilpatrick (ed.) *Explorations in Transactional Psychology.* New York: New York University Press.

Kirby v. Illinois (1972) 40 U.S.L.W. 4607 (U.S.).

Langer, J., S. Wapner and H. Werner (1961) "The effect of danger upon the experience of time." Amer. J. of Psychology 74, 1: 94–97.

Leary v. United States (1969) 395 U.S. 6, 89 S.Ct. 1532.

Luh, C. W. (1922) "The conditions of retention." Psych. Monographs 31, 3(No. 142).

Lund, F. H. (1925) "The psychology of belief." J. of Abnormal and Social Psychology 20, 2: 174–196.

Marshall, J. (1968) *Intention in Law and Society.* New York: Funk & Wagnalls.

—— (1966a) *Law and Psychology in Conflict.* Indianapolis: Bobbs-Merrill.

—— (1966b) "Relation of the unconscious to intention." Virginia Law Rev. 52, 7: 1256–1282.

—— and H. Mansson (1966) "Punitiveness, recall and the police." J. of Research in Crime and Delinquency 1966 (July): 129–139.

Marshall, J., K. H. Marquis, and S. Oskamp (1971) "Effects of kinds of question and atmosphere of interrogation on accuracy and completeness of testimony." Harvard Law Rev. 84, 7: 1620–1643.

Marston, W. M. (1924) "Studies in testimony." J. of Criminal Law and Criminology 15: 5–31.

McCarty, D. G. (1960) *Psychology and the Law.* Englewood Cliffs, N.J.: Prentice-Hall.

Melville, H. (1961) *Billy Budd and the Piazza Tales.* New York: Dolphin Books.

Milgrim, S. (1965) "Some conditions of obedience and disobedience to authority." Human Relations 18, 1: 57–76.

Miller, D. R. and G. E. Swanson (1956) "The study of conflict," pp. 131–174 in M. R. Jones (ed.) *Nebraska Symposium on Motivation.* Lincoln: University of Nebraska Press.

Miranda v. Arizona (1966) 384 U.S. 436, 86 S.Ct. 1602.

Moore v. Dempsey (1923) 261 U.S. 86, 43 S.Ct. 265.

Morisette v. United States (1952) 342 U.S. 246, 72 S.Ct. 240.

Morris, R. E. (1957) "Witness performance under stress: a sociological approach." J. of Social Issues 13, 2: 17–22.

Munsterberg, H. (1923) *On The Witness Stand: Essays in Psychology and Crime.* New York: Doubleday, Page.

Namet v. United States (1963) 373 U.S. 179, 83 S.Ct. 1151.

New York Times (May 26, 1971): 1, col. 5.

Padawer-Singer, A. M. (1970) "Free press-fair trial:" Paper presented at the Symposium on Psychological Research in Legal Settings of the American Psychological Association.

Plato (1938) *Phaedo* (Sir R. W. Livingstone, trans.) London: Oxford University Press.

Pointer v. Texas (1965) 380 U.S. 400, 85 S.Ct. 1065.

Pollock, F. (1941) *Holmes-Pollock Letters* (Vol. 2, M. Howe, ed.). Cambridge: Harvard University Press.

—— and F. W. Maitland (1911) *The History of English Law,* Vol. 2. Cambridge: Cambridge University Press.

Reed v. Anderson (1972) 40 U.S.L.W. 2736 (3rd Cir.).

Regina v. Smyth (1957) 92 C.L.R. 163.

Remmer v. United States (1954) 347 U.S. 227, 74 S.Ct. 450.

Rock, I. and L. Kaufman (1962) "The moon illusion." Science 136 (June 22):1023.

Sarnoff, I. (1962) *Personality Dynamics and Development.* New York: John Wiley.

Sherif, M. (1936) *Psychology of Social Norms.* New York: Harper and Brothers.

Simeon Ben Shatach, *Talmud,* first Chapter, ninth citation, Tractate, Sayings of the Fathers.

Simon, R. J. (1967) *The Jury and the Defense of Insanity.* Boston: Little, Brown.

Snee, T. J. and D. E. Lush (1941) "Interaction of the narrative and interrogatory methods of obtaining testimony." J. of Psychology 11: 229–236.

Spiegel, H. (1967) "Hypnosis and invasion of privacy," pp. 355–364 in V. Lawyer and B. George, Jr. (eds.) *How to Defend a Criminal Case—From Arrest to Verdict.* Boston: American Trial Lawyers Association.

Stern, W. (1939) "Psychology of testimony." J. of Abnormal and Social Psychology 34, 1: 3–20.

———— (1910) "Abstracts of lectures on the psychology of testimony and on the study of individuality." Amer. J. of Psychology 21, 2: 270–282.

Stovall v. Denno (1967) 388 U.S. 293, 87 S.Ct. 1967.

Thucydides (1934) *The Complete Writings of Thucydides* (R. Crawley Translation). New York: Modern Library.

Tot v. United States (1943) 319 U.S. 463, 63 S.Ct. 1241.

Travers, J. L. and N. Morris (1961) "Imputed intent in murder, or *Smith v. Smyth.*" Australian Law J. 35, (August 31): 154–176.

Turner v. Louisiana (1965) 379 U.S. 466, 85 S.Ct. 546

United States v. Ash (1972) 40 U.S.L.W. 2568 (D.C Cir.), cert. granted, 40 U.S.L.W. 3581 (U.S. June 12 1972).

United States v. Wade (1967) 388 U.S. 218, 87 S.Ct 1926.

Wall, P. (1965) *Eye-Witness Identification in Criminal Cases.* Springfield: C. C. Thomas.

Washington v. Texas (1967) 388 U.S. 14, 87 S.Ct. 1920.

Wellman, F. L. (1923) *The Art of Cross-Examination.* New York: Macmillan.

Wigmore, J. H. (1931) *The Principles of Judicial Proof.* Boston: Little, Brown.

Williams, G. L. (1965) *The Mental Element in Crime.* Jerusalem: Magnes Press.

Winter, R. K. Jr. (1971) "The jury and the risk of non persuasion." Law and Society Rev. 5, 3: 335–344.

Zimbardo, P. G. (1969) "The human choice: individuation, reason and order versus deindividuation, impulse, and chaos," pp. 237–307 in W. Arnold and D. Levine (eds.) *Nebraska Symposium on Motivation.* Lincoln: University of Nebraska Press.

24. The Trial of a Rape Case

RICHARD A. HIBEY

THERE IS TRUTH IN THE OLD PLATITUDE WHICH traditionally begins discussions about the crime of rape—that it is a charge which is easy to make, difficult to prove, and even more difficult to defend.[1] Accordingly, the advocate finds no phase of an investigation and trial of such a case unimportant. However, there are certain aspects of a rape case which require special analysis, including corroboration, consent, and character.[2] The primary task for both the prosecutor and defense counsel is to unite these factors into probative and credible evidence supporting their respective cases.

Experience on both sides of a rape trial will attest that proof of these elements indicating either a verdict of guilty beyond a reasonable doubt or an acquittal does not assure that result, or even render it predictable, because the jury's assessment of the credibility of the witnesses and their evidence is not always rational.[3] This phenomenon stems in large part from certain ideas jurors have about the crime of rape, some of which are believed with such ferocity that jury verdicts are often examples of outright nullification—the ultimate and extreme exercise of the fact finder's prerogative.[4]

These notions may include the following:

(a) Black men are more likely to attack white women than black women;[5]

(b) The only cases that are seriously prosecuted are the rapes of white women;

(c) The punishment for a black man raping a white woman is death, or mandatory life imprisonment, or some form of corporal punishment in addition to incarceration;

(d) A hitchhiking girl impliedly consents to intercourse however "imperfectly selected" her sexual partner might be;

▶SOURCE: *"The Trial of a Rape Case: An Advocate's Analysis of Corroboration, Consent and Character,"* Criminal Law Bulletin *(1973), 11:309–334. Copyright 1973, Warren, Gorham, and Lamont, Inc., 210 South St., Boston, Mass. 02111, all rights reserved. Reprinted by Permission.*

[1]"It is true rape is a most detestable crime, and therefore ought severely and impartially to be punished with death; but it must be remembered, that it is an accusation easily to be made and hard to be proved, and harder to be defended by the party accused, tho never so innocent." 1 M. Hale, Pleas of the Crown *635.

[2]This article will not discuss the lesser included offenses of rape, carnal knowledge of a minor and its lesser included offenses, the alibi, mistake of age, or insanity defenses. The principal text will examine the rape case as it is tried in the District of Columbia. The law of other jurisdictions as it affects this discussion will be footnoted.

[3]The problem of credibility in rape cases was well recognized as early as the 17th century:

"The party ravished may give evidence upon oath, and is in law a competent witness; but the credibility of her testimony, and how far forth she is to be believed, must be left to the jury, and is more or less credible according to the circumstances of fact that concur in that testimony. . . . It is one thing whether a witness be admissible to be heard, another thing, whether they are to be believed when heard."
1 M. Hale, Pleas of the Crown *633, *635.

[4]*Dougherty v. United States*, No. 24318 (D.C. Cir., June 30, 1972).

[5]Amir, "Forcible Rape," 31 *Fed. Prob.* 51 (1967).

(e) A girl who sleeps in the nude is "looking for" intercourse even when her sexual partner arrives surreptitiously and without invitation through a window in the middle of the night;

(f) A victim who does not wear undergarments at the time she was attacked in all likelihood was not attacked at all.

Regardless of the effect of these impressions, counsel for each side must objectively assess the rational qualities supporting the credibility of his case in order to advocate effectively.

In view of the touchstone of credibility, that elusive ingredient in a criminal trial made more elusive by the nature of a rape case, this discussion will focus on the elements of corroboration of the crime of rape, the victim's consent, and character evidence. Effective advocacy demands that evidence relating to these three elements be marshalled according to the adversary's theory of the case.

CORROBORATION[6]

Rape involves sexual intercourse with a woman (not one's wife) which is forcible and against her will.[7] In those jurisdictions which require cor-

[6]For purposes of this discussion, corroboration may be defined as support of a fact by evidence independent of the mere assertion of that fact. "In rape prosecutions, 'corroboration, in the sense that there must be circumstances in proof which tend to support the prosecutrix' story is required.'" *Borum v. United States*, 409 F.2d 433, 438 (D.C. Cir. 1967), *quoting Ewing v. United States*, 135F.2d 633, 636 (D.C. Cir. 1942), *cert. denied*, 318 U.S. 776, *rehearing denied*, 318 U.S. 803 (1943).

[7]*See, e.g.,* Ala. Code tit. 14, § 396 (1958); Alaska Stat. § 11.15.120 (1962); Cal. Penal Code § 261 (West 1970); Iowa Code § 698.1 (1971); Kan. Stat. Ann. § 21–3502 (Supp. 1970); Mo. Rev. Stat. § 559.260 (Supp. 1970); Neb. Rev. Stat. § 28–408 (1964); N.J. Rev. Stat. § 2A:138–1 (Supp. 1972); N.M. Stat. Ann. § 40A–9–2 (1953); N.D. Cent. Code § 12–30–01 (Supp. 1971); Ohio Rev. Code § 2905.01(Supp. 1970); Okla. Stat. Ann. tit. 21, § 1111 (1951); Pa. Stat. Ann. tit. 18, § 4721 (1972); R.I. Gen Laws Ann. § 11–37–1 (1969); S.C. Code Ann. § 16–71 (1962); Tex. Penal Code art. 1183 (1963); Utah Code Ann. § 76–53–15 (1953); W. Va. Code Ann. § 61–2–15 (1966); Wis. Stat. § 944.01 (1969).

roboration,[8] there are two aspects of the crime

[8]See Note, *Forcible and Statutory Rape,* 62 Yale L. J. 55,61–62 n.44 (1952). For more recent decisions for the necessity of corroboration see, e.g., *United States v. Jenkins,* 436 F.2d 140 (D.C. Cir. 1970) (testimony of the victim must be corroborated both as to the corpus delecti and the identity of the accused); *Wesley v. State,* 225 Ga. 22, 165 S.E.2d 719 (1969) (requires that the victim's testimony be corroborated); *Territory of Hawaii v. Hays,* 43 Haw. 58 (1958) (testimony must be clear and convincing and supported by surrounding circumstances); *State v. Hunt,* 178 Neb. 783, 135 N.W.2d 475 (1965) (prosecutrix's testimony must be corroborated as to material facts and circumstances which support her principle testimony); *Texter v. State,* 170 Neb. 426, 102 N.W.2d 655 (1960) (testimony of prosecutrix alone is not sufficient to warrant a conviction but must be corroborated by other evidence on material points); *People v. Augustine,* 35 App. Div. 2d 313 N.Y.S.2d, 323, 527 (1970) (need legally sufficient corroborative evidence of every material fact essential to constitute crime of rape); *People v. Tellers,* 40 Misc. 2d 551, 243 N.Y.S.2d 440 (Sup. Ct. King's County 1963) (independent supporting evidence is required). A number of jurisdictions have held corroboration unnecessary. See *Blackmon v. State,* 240 So. 2d 696, *cert. denied*, 240 So. 2d 699 (Ala. Ct. Crim. App. 1970) (the fact that appellant's convictions rest upon her uncorroborated testimony is of no consequence); *Bakken v. State,* 489 P.2d 120 (Alaska 1971) (statutory rape has no corroboration requirement); *State v. Dutton,* 106 Ariz. 463,478 P.2d 87 (1970) (testimony of prosecuting witness alone is sufficient to support a conviction); *Lacy v. State,* 240 Ark. 84, 398 S.W.2d 508 (1966); *People v. Stevenson.* 275 Cal. App. 2d 645, 80 Cal. Rptr. 392 (1969) (the victim's testimony does not require corroboration); *People v. Burroughs,* 200 Cal. App. 2d 629, 19 Cal. Rptr. 344(Dist. Ct. App. 2d, 1962); *Smith v. State,* 239 So. 2d 284 (Fla. 1970) (corroboration of Prosecutrix's testimony is not necessary to authorize conviction for rape); *State v. Gee,* 93 Idaho 636, 470 P.2d 296 (1970); *State v. Rassmussen,* 92Idaho 731, 449 P.2d 837 (1970); *People v. Griggs,* 266 N.E.2d 398 (Ill. App. Ct. 1970) (if the testimony of prosecutrix is clear and convincing no corroboration is needed); *People v. White,* 26 Ill. 2d 199, 186 N.E.2d 351 (1962) (must be clear and convincing, if it is not, other corroborative evidence must be produced); *Douglas v. State,* 254Ind. 517, 261 N.E.2d 567 (1970) (uncorroborated testimony of the victim is sufficient to sustain the judgment of conviction); *Grimm v. State,* 254 Ind. 150, 258 N.E.2d 407 (1970); *Robinson v. Commonwealth,* 459 S.W.2d 147 (Ky. Ct. App. 1970) (unsupported testimony of prosecutrix if not contradictory or incredible, or inherently improbable, may be sufficient to sustain a conviction of rape); *State v. Dipietrantonio,*152 Me. 41, 122 A.2d 414 (1956) (corroboration must be probable and credible); *Coward v. State,* 10 Md. App. 127, 268 A.2d 508 (1970) (testimony of victim, if believed, including her positive

the study of which, in the light of such a rule, requires careful analysis: identification of the defendant as the perpetrator of the act complained of and penetration.[9]

identification of accused as perpetrator of the crime, is sufficient to support conviction of rape); *Johnson v. State*, 238 Md. 528, 209 A.2d 414 (1965); *Goode v. State*, 245 Miss. 391, 146 So. 2d 74 (1962) (sufficient, but should be scrutinized with caution); *State v. Gray*, 423 S.W.2d 776 (Mo. 1968) (corroboration of prosecutrix's version of incident is not required, where evidence was not contradictory in nature or unbelievable); *State v. Warren*, 366 S.W.2d 311 (Mo. 1963) (sufficient unless inherently contradictory or unconvincing when applied to admitted facts); *State v. Bouldin*, 153 Mont. 276, 456 P.2d 830 (1969); Application of Bennett, 77 Nev. 429, 266 P.2d 343 (1961); *Strunk v. State*, 450 P.2d 216 (Okla. Ct. Crim. App. 1969) (conviction for rape may be had on the uncorroborated testimony of the prosecutrix, or on slight corroboration where testimony of prosecutrix is not inherently improbable or unworthy of credence); *State v. Fitzmaurice*, 475 P.2d 426 (Ore. Ct. App. 1970) (rape conviction may be had on the uncorroborated testimony of the prosecutrix); *State v. Fulks*, 83 S.D. 433, 160 N.W.2d 418 (1968) (it is not essential to conviction of statutory rape that testimony of complaining witness be corroborated); *Carroll v. State*, 212 Tenn. 464, 370 S.W.2d 523 (1963); *Thomas v. State*, 466 S.W.2d 783 (Texas Ct. Crim. App. 1971) (prosecutrix's testimony in prosecution for assault with intent to rape need not be corroborated); *Johnson v. State*, 449 S.W.2d 65 (Texas Ct. Crim. App. 1969); *State v. Hodges*, 14 Utah 2d 197, 381 P.2d 81 (1963); *Fogg v. Commonwealth*, 208 Va. 541, 159 S.E.2d 616 (1968); *State v. Jennen*, 58 Wash. 2d 171, 361 P. 2d 739 (1961).

At common law, "the testimony of the prosecutrix or injured person, in the trial of all offenses against the chastity of women, was alone sufficient evidence to support a conviction . . ." 7 J. Wigmore, Evidence § 2061(3d ed. 1940).

[9]Merely the slightest penetration of the *labia maiora* by the penis is sufficient: "The crime of rape is committed if it [the male sex organ] enters only the labia of the female organ." *Holmes v. United States*, 171 F.2d 1022, 1023(D.C. Cir. 1948).

There have been a number of cases in the District of Columbia which have focused on the corroboration requirements of these two elements. E.g., *United States v. Terry*, 422 F.2d 704 (D.C. Cir. 1970); *Allison v. United States*, 409 F.2d 445 (D.C. Cir. 1969); *Thomas v. United States*, 387 F.2d 191 (D.C. Cir. 1967); *Franklin v. United States*, 330 F.2d 205 (D.C. Cir. 1964); *Wheeler v. United Stetes*, 211 F.2d 19 (D.C. Cir.), *cert. denied*, 347 U.S. 1019 (1954); *Ewing v. United States*, 135 F.2d 633 (D.C. Cir. 1942), *cert. denied*, 318 U.S. 776, *rehearing denied*, 318 U.S. 803 (1943); *Kidwell v. United States*, 38 App. D.C. 566 (1912). For cases in other jurisdictions focusing upon corroboration requirements, see Annot., 60 A.L.R. 1124 (1929).

Identification

At common law, rape was a heinous crime, punishable by death or by both castration and putting one's eyes out.[10] Through the centuries rape retained its capital character and slowly the common law began to recognize exceptions to the general proposition that no corroboration of the elements of rape was required.[11] While it is difficult to say with accuracy what uniformly constituted corroborated proof of rape, it does not do violence to logic and the human experience to appreciate why many jurisdictions have come to require corroboration under certain circumstances.[12]

The element of identification, for example, has a long history of its erroneous proof in criminal cases.[13] The combination of this historical truth with the emotion-laden cir-

[10]As Mathew Hale described it, "Rape was anciently a felony . . . and was punished by loss of life. But in the process of time that punishment seemed too hard; but the truth is, a severe punishment succeeded in the place thereof; viz. castration and the loss of eyes . . ." 1 M. Hale, Pleas of the Crown *626. See Neville, "Rape in Early English Law," 121 *Just. P.* 223 (1957).

[11]*Cf.* note 8 *supra*.

[12]One court has concluded:
"Today, in the absence of a statute requiring corroboration, it is generally held that the unsupported testimony of the prosecutrix, if not contradictory or incredible, or inherently improbable, may be sufficient to sustain a conviction of rape . . . but where such testimony bears on its face indications of unreliability or improbability, and is contradicted by other evidence, it is insufficient to support a verdict without corroboration."

In re F., 68 Misc. 2d 244, 247, 327 N.Y.S.2d 237, 240 (Family Ct. 1971). See *Robinson v. Commonwealth*, 459 S.W.2d 147 (Ky. 1970) (sufficient if not contradictory or inherently improbable); *State v. Dipietrantonio*, 152 Me. 41, 122 A.2d 414 (1956) (must be probable and credible); *State v. Warren*, 366 S.W.2d 311 (Mo. 1963) (sufficient unless inherently contradictory or unconvincing when applied to admitted facts); *People v. Linzy*, 38 App. Div. 2d 648, 327 N.Y.S.2d 267 (1971); *In re* G., 71 Misc. 2d 312, 328 N.Y.S.2d 777 (Family Ct. 1972); *Strunk v. State*, 450 P.2d 216 (Okla. 1969) (sufficient unless inherently improbable or unworthy of belief).

[13]See generally E. Borchard, *Convicting the Innocent* (1932); P. Wall, *Eyewitness Identification in Criminal Cases* (1965).

cumstances peculiar to instances of rape infect the identification experience instinct with unreliability. It goes without saying that the adversaries in a rape trial must probe the identity element with great care.

Corroboration of Identification: The Prosecutor's Role. The prosecutor's interviews with the complaining witness provide the basis for his assessment of the proof. These conferences are often viewed by the victim as part of the continuum of horror she has experienced since she was attacked. This distress can be attributed to a number of factors. The complainant is often skeptical of the prosecutor's representation that the matters discussed will be kept in confidence until the criminal process requires their publication. She may also be upset by his persistent delving questions about her assailant's face, his features, her general opportunity to observe, the lighting, location, the length of time they were together, the immediacy of her complaint, his penis, its placement, her position, her reaction, and her examination by hospital authorities and medical personnel. Unnerving questions, which she takes as sinister suggestions, concerning what cooperation, if any, she gave her assailant and inquiries into her past, particularly those concerning prior acts of consensual intercourse and the sources who would attest to her reputation in the community for veracity and chastity, add to the tension.

The majority of jurisdictions do not require corroboration of the victim's complaint in order to establish a *prima facie* case for rape.[14] Yet cases in those jurisdictions never fail to recite the litany of facts which support the victim's testimony and, thus in reality, to evidence corroboration of identification and/or penetration.[15] One must conclude that while the articulation of the rule speaks in terms of the sufficiency of uncorroborated proof, the fact remains that proof of rape in most cases is sufficient only when the evidence is corroborated.

The quality and/or quantity of evidence necessary to corroborate identification depends upon the "danger of falsification"[16] by the victim. Thus, where the sole issue in the case is identification, no further corroboration beyond a showing that the complainant had an adequate opportunity to observe her attacker may be needed.[17] Where consent, penetration, or the trustworthiness of the complainant is at issue, the danger of falsification of rape increases and, accordingly, more proof on the element of identification is required.[18]

As an essential element of every crime, identification has been the subject of innumerable decisions and treatises dating from the earliest days of our jurisprudence.[19] Yet the most profound impact upon the treatment of identification as an element of all crime is of recent vintage. The entire shape of the criminal trial was altered by the trilogy of identification cases decided by the Supreme Court in 1967.[20] As a result of the *Wade-Gilbert-Stovall* cases and their flourishing progeny,[21] identification

---

[14]See Annot., 60 A.L.R. 1124, 1125 (1929); *cf.* notes 8 & 12 *supra.*

[15]See Annot., 60 A.L.R. 1124, 1141 (1929).

[16]*Thomas v. United States* 387 F.2d 191, 192 (D.C. Cir. 1967); *Franklin v. United States,* 330 F.2d 205, 208 (D.C. Cir. 1964); *Alvarado v. State,* 63 Ariz. 511, 164 P.2d 460 (1945); *People v. Silva,* 405 Ill. 158, 89 N.E.2d 800 (1950); *State v. Wood,* 355 Mo. 1008, 199 S.W.2d 396 (1947); *Lee v. State,* 485 P.2d 482 (Okla. 1971); *Commonwealth v. Oyler,* 130 Pa. Super. 405, 197 A. 508 (1939); *Young v. Commonwealth,* 185 Va. 1032, 40 S.E.2d 805 (1947); *Cleaveland v. State,* 211 Wis. 565, 248 N.W.408 (1933).

[17]*Thomas v. United States,* 387 F.2d 191, 192 (D.C. Cir. 1967).

[18]The "danger of an erroneous identification in a rape case is not of the same magnitude as the danger of a fabricated rape. . . ." *Franklin v. United States,* 330 F.2d 205, 208 (D.C. Cir. 1964).

[19]P. Wall, *Eyewitness Identification in Criminal Cases* (1965); 1–2 F. Wharton, *Evidence in Criminal Issues* (10th ed. 1912).

[20]*Stovall v. Denno,* 388 U.S. 293 (1967) (*United States v. Wade* is not retroactive); *Gilbert v. California,* 388 U.S. 263 (1967) (in court identification is inadmissible unless it is untainted from the illegal lineup identification); *United States v. Wade,* 388 U.S. 218 (1967) (post indictment lineup held to be critical stage thereby entitling accused to presence of counsel).

[21]See, e.g., *Biggers v. Tennessee,* 390 U.S. 404 (1968) (requiring defendant to repeat words allegedly used at time of rape of complaining witness upheld when witness was

undergoes the closest scrutiny according to standards of fairness, procedural due process, and the absolute requirements of counsel's assistance. Therefore, evidence which proves or disproves the elements of fairness surrounding each identification for purposes of the trilogical inquiry comprises the substantive proof of corroboration of the victim's identification of her assailant. Thus, factors bearing on the physical capacity of the witness to observe fairly[22] also go to the question of whether she observed accurately. The same considerations hold true for the conditions surrounding the observation[23] and the description of the features of her assailant.[24]

In addition to the vital sensations of the identification experience, the inquiry focuses on fundamental questions of the bias, interest, and motivation of the witness to falsify[25] as well as the suggestivity of the process by which identification for law enforcement purposes is formalized. Thus, if the identification is the result of an on-the-street confrontation,[26] a police cellblock "show up,"[27] a court ordered line up,[28] or a photographic identification[29] an inquiry of constitutional magnitude is required to establish

thought able to identify defendant based on that and other elements); *Simmons v. United States*, 390 U.S. 377 (1968) (showing of photographs to a witness held proper means of acquiring identification); *Russell v. United States*,408 F.2d 1280 (D.C. Cir. 1969) (identification is proper when made by witness after police returned subject to scene of alleged crime shortly thereafter). See also Annot., 39 A.L.R.3d 487 (1971) (admissibility of evidence of lineup identification as affected by allegedly suggestive lineup procedures); 39 A.L.R.3d 791 (1971) (admissibility of evidence of showup identification as affected by allegedly suggestive showup procedures); 39 A.L.R.3d 1000(1971) (admissibility of evidence of photographic identification as affected by allegedly suggestive identification procedures).

[22]For example, fright, fatigue, preoccupation, age, health, impairment to the senses, ethical medication, drugs, intoxication. See, e.g., *United States v. Hiss*, 88 F. Supp. 559 (S.D.N.Y. 1950) (insanity); *Lester v. Gay*, 217 Ala. 585, 117 So. 211 (1928) (hallucinations caused by fainting); *State v. Ballestros*, 100 Ariz. 262, 413 P.2d 739 (1966) (narcotics); *People v. Smith*, 4 Cal. App. 3d 403, 84Cal. Rptr. 412 (1970) (narcotics); *People v. McGuire*, 118Ill. 2d 257, 163 N.E.2d 832 (1960) (intoxication); *State v. Muskell,*161 N.W.2d 732 (Iowa 1968) (senility); *Mosley v. Commonwealth,*420 S.W.2d 679 (Ky. 1967) (schizophrenic fantasies).

[23]For example, distance, duration, direction, angle of view, weather, daytime, night time, lighting, and obstruction to vision. See, e.g., *People v. Loar*, 165 Cal. App. 2d 765, 333 P.2d 49(1958) (darkness); *People v. Capon*, 23 Ill. 2d 254, 178 N.E. 2d 296 (1961), *cert. denied*, 369 U.S. 878 (1962) (fluorescent light).

[24]For example, age, height, weight, build, race, skin tone, hair, facial features, voice, and clothing. See, e.g., *People v. Loar*, 165Cal. App. 2d 765, 333 P.2d 49 (1958) (identification made by voice, general appearance and clothing); *People v. Glab*, 15 Cal. App. 2d 120, 59 P.2d 195 (1936) (sound of

footsteps); *People v. Bealey*, 81 Cal. App. 648, 254 P. 628 (1927) (silhouettes); *People v. Capon*, 23 Ill. 2d 254, 178 N.E.2d 296 (1961), *cert. denied*, 369U.S. 878 (1962) (identification made by limp, clothing and general description); *People v. McGee*, 21 Ill. 2d 440, 173 N.E.2d 434 (1961) (profile in dark).

[25]*Mason v. United States*, 408 F.2d 903 (D.C. Cir. 1969).

[26]*Russell v. United States*, 408 F.2d 1280 (D.C. Cir. 1969).

[27]*Clemens v. United States*, 408 F.2d 1230 (D.C. Cir. 1968), *cert. denied,* 394 U.S. 964 (jail cell showup held suggestive); *In re* Hill, 71 Cal. App. 2d 997, 458 P.2d 449, 80 Cal. Rptr. 537, *cert denied*, 397 U.S. 1017 (1969). *Contra, Commonwealth v. Biancone*, 175 Pa. Super. 6, 102 A.2d 199 (1954) (jail cell showup held not suggestive).

[28]The prevailing view in many jurisdictions is that the circumstances attending a lineup may be so unfair or so suggestive as to render evidence of any resulting identification inadmissible. *Adams v. United States*, 399 F.2d 574 (D.C. Cir. 1968); *Bowman v. State*, 44 Ala. App. 331, 208 So. 2d 241 (1968) (lineup in which defendant and his companion were the only blacks); *People v. Caruso*, 68 Cal. App. 2d 183, 436 P.2d 336, 65 Cal. Rptr. 336 (1968); *People v. Blumenshine*, 42 Ill. 2d 508, 250 N.E.2d 152 (1969). There is some support for the view that the manner in which a lineup was held goes only to the weight of the identification evidence, rather than to its admissibility. *State v. le Vier*, 202Kan. 544, 451 P.2d 142 (1969).

[29]The presentation to witnesses of several photographs, including that of the defendant, has generally been held proper, in the absence of evidence of any unfairness in the conduct of the exhibit. *Simmons v. United States*, 390 U.S. 377 (1968); *United States v. Clark*, 289 F. Supp. 610 (E.D. Pa. 1968); *McClain v. State*, 444 S.W.2d 99 (Ark. 1969); *People v. Blackburn*, 260 Cal. App. 2d 35, 66 Cal. Rptr. 845 (1968); *Tafero v. State*, 223 So. 2d 564 (Fla. App. 1969); *People v. Williams,*117 Ill. App. 2d 34, 254 N.E.2d 81 (1969); *Basaff v. State*, 208 Md. 643, 119 A.2d 917 (1956); *Commonwealth v. Geraway*, 355Mass. 433, 245 N.E.2d 423, *cert. denied*, 396 U.S. 911 (1969); *State v. Balle*, 442 S.W.2d (Mo. 1969); *People v. Ralming,*26 N.Y.2d 411, 259 N.E.2d 727, 311 N.Y.S.2d 292 (1970).

fairness of the identification process. But upon a finding of admissibility, the evidence upon which the ruling is made becomes substantive proof that the complainant's in-court identification has been corroborated.

This practice is especially helpful in cases where the court has found an "independent source" of identification to exist. By producing such a source the witness' in-court identification can be admitted as free from the primary taint of her illegal or unfair out-of-court recognition. Independent source evidence focuses on the indicia of reliability which, in effect, corroborate identification.[30]

There are, of course, other forms of evidence, extrinsic in nature, that corroborate identification. Thus, eye-witnesses to the attack itself or to circumstances which support testimony of the complainant fulfill the corroboration requirement. Likewise, fingerprints,[31] shoe prints, tire treads, firearms, toolmarks, wood, glass, soil and minerals, hair and fibers, blood and other body fluids are sources of corroborative evidence which should be examined before the case for identification can be laid to rest.[32]

Defense Counsel's Attack upon Corroboration of Identification. Defense counsel's inquiry into corroboration begins with two sources or information available to him: the formal and informal discovery process,[33] and the defendant himself.

---

[30]*United States v. Wade,* 388 U.S. 218, 241 (1967), *quoting Wong Sun v. United States,* 371 U.S. 471, 488 (1963).

[31]While the presence of a defendant's fingerprints at the scene of a crime is, procedural problems aside, admissible, it remains equivocal evidence if it cannot be shown that the defendant did not otherwise have access to the location at the scene where his fingerprints were recovered. *Stevenson v. United States,* 380 F.2d 590 (D.C. Cir. 1967).

In *Borum v. United States,* 380 F.2d 595 (D.C. Cir. 1967), a burglary defendant's fingerprints were found on jars that were in the home at the time of the crime. The Government offered no evidence that the fingerprints were left on the jars during the course of the burglary. Thus, where the prints could have been there "indefinitely", maybe even "for a period of years"the jury was left without a way of determining how they got on the jar. Such speculation was held to be impermissible. It should be noted, however, that in the District of Columbia the defendant was not obliged to explain the presence of his prints on the premises. *Id.* at 596. The applicability of this case to the corroboration requirement in rape trials is obvious. The equivocal nature of certain evidence could strip it of its corroborative force. For cases discussing the sufficiency of fingerprints evidence in a criminal case see Annot., 28 A.L.R.2d 1150–56 (1953); Annot., 63 A.L.R. 1325 (1929); Annot., 16 A.L.R. 370–71 (1922).

[32]The forensic sciences have reached high levels of sophistication in developing reliable tests which provide evidence for use in all trials. The prosecutor, state or federal, holds a distinct advantage over his adversary in developing scientific evidence for his case. In addition to the police laboratories, an integral part of the operation of every major metropolitan police department, the laboratory of the Federal Bureau of Investigation provides, free of cost, testing services in all technical subject areas mentioned in the text as well as in areas such as document identification, photograph analysis, cryptanalysis, gambling deciphering, typewriter standards, and safe insulation. Moreover, the scientists of the FBI laboratory are prepared to testify to their findings in state and federal criminal trials. For an explanation of the nature and scope of the service provided by this law enforcement agency, see Federal Bureau of Investigation, U.S. Dept. of Justice, *Scientific Aids* (1970).

[33]The informal discovery process includes: examination of the scene of the crime, conferences with the prosecutor, and interviews with the witnesses and police. Interviewing witnesses, especially the complainant, is not without difficulties, for the prosecutor may insist that defense counsel (or his investigator) identify himself and explain the purpose of the interview. Defense attorneys complain that this introduction permits the witness the choice of refusing to discuss the case, thus depriving them of a most critical means of discovery.

If such a practice effectively denies counsel the free access to witnesses which the prosecutor has, it is clearly indefensible. This principle is supported by *Gregory v. United States,* 369 F.2d 185 (D.C. Cir. 1966), where the prosecutor told murder witnesses that they were free to talk to defense counsel, but he advised them not to talk to anyone unless he (the prosecutor) was present. The Court of Appeals reversed the conviction and stated:

"Witnesses, particularly eyewitnesses, to a crime are the property neither of the prosecution nor the defense. Both sides have an equal right, and should have an equal opportunity, to interview them. . . . [W]e know of nothing in the law which gives the prosecutor the right to interfere with the preparation of the defense by effectively denying defense counsel access to the witnesses except in his presence. . . . . In fact, Canon 39 of the

Through discovery counsel may learn of weaknesses in the Government's case on the issues of corroboration of identification and penetration. At the same time, he may also learn from his client that the complainant consented to sexual intercourse. While this will present difficult choices at the time of trial[34] his functions at this stage of the case are clear.

Counsel for the defendant can expect no less discovery than that which the Federal Rules of Criminal Procedure (or his state's equivalent) and the case law require. It is only upon a full disclosure under the law that he will be able to focus on the elements of corroboration, consent and character. Thus, where available and appropriate, counsel should formally seek a Bill of Particulars,[35] discovery and inspection of evidence,[36] production of grand jury minutes,[37]

and production of the preliminary hearing transcript.[38] In addition, the Government is obliged to produce evidence favorable to the accused under the doctrine of *Brady v. Maryland*.[39]

Canons of Professional Ethics makes explicit the propriety [of the conduct which the prosecutor sought to impair]: 'A lawyer may properly interview any witness or prospective witness . . . without the consent of opposing counsel.

. . . . The current tendency in the criminal law is in the direction of discovery of the facts before trial and elimination of surprise at trial. A related development in the criminal law is the requirement that the prosecution not frustrate the defense in the preparation of its case. Information favorable to the defense must be made available to the defense. *Brady v. Maryland*, 373 U.S.83 (1963). . . . It is not suggested here that there was any direct suppression of evidence. But there was unquestionably a suppression of the means by which the defense could obtain evidence. . . . [T]he prosecutor's advice to these eyewitnesses . . . denied appellant a fair trial.' "

Id. at 188.

[34]*See* discussion, *infra* at 322.

[35]There is some question as to whether a Bill of Particulars is a recognized discovery device. See *United States v. Tolub*, 187 F. Supp. 705(S.D.N.Y. 1960), *aff'd,* 309 F.2d 286 (2d Cir. 1962). Nevertheless, the disclosures incident to the issuance of a bill are helpful to counsel. See G. Shadoan, *Laws and Tactics in Federal Criminal Cases* 166–76 (1964).

[36]Rule 16 of the Federal Rules of Criminal Procedure provides defense counsel, at the court's discretion, with the pretrial opportunity to inspect, examine, and subject to his own test-analysis, all tangible evidence the government intends to use in its case in chief as well as the defendant's statements. However, this rule specifically excludes pretrial

discovery of statements of trial witnesses to government agents that are written by the witness himself, or substantially verbatim recitals of his oral statements, or his grand jury testimony. The disclosure of these statements is made available after the witness has testified for the government on direct examination, but before his cross-examination. 18 U.S.C. § 3500 (1970).

State rules are similar. See, e.g., *Peel v. State,* 154 So. 2d 910 (Ct. App. Fla. 1963), *cert. denied,* 380 U.S. 986 (1964); Fla. R. Crim. P. 1.220(b) (1967) (tangible objects may be discovered, but not the pretrial statements of a defendant or those who will testify against him); Md. R. P. 728 (1971) (upon defendant's motion, a court may order the state's attorney to produce designated books, papers, documents, or tangible objects in connection with the defendant's case for inspection); *Glaros v. State,* 223 Md. 272, 164 A.2d 461, 463 (1960) (defendant may not inspect trial notes made by officers after their conversations with him); Mo. R.Crim. P. 25.19 (1971) (upon motion, a subpoena may be issued for production of objects, books, documents, and other tangible evidence); *State v. Engberg,* 377 S.W.2d 282, 286 (Mo. 1964) (motion for production of the statement of a chief prosecution witness denied). *State v. Anair,* 123 Vt. 80, 181 A.2d 61 (1962); Vt. Stat. Ann., tit. 13, § 6727 (Supp. 1971) (provides for discovery of tangible evidence, but not statements other than those of the defendant). See generally 73 A.L.R.2d 28,74, 102–14, 119–26 (1960).

[37]In the federal practice, the grand jury testimony of government witnesses is discoverable at trial because such testimony is a Jencks Statement. 18 U.S.C. §3500(e)(3) (1970). In *Young v. United States,* 406 F.2d 960 (D.C. Cir. 1968), the court held that the grand jury testimony of nontrial witnesses is discoverable by the defense where the trial court, in its discretion, determines that quest for truth is best served by disclosure. State practice is similar. See, e.g., *People v. Johnson,* 31 Ill. 2d 602, 203 N.E.2d 399 (1965) (in its discretion, a court may permit disclosure of grand jury testimony of a witness who testifies at trial); *People v. Di Napoli,* 27N.Y.2d 229, 265 N.E.2d 622, 316 N.Y.S.2d 622 (1970); N.Y. Crim. P. § 952 (McKinney 1970) (an order for the inspection of grand jury testimony is in the discretion of the trial judge).

[38]18 U.S.C. § 3006 A(e)(1) (1970).

[39]373 U.S. 83 (1963). In that case, the prosecutor withheld the confession of an accomplice for the murder for which Brady was being tried. The Supreme Court reversed, holding that "suppression by the prosecution of evidence favorable to the accused upon request violates due process where the evidence is either material to guilt or to punishment,

Accordingly, counsel for the defendant must receive from the Government all evidence, including testimony of any witness and the complainant, which specifically exonerates the defendant or negates the suggestion of his guilt. Moreover, counsel is entitled to any physical evidence pointing to other suspects, records of scientific testing which yielded negative results as to his client or the complainant, evidence that complainant has a mental history which would require a psychiatric examination for purposes of the case, recantations of complainant's story, her false accusations of others, and evidence of her prior acts of consensual intercourse, or her reputation for unchastity and her consent.[40] Armed with discovered evidence, counsel is in a position to analyze the weaknesses of the Government's case and make judgments about the theories of his defense.

Challenges to identification should be considered on both procedural and substantive grounds. Accordingly, defense counsel must review the history of the identification process in the same way as the prosecutor. Through discovery and motions, the defense attorney will begin to secure definition of the Government's case through written responses, courtroom statements by the Government attorney, and, most importantly, through the testimony of witnesses at pretrial hearings on those aspects of the case which place the issue of identification more sharply into focus.

Penetration

Where corroboration of penetration is required, the prosecutor should examine the following sources for his proof: complainant's account of the offense; medical examination of the complainant; physical examination of the accused; results of any scientific tests performed on the evidence; and direct eyewitness evidence.

Experience indicates that the vast majority of cases present circumstantial evidence of penetration as opposed to direct eyewitness evidence. In *Allison v. United States,*[41] the United States Court of Appeals for the District of Columbia recited a list of "circumstances in proof which tend to support the prosecutrix' story":

"Among the 'circumstances' we have deemed corroborative are the following: (1) medical evidence and testimony, (2) evidence of breaking and entering the prosecutrix' apartment, (3) condition of clothing, (4) bruises and scratches, (5) emotional condition of prosecutrix, (6) opportunity of accused, (7) conduct of accused at time of arrest, (8) presence of semen or blood on clothing of accused or victim, (9) promptness of complaints to friends and police, (10) lack of motive to falsify. This list, of course, is not exhaustive, and the corroboration in such cases 'must be evaluated on its own merits.' *Bailey & Humphries v. United States,* 405 F. 2d 1352 (D.C. Cir. 1968)."[42]

Many of the sources of corroboration for identification described earlier likewise serve to establish the proof of corroboration for penetration.[43] For example, hairs found in the complainant's vaginal area are subject both to classification as to kind (animal or human), type (head, body, pubic), race (Negroid, Mongoloid or Caucasoid), and to microscopic comparison with hairs taken from defendant for examination. A simple serological test, performed by a trained police technician who applies benzidine to the penis of the accused, may yield a reaction indicating the possible presence of blood.[44]

---

irrespective of the good faith or bad faith of the prosecution." *Id.* at 87. In *Levin v. Katzenbach,* 363 F.2d 287 (D.C. Cir. 1966), a new trial was ordered for the non-disclosure of a witness whose testimony might have raised a reasonable doubt even though defense counsel would have discovered the exculpatory evidence on his own. See also *Ellis v. United States,* 345 F.2d 961 (D.C. Cir. 1965).

[40] *Giles v. Maryland,* 386 U.S. 66 (1967).

[41] 409 F.2d 445 (D.C. Cir. 1969).

[42] *Id.* at 448, n.8.

[43] It should be noted that corroborated evidence of identification does not *per se* constitute corroborated evidence of penetration and vice versa. *Franklin v. United States,* 330 F.2d 205, 209 (D.C. Cir. 1964). Thus, while pregnancy will corroborate intercourse, it does not establish force or the identity of the sexual partner. *Kidwell v. United States,* 38 App. D.C. 566 (1912).

[44] In *Schmerber v. California,* 384 U.S. 757 (1966), the Supreme Court held that the fourth, fifth, and sixth amendment

Counsel for defendant must satisfy himself as to the probity of the evidence corroborating penetration. In the absence of independent eye-witness testimony on the issue, the discovery process is particularly effective in compelling the disclosure of medical and other forensic scientific evidence.[45] Under the Federal Rules of Criminal Procedure, counsel may submit all tangible evidence in the case for examination by experts of his own choosing. To the extent that he uses "outside" experts the Government has an equivalent right to discover the reports or conclusions which those experts make.[46]

rights were not violated when, upon refusal to take a "breathalizer" test, a sample of the accused's blood was taken. In discussing the fifth amendment implications of the case, the Court, citing *Hold v. United States,* 218 U.S. 245 (1910), found that there was no evidence of "testimonial compulsion" and that, accordingly, the petitioner's body is properly a source of real or physical evidence which may be used against him.

The benzidine test demonstrates a positive reaction for the presence of peroxydase, an enzyme found in human blood. Peroxydase, however, is present in many other items, including fruit juices, cabbage and potatoes. Thus, the benzidine test cannot in all circumstances be definitive. However, when examining the result of such a test administered on the defendant's penis, the inference is strong that the positive reaction is the result of his penis having a bloody contact rather than a vegetarian one. In *United States v. Sheard,* No. 71–1250 (D.D.C., Nov. 16, 1972) (Slip op. 19), the court discussed the results of benzidine tests and the possible causal factors contributing thereto, but nevertheless determined that the test results had sufficient probative value to be admissible.

There are other serological tests which are used to test garments for the presence of blood. The equivocal nature of a benzidine test on clothing which could have come in contact with many substances totally discredits the value of the test on such articles. For discussion of the forensic application of hair and serological analyses see T. Gonzales et al., *Legal Medicine, Pathology and Toxicology* (2d ed. 1954); R. Geadwohl, *Legal Medicine* (2d ed. 1968); 1–4 F. Lundquist, *Methods of Forensic Science* (1962–65).

[45]*Cf.* note 36 *supra* and accompanying text.

[46]Fed. R. Crim. P. 16(c). Only a few states have provisions for discovery of experts'names or testimony in criminal proceedings. See Ill. Ann. Stat. ch. 38, §§ 114–9 (Smith-Hurd 1971) (motion for list of witnesses); Annot., 96 A.L.R.2d 1224 (criminal discovery).

CONSENT

In criminal cases an affirmative defense is one which does not dispute the occurrence of a certain event or transaction; it attempts to legitimize it (consent), specially excuse it (duress, self defense, insanity, mistake), condemn it (entrapment), or establish that it transpired without action by the defendant (alibi). Consent, as an affirmative defense to rape, concedes essential facts of time, place, persons involved and the act of sexual intercourse in an effort to legitimize the act.

Consent must be affirmatively asserted. In terms of presentation, therefore, the organization and quality surrounding its assertion must not be inferior to the presentation of the Government's case. In the final analysis, however, its success depends upon which version of the facts the jury will believe. Thus, the advocates must not only make their cases believable, they must also make the other side's case unbelievable.

Defense counsel must, above all, determine when the process of discreditation should begin and what form it should take. This problem is most difficult to solve where the Government's case-in-chief appears weak as to one or more elements of the crime and where the defendant claims that the complainant consented. The problem is obvious: on the one hand if counsel vigorously challenges the Government's proof of the elements, the likelihood of the jury believing a consent defense, later raised in the defendant's case, is remote. On the other hand, if counsel lays the foundation for a consent defense on cross-examination of the complainant, he will be hard put, to say the least, to urge upon a jury that his client was not the man who raped her or that she was not penetrated at all.

Trial Tactics and the Consent Defense. At the trial stage itself counsel for the defendant must be flexible enough to choose the theory which is best suited to the facts of the case. As he hears the evidence and while he cross-examines on it, he must ask himself whether a case-in-chief which attacks the essential elements of the crime of rape is all that he thinks need be presented to prevail on motion or before the jury. He must ask himself whether he should lay the foundation of the defense of consent during the Government's presentation. In such circumstances, counsel might find that his best alternative is to rely on the record he made, presumably out of the presence of the jury, on the identification issue and to abandon the substantive question of iden.ification before the jury. On cross-examination counsel may also be able to refute the corroborative evidence of penetration, especially if it is circumstantial and scientific, without declaring to the jury an all-out assault on that element. Moreover, he might also cross-examine the complainant on the question of her consent.

This cross-examination is foundational in nature and as such does not jeopardize counsel's motion for judgment of acquittal at the close of the Government's case.[47] If, by her answer, the victim affirms the theory of consent, then consent is in the Government's case-in-chief and may be enough to take the case away from the jury. If she denies that she consented, the stage has been set for a full ventilation of the consent defense. In any event, the merit of motion for judgment of acquittal would remain intact.

The form of cross-examination depends upon the strength of the consent issue. To the extent that the theory of consent can be woven into the testimony of the complainant, an ideal cross-examination can be fashioned. It may be, however, that counsel will be forced to limit his questions to those which will merely give the jury an idea of what to expect in the defendant's case and bring into sharp focus the fundamental factual controversy for its resolution.[48]

---

[47]Cross-examination can destroy any element of the Government's case-in-chief. When this is accomplished, a motion for judgment of acquittal at the close of the Government's case should end the trial. See, e.g., *Farrar v. United States*, 275F.2d 868 (D.C. Cir. 1960).

[48]The following dialogue will serve as an illustration of the approach counsel may take on cross-examination:

Q. Isn't it a fact that at the point when your girdle came off, you *assisted* in the taking of that girdle off?

A. *Assisted?* I wouldn't use the word "assisted."

Q. Did you participate in taking that girdle off?

A. No. I might have had my hands down there, yes, but I didn't participate.

Q. Did you in any way pull that girdle down?

A. No, I wouldn't say that, sir.

Q. The girdle wasn't ripped, was it?

A. No, it wasn't.

Q. Your dress wasn't ripped, either was it?

A. No.

Q. Nor were your underpants ripped?

A. No, they were not ripped.

Q. Isn't it a fact that you helped those men take that girdle off your body?

A. That's not true.

Q. Isn't it a fact, further, that you did not resist their taking off those underpants from your body?

A. That's not true. That's not true.

Q. Isn't it a fact, at least certainly between the second and third intercourse you took time out to brush away the excesses of fluid that were around your vaginal area?

A. No, that's not true.

Q. Isn't it a fact that upon the occasion of at least the third intercourse you assisted the third man in the completion of the sexual act to the extent of assisting him in penetrating you?

A. No, that's not true, sir.

Q. Is it not a fact that on the occasion of the third intercourse, you said to the man "come on, come on"? (Short pause) Did you hear my question?

A. Yes, I heard your question, sir.

Q. Do you have an answer?

A. No, no. If I used the words "come on," it meant please leave me alone, come on, don't do this to me. I don't know whether I didn't say that. But I didn't say "come on" in the sense the other way.

Q. Did there come a time during the course of your intercourse with these men that you did not resist in any way?

A. I was always resisting.

Q. I am talking now about beyond the resistance within your own mind. Was there ever a time when there was a physical non-resistance?

A. Physical non-resistance? Sir, I cannot remember every minute.

The accusatory form, "isn't it a fact", has been held permissible even though counsel did not have a foundation in fact for asking the question. In *United States v. Pugh*, 436 F.2d 222 (D.C. Cir. 1970), for example, the court found that counsel should have been permitted to ask a witness in a robbery prosecution whether, at the time of a post midnight robbery, he was taking the victim to see a girl rather than a "fellow," as testified to, even though counsel admittedly had no factual foundation for asking the question. The court found that the question was relevant and material because

In the absence of establishing consent by cross-examination of Government witnesses, experience has shown that this defense may succeed only if the defendant testifies in his own behalf. In the confidence of the attorney-client relationship, all elements of the complaint of the intercourse will be admitted save for the element of force or non-consent.[49] Nevertheless,

no presentation of a consent defense will be effective unless full discovery by counsel is conducted. All evidence—testimonial and non-testimonial—which can rationally be argued as indicating a non-consensual "connection" must be shown because such evidence will be a cornerstone of the prosecutor's proof and cross-examination.

For the prosecutor, his access to facts bearing on consent flows from familiarity with the facts during preparation and insights that those facts inspire. The thoroughness of his interviews of the complainant, witnesses and the police must

the government had first queried the witness about the purpose of their early morning presence at the scene of the crime. Further the court found that "[a] second legitimate objective of the question could have been to discover an additional witness to the robbery." *Id.* at 224. The court stated that "[t]rial counsel in many cases cannot possibly have a foundation in fact for all questions, only a well-reasoned suspicion that a circumstance might be true." *Id.* at 225. The court neither found the question to be anything more than exploratory thereof, nor to be instinct with false insinuation and, thus, improper.

In *United States v. Fowler,* No. 71–1330 (D.C. Cir., July 6, 1972), the court held that an undercover narcotics officer (the principal prosecution witness in a narcotics case) could be asked the reasons for his dismissal from the police department (which occurred prior to trial) and whether he was using narcotics at the time he observed the defendant committing the alleged crime. "The obvious ground for such cross-examination would be to determine the witness' credibility and his powers of observation at the time he observed the offense." Slip op. at 2. The court once again recognized the permissibility of asking questions without factual foundation when circumstances at trial make it necessary to do so. But then the court issued this caveat:

"We do not mean to indicate that either counsel on cross-examination may, without a reasonable basis therefor, ask direct questions which tend to incriminate or degrade the witness and thus plant an unfounded bias in the minds of jurors which subsequent testimony cannot entirely displace. To authorize such cross-examination the general rule is that the questioner must be in possession of some facts which support a genuine belief that the witness committed the offense or the degrading act to which the questioning relates. If this rule is breached, the violator should be severely censured. Such practice is impermissible and should not be tolerated. At the same time where counsel has some basis, even though it may be very slight, he may ask nonaccusatory questions regarding convictions or conduct of this type in a good faith attempt to impeach the witness."

Slip op. at 4.

[49] Counsel should also inquire into his client's prior history of sexual misconduct or of accusations against him for sex-

ual misconduct. The theory of this questioning should not be limited to anticipating an attack on the defenses of consent and character; it embraces the substantive proof of the government's case.

It is established that evidence of other similar crimes is inadmissible to prove that the defendant was disposed to commit the crime in question and therefore committed it. 1 J. Wigmore, *Evidence* § 192–194 (3d ed. 1940); Note, *Other Crimes: Evidence at Trial,* 70 Yale L.J. 763 (1961). However, evidence of other crimes may be admissible on other grounds:

"Evidence of other crimes is admissible when relevant to (1) motive, (2) intent, (3) absence of mistake or accident, (4) a common scheme or plan embracing the commission of two or more crimes so related to each other that proof of one tends to establish the other, and (5) the identity of the person charged with the commission of the crime on trial."

Drew v. United States, 331 F.2d 85, 90 (D.C. Cir. 1964). See *Wakaksan v. United States,* 367 F.2d 639, 645 (8th Cir. 1966); C. McCormick, Handbook of the Law of Evidence 328–30 (1954).

Admissibility of such evidence as relevant is governed by the "purpose of the proof and the probabilities." *United States v. Bobbitt,* 450 F.2d 685 (D.C. Cir. 1971). Where identification is controverted and the defendant's presence at the scene is in issue, for example, proof of other similar crimes may be relevant to the question of identity in the case on trial. Where the defendant exhibits patterns of behavior so as to demonstrate a modus operandi, the "signature" of his method may be relevant in identifying him in the instant case. *Id.* at 690; *United States v. Bussey,* 432 F.2d 1330 (D.C. Cir. 1970). But care must be taken to determine whether "the crimes charged are of such a nature that the jury might regard one as corroborative of the other, when, in fact, no corroboration exists." *Kidwell v. United States,* 38 App. D.C. 566 (1912). Rape was the crime in *Kidwell* and accordingly the caution of that case is well taken where corroboration is an essential element of the crime.

offset the depth of his adversary's cross-examination of these witnesses.

For both advocates, however, the function of discreditation must take them beyond the immediate facts of the alleged incident. The character and reputation of the complainant and of the defendant must be explored.[50]

CHARACTER AND REPUTATION

Evidence of Complainant's Character

In the majority of jurisdictions which have considered the question, evidence of the complainant's general character or reputation for unchastity is admissible upon the issue of her consent.[51]

The more controverted question is whether specific acts of unchastity should be admissible as evidence of that character. The prosecutor will argue that specific acts of unchastity are inadmissible because they fail to evidence a *character* predisposed to consenting to intercourse; because she has consented to intercourse on previous occasions, complainant has not forfeited her right to choose her sexual partner. Defense counsel will argue that this prior act of consensual intercourse must in fairness be disclosed to the jury so that they might evaluate the act of intercourse on trial which is, likewise, claimed to be consensual.

No flat rule of admission or exclusion of this evidence would enhance the integrity of the fact-finding effort of the jury. Under such a rule counsel's arguments would not advance much beyond preliminary offerings noted above and

the judge's decision would almost amount to a flip of the coin. The ultimate decision as to admissibility should be left to the exercise of the court's discretion after it has considered the circumstance of the particular case. Thus, the court would be asked to weigh the prejudicial impact of such evidence against its probative value in the context of the total evidence before the jury.[52] In applying this interest-balancing analysis to the proof, counsel should address himself to the questions of time, place, persons involved, and circumstances of the act to determine whether it is too vague to be identified, too remote in time to be probative, or so dissimilar[53] to the circumstances of the present case as to lose probative force, confuse and otherwise prejudice the jury.

Where consent is not an issue, prior *specific acts* of unchastity seem to be irrelevant to the question of whether defendant committed the crime of rape. Absent a showing of patterned, indiscriminate, or notorious misbehavior by the complainant it would seem that such evidence

---

[50]*Giles v. Maryland,* 386 U.S. 66 (1967), is a startling example, not only of the significance of the *Brady* doctrine, but also of the impact evidence of the complainant's character and reputation can have on the outcome of a case.

[51]1 J. Wigmore, *Evidence* § 62 (3d ed. 1940). The fourth circuit has held that an attorney's failure to investigate the character of a complainant in a rape case constitutes ineffective assistance of counsel. *Coles v. Peyton,* 389 F.2d 224 (4th Cir. 1968). See *Packineau v. United States,* 202 F.2d 681 (8th Cir. 1953), where prior acts of unchastity were considered evidence going not only to consent but to the complainant's credibility.

[52]This is the approach used in cases discussing the admissibility of cross-examination questions directed to the defendant's character witnesses. In *Awkard v. United States,* 352 F.2d 641 (D.C. Cir. 1965), the court of appeals rejected the mechanical rigidity of the techniques for presenting and rebutting character evidence and focused on the need for judicial discretion in overseeing the line of cross-examination of character witnesses in order to prevent prejudice.

The need is no less where the character of the complainant is put in issue by the defendant's cross-examination. The discretionary action by the court gives it the opportunity to sharpen the issue according to the theory which supports the attack. Thus, if the character evidence demonstrates lack of credibility or consent, the court could rule according to the evidence in the case and instruct the jury as to the limitations of the proof. *Michelson v. United States,* 335 U.S. 469 (1948). The usual apprehensions about the uselessness of cautionary instructions to the jury practically disappear because the exercise of judicial discretion on the admissibility of the evidence, which precedes the instruction, is done out of the presence of the jury. The jurors therefore hear only that evidence which the trial judge has admitted.

[53]Prior consensual intercourse with one who is a friend or a lover, for example, would be irrelevant on the issue of consent where the evidence establishes that the defendant and the complainant are strangers.

would shed little light on her credibility.[54] On the other hand, where the key issue in the case is

[54]The value of psychological and psychiatric testing for testimonial competency has long been recognized. See Hutchins & Slesinger, *Some Observations on the Law of Evidence—The Competency of Witnesses*, 37 *Yale L.J.* 1017, 1019 (1928). It is also clear that psychiatric and psychological testimony on the question of the competency of a witness is admissible. In *District of Columbia v. Armes*, 107 U.S. 519 (1882), the Supreme Court stated that the trial court should resolve the question of the competency of a "lunatic" after examination by the court of the witness himself and *"any competent witnesses* who can speak to the nature and extent of his insanity." (Emphasis added.) *Id.* at 522. Moreover, in *Peckham v. United States*, 210 F.2d 693 (D.C. Cir. 1953), the court of appeals suggested that although evidence of prior psychiatric treatment of a witness was properly excluded on the issue of the witness' *credibility*, it might have been admitted on the issue of *competency* if the latter question had been raised in a timely fashion. *Id.* at 698 n.5. See also *People v. Hudson*, 341 Ill. 187, 173 N.E. 278 (1930).

It has long been recognized by the medical profession, the courts, and legal commentators that such an examination is most desirable in cases involving sex offenses. In *Wilson v. United States*, 271 F.2d 492 (D.C. Cir. 1959), the court, in dictum, quoted Professor Wigmore:

> "No judge should ever let a sex-offense charge go to the jury unless the female complainant's social history and mental makeup have been examined and testified to by a qualified physician. 3 J. Wigmore, Evidence, § 924(a) (3d ed. 1940)."

Id. and the 1937–38 Report of the ABA Committee on the Improvement of the Law of Evidence:

> "Today it is *unanimously* held (and we say "unanimously" advisedly) by experienced psychiatrists that the complainant woman in a sex offense should *always* be examined by competent experts to ascertain whether she suffers from some mental or moral delusion or tendency, frequently found especially in young girls, causing distortion of the imagination in sex cases."

Id.

˙ Similar views are held by leading medical figures. The late Dr. Manfred Guttmacher has commented:

> "Women frequently have fantasies of being raped. Dr. Karl A. Menninger has said that such fantasies might almost be said to be universal. And in a hysterical female, these fantasies are all too easily translated into actual belief and memory falsification. It is fairly certain that many innocent men have gone to prison on the plausible tale of some innocent looking girl because the orthodox rules of evidence (and the chivalry of judges unversed in psychiatry) did not permit adequate probing of her veracity."

M. Guttmacher & H. Weihoffen, *Psychiatry and the Law* 375

credibility, uncomplicated by a consent defense, the jury should be allowed to hear *general* reputation evidence of complainant's unchastity in order to weigh and credit her testimony in the context of the character of person she is reputed to be.[55] The court's exercise of discretion in ruling on these evidentiary problems promotes a flexible standard which takes into consideration all of the aspects of the case and provides for a balance in the deliberative process that is fair to adversary interests involved.

Evidence of Defendant's Character

The character of the defendant becomes an evidentiary matter only when he chooses to place it in issue.[56] Defense counsel must deter-

(1952). See W. Overholser, *The Psychiatrist and the Law* 50–56 (1953); Overholser, "Psychiatry's Contributions to Criminal Law and Procedure," 12 *Okla. L. Rev.* 13, 22–23, (1959).

For further views, on this question see Note, "Psychiatric Examination of the Mentally Abnormal Witness," 59 *Yale L.J.* 1324, 1341 (1958), where the author suggests that the only serious objection to this type of compulsory examination is the attendant invasion of privacy, but notes that this might be outweighed by the need to seek the truth in this type of case. Furthermore, "if the witness is normal, his privacy will remain intact, since nobody but the psychiatrist will have heard the witness' life history." *Id.* 1341. See also *United States v. Dildy*, 39 F.R.D. 340 (D.D.C. 1966); C. McCormick, *Evidence* § 45 at 99-100 (1954); Note, "Psychiatric Examination of Prosecutrix in Rape Case," *N.C.L. Rev.* 234 (1966).

[55]Wigmore has suggested that such evidence is admissible

> "because a certain type of feminine character predisposes to imaginary or false charges of this sort and is psychologically inseparable from a tendency to make advances, and its admissibility to discredit credibility . . . cannot in practice be distinguished from its present bearing."

1 J. Wigmore, *Evidence* § 62 at 467 (3d ed. 1940).

In the Chadbourn Revision of Wigmore's treatise, the author urges modification of rules governing the admissibility of evidence bearing on general reputation and specific acts of unchastity so that the life history of a rape complainant may be adequately portrayed, thus assuring protection against "injustices that may be caused by such unprobed testimony . . ." 3A J. Wigmore, *Evidence* § 924b at 747 (Chadbourn Rev. 1970).

[56]*Michelson v. United States*, 335 U.S. 469 (1948). "The rule, then, firmly and universally established in policy and tradition, is that the prosecution may not initially attack the defendant's character." 1 J. Wigmore, *Evidence* § 57 at 456 (3d ed. 1940).

mine whether, on the facts of his case, a character defense *per se* or in combination with the consent defense is likely to create a reasonable doubt as to the defendant's guilt.[57]

In considering whether to interpose the character defense, counsel should be aware of several factors which will have a bearing on its merits:

(a)   sources of testimony

(b)   hearsay nature of the testimony

(c)   character traits in issue

(d)   negative evidence of character

(e)   cross-examination of character witnesses

Counsel's examination of defendant's family, friends, work associates, teachers, classmates, fellow-parishioners, and members of other social groups of which he is a member should provide him with information concerning his client's character and reputation in the community. Interviews with these persons should explore the duration of their relationship with the defendant and the period of the defendant's life which it covered. In turn, these temporal elements must be tied to the crime in question.[58] Thus, a person who knew the defendant's reputation when he was a child is not likely to enlighten the jury concerning his character at the time of the alleged incident.

[57]D.C. Bar Association, *Model Jury Instructions* (1966) state:
"The circumstances may be such that evidence of good character may alone create a reasonable doubt of the defendant's guilt, although without it other evidence would be convincing. Notwithstanding evidence of good character and reputation, however, you may convict the defendant if, after weighing all the evidence, including evidence of good character, you are convinced that the defendant is guilty of the crime charged."
See *Michelson v. United States*, 335 U.S. 469, 476 (1948); *Edington v. United States*, 164 U.S. 361, 366 (1896); *Villaroman v. United States*, 184 F.2d 261, 263 (D.C. Cir. 1950).

[58]The reputation to be proved should be the defendant's reputation in the community in which he lives at the time of the alleged crime or shortly preceding that time. *Lomax v. United States*, 37 App. D.C. 414, 418 (1911). See also *Awkard v. United States*, 352 F.2d 641, 642 n.1 (D.C. Cir. 1965).

Counsel's inquiry must focus upon his client's reputation as exhibited by hearsay statements of the witnesses and not by their individual opinions. In most jurisdictions, it matters not what these witnesses personally think of the defendant's character; rather it is what the community, as the witness knows it, thinks is the measure of the man.[59]

The commission of crime is said to evidence certain flaws of character in the criminal. Where the accused seeks to demonstrate his good character, he may do so only insofar as particular character traits are placed in supposition by the kind of crime which he allegedly committed.[60] Thus, a non-violent act of larceny raises questions concerning the felon's reputation for truthfulness and honesty but it does not evoke an inquiry as to his reputation for peacefulness

[59]In *Shimon v. United States*, 352 F.2d 449 (D.C. Cir. 1965) the court, explaining *Michelson v. United States*, 335 U.S. 469 (1948), stated:
"It is not what the speaker knows as to the defendant's personal habits, character, family, or business integrity but what he has heard about his reputation in this regard. It is not the substance but 'the shadow his daily life has cast in his neighborhood' which is the subject of inquiry."
352 F.2d at 453.
There are some jurisdictions, however, which allow personal opinion evidence or evidence going to the defendant's character. *See* Note, "Other Crimes Evidence at Trial: Of Balancing and Other Matters," 70 *Yale L.J.* 763, 779 (1961).
Rule 405 of the Federal Rules of Evidence, effective July 1, 1973 provides:

(a) Reputation or opinion.—In all cases in which evidence of character or a trait of character of a person is admissible, proof may be made by testimony as to reputation or by testimony in the form of an opinion. On cross-examination, inquiry is allowable into relevant specific instances of conduct.

(b) Specific instances of conduct.—In cases in which character or a trait of character of a person is an essential element of a charge, claim, or defense, proof may also be made of specific instances of his conduct.

If this rule of evidence is adopted it would change the Michelson Rule which governed this evidentiary proposition in the Federal system.

[60]*Morris v. District of Columbia*, 124 F.2d 284 (D.C. Cir. 1941); C. McCormick, *Evidence* § 158 at 334 (1954).

and good order (that is, non-violence). Rape (simple or armed) is a crime of violence. Therefore, the character traits of peace and good order may be put in issue by the defendant.

A reading of the questions asked of a character witness[61] should convince anyone that persons who have specifically discussed the reputation of a defendant for given character traits are not numerous. On the other hand, there may be a number of individuals who have "never heard anything bad about" the defendant. This type of negative character evidence is admissible in some jurisdictions[62] and can be argued in support of the proposition that it is only when people are in trouble or associated with trouble that their character traits are openly assessed.

[61]The following are typical of the questions asked:

Q. Do you know the defendant, X?

Q. How long have you known him?

Q. How or in what capacity have you known him?

Q. Do you know other people who know him?

Q. Have you ever heard these people discuss his reputation in the community for being a peaceful and orderly person?

Q. What is Mr. X's reputation in the community for peacefulness and orderly conduct?

Under Rule 405 of the Federal Rules of Evidence, the questions put to the witness would not necessarily include those dealing with other peoples' assessment of the defendant. The question to be asked of the witness would be:

Q. Do you have an opinion as to whether the defendant is a peaceful and orderly person?

Q. What is your opinion?

[62]In *Harrison v. District of Columbia*, 95 A.2d 332 (D.C. Mun. Ct. App. 1953), a character witness in a paternity suit testified that he had never heard anything bad about the defendant. The court held that he was properly cross examined as to whether he had heard of defendant's having been arrested for assault. See also *People v. Van Gaasbeck*, 189 N.Y. 408, 82 N.E. 718 (1907); *State v. Axelson*, 37 Wash. 2d 393, 223 P.2d 1059 (1950). As an evidentiary prerequisite, the character witness must be shown to be in such a position that he would have heard anything that was said concerning the persons's character or reputation. *State v. Cavener*, 356 Mo. 602, 202 S.W.2d 869 (1947).

Non-discussion is the greatest compliment to a man's character.[63]

In the final analysis, however, the probability of success of the character defense depends upon the prosecutor's cross-examination of the witnesses. Cross-examination will attack the sources of the hearsay testimony by requiring a basis for each assertion the witness makes, not only for the ultimate hearsay opinion, but also for the answers to foundation questions which lead up to it.[64]

Experience teaches that juries evaluate the character witness' testimony as if it were his personal opinion. The credit the jury attaches to his testimony is measured according to the interest he has in the outcome of the case. Moreover, since the jury views the testimony as the character witness' own opinion, his demeanor on the stand becomes a vital element of his credibility. The witness' status as an objective reporter is yet to be determined.

The Prosecution's Attack on Defendant's Character Evidence

As cross-examination proceeds to foundational questions designed to rebut the evidence of defendant's good character, technique and effect operate to require a balance between the probity of the evidence and its prejudicial impact on the

[63]In *Deschenes v. United States*, 224 F.2d 688 (10th Cir. 1955), the court sustained the use of negative character evidence only to the extent the witness stated that he had never heard anything said ill of the defendant. The court further held, however, that the witness was incompetent to testify as to whether the defendant's reputation for truth and honesty was good or bad because he had never heard it discussed. The Missouri Supreme Court, however, considered negative character evidence as the most cogent evidence of a person's good character and reputation. In the absence of any discussion about good character, the court asserted, it may reasonably be presumed that the person's character is good. *State v. Cavener*, 356 Mo. 602, 202 S.W.2d 869, 875(1947). *Accord*, 5 J. Wigmore, *Evidence* § 1614 (3d ed. 1940).

[64]The following questions are indicative of the approach counsel should adopt:

Direct Examination	Cross Examination
Q. How or in what capacity have you known him?	Q. You do not know him in [specify other social settings], do you?

jury. The prosecutor is permitted to ask the witness whether he or she "has heard" that defendant was previously arrested for or convicted of the commission of a named crime.[65] In theory, this question goes to the credibility of the witness, testing the scope and reliability of his hearsay information. The fundamental factual question to be answered by the query is not whether the defendant committed the crime for which he had been previously arrested or convicted but rather, "Does this witness know what he is talking about."[66] Since it is the defendant's reputation in the eyes of the community rather than the defendant's credibility as a witness which is put in issue by this evidence, cross-examination may query as to the defendant's arrests as well as his convictions.[67]

In practice, the effect of this type of cross-examination can prejudice a defendant's right to a fair trial. Proof of other crimes may tend to show the defendant to be a "bad man" and deserving of conviction or may encourage the jury to conclude that commission of a crime in the past is decisive of the issue of guilt in the present trial.[68] The cross-examination therefore could become a method of attacking the defendant rather than his witness' credibility.

Defense counsel's task is to overcome this kind of cross-examination, beginning with pre-trial discovery. Through discovery, defense counsel should have received a copy of the defendant's arrest record. He should study the record to determine what arrest or conviction, if any, is probative evidence rebutting the propos-

---

Q. Do you know other people who know him?

Q. Have you heard those people discuss his reputation for peace and order?

Q. You do not now him [if applicable]—the setting in which this incident took place, do you?
Q. Who are the people you say know the defendant?
Q. How do they know him?
Q. When, why?
Q. Where?
Q. Why was his reputation discussed?
Q. What did they say?
Q. How many other occasions was his reputation discussed?
Q. What were the reasons for the discussion on each of those occasions?
Q. When was the last time you heard the defendant's reputation being discussed?

Each of these questions provides a springboard for further questions as the responses of the witness indicate.

---

[65]*Michelson v. United States*, 335 U.S. 469, 477 (1948); *Flournoy v. State*, 34 Ala. App. 23, 37 So. 2d 218, *cert. denied*, 215 Ala. 285, 37 So. 2d 323 (1948); *People v. Logan*, 41 Cal. 2d 279, 260 P.2d 20 (1953); *State v. Blake*, 157 Conn. 99, 249 A.2d 232 (1969); *Jordan v. State*, 232 Ind. 265, 110 N.E.2d 751 (1953); *Broyles v. Commonwealth*, 267 S.W.2d 73 (Ky. 1954); *Raimondi v. State*, 12 Md. App. 322, 278 A.2d 664 (1971); *State v. Steensen*, 35 N.J. Super. 103, 113 A.2d 203 (1955); *Commonwealth v. Amos*, 445 Pa. 297, 284 A.2d 748 (1971); *Lutz v. State*, 146 Tex. Crim. 503, 176 S.W.2d 317 (1943).

Under Rule 405 of the Federal Rules of Evidence, the central theory of cross-examination of a witness giving his opinion as to the defendant's character would be to inquire whether the witness' opinion would change if he were informed that the defendant was arrested or convicted of the particular crime on a particular date.

[66] "The rationale given for allowing such questions is that, if answered affirmatively, they might cast serious

doubt on the witness' testimony, thus serving a legitimate rebuttal function, and that, if answered negatively, they would show that the witness did not know enough about the accused's reputation to testify."
Note, "Other Crimes Evidence at Trial: Of Balancing and Other Matters," *supra* note 59, at 779.

[67]*Michelson v. United States*, 335 U.S. 469 (1948); *Awkard v. United States*, 352 F.2d 641 (D.C. Cir. 1965). See C. McCormick, *Evidence* § 158 (1954).

[68]*People v. Molineaux*, 168 N.Y. 264, 61 N.E. 286 (1901); *State v. Zimmerlee*, 492 P.2d 795, u98 (Ore. 1972); *Shaffner v. Commonwealth*, 72 Pa. 60, 65 (1872).

As noted by Wigmore in his treatise on evidence:

"The rumor of the misconduct, when admitted, goes far, in spite of all theory and of the judge's charge, towards fixing the misconduct as fact upon the other person (defendant), and thus does three improper things,—(1) it violates the fundamental rule of fairness (ante, § 979) that prohibits the use of such facts, (2) it

ition that the defendant has a good reputation for peace and good order. In doing so, he should consider whether the impeaching matter bears a relationship to the nature of the charge against the defendant;[69] whether it would be inconsistent with the character traits of peace and good order;[70] and whether the matter is identical with or similar to the crime on trial.[71] The

gets at them by hearsay only, and not by trustworthy testimony and (3) it leaves the other person (defendant) no means of defending himself by denial or explanation, such as he would otherwise have had if the rule had allowed that conduct to be made the subject of an issue. Moreover, these are not occurrences of possibility, but of daily practice. This method of inquiry or cross-examined is frequently resorted to by counsel for the very purpose of injuring by indirection a character which they are forbidden directly to attack in that way; they rely upon the mere putting of the question (not caring that it is answered negatively) to convey their covert insinuation. The value of the inquiry for testing purposes is often so small and the opportunities of its abuse by underhand ways are so great that the practice may amount to little more than a mere subterfuge, and should be strictly supervised by forbidding it to counsel who do not use it in good faith."

3A J. Wigmore, *Evidence* § 988 (Chadbourn Rev. 1970). See Note, "Other Crimes Evidence At Trial: Of Balancing and Other Matters," *supra* note 59, at 773.

[69]*United States v. Wooden*, 420 F.2d 251, 253 (D.C. Cir. 1969); *Awkard v. United States*, 352 F.2d 641 (D.C. Cir. 1965); *Clark v. United States*, 23 F.2d 756, 757 (D.C. Cir. 1927); *Sacks v. United States*, 41 App. D.C. 34, 36 (D.C. Ct. App. 1913).

[70]*Awkard v. United States*, 352 F.2d 641 (D.C. Cir. 1965); *Josey v. United States*, 135 F.2d 809, 811 (D.C. Cir. 1943); *Harrison v. District of Columbia*, 95 A.2d 332, 335 (D.C. Mun. Ct. App. 1953).

[71]In *Shimon v. United States*, 352 F.2d 449, 454 (D.C. Cir. 1965), the court warned:

"The prejudicial impact of impeachment questions

analysis of these objective criteria, as they apply in the given case, will help the trial judge to exercise properly his discretion in ruling on the admissibility of the impeaching matter.[72]

CONCLUSION

The trial of a rape case imposes inordinate demands on the advocates' abilities to prepare and present the evidence. While this discussion could not hope to be compendious in its coverage of the problems facing both the prosecutor and defense counsel in all cases, it should have provided the advocates with an insight into issues which, more often than not, will appear in most rape cases. The emphasis of this article, therefore, is on the role of the attorney as an advocate addressing himself to the issues of rape prosecution. To the extent that these ends might have been accomplished, it is hoped that the spirit of the fair and impartial administration of justice has been served.

involving the same kind of offense might in some cases so outweigh the legitimate probative value of impeachment that they should not be allowed or if allowed should be limited in scope so as not to strike the accused under the cloak of impeachment of the witness."

[72]The Supreme Court has recognized the difficulties inherent in ruling on the admissibility of character evidence:

"Both propriety and abuse of hearsay reputation testimony, on both sides, depend on numerous and subtle considerations difficult to detect or appraise from a cold record, and therefore rarely and only on a clear showing of prejudicial abuse of discretion will Courts of Appeals disturb rulings of trial courts on this subject." *Michelson v. United States*, 335 U.S. 469, 480 (1948).

25. The American Jury Study

HARRY KALVEN, JR.
HANS ZEISEL

AS A MATTER OF BOTH THEORETICAL INTEREST and methodological convenience, we study the performance of the jury measured against the performance of the judge as a baseline. Our material is a massive sample of actual criminal jury trials conducted in the United States in recent years. For each of these trials we have the actual decision of the jury and a communication from the trial judge, telling how he would have disposed of that case had it been tried before him without a jury. In this sense, we have been able to execute the grand experiment of having each case, over the wide universe of contemporary jury business in the criminal law, tried by a jury and also by a judge, thus obtaining matched verdicts for study. The result is a systematic view of how often the jury disagrees with the judge, of the direction of such disagreement, and an assessment of the reasons for it. . . .

It was not possible to compile a complete list of judges engaged in jury trials throughout the United States, although we did our best to approximate such a list by using the latest directories. Nor did we send invitations to a random sample of judges from our list; instead we approached all judges. Finally, since these respondents were judges, there was of course no way of insisting that they cooperate; thus, the self-selection of the judges, and not a lottery design of ours, determined the composition of the sample. To be then, for the moment, but only for the moment, as harsh to ourselves as possible, our sample is simply the residue of self-selected judges, derived from a list imperfect to begin with.

The original list contained some 3500 judges[1] of whom we knew only that they *might* preside over criminal jury trials, since they were members of a court that had the necessary jurisdiction. Close to ten percent of our letters were returned because the judge was deceased or was no longer a member of the court. To about forty percent of the letters there was no reply, and we do not know whether this was so because of an imperfect address or because the judge had no criminal jury trials or did not want to cooperate. The remaining judges, a little under half of those on the original list, answered with the following results:

No criminal jury trials		840
No jury trials	735	
Only civil jury trials	105	
Refused to cooperate		68
Unable to cooperate		72
Agreed to cooperate but failed		111
Sent no reports	71	
Sent incomplete reports	40	
Cooperated effectively		555
		1646

▶SOURCE: *The American Jury. Boston: Little, Brown and Company, 1966, Pp. 10, 35–36, 45–47, 50–52, and 149–162.* Reprinted by permission.

[1] We attempted a census, knowing that it would fail. The list included all state judges in courts listed as having criminal jurisdiction and all U.S. District Court Judges.

By mail questionnaire trial judges were asked to report, for cases tried before them, how the jury decided the case, and how they would have decided it, had it been tried before them without a jury. In addition, the judge was asked to give some descriptive and evaluative material about the case, the parties, and counsel.

We might reflect for a moment on the reasons that led to this particular research design. Even in theory, alternative approaches to the special problem of jury-judge disagreement are severely limited. The ideal method for exploring it—trying each case twice, once to a judge and once to a jury—is grossly impractical. The easiest and most practical method would be simply to compare cases actually tried to a judge with cases actually tried to a jury, but such a comparison would not be very helpful. Criminal cases before a judge differ in significant ways from those that go to a jury. It is of small interest to learn how judge and jury decide *different cases;* the question is how judge and jury would decide the *same* case.

Again one might have stepped back from the particularity of the case, and essayed a general opinion poll of the bar and the judiciary on when and why they thought judge and jury would differ. Given the undeniable expertise of lawyers and judges, whose business it is to try cases with and without juries, such a study would have had some value, but it would necessarily have been bland and lacking secure foundation. In the light then of available alternatives, the design of matching a real jury verdict and a hypothetical judge verdict[2] for a great number of actual cases emerges as the most rigorous practicable approach.

The use of the mail questionnaire requires perhaps an additional word of explanation, since the mail questionnaire is not often the preferred instrument of research.[3] It makes it difficult to achieve a sufficient level of cooperation and creates the problem of self-selection. Moreover, the reporting is usually done by an inexpert respondent without assistance from a trained interviewer. It requires further that the questions be rigidly framed once and for all in advance.

For this study, however, the mail questionnaire proved to be the most efficient approach. It would have been extravagant to arrange for a staff of interviewers throughout the United States to personally interview a judge each time he finished a jury trial. And our respondents were anything but inexpert; they were judges being asked about a matter in which they had the greatest interest and the greatest professional competence.

In the end, the mail questionnaire had a decisive advantage for a study that made great demands on confidential information. The elimination of the personal interviewer made it possible for the judge to report to the Jury Project, in confidence, information about his disagreements with the jury in particular cases which he might understandably have been reluctant to disclose face to face.

A distinctive feature of the research design is that it was able to use two questionnaire forms, building a second on experience with the first. The original form, the Sample I questionnaire, was a relatively open, unstructured effort. After considerable experience with its analysis, a second version more tightly controlled and more detailed, was designed and put into the field. The total sample is distributed between the two questionnaires as follows:

	Trials	Percent
Sample I	2385	67
Sample II	1191	33
Total	3576	100%

[2]The judge was asked for the jury trial he was conducting and reporting on: "How would *you* have decided the case had you tried it *without* a jury?" As a matter of convenience we shall call the judge's hypothetical decision "the judge's verdict," in contrast to the jury's verdict, although in strict legal terminology a judge sitting without a jury renders not a verdict but a "judgment."

[3]For a list of the manifold problems in the use of the mail questionnaire, see Wales and Ferber, *A Basic Bibliography on Marketing Research* § 7.3 (2d ed., Chicago, 1963).

Many questions were identical on both questionnaires, and for such items the two samples can be treated as one. At times, however, Sample II recruited special information, and thus for some points we rely on it exclusively. . . .

It may be helpful at the start to recall four types of information requested from the trial judge:

1.   Reports on such routine objective facts as the nature of the case, the types of evidence presented, the demographic characteristics of the defendant and the victim, etc. Here there can be no problem about the reliability of the judge's reporting, except for an occasional lapse in accuracy that could befall any reporter.

2.   Facts about the trial which require some judgment or evaluation on the part of the judge. He was asked to report whether the case was difficult to comprehend, whether defense counsel was superior, and whether the defendant was sympathetic. The issue here is whether the judge's subjective judgment corresponds to some reality. Can we be sure, in other words, that one counsel *is* better than his adversary if the judge has rated him so?

The important safeguard is the special experience and competence of the reporter. If anyone can make a meaningful judgment on a question such as the quality of counsel, the trial judge can. In fact, because he is likely to have seen many jury trials in his career, he is in a position far superior to any independent staff member in making such a judgment. Thus, it is reasonable to rely on the judge on points like these, which are peculiarly within his special experience.[4]

[4]The operational theory can be put this way: If it had been possible to assign these tasks of classification to more than one judge in each case, they would have come to the same result in the great majority of the cases and, not unexpectedly, would have disagreed in some borderline cases. Such borderline disagreement does not derive from any unreliability of the reporter but from an inherent ambiguity in all questions that contain broad gradations. Fortunately, ambiguities at the borderline do little harm; it is the extreme cases that produce significant differences, not the borderline cases which fall now to this side and now to that. Hence we

3.   The reasons the judge gives for his disagreement with the jury. Two points are here involved: whether the judge was candid in telling why he thinks the disagreement arose, and whether the judge's explanation is likely to be correct. For the moment, we confront only the issue of whether there is reason to doubt the judge's candor. The issue need not detain us: a judge interested enough and serious enough to cooperate in the survey, and trusting the research venture enough to supply it with confidential information, would not dissemble on this point.

4.   Lastly, we come to the judge's statement of how he would have decided the case had it been tried before him without a jury. Since the judge's verdict is hypothetical, justification is needed for relying on it. Several considerations suggest that this "verdict" represents a sober act of judgment on the part of the judge. The matter lies somewhat differently for agreements and disagreements. Presumably the judge, in general, would find it more comfortable to report agreement. If, therefore, he nevertheless reports disagreement, it seems only reasonable to accept his statement. In addition, when he states a disagreement he corroborates it in a variety of important ways. In cases where he would have convicted, he states the sentence he would have imposed. He also given reasons for his disagreement, and, he exercises the opportunity afforded to show the intensity of his disagreement by grading the merits of the jury verdict. Most important, the judge, in the course of an ordinary jury trial, comes to some conclusion in his own mind as he listens to the case. Therefore, when the research operation intrudes into the trial process, it is not really asking the judge to make a decision he otherwise would not have made, but rather simply to report a judgment he probably has made anyway. Hence, again it seems certain that the disagreements reported by the judges indicate real differences. . . .

conclude that the margin of error in these evaluative items is self-correcting. See Kendall, *Conflict and Mood: Factors Affecting Stability of Response* (1954).

We begin our inquiry into what the jury makes of the evidence by establishing two basic propositions. The first is simply that, contrary to an often voiced suspicion, the jury does by and large understand the facts and get the case straight. The second proposition is that the jury's decision by and large moves with the weight and direction of the evidence. Taken together, these propositions provide a background against which to evaluate situations in which the jury disagrees with the judge on the handling of evidence.

The hypothesis that the jury does *not* understand the case had loomed large in the debate over the jury. It has not infrequently been charged that the modern jury is asked to perform heroic feats of attention and recall well beyond the capacities of ordinary men. A trial, it has been argued, presents to the jury a mass of material which it cannot possibly absorb, and presents it in an artificial sequence which aggravates the jury's intellectual problem. The upshot is said to be that the jury often does not get the case straight and, therefore, is deciding a case different from the one actually before it.

Perhaps the most vivid spokesman in recent years for this challenge to the jury system was the late Judge Jerome Frank. In the course of a long criticism of the jury system, centered primarily on the jury's freedom to disregard the law totally and to do what it pleases, Judge Frank offers serious criticism of the jury's capacity to follow the facts. We quote here at some length his statement of the jury's difficulties.

"Suppose, however, that the jurors always did understand the *R's* [rules]. Nevertheless, often they would face amazing obstacles to ascertaining the *F's* [facts]. For the evidence is not presented all at once or in an orderly fashion. The very mode of its presentation is confusing. The jurors are supposed to keep their minds in suspense until all of the evidence is in.

"Can a jury perform such a task? Has it the means and capacity? Are the conditions of a jury trial such as to make for the required calm deliberations by the jurors? Wigmore, who defends the jury system, himself tells us that the courtroom is 'a place of surging emotions, distracting episodes, and sensational surprises. The parties are keyed up to the contest; and the topics are often calculated to stir up the sympathy, or prejudice, or ridicule of the tribunal.'

"We may, therefore, seriously question the statement of Professors Michael and Adler that, unlike the witnesses, the jury 'observes the things and events exhibited to its senses under conditions designed to make the observation reliable and accurate. In the case of what (the jury) observes directly the factor of memory is negligible.' As shown by Wigmore, Green, and Burrill, the first of those comments surely does not square with observable courtroom realities. As to the second—that the factor of the jurors' memory is negligible—consider the following: theoretically, as we saw, the jury, in its process of fact-finding, applies to the evidence the legal rules it learns from the judge. If the jury actually did conduct itself according to this theory, it would be unable to comprehend the evidence intelligently until it received those instructions about the rules. But those instructions are given, not before the jury hears the evidence, but only after all the witnesses have left the stand. Then, for the first time, are the jurors asked to consider the testimony in the light of the rules. In other words, if jurors are to do their duty, they must now recollect and assemble the separate fragments of the evidence (including the demeanor of the several witnesses) and fit them into the rules. If the trial has lasted for many days or weeks, the required feat of memory is prodigious. . . .

"The surroundings of inquiry during a jury trial differ extraordinarily from those in which the juryman conducts his ordinary affairs. At a trial, the jurors hear the evidence in a public place, under conditions of a kind to which they are unaccustomed: No juror is able to withdraw to his own room, or office, for private individual reflection. And, at the close of the trial, the jurors are pressed for time in reaching their joint decision. Even twelve experienced judges, deliberating together, would probably not function well under the conditions we impose on the twelve inexperienced laymen."[5]

In the counterpoint of the debate over the jury, its defenders have suggested several offsetting considerations. First, although the trial is not a perfectly logical enterprise, it nevertheless is based upon a highly structured argument. Again, it is not necessary that every member of

[5]*Courts on Trial*, pp. 118–120 (1949).

the jury recall every fact of the trial record. In many instances it will suffice if only some members are able to do so and then make these facts available to the other jurors. The collective recall of the jury, it is argued, is certain to be superior to the average recall of the individual juror.[6]

When the challenge of not understanding is put most strongly, it becomes apparent that it goes to the heart of the jury system. If the jury with any great degree of frequency does not understand the facts, it is difficult to defend it. Further, even when the challenge is put somewhat less strongly, it becomes, at the least, a plea for blue ribbon juries, that is for recruiting the jury, not from a representative sample of the people at large, but from an educated elite, who would be intelligent enough to handle the difficult, intellectual job.

Our concern is not to debate these points a priori, but rather to look to the data to see what we can learn about whether the jury does in fact understand.

It may come as something of a surprise that a survey of judge-jury disagreements can throw light on this particular issue.[7] One might have thought that the jury's understanding could be ascertained only by directly interviewing the jurors and conceivably by giving them some sort of test to measure their recall. Actually, however, the data yield powerful inferences concerning the jury's understanding. There are several converging lines of analysis.

The first runs as follows. If the jury misunderstands the facts of a case, it will then, of necessity, be deciding a different case from the judge, who presumably does understand the facts. And, if the jury is deciding a different case, whether or not it agrees with the judge will

be a matter of chance. To the extent that, in actual fact, jury and judge agree considerably more often than chance would dictate, the hypothesis of substantial jury misunderstanding would seem defeated. The basic table of disagreements provides critical evidence on this issue in two respects. The amount of agreement, 75 percent of all cases, is so substantial as to make it highly improbable that much of it was caused by chance. Equally important, the disagreement, as we have seen, is highly directional, thus compelling the conclusion that misunderstanding cannot in and of itself be a major factor in causing judge-jury disagreement and, hence, cannot be a major determinant of the jury's behavior.

A second line of analysis is based on the reason-assessment materials previously summarized. Two important points emerged. First, in 90 percent of the disagreements it is possible to find a reason or reasons for the disagreement without recourse to misunderstanding of the case; hence, in the great majority of disagreements there is a plausible explanation which, by its nature, precludes the notion that the jury did not understand the case. More significant, the judge almost never advances the inability of the jury to understand as a reason for disagreement. Actually there is only one clear instance out of all of the disagreements where the judge states outright that the reason the jury disagreed with him was because of its inability to understand.[8] In this case the charge was embezzlement

---

[6]This point was brilliantly realized in the Reginald Rose film, "Twelve Angry Men" (1957).

[7]It is one of the chief advantages of a broadly gauged study that there is always more "take" from the design than one may at first intend. For example, the comprehensibility index, Q. 11 of the Sample II questionnaire, was aimed at classifying the cases in terms of evidentiary difficulty. Its use in Tables I through V is one of these happy byproducts.

[8]Even in this case, the misunderstanding appears not to have been the sole explanation; there were other reasons for the jury's disagreement, such as several sentiments about the defendant who was "an attractive woman" with a "loyal husband who was well liked," the "mother of a fine 12-year old boy," and "provided for her mother." Further, the judge notes that the defendant's expert witness offered testimony which "bordered on perjury," and that he was at the time of the trial up for disciplinary action.

In six other cases there is at most a suggestion that the jury did not understand the case in some aspect, e.g., "It's doubtful the jury caught this"; "Many documents were offered and there was a likelihood of confusion"; in a narcotics case "Jury was too naive and lacked the worldly experience." Perhaps most significant, in five of these seven cases the jury hangs.

by a city bookkeeper who had worked out an involved system to cover withdrawals. The trial lasted some ten days, and at the end the jury, after three hours of deliberation, acquits. While the judge notes that the jurors "all were poorly educated and an expert witness had to carry them through many steps of bookkeeping," he explicitly tells us:

"The jury simply was not able to understand the case which was perfectly presented."

The uniqueness of this case among the thousand instances of disagreement argues impellingly against any general hypothesis that the jury does not understand the case.

The matter need not rest on inferences, good as these are. The Sample II questionnaire furnishes data permitting a more direct approach to the problem. The judge was asked the following questions: Compared to the average criminal case, was the evidence as a whole easy to comprehend? somewhat difficult? very difficult to comprehend? Table I provides an important map of how difficult the criminal case that goes to the jury actually is.

Despite its simplicity the table makes an important contribution to the solution of the problem: it shows that the great bulk of cases are routine as to comprehension and hence unlikely to be misunderstood.[9]

We now make a critical analytic use of this distinction between difficult and easy cases. The analysis involves two steps: First, it will appear that the jury in several ways sufficiently acknowledges the difference between easy and difficult cases, so that we can be sure that the jury perceives the difficult cases as difficult. Second, if the jury has a propensity not to understand, it must be assumed that the propensity is greater for difficult cases than for easy cases. We thus reach a prediction that, *if the jury does not under-*

[9]There is other evidence that the bulk of cases are easy to comprehend. Only 43 percent of the cases are classed by the judge as close on the evidence. Again, the average number of witnesses is seven. Lastly, a great many of the trials are short; 42 percent of the trials take one day or less.

Table I. Difficulty of Case as Graded by the Judge

	Percent
Easy to comprehend	86
Somewhat difficult	12
Very difficult	2
Total	100%
Number of cases*	1191

*Sample II only.

stand the case, it will disagree with the judge more often in difficult cases than it does in easy cases.

There are at least two ways to test the jury's sensitivity to the difficulty of the case. There are the data of how often the jury comes back to the court during its deliberations with an inquiry or a question. In the majority of cases the jury does not come back at all, once the deliberation starts. But there are enough cases in which it does, to provide a helpful reading on whether the jury perceives the difference between easy and difficult cases. Table II shows that in difficult cases the jury comes back with questions about twice as often as in easy cases.

A second line of proof is a bit more complicated; it comes from data on jury deliberation time. One test of the jury's perception of the difference between difficult and easy cases is whether the jury deliberates longer in the difficult cases.

Table III shows in graphic form the general relationship between trial length and length of deliberation. The points on this graph represent cases, grouped according to their average trial length, as indicated by the scale at the base; their height, indicated by the scale on the margin, gives the corresponding average length of deliberation for each group.[10] The line, as expected, has a rising slope; the deliberation time increases with the trial length. Specifically, the jury deliberates a little more than one hour for every trial day, except for the very brief trials, for which the deliberation lasts relatively longer,

[10]Theoretically, each individual trial could have been represented by a separate point, but for the purpose at hand this short cut suffices.

Table II. Frequency of Jury's Coming Back with Questions by Difficulty of Case

	Easy Cases	Difficult Cases*
Jury comes back	14%	27%
Number of cases	1024	167

*Somewhat Difficult and Very Difficult combined.

Table III. Trial Length and Deliberation Time (All Cases)*

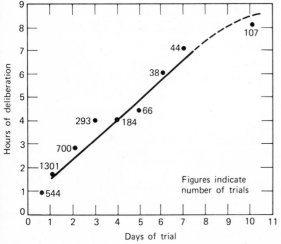

*In bringing days and hours to a common denominator, we assumed the trial days to have 4 hours.

and for very long trials, which require a relatively shorter deliberation than one hour per trial day.

Table IV then brings this segment of the analysis into sharper focus by showing the average length of deliberation time for cases of different degrees of difficulty when the trial length is held constant. For the purposes of this table we distinguish three degrees of difficulty: clear and easy, close and easy, and difficult, irrespective of whether clear or close on the evidence.

For any given length of trial, the jury deliberates longer in the difficult cases than it does in the easy case. The conclusion is therefore justified that the jury does indeed perceive sensitively the different degrees of difficulty in the cases presented to it.

We are now ready to take the final step and present the judge-jury disagreement figures for the easy and difficult cases. The hypothesis is that *if the jury has any propensity to misunderstand the case,* it will be more likely to disagree with the judge in those cases it perceives as difficult. Table V provides the relevant data.

The result is a stunning refutation of the hypothesis that the jury does not understand. While, as we can see, jury disagreement is greater in close cases than in clear ones, there is virtually no difference between the frequency of disagreement when the case is easy and when the case is difficult; this holds true for the cases that are clear as well as for the close ones.

Finally, we pause to note that Table V offers the first opportunity to confront the results of reason assessment with the results of cross tabulation and to take the compatibility of the one with the other as an important corroboration of both. Reason assessment yielded almost no cases in which failure to understand was a reason for disagreement. The cross tabulation presented in Table V yields the same results by revealing virtually identical frequencies of disagreement in easy and difficult cases. Thus, in our first try at confrontation we see that two methods of analysis–reason assessment and cross tabulation–working independently of each other, yield congruent results.[11] We conclude, therefore, that for the law's practical purposes the jury does understand the case.

The discussion turns now from consideration of the jury's understanding of the facts to a first look at what the jury does with them. What can be said of the degree to which the jury follows the weight and direction of the evidence? To what degree is the evidence a determinant of the jury's decision? If some way could be found to organize or map the evidence in terms of the

[11]In this instance a negative finding is supported by the confrontation of reason assessment and cross-tabulation. Elsewhere, affirmative findings will be tested.

Table IV. Average Length of Deliberation by
Difficulty of Case

Length of Trial	Clear and Easy Hours	Close and Easy Hours	Difficult Hours
Under two complete days	1.5	1.9	2.2
Two to four days	2.5	4.6	3.9
One week or more	4.0	5.5	9.0
Average deliberation	2.1	3.3	4.5
Number of cases	618	406	167

Table V. Judge-Jury Disagreement as Affected by Difficulty of Case

	Clear Cases		Close Cases	
	Easy	Difficult	Easy	Difficult
Judge and jury disagree	9%	8%	41%	39%
Number of cases	618	57	406	110

evidentiary strength or weakness of the cases, one could test the jury's response by running its decisions across such an evidence map.

There is, of course, no ideal way of determining the strength of the evidence in each case, but we can make two approximations: one, very simple, the other, fairly intricate. The simple approximation utilizes the judge's classification of cases as either clear or close. Using this distinction and adding as another dimension the way the judge himself decides the case, one can draw an evidential map in four gross categories:

1	2
Clear cases where the judge acquits	Close cases where the judge acquits
3	4
Close cases where the judge convicts	Clear cases where the judge convicts

This evidence map goes from the cases most favorable to the defendant to the cases least favorable to him. If the jury's judgment is in large part determined by the strength and direction of the evidence, one would predict that it would acquit most often in category 1 and least often in category 4, and that there would be a marked difference in its acquittal rate as we go from one category to the next. Table VI, which shows the jury's acquittal rate, indicates that this is indeed the case.

In the strongest evidence category for the defendant, the jury acquits in 95 percent of the cases; in the weakest category for the defendant it acquits in only 10 percent of the cases; and in the middle categories, in terms of the strength of the case for the defendant, the jury, appropriately, acquits in 74 and 46 percent of the cases respectively. Thus, in these very broad terms, it is apparent that the jury's judgment does follow the direction of the evidence.[12]

A more complex map of the weight and direction of the evidence can be plotted by using various objective items of evidence information. Table VII employs three variables in grading the evidence: (1) the strength of the prosecution's evidence (very strong, strong, normal); (2) the balance of contradictions (pro-defendant

[12]One other aspect of Table VI will be of considerable interest. Even in the clear-convict cases the jury disagrees one tenth of the time, indicating that values or sentiments also mold its judgment.

Table VI. Jury Acquittal in Clear and Close Cases

	1 Clear Cases— Judge Acquits	2 Close Cases— Judge Acquits	3 Close Cases— Judge Convicts	4 Clear Cases— Judge Convicts
Jury acquits	95%	74%	46%	10%
Number of cases	60	142	374	615

Table VII. Jury Acquittal Rate and Strength of Evidence
(Percent Jury acquittals of all verdicts in each cell)*

	Balance of Contradictions						
	Pro-defendant		Neutral		Pro-prosecution		
Strength of prosecution's case	No Record/ Stand	Record/ No Stand	No Record/ Stand	Record/ No Stand	No Record/ Stand	Record/ No Stand	Average
Normal	65	38	49	30	26	28	40
Strong	45	44	40	21	18	9	30
Very strong (Confession)	31	13	30	17	21	12	21
Average	44		35		20		

Total No Record/Stand
42

Total Record/No Stand
25

*Sample II, only.

neutral, pro-prosecution); and (3) the presence or absence of a criminal record.[13]

Looking initially just at the design of Table VII, we see that the strongest defense case is found in the upper lefthand cell where the defendant has no record, prosecution strength is normal, and there are contradictions in the prosecution's case; conversely, the weakest defense case is found in the extreme lower righthand cell, where the defendant has a record, the prosecution's evidence is very strong, and there are contradictions in the defendant's case. In a

model, where (D) indicates an imbalance in favor of the defense and (P) an imbalance in favor of the prosecution:

[13] A word in explanation of these variables is necessary. The *record index* is comprised of three factors: Did the defendant have a criminal record? Did he take the stand? Did the jury learn of the record? We group in one class those defendants who take the stand and either have no record or are able to hide it from the jury; to these we add the special group of defendants who do not take the stand, but of whom the jury learns, as it sometimes happens, that they have no record. All other defendants are classed in the other group on the rationale that either the record of which the jury learns or the suspicion of a record because of the refusal to take the stand may evoke a negative reaction.

The *contradictions balance* is derived from the following

		Defendant Contradictions		
		Major	Minor	None
Prosecution Contradictions	Major	—	D	D
	Minor	P	—	D
	None	P	P	—

The strength of the prosecution evidence is gauged "very strong" if there is a confession, "strong" when—although no confession is present—there is an eyewitness or expert or objective evidence, and "normal" when the prosecution offers simply the complainant and/or police.

rough way the evidence can be said to move between these points of maximum strength for the defense and maximum strength for the prosecution.

Further, as one follows a row downwards, the strength of the prosecution's case increases, and, again, as one moves from left to right the strength of the prosecution increases as contradictions in favor of the defendant shift to contradictions that favor the prosecution's case. And, finally, moving from "no record" to "record"one expects the strength of the prosecution's case to increase. If then we accept Table VII, as a reasonable pattern of the weight and direction of the evidence, we can test once more the jury's response to the evidence by tracing the jury acquittal rates across the cells of the table.

The results corroborate strikingly the hypothesis that the jury follows the direction of the evidence. The highest acquittal rate (65 percent) is in the upper extreme lefthand cell, where the defense case is the strongest, and one of the two lowest acquittal rates is in the extreme righthand cell, where the prosecution evidence is the strongest. Further, if one reads across the

bottom row, the jury's average acquittal rate moves from 44 percent to 35 percent to 20 percent, going, in terms of contradictions, from strong defense to strong prosecution; and, if one reads down the outer column, the jury's average acquittal rate declines from 40 to 30 to 21 percent, as the strength of the prosecution's case increases. Finally, if we take the average of the cases where the defendant has no record as against the case where he has a record, the acquittal rate declines from 42 to 25 percent.

Both the simple and the more complex evidence maps then tell the same story about the jury's performance, namely, that its verdicts move basically with the weight and direction of the evidence.[14]

The evidence involved in the criminal jury trial, shows that the jury by and large does understand the case and get it straight, and the evidence itself is a major determinant of the decision of both judge and jury.

[14]The *judge's* acquittal rate also moves with the direction of the evidence, a circumstance which happily lends reality to Table VII as an evidence map.

Judge Acquittal Rate and Strength of the Evidence (Percent Judge Acquittals of all Verdicts in each Cell)

	Balance of Contradictions						
	Pro defendant		Neutral		Pro-prosecution		
Strength of Prosecution Case	No Record	Record	No Record	Record	No Record	Record	Average
Normal	29	37	31	22	6	6	24
Strong	17	28	20	11	4	5	15
Very Strong	13	0	10	3	3	0	5
Average	25		21		14		17
			No Record		Record		
Total			21		14		

26. Physical Attractiveness and Jury Decisions

HAROLD SIGALL
NANCY OSTROVE

RECENT RESEARCH CLEARLY DEMONSTRATES THAT physically attractive people benefit greatly from their appearance in many ways. For example, Miller (1970) and Dion, Berscheid, and Walster (1972) have found evidence for a "physical attractiveness stereotype": Compared to unattractive individuals, good-looking people are seen as possessing more socially desirable traits and as having more future potential for happiness and success. Not surprisingly, physically attractive people are also liked better than their unattractive counterparts (see, e.g., Byrne, London & Reeves, 1968).

Given this background, consider a stimulus person who has committed a crime. What effects might the physical attractiveness of a criminal defendant have on jurors' judgments? One might expect that even though extralegal factors such as appearance should not influence juridic judgment, that good-looking defendants would benefit and receive relatively lenient treatment. Various investigators have shown that *generally* attractive (likeable) defendants are treated more leniently; that a physically unattractive transgressor is viewed as more likely to transgress in the future, and that judgments are more severe when made against physically unattractive as opposed to good-looking offenders. One way to

account for these results is in terms of reinforcement theory: Since physical attractiveness is a conditioned positive stimulus, those who possess it are viewed favorably, and we like them better and treat them more kindly. A more cognitive approach, one that searches for a "rational" explanation for the generous treatment of beautiful people, might suppose that since we believe (*a*) good-looking individuals are "better" in other ways, (*b*) they have more potential, and (*c*) they are less likely to transgress again, it makes "sense" to go easy on them, to give them a second chance, etc. Such an approach suggests that physical attractiveness will not always benefit an offender. When, for example, it is reasonable to infer that an individual used his appearance for illicit ends and that physical attractiveness is positively related to the successful enactment of the offense, the individual should be viewed as relatively more dangerous. Not only is he more capable of committing the crime again in the future, but he also may arouse our animosity for having misappropriated his God-given fortune.

In this experiment the physical attractiveness of a criminal defendant was varied along with the nature of the crime, and simulated jurors passed sentences. An interaction was predicted: when the crime was unrelated to attractiveness, as in Efran's (1972) study, sentences would be greater for the unattractive than the attractive defendant; when the crime was attractiveness-related, the attractive defendant would receive severer judgments.

▶SOURCE: *"Effects of the Physical Attractiveness of the Defendant and Nature of the Crime on Juridic Judgment,"* Proceedings, *81st Annual Convention, American Psychological Association* (1973). Pp. 267–268. Copyright 1973 by the American Psychological Association. Reprinted by permission.

METHOD

Overview and subjects

60 male and 60 female undergraduate Ss acting as simulated jurors were presented with biographical material and a criminal case account. One-third of the Ss believed the defendant was physically attractive, another third that she was unattractive, and the remainder were not given any information concerning appearance. Crosscutting the attractiveness variable, half of the Ss read a burglary case (Attractiveness Unrelated) and the rest an account of a confidence game episode (Attractiveness Related). After reading the materials, Ss sentenced the defendant to a term of imprisonment. The Ss were assigned randomly to one of the six resulting conditions, the only restriction on randomization being that an equal number of men and women appeared in each cell.

Procedure

Upon arrival each S received a folder containing the stimulus materials. An instruction sheet informed S that he or she would read an account of a criminal case along with biographical information concerning the defendant. The Ss were instructed to consider the case carefully and told that later they would be asked to answer questions. An index card containing biographical information was presented next. This information included the defendant's name, Barbara Helm, her race (Caucasian), religion (Protestant), age (23), education (one semester college), and previous record (traffic violations and an earlier arrest, without conviction, for suspicion, "circumstances similar to present case"). All Ss received this identical information. In addition, a photograph of an attractive woman was affixed to the card in the Attractive conditions, while an unattractive photograph was presented in the Unattractive conditions. The Ss then read the case account: Half of the Ss read an account of a burglary (Attractiveness-Unrelated condition); the remainder read an account of a swindle (Attractiveness-Related

condition). Miss Helm was charged with breaking and entering, and grand larceny in the burglary version. She was alleged to have illegally obtained a pass key, and to have watched the movements of her victim, a 46-yr.-old bachelor who resided in the same high-rise building into which she had recently moved. While he was out, she entered his apartment and stole $2,200 in cash and merchandise. In the swindle, Miss Helm allegedly contrived to develop contact with the victim, and after solidifying her initial contacts induced him to invest $2,200 in a nonexistent corporation. She was charged with obtaining money under false pretenses and grand larceny. In each case, the evidence overwhelmingly indicated her guilt. The Ss then sentenced the defendant to a term of imprisonment which could range from 1 to 15 yr. After S passed sentence, E produced another form, which asked S to recall certain facts, to rate the seriousness of the offense, and to rate the defendant on a series of bipolar adjectives, the critical one being a rating of the defendant's physical attractiveness on a 9-point scale. Upon completion of this form, Ss were debriefed.

RESULTS AND DISCUSSION

The physical attractiveness manipulation was successful: The mean physical attractiveness rating was 7.53 for the attractive defendant and 3.22 for the unattractive defendant ($F = 184.29$, $df = 1/108$, $p < .001$). These ratings were not affected by the nature of the crime.

That the swindle and burglary would be perceived as attractiveness-related and unrelated, respectively, was based on intuition and no direct check was obtained. Nevertheless, indirect evidence supports this contention: Ss given no information concerning the defendant's beauty attributed greater physical attractiveness to her in the swindle condition ($\overline{X} = 6.65$) than in the burglary condition ($\overline{X} = 5.65$; $F = 4.93$, $df = 1/108$, $p < .05$). To preclude alternative explanations based on differential seriousness of the two crimes, the case accounts were designed to describe offenses roughly equal in seriousness. Ratings of the seriousness of the crime indicated that this aim was achieved. There was a slight nonsignificant tendency for the attractive swindler's offense to be viewed more seriously than the unattractive swindler's, and for the unattractive burglar's offense to be viewed as more serious than the attractive burglar's. There were no main effects, and when attractiveness information was withheld ratings of seriousness were nearly identical. A final preliminary analysis indicated that there were no differences in responses by men and women, and S sex was therefore ignored as a variable.

Table I summarizes the results on the main dependent measure. The hypothesized interaction materialized:The attractive swindler received greater punishment than the unattractive swindler, and the unattractive burglar was treated more harshly than the attractive burglar ($F = 7.02$, $df = 1/108$, $p < .01$). It should be pointed out that sentences administered in the Unattractive and Control conditions were almost identical. Thus it seems reasonable to suggest that being unattractive did not produce discriminatory responses per se. Rather, it seems that it was the appearance of the defendant in the Attractive conditions which had the major impact. The beautiful burglar "got off easy,"while the beautiful swindler paid a little more.

The findings of this experiment may be taken as evidence supporting a cognitive interpretation for the previous finding that attractive offenders are dealt with leniently. The notion that good-looking criminals are usually treated gently because they are seen as generally less dangerous and more capable of virtue, remains tenable. The position that physical attractiveness is a positive trait and will therefore have a unidirectionally favorable effect on judgments of those who have it would have led to accurate predictions of the results in the burglar condition but not those in the swindle condition.

While our cognitive approach implies that

Table I. Mean Sentence Assigned (in Yr.)

Offense	Defendant's Physical Attractiveness		
	Attractive	Unattractive	Control
Swindle	5.45	4.35	4.35
Burglary	2.80	5.20	5.10

Note: $n = 20$ per cell.

perceivers respond "rationally," we use quotation marks because it is clear that they do not necessarily respond logically. It may be seen easily that even if reliable correlations between appearance and actual virtue had been established (which they have not), it would not follow that punitive judgments should be made simply on the basis of looks. This experimental situation, in which college students acting as simulated jurors made individual judgments, obviously is quite different from the jury-room situation in an actual trial. Whether similar results would obtain under real courtroom conditions is a moot question. Perhaps, e.g., if even 1 among 12 people noticed the illogical relationship between beauty and judgment, and pointed this out to fellow jurors, the effects of attractiveness would disappear. Nevertheless, our results contribute to an accumulating body of findings that indicate that extralegal factors do influence judgments of simulated jurors. At the very least this points to the *possibility* that similar processes and outcomes would manifest themselves in actual jury deliberations. Our feeling is that increased knowledge concerning person-perception processes potentially can contribute to a better understanding of the jury system, which is currently under scrutiny.

REFERENCES

Byrne, D., London, O., & Reeves, K. The effects of physical attractiveness, sex, and attitude similarity on interpersonal attraction. *Journal of Personality,* 1968, **36,** 259–271.

Dion, K., Berscheid, E., & Walster, E. What is beautiful is good. *Journal of Personality and Social Psychology,* 1972, **24,** 285–290.

Efran, M. G. The effect of physical appearance on the judgment of guilt, interpersonal interaction, and severity of recommended punishment in a simulated jury task. Unpublished manuscript, University of Toronto, 1972.

Miller, A. G. Role of physical attractiveness in impression formation. *Psychonomic Science,* 1970, **19,** 241–243.

27. Analyzing Postarrest Dispositions

PETER J. BURKE
AUSTIN T. TURK

ALTHOUGH THERE IS A CONTINUING DEBATE OVER the extent to which such differences are attributable to behavioral differences or to discriminatory treatment, the conventional wisdom of criminology has long been that socially disadvantaged persons (usually specified as those having one or more of such characteristics as lower socio-economic status, minority racial or ethnic membership, teenage or young adult, and a prior criminal record) generally have higher criminality rates and are more likely than the advantaged to be prosecuted, tried, and convicted, and to be more severely penalized upon conviction (Chambliss, 1969:86; Sutherland and Cressey, 1970:132–151,219–227; Turk, 1969:108–173).

However, the available evidence is at best ambiguous. While recent studies (e.g., Green, 1970; Weiner and Willie, 1971; Arnold, 1971; Chiricos, Jackson, and Waldo, 1972; Thornberry, 1973) have confirmed the generally higher official rates and legal risks of the socially disadvantaged, they have raised more questions than have been answered regarding the relative significance of particular variables and the importance of interactions among them in accounting for differential risks in the criminalization process. The available studies have (a) been limited to juveniles; (b) considered only a few nonlegal and legal variables, with

▶SOURCE: *"Factors Affecting Postarrest Dispositions: A Model for Analysis," Social Problems (February, 1975) 22:313–332. Reprinted by permission.*

especially little attention to specific offense categories and to separate features of prior criminal records; (c) reported no follow-up or time-series data; and/or (d) provided only minimal data analyses—a deficiency largely attributable to the lack until very recently of adequate techniques for analyzing the nominal and ordinal data generated in most criminological research.

PURPOSE

The objective of the present report is primarily methodological rather than substantive: to provide an illustrative application of log-linear analysis for hierarchical models (Goodman, 1970, 1971a, 1971b, 1972a, 1972b, 1973) to the complex analytical problems encountered by criminologists in research on the relationship between social disadvantage and criminalization. In addition to showing the utility of this technique for revealing partial relationships and net effects in contingency tables, we also use this occasion to show how the technique of standardization can be used to "control for" the possible effects of certain variables without contending with either an excessive number of variables or inordinately reduced cell frequencies.

Substantively, we are interested in what this analysis tells us about (1) whether and to what extent such variables as an arrested individual's age, race, occupational status, and record of incarceration influence the type and severity of the case disposition; and (2) if such variables are found to have effects, whether their influence is direct or else indirect through effects of the nature of the offenses charged. However, we must emphasize that this is a very limited, illustrative analysis in that we deal here with only a few selected variables and do not take up such crucial substantive problems as those of specifying variations in case disposition by offense type and of determining the specific distribution of cases across offense categories by age, race, occupational status, record of prior incarceration, and other variables to be considered. Therefore, the findings are to be viewed as illustrative of the kinds of conclusions that may result from the use of log-linear analysis.

DATA

The data consist of information on a 20 percent random sample of adults arrested in Indianapolis in 1964 (N = 3941). In this illustrative analysis we consider only the following variables: *Age* (Under 25; 25–34; 35–49; over 49), *Race* (White; Non-white), *Occupational Status* (High; Medium; Low), *Prior Incarceration* (Yes; No)—the measure representing prior arrest history in this analysis—*Offense Category* of the most serious charge in the current (last 1964) arrest (Violence; Theft; Vice; Disorderly Conduct; Traffic; Other), and *Disposition of the Case* (No Court; Dismissed or Not Guilty; Judgment Withheld; Suspended Sentence or Probation; Fine; Prison); and we confine our analysis to males.

PROCEDURES

One of the major problems with much previous research on the possibility of discriminatory treatment of socially disadvantaged persons in the arrest and disposition process has been the inability to deal meaningfully with more than two or three nonintervally scaled variables at a time, even though the state of knowledge indicated clearly that it was necessary to partial out the relationship among several such variables.

The advent of the Goodman technique of log-linear fits for hierarchical models seems to solve many of the analytic problems in dealing with several categoric variables at once meaningfully and systematically. In this analysis we focus on the net effects of age, race, occupational status, and prior incarceration on the disposition of an arrest. Since we are interested not in the gross effect of age or race or status, but rather in the effects of each net of the others as well as net of prior incarceration, it is necessary that we put all of this information into one large five-way contingency table of *disposition of the case* by *age* by *race* by *occupational status* by *prior incarceration*. In fact we do this twice: once on the raw frequencies and once on frequencies adjusted, by standardization, to remove the effects of the category of offense charged in the arrest. Our first analysis intentionally ignores the category of offense charged in the arrest and can be thought of as a "zero order" analysis of the effects of social characteristics on disposition. A second analysis of the same data is then performed with offense category controlled by standardization, and comparisons between the two analyses will give information about the gross and net effects of the social characteristics, and allow us to interpret the differences (if any) as the result of different offenses being charged to persons with different characteristics. The remaining net effects then represent our best estimates for the existence of possible direct effects of social characteristics on disposition, independent of category of offense (and independent of other controls in the model).

ANALYSIS AND RESULTS

Before beginning the analysis, it should be pointed out that unlike most statistical analyses of contingency tables, the procedure used here deals not with actual frequency counts but with the natural logarithms of those frequency counts. The reason for this transformation of the basic data is to conceptually simplify the models of analysis. It would be possible, using a multiplicative model, to obtain the same substantive results analyzing raw frequencies and ratios of such frequencies.However, most people find it intuitively easier to understand the kind of additive model obtained when one transforms frequencies to their logarithms. Thus, the first step in the analysis of the five-way table of disposition of the case (D) by age (A) by occupational status (S) by race (R) by prior incarceration (I) is to transform the cell frequencies to their natural logarithms (this actually is done by the computer program ECTA). The data in the five-way table, when logged, can be represented by the following full or saturated model:

categories of disposition of the case. All of these interpretations are equivalent, and as the number of items or factors present in an interaction term in the model increases, the number of possible interpretations increases. The saturated model below, (1), contains 32 possible effects (actually 1260 parameters); and considerable economy in understanding the explanation would be brought about if most of these effect parameters, especially the higher order interaction effects, could be assumed to be zero without doing injustice to the fit of the model to the data.

There are, at this point, two ways we can proceed, which might be termed confirmatory and

$$
\begin{aligned}
G_{ijklm} = \theta_{ijklm} \quad a\, & \lambda_i^D + \lambda_j^A + \lambda_k^S + \lambda_l^R + \lambda_m^I \\
& + \lambda_{ij}^{DA} + \lambda_{ik}^{DS} + \dots \text{(eight other two-factor effects)} \\
& + \lambda_{ijk}^{DAS} + \lambda_{jijl}^{DAR} + \dots \text{(eight other three-factor effects)} \\
& + \lambda_{ijkl}^{DASR} + \lambda_{ijkm}^{DASI} + \text{(three other four-factor effects)} \\
& + \lambda_{ijklm}^{DASRI}
\end{aligned}
\tag{1}
$$

The G_{ijklm} represents the log of the expected frequency in cell (i,j,k,l,m) of our five-way table and the λ's represent possible "effects" of the five variables, their associations and interactions on G_{ijklm}. The superscripts on the effect parameters refer to the variable whose effect is being considered. Thus λ_i^D represents the main effect in category i of the variable disposition of the case. This one factor or "main" effect exists if there is an unequal distribution of cases across the categories of the variable, disposition of the case. λ_{ij}^{DA} represents the two-factor association effect in category i, j of disposition of the case and age. This effect exists if there is any net or partial relationship between age and disposition with all other effects controlled. Similarly λ_{ijk}^{DAS} and other higher order effects represent the interaction effect in the designated categories of the designated variables. λ_{ijk}^{DAS} may be interpreted as being due either to the varying relationship between age and disposition across categories of status, or to the varying relationship between status and disposition across categories of age, or alternatively to the varying relationship between age and status across

exploratory analyses. On the confirmatory side, for example, one may have a particular model derived from theory which includes only certain relationships and interactions, which one wants to test in order to see whether such a model adequately reproduces the data; or one might want for theoretical reasons to test the significance of the net effect of one variable on another with all other variables controlled. In either case prior hypotheses are being tested. On the other hand one may not have any prior hypotheses and may wish to follow exploratory procedures, trying out a series of models until one is found that does fit the data. Our plan is to illustrate both procedures. We begin with the exploratory approach, while in the second part of the paper we deal briefly with the procedures of a confirmatory analysis.

Given our initial exploratory approach, there are still a couple of ways in which we might proceed to find the model which best fits the data. One way would be systematically to go through and test all possible models. That is, test all possible combinations of factors taken one, two, three, four, etc., at a time. This would result in the testing of several thousands of logically possible models with the present data; however, there is a simpler though perhaps less systematic way to proceed.

We begin a step-by-step procedure which starts by computing the effect parameters of the saturated model, M_0, containing all factors as outlined in equation (1). This was done using Goodman and Fay's program ECTA (Everyman's Contingency Table Analyzer). This model, because it contains all the factors, fits the data perfectly, although not all of the coefficients are statistically significant. As our next step, we chose from these results an initial model, M_1, which contains *only* two-factor associations, and only those two-factor associations which were highly significant. These factors (see Table I) were age by disposition, age by prior incarceration, disposition by prior incarceration, status by race, and status by prior incarceration.

To say we included only the significant two-factor associations in the model, we are speaking a little loosely, since with the hierarchical models being investigated here, if we include any higher order effect, such as a two- or three-factor component of the model, we necessarily include a certain set of the lower order components. Thus if we include a three-factor effect like λ_{ijk}^{DAS}, we necessarily include three two-factor effects, λ_{ij}^{DA}, λ_{ik}^{DS}, λ_{jk}^{AS}, and three one-factor effects, λ_i^D, λ_j^A, and λ_k^S. Having included the five two-factor associations that we did for Model M_1, we also have included all the one-factor marginal effects. This, we feel, is somewhat a drawback; the development of nonhierarchical models is potentially more useful because of the freedom to insert or not to insert effects at any level without restriction.

How well does Model M_1 fit the data? To test this model, we compute chi-square and degrees of freedom.[1] If the value of chi-square (relative to degrees of freedom) is small enough, then the

observed and expected cell frequencies in the five-way table are close together and we can say the model fits the data. On the other hand, if we obtain a large value of chi-square (indicating a lack of fit of the model to the data), the model is rejected. In this particular case, as indicated in Table I, Model M_1 has 248 degrees of freedom and a chi-square value of 359.05, indicating that it is not sufficient to adequately represent the data in the five-way table.

By altering the model to include additional factors, the fit can be improved, though at the cost of making the model more complex. Our procedure (forward-selection) is to add factors, one at a time, each time noting the effect of such an addition on the chi-square value. Factors which significantly reduce chi-square will be included in the model. Hopefully we can obtain a good fit (no significant difference between the expected frequencies based on the model and the actual frequencies of the five-way table) by introducing only a few additional factors. Of course, at the extreme, if we introduce all the factors we are back to Model M_0 which fits the data perfectly but incorporates all the information available in the five-way table without any parsimony.

Using this forward-selection procedure three additional two-factor associations (again suggested by the analysis of M_0) were next identified in Models M_2 through M_4 (Table I) as making potentially significant contributions. That is, by comparing Model M_1 in turn with M_2, M_3 and M_4, each of the two-factor associations added can be seen to significantly reduce the value of chi-square (relative to degrees of freedom); and these were all added to Model M_1, thus giving rise to Model M_5. These new factors are disposition by race, disposition by occupational status, and age by status. Our model, M_5, in Table I, now contains eight of ten possible two-factor associations. Adding the two remaining two-factor associations (age by race and race by prior incarceration) as in Model M_6, helps contribute to the fit of the model to the data; however, the model still does not adequately fit the data in the five-way table ($\chi^2 = 261.18$, DF =

---

[1] Although traditional goodness-of-fit chi-square can be used in this context, Goodman (1970:247) suggests the likelihood-ratio chi-square is better; it is this estimate of chi-square that we use throughout this analysis.

Table I. Chi-Square Values for Some Hypothesized Models
Pertaining to the Data in the Five-Way Table of Disposition (D),
by Age (A) by Occupational Status (S), by Race (R),
by Prior Incarceration (I)

Hypothesized Model		Degrees of Freedom	Likelihood Ratio Chi-Square	$p \leqslant$
M_0	(DASRI)	0	0.00	—
M_1	(DA) (DI) (AI) (SR) (SI)	248	359.05	.001
M_2	M_1 + (DR)	243	341.27	.001
M_3	M_1 + (DS)	238	329.23	.001
M_4	M_1 + (AS)	242	341.77	.001
M_5	M_1 + (DR) (DS) (AS)	227	289.36	.003
M_6	all two-factor effects	223	261.18	.040
M_7	M_6 + (ARI)	220	234.28	.242
M_8	M_7 − (DA)	235	332.43	.001
M_9	M_7 − (DS)	230	269.17	.039
M_{10}	M_7 − (DR)	225	258.11	.064
M_{11}	M_7 − (DI)	225	506.73	.001
M_{12}	M_7 − (AS)	226	253.97	.097
M_{13}	M_6 − (AR)	226	260.96	.055
M_{14}	M_6 − (AI)	226	483.94	.001
M_{15}	M_7 − (SR)	222	446.86	.001
M_{16}	M_7 − (SI)	222	289.69	.002
M_{17}	M_6 − (RI)	224	235.34	.288
M_{18}	M_6	223	261.18	.040

223, $p \leqslant .040$). Up to this point we have avoided three-factor and higher-order interactions because they are less simple or parsimonious. Given the results so far, however, it is clear that the simple model does not "account for" the data in the five-way table; and we therefore move up one level of complexity to consider the possible contributions of some of the three-factor interactions. Model M_7 adds the Age by Race by Prior Incarceration factor to Model M_6. This particular factor was considered because it had the largest effect as suggested by the results of the analysis of the saturated model, M_0.

Comparing Model M_7 with M_6 shows that the three-factor interaction (ARI) does add significantly to the fit between the model and the data, and results in a model which does not differ significantly from the data. Additionally, no other three-factor effect was found to contribute significantly to the reduction of chi-square;

and we therefore tentatively suggest Model M_7 as the best representation of the data. It still remains, however, to test the net contribution of each of the components in Model M_7 to be sure each is still carrying a significant part of the load. It may be that as we added new factors the net contributions of some of the factors added earlier have diminished to less than significant magnitudes.

To test this possibility eleven new models are considered (M_8 through M_{18}), each of which leaves out a single factor as compared with Model M_7. The difference in chi-square and degrees of freedom values between each of the new models and M_7 may be used to test the net contribution of the factor left out. The procedure is analogous to that used in multiple regression for the testing of net effects, with differences in chi-square values here being used instead of differences in R^2 values. Table II pre-

Table II. Tests of the Net Contribution of Each of the Factors
Included in Model M_7. Data from Table I

Comparison	Source of Difference Tested	Net Contribution		
		df	Chi-Square	$p \leqslant$
$M_7 : M_8$	(DA)	15	98.15	.001
$M_7 : \checkmark_9$	(DS)	10	34.89	.001
$M_7 : M_{10}$	(DR)	5	23.83	.001
$M_7 : M_{11}$	(DI)	5	272.45	.001
$M_7 : M_{12}$	(AS)	6	19.69	.01
$M_6 : M_{13}$	(AR)	3	26.68	.001
$M_6 : M_{14}$	(AI)	3	249.66	.001
$M_7 : M_{15}$	(SR)	2	212.58	.001
$M_7 : M_{16}$	(SI)	2	55.41	.001
$M_6 : M_{17}$	(RI)	1	1.06	.28
$M_7 : M_{18}$	(ARI)	3	26.90	.001

sents the results of this analysis as derived from the chi-square and degrees of freedom values given in Table I. In this case all but one of the included components have significant net contributions; and that one, race by prior incarceration, must be included because it is part of a significant interaction among age, race, and prior incarceration. Model M_7 is therefore accepted as our best understanding of what is going on in the data of the five-way table.

What does Model M_7 tell us? It says, basically, that in order to reproduce the data in the five-way table one need consider (in addition to the marginal distributions for each variable) only the marginal distributions of the two-factor and three-factor associations and interactions included in the model, i.e., the relationships between ten pairs of variables and the interaction among one set of three variables. The remaining three-factor interactions, the four-factor interactions, and the five-factor interaction may be ignored. On the assumption that the relationships which must be considered are due to causal forces, Figure 1 represents a summary of Model M_7.

For illustrative purposes we next discuss four

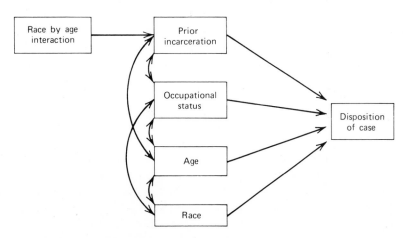

Figure 1. Causal diagram representing model M_7.

Table III. Effect Parameters for Disposition of Case
by Age Under M_7

	Age			
Disposition of the Case	Under 25	25–34	35–49	Over 49
No court	.407**	.229*	−1.64	−.473**
Dismissed, not guilty	−.188	−.018	.108	.099
Judgment withheld	−.257†	−.214†	.129	.342**
Suspended sentence, probation	−.195	.033	.021	.140
Fine	−.013	.174*	−.066	−.096
Prison	.245*	−.204†	−.028	−.013

**p ≤ .01.
*p ≤ .05.
†p ≤ .10.

of the two-factor effects which went with the model: the ones which include the variable, disposition of the case. We begin by looking at the effect of age on disposition of the case. These are the λ_{ij}^{DA} in Model M_7, of which there are 6 × 4 or 24 coefficients presented in Table III. In looking at this table of effects, it should be clear that we are examining a table which consists of parameter estimates for only part of the complete Model M_7. It should also be made clear that all of the coefficients in this table are *partial* coefficients, and may be thought of as measuring the effect of age on disposition while controlling for all other parts of the model.

These effect parameters may be interpreted as follows: a zero coefficient represents no deviation from what would be expected in a model that did not include the effect parameter being considered (in this case age by disposition). A positive coefficient represents a situation in which there are more cases in the cells than would be expected. Similarly, a negative coefficient represents a situation where there are fewer than expected cases in the cells. With this in mind, as we inspect the table, we see a number of coefficients which differ significantly from zero in either a positive or a negative direction.

Thus, it would appear that the two-factor ef-

fect of age by disposition is included in Model M_7 because age and disposition of the cases are related in the following way: first, there is a disproportionate tendency for people in the under age 35 groups to have their arrest *not* result in court processing—that is, there are more cases than expected in these two cells—(while those over 49 are *more* likely to have their arrest result in court processing). Second, there are greater than average tendencies for persons under 25 to be sent to prison, and less than average tendencies for persons between 25 and 35 to be sent to prison, though this latter group has a greater tendency than others to receive a fine. Third, there is a greater tendency for persons over 49 to have the court withhold judgment in their cases compared with the under age 35 group. All of these tendencies together are the content of the relationship between age and disposition of the case; and there is no convenient way to summarize them in a single sentence or coefficient. This perhaps is one of the disadvantages of having polytomous as opposed to dichotomous variables, but it is not a serious handicap inasmuch as the content of the relationship can be interpreted and understood.

Table IV presents the effect parameters for the relationship between disposition and prior incarceration. It can be seen that if the person

Table IV. Effect Parameters for Disposition of Case by Prior Incarceration under M_7

Disposition of the Case	Prior Incarceration	
	Yes	No
No court	.002	−.002
Dismissed, not guilty	−.319**	.319**
Judgment withheld	−.145*	.145*
Suspended sentence, probation	−.115†	.115†
Fine	−.029	.029
Prison	.610**	−.610**

**p ≤ .01.
*p ≤ .05.
†p ≤ .10.

arrested has been previously incarcerated, the chances are much greater that he/she will be sentenced to prison, and much less that the case will be "dismissed,"[2] that judgment will be withheld, or that he/she will receive a suspended sentence or probation. Conversely, of course, if the person arrested has not been previously incarcerated, he/she is much less likely to be sent to prison and much more likely to have the case "dismissed."

Table V. Effect Parameters for Disposition of Case by Race under M_7

Disposition of the Case	Race	
	White	Nonwhite
No court	−.069	.069
Dismissed, not guilty	−.167**	.167**
Judgment withheld	.120†	−.120†
Suspended sentence, probation	.029	−.029
Fine	.047	−.047
Prison	.039	−.039

**p ≤ .01.
†p ≤ .10.

[2]We shall use the term "dismissed" to indicate the category of dispositions which includes not only cases that were dismissed but also cases judged not guilty.

Table V shows the effect parameters for the relationship between disposition and race, indicating that the major effect is with respect to the two categories of "dismissed" and judgment withheld. Whites are less likely to have the case "dismissed" and more likely to have judgment withheld. Conversely, blacks are more likely to have the case "dismissed."

Finally, Table VI shows the effect parameters for the relationship between disposition and occupational status. It will be recalled that occupational status was coded into three categories: high, medium, and low. In calculating the effect parameters for this model we used the option of coding these categories to yield the linear and quadratic components of the status effects (Goodman, 1971a).[3] The existence of a linear component implies that there is a constant proportional increase (or decrease) in levels of the dependent variable as we move across status categories. The existence of a quadratic component implies a nonlinear relationship. The presence of both components implies that there is an increase (or decrease) in the level of the dependent variable comparing high and low status groups, but that the middle status group is higher (or lower) than would be expected under a linear model. In the present data we see only significant linear components of the status effects; and these occur for the categories of "dismissed" and of "prison," thus indicating a constant proportional decrease in the chances of having the case "dismissed" as we move from high to low status groups, and a constant proportional increase in the chance of going to prison.

The remaining seven marginal relationships included in the model can be interpreted in similar fashion. Methodologically there is nothing new, and substantively they do not deal

[3]Age was not dealt with in this fashion here since an earlier analysis of these data (not reported here) suggested that quadratic and cubic effects rather than linear effects were the rule. The analysis was, therefore, more easily handled and interpreted with age coded simply as a nominal scale, categoric variable.

Table VI. Effect Parameters for Disposition of Case by Occupational Status Under M₇

Disposition of the Case	Occupational Status Effects	
	Linear	Quadratic
No court	−.015	−.032
Dismissed, not guilty	.260**	.052
Judgment withheld	−.079	−.049
Suspended sentence, probation	−.027	−.045
Fine	.020	−.038
Prison	−.162**	−.005

**p ≤ .01.

with the outcome variable of concern, disposition of the case; we therefore will not consider them further here. All of the effects included in Model M₇, however, are based on data which has not been standardized for category of offense charged in the arrest, so that although the effects of age, race, and occupational status on dispositions described above are net of each other as well as of prior incarceration, they may be in part the result of differences in types of offenses committed or charged. For this reason we next analyzed the same data after standardizing for category of offense charged in the arrest.

To standardize the data, using the procedure of direct standardization, an expected distribution of cases in the five-way table was computed on the assumption that each subset (by age, race, status, and prior incarceration) had the same distribution of cases across offense categories. The common distribution that was used in these calculations was the distribution for the total sample. The logs of these expected frequencies were then analyzed as were the logs of the raw frequencies, using the method of log-linear fits for hierarchical models. At this point, we switch to a confirmatory mode of analysis, beginning with a test of model M₇—which we shall now refer to as model SM₇ to designate that we are working with the standardized data.

With the standardized data, model SM₇, with 220 degrees of freedom, has a chi-square of 230.37 (associated p = .302) and the model thus fits the data quite well. Testing the components of this model one at a time for the significance of their contribution to the fit of the model to the data we find that two components previously significant no longer make significant contributions (see Table VII).

The two components which are not significant are the status by disposition association (Table IX) and the race by disposition association (Table X). All other effects are significant,

Table VII. Tests of the Net Contribution of Each of the Factors Included in Model SM₇

Comparison	Sources of Difference Tested	Net Contribution		
		df	Chi-Square	p ≤
$SM_7 : SM_8$	(DA)	15	53.83	.001
$SM_7 : SM_9$	(DS)	10	14.57	.20
$SM_7 : SM_{10}$	(DR)	5	0.79	.98
$SM_7 : SM_{11}$	(DI)	5	189.96	.001
$SM_7 : SM_{12}$	(AS)	6	22.09	.01
$SM_6 : SM_{13}$	(AR)	3	29.37	.001
$SM_6 : SM_{14}$	(AI)	3	225.27	.001
$SM_7 : SM_{15}$	(SR)	2	204.57	.001
$SM_7 : SM_{16}$	(SI)	2	66.04	.001
$SM_8 : SM_{17}$	(RI)	1	0.18	.70
$SM_7 : SM_{18}$	(ARI)	3	27.16	.001

as they were with the unstandardized data. We thus conclude that the race and occupational status effects on disposition of the case, which were observed in the unstandardized data, are indirect rather than direct. Race and status directly affect the type of offense committed or charged, and the type of offense charged affects the disposition of the case. Put another way, this analysis suggests that the reason for the differential disposition of persons by race or occupational status is the differential offenses committed or charged by race or status groups. On the assumption that the relationships which must be considered in Model SM7 are due to causal forces, Figure 2 represents a summary of the model. Tables VIII through XI present the effect parameters which include the outcome variable, disposition of the case. These may be compared directly with Tables III to VI. The remaining effect parameters are not reported here.

Before getting into a substantive discussion of these results, perhaps we should note that the largest changes in the parameters of the model (aside from failure of the disposition by race and disposition by status effects to achieve sig-

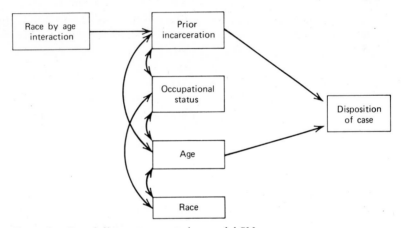

Figure 2. Causal diagram representing model SM7.

Table VIII. Effect Parameters for Disposition of the Case by Age Under SM^7

	Age			
Disposition of the Case	Under 25	25–34	35-49	Over 49
No court	.154	.142	.068	−.364**
Dismissed, not guilty	−.097	−.087	−.033	.216*
Judgment withheld	−.057	−.101	.042	.115
Suspended sentence, probation	−.123	.049	.009	.065
Fine	.050	.168*	−.203**	−.014
Prison	.073	−.171†	.117	−.019

**p ≤ .01.
*p ≤ .05.
†p ≤ .10.

Table IX. Effect Parameters for Disposition of Case by Occupational Status under SM_7

| Disposition of the Case | Occupational Status Effects | |
	Linear	Quadratic
No court	−.032	−.028
Dismissed, not guilty	.144	.976
Judgment withheld	−.033	−.053
Suspended sentence, probation	.040	.010
Fine	.003	−.009
Prison	−.116	.004

Table X. Effect Parameters for Disposition of Case by Race under SM_7

| Disposition of the Case | Race | |
	White	Nonwhite
No court	.008	−.008
Dismissed, not guilty	.008	−.008
Judgment withheld	.030	−.030
Suspended sentence, probation	−.021	.021
Fine	−.016	.016
Prison	−.009	.009

nificance) are in the nature of the relationship between Age and Disposition as shown in Table VIII. Where we had previously noted a greater than expected tendency for arrested persons under the age of 25 to be sent to prison, there is, with standardization by category of offense, no such tendency. Evidently the effect in the unstandardized data is due to the younger being charged with more serious offenses. Also the previously noted tendency for those under age 35 not to go to court, though still in that direction, is no longer significant. The tendency for those over age 49 to have their cases go to court remains, though the disposition once in court now (with standardization) appears to be more likely to be in the category "dismissed or not guilty" rather than the previously noted "judgment withheld." Also the previously noted tendency for those between 25 and 35 to be not sent to prison does remain after standardization, as does their greater than expected chances of being fined, while the chances of being fined for those in the 35 to 49 age bracket have diminished to be significantly less than expected.

In sum, though the nature of the relationship between disposition and age seems to have shifted slightly, age continues to have an effect on the disposition of the case independently of the category of offense charged in the arrest. The effect of prior incarceration on disposition remains virtually unaltered after standardizing on category of offense (Table XI), as do the relationships between race and status, age and status, prior incarceration and status, and the interaction between race, age, and prior incarceration (tables not shown here).

DISCUSSION

Turning first to the substantive results of this illustrative analysis, we find several ways in which log-linear analysis has both increased the specificity of some empirical generalizations familiar to criminologists and produced some provocative leads for further research on the extent and nature of discriminatory criminalization.

Perhaps the most familiar and expected finding is that men who have been in-

Table XI. Effect Parameters for Disposition of the Case by Prior Incarceration under SM_7

| Disposition of the Case | Prior Incarceration | |
	Yes	No
No court	−.010	.010
Dismissed, not guilty	−.205**	.205**
Judgment withheld	−.183**	.183**
Suspended sentence, probation	−.145*	.145*
Fine	−.004	.004
Prison	.546**	−.546**

**$p \leqslant .01$.
*$p \leqslant .05$.

stitutionalized before are significantly more likely to be brought to court, to be convicted, and to be given a prison sentence instead of some less severe disposition. However, against the frequent argument that this is because ex-convicts are more likely to commit relatively serious offenses (whether this is blamed upon their incorrigibility, prison socialization, or disillusionment caused by postprison harassment and lack of rehabilitative help), these data show that the effect exists even when nature of the offense is controlled (compare effect parameters in Tables VI and XI). This suggests that those who attempt to explain the greater risk for ex-convicts in terms of their vulnerability to the biases of legal control agents may be on firmer ground than are those who attribute the differential risk to the greater propensity of ex-convicts for relatively serious crimes.

Although young male offenders are most likely to be given a precourt "break," those who are brought to trial are more likely than older offenders to receive prison sentences, because they are more likely to have been charged with relatively serious crimes. This common generalization *cum* interpretation was given some support by the finding that both the significantly higher chance of a "no court" disposition and the greater risk of imprisonment for males under 25 were eliminated when we controlled for type of offense (Tables III and VIII).

Other findings relating age and disposition are less easily, or plausibly, explained. One may speculate that males 25–34 were, regardless of offense, most likely to be fined and least likely to be imprisoned because they are the backbone of the labor force. Or it may be that males 35–49 are least likely to be fined when offense is controlled because of their greater ability—by virtue of greater experience, established reputations, and higher incomes—to negotiate relatively lenient treatment by the court. And perhaps older males are most likely to have to go to court, yet unlikely to be severely treated, because they are disproportionately lower-class petty offenders—though opposing this rather

plausible interpretation are the facts (a) that occupational status was controlled, and (b) that the disposition pattern for the older males was not changed by controlling for offense type.

The effect of occupational status upon disposition is generally in the usual direction, i.e., the lower the status, the more severe the disposition. Moreover, the disappearance of this effect when offense is controlled tends to support the view that class-linked behavior variations rather than discriminatory treatment produce class differences in case disposition. But a possibly confounding factor is the highly significant relationship between prior incarceration and occupational status (tables not shown here), since the greater chance that lower-class males have been previously incarcerated implies that some part of their risk arises from a factor already shown to generate a higher probability of imprisonment irrespective of offense. In addition, the strong relationship between race and occupational status (tables not shown here) introduces still another complication for any simple behavioral interpretation in terms of class culture differences.

Contrary to expectations derived from the available literature, race appears to have little detectable effect upon disposition; and even that effect tends to be the reverse of what might be expected under the presumption of discriminatory treatment of nonwhites. When type of offense is not controlled, it appears that nonwhites are more likely than whites to have their cases dismissed, etc., and somewhat less likely to have judgment withheld. But even these effects disappear when type of offense is controlled, leaving us with the finding that race has no independent effect upon case disposition. It would, however, be premature to conclude that race has nothing to do with disposition, for the significance, regardless of offense, of the race by occupational status association and of the three-factor interaction of age by race by prior incarceration suggests that the race effect may be masked by its complex relations with other factors, and that there may indeed be some discrimination operating in ways not readily described by the simplifying rhetoric characteristic of most debates over racism in law enforcement.

The unsurprising finding that race and occupational status are significantly related emphasizes the need not only to test for discriminatory legal processing but also to test the relative validity of explanations, for whatever bias may be found, emphasizing racism, on the one hand, or class discrimination, on the other.

To complicate the research task even further, how does one account for the complex interaction of race with age and prior incarceration? Young nonwhites may be more likely than their white age peers to have been previously institutionalized because they commit more serious offenses (Black and Reis, 1970); but controlling for current offense, at least, does not change the relationship. Another possibility is that the home situation of nonwhite youths is perceived by authorities as less adequate than that of whites, so that nonwhites are institutionalized where whites would be released to the custody of their parents. Perhaps there is discrimination, in such terms; but then we must also explain the similar differences found for males 25–34. The standard argument that differential disposition in this case is a function of differences in type of offense—i.e., nonwhite men commit more serious crimes—is questioned by our finding that this pattern is unaffected by controlling for offense, so that the discrimination argument is given some support. Finally, the reversal of the pattern as we move from the younger to the older age categories is especially hard to explain; possibly there is some association here with the apparently greater use in the past of summary, unofficial punishment in the legal control of nonwhites than in the control of whites—i.e., formal, recorded incarcerations were, at least in some Southern locales, often dispensed with in cases (especially minor ones) where the offender was thought to be a politically and economically inconsequential nonwhite.

Clearly, our illustrative analysis has done little more than to point up the difficulties of determining, much less explaining, the extent and nature of discrimination against the socially disadvantaged in postarrest proceedings. Nonetheless, even this limited exploration demonstrates that assertions of such bias in the legal system require better evidence than has so far been offered in their support.

On the methodological side, we have distinguished between an exploratory approach and the alternative of a confirmatory or hypothesis-testing approach to the analysis of these tables; and we also distinguished between the analysis of hierarchical models as in the present paper and the potentially more useful approach of nonhierarchical models. With the version of the ECTA program available to us at the time, such nonhierarchical analyses were beyond us.

While the computations themselves are fairly straightforward, it does appear that application of log-linear analysis of polytomous variables as in the present study (1) is somewhat more cumbersome than when the analysis is limited to dichotomous variables, as in most of Goodman's examples, and (2) generates results not easily condensed into simple statements—as the multitude of tables and descriptions here attest.

1. With polytomous variables in an exploratory approach,[4] the search for an unsaturated model that adequately describes the data in a multivariable contingency table does require more work than with dichotomous variables alone because the selection of effects to be included in any model to be tested is less easily decided. For instance, a large number of distinct coefficients may be needed to describe a single effect parameter such as the λ_{ij}^{DA} described in Tables III and VIII. Since the subscript i takes on values from 1 to 6 (for the six possible dispositions), while the subscript j takes on values from 1 to 4 (for the four age categories), there are 24 different values for λ^{DA}: one for each cell. In-

---

[4]Of course, none of these problems occur in a confirmatory analysis, since we proceed directly to the test of an *a priori* model.

spection of the results for the saturated model with an eye to finding effects which ought to be included in an unsaturated, or reduced, model, one must decide whether an effect such as λ_{ij}^{DA} should be included if one or two or three or five of the twenty-four coefficients are significantly different from zero, knowing that some of a large number of coefficients are going to differ from zero by chance.[5] Also, does one include a factor with three significant coefficients at the .05 level *before* including a factor with one significant coefficient at the .01 level, since the net contribution of the second factor to be included may be nonsignificant once the other factor has been included?

The only solution to the problem of choosing appropriate effects is to try more models. Should an effect be included if only one of the 24 coefficients is significant at the .05 level in the saturated model? One can only try it and see what the net contribution is to the particular model being considered. To decide which of two effects should be included first, one must try it both ways. The only rule—equally applicable to the case of dichotomous variables—is to include simpler effects first, i.e., two-factor effects before three-factor effects, three-factor effects before four-factor effects, etc., because in working with hierarchical models the inclusion of an n-factor effect presumes the inclusion of the (n − 1)-factor effects for the variables in question. It follows that, for example, the two-factor models should be explored prior to including three-factor effects. An important additional consideration is that this rule minimizes the need to deal with the more complex factors,

which makes the analysis easier both to do and to follow.

One caveat of this exploratory approach, however, is in order. As one proceeds to try alternative models in the absence of theoretical justification, there is increasing likelihood to include some relationships in the model which are simply the result of sampling error. In that situation the results could be quite misleading; and for this reason, confirmatory analyses testing theoretically derived hypotheses are recommended whenever possible.

2. In large contingency tables the relationships obviously may be exceedingly complex, so that although it is easy with the Goodman procedure to test for the significance of such relationships, it may be difficult to describe them—as in our description of the relationship between age and disposition and our comparison of that relationship before and after standardization (Tables III and VIII). Discussion is, of course, facilitated by knowing which of the coefficients (i.e., which of the cells in the table) are different from others. In this way we can locate the source of the statistical association which exists for the table considered as a whole. The fact remains, however, that the relationship itself may well be too complex to be conveniently and easily described.

Some economy can be had if one or more of the variables can be coded to show linear, quadratic, etc., effects, as in the case of occupational status in this paper, where we observed the relationship between status and disposition simply described by the linear effects of status on two disposition outcomes (Table VI). This economy and parsimony, however, depends upon the relationship remaining simple and linear, as was clearly not the case in the age by disposition relationship (see footnote 4).

Our last point concerns the use of standardization (in this case on type of offense) to achieve control over some variable not included directly in the analysis. There may be several motivations for doing this, though two that may occur fairly frequently are (1) that the factor on which

---

[5] Such questions do not arise when dealing only with dichotomous variables, since in that case, though there are four coefficients for each factor, numerically (in absolute value) and statistically (in terms of significance) they are identical; and there is then only a single coefficient which needs to be considered for each effect considered for inclusion in the model. In this case it becomes easy to include the more significant effects prior to the less significant (though it is always possible that the net effects of the factors in the reduced model are not ranked in the same order as they are in the saturated model).

standardization occurs is (a) statistically but not substantively important or (b) so overwhelmingly important and obvious that it needs no discussion but does need to be taken into account, and (2) that the data for a complete n-way table may not be available, but that there are data to effect indirect standardization of a control factor, and one wants to use this limited information to the best advantage possible (Kitagawa, 1964). In any case, the application of the log-linear analysis to expected frequencies is straightforward as long as one remembers two things: (1) that in standardizing one is dealing with expected distributions and not actual distributions, and the data are always, therefore, hypothetical; (2) and perhaps more important, that standardization may obscure information about possible interaction among the variables, and some caution, therefore, is warranted in interpreting results (Atchley, 1968).

To conclude, further research on the relationship between social disadvantage and criminalization must recognize the complexity of that relationship not only in theory but equally in the design and execution of research. We have tried in this paper to demonstrate that the use of log-linear analysis, as proposed by Goodman, does give criminologists and other deviance researchers concerned with categoric outcomes a far more powerful means for analyzing the complex contingency tables which generally arise in this area than has so far been available, thus enabling us to overcome the constraints imposed on previous studies by analytical tools inadequate to the task.

REFERENCES

Arnold, William R.
  1971 "Race and ethnicity relative to other factors in juvenile court dispositons,"American Journal of Sociology 77(September): 211–227.

Atchley, Robert
  1968 "A qualification of test factor standardization," Social Forces 47(September):84–85.

Black, Donald J.
  1970 "The production of crime rates." American Sociological Review 35(August): 733–748.

Black, Donald J. and Albert J. Reiss, Jr.
  1970 "Police control of juveniles." American Sociological Review 35(February): 63–77.

Chambliss, William J., ed.
  1969 Crime and the Legal Processes. New York: McGraw-Hill.

Chiricos, Theodore G., Phillips D. Jackson, and Gordon P. Waldo
  1974 "Inequality in the imposition of a criminal label." Social Problems 19(Spring): 553–572.

Goodman, L. A.
  1970 "The multivariate analysis of qualitative data: interactions among multiple classifications." Journal of American Statistical Association 65:226–256.
  1971a "The analysis of multidimensional contingency tables: Stepwise procedures and direct estimation methods for building models for multiple classifications." Technometrics 13:33–61.
  1971b "Partitioning of chi-square, analysis of marginal contingency tables, and estimations of expected frequencies in multidimensional contingency tables." Journal of the American Statistical Association 66:339–344.
  1972a "A general model for the analysis of surveys." American Journal of Sociology 77:1035–1086.
  1972b "A modified multiple regression approach to the analysis of dichotomous variables." American Sociological Review 37:28–46.
  1973 "Causal analysis of data from panel studies and other kinds of surveys."American Journal of Sociology 78:1135–1191.

Green, Edward
  1970 "Race, social status, and criminal arrest." American Sociological Review 35(June): 476–490.

Kitagawa, Evelyn M.
  1964 "Standardized comparisons in population research." Demography 1:296–315.

Reiss, Albert J., Jr.
  1968 "Police brutality—answers to key questions." Transaction July/August.
  1971 The Police and the Public. New Haven and London: Yale University Press.

Sutherland, Edwin H. and Donald R. Cressey
  1970 Criminology. New York: J. B. Lippincott Co., 8th Edition.

Thornberry, Terence P.
  1973 "Race, socioeconomic status, and sentencing in the juvenile justice system" Journal of Criminal Law and Criminology 64(March): 90–98.

Turk, Austin T.
  1969 Criminality and Legal Order. Chicago: Rand McNally.

Weiner, Norman L. and Charles V. Willie
  1971 "Decisions by juvenile officers." American Journal of Sociology 77 (September): 199–210.

28. Extra-Legal Attributes and Criminal Sentencing

JOHN HAGAN

INTRODUCTION

Nearly half a century after Thorsten Sellin (1928) first introduced the topic for research, the issue of discrimination in judicial sentencing is still very much with us. Thus, Richard Quinney (1970: 142), among the more provocative critics of our system of criminal justice, observes that

"Obviously judicial decisions are not made uniformly. Decisions are made according to a host of extra-legal factors, including the age of the offender, his race, and social class.

"Perhaps the most obvious example of judicial discretion occurs in the handling of cases of persons from minority groups. Negroes, in comparison to whites, are convicted with lesser evidence and sentenced to more severe punishments."

A more detailed version of this argument is presented in the work of Chambliss and Seidman (1971). A propositional theory of the legal process is formulated which focuses on the bureaucratic character of criminal justice and the use of discretion within this context. The key postulate in this theory assumes that legal decision-making will be motivated by the desire to maximize institutional benefits, while minimizing organizational strains. It is also assumed that political power, in its close association with social class position, is the basic deter-minant of organizational rewards and constraints. Two testable deductions follow (Chambliss and Seidman, 1971: 475):

1. Where laws are so stated that people of all classes are equally likely to violate them, the lower the social position of the offender, the greater is the likelihood that sanctions will be imposed on him.

2. When sanctions are imposed, the most severe sanctions will be imposed on persons in the lowest social class.

Leaving no doubt as to the meaning of these propositions for judicial decision-making, Chambliss and Seidman (1971: 468) observe that, "[t]he judge's role in Anglo-American law in sentencing allows for at least as great discretion as do the roles of the prosecutor and the police. . . . The demands for efficient and orderly performance of the court take priority and create a propensity on the part of the courts to dispose of cases in ways that ensure the continued smooth functioning of the system. The consequence of such a policy is to systematically select certain categories of offenders (specifically the poor and the black) for the most severe treatment."

The discussion that follows reviews research relating to the charge of discrimination in sentencing. In the studies reviewed, answers are sought to the following questions:

i. *Are* extra-legal attributes of the defendant a basis of differential sentencing?

▶SOURCE: *"Extra-Legal Attributes and Criminal Sentencing: An Assessment of a Sociological Viewpoint," Law and Society Review (Spring, 1974) 8:357–383. Reprinted by permission.*

ii. If so, *how much* differential sentencing occurs?

iii. In *what particular settings,* if any, does the differential sentencing occur?

STUDIES OF JUDICIAL SENTENCING

Studies of judicial sentencing have tended to adopt a "sociological viewpoint," emphasizing the role of "extra-legal attributes" of the offender in the determination of judicial dispositions.[1] The independent variables given prominence by this approach include the race, sex, age, and socio-economic status of the defendant. Although such variables are *presumably* legally irrelevant to the imposition of sentence, sociologically-oriented studies have attempted to detect their extra-legal influence.

An alternative view of sentencing, which attends to factors emphasized in official-normative descriptions of the criminal justice system, may be referred to as the "legalistic" viewpoint. The variables of interest here include the defendant's prior conviction record and the nature and number of the charges presently brought against him.

Table I provides an overview of the manner in which the two viewpoints have been incorporated in twenty studies of judicial sentencing patterns.[2] All twenty treat one or more of the extra-legal offender characteristics as the independent variable(s); sixteen also hold constant at

---

[1] The term "extra-legal attributes" is used in this discussion to refer to perceived characteristics of the offender that are legally irrelevant to the imposition of sentence.

The term "sociological viewpoint" is used in a restrictive sense to refer to an emphasis on extra-legal attributes in studies of sentencing. There are, of course, other sociological views on sentencing, and some of these are considered in the conclusion to this paper.

[2] Studies were originally located by consulting previous discussions of the sentencing literature (Green, 1971; Overby, 1971; Mannheim, 1968), a bibliography on sentencing research (Tompkins, 1971), *Abstracts on Criminology and Penology,* and *Sociological Abstracts.* A purposive sample of 20 studies, and tables therein was then selected on the basis of three criteria: (1) public availability, (2) attention to variables of concern, and (3) frequency of citation in the literature.

---

least one legal aspect of the defendant and his offense. There is, then, in sixteen studies, an acknowledgment of legal factors when testing sociological hypotheses. However, the *degree* to which each incorporates controls for legal considerations is an important source of variation. The nature and degree of this variation, and its apparent consequences, will be a continuing concern in the remaining portions of this paper.

To understand the patterns of analysis commonly found in studies of judicial sentencing, it will be helpful to briefly consider the statistical techniques frequently used in this type of research. Of the twenty studies cited in Table I, eleven incorporated tests of significance, four computed summary measures of association, and eight used neither form of analysis. The frequent reliance on tests of significance in these studies is troubling, considering the extensive debate regarding the merits of such tests (for example, see Selvin, 1957; Selvin and Stuart, 1966; Kish, 1959; Camilleri, 1962; and Labovitz, 1969). In the context of the current discussion, several difficulties associated with the use of significance tests need to be examined.

A basic problem in the use of significance tests is the frequency with which their results are misinterpreted. One source of this problem is a tendency to confuse the meanings of *substantive* and *statistical* significance. A relationship is considered statistically significant when we have established, subject to an accepted risk of error, that *there is* a relationship between two variables. Separate from the issue of whether or not a relationship exists is the question of *how strong* the relationship is. The strength of a relationship is indicated by a measure of association. Tests of significance are inappropriate for this purpose because they are markedly influenced by the size of the sample involved. For example, when the sample size is large, as is usually the case in studies of sentencing,[3] it is generally quite easy

---

[3] One misguided reason for the use of large samples in sentencing studies is the assumption that such a procedure will randomize the affects of extraneous variables. This assumption is, of course, false.

Table I. Studies Relating Extra-Legal Offender Characteristics to Judicial Sentencing

Study	Primary Sample	Salient Independent Variables	Salient Dependent Variables	Legal Variables Controlled	Test of Significance	Summary Measure of Association
Sellin (1928)	18,239 cases in Detroit	race	sentence, conviction	offense	no	no
Martin (1934)	927 cases, Texas, 1930	race, occupation, sex, age	sentence	none	no	no
Johnson (1941)	122 death sentences, N. Carolina, 1933-39	race of offender & victim	appellate review	murder cases only	no	no
Lemert et al. (1948)	914 cases, Los Angeles, 1930	race	sentence	offense, prior record	yes	no
Garfinkel (1949)	821 offenders, homicide, No. Carolina	race of offender & victim	sentence, charge reduction	type of murder	no	no
Johnson (1957)	650 admissions, death row. North Carolina: 1930-40	race, education, occupation	execution	offense type	yes	no
Green (1961)	1,437 cases, Philadelphia	sex, age, race	sentence	offense, prior record, number of charges	yes	yes
Bullock (1961)	3,644 Texas prison inmates	race	sentence	offense type	yes	yes
Jacob (1962)	1,864 court cases, New Orleans	race	sentence	offense type	yes	no
Bedau (1964)	235 capital cases, New Jersey, 1907-60	race, age, sex, SES	execution	none	yes	no

Study	Sample	Variables	Dependent Variable	Controls		
Green (1964)	118 robbery cases, 291 burglary cases, Philadelphia	race of offender & victim	sentence	type of offense, number of charges, prior record	no	no
Partington (1965)	2,798 rape cases, Virginia	race	sentence & appellate review	type of rape	no	no
Wolfgang et al. (1962)	439 death sentences, murder, Pennsylvania	age, race, occupation	appellate review	offense type	yes	no
Wolf (1965)	159 capital cases, New Jersey: 1937-61	age, race	sentence	offense type	yes	no
Bedau (1965)	92 capital cases, Oregon, 1903-64	race, age, SES	execution	none	no	no
Forslund (1969)	3,882 arrests, Samford, Conn.	race, occupation, age	conviction, dismissal	none	yes	no
Southern Regional Council (1969)	1,207 cases, 7 southern states	race of offender & victim	sentence	offense, prior record	no	no
Nagel (1969)	2,930 larceny & assault cases	income, sex, race, age	sentence & conviction	offense, number of charges, prior record	no	yes
Judson et al (1969)	238 First Degree Murder cases, sentenced by Jury	race, age, sex, SES	execution	prior record, characteristics of offense	yes	yes
Wolfgang et al (1973)	3,000 rape cases, from 11 southern states, 1945-65	race of offender & victim	execution	prior record, contemporaneous offense, and others	yes	no

to establish statistical significance for even a very small relationship.[4] Within the context of large samples, then, one says very little by indicating that a relationship is "statistically significant" (Blalock, 1960: 225).

A second problem with tests of significance is the confusion of the meanings of *causal* and *statistical* significance. This confusion is particularly worrysome in the type of nonexperimental research used in sentencing studies. The error consists of a failure to acknowledge that a statistically significant relationship between an independent and dependent variable may often be alternatively explained (i.e., shown spurious) by controlling for antecedent variables associated with the independent variable. The tendency to mix the meanings of causal and statistical significance may thus misguidedly encourage a premature end to the data analysis process, and result in the assignment of false importance to spurious findings.[5] This failure to consider alternative explanatory hypotheses is recognizable in the inadequate manner in which many sociologically oriented studies of judicial sentencing have held constant the influence of legally relevant variables.

One final point should be made regarding the samples utilized in the studies cited in Table I. Ten of these (Johnson, 1941; Garfinkel, 1949; Johnson, 1957; Bedau, 1964; Partington, 1965; Wolfgang et al., 1962; Wolf, 1965; Bedau, 1965; Judson et al., 1969; and Wolfgang and Riedel,

1973) deal primarily with capital cases, while the remaining ten (Sellin, 1928; Martin, 1934; Lemert and Rosberg, 1948; Green, 1961; Bullock, 1961; Jacob, 1962; Green, 1964; Forslund, 1969; Southern Regional Council, 1969; Nagel, 1969) focus largely on non-capital offenses. Because capital cases may more directly involve an expression of social mores, because they are more often tried before juries, and because sentencing decisions in these cases usually follow protracted litigation, it seems reasonable to expect different patterns of disposition in samples made up of capital cases.

Succeeding sections of this paper will examine our sample of twenty studies in terms of the points emphasized above. Thus, we shall, in turn, investigate the relationship between race, socio-economic status, age, and sex of the offender, and the nature of judicial dispositions. In each study, we shall consider not only the statistical significance of the relationship, but also the strength and form of the association, the extent to which controls are introduced for the influence of legally relevant factors, and the type of sample used in the investigation.

RACE AS THE INDEPENDENT VARIABLE

The most frequently considered offender characteristic in studies of sentencing is race. Sociologically-oriented studies have been concerned that the judicial process may be either excessively harsh, or, alternatively, unduly lenient, in the handling of minority group defendants. The assumption has been that relationships observed in either direction would reflect negatively on the attainment of equality before the law.

To evaluate the hypothesis that "race makes a difference," relevant data from seventeen studies (Tables II, III, IV and V) have been reanalyzed.[6] Because most of the studies did not compute a measure of association, and because

[4]Labovitz (1969: 143) makes a similar point in the following manner:

"It may be argued that significance tests at best provide the absolute minimum of knowledge, e.g., whether or not 'r' is significantly different from zero. . . . But a zero relation . . . is useless to refute. Most things (and perhaps all things) are statistically related, if only to a very small degree. The surprising case is the zero relation, which is more likely in small samples than in large."

[5]For an excellent discussion of the techniques of causal analysis and the use of statistical controls for the test of alternative explanatory hypotheses, see Hirschi and Selvin (1967: 35–174). Their discussion will also be useful in distinguishing the different techniques used in introducing statistical controls in tabular, as contrasted with multivariate analysis.

[6]One of the studies (Jacob, 1962) did not present data in a manner suited to inclusion in this table; two other studies (Green, 1964; Wolfgang and Riedel, 1973) are reserved for consideration in Tables VI and VII.

some of them also did not include a test of significance, it was necessary to perform additional computations on the data provided in the original tables. Where additional computations have been performed, the results are presented in brackets. In addition, there were instances where tables useful for comparative purposes were not included in the final presentation of a study's findings. It was often possible, however, to reconstruct many of these tables from the text.[7] Summary statistics derived from these reconstructed tables are shown in brackets. The test of significance used is chi-square (χ^2), and the measure of association presented is Goodman and Kruskal's tau-b (tb).[8] An advantage of the latter measure is its interpretation in terms of the increase in accuracy, beyond that provided by chance alone, that knowledge of an independent variable makes possible in the prediction of a dependent variable. In this discussion, we shall be concerned with the extent to which knowledge of the extra-legal attributes of the defendants improves our accuracy in predicting judicial dispositions.

An examination of Table II, containing studies focusing on non-capital cases, reveals a number of interesting findings. Perhaps the most striking aspect of the table is the small magnitude of many of the relationships observed. Thus, the largest tb indicated is .08 (Lemert and Rosberg, 1948), with the majority of the studies revealing relationships much lower in strength. It is particularly noteworthy that this is often the case regardless of the degree to which the findings are statistically significant. Thus, there are several statistically significant relationships in the table where tb is smaller than .01. This indicates that knowledge of race increases the accuracy of the prediction of sentencing outcome by less than one percent.

Attention is next given to the effect of controlling for the type of offense charged. Although there is some evidence in Table II of a strengthening of tb relationships when offense is held constant, the more notable result is to emphasize the relatively small relationships involved in many of these studies. Thus, while many of the findings reported in Table II are statistically significant, the median value of tb reported in the offense column of this table is .014. That is, when one controls for type of offense, the median increase in the accuracy of prediction of judicial disposition from knowledge of the defendant's race is 1.4 percent.

A useful illustration of the uninformativeness of significance tests is found in Bullock's (1969) data. Bullock presents several tables showing relationships between race and sentencing that are statistically significant at the .01 level. Unfortunately, these tables were percentaged within categories of the *dependent variable*, "length of sentence." Although handling the data in this manner has no effect on calculations of statistical significance, presentation in this form makes interpretation of the results difficult (Zeisel, 1957; Hirschi and Selvin, 1967). In Table III, the original data have been recalculated within categories of the *independent* variable, "race." The results are instructive.

The first section of Table III contains all cases in the original sample, with the dependent variable dichotomized into "short" and "long" sentences. The percentage difference between blacks and whites receiving short and long sentences is only four percent, yet this finding is statistically significant at the .01 level. When the type of offense is controlled in the remaining sections of Table III, the percentage differences increase somewhat, but fluctuate in direction. Thus, while eight percent of the blacks receive *longer* sentences for burglary, seven percent receive *shorter* sentences for rape and murder. Fluctuations of this size in the direction of the

---

[7] A copy of the tables used in this article is available, on request, from the author. For a discussion of the methods of secondary analysis used in this review, see Hirschi and Selvin (1967: Ch. 3).

[8] Chi square was chosen as the test of significance in this review because of its frequent use in the original studies. For a discussion of the chi square test of significance, see Blalock (1960: 212–21). Tau-b was selected as the measure of association on the basis of its proportional-reduction-in-error (PRE) interpretation (see Costner, 1965) and, further, on its performance in a recent "test of validity" by Hunter (1973). For a discussion of tau-b, see Blalock (1960: 232–34).

Table II. Race as an Independent Variable (Non-Capital Cases)

Stduy	Dependent Variable	X^2	t_b	Offense	Controls for Legally Significant Variables X^2	t_b	Prior Record	X^2	t_b
Sellin (1928)	sentence	(392.4) (P<.01)	(.008)	felonies	(119.6) (P<.01)	(.036)			
				misdemenor	(266.4) (P<.01)	(.010)			
Martin (1934)	sentence	(31.97) (P=.01)	(.007)						
Lemert et al (1948)	sentence	(20.41) (P<.01)	(.008)	burglary	19.16 P<.01	(.021)	none	3.21 P>.50	(.016)
				2nd degree auto theft	15.16 P<.05	(.014)	some	15.98 P<.01	(.080)
				narcotics	7.85 P<.05	(.047)			
				assault	10.09 P>.10	(.035)			
				rape	3.06 P>.10	(.017)			
Bullock (1961)	sentence	(8.37) (P<.01)	(.002)	murder	8.10 P<.01	(.004)			
				rape	1.92 P<.25	(.005)			
				burglary	14.45 P<.01	(.010)			

Study				
Green (1961)	sentence	20.5 P<.01 (.002)	burglary 4.79 P=.19 (.006)	none 1.00 P>.80 (.003)
				some 4.90 P>.10 (.015)
Forslund (1969)	conviction (43.33) (P<.01) (.011)			
Southern Regional Council (1969)	sentence (25.66) (P<.01) (.025)			none (10.14) (P<.01) (.024)
				some (13.74) (P<.01) (.022)
Nagel (1969)	sentence —state cases (3.53) (P>.01) (.004) —federal cases (7.73) (P<.01) (.013) (larceny & assault cases)	state assault (1.08) (P=.30) (.003) state larceny (26.48) (P<.01) (.056) federal assault (.29) (P<.59) (.003) federal larceny (8.20) (P<.01) (.017)		none (.52) (P=.47) (.003)
				some (7.51) (P<.01) (.025)

relationship could easily result from a distortion introduced in the original research when the continuous dependent variable, length of sentence, was dichotomized into the categories "short" and "long." There is the additional possibility that these findings result from the failure to hold constant prior record and number of charges. Notwithstanding these possibilities, three of the four relationships illustrated in Table III are *statistically* significant.

Returning to Table II, we consider next the effects of controlling both for the type of offense charged *and* the previous record of the offender. Three studies (Lemert and Rosberg, 1948; Green, 1961; and Nagel, 1969) have utilized this type of simultaneous control.[9] Each of the three dichotomizes the previous record of the offenders in terms of either no previous convictions, or, one or more previous convictions. When one controls for both offense and prior record, the results are strikingly consistent. In all three studies, considering first only those offenders with no previous convictions, the relationship between race and sentencing becomes statistically insignificant (at the .05 level), with the median t_b only .003. Thus, the increase in the accuracy of predicting judicial outcome on the basis of knowledge of race is less than one percent. Alternatively, when those cases of offenders with "some"previous convictions are considered, the relationships between race and sentencing in two of the three studies remain statistically significant. Tau$_b$ ranges between a high value in Lemert and Rosberg's (1948) study of .08 to a low value in Green's (1961) research of .015. The median t_b is .025, representing a 2.5 percent increase in the accuracy of predicting judicial outcome on the basis of knowledge of race.

An example of the interaction effect just described, undiscussed in the original study, can

be illustrated by reconstructing several tables from Nagel's (1969) research. The reconstructed data is presented in Table IV. The first section of this table indicates a 14 percent difference in the rate of imprisonment of black and white offenders. However, when the presence or absence of prior convictions is controlled, the outcome changes. Thus, among offenders with no prior convictions, the difference in the rate of imprisonment for blacks and whites shrinks to six percent and loses statistical significance at conventional levels. In contrast, among offenders with "some" prior convictions, the racial difference in the rate of incarceration increases to 16 percent and retains statistical significance.

It is interesting to note two of the interpretations given to the type of findings just reported. Lemert and Rosberg (1948: 18) conclude that the statistically significant relationship between race and sentencing for offenders with "some" previous convictions indicates that, ". . . race prejudice is a more significantly operating variable when groups concerned are definitely stereotyped as criminal." In contrast, Green (1961: 11) suggests that the control implied in "one or more" previous convictions, ". . . is insensitive to possible differences between whites and racial minorities in the *number* of prior felony convictions, a factor which is very likely to influence the judge's determination of the sentence" (emphasis in the original). Clearly, additional data providing a more systematic control for the number of prior convictions will be necessary before any definitive conclusions can be reached. For the moment, we can only conclude that this version of the "racial hypothesis"remains open to some doubt.

Attention is directed, next, to Table V, containing studies concerned primarily with sentencing in capital cases. Findings reported in this table parallel those in Table II.Again, the relationships observed are not large. Thus, the median value of t_b, before controlling for offense, is .012, and .015 after holding offense constant. Knowing the race of the offender in capital cases, then, increases the accuracy of

---

[9]It should be noted that Lemert and Rosberg's study additionally involves a control for occupational status. A fourth study (Southern Regional Council, 1969) did not control for previous record simultaneously with offense, and therefore is not included in this discussion.

Table III. Race and Sentencing (Bullock, 1961)

	Total Cases			Burglary Cases			Rape Cases			Murder Cases		
Race	Per Cent Short Sentences	Per Cent Long Sentences	N	Per Cent Short Sentences	Per Cent Long Sentences	N	Per Cent Short Sentences	Per Cent Long Sentences	N	Per Cent Short Sentences	Per Cent Long Sentences	N
Black	52%	48%	1727	72%	28%	572	41%	59%	119	42%	58%	1037
White	56%	44%	1917	80%	20%	910	34%	66%	255	35%	65%	751
X^2	8.37			14.45			1.92			8.10		
P	<.01			<.01			<.25			<.01		
t_b	.002			.010			.005			.004		

Table IV. The Effects of Controlling for Prior Convictions (Nagel, 1969)

	Total Federal Larceny Cases			Federal Larceny Cases, No Prior Convictions			Federal Larceny Cases, Some Prior Convictions		
Race	Per Cent Suspended Sentence or Probation	Per Cent Imprisoned	N	Per Cent Suspended Sentence or Probation	Per Cent Imprisoned	N	Per Cent Suspended Sentence or Probation	Per Cent Imprisoned	N
Black	46%	54%	152	80%	20%	37	34%	66%	110
White	60%	40%	330	86%	14%	114	50%	50%	186
X^2	8.20			.52			7.51		
P	<.01			.47			<.01		
t_b	.017			.003			.025		

Table V. Race as the Independent Variable (Capital Cases)

Study	Dependent Variable	X^2	t_b	Controls for Legally Significant Variables Offense	X^2	t_b	Prior Record X^2	t_b
Johnson (1941)	appellate review	(.09) (P=.76)	(.001)	Sample contains capital cases only				
Garfinkel (1949)	sentence (murder cases only)	(7.57) (P=.02)	(.008)	1st degree murder	(9.83) (P<.01)	(.015)		
				2nd degree murder & manslaughter	(.00) (P=.96)	(.001)		
Johnson (1957)	appellate review (capital cases only)	(11.33) (P<.01)	(0.17)	murder	(14.19) (P<.01)	(.029)		
				rape	(.92) (P>.30)	(.007)		
				burglary	(1.04) (P>.30)	(.025)		
Bedau (1964)	execution	(8.20) (P=.02)	(.012)	sample contains capital cases only				
Partington (1965)	sentence (rape cases only)	(46.06) (P<.01)	(.001)	Att'd rape	(30.26) (P<.01)	(.021)		
				Att'd stat. rape	(P=.14) (P=.14)	(.128)		
				Stat. rape	(5.48) (P=.02)	(.013)		
				Rape	(34.30) (P<.01)	(.006)		

Wolfgang et al. (1962)	appellate review (capital cases only)	4.33 P<.05	(.012)	felony murder	4.27 P=.04 .87 P=.35	(.023)	
				non-felony murder		(.007)	
Wolf (1965)	sentence (capital cases only)	4.157 P=.05	(.031)	felony murder	2.23 P=.14 .23 P=.63	(.036)	
				non-felony murder		(.004)	
Bedau (1965)	execution	(.06) (P=.97)	(.001)	sample contains capital cases only			
Judson et al (1969)	execution	(10.34) (P=.02)	(.043)	sample contains capital cases only	interval (P>.05) measure		.001*

*The value reported in this column is r^2, a measure analogous to t_b, at an interval level of measurement (see Costner, 1965).

predicting judicial disposition by 1.5 percent. The causal importance of this relationship, however, is called into doubt by the single study controlling simultaneously for charge, and related "third" variables. Thus, Judson et al. (1969) report a partial r^2 in this context of .001.[10] This relationship is not statistically significant at the .05 level.

INTER-RACIAL OFFENSES

Findings reviewed to this point suggest some reason to doubt the charge of racial discrimination in sentencing. One plausible path of analysis, however, remains to be examined. The hypothesis which we shall next examine is that it is in the context of *inter-racial* offenses, particularly those involving blacks victimizing whites, that differential sentencing is most likely to occur. This proposition has been tested in samples of both capital and non-capital offenses.

Table VI contains the single study (Green, 1964) offering a test of the inter-racial hypothesis in a sample of non-capital cases. Using a mode of analysis somewhat different from that of other studies considered in this review, Green first established the mean sentence received for robbery and burglary offenses in each of three offender-victim groupings. Next, "expected" means were calculated for each of the groupings on the basis of the specific offense, number of bills of indictment, and prior convictions characterizing the cases in each grouping. Comparisons of the observed and expected means, presented in Table VI, reveal that the discrepancies are small and in no consistent direction. The inter-racial hypothesis thus receives little support from this set of findings.

The implications of the findings in Table VII, containing samples of capital cases, are more disturbing. In this table, three of the five studies

report findings statistically significant at the .05 level, with a median tb of .021. The finding causing the most concern, however, is the relationship between race and sentence reported by Wolfgang and Riedel (1973). In this study of inter- and intra-racial rape in eleven southern states, the zero-order relationship between race and sentence produces a tb of .226. In other words, knowing the inter- and/or intra-racial make-up of rape cases, allows a 22.6 percent increase in the accuracy of predicting a life or death outcome for the defendants.

Unfortunately, Wolfgang and Riedel have not yet published data relating to a further control for the prior records of the offenders. Instead, they have simply indicated that such a control does not eliminate the statistical significance of the original relationship. Given our earlier discussion of the influence of sample size on the results of significance tests, we clearly cannot base any final conclusions on this information alone. Nevertheless, given the strength of the original relationship, it is safe to conclude that this study raises the definite suspicion of differential sentencing, even if it does not definitively establish its existence.[11]

Finally, it should be noted that four of the five studies reported in Table VII were carried out in the southern United States. The single study of sentencing in inter-racial capital cases conducted outside of the south (Judson et al., 1969), does not report statistically significant differences in the use of the death penalty by the race of offender and victim. The authors note in the text that this relationship remains non-significant in the presence of a control for prior record and several other possible suppressor variables.

---

[10]For a discussion of the techniques of partial correlation, see Blalock (1960: Ch. 19). For a discussion of the particular partial correlation used in this instance, see Judson et. al. (1969).

[11]A more convincing demonstration of the causal basis of the relationship would involve presentation of data including a *simultaneous* control for prior record, contemporaneous offenses, and type of rape charged (e.g., rape, attempted rape, statutory rape, attempted statutory rape). Presentation of this data would illustrate in more definitive terms what is suggested in the material already published.

Table VI. Inter-Racial Robbery and Burglary*

Robbery cases:	B-W	W-W	B-B	Total
Observed Means†	27.5	22.4	14.3	21.5
	(51)	(22)	(45)	(118)
Expected Means†	27.1	21.9	15.0	21.5
Burglary cases:	B-W	W—W	B—B	Total
Observed Means†	10.62	12.28	6.96	10.3
	(149)	(80)	(66)	(295)
Expected Means†	10.44	11.88	8.30	10.3

*This table is adapted from Green (1964); B-W = black defendant-white victim; W-W = white defendant-white victim; B-B = black defendant-black victim.

†"Means" refer to average sentence length in months.

SOCIO-ECONOMIC STATUS AS THE INDEPENDENT VARIABLE

Next to race, socio-economic status of the defendant is probably the most common suspect variable in studies of sentencing. Six of the studies available to this review have focused on the socio-economic status of the offender as an independent variable. Their findings are summarized in Tables VIII and IX.[12]

Looking at Table VIII, containing samples primarily of non-capital cases, we find statistically significant findings both before and after controls for the type of offense are introduced. The median t_b before controlling for type of offense is .020, and .024 after its introduction as a control. Holding offense constant, then, the median increase in the accuracy of predicting disposition, knowing socio-economic status, is 2.4 percent.

The most important findings in Table VIII, however, are found in Nagel's analysis of larcency cases in the federal courts. It was in federal larceny cases only that Nagel was able to control for both offense type and prior record

[12]In five of these studies (Martin, 1934; Forslund, 1969; Bedau, 1964; 1965; and Judson et al., 1969), the indicator of socio-economic status is occupation; in the sixth study (Nagel, 1969), the indicator is "indigent"or "non-indigent" financial status.

of the offender. Controlling only for the offense, Nagel's data indicate a statistically significant (P<.01) relationship between socio-economic status and sentencing (t_b=.024). However, when one controls for prior record, the relationship becomes statistically insignificant (at the .05 level) and diminished in strength (t_b=.008 and .009). When legally relevant factors are held constant, then, knowledge of social class increases accuracy in predicting the sentencing decision by less than one percent.

Somewhat different findings emerge from Table IX, containing studies in which the samples consist mainly of capital cases. While the first two studies in this table (Bedau, 1964; 1965) report findings that are statistically non-significant at the .05 level and weak in strength (t_b=.002 and .022), the final study (Judson et al., 1969), reports a relationship between socio-economic status and disposition which is statistically significant at the .001 level, and somewhat stronger in strength (r²=.048). This relationship remains substantially unchanged (r²=.032), and statistically significant (P<.01), following the introduction of controls for prior record and a series of other potentially contaminating variables. There is, then, evidence of differential sentencing by social class in the disposition of capital cases, in this study of jury sentencing in a non-southern state.

Table VII. Inter-Racial Capital Crimes

Study	Dependent Variable	Offense	Controls for Legally Significant Variables		Prior Record	
			X^2	t_b	X^2	t_b
Johnson (1941)	Appellate Review	Capital cases	(2.37) (P=.12)	(.019)		
Garfinkel (1949)	Sentence	1st Degree Murder	(8.38) (P<.01)	(.022)		
		2nd Degree Murder & Manslaughter	(.167) (P=.68)	(.001)		
Partington (1965)	Sentence	Rape Cases Only	(5.68) (P=.02)	(.063)		
Wolfgang et al. (1973)	Sentence	Rape Cases Only	275.71 P<.05	(.226)		
Judson et al. (1969)	Sentence	Capital Cases	(.008) (P=.93)	(.001)		

356

Table VIII. Socio-Economic Status as an Independent Variable (Non-Capital Cases)

Study	Dependent Variable	X^2	t_b	Controls for Legally Significant Variables					
				Offense	X^2	t_b	Prior Record	X^2	t_b
Martin (1934)	sentence	(180.63) (P<.01)	(.004)						
Forslund (1969)	conviction	(58.41) (P<.01)	(.016)						
Nagel (1969)	sentence			federal	(8.84) (P<.01)	(.024)			
	—state cases	(30.88) (P<.01)	(.030)	state assault	(23.75) (P<.01)	(.040)			
	—federal cases	(15.10) (P<.01)	(.023)	state larceny	(2.09) (P=.14)	(.017)			
	(larceny & assault cases)			federal assault	(12.70) (P<.01)	(.024)			
				federal larceny			none	(.124) (P=.26)	(.008)
							some	(2.76) (P=.10)	(.009)

Table IX. Socio-Economic Status as the Independent Variable (Capital Cases)

Controls for Legally Significant Variables

Study	Dependent Variable	Offense	X²	t_b	Prior Record	X²	t_b
Bedau (1964)	execution	capital cases	(.73) (P=.69)	(.002)			
Bedau (1965)	execution	capital cases	(3.23) (P=.20)	(.022)			
Judson et al (1969)	execution	first degree murder	(17.77) (P=.001)	(.048)*	interval measure	(P<.01)	(.032)*

*The value reported in this column is r^2, a measure analogous to t_b, at an interval level of measurement (see Costner, 1965).

Table X. Age as an Independent Variable (Non-Capital Cases)

Controls for Legally Significant Variables

Study	Dependent Variable	Offense	X²	t_b	Prior Record	X²	t_b
Martin (1934)	sentence		(14.01) (P<.01)	(.015)			
Green (1961)	sentence	burglary	60.30 P<.01	(.007)	none	4.0 P>.20	(.011)
Forslund (1969)	conviction		(22.49) (P<.01)	(.006)			
Nagel (1969)	sentence —state cases (1.92)(P=.17) —federal cases (1.38)(P=.24) (larceny & assault cases)	state assault / state larceny / federal assault / federal larceny	(1.33)(P=.25) / (4.61)(P=.03) / (.07)(P=.79) / (1.82)(P=.18)	(.004) / (.011) / (.001) / (.003)			

(state cases t_b (.002); federal cases t_b (.001))

AGE AND SEX AS THE INDEPENDENT VARIABLES

A final set of tables considers the role of age and sex as independent variables in the sentencing decision. Looking first at Tables X and XI, we find a number of studies reporting data on the role of age. Although three of the four studies in Table X initially report statistically significant relationships between age and disposition, these relationships are consistently small. The median value of t_b, before controlling for offense type and prior record, is .006. Following the introduction of these controls, Green reports that the relationship loses statistical significance (at the .05 level), and attains a value of t_b equal to .011. Similarly small relationships are the norm in Table XI, where studies involving capital cases are summarized.

Tables XII and XIII contain data from three studies which have considered the role of sex as an independent variable in judicial dispositions. The pattern of findings recorded in these tables is consistent with that contained in the findings derived from Green's (1961) research. Green's data indicate that when sex of the offender and final sentencing decision are related, without controlling for additional legal variables, the result is a t_b of .005, a finding significant at the .02 level. However, when offense type is held constant, and when only those cases of offenders with no previous convictions are considered, the resulting relationships are reduced below statistical significance, and the values attained by t_b are .001 and .004. This pattern is repeated in a study of capital cases by Judson et al. (1969). Thus, it may be concluded tentatively that the sex of the defendant plays a negligible role in the sentencing decision.

DISCUSSION

The central finding of this review of past research is that there is generally a small relationship between extra-legal attributes of the offender and sentencing decisions. In more concrete terms, the findings of this review can be summarized with reference to each of the four attributes considered:

(a) *Race*: Evidence of differential sentencing was found in inter-racial *capital cases* in the southern United States. In samples of *non-capital cases*, however, when offense type was held constant among offenders with *no* prior record, the relationship between race and disposition was diminished below statistical significance. Holding offense type constant, among offenders with "some" previous convictions, a modest, statistically significant relationship between race and disposition was sustained in two of three studies. The need for stricter control over the *number* of previous convictions was indicated.

(b) *Socio-Economic Status*: With social class as the relevant variable, some evidence of differential sentencing was again found in *capital cases* in a non-southern state. This finding withstood controls for legally significant factors. In a sample of *non-capital cases*, however, the relationship between class and disposition was diminished in strength, and reduced below statistical significance, by holding constant the effects of offense type and prior record.

(c) *Age and Sex*: In *capital and non-capital cases* alike, initial relationships between both age and sex, and judicial disposition, were reduced below statistical significance by the introduction of controls for legally relevant factors.

Several comments regarding these conclusions may be helpful in placing them in proper context. First, it should be noted that capital cases constitute a relatively small proportion of criminal cases. Second, samples of capital cases used in the studies we have considered often have included sentencing decisions made as far back as the turn of the century. Third, capital cases are frequently tried before juries, rather than judges. Several of the studies of sentencing in capital cases deal with jury dispositions only (Wolff, 1965; Judson et al., 1969), while others

Table XI. Age as the Independent Variable (Capital Cases)

Study	Dependent Variable	Offense	Controls for Legally Significant Variables				
			X^2	t_b	Prior Record	X^2	t_b
Bedau (1964)	execution	capital cases	(3.84) (P=.15)	(.008)			
Wolfgang et al. (1962)	appellate review	capital cases	(27.44) (P<.01)	(.067)			
Wolf (1965)	sentence	capital cases	.43 P=.51	(.008)			
Bedau (1965)	execution	capital cases	(1.24) (P=.54)	(.005)			
Judson et al. (1969)	execution	first degree murder	(.35) (P=.56)	(.001)			

Table XII. Sex as an Independent Variable (Non-Capital Cases)

				Controls for Legally Significant Variables					
Study	Dependent Variable	X^2	t_b	Offense	X^2	t_b	Prior Record	X^2	t_b
Martin (1934)	sentence	(3.29) (P=.99)	(.001)						
Green (1961)	sentence	9.1 P<.02	(.005)	felony			none	.02 P=.99	(.001)
				misdemeanor			none	1.45 P>.30	(.004)
Nagel (1969)	sentence —state cases	(2.77) (P=.10)	(.006)	state assault	(.66) (P=.42)	(.002)			
				state larceny	(6.46) (P=.01)	(.011)			
	—federal cases (larceny & assault cases)	(.37) (P=.54)	(.001)	federal assault	(.08) (P=.78)	(.001)			
				federal larceny	(1.54) (P=.21)	(.003)			

Table XIII. Sex as the Independent Variable (Capital Cases)

Study	Dependent Variable	Controls for Legally Significant Variables					
		Offense	X^2	t_b	Prior Record	X^2	t_b
Bedau (1964)	execution	capital cases	7.52 P<.01	(.033)			
Judson et al. (1969)	execution	first degree murder	(10.49) (P=.001)	(.041)	interval measure	P>.05	(.006)*

*The value reported in this colum is r^2, a measure analogous to t_b, at an interval level of measurement (see Costner, 1965).

concerned with inter-racial offenses focus *primarily* on jury decisions (*see* Garfinkel, 1949: 403). Such studies may, then, say more about the inadequacies of the jury system, particularly as it has been involved in the invocation of the death penalty, than about the general operations of the courts.

In commenting on the findings recorded in this review, it is also important to note that the authors of the original articles often suggested the occurrence of unjust discrimination, where our analysis has frequently indicated the weakness of the evidence "supporting" such inferences. One plausible explanation of this discrepancy returns us to a concern, voiced at the outset of this paper, regarding the uncritical use of tests of significance. It was noted that a problem with conclusions formed solely on the basis of significance tests is the tendency to confuse substantive and causal significance with statistical significance, thus short-circuiting the search for alternative explanations of relationships. In the studies here reviewed, analysis frequently stopped short of the consideration of important legal variables, while at the same time overlooking the size of the relationships reported.

Finally, the central finding of this discussion must be reemphasized. Review of the data from twenty studies of judicial sentencing indicates that, while there may be evidence of differential sentencing, knowledge of extra-legal offender characteristics contributes relatively little to our ability to predict judicial dispositions. Only in rare instances did knowledge of extra-legal attributes of the offender increase our accuracy in predicting judicial disposition by more than five percent.

CONCLUSIONS

The findings of this review have several important implications. One plausible response to the data reviewed would be the suggestion that official, fragmentary sources of data are necessarily inadequate to the question at issue. It could be suggested that what is required is longitudinal data, based on observations of defendants' experiences in transit through the criminal justice system. Attention would here be given to such factors as the circumstances of police-suspect encounters, arrest procedures, charge considerations, plea-negotiation, legal representation, bail arrangements and pre-sentence investigations.[13] These factors may operate cumulatively to the disadvantage of minority group defendants. A longitudinal approach might, then, make visible a sequence of events that seriously detracts from equality in sentencing.

It should be noted, however, that there is some research on earlier stages in the legal pro-

[13]Perhaps the most important of these factors is pre-trial incarceration and the use of bail (for example, see Engle, 1971).

cess that suggests conclusions surprisingly similar to those reported in this review (*see particularly* Bordua, 1969; Black, 1971). While such findings could hardly be interpreted as disputing the value of a vigilant concern for social justice, at the same time they do suggest the need for "new directions" in sentencing research (*cf.* Blumberg, 1967: 19; Lemert, 1971: 62).

A partial list of other approaches yet to be fully developed would include attention to the following: (a) the effects of such organizational constraints as case-loads, court referral rates, and fluctuations of space in treatment institutions; (b) the role of such community factors as recidivism rates, variation in offense patterns, and the publicity given to certain types of crimes; and (c) the importance of characteristics of those doing the judging, such as their cognitive styles, attitude sets, and perceptual patterns. Study of these variables will require an awareness of movement between different levels of analysis, and also use of some of the multivariate techniques that have to date received relatively little attention from those concerned with sentencing patterns in the criminal courts.[14]

There is, finally, one remaining possibility to be considered. It could be argued that extra-legal attributes of the offender are likely to exercise their influence at each stage of the legal process in *interaction* with the types of variables we have just discussed. For example, it is certainly plausible to expect variation in the attitudes of judges toward different groups of offenders. Variation in attitudes, in association with corresponding patterns in sentencing, could plausibly lead to a suppression effect, with the harsh sentences of less tolerant judges canceling out the lenient sentences of those judges more sympathetic to the group involved. A test of this hypothesis will require the researcher to go beyond the confines of official court data to obtain independent measures of judicial attitudes and related variables. Once again, then, official, fragmentary sources of data seem unable by themselves to provide the evidence sufficient to resolve important questions about the sentencing process. Definitive answers, it seems, must await the collection and analysis of new kinds of data on sentencing.

---

[14]Recent research by John Hogarth (1971) represents an important reconceptualization of the study of sentencing along many of the lines suggested in this discussion.

REFERENCES

Bedau, Hugo A. (1964) "Death Sentences in New Jersey," 19 Rutgers Law Review 1.

———— (1965) "Capital Punishment in Oregon, 1903–64," 45 Oregon Law Review 1.

Black, Donald (1971) "The Social Organization of Arrest," 23 Stanford Law Review 1087.

Blalock, Hubert A. (1960) Social Statistics. New York: McGraw-Hill.

Blumberg, Abraham (1967) Criminal Justice. Chicago: Quadrangle Books.

Bordua, David J. (1969) "Recent Trends: Deviant Behavior and Social Control," 369 The Annals of the American Academy of Political and Social Science 149.

Bullock, Henry (1961) "Significance of the Racial Factor in the Length of Prison Sentences," 52 Journal of Criminal Law, Criminology, and Police Science 411.

Camilleri, Santo F. (1962) "Theory, Probability, and Induction in Social Research," 27 American Sociological Review 170.

Chambliss, William J. and Robert B. Seidman (1971) Law, Order, and Power. Reading, Massachusetts: Addison-Wesley Publishing Co.

Costner, Hubert L. (1965) "Criteria for Measures of Association," 30 American Sociological Review 341.

Engle, C. Donald (1971) Criminal Justice in the City. Unpublished Ph.D. Dissertation: Temple University.

Forslund, Morris A. (1969) "Age, Occupation, and Conviction Rates of White and Negro Males: A Case Study," 6 Rocky Mountain Social Science Journal 141.

Garfinkel, Harold (1949) "Research Note on Inter- and Intra-Racial Homicides," 27 Social Forces 369.

Green, Edward (1961) Judicial Attitudes in Sentencing. London: Mac-Millan and Company Ltd.

—— (1964) "Inter- and Intra-Racial Crime Relative to Sentencing," 55 Journal of Criminal Law, Criminology and Police Science 348.

—— (1971) "Research on Disparities," in Leon Radzinowicz and Marvin Wolfgang (editors) Crime and Justice, Vol. II, The Criminal in the Arms of the Law. New York: Basic Books.

Hirschi, Travis and Hannan C. Selvin (1967) Delinquency Research: An appraisal of Analytic Methods. New York: Free Press.

Hogarth, John (1971) Sentencing as a Human Process. Toronto: University of Toronto Press.

Hunter, A. A. (1973) "On the Validity of Measures of Association: The Nominal-Nominal, Two-by-Two Case," 79 American Journal of Sociology 99.

Jacob, Hubert (1962) "Politics and Criminal Prosecutions in New Orleans,"8 Tulane Studies in Political Science 77.

Johnson, Guy (1941) "The Negro and Crime," 217 The Annals of the American Academy of Political and Social Science 93.

Johnson, Elmer H. (1957) "Selective Factors in Capital Punishment," 36 Social Forces 165.

Judson, Charles J., James J. Pandell, Jack B. Owens, James L. McIntosh, Dale L. Matschullat (1969) "A Study of the California Penalty Jury in First Degree Murder Cases," 21 Stanford Law Review 1297.

Kish, Leslie (1959) "Some Statistical Problems in Research design," 24 American Sociological Review 328.

Labovitz, Sanford (1969) "The Nonutility of Significance Tests: The Significance of Tests of Significance Reconsidered," 13 Pacific Sociological Review 141.

Lemert, Edwin M. and Judy Rosberg (1948) "The Administration of Justice to Minority Groups in Los Angeles County," 11 University of California Publications in Culture and Society 1.

Lemert, Edwin M. (1971) Instead of Court: Diversion in Juvenile Justice. Washington: U.S. Government Printing Office.

Mannheim, Hermann (1968) "Sentencing Revisited," in Marvin Wolfgang (editor) Crime and Culture. New York: John Wiley and Sons Inc.

Martin, Roscoe (1934) The Defendant and Criminal Justice. University of Texas Bulletin No. 3437: Bureau of Research in the Social Sciences.

Nagel, Stuart (1969) The Legal Process from a Behavioral Perspective. Homewood, Illinois: The Dorsey Press.

Overby, Andrew (1971) "Discrimination Against Minority Groups," in Leon Radzinowicz and Marvin E. Wolfgang (editors) Crime and Justice, Vol. II, The Criminal in the Arms of the Law. New York: Basic Books, Inc.

Partington, Donald (1965) "The Incidence of the Death Penalty for Rape in Virginia," 22 Washington and Lee Law Review 43.

Quinney, Richard (1970) The Social Reality of Crime. Boston: Little, Brown, and Company.

Sellin, Thorsten (1928) "The Negro Criminal: A Statistical Note," 140 The Annals of the American Academy of Political and Social Science 52.

Selvin, Hanan C. (1957) "A Critique of Tests of Significance in Survey Research,"22 American Sociological Review 519.

Selvin, Hanan C. and Alan Stuart (1966) "Data Dredging Procedures in Survey Analysis," 20 The American Statistician 20.

Southern Regional Council (1969) Race Makes the Difference. Atlanta.

Tompkins, Dorthy L. (1971) Sentencing the Offender: A Bibliography. University of California at Berkeley: Institute of Governmental Studies.

Wolf, Edwin (1965) "Abstract of Analysis of Jury Sentencing in Capital Cases: New Jersey: 1937–1961," 19 Rutgers Law Review 56.

Wolfgang, Marvin E., Arlene Kelly and Hans C. Nolde (1962) "Comparison of Executed and Convicted Among Admissions to Death Row," 53 Journal of Criminal Law, Criminology, and Police Science 301.

Wolfgang, Marvin E. and Marc Riedel (1973) "Race, Judicial Discretion, and the Death Penalty," 407 The Annals of the American Academy of Political and Social Science 119.

Zeisel, Hans (1957) Say it with Figures. New York: Harper & Row.

Rationales of Legal Intervention

WHEN AN INDIVIDUAL COMMITS A PUNISHABLE OFFENSE, IS DETECTED BY LAW enforcement personnel, and is found guilty in a court of law, he or she must somehow be punished within some formally prescribed, legislatively determined constraints. In this section we consider some of the social and philosophical rationales that seem to justify the pain inflicted upon the convicted offender and the evidence that exists to buttress each of these positions. The currently dominant rationale—rehabilitation/treatment/correction—is treated in detail in section six.

There has been a significant increase of interest and research in the area of deterrence. Will more severe and certain penalties prevent or reduce recidivism, or reduce the chances that a potential offender will engage in crime? It would be most instructive to gain an overview of the research regarding punishment and deterrence. Tittle's selection is a summary of deterrence research, with particular emphasis on the issue of the death penalty. Viewing direct and indirect investigative data, he points out methodological problems, defects of logic, and interpretive difficulties. The impact of certainty and severity of punishment is examined by Antunes and Hunt. They compare per capita crime rates in 49 states as to severity and certainty of punishment.

The risk of an individual committing a major offense is not extraordinarily high, while there is much greater probability that otherwise "good citizens" may well drink and drive. The problems associated with driving while intoxicated were of such importance that the city of Chicago instituted changes in court practices regarding this crime and made a short penal sentence mandatory. Superficial examination of what happened afterward seemed to indicate the success of this program, but Robertson shows that while drunken driving fatalities fell, when comparable data from Milwaukee were used for the same period, the best evaluation of the Chicago approach seems to indicate that it failed.

The unique nature of capital punishment as a legal penalty, and the manner in which recent Supreme Court decisions have affected it (as violating the Constitutional prohibition against "cruel and unusual punishment"), is studied by Bower. He investigates the deterrent effect of the death penalty by examining murder rates in adjacent states with and without capital punishment. Public reaction and support of capital punishment has often been said to be based on a belief in its punitiveness by persons who are authoritarian, politically conservative, and who desire revenge. Thomas and Foster propose, on the contrary, that the real factors underlying public support of the death penalty are fear of crime, a perception of the increasing crime rate, a belief in punishment as a deterrent, and a willingness to forcefully punish the criminal.

If evidence is not clear on the effectiveness of deterrence, an alternative model or rationale of punishment may be that of incapacitation, which in modern times means mandatory imprisonment for long periods, especially for career and repetitively violent offenders, who, at least while imprisoned, are not attacking the general public. Van Dine, working with data on adult offenders indicted in a one-year period, found that the most stringent penalties would have prevented relatively little violent crime.

In contrast to proposals for increased severity or extended use of incapacitating techniques, there is a current wave of sentiment and legislative proposals aimed at decriminalizing minor offenses now prohibited, usually in the areas of vice, gambling, and sex. Some of these crimes have become more or less socially acceptable forms of behavior. Geis's survey of criminal justice personnel and homosexual groups in seven states goes beyond the theoretical issues involved, and examines the consequences of decriminalization of consensual adult homosexuality. None of the predicted dire consequences, such as an increase of homosexual attacks or adult-juvenile homosexual seductions, seems to have occurred.

29. Punishment and Deterrence

CHARLES R. TITTLE

FEW ISSUES IN SOCIAL SCIENCE HAVE EVOKED SO much ideological debate as the question of whether punishment deters deviance. This controversy has been a two-edged sword. While it has kept alive an interest in the problem, it has at the same time inhibited thorough empirical investigation and has led to premature conclusions. Despite the fact that the question is essentially an empirical one, comparatively little research has been undertaken. As a result, social-scientific and lay opinion has always rested on a tenuous base, and the criminal law has been founded on a set of unproven assumptions.

For most of this century social scientists have been generally persuaded that punishment is relatively unimportant as a behavioral influence. For instance, a well-known criminological classic declares that punishment "does not deter . . . [nor] does it act as a deterrent upon others . . . ,"[1] and a popular contemporary text concludes that legal punishment is of limited effectiveness because "it does not prevent crime in others or prevent relapse into crime."[2] But recent changes in perspective have led to some reassessment of that position, and research since 1960 has provided empirical challenge to the orthodox view.

▶SOURCE: *"Punishment and Deterrence of Deviants,"* in Simon Rottenberg (Ed.) *The Economics of Crime and Punishment. Washington: The American Enterprise Institute for American Policy Research, 1973. Pp. 85–102. Reprinted by permission.*

[1]Frank Tannenbaum, *Crime and the Community* (Boston: Ginn and Co., 1938), p. 478.

[2]Walter C. Reckless, *The Crime Problem*, 4th ed. (New York: Appleton-Century-Crofts, 1967), p. 508.

I. PREVIOUS RESEARCH

The argument that punishment has little or no deterrent effect typically stems from two kinds of evidence. The best known concerns the relationship between capital punishment and homicide.[3] Included in this literature are investigations comparing crime rates of political units which differ in legal provision for the death penalty,[4] comparisons over a period of time of political units which use capital punishment for some periods but not others,[5] sequence studies focusing on the frequency of homicide following publicity about executions,[6] and illustrative case or historical episodes.[7] These investigations

[3]Edwin H. Sutherland and Donald R. Cressey, *Principles of Criminology* (Philadelphia: J. B. Lippincott, 1966), pp. 335–53.

[4]Karl F. Schuessler, "The Deterrent Influence of the Death Penalty," *The Annals*, vol. 284 (November 1952), pp. 54–62, and Thorsten Sellin, "Homicides in Retentionist and Abolitionist States," in *Capital Punishment* (New York: Harper and Row, 1967), pp. 135–38.

[5]Schuessler, "The Deterrent Influence"; Nigel Walker, *Crime and Punishment in Britain* (Edinburgh: University of Edinburgh Press, 1965), pp. 238–41; and Hans Mattick, *The Unexamined Death* (Chicago: John Howard Association, 1963).

[6]Leonard Savitz, "A Study in Capital Punishment," *Journal of Criminal Law, Criminology, and Police Science*, vol. 49 (November-December 1958), pp. 328–48; and Robert H. Dann, "The Deterrent Effect of Capital Punishment," *Friends Social Science Bulletin*, no. 29 (Philadelphia, 1935), as described in Mattick, *The Unexamined Death.*

[7]See Paul B. Horton and Gerald R. Leslie, *The Sociology of Social Problems* (New York: Appleton-Century-Crofts, 1965), pp. 165–69; and Harry E. Barnes and Negley K. Teeters, *New Horizons in Criminology* (Englewood Cliffs, N.J.: Prentice-Hall, 1959), pp. 315–17.

all indicate that capital punishment, at least as it has been practiced in recent decades, adds nothing in deterrent power beyond what is already accomplished by the next most severe penalty. From this base, many generalize that punishment per se must be ineffective.

A second well-known body of data is relevant to whether punishment other than death or permanent separation from society deters those punished from future offenses. In one study, corporal punishment was found to be unrelated to further offense,[8] and a study of the relationship between cumulative time in prison (days in) and cumulative time between discharges and reconvictions (days out) reported no correlation between the two.[9] Recidivism rates for releasees were also generally reported to be very high.[10] In addition, experimental animal studies provided a basis for discounting the deterrent power of negative sanctions. Although the effectiveness of punishment as a conditioning tool has been controversial, the typical interpretation in the past was that negative reinforcement was at best inefficient.[11]

Some information prior to 1960 supported the view that the threat of detection and punishment had some influence on deviance. For example, historical case material showed that crime sometimes increased when police were immobilized, and that it tended to decrease when police surveillance was increased or when technical innovations were employed.[12]

Nevertheless, most students of the subject interpreted the bulk of the data as contrary to a deterrent hypothesis.[13]

II. CONTEMPORARY VIEWPOINTS

Within the past few years, students of deviance have turned their attention away from the deviant act and have focused on social reaction to deviance.[14] Interest in negative sanctions as independent variables has blossomed, and many have come to question earlier interpretations and assumptions. Consequently, critical reassessment of the death penalty and recidivism research has taken place, and we now have a body of research concerned with the role of sanctions in generating conformity.

Review of the capital punishment research has identified a number of deficiencies that make it less useful in resolving the deterrence issue than previously thought.[15] One of the most important defects of that body of work is its inattention to the probability, or perceived probability, of imposition of the penalty. It has been noted that the effect of a legal provision for a death penalty may not be the same as the effect of a death penalty that is imposed with a reasonably high degree of certainty. Only Karl F. Schuessler attempted to take this dimension into

---

[8]See Robert G. Caldwell, "The Deterrent Influence of Corporal Punishment upon Prisoners Who Have Been Whipped," *American Sociological Review*, vol. 2 (April 1944), pp. 171–77.

[9]Norval Morris, *The Habitual Offender* (Cambridge, Mass.: Harvard University Press, 1951).

[10]Eleanor and Sheldon Glueck, *Criminal Careers in Retrospect* (New York: The Commonwealth Fund, 1943), p. 121; George B. Vold, "Does the Prison Reform?" *The Annals,* vol. 293 (May 1954), pp. 42–50; and Harry C. Westover, "Is Prison Rehabilitation Successful?" *Federal Probation,* vol. 22 (March 1958), pp. 3–6.

[11]B. F. Skinner, *Science and Human Behavior* (New York: Macmillan, 1953); Albert Bandura. "Punishment Revisited," *Journal of Consulting Psychology,* vol. 26 (1962), pp. 298–301.

[12]Jackson Toby, "Is Punishment Necessary?" *Journal of*

Criminal Law, Criminology, and Police Science, vol. 55 (September 1964), pp. 332–37; Johs Andenaes, "General Prevention—Illusion or Reality?" *Journal of Criminal Law, Criminology, and Police Science*, vol. 43 (1952), pp. 176–98; and Jerome Hall, *Theft, Law, and Society*, 2nd ed. (Indianapolis: Bobbs-Merrill, 1952), pp. 284–87.

[13]John C. Ball, "The Deterrence Concept in Criminology and Law," *Journal of Criminal Law, Criminology, and Police Science*, vol. 46 (September-October 1955), pp. 347–54.

[14]Jack P. Gibbs, "Conceptions of Deviant Behavior: The Old and the New," *Pacific Sociological Review*, vol. 9 (Spring 1966), pp. 9–14.

[15]See Paul W. Tappan, *Crime, Justice, and Correction* (New York: McGraw-Hill, 1960), pp. 253–55; Walker, *Crime and Punishment*, p. 241; Frank E. Zimring, *Perspectives on Deterrence*, Public Health Service Publication No. 2056, NIMH Center for Studies of Crime and Delinquency (Washington, D.C.: U.S. Government Printing Office, 1971); and Charles H. Logan, "Legal Sanctions and Deterrence from Crime" (Ph.D. diss., Indiana University, 1971).

account. Using a crude index of the certainty of execution, he found a negative ($-.29$), although nonsignificant, correlation between certainty of execution and the homicide rate—even though he was dealing with an attenuated distribution and a collection of low probability cases.[16] It is possible that if capital punishment were inflicted in a large proportion of the cases in which homicides occur, it would prove to be a deterrent. But since there are no systematic data from societies which have been both efficient in apprehension of offenders and willing to impose the death penalty, it is impossible to know whether it would be a deterrent under such conditions.

A second weakness of the capital punishment literature is its reliance upon anecdotal material.[17] The prevalence of crime in the face of possible capital punishment tells only how many offenses were not deterred; it does not indicate the number of contemplated deviant acts that may have been deterred. Similarly the number of convicted murderers who maintain that they did not consider the penalty before committing homicide reveals nothing about the number of potential murderers who may have taken it into account.

Finally, even if the death penalty research were impeccably valid, it would still reveal little about the deterrent power of punishment. The studies, without exception, really test whether capital punishment, as it is practiced in the modern world (that is, with a low probability of being used), adds anything additional to imprisonment as a deterrent. A valid test of the deterrent effect of capital punishment would be to pit it against the alternative of no punishment. We cannot interpret the fact that the threat of death apparently deters murder to no greater extent than the simple threat of imprisonment to mean that capital punishment does not deter at all; nor can we interpret it to mean that sanctions of all types are poor deterrents for all types of deviance. This latter point is especially applicable, since homicide is usually considered to be a unique kind of deviance.[18] Thus, although the death penalty literature provides sufficient justification for dispensing with capital punishment in modern society, it affords little basis for conclusions about the general question of whether sanctions influence behavior.

The use of recidivism literature as support for the pessimistic view of punishment has also undergone critical review. Among the most important problems in drawing general conclusions from this material is simply that recidivism data are applicable only to the question of specific deterrence (effect on the one punished) and not to general deterrence (effect on behavior in a population). Not only is it inappropriate to generalize from one level to the other, but it is actually reasonable to postulate that punishment might stimulate further deviance by the victim at the same time that it serves as a deterrent to those not punished.[19] The same mechanisms that labeling theorists point to as generators of secondary deviance, stigmatization, and rejection,[20] may also deter the nonstigmatized from engaging in the behavior that resulted in the label. In any case, specific deterrence is of far less importance than is general deterrence. Even complete specific deterrence would have little effect upon crime rates because only a small proportion of offenders are ever in a position to become recidivists.[21]

[16]See Schuessler, "The Deterrent Influence," and Quinn McNemar, *Psychological Statistics* (New York: John Wiley and Sons, 1955), pp. 149–50.

[17]See Walker, *Crime and Punishment*, p. 238, and Zimring, *Perspectives.*

[18]William J. Chambliss, "Types of Deviance and the Effectiveness of Legal Sanctions," *Wisconsin Law Review*, Summer 1967, pp. 703–19.

[19]Charles R. Tittle, "Crime Rates and Legal Sanctions," *Social Problems*, vol. 16 (Spring 1969), pp. 409–23; and Bernard A. Thorsell and Lloyd W. Klemke, "The Labeling Process: Reinforcement and Deterrent?" *Law and Society Review*, vol. 6 (February 1972), pp. 393–403.

[20]Edwin M. Lemert, "The Concept of Secondary Deviation," in *Human Deviance, Social Problems, and Social Control* (Englewood Cliffs, N.J.: Prentice-Hall, 1967), pp. 40–60.

[21]Leroy Gould and Zvi Namenwirth, "Contrary Objectives: Crime Control and Rehabilitation of Criminals," in Jack Douglas, *Crime and Justice in American Society* (Indianapolis: Bobbs-Merrill, 1971), pp. 256–57.

A second problem in drawing conclusions from recidivism studies, particularly studies of prison releasees, is that recidivism may be a by-product of prison life itself. These ancillary conditions may negate the effect of the punishment. For instance, the deterrent objective of incarceration—to increase fear of sanction—may be undermined by socialization into deviant subcultures and by exposure to deviant role models while incarcerated.[22] On the other hand, future conformity may be the product of rehabilitative efforts undertaken during incarceration rather than deterrence based on fear of punishment. Recidivism rates may, therefore, indicate more about the conditions under which the punishment is administered than about the punishment itself.

Further, a valid test of the specific deterrent effect of legal sanctions would involve comparisons of the recidivism of those punished with the recidivism of offenders who had experienced no contact with the law at all. Although there are really no data on this point (the government crime reports reveal, however, that rearrest is highest for those whose cases were previously dismissed or who were acquitted),[23] it hardly seems plausible that offenders who go undetected will be less likely to repeat an offense than those who are caught and punished.[24] True, comparison of recidivism of probationers with incarcerees suggests less effect for incarceration,[25] but there may well be a selective factor involved,[26] and probation is itself a form of legal punishment. Hence, one would conclude most appropriately from such comparisons that incarceration adds nothing in deterrent power to that which is achieved with the lesser penalty—rather than that incarceration or punishment in general fails to deter.

But even if these three considerations were not relevant, the recidivism literature would still not justify an antideterrent conclusion. Logical defects and interpretive difficulties have always plagued this type of work.[27] Moreover, the data are not so contrary to the deterrence argument as is usually assumed. While there are many variations and complexities, the available follow-up data suggest that instead of the widely believed 65 percent to 85 percent return-to-prison rate, only about 35 percent actually return.[28] And, a recent FBI study suggests that legal sanction may be more of a specific deterrent than even the FBI is willing to admit. By means of arrest reports, all offenders released from custody in 1963 were followed for six years. Although 65 percent were re-arrested on some charge during the follow-up period, only 23 percent, or 40 percent of those rearrested during the first four years, had been reconvicted by the end of the fourth year. Furthermore, extrapolation indicates an overall reconviction rate for the remainder of the offenders' lives somewhat below 35 percent.[29]

[22]Donald Clemmer, *The Prison Community* (Boston: Christopher Publishing Company, 1940), and Stanton Wheeler, "Socialization in Correctional Communities,"*American Sociological Review*, vol. 26 (October 1961), pp. 697–712.

[23]See United States Department of Justice, *Uniform Crime Reports* (Washington, D.C.: U.S. Government Printing Office, 1967), p. 37.

[24]Herbert L. Packer, *The Limits of the Criminal Sanction* (Stanford: Stanford University Press, 1968), p. 46.

[25]Martin A. Levin, "Policy Evaluation and Recidivism," *Law and Society Review*, vol. 6 (August 1971), pp. 17–46.

[26]Leslie T. Wilkins, *Evaluation of Penal Measures* (New York: Random House, 1969).

[27]See Walker, *Crime and Punishment*, pp. 242–60, and Wilkins, *Evaluation*.

[28]Daniel Glaser, *The Effectiveness of a Prison and Parole System* (Indianapolis: Bobbs-Merrill, 1964), pp. 13–35; and Wilkins, *Evaluation*.

[29]FBI, *Uniform Crime Reports*, p. 41. Since the *Uniform Crime Reports* neglect to report reconvictions in subsequent years, one must extrapolate. In so doing, however, we must take note of the possibility that the number of reconvicted may have risen as people arrested during the first four years came to trial at a later date and as additional arrests were made. Given that lag time in the judicial process is rarely more than two years, and that most of those rearrested during the six years covered by the follow-up were taken into custody during the first two years (66 percent), it is reasonable to assume that the vast majority of rearrestees had been tried by the end of the fourth year. If we assume, moreover, that the 40 percent rate of reconviction of arrestees applies only to those arrested during the first two years of the

Finally, recent comprehensive reviews of the experimental evidence concerning punishment conclude that, contrary to earlier beliefs, and even some current ones,[30] punishment can be highly effective in eliminating behavioral responses.[31] But more important, contemporary laboratory work points up the limitations of conditioning principles for human beings, and suggests that vicarious reinforcement (social learning) rather than operant conditioning, is more likely to be operative. Research on social learning has shown that vicarious negative reinforcement may play a very important role in the determination of human behavior.[32]

The research undertaken before 1960, therefore, provides little basis for judging the deterrent power of sanctions. At best, the evidence indicates that the issue is problematic. Certainly the data do not justify sweeping conclusions as to the inefficacy of sanctions.

III. RECENT RESEARCH

Along with a critical review of past research, contemporary perspectives have spawned a series of studies, most of which contradict previ-

ously held views that negative sanctions have little effect on behavior.

Direct Investigative Evidence

The experimental researchers working on the problem of vicarious learning have compiled some of the most interesting data on this subject. Numerous experiments have shown that observing others being rewarded or punished can influence the future behavior of the observers just as if they had been directly reinforced. Apparently this is the result of the individuals' having psychically experienced the feelings of those whom they observed being rewarded or punished. Presumably this same process is operative in nonlaboratory contexts, and it may even extend to vicarious conditioning from verbal reports. If so, it implies that general deterrence, to the extent that it occurs, is possible because citizens vicariously identify with punished individuals. And of course the same process might account for the failure or weakness of general deterrence, since much deviance is actually rewarded and most goes unpunished.

Other relevant data have been reported in a series of sociological and sociopsychological studies. The first involved an investigation by William J. Chambliss of obedience to parking regulations on a midwestern university campus in 1966. He found that significant reductions in parking violations by faculty members followed an increase in the certainty of apprehension and severity of penalties. The effect was especially strong for those who were frequent violators, but a significant proportion of the professors were unaffected because they seldom or never violated the rules.[33]

The second study was an attempt to assess the effects of a "sanction threat" and a "conscience appeal" on compliance with income tax laws. Taxpayers were randomly assigned to treatment and control groups. Before tax returns were submitted, one group was interviewed and asked questions suggesting the possibility that

---

follow-up, and if we project this conviction rate to cover all those arrested from the third through the sixth years, we arrive at a total reconviction rate of 26 percent for the original sample of releasees. Furthermore, during the fifth and sixth years an increment of only about 2 percent per year in additional arrests was added. Hence the reconviction rate of offenders released in 1963 would appear to be well below 35 percent even if one projects the follow-up far beyond the original six years.

[30] For example, see James B. Appel and Neil J. Peterson, "What's Wrong with Punishment?" *Journal of Criminal Law, Criminology, and Police Science*, vol. 56 (1965), pp. 450–53.

[31] See N. H. Azrin and W. C. Holz, "Punishment," in *Operant Behavior: Areas of Research and Application*, ed. Werner K. Honig (New York: Appleton-Century-Crofts, 1966), pp. 380–447; Albert Bandura, *Principles of Behavior Modification* (New York: Holt, Rinehart and Winston, 1969), pp. 293–353.

[32] Bandura, *Behavior Modification*, pp. 118–216, and Albert Bandura and Richard H. Walters, *Social Learning and Personality Development* (New York: Holt, Rinehart and Winston, 1963).

[33] See Chambliss, "The Deterrent Influence."

they might be punished if they misreported their incomes. A second group was reminded of their moral responsibility, while a third group was interviewed but asked none of the questions suggesting a "sanction threat" or a "conscience appeal." A fourth group was not interviewed. The "sanction appeal"and "conscience appeal" groups both reported significantly higher incomes than the control groups, but the appeal to conscience was found to produce greater reported income than the sanction threat. The effectiveness of the inducements was also found to vary by social characteristics of the subjects, particularly socioeconomic status. It was also discovered that among some subjects (35 percent) the "sanction threat" led to greater deduction claims, apparently as a result of attempts to recover "losses" suffered from more honest reporting.[34]

Although this particular study can be criticized because the "threat" and "conscience appeal" were not clearly expressed as such and because no attention was paid to how probable the subjects might have thought the sanction was, it provides powerful evidence in favor of a deterrent hypothesis. Still, it suggests that other variables may be more important in some instances than sanctions and that sanction threats may have produced countertendencies.

In 1967, Jai B. P. Sinha required pairs of experimental subjects to perform a difficult task with a financial reward as an incentive to successful completion. One member of each pair was a stooge. The test subjects were told not to help each other in performing the task, but they were allowed to give instructions to each other. Actual aid in response to the pleas of the stooges, therefore, represented cheating. In one condition the subjects were threatened with punishment, while in the other, no mention of punishment was made. Significantly less cheating occurred in the threat condition than the free condition. But among those who broke the rules, the number of violations was similar in each of the conditions. These data suggest that deterrence is likely to operate among those who have not transgressed, but that once violation occurs, the threat of sanction is less likely to inhibit further evidence.[35]

These studies were followed by two similar, but independently undertaken, investigations using official statistics. In 1968, Jack P. Gibbs constructed indexes of severity and certainty of punishment for homicide in each of the United States using FBI and prisoner statistics. He then examined the relationship between these indexes and homicide rates. The data showed strong negative associations which suggested that the greater the certainty of imprisonment and the greater the length of time in prison, the lower the homicide rate.[36]

In my own research in 1969, I used official statistics to develop indexes of the certainty of imprisonment and the severity of punishment for seven major offense categories and a category of total felonies.[37] The actual content of the indexes differed from those used by Gibbs, although they employed the same logic. Again the relationship between these indexes and crime rates indicated that low crime rates were likely to be present when there was a high probability of imprisonment for any offense. A negative relationship between the average length of prison time served and the crime rate, however, was present only for the offense of homicide. Other analysis highlighted a complex interaction, in their relationship to crime rate, between certainty of imprisonment and length of time spent in prison. Certainty generally corresponded to

---

[34]Richard D. Schwartz and Sonya Orleans, "On Legal Sanctions," *The University of Chicago Law Review*, vol. 34 (Winter 1967), pp. 274–300, and Richard D. Schwartz, "Sanctions and Compliance," Paper delivered at the Annual Meeting of the American Sociological Association, San Francisco, 1969.

[35]Jai B. P. Sinha, "Ethical Risk and Censure-avoiding Behavior," *Journal of Social Psychology*, vol. 71 (April 1967), pp. 267–75.

[36]Jack P. Gibbs, "Crime, Punishment and Deterrence," *Southwestern Social Science Quarterly*, vol. 48 (March 1968), pp. 515–30.

[37]Tittle, "Crime Rates."

lower crime rates regardless of the level of severity, but severity seemed to be associated with lower crime rates only when particular levels of certainty were extant.

The work by Gibbs and myself, described above, immediately led to research and commentary by others. In 1969, Louis N. Gray and J. David Martin reanalyzed Gibbs's data; in 1971 William C. Bailey, working with Martin and Gray, and Charles H. Logan, working separately, reanalyzed my data using more precise and rigorous statistical techniques. In all three instances the original findings were confirmed with the exception that Logan's results suggested a more important influence for severity of punishment than the original analysis.[38] In 1970 Theodore G. Chiricos and Gordon P. Waldo, however, employed similar indexes in studying, on the one hand, the association among certainty of imprisonment, severity of punishment and crime rates at different points in time, and, on the other hand, in looking at percentage changes in the indexes from time period to time period. Their analysis suggested to them that the evidence was too inconsistent to be accepted in support of deterrence theory. Furthermore, they challenged the original findings of Gibbs and myself on methodological grounds, with charges that the results were spurious and artificially produced.[39]

Logan, in turn, criticized the Chiricos and Waldo paper, arguing first, that their data concerning certainty of imprisonment were in fact remarkably consistent and even impressive (the authors observed this themselves but dismissed it because they believed it was an artifact); second, that their technique of studying the relationship between percentage change in two indexes was deceptive and unreliable since the base on which the percentages were calculated was so small; third, that it was inappropriate to relate measures of change in indexes selected arbitrarily at widely separated points in time; and fourth, that they maximized the likelihood of finding inconsistent results by using specific offenses only (excluding a category of total offenses), and by considering only small time periods.[40] Bailey, Gray, and Martin in another critique pointed out that much of the data used by Chiricos and Waldo were incomparable and incomplete.[41] Moreover, both critiques demonstrated that the Chiricos and Waldo methodological attack was without merit. Thus, my conclusions and those of Gibbs in support of deterrence theory appear to be well grounded, and some basis has been established for interpreting the Chiricos and Waldo findings concerning certainty of punishment as supportive of the deterrence notion.

In the same research vein, Logan in 1972 used higher order statistical techniques to analyze original arrest data provided by the FBI. The results were consistent with deterrence theory in revealing a generally negative relationship between arrest probability and crime rate for the states of the United States for all offenses except homicide.

Research of a different type was conducted by Richard G. Salem and William J. Bowers. In 1970, they examined the relationship between the severity of sanctioning policy in universities and the frequency of self-reported academic rule breaking by samples of students. In one analysis they found negative relationships which they interpreted as being indirect.[42] Their statistical elaboration suggested that peer disapproval

---

[38]Louis N. Gray and J. David Martin, "Punishment and Deterrence: Another Analysis of Gibbs' Data," *Social Science Quarterly*, vol. 50 (1969), pp. 389–95; William C. Bailey, J. David Martin and Louis N. Gray, "Crime and Deterrence: A Correlation Analysis," mimeographed, 1971; Charles H. Logan, "Legal Sanctions"; and idem, "General Deterrent Effects of Imprisonment," *Social Forces*, vol. 51 (September 1972), pp. 64–73.

[39]Theodore G. Chiricos and Gordon P. Waldo, "Punishment and Crime: An Examination of Some Empirical Evidence," *Social Problems*, vol. 18 (Fall 1970), pp. 200–17.

[40]Charles H. Logan, "On Punishment and Crime (Chiricos and Waldo, 1970): Some Methodological Commentary," *Social Problems*, vol. 19 (Fall 1971), pp. 280–84.

[41]William C. Bailey, Louis N. Gray, and J. David Martin in ibid., pp. 284–89.

[42]Richard G. Salem and William J. Bowers, "Severity of

may have intervened as the interpretive link between formal sanctioning policy and rule breaking. But in a later, more careful analysis, they concluded that the sanctioning policy did not have even an indirect effect, but was instead a dependent variable representing response to deviant behavior.[43] If it can be assumed that the later analysis using only one type of deviance is representative of all of the deviances considered in their earlier analysis, the Salem and Bowers data are contrary to deterrence theory. However, had the investigators taken into account the actual or perceived certainty that the university sanctioning policies would have been carried out, the results might have been different. Just as in the case of the capital punishment research, we find that a policy may differ considerably from what is usually done, and perceptions of either or both might be different still.

The importance of perceptions of the probability of experiencing a sanction is shown by two studies. In 1969, Gary F. Jensen examined the relationship between beliefs concerning the likelihood of being caught and punished and delinquency (self-reported and officially recorded). His measure of perceived certainty was quite crude—an expression of agreement with a statement implying high probability of apprehension/punishment for delinquent behavior generally—but the data still revealed negative associations.[44] Although those associations were not overpowering in magnitude, they are especially interesting because they deal with the question of deterrence at the level of cognition. Jensen's work confirms that many people misperceive the actual probability of apprehension and punishment, though delinquency was

directly related to perceptions. This is consistent with common sense reasoning that the effectiveness of sanctions actually depends upon perceptions about those sanctions—perceptions which may bear little relationship to reality but which may vary from individual to individual and from social group to social group as a result of other variables.

Further support for this notion is provided by Waldo and Chiricos. In a sample survey of students at a southern university, they found that perceived certainty of apprehension and penalty were negatively related to probability of marijuana use and theft, but more strongly to marijuana use than theft. The authors interpreted the findings as supportive of deterrence ideas but pointed out that such deterrence is most likely for crimes lacking moral endorsement in the population. They argue that for rules rooted in moral imperatives, official sanctions are secondary to informal pressures imposed by peers and others, or to control by internalized inhibitions. The authors found no support, however, for the proposition that perceived severity of sanction had any deterrent effect.[45]

Finally, an experimental test of the effect of a sanction threat and a moral appeal demonstrated that while college classroom cheating could be substantially deterred by a threat of detection and punishment, a moral appeal had no effect whatsoever.[46] The study also showed that the sanction threat produced greater deterrence among females than males and also among those who had less need to cheat than among those who had greater need. The evidence was interpreted as strongly supportive of deterrence theory, at least in a situation involving instrumental behavior, low commitment to

Formal Sanctions as a Deterrent to Deviant Behavior," *Law and Society Review*, vol. 5 (August 1970), pp. 21–40.

[43]William J. Bowers and Richard G. Salem, "Severity of Formal Sanctions as a Repressive Response to Deviant Behavior," *Law and Society Review*, vol. 6 (February 1972), pp. 427–41.

[44]Gary F. Jensen, " 'Crime Doesn't Pay': Correlates of a Shared Misunderstanding," *Social Problems*, vol. 17 (Fall 1969), pp. 189–201.

[45]Gordon P. Waldo and Theodore G. Chiricos, "Perceived Penal Sanction and Self-Reported Criminality: A Neglected Approach to Deterrence Research," *Social Problems*, vol. 19 (Spring 1972), pp. 522–40.

[46]Charles R. Tittle and Alan R. Rowe, "Moral Appeal, Sanction Threat, and Deviance: An Experimental Test," *Social Problems*, vol. 20 (Spring 1973).

the deviance, and a norm with little moral support.

Indirect Investigative Evidence

Other recent research is relevant to the deterrence question but is less directly applicable. In one 1963 study, Salomon Rettig and Harve E. Rawson asked students to judge the probability that hypothetical persons would perform unethical behavior in various kinds of situations. The situations varied with regard to the intent of the act, the type of victim, the certainty of apprehension, the severity of punishment, and the value of the behavior to the individual. Of the six variables, the one that most influenced the predictions of the actions of the hypothetical characters was the severity of punishment.[47]

In another piece of research the same questionnaire was answered by students who had participated one year earlier in an experiment. The experimental subjects had been paid to complete an essentially impossible task so that any reported success represented deviance. The results showed that those who had cheated in the experiment were far less sensitive to punishment as a behavioral influence on the hypothetical person than were those who had not cheated. Assuming that the judges were reflecting their own sensitivities in predicting the behavior of the hypothetical individuals, the authors concluded that "the reinforcement value of a censure is the most significant determinant which predicts unethical behavior."[48]

The same approach was used again by Rettig in 1964 when he compared the "ethical risk sensitivity" of reformatory inmates and a sample of college students. In predicting whether a hypothetical bank teller would embezzle funds, the prisoners more often took into account the teller's perception of the severity of censure than his consideration of gain, expectation of discovery, or intention to steal rather than borrow. The students also placed first priority on the severity of censure, but their predictions were more affected by considerations of gain and probability of detection than were the prisoners' predictions.[49]

In 1968, the original Rawson and Rettig technique was refined by Sinha, who changed the scale and included different ethically dubious behaviors in the hypothetical situations. He concluded that behavioral decisions involve different sets of considerations for various ethical situations and types of deviance. Unlike the previous researchers, he found that expectation for censure was the most important factor taken into account by the respondents, but he concluded that probability of censure and reinforcement value of the censure (severity) were interrelated in such a way that the effect of severity is contingent upon certainty,[50] a conclusion similar to one I reached in 1969 in another kind of study.[51]

In 1967, Daniel S. Claster compared a sample of incarcerated delinquents with a sample of nondelinquents with respect to the accuracy of their knowledge concerning probability of arrest and conviction for different crimes, the self-reported likelihood that they might engage in the various criminal behaviors, and for those who could conceptualize themselves as committing crimes, their perceptions of the probability that they might be arrested and convicted. The data showed no significant differences between the delinquents and nondelinquents in knowledge about the actual general certainty of arrest and conviction, but they did reveal that delin-

[47]Salomon Rettig and Harve E. Rawson, "The Risk Hypothesis in Predictive Judgments of Unethical Behavior," *Journal of Abnormal and Social Psychology*, vol. 66 (March 1963), pp. 243–48.

[48]Salomon Rettig and Benjamin Pasamanick, "Differential Judgment of Ethical Risk by Cheaters and Non-cheaters," *Journal of Abnormal and Social Psychology*, vol. 69 (July 1964), p. 112.

[49]Salomon Rettig, "Ethical Risk Sensitivity in Male Prisoners," *British Journal of Criminology*, vol. 4 (October 1964), 582–90.

[50]Jai B. P. Sinha, "A Note on Ethical Risk Hypothesis," *Journal of Social Psychology*, vol. 76 (October 1968), pp. 117–22.

[51]Tittle, "Crime Rates."

quents who said they might engage in different crimes perceived the likelihood of personal arrest and conviction to be lower than did the nondelinquents who admitted that they might do the deviant things.[52]

Irving M. Piliavin and his associates were concerned with whether potential informal sanctions ("personal costs") differentiated delinquents from nondelinquents[53] and whether concern with informal personal costs was predictive of laboratory cheating.[54] Perceived personal costs were measured by questionnaire responses to items concerning the importance to the individual of favorable opinions from significant others such as parents or teachers. A survey revealed a negative association between perceived personal costs and delinquency, while the experiment demonstrated that "low cost" boys cheated more than "high cost" boys.

There is also a series of studies focusing on the use of sanctions by one person to induce obedience by another individual to commands. In 1969 J. Horai and James T. Tedeschi had college students play an interpersonal game ("prisoner's dilemma") in an experimental situation. One player was allowed to use sanctions in an effort to get the other player to act against his self-interest. They varied the credibility of the sanctions (probability of imposition) as well as the severity. Both were observed to be instrumental in generating compliance.[55] The next year Tedeschi repeated the experiment with Thomas Faley using ROTC cadets and varying the status of the threatener as well as the severity and credibility of the threats. Again certainty and severity of the sanction threat were found to influence the degree of compliance, and the results showed greater compliance to threats by high status persons than to threats by low-status individuals.[56] In 1970, James Gahagan and others conducted a similar experiment in which they varied the pattern of punishment as well as the credibility of threat. They were able to confirm the importance of certainty of sanction but found no effect for patterning.[57] All three experiments suggest that compliance with interpersonal commands is affected by sanction threats.

These indirect studies are all consistent with the proposition that negative sanctions bear importantly upon behavior. But the data are too oblique and involve too many dubious assumptions to permit anything more than tenuous suggestions. Rettig and Rawson did not ask their subjects how they would behave in the various situations; they asked them how they thought a hypothetical person would behave. Thus, while they probably measured the variables which the subjects thought were generally operative in behavioral decisions, these might not be the variables which are operative. Similarly Claster failed to examine the relationship between self-assessed likelihood of deviant behavior and perceived probability of personal arrest and conviction. He reported only how the delinquents and nondelinquents who thought they might commit deviant acts differed in perceptions of the probability of personally experiencing sanctions. And the Piliavin studies neglected the subjects' perceptions of the probability of their de-

[52]Daniel S. Claster, "Comparison of Risk Perception Between Delinquents and Non-delinquents," *Journal of Criminal Law, Criminology, and Police Science*, vol. 58 (March 1967), pp. 80–86.

[53]Irving M. Piliavin, Jane Allyn Hardyck, and Arlene C Vadum, "Constraining Effects of Personal Costs on the Transgressions of Juveniles," *Journal of Personality and Social Psychology*, vol. 10 (1968), pp. 227–31.

[54]Irving M. Piliavin, Arlene C. Vadum, and Jane Allyn Hardyck, "Delinquency, Personal Costs, and Parental Treatment: A Test of a Cost-Reward Model," *Journal of Criminal Law, Criminology, and Police Science*, vol. 60 (July 1969), pp. 165–72.

[55]J. Horai and James T. Tedeschi, "Effects of Credibility and Magnitude of Punishment on Compliance to Threats," *Journal of Personality and Social Psychology*, vol. 12 (February 1969), pp. 164–69.

[56]Thomas Faley and James T. Tedeschi, "Status and Reactions to Threats," *Journal of Personality and Social Psychology*, vol. 17 (February 1971), pp. 192–99.

[57]James Gahagan, James T. Tedeschi, Thomas Faley and Svenn Lindskold, "Patterns of Punishment and Reactions to Threats," *Journal of Social Psychology*, vol. 80 (February 1970), pp. 115–16.

viance being found out by others significant to them, perceptions of the probability that "costs" would result from discovery, or even perceptions of the probability of getting caught. They just assumed that all these probabilities were perceived as high, or at least high enough to generate an effect. Finally, the experiments about interpersonal control did not involve real rewards for winning; they also are restricted in applicability because obedience to individual orders may not be comparable to conformity with social norms or laws.

Case Materials

Other evidence comes from contemporary case material. Increases in some types of crimes have been recorded in situations where police were immobilized,[58] and decreases in crime following greater police surveillance or improvements in police techniques have been registered.[59] Perhaps the best data of this type are those presented by H. Lawrence Ross and his associates in 1970. They employed a time-series design to study the effect of the British breathalyser law of 1967. This legislation made it possible for suspected drinkers or traffic offenders to be tested immediately, and under the law a person who was ultimately convicted would receive a mandatory penalty. If it can be assumed that fewer traffic casualties indicates fewer cases of drinking while driving, then the data clearly demonstrate that the law had a substantial impact. Since the purpose of the law was to increase the probability of detection and penalty for driving while drinking, its effect strongly supports a deterrent interpretation.[60]

Case material concerning situations in which severity of penalty was varied, however, have not supported a deterrent hypothesis. Although most of these studies have equivocal interpretations,[61] one clear-cut investigation was conducted by Barry Schwartz in 1968. He found no basis for concluding that the amount of rape in Philadelphia was significantly affected by increased penalties.[62]

In general, recent case material is consistent with the other research in suggesting that sanctions have some deterrent effect when the probability of imposition is reasonably high, but that the severity of sanctions in the absence of certainty seems to bear little relationship to future deviance.

IV. SYNTHESIS

What, then, can be concluded from the recent research? It seems quite clear from this work that social scientists must at least take the deterrence question seriously. Almost all research since 1960 suggests that the deterrence hypothesis is worth considering, at least as far as certainty of sanction is concerned. Enough suggestive data have been reported to mandate systematic research efforts and to compel theoretical consideration of sanctions in the search for explanations of human behavior and social organization. But it is equally obvious that the research conducted so far is not definitive.

---

[58]Gerald Clark, "Black Tuesday in Montreal: What Happens when the Police Strike," *New York Times Magazine*, November 16, 1969, p. 45ff.; and Johs Andenaes, "The General Preventive Effects of Punishment," *University of Pennsylvania Law Review*, vol. 114 (1966), pp. 949–83.

[59]See Zimring, *Perspectives*, pp. 68–73; Walker, *Crime and Punishment*, pp. 241–42; John E. Conklin, *Robbery and the Criminal Justice System* (Philadelphia: J. B. Lippincott, 1972), p. 143.

[60]H. Laurence Ross, Donald T. Campbell, and Gene V. Glass, "Determining the Social Effects of a Legal Reform:

The British 'Breathalyser' Crackdown of 1967," *American Behavioral Scientist*, vol. 13 (March-April 1970), pp. 493–509.

[61]See Patrik Tornudd, "The Preventive Effect of Fines for Drunkenness," in *Scandinavian Studies in Criminology*, vol. 2 (Oslo: Univereitetsforlaget, 1968), pp. 109–24; Donald T. Campbell and H. Laurence Ross, "The Connecticut Crackdown on Speeding: Time-Series Data in Quasi-Experimental Analysis," *Law and Society Review*, vol. 3 (1968), pp. 33–53, and Gene V. Glass, "Analysis of Data on the Connecticut Speeding Crackdown as a Time-Series Quasi-Experiment," *Law and Society Review*, vol. 3 (1968), pp. 55–76.

[62]Barry Schwartz, "The Effect in Philadelphia of Pennsylvania's Increased Penalties for Rape and Attempted Rape," *Journal of Criminal Law, Criminology, and Police Science*, vol. 59 (December 1968), pp. 509–15.

The only safe conclusion it permits is that sanctions probably have some deterrent capability under some circumstances. There are many gaps in our knowledge which must be filled before we can speak with confidence on the subject.

First, we do not know what influence the type of norm has on the degree of deterrence that is possible. Sociological literature suggests that the type of norm ought to make a difference. Some norms are thought to provoke obedience irrespective of sanctions while others seem to invite disobedience despite provisions for sanctions.[63] Research has dealt with a wide variety of norms, from parking regulations and arbitrary rules to serious felonies. Yet so many other variables have been involved and the measurement of the degree of deterrence achieved has been so crude that specifying variation by type of norm is impossible with present data. Adequate data would demonstrate the relative degree of deterrence for norms that vary in specificity, importance, legitimacy, legality, formality, and moral status.

Second, it is presently unknown how much difference the type of behavior makes with respect to effectiveness of deterrence. Some behaviors are intrinsically rewarding while others are rewarding only for purposes of achieving long-range goals. Furthermore, the same behavior may have high utility for one person but low utility for another, or it may have high utility for the same person in one situation but not another. Thus, deterrence may be more or less possible depending upon the strength of motivations involved; it may also be dependent upon the kind of motivations that are operative. It is reasonable to imagine that acts of rebellion, behavior in search of martyrdom, behavior undertaken to reinforce a deviant identity, or deviance in protest of injustice would be less deterrable than deviance undertaken for other purposes.

The value of an act to the actors has always been of key importance in deterrence theory. Yet few studies have attempted to take this into account. Most assume that motivation is equal across behaviors and individuals. But without some control of this variable, knowledge of the effects of sanctions will always be incomplete.

The type of behavior may be important in other ways as well. Sanctions may have more influence upon behavior that is subject to reasoned calculation than on emotional or impulsive behavior.[64] Finally, a distinction might have to be made concerning the position of an act in a series of potential deviant acts. Sinha's 1967 experiment and much of the recidivism research suggests that once a sanction threat fails to deter an act, its potency as a deterrent to further deviant acts by that person may be eroded.

Third, evidence is especially lacking concerning the impact of sanction threats upon various types of people. Social class, age, sex, race, social visibility of occupation, personal alienation from the political and social system, and moral commitments to the norms may all be major determinants of the probability that deterrent effects will be possible in various situations. But there are presently no systematic data to assess this possibility or to establish how much relative difference these various social characteristics might make.

Fourth, aspects of the sanctions themselves, no doubt, have a great deal to do with deterrence. Several studies have indicated that the certainty of experiencing a threatened sanction is a key variable, although the importance of severity has been shown to be more problematic. Other dimensions of probable importance include whether the sanction is to be imposed on a formal or an informal level, the status of the sanctioner, the celerity with which the sanction is applied, and the universality of imposition.[65] But again one must rely on theoretical, rather

---

[63]See William J. Chambliss, "Types of Deviance and the Effectiveness of Legal Sanctions," *Wisconsin Law Review*, Summer 1967, pp. 703–19; and H. Taylor Buckner, *Deviance, Reality, and Change* (New York: Random House, 1971).

[64]See Chambliss, "Types of Deviance."

[65]Alexander L. Clark and Jack P. Gibbs, "Social Control: A Reformulation," *Social Problems*, vol. 12 (Spring 1965), pp. 398–415.

than empirical, guidelines in considering these dimensions. One is especially handicapped in trying to answer questions about the interrelationship of these dimensions in their impact upon conformity. It has been suggested that some sanction characteristics are contingent upon others. Formal sanctions may be generally effective only when reinforced by informal sanctions or when the certainty of punishment is high.[66] Similarly, severity of sanction may come into play only after certain levels of certainty have been achieved.[67]

But beliefs or perceptions about sanctions may be more important than actual sanction characteristics. Ignorance probably constitutes the major component of deterrence. Anxiety probably influences behavior more than raw fear, at least as far as legal norms are concerned. After all, the chance of experiencing a sanction for most crimes is miniscule,[68] and the severity of punishment frequently turns out to be relatively light.[69]

If individual fear of sanction has a bearing on behavior, surely cognitions are key linkages; since cognitions probably vary somewhat independently of reality, then the most useful knowledge is not actual sanction characteristics, but what those characteristics are perceived to be by different categories of people. For instance, the propensity of middle-class people to refrain from ordinary crime may be at least partly a result of their gross overestimate of the probability that they would be caught, and of their perception of punishment as more severe than it might actually turn out to be. Middle-class people usually have little personal experience with law enforcement processes, and they therefore are in no position to judge accurately.

Lower class individuals, however, often have frequent contact with the legal system and consequently know that the probability of being caught and punished is really not great and that being legally sanctioned is not unbearable. But even if objective knowledge about sanctions were available to all, people would still perceive the personal costs differently.

It is important to note that the relationship between perceptions of sanction characteristics and deviance might not be simple or linear. It is possible that some people may be stimulated to engage in deviance by a certain amount of risk,[70] but that this incentive diminishes when the risk becomes so great that it is no longer a gamble. The relationship for such people would be curvilinear, while for others it might be linear or log linear. Unfortunately there are very few data about these matters, so we are left to speculation.

Not only may sanctions influence the amount and kind of deviance, but the relationship is probably reciprocal, at least for legal sanctions. Once we can identify and describe the causal influence of sanctions under various conditions, we will then have to attack the problem of separating the effects of sanctions on deviance from the effects of deviance upon sanction reactions.

Fifth, it is a total mystery how the various factors that have been discussed are interrelated in the generation of conformity. Surely these variables do not operate in a vacuum; they occur in combinations, and the effect of each is probably influenced by the presence of the others. Some evidence already suggests that dimensions of sanctions interact in crucial ways. But when it is recognized that characteristics of norms, of the subject population, and of the behavior may all mesh in endless varieties, it becomes clear that theoretical questions about deterrence have not even been addressed, much less resolved.

Finally, other variables may affect conformity

---

[66]Jackson Toby, "Is Punishment Necessary?" *Journal of Criminal Law, Criminology, and Police Science*, vol. 55 (September 1964), pp. 332–37, and Ernst W. Puttkammer, *Administration of Criminal Law* (Chicago: University of Chicago Press, 1953).

[67]Tittle, "Crime Rates."

[68]Logan, "Legal Sanctions," pp. 80–81.

[69]See the National Prisoner Statistics, "Prisoners Released from State and Federal Institutions" (Washington, D.C.: Bureau of Prisons, U.S. Justice Department, 1960).

[70]Carl Werthman, "Delinquency and Moral Character," in *Delinquency, Crime, and Social Process*, ed. Donald R. Cressey and David A. Ward (New York: Harper and Row, 1969), pp. 613–32.

independently or they may combine with sanction variables in influencing behavior. Social scientists have at one time or another attributed significance to biological propensities, internalization of moral standards, beliefs about the amount of deviance that is occurring, imputed legitimacy of the general normative system, peer acceptance or rejection, relative deprivation, self-concepts, and symbolically learned motivations.[71] But we don't know how important each of these is, how important they are relative to sanctions, or how they might influence sanction-related variables. Understanding of conformity/deviance will not be complete until statements can be made about how each of the factors discussed here is generally and specifically operative in the production of conformity.

V. CONCLUSION

Despite the confidence expressed by some, it is clear that very little is known about the role of

[71]See Albert K. Cohen, *Deviance and Control* (Englewood Cliffs, N.J.:Prentice-Hall, 1966).

sanctions in generating social order. Enough research evidence has accumulated to justify serious consideration of the question. But this paper has outlined so many gaps in knowledge that need to be filled that closing them would require decades of full-time work by hundreds of social scientists. It is time that we begin in earnest to supply that information, remembering that the task is not an easy one. The job requires many kinds of data gathered in a wide variety of circumstances, with numerous research methods. Productive outcomes will depend upon clearer definitions and conceptual formulations than have been found in the past. In an area so prone to ideological contamination, moreover, we must exercise great effort to generate and preserve a spirit of objective inquiry. Nevertheless, if social order is to be understood and if fundamental assumptions on which so many social institutions rest are to be evaluated, we must turn our attention to this long-neglected problem.

30. Certainty and Severity of Punishment

GEORGE ANTUNES
A. LEE HUNT

"THE ABSENCE OF INFORMATION CAN ITSELF both give rise to and ensure the continued dominance of irrational modes of thought and action. For a vacuum created by the absence of surmise, random speculation and unsupported assumption."[1]

It is generally agreed that a legitimate reason for the existence of governments is to procure for the citizenry the safety and security of their persons and possessions. Unfortunately, governments are never fully successful in this regard, with the result that they have as a major problem the task of reducing dangerous crime. Many public officials in the United States have advocated the use of more severe penal sanctions as a means of deterring crime.[2] Unfortu-

nately, very little research has been conducted to ascertain the deterrent effect of criminal sanctions, or to determine the possible impact of longer prison sentences on levels of serious crime. The preponderance of arguments both for and against punitive sanctions are founded on ethical grounds or "common sense," and generally have been advanced without scientific support.[3] Indeed, implicit in our criminal justice policies are the hypotheses that the certainty and severity of punishment will deter crime.[4] However, scholars have undertaken relatively little systematic research to discover the extent to which these hypotheses enjoy empirical support.

The relevant research can be covered briefly. First, however, it will be helpful to distinguish two types of deterrence: *special* (the specific deterrence of a given individual), and *general* (the overall reduction in crime due to the inhibitory effect of sanctions on an aggregate of persons). As Packer notes:

"These two are quite different although they are

▶SOURCE: *"The Impact of Certainty and Severity of Punishment on Levels of Crime in American States; An Extended Analysis. The Journal of Criminal Law and Criminology* (1973) 64:486–493. Reprinted by permission.

[1]F. Zimring and G. Hawkins, *Deterrence: The Legal Threat in Crime Control* 17 (1973).

[2]Former FBI Chief J. Edgar Hoover once noted:
"I warn you to stay unswerving to your task—that of standing by the man on the firing line—the practical, hard-headed, experienced honest policemen who have shown by their efforts that they, and they alone, know the answer to the crime problem. That answer can be summed up in one sentence—adequate detection, swift apprehension, and certain, unrelenting punishment. That is what the criminal fears. That is what he understands, and nothing else, and that fear is the only thing which will force him into the ranks of the law-abiding."
E. Sutherland and D. Cressey, *Criminology* 347 (8th ed. 1970). For more recent statements by President Richard Nixon on the same theme, *see* R. Harris, *Justice* (1970).

[3]See Levin, "Crime as a Deterrent," 72 New Statesman 9 (1966). See also Van Den Haag, "On Deterrence and the Death Penalty," 78 *Ethics* 280 (1968).

[4]For example, over twenty years ago Edwin Sutherland observed the following:
"The conventional policy has been to punish those who are convicted of crimes, on the hypothesis that this both reforms those who are punished and deters others from crimes in the future. Also, according to this hypothesis, crime rates can be reduced by increasing the severity, certainty, and speed of punishment."
E. Sutherland, *Principles of Criminology* 613 (4th ed. 1947).

often confused in discussion of problems of punishment. For example, it is sometimes said that a high rate of repeat offenses, or recidivism as it is technically known, among persons who have already been once subjected to criminal punishment shows that deterrence does not work. The fact of recidivism may throw some doubt on the efficacy of *special* deterrence, but a moment's reflection will show that it says nothing about the effect of *general* deterrence."[5]

It is general deterrence which we wish to examine in this paper. Thus, we may safely disregard the rather extensive literature indicating that both incarceration and "treatment" intended to reform are often markedly unsuccessful in attaining that goal.[6]

We may also disregard the studies focusing on the deterrent effect of capital punishment.[7] We do so because capital punishment, although quite severe, is remarkably uncertain. Murder is the only crime for which execution has been employed enough to be statistically meaningful. However, whatever the findings of research on the deterrent effect of capital punishment may be, they cannot be generalized to crimes other than murder. Further, it should be noted that there are some problems in generalizing the deterrent effect of capital punishment even to the set of all murders. The vast bulk of persons convicted of homicide are incarcerated, not executed. In fact, the death penalty rarely has been imposed in recent years. Even those sentenced to death are able to delay execution through lengthy, and often successful, appeals.[8]

[5]H. Packer, *The Limits of the Criminal Sanction* 39 (1968).

[6]For a general overview of much of this work, see Sutherland and Cressey, *supra* note 2, at 607–36. See also Schur, "The New Penology: Fact or Fiction? 49 *J. Crim. L.C. & P.S.*331 (1958).

[7]It should be obvious that the capital punishment literature must, of necessity, focus on the question of general deterrence, since the excuted person is incapable of future behavior which would indicate successful individual deterrence. The various studies of capital punishment have revealed no evidence of deterrent impact beyond that obtained from lengthy incarceration. For a good collection of articles and research bearing on this topic, see *Capital Punishment* (T. Sellin ed. 1967).

[8]For example, in the state of Maryland, during the period

We now turn our attention to other empirical studies of the deterrent impact of sanctions.[9] One major thrust in the empirical literature involving the study of murder is an initial work by Gibbs.[10] He constructed aggregate measures of certainty of punishment based on the number of state prison admissions for homicide in 1960, divided by the mean number of homicides known to police for 1959 and 1960. Severity of punishment was measured as the median number of months served by all persons in prison on December 31, 1960. Although some may take exception to the respective measures of these variables, we find the operations adequate. Utilizing data from the Federal Bureau of Investigation's *Uniform Crime Reports*[11] and the *National Prisoner Statistics*,[12] Gibbs computed certainty and severity values for each of the forty-eight states *circa* 1960.[13] Dichotomizing this data, Gibbs used Chi-square tests and phi correlations to assess the impact of certainty and severity of punishment on rates of homicide known to the police in 1960.

Gibbs reported an inverse relationship be-

1936–1961, only 59 percent of those sentenced to death for rape were actually executed. See Sutherland and Cressey, *supra* note 2, at 35.

[9]Empirical research on general deterrence falls into three areas: violations of college rules, homicide and other crimes. For a look at the deterrent impact of sanctions on violations of college rules, see Chamblis, "The Deterrent Influence of Punishment," 12 *Crime and Delinquency*70 (1966); Salem and Bowers, "Severity of Formal Sanctions as a Deterrent to Deviant Behavior," 5 *Law and Society Rev.* 21 (1970). However, the validity of generalizing from these particular offenses and sanctions to more serious crimes involving long prison sentences can be questioned. Thus, this literature review shall focus on the remaining two sets of studies.

[10]Gibbs, "Crime, Punishment, and Deterrence," 48 *Soc. Sci. Q.* 515 (1968).

[11]FBI, *Uniform Crime Reports* (1960).

[12]Bureau of Prisons, U.S. Dept. of Justice, *Prisoners Released from State and Federal Institutions*1960 (National Prisoner Statistic Series).

[13]Gibbs actually computes values for only 47 states. His certainty and severity values for the New Jersey area are computed as the average of the values obtained for New York and Connecticut. (New Jersey does not cooperate with the Federal Bureau of Prison's statistical reporting effort).

tween the homicide rate and both independent variables, and concluded that his findings, contrary to common assertion, demonstrated evidence of a relationship between the crime rate and legal reactions to crime.

Following Gibbs, and utilizing the same data, Gray and Martin[14] reported a series of regression models which also demonstrated moderate, inverse associations between the variables. Specifically, the homicide rate correlated −.37 with severity, and −.28 with certainty. The multiple correlation indicating the combined effects of both certainty and severity on homicide was .47, thus accounting for 22 percent of the variance. Gray and Martin also computed several regression analyses in which the data were subjected to a natural logarithm transformation. This produced no change in the correlation between certainty and homicide, but the correlation of the latter with severity increased to −.51. The multiple correlation of the transformed data increased to .61, accounting for 38 percent of the variance.[15] Gray and Martin concluded that the independent variables have a demonstrable, and equally weighted, impact on the homicide rate.

Attempting to clarify methodological issues raised in these studies, Bean and Cushing[16] performed a second re-analysis of Gibbs' data. They found that the data did not violate assumptions of normality, and therefore did not need to be transformed in order to meet the assumptions for using multiple regression. They also tested the data for departures from linearity. When no significant departures were found, they con-

cluded that the logarithmic transformation models presented by Gray and Martin did not result in a significant increase in prediction and, thus, the models must be ruled out on the grounds of parsimony.

Bean and Cushing extended the Gray and Martin model by incorporating an etiological variable. Examining the residuals of the multiple regression of certainty and severity on homicide rate, they found that "most of the large positive residuals occurred for southern states and most of the large negative residuals for non-southern states."[17] To investigate the hypothesis that the effects of certainty and severity are contingent upon region, a revised regression model incorporating "region" as a variable was tested.[18] This resulted in the squared multiple correlation increasing from .22 to .69. Indeed, the squared correlation between region and homicide rate was a startling .62.

The concept "region" is a surrogate for various unmeasured variables.[19] To demonstrate the theoretical importance of "region," Bean and Cushing replace this variable with a measure of "percent black population."[20] Utilizing this variable and measures of certainty and severity as the independent variables, they observe a squared multiple correlation of .76. Examining the slopes of the certainty and severity variables in this regression, they conclude that when

---

[17]*Id.* at 283.

[18]This was done with standard "dummy variable" techniques. Those unfamiliar with these procedures should refer to Suits, "Use of Dummy Variables in Regression Equations,"52 *J. Amer. Stat. Ass'n.* 548 (1957).

[19]See D. Campbell and J. Stanley, *Experimental and Quasi-Experimental Designs for Research* (1963), where the authors discuss the fact that including "region" as a variable is an attempt to control for differences in specific history.

[20]Bean and Cushing note that:

"the findings elsewhere that there is a higher homicide rate among blacks than whites and the fact that the southern states in general have a higher proportion of black population than do the nonsouthern states, [thus presents] a reasonable hypothesis that the etiological significance of region consists in differences in the proportion black among state populations."

Bean and Cushing, *supra* note 16, at 287.

---

[14]Gray and Martin, "Punishment and Deterrence: Another Analysis of Gibbs' Data,"50 *Soc. Sci. Q.* 389 (1969).

[15]It should be noted that because of the log transformation, the form of the regression equation is nonlinear. Expressed in terms of the raw variables, the "multiple regression" equation is of the form

$$Y = aX_1^{b_1}X_2^{b_2} + e, \text{ where "a" is a constant,}$$

X_1 is certainty, X_2 is severity, b_1 and b_2 are least squares coefficients and "e" is an error term.

[16]Bean and Cushing, "Criminal Homicide, Punishment, and Deterrence: Methodological and Substantive Reconsiderations," 52 *Soc. Sci. Q.* 277 (1971).

percent black population is controlled as an etiological variable, "the variable measuring legal reactions to crime retained its association with criminal homicide rate in a direction consistent with the deterrence hypothesis."[21]

These studies of homicide converge on the finding that certainty and severity of punishment exhibit a moderate deterrent impact. One might ask, however, whether this is typical of the relationship between these two independent variables and other types of crimes. A separate set of deterrence studies examines this question, primarily by utilizing the seven FBI Index crime categories.

Tittle[22] analyzed data on the FBI Index crimes, including homicide.[23] Although his operational measures of certainty and severity differed slightly from those employed in previous studies, this work seems generally comparable.[24] All the variables were grouped into rank categories and the ordinal statistic Tau c was employed to assess the impact of certainty and severity on crime rates for each of the seven crime categories. This analysis produced a moderate to weak inverse association between certainty and crime rates for each of the seven crimes. These ranged from a high of $-.57$ for sex offenses to a low of $-.08$ for auto theft. The correlation between murder and certainty was $-.17$. However, when the severity variable was examined a *negative* association, $-.45$, was

found *only* between severity and homicide. The relationship between severity and each of the six other crime categories was *positive*, ranging from a high of .26 for sex offenses to a low of .04 for auto theft. These findings are contrary to the commonly proposed deterrence hypothesis.[25]

Waldo and Chiricos also incorporated the seven FBI Index crimes in an examination of the impact of certainty on crime rates across three time points: 1950, 1960 and 1963.[26] Two time points were utilized in testing the impact of severity: 1960 and 1964. This analysis further sought to assess the impact of changes in levels of certainty and severity on two dependent variables: crime rates and changes in crime rates. All the data were dichotomized, and phi correlations were computed as measures of impact. With respect to certainty, the results for all three time periods generally supported the findings of Tittle and others. All the correlations were negative and low to moderate in magnitude, with the exception of homicide in 1950, which was $+.02$.[27]

No pattern emerged from the analysis of changes in levels of certainty and severity on changes in crime rates. Waldo and Chiricos conclude that evidence in support of a deterrent impact for levels of certainty or severity on crime rates is not sufficiently demonstrated in

---

[21]Bean and Cushing, *supra* note 16, at 289.

[22]Tittle, "Crime Rates and Legal Sanction," 16 *Social Problems* 409 (1969).

[23]In addition to homicide, the FBI collects data on six other categories of serious crimes: rape, assault, larceny, robbery, burglary and auto theft. FBI reports often combine crimes in all seven categories to obtain an overall index of serious crime, hence the designation of these seven crimes in the scholarly literature as "index" crimes.

[24]Tittle combines data from two time points, 1960–1963. Certainty for each category of crime is as follows: the number admitted to prison for crime "x" in 1960 and 1963 divided by the number of crime "x" known to police in 1959 and 1962. Severity is defined as the mean length of sentence served for crime "x" by those released from state prisons in 1960. Crime rates for each category were obtained by averaging data from 1959 and 1962.

[25]Observing that controls for urbanization all but eliminate the association between severity and crime rate, Tittle remarked:

"Severity alone is simply irrelevant to the control of deviance. Severity of punishment may serve other functions, of course, and high degrees of severity might be explained as reactive responses by legislatures and judicial personnel to high offense rates, particularly where the certainty of punishment is likely to be low—as in urban areas (where the association between certainty and urbanization is $-.52$)."

Tittle, *supra* note 22, at 416.

[26]Chiricos and Waldo, "Punishment and Crime: An Examination of Some Empirical Evidence," 18 *Social Problems* 200 (1970).

[27]For the time period 1964, Chiricos and Waldo reported negative correlations of severity with homicide ($-.03$), assault ($-.08$) and larceny ($-.09$). Chiricos and Waldo, *supra* note 26.

their analysis to justify acceptance of the deterrence hypothesis.[28]

SUMMARY OF CONCLUSIONS FROM EMPIRICAL RESEARCH ON DETERRENCE

First, it is evident that certainty of punishment has a mild deterrent impact on crime rates. This is demonstrated in all the studies reviewed, in spite of varying measurement operations, time points and methods of analysis. At least in this respect, the theory of deterrence receives some support.

Secondly, severity of punishment exhibits a moderate deterrent impact on homicide rates, but is unrelated to crime rates for other types of crimes. If this is the case, what attributes distinguish homicide from the other six crime categories which would account for the differential deterrent impact of severity? Several aspects of homicide can be considered in this regard. From studies of the etiology of crime we know that murder, in contrast to other types of crime, occurs in or near the home. The murderer is usually a member of the family or someone well known to the victim. Finally, in contrast to many other crimes, murder is usually done without reflection in a moment of high passion.[29] From this, the following points can be drawn:

1.   All other things being equal, the deterrent impact of certainty and severity should be greater for a rational, economic crime like burglary, than for a spontaneous emotional crime like murder.

2.   Since there is frequently a connection between murderer and victim, most murders are "solved." This means that the certainty rate for murders as a category of crime should be much higher than the certainty rate for other types of crime. This is borne out by the data reviewed above.[30]

With respect to the existing research findings, these two points imply the following:

1.   Certainty, acting alone, has a deterrent impact on crime rates.

2.   Given the impact of severity on murder, severity should have an even greater impact on other crimes. Since it does not, it is plausible to hypothesize that *severity only has a deterrent impact when the certainty level is high enough to make severity salient.* Any deterrent impact from severity depends on the level of certainty.[31]

Severity can be most effectively integrated into a deterrence theory by formulation of a model in which the effects of severity operate interactively with the effects of certainty. The basic hypothesis would be that deterrence, as measured by crime rate, is some function of the product of certainty and severity. A more complicated model allows a separate causal link between deterrence and certainty, as well as that between the product of certainty and severity. (These models are described in greater detail, as models 3 and 2 respectively, in Figure 1.)

Figure 1.   Alternative Regression Models

$$(1)\ y = a + b_1C + b_2S + e$$
$$(2)\ y = a + b_1C + b_2CS + e$$
$$(3)\ y = a + b_1CS + e$$
$$(4)\ y = a + b_1C + e$$
$$(5)\ y = a + b_1S + e$$

[28]Chiricos and Waldo, *supra* note 26, at 211–213. This contention is refuted by Bean and Cushing, *supra* note 16, at 279.

[29]See the discussion in an excellent review by Wolfgang, *Homicide,* in 3 *International Encyclopedia of the Social Sciences* 490 (1968).

[30]Tittle found that mean certainty ranged from a high of .47 for homicide to a low of .015 for auto theft. Over half of all offense categories had a mean certainty value below .1. Our analysis yielded similar figures.

[31]How high is "high enough" is an empirical question. It may also be the case that this parameter will differ across types of crime. However, the general functional relationship can be expressed as a function of the product of certainty and severity.

RESEARCH DESIGN

The dependent variable in the analysis performed in this paper is "crime rate." This is a *per capita* measurement of the number of crimes per 100,000 inhabitants in each of 49 states.[32] Seven categories of crime are examined as dependent variables: homicide, sex crimes, robbery, assault, burglary, larceny and auto theft.

Certainty of imprisonment and severity of sentence are determined for each of these crime categories and are treated as independent variables. The "certainty" variable is calculated by dividing the number of persons admitted to prison for a given crime in year "x" by the number of the type of crime known to police in year "x-1." The measure of "severity of sentence" is the median length of sentence served by all those in prison for a given crime on any specified reporting date.

The number of crimes known to police in 1959 and 1960 and the crime rates for 1960 were collected from the FBI's *Uniform Crime Reports, 1960*. Information about admission to state prisons and median sentence length were obtained from the Federal Bureau of Prisons'*Characteristics of State Prisoners.*[33] Thus, in this analysis, "certainty" will be indicated by the number of persons admitted to state prisons in 1960 divided by the number of crimes known to the state police in 1959. "Severity" is the median sentence served by persons incarcerated on December 31, 1960.

One aim of this study is to extend the analyses of Tittle and of Chiricos and Waldo through the application of interval level statistics to similar data. We thereby avoid the limitations imposed by collapsing data into ordinal or nominal categories, and instead, may retain information about relationships which is frequently lost by the use of the less powerful nonparametric techniques.

Accordingly, we employ the following techniques in our analysis: First, we replicate Tittle's work by computing the bivariate relationships between certainty and crime rate for each of the seven index crime categories. Then, we make the additional comparison of crime rates and severity. The combined predictive effects of certainty and severity considered simultaneously are then explored through a series of linear multiple regressions.

To examine the hypothesis that severity has a deterrent impact on crime rates only under conditions of high certainty, we compute for each type of index crime a regression model of the following form:[34]

$$y = a + b_1CS + e$$

where: y is a crime rate
   a is a constant
   b_1 is a least squares regression coefficient
   C is certainty of imprisonment
   S is severity of sentence
   e is the residual error

In this equation, note that severity, whatever its value, will have a predictive impact only when certainty is greater than zero. As certainty approaches one, severity approaches its maximum impact value. The second hypothesis—that certainty has an independent deterrent effect in addition to the effect of its interaction with severity—is explored through a regression equation of the form:

$$y = a + b_1C + b_2CS + e$$

where: y is a crime rate
   a is a constant
   b_1 and b_2 are least squares regression coefficients
   C is certainty of imprisonment
   S is severity of sentence
   e is the residual error

---

[32]The list of states examined include the District of Columbia and Hawaii. New Jersey and Alaska are omitted due to lack of information in the data source.

[33]Federal Bureau of Prisons, U.S. Dep't of Justice, *Characteristics of State Prisoners* (1960).

[34]For an elementary discussion of bivariate and multiple regression, see H. Blalock, *Social Statistics* (2d ed. 1972). The use of non-linear regression models is discussed in Hamblin, "Mathematical Experimentation and Sociological Theory: A Critical Analysis," 34 *Sociometry* 423 (1971).

A listing of the five alternative regression models to be examined is provided in Figure 1. We turn now to an analysis of our data in order to ascertain the empirical viability of the alternative models.

ANALYSIS OF THE DATA

The first step in the analysis consists of a series of bivariate regressions between certainty and severity (as independent variables), and crime rates (as the dependent variable) for the seven index crimes. Table I presents the product-moment correlations and the regression slopes from these equations.

Turning to these results, we observe that the correlations on "murder" agree with other findings reported, i.e., certainty and severity demonstrate a slight negative relationship with homicide rates. Furthermore, for all seven categories of index crimes, these results generally agree with those reported by Tittle and also by Waldo and Chiricos. Certainty exhibits a slight to moderate negative relationship with each of the seven types of crime rate, while severity demonstrates a weak positive relationship (with the exception of homicide). In our analysis, we found, unlike Tittle, a negative relationship between the crime rate for larceny and severity. However, the magnitude of the correlation is so slight (−.06) that no inference about the sign is allowable.

On the basis of the findings presented in Table I we, too, would be led to reject the hypothesis that both certainty and severity have a deterrent effect on crime. The evidence mustered at this point would suggest a policy direction which aims at increasing the certainty of punishment. The commonly held opinion that severe sentencing will lead to a reduction in crime rates simply finds no empirical support in these data.

Noting the anomalous results with regard to the relationship between homicide rate and severity, we were led to our original hypothesis that severity would have a deterrent impact on crime rates only under conditions of high certainty. Accordingly, we outlined two possible configurations of this interactive relationship in the regression models presented in Figure 1. These models represent an exploratory attempt to create a viable, parsimonious theory of deterrence in which predictive capabilities are enhanced without the necessity of including additional variables.

The usefulness of these regression models with respect to each of the seven crime categories may be ascertained by examination of Table II, which offers a summary of the explanatory capabilities (as expressed by R^2) for each of these models for each type of crime.

In the summary presented in Table II, models 4 and 5 represent, respectively, the simple linear effects of certainty of punishment and

Table I. Bivariate Regressions of Crime Rates in States (1960) on Certainty and Severity for Seven Categories of Crime

Crime Category	Certainty			Severity		
	Slope	r	r^2	Slope	r	r^2
Murder	−4.3	−.19	.04	−.07	−.39	.15
Rape	−8.1	−.56	.31	.13	.30	.09
Robbery	−75.0	−.32	.10	.48	.10	.01
Assault	−118.2	−.27	.07	2.10	.18	.03
Burglary	−3639.8	−.40	.13	5.10	.09	.01
Larceny	−1441.7	−.36	.13	1.36	−.06	.00
Auto-theft	−1807.3	−.30	.09	.09	.03	.00

Table II. Summary of Predictive Models (R^2)

Regression Model	1 (C + S)	2 (C + CS)	3 (CS)	4 (C)	5 (S)
Dependent variable:					
Homicide	.21*	.19	.19*	.04*	.15*
Rape	.31	.31*	.20*	.31*	.09
Robbery	.11*	.16*	.07*	.10*	.01
Assault	.08	.15	.13*	.07*	.03
Burglary	.16	.16	.12*	.13*	.01
Larceny	.14*	.18*	.18*	.13*	.00
Auto-theft	.10	.09	.06*	.09*	.00
Average R^2	.16	.18	.14	.12	.04

*Slope(s) of the regression equation negative.

severity of sentence actually served acting alone on actual crime rates. In these models we make observations which are consistent with our initial bivariate observations, that is, severity, acting alone, accounts for very little of the explained variation in crime rates, regardless of type of crime. Furthermore, the regression coefficients for model 5 are almost all positive in sign (the exceptions being homicide and larceny), indicating that higher levels of severity are associated with *higher* levels of crime. The positive nature of this association is worthy of only passing notice, since the strength of association is generally slight. With the single exception of homicide rate, the severity variable consistently accounts for less than ten percent explained variation, and, in four types of crime, predicts less than one percent. Of the five alternative regression models, the severity model (number 5) is the weakest predictive scheme.

Considering the effects of the certainty variable acting independently, the average variance explained increases to 12 percent. For all seven categories, the slope of the regression equation is negative. Thus, these correlations are interpretable as demonstrating a consistent deterrent effect on levels of crime.

In the simple multiplicative model 3, the average amount of explained variance is fourteen percent. More importantly, every regression

slope in this model is negative in direction, supporting a deterrence interpretation.

Model 1 considers the linear, additive effects of certainty and severity. For homicide, burglary and auto theft this model is one of the strongest predictors, with an average R-square of .16. However, only three of the seven equations have the requisite negative regression slopes. Thus, the increased predictive power is of little use because the model cannot provide interpretations to consistently support the deterrence hypothesis.

In model 2, the effects of severity are not only examined in an interactive context with certainty (as in model 3), but allowance is made for an additional, separate link between certainty and crime rates.[35] This model articulates the more elaborate hypothesis about the conditions under which severity may combine with certainty to influence crime rates. However, from the data analysis, we see that model 2 is not markedly better in predictive power than either the simple additive or simple multiplicative models (models 1 and 3 respectively). Moreover, the regression slopes in model 2 are negative for

[35] Two related models, $y = a + b_1C + b_2C^2S + e$ and $y = a + b_1C + b_2C^3S + e$, were also computed. There proved to be little difference between these and the simpler Model 2. To simplify the presentation, only the results from Model 2 are reported.

only three of the seven dependent variables.[36] Thus, model 2, although viable in terms of predictive power, generally does not conform to the requirements of a deterrence model.

SUMMARY AND CONCLUSION

In this paper we have attempted to distinguish the independent and interactive effects of certainty of punishment and severity of sentence on the level of crime rates in the American states. We have applied several regression models in a test of the effects of these variables in the general deterrence of crime.

From this analysis we find no support for severity of sentence acting alone as a deterrent to crime. However, we find a consistent, moderate effect for certainty of punishment acting to reduce crime rates. Attempts to improve predictive capability through a theoretically formulated model, in which severity exerts an impact on crime rates only under conditions of high certainty, are partially successful. The more complicated version of this model, which hypothesizes both an effect from certainty and severity combined, and a separate effect from certainty acting alone, is the best predictor of crime rates. Nevertheless, it is theoretically uninterpretable. The simpler model, in which certainty and severity combine to jointly influence crime rates, demonstrates good prediction relative to the alternative arrangements of the independent variables. It is theoretically interpretable. In our judgment, this model plausibly demonstrates that certainty and severity do have a moderate deterrent effect upon rates of crime. However, it should be kept in mind that certainty, considered by itself, has a moderate deterrent effect for all crimes, while severity acting

alone is not associated with lower rates of crime. When certainty and severity are combined, as is the case of our model, then the impact of severity is filtered through the certainty value. This means that increasing severity in a condition of low certainty will have little effect on crime rates.

As Zimring and Hawkins have noted, sentences in the United States are currently quite severe in comparison to those imposed in Western Europe.[37] It is quite likely that spending additional funds to keep convicts in prison for longer periods of time will not result in any meaningful increase in general deterrence. Monies spent in this fashion will simply be wasted. Indeed, increasing the severity of sentences may have the unintended consequence of reducing the level of special deterrence through increased recidivism. There are a number of reasons why more severe sentences might cause higher rates of recidivism. Among them are the increased social stigmatization associated with longer sentences, the inability of those sanctioned and released to live normally in society after prolonged incarceration and a heightened sense of alienation and injustice caused by lengthy incarceration under a condition of low certainty of imprisonment. In our opinion, the appropriate criminal justice policy is one which attempts to reduce crime by increasing the probability of apprehension and prosecution.[38] This would have the advantage of not only increasing the level of general deterrence, but might also result in an increased sense of the fairness of punishment and lower rates of recidivism.

[37]E. Zimring and G. Hawkins, *supra* note 1, at 56.

[38]Such a policy runs contrary to the commonly held opinion that crime can be reduced by dealing more harshly with those convicted of crimes. For a discussion of some of the difficulties involved in attempting to implement a policy of increasing certainty rather than severity see Antunes and Hunt, "The Deterrent Impact of Criminal Sanctions: Some Implications for Criminal Justice Policy," 51 *J. Urban Law* 145 (1973).

[36]Although not reported in Table 2, an inspection of the four non-conforming regression equations for Model 2 indicates that in two equations certainty slopes are positive, while in the other two equations the slopes of the product terms combining certainty and severity are positive.

31. Deterring the Drunk Driver

LEON S. ROBERTSON
ROBERT F. RICH
H. LAURENCE ROSS

EXCESSIVE DRINKING IS INVOLVED IN OVER ONE-half of the motor vehicle associated fatalities in the United States (Department of Transportation, 1968). Various means have been suggested, and some tried, to curb these losses. In only a few cases have countermeasures against driving while intoxicated been subjected to scientifically acceptable evaluation as to effectiveness.

In one such study, Barmack and Payne (1964b) used an information program with administrative review and psychiatric referral in an attempt to reduce alcohol-related crashes by airmen at an Air Force base. Based on their earlier studies (1964a) showing various types of stress-related and deviant behavior associated with driving while intoxicated, the image of the intoxicated driver as "sick" was communicated in meetings, on bulletin boards, and in the base newspaper. Airmen who lost time because of injury in a privately-owned vehicle had their service records reviewed, and evidence of "ineffective behavior" could result in discharge or psychiatric referral. The psychiatrist could then recommend a medical discharge, suggest psychiatric therapy, or take no action.

Comparison of the injury rate in the year preceding and the year of the program showed a significantly lower injury rate after three months of the program, and for the remainder of the year of the study. Comparison of the injury rate over the year of the study with national data and with comparable data from another Air Force base during the same time period as the program showed a significantly lower rate on the Air Force base where the program was conducted.

These findings suggest that alcohol countermeasures can be effective. However, it is undoubtedly more difficult to initiate and administer a program such as this where people are not under as wide an administrative control as is the case in the military. The most commonly employed approach in civilian jurisdictions has been the imposition of legal sanctions through the police and court systems.

An example of good research to evaluate the effects of legal countermeasures is the use of the interrupted time series (Ross, et al., 1970) to show successfully that alcohol countermeasures adopted by the British Government significantly reduced the incidence of fatalities during certain times of the day and week. The British Road Safety Act, effective October 9, 1967, authorized the police to subject a suspect to a breath test for alcohol *prior* to arrest. (The pre-arrest test has not been legislated in most U.S. jurisdictions although every state now has an "implied consent" law which is uniformly applied subsequent to arrest.) Those drives with blood alcohol concentration above 0.08% by weight as indicated by a breath test were taken to a police station for further tests. If the first

▶SOURCE: *"Jail Sentences for Driving While Intoxicated in Chicago: A Judicial Policy That Failed," Law and Society Review (Fall, 1973), 8:55–67. Reprinted by permission.*

test was corroborated by a second breath test and, then, a blood or urine test, the driver was arrested and was subject to a one-year driving license suspension, and a fine of £100 or imprisonment for up to four months or both. The Act was widely publicized before it was put into effect. Ross, Campbell, and Glass showed that the level of the time series of fatalities and "serious casualties" was reduced significantly in England beginning in October 1967, particularly in late night hours when alcohol is most often involved in crashes (Department of Transportation, 1968). These findings have led to legislation providing for pre-arrest breath testing in a few jurisdictions in the United States (Insurance Institute for Highway Safety, 1971).

The purpose of this paper is to use the interrupted time series to study the effect on fatalities in Chicago of the highly publicized use of 7-day jail sentences as a countermeasure against driving while intoxicated during the winter and spring of 1971. Arrests and processing of cases are also examined. We emphasize that we were not involved in the planning or implementation of the Chicago "crackdown." This study is based on data collected from police, coroner, and court records.

JAIL SENTENCES IN CHICAGO

In late December 1970 and the first six months of 1971, magistrates in Chicago's traffic courts were directed by the supervising judge to sentence persons convicted of driving while intoxicated (DWI) to seven days in jail and to recommend to the Secretary of State's office that such drivers' licenses be suspended for one year. This policy was publicly announced and widely publicized on December 15 and implemented beginning on December 18, 1970. The policy was at first announced as ending January 2, 1971, but subsequent extensions through midsummer were announced based on claims that fatalities had been greatly reduced (Field, 1971). These claims were based on a percentage change in fatalities during the holiday period from the previous year.

The rationale for the Chicago crackdown was based on a study of convictions for DWI conducted by the Circuit Court's Psychiatric Institute. From April 6, 1970 to the end of July 1970, the first ten persons convicted of DWI each day were placed on probation and referred to the Circuit Court's Psychiatric Institute for examination and diagnosis. Of the cases examined, 8% admitted being "alcoholics" and an additional 12% were diagnosed as alcoholics. On the basis of the psychiatric examinations, it was concluded that "80% of the new arrests will involve social drinkers *only*" (Kelleher, 1970).[1] Chicago officials concluded that the fatalities involving alcohol resulted mainly from social drinking and that 7-day jail sentences for persons convicted of DWI would deter social drinkers from drinking an amount likely to involve them in fatal crashes (Field, 1971). Note that no attempt was made to change the method of detecting impaired drivers by police, as was provided in the British law. Indeed, Illinois at that time had no implied consent law providing penalties if a driver refused to be tested for alcohol after he was arrested.[2]

INTERRUPTED TIME-SERIES ANALYSIS

The interrupted time-series model has been revised since its use on the British data to test for a change in upward or downward slope of the curve in addition to the changes in its general level as illustrated in the British data (Ross, et al., 1970). Using the revised model, it is possible to test whether either of these types of changes in the time series can be attributed to chance.

A short-term change in a time series, such as the reduction in fatalities observed by Chicago officials, may occur for a number of reasons. Events simultaneous with those intended to evoke the change, e.g., favorable weather condi-

---

[1]We reserve critique of this study and its conclusions for the discussion.

[2]Such laws are required in order to meet the Highway Safety Program Standards issued in 1967 by the Secretary of Transportation as authorized by the Federal Highway Safety Act of 1966.

tions, may actually produce the outcome. A long-term trend, unrelated to the action taken, may have developed and the short-term change may be only a part of it. The methods used to measure the outcome, i.e., police statistics, may have changed or initial measurement, e.g., publicity regarding a high crash rate prior to the action, may have produced the change. The assumed change may only be a chance variation or, in the case where the "before" observation was an extreme case, the change could reflect a statistical phenomenon called regression toward the mean (Ross, et al., 1970). To attribute change to some action, such as jail sentences, one must rule out the possibility that one or more of these explanations account for the observed change.

To measure the possible effect of simultaneous events, we collected data from Milwaukee as well as Chicago to see if comparable trends were found in a neighboring city where there was no special program beyond the usual effort to curb driving while intoxicated in the period under study. Milwaukee is comparable to Chicago in weather conditions and police-court systems. Milwaukee, of course, has a smaller population, but this was controlled in part by calculating the fatality rate per 100,000 population.[3] There was no evidence of a change in the method of compiling the data in either city during the period studied.

FATALITIES IN CHICAGO AND MILWAUKEE

Motor vehicle related fatalities per 100,000 population per month and various subcategories (pedestrians, etc.) were calculated for all such fatalities recorded by the police from January 1966 through June 1971. Changes in population from the 1960 and 1970 censuses were prorated monthly over the decade. Correc-

[3]The product moment correlation between fatality rate and population size of cities is low, for example, it was −0.29 for the 39 largest cities of the U.S. in 1969.

tions for variation in length of month were made by multiplying the rate for a given month by 31 divided by the number of days in the month. A Fourier analysis, which reveals seasonal variation (Tintner, 1952: 217–22), was performed and no statistically significant seasonal variation was found in any of the data to be presented. Therefore, no seasonal corrections were made.

Total motor vehicle related fatalities per 100,000 population for Chicago are shown monthly by the darker curve in Figure 1. The vertical line indicates the time of the crackdown. Although the rates in the early months of 1971 are somewhat lower than the same months in previous years the statistical analysis indicates that the difference between the series from December 1970 through June 1971, and that for the previous years could very commonly have occurred by chance. The statistical significance test shows that t for change in level was 0.87 (df = 62, p > 0.20) and the t for change in slope was 0.79 (df = 62, p > 0.40), clearly offering no reason to reject the null hypothesis that the change was a chance variation. The Milwaukee data, shown in Figure 2, indicate a much sharper drop in rate of fatalities after November 1970 than that in Chicago during the same period but the statistical test showed that this change, too, could very commonly have occurred by chance; t for change in level was 0.58 (df = 62, p > 0.40) and t for change in slope was 0.70 (df = 62, p > 0.40).

There appears to the eye to be a downward drift in the fatality rates in both cities beginning in 1969, some two years before the "crackdown." Comparison of the time series before and after January 1969 does reveal a statistically significant reduction in fatalities in both Chicago and Milwaukee after January 1969. However, examination of categories of types of fatalities showed that this reduction occurred for pedestrians only. The lighter curve in Figures 1 and 2 indicate pedestrian fatalities per 100,000 population in Chicago and Milwaukee respectively. There was a significant change in

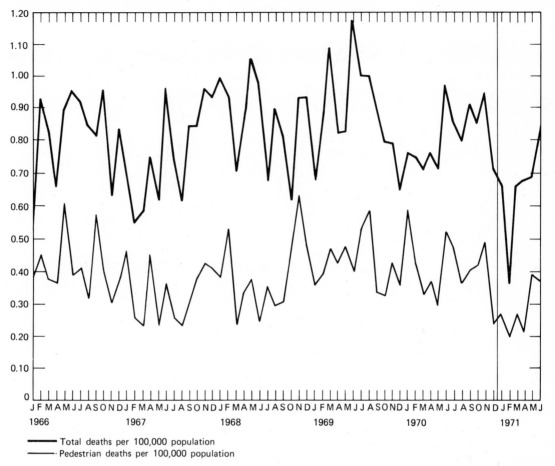

Figure 1.   Chicago fatality rate.

level of pedestrian fatalities in both cities after December 1968 (t = 1.99, df = 62,p < .05 in Chicago; t = 2.86, df = 62, p < .01 in Milwaukee) and a significant change in slope in Milwaukee (t = 2.89, df = 62,p < .01) but not Chicago (t = 1.71, df = 62, p > .05). The changes in nonpedestrian fatalities were within the bounds of usually accepted standards for chance variation.

OTHER CHANGES DURING THE CRACKDOWN

There were at least 17 articles in Chicago newspapers and eight television newsfilms during the

six months of the crackdown that were studied. However, there was no survey of public awareness or behavior during the crackdown so we cannot assess the degree to which the public knew about it or modified drinking or driving behavior. In light of the lack of demonstrated effect of the crackdown, one may question the degree to which a crackdown occurred and what repercussions, if any, the crackdown had on arrests and processing of cases. One study found that a crackdown on speeding in Connecticut had less effect on fatalities than on arrests and dispositions of cases (Campbell and Ross, 1968). Although data on actual sentences for DWI are not available, the number of 7-day sentences for

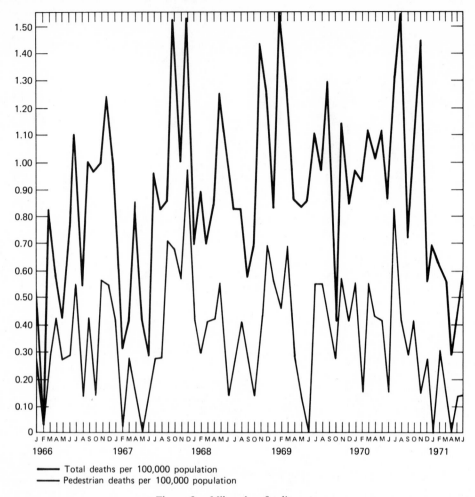

Total deaths per 100,000 population
Pedestrian deaths per 100,000 population

Figure 2. Milwaukee fatality rate.

all traffic-related offenses were 317,357, and 557 for the first six months of 1969, 1970, and 1971 respectively. We were told by Chicago officials that "most" of these sentences were for DWI.

The time series of number of total arrests for DWI is shown in Figure 3. There is no statistically significant difference in level (t = 0.38, df = 26, p > 0.50) or slope (t = 0.42, df = 26, p > 0.50) between the pre- and post-crackdown periods. The time series of percentage of arrestees tested for blood alcohol concentration (not shown) was almost a flat line varying between

26% and 37%. Again, comparison of the series before and after the crackdown reveals no change in level (t = 0.52, df = 26, p > 0.50) or slope (t = 0.57, df = 26, p > 0.50). Figure 4 displays the percentage of those arrested who were found guilty categorized by blood alcohol concentration. The percent found guilty of those whose blood alcohol was less then 0.10% is shown by the bottom curve. The top curve represents the percent found guilty of those whose blood alcohol was 0.10% or greater. The percent found guilty of those not tested is shown by the middle curve. There was no significant

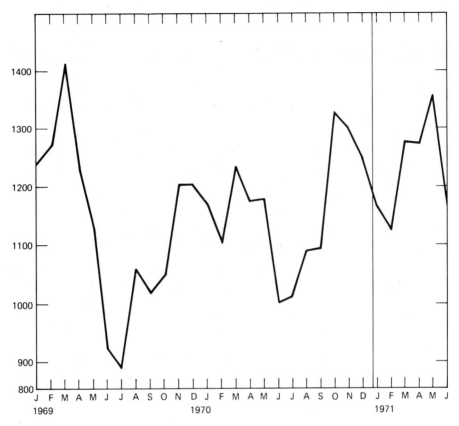

Figure 3. Chicago arrests for DWI.

change in the time series for those tested, whether below 0.10% (t for level = 1.65, df = 26, p > 0.10; t for slope = 1.76, df = 36, p > 0.05) or 0.10% or above (t for level = 1.87, df = 26, p > 0.05; t for slope = 1.94, df = 26, p > 0.05). There was a significant decrease in level (t = 4.02, df = 26, p < .01) and slope (t = 4.20, df = 26, p < .01) of convictions for those who were arrested but not tested.

DISCUSSION

We conclude from the analysis that the change in motor vehicle fatalities that occurred during the Chicago crackdown on drivers convicted of driving while intoxicated was only a chance variation from the fatality rate over the preceding five years. However, there was a significant de-

crease in pedestrian fatalities beginning in 1969 both in Chicago and Milwaukee. By comparing 1971 with 1970 figures, Chicago officials mistakenly concluded that the decrease occurred because of the crackdown rather than because it was part of a more general downward trend which occurred outside Chicago as well.

The reason for the more general decrease in fatalities is unknown. There is a high correlation between various economic indicators and fatality rates (Joksch and Wuerdemann, 1970). Since there was an economic recession during the period of the decrease in pedestrian fatalities seen here, we can speculate that the search for the concomitants of economic indicators that affect fatality rates should concentrate on pedestrian fatalities.

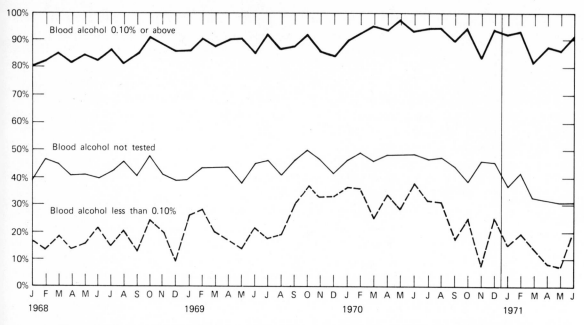

Figure 4.   Percent of arrests that resulted in convictions for DWI by blood alcohol concentration.

Why did the Chicago crackdown fail to influence the fatality rate significantly? The threat of 7-day jail sentences as a countermeasure against DWI involves a number of assumptions, any one of which may be incorrect. On the basis of a study of convicted DWIs, Chicago officials assumed that most drinking-related fatalities are caused by social drinkers. They also assumed, at least implicitly, that their sample was valid and that convicted DWIs are the same type of drinkers as those who get into fatal crashes.

The validity of the Chicago court's study of convicted DWIs is questionable because of the sampling employed and the over-simplification of its conclusion that the convicted DWIs can be divided into alcoholics and social drinkers. The sample may have been biased by taking the first 10 cases each day rather than sampling at random. Even if the sample were representative of convictions, the convicted drivers in the period sampled included 2% whose blood alcohol was below 0.10% and 45% whose blood alcohol was

not tested. There is no way of knowing the degree to which such a sample statistically represents drivers who are involved in alcohol-related fatalities. In light of studies which indicate that there are a number of different types of problem drinkers (Calahan, 1970), and that problem drinkers are a major factor in fatalities (Department of Transportation, 1968), the simple classification of the sample into alcoholics and social drinkers suggests that either the sample was unrepresentative or the diagnoses were invalid.

Assuming that the publicity received by the crackdown was effective in reaching those who subsequently were involved in fatal crashes, it appears that the punitive threat of 7-day jail sentences did not deter them from getting into crashes. Ideally we would like to present the degree of alcohol involvement in these fatalities, but many of the fatally injured drivers involved in these crashes were not tested and some who survived up to 24 hours were tested more than six hours after the crash, which may result in a low estimate of alcohol involvement. Therefore, adequate data on alcohol involvement are not available. We can only speculate that, since the fatality rate did not change significantly during the crackdown, alcohol involvement remained the same as before the crackdown.

There are a number of points in the processing of violators of the law which may change as a result of changes at other points. Arrest may increase or decrease. Plea bargaining may change the disposition of cases. Judges or juries may become more or less lenient in convictions and sentencing. Penal, rehabilitative, probation and parole arrangements may or may not change. At any one of these points the effect of a given change may be undermined (Campbell and Ross, 1968). If a particular effort fails, it is necessary to ask whether the effort itself is ineffective or whether it failed because of a change somewhere else in the system.

We found no evidence of a significant change in arrests for DWI. The number of drivers tested for blood alcohol after arrests also did not change significantly, and the proportion convicted of those tested did not change significantly. There was a significant decrease in convictions of those who were not tested. Since the number tested did not decrease, this change appears to be a result of changes in plea bargaining or reluctance of judges or juries to convict and sentence to seven days in jail those drivers for whom objective evidence of impairment was not available. If the drivers had perceived that they were less likely to be convicted by refusing the test, there should have been a decrease in the number tested, which did not occur.

Whether or not the Chicago crackdown would have been effective in reducing fatalities had it been given more publicity, been accompanied by more arrests, or included more convictions, is problematic. A major difference between the Chicago crackdown and the Lackland and British efforts is the greater emphasis on apprehension of the drinking driver in the latter two cases. It is reasonable to hypothesize that countermeasures which increase the probability of apprehension may deter a subset of drinkers from driving while impaired but that strictly punitive countermeasures will have little, if any, effect.

The general pattern of stress, deviancy, and multiple convictions in the backgrounds of a large proportion of persons convicted of driving while intoxicated and those involved in crashes after excessive drinking (Waller, 1967) suggests that a strictly punitive approach is not likely to be successful in deterring many of these persons from repeat performances. Most of these persons are known to the police and other community agencies. The collaboration and cooperation of the police, courts, social agencies in the community, and scientists knowledgeable in the multiple facets of the alcohol-impaired driver problem will be required if effective countermeasures directed to identified subgroups of drinkers are to be developed.

If we, as a society, are to develop effective reforms and avoid repeating our mistakes, those who administer attempts at social reform must be convinced of the value of careful evaluation of the effort, from basic assumptions through final outcomes (Campbell, 1969). If we are to reduce the tragic losses incurred from drivers impaired by drinking, it is necessary that various countermeasures be tried and evaluated as to effectiveness. However, if we are not judicious in careful analysis of assumptions and the evidence on which they are based, we shall continue to mount campaigns which are costly in money, time, and effort and which preclude development and application of effective ones.

REFERENCES

Barmack, J. E. and D. E. Payne (1964b) "The Lackland Accident Countermeasure Experiment," pp. 665–673 in W. Haddon, Jr., E. A. Suchman, and D. Klein (eds.) *Accident Research*. Harper and Row.

——— (1964a) "Injury-Producing Motor Vehicle Accidents Among Airmen," pp. 504–522 in W. Haddon, Jr., E. A. Suchman, and D. Klein (eds.) *Accident Research*. Harper and Row.

Calahan, D. (1970) *Problem Drinkers*, New York: Jossey-Bass.

Campbell, D. T. (1969) "Reforms as Experiments," 24 *American Psychologist* 409.

—— and H. L. Ross (1968) "The Connecticut Crackdown on Speeding," 3 *Law and Society Review* 55.

Department of Transportation (1968) "1968 Alcohol and Highway Safety Report," Committee Print (Committee on Public Works U.S. House of Representatives), 90th Congress, Second Session, U.S. Government Printing Office.

Field, A. C., Jr. (1971) "The Drinking Driver: Chicago's Quest for a New Ethic," 19 Traffic Digest and Review 1.

Insurance Institute for Highway Safety (1971) "Pre-arrest Testing Now Allowed in Seven States," 17 *Status Report* 6.

Joksch, H. C. and H. Wuerdemann (1970) "Estimating the Effects of Crash Phase Injury Countermeasures," Hartford: The Travelers Research Corporation.

Kelleher, E. J. (1970) "A Diagnostic Evaluation of Four Hundred Drinking Drivers," The Psychiatric Institute, Circuit Court of Cook County.

Ross, H. L., D. T. Campbell, and G. V. Glass (1970) "Determining the Social Effects of a Legal Reform: The British 'Breathalyser' Crackdown of 1967," 13 *American Behavioral Scientist* 493.

Tintner, G. (1952) *Econometrics*. New York: John Wiley & Sons, Inc.

Waller, J. A. (1967) "Drinking Drivers and Driving Drinkers: The Need for Multiple Approaches to Accidents Involving Alcohol," in M. Selzer, P. Gikas and D. F. Huelke (eds.) *The Prevention of Highway Injury*. Highway Safety Research Institute.

32. Executions in America

WILLIAM J. BOWERS

IN THE RECENTLY RENEWED DEBATE OVER CAPITAL punishment, proponents of the death penalty have used two arguments relating to the presumed deterrent power of the death penalty to bolster their case for a return to capital punishment. The first is that the nationwide judicial moratorium on executions in America in the 1960s was, in part, responsible for the recent rise in murder rates in this country. They assert that the growing awareness in the late 1960s that death would no longer be imposed as a punishment for criminal homicide removed an effective constraint on would-be murderers. And secondly, they claim that a return to mandatory capital punishment upon conviction for capital offenses would harness the deterrent power of the death penalty. The fact that as many as nine out of ten convicted murderers have escaped death under discretionary capital punishment in

▶SOURCE: *Executions in America. Lexington, Mass.: Lexington Books, 1974. Pp. 137–147. Reprinted by permission of the publisher.*

Our analysis of the effects of the 1967 judicial moratorium on executions in the United States draws on the work of Marvin E. Wolfgang as reported in his testimony before Subcommittee No. 3 of the Committee on the Judiciary of the United States House of Representatives, on proposed legislation for a moratorium on capital punishment (Hart-Celler Hearings, March 16, 1972, pp. 181, 183–189). Our analysis of the effect of the mandatory death sentence was first suggested to me by Jack Himmelstein of the NAACP Legal Defense and Education Fund, Inc. In the preparation and analysis of the data in this chapter Andréa Carr and Glenn Pierce made a substantial contribution. To each of these four, I wish to express my appreciation.

recent years, they argue, robbed the death penalty of its deterrent potential.

While previous research gives no indication that the death penalty has greater deterrent power than imprisonment, it is true that these investigations have typically examined the de jure existence of the death penalty rather than the extensiveness of its use. In particular, there are no investigations directed specifically at the effect of the de facto cessation of executions, as in the case of the 1967 moratorium on executions in America. It might be argued that existing studies of differential use of the death penalty (Schuessler 1952; Ohio Legislative Service Commission 1961), of the impact of discrete executions (Dann 1935; Graves 1956), and of sentencing of death (Savitz 1958) should show some evidence of deterrence if the actual application of the death penalty, apart from its existence, acts as a constraint on homicide. Admittedly, however, none of these investigations focus directly on the cessation of executions. The impact of the nationwide moratorium of executions may, therefore, be regarded as an open question from the viewpoint of existing evidence on deterrence. And, certainly it is an important issue for investigation in view of the claim that it has led to a precipitous rise in homicide in the United States.

Nor do any existing studies direct themselves specifically to the possible deterrent effects of the mandatory death sentence. Research has not been able to establish that increased risk or certainty of execution for capital crimes contributes to the deterrent value of the death penalty (Schuessler 1952; Ohio Legislature Service Commission 1961). It is conceivable, however, that the states under investigation imposed discretionary capital punishment, and that the certainty of execution under this alternative simply did not reach a high enough level to produce demonstrable deterrent effects. It might be argued that if the mandatory death penalty were a distinctly potent deterrent, this should have been reflected in at least some of the comparisons that have been made between abolition and death penalty states (Sellin 1959). But without knowing in which, if any, of the death penalty states its use was mandatory, we cannot be sure that it was associated with lower homicide rates. The possibility remains, therefore, that mandatory capital punishment may have a deterrent advantage over its discretionary use or imprisonment as alternatives.

Our purpose in this chapter is to make a direct assessment of these two claims—that the judicial moratorium on executions has contributed to increased homicide rates and that mandatory capital punishment would tend to reduce the incidence of homicide. We shall adapt the form of analysis used by Professor Thorsten Sellin in his pioneering work on the deterrent effects of capital punishment. Sellin has compared homicide rates for contiguous death penalty and abolition states and for a given state at varying points in time to determine whether its availability bears any relationship to the level of homicide in the state.

For such comparisons to be an adequate test of deterrence, it must be assumed (1) that the proportion of capital murders among all homicides remains reasonably constant over time and from one jurisdiction to the next, (2) that the effects are felt primarily within the jurisdiction in which the existence or imposition of the death penalty occurs, and (3) that the effect of other factors (i.e., population characteristics and socio-cultural environment) known to influence murder rates in a serious manner are eliminated or taken into account or assumed to be constant across state lines. For this purpose,

Sellin has used one or more *contiguous* states as controls. In the analysis that follows, we too rely heavily on this procedure of comparing states of primary interest with one or more contiguous states serving as controls.

The first empirical section of this chapter examines selected states before and after the judicial moratorium on executions in America. It reports data initially presented in 1972 by Professor Marvin E. Wolfgang in his testimony before the House Subcommittee on the Judiciary then considering legislation for a continuation of the existing moratorium. (Hart-Celler Hearings, March 16, 1972,181, 183–189). Professor Wolfgang's analysis covered the eight-year period from 1963 through 1970 (four years before and three years after the nationwide moratorium in 1967) and included all states in which the death penalty was abolished throughout this eight-year period, together with contiguous death penalty states.

We have extended the scope of his analysis (1) by including additional states which abolished the death penalty within the four-year period prior to the nationwide moratorium on executions, and (2) by adding 1971 homicide rates, not available from the *Uniform Crime Reports* of the F.B.I. at the time of Wolfgang's analysis, to cover four-year periods both before and after the moratorium in 1967. As a result, our analysis will cover a nine-year period and include *every* state in which the death penalty was not legally available throughout the period of the moratorium, with at least one contiguous death penalty state as a control. (We exclude Alaska and Hawaii for lack of contiguous jurisdictions.)

In the second empirical section, we examine states which have made a change from mandatory to discretionary capital punishment for first degree murder. This move to discretionary use of the death penalty has occurred in all death penalty jurisdictions over the course of the last century or so. Until very recently, however, information on the timing of such changes was available only for states that made this move since the second World War (Bedau 1967b,

27-30; S. Ehrmann 1961). Our analysis was begun with this more restricted information on recent moves to discretionary capital punishment. Fortunately, a complete inventory of the changes from mandatory to discretionary capital punishment was recently compiled (Garin 1973) in time for us to extend the analysis to include states that made this move prior to World War II. The analysis as it now stands, includes *every* state for which data on homicide rates can be obtained for a period of four years before and after the move to discretionary capital punishment. (The one exception to this rule is New Hampshire, for which data are available for three years before and four years after its move to discretionary capital punishment.)

THE EFFECT OF THE JUDICIAL MORATORIUM

As in the case of the Canadian experiment with abolition, the judicial moratorium on executions in the United States was also a nationwide phenomenon which can be given a specific beginning point. In the Canadian experiment, however, the change was relatively abrupt in the sense that no further executions (except for the killing of a law officer) could be performed according to legislative decree. In the case of the judicial moratorium in the United States, the awareness that executions had come to an end was undoubtedly less immediate and widespread. Indeed, convicted offenders were still being sentenced to death after June 1967, and there was no legislative assurance that these sentences would not eventually be carried out. Thus, growing recognition that the death penalty would not be imposed might be expected to produce *gradually* increasing levels of homicide in death penalty states after the moratorium, *relative* to the levels of homicide in abolition states.

More specifically, if the death penalty exercises a greater deterrent effect on prospective murderers than does imprisonment, the following propositions ought to be true:

1. Death penalty states should show increased levels of homicide after the 1967 judicial moratorium. Growing public awareness that the death penalty was no longer being employed in practice should have resulted in progressively increasing homicide rates among states that previously imposed the death penalty.

2. There should be no noticeable change (upturn) in the level of homicides for abolition states subsequent to the cessation of executions. Any changes in the homicide rates of abolition states should be the result of ongoing trends over time.

3. States which abolish capital punishment in the period immediately before the judicial moratorium should show increased levels of homicide relative to contiguous death penalty states prior to the moratorium; but death penalty states should tend to narrow any gap in homicide rates previously opened by recent abolition states after the cessation of executions.

Figures 1 through 8 present eight graphs comparing the homicide rates of abolition states and contiguous death penalty states, for the four years prior to the judicial moratorium on capital punishment and the four years subsequent to it. The first four figures in our analysis compare death penalty states with states which were abolitionist for the entire nine-year period under investigation—1963 through 1971.

The homicide rates for Michigan, an abolition state, with its contiguous death penalty state, Illinois, are shown in Figure 1. The graph directly contradicts the argument that the death penalty is a uniquely effective deterrent. Prior to 1967 the homicide rates of abolitionist Michigan were consistently lower than those of Illinois. And, after 1967, it is the abolitionist state and not the death penalty state, as the deterrence perspective would predict, that experiences the greater rise.

Figures 2 and 3 permit comparisons among the New England states of Maine, New Hampshire, Vermont, Massachusetts, Rhode Island,

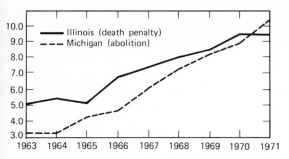

Figure 1. Annual homicide rates before and after the judicial moratorium on executions in Michigan and Illinois. Source: Annual state homicide rates from Federal Bureau of Investigation, Uniform Crime Reports (annual).

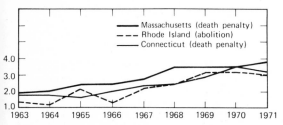

Figure 2. Annual homicide rates before and after the judicial moratorium on executions in Rhode Island, Connecticut, and Massachusetts. Source: See source footnote Figure 1.

and Connecticut. Of these states, Maine and Rhode Island had no death penalty for the entire period under study, and Vermont abolished its death penalty in 1965. In Figure 2 we can see an obvious similarity of homicide rates and trends for Massachusetts, Connecticut, and Rhode Island. All three states, regardless of their punishment for murder, show a general and gradual increase in homicide throughout the period, the ranking of the three states in terms of homicide rate is the same in 1971 as it was in 1963.

The homicide rates for Maine, New Hampshire, and Vermont are shown in Figure 3. As might be expected, these states showed greater instability of rates from year to year than did their more populous New England counterparts. However, New Hampshire, with the death penalty, showed little overall increase in

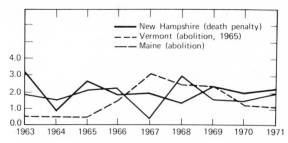

Figure 3. Annual homicide rates before and after the judicial moratorium on executions in Maine, Vermont, and New Hampshire. Source: See source footnote Figure 1.

its homicide rate after 1967, while the abolitionist states of Maine and Vermont showed an increase and a decrease, respectively. The only evidence in the graph to suggest that the death penalty may be a more effective deterrent than imprisonment is the rise of Vermont's homicide rate in the two years following abolition of the death penalty. Yet, further examination of the graph reveals that after 1967 Vermont's upward homicide trend is completely reversed and that by 1971 its homicide rate is almost back to the 1963 level.

Figure 4 presents the homicide rate for North Dakota, an abolition state, and two contiguous death penalty states, South Dakota, and Nebraska. Like the less populous New England states, these three states show substantial fluctuations in homicide rates; but here again we find no evidence supporting the death penalty as a more effective deterrent. Note that during the period 1963 to 1967 the homicide rate for

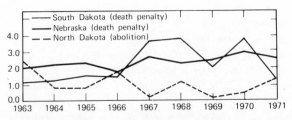

Figure 4. Annual homicide rates before and after the judicial moratorium on executions in North Dakota, Nebraska, and South Dakota. Source: See source footnote Figure 1.

North Dakota dropped, while the corresponding rates of Nebraska and South Dakota increased. After the moratorium, however, North Dakota's homicide rate climbed gradually, while the rates for the two contiguous death penalty states display contrasting trends. Homicides in Nebraska rose slightly, while those in South Dakota generally, though irregularly, declined.

Figures 5 through 7 present three states which recently abolished the death penalty—Oregon (1964), New York (1965), and West Virginia (1965)—together with their respective contiguous death penalty states.

Figure 5 compares recently abolitionist Oregon with Washington and Idaho, both death penalty states. Comparison of these three states is difficult because of the relative instability of their homicide rates, but it does appear that all three states, irrespective of their mode of punishment, experienced similar homicide trends over the 1963–1971 period. The state showing the most stability in its trend, Washington, did experience a rising homicide rate after 1967, but this pattern clearly seems to have been established prior to the judicial moratorium.

Special note should be made that Oregon's abolition of the death penalty in 1964 was accomplished by public referendum—the only state in the Union to have done so—and consequently there was considerable public awareness of the change. This is significant because it bears on the argument that the residents in abolition jurisdictions are typically unaware that the death penalty cannot be imposed in their state.

With reference to Oregon's abolition of the death penalty, Figure 5 shows that homicide did increase in the year immediately after abolition but this rise was not much greater than the drop in homicide occurring the year before. Moreover, if the analysis is extended to include the three years prior to abolition (two of which do not appear in the graph), and the three years after (to the beginning of the judicial moratorium) Oregon's homicide rate increased no more than the rates of its two contiguous death penalty states. The average of Oregon's homicide rate for the 1961 to 1963 period was 2.9 and for 1965–67, 3.1, an increase of 0.2; whereas the average for Washington and Idaho over the same period increased 0.2 and 0.6 respectively.

Notice in the next graph, Figure 6, that West Virginia's homicide rate rose gradually between

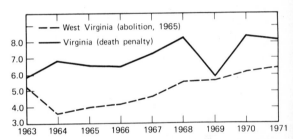

Figure 6. Annual homicide rates before and after the judicial moratorium on executions in West Virginia and Virginia. Source: See source footnote Figure 1.

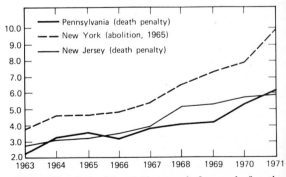

Figure 7. Annual homicide rates before and after the judicial moratorium on executions in New York, New Jersey, and Pennsylvania. Source: See source footnote Figure 1.

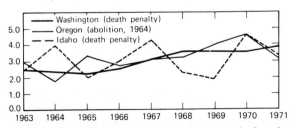

Figure 5. Annual homicide rates before and after the judicial moratorium on executions in Oregon, Idaho, and Washington. Source: See source footnote Figure 1.

1965 when it abolished the death penalty, and 1967. Yet, the increase was no greater than Virginia's, the contiguous death penalty state. After the judicial moratorium both states continued to show similar increases in homicide rates. In 1969 Virginia experienced a sharp drop in homicide; the following year Virginia's rate returned to its previous level. When the entire 1967 to 1971 period is considered, we find no evidence to suggest that Virginia's homicide rate had risen more than West Virginia's.

Figure 7 compares New York, which abolished the death penalty in 1965,with Pennsylvania and New Jersey, both death penalty states. In the two years after New York's abolition, its homicide rate rose from 4.6 to 5.4, or a 17 percent increase, while the corresponding rates for New Jersey and Pennsylvania rose 22 percent and 9 percent respectively. This pattern continued in the year immediately after the moratorium. Starting in 1969, however, we find a more precipitous increase in New York's homicide rate than in either New Jersey's or Pennsylvania's—precisely the opposite of what we should expect if the death penalty were having a unique deterrent effect that was forfeited by the moratorium.

The final graph, Figure 8, contains the North Central states of Minnesota, Wisconsin, and Iowa. The first two are abolition states for the entire period, and the third, Iowa, abolished the death penalty in 1965. Since all three states had abolished the death penalty by 1967, we should not expect the moratorium to affect their

homicide rates. However, we should expect Iowa, after its abolition in 1965, to exhibit an increase in homicide relative to Wisconsin and Minnesota (see proposition 3 above). However, the graph reveals the opposite to be true. Iowa's homicide rate rose 0.5 between 1965 and 1971, whereas the rates for Wisconsin and Minnesota increased 1.3 and 1.0 respectively.

Our analysis to this point has uncovered no evidence suggesting that the death penalty is a more effective deterrent than imprisonment. However, chance fluctuations in the homicide rates of the individual states examined so far have, in some cases, made it difficult to assess the effects of the judicial moratorium. In order to minimize the problem of random instability and focus more specifically on the differential effect of the moratorium on abolition and death penalty states, we have prepared a summary graph in Figure 9, which includes only those states which were abolitionist for the entire period of analysis and their contiguous death penalty states (data from Figures 1 through 4 excluding Vermont in 3).

The summary graph in Figure 9 shows the average homicide rates for states which

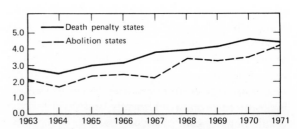

Figure 9.   Average homicide rates of abolition states with corresponding contiguous death penalty states examined in Figures 1 through 8.

Since each comparison of an abolition state with contiguous death penalty states was a unique test of the effect of the judicial moratorium, the average annual homicide rates in Figure 9 were not weighted according to state population. Where an abolition state had more than one contiguous death penalty state the homicide rates of the latter jurisdictions were averaged to provide single annual estimates. Finally, the values for Figures 5 through 8 and for Vermont from Figure 3 were omitted from this figure in order to avoid the possible confounding effects of recent abolition.

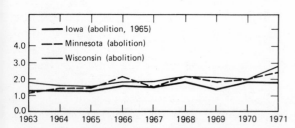

Figure 8.   Annual homicide rates before and after the judicial moratorium on executions in Iowa, Minnesota, and Wisconsin. Source: See source footnote Figure 1.

abolished the death penalty for the entire 1963–1971 period and the average rates for their contiguous death penalty states. The graph supports our previous analysis of individual states. Notice that it is the abolition states which show a somewhat greater increase in homicide after the cessation of executions in 1967.

In summary, we can find no evidence to suggest that the death penalty is a uniquely deterrent form of punishment. With regard to the specific issue of the judicial moratorium, none of our findings support the proposition that its *de facto* suspension in 1967 has been responsible for increasing homicide rates in those states which impose the death penalty.

One of the assumptions in the foregoing analysis, as we have noted, is that the effect of the death penalty will be felt primarily in the jurisdiction where it exists and is applied; hence, our inference that death penalty states would be more seriously affected than abolition states by the moratorium on executions. . . . The various Canadian provinces all had the death penalty available prior to the nationwide experiment with abolition beginning in December 1967.

To show that rising homicide rates in the late 1960s in Canada were not a response to this experiment with abolition, Professor Fattah compared the trends in homicide with those for other serious crimes in Canada. The analysis revealed that, in fact, homicide rates increased at a slower pace than did the rates of other serious and violent crimes, for which death was not an available punishment before the period of abolition began.

It is likewise instructive to turn briefly to national trends in homicide and other offenses in assessing the impact of the moratorium in the United States. Thus, in addition to comparing selected jurisdictions within the United States, Professor Wolfgang in his original analysis also examined the national pattern of homicide rates from 1963 to 1970 and compared it with the patterns for other major crimes over the same period. The following excerpt from his testimony before the House Subcommittee on the Judiciary summarizes his findings and presents his conclusions:

"We have examined homicide rates in the United States four years prior to the judicial moratorium and four years subsequent to it. In general, during the past four years, the criminal homicide rate has increased at a slower pace than any of the seven major crimes in the crime index, according to the *Uniform Crime Reports* of the F.B.I. For all serious crimes (homicide, rape, robbery, aggravated assault and battery, burglary, larceny, auto theft) there was a 42.6 per cent increase between 1967–1970, but for criminal homicide there was only a 27.8 per cent increase. Moreover, the increase in the homicide rate from 1963 (4.5 per 100,000) to 1967 (6.1) was 35.5 per cent; while the increase from 1967 (6.1) to 1970 (7.8) was lower, or 27.8 per cent. In short, the rate of the incline of homicide was less in the four years since the judicial moratorium than before the judicial moratorium."

Wolfgang concludes his analysis:

"In sum, there is no evidence to indicate that an additional two year moratorium by legislative enactment would have any untoward effect on the homicide rate . . . The absence of a moratorium would, however, continue racially discriminatory and cruel and unusual sentencing and application of the death penalty."

Thus, while it is true that Canada and the United States both experienced rising homicide rates in the late 1960s, these rates increased at a slower pace than did the rates of other serious crimes for which the death penalty was never available. It is also true that both nations entered periods of reduced use and/or availability of the death penalty in 1967, but it should be noted that a moratorium on executions in Canada, comparable to the one in the United States, actually occurred with the last Canadian execution in 1962. If a moratorium on executions were responsible for subsequently increasing levels of homicide, such increases should have occurred some five years earlier in Canada than in the United States. The fact that increasing homicide rates were closely associated with increasing levels of other major and particularly violent crimes in Canada and the United States plainly suggests that it is not the suspension or abolition of the death penalty, but broader social forces contributing to violent criminal behavior that account for the variations in criminal homicide rates in these two contiguous nations.

REFERENCES

1. Bedau H. (ed.). *The Death Penalty in America.* Garden City, New York: Anchor, 1967.

2. Dann, R. H. "The Deterrent Effect of Capital Punishment." *Friends Social Service Series* 29 (1935): 1.

3. Ehrmann, S. R. "Capital Punishment Today—Why?" in Herbert Bloch (ed.), *Crime in America*, N.Y.: Philosophical Library, Inc., 1961 pp. 81, 91.

4. NAACP Legal Defense and Educational Fund, Inc. Memorandum on Mandatory and Discretionary Capital Statutes, by N. Garin (prepared for J. Himmelstein), 1973.

5. Graves, W. F. "A Doctor Looks at Capital Punishment." *J. of the Loma Linda U. School of Med.* 10 (1956): 137.

6. Ohio Legislative Service Commission. "Capital Punishment." Staff Research Report no. 46 (1961).

7. Savitz, L. "A Brief History of Capital Punishment in Pennsylvania." *Prison J.* 38 (1958): 50.

8. Scheussler, K. F. "The Deterrent Influence of the Death Penalty." *The Annals* 284 (1952): 54.

9. Sellin, T. *The Death Penalty.* Phila., Pa.: American Law Institute, 1959.

33. Public Attitudes Toward Capital Punishment

CHARLES W. THOMAS
ROBERT G. HOWARD

PARTLY AS A REFLECTION OF THE ISSUES POSED IN such landmark Supreme Court cases as *Witherspoon v. Illinois* (30), *Furman v. Georgia* (11), and *Gregg v. Georgia* (12), most quantitative research on capital punishment focuses on two general kinds of problems. First, a relatively large literature has examined the manner in which the criminal justice system, especially juries and trial judges, process capital cases (3, 15, 16, 18, 31, 32). These studies have attempted to determine whether capital punishment is imposed in a discriminatory fashion and, if so, to identify the correlates of such improper discretionary decision making. Second, an increasingly sophisticated series of studies has examined the consequences of varying degrees of reliance on capital punishment (1, 2, 6, 8, 9, 20, 33). That body of research has attempted to determine whether the imposition of the death penalty serves the goal of general deterrence.

The fact that the preponderance of the quantitative evidence shows that there are significant abuses of discretionary powers in the determination of who will be sentenced to death and that, notwithstanding a very small body of contrary evidence (9, 33), capital punishment for homicide has no deterrent effect is not immediately relevant to the goals of this study. The point is simply that most of the research literature concerns itself with how we impose so severe a sanction on criminal offenders and if doing so serves any purpose beyond its obvious ability to incapacitate a particular offender.

Those kinds of questions are important, but they tend to direct our attention away from a paradox of rather considerable proportion. Specifically, the worldwide trend away from capital punishment, regardless of the procedures by means of which it is applied or any societal purpose it might serve, has been pronounced throughout the twentieth century. Despite this, between June of 1972, when the Supreme Court, in *Furman v. Georgia,* ruled that capital punishment was unconstitutional, and July of 1976, when it held, in *Gregg v. Georgia,* that guided discretion statutes had overcome the constitutional flaws identified in *Furman,* thirty-five states and the Congress of the United States had enacted revised death penalty statutes. Then, on January 17, 1977, Gary Mark Gilmore was executed by a firing squad in Utah, thus becoming the first person to be put to death in the United States in almost a decade. Further, and not unimportantly given the problem to be addressed here, the level of public support for capital punishment has been increasing since the mid-1960's (10).

What we see, then, is the emergence of a worldwide movement away from any reliance on capital punishment, but an increasing willingness on the part of both American citizens and their elected representatives to retain death

▶SOURCE: *"Public Attitudes Toward the Death Penalty: A Comparative Analysis,"Journal of Behavioral Economics, Vol. 6, No. 1. (forthcoming) Reprinted by permission.*

as a sanction for criminal behavior. The most obvious question, therefore, does not revolve around the equity of the procedures we may fashion to process criminal offenders or the efficacy of putting them to death. Neither of these issues could be of any concern whatsoever were it not for our continued willingness to adopt capital punishment statutes and, presumably, to actually put convicted offenders to death. Thus, the real issue appears to be why such a large proportion of the population remains supportive of capital punishment.

That is precisely what this study is directed toward. Based on an analysis of data obtained from a randomly selected sample of 3,334 adult residents of one southeastern Standard Metropolitan Statistical Area, we will examine several attitudinal characteristics and personality traits that have been related to support for capital punishment in previous research. The purposes of the multiple regression analysis presented are two-fold. First, and partly because much of the prior research employed types of statistical analysis that do not specify what proportion of the variance in capital punishment attitudes is explained by the predictor variables which were employed, the determination of the variance explained by the variables used here is important. Second, and more importantly from our point of view, it is imperative that we move toward a more complete understanding of the relative importance of the several independent variables.

PRIOR RESEARCH

Because thorough reviews of prior research on determinants of public attitudes toward capital punishment are readily available elsewhere (4, 28), no detailed commentary is necessary here. Still, it is important to identify three general categories into which the majority of studies fall. The first of these consists of relatively superficial kinds of public opinion polls which have examined variations in support for capital punishment across segments of the population which differ in their social and demographic characteristics. Although these studies are not of direct relevance to this research, their findings do provide some indirectly important information. As noted previously, they consistently show that support for capital punishment declined to the point that during the mid-1960's the proportion of the population which was opposed to capital punishment was larger than that which was supportive, but that by the early 1970's a significant majority were in favor of the death penalty (10, 13, 28). They also show that levels of support are not constant across categories of the population or between different geographical areas of the country (13, 28). Thus, Vidmar and Ellsworth (28, p. 131) observe that:

"Generally, people who support the death penalty tend to be older, less educated, male, more wealthy, white, and from urban areas. A greater percentage of white collar workers, manual laborers, and farmers favor capital punishment than do professionals and businesspersons."

At the same time, however, an inspection of these poll data also reveals something else. Despite some percentage differences between levels of support when one segment of the population is compared with another, the magnitude of these differences, with the exception of race (blacks almost invariably being far less supportive than whites), is quite small. Recent statistics cited by Hindelang et al. (13, p. 327) are instructive in this regard. For example, the data they summarize, which were drawn from a nationwide sample as part of a study conducted by the American Institute of Public Opinion, show that, consistent with the Vidmar and Ellsworth interpretation of the general poll literature, support was higher among the older, less educated, and so on. However, the percentage differences are so small in most instances that it is clear that these general characteristics are capable of accounting for only a very small portion of the variation in public sentiments.

Partly because public support for the death

penalty cannot be adequately explained by traditional social, demographic, and economic factors, two other types of research have drawn an increasing amount of attention. Without wishing to oversimplify the thrust of either or to raise any disciplinary hackles unnecessarily, one type offers more of a psychological view, in the sense that it is relatively more concerned with something akin to personality attributes, while the other is a good deal more social psychological or sociological, in the sense that individual characteristics are far less emphasized. Also, at least from our vantage point, the psychological perspective often offers a quasi-clinical explanation of capital punishment attitudes, but the social psychological orientation is generally more cautious about things clinical.

However crude this distinction may be, what we have termed a psychological point of view is associated with research that implicitly or explicitly approaches attitudes supportive of capital punishment in something like the following fashion. Killing people who have been convicted of a criminal offense is a uniquely severe response. Those who support such a response may very well do so because of personality characteristics that are essentially unrelated to any rational consideration of what is right or wrong, just or unjust, useful or not useful. If so, they are certainly different from normal people who, at least hypothetically, are relatively rational, calculative, and pragmatic. Thus, research grounded in this point of view has related such variables at punitiveness, authoritarianism, dogmatism, rigidity, intolerance, fascism, and other similar factors to support for capital punishment and, by and large, significant correlations have been found (5, 7, 16, 21, 27).

While the point should not be pushed too far, the implication of much of this literature is that there is something wrong with someone who supports capital punishment. After all, being labeled as punitive, dogmatic, intolerant, or authoritarian is not the sort of thing that many of us hope for. All imply some personality defect. There is one glaring problem with this point of view. As has been noted elsewhere (23), casting support for capital punishment as a manifestation of a personality trait or disorder tends to place us on some pretty thin ice when we consider the fact that recent public opinion polls suggest that more than two-thirds of the population support the death penalty under some circumstances. Thus, at least in a statistical sense, the abolitionists appear to be more deviant than the retentionists.

This difficulty has done much to stimulate a somewhat different approach to research in this area. Prior research reported by the senior author of this paper provides one clear illustration of this alternative to a clinical view (22, 23, 24). Specifically, support for capital punishment may be viewed as a most unusual phenomenon in at least two regards. First, as has already been noted, it is so pervasive that attempts to explain it with such traditional variables as sex, religious affiliation, place of residence, education, income, occupational prestige, and so on are altogether unsatisfactory. Second, as was also pointed out already, one is most unlikely to explain support for the death penalty as a manifestation of some aberrant personality characteristic. Instead, at least by implication, we must look for far more general influences, influences that are at once sufficiently pervasive and positively oriented toward punishment that they could account for a significant portion of the variance in attitudes toward capital punishment.

Two such influences have been emphasized in earlier research (19, 22, 23, 24, 27). One deals with the extent to which individuals believe that punishment can serve the goals of general and specific deterrence. This variable may be termed utilitarian sentiments in the sense that it reflects the "forward looking" character of the utilitarian position by emphasizing the efficacy of sanctions. The other focuses attention on whether individuals endorse the notion that sanctions should be imposed on criminal offenders simply because doing so is just. Because such views have the "backward looking" character commonly associated with the retributive perspective in philosophy, it is convenient to term this variable retributive sentiments.

The important point is that both of these justifications for punishment are so deeply ingrained in our cultural system that individuals in all sectors of our society can be expected to acquire an appreciation for these sentiments through their involvement in an entirely normal socialization process. Further, once these sentiments have become a part of our world-views, they clearly play a significant role in shaping our responses to criminality: criminals should be punished in proportion to the magnitude of their wrong doing because it is just (retributive sentiments) and because doing so will have the pragmatic consequence of lessening the magnitude of the problem posed by criminality (utilitarian sentiments).

Taken together, the psychological and social psychological views described above imply two rather different explanations of public support for capital punishment, and both perspectives are of very direct relevance to many of the issues being argued in the courts. Interpreted in terms of their legal relevance, it seems fair to say that both have a bearing on any determination of whether capital punishment is violative of Eighth Amendment guarantees against cruel and unusual punishment, at least as those guarantees have been interpreted in *Weems v. United States* (29), *Trop v. Dulles* (26), *Furman v. Georgia* (11), and *Gregg v. Georgia* (12). The most basic premise is that the meaning of cruel and unusual punishment is necessarily linked to "evolving standards of decency that mark the progress of a maturing society" (26, p. 101). Confronted with public opinion poll data that reflect continuing public support for the death penalty, the psychological view has produced evidence that some fraction of that support is the product of negatively valued personality characteristics or of attitudes, such as intolerance, racial bias, and antidemocratic sentiments, which are so at odds with other constitutional guarantees that it should not be considered in any measure of evolving societal standards. The

social psychological research is generally less condemning of those who support capital punishment, but it leads to an essentially similar conclusion. Particularly to the extent that utilitarian sentiments play a determinative role, the contention has typically been that public sentiments are so contrary to the preponderance of the available empirical evidence that care must be taken to discriminate between informed and uninformed opinion. In other words, if large numbers of people are willing to support the death penalty because they believe that the imposition of that penalty will lessen the crime problem through deterring offenders, much evidence suggests that their support flows from an entirely too optimistic understanding of the efficacy of punishment.

These and other legal issues notwithstanding, only infrequently have researchers attempted to determine how much of the variation in public support for capital punishment can be attributed to the kinds of variables that have been hypothesized as being of relevance. Further, they have almost never gone on to evaluate the relative effects of those variables (but see 19, 23, 27). It is toward those two concerns that our attention now turns.

RESEARCH METHODOLOGY

The data employed here were obtained during the course of a larger study conducted in Chesapeake, Norfolk, Portsmouth, and Virginia Beach, Virginia during the Winter of 1973–1974. The purposes of the study dictated that those included in a systematic random sample drawn from the most current telephone directory for that SMSA ($N = 9,178$) who were no longer residents of those cities be excluded, and 1,949 could not be reached at the addresses we had obtained. Of the 7,229 households contacted, properly completed questionnaires were returned by 3,334 (46.1 percent of those contacted). This rate of return is within the normal range for studies of this type, but care should be taken in interpreting the results of the analysis because of the response biases common to such studies. Specifically, a comparison of the social and demographic characteristics of those who returned questionnaires with the 1970 census information for these cities revealed that the sample includes disproportionately large numbers of citizens who were older, white, relatively well-educated, higher in occupational prestige, and male. Although there is no reasonable way to adjust for these biases, it should be noted that, with the exception of race, none of these characteristics have been strongly related to the dependent variable under consideration here in previous research.

The manner in which the major variables included in the analysis were operationalized is summarized below.

Dogmatism

As Vidmar (27, p. 341) has noted, "there is a substantial body of literature showing that samples of U.S. adults who favor the death penalty are more likely to score high on measures of authoritarianism and dogmatism and are more likely to be 'conservative' in their social and political views than persons who are opposed to the death penalty." Hollander (14, p. 411) provides an adequately clear conceptual definition of the term: "The highly dogmatic individual has a set of tightly organized beliefs, usually derived from authority. A feature of dogmatism is rigidity in the psychological field, which takes the form of resistance to the acceptance of information that is contradictory to the individual's system of beliefs." Unlike the other measures employed here, the items in the dogmatism scale tend to lack face validity, but they are comparable to those employed in previous research. For this and each of the other scales, care was taken to exclude potential attitude items that did not reflect a single underlying construct. Toward this end, each scale was factor analyzed, and any item that did not yield a factor loading of .40 or higher on the first factor of the unrotated factor matrix was excluded from the final scale. The items, factor loadings, response distributions,

means, and standard deviations of all of the measures are provided in Appendix A. High scale scores on the dogmatism measure reflect high levels of dogmatism.

Civil Liberties

Although the rigidity associated with dogmatism has often been linked to conservative attitudes of one kind or another, it is not a measure of conservatism itself. Further, general measures of liberalism or conservatism appear to be both too vague and too multidimensional to be of special relevance here. On the other hand, there is at least one area where those who vary on this dimension quite clearly differ with another. Conservatives typically contend that we have been so careful to protect the rights of the guilty that we have ignored those of the innocent; liberals argue that few things are of more pressing relevance than the protection of basic constitutionally guaranteed civil liberties. Thus, the eight-item Likert-type measure developed here was designed to measure variations in support for fundamental civil liberties. High scale scores on the civil liberties measure reflect high levels of support for civil liberties.

Utilitarian Sentiments

One of the major variables identified in previous research as a determinant of support for capital punishment is the extent to which individuals feel that punishment serves the related goals of specific and general deterrence. The basic notion is that those who view punishment as a useful means of controlling or shaping human behavior are more likely to accept the death penalty as a useful means of controlling especially threatening types of criminal behavior rather than defining it as a uniquely severe form of punishment that is qualitatively different from other penalties. High scale scores on the utilitarian sentiments measure reflect positive assessments of the efficacy of punishment.

Retributive Sentiments

Although recent research has shown that retributive and utilitarian sentiments are positively related to one another, this perspective on punishment is quite different from the utilitarian point of view. The contention that we are morally obligated to abide by the law and to punish law violators is central to this position, and this provides the focus for the scale employed here. High scale scores on the retributive sentiments measure reflect highly retributive feelings.

Support for Capital Punishment

Finally, a four-item measure of attitudes toward capital punishment was derived by the factor analytic method described earlier. This scale was designed to measure whether those in the sample felt we should retain the death penalty, and particular care was taken to avoid employing items which reflected any opinions regarding the utility of the penalty. High scale scores reflect support for capital punishment.

ANALYSIS AND FINDINGS

Prior research suggests that each of the four predictor variables will be significantly related to support for capital punishment and, implicitly or explicitly, that they will be related to one another. As was indicated earlier, the generally supportive attitudes reflected in a large number of public opinion polls also provide a reasonably sound basis for stating some hypotheses regarding which of the independent variables are likely to be most influential. Specifically, while such personality characteristics as dogmatism may

play a significant role in encouraging the adoption of attitudes which, in turn, produce support for capital punishment, we see little justification for viewing dogmatism as a major determinant of support for the death penalty. A somewhat stronger case, however, can be made for a linkage between attitudes toward civil liberties and capital punishment. Still, recent research on the topic strongly suggests that utilitarian and retributive sentiments will play the most influential role.

Although the primary research questions cannot be pursued with simple zero-order correlations, the intercorrelation matrix reported in Table I merits some preliminary consideration. First, with the exception of the substantively trivial correlation between dogmatism and support for capital punishment ($r = .036$), utilitarian sentiments ($r = .452$), retributive sentiments ($r = .336$), and support for civil liberties ($r = -.296$) are significantly correlated with the dependent variable, and all of the correlations are in the predicted direction. Second, excepting the weak linkage between dogmatism and retributive sentiments ($r = .077$), they are related to one another. Of special importance in that regard is the finding that those who view punishment in a retributive manner are also likely to view it as serving some utilitarian end ($r = .408$). Further, although dogmatism was insignificantly related to the death penalty variable, it has a relatively strong correlation with support for civil liberties ($r = -.496$), with those who are most dogmatic being least likely to en-

Table I. Intercorrelations Between Capital Punishment (X1), Utilitarian Sentiments (X2), Attitudes Toward Civil Liverties (X3), Dogmatism (X4), and Retributive Sentiments (X5)

	X1	X2	X3	X4	X5
X1	1.000	.452	−.296	.036	.336
X2		1.000	−.458	.275	.408
X3			1.000	−.496	−.242
X4				1.000	.077
X5					1.000

dorse constitutionally guaranteed civil liberties.

While these bivariate correlations provide tentative support for several of our expectations, they obviously do not provide information on the proportion of variance in support for capital punishment which is explained by the combined influence of all four predictors. In addition, it would be inappropriate to attempt any ordering of the four independent variables on the basis of the correlations presented in Table I. Those issues can be pursued, however, through a multiple regression analysis which incorporates all four predictors. A summary of the relevant statistical information from that analysis is provided in Table II.

An examination of Table II, which is derived from a standard stepwise regression analysis, shows that the four predictor variables are able to explain 25.8 percent of the variation in attitudes toward capital punishment ($R^2 = .258$). Further, to the extent that the magnitude of the standardized regression coefficients provides the most common means of determining the relative importance of predictor variables, the expectations advanced earlier are generally supported. The single best predictor is clearly utilitarian sentiments ($\beta = .350$), followed by support for civil liberties ($\beta = -.171$), retributive sentiments ($\beta = .164$), and dogmatism ($\beta = -.157$).

A closer inspection of these findings, however, reveals one interpretive problem. The dogmatism variable which, taken by itself, explains only an insignificant fraction of the variance in the dependent variable ($r^2 = .001$) adds almost two percent to the explained variance when it enters the regression equation as the last variable (R^2 increment = .185). In addition, the sign of the regression coefficient for the dogmatism scale is negative, and, like those of the other independent variables, it is statistically significant at less than the .001 level. In other words, while the zero-order correlation between dogmatism and the capital punishment variable is very weak and positive, its influence becomes significant and negative when it is employed with the other three variables in a single regression equation. Thus, taken at face value, we would have to conclude that, quite contrary to previous research, those who are most dogmatic are opposed to capital punishment after the influence of utilitarian sentiments, retributive sentiments, and attitudes toward civil liberties are removed.

The interpretation of this finding poses both statistical and substantive problems. Apart from any consideration of the sign of the coefficient for the dogmatism variable, ranking the importance of all of these independent variables in terms of their regression coefficients or the R^2 increments presented in Table II is inherently ambiguous when the variables are intercorrelated. For example, Kerlinger and Pedhazur (17, p. 296) note that:

"In nonexperimental research . . . the independent variables are generally correlated, sometimes substantially. This makes it difficult, if not impossible, to untangle the variance accounted for in the dependent variable and to attribute it to individual independent variables."

Table II. Summary of Multiple Regression Analysis on Determinants of Attitudes Toward Capital Punishment

Independent Variable	R Square	RSQ Change	Simple r	b	β	F Ratio
Utilitarian sentiments	.204	.204	.452	.319	.350	379.504[a]
Retributive sentiments	.323	.028	.336	.301	.164	99.717[a]
Attitudes toward civil liberties	.239	.007	−.293	−.111	−.171	83.335[a]
Dogmatism	.258	.019	.036	−.147	−.157	82.904[a]

[a]Significant at $p < .001$

This is at least one aspect of the problem we confront with these variables. The average intercorrelation of the four independent variables is .307. Further, some are a good deal more highly intercorrelated, particularly dogmatism and the civil liberties variable ($r = -.496$). One way to deal with this is to seek additional evidence on the relative importance of the independent variables. This was accomplished by computing four separate regression equations so that we could determine the R^2 increment associated with each variable when it is forced into the regression equation as the last variable, thus providing an estimate of its unique contribution to the explained variance. The R^2 increments we obtained provided a ranking of the variables that was slightly different from that based on the regression coefficients: utilitarian sentiments (R^2 increment = .085), retributive sentiments (R^2 increment = .022), attitudes toward civil liberties (R^2 increment = .019), and dogmatism (R^2 increment = .018).

This extension of the analysis, however, does not resolve the problem posed by the negative sign of the dogmatism regression coefficient, but the statistical and substantive issues are closely intertwined in that regard. Specifically, it seems likely that the civil liberties measure is exerting a suppressor effect on the relationship between dogmatism and support for capital punishment. Thus, once the civil liberties measure is taken into account, as it is in the computation of the standardized regression coefficient for dogmatism which is presented in Table II, the initially weak effect of dogmatism becomes more significant. That certainly makes substantive sense. It is akin to correlating rigidity, a personality trait that has been related to both highly liberal and highly conservative attitudes in prior research, with support for capital punishment, which has also been related to liberal-conservative attitudes, while holding a measure of liberal-conservative attitudes constant. Stated more simply, it is likely that the dogmatism variable would be substantively insignificant were the civil liberties variable to be removed from the regression equation. This is precisely what happens when that is done. In the three-variable equation we find that utilitarian sentiments are of major importance ($\beta = .404$, R^2 increment = .204), that retributive sentiments are less important ($\beta = .178$, R^2 increment = .028), and that, while still statistically significant, dogmatism adds virtually nothing to the explained variance ($\beta = -.088$, R^2 increment = .007).

On balance, and despite the unanticipated problem posed by the effect of the dogmatism measure, we interpret these findings as supportive of our expectations. Relative to prior research, these independent variables allow us to explain a statistically and substantively significant portion of the variance in public attitudes toward capital punishment. Further, the suggestion that those who support capital punishment because they are rigid, intolerant, and excessively conservative finds only partial support here. The effect of dogmatism, particularly when taken by itself, is trivial, and the effect of attitudes toward civil liberties, our measure of a relevant aspect of conservative-liberal attitudes, is less than that associated with either retributive or utilitarian sentiments. Indeed, without any intent to gloss over the fact that each of the four predictor variables proved to have a statistically significant effect on attitudes toward capital punishment, the most impressive finding is the dominant role played by the utilitarian belief that punishment has a deterrent effect. Further, the regression analysis shows that 89.99 percent of the explained variance ($R^2 = .232$) attributable to the four variables could be accounted for if only the utilitarian and retributive sentiments variables had been employed in the analysis.

SUMMARY AND CONCLUSIONS

Prior research has devoted a good deal of attention to studies of abuses of discretionary decision making in the processing of capital cases and assessments of the deterrent efficacy of capital punishment. While such research is of considerable importance, it has often had the effect of diverting attention from examinations of why so many citizens are willing to support the retention of capital punishment in the face of a worldwide movement away from any reliance on so extreme a sanction. Further, the relatively small number of studies that have taken public attitudes toward the death penalty as their primary concern have produced rather contrary conclusions regarding the variables that are determinants of these attitudes. Some have taken the view that those who support capital punishment are characteristically punitive, authoritarian, dogmatic, excessively conservative, or are, in some other clinical or quasi-clinical sense, willing to retain the death penalty for reason related to their defective personalities. Others have taken the quite different view that support for capital punishment is an entirely normal attitude among those who have been socialized to believe that the punishment of criminal offenders is both just (retributive sentiments) and a useful means of controlling or resolving a social problem that many agree is of increasing proportions (utilitarian sentiments).

The goal of this analysis, which is based on questionnaire data obtained from a sample of 3,334 adults who were randomly selected from one southeastern metropolitan area, has been to determine (1) the proportion of variance in attitudes toward capital punishment which should be explained by variables employed in earlier studies; (2) the relative importance of each of those variables; and (3) the relative merits of what have been described earlier as psychological and social psychological interpretations of support for the death penalty. Our multiple regression analysis showed that a relatively large proportion of the variance in attitudes toward capital punishment could be explained by the variables we employed. Further, while the moderate intercorrelations between the independent variables makes any determination of their relative importance somewhat ambiguous, an assessment of their importance based on an estimate of their unique contributions to the explained variance showed that utilitarian and retributive sentiments, our indicators of social psychological variables, were more influential than attitudes toward civil liberties and dogmatism, our indicators of types of variables more common in psychological explanations.

Because we found that almost eighty percent of the explained variance in support for capital punishment could have been accounted for had we relied exclusively on our measure of the perceived utility of punishment, our feeling is that the implications of this study for those concerned with social policy can be summarized in a straightforward fashion. Specifically, it seems clear that large numbers of citizens remain willing to retain the death penalty because of their feeling that doing so serves a useful purpose, that it may well be capable of deterring offenders from involvement in the kinds of behavior which are defined as capital crimes. Although reviews of the literature on the deterrent efficacy of sanctions quite clearly show that sanctions of some types can effectively deter some types of behavior (25, 34), the preponderance of the evidence on the deterrent effect of capital punishment shows that its impact is either weak or nonexistent. The implication is that private citizens may be willing to retain the death penalty because of entirely unrealistic expectations regarding its ability to deter criminal behavior. Indeed, to the extent that the constitutionality of capital punishment statutes is premised on informed public opinion, our conclusion is that a substantial fraction of support for capital punishment flows from such inadequately informed opinions that those statutes do not have the necessary support.

REFERENCES

1. Bailey, W. C. "Murder and Capital Punishment: Some Further Evidence,"*American Journal of Orthopsychiatry*, 45, 1975, 669–688.

2. Becker, G. S. "Crime and Punishment: An Economic Approach," *Journal of Political Economy*, 72, 1968, 169–217.

3.   Bedau, H. A. "Felony Murder Rape and the Mandatory Death Penalty," *Suffolk University Law Review*, 10, 1976, 493–520.

4.   Bedau, H. A. and C. M. Pierce (eds.) *Capital Punishment in the United States.* New York: AMS Press, 1976.

5.   Boehm, V. "Mr. Prejudice, Miss Sympathy and the Authoritarian Personality." *Wisconsin Law Review*, 1968, 736–750.

6.   Bowers, W. J. and G. L. Pierce. "The Illusion of Deterrence in Issac Ehrlich's Research on Capital Punishment," *Yale Law Journal*, 85, 1975, 187–208.

7.   Comrey, S. and J. Newmeyer. "Measurement of Radicalism and Conservatism." *Journal of Social Psychology*, 67, 1965, 357–369.

8.   Ehrlich, I. "Deterrence: Evidence and Inference," *Yale Law Journal*, 85, 1975, 209–227.

9.   Ehrlich, I. "The Deterrent Effect of Capital Punishment: A Question of Life and Death," *American Economic Review*, 65, 1975, 397–417.

10.   Erskine, H. "The Polls: Capital Punishment," *Public Opinion Quarterly*, 34, 1970, 290–307.

11.   *Furman v. Georgia,* 408 U.S. 238 (1972).

12.   *Gregg v. Georgia,* 49 L.Ed. 2d 859 (1976).

13.   Hindelang, M. J., M. R. Gottfredson, C. S. Dunn, and N. Parisi. *Sourcebook of Criminal Justice Statistics, 1976.* Washington, D.C.: U.S. Government Printing Office, 1977.

14.   Hollander, E. P. *Principles and Methods of Social Psychology,* 2nd edition. New York: Oxford University Press, 1971.

15.   Johnson, E. "Selective Factors in Capital Punishment," *Social Forces,* 36, 1957, 165–169.

16.   Jurow, G. L. "New Data on the Effect of a 'Death Qualified' Jury on the Guilt Determination Process," *Harvard Law Review,* 84, 1971, 567–611.

17.   Kerlinger, F. N. and E. J. Pedhazur. *Multiple Regression in Behavioral Research.* New York: Holt, Rinehart and Winston, 1973.

18.   Riedel, M. "Discrimination in the Imposition of the Death Penalty: A Comparison of the Characteristics of Offenders Sentenced Pre-Furman and Post-Furman," *Temple Law Quarterly,* 49, 1976, 261–287.

19.   Sarat, A. D. and N. Vidmar. "The Public and the Death Penalty: Testing the Marshall Hypothesis," Pp. 190–226 in H. A. Bedau and C. M. Pierce (eds.), *Capital Punishment in the United States.* New York: AMS Press, 1976.

20.   Schuessler, K. "The Deterrent Influence of the Death Penalty," *The Annals,* 284, 1952, 54–63.

21.   Snortum, J. and V. Ashear. "Prejudice, Punitiveness and Personality," *Journal of Personality Assessment,* 36, 1972, 291–301.

22.   Thomas, C. W. "Eighth Amendment Challenges to the Death Penalty," Unpublished paper presented to the Southern Sociological Society convention, April, 1977.

23.   Thomas, C. W. and S. C. Foster. "A Sociological Perspective on Public Support for Capital Punishment," *American Journal of Orthopsychiatry,* 45, 1975, 641–657.

24.   Thomas, C. W. and D. T. Mason. "Correlates of Public Support for Capital Punishment," *Social Problems,* forthcoming.

25.   Tittle, C. R. and C. H. Logan. "Sanctions and Deviance: Evidence and Remaining Questions," *Law and Society Review,* 7, 1973, 371–392.

26.   *Trop v. Dulles,* 356 U.S. 86 (1958).

27.   Vidmar, N. "Retributive and Utilitarian Motive and Other Correlates of Canadian Attitudes Toward the Death Penalty." *The Canadian Psychologist,* 15, 1974, 337–356.

28.   Vidmar, N. and P. C. Ellsworth. "Public Opinion and the Death Penalty," Pp. 125–151 in H. A. Bedau and C. M. Pierce (eds.), *Capital Punishment in the United States.* New York: AMS Press, 1976.

29.   *Weems v. United States,* 217 U.S. 349 (1910).

30.   *Witherspoon v. Illinois,* 391 U.S. 510 (1968).

31.   Wolfgang, M., A. Kelly and H. Nolde. "Comparison of the Executed and the Commuted Among Admissions to Death Row," *Journal of Criminal Law, Criminology and Police Science,* 53, 1962, 301–311.

32.   Wolfgang, M. and M. Reidel. "Race, Judicial

Discretion and the Death penalty," *The Annals*, 407, 1973, 119–133.

33.   Yunker, J. A. "Is the Death Penalty a Deterrent to Homicide? Some Time Series Evidence," *Journal of Behavioral Economics*, 5, 1976, 45–82.

34.   Zimring, F. E. and G. Hawkins. *Deterrence: The Legal Threat in Crime Control.* Chicago: The University of Chicago Press, 1973.

Appendix A

	SA	A	U	D	SD	Factor Loading
Attitudes Toward Civil Liberties						
The police should have the right to listen to and record telephone conversations if they believe that they need to do so.	11.8	30.0	11.8	26.0	20.3	.643
Convicted criminals should not have the right to appeal their convictions to a higher court.	5.9	10.4	8.1	46.8	28.7	.515
Tax money should not be used to pay for jury trials when the offender is obviously guilty.	8.0	16.2	11.2	43.8	20.8	.546
People who do not believe in and support our form of government should be punished.	5.6	13.6	14.2	46.9	19.8	.532
If there is evidence that proves that someone is guilty, it should be used in court regardless of how it was obtained by the police.	19.7	41.0	10.6	20.6	8.1	.614
Protests and demonstrations against our government, even if peaceful, should not be allowed in such troubled times as these.	8.2	17.8	11.2	44.7	18.1	.620
When a person is arrested, he should be held in jail until his case comes to trial if the police and prosecutors believe this is necessary.	10.8	48.9	11.9	22.5	6.0	.454
The police should be allowed to stop and search persons on the street if they feel it is necessary.	8.9	34.3	12.8	27.6	16.4	.569

Scale Mean = 25.849   Standard Deviation = 6.060

	SA	A	U	D	SD	Factor Loading
Dogmatism						
Most people just don't know what's good for them.	1.5	20.9	10.3	43.4	23.8	.430
Man on his own is a helpless and miserable creature.	2.9	36.8	20.9	33.2	6.2	.606
An insult to your name should not be forgotten.	8.0	39.7	16.5	27.7	8.1	.423
Of all the different philosophies which exist in this world there is probably only one which is correct.	2.1	35.7	17.4	37.7	7.2	.433

	SA	A	U	D	SD	*Factor Loading*
Dogmatism (continued)						
The highest form of government is a democracy and the highest form of democracy is a government run by those who are most intelligent.	15.5	57.8	14.4	10.0	2.3	.518
Most of the ideas which get printed today aren't worth the paper they're printed on.	9.2	40.8	18.0	26.5	5.5	.401
In this complicated would of ours the only way we can know what's going on is to rely on leaders or experts who can be trusted.	6.0	55.5	16.1	19.0	3.3	.529

Scale Mean = 20.325 Standard Deviation = 4.237

Utilitarian Sentiments

	SA	A	U	D	SD	*Factor Loading*
If judges would give longer sentences to criminals fewer of them would break the law again.	4.6	18.5	14.0	33.4	29.5	.719
A firm response to those who violate the law would soon reduce the crime rate in our society.	1.5	6.1	10.8	47.4	34.2	.615
The more seriously we punish someone for a crime the less likely he will be to break the law again.	4.9	20.6	17.8	36.5	20.2	.752
Punishing a criminal does little to keep him from committing another crime.	4.9	22.4	14.9	44.1	13.7	.469
Regardless of whether prison sentences keep the person who received the sentence from breaking the law again, they do show others in out society that crime does *not* pay.	1.9	8.4	7.4	61.2	21.1	.480
If people were certain that they would be punished for their actions, there would be far less crime.	1.6	11.5	7.5	52.9	26.6	.604

Scale Mean = 22.395 Standard Deviation = 4.330

Attitudes Toward Capital Punishment

	SA	A	U	D	SD	*Factor Loading*
I think that we should have a mandatory death penalty for some types of very serious criminal offenses.	6.2	8.3	5.1	26.4	53.9	.855

	SA	A	U	D	SD	Factor Loading
Attitudes Toward Capital Punishment (continued)						
Regardless of whether we actually use the death penalty, I think our laws should allow us to put someone to death should the need ever arise.	6.3	11.0	8.1	39.8	34.8	.794
No offense is so serious that it deserved to be punished by death.	4.8	6.6	7.8	40.4	40.4	.853
The execution of criminals is a disgrace to a civilized society.	4.3	9.0	9.6	50.8	26.2	.793

Scale Mean = 15.898 Standard Deviation = 3.948

	SA	A	U	D	SD	Factor Loading
Retributive Sentiments						
It is our duty to obey the law even though we may not always agree with it.	.7	3.2	3.5	55.8	36.7	.689
If a law is not fair and just, I feel no responsibility to abide by it.	2.1	8.0	10.4	58.8	20.6	.410
We have a moral obligation to punish people who break the law	1.0	9.0	8.0	62.6	19.3	.470
All citizens should show respect for the laws.	1.6	.5	1.2	44.2	52.6	.594

Scale Mean = 16.483 Standard Deviation = 2.154

34. Incapacitation of the Dangerous Offender

STEPHAN VAN DINE
SIMON DINITZ
JOHN CONRAD

OF THE POSSIBLE BENEFITS OF INCARCERATION, the protection of the public from violent crime is receiving considerable speculative attention from social critics. By restraining men disposed to the commission of violence, it is argued, the streets will become safer for as long as the restraint is in effect. Wilson (1975) and van den Haag (1975) have both made this point vigorously, referring to the landmark cohort study of Wolfgang, Figlio and Sellin (1972) and the less well known work of Shlomo and Reuel Shinnar (1975). This argument has been persuasive in many quarters, leading to the advocacy on a "hard line" in sentencing adult offenders convicted of crimes against the person. The call for long and mandatory sentences for these offenders is increasingly insistent.

Recent attempts to provide empirical evidence in support of an incapacitation policy have led to conflicting conclusions. In a marginal reference to the measurement of the incapacitation effect of punishment, Ehrlich (1973) found that less than 10 percent of the impact of imprisonment on the crime rate could be attributed to the restraint of offenders. Ehrlich's analysis included all seven index offenses and was based on a regression model for the study of the effects of deterrence; he did not

▶SOURCE: *"The Incapacitation of the Dangerous Offender: A Statistical Experiment," Journal of Research in Crime and Delinquency (January, 1977) 14: 22–34. Reprinted by permission.*

derive a more specific value for incapacitation as it related to the four violent index crimes.

Clark (1974) used data produced by the Philadelphia Birth Cohort study (Wolfgang et al., 1972) to estimate the extent to which crime would have increased if no juvenile had been confined. He computed a yearly average of index crimes committed by each chronic juvenile recidivist, and multiplied that average by the number of serious offenders incarcerated each year. The result is an increase of five to 15 percent in crime committed by the Wolfgang 1945 Birth Cohort; a similar increase in crime for all juveniles would have been reflected in an increase of one to four percent in reported crimes in Philadelphia.

Relying principally on California data, Greenberg (1975) estimated that each one year reduction in average sentence length would result in increases in the index crime rates of from 1.2 to 8.0 percent. This study rests on debatable assumptions. Greenberg estimates that the true figure for return to prison with convictions for new crimes during the first year after release will approximate eight percent, a much lower figure than usually suggested. The discrepancy is attributable to the exclusion of technical parole violations. Greenberg finally arrives at an average rate of index crimes committed by recidivists within a range of 0.5 to 4.3 crimes per recidivist per year. His calculation also rests on the dubious assumption that the average duration of a criminal career is five years, arguing that the higher averages usually accepted underrepresent one-crime offenders. He also inflates the crime rates reported in the Uniform Crime Reports by a multiplier derived from victimization studies. Greenberg's analysis concludes with two important and credible speculations: first, the low level of incapacitation which he infers from the data is attributable in part to the low rate of commission of serious crime by parolees. His second speculation points to the low rate of incarceration for index crimes. Obviously, if a more severe policy of restraint were applied, the incapacitative effects of imprisonment would substantially increase.

Ehrlich, Clarke, and Greenberg all conclude that incapacitation, as presently administered, has a relatively modest impact on the crime rate. The study by Shlomo and Reuel Shinnar (1975) approaches the problem from a different perspective and set of assumptions. Using data from the Uniform Crime Reports, they attempt to arrive at an estimate of the amount of crime which might be prevented by a much more severe sentencing policy. They estimate that the average number of crimes committed in the course of a criminal career is about 25 and that recidivists constitute 16 percent of the criminal population but commit about 90 percent of the crimes. The significant estimate derived from this analysis is that the career criminal commits six to 14 offenses per year while getting caught once. Therefore, the Shinnars boldly project that mandatory sentences, five years for violent index crimes and three years for burglary, could reduce the incidence of these crimes by 80 percent.

The studies discussed here are applications of various explanatory models to existing statistics of crime and delinquency. The investigation which will be described in this article attempts to fill an empirical gap. The basic question which we wish to address is: How many actual offenses might have been prevented by sentencing policies which are designed for the purpose of incapacitating the dangerous offender? In the next section, we shall set forth the methodology by which we arrive at an estimate based on an extensive case-by-case review of the histories of all violent offenders indicted in the Court of Common Pleas for Franklin County, (Columbus), Ohio during the year 1973.

METHODOLOGY

Our fundamental question cannot be answered without addressing subsidiary problems. The two primary issues can be formulated as follows:

1. How much violent crime will be prevented by an explicit policy of sentencing for incapacitation?

2. How long must sentences be if incapacitation is to make a significant impact on the violent crime rates?

Breaking these questions down to produce answers relevant to policy, we tried to design a study which would settle, so far as possible, the specific issues confronting the legislature in establishing sentencing limits and the courts in establishing actual terms of custodial confinement for offenders to be sentenced. We need to know the specific consequences of varying incapacitation policies on the incidence of homicide, robbery, aggravated assault, and forcible rape. How many of these crimes would be prevented by the restraint of repetitively violent criminals for periods of three or five years? Of violators with previous histories of non-violent offenses only? Of those under some specific age level reserved for the juvenile court? In short, what can the criminal histories of actual offenders tell us about the optimal sentencing policies if the reduction of violent crime is to be the object of a policy of incapacitation?

The 1973 Indictment and Conviction File

To address these and related questions, we collected all recorded data on every person charged with each of the violent crimes enumerated above in Franklin County (Columbus), Ohio in 1973.[1] In 1973, 364 adults were arrested and charged with one or more murders and manslaughters, robberies, aggravated assaults, and violent sex offenses. Of these 364 persons, 14 were charged with violent crimes committed while in prison or as escapees from a penal institution. These 14 cases were eliminated from the universe of eligible subjects. Also excluded were eight subjects for whom no previous criminal histories could be found in the files of the Columbus Police Department, the Franklin County Sheriff's Department, the Ohio Bureau of Criminal Identification, the F.B.I., or the Ohio Department of Rehabilitation and Corrections. Elimination of the 14 prison inmates and escapees and the eight persons with missing files reduced the cohort to 342 subjects.

The 342 remaining individuals met the following criteria. All were adults or juveniles bound over and charged as adults. All had been indicted or arraigned for one of the major personal crimes. All were listed by the Franklin County Prosecutor as "disposed of" (cases completed) during the 1973 calendar year. The Prosecutor "disposes of" a person charged with a crime in one of three ways: a plea of *nolle prosequi* is entered, usually because the prosecutor lacks sufficient evidence; the case proceeds to trial and the defendant is acquitted; or the defendant pleads guilty or is so found in the trial. A case is not considered complete until the immediate appeals are concluded.

Of our cohort of 342 Franklin County violent offenders in 1973, 166 were found guilty as charged. The remainder, 176 cases, were distributed between the two-thirds who were released on writs of *nolle prosequi* and "no bills," and the

[1]The cohort consists of all violent felony cases completed in 1973. Not all the cases began in 1973. Half the individuals were first booked in 1973 (50.0 percent), most of the rest in 1972 (45.6 percent) and the remainder in 1971 or before (4.4 percent). For simplicity in the study, the population is called the 1973 cohort and treated as if all cases began in 1973. This determination does not influence the results of the study, since the hypothetical incapacitation sentence is imposed on each person's record individually.

other third, who, after plea-bargaining, pled guilty to a lesser offense. We have divided our cohort accordingly into two groups, those who were found guilty as charged, and those who were indicted but not convicted on the violent crime charge. Our analysis separates these two groups, as will be seen in the tables we present in this paper.

Nevertheless it is essential to understand that our basic assumption holds that *all subjects in the cohort, whether found guilty or not of the crimes with which they were charged, did in fact commit all the crimes for which they were arrested.* Thus a man who was arrested for 14 robberies but tried and convicted on only three, is assumed, for the purpose of this study, to have committed all 14. If he had been subjected to a mandatory sentence on his last previous conviction of a felony, the resulting incapacitation would be counted as preventing all 14 offenses. This assumption deliberately overstates the effectiveness of an incapacitation policy. We are interested here in exploring the maximum potential of imprisonment in the prevention of crime; this assumption yields a maximum estimate of the effectiveness of adult incapacitation policies, as far as our data will let us go. To develop a minimum estimate of effectiveness, we compare convictions prevented to the number of crimes committed.

The uses of official records have limitations well known to criminologists. It would have been desirable to complete our analysis by presenting the influence of the variables of socioeconomic status, educational level, employment histories and other items of social differentiation, but the only uniform social information available identified those under study by age and race.

To test the effectiveness of incapacitation, we needed to determine how many of the 1973 offenses would have been prevented if an incapacitating sentence had been imposed at the last previous conviction. We tested five hypothetical sentencing policies, as follows:

Sentencing Option I: Assume that on any felony

conviction, whether violent or not, a five year net mandatory prison term was imposed.

Sentencing Option II: Assume that on any felony conviction after the first (second and following), whether violent or not, a five year net mandatory prison term was imposed. On the first conviction the penalty structure continues as under present law.

Sentencing Option III: Assume that on any felony conviction after the second (third and following), whether violent or not, a five year net mandatory prison term was imposed. On the first two convictions the penalty structure continues as under present law.

Sentencing Option IV: Assume that on any felony conviction, whether violent or not, a three year net mandatory prison term was imposed.

Sentencing Option V: Assume that on any first violent felony conviction, a five year net mandatory prison term was imposed. For any subsequent violent or non-violent felony by the same offender, a five year net mandatory prison term was imposed. For offenders convicted of only non-violent felonies, the penalty structure continues as under present law.

The adult histories of the 342 convicted 1973 violent offenders were examined to obtain the following information:

1. Did they have any previous felony conviction?

2. Were any such convictions for prior violent crimes?

3. When was the last felony conviction recorded prior to the 1973 conviction?

4. Would the imposition of a three or five year sentence for the earlier violation have prevented the 1973 offense? Would any of the 342 have been in prison under a stiffer earlier sentence and consequently been incapable of the 1973 murder/manslaughter, robbery, aggravated assault or violent sex offense?

Each case in the cohort was reviewed to provide an answer to each of these questions. In addition to arrest and court records, the F.B.I. arrest histories were also examined and coded. In this way each criminal career represented in the sample could be charted to determine the effect of a mandatory sentence of the length called for in each option for each offender meeting the criteria of the options under evaluation.

RESULTS

Table I presents our cohort in a distribution of the offenses for which they were indicted, the number of crimes with which they were charged, and the number of crimes charged per defendant. Robbery is by far the most frequent crime, and although this offense may be brutally violent, it may also be without violence inflicted or intended. Note also that if the robberies included under the separate heading of multiple offense category are combined with the robbery category, the total number of robbers would be 168, nearly half our sample. By the nature of this multiple offense category group, the robbers included in it must be presumed to be especially dangerous.

Attrition of the indictment sample is evident in Table II, which shows that only 166, or 48 percent, of the 342 persons indicted were convicted on violent charges for which they were indicted. Plea bargaining played an important role. Most of those convicted of a violent offense were convicted of fewer counts than the number for which they were indicted. Reduction of charges were quantitative as well as qualitative; it was not uncommon to find that 11 of 14 robbery counts, for example, were dismissed, leaving three counts for the actual conviction. A robbery and rape in the indictment resulted in a rape conviction. As previously indicated, where charges were dismissed in this manner, we counted them as actual offenses which might have been prevented by a policy of incapacitation.

As indicated in Table III, the 342 original

Table I. Distribution of Cohort by Crime of Indictment, Numbers of Crimes, and Number of Crimes per Indictee

	Persons Indicted	Crimes Charged by Categories of Persons Indicted	Charges/Person
Murder/manslaughter	36	45	1.2
Robbery	128	269	2.1
Sex offenses (violent)	79	111	1.4
Assault	49	66	1.3
Multiple offense (two of the above)	50[a]	147[b]	2.9
Total	342	638	1.9

[a]Of the 50 persons, 22 were charged with robbery-assault offenses, 12 with robbery-sex offenses, 6 with murder/manslaughter-robbery offenses, 6 with murder/manslaughter-assault offenses, 3 with assault-sex offenses, and 1 with murder/manslaughter-sex offenses.

[b]The 50 persons charged with multiple offenses generated 147 charges, of wheich there were 17 murder charges, 55 robbery charges, 32 sex offenses, and 43 assault offenses.

Table II. Distribution of Cohort by Crime of Conviction, Number of Convictions, and Number of Conviction-Counts per Offender

	Persons Convicted	Conviction-Counts	Conviction-Counts per Offender
Murder/manslaughter	18	20	1.1
Robbery	77	100	1.3
Sex offenses (violent)	23	24	1.0
Assault	28	30	1.1
Multiple offense (two of the above)	20[a]	57[b]	2.8
Total	166	231	1.4

[a]Of the 20 persons with multiple offenses, 6 each were convicted for robbery-assault offenses and with murder/manslaughter-assault offenses, 5 for murder/manslaughter-robbery offenses, and 1 offender for each of three combinations: murder/manslaughter-sex offenses, robbery-sex offenses, assault-sex offenses.

[b]The 20 offenders convicted on multiple offenses generated 57 conviction-counts, of which there were 14 murder conviction-counts, 20 robbery conviction-counts, 5 sex offense conviction-counts, and 18 assault conviction-counts.

Table III. Total Recorded Violent Offenses and Violent Offenses Cleared, Franklin County 1973

	Reported Violent UCR Crimes Franklin County, 1973[a]	Cleared by Arrest		Cleared by Conviction	
		N	% of UCR	N	% of UCR
Murder/manslaughter	65	62	95.4	34	52.3
Robbery	1,554	324	20.8	120	7.7
Sex offenses (violent)	326	143	43.9	29	8.9
Assault	947	109	11.5	48	5.1
Total	2,892	638	22.1	231	8.0

[a]UCR denotes Uniform Crime Reports.

members of the cohort were responsible for 638 offenses, which were cleared by their arrest. The 166 men who were convicted cleared only 231 offenses. These figures compare with the 2,892 violent index offenses reported in Franklin County in the 1973 *Uniform Crime Reports*. At the arrest level, the 638 charges represent 22.1 percent clearance on the reported violent crimes, but at the conviction level only 8.0 percent of these crimes finally resulted in a conviction. There was the usual variation in clearance rates. Clearance by arrest for murder/manslaughter amounted to 95.4 percent and by conviction to 52.3 percent; this compares with national clearances for these crimes for 1973 of 81.0 percent and 26.4 percent respectively. Clearance rates for Franklin County aggravated assaults were 11.5 percent by arrest and 5.1 percent by conviction. Although 43.9 percent of the violent sex offenses were cleared by arrest, only 8.9 percent resulted in convictions, which probably reflects the difficulty in prosecuting such cases to a conclusion.

The Frequency of Prior Felony Convictions

Of our 342 cohort members, only 107 had prior felony convictions. It is important to note that the average interval between the 1973 offense and the immediately previous felony conviction was 5.56 years, although the median interval

was 3.6 years. Examining the interval between convictions of the 107 recidivists, we found that an incapacitation period of three years would have prevented, at the most, only 42.4 percent of these persons from committing their 1973 offenses. With a five year incapacitation, 63.7 percent of the recidivists might have been prevented from the commission of the 1973 violent offenses.

THE TESTS OF INCAPACITATION

Our most severe sentencing option, designated here as Option I, provides that every convicted felon, regardless of the nature of the offense, will receive a sentence of five years net imprisonment. To re-state Option I, if any member of the cohort had an adult felony conviction of any sort in the five year period before 1973, then the charges and convictions recorded in that year would be considered to have been prevented.

Under Option I, we find that 68 offenders would have been prevented from committing an offense in 1973, which is 19.9 percent of the cohort. These individuals were responsible for 115 counts of violent crime. But at the conviction level, only 54 counts of violence would have been prevented by the Option I sentencing policy. Note that these 68 persons committed 115 offenses which would not have been carried out

Table IV. Persons Indicted by Number of Prior Offenses

Number of Prior Offenses	Total[a]		Violent		Non-Violent	
	N	%	N	%	N	%
0	235	68.7	307	89.8	262	76.6
1	57	16.7	29	8.5	54	15.8
2	31	9.1	3	0.9	19	5.6
3	11	3.2	2	0.6	9	2.6
4	5	1.5	1	0.3	1	0.3
5	2	0.6	–	–	1	0.3
6	1	0.3	–	–	–	–
Totals	342	100.0	342	100.0	342	100.0

[a]The non-violent and violent offender columns are not mutually exclusive. The total is not a sum of those columns.

Table V. The Impact of Option I[a] on the Amount of Crime Prevented, Arrest Level, and Conviction Level

	Persons Indicted	Persons Prevented		1973 UCR, Violent Crimes	Counts Prevented			
					Arrest Level		Conviction Level	
		N	% of Indicted		N	% of UCR	N	% of UCR
Murder/manslaughter	36	7	19.4	65	18	27.7	9	13.8
Robbery	128	36	28.1	1,554	64	4.1	30	1.9
Sex offenses (violent)	79	8	10.1	326	21	6.4	6	1.8
Assault	49	4	8.2	927	12	1.3	9	1.0
Multiple offenses (two of the above)	50	13	26.0	—	—	—	—	—
Totals	342	68	19.9	2,892	115	4.0	54	1.9

[a]Option I: a five year net prison term imposed after any felony conviction; no violent felonies are required.

if the Option I sentencing policy were applied; this modest total represents 4.0 percent of the 2,892 crimes of violence reported during 1973. But there were only 54 of these 115 preventable counts which resulted in convictions, or 1.9 percent of the reported crimes.

These findings are well within the ranges suggested by the models proposed by Clarke, Greenberg, and Ehrlich. The Shinnars' estimate cannot be reconciled with our findings, especially since for adults Option I is more severe than any policy they suggest.

Option II also calls for a mandatory sentence of five years, but it focuses on recidivist offenders. It is the most severe sentence applicable only to recidivists among the options considered here.

Under this option, 28 of the 342 indictees, charged with 43 violent offenses, would have been prevented from committing these offenses in 1973 if this sentencing policy had been in effect. The percentage of Franklin County violence would have been reduced by 1.5 percent.

The results of Option III-V are shown in Table VII. It is apparent that none of these variants on the severe sentencing policy of Option I would have prevented as much as the 4.0 percent of violent crime which our most drastic sentencing policy would have averted. But if Option I were mandated by the statutes, every felon would serve a five year sentence, even if the offense involved nothing more serious than bad checks, larceny, or auto theft. The absurd results to which such a policy would lead are hardly offset by the preventive effect described here. But any more specific option would be even less effective in the prevention of violent crime.

CONCLUSIONS

Based then, on this research, it would seem that the conclusions of Ehrlich, Clarke and Greenberg are supported. This study strongly suggests that incapacitation makes only a small and modest impact on the violent crime rate; a 4.0 percent drop is the highest estimate obtained in this research, utilizing the impractically harsh Option I.

Why doesn't incapacitation prevent more crime? This analysis suggests three reasons. First, our study did not assume the incapacitation of juveniles. Since in 1973 about one-fourth the persons arrested for violent crimes were juveniles, (Table 30, 1973 *Uniform Crime Reports*), stiffer policies which leave the juvenile system unaffected can have no impact on the incidence of juvenile violence. Certainly incapacitation of juvenile felony offenders would have prevented some violent crimes. Incapacitation policies applied to juvenile offenders would require a drastic modification of juvenile court legislation and the disposition of juvenile offenders.

Second, at least according to this study, the pool of violent recidivists who would have been immobilized through incapacitation is comparatively small in comparison to all those indicted for violent offenses. *Over two-thirds of the persons in this study were first time felony offenders. Incapacitation could not have prevented their 1973 crimes.* Only 31 percent of the cohort had any previous felony conviction. Only 11 percent of the cohort had any previous *violent* felony conviction. Fourteen percent of the cohort had two or more felonies of any type. The potential target groups are too small for incapacitation to be truly effective.

Third, the rate of repetition for the recidivist group is too low to provide significant reductions in the incidence of crime through an incapacitation policy. The average interval between violent incidents for a repeat offender was 5.6 years; the median was 3.6 years. Probably some of this delay was caused by imprisonment; some was caused by difficulties in apprehending an offender after his return to crime. Nonetheless, the typical offender in this cohort probably committed violent crime infrequently; at the least he was arrested infrequently. The clearest example is the case of the most frequent offender. This man had six prior felony offenses and

Table VI. The Impact of Option II[a] on the Amount of Crime Prevented, Arrest Level, and Conviction Level

	Persons Indicted	Persons Prevented		1973 UCR, Violent Crimes	Counts Prevented			
					Arrest Level		Conviction Level	
		N	% of Indicted		N	% of UCR	N	% of UCR
Murder/manslaughter	36	0	—	65	2	3.1	1	1.5
Robbery	128	18	14.1	1,554	28	1.8	15	1.0
Sex offenses (violent)	79	4	5.1	326	7	2.2	1	0.3
Assault	49	2	4.1	947	6	0.6	3	0.3
Multiple offenses (two of the above)	50	4	8.0	—	—	—	—	—
Totals	342	28	8.2	2,892	43	1.5	20	0.7

[a]Option II: a five year net prison term imposed after any second felony conviction; no violent felonies are required.

Table VII. Summary of the Impact of Five Sentencing Options

Measure of Prevention Sentencing Option Number	Persons Prevented	% of[a] Cohort	Indictment Charges Prevented	% of[b] UCR	Conviction Counts Prevented	% of[b] UCR
I	68	19.9	115	4.0	54	1.9
II	28	8.2	43	1.5	20	0.7
III	12	3.5	21	0.7	11	0.4
IV	44	12.9	71	2.5	28	1.0
V	21	6.1	41	1.4	24	0.8

[a]The cohort consisted of 342 indictees.
[b]There was a total of 2,892 violent felonies in Franklin County in 1973.
Option I: One or more convictions, no prior violent felony, five year mandatory sentence.
Option II: Two or more convictions, no prior violent felony, five year mandatory sentence.
Option III: Three or more convictions, no prior violent felony, five year mandatory sentence.
Option IV: One or more convictions, no prior violent felony, three year mandatory sentence.
Option V: One or more convictions, one violent felony required, five year mandatory sentence.

was convicted in 1973 of a seventh. Yet it took him 40 years to acquire such a record. Two persons had five convictions; one began his felony career in 1937, the other in 1945. The implication is that career violent offenders commit their crimes slowly, if persistently.

Only about 40–50 percent of Columbus' reported violent crime is cleared each year by an adult or juvenile arrest. The Shinnars premise their study on the belief that most uncleared crime is committed by those arrested. Following these writers, a strict incapacitation policy would prevent more crime than is actually cleared by arrest. A reduction of the "safety" crime rate (violent crime plus burglary) by 80 percent as postulated by the Shinnars contrasts markedly with the national clearance rate of less than half of the crimes reported to the UCR. This reduction also seems unlikely since police seek to "clear" as many crimes as possible on those arrested. Certainly our study illustrates this practice, i.e., persons who are arrested are frequently charged and even over-charged with multiple incidents; some of our subjects were charged with as many as 17 robberies.

The Shinnars assume that those arrested for

violent offenses also committed the uncleared violent offenses. In the data in our study, the 342 adults arrested accounted for 638 crimes, or 22.1 percent of the reported violent crimes in the country; three and one-half times as many as were actually cleared by arrest. In a simple calculation the crimes prevented by incapacitation, 4.0 percent of the total reported, would also be increased three and one-half times, to a total of about 18 percent. In other words, if:

1. every arrest was proper and yielded a conviction,

2. juveniles committed crimes at the same rate as adults,

3. all convicted felons had received a five year net prison sentence, and

4. every crime was committed by a person later arrested,

then the violent crime rate might be reduced by the 18 percent calculated above. Given the improbability of such a set of conditions, the Shinnars' estimate of an 80 percent reduction in safety crime stretches the imagination.

The implication of this analysis is clear. The characteristics of the criminal population and the limits of the criminal justice process minimize the potential of incapacitation. Our findings show that those arrested for violent crime are primarily first offenders. The repeaters are recidivating at a much slower rate than the Shinnars assume. We conclude from our data that incapacitation is a much less effective tool in the reduction of crime than Wilson and van den Haag believe.

Wilson's recommendations for an incapacitation policy as a means of crime control are based on the Shinnar extrapolations and on the Wolfgang cohort study. Superficially, Wilson's suggestion has face validity. If, indeed, as Wolfgang noted, a certain small population of repeaters commit a large number of crimes in a short period, then simply slowing them down with incapacitation-oriented sentences ought to cut the crime rate.

This suggestion fails, however, when tested on an adult population. It seems likely that no matter how lax the adult criminal justice system may be, convicted felons do not return to crime as quickly as the repetitive juveniles in the Wolfgang study.

The possibility exists that this cohort, a collection of people in one county in one year, is atypical. Perhaps, for cities other than Columbus, the typical criminal population consists of a larger proportion of repeat offenders. We encourage replication of this study to test that possibility.

For incapacitation to be effective, two conditions must exist. First, the apprehension rate must be greatly increased, unless it can be shown that a very large percentage of uncleared crimes are committed by those who are arrested. Second, a large percentage of crimes must be committed by repeat offenders, much higher than has been found in this study. This second condition depends upon the assumption that convicted offenders spend very little time in prison. Advocates of an incapacitation policy assume that both of these conditions are largely true. This study suggests that they are not.

A FINAL CAUTION

We plan to make a parallel study of the effect of incapacitation sentences on the incidence of juvenile violence. We cannot now safely generalize about the impact of incapacitating sentences on juvenile offenders. The impediment is the limited number of juvenile offense records we have been able to accumulate for our cohort of 342. So far, we have been able to locate only 90 juvenile crime histories for the total group. This number is much too small for a firm conclusion.

Nevertheless, it is legitimate to make an estimate, and we have done so, using two kinds of assumption. Proceeding with sentencing Option I, in which persons are incarcerated for a full five years on conviction of any felony, we have applied this policy to members of the cohort using these assumptions, which, as will be seen, demonstrate the limits of the impact of incapacitation without clearly establishing its actual effect.

We begin by making a simple extrapolation from the records of the 90 cohort members we have. When sentencing Option I is applied without including the juvenile records, 115 crimes were prevented, 4.0 percent of the 2,892 violent offenses committed in the county. When the 90 juvenile records are included in the data, 122 crimes, or 4.2 percent of the total, are prevented. If we extrapolate the experience of the 90 records to all 342 members of the cohort, thus assuming that the incidence of juvenile commission of felonies for the total cohort is the same as for the 90 on whom we have records, we find that 142—or 4.9 percent—of the 2,892 reported crimes would have been prevented. If this estimate is close to reality—and we do not know what its distance from the truth may be—the reduction of adult violence by a policy of incapacitation of the juvenile felony offenders will be slight. It must be stressed that this conclusion does not apply to the prevention of juvenile violence by incapacitating policies imposed on juvenile felony offenders. This estimate is placed in perspective when it is noted that the Uniform Crime Reports for 1973 indicate that 22.7 percent of arrests for violent offenses involved juveniles.

Another basis for estimate assumes the worst case to prevail. We tried the supposition that every member of the cohort whose juvenile record is missing had committed a felony offense as a juvenile. Thus, all 1973 offenses committed by persons who were juveniles between 1968 and 1973 would have been prevented. Obviously this distorts reality, since of the available 90 juvenile records, 76 were clear of felony convictions. But when we use this assumption we find that the impact of incapacitation is more than doubled. The number of violent crimes rises from 142 to 303—10.5 percent of the 2,892 violent crimes in the crimes in the country in 1973. Given the obvious exaggeration of this assumption, the reduction of crime by incapacitation still seems unimpressive.

35. Decriminalization of Consensual Homosexuality

GILBERT GEIS
RICHARD WRIGHT
THOMAS GARRETT
PAUL R. WILSON

STATE LEGISLATURES INCREASINGLY ARE CONSID-
ering legal reforms that would remove criminal
penalties from homosexual activities in private
between consenting adults. In part, this response
has emerged with the growing demands of other
minorities for legal rights. In addition, as Edwin Schur (1965, p. 110) has noted, there has
been a "general breakdown of the conspiracy of
silence that has traditionally surrounded
[homosexuality]." Nevertheless, the great majority of American jurisdictions continue to outlaw
any type of homosexual act, whether consensual
or not.

Widespread controversy exists concerning
the impact of the altered statutes. The controversy centers most fundamentally on the
question of whether decriminalization will encourage homosexual behavior and/or increase
its visibility. Similarly, debate has been concerned with the effect that decriminalization
might have on other forms of criminal behavior
and upon law enforcement procedures (cf. Geis,
1972, pp. 15–52).

There are some bits of information that bear
upon these issues. In Holland, a study conducted at the University of Utrecht indicated no
change in the incidence of homosexuality following its decriminalization (Wilson & Chappell,
1968). Reports regarding the pioneering 1962
Illinois decriminalization statute, however,
maintain that it has not been effective in providing protection for homosexuals. Martin
Hoffman (1969, p. 95) notes that "homosexuals
in Chicago have had somewhat more trouble
with the law since enactment of the new penal
code than have homosexuals in San Francisco
during the same period of time," an observation
that underlines the fact that decriminalization is
no panacea, though it fails to address the question of whether Illinois homosexuals have been
better or worse off following enactment of the
new law. Others believe that removal of sodomy
from the Illinois code caused the police to become more intense in their pursuit of homosexuals under the state's solicitation law (Gunnison,
1969).

However, commentators (cf. Abse, 1968, p.
87) on the drive in England that led to the decriminalization of homosexual acts note that debates there "helped to make the country a little
more rational. Persistent educational campaigns
of this kind assist both the nation and its leaders
to gain insights and to come to terms with sexu-
ality and aggression." This last may be, in fact,
the most significant correlate of decriminalization, for it is not only the law on the statute
books that bears upon homosexuals but also the
views put forward by persons all about them.
And such persons inevitably have formed their

▶SOURCE: *"Reported Consequences of Decriminalization of
Consensual Adult Homosexuality in Seven American States," Journal of Homosexuality (Summer, 1976) 1 (4): 419–426. Reprinted by
permission.*

own opinions to a great extent on the basis of legal dictates.

Individuals opposing decriminalization of homosexuality generally maintain that such a move would produce a corrosive effect on society. They feel that if criminal sanctions are removed there will be not only more private homosexual activity but also an increase in homosexual acts in public places. This they regard as undesirable for a variety of reasons, some theological, some pragmatic (e.g., the birth rate will decline and jeopardize national defense), and some aesthetic. They also argue that without the criminal law to control homosexuality there will be an increase in crimes said to be associated with the homosexual subculture, such as solicitation, child molestation, and sadistic crimes of violence (Davis, 1973).

Proponents of revision of the law assert that in a democratic society all persons should be allowed to do as they please, so long as they do not harm others. They insist that homosexuality probably leads to no more undesirable consequences, such as child molestation, than does heterosexuality, and that if it is the consequences that are undesirable, then *they* ought to be outlawed, and not homosexual acts themselves. Criminal law in general is said to be brought into disrepute by allowing statutes that are fundamentally unenforceable to remain on the books. Blackmail is one consequence of homosexual statutes. Another is the violation of the law by police officers as well as their employment in matters that divert their attention from serious criminal activity. Homosexuals also find themselves disproportionately the victims of criminal violence, since they are inhibited from access to legal redress because of the jeopardy of their own position (Sagarin & MacNamara, 1975).

No attempt has been made to date to document the reasonableness of these varying views by examining the experiences of the states that have changed the law regarding homosexuality. Information of this sort, we believe, could suggest to persons in jurisdictions contemplating a change in their codes some likely consequences of such action.

METHOD

At the time of our survey, seven states—Colorado, Delaware, Oregon, Hawaii, Ohio, Illinois, and Connecticut—had decriminalized private homosexual behavior between consenting adults. Questionnaires were sent to the police departments in cities in each of these states with populations of 50,000 or more persons—a total of 70 departments in all. One questionnaire was directed to the department chief, and the second was to be routed to the officer in the department responsible for offenses such as homosexual activity. Similarly, the prosecuting attorneys for the counties in which the cities were located received a pair of questionnaires. Exceptions occurred in Delaware, where the sole prosecutor, the attorney general, received the inquiries, and in Colorado, where prosecution is arranged by districts rather than by counties. We also sent five questionnaires each to 47 homosexual groups listed in a national directory, asking that they be distributed to members.

Each questionnaire was accompanied by a letter describing the purpose of our survey and stressing its confidentiality and anonymity. A stamped, preaddressed envelope was provided for return of the questionnaires.

The response rate, as we had anticipated, was relatively low for each group. Seventeen police departments (24%) responded, returning a total of 26 questionnaires (19%). Thirteen prosecuting attorney offices answered (33%), sending back 21 questionnaires (26%). The return from members of homosexual groups was particularly low; six groups were represented (13%), and they forwarded a total of 27 questionnaires (12%). The rather low percentage of returns should not be regarded as a serious shortcoming of the study, we believe. We were not aiming at total coverage, but rather at determining how officials and persons closely acquainted with the situation found things after decriminalization. We wanted to acquire a sense of what seemed to have occurred, not a numerical inventory of what, under any circumstances, would be idiosyncratic results in different cities and counties.

FINDINGS

The questionnaire responses indicated a consistent belief among those replying that the decriminalization of homosexuality had not produced the kinds of deleterious consequences that had been warned against. There were differences among the respondent groups in regard to particular matters, but the agreement was more pronounced than the distinctions.

In regard to the use of force by homosexuals, for instance, a large majority of the members of all groups felt that there had been no increase in such behavior since the enactment of the decriminalization measure. Surprisingly, more police officers (20, or 88%) and prosecuting attorneys (17, or 90%) than homosexuals (19, or 73%) felt this way. (Percentages will vary at times because of different numbers of persons answering each question. This is the reason we report both numerical and percentage figures.) Additionally, 20 police officers (96%) and 16 prosecuting attorneys (65%) replied that the involvement of homosexuals in non-sex-related crimes had not risen.

Fear of "corrupting" relationships between adult homosexuals and minors constitutes a matter that often is alleged to lie behind criminal statutes. In this regard, it is noteworthy that 16 prosecuting attorneys (80%), 25 homosexuals (96%), and 18 police officers (69%) stated that the involvement of homosexuals with minors was no more prevalent today than before the change in the law. The discrepancy between the law enforcement response and the homosexual response to this question might be regarded as an indicator of an arena of intense debate. Indeed, in their written comments, a large number of policemen, while grudgingly granting the reasonableness of decriminalization, nonetheless felt compelled to suggest a particular need for measures protecting young persons from homosexual solicitation.

A majority of each group (17 homosexuals, or 63%; 12 prosecutors, or 71%; and 14 police officers, or 54%) believed that despite decriminalization private homosexual behavior had not increased notably. With the exception of fewer than a handful of respondents who believed that there had been an increase, the remaining respondents said they thought the amount of homosexual behavior had remained essentially the same following decriminalization.

There were striking differences in the manner in which the respondents replied to the question regarding public displays of homosexual behavior in the wake of the law's revision. The police (17, or 65%) and the homosexuals (15, or 58%) both saw an increase in such behavior, but only 6 prosecutors (33%) saw things the same way. This may indicate, perhaps, that persons most conversant with the behavior will become aware of consequences of the law's changes while such changes will have no particular impact upon persons more removed from the foci of the activity.

About half of the respondents in each category noted an increase in gay bars, but the members of the groups sharply disagreed on the question of whether there had been an increase in public solicitation by homosexuals. Only 3 homosexuals (12%), compared to 5 attorneys (26%) and 15 policemen (59%), thought that such an increase had taken place.

A large majority of policemen (21, or 81%) felt that the homosexual subculture had become more unified since decriminalization, a response that found agreement from 12 (60%) of the prosecuting attorneys but only 11 (42%) of the homosexuals.

A notable finding was that a sizable proportion of each group responded that social condemnation of homosexuals had decreased after the law's revision: 11 homosexuals (44%), 13 police officials (52%), and 9 prosecuting attorneys (45%). Only 3 respondents felt that social condemnation was greater—2 police officers and 1 homosexual. Similarly, only 1 person, a police official, noted an increase in blackmail of homosexuals. In fact, 8 homosexuals (31%), 2 prosecuting attorneys (11%), and 4 police officers (17%) reported an apparent decrease.

Predictably, the police and prosecuting attorneys disagreed with the homosexuals when asked if they believed as many homosexuals are arrested today as before, but charged under different statutes. Only 3 police officers (12%) and 2 prosecuting attorneys (11%) thought that this was the case, compared to 18 homosexuals (75%). Some of the arresting statutes cited by the homosexuals included loitering, jaywalking, disturbing the peace, vagrancy, and disorderly conduct. As stated by one of the homosexual respondents: "Cops still wait for us to do something wrong."

Another particularly important finding, given the present concern for crime control, was that 13 police officers (50%) reported that decriminalizing private homosexual behavior allowed them to spend more time on serious crimes. We did not specifically ask the prosecuting attorneys if the legislative change had helped to cut caseloads, but 1 attorney volunteered: "I basically have no interest in prosecuting victimless crimes. We are overburdened with more property crimes and crimes of violence than we can handle."

The police and prosecuting attorneys, when asked what penalty they would prescribe for homosexual conduct, were it still illegal, generally replied that it was a psychiatric problem and should be treated accordingly. Nineteen police officers (70%) specified psychiatric care, as did 10 prosecuting attorneys (48%). One police chief recommended "forced attendance in a class showing the results of what happens to fags as they grow older and lonely."

The results also showed, not surprisingly, that the vast majority of homosexual respondents (24, or 88%) were in favor of the change in the legislation when it took place. Prosecuting attorneys also generally said that they were supportive of the revision at its inception (16, or 84%). Only 11 police officers (44%) said that they were in agreement with the decriminalization when it occurred. When questioned about their current feelings about the legal change, however, the police and the homosexuals offered a more positive evaluation. The homosexuals were now in unanimous support, and police approval had risen significantly to 57% (13 officers). There was a rather surprising decline in the number of prosecuting attorneys now noting approval (14, or 77%).

The three groups also were questioned about their feelings toward other victimless crimes in light of their experience with the decriminalization of homosexual acts. Fifty percent of the officers (13 persons) reported that they were less in favor now of decriminalizing prostitution, gambling, pornography, and marijuana use. The homosexuals, however, were considerably more liberal. They were presently more supportive of decriminalizing these offenses by a majority ranging from 53% to 60%, depending upon the specific offense. Prosecuting attorneys' response to the question were less homogeneous. There was a reported increase in support for decriminalizing prostitution, with 10 of 21 respondents, or 48%, taking this position now. But there was reportedly less support now than earlier for decriminalizing marijuana use, and the same level of support for proscription of gambling and pornography. For these offenses decriminalization was favored by 48%, 38%, and 38% of the respondents, respectively.

DISCUSSION

The responses we elicited from the members of our sample obviously combine, in inextricable ways, facts and perceptions. Each of us has a tendency to see what it is that we are seeking. Nonetheless, the responses indicate with some force that in those states where homosexuality has been removed from the criminal codes the consequences, as perceived by persons in law enforcement and in the homosexual community, generally have been quite benign. The police, for instance, report an initial opposition to decriminalization (44% agreed with it) that has now changed to 57% approval. The number of persons involved may be small, but it can be presumed that the enactment of the statutes, if the results had been disruptive, would have whittled away any original support in law enforcement circles. The change toward more favorable views by the police is tied to reports of more time to enforce laws against more serious crimes, less blackmail, and no notable increases in the kinds of behavior that the police regard as particularly heinous—use of force by homosexuals, involvement of homosexuals in other kinds of crime, and child molestation.

The changes in the laws received only mild approval from the homosexual respondents. Many, in response to open-ended questions, noted that the matter represented only a partial step toward social equality and justice. "We need legislation to end discrimination in employment, housing, and [to allow] us to be open about our feelings toward each other," one respondent noted. Another observed succinctly: "The law is necessary and good, but it doesn't change society's prejudices, fears, and ignorance." A large number of the homosexual group expressed a particular need for some mechanism whereby public attitudes toward them would be altered. Nonetheless, there were many strong expressions of approval of the change that had taken place. "I thank God(dess)," wrote one respondent, "for the law because, speaking for myself, I feel somewhat free from *real* police harassment."

For other states that are now debating their statutes regarding homosexuality, our pilot survey would seem to indicate that they ought not to take very seriously Cassandra-like pronouncements regarding dire consequences if they join the handful of states now operating without statutes outlawing consensual adult homosexuality. In Oregon, for instance, one legislator suggested during debate on the state's law that Oregon would become "a playground for these kinds of people" (Fadeley, 1972, p. 522). The facts hardly seem to support such a scare tactic.

We suspect, most fundamentally, that attitudes toward and activities of homosexuals largely will be conditioned by matters beyond the ken of the criminal law. Homosexuality may increase significantly as a consequence of the imperatives of the ethos of women's liberation; some psychiatrists (Ginsberg, Frosch, & Shapiro, 1972) now maintain, for instance, that that ethos has been responsible for a dramatic rise in impotence among males. Conversely, homosexuality may decline, as Charles Winick (1968) suggests, because of the growing freedom of heterosexual activity and, in particular, the use in heterosexual relations of acts that in the past were more exclusively confined to the homosexual domain, such as oral copulation.

In the final analysis, though, decriminalization ought not be undervalued. It is likely to have a long-range impact upon homosexual self-concepts. "Affirmation through law and governmental acts expresses the public worth of one's subculture's norms relative to those of others," Gusfield (1968, p. 58) noted in a study of social movements. Similarly, Donald Webster Cory (1951, p. 12) has observed that "a person cannot live in . . . a society that outlaws and banishes his activities and desires . . . without a fundamental influence on his personality." The point may be somewhat overstated, but its basic thrust seems accurate and important.

REFERENCES

Abse, L. The Sexual Offences Act. *British Journal of Criminology*, 1968, *8,* 86–88.

Cory, D. W. *The homosexual in America.* New York: Greenberg, 1951.

Davis, E. Victimless crime: The case for continued enforcement. *Police Science and Administration,* 1973, *1,* 11–20.

Fadeley, E. N. Sex in the new code. *Oregon Law Review,* 1972, *51,* 517–524.

Geis, G. *Not the law's business? An examination of homosexuality, abortion, prostitution, narcotics, and gambling in the United States.* Washington, D.C.: United States Government Printing Office, 1972.

Ginsberg, G. L., Frosch, W. A., & Shapiro, T. The new impotence. *Archives of General Psychiatry,* 1972, *26,* 218–220.

Gunnison, F. The homophile movement in America. In R. W. Weltge (Ed.), *The same sex: An appraisal of homosexuality.* Philadelphia: Pilgrim Press, 1969.

Gusfield, J. On legislating morals: The symbolic process of designating deviancy. *California Law Review,* 1968, *56*, 54–68.

Hoffman, M. *The gay world: Homosexuality and the social creation of evil.* New York: Bantam, 1969.

Sagarin, E., & MacNamara, D. E. J. The homosexual as a crime victim. *International Journal of Criminology and Penology,* 1975, *3*, 14–25.

Schur, E. M. *Crimes without victims: Deviant behavior and public policy.* Englewood Cliffs, N.J.: Prentice-Hall, 1965.

Wilson, P. R., & Chappell, D. Australian attitudes toward abortion, prostitution, and homosexuality. *Australian Quarterly,* 1968, *40,* 7–17.

Winick, C. *The new people: Desexualization in American life.* New York: Pegasus, 1968.

SECTION IV

Custodial Institutions

PENAL INSTITUTIONS, OFTEN HOPEFULLY AND EUPHEMISTICALLY RENAMED "correctional facilities," have undergone enormous transformations within the last decade. Under pressure of court decisions, professional criminologists, and a public disillusioned with older methods of prison management, many states have made significant changes intended to lessen the inherent cruelty of incarceration and facilitate the rehabilitation of an increasing proportion of prisoners. We attempt in this section to present selections that describe the business of prison management. This examination of the formal organization of custodial life will serve as a backdrop for the material encountered later in this volume.

The first selection describes a unique institutional setting, a coed prison at the Federal Correctional Institution at Fort Worth, Texas. Here are found men and women offenders of specified types who have usually transferred from some other facilities. Within an atmosphere of normalcy, male prisoners eat and work with female offenders, while still operating under severe official restrictions on "physical contact." In an article especially written for this volume by Hopper, the Mississippi State Penitentiary is described, a less "free" setting, but one approaching sexual normalcy because of conjugal visiting. Married male prisoners have sexual access to their wives in special prison facilities, and, in recent years, conjugal visiting is even permitted married female offenders and the visits have been extended to three days duration.

One of the results of recent prisoner agitation and legal action has been the overturning in most states of rigid and unreasonable rules and disciplinary machinery. The Inmate Reference Manual of Arizona State Prison, a rather typical prison rule book, is examined in our next selection. It details a remarkably reasonable procedure for handling disciplinary cases, possible sanctions and penalties, and safeguards of prisoners' rights.

It does not follow of course that penal institutions have suddenly become humane institutions. The "Hole" at San Quentin, a prison in one of the most progressive of our state systems, is next depicted in ruthless detail. We learn, through the eyes of an anthropologist who worked in the prison, of the corrosive nature of the punishment section and the role of the staff in this setting. Can these conditions continue? Perhaps the most important development relating to penal institutions in recent years involves the legal rights of prisoners. The selections from Fogel touch on a range of problems and the legal aspects of each—corporal punishment and guard brutality, solitary confinement, denial of medical care, and even constitutional issues regarding the prisoners' religious rights and access to mail and publications.

The final selection in this section describes prison furloughs, the release of inmates to visit their homes for one or two days. This practice, which remained relately rare until the last few years, now involves perhaps a quarter of a million unescorted trips into the community each year. Although its specific effect on rehabilitation remains conjectural at this time, there is no doubt that it improves prisoner morale, strengthens family ties, and facilitates a search for employment when release is imminent.

36. A Coed Prison

ESTHER HEFFERNAN
ELIZABETH KRIPPEL

THE BASIC CRITERIA FOR ADMISSION TO FEDERAL Correctional Institution (F.C.I.), Fort Worth, are that a man or woman be within two years of a probable release date, qualify for participation in one of the functional Unit Programs, have no record of violent behavior and be from the South-Central region of the United States. Exceptions have been made, however, in regard to each of these criteria, most notably the last. Within these guidelines, the roads to F.C.I. are many and varied.

In the summer of 1973, approximately 60 per cent of the residents were "transfers" from other institutions in the Federal System. Most had applied for admission to Fort Worth in order to take part in one of the treatment programs or simply to be closer to home. For a few, these officially "acceptable" reasons masked the hope of "doing easy time." In other cases, transfers were initiated by the staff at the other institutions, primarily for reasons of health and age. The other 40 per cent of the resident population were committed to Fort Worth directly from Federal Courts. For many of these, it was their first commitment to a correctional facility.

*

Few residents arriving at Fort Worth are to-tally unaware of the fact that the institution is unique in many respects. Widely reputed along the grapevine as "the best place to do time—if you have to do time," F.C.I.'s coed setting, its opportunities for passes, furloughs, and work or study release, and sometimes the treatment orientation of its programs are discussed with prospective residents in county jails and Federal prisons across the country. Nothing, however, seems to prepare them fully for the reality which greets them.

In terms of physical layout and security measures, the Federal Correctional Institution at Fort Worth, Texas, seems typical of institutions officially listed by the Federal Bureau of Prisons as "intermediate term facilities for adults." Located on the fringes of the city's southwest side, its yellow stone buildings with their red tile roofs are easily visible from Interstate 820 to the south or Seminary Drive which borders it on the north. An eight-foot fence rims the property and encloses within its protective shield not only the main institution but two groups of staff housing and the remnants of the dairy farm which once gave the facility its still more widely known name as the "narcotics farm." The five main buildings cluster around a pleasant yard with a healthy and surprisingly undisturbed flower garden in the center and colorful park benches located at various points in the yard. A twelve-foot fence surrounds these buildings and is topped with electrical wiring which allows for surveillance from a large panel in the Control

▶SOURCE: *Interim Report on Research, Fort Worth Federal Correctional Institution (February 1973–May, 1974), pp. 23–26; and Final Report on Research, Fort Worth Federal Correctional Institution (February 1973–March, 1975), pp. 3–4, 25–26, 33–38 (Editorial adaptations). Reprinted by permission of the authors.*

441

Room. Just outside the fence at intervals of about fifty yards there are powerful perimeter lights for use in guarding the institution at night. To almost no one's displeasure these have never been fully utilized because of the energy crisis which surfaced just as the installation was completed. Standard security measures also include closed-circuit television cameras which keep a watchful eye on all who pass into or out of the Administration Building. Residents expressed some initial dismay and fear that "this is going to be just like any other joint" when these were installed. Now they have forgotten that such security measures are present.

*

SOCIAL RELATIONSHIPS

Social relationships, especially with one's fellow residents, play a significant role in the life of almost every resident. Eighty-five per cent of those interviewed maintain that "going it alone" is just not possible at F.C.I. ". . . a lot of people come here with the idea that that's how they'll do their time, but they change. Only those who are real loners on the 'outside' stick with it." "You can't go it alone here—at least not for very long . . . the atmosphere is such that you really can't keep to yourself." While acknowledging the need for people in their lives, most residents are very cautious in picking their associates. Many, in fact, state that they prefer to use the term "acquaintances" rather than "friends" to describe their relationships. In some instances, this is simply one of the realities of prison existence. "It's pretty hard to make real friends in prison . . . people are never the kind of people 'inside' that they are 'outside.'" For others, having "acquaintances only" is a protective device.

"There are people I talk to, but I don't tell anyone my business and I *certainly* don't want to know anyone else's—that will get you into trouble every time. Suppose a guy tells you that he's messing with drugs and then he gets caught—he'll accuse *you* of being the 'snitch.'"

It is also seen as a way of protecting oneself from another "danger."

"I wouldn't say I have friends here but there are a couple of people I can talk to. . . . I think one of the big reasons why so many people leave and come right back is that they miss their old friends. . . . That's one reason I don't want to get too close to anyone here."

Even in the case of "acquaintanceships," however, there is some degree of involvement and the question which needs to be answered is: What is it about Fort Worth that makes "going it alone" almost impossible even for people who came with the intention of doing so? Undoubtedly, the answer is found in the multiplicity of relationships which are available in an environment which not only allows for but encourages their development. Unlike other institutional settings in which relationships tend to be structured by adaptive patterns to the *deprivation* of "normal" affective relationships, Fort Worth provides normal relational opportunities because of its heterogeneous population, its co-correctional environment, and its extensive contact with the outside community.

CO-CORRECTIONS

This quality is most clearly reflected in the comments made by some residents who see the presence of members of the opposite sex as a definite "plus." "It makes it more like the 'outside' world to talk with the men and to see them around all the time." "It makes time go faster and easier because you don't think about the streets and home so much." "It's good to see all the pretty ladies around—it helps morale!" Not only does it contribute to a generally pleasant and "normal" atmosphere, but the coed setting is also seen as a key factor in the reduction of problematic relationships traditionally associated with prison life. "Anyone who has done time in a real joint will tell you that homosexuality is the biggest source of trouble—here that seems to be almost completely eliminated." "Having women around just makes the place alive—you don't see the dudes dragging along, not caring how they look, always on edge or looking for a fight over some little thing." Seventy per cent of the residents think the co-correctional setting is clearly a positive factor.

Although not actually negative in their reactions, 19 per cent of the residents indicate that they have mixed feelings about the coed setting.

"For some it's a very good thing; for others it simply opens up a whole new set of problems. People like _____ can gain a great deal—women have always been the source of his problems and here he has had to learn new patterns of behavior and new types of relationships with women. . . . I'm sure there are women who need the same kind of help in their relationships with men."

Where strongly negative feelings are expressed, the reasons are almost invariably related to the difficulties of adhering to the rules regarding physical contact; in effect, these "normal relationships" are not "normal" enough! "It's a bad scene, man! The women are like the flowers out on the yard—for decorative purposes only! It's one of the things that beats you for your brains around here." A woman expresses much the same feeling: "I like being around the men but it's just too hard . . . the rules on physical contact are 'unreal' and they change from one policeman to another."

There are a few, of course, who maintain that the limitations on association are not strict enough.

"Eating with them [the women] is O.K., I guess, and things like that, but that should be ALL. . . . There'd be a lot less drugs and alcohol around here if this wasn't coed—the women are always egging the men on to get stuff for them."

*

If the co-correctional setting provides an atmosphere of normalcy, it does so because it multiplies the number of affective relational opportunities usually available within a prison environment; acquaintanceships, friendships or group affiliation may be either single-sex or heterosexual relationships.

Single-sex relationships, whether among men or among women, tend to develop between those who are of the same race, approximately the same age, and who share a similar background in offense history, previous commitment experience and social status.

*

A resident's approval of the co-correctional environment at Fort Worth does not necessarily mean that he or she is involved in any of the various forms heterosexual relationships may take. Nor, on the other hand, does a resident's disapproval of the coed setting imply non-involvement in such relationships. Only 11 per cent of the residents, all of them men, state that they have "steered clear" of any contact with the opposite sex. Another 21 per cent, one of whom is a woman, indicate that their communication is generally limited to "passing the time of day" with those they happen to meet on their jobs, in class, or waiting in line in the "mess hall." For 68 per cent, however, the relationships which exist between men and women play an integral role in their lives at Fort Worth.

*

FORMS OF RELATIONSHIPS

In general, six forms of heterosexual relationships appear at Fort Worth. The first is one of friendship. Interestingly enough it appears that there are two major recruitment sources for the friendship relationship between a man or woman or in a group situation. For men and women with intact marriages, co-corrections provide a more "real" atmosphere where they can enjoy the supportive companionship of the other sex while the control structures provide a normative support which protects the marital status of the participants. For women who have had a history of prostitution, and for men who have served long periods of time without contact with women or in the role of pimp, the friendship relationship provides a comfortable means of exploring non-exploitive ways of relating to the other sex. The second set of roles might be described as "protective uncle" or "mothering aunt" relationships. When a young woman arrives at Fort Worth she frequently is rather overwhelmed with the advances offered, and will accept the support of an older man in an "uncle" role. The support is mutual, since like the friendship role, the "uncle" role provides an older man with an opportunity to move into relationships with women in a non-competitive and non-demanding way, while for the younger woman it allows a breathing space and a time to determine if there are younger men with whom she would like to associate, or would prefer to remain in a companionship role. The "mothering role" was described by one of the women as follows:"There are some very lonely people here, especially older men. I have all the romance I need outside, so I spend quite a lot of my time with the older fellows."Again, it provides mutual support without any obligations. The third relational form is the direct one of "dating" and like its counterpart on the outside, is entered into by both partners with a variety of intentions. In some cases friendship relationships develop into "dating" relationships, and rather casual companionships become very intense without either partner originally intending it to occur. However, among the residents there are a set of cautionary norms about becoming too emotionally involved, since "prison romances never work." Persons are warned that when "the other" goes out ahead the relationship ceases, since "they want to forget what went on inside" or "they have so many other choices on the street." One of the women who was in the original Alderson transfer mentioned that it is necessary to "lay it on" to the women that "most guys are married, the chance of meeting and marrying is slim, and the 'getting down' here is humiliating and degrading, and women are just being used." From several of the interviews it appears that as the balance shifts from the predominence of women who transferred from other institutions to those who come directly from the courts, there is an increase in the amount and intensity of sexual involvement.

This is another area of "messing around" in which the presence of older transfer residents play a critical role, since it is their pressure on new residents not to jeopardize the "good things going at Fort Worth," rather than external controls, which are the most effective.

The fourth form of relationship involves the residents at Fort Worth who are married. In an effort to keep marital bonds intact, a real effort is made to affect the transfer of the other partner to the institution. In some cases the transfer has had the desired outcome, but in others the presence of intervening relationships may set the stage for another transfer, or a very strained situation. This is an area in which the adaptive norms to control heterosexual behavior within the institution are not clear-cut:

"Here there is a direct normative conflict between the institutional regulations (which have been developed with the legal and community moral standards in mind regarding both pre-marital and extra-marital relations) and the whole question of marital rights. This is a critical question which has not been resolved in single sex institutions either, and state legislatures vary in their willingness to allow visitation privileges and furloughs. Are marital rights forfeited with the commission of an offense? Can institutions for internal regulatory reasons have the right to restrict family contacts? There have not been any precise answers to these questions within either the State or Federal systems, and they pose an even greater problem at Fort Worth. The staff, the couples involved and the other residents are normatively ambivalent. Generally conjugal relations are seen as a violation of regulations—and therefore serious—but at the same time as not "wrong"—and therefore not subject to the same formal and informal sanctions which cover other violations. As a result an informal "double standard" seems to have evolved which does not appear to be destructive of the normative structures, but which will remain a point of tension until there is some resolution of this conflict of rights."

The fifth and sixth relational roles are exploitive and appear to be played by relatively few residents. The first is a "commissary companionship" where older men are willing to "pay for" a companion to sit with in the dining room and chat with in the yard. In reality it may not be as exploitive as some observers assume, since in time it may move to a form of "uncle" relationship. For women who have lived by prostitution it represents a very non-demanding trick and for the men it provides enough practice in talking to women to establish a confidence to move to a relationship with a non-economic basis. And finally, there is a very limited amount of prostitution at Fort Worth, which appears in most cases to be part of the reaction of women committed directly from the courts with a background of prostitution who respond initially to a ready market, and only later are able to shift to one of the alternative life styles available.

In addition to the heterosexual relationships arising in a co-correctional situation, some of the men and women who have been involved for a relatively long time in prison homosexuality continue their relationships at Fort Worth, but without the coercive physical or psychological pressures that occur in a single-sex institution. However, one of the women noted that "there were very few lesbians, the ones that are here have men who are helping them turn around."

That final comment, however, on "men helping them turn around," leads to a more critical aspect of the effect of co-corrections on the women at Fort Worth. While to some extent the situation at Fort Worth is simply an extension of the larger question of the role of women in society, there are certain ways in which the prison situation intensifies these issues. As a result of the sex ratio, there is a pressure for each women to become a walk-partner. Women who do not wish to participate tend to withdraw to the unit, but in insufficient numbers to develop any cooperative or cohesive programs within the women's unit itself. As the women move into the walk-partner relationship, they also tend to enter programs in terms of the interests of the men with whom they are involved. While the programs themselves may be valuable, in many cases the women's history of criminal involvement related to the activities of their husbands or lovers, and this dependency relationship is simply continued within the prison. While one of the values of co-corrections in a situation like Fort Worth is that men and women can relate to each other in a diversity of settings, it unintentionally results in a situation where women do not have a "program" of their own where they can develop leadership roles and cohesive structures which would provide them with alternate life styles.

37. Conjugal Visiting

COLUMBUS B. HOPPER

ALTHOUGH CONJUGAL VISITING HAS FOUND LITTLE favor in American corrections generally, it is considered important in Mississippi's correctional facility at Parchman.[1] While some correctional authorities have learned that conjugal visiting is allowed in Mississippi's prison,[2] they have considered it a quaint practice in an old penal plantation system which allowed the visits as a concession to male prisoners for their labor. Thus conjugal visiting at Parchman often has been evaluated as a temporary aberration that would cease when modern ideas such as furloughs, work release, and community corrections moved into Mississippi. In recent years, Mississippi has adopted these programs along with others thought to be in the vanguard of corrections. Instead of dying out, conjugal visiting has continued to develop and has emerged as a feature that seems impervious to fads and fashions. It is now firmly established and is likely to remain so in the future.

THE INFORMAL BEGINNING

Conjugal visiting began in the dim past of Mississippi penology. It started at least as early as 1918 when Parchman was a racially segregated penal farm where inmates worked from daylight to dark to make a profit for the state. The only contribution the penitentiary made to the beginning of the practice was to allow it. In each of the individual camps scattered over the penitentiary farmland, the inmates built their own conjugal visiting facilities out of scrap lumber and gave them the name of "red houses." In the early days, the practice was confined largely to the negro camps. Moreover, there was little or no institutional control over the privilege except that it was limited to male prisoners. A sergeant of one camp said, for example, that when he became sergeant of his camp in 1940, conjugal visiting was being practiced but no facilities were provided. The usual practice, he added, was for an inmate to take his wife or girl friend into the sleeping quarters of the inmates and to secure whatever privacy he could by hanging up blankets over beds. Upon gaining control of his camp, the sergeant allowed the men to construct a small building for conjugal visits.

FORMAL ACCEPTANCE

The first conjugal visiting facilities at Parchman planned and specifically provided by the penitentiary were those at the original first offenders unit, opened in 1965. In this unit, the red house was included in the plan from the beginning and it was made of the same red brick as the main building itself. The planning and

▶SOURCE: *Paper written especially for this volume.*

[1]Conjugal visiting is now allowed in California and in Alaska on a limited basis. Mississippi remains, however, the only state to make a major commitment to the practice throughout an inmate's entire imprisonment.

[2]The first detailed description of the program was in Columbus B. Hopper, "The Conjugal Visit at the Mississippi State Penitentiary," *The Journal of Criminal Law, Criminology and Police Science*, Vol. 53, No. 3, September, 1962, pp. 340–343.

institutional construction of the conjugal visiting facilities at this unit marked the beginning of formal acceptance of the practice by the institutional administration. All new camps constructed since 1965 have included conjugal visiting facilities, still referred to as red houses.

Although conjugal visiting at Parchman received formal recognition in 1965, it continued for several years as an informal practice with little supervision or support. The red houses in the older camps remained eyesores because no money was allotted to them. In spite of a lack of funding, conjugal visiting slowly became respected. By 1969, both staff members and inmates were convinced that the visits were important to inmate morale and that they helped to reduce homosexuality. Above all, their value in retaining marriages was appreciated.[3]

When the staff members began to appreciate the conjugal visiting program, the old accommodative attitude was replaced by a cooperative spirit. Whereas in earlier days the privilege was permitted in an indifferent manner, it now became something staff members supported. All visitors were greeted warmly and effort was made to give to the inmates and their wives as much privacy as possible. Facilities for the visits remained a problem until 1972 when major improvements were made at the Delta prison farm, including renovation of physical facilities, a reduction of overcrowding and an end to the use of armed inmate guards.

THE MODERN PROGRAM

As a result of sweeping changes, Parchman is greatly different today. The conjugal visiting program has been improved along with the general revamping. The make-shift red houses have been replaced in each regular camp for men by modern units made of red brick.[4] The

---

[3]See Columbus B. Hopper, *Sex In Prison* (Baton Rouge: Louisiana State University Press, 1969).

[4]Conjugal visits are not allowed in the Maximum Security Unit which houses inmates who are sentenced to death and those who have been temporarily removed from the general population for infraction of rules.

---

rooms have paneled walls and tile floors. Each has rest rooms and some are air conditioned. The rooms are attractively painted and furnished with beds and chairs and whatever else an inmate may want to decorate a room with as long as it is not against the rules of the prison. An inmate must sign in a book before he is allowed in the red house and all must give proof of marriage. Conjugal visits are allowed every other Sunday in the afternoon from one o'clock until five.

Conjugal visiting was initiated for the women inmates in July of 1972. The women's program is under the supervision of the local health department and birth control practices are required. The main building in the Women's Camp was previously a motel in a nearby town. The penitentiary bought it and moved it to Parchman when the motel chain decided to build a larger motel to replace it. The lobby is used as a day room and lounging area. It is also used as a general visiting area on Sundays. The offices are used as counseling rooms and medical rooms. The kitchen and dining rooms serve their original functions. The private rooms house the inmates.

The rooms are essentially the same as they were before the facility was moved to the prison. Each room has a bath and shower, a sink, dressing table, window curtains and closets for clothes. An inmate may decorate her room any way she wants to with the exception of driving nails into the walls. When a woman's husband comes to see her, they visit within the privacy of her room. As in the program for men, the female inmates are eligible for conjugal visits on the first visiting day after they arrive at the camp. The entire camp has a high wire fence around it.

THREE-DAY VISITS

In 1974, the biweekly conjugal visiting program for both men and women was expanded by the addition of a three-day family visitation program. It is a simple program which allows an inmate's family to spend three days and two nights with him or her in the penitentiary. Usually the family visits are from Friday through Sunday.

Upon arrival at Parchman, the family moves into a housing unit designated for the program. There currently are five efficiency apartments and four houses used in family visitation. These facilities were furnished through contributions from furniture stores in the surrounding area and also by donations from the inmates' families. Everything is furnished except food and bed linen which the individual family must bring when they come to visit.

Although the family visitation program is not limited to the married inmates, the great majority of those who participate in it also have conjugal visits. While no restrictions other than marriage are made on those who are eligible for conjugal visits, the family visitation program is limited to those who have achieved half-trusty or "B" status. This restriction is necessary because the family visitation units are, in some cases, a mile or two removed from the regular camps and the inmates and their families are on their own and unguarded during the three-day visits. The typical married inmate of half-trusty or trusty status is able to have a family visit every two months.

The family visitation and conjugal visiting programs reflect the emphasis which the Mississippi correctional authorities place on positive family relationships. They believe that an inmate who has a stable marriage should be allowed to retain it. They feel that whatever help they might give an individual would be negated if his or her marriage failed. Therefore, they make effort to assure contact between inmates and their families in several ways. Ten-day furloughs are granted to approximately four-hundred inmates each year. Furthermore, three-day passes are given during periods of family crisis. A crisis is defined more broadly than illness or death of a family member. In some instances, for example, individual inmates have been given passes to help repair their homes which were damaged by storms.

The high regard which Mississippi prison officials have for marital relationships is also demonstrated in the rare instances in which both marital partners are imprisoned. When a husband and wife are both in Parchman, the husband is allowed to visit his wife in the Women's Camp on visiting days and have conjugal visits. If both partners are trusties or half-trusties, they are allowed to have the three-day visits in the family visitation units. The couple is driven to and from the family visitation unit by a prison employee.

INMATE AND STAFF OPINIONS

When one talks to the inmates at Parchman, the impact of the conjugal and family visitation programs is striking. A thirty-year-old woman who had served two years described her experience as follows:

"The relationship I have with my husband is very precious to me. He and my children are my life. I don't believe I could make it without the program. The fact that I have a room that I can identify with means so much to me. My husband knows my room, where I live and we can visit in private when he comes to see me here. I've also been to the family units a number of times. Once you are there, you are on your own. You almost forget you are in prison. You are cooking, preparing meals, putting your children to bed at night. My husband sometimes brings a grill and we cook out just like we did at home. It makes me feel like a complete woman again.

There's only one bad thing—the pain of leaving and having to go back to the camp. But of course it is worth it. It is really wonderful. You can get outside as long as you stay in the yard. Last summer we played softball all afternoon and fixed steaks on the grill. My daughter fixed the salad. I can't tell you how much it meant to me."

A woman who had been married two years and who had served only eight months said:

"When I first got here I didn't think I could make it. I hadn't heard of conjugal visiting but the other married girls told me about it. I really enjoy the program and my husband thinks it's great. He visits me every visiting day and we had a three-day visit last month. I don't worry about my husband going out with other women. I don't think my husband would be untrue even if he couldn't visit. I've got a lot of confidence in my man. It's a normal sex relationship when he visits, about like at home.

"I was scared to death when I first came in. A homosexual approached me. She said I was small and cute. I didn't say nothing; I just got away from her. She didn't bother me any more. They hollered 'new meat' when I came in and it scared me. But I'm not afraid now. Once you let them know you have a husband and are not interested, the homosexuals don't bother you any more. I wish the married women had a special camp of their own but I don't guess it can be done."

The male inmates who participate in the program sound similar to the women in their praise of it. Speaking of his reaction to conjugal visits, a twenty-eight-year-old man with a wife and two children said:

"It's the one thing that lets me keep my sanity in here. I write to my wife every day and I look forward to visiting days more than I did to Christmas when I was a boy. We all dress up and try to look as nice as we can. I've got a family that I love as much as you do yours. Just put yourself in my place and imagine what it would mean to you. I've just had a three-day visit with my wife and my two little boys. My wife fixed my favorite meals and we played with the kids, watched television. I felt like a human being again. There's no way I'd mess up and lose this by being sent to Maximum Security."

The number of inmates participating in the conjugal visiting program at Parchman is extensive. The wives of approximately 470 men—almost 60 percent of those with legal marriages—visit regularly or occasionally. Twenty-four of the 83 women confined at Parchman in February of 1976 were married and 17 of them were receiving conjugal visits. Although there are proportionately fewer intact marriages among women in Parchman than among the men, 70 percent of the women who are married participate in conjugal visits.

Staff support for the conjugal and family visitation programs is consistent. Not only do the staff members feel that it is the right thing to do, they also feel that it makes their jobs easier by increasing inmate morale.

Unmarried inmates also favor conjugal visiting. Although some say they think all individuals married or not should be allowed them, it is difficult to find a prisoner who doesn't praise the visits. It is easy to find criticism of other programs such as basic education, vocational education, counseling, work release, or pre-release. Parchman inmates are not reluctant to gripe, complain and to file suits. Their praise of conjugal visiting must, therefore, be considered genuine. The attitude of the majority of single inmates at Parchman can be summed up in the words of a young woman who said:

"I think the conjugal visiting program is wonderful. I really do. I feel no hostility because I can't and married women can. That's the way society is. I'd like to have a man visit me but I can't. I can see why they don't do that."

Some single inmates in the camps for men even volunteer to help keep the red houses clean. Even inmates who receive no visitors at all enjoy visiting day. They like to see new faces, especially children. If nothing else, it is a change from the daily routine.

CONCLUSION

Those who oppose conjugal visits offer several objections.[5] The chief complaint is that the visits seem degrading and emphasize only the physical satisfactions of sex. Other people believe that married inmates who engage in conjugal visits are those who would adjust best to prison life even without sexual relations. Additional criticisms are that conjugal visits offer no solution to the sexual tension of single prisoners and that wives may become pregnant, creating further

[5]A good summary of the arguments for and against conjugal visiting may be found in Sue Titus Reid, *Crime and Criminology* (Hinsdale, Illinois: The Dryden Press, 1976) pp. 617–619.

problems for the state and the inmate. Some people argue that conjugal visiting does not decrease homosexuality and that it is contrary to community oriented programs.

The current program of conjugal and family visitation in Mississippi does not seem degrading. In fact, it appears less degrading than visitation in prisons where inmates and their spouses furtively kiss in a crowded room while a guard's head is turned. The Mississippi officials do not claim that conjugal visits will solve prison problems. They are convinced, however, that their program helps and they are content to evaluate it on their own terms. They feel that it is right for them. They do not ask that it be subjected to rigorous empirical tests. It is enough that they feel good in allowing it and that individual inmates whom they know personally are grateful for it.

Conjugal visiting at Parchman also reveals a degree of community involvement which should be a lesson to correctional administrators elsewhere. Private citizens have been asked to contribute furniture and money to the program. Many authorities feel that the public would criticize conjugal visits, but the experience in Mississippi suggests the opposite. In addition, the argument that the Mississippi population is more liberal than the people in other states does not seem tenable. Although most of them would not admit it, it is likely that correctional administrators in other states are less willing to adopt conjugal visits than are the publics that they serve.

38. Inmate Rules

ARIZONA STATE PRISON

PROCEDURES FOR ADMINISTRATION OF THE DISCIPLINE PROGRAM

A. Informal Disposition of Violations

VIOLATIONS OF THE RULES WHICH ARE MINOR IN nature may, at the discretion of the staff member observing it, be resolved and disposed of in an informal manner by counseling, warning or admonishment of the prisoner in question. If such is the case, an informational notation, not an official entry of disciplinary action taken, may be entered in the prisoner's file as part of a chronological record of the prisoner's overall adjustment and progress.

B. Formal Disposition of Violations

If the violation is of a serious nature or, in the judgment of the staff member observing it, the violation should be handled in a formal manner, the procedures listed below shall be followed:

1. The staff member shall write, sign and submit to the Associate Warden in charge of custody or his assistant a Preliminary Report of a Rule Violation giving the time, place and nature of the violation, and will verbally inform the prisoner that he has done so.

2. At the time of the violation, the staff member may restrict a prisoner to his cell or dormitory or release him from his work or training assignment to be placed in his cell or dor-

▶SOURCE: *Arizona State Prison Inmate Reference Manual. Florence, Arizona. n.d. Pp. 4–30 (Editorial adaptations.)*

mitory. If the violation or prisoner involved in the violation constitutes a threat or danger to any person, or to the orderly operation of the prison, the prisoner may be confined in an appropriate location by the Associate Warden in charge or his assistant pending further disposition of the matter.

3. Upon receiving the Preliminary Report of a Rule Violation, the Associate Warden in charge of custody or his assistant will, if necessary, conduct or initiate a preliminary investigation and make one of the following determinations:

a. The violation need not be referred to the Discipline Committee but instead can be handled and disposed of with no loss of time credits, loss of major privilege or confinement imposed on the prisoner. He will indicate this disposition of the matter on the Preliminary Report of a Rule Violation and cause it to be placed in the prisoner's file.

b. The violation should be referred to the Discipline Committee for a hearing and disposition, but the prisoner need not be confined pending the hearing.

c. The violation should be referred to the Discipline Committee for hearing and disposition, and the prisoner is confined pending the hearing.

d. The violation should be dismissed, and no record made of the incident.

4. If the Associate Warden in charge of custody or his assistant refers the violation to the

Discipline Committee, he shall conduct or initiate an investigation and determine the facts and circumstances of the incident and prepare and forward formal disciplinary charges to the Chairman of the Discipline Committee.

5. If the accused prisoner is not confined in lockup status pending the hearing before the Discipline Committee, he shall be provided a copy of the formal disciplinary charges within 5 working days after the date the alleged offender is discovered, and he shall be provided a hearing before the Discipline Committee within a reasonable time after receiving the charges.

6. If the accused prisoner is confined in lockup status as a result of his alleged violation of a rule, he shall be provided a copy of the Formal Disciplinary Charges within 5 working days after the alleged offender is discovered, and he shall be granted a hearing before the Discipline Committee within 5 working days after receiving the charges. However, in serious cases where the nature or scope of the offense is complex and complicated, a prisoner may be held in lockup status pending an investigation for longer than 10 days providing that the Director of the Department of Corrections specifically authorizes such detention.

7. Upon a showing of good cause and in order to provide and facilitate a fair hearing, the Committee may, upon request of either the accused inmate or the complaining witness, grant a continuance; however, each side is limited to one continuance. In no event will a continuance be for longer than 2 calendar weeks.

8. In no event will placing the alleged offender in lockup status pending a hearing or during a continuance affect his earning of two for one time, provided he is in a two for one position at the time of the lockup. Two for one time is only lost for disciplinary reasons pursuant to an action of the Disciplinary Committee.

C. The Discipline Committee

The Superintendent shall designate or appoint any staff member to sit as a member of the Discipline Committee to hear and make dispositions in all matters of discipline or violation of rules referred to it.

1. Membership. The individual members may vary from meeting to meeting, but in formal meetings there shall be 3 members. One shall be from the Custody Staff, one from the Care and Treatment Staff and, whenever possible, one from other than the Custody Staff. No staff member shall serve on the Committee who has been involved in the making or investigation of the charges.

2. Jurisdiction. The Committee shall hear and dispose of violations or other matters where a prisoner faces the following sanctions or penalties:

    a. Denial of good time credits ("copper time") under the provisions of A.R.S. § 31–251.

    b. Denial of two for one time credits under the provisions of A.R.S. §31–252.

    c. Confinement in disciplinary isolation.

D. The Conduct of Disciplinary Hearings

1. The Committee hearing shall begin with a reading and a clear explanation of the charges to the prisoner, and the prisoner shall plead guilty or not guilty to the charges.

2. The prisoner, if he desires, is entitled to be represented by private counsel supplied and arranged for at his own expense, or he may designate another prisoner or a staff member willing to serve in the capacity of counsel or representative. The prisoner shall be given reasonable opportunity to consult with his counsel for the purpose of preparing his defense.

3. The prisoner is entitled to hear all witnesses against him, and his counsel or representative is entitled to examine such witnesses. If the prisoner is either representing himself or is represented by another prisoner, he shall present his questions through a staff member designated by the Discipline Committee, who is willing to serve in that capacity and who can be relieved of his duties at the time of the hearing.

4.   The prisoner is entitled to call other prisoners or staff members as witnesses, but in such a case the prisoner must provide the Chairman of the Discipline Committee a list of the names of such witnesses no later than 2 working days prior to the hearing, on a form provided by the institution, so that adequate arrangements can be made for the witnesses to be present. Inmates must be willing to serve as witnesses. (See Form #2.)

5.   All witnesses may be questioned by the members of the Committee.

6.   The number of witnesses to be called and heard shall be at the discretion of the Committee in order to prevent cumulative or irrelevant testimony.

7.   All hearings shall be recorded by a mechanical transcription device, and a written list, summary or minutes of the cases heard and disposed of shall be prepared.

E. Decisions and Actions of the Committee

1.   After hearing testimony, examining evidence and considering facts and circumstances, the Committee, by majority vote, may:

    a.   Find the prisoner not guilty of the charges, dismiss them, and order that no record of them be placed in the prisoner's file.

    b.   Find the prisoner guilty of the charges, and impose appropriate sanctions or penalties to be executed either immediately or stayed pending appeal.

    c.   Find the prisoner guilty of the charges and impose appropriate sanctions or penalties, but suspend execution of the sanctions or penal-ties for any period of time, not exceeding 90 calendar days, contingent on the prisoner's meeting such terms and conditions as are established and determined by the Committee.

    d.   Refer the prisoner, whether guilty or not guilty, to the Reclassification Committee for a review and evaluation and, if necessary, a change in his custody status, work or training assignment or housing location.

    e.   Refer the prisoner, whether guilty or not guilty, to the appropriate staff member, office or department for treatment services.

2.   Upon conclusion of the hearing, the Committee will inform the prisoner in writing of its findings or decision (see Form #3). If he is found guilty, he will be informed and provided with written notice of the sanctions and penalties to be imposed and of his right to appeal the Committee's actions.

F. Sanctions and Penalties

Upon finding that the prisoner is guilty of the charges, the Committee is authorized to impose, or to impose but suspend execution for no longer than 90 days, any or all of the following sanctions or penalties which shall be made a matter of record in the prisoner's file. Where more than one charge is filed against the prisoner and he is found guilty on any two or more charges, the sanction or penalty imposed shall be served concurrently unless otherwise specifically provided by the Committee, but in no event to exceed 30 calendar days. The sanctions and penalties are:

1.   Verbal or written reprimand, admonishment, censure or warning.

2.   Confinement of the prisoner in lockup status for a period not to exceed 30 calendar days.

3.   Confinement of the prisoner in a cell or other place designated as disciplinary isolation for a period not to exceed 30 calendar days.

4. Order and direct that any application of good time credits which had accrued or would otherwise accrue and be applied at the next anniversary date of the prisoner's sentence under the provisions of A.R.S § 31–251 be denied.

5. Recommend to the Reclassification Committee that the prisoner be removed from any assignment for which he has been receiving two for one time credits under the provisions of A.R.S. § 31–252.

6. Make a recommendation to the Board of Pardons and Paroles that good time credits already earned and applied to the prisoner's sentence be forfeited.

7. Order and direct that the prisoner be denied any or all privileges, including recreational and entertainment activities, but excluding food and exercise.

8. Order and direct the return of property of another prisoner, staff member or the State of Arizona which is in his possession without proper authorization.

9. Order and direct that the prisoner make monetary restitution for the damage to or destruction of the property of another prisoner, a staff member or the State of Arizona caused by the deliberate, intentional, careless or negligent acts of the prisoner.

G. Disciplinary Isolation

Prisoners can be confined in cells or other appropriate facilities designated as disciplinary isolation as a result of being found guilty of preferred charges by the Discipline Committee, but only under the procedures and conditions listed below.

1. No prisoner shall be confined in disciplinary isolation for more than 15 calendar days on a single charge; however, separate sanctions and penalties may be imposed for separate violations which are handled and disposed of at a single meeting of the Committee.

2. Violations by a prisoner confined in disciplinary isolation status can result in the filing of new and additional charges which will be disposed of in a new hearing in the manner already described above. If a prisoner is found guilty of a violation while serving a disciplinary penalty, the sanction or penalty imposed on the new violation shall be served concurrently with the prior penalty unless otherwise specifically provided by the Committee.

3. Prisoners confined in disciplinary isolation status will be provided the following:

a. Three regular meals per day consisting of the same food and drink in the same proportions as provided other inmates not so confined, but not to include desserts.

b. Medical care as needed and authorized by medical technicians and physicians.

c. Showers on three occasions per week, on different days of the week, when such facilities are available in the immediate area and when the number of officers necessary to maintain appropriate security and control are available. The use of showers may be denied to any individual prisoner or group of prisoners by the Shift Commander, Area Captain or Senior Captain if he determines such use would constitute a threat or danger to any person or to the security and orderly operation of the Prison. In such an instance, the staff member denying the scheduled use of showers shall file a brief written report to that effect with the Assistant Superintendent for Custody by no later than the next business day (excluding weekends and holidays).

d. Exercise outside the isolation cell, but not necessarily outside the immediate area within the building, on three scheduled occasions per week, of no less than one hour on each occasion on three different days of the week. Scheduled exercise may be denied to any individual prisoner or group of prisoners by the Shift Commander, Area Captain or Senior Captain if he determines such exercise would constitute a threat or danger to any person or to the security and orderly operation of the Prison. In such an instance, the staff member denying the exercise shall file a brief written report to that effect with the Assistant Superintendent for Custody by not later than the next business day (excluding weekends and holidays).

e. Change of clothing as needed, but no less than one per week.

4. No activities or items generally considered as privileges enjoyed by prisoners in the general population will be afforded prisoners in disciplinary isolation, except visitation by persons on the prisoner's approved visiting list.

*

APPEAL OF ACTION BY THE DISCIPLINE COMMITTEE

Any prisoner found to be guilty of a rule violation by the Discipline Committee may appeal such finding or any sanctions or penalties imposed as a result of the finding to a person designated as an Appeals Officer appointed by the Arizona Department of Corrections.

*

RULES AND REGULATIONS

A. Violations of Statutes

Prisoners of the Arizona State Prison are subject to all laws of the United States and of the State of Arizona. Any prisoner violating these laws may be charged and tried for that violation in the same manner as any other citizen in the appropriate state or federal court. The filing of charges in a judicial court of record for a violation of state or federal laws does not in any way prevent or preclude the administrative handling of that same act as a prison disciplinary matter or of the taking of disciplinary action against the prisoner in question. These violations are:

1. Violation of any law or statute of the State of Arizona.

2. Violation of any law or statute of the United States.

B. Violations Against Persons

1. Intentionally causing the death or bodily injury of any person.

2. Striking any person with hands, fists, feet or with any weapon or object.

3. Shooting or shooting at any person with any type of firearm.

4. Intentionally projecting any item at another person by the use of the hands or by any mechanical device.

5. Verbally threatening any person with death, violence or injury.

6. Threatening or menacing any person with a weapon or any other item.

7. Fighting, boxing, wrestling and any other form of physical encounter which causes or could cause injury to another person, except as part of an approved recreational or athletic activity.

8. Participating in homosexual or any sexual behavior or activity with any person, male or female.

9. Requesting, demanding, threatening or in any other way inducing any other person to participate in homosexual or any other sexual behavior or activity.

10. Indecent or unnecessary exposure or exhibition of the genital organs.

11. Use of written or verbal profane, obscene (as prescribed by applicable constitutional standards) or abusive words, language or gestures to another person.

12. Insubordination to a staff member.

13. Offering or giving of any gift, personal service, favor, money or anything else of value to any person as a bribe, or in any other way attempting to influence that person to do anything prohibited by these rules or the laws of the United States or the State of Arizona.

14.   Requesting, demanding, inducing and/or receiving any goods, property, personal service, favor, gift or any item of value in return for protection or other services or considerations.

15.   Individually, or in participation with others, taking and holding of a staff member or of any other person as a hostage or in any way restraining, holding or confining any person against his will.

16.   Obstructing, interfering with or preventing any staff member from carrying out his orders, duties or assignments.

C. Violations Pertaining to the Security and the Orderly Operation of the Prison

1.   Participation in any meeting or gathering which has not been specifically authorized by the Prison staff or an individual staff member.

2.   Participation in any group demonstration, disturbance, riot, strike, refusal to work, work stoppage or work slow down.

3.   Escaping, walking away or otherwise absenting oneself from the institution without prior specific authorization and permission from a staff member.

4.   Escaping, walking away or otherwise absenting oneself from the immediate jurisdiction, control or supervision of a staff member or other legally constituted authority.

5.   Participating in the planning of, or otherwise conspiring with another person to aid, abet or prevent discovery of the escape or walk-away of another prisoner from the institution, or from the immediate jurisdiction, control or supervision of a staff member or other legally constituted authority.

6.   Unauthorized possession on one's person, in one's cell, immediate sleeping area, locker or immediate place of work assignment; unauthorized receiving from or giving to another person; unauthorized fashioning or manufacturing; unauthorized introduction or arrangement for the introduction into the institution of:

    a.   Any key, lock, locking device, chain, rope, ladder, tool or other items which could be used to effect an escape.

    b.   Any mannequin, dummy, replica of a human body, or any item or device which would cause any prisoner to be counted as being present at the designated time and place when, in fact, he would be absent; or in any way would aid or abet the escape or walk-away of a prisoner.

    c.   Any mask, wig or disguise, or any other means of altering normal physical appearance which would make ready identification of a prisoner difficult.

7.   Tampering with, removal of, damage to, destruction of, blocking of or in any way making inoperable any lock, door, blocking device or allied equipment, or any fire or safety equipment.

8.   Knowingly not being physically present at the designated time and place of a count of all of the prisoner population or that part of the population of which the prisoner is a member without the prior knowledge and permission of a staff member.

9.   Causing or participating in any interference, delay, disruption or deception with regard to the process of counting part or all of the prisoner population.

10.   Wearing of any mask, wig, or disguise, or any other alteration of the normal physical appearance which would make ready identification of the prisoner difficult.

11.   Causing, through carelessness or neglect, a fire or the setting of any fire without the prior permission of a staff member.

12.   Absence from one's cell or immediate

housing area, place of work, training assignment, or other area designated by a staff member, without the specific prior knowledge and permission of a staff member.

13. Unauthorized presence or being out of place in any building, facility, area, location, vehicle or restricted place.

14. Failure to follow, or to carry out, any lawful and reasonable direction, instruction or order of a staff member or other legally constituted authority.

15. Failure to perform or complete any work, training or other assignment, as ordered, directed or instructed, either verbally or in writing by a staff member.

16. Being under the influence of alcohol, drugs, narcotics, or any intoxicant, depressant or stimulant not specifically authorized, prescribed or issued by a staff member of the institution.

17. Refusal to allow, hindering of, or obstruction of the search of a prisoner, his cell or his property by a staff member.

18. Hanging, fastening or attaching of any sheet, blanket, curtain, drapery or other materials, whether transparent or not, on any part or all of the front, or door, of a cell or around a dormitory bed or other immediate sleeping area without the prior permission of a staff member.

D. Violations Pertaining to Possession, Manufacture and Introduction of Contraband

1. Unauthorized possession on his person, in his cell, immediate sleeping area, locker or immediate place of work or assignment; unauthorized receiving from, or giving to another person; unauthorized fashioning or manufacturing; unauthorized introduction, or in any way arranging for the introduction on state property of any item; unauthorized mailing, shipping, dispatching or smuggling, or in any way arranging to mail, ship, dispatch or smuggle away from state property of any item considered contraband by the institution, not sold in the institution's Canteen, not permitted by the established policy of the institution, or by these rules or which is otherwise not expressly authorized and approved for receipt and retention by the individual prisoner.

2. Possession on one's person, in one's cell, immediate sleeping area, locker or immediate place of work or assignment; receiving from or giving to another person; fashioning or manufacturing; introduction or arranging for the introduction into the institution without the prior knowledge and permission of a staff member of:

    a. Any gun, knife, pointed or sharpened instrument, club or weapon capable of causing or inflicting bodily injury to another person.

    b. Any flammable, poisonous or explosive material or device, or any type of ammunition.

    c. Any drug, narcotic, intoxicant, depressant or stimulant, including alcohol and alcoholic beverages.

    d. Any device, equipment, paraphernalia or any other item which can be used for the injection, inhalation or absorption of drugs, narcotics, intoxicants or medicines, not specifically prescribed, authorized or issued to the individual prisoner by a staff member.

    e. Any form of securities, bonds, coins, currency, legal tender, official papers or documents or articles of identification.

    f. Any item of an officer's uniform, civilian clothing, or staff clothing, including badges, buttons, name tags or items or personal identification.

    g. Any permitted or issued clothing, tools, equipment, goods, property, materials or items in excess of the number and amount authorized or issued to the individual prisoner.

    h. Any obscene material, as defined by A.R.S. § 13–531.01.2:

"Obscene" means that which considered as a whole has as its dominant theme or purpose an appeal to prurient interest or a shameful or morbid interest in nudity, sex or lewdness going substantially beyond customary limits of candor in description or representation of such matters and is utterly without redeeming social importance.

i. Any contraband, illegally manufactured, or altered food or drink.

3. Selling, giving, bartering, disposing of or administering any medicine, drug, narcotic, intoxicant, stimulant, depressant or medical supply other than as expressly instructed by a staff member.

4. Possession in his cell, immediate sleeping area or locker of an excessive amount of personal goods, property, materials or items to the degree that his sleeping or living area or locker presents unkept, untidy, excessively cluttered or offensive appearance, or to the degree that it restricts or interferes with the free movement of another prisoner, with officers' visual observation of the cell or sleeping area or creates a fire or safety hazard.

5. Possession on one's person, in one's cell or immediate sleeping area, immediate place of work or assignment or a locker of more than 3 cartons of tailor-made cigarettes, 30 cigars or other smoking materials in excess of the amount allotted under these rules, without the prior knowledge and permission of a staff member.

E. Violations Pertaining to Property and Involving Fraud

1. Receiving from or giving to another person; possession on one's person, in one's cell, immediate sleeping area, locker or immediate place of work or assignment of any goods, property or item of value of another prisoner without the prior knowledge and approval of a staff member.

2. Theft or otherwise taking possession of any goods, property or item of value of another prisoner, staff member or the State of Arizona without the prior authorization of a staff member or by the use of threats, duress, deception or force.

3. Altering, damaging or destroying goods, property or item of value of another person or the State of Arizona.

4. Giving, loaning or otherwise providing money, goods, property or any item of value to another person for profit or increased return.

5. Providing false reports, giving false statements, lying, misrepresenting or distorting the truth, or otherwise communicating inaccurate, untrue or misleading information to a staff member.

6. Counterfeiting, manufacture or reproduction, forgery or possession of any official paper or document, money, currency, coins or articles of identification without the prior knowledge and permission of a staff member.

7. Transfer or attempt to transfer funds from the trust account of one prisoner to that of another without the prior knowledge and permission of a staff member.

8. Exchanging, trading, bartering, giving, receiving or other participation in the transfer of money, personal property or any other item of value from one prisoner to another without the prior knowledge and permission of a staff member.

9. Contracting or arranging to fashion, design, construct or manufacture any hobby item, art work, craft item or any other item for another prisoner without the prior knowledge and permission of a staff member.

F. Violations Pertaining to Policy and Procedures

1. Participation in any betting, gambling or games of chance, or preparing or conducting games of chance or a gambling pool.

2. Possession on one's person, in one's cell, locker, sleeping area, immediate place of work or assignment; fashioning, designing or manufacturing, introducing or attempting to introduce into the Prison any betting or gambling items without the prior knowledge and permission of a staff member.

3. Transmitting or attempting to transmit through the mail threats, demands or obscene materials (as defined by A.R.S. § 13–531.01.2).

4. Violation of any United States postal laws or regulations.

5. Violating or attempting to violate any Prison mailing regulation.

6. Violating or attempting to violate any Prison visiting regulation.

7. Use of any telephone without the prior specific knowledge and permission of a staff member.

8. Contacting or attempting to contact any person or persons outside the Prison, except as specifically authorized by the mail or visiting regulations or with the prior knowledge and permission of a staff member.

9. Feigning or misrepresenting illness, injury or physical condition.

G. Violations Pertaining to Personal Appearance and Sanitation

1. Willful failure of a prisoner to keep his body, hair and clothes in as clean, sanitary, neat and odor-free condition as is possible under the circumstances of his particular custody.

2. Failure of a prisoner to keep his cell or immediate sleeping area clean, odor-free, sanitary, free of trash and debris and available to the visual observation of a staff member.

3. The growing or wearing of a beard, mustache, goatee or otherwise not being clean shaven.

4. The growing or wearing of thick or untrimmed sideburns or sideburns extending below the bottom lobe of the ear.

5. The growing or wearing of the hair on the head long enough to extend onto the collar of an ordinary shirt, cover any part of the ears or eyebrows, or to be longer than 3 inches on top, except as otherwise prescribed by A.R.S. § 31–228.C, as follows: "One month prior to date of discharge, the prisoner shall be permitted to allow his hair to grow." Prisoners allowed to permit their hair to grow beyond the limits established in these rules, under the provisions of the statute, are those whose maximum sentence will expire within 30 days or those who have already had a hearing before the Arizona Board of Pardons and Paroles and have a definite minimum release data scheduled. Prisoners waiting for a hearing before the Board of Pardons and Paroles are **not** authorized to permit their hair to grow beyond the limits established in these rules.

6. Wearing on the person, body or clothing of earrings, beads, pendants, medallions or other items of decoration or jewelry. Watches, finger rings, religious medals or crosses are excepted.

H. Violations Pertaining to Safety

1. Failure to observe, follow and comply with any Prison safety policies or rules and regulations.

2. Operation or use of any tool, equipment, machinery or vehicle without the permission of a staff member.

3. Careless, reckless or negligent operation or use of any Prison tool, equipment, machinery or vehicle.

4. Use, handling of, tampering with, or carelessly, negligently, recklessly or willfully causing damage or destruction to any piece of safety equipment or safety device, except in the case of an emergency or with the prior knowledge and permission of a staff member.

5. Repair, alteration, modification, tampering with or carelessly, negligently, recklessly or willfully causing damage to or destruction of any part of the electrical, plumbing, water, sewerage, communications and other utilities without the prior knowledge and permission of a staff member.

6.   Any careless, reckless, negligent or willful act or behavior which causes or could cause death or injury to another person.

7.   Smoking in any area or building when or where smoking is restricted or prohibited.

I. Disposition of Violations of Rules Which Are Also Violations of State or Federal Statutes

When a prisoner is alleged to have committed a violation of rules which is also a violation of the laws or statutes of the State of Arizona or of the United States, the processing and disposition of that violation will be handled in the same manner as described above in regard to acts which are not necessarily violations of statutes or laws.

In the case of such concurrent violations, the Superintendent, at his discretion, may order an investigation into the matter and that it be referred to the appropriate state or federal authorities.

39. The Hole

R. THEODORE DAVIDSON

A SMALL, YET SIGNIFICANT GROUP OF PRISONERS IS kept in what is euphemistically called the Adjustment Center. This is a small, somewhat self-contained prison within the prison. Here, men who the staff think are habitual troublemakers within the prison or men who are suspected of committing serious crimes inside the prison are brought for long-term punishment. Also, about 30 percent of the men in the Adjustment Center (commonly called "AC") are there for long-term protective custody (protection of a prisoner from other prisoners who may have reason to bring physical harm to him). The Adjustment Center is a relatively new building with staff offices and a small mess hall on one end of the building. The prisoners in AC are subjected to a rigorous routine which entails sharply reduced privileges, severely restricted movement inside AC, and isolation from the rest of the prison and prisoners. A much tighter security is imposed over these prisoners by the staff with the aid of newer facilities—such as a mechanism permitting them to independently lock and unlock cells from the staff portion of the building, outside the cell block area. The floor of each tier extends to the reinforced concrete wall of the building. Therefore, AC does not have an outer shell like the other four cell blocks do. There are 34 cells on each tier, but the cell block area is constructed so that each side, with its 17 cells, is

▶SOURCE: *Chicano Prisoners: The Key to San Quentin.* New York: Holt, Rinehart and Winston, 1974. Pp. 11–12, 25–27, 29. *(Editorial adaptations). Reprinted by permission of Holt, Rinehart and Winston.*

isolated from all other parts of AC. Since the last execution in San Quentin's gas chamber, in 1967, the moratorium on executions led to over 100 prisoners being held under sentence of death. To accommodate these prisoners, the top two tiers of AC were converted into an additional Death Row. This has reduced AC to three tiers which hold about 102 prisoners. Consequently, B Section in South Block (commonly referred to as "the hole"—where prisoners are sent for short-term, in-prison punishment) has been expanded into A Section to accommodate the overflow from AC.

*

ROUTINE ACTIVITIES IN AC AND "THE HOLE"

A prisoner constantly faces the potential of getting into trouble with the staff or with his fellow prisoners. If this should happen, the prisoner may be subjected to the very different routine of the Adjustment Center (AC) or B Section ("the hole"). The Adjustment Center is a prison within the prison. . . . A prisoner will be kept in AC for at least the major portion of a year, if not several years; for the AC is not used for short-term punishment. Upon entry into AC, a prisoner usually is first put in "isolation." Later he enters grade 3 segregation and potentially may work his way up to grade 1 segregation.

Legally, a man cannot be kept in isolation for more than 29 days. However, there are ways that the staff can technically (on paper) get around this limitation if they have strong, negative feelings against the prisoner. The most extreme type of isolation occurs when a man is put in a "quiet cell." Here the prisoner finds himself in a stripped cell, with just a mattress on a cement block and a metal toilet and sink. He is allowed no personal property other than the clothes on his back. There is a small cement block entryway with a solid steel door outside his regular barred door. He can see and hear nothing that is happening outside his cell. The lights are controlled from the outside (as they are in all isolation and grade 1 and 2 segregation cells); and, if the guards are really down on the prisoner, they will shut the door and keep the lights off—except during meals. If their feelings are extreme, they may not even turn the lights on at meal time, when the food is pushed in to the prisoner through the slot in the bars. The previous maximum of 29 days in a quiet cell has legally been reduced to 10 days, but staff are still able to circumvent the rule by letting the prisoner out for less than an hour and then putting him right back in.

For regular isolation, a prisoner is not put in a quiet cell. However, the prisoner still is locked in 24 hours a day, with no personal property, and with no smoking permitted. Technically, the prison rules allow prisoners in isolation to have pencil and paper for corresponding with an attorney or for preparing a petition to the court. However, in reality this depends on the guard. The prisoner may get a pencil and no paper, or vice versa, with some excuse being given about not being able to find the other. Or, the word may come down from the captain that the prisoner is not to have any. Even if he is given both pencil and paper, there is no way for him to check that the guards mail his correspondence.

After a prisoner serves his isolation time, he is put into grade 3 segregation. Occasionally a prisoner who is being held for investigation (not for punishment) will go directly into grade 3. At grade 3 segregation, the prisoner is kept in his cell 23½ hours a day. He is allowed outside, in the corridor in front of his cell, for exercise for a half hour every day; but he is not allowed to go

to the AC exercise yard. He eats in his cell. Most of his personal property is kept from him; but he is allowed to use the state-issued tobacco (which prisoners claim is a very poor roll-your-own variety). He is not allowed to listen to either of the two prison-monitored commercial radio stations.

When the staff decide the prisoner is ready, he is graduated into grade 2 segregation. Now the prisoner's lot improves. He is allowed to have his wallet, comb, toothbrush, and toothpaste. He may exercise in the AC yard for an hour a day. Also, he goes to eat in the small AC mess hall. He is allowed to have earphones and access to the library cart that brings books through the AC. In addition, he can order canteen items (if he legally has the money in his prisoner account)—within a $12 monthly limit.

At grade 1 segregation, a prisoner is out of his cell for longer periods. He is allowed to go to the AC yard for one hour in the morning and one and a half hours in the afternoon. He is given the freedom of having an AC job—such as pushing carts, cleaning up, and such. He is allowed to order almost a full draw each month from the canteen. He may have all of his personal property, except for those items in glass containers. When the staff decide it is time, the prisoner's next graduation will be from AC to the "mainline" population where he will probably be celled in C Section of South Block for a while.

The AC is directly inaccessible to the mainline. It is harder for mainline prisoners to get illegal goods in to prisoners in AC than it is to those in B Section, for there is less movement of prisoners in and out. However, there are ways—such as a guard bringing a carton of cigarettes in each time he comes inside. The mainline prisoners who make the arrangements will give the guard 20 or 40 dollars every so often for his effort.

In the southwest quarter of South Block, B Section stands in grim contrast to the new and relatively clean Adjustment Center. Commonly called "the hole" by prisoners, B Section is used for short-term punishment of prisoners, for holding a man for short-term investigation, or for holding a man under protective custody. Many prisoners claim that this is the worst place to be locked up in all of CDC. Chain link fencing is welded outside the rails of the walkways that run along the second through fifth tiers, making an additional cage that is used to control prisoners and prevent them from throwing guards or other prisoners over the railing when they are moving to or from their cells. In certain places, concertina wire (coiled barbed wire) is a grotesque reminder that prisoners are not to try to get to certain places. When a prisoner is taken to B Section, other prisoners generally refer to his being "thrown into the hole." Technically a prisoner is either in isolation or in one of the 3 grades of segregation. When pressed for further distinctions, prisoners acknowledge that only the quiet cells are actually the hole.

The six quiet cells on the ground tier in B Section are strip cells similar to those in AC. However, these have no cement block—the mattress is just put on the floor. In the mid 1960s, there was only a hole in the floor where the toilet had been and no wash basin; the prisoner was given a bucket of clean water for drinking and washing, and an empty bucket in which to perform bodily functions. The buckets were changed daily. Now there are metal toilets and sinks in most of them. However, they are not much better than the bucket routine; for the guards flush the toilets from the outside only once a day; and they "stink to high heaven" and are almost impossible to clean (the prisoner has nothing with which to clean them)—especially in the dark. Occasionally, when guards have very strong feelings against a prisoner, they actually go beyond the limits of punishment prescribed for isolation. In these instances a prisoner may find himself stark naked, in a totally stripped cell, where even the metal toilet and sink are removed—"for his protection." Utter darkness, profound silence, foul odors, bare skin, and cold concrete prevail.

The rest of the cells in B Section are strip cells, with the remainder of the cells on the bottom tier being regular isolation cells. The routine in regular isolation is the same as in AC. In B Section though, a man may just serve isolation time, without even being graduated to grade 3 segregation, for the lengths of punishment are shorter than in AC, and perhaps there is no time left for working up through the 3 grades of segregation.

The routine of segregation in B Section corresponds with the three grades described for AC. As in AC, a prisoner under investigation (who is not being punished) will immediately be put into grade 3 segregation, without going before disciplinary court and without serving isolation time. In B Section, all three grades are shuttled to meals in small groups—usually a tier and a half at a time, with only half of each group eating together, because they use two of the four sections of the south mess hall. Grades 2 and 1 have access to a small exercise yard next to the hospital. Once in segregation, if a prisoner has no bad reports, disciplinary court will graduate him to the next grade after 30 days, except for the move from grade 1 to the mainline population.

A special group of prisoners are those who are held in B Section under protective custody. These men are not being punished for breaking rules or laws. They are being held for their own protection, to keep them from getting hurt by other prisoners who may have reason to do so. For example, if a man has overextended his credit and cannot pay his debts, he may go to the guards and request that they lock him up so that those to whom he owes money cannot get to him. The guards oblige if they think the case merits such action; however, they do not want the situation to be too pleasurable. If it were, they might be deluged with such requests. Therefore, these prisoners are put into segregation; and they have to work their way up to grade 1, as do those who are being punished. The only difference is that these men usually are double celled, and the bunk beds are not stripped from the cells. During the last 30 days in grade 1, the guards consider the man's situation as it relates to the yard. If it is relatively safe (such as those to whom he owed money having been transferred to another prison), he is released to the yard (the mainline population). If not, staff may transfer him to another prison, hoping that he will make it better there.

B Section is more readily accessible to the mainline than AC is, and therefore illegal goods can be brought in to those prisoners who are being kept there. In this way, prisoners are often able to mitigate some of the punishment that is imposed on them. However, there is no question that the daily routine of B Section is punishment. And, prisoners have very strong feelings about the negative "extras" that may be imposed by a guard who feels in a punitive mood. Prisoners see much of this "extra" punishment as being more humanly degrading than the actual physical punishment.

*

40. Legal Rights of Prisoners

DAVID FOGEL

THE COURTS HAVE TRADITIONALLY KEPT A RE-spectable distance from prisons with a "hands-off" posture, displaying a great reluctance to interfere with prison management. "Hands-off" is a doctrine—not a rule of law. Its policy implication is one of judicial abstention.[1]

"The rationale behind the doctrine is that prison officials should have a wide area of discretion in the administration of their institutions. It was felt that the court should not interfere in areas where it lacked the expertise that prison administrators possessed, that the operation of prisons was an administrative function, and that judicial interference might detract from penal goals. As the primary goal of incarceration has moved toward rehabilitation, judicial reluctance to intrude into areas of prison administration has eased. Initially courts would act only in rare and exceptional circumstances. Today the view is that 'under our constitutional system, the payment which society exacts for the transgression of the law does not include regulating the transgressor to arbitrary and capricious action.'"[2]

The consequence of the "hands-off doctrine" had been to place the "prison officials in a position of virtual invulnerability and absolute power."[3]

▶SOURCE: "... We Are the Living Proof...": The Justice Model for Corrections. Cincinnati: W. H. Anderson Co., 1975. Pp. 127–133, 136–143, 145–148, 151–153, 169–172. (Editorial adaptations) Reprinted with permission of the publishers.

[1]Philip J. Hirschkop and Michael A. Milleman, "The Unconstitutionality of Prison Life," *Virginia Law Review*, Vol 55, June 1969, p. 812.

[2]*Landman v. Peyton*, 370 F. 2d 135, 141 (4th Cir. 1966).

[3]*Op. cit.*, n 66, Hirschkop and Milleman, p. 813.

We turn now to an examination of some major substantive areas to see how prisoners have attacked this "absolute power." ...

CHALLENGES TO THE CONDITIONS OF CONFINEMENT

Definition

Conditions of confinement encompass all aspects of prison life, and the cases are correspondingly numerous. We present a sample. The most usual means of challenging prison conditions is in federal court in a 42 U.S.C. § 1983 suit for deprivation of a federally-protected right under color of state law.[4]

Usually, the constitutional basis for these suits is the Eighth Amendment's ban on cruel and unusual punishment, though the due process clause of the Fourteenth Amendment is sometimes invoked. Using these constitutional provisions, prisoners have challenged, *inter alia*, physical brutality, conditions in solitary confinement, punishment for improper reasons, failure of prison personnel to protect inmates from assault and other injuries, and failure to provide needed medical care.

These suits have been faciliated by legal developments which have broadened the scope of the Eighth Amendment. Once considered to apply only to physical tortures used in England

[4]However, it has recently been held that federal habeas corpus is available to state prisoners to challenge the conditions of confinement even where the remedy sought is not release. *Wilwording v. Swenson*, 404 U.S. 249 (1971).

and Colonial America, the Eighth Amendment was regarded as essentially a dead letter throughout the nineteenth century. But in 1910, the Supreme Court articulated a more flexible view of the amendment: "Time works changes, brings into existence new conditions and purposes. Therefore, a principle to be vital must be capable of wider application than the mischief which gave it birth." *Weems v. United States,* 217 U.S. 349, 373 (1910). And in *Trop v. Dulles,* 356 U.S. 86 (1958), the Court determined that a punishment may violate the Eighth Amendment even though no physical mistreatment is involved. In his majority opinion, Chief Justice Warren said the Eighth Amendment "must draw its meaning from the evolving standards of decency that mark the progress of a maturing society. . . ." (At 101.)

Today, a punishment may be deemed cruel and unusual on several grounds. First, it may be so inhumane in itself as to "shock the conscience"; this conforms to the original meaning of the Eighth Amendment. Second, the punishment may violate the Eighth Amendment even though it is not cruel and unusual in itself, if it is disproportionate to the gravity of the offense for which it is imposed. Finally, a court may find a particular penal measure violative of the Eighth Amendment if it is more severe than necessary to achieve a legitimate penal goal.

Corporal Punishment and Physical brutality

The two major cases in the area of corporal punishment are *Talley v. Stephens,* 247 F. Supp. 683 (E.D. Ark. 1965) and *Jackson v. Bishop,* 404 F. 2d 571 (8th Cir. 1968). Both cases examined the constitutionality of whipping as punishment in the Arkansas prison system. By the time these cases were adjudicated, flogging as a means of disciplining prisoners had been outlawed by statute in most of the other states.

In *Talley v. Stephens, supra,* three Arkansas state prisoners brought a suit under § 1983 of the Civil Rights Act to enjoin, among other things, the use of the strap as punishment for rule infractions. The record in the case indicated that the offenses for which whipping could be imposed were not specified in prison regulations, nor were the number of blows which could be inflicted. As a result, both matters were left within the discretion of the administering officer. Predictably, abuses were frequent.

The plaintiffs contended that whipping was, *per se,* violative of the Eighth Amendment. The Court, with Judge Henley writing the majority opinion, was unwilling to go that far. However, Judge Henley enjoined the whippings as they were then administered, ordering the State Penitentiary Board to promulgate safeguards, e.g., limitations on the number of blows to be administered and fair warning to the inmates of the offenses that may result in whipping.

Following the decision in *Talley v. Stephens,* the Board did draw up some standards for the administration of corporal punishment in Arkansas. They failed to prevent abuse and the constitutionality of whipping was challenged again in *Jackson v. Bishop,* 404 F. 2d 571 (8th Cir. 1968).

In the majority opinion, Judge Blackmun, now Justice Blackmun of the Supreme Court, addressed the issue of the constitutionality of whipping, noting that prisoners do not forfeit their Eighth Amendment rights when they are incarcerated. Citing *Trop v. Dulles,* 356 U.S. 86 (1958), Judge Blackmun pointed out the flexible nature of the "cruel and unusual" concept. He wrote, "In determining whether a particular punishment violates the Eighth Amendment, notions of decency and civilized standards are relevant factors."

In reaching its decision, the Court considered the following factors: (1) that no conceivable safeguards could prevent abuse if whipping were permitted; (2) that existing safeguards were not followed; (3) that rules are easily circumvented; (4) that control of low-level personnel presents a difficult problem in this context; (5) that drawing the line between whipping and other forms of corporal punishment is very difficult once the former is permitted; (6) that corporal punishment frustrates correctional goals and engenders hatred among the inmates; and (7) that the use of the strap is opposed by public opinion. Considering all these factors, Judge Blackmun said: ". . . we have no difficulty in reaching the conclusion that the use of the strap in [the] penitentiaries of Arkansas in the 20th century, runs afoul of the Eighth Amendment. . . ." (At 579).

A more recent case, *Inmates of Attica Correctional Facility v. Rockefeller*, 453 F. 2d 12 (2d Cir. 1971), challenged physical brutality in another context. Following the riot, the prisoners' complaints alleged that guards at the prison retaliated against the inmates with brutal and abusive treatment, including the beatings, forcing the inmates to run the gauntlet, and verbal abuse such as threats and racial slurs. These sorts of occurrences are common enough following prison riots as to be reasonably predictable.

Judge Mansfield's opinion for the majority reversed the District Court's denial of a preliminary and permanent injunction against such abuse. Where, as here, the physical force used went far beyond what was necessary to keep order, the guards' conduct amounted to a violation of the Eighth Amendment. And, Judge Mansfield concluded, since there was no adequate assurance in the record that inmates would be protected from future assaults, a permanent injunction was found to be the appropriate form of relief.

One of the major cases challenging treatment allegedly violative of the Eighth Amendment, *Holt v. Sarver*, 309 F. Supp. 362 (E.D. Ark. 1970), *aff'd* 442 F. 2d 304 (8th Cir. 1971), defies classification and therefore is included here. In this case, the Court considered the Arkansas penitentiary system and found that, in cumulative effect, the conditions existing therein constituted cruel and unusual punishment. In reaching its decision, the Court considered the extensive use of prisoners as guards, the lack of rehabilitation program, the open barracks system, and the conditions in solitary confinement. Judge Henley, in ordering injunctive relief, said:

"Apart from physical danger, confinement in the Penitentiary involves living under degrading and disgusting conditions. This Court has no patience with those who still say, even when they ought to know better, that to change those conditions will convert the prison into a country club. . . . Let there be no mistake in the matter; the obligation of the Respondents [correctional administrators] to eliminate existing unconstitutionalities does not depend upon what the Legislature may do or upon what the Governor may do. . . ." (At 381.)

Solitary Confinement

A large class of cases in which prisoners have invoked the Eighth Amendment to challenge prison conditions has concerned solitary confinement. None of these cases has declared solitary confinement to be cruel and unusual in itself (though this may be a future development), but they have prohibited some of its more inhumane applications.

In *Jordon v. Fitzharris*, 257 F. Supp. 674 (N.D. Cal. 1966), the Court considered the constitutionality of facilities for solitary confinement at Soledad Prison. The plaintiff had been confined in a "strip cell" which was never cleaned despite the convict-occupant's repeated vomiting. He was provided with no means of maintaining personal cleanliness, completely deprived of clothing for the first eight days of confinement, and given only a canvas mat on which to sleep. Granting an injunction preventing prison officials from confining the convict in this cell, the Court said:

". . . when, as it appears in the case at bar, the responsible prison authorities in the use of the strip cells have abandoned elemental concepts of decency by permitting conditions to prevail of a shocking and debased nature, then the courts must intervene—and intervene promptly—to restore the primal rules of a civilized community in accord with the mandate of the Constitution of the United States." (At 680).

Four years later, in *Landman v. Royster*, 333 F. Supp. 621 (E.D.Va. 1971), the following aspects of solitary confinement were enjoined: bread and water diet, use of chains and handcuffs as restraining devices, deprivation of clothing in unheated cells with open windows, putting more than one man in an isolation cell—unless justified by emergency conditions, and the use of tear gas against non-threatening inmates.

In *LaReau v. MacDougall,* 473 F. 2d 974 (2d Cir. 1972), an inmate at the Connecticut Correctional Institution brought a § 1983 suit seeking an injunction against certain conditions in the prison's strip cells. The Court enjoined the practice of keeping the cell dark except for meals and writing as threatening to the inmate's sanity and violative of the Eighth Amendment. It also ruled the "Chinese toilet," i.e., a hole in the floor flushed from the outside, to be too degrading to pass constitutional standards.

Sinclair v. Henderson, 435 F. 2d 125 (5th Cir. 1970), involved a prisoner's challenge to conditions on Death Row. He alleged that the inmates had only fifteen minutes per day to wash, shave, and exercise; the toilets in the cells overflowed frequently; the drinking water contained rust; the food was contaminated with roaches and hair and served from filthy food carts on greasy trays. Claiming that these conditions violated the Eighth Amendment, the Fifth Circuit Court reversed the dismissal of the complaint by the District Court, holding that it stated a claim and remanding it for consideration on the merits.

There is a high degree of similarity in the approach the courts used in these cases. They attack conditions in solitary confinement on a hit-or-miss basis but refrain from declaring this form of confinement unconstitutional. Logically, however, if a court were satisfied that solitary confinement, even without the degrading and brutal conditions and practices, threatened sanity or was unnecessarily severe for the purpose it was designed to serve, the court should have had no scruples about declaring it unconstitutional *per se.*[5] But more to the point, it was not declared unconstitutional, and "hands off" now meant cautious warnings to the correctional administrator.

*

[5]"The Constitutional Status of Solitary Confinement," *Cornell Law Review,* Vol. 57, 1972, p. 476.

The Denial of Medical Care

Prison medical facilities and personnel are frequently inadequate. When a prisoner brings suit for damages or injunctive relief because of failure to provide adequate medical treatment, he may either sue the prison doctor or other responsible officials in a state tort or bring a suit in federal court in a § 1983 action under the Civil Rights Act. His chances of winning on the latter are slim, however, for he must show denial of treatment or mistreatment beyond what must be shown in a civil malpractice suit. In an addendum to *Ramsey v. Ciccone,* 310 F. Supp. 600(M.D. Mo. 1970), Judge Becker outlined the kinds of inadequate medical treatment that must be shown to rise to the level of an Eighth Amendment violation. For instance, where a statutory duty to provide treatment exists, then an intentional denial constitutes a violation of the Eighth Amendment. Similarly, gross negligence leading to injury is a claim cognizable under § 1983. On the other hand, simple negligence, even when it causes injury, was not found to be a constitutional violation and the prisoner had to seek relief in a state tort suit. Mere faulty judgment by a physician resulting in injury may not be made a constitutional claim.

An example of the egregious negligence that must be demonstrated to recover under § 1983 is *Martinez v. Mancusi,* 443 F. 2d 921 (2d Cir. 1970). In this case the plaintiff, an inmate of Attica Correctional Facility and a victim of infantile paralysis, had been taken to a hospital for a delicate operation. Shortly thereafter, the warden ordered him returned to Attica without a surgeon's discharge. The guards in charge of his return forced him to walk from the hospital, against the surgeon's orders. Upon return to Attica, he was kept in the prison hospital for one day, then returned to his cell with no facilities for medical care.

The District Court dismissed the complaint, but the Second Circuit Court reversed the dismissal, holding that the allegations here do state a cause of action under § 1983. The warden's failure to check with the surgeon before returning Martinez to prison, when he knew that the operation was delicate, and the prison doctor's failure to inquire of the surgeon about proper post-operative treatment amounted to *deliberate* indifference.

In *Tolbert v. Eyman*, 434 F. 2d 625 (9th Cir. 1970), the Ninth Circuit Court, in a *per curiam* opinion, reversed the District Court's decision of a § 1983 petition alleging inadequate medical care. The prisoner had an eye disease related to diabetes. Medicine for the disease sent by his wife and a druggist was repeatedly refused by the prison administration. As a result, the prisoner's condition worsened to the point of near blindness. The Court held that these facts constituted a *prima facie* case under § 1983.

Recovery in these cases is rare. A number of cases either dismiss the complaints or deny relief. In *Matthews v. Brown*, 362 F. Supp. 622 (E.D. Va. 1973), no negligence was shown in treatment received by a prisoner after an accident in the prison machine shop; in *Church v. Hegstrom*, 416 F. 2d 449 (2d Cir. 1969), no claim for relief was stated when there was no allegation that officials knew of inmate's need for treatment; in *Ramsey v. Ciccone*, 310 F. Supp. 600 (M.D. Mo. 1970), no claim for federal relief was stated where the alleged mistreatment was not continuing or was unsupported by recognized medical opinion; in *Coppinger v. Townsend*, 398 F. 2d 392 (10th Cir. 1968), no claim was stated when alleged mistreatment was only a difference of opinion between the doctor and the inmate; in *Reynolds v. Swenson*, 313 F. Supp. 328 (W.D. Mo. 1970), no claim was stated where there was no allegation that needed treatment was knowingly withheld.

The cases demonstrate great reluctance to award relief for inadequate medical care. The reason for this may be a recognition of the inherently discretionary nature of medical judgments, as well as deference, perhaps excessive, to the expertise of the medical profession. Recoveries are possible, however, when extreme negligence or total disregard of medical needs is demonstrated. If the courts showed timidity in

relation to some conditions of confinement, the tenacity of the "hands off" doctrine was more visible when the judiciary had the medical profession, rather than correctional officials, before the bar.

FIRST AMENDMENT RELIGIOUS RIGHTS

Definition

The religious rights of American citizens are grounded in the First Amendment to the U.S. Constitution: "Congress shall make no law respecting an establishment of religion, or prohibiting the free exercise thereof. . . ." Because freedom of religion is considered one of the fundamental or "preferred" freedoms, the federal courts have shown greater willingness to scrutinize prison practices allegedly burdening religious rights than they have in other areas of prison life. Federal courts have reiterated the importance of the First Amendment guarantee of freedom of religion and declared it a proper area for intervention. *Cruz v. Beto*, 405 U.S. 319 (1972); *Pierce v. La Vallee*, 293 F. 2d 233 (2d Cir. 1961); *Gittlemacker v. Prasse*, 428 F. 2d 1 (3rd Cir. 1970); *Brown v. Peyton*, 437 F. 2d 1228 (4th Cir. 1971).

This is not meant to imply that courts have denied correctional officials the ability to impose restrictions on religious expression. As in free society, a person's beliefs cannot be regulated, but reasonable restrictions on expression may be imposed if certain criteria are met. The test that the courts apply most frequently in evaluating the constitutionality of rules limiting the expression of religion is a two-fold one. First, the state must show a "compelling interest" in restricting the conduct. Second, the state's goal must be achieved by means which burden religious freedom as little as possible. *Brown v. Peyton, supra; Barnett v. Rodgers*, 410 F.2d 995 (D.C. Cir. 1969); *Remmers v. Brewer*, 361 F. Supp. 537 (S.D. Iowa 1973), *aff'd* 494 F. 2d 1277 (8th Cir. 1974). If a given rule fails either of these tests, it will frequently be invalidated by the courts.

Defining religion for constitutional purposes is difficult. Technically, courts, in their wisdom, decline to examine the tenets of a religion and "validate" it as meriting constitutional protection; such an examination is not the business of a governmental body. But if no inquiries into the nature of an alleged religion were made, the opportunities for abuse are obvious, especially as might be expected in prison. Therefore, courts have made tentative inquiries into the nature of new sects before applying First Amendment guarantees. In *Theriault v. Carlson,* 339 F. Supp. 375 (N.D. Ga. 1972), for example, the District Court found that the prisoner-founded Church of the New Song had as one of its tenets a belief in a Supreme Being and other attributes of a religion, and therefore the state could not restrict its exercise without meeting constitutional criteria. (But later it did not go along with the wine, steak, etc. claimed by its adherents to be necessary for worship services.)

Similarly, courts distinguish between essential religious practices and those of more marginal importance, requiring less justification by the state for regulation of the latter. In *Rinehart v. Brewer,* 360 F. Supp. 105 (S.D. Iowa 1973), an inmate member of the Church of the New Song challenged the prison rules requiring shaving and periodic haircuts on the ground that his religion mandated the wearing of hair in a style conducive to "inner peace." The District Court upheld the regulations, declaring that, since no particular hair length was religiously required, the rules did not render practice of his religion impossible. In *Walker v. Blackwell,* 411 F. 2d 23 (5th Cir. 1969), the Black Muslim prisoners' request to listen to Elijah Muhammed's weekly radio program was denied, partly because they had not shown that it was essential to the practice of Islam.

Dietary Laws

As with many other issues in the courts' treatment of prisoners' religious rights, the question of the obligation of the prison to provide for the religiously-mandated dietary requirements of its inmates arose in Black Muslim cases. The Islamic faith prohibits consumption of pork and sets aside the month of December (Ramadan) during which no food may be taken between sunrise and sunset. Challenges to prison practices which frustrate these requirements make up most of the dietary law cases.

In most of the cases, the courts assume that dietary practices impinging on religious rights are reviewable. One case, *Childs v. Pegelow,* 321 F. 2d 487 (4th Cir. 1963), held that arranging mealtimes is a matter of routine prison administration, so that a challenge to an official decision is nonjusticiable. However, other cases proceed by applying a "balancing" test, weighing the extent of the burden on religious freedom against the administrative burden of providing for the dietary requirements. Because of this mode of analysis, the result depends largely on the facts of the particular case or court.

In *Abernathy v. Cunningham,* 393 F. 2d 775 (4th Cir. 1968), the Black Muslims challenged the prison's failure to provide a pork-free noon meal. The court denied relief, finding that the petitioners could meet their nutritional needs by skipping the dishes containing pork. It is unclear what the outcome would be under different facts. Similarly, the court in *Walker v. Blackwell,* 411 F. 2d 23 (5th Cir. 1969), denied relief to Black Muslim petitioners seeking a nightly meal of coffee and pastry, both of a special type, during Ramadan. After applying the balancing test, the court concluded that the administrative burden and extra expense outweighed the deprivation of the unbridled exercise of this religion practice.

In a similar case, *Barnett v. Rodgers,* 410 F. 2d 995 (D.C. Cir. 1969), the Court of Appeals for the District of Columbia Circuit put a heavier burden on the state, applying the two-fold "compelling state interest" and "least restrictive" means test. It remanded the lower court's denial of relief where the petitioners wanted one pork-free meal a day. The Court of Appeals noted that the state had made no showing of a compelling state interest in an extensive use of pork in the prisoners' diet, nor had it shown that such interest could be served by means less burdensome to petitioners' right of free exercise.

Religious Literature and Correspondence with a Spiritual Advisor

During the 1960s, Black Muslims in prison sought permission to receive religious literature like "Muhammed Speaks" and "Message to the Black Man in America." Because of their alleged black supremacist ideology, courts were at first inclined to support the prison officials' decision to ban them, either deferring to the administrator's discretion or finding on the merits that the publications posed a danger to prison security. Now the trend is toward allowing such literature, or at least requiring a careful scrutiny of the material to determine whether it can be provided under conditions mitigating its alleged potential disruptive effect. The Fourth Circuit Court, for example, ordered a reconsideration of whether or not "Muhammed Speaks" and "Message to the Black Man" constitute a danger to prison security in *Brown v. Peyton,* 437 F. 2d 1228 (4th Cir. 1971), after it had, three years earlier, decided to uphold a denial of the very same publications.

Other courts have also tended to carefully examine bans on religious literature, though it is not always clear which test they apply to determine the prison rule's constitutionality. In *Long v. Parker,* 390 F. 2d 816 (3d Cir. 1968), the court overturned the decision of the lower court, upholding a rule forbidding prisoners to subscribe to "Muhammed Speaks" because of the dangerous effect of its alleged racist content. Where religious literature is concerned, said Judge Forman for the court, the test must be whether it creates a "clear and present danger" of a breach in prison security. The court in *Walker v. Blackwell,* 411F. 2d 23 (5th Cir. 1969), overturned a lower court holding on the merits, finding that the overall tone of "Muhammed Speaks" was not inflammatory, but encouraged blacks to improve themselves through work and study. However, in a Tenth Circuit Court case,

Hoggro v. Pontesso, 456 F. 2d 917 (10th Cir. 1972), the court upheld the denial of Black Muslim religious publications on the basis of an earlier case in which, after a hearing, they were found to be inflammatory. Since we do not know the facts of the earlier case we cannot tell whether this case is distinguishable; conditions in the prison may have been, for example, unusually tense.

Related to the right to receive religious literature is the right to correspond with a spiritual advisor. Since this right also receives First Amendment protection, the state must show a compelling interest to constitutionally prohibit such correspondence. In *Walker v. Blackwell,* 411 F. 2d 23 (5th Cir. 1969), the lower court had upheld a rule prohibiting correspondence by Black Muslims with Elijah Muhammed. The Court of Appeals reversed the decision, ruling that the prison must allow inmates to write to Elijah Muhammed for the limited purpose of spiritual guidance. In a similar case, *Cooper v. Pate,* 382 F. 2d 518 (7th Cir. 1967), the Court of Appeals upheld the lower court's ruling that the prison could not constitutionally bar prisoners from writing to Elijah Muhammed for spiritual guidance unless the communication presents a "clear and present danger" to prison security. *Neal v. State of Georgia,* 469 F. 2d 446 (5th Cir. 1972), dealt with the same issue in a non-Black Muslim context. The Court of Appeals reversed and remanded the lower court dismissal of the petitioner's § 1983 complaint, in which he alleged that he had been denied correspondence with his spiritual advisor. Judge Wisdom said that the state must show either a compelling interest or the existence of a security or discipline problem to curtail First Amendment rights.

*

MAIL AND MEDIA RIGHTS OF PRISONERS

Definition

An often-noted characteristic of prison life is the inmates' sense of isolation from the world outside the walls. Their avenues of communication with people and events in the nonprison society are severely limited by incarceration. Historically, prisoners had not been permitted to correspond with family, friends, and legal counsel, ("buried from the world") and then grudgingly permitted to do so; albeit under carefully circumscribed conditions. In the past, prison officials have freely censored both incoming and outgoing mail, a practice which they contended was necessary to intercept contraband, weapons, plans of escape, and blueprints for future criminal activity, to say nothing of manuscripts, letters to newspaper editors, and criticisms of the prison officials themselves.

Recently, the necessity and constitutional validity of extensive censorship have been questioned by the courts. Written communication is protected under the free speech clause of the First Amendment, which means that it is a "preferred" freedom. Like freedom of religion, freedom of speech in the non-prison world may not be curtailed unless the state demonstrates both that a *compelling state interest* exists and that the interest is being served by the *means least restrictive* of individual liberty.

However, this constitutional standard has not always been applied to the mail rights of prisoners because the extent of their rights under the free speech clause of the First Amendment is unclear. There is general recognition that imprisonment necessitates *some* curtailment of these rights of expression, but *how much* curtailment is a matter of disagreement and is still evolving.

Right of access to the media is a vital one for prisoners in several respects. First, since the average citizen is unlikely to experience prison conditions first-hand, the public depends heavily on the news media for its information about the penal system. Prisoners depend on journalists too, to publicize their grievances and to increase pressure for reform. Second, it is important that prisoners have access to news publications. A characteristic of prison life is the sense of isolation and alienation it breeds among the inmates. A prisoner with a subscription to

magazines and newspapers of significance to him may feel less cut-off from the outside world.

Here too, rights of communication with the press are "preferred" First Amendment freedoms, implicating both the free speech and free press clauses. Despite fairly numerous cases on the subject, the First Amendment rights of prisoners to communicate with the media remain unclear. Several cases analyze the issues in terms of the free addressee's right to receive correspondence, or the public interest in free and open debate, or the public's "right to know," rather than facing the questions of the *prisoner's* rights.

The access to media cases are divided into three subject areas; the right of access to the media, interviews with the press, and the right to receive publications. They follow the prisoner mail rights discussion.

Mail

The United States Supreme Court recently decided *Procunier v. Martinez*,—U.S.—, 40 L. Ed. 2d 224 (1974), a case challenging California's regulations for the censorship of general prisoner correspondence. The regulations applied to all non-legal correspondence, prohibited any material tending to "agitate, unduly complain, or magnify grievances." The regulations authorized prison officials to delete anything they considered to be "lewd, obscene, or defamatory; to contain foreign matter, or [to be] otherwise inappropriate." In addition, any material "expressing inflammatory political, racial, religious or other views or beliefs . . ." was declared to be contraband. In practice, these regulations allowed censoring officials to delete anything critical of the institution or its personnel. The District Court declared the regulations unconstitutional because they interfered with protected expression without adequate justification; further, the Court declared them void for vagueness.

The Supreme Court affirmed the District Court's decision, with Justice Powell writing the majority opinion. Noting the courts' traditional deference to the judgment of correctional personnel in this area, Powell nevertheless said: "[w]hen a prison regulation or practice offends a fundamental constitutional guarantee, federal courts will discharge their duty to protect constitutional rights. . . . The issue before us is the appropriate standard of review for prison regulations restricting freedom of speech." (At 40 L. Ed. 2d 236.) Mr. Justice Powell avoided reaching the issue of the prisoner's First Amendment rights in the mail area. Instead, he chose to decide the case on the narrower ground of the free addressee/sender's rights to unfettered communication. These regulations fairly invited prison officials and employees to apply their own personal judgments as standards for prisoner mail censorship. (At 40 L. Ed. 2d 241.) Further, when a letter is censored or rejected, the Court ruled that certain minimum procedural safeguards must be afforded the inmate: notification, an opportunity to protest, and referral of the matter to a non-censoring official.

Justice Marshall, though concurring in the result, did not agree with the majority's avoidance of the prisoner's First Amendment right to send and receive mail. He rejected the opinion's necessary implication that prison officials possess the general right to open and read all mail. Such wholesale reading of mail might well chill the inmate's free expression of ideas, A prisoner's free and open expression will surely be restrained by the knowledge that his every word may be read by his jailers and that his message could well find its way into a disciplinary file, be the object of ridicule or even lead to reprisals. (At 40 L. Ed. 2d 246.) Justice Marshall also found the state's justifications for reading all incoming and outgoing mail inadequate. The fears of transmission of contraband and escape plans were simply too speculative to permit all mail to be read. When prison authorities have reason to believe that an escape plot is being hatched by a particular inmate through his correspondence, they may well have an adequate basis to seize that inmate's letters; but there is no

such justification for a blanket policy of reading all prison mail. (At 40 L. Ed. 2d 247.)

Finally, Justice Marshall disagreed with the state's contention that reading all mail was necessary to further rehabilitative goals. On the contrary, the inhibiting effect on communication of the knowledge that every word will be read by prison officials runs counter to true rehabilitation. "To suppress expression is to reject the basic human desire for recognition and affront the individual's worth and dignity." (At 40 L. Ed. 2d 248.)

*

Access to Publications

Since First Amendment freedoms are involved, courts have been willing to scrutinize with care prison regulations that deny inmates access to news publications. As with infringement of religious rights, the state must show a compelling interest in defense of its regulations limiting access. Sometimes, the court requires the state to demonstrate that the publication creates a clear and present danger to prison security.

Where regulations on receiving publications are arbitrarily applied or inherently discriminatory, the courts have ruled on the basis of the equal protection clause of the 14th Amendment. Courts have been particularly solicitous if they suspect racial discrimination.

In *Fortune Society v. McGinnis,* 319 F. Supp. 901 (S.D.N.Y. 1970), the Fortune Society, a prisoner aid and reform group, and a group of state prisoners brought a class action seeking a cease and desist order against the Commissioner of Corrections of New York State and the Superintendent of a prison for preventing inmates from receiving the *Fortune Society Newsletter.*

Judge Weinfeld, in granting a preliminary injunction, found that the prison administration had presented no justification for banning the newsletter, other than a statement to the Fortune Society that its publication misrepresented the prison system. Even if true, he said, this would not be sufficient to ban the newsletter, for the First Amendment requires a showing of a *compelling* state interest. Here, the state must demonstrate that the material it seeks to exclude creates a "clear and present danger" to prison security.

Jackson v. Godwin, 400 F. 2d 529 (5th Cir. 1968), is another case in which exclusion of publications was overturned by the court. It was decided on equal protection grounds. Florida state prisoners brought a § 1983 action alleging denial of access to black-oriented, "non-subversive" publications, while white prisoners were permitted white-oriented material. The regulations permitted the inmate to subscribe only to his hometown newspaper and to magazines on a restrictive list. The Court of Appeals, through Judge Tuttle, first said that the court has "a duty to protect the prisoner from unlawful and onerous treatment of a nature that, of itself, adds punitive measures to those legally meted out by the court." (At 532.) Noting that constitutional rights attach to all persons, the court found that the rules in question had been arbitrarily applied and were racially discriminatory, in effect, even when applied equitably. The "hometown rule" had not been fully enforced since white prisoners were afforded easy access to white-oriented newspapers not published in their hometowns. In addition, non-inflammatory black-oriented publications like *Sepia* and *Ebony* were regularly excluded from the approved list as "unhealthy" (a medical model term borrowed by custody officials, herein referring not to physical health but rather to political unhealthiness as they viewed it.) Considering the 50% black composition of the prison population, the court hinted that conscious discrimination might be at work. Further, the "hometown rule" was inherently discriminatory because few black inmates were likely to be from a town that published a black-oriented newspaper. Judge Tuttle therefore ordered that all black inmates might not have their health impaired by permitting them to subscribe to one black newspaper and that at least one black-oriented magazine be placed on the list of approved publications.

*

SUMMARY

For a free-wheeling *keeper* or *treater* to suddenly become a *defendant* is status-costly. Inside the walls his discretion reigned supreme, but it looked odd when it had to be explained in a courtroom. The prisoner as plaintiff enjoys the status of "equality" before the bench. The judge, however, was not likely to listen as sympathetically to a latter-day Elam Lynds in the person of James Park, Associate Warden of San Quentin (1971), explaining how he "knew" he had his culprit.

"That's simple; we know who did it from the other inmates. . . . If several reliable inmates point to this guy, or refuse to clear him, we know he's guilty. We don't have the type of case we could take to court: it would be too dangerous for our inmate-informers to have to testify. You middle-class due-processors don't understand; it's an administrative matter, not judicial."[6]

In another strange notion of due process in New York, deputy warden Perry DeLong, after taking 100 days of good-time from an inmate, explains the process of forfeiture in this excerpt:

Q. At the disciplinary hearings, are inmates entitled to call witness in their behalf?

A. No.

Q. Are they entitled to cross examine guards?

A. They are not.

Q. What record is made of the proceeding at a disciplinary hearing?

A. As you see here, on the disciplinary report, the punishment is noted. This disciplinary

---

[6]Jessica Mitford, "Kind and Usual Punishment in California," in Burton M. Atkins and Henry R. Glick, eds., *Prison, Protests and Politics*, Englewood Cliffs, N.J.: Prentice-Hall, Inc., 1972, p. 159.

hearing is not a judicial hearing, it corresponds to, I believe, a *potter familus*[sic]. I could be wrong on the *potter familus.*

Q. *Potter familus?*

A. It is probably known as the authority figure, as meting out what is family punishment, or family discipline. This is not a judicial thing in the sense of a court of record, and there is no provision for it as a court of record, and this is an internal disciplinary thing, very much as a father and mother in the home say, 'Johnny, you have done so and so, and you are forbidden to do it, and therefore you will stay in your room.'[7]

With the unlimited ability to defend themselves, correctional administrators dug in on even minor issues. In *Conklin v. Wainwright,* 424 F. 2d 516 (5th Cir. 1970), the court decided against the prisoner who wanted more than ten sheets of paper a day for preparing a legal argument. Presumably, if the allotment was less than ten sheets, the case may have been decided in the plaintiff's favor!

Moving along the continuum of pariah-penitent-prisoner-patient-plaintiff, we see increasing activity on the part of the offender. Being a pariah merely entailed leaving the community, having a punishment performed upon the body, or execution—one-time summary acts. Becoming a penitent began to involve the offender in a moral venture. It was minimal and sedentary, but it did require a response. Being a prisoner, in the common-sense meaning of the term, began to require active and even more rigorous responses—marching, working, obedience to routine. The patient status (as with the penitent) engaged the convict on an inner level. In addition to the normal burdens incumbent upon occupants of prison cells, the convict

now could, by a display of insight, climb a clinical ladder to improve his status. If the treaters looked at the treated through a prism of determinism the prisoner, in peering back, was refracting free will. Heeding their admonishment to change, he simply chose another path to change. The course turned out to be a legal one in which the prisoner wished to be seen as a competent (political) being. Correctional administrators were not ready to accept it. Sol Rubin describes the foot-dragging by the correctional establishment:

"Aside from what they do or do not do in regard to sentencing, the rights of prisoners, and the rights of probationers and parolees, court decisions have had an impact on the correctional process that is clearly discernible in the reactions of correctional administration. Administrative responses to court decisions may be classified into three self-explanatory categories—the positive response, the provocative response, and the defensive response. From all that I can discover, there is little in administrative behavior that is positive and somewhat more that is provocative; the great bulk of administrative behavior is defensive. By that I mean administrators sit tight on those they are dealing with until they are forced by a court decision or a legislature to change their pattern. And even then, they resist compliance."[8]

The net result of the correctional case law development to date seems to be the construction of an uncertain "shield against authority, or zone of inviolability" for convicts. More specifically it has simply condemned conditions of

"lengthy solitary confinement, dark cells where no light burns, . . . no bed or mattress, bad or no food, being kept nude, being kept in cells which are full of filth and excrement, cells otherwise unhygienic, as well as the use of physical force . . . [requiring] some kind of notice or statement of the case against them, and some kind of opportunity to respond."[9]

---

[7]Deposition of Perry J. DeLong, Jan. 10, 1969, at 39–41 *Visconti v. LaVallee,* No. 68 Civil 403(N.D.N.Y., filed Nov. 1968). (As cited in Turner, *Stanford Law Review* Vol. 23 p. 500).

[8]Sol Rubin, "The Impact of Court Decisions on the Correctional Process," *Crime and Delinquency,* Vol. 20, No. 2, p. 133.

[9]Annual Chief Justice Earl Warren Conference sponsored by the Roscoe Pound-American Trial Lawyers Foundation, *A Program for Prison Reform,* June 9–10, 1972, pp. 51, 52.

Why did we have to undergo torturous and lengthy litigation to be forced to accede to such amelioratives? Why were they not simply administratively ordered! Perhaps in the last analysis it was administrative resistance to the prisoner's micro-world concerns which generated counter-resistance in the form of litigation.

The irony of this chapter of correctional history lies in the fact that the unlawful, in bringing the agents of law to court, received more lawful treatment. The offender demonstrated that he was quite volitional. Indeed the idea of the offender-as-responsible opened a frightening Pandora's Box.

41. Prison Furloughs

MICHAEL S. SERRILL

EVERY MONTH ACROSS THE UNITED STATES, MORE than 30,000 furloughs are granted to adult inmates, and more than 6,000 to juveniles. During the 1973–74 fiscal year, more than 250,000 unescorted trips into the community were made by adult inmates and more than 70,000 by juveniles (*see chart*). How many individual inmates participated is difficult to determine. Most states only keep raw statistics on the number of leaves granted, without attempting to determine how many individuals were involved. A single offender may be granted only one furlough, or a dozen, in the course of a year, depending on the program. For instance, the District of Columbia and the state of California each released about 1,000 different men on furlough last year. Many of the D.C. inmates were released several times a week and by the year's end the 1,000 men accumulated 38,000 furloughs among them. In California, the offenders accumulated only 1,100 furloughs.

A furlough is defined by prison officials as a release to visit the family, to apply for a job or school, to attend public functions, or to visit sick or dying relatives. Education- and work-release activities are not included.

Most furloughs last from forty-eight to seventy-two hours and are taken on weekends.

The recent rapid expansion of furlough programs represents a veritable revolution in

►SOURCE: *"Prison Furloughs in America,"* *Corrections Magazine* *(July/August, 1975), 1(6): 3–7. Reprinted with permission of Corrections Magazine, 801 Second Avenue, New York, NY 10017.*

correctional thinking around the country, especially since in most states there was no such thing as a furlough program prior to 1969. Before then, such programs, at least for adults, were either proscribed by law or used very cautiously and infrequently for carefully screened inmates who needed to go out for some special reason, like death-bed visits, funerals, or medical treatment.

In the case of juveniles, home visiting programs have been in effect for years in some states, though the practice has expanded dramatically in recent years. Juvenile corrections administrators are generally empowered by law with broad authority to act in the "best interest" of the child. In most states it has therefore been unnecessary to pass special legislation permitting home visits for juveniles.

Only a handful of states remain without any provision for adult furloughs, other than for death-bed visits and funerals.

*

Once adult furlough programs were initiated, they grew with almost incredible speed. In Oregon, officials say that in 1968, a year after their furlough law was passed, 9 furloughs were granted. Last year, a total of 27,000 such leaves were granted. Florida's program was initiated in November, 1971. Since then, a total of 166,000 furloughs have been awarded. Between July, 1974, and April, 1975, the total was 42,000. In Massachusetts, the program began on November 6, 1972. Between November 6 and December 31, 1,150 furloughs were granted.

477

During 1973, the total was 7,204. During 1974, adult inmates took 8,115 furloughs.

Why the idea of furloughs has come into favor so suddenly and the programs have expanded so rapidly is a matter of speculation among prison administrators and other corrections experts. Some say it is a natural outgrowth of the popularity and widespread use of work-release programs, which are now operating in all but two or three states. Administrators reason that if inmates are responsible enough to leave institutions or work-release centers unsupervised every day to go to work, then they certainly can be trusted to spend a few hours, or a few days, at home without heading for the nearest airport. Many furloughs—perhaps more than half—are awarded to inmates who live in work-release or other community correctional centers. Of the approximately 53,000 furloughs granted to Florida inmates last year, only 12,000 were for those in institutions. The rest went to residents of Florida's network of community correctional centers. Of the 3,700 "temporary leaves" given to Oregon inmates every month, all but about 250 go to inmates in work-release centers. And there are only about 220 inmates in the centers at any given time, meaning that a single inmate may be given leaves several times a week.

Most states, and the federal government, have given correctional agencies open-ended authority to establish their own rules and regulations for furloughs. The most common restriction in the various laws is simply that no furlough last more than thirty days.

The administrative regulations governing the programs vary widely from state to state; sometimes they seem to be based more on the political climate than on considerations of security. Some agencies ban from consideration all offenders convicted of violent crimes, while others include them. Some only consider those who are in the last sixty days, or six months, or one year, before their expected release date, while others will consider anyone whom they judge to have

proven himself trustworthy. Two almost universal requirements are that the offender first achieve minimum-custody status, and have a clean disciplinary record for a period of time, sometimes six months, sometimes a year. Sex offenders are almost always excluded.

The reasons for which inmates are permitted furloughs also vary from state to state. In a number of jurisdictions, an inmate must give a specific reason for wanting a furlough, such as an employment interview, college or vocational school application, to attend church, to give a talk before some community group, to visit a sick relative, or to attend a son's or daughter's graduation or wedding.

Those agencies with the largest furlough programs, however, send the greatest number of offenders home simply to visit their families. In Florida, for instance, of the 4,388 furloughs approved in April, 2,242 were for family visiting. In the federal prison system, well over half of the 14,000 overnight furloughs approved last year were for "release transition," meaning a general furlough designed to help the offender reintroduce himself to his family and refamiliarize himself with non-prison life.

Prison administrators do not defend their furlough programs simply as another "goodie" to offer to inmates as a reward for staying out of trouble. Neither are they considered to be solely a means for relieving inmates' pent-up sexual urges. Instead, the programs are generally proposed and defended as a means of gradually "reintegrating"an offender into a society that may have become alien to him while he was locked up. In fact, as some administrators have become disillusioned with the value of their institutional programs, they have turned to theories of "reintegration" as the main thrust of their programming. The corrections directors in Connecticut, Illinois, Michigan, and other states with large furlough programs all say that furloughs are only one part of an overall program designed to build up a solid base of community and family support for an inmate *before* he walks out the front gate of the prison. Subsidiary benefits of furloughs, they say, are that they improve morale in institutions and give parole boards something tangible to look at when deciding whether an offender should be released.

To many people, the fact that a man has committed a serious enough crime to be sent to prison automatically designates him as dangerous. Too many old movies and new television shows, officials say, have given the public the impression that the first impulse of a large number of offenders released from prison is to rape and rob. The idea of letting prisoners out unsupervised for a weekend, or even for an hour, thus strikes some laymen as utter lunacy.

The negative feelings held by many people about furloughs are often reinforced by media coverage, which is sometimes confined to the more spectacular failures. The New York State program, for instance, has gotten relatively little news coverage and caused little public controversy, though the Department of Correctional Services grants more than 16,000 furloughs a year, and claims a 98 per cent success rate. But in late June, the program made headlines all over the country. An inmate in prison for throwing his two young daughters through a second-story window was released on furlough. He went home to Brooklyn and allegedly hurled the same two girls off the roof of a four-story building, critically injuring them.

Some police officials and district attorneys, already angry that many of the suspects they apprehend and prosecute never go to prison, are infuriated when those who are locked up are released on furlough. And when police and prosecutors begin to attack a furlough program, they often get ample assistance from conservative legislators, especially if it is an election year.

These facts make the various furlough programs perhaps the most vulnerable experiment ever undertaken in corrections. It is often said by corrections officials that the worst thing that can happen to a furlough program is for the media to find out about it. Even if the news coverage is positive, they point out, it is almost sure to bring a flurry of press releases from the program's opponents. And if there is an incident involving a furloughee while the media is focusing its attention on the program, the entire effort may be endangered, say corrections officials.

Corrections agencies whose furlough programs come under attack can usually come up with statistics showing substantial "success." When the number of furloughs given is compared to the number of escapes and new crimes by furloughees, most agencies show success rates of 98 per cent or better. Corrections officials defend this measurement by maintaining that the proper way to measure the success of a program is to compare the number of potential incidents—that is, the number of furloughs—to the number of actual incidents. Critics say that a better measure would be to compare the number of individual people furloughed with the number of incidents. But even using this measurement, most agencies still have return rates of over 90 per cent.

Furlough critics respond that if even one man on furlough commits a serious crime, then the corrections officials have abdicated their primary responsibility—to protect the public from the men in their charge.

NATIONAL SURVEY ON PRISON
FURLOUGH PROGRAMS *

| | Number of Furloughs | | | |
| | Adults | | Juveniles | |
	Per Month	Fiscal 1974	Per Month	Fiscal 1974
Alabama	90	1,805	NA[1]	NA
Alaska	NA	NA	NA	NA
Arizona	NA	77[2]	NA	NA
Arkansas	14[3]	170[3]	NA	NA
California	93[3]	1,121[3]	25	960
Colorado	190	2,300	150	1,800
Connecticut	550	6,600	235	2,800
Delaware	25	450	75-80	800-1,000
D.C.	3,000[4]	38,000[4]	NA	NA
Florida	4,388[5]	53,000	84	1,011
Georgia	230	2,800	137	1,643
Hawaii	Not permitted		27	499
Idaho	21	200	43	300
Illinois	375[3]	4,500[3]	1,400	16,300
Indiana	38	425[6]	110	1,300
Iowa	186	2,238	NA	NA
Kansas	25	302	122	1,346
Kentucky	45	500	7	78
Louisiana	NA	1,671	NA	NA
Maine	78	935	64	767
Maryland	500-700	5,000	210	2,100
Massachusetts	651[5]	8,115	No juvenile institutions	
Michigan	400-500	5,282	45	500
Minnesota	33	393	NA	600
Mississippi	40	490	60-75	800-900

*This chart reflects the results of a national survey of furlough programs conducted by *Corrections Magazine.* Most of the statistics were solicited by letter. Many state correctional agencies had no statistics available on their furlough programs. In some cases, they were able only to estimate the number of furloughs granted in a typical month and in all of fiscal 1974. In some cases, the annual total was divided by twelve to provide an approximate monthly figure. In general, rounded-off figures are estimates. In all cases, these figures represent the number of furloughs granted, not the number of individuals involved. Most agencies could not supply the latter figure. Many inmates receive multiple furloughs.

[1] NA = Figures not available.

National Survey on Prison Furlough Programs *(continued)*

| | Number of Furloughs | | | |
| | Adults | | Juveniles | |
	Per Month	Fiscal 1974	Per Month	Fiscal 1974
Missouri	NA	934	Not permitted	
Montana	Not permitted		34	402
Nebraska	194	2,322	Included in adult figures	
Nevada	Furlough program just approved		1-2	8-10
New Hampshire	Furlough program just approved		100	1,200
New Jersey	8,352	696	NA	NA
New Mexico	NA	135	Included in adult figures	
New York	1,352	16,226	188	2,250
North Carolina	2,918	35,020	130[7]	1,560
North Dakota	6	29	7	168
Ohio	Furlough program just approved		200-300	3,160
Oklahoma	Not permitted		106	1,282
Oregon	3,716	27,000	NA	NA
Pennsylvania	350	1,506	1,500	18,000
Rhode Island	Furlough program just approved		150	1,800
South Carolina	753	9,877	Not permitted	
South Dakota	1	10	Included in adult figures	
Tennessee	105	1,300	459	5,508
Texas	Not permitted		200	2,400
Utah	45	540	25-40	350-400
Vermont	778	9,340	50	700
Virginia	NA	4,500	127[8]	2,000
Washington	239	2,865	86	1,040
West Virginia	Not permitted		Not permitted	
Wisconsin	Not permitted		NA	NA
Wyoming	Not permitted		Not permitted	
Federal System	1,450	17,400	No juvenile institutions	

[2] From December, 1974, through April, 1975.
[3] Excludes furloughs from work-release centers.
[4] Includes some work- and study-release.
   Program recently cut back sharply.
[5] For April, 1975.
[6] From July, 1974, through May,1975
[7] From January, 1975, through May, 1975.
[8] For May, 1975

The Prison Community: Informal Inmate Social Structure

THE STUDY OF THE PRISON AS A SOCIAL SYSTEM BEGAN IN THE 1940s AND BOTH research and the inmate community being studied seem to have become more complex during the ensuing years. The world of the custodial/correctional institution is a relatively closed world, a "total institution" as Erving Goffman has phrased it. Because men and women confined in such relatively closed settings develop an informal social system with levels of caste, firmly held values, and methods of enforcing those values, these settings are of particular interest to sociologists, social psychologists, and occasionally anthropologists. The results of their studies throw considerable light on the strength and viability of this sub-rosa social system and its pervasive effects upon the occupants of such total institutions. These investigations do much to explain why such influences seem to largely neutralize the alleged positive consequences of incarceration and rehabilitative measures.

One of the most ingenious and devastating studies of the climate of interpersonal relationships that is generated in a total institution was carried out by Haney and his colleagues. A simulated prison was set up with volunteer students playing the roles of guards or inmates. Initially normal interaction occurred, but over time the "guards" turned sadistic and threatening and began to dehumanize their peers who were playing the inmate roles. The "prisoners" became increasingly passive, dependent, and depressed. A study of actual guard–inmate relationships by McCorkle describes in subtle detail the corruption that occurs when, to secure a smooth-working relationship between prisoners and their custodians, friendship and reciprocity result in rule violation and an erosion of guard authority. A quite different and more recent view of guard–prisoner relationships is found in Miller's selection. Using Transactional Analysis this selection describes the manner in which the staff is victimized by means of physical games, therapeutic games, and other sorts of strategies engaged in by "street-wise" and "institution-wise" prisoners.

A dominant, almost irresistable, socializing feature of prison life is an inmate code of appropriate and expected behavior. Wieder approaches the problem as a student of language; he suggests that in a community facility housing young delinquents there had evolved an unwritten moral and behavioral code with clear and certain sanctions. This code emphasized loyalty, sharing, and helping one another, as well as noninvolvement and noncooperation with staff (values which have been found in other studies of adult and juvenile institutions).

Social systems are not held together by values alone. As the Marxists are fond of pointing out, strong mutual influences exist between values and the economic system. Because prisons have traditionally been settings where creature comforts and consumer goods were meager or nonexistent, it is hardly surprising that an underground market system for illicit goods and services inevitably is part of every prison. Such an arrangement reinforces the status system among inmates and helps not only to fill idle time in the planning and actualizing of illicit transactions but also gives satisfaction to the prisoner underclass which has "beaten the system." The selection by Guenther describes rackets such as loan sharking, illicit currency, storekeeping, gambling, pornography, homebrew, and drugs as part of the covert economics of a large federal prison.

Social settings or occupational groups with unique experiences evolve special vocabularies, sometimes referred to as "argot." Another selection from Guenther describes the special words associated with recurring experiences of prison life that require argot.

The next three articles deal with special groups that are formed in particular institutions. Williams and Fish detail the phenomenon of homosexual "families" that develop within female institutions. Courtship, marriage, and divorce are described, and the authors attempt to identify the emotional needs of imprisoned girls and women. These needs are reflected in the creation of synthetic family networks in spite of opposition from staff.

In the next selection, Leo Carroll studies social types among white prisoners, and various roles associated with sexual behavior, drug use, and informing—all within the context of a large male prison. In his second selection, Carroll details the very different social types that he identified among black inmates in the same prison. They became "brothers" and "partners" versus "Toms," and revolutionaries versus "half-steppers." The strains of these different roles often led to heavy conflict. Inmates often do not interact with one another because of political and religious stratification as well as the more obvious splits along racial or ethnic lines. Jacobs, in his study of the Illinois penitentiary near Chicago, describes the strong, largely unmodifiable racial coteries among the "super gangs" of different races and the more newly developed stratification and conflict relating to religious dissimilarities within racial groups.

Students of prison life have rarely been in prison themselves. In viewing new buildings, gleaming medical facilities, neat libraries, and the presence of many therapists and programs, the outsider may well conclude that incarceration can't be all that bad—especially when compared with ghetto living. But what Sykes has referred to as the "pains of imprisonment" are more subtle and by no means inconsequential. In a classic statement, now twenty years old but still essentially valid, Sykes from his study of the Trenton, New Jersey prison argues forcefully about the deprivation of liberty, goods, and services; the denial of heterosexual relationships; and the lack of autonomy and personal security. A more recent analysis of the routinization, debasement, and dehumanization of confinement, taken from Guenther's study of the Atlanta penitentiary, suggests that the many reforms of intervening years between the Sykes and Guenther studies have done little to lessen the punitive nature of incarceration in this country.

No matter how benign a prison administration may be, perhaps the core preoccupation of most employees is the problem of security and potential escapes. Once more Guenther investigates this problem in Atlanta and describes the types of escape attempts, the reasons for escape, and the attendant concern shown by staff regarding all contraband that might facilitate such attempts.

42. Interpersonal Dynamics in a Simulated Prison

CRAIG HANEY
CURTIS BANKS
PHILIP ZIMBARDO

THE APPROACH TAKEN IN THE PRESENT EMPIRICAL study attempted to create a prison-like situation in which the guards and inmates were initially comparable and characterized as being "normal-average," and then to observe the patterns of behavior that resulted, as well as the cognitive, emotional and attitudinal reactions that emerged. Thus, we began our experiment with a sample of individuals who did not deviate from the normal range of the general population on a variety of dimensions we were able to measure. Half were randomly assigned to the role of "prisoner,"the others to that of "guard," neither group having any history of crime, emotional disability, physical handicap nor even intellectual or social disadvantage.

The environment created was that of a "mock" prison that physically constrained the prisoners in barred cells and psychologically conveyed the sense of imprisonment to all participants. Our intention was not to create a *literal* simulation of an American prison, but rather a functional representation of one. For ethical, moral, and pragmatic reasons we could not detain our subjects for extended or indefinite periods of time, we could not exercise the threat and promise of severe physical punishment, we could not allow homosexual or racist practices to flourish, nor could we dupli-

▶SOURCE: *"Interpersonal Dynamics in a Simulated Prison,"* *International Journal of Criminology and Penology, (1973), 1 (1):* *67–82, 83–92. Reprinted by permission.*

cate certain other specific aspects of prison life. Nevertheless, we believed that we could create a situation with sufficient mundane realism to allow the role-playing participants to go beyond the superficial demands of their assignment into the deep structure of the characters they represented. To do so, we established functional equivalents for the activities and experiences of actual prison life that were expected to produce qualitatively similar psychological reactions in our subjects—feelings of power and powerlessness, of control and oppression, of satisfaction and frustration, of arbitrary rule and resistance to authority, of status and anonymity, of machismo and emasculation. In the conventional terminology of experimental social psychology, we first identified a number of relevant conceptual variables through analysis of existing prison situations, then designed a setting in which these variables were operationalized. No specific hypotheses were advanced other than that the assignment to the treatment of "guard"or "prisoner" would result in significantly different reactions on behavioral measures of interaction, emotional measures of mood state and pathology, attitudes toward self, as well as other indices of coping and adaptation to this novel situation. What follows is the mechanics of how we created and peopled our prison, what we observed, what our subjects reported, and, finally, what we can conclude about the nature of the prison environment and the psychology of imprisonment which can account for the failure of our prisons.

METHOD

Overview

The effects of playing the role of "guard" or "prisoner" were studied in the context of an experimental simulation of a prison environment. The research design was a relatively simple one, involving as it did only a single treatment variable, the random assignment to either a "guard" or "prisoner" condition. These roles were enacted over an extended period of time (nearly one week) within an environment that was physically constructed to resemble a prison. Central to the methodology of creating and maintaining a psychological state of imprisonment was the functional simulation of significant properties of "real prison life"(established through information from former inmates, correctional personnel, and texts).

The "guards" were free within certain limits to implement the procedures of induction into the prison setting and maintenance of custodial retention of the "prisoners." These inmates, having voluntarily submitted to the conditions of this total institution in which they now lived, coped in various ways with its stresses and its challenges. The behavior of both groups of subjects was observed, recorded, and analyzed. The dependent measures were of two general types: transactions between and within each group of subjects, recorded on video and audio tape as well as directly observed; individual reactions on questionnaires, mood inventories, personality tests, daily guard shift reports, and post experimental interviews.

Subjects

The 22 subjects who participated in the experiment were selected from an initial pool of 75 respondents, who answered a newspaper ad asking for male volunteers to participate in a psychological study of "prison life" in return for payment of $15 per day. Those who responded to the notice completed an extensive questionnaire concerning their family background, physical and mental health history, prior experience, and attitudinal propensities with respect to sources of psychopathology (including their involvements in crime). Each respondent who completed the background questionnaire was interviewed by one of two experimenters. Finally, the 24 subjects who were judged to be most stable (physically and mentally), most mature, and least involved in anti-social behaviors were selected to participate in the study. On a random basis, half of the subjects were assigned the role of "guard," half were assigned to the role of "prisoner."

The subjects were normal, healthy males attending colleges throughout the United States who were in the Stanford area during the summer. They were largely of middle class socioeconomic status, Caucasians (with the exception of one Oriental subject). Initially they were strangers to each other, a selection precaution taken to avoid the disruption of any pre-existing friendship patterns and to mitigate against any transfer into the experimental situation of previously established relationships or patterns of behavior.

This final sample of subjects was administered a battery of psychological tests on the day prior to the start of the simulation, but to avoid any selective bias on the part of the experimenter-observers, scores were not tabulated until the study was completed.

Two subjects who were assigned to be a "stand-by" in case an additional "prisoner" was needed were not called, and one subject assigned to be a "stand-by" guard decided against participating just before the simulation phase began—thus, our data analysis is based upon ten prisoners and eleven guards in our experimental conditions.

PROCEDURE

Physical Aspects of the Prison

The prison was built in a 35-foot section of a basement corridor in the psychology building at

Stanford University. It was partitioned by two fabricated walls, one of which was fitted with the only entrance door to the cell block, the other contained a small observation screen. Three small cells (6 × 9 ft) were made from converted laboratory rooms by replacing the usual doors with steel barred, black painted ones, and removing all furniture.

A cot (with mattress, sheet, and pillow) for each prisoner was the only furniture in the cells. A small closet across from the cells served as a solitary confinement facility; its dimension were extremely small (2 × 2 × 7 ft), and it was unlit.

In addition, several rooms in an adjacent wing of the building were used as guard's quarters (to change in and out of uniform or for rest and relaxation), a bedroom for the "warden" and "superintendent," and an interview-testing room. Behind the observation screen at one end of the "yard" were video recording equipment and sufficient space for several observers.

Operational Details

The "prisoner" subjects remained in the mock-prison 24 hours per day for the duration of the study. Three were arbitrarily assigned to each of the three cells; the others were on stand-by call at their homes. The "guard" subjects worked on three-man, eight-hour shifts; remaining in the prison environment only during their work shift, going about their usual lives at other times.

Role Instructions

All subjects had been told that they would be assigned either the guard or the prisoner role on a completely random basis and all had voluntarily agreed to play either role for $15.00 per day for up to two weeks. They signed a contract guaranteeing a minimally adequate diet, clothing, housing, and medical care as well as the financial remuneration in return for their stated "intention" of serving in the assigned role for the duration of the study.

It was made explicit in the contract that those assigned to be prisoners should expect to be under surveillance (have little or no privacy) and

to have some of their basic civil rights suspended during their imprisonment, excluding physical abuse. They were given no other information about what to expect nor instructions about behavior appropriate for a prisoner role. Those actually assigned to this treatment were informed by phone to be available at their place of residence on a given Sunday when we would start the experiment.

The subjects assigned to be guards attended an orientation meeting on the day prior to the induction of the prisoners. At this time they were introduced to the principal investigators, the "Superintendent" of the prison (P.G.Z.) and an undergraduate research assistant who assumed the administrative role of "Warden." they were told that we wanted to try to simulate a prison environment within the limits imposed by pragmatic and ethical considerations. Their assigned task was to "maintain the reasonable degree of order within the prison necessary for its effective functioning,"although the specifics of how this duty might be implemented were not explicitly detailed. They were made aware of the fact that while many of the contingencies with which they might be confronted were essentially unpredictable (e.g., prisoner escape attempts), part of their task was to be prepared for such eventualities and to be able to deal appropriately with the variety of situations that might arise. The "Warden" instructed the guards in the administrative details, including: the work-shifts, the mandatory daily completion of shift reports concerning the activity of guards and prisoners, the completion of "critical incident" reports which detailed unusual occurrences, and the administration of meals, work, and recreation programs for the prisoners. In order to begin to involve these subjects in their roles even before the first prisoner was incarcerated, the guards assisted in the final phases of completing the prison complex—putting the cots in the cells, signs on the walls, setting up the guards' quarters, moving furniture, water coolers, refrigerators, and so on.

The guards generally believed that we were

primarily interested in studying the behavior of the prisoners. Of course, we were as interested in the effects that enacting the role of guard in this environment would have on their behavior and subjective states.

To optimize the extent to which their behavior would reflect their genuine reactions to the experimental prison situation and not simply their ability to follow instructions, they were intentionally given only minimal guidelines for what it meant to be a guard. An explicit and categorical prohibition against the use of physical punishment or physical aggression was, however, emphasized by the experimenters. Thus, with this single notable exception, their roles were relatively unstructured initially, requiring each "guard" to carry out activities necessary for interacting with a group of "prisoners" as well as with other "guards" and the "correctional staff."

Uniforms

In order to promote feelings of anonymity in the subjects each group was issued identical uniforms. For the guards, the uniform consisted of: plain khaki shirts and trousers, a whistle, a police night stick (wooden batons), and reflecting sunglasses that made eye contact impossible. The prisoners' uniform consisted of loosely fitting muslin smocks with an identification number on front and back. No underclothes were worn beneath these "dresses," a light chain and lock were placed around one ankle. On their feet they wore rubber sandals and their hair was covered with a nylon stocking made into a cap. Each prisoner was also issued a toothbrush, soap, soapdish, towel, and bed linen. No personal belongings were allowed in the cells.

The outfitting of both prisoners and guards in this manner served to enhance group identity and reduce individual uniqueness within the two groups. The khaki uniforms were intended to convey a military attitude, while the whistle and night-stick were carried as symbols of control and power. The prisoners'uniforms were designed not only to deindividuate the prisoners but to be humiliating and serve as symbols of their dependence and subservience. The ankle chain was a constant reminder (even during their sleep when it hit the other ankle) of the oppressiveness of the environment. The stocking cap removed any distinctiveness associated with hair length, color, or style (as does shaving of heads in some "real" prisons and the military). The ill-fitting uniforms made the prisoners feel awkward in their movements; since these dresses were worn without undergarments, the uniforms forced them to assume unfamiliar postures, more like those of a woman than a man—another part of the emasculating process of becoming a prisoner.

Induction Procedure

With the cooperation of the Palo Alto City Police Department all of the subjects assigned to the prisoner treatment were unexpectedly "arrested" at their residences. A police officer charged them with suspicion of burglary or armed robbery, advised them of their legal rights, handcuffed them, thoroughly searched them (often as curious neighbors looked on), and carried them off to the police station in the rear of the police car. At the station they went through the standard routines of being fingerprinted, having an identification file prepared, and then being placed in a detention cell. Each prisoner was blindfolded and subsequently driven by one of the experimenters and a subject-guard to our mock prison. Throughout the entire arrest procedure, the police officers involved maintained a formal, serious attitude, avoiding answering any questions of clarification as to the relation of this "arrest" to the mock prison study.

Upon arrival at our experimental prison, each prisoner was stripped, sprayed with a delousing preparation (a deodorant spray) and made to stand alone naked for a while in the cell yard. After being given the uniform described previously and having an I.D. picture taken ("mug shot"), the prisoner was put in his cell and ordered to remain silent.

Administrative Routine

When all the cells were occupied, the warden greeted the prisoners and read them the rules of the institution (developed by the guards and the warden). They were to be memorized and to be followed. Prisoners were to be referred to only by the number on their uniforms, also in an effort to depersonalize them.

The prisoners were to be served three bland meals per day, were allowed three supervised toilet visits, and given two hours daily for the privilege of reading or letterwriting. Work assignments were issued for which the prisoners were to receive as hourly wage to constitute their $15 daily payment. Two visiting periods per week were scheduled, as were movie rights and exercise periods. Three times a day all prisoners were lined up for a "count" (one on each guard work-shift). The initial purpose of the "count" was to ascertain that all prisoners were present, and to test them on their knowledge of the rules and their I.D. numbers. The first perfunctory counts lasted only about ten minutes, but on each successive day (or night) they were spontaneously increased in duration until some lasted several hours. Many of the pre-established features of administrative routine were modified or abandoned by the guards, and some privileges were forgotten by the staff over the course of study.

DATA COLLECTION (DEPENDENT MEASURES)

The exploratory nature of this investigation and the absence of specific hypotheses led us to adopt the strategy of surveying as many as possible behavioral and psychological manifestations of the prison experience on the guards and the prisoners. In fact, one major methodological problem in a study of this kind is defining the limits of the "data," since relevant data emerged from virtually every interaction between any of the participants, as well as from subjective and behavioral reactions of individual prisoners, guards, the warden, superintendent, research assistants, and visitors to the prison. It will also be clear when the results are presented that causal direction cannot always be established in the patterns of interaction where any given behavior might be the consequence of a current or prior instigation by another subject and, in turn, might serve as impetus for eliciting reactions from others.

Data collection was organized around the following sources:

1. *Videotaping.* About 12 hours of recordings were made of daily, regularly occurring events, such as the counts and meals, as well as unusual interactions, such as a prisoner rebellion, visits from a priest, a lawyer and parents, Parole Board meetings, and others. Concealed video equipment recorded these events through a screen in the partition at one end of the cellblock yard or in a conference room (for parole meetings).

2. *Audio recording.* Over 30 hours of recordings were made of verbal interactions between guards and prisoners on the prison yard. Concealed microphones picked up all conversation taking place in the yard as well as some within the cells. Other concealed recordings were made in the testing-interview room on selected occasions—interactions between the warden, superintendent, and the prisoners' Grievance Committee, parents, other visitors, and prisoners released early. In addition, each subject was interviewed by one of the experimenters (or by other research associates) during the study, and most just prior to its termination.

3. *Rating Scales.* Mood adjective checklists and sociometric measures were administered on several occasions to assess emotional changes in affective state and interpersonal dynamics among the guard and prisoner groups.

4. *Individual Difference Scales.* One day prior to the start of the simulation all subjects completed a series of paper and pencil personality tests. Theses tests were selected to provide dispositional indicators of interpersonal bahavior styles—the F scale of Authoritarian Personality (Adorno, et al., 1950), and the Machiavellianism Scale (Christie and Geis, 1970)—as well as areas of possible personality pathology through the newly developed Comrey Personality Scale (Comrey, 1970). The subscales of this latter test consist of:

a. trustworthiness   e. stability
b. orderliness   f. extroversion
c. conformity   g. masculinity
d. activity   h. empathy

5. *Personal Observations.* The guards made daily reports of their observations after each shift, the experimenters kept informal diaries and all subjects completed post-experimental questionnaires of their reactions to the experience about a month after the study was over.

Data analysis presented problems of several kinds. First, some of the data was subject to possible artifacts due to selective sampling. The video and audio recordings tended to be focused upon the more interesting, dramatic events that occurred. Over time, the experimenters became more personally involved in the transactions, and were not as distant and objective as they should have been. Second, there are not complete data on all subjects for each measure because of prisoners being released at different times and because of unexpected disruptions, conflicts, and administrative problems. Finally, we have a relatively small sample on which to make cross-tabulations by possible independent and individual difference variables.

However, despite these shortcomings some of the overall effects in the data are powerful enough to reveal clear, reliable results. Also, some of the more subtle analyses were able to yield statistically significant results even with the small sample size. Most crucial for the conclusions generated by this exploratory study is the consistency in the pattern of relationships which emerge across a wide range of measuring instruments and different observers. Special analyses were required only of the video and

audio material; the other data sources were analyzed following established scoring procedures.

Video Analysis

There were 25 relatively discrete incidents identifiable on the tapes of prisoner-guard interactions. Each incident or scene was scored for the presence of nine behavioral (and verbal) categories. Two judges who had not been involved with the simulation study scored these tapes. These categories were defined as follows:

Question. All questions asked, requests for information or assistance (excluding rhetorical questions).

Command. An order to commence or abstain from a specific behavior, directed either to individuals or groups. Also generalized orders, e.g., "Settle down."

Information. A specific piece of information proferred by anyone whether requested or not, dealing with any contingency of the simulation.

Individuating reference. Positive: use of a person's real name, nickname, or allusion to special positive physical characteristics. Negative: use of prison number, title, generalized "you," or reference to derogatory characteristic.

Threat. Verbal statement of contingent negative consequences of a wide variety, e.g., no meal, long count pushups, lock-up in hole, no visitors, etc.

Deprecation/insult. Use of obscenity, slander, malicious statement directed toward individuals or group, e.g., "You lead a life of mendacity," or "You guys are really stupid."

Resistance. Any physical resistance, usually prisoners to guards, such as holding onto beds, blocking doors, shoving guard or prisoner, taking off stocking caps, refusing to carry out orders.

Help. Person physically assisting another (i.e., excludes verbal statements of support), e.g., guard helping another to open door, prisoner helping another prisoner in cleanup duties.

Use of instruments.   Use of any physical instrument to either intimidate, threaten, or achieve specific end, e.g., fire extinguisher, batons, whistles.

Audio Analysis
For purposes of classifying the verbal behavior recorded from interviews with guards and prisoners, eleven categories were devised. Each statement made by the interviewee was assigned to the appropriate category by judges. At the end of this process for any given interview analysis, a list had been compiled of the nature and frequencies of the interviewee's discourse. The eleven categories for assignment of verbal expressions were:

Questions.   All questions asked, requests for information or assistance (excluding rhetorical questions).

Informative statements.   A specific piece of information proferred by anyone whether requested or not, dealing with any contingency of the simulation.

Demands.   Declarative statements of need or imperative requests.

Requests.   Deferential statements for material or personal consideration.

Commands.   Orders to commence or abstain from a specific behavior, directed either to individuals or groups.

Outlook, positive/negative.   Expression of expectancies for future experiences or future events; either negative or positive in tone, e.g., "I don't think I can make it" vs. "I believe I will feel better."

Criticism.   Expressions of critical evaluation concerning other subjects, the experimenters, or the experiment itself.

Statements of identifying reference, deindividuating/individuating.   Statements wherein subject makes some reference to another subject specifically by allusion to given name or distinctive characteristics (individuating reference), or by allusion to nonspecific identity or institutional number (deindividuating reference).

Desire to continue.   Any expression of subject's wish to continue or to curtail participation in the experiment.

Self-evaluation, positive/negative.   Statements of self-esteem or self-degradation, e.g., "I feel pretty good about the way I've adjusted"vs. "I hate myself for being so oppressive."

Action intentions, positive/negative including "intent to aggress."   Statements concerning interviewees' intentions to do something in the future, either of a positive, constructive nature or a negative, destructive nature, e.g., "I'm not going to be so mean from now on" vs. "I'll break the door down."

RESULTS

Overview
The results of the present experiment support many commonly held conceptions of prison life and validate anecdotal evidence supplied by articulate ex-convicts. The simulated prison environment had great impact upon the affective states of both guards and prisoners as well as upon the interpersonal interactions between and within those role-groups. In general, guards and prisoners showed a marked tendency toward increased negativity of affect as their overall outlook became increasingly bleak. As the experiment progressed, prisoners expressed intentions to do harm to others more frequently. For both prisoners and guards, self-evaluations were more deprecating as the experience of the prison environment became internalized.

Overt behavior was generally consistent with the subjective self-reports and affective expressions of the subjects. Despite the fact that guards and prisoners were essentially free to engage in any form of interaction (positive or negative, supportive or affrontive, etc.), the characteristic nature of their encounters tended to be negative, hostile, affrontive, and dehumanizing. Prisoners immediately adopted a generally passive response mode while guards assumed a very active initiative role in all interactions. Throughout the experiment, commands were the most frequent form of verbal behavior and, generally, verbal exchanges were strikingly impersonal, with few references to individual identity. Although it was clear to all subjects that the experimenters would not permit physical violence to take place, varieties of less direct aggressive behavior were observed frequently (especially on the part of guards). In lieu of physical violence, verbal affronts were used as one of the most frequent forms of interpersonal contact between guards and prisoners.

The most dramatic evidence of the impact of this situation upon the participants was seen in the gross reactions of five prisoners who had to be released because of extreme emotional depression, crying, rage, and acute anxiety. The pattern of symptoms was quite similar in four of the subjects and began as early as the second day of imprisonment. The fifth subject was released after being treated for a psychosomatic rash that covered portions of his body. Of the remaining prisoners, only two said they were not willing to forfeit the money they had earned in return for being "paroled."when the experiment was terminated prematurely after only six days, all the remaining prisoners were delighted by their unexpected good fortune. In contrast most of the guards seemed to be distressed by the decision to stop the experiment and it appeared to us that they had become sufficiently involved in their roles so that they now enjoyed the extreme control and power that they exercised and were reluctant to give it up. One guard did report being personally upset at the suffering of the prisoners, and claimed to have considered asking to change his role to become one of them—but never did so. None of the guards ever failed

to come to work on time for their shift, and indeed, on several occasions guards remained on duty voluntarily and uncomplaining for extra hours—without additional pay.

The extremely pathological reactions that emerged in both groups of subjects testify to the power of the social forces operating, but still there were individual differences seen in styles of coping with this novel experience and in degrees of successful adaptation to it. Half the prisoners did endure the oppressive atmosphere, and not all the guards resorted to hostility. Some guards were tough but fair ("played by the rules"), some went far beyond their roles to engage in creative cruelty and harassment, while a few were passive and rarely instigated any coercive control over the prisoners.

These differential reactions to the experience of imprisonment were not suggested by or predictable from the self-report measures of personality and attitude or the interviews taken before the experiment began. The standardized tests employed indicated that a perfectly normal emotionally stable sample of subjects had been selected. In those few instances where differential test scores do discriminate between subjects, there is an opportunity to partially discern some of the personality variables which may be critical in the adaptation to and tolerance of prison confinement.

Initial Personality and Attitude Measures

Overall, it is apparent that initial personality-attitude dispositions account for an extremely small part of the variance in reactions to this mock prison experience. However, in a few select instances, such dispositions do seem to be correlated with the prisoner's ability to adjust to the experimental prison environment.

Comrey Scale. The Comrey Personality Inventory (Comrey, 1970) was the primary personality scale administered to both guards and prisoners. The mean scores for prisoners and guards on the eight sub-scales of the test are shown in Table I. No differences between pris-

Table I. Mean Scores for Prisoners and Guards on 8 Comrey Subscales

Scale	Prisoners	Guards
Trustworthiness-high score indicates belief in the basic honesty and good intentions of others.	$\overline{X} = 92.56$	$\overline{X} = 89.64$
Orderliness-extent to which person is meticulous and concerned with neatness and orderliness.	$\overline{X} = 75.67$	$\overline{X} = 73.82$
Conformity-indicates belief in law enforcement, acceptance of society as it is, resentment of nonconformity in others.	$\overline{X} = 65.67$	$\overline{X} = 63.18$
Activity-liking for physical activity, hard work, and exercise.	$\overline{X} = 89.78$	$\overline{X} = 91.73$
Stability-high score indicates calm, optimistic, stable, confident individual.	$\overline{X} = 98.33$	$\overline{X} = 101.45$
Extroversion-suggests outgoing, easy to meet person.	$\overline{X} = 83.22$	$\overline{X} = 81.91$
Masculinity- "people who are not bothered by crawling creatures, the sight of blood, vulgarity, who do not cry easily, and are not interested in love stories."	$\overline{X} = 88.44$	$\overline{X} = 87.00$
P-(Empathy) - high score indicates "individuals who are sympathetic, helpful, generous, and interested in devoting their lives to the service of others."	$\overline{X} = 91.78$	$\overline{X} = 95.36$

oner and guard mean scores on any scale even approach statistical significance. Furthermore, in no case does any group mean fall outside of the 40 to 60 centile range of the normative male population reported by Comrey.

Table II shows the mean scores on the Comrey sub-scales for prisoners who remained compared with prisoners who were released early due to severe emotional reactions to the environment. Although none of the comparisons achieved statistical significance, three seemed at least suggestive as possible discriminators of those who were able to tolerate this type of confinement and those who were not. Compared with those who had to be released, prisoners who remained in prison until the termination of the study: scored higher on conformity ("acceptance of society as it is"), showed substantially higher average scores on Comrey's measure of extroversion, and also scored higher on a scale of empathy (helpfulness, sympathy and generosity).

F-Scale. The F-Scale is designed to measure rigid adherence to conventional values, and a submissive, uncritical attitude towards authority. There was no difference between the mean score for prisoners (4.78) and the mean score for guards (4.36) on this scale.

Again, comparing those prisoners who remained with those who were released early, we notice an interesting trend. This intragroup comparison shows remaining prisoners scoring more than twice as high on conventionality and authoritarianism ($\overline{X} = 7.78$) than those prisoners released early ($\overline{X} = 3.20$). While the difference between these means fails to reach acceptable levels of significance, it is striking to note that a rank-ordering of prisoners on the F-scale correlates highly with the duration of their stay in the experiment ($r_s = .898$, $p < .005$). To the extent that a prisoner rated high in rigidity, in adherence to conventional values, and in the acceptance of authority, he was likely to remain longer and adjust more effectively to this authoritarian prison environment.

Machiavellianism. There were no significant mean differences found between guards ($\overline{X} = 7.73$) and prisoners ($\overline{X} = 8.77$) on this measure

Table II. Mean Scores for "Remaining" vs. "Early Released"
Prisoners on Comrey Subscales

Scale	Remaining Prisoners	Early Released Prisoners	Mean Difference
Trustworthiness	93.4	90.8	+ 2.6
Orderliness	76.6	78.0	− 1.4
Conformity	67.2	59.4	+ 7.8
Activity	91.4	86.8	+ 4.6
Stability	99.2	99.6	− .4
Extroversion	98.4	76.2	+22.2
Masculinity	91.6	86.0	+ 5.6
Empathy	103.8	85.6	+17.2

of effective interpersonal manipulation. In addition, the Mach Scale was of no help in predicting the likelihood that a prisoner would tolerate the prison situation and remain in the study until its termination.

This latter finding, the lack of any mean differences between prisoners who remained versus those who were released from the study, is somewhat surprising since one might expect the Hi Mach's skill at manipulating social interaction and mediating favorable outcomes for himself might be acutely relevant to the simulated prison environment. Indeed, the two prisoners who scored highest on the Machiavellianism scale were also among those adjudged by the experimenters to have made unusually effective adaptations to their confinement. Yet, paradoxically (and this may give the reader some feeling for the anomalies we encountered in attempting to predict in-prison behavior from personality measures), the other two prisoners whom we categorized as having effectively adjusted to confinement actually obtained the lowest Mach scores of any prisoners.

Video Recordings

An analysis of the video recordings indicates a preponderance of genuinely negative interactions, that is, physical aggression, threats, deprecations, and so on. It is also clear that any assertive activity was largely the prerogative of the guards, while prisoners generally assumed a decidedly passive demeanor. Guards more often aggressed, more often insulted, more often threatened. Prisoners, when they reacted at all, engaged primarily in resistance to these guard behaviors.

For guards, the most frequent verbal behavior was the giving of commands and their most frequent form of physical behavior was aggression. The most frequent form of prisoners' verbal behavior was question-asking, their most frequent form of physical behavior was resistance. On the other hand, the most *in*frequent behavior engaged in overall throughout the experiment was "helping"—only one such incident was noted from all the video recordings collected. That solitary sign of human concern for a fellow occurred between two prisoners.

Although question-asking was the most frequent form of verbal behavior for the prisoners, guards actually asked questions more frequently overall than did prisoners (but not significantly so). This is reflective of the fact that the overall level of behavior emitted was much higher for the guards than for the prisoners. All of those verbal acts categorized as commands were engaged in by guards. Obviously, prisoners had no opportunity to give commands at all, that behavior becoming the exclusive "right" of guards.

Of a total 61 incidents of direct interpersonal reference observed (incidents in which one subject spoke directly to another with the use of some identifying reference, i.e., "Hey, Peter";

"you there," etc.), 58 involved the use of some deindividuating rather than some individuating form of reference. (Recall that we characterized this distinction as follows: an individuating reference involved the use of a person's actual name, nickname, or allusion to special physical characteristics, whereas a deindividuating reference involved the use of a prison number or a generalized "you"—thus being a very depersonalizing form of reference.) Since all subjects were at liberty to refer to one another in either mode, it is significant that such a large proportion of the references noted were in the deindividuating mode ($Z = 6.9$, $p < .01$). Deindividuating references were made more often by guards in speaking to prisoners than the reverse ($Z = 3.67$, $p < .01$). (This finding, as all prisoner–guard comparisons for specific categories, may be somewhat confounded by the fact that guards apparently enjoyed a greater freedom to initiate verbal as well as other forms of behavior. Note, however, that the existence of this greater "freedom" on the part of the guards is itself an empirical finding since it was not prescribed *a priori*.) It is of additional interest to point out that in the only 3 cases in which verbal exchange involved some individuating reference, it was prisoners who personalized guards.

A total of 32 incidents were observed that involved a verbal threat spoken by one subject to another. Of these, 27 such incidents involved a guard threatening a prisoner. Again, the indulgence of guards in this form of behavior was significantly greater than the indulgence of prisoners, the observed frequencies deviating significantly from an equal distribution of threats across both groups ($Z = 3.88$, $p < .01$).

Guards more often deprecated and insulted prisoners than prisoners did to guards. Of a total of 67 observed incidents, the deprecation insult was expressed disproportionately by guards to prisoners 61 times; ($Z = 6.72$, $p < .01$).

Physical resistance was observed 34 different times. Of these, 32 incidents involved resistance by a prisoner. Thus, as we might expect, at least in this reactive behavior domain, prisoner responses far exceeded those of the guards ($Z = 5.14$, $p < .01$).

The use of some object or instrument in the achievement of an intended purpose or in some interpersonal interaction was observed 29 times. Twenty-three such incidents involved the use of an instrument by a guard rather than a prisoner. This disproportionate frequency is significantly variant from an equal random use by both prisoners and guards ($Z = 3.16$, $p < .01$).

Over time, from day to day, guards were observed to generally escalate their harassment of the prisoners. In particular, a comparison of two of the first prisoner–guard interactions (during the counts) with two of the last counts in the experiment yielded significant differences in: the use of deindividuating references per unit time ($\overline{X}_{t1} = 0.0$ and $\overline{X}_{t2} = 5.40$, respectively; $t = 3.65$, $p < .10$); the incidence of deprecation-insult per unit time ($\overline{X}_{t1} = .3$ and $\overline{X}_{t2} = 5.70$, respectively; $t = 3.16$, $p < .10$). On the other hand, a temporal analysis of the prisoner video data indicated a general decrease across all categories over time: prisoners came to initiate acts far less frequently and responded (if at all) more passively to the acts of others—they simply *behaved less*.

Although the harassment by the guards escalated overall as the experiment wore on, there was some variation in the extent to which the three different guard shifts contributed to the harassment in general. With the exception of the 2:30 A.M. count, prisoners enjoyed some respite during the late night guard shift (10:00 P.M. to 6:00 A.M.). But they really were "under the gun" during the evening shift. This was obvious in our observations and in subsequent interviews with the prisoners, and was also confirmed in analysis of the video taped interactions. Comparing the three different guard shifts, the evening shift was significantly different from the other two in resorting to command; the means being 9.30 and 4.04, respectively, for standardized units of time ($t = 2.50$, $p < .05$). In addition, the guards on this "tough and cruel" shift showed more than twice as many deprecation insults toward the prisoners (means of 5.17 and 2.29, respectively, $p < .20$). They also tended to use instruments more often than other shifts to keep the prisoners in line.

Audio Recordings

The audio recordings made throughout the prison simulation afforded one opportunity to systematically collect self-report data from prisoners and guards regarding (among other things) their emotional reactions, their outlook, and their interpersonal evaluations and activities within the experimental setting. Recorded interviews with both prisoners and guards offered evidence that: guards tended to express nearly as much negative outlook and negative self-regard as most prisoners (one concerned guard, in fact, expressed more negative self-regard than any prisoner and more general negative affect than all but one of the prisoners); prisoner interviews were marked by negativity in expressions of affect, self-regard, and action intentions (including intent to aggress, and negative outlook).

Analysis of the prisoner interviews also gave *post hoc* support to our informal impressions and subjective decisions concerning the differential emotional effects of the experiment upon those prisoners who remained and those who were released early from the study. A comparison of the mean number of expressions of negative outlook, negative affect, negative self-regard, and intentions to aggress made by remaining versus released prisoners (per interview) yielded the following results: prisoners released early expressed more negative expectations during interviews than those who remained ($t = 2.32$, $p < .10$) and also more negative affect ($t = 2.17$, $p < .10$); prisoners released early expressed more negative self-regard, and four times as many "intentions to aggress" as prisoners who remained (although those comparisons fail to reach an acceptable level of significance).

Since we could video-record only public interactions on the "yard," it was of special interest to discover what was occurring among prisoners

in private. What were they talking about in the cells—their college life, their vocation, girl friends, what they would do for the remainder of the summer once the experiment was over? We were surprised to discover that fully 90 percent of all conversations among prisoners were related to prison topics, while only 10 percent to nonprison topics such as the above. They were most concerned about food, guard harassment, setting up a grievance committee, escape plans, visitors, reactions of prisoners in the other cells, and in solitary. Thus, in their private conversations when they might escape the roles they were playing in public, they did not. There was no discontinuity between their presentation of self when under surveillance and when alone.

Even more remarkable was the discovery that the prisoners had begun to adopt and accept the guards' negative attitude toward them. Half of all reported private interactions between prisoners could be classified as nonsupportive and noncooperative. Moreover, when prisoners made evaluative statements of or expressed regard for, their fellow prisoners, 85 percent of the time they were uncomplimentary and deprecating. This set of observed frequencies departs significantly from chance expectations based on a conservative binominal probability frequency ($p < .01$) for prison vs. nonprison topics; ($p < .05$) for negative vs. positive or neutral regard.

Mood Adjective Self-Reports

Twice during the progress of the experiment each subject was asked to complete a mood adjective checklist and indicate his current affective state. The data gleaned from these self-reports did not lend themselves readily to statistical analysis. However, the trends suggested by simple enumeration are important enough to include without reference to statistical significance. In these written self-reports, prisoners expressed nearly three times as much negative as positive affect. Prisoners roughly expressed three times as much negative affect as guards. Guards expressed slightly more negative than positive affect. While prisoners expressed about twice as much emotionality as did guards, a comparison of mood self-reports over time reveals that the prisoners showed two to three times as much mood fluctuation as did the relatively stable guards. On the dimension of activity-passivity, prisoners tended to score twice as high, indicating twice as much internal "agitation" as guards (although, as stated above, prisoners were seen to be markedly less active than guards in terms of overt behavior).

It would seem from these results that while the experience had a categorically negative emotional impact upon both guards and prisoners, the effects upon prisoners were more profound and unstable.

When the mood scales were administered for a third time, just after the subjects were told the study had been terminated (and the early released subjects returned for the debriefing encounter session), marked changes in mood were evident. All of the now "ex-convicts" selected self-descriptive adjectives that characterized their mood as less negative and much more positive. In addition, they now felt less passive than before. There were no longer any differences on the sub-scales of this test between prisoners released early and those who remained throughout. Both groups of subjects had returned to their pre-experimental baselines of emotional responsiveness. This seems to reflect the situational specificity of the depression and stress reactions experienced while in the role of prisoner.

*

CONCLUSIONS AND DISCUSSION

It should be apparent that the elaborate procedures (and staging) employed by the experimenters to ensure a high degree of mundane realism in this mock prison contributed to its effective functional simulation of the psychological dynamics operating in "real" prisons. We observed empirical relationships in the simulated prison environment that were strikingly isomorphic to the internal relations of real prisons, corroborating many of the documented reports of what occurs behind prison walls.

The conferring of differential power on the status of "guard" and "prisoner" constituted, in effect, the institutional validation of those roles. But further, many of the subjects ceased distinguishing between prison role and their prior self-identities. When this occurred, within what was a surprisingly short period of time, we witnessed a sample of normal, healthy American college students fractionate into a group of prison guards who seemed to derive pleasure from insulting, threatening, humiliating, and dehumanizing their peers—those who by chance selection had been assigned to the "prisoner" role. The typical prisoner syndrome was one of passivity, dependency, depression, helplessness, and self-depreciaton. Prisoner participation in the social reality that the guards had structured for them lent increasing validity to it. As the prisoners became resigned to their treatment over time, many acted in ways to justify their fate at the hands of the guards, adopting attitudes and behaviors that helped to sanction their victimization. Most dramatic and distressing to us was the ease with which sadistic behavior could be elicited in individuals who were not "sadistic types," and the frequency with which acute emotional breakdowns could occur in men selected precisely for their emotional stability.

Situational Versus Dispositional Attribution

To what can we attribute these deviant behavior patterns? If these reactions had been observed within the confines of an existing penal institution, it is probable that a dispositional hypothesis would be invoked as an explanation. Some cruel guards might be singled out as sadistic or passive-aggressive personality types who chose to work in a correctional institution because of the outlets provided for sanctioned aggression. Aberrant reactions on the part of the inmate population would likewise be viewed as an extrapolation from the prior social histories of these men as violent, anti-social, psychopathic, unstable character types.

Existing penal institutions may be viewed as *natural experiments* in social control in which any attempts at providing a causal attribution for observed behavior hopelessly confound dispositional and situational causes. In contrast, the design of our study minimized the utility of trait or prior social history explanations by means of judicious subject selection and random assignment to roles. Considerable effort and care went into determining the composition of the final subject population from which our guards and prisoners were drawn. Through case histories, personal interviews, and a battery of personality tests, the subjects chosen to participate manifested no apparent abnormalities, anti-social tendencies, or social backgrounds that were other than exemplary. On every one of the scores of the diagnostic tests each subject scored within the normal-average range. Our subjects, then, were highly representative of middleclass, Caucasian American society (17 to 30 years in age), although above average in both intelligence and emotional stability.

Nevertheless, in less than one week their *behavior* in this simulated prison could be characterized as pathological and anti-social. The negative, anti-social reactions observed were not the product of an environment created by combining a collection of deviant personalities, but rather, the result of an intrinsically pathological situation that could distort and rechannel the behavior of essentially normal individuals. The abnormality here resided in the psychological nature of the situation and not in those who passed through it. Thus, we offer another instance in support of Mischel's (1968) social-learning analysis of the power of situational variables to shape complex social behavior. Our results are also congruent with those of Milgram (1965) who most convincingly demonstrated the proposition that evil acts are not necessarily the deeds of evil men, but may be attributable to the operation of powerful social forces. Our findings go one step further, however, in removing the immediate presence of the dominant experimenter-authority figure, giving the subjects-as-guards a freer range of behavioral alternatives, and involving the participants for a much more extended period of time.

Despite the evidence favoring a situational causal analysis in this experiment, it should be clear that the research design actually *minimized* the effects of individual differences by use of a homogeneous middle-range subject population. It did not allow the strongest possible test of the relative utility of the two types of explanation. We cannot say that personality differences have no effect on behavior in situations such as the one reported here. Rather, we may assert that the variance in behavior observed could be reliably attributed to variations in situational rather than personality variables. The inherently pathological characteristics of the prison situation itself, at least as functionally simulated in our study, were a *sufficient* condition to produce aberrant, anti-social behavior. (An alternative design that would maximize the potential operation of personality or dispositional variables would assign subjects who were extreme on preselected personality dimensions to each of the two experimental treatments. Such a design would, however, require a larger subject population and more resources than we had available).

The failure of personality assessment variables to reliably discriminate the various patterns of prison behavior, guard reactions as well as prisoner coping styles, is reminiscent of the inability of personality tests to contribute to an understanding of the psychological differences between American P.O.W.s in Korea who succumbed to alleged Chinese Communist brainwashing by "collaborating with the enemy" and those who resisted (cf. Schein, 1961). It seems to us that there is little reason to expect paper-and-pencil behavioral reactions on personality tests taken under "normal" conditions to generalize to coping behaviors under novel, stressful, or abnormal environmental conditions. It may be that the best predictor of behavior in situations of stress and power, as occurs in prisons, is overt behavior in functionally comparable simulated environments.

In the situation of imprisonment faced by our subjects, despite the potent situational control, individual differences were nevertheless manifested both in coping styles among the prisoners and in the extent and type of aggression and exercise of power among the guards. Personality variables, conceived of as learned behavior styles can act as moderator variables in allaying or intensifying the impact of social situational variables. Their predictive utility depends upon acknowledging the interactive relationship of such learned dispositional tendencies with the eliciting force of the situational variables.

Reality of the Simulation

At this point it seems necessary to confront the critical question of "reality" in the simulated prison environment: were the behaviors observed more than the mere acting out of assigned roles convincingly? To be sure, ethical, legal, and practical considerations set limits upon the degree to which this situation could approach the conditions existing in actual prisons and penitentiaries. Necessarily absent were some of the most salient aspects of prison life reported by criminologists and documented in the writing of prisoners (such as in George Jackson's *Soledad Letters,* 1970, and by Charrière, 1969). There was no involuntary homosexuality, no racism, no physical beatings, no threat to life by prisoners against each other or the guards. Moreover, the maximum anticipated "sentence" was only two weeks and, unlike some prison systems, could not be extended indefinitely for infractions of the internal operating rules of the prison.

In one sense, the profound psychological effects we observed under the relatively minimal prison-like conditions which existed in our mock prison make the results even more dramatic, and should force us to consider the devastating impact of chronic incarceration in real prisons. On the other hand, we must contend with the criticism that the conditions that prevailed in this mock prison were too minimal to provide a meaningful analogue to existing prisons. It is necessary to demonstrate that the participants in this experiment transcended the conscious limits of their preconceived stereotyped roles and their awareness of the artificiality and limited duration of imprisonment. We feel there is abundant evidence that virtually all of the subjects at one time or another experienced reactions that went well beyond the surface demands of role-playing and penetrated the deep structure of the psychology of imprisonment.

Although instructions about how to behave in the roles of guard or prisoner were not explicitly defined, demand characteristics in the experiment obviously exerted some directing influence. Therefore, it is enlightening to look to circumstances where role demands were minimal, where the subjects believed they were not being observed, or where they should not have been behaving under the constraints imposed by their roles (as in "private" situations), in order to assess whether the role behaviors reflected anything more than public conformity or good acting.

When the private conversations of the prisoners were monitored, we learned that almost all (a full 90 percent) of what they talked about was directly related to immediate prison conditions, that is, food, privileges, punishment, guard harassment, and so on. Only one-tenth of the time did their conversations deal with their life outside the prison. Consequently, although they had lived together under such intense conditions, the prisoners knew surprisingly little about each other's past history or future plans. This excessive concentration on the vicissitudes of their current situation helped to make the prison experience more oppressive for the prisoners because, instead of escaping from it when they had a chance to do so in the privacy of their cells, the prisoners continued to allow it to dominate their thoughts and social relations. The guards also rarely exchanged personal information during their relaxation breaks. They either talked about "problem prisoners," other prison topics, or did not talk at all. There were few instances of any personal communication across the two role groups. Moreover, when prisoners referred to other prisoners during interviews, they typically deprecated each other, seemingly adopting the guards' negative attitude.

From post experimental data, we discovered that when individual guards were alone with solitary prisoners and out of range of any recording equipment, as on the way to or in the toilet, harassment often was greater than it was on the "Yard." Similarly, video-taped analyses of total guard aggression showed a daily escalation even after most prisoners had ceased resisting and prisoner deterioration had become visibly obvious to them. Thus guard aggression was no longer elicited as it was initially in response to perceived threats, but was emitted simply as a "natural" consequence of being in the uniform of a "guard" and asserting the power inherent in that role. In specific instances we noted cases of a guard (who did not know he was being observed) in the early morning hours pacing the Yard as the prisoners slept—vigorously pounding his night stick into his hand while he "kept watch" over his captives. Or another guard who detained an "incorrigible" prisoner in solitary confinement beyond the duration set by the guards' own rules, and then he conspired to keep him in the hole all night while attempting to conceal this information from the experimenters who were thought to be too soft on the prisoners.

In passing we may note an additional point about the nature of role-playing and the extent to which actual behavior is "explained away" by reference to it. It will be recalled that many guards continued to intensify their harassment and aggressive behavior even after the second day of the study, when prisoner deterioration became marked and visible and emotional breakdowns began to occur (in the presence of the guards). When questioned after the study about their persistent affrontive and harassing

behavior in the face of prisoner emotional trauma, most guards replied that they were "just playing the role" of a tough guard, although none ever doubted the magnitude or validity of the prisoners' emotional response. The reader may wish to consider to what extremes an individual may go, how great must be the consequences of his behavior for others, before he can no longer rightfully attribute his actions to "playing a role" and thereby abdicate responsibility.

When introduced to a Catholic priest, many of the role-playing prisoners referred to themselves by their prison number rather than their Christian names. Some even asked him to get a lawyer to help them get out. When a public defender was summoned to interview those prisoners who had not yet been released, almost all of them strenuously demanded that he "bail" them out immediately.

One of the most remarkable incidents of the study occurred during a parole board hearing when each of five prisoners eligible for parole was asked by the senior author whether he would be willing to forfeit all the money earned as a prisoner if he were to be paroled (released from the study). Three of the five prisoners said, "yes," they would be willing to do this. Notice that the original incentive for participating in the study had been the promise of money, and they were, after only four days, prepared to give this up completely. And, more surprisingly, when told that this possibility would have to be discussed with the members of the staff before a decision could be made, each prisoner got up quietly and was escorted by a guard back to his cell. If they had regarded themselves simply as "subjects" participating in an experiment for money, then there was no longer any incentive to remain in the study and they could have easily escaped this situation that had so clearly become aversive for them by quitting. Yet, so powerful was the control that the situation had come to have over them, so much a reality had this simulated environment become, that they were unable to see that their original and singular motive for remaining no longer obtained, and they returned to their cells to await a "parole" decision by their captors.

The reality of the prison was also attested to by our prison consultant who had spent over 16 years in prison, as well as the priest who had been a prison chaplain and the public defender who were all brought into direct contact with our simulated prison environment. Further, the depressed affect of the prisoners, the guards' willingness to work overtime for no additional pay, the spontaneous use of prison titles and ID numbers in nonrole-related situations all point to a level of reality as real as any other in the lives of all those who shared this experience.

To understand how an illusion of imprisonment could have become so real, we need now to consider the uses of power by the guards as well as the effects of such power in shaping the prisoner mentality.

Pathology of Power
Being a guard carried with it social status within the prison, a group identity (when wearing the uniform), and above all, the freedom to exercise an unprecedented degree of control over the lives of other human beings. This control was invariably expressed in terms of sanctions, punishment, demands, and with the threat of manifest physical power. There was no need for the guards to rationally justify a request as they did their ordinary life, and merely to make a demand was sufficient to have it carried out. Many of the guards showed in their behavior and revealed in post-experimental statements that this sense of power was exhilarating.

The use of power was self-aggrandizing and self-perpetuating. The guard power, derived initially from an arbitrary and randomly assigned label, was intensified whenever there was any perceived threat by the prisoners and this new level subsequently became the baseline from which further hostility and harassment would begin. The most hostile guards on each shift moved spontaneously into the leadership roles of giving orders and deciding on punishments.

They became role models whose behavior was emulated by other members of the shift. Despite minimal contact between the three separate guard shifts and nearly 16 hours a day spent away from the prison, the absolute level of aggression, as well as more subtle and "creative" forms of aggression manifested, increased in a spiralling function. Not to be tough and arrogant was to be seen as a sign of weakness by the guards, and even those "good" guards who did not get as drawn into the power syndrome as the others respected the implicit norm of *never* contradicting or even interfering with an action of a more hostile guard on their shift.

After the first day of the study, practically all prisoner rights (even such things as the time and conditions of sleeping and eating) came to be redefined by the guards as "privileges" which were to be earned for obedient behavior. Constructive activities such as watching movies or reading (previously planned and suggested by the experimenters) were arbitrarily cancelled until further notice by the guards—and were subsequently never allowed. "Reward" then became granting approval for prisoners to eat, sleep, go to the toilet, talk, smoke a cigarette, wear eyeglasses, or the temporary diminution of harassment. One wonders about the conceptual nature of "positive" reinforcement when subjects are in such conditions of deprivation, and the extent to which even minimally acceptable conditions become rewarding when experienced in the context of such an impoverished environment.

We might also question whether there are meaningful nonviolent alternatives as models for behavior modification in real prisons. In a world where men are either powerful or powerless, everyone learns to despise the lack of power in others and in oneself. It seems to us that prisoners learn to admire power for its own sake—power becoming the ultimate reward. Real prisoners soon learn the means to gain power whether through ingratiation, informing, sexual control of other prisoners or development of powerful cliques. When they are released from prison, it is unlikely they will ever want to feel so powerless again and will take action to establish and assert a sense of power.

The Pathological Prisoner Syndrome

Various coping strategies were employed by our prisoners as they began to react to their perceived loss of personal identity and the arbitrary control of their lives. At first they exhibited disbelief at the total invasion of their privacy, constant surveillance, and atmosphere of oppression in which they were living. Their next response was rebellion, first by the use of direct force, and later with subtle divisive tactics designed to foster distrust among the prisoners. They then tried to work within the system by setting up an elected grievance committee. When that collective action failed to produce meaningful changes in their existence, individual self-interests emerged. The breakdown in prisoner cohesion was the start of social disintegration that gave rise not only to feelings of isolation, but deprecation of other prisoners as well. As noted before, half the prisoners coped with the prison situation by becoming "sick"—extremely disturbed emotionally—as a passive way of demanding attention and help. Others became excessively obedient in trying to be "good" prisoners. They sided with the guards against a solitary fellow prisoner who coped with his situation by refusing to eat. Instead of supporting this final and major act of rebellion, the prisoners treated him as a trouble-maker who deserved to be punished for his disobedience. It is likely that the negative self-regard among the prisoners noted by the end of the study was the product of their coming to believe that the continued hostility toward all of them was justified because they "deserved it" (following Walster, 1966). As the days wore on, the modal prisoner reaction was one of passivity, dependence, and flattened affect.

Let us briefly consider some of the relevant processes involved in bringing about these reactions.

Loss of Personal Identity.   Identity is, for most people, conferred by social recognition of one's uniqueness, and established through one's name, dress, appearance, behavior style, and history. Living among strangers who do not know your name or history (who refer to you only by number), dressed in a uniform exactly like all other prisoners, not wanting to call attention to one's self because of the unpredictable consequences it might provoke—all led to a weakening of self identity among the prisoners. As they began to lose initiative and emotional responsivity, while acting ever more compliantly, indeed, the prisoners became deindividuated not only to the guards and the observers, but also to themselves.

Arbitrary Control.   On post-experimental questionnaires, the most frequently mentioned aversive aspect of the prison experience was that of being subjugated to the patently arbitrary, capricious decisions, and rules of the guards. A question by a prisoner as often elicited derogation and aggression as it did a rational answer. Smiling at a joke could be punished in the same way that failing to smile might be. An individual acting in defiance of the rules could bring punishment to innocent cell partners (who became, in effect, "mutually yoked controls"), to himself, or to all.

As the environment became more unpredictable, and previously learned assumptions about a just and orderly world were no longer functional, prisoners ceased to initiate any action. They moved about on orders and when in their cells rarely engaged in any purposeful activity. Their zombie-like reaction was the functional equivalent of the learned helplessness phenomenon reported by Seligman and Grove (1970). Since their behavior did not seem to have any contingent relationship to environmental consequences, the prisoners essentially gave up and stopped behaving. Thus the subjective magnitude of aversiveness was manipulated by the guards not in terms of physical punishment but rather by controlling the psychological dimension of environmental predictability (Singer and Glass, 1972).

Dependency and Emasculation. The network of dependency relations established by the guards not only promoted helplessness in the prisoners but served to emasculate them as well. The arbitrary control by the guards put the prisoners at their mercy for even the daily, commonplace functions like going to the toilet. To do so required publicly obtained permission (not always granted) and then a personal escort to the toilet while blindfolded and handcuffed. The same was true for many other activities ordinarily practiced spontaneously without thought, such as lighting up a cigarette, reading a novel, writing a letter, drinking a glass of water, or brushing one's teeth. These were all privileged activities requiring permission and necessitating a prior show of good behavior. These low level dependencies engendered a regressive orientation in the prisoners. Their dependency was defined in terms of the extent of the domain of control over all aspects of their lives which they allowed other individuals (the guards and prison staff) to exercise.

As in real prisons, the assertive, independent, aggressive nature of male prisoners posed a threat which was overcome by a variety of tactics. The prisoner uniforms resembled smocks or dresses, which made them look silly and enabled the guards to refer to them as "sissies" or "girls." wearing these uniforms without any underclothes forced the prisoners to move and sit in unfamiliar, feminine postures. Any sign of individual rebellion was labelled as indicative of "incorrigibility" and resulted in loss of privileges, solitary confinement, humiliation or punishment of cell mates. Physically smaller guards were able to induce stronger prisoners to act foolishly and obediently. Prisoners were encouraged to belittle each other publicly during the counts. These and other tactics all served to engender in the prisoners a lessened sense of their masculinity (as defined by their external culture). It followed then, that although the

prisoners usually outnumbered the guards during line-ups and counts (nine vs. three), there never was an attempt to directly overpower them. (Interestingly, after the study was terminated, the prisoners expressed the belief that the basis for assignment to guard and prisoner groups was physical size. They perceived the guards as "bigger," when, in fact, there was no difference in average height or weight between these randomly determined groups.)

In conclusion, we believe this demonstration reveals new dimensions in the social psychology of imprisonment worth pursuing in future research. In addition, this research provides a paradigm and information base for studying alternatives to existing guard training, as well as for questioning the basic operating principles on which penal institutions rest. If our mock prison could generate the extent of pathology it did in such a short time, then the punishment of being imprisoned in a real prison does not "fit the crime" for most prisoners—indeed, it far exceeds it! Moreover, since both prisoners and guards are locked into a dynamic, symbiotic relationship which is destructive to their human nature, guards are also society's prisoners.

Shortly after our study was terminated, the indiscriminate killings at San Quentin and Attica occurred, emphasizing the urgency for prison reforms that recognize the dignity and humanity of both prisoners and guards who are constantly forced into one of the most intimate and potentially deadly encounters known to man.

REFERENCES

Adorno, T. W., Frenkel-Brunswik, E., Levinson, D. J., and Sanford, R. N. *The Authoritarian Personality.* New York: Harper, 1950.

Charrière, H. *Papillion.* Robert Laffont, 1969.

Christie, R. and Geis, F. L. (Eds.). *Studies in Machiavellianism.* New York: Academic Press, 1970.

Comrey, A. L. *Comrey Personality Scales.* San Diego: Educational and Industrial Testing Service, 1970.

Glass, D. C. and Singer, J. E. "Behavioral after effects of unpredictable and uncontrollable aversive events." *American Scientist,* 1972, *6*, (4), 457–465.

Jackson, G. *Soledad Brother: the Prison Letters of George Jackson.* New York: Bantam Books, 1970.

Milgram, S. "Some conditions of obedience and disobedience to authority." *Human Relations,* 1965, *18* (1), 57–76.

Mischel, W. *Personality and Assessment.* New York: Wiley, 1968.

Schein, E. *Coercive Persuasion.* New York: Norton, 1961.

Seligman, M. E. and Groves, D. P. "Nontransient learned helplessness." *Psychonomic Science,* 1970, *19* (3), 191–192.

Walster, E. "Assignment of responsibility for an accident." *Journal of Personality and Social Psychology,* 1966, *3* (1), 73–79.

43. Guard-Inmate Relationships

LLOYD W. McCORKLE*

IN THE MIND OF THE MANY, CUSTODY AND INMATE treatment and welfare are viewed as contrasting, if not opposing, objectives of the prison. Custody is frequently dismissed as a rather sordid and punitive operation, consisting chiefly of keeping inmates perpetually locked, counted and controlled. Almost as if in opposition to this, treatment and welfare are described as attempts to introduce freedom and dignity into custody's restrictive, punitive context by the provision of recreation, education and counselling. This traditional contrast, disfigured by bias and half-truth, misses the central reality of the inmate's life in prison.

The reality is simply this: the welfare of the individual inmate, to say nothing of his psychological freedom and dignity, does not importantly depend on how much education, recreation, and consultation he receives but rather depends on how he manages to live and relate with the other inmates who constitute his crucial and only meaningful world. It is what he experiences in this world; how he attains satisfactions from it, how he avoids its pernicious effects—how, in a word, he survives in it that determines his adjustment and decides whether he will emerge from prison with an intact or shattered integrity. The significant impact of in-

▶SOURCE: *"Social Structure in a Prison," Welfare Reporter* (December, 1956), 8: 5–6, 13, 15. (Editorial adaptations.) Reprinted with permission.

*The author informs the editors that he wishes to acknowledge his indebtedness to Gresham Sykes for portions of this article.

stitutional officials is, therefore, not in terms of their relations with the inmate alone, but in terms of a total effect on the social world in which he is inextricably enmeshed. In these terms, an evaluation of the institution's contribution to the welfare of its inmates may not realistically be made with the typical institutional platitudes and statistics about hours of recreation, treatment, and education. The evaluation must rather be made in terms of how the prison authorities are affecting the total social climate, how successfully they are enabling the less hostile persons to advance themselves, how successfully they are protecting these people from intimidation or exploitation by the more antisocial inmates, how effectively they curb and frustrate the lying, swindling, and covert violence which is always under the surface of the inmate social world.

The efficient custodian now emerges from the role of restrictor and becomes the one who safeguards inmate welfare. Most inmates will admit and even require the keeper to assume this function. They understand that the metal detector which uncovers a file intended for an escape attempt will also detect a knife intended for the unsuspecting back of a friend. Inmates will privately express their relief at the construction of a segregation wing which protects them from the depredations of men who are outlaws even in the prison world. Much as they complain of the disciplinary court which punishes them for their infractions, they are grateful for the swift and stern justice meted out to inmates who loot their cells. In short, these men realize, sometimes dimly, sometimes keenly, that a control system which is lax enough to permit widespread thievery and intimidation must eventually result in a deteriorating and vicious circle.

An accurate, moment-to-moment knowledge of, and control over, the whereabouts and destinations of all inmates moving about the institution is essential to the operation of a maximum security prison. These twin objectives, knowledge and control, are mutually indispensable, since it is impossible to exercise either without the other. But it would be a narrow view to consider movement-control a purely custodial objective. No matter how irksome and "petty" it seems to the inmates whose activities are curtailed, there is probably no other single custodial goal which is more crucially tied up with the general welfare of inmates.

The organization of the 1952 riots was, in large part, a result of the inmates' ability to roam about the institution and select individuals for cooperation and intimidation. Ironically, the inmates most frequently selected for intimidation were those who obeyed prison regulations. A general tightening of discipline has greatly ameliorated this problem, but it is still a threat for certain inmates, and it remains a chronic control problem. Short of an undesirable return to the Pennsylvania system of isolation, inmate contact for illegal purposes will remain a problem which may be controlled but never eradicated.

The most serious obstacle to the achievement of the above objective is the breakdown of institutional policy at the point of officer-inmate contact. In the *New Jersey State Prison-Princeton University Study of Prison Social Structure,* the failures at this point were lumped under three general headings: Corruption through Friendship, Corruption through Reciprocity, and Corruption through Default.

CORRUPTION THROUGH FRIENDSHIP

The correction officer is in close and intimate association with his prisoners throughout the course of the working day. He can remain aloof only with difficulty for he possesses few of those devices which normally serve to separate rulers and the ruled. He cannot withdraw physically in symbolic affirmation of social distance; he has no intermediaries to bear the brunt of resentment springing from orders which are disliked; he cannot fall back on a dignity adhering to his office—he is a "hack" or "screw" in the eyes of those he controls and an unwelcome display of officiousness evokes that great destroyer of respect, the ribald humor of the dispossessed.

There are many pressures in American culture to "be nice," to "be a good Joe," and the guard in the maximum security prison is not immune. The guard is constantly exposed to a sort of moral blackmail in which the first signs of condemnation or estrangement are immediately countered by the inmates with the threat of ridicule or hostility. In this complex interplay, the guard does not always start from a position of determined opposition to "being friendly." The cell-block officer holds an intermediate post in a bureaucratic structure between top prison officials—his captains, lieutenants, and sergeants—and the prisoners in his charge. Like many "unlucky" Pierres always in the middle, the guard is caught in a conflict of loyalties. He resents many of the actions of his superiors—the reprimands, the lack of ready appreciation, the incomprehensible order—and in the inmates he finds willing sympathizers; they too claim to suffer from the unreasonable caprice of power. Furthermore, the guard in many cases is marked by a basic ambivalence towards the criminals under his supervision. Although condemned by society through its instrument, the law, many criminals are a "success" in terms of a mundane system of values which places a high degree of prestige on notoriety and wealth even though won by devious means; the poorly-paid guard may be gratified to associate with a famous racketeer. This ambivalence in the correctional officer's attitudes towards his captives cuts deeper than a discrepancy between the inmate's position in the power structure of the prison and his possible status in a *sub rosa* stratification system. There may also be a discrepancy between the judgments of society and the guard's work-a-day values as far as the "criminality" of the inmate is concerned. The bookie, the man convicted of deserting his wife, the inmate who stridently proclaims his innocence and is believed—the guard often believes that these men are not seriously to be viewed as criminals, as desperate prisoners to be rigidly suppressed.

CORRUPTION THROUGH RECIPROCITY

To a large extent the guard is dependent on inmates for the satisfactory performance of his duties and, like many figures of authority, the guard is evaluated in terms of the conduct of the men he controls—a troublesome, noisy, dirty cell-block reflects on the guard's ability to "handle prisoners" and this forms an important component of the merit rating which is used as the basis for pay raises and promotions. A guard cannot rely on the direct application of force to achieve compliance, for he is one man against hundreds; and if he continually calls for additional help he becomes a major problem for the short-handed prison administration. A guard cannot easily rely on threats of punishment, for he is dealing with men who are already being punished near the limits permitted by society; and if the guard insists on constantly using the last few negative sanctions available to the institution—the withdrawal of recreation facilities and other privileges, solitary confinement, or loss of good time—he again becomes burdensome to the prison administration which realizes that its apparent dominance rests on some degree of uncoerced cooperation. The guard, then, is under pressure to achieve a smoothly running cell-block not with the stick but with the carrot, but here again his stock of rewards is limited. One of the best "offers" he can make is ignoring minor offenses or making sure that he never places himself in a position to discover infractions of the rules.

Aside from winning routine and superficial compliance, the guard has another "favor" to be secured from inmates which makes him willing to forego strict enforcement of prison regulations. Many prisons have experienced a riot in which the tables are momentarily turned and the captives hold sway over their quondam captors. The guard knows that he may some day be a hostage and that his life may turn on the settling of old accounts; a fund of good will becomes a valuable form of insurance.

CORRUPTION THROUGH DEFAULT

Finally, much of the guard's authority tends to be destroyed by the innocuous encroachment of inmates on the guard's duties. Making out reports, checking cells at the periodic count, locking and unlocking doors—in short, all the minor chores which the guard is called on to perform during the course of the day—may gradually be transferred into the hands of inmates whom the guard has come to trust. The cell-block "runner," formally assigned the tasks of delivering mail, housekeeping duties, and similar jobs, is of particular importance in this respect. Inmates in this position function in a manner analogous to that of the company clerk in the armed forces and at times they may wield great power and influence in the life of the cell-block. For reasons of indifference, laziness, or naiveté, the guard may find much of his authority whittled away; nonfeasance, rather than malfeasance, has corrupted the theoretical guard-inmate relationship.

Authority, like a woman's virtue, once lost is hard to regain. The measures to break up an established pattern of abdication need be much more severe than those required to stop the first steps in the corruption of authority. In the first place, a guard assigned to a cell-block in which a large portion of control has been transferred in the past from the correctional officer to the inmates is faced with the weight of precedent; it requires a good deal of moral courage on his part to face the gibes and aggression of inmates who fiercely defend the legitimacy of the *status quo* established by custom. In the second place, if the guard himself has allowed his authority to be subverted, he may find his attempts to rectify his error checked by a threat from the inmates to send a "snitch-kite"—an anonymous note—to the guard's superior officers explaining his past derelictions in detail; this simple form of blackmail may on occasion be sufficient to maintain the existing balance of power.

44. Games Inmates Play

STUART J. MILLER
CLEMENS BARTOLLAS
DONALD JENNIFER
EDWARD REDD
SIMON DINITZ

TRANSACTIONAL ANALYSIS HAS DIRECTED OUR AT-
tention to the interpersonal games people play.[1]
These games are defined as ". . . ongoing series
of complementary ulterior transactions progres-
sing to a well-defined, predictable outcome."[2]
Every game is basically dishonest and may be
used not only to keep individuals from becoming intimate with others, but also, to escape
boredom. The payoff to these games is for participants to manipulate others to gain an advantage.[3]

Utilizing the Game Formula of Transactional
Analysis $(C + G = R \rightarrow S \rightarrow X \rightarrow P)$, the intent of
this article is to examine games inmates play
with the staff in an end-of-the-line juvenile institution.[4] The deprivations of institutional life

appear to attenuate the possibility of normal social interaction among inmates and staff. In addition, the custodial orientation of the staff contributes to social distance between the keepers
and the kept.[5] Victimized both by the coercive
nature of the institution and the self-serving
needs of the staff, boys in this training school
attempt to survive by playing games.

The weakening of staff control is one result of
this apparent role reversal. If staff members
were in complete control, it is doubtful they
would permit themselves to be victimized.[6] It is

►SOURCE: *"Games Inmates Play: Notes on Staff Victimiza-
tion,"* in Israel Drapkin and Emilio Viano (Eds.) *Victimology: A
New Focus. Volume V. Exploiters and Exploited: The Dynamics of
Victimization.* Lexington, Mass.: Lexington Books, D. C. Heath,
Inc., 1974. Pp. 143–155. Reprinted with permission.

[1]Eric Berne, *Games People Play* (New York: Grove Press,
Inc., 1964).

[2]Ibid., p. 48.

[3]Ibid., p. 48. Other books taking the Transactional
Analysis perspective are Eric Berne, *Transactional Analysis in
Psychotherapy*; Eric Berne, *What Do You Say After You Say
Hello*; Thomas Harris, *I'm OK—You're OK*; and Muriel James
and Dorothy Jongeward, *Born to Win: Transactional Analysis
with Gestalt Experiments.*

[4]This formula is found in Eric Berne, *What Do You Say
After You Say Hello* (New York: Grove Press, Inc., 1972), p.

23. Berne explains this formula by saying "C + G means that
the con hooks into a gimmick, so that the respondent responds (R). The player then pulls the switch (S), and that is
followed by a moment of confusion or crossup (X), after
which both players collect their payoffs (P). Whatever fits
this formula is a game, and whatever does not fit it is not a
game."

[5]For a discussion of the effects of institutional life on its
residents, see the following: Donald Clemmer, *The Prison
Community* (New York: Holt, Rinehart and Winston, 1966);
Gresham M. Sykes, *The Society of Captives* (Princeton, N.J.:
Princeton University Press, 1958); Alan Davis, "Sexual As-
saults in the Philadelphia Prison System and Sheriff's Vans,"
Transaction 12 (1968); Clarence Schrag, "Leadership among
Prison Inmates," *American Sociological Review* 19 (February
1954): 37–42; Erving Goffman, "The Characteristics of
Total Institutions," in Amitai Etzioni (ed.), *Complex Organiza-
tions: A Sociological Reader* (New York: Holt, Rinehart and
Winston, Inc., 1961), pp. 312–40.

[6]For a discussion of the origins of victimology, see: B.
Mendelsohn, "The Origin of Victimology," *Excerpta*

also obvious that such exploitation by inmates does militate against rehabilitation, since they are only continuing the patterns of behavior which resulted in their incarceration in the first place. Therefore, the process of inmates exploiting the staff is another critical factor moving our penal institutions away from being a therapeutic milieu.

THE INSTITUTIONAL SETTING

The institution involved in this study is considered end-of-the-line and is reserved for overly hostile and aggressive males who range in age from fifteen to twenty years. The institution's capacity is 192 boys, although only 150 were in residence at the time of the study. The boys are housed in eight cottages joined by corridors connecting school, vocational, and recreational areas. Each cottage contains sixteen single rooms and two four-bed dormitories. In addition to this sleeping area, a cottage includes dining and recreational areas, a shower and bathroom, and two offices for staff. These offices, with large picture windows, are located at the juncture of the dormitory, shower, recreation and dining areas. Thus, both boys and staff have ample opportunity to keep each other under surveillance. The cottage staff is composed of one social worker and six youth leaders. It is these staff members who are in the closest contact with inmates and who are most likely to be the subject of inmate games.

Inmates, known to be some of the hardest core delinquents in the state, are experts in how to survive in institutions. The population of this study averaged 16.9 years of age, one-half were black and over two-thirds were lower class. They were primarily from the ghettos of Ohio's largest cities, with their crimes including both serious personal and property offenses. One-half had been diagnosed as dangerous to others and one-fifth more as emotionally disturbed. For many, their experience in the ghettos primed them for cottage life, which can most accurately be described as an exploitation matrix.

This matrix is well known in social psychology as a pecking order. Each youth, on the basis of his physical strength, intelligence and personal characteristics ends up somewhere in this social hierarchy. Additionally, his placement in the peer hierarchy greatly affects the number and types of games he will play with the staff. If he is especially strong and capable, for example, he may become the group leader or "heavy."[7] This heavy is concerned about staying on the staff members' good side because he knows that his position of leadership is dependent on their good will, therefore, he plays games to convince them of his pro-social involvement. If the youth is in a second group of boys immediately below the heavy, he is usually engaged in a power struggle for the top position, and must utilize all the manipulative abilities he has to gain his "rep." If he is still further down the line, he generally does not have much hope in moving up the "ladder," even though he is very much interested in being accepted on an equal basis with other peers. To gain this acceptance and for the strength of his own ego, he, too, must be able to play games to the staff's disadvantage. Finally, and at the bottom of the hierarchy, are the cottage scapegoats, often sexually exploited boys who receive little respect from anyone and who are desperately trying to get off the bottom. They are interested in exploiting the staff because they know that "putting things over" on them is often one key to their successful escape from their lowly status. All boys, therefore, are interested in playing games, since they know that their game playing ability can affect where they fit in the peer social structure.

Criminologica 3 (May–June 1963): 239–41; Hans von Hentig, *The Criminal and His Victim* (New Haven: Yale University Press, 1948); Henri Ellenberger, "Relations psychologiques entre le criminel et la victime," *Revue internationale de criminologie et de police technique*, 3 (April–June 1954).

[7]Stuart J. Miller, Clemens Bartollas, James Roberts, and Simon Dinitz, "The Heavy and Social Control," in *Proceedings of the Alpha Kappa Delta Sociological Research Symposium*, forthcoming.

THE PRESENT STUDY

Participant observation and a series of tape recorded interviews with both the staff and boys were used to clarify the dynamics of interaction between staff and boys. Participant observation was used principally to capture and depict the process of interaction, and in-depth interviews with three staff members were especially helpful in understanding the nature of staff exploitation.[8]

Experienced staff members seem to feel that all staff members are victimized, whether they know it or not. Some, especially early in their career, are overtly victimized. Contraband (money, food, clothing, and radios) may be stolen from them, they may be physically pushed around by aggressive students, or perhaps even violently assaulted by students.[9] But the much more frequent means of exploitation involves game playing, which is done in such a way that staff members may not be aware they are being victimized. Apparently, the only staff members readily able to recognize games and thus reduce the chances of being victimized are lower class blacks who have worked at this institution for several years.

The background of these lower class blacks appears to sensitize them more to the dynamics of exploitative games. The experience of ghetto living seems to make them more aware when someone is coming on straight or conning them, and they are therefore able to call the boys on their games. On the other hand, middle class black or white staff members are much less sensitive to boys "putting them on," since they have not had the experience of struggling for their survival on the streets. They also have not been exposed to the everyday transactions of ghetto living. Subsequently, exploitation by students may either not be recognized or its importance ignored. Paradoxically, while these middle class staff members may be more likely to leave the boys alone, they are more likely to be confronted by inmates who are testing them both mentally and physically. Inmates want to see how much pressure can be placed on these leaders and to what extent they will be permitted to run their own lives.

THESAURUS OF GAMES

In this institution, boys play physical, psychological, therapeutic, theological, and materialistic games. Each of these categories is made up of concrete games played by boys. As previously noted, the games are analyzed using the Game Formula of Transactional Analysis. This formula means that "the con hooks into a gimmick, so that the respondent responds. The player then pulls the switch, and that is followed by a moment of confusion or crossup, after which both players collect their payoffs."[10]

Physical Games

Since out and out physical attacks on staff members are generally doomed to failure, it is necessary for these youths to invent other means of maneuvering into a dominant position over the staff.[11] These games are used to put pressure on leaders so that they have less control over inmates.

---

[8]Mr. Edward Redd, Donald Jennifer, and James Roberts were these three staff members.

[9]To illustrate, one weak staff member, coming upon a group of boys having sex with another, was told to leave the area until they were finished. Another staff member was dragged by his heels around the cottage. Other staff have been locked in rooms during escapes. A timid staff member was kept with three students while they took the food cart into a back corridor, rammed it into an exit door until it broke, and then escaped. Sometimes, a fearful staff member will literally have kids turn their noses up to him, sneer at him, and then tell him to "go get lost."

[10]There are several ways in which this paper fails to operationalize this formula. The payoff, for example, is generally collected more by the inmate than by the staff in these institutional games. These games are also more intentional (overt) and less psychological (covert) than the games found in *Games People Play*.

[11]Attacking a staff member can result in a transfer to the adult reformitory, which severely reduces the popularity of a physical altercation with staff. In addition, while one staff member is being attacked, the other one can phone for help.

"You Ain't Shit"

Con: New youth leaders sometimes receive considerable attention from one of the most aggressive youths in the cottage. This youth frequently "raps" with the leader in his office, telling him how glad they are that he came to work in the cottage. The game's purpose is to physically intimidate the leader so that he can be controlled.

Hook or Gimmick: The new leader readily responds to the boy because he wants acceptance from the cottage's aggressive youths.

Switch: The inmate suddenly picks an argument for no apparent reason and challenges the youth leader to fight it out in the bathroom. He baits the leader by telling him, "You ain't shit." The leader or mark is confused by this crossup; he just cannot understand the youth's reaction.

Payoff: If the youth leader agrees to go to the bathroom, the boy will go in with him. However, he will quickly quit after a punch or two has been thrown—before either he or the youth leader are hurt. In this case, the game has been foiled, and there is no payoff. But if he does not go, then inmates gain the payoff of his physical intimidation. If the staff member has played the game, he, in turn, is able to nurture his hurt feelings.

"Excuse Me. You're in My Way"

Con: The very negative, sullen youth who is extremely aggressive does not always need to confront the staff directly in order to gain the upper hand. One way this can be done is for the inmate to brush angrily past a staff member, catching him by the shoulder, but never slowing down or apologizing. The purpose of the game is for the boy to be able to establish himself in a superior position, and he can, providing he is able successfully to couple his "presentation of self" with occasional indirect acts of defiance.

Hook or Gimmick: His very demeanor and activities are observed by the staff members, and it is from this that they get the impression that he is too strong for them to handle. Therefore, the staff member chooses to ignore the youth bumping into him.

Switch: Here, the aggressive youth decides to increase his aggression. In an actual instance, a staff member had his key in the door and had the door partially closed when the aggressive youth barged through the door and, with complete lack of ceremony and disregard for the staff, started to search a room for cigarettes he thought had been stolen. This staff member had permitted small liberties with this youth in the past, but was surprised and confused by this overt defiance.

Payoff: Permitting this increased act of defiance usually means that staff members have lost their ability to control the youth. If challenged, the youth has two options: he can either rationalize the act away, saying he was so angry with another inmate that he was not aware what he was doing or he can throw up his fists, daring the staff member to move into him. Nevertheless, either choice generally means that he has failed in his attaining the payoff of greater power over staff.

"What's Wrong With a Little Horseplay?"

Con: A more desirable and less risky way for youths to test the staff is to engage them in "horseplay." If the youth can get the staff member to play with him in such a way that it tests his strength, then the physical strength of this youth leader becomes known.

Hook or Gimmick: The leader feels he is "The Man" and therefore is reluctant to back down from arm or leg wrestling.

Switch: The staff member loses this test of strength, and discovers to his chagrin that much is being made of his defeat.

Payoff: The payoff is to become aware of a

weak youth leader and to use this weakness against him. Students then become more defiant in their demeanor, more blatant in their refusals to comply with instructions, and more vocal in their threats of force. Feeling humiliated by his loss of respect, the leader receives his payoff by becoming more fearful in his interactions with inmates.

"I Will Get You"

Con: Social workers have a great deal of power over how long a youth stays in the institution. Thus, boys are constantly seeking ways to control a social worker and physical intimidation is a very popular way.

Hook or Gimmick: Since social workers are usually afraid of the boys, a direct threat on their lives generally creates considerable anxiety.

Switch: After warning the social worker that he will "get him" following his release or escape, the youth then becomes extremely friendly. The social worker or mark is confused by this crossup. He cannot understand why the hostile youth has become so amicable.

Payoff: The game is successful if the social worker begins to go out of his way to please the youth. The social worker's payoff is to feel that the youth has become more pro-social in his attitudes and behavior.

Psychological Games

As one moves away from physical confrontations, the risks and rewards are reduced because inmates are more concerned about emotionally upsetting youth leaders and social workers than they are in controlling them. Once the staff members are upset, however, they may neglect their jobs, overreact to the boys, and eventually lose control.

"You're Not Quite Yourself Today"

Con: This game involves the process of getting to know the moods and temperaments of the staff members so well that boys know as soon as a staff member walks in the cottage door what mood he is in that day. If it appears that he does not feel well or it looks like he has a hangover from the night before, then this gives inmates their opportunity.

Hook or Gimmick: The social worker or youth who is already uncomfortable because he does not feel well is not able to deal with much frustration. Aware of this, inmates go out of their way to place demands on their leaders. Nearly every boy in the cottage, for example, will insist on talking with them.

Switch: The crossup arises when problems are brought to the harassed youth leader or social worker which he thought were resolved. To illustrate, the social worker is informed by an inmate—for whom he has worked on his home placement for some time—that he no longer wants to go to the group home. Or one of the leader's favorite students begins "acting out." In the midst of a bad day, this unexpected event is more than a little overwhelming.

Payoff: The game is successful if the social worker or youth leader's "not-OK child" is hooked, and he becomes upset and disappointed, wearing his feelings on his sleeve for a few days. The staff member's payoff is to have these angry feelings toward his boys.

"He's Stupid: How Did He Ever Get to Be a Youth Leader Here?"

Con: The intelligence of the youth leader is an area where boys try to "run game" on their cottage leaders. They will, for example, make the following statement about one of the leaders, "He's stupid; he's dumber than anybody in the cottage." If the staff member has not overheard this, inmates make certain that this label filters back to him.

Hook or Gimmick: Many youth leaders have had difficulty in school and have developed some inferiority concerning their acumen. Intelligence, therefore, is a sensitive area.

Switch: Inmates make certain that a leader is aware that they feel he is "stupid." Then, in the midst of a cottage meeting in which everyone in the cottage is present, an inmate calls this leader "stupid" or "dumb." All the boys (and sometimes even some of the staff members if they feel the label is true) laugh, and this infuriates the youth leader.

Payoff: The game is successful if the label begins to bother the youth leader. While inmates feel a strong sense of revenge when they are able to pull it off, the staff member usually uses this game as a justification for withdrawing from his involvement with inmates.

"I've a 'Wooden Leg': Don't Expect
too Much from Me"

Con: Inmates also find it useful to play up physical or psychological labels they have been given. Physical ailments or psychological problems, for example, may be used to escape legitimate tasks demanded of them in their institutional living.[12]

Hook or Gimmick: When the youth who is labeled as a suicide risk says, "Hey man, I'm a psycho. You can't make me do that," staff members are under pressure because they know that the label exists and they do not want to be responsible for driving him to suicide.[13]

Switch: The youth proceeds to cut a surface wound on his arm. Upset by this action and fearful of an eventually successful suicide, leaders frequently react, "Lets get him the hell out of the cottage."

[12]This game is similar to "Wooden Leg" found in Berne, *Games People Play,* pp. 159–63.

[13]Several years ago a boy hanged himself, and had to be cut down by a staff member. Another youth recently burned to death in a fire. The memories of these events are still fresh in the minds of those in the institution.

Payoff: If boys can convince staff that they have a "wooden leg" and are unable "to make it" at this institution, then behavior, such as suicide attempts, is able to elicit preferred treatment from staff. The best payoff is when a boy is transferred out of this maximum security institution because staff are afraid of his "wooden leg." Staff members, in turn, receive additional reinforcement to the feeling that they are working with "losers."

Therapeutic Games

While boys sometimes play therapeutic games in order to amuse themselves, they most frequently are played to make the staff feel that the inmates are deriving maximum benefit from the institution's treatment program.

"You've Really Helped Me"

Con: A boy will go to a staff member and tell him how much he has been helping him. Particularly resourceful boys even use what staff members in other institutions have told them about themselves and claim that they received this "valuable" insight from a staff member in this institution. The motive is to receive positive reinforcement at the next review.

Hook or Gimmick: This tends to hook the egos of staff members, especially if they are new.

Switch: The crossup arises when the inmate tells all the staff members at the review how much this one staff member has helped him. What frequently happens then is that the particular staff member becomes so determined to support the boy in question that he challenges negative comments from other staff members.

Payoff: The game is successful providing the inmate is able to use the one staff member to attain what he had hoped to attain from his review. The staff member usually ends up feeling that he is the only leader in the cottage who really understands the youth.

"I'm With You All the Way, I Really Am"

Con: Some youths are extremely skillful in figuring out what staff members want, and are equally skillful in fulfilling their expectations. Although this may indicate genuine change in attitude, it may also simply be a con game in which the boy is more interested in a short stay and special institutional privileges than positive adjustment to the community following release.

Hook or Gimmick: The boy tries to communicate to staff members that he has taken over their point of view—which is what they want to hear.

Switch: When a youth arrives at the institution with a turbulent prior institutional history, staff members anticipate that they will have trouble with him. If he does well, cottage youth leaders may be initially confused by his positive behavior, but are likely to give themselves the credit for the inmate's positive institutional adjustment.

Payoff: The game is successful providing the boy receives all the positive reinforcement the staff can give (extra institutional privileges and short stay), and staff members feel that this changed behavior on the boy's part was because of their impact.

"What Did You Think of the Group Meeting?"

Con: Group leaders are evaluated partially on the basis of audiovisual tapes they have made on their group meetings; and to get positive support from the group leader, inmates sometimes try to make him look good in these taped group sessions. They do this by creating the type of group interaction they have learned the group leader wants.[14]

[14]Transactional Analysis is the group modality which is being used at the present time.

Hook or Gimmick: The group leader, of course, is pleased with his boys. He is also pleased with the positive evaluation he has received from his supervisor for the good group session.

Switch: Inmate communicate on a sub-rosa level to their group leader that he is dependent on them for their support. If he scratches their backs, they will continue to stratch his. The crossup arises when the group leader realizes that he is being co-opted.

Payoff: The game is successful if the group leader supports his group members at reviews, disciplinary meetings, and before other staff members. His payoff has to do with the feeling that he is a positive factor in their "successful" adjustment to the institution.

Theological Games

Boys occasionally have profound spiritual experiences in the institution which may have lasting influence on their lives. However, there are more youths who feign religious interest or conversion because of the effect it will have on the chaplain and other treatment staff members.

"Are You Saved?"

Con: Boys know that an interest in religious phenomena is considered desirable by staff. They also know that the chaplain has considerable power and that he will support those who have had religious experiences during their stay.

Hook or Gimmick: The hook involves making the chaplain feel that he has been instrumental in this spiritual discovery.

Switch: The crossup occurs when the youth goes to the chaplain's office and tells him how he has been getting exploited by cottage staff and institutional peers. The chaplain, who has already been supportive of the youth because of his spiritual discovery and commitment, now is petitioned by the youth to intervene in some of the problems he has in the cottage.

Payoff: The game has a successful outcome for the inmate if the chaplain intervenes and helps expedite his release from the institution. The payoff for the chaplain, of course, relates to his feeling that he is being an effective instrument of Christianity at the institution.

Material Games

The purpose of these games is to improve the inmates' lot in the institution and to make their stay as pleasureable as possible. Since many items, such as food, candy, and cigarettes are scarce, and the bureaucratic rules reduce freedom, boys are continually trying to manipulate to staff to their own advantage.

"If Not that One, How About this One?"

Con: Youths who are difficult to control realize that they can get staff members to compromise and permit behavior which would be normally rejected.

Hook or Gimmick: Staff members find the emotional outbursts of strong inmates who have considerable power in the cottage distasteful.

Switch: A boy approaches a staff member with a request. He is aware that this request is out of line and will not be approved; but after it is turned down, he then makes a second request which is more feasible. Since this youth is strong and has a violent temper, he is aware that the staff member will jump at the second request in order to avoid his acting out behavior.

Payoff: If, in fact, the inmate is able to improve his living conditions and to make life more enjoyable, then this game has been successful. Granting the inmate's request makes the youth leader or social worker feel good because he has been able to control the inmate

(turned down his first request) but yet avoided his emotional reaction (granted his second request).

"Excuse Me. I Have a Problem"

Con: Another game to improve one's lot is where one youth engages a staff member in conversation while other peers are involved in deviant activity.[15]

Hook or Gimmick: A boy requests permission to talk with a youth leader about a serious problem, involving school, girl friend, goals in life, or family. The leader's ego is flattered, diverting his attention from supervising the other students in the cottage.

Switch: Meanwhile, back in the shower, dormitory, or private room, sexual exploitation, escape, or assault is taking place.

Payoff: To be able to participate in deviant activity is the payoff of this transaction. Unaware of what is going on in the cottage, the staff's payoff is to feel good about helping this inmate.

CONCLUSION

The use of qualitative techniques including participant observation and interviews enabled this analysis of staff-inmate conflict to be focused through the viewpoint of interpersonal games. While there is no challenging the fact that staff members are in control, it is also clear that inmates are using every means at hand to salvage whatever control possible. Extensive violence, while rare, does remain a possibility. Most institutional games, however, are of the more subtle type in which one intellect is pitted against another or in which one person's slightly greater understanding of self and others is used to try to gain an advantage.

[15]This was easier to do when only one staff member worked each shift.

The games elaborated upon here take several forms. Physical games are designed to control the staff which, in turn, gives peers more freedom in the institution. Psychological games are played in a passive-aggressive way to direct hostility toward the staff. Therapeutic and theological games are played primarily to expedite one's release. But equally as important are the material games designed to improve one's lot and to make institutional living as pleasurable as possible.

Finally, it has been argued by Clemmer and others that the custodial goals of our institutions contribute to the staff-inmate split and result in each side directing hostilities toward the other.[16]

In addition, observers say that in treatment-oriented institutions relations between staff and inmates are of a more cooperative, trusting, and friendly nature than in custodial institutions. Although speculative, the type of institutional goal orientation should be reflected in the types of games their inmates play. If this turns out to be the case, an analysis of institutional goals in conjunction with inmate games should yield significant insights into our institutional processes.

[16]Oscar Grusky, "Organizational Goals and the Behavior of Informal Leaders," *American Journal of Sociology* 65 (July–May 1959–60): 59–67; Oscar Grusky, "Role Conflict in Organization: A Study of Prison Camp Officials,"*Administrative Science Quarterly* 3 (June–March 1958–59): 452–72; David Street, Robert Vinter, and Charles Perrow, *Organization for Treatment* (New York: The Free Press, 1960); Bernard Berk, "Organizational Goals and Inmate Organization," *The American Journal of Sociology* 71 (March 1966): 522–32; Richard McCleery, "Policy Change in Prison Management," in Amitai Etzioni (ed.), *Complex Organizations: A Sociological Reader* (New York: Holt, Rinehart and Winston, Inc., 1961), pp. 376–400; Richard McCleery, "Authoritarianism and the Belief System of Incorrigibles," in Cressey (ed.), *The Prison: Studies in Institutional Organization and Change* (New York: Holt, Rinehart and Winston, 1961); Terrence Morris, Pauline Morris, and Barbara Biely, "It's the Prisoners Who Run This Prison," *Prison Service Journal* 3 (January 1961): 3–11; Joseph C. Mouledous, "Organizational Goals and Structure Change: A Study of the Organization of a Prison Social System," *Social Forces* 41 (March 1963): 283–90.

45. The Inmate Code in a Halfway House

D. L. WIEDER

THE EAST LOS ANGELES HALFWAY HOUSE WAS LO-
cated on Breed Street near Brooklyn and Soto in
Boyle Heights, in the eastern section of Los
Angeles. The neighborhood was once a Jewish
community, but is now a Mexican-American
ghetto. The area is the largest debarcation point
in the state for Mexicans coming into this country. Mexican foods are prominent in the mar-
kets. Almost all restaurants in the area are Mexican. One is often first spoken to in Spanish when
in a store or restaurant, and only if that attempt
fails is English tried. Papers and literature in
Spanish are available on the street corners. Both
men and women dress "typically chicano," with
many, perhaps most, of the men sporting full
mustaches. Although many non-Mexicans live
in the neighborhood, people visible on the street
are almost exclusively Mexican. The area is reputed by the police and correctional workers to
be one of the highest narcotic traffic areas in the
state. During the day, on Brooklyn Avenue, one
sees the "harness bulls" or "black and whites"
(motorcycle police and police cruisers) pass by
once every ten minutes. At night, the police pass
by perhaps once every three minutes.

East Los Angeles was chosen as the location
for the halfway house, at least in part, in response to a community request that a program
of this type be placed in this high narcotic traffic
area.

The halfway house was located in a thirty-

year-old stucco building that was previously
used as a children's day-care center. A portion
of the building also housed the Halfway House
Parole District Office. The remainder of the
building was used as the residential area. It contained five dormitories (each housing a
maximum of six men), a kitchen, a spacious dining room, a large recreation-meeting room, and
a sitting or reception room.

*

This selection examines the convict code,
which is the classical or traditional explanation
of those forms of deviant behavior engaged in
by inmates, convicts, or residents of rehabilitative organizations. In traditional analyses of deviant behavior, some subversive or contra-
culture normative order is searched out by the
analyst and utilized by him as an explanation for
the behavior patterns he has observed. In the
case of prisons and related organizations, the
"convict code" is typically encountered by the
researcher and employed as such an explanation.

THE CODE AS AN EXPLICITLY VERBALIZED MORAL ORDER

My participant observation detected a code
which was operative at halfway house. My principal resident informants, whom I came to know
over a period of several months, and with whom
I had at least several conversations a week and
often several a day, spoke readily of a code.
They called this code *the code* and told of a set of

▶SOURCE: *Language and Social Reality: Approaches to Semio-
tics. # 10. The Hague: Mouton, 1974, Pp. 52–53, 113–126.
Reprinted by permission.*

activities that they *should* and *should not* engage in. They also spoke of "regular guys" (followers of the code) and said that every one of the residents at the halfway house was a regular guy. They explained to me that everyone there had "done a lot of time" and had even learned the code much earlier than their prison experiences, as hypes on the street.

THE CODE AND EXPLICITLY
VERBALIZED SANCTIONS

Residents of the halfway house, like inmates as they are described in the literature on prisons, spoke clearly about the ways in which the code was enforced. As traditionally reported, and as I observed in the case of the halfway house, enforcement of the code by inmates or residents is closely related to the use of social types. The code is generally enforced by inmates through their application of a label or social-type name to those inmates who are seen by members of the group as deviating from the code.

In the case of the halfway house, the only deviant types or labels that I regularly heard were "kiss ass," "snitch," and "sniveler." To be called a "kiss ass" meant that one was too close to staff. The title "snitch" was employed to designate another as an informer. "Sniveler" was employed to designate another resident as one who chronically complained to staff and pleaded with staff for better treatment. Residents spoke of kissing ass, snitching, and sniveling as clearly moral matters which required their attention and intervention.

Sanctions directed against the sniveler were minor when compared with the measures taken against the snitch and kiss ass. A sniveler would be spoken of as a "fool" and "not like one of us." Sanctions directed against kiss asses and snitches, while more potent, were spoken of with less clarity and uniformity. At times, residents said that kiss asses would be frozen out of contact with the other "guys" and that immediate violence would be done against snitches. At other times, residents spoke of the

"fact" that violations of the code would be remembered and dealt with later. That is, the reprehensible one would, like all other residents, at some time return to the "joint" (prison). In the joint, his reprehensible reputation would be spread, and at that point he would not be trusted by the other cons and would be suspected by the other cons on each occasion in which they thought someone had snitched.

THE SPECIFICS OF THE CODE AT
HALFWAY HOUSE

The code was often spoken of by residents as containing a set of maxims. While a specific resident could not recite all of the maxims, what residents said about the code can be formulated in that fashion. As a set of maxims, the code in its specifics is as follows:

1. *Above all else, do not snitch.* Informing was regarded as an act directed not simply against an individual, but against the whole collection of deviant colleagues. Snitching would permanently jeopardize a resident's standing with other hypes, residents, and inmates. His reputation would be spread throughout the whole deviant community, and he would find that he could no longer operate with other deviants. There was only one actual case in which I observed snitching or possible snitching as a real issue (as compared to a potential or hypothetical issue) at the halfway house. And the only reason this case was observable to me was because a resident who was fearful that others regarded him as a snitch told the following story to his parole agent, who in turn told me. "Pablo" came to his parole agent, telling him of his anxiety about a parolee who was about to move into the halfway house. Years before, the two men had used and sold drugs together. Both were arrested, but charges were dropped against Pablo, while the other man was tried. Pablo said that the other man thought Pablo had informed on him, though Pablo told him he had not. Now Pablo wanted release from the halfway house because of what that man might do and how the other residents might treat him if the other man ever talked about him. Except for this incident, I observed no cases of residents' being identified as snitches. I did, however, hear talk about specific snitches who were not residents (other men in prison or in the community), as well as much talk about snitches and snitching in general.

2. *Do not cop out.* That is, do not admit that you have done something illegal or illegitimate. Someone who turned himself in willingly would be regarded as strange, "not like us," dumb, and probably not trustworthy, because to "cop out" was a form of defecting to the other side. To turn oneself in could be viewed as a form of defection, because it implied agreement with the standards that one had violated. To turn oneself in to a parole agent when one was about to be caught anyway or when one was "tired of running" and likely to get caught by the police, however, was not talked about as "copping out."

3. *Do not take advantage of other residents.* This maxim was principally directed against thievery among residents. However, if a resident had something stolen from him, it was his own responsibility to take care of the thief. Unlike the case of the snitch, a resident could not count on others to negatively sanction the thief. Residents were prohibited by the code from appealing to staff for assistance in locating the stolen goods.

4. *Share what you have.* A regular resident should be relatively generous with other residents in terms of his money, clothes, and wine. If he used drugs, he should offer a "taste" to others that were around when he "geezed." He should share drugs with his closest friends and sell drugs to others, if he had more than he needed. He should share his "fit" (syringe and spoon) with others and "score" (purchase drugs) for those who could not find a connection (source of drugs).

5. *Help other residents.* This maxim was principally a directive to help one's fellows avoid de-

tection and punishment. It included "standing point" for them (being a lookout for staff or the police when the other was involved in a compromising activity, such as injecting drugs), warning them about suspicions that staff had, telling staff that they were ignorant about the activities of other residents, so as not to help staff indirectly investigate another guy,[1] arguing with staff on the behalf of another resident, providing cover stories for other residents, helping another resident sneak into the house after curfew, etc.

6. *Do not mess with other residents' interests.* A resident should not prevent others from enjoying their deviance, should not disapprove of it, and should not in any way draw staff's attention to it. This includes not "bringing the heat" by engaging in suspicious actions or by getting into an unnecessary altercation with staff. For example, one could "bring the heat" by leaving evidence of drug use around the house which would lead staff to suspect everybody.

7. *Do not trust staff—staff is heat.* This maxim simply says that in the final analysis staff cannot be trusted, because one of staff's principal occupational duties is to detect deviance. Anything a resident might let them know about himself or others could, in some presently unknown fashion, be used by them to send him or someone else back to the joint. So, if a resident has anything deviant going for him at all (like having a common law wife, occasionally using heroin, having user friends in his house, or even using marijuana), he is well advised not to let his agent know his real residence and to give his mother's address instead. In this way he avoids letting his agent know anything that might lead to the discovery of his deviant doings. This advice holds even if a resident is on the best of terms with his agent.

8. *Show your loyalty to the residents.* Staff, in fact, is "the enemy," and a resident's actions should show that he recognizes this. He should

---

[1] Also included generally under the rule, "do not snitch."

not "kiss ass," do favors for staff, be friendly to staff, take their side in an argument, or accept the legitimacy of their rules. Any of these acts can be understood as a defection to their side, and makes a resident suspect of being the kind of "guy" that would snitch. It is not that being friendly to staff or complying with staff's regulations is intrinsically illegitimate, but these matters indicate what kind of person one is and that one, thereby, may not be trustworthy in protecting residents and their interests. If a resident makes it clear in other ways (as, for example, in his private dealings with other residents) that he indeed is on the residents' side, these signalizing activities may then be understood in other ways by the other residents. They may be understood as efforts to manipulate staff in some concrete way, e.g., a resident wants them to give him the best jobs they have, or wants to make the kind of impression on his parole agent that will lead the agent away from suspecting him when he otherwise might.

THE CODE AS EXPLANATION FOR RESIDENT BEHAVIOR

Treating the rules of the code as maxims of conduct that residents follow and enforce upon one another provides a traditional sociological explanation for the regular patterns of deviant behavior that were observed in the halfway house. The rules account for that behavior in the following specific ways.

If residents comply with the maxim, "Show your loyalty to the residents," then they would be motivated to avoid spending time with staff, avoid lively conversation with staff, and, by the use of Spanish and other conversational devices, would exclude staff from their conversations. The injunction against trusting staff, not letting staff know about residents' doings as a way of protecting other residents, and even the injunction against "snitching"[2] are also fulfilled (in

part) in the avoidance behavior "doing distance."

Further, residents can show their loyalty to each other by displaying a lack of enthusiasm for what staff proposes in group, by not paying attention in group, by verbally demeaning the program in group, and by not staying around after group to talk with staff about the program. That is, showing where one's loyalties are can be accomplished by displaying the behaviors "disinterest and disrespect." Similarly, by complying with no more than what staff demands and explicitly sanctions ("passive compliance") and by attempting to get staff to do what they hope a resident will do for himself ("demands and requests"), one can, thereby, also show his loyalties by doing as little as possible for "the enemy" and taking him for whatever one can get.

Patterns of lying and generally being a bad informant, which left staff ignorant of what was actually happening at the moment, ignorant of what a resident would do, and ignorant of whether or not he would do as he had promised, are provided for in the maxims, "Do not snitch," "Do not cop out," "Do not trust staff," "Help other inmates," and "Do not mess with other residents' interests." The maxim, "Do not snitch," directs the resident to avoid letting staff share any of his knowledge of other residents. "Do not cop out" directs him to prevent staff from knowing about his own activities. These same maxims would lead residents to prevent staff from hearing anything about what residents were doing, including who is friends with whom, who is physically in the house, that drugs are being used (which is different from snitching, which would be that "Jones" is using drugs), and often whether or not one resident even knows another.

Patterns of violating rules and routines are protected, supported, and encouraged by the code, though they are not directly prescribed. While there is nothing in the code which says

---

[2]The relationship of "doing distance" to "snitching" requires further explanation. Residents explained to me that being aloof from staff, which can be accomplished by "doing distance," indicates to others that one would not snitch. If one did not stay aloof, then special effort would be required to retain the trust of other residents.

"miss group," "be late for curfew," "bring wine into the house," or "use drugs," any of these activities, especially the use of drugs, is a relatively clear sign of one's loyalties. Residents sometimes told me that they took drugs that were offered to them, because refusing would indicate that they disapproved of drug use or were "taking to heart" staff hopes that they would not use drugs.

Patterns of deviant behavior were protected by maxims of the code which required that (a) other residents help those who chose to violate the "rules" and "routines," (b) other residents cover for those who needed it (standing point, providing excuses and alibis, sneaking them into the house when the "night watchman" [SPA] was not looking, etc.), and (c) no resident let staff verbally know about deviant activities. Deviant activities were further supported by the set of rules which said that residents should let each other do whatever deviant (from staff's point of view) thing they chose, and if they were to engage in deviant consumption of wine and drugs, that these should be shared with others.

In this fashion, the code as I found it at halfway house would explain the patterns of deviance that I observed there. The code provides the motivations to engage in those patterns, to positively sanction those patterns, and to not interfere with those patterns even if a resident were to find it in his own interest to do so. This form of explanation is traditional in the analysis of correctional organizations and has its direct analog in traditional analyses of other forms of deviant behavior.

THE SOCIOLOGICAL LITERATURE ON THE CONVICT CODE

Although patterns of deviant behavior are traditionally explained by reference to a set of rules like the convict code, explanations are often not the focus of traditional research. In many areas of sociology, including the analysis of subcultures or contra-cultures in the prison setting, only the earliest studies focus on explaining observed patterns of behavior in terms of rules.

Later studies explore such matters as the functional relationships between the rules or normative culture detected in early studies and other elements of organization. Therefore, in the research on the prison, many studies report variations in normative orders without indicating any patterns of behavior that inmate compliance to such contra-normative orders would produce (e.g., Weinberg, 1942; Caldwell, 1956; Galtung, 1958). Other studies show the ways that the code and the social types that revolve around it make inmates' behavior understandable (e.g., Sykes and Messinger, 1960), predictable (e.g., Schragg, 1944), and characterizable as repudiating institutional norms (e.g., Cloward, 1960) without specifying observed patterns of behavior which would be produced by the rules under consideration.

Most recent research is concerned with the practical import of the convict code as an impediment to rehabilitation and/or treatment. One set of studies explores the relationship between types of prison administration and the extent to which the code is elaborated and enforced (e.g., Grusky, 1959; McLeery, 1961 a, b; Street, 1965; Berk, 1966; Street, Vintner, and Perrow, 1966; and Studt, Messinger, and Wilson, 1968). Another set of studies is directed at detecting the conditions under which varying degrees of compliance with the code are fostered (Wheeler, 1961; Garabedian, 1963; Tittle and Tittle, 1964; and Ward and Kassebaum, 1965). For the interests of my research, these studies document the fact that the code, although varied in the extent of its elaboration and enforceability, is widely found. Another set of studies, to be reviewed below, is considerably more detailed in the ways the code is used to analyze and account for inmate behavior.

STUDIES WHICH EMPLOY THE CODE TO ANALYZE AND ACCOUNT FOR INMATE BEHAVIOR

In what is generally regarded as the first major study of prisons, Clemmer, in *The Prison Community* (1940), portrays the formal organization of the prison, the daily round of life in prison, and the prison "culture." His principal thesis is that this prison culture, which is partially assimilated by all prisoners and wholly assimilated by twenty to forty percent, turns those convicted of crimes into even more anti-social persons.

The code detected at the halfway house was strikingly similar to that described by Clemmer. He counts the code as one of the fundamental social controls among the inmate population. It revolves around two propositions: "Don't help the officials"and "Do help your fellow inmates." Thus, Clemmer's prisonized inmate would not snitch, would regard officials as his enemy and would show this by, for example, not talking to them except about "business," and would assist his fellow inmates by helping them avoid detection in their deviance. He proposed that the code "does control conduct in many instances and tends to control it in other instances" (p. 140). Throughout the rest of the volume, interspersed in his discussion of rules, patterns of leisure, patterns of work, and sexual patterns, he cites a variety of examples of complying with the code. He recites incidents in which one inmate would not inform on two other inmates who stole his cat (p. 158) and another who would not inform on an inmate who knifed him (p. 164) as instances of complying with the code. He cites stealing food from the institution (p. 160) and sharing that stolen food with inmates who have just gotten off bread and water (p. 164) as further instances.

In a variety of contexts, he shows patterns of hostility (exhibited toward the guards) which are produced by inmates complying with the code. Cursing and denouncing the guards is described as necessary for the inmate who wishes to retain the respect of his fellows. Being insolent to the guards and threatening them is depicted as giving the inmate prestige among his fellows (pp. 196, 304). Other patterns of behavior and attitude associated with compliance to the code include not respecting prison rules (p. 195), talking about criminal exploits, stealing from the prison, gambling, and engaging in homosexual behavior (p. 304). Though Clemmer's analysis

of the code is scattered throughout this work, he does analyze patterns of deviant behavior as the outcome of what he calls "prisonization," which is principally socialization to the convict code.

Historically, the next major piece of prison research was Sykes' *The Society of Captives*. Sykes' strategy was to account for the inmate social system by proposing that it developed as a protective device to insulate the inmate from the pains of imprisonment which amount to an attack on his self-conception. The inmate social system protects the self-conception by providing a social world in which the inmate can have status and in which he can believe that it is his captors who are immoral and incompetent rather than himself. Sykes' analysis of the code is embedded in this thesis, and his presentation of the code is embedded in a system of social types which revolve around the code, each social type representing a pattern of compliance with or deviance from the code.

In Sykes' description, the staff of the maximum security prison he studied, like the staff of the halfway house, was "engaged in a continuous struggle to maintain order" (Sykes, 1958: 42). He lists fifteen rule violations which were reported during one week, indicating that both inmates and officials agreed that the actual offense rate was much higher. Sykes argues that inmates violate rules because they lack a sense of duty to comply with them (p. 47). They lack this sense of duty because of the nature of the inmate social world (p. 62), which leads them to violate institutional regulations by coercion of fellow prisoners, fraud, gambling, homosexuality, sharing of stolen supplies, and so on. That social world is characterized in terms of a set of argot roles (pp. 84–108) which simultaneously deal with the major problems of prison life and are the devices for indicating inmate admiration for and disapproval of the behavior of their fellow inmates. Thus, each type represents the moral standing of the inmate to which it is applied. The term "rat" is applied to inmates who have betrayed their fellows by violating the rule, "Do not snitch." The "center man" would correspond to the kiss-ass in the halfway house, for he is disloyal to his fellow inmates by displaying the attitudes of the custodians—frequently not because he agrees with them, but in order to manipulate them. The "gorilla" exploits his fellow inmates by use or threat of violence, while the "merchant" exploits them by inappropriately selling goods stolen from the prison, which in terms of the code should be freely shared. Both gorillas and merchants are despised for their violation of the ideals of inmate solidarity. Inmates who react with violence toward the officials are referred to as "ball busters," while those who are quick to fight with their fellow inmates are called "toughs." Though inmates are ambivalent toward both types, they have more respect for the "tough," because the "ball buster"brings the "heat" (more surveillance and stricter enforcement of the rules) down on the whole inmate population. He violates the maxim, "don't cause unnecessary trouble." The one type that inmates unequivocally admire is the "real man," who exemplifies compliance with the convict code. He is able to "take it." He has strength. He exemplifies "masculine mannerisms and inward stamina" (p. 101) and "confronts his captors with neither subservience nor aggression" (p. 102). Sykes proposes that by responding to one another as "real men" (complying with the code), inmates reduce the pains of imprisonment and can achieve a sense of self-respect. They would thereby have no sense of duty toward the institutional rules and in turn would enact the patterns of deviant behavior he observed.[3]

In a more recent study, Garabedian follows Sykes by treating the code in terms of the social types that revolve around it. Using attitudinal items on an anonymous questionnaire submitted to a sample of inmates of a maximum security prison, Garabedian was able to detect the social types of "square Johns," "politicians," "right guys," and "outlaws." He reports a series of behaviors associated with the types that are similar to the patterns of deviant behavior detected at halfway house. Extent of participation in staff-sponsored programs, amount of contact with staff, knowledge of the therapeutic program of the institution, and numbers of rule violations committed all vary with social type. Similar to Sykes' findings, the rank order of compliance to staff's regulations and "hopes" was "square Johns," "politicians," "right guys, "and "outlaws." This finding indicates that the activities of nonparticipation in staff programs, not having contacts with staff, not having knowledge of the therapeutic programs, and committing rule violations were all associated with commitment to the code.

A further example of behaviors caused by the code is the open display of hostility toward staff which often occurs when inmates attend group therapy. Ohlin's *Sociology and the Field of Corrections* (1956) proposes that the act of going to therapy is viewed by nonparticipating inmates as violating those tenets of the code which prohibit contact with staff. In turn, those inmates put pressure on the inmate who goes to therapy "to reaffirm his continued allegiance and identification with the inmate value system. The participating inmate can handle this kind of pressure for a time by displaying conspicuous acts of aggression against authorities both within and outside the therapy group" (Ohlin, 1956: 36).

It appears, however, that this is not an easy solution. More typical is avoidance of therapy in the first place. Using an attitudinal device on a questionnaire to detect sentiments supportive of the code, studies find that those who most strongly support the code least frequently appear at group therapy sessions and that when they do participate, their involvement is superficial.

Other abbreviated accounts of behavior analyzable as produced through conformity to

[3]However, in another account of the same research in which Sykes contrasts "real men," "merchants," and "toughs," he finds that while all three types commit violations of prison rules, "toughs" do so at a higher rate than do "real men" and "merchants" (Sykes, 1956).

the code is available, but it only repeats the findings which have been cited.

SUMMARY AND IMPLICATIONS

Essentially the same code has been found in a variety of settings and has been utilized by sociologists to account for a variety of deviant behavior: violation of institutional rules, refusal to give information to officers, hostile gestures and talk toward officers, threats against officers, gambling, stealing from the institution, sharing stolen goods, engaging in homosexuality, avoidance of contact with staff, and avoidance of participation in group therapy programs. These behaviors have been traditionally analyzed as produced by compliance to the convict code. It has been found that these behaviors are prescribed by the code, or supported by the code in the sense that other inmates are prohibited from interfering or disapproving of the activity by maxims of the code, or they are encouraged by the code, since one shows his compliance with the code and loyalty to its underlying values by engaging in the deviant behavior.

46. The Language of Prison Life

ANTHONY GUENTHER

ONE OF THE CENTRAL CHARACTERISTICS OF SUB-cultures generally and prison society in particular is their distinctive language systems. Most human aggregates which endure long enough to develop a cultural history generate a terminology that is exclusive to its own purposes and group membership. . . .

Sociologists of language and anthropological linguists have suggested that language is probably the most important medium by which culture is transmitted. Its use among participants of any group, prisoners included, signifies how and why communication takes place. For this reason studies of prison systems often include a discussion of argot, usually as a description of its unique attributes. One authority, Joyce Hertzler, refers to the language of the prison as *cant*, which he considers:

"[A] more or less barbarous *secret* language used by the halfworld and the underworld . . . especially prison inmates, thieves, pickpockets, shoplifters, beggars, hoboes, card-sharpers, confidence men, swindlers, safe-crackers, drug addicts and drug traffickers, racketeers, gangsters, white slavers and prostitutes, and other criminal elements and their associates."[1]

Hertzler says further:

"These special terminologies include words used to refer to types of crime and criminals, to the techniques and tools used in their activities and the materials involved, and especially to the other categories of persons and the social institutions to which they become related in their nefarious activities—'fences,' the victims or customers, the law, the police."[2]

The earliest work on argot appears to have been done by Clemmer,[3] although earlier accounts of language systems among incarcerated persons may be found.[4] In his study Clemmer identified 1,063 words and terms which enjoyed common usage in the 1930s prison and classified them according to the following schema:[5]

[2]*Ibid.*, p. 329.

[3]Clemmer, *The Prison Community*, New York: Rinehart, 1958, pp. 88–100.

[4]See, for example, H. L. Mencken, *The American Language*, New York: Alfred A. Knopf, 1936, pp. 580–581. I am indebted to Mary Mays for her unpublished paper, "Prison Argot: Meaning and Function,"1973, in which she calls attention to Mencken's work. Of particular value is Mencken's reference to early sources on prison terminology, duplicated here for those who have an interest in the topic: Herbert Yenne, "Prison Lingo," *American Speech* (March, 1927); "Table Talk," *San Quentin Bulletin* (January, 1931); George Milburn, "Convicts' Jargon," *American Speech* (August, 1931); J. Louis Kuethe, "Can Cant," *Baltimore Evening Sun* (December 9, 1932); "A Prison Dictionary (Expurgated)," *American Speech* (October, 1933); and J. Louis Kuethe, "Prison Parlance," *American Speech* (February, 1934). A splendid work, largely neglected because it is an out-of-print and obscure document, is Noel Ersine, *Underworld and Prison Slang*. Upland, Indiana: A. D. Freese and Son, 1933. This source includes a commentary on argot and a listing of 1,403 terms.

[5]This is derived from Clemmer, *op. cit.*, Table VIII, p. 89.

▶SOURCE: *The Social Dimensions of a Penitentiary. Report to the National Institute of Law Enforcement and Criminal Justice (1975), unpublished mimeo. 5:81–87. Reprinted by permission of author.*

[1]Joyce O. Hertzler, *A Sociology of Language*, New York: Random House, 1965, p. 328.

Prison (equipment, authorities,
articles of daily commerce,
mental status, punishment,
sentence)   32.4%

Crime (technique, police, loot,
escape, guns)   30.1

Sex (homosexual, heterosexual)   10.9

Description of individuals   7.8

Body parts   5.5

Vagabondage   5.4

Drugs and narcotics   3.5

Alcohol   3.2

Gambling   1.2

In his discussion of prison argot Clemmer makes several observations which in part account for its development in prison: (1) the vocabulary is socially transmitted from resident offenders to newly-committed persons; (2) profanity, slang, and argot substitute for the limited vocabulary (especially adjectives) among many prisoners; (3) some terms convey elements of humor; (4) the use of uncommon language excluding others from participation is a familiar device for promoting group cohesion; and (5) jargon is a means of aggrandizing one's position and impressing others.[6]

Prison argot, then, appears to reflect the sentiments of criminal culture. Although the language system prevailing in a given prison may differ from those in other institutions or may not closely correspond with linguistic patterns in past years, the differences are largely a matter of degree. The reason for this has been aptly put by Stephenson and Scarpitti:

"Theoretical analysis has been directed largely to the social functions of argot. Analysts have ascribed to argot such functions as expression of solidarity, identification of in-group members, utilitarian symbolization of the complexities and subtleties of group life, exclusion of non-members, maintenance of secrecy, and veiled expressions of hostility."[7]

There is little reason to believe that the conditions of prison life which historically gave rise to its language structure have been dramatically altered. To be sure, many terms that had underworld origins and were assimilated by prison culture are rarely heard,[8] e.g., the *can* (police station), *punk* (bread), *big house* (penitentiary), *fish* (new prisoner), or to *crash out* (escape), to *get the book* or to *do it all* (life imprisonment), to *go stir-bug* (crazy), to *burn* or get the *hot seat* (electrocution). But it is probably a significant indicator of the separation of prison and society that a special vocabulary with its own nuances and overtones persists. There continue to be several categories of terms which refer to crime, law enforcement, criminal procedure, conviction, prison staff, institutional facilities, inmate personalities, and prison routine which are found in one form or another throughout prison systems.

Many of the actual terms which are in the daily usage of prisoners are obscene by community standards, and no small number are derisory. In both senses the world of incarceration is made out to be picturesque and unique; it is also a world of opposites—humor and tragedy, loyalty and subversion, value and worthlessness. Data on argot from the Atlanta penitentiary are similar in this respect to other works which have appeared recently.[9]

---

[6]*Ibid.*, p. 90.

[7]Richard M. Stephenson and Frank R. Scarpitti, "Argot in a Therapeutic Correctional Milieu," *Social Problems*, 15 (Winter, 1968), p. 384.

[8]Many words and terms, as Hertzler, *op. cit.*, p. 329 has shown, are absorbed into everyday vocabularies, thus no longer requiring explanation for most people: "trigger man," "muscle," to "hijack," "take for a ride," give the "third degree" or "bum rap."

[9]A glossary of prison terminology is found in Clemmer, *op. cit.*, Appendix B, pp. 330–336; three other accounts published in the last ten years are Giallombardo, *Society of Women*, New York: John Wiley & Sons, 1966, Appendix B, pp. 200–209; Fred T. Wilkinson (with Fred DeArmond), "Lingo of the Con Fraternity," *The Realities of Crime and Punishment: A Prison Administrator's Testament*, Springfield,

The obscene properties of prison language systems have been commented upon by many writers.[10] Terms which refer to sexual relations, whether homosexual or heterosexual, tend to be more crudely drawn than their counterparts outside. Thus to "cop a joint" or get a "head job" refers to fellatio, and "getting a little round-eye" is anal intercourse. A dish consisting of ground beef or chipped beef on toast served in the dining hall may be called "shit on a shingle." Old timers sometimes make nostalgic reference to "piss and punk" (bread and water) days when the diet in solitary confinement was restricted. But the expression whose blatant profanity can most often be encountered in the Atlanta penitentiary is "motherfucker." It is a term used ubiquitously by blacks, but also by many whites, in reference to staff, other inmates, physical objects and events. There are even gradations of motherfuckers.[11] Special significance is attached to the term as an instance of "doing the dozens" (insulting one's relatives or spouse), but the fact that it describes an incestuous act appears to mean little to confined felons.

Beginning with the commission of a crime, argot terms may be discerned at nearly every stage of the conviction and incarceration process. The offender takes a "fall" as a result of arrest by the "Feds." He "cops a plea" to a lesser offense, or one of a series of "counts" (charges) in exchange for partial immunity from prosecution. He is sentenced to a "bit" or "beef," and occasionally his time is "running wild" or "stacked" (two or more consecutive sentences). If he is confronted with problems while serving his sentence, he does "hard time;" those with

chronic problems say that prison is "like going through hell backwards." If he conducts himself according to regulations, thus avoiding homosexual liaisons and participating in rackets, or if he gets in trouble and is "burped" (discreetly handled) by an officer who does not want to issue a "shot" (disciplinary report), he may "make" parole. By doing most of his time he can "hit the streets" on "M.R." (mandatory release). Nearing release he "gets so short he can hardly walk." No one, however, aspires to a "back door parole" (dying in prison).

Inmates under ordinary circumstances interact with a large number of persons who are employed by the institution. Foremost among these is the "screw" or "hack" already described. Special needs of inmates are met by the "croaker" (doctor), the "shrink" or "bug doctor" (psychiatrist), and the "sky pilot" (minister).

A final important aspect of communication in the prison, apart from the vernacular, is nicknames. Identities at Atlanta consist formally of one's last name and a number. The close associations prisoners develop with one another will be on a first-name basis, with nicknames (unless preferred by the inmate) reserved for those who are known more superficially. Like nicknames in the home world, some are not designed for face-to-face usage. A few, such as "Red," "Slim," or "Shorty" are not very distinctive. The preponderance of nicknames among Atlanta prisoners are derived from one of three cues. The first group is based upon physical features or movements. Included are "Snake Eye," "Wide Track," "Grasshopper," "Jeep," "Peckernose," "Casper the Ghost," "Mr. Clean," and "Bad Eye." The second category takes into account distinctive personality features. Examples are "Revolutionary Red," "007" ("Double-oh-Seven"), "Time Clock," "Motor Mouth," and "Killer." Finally some nicknames are derived from presumed homosexual inclinations. A few illustrative cases are "Sweet Lips," "Big Mama," "The Asshole Bandit," "Honey Buns," and "Gwendolyn."

Missouri, 1972, pp. 239–248; and "Glossary" (compiled by Inmate Thomas Green), in Doe H. Chang and Warren B. Armstrong (eds.), *The Prison: Voices from the Inside*, Cambridge, Massachusetts: Schenkman, 1972, pp. 325–331.

[10] See Ersine, *op. cit.*, p. 7, and Clemmer, *op. cit.*, pp. 90–91.

[11] *Viz.*, (1) standard motherfucker; (2) double-barreled motherfucker; (3) nine-barreled motherfucker; and (4) *rotating* motherfucker.

47. Prison Rackets

ANTHONY GUENTHER

"I'M JUST UP FROM ATLANTA. THAT WAS A HOTEL, I'VE been in a lot worse. . . . But Atlanta was just fine. I ran two poker games . . . the guy who had the games liked me, so when he left he gave them to me. Now my partner has them. There's no money, it's all done in cigarettes. A guy may owe you forty or fifty boxes."[1]

Recent interest in the prisoner's market system[2] has brought to light its effect upon relationships among various sectors of the institution. From the moment of commitment to a penitentiary a new man will be thrust into a system of economic exchange in which his possessions, his commissary account—indeed, his own body—are subjected to the wants, needs and desires of others. Those who know how to do time quickly establish themselves as independent operators or find their niche in the exchange system. Those who are new to the penitentiary go through a period of reconnaissance even as they find themselves scrutinized by the inmate population. They discover that a Spartan existence is ahead for those who are not affluent when they enter the prison, but that oppor-

tunities for getting ahead financially are abundant. Almost no one in the institution needs to experience poverty, assuming, of course, he is willing to incur some possible costs. This section examines at close range the major types of "hustles" in the prison community and the artifacts of their operation.

CURRENCY, LOAN SHARKING AND STOREKEEPING

Since currency and coins are contraband in the prison an illicit medium of exchange arises to take their place. This medium is cigarettes, which appear to be a universal form of currency in total institutions. . . .

Williams and Fish[3] have pointed out that cigarettes come in three levels of buying power resembling denominations. Small purchases and minor favors can be repaid with individual cigarettes, moderately large purchases and slightly greater services can be secured with packs of twenty cigarettes, and large transactions can be made with a carton ("box") of ten packs.

Equally universal are the proclivities of inmates to borrow and loan cigarettes and to operate businesses of loaning "money" within the prison. A person who engages in these activities is referred to by Sykes and Messinger as a merchant or peddler who "exploits his fellow captives not by force but by manipulation and trickery, and who typically sells or trades goods that

▶SOURCE: *The Social Dimensions of a Penitentiary. Report to the National Institute of Law Enforcement and Criminal Justice (1975), unpublished mimeo. 7:64–71, 78–92. Reprinted by permission of the author.*

[1]M. Yanow, *Observations from the Treadmill*, New York: Viking, 1973, pp. 64–65.

[2]A very fine account of this marketplace is Heather Strange and Joseph McCrory, "Bulls and Bears in the Cellblock," *Society*, 11 (July/August, 1974), pp. 51–59. A more lengthy account is Vergil L. Williams and Mary Fish, *Convicts, Codes, and Contraband: The Prison Life of Men and Women*, Cambridge, Massachusetts: Ballinger, 1974.

[3]Williams and Fish, *op. cit.*, p. 55.

are in short supply."[4] Merchants, then, may operate a "store," usually from their cells, which supplies at inflated rates the goods ordinarily available from the commissary.[5] Credit is generally extended to prisoners who have drawn the full month's allotment from their commissary accounts. Although records of financial transactions pose a risk for the storekeeper, they are essential if the size of his operation is very large. A merchant may also engage in loan sharking, which works behind walls almost identically to its counterpart in the home world. The loan shark preys upon those who are unable to obtain credit elsewhere. In exchange for the risk he takes, the lender charges a widely known interest rate, often expressed as a "two for one," or a "three for two." The loan's duration is short, for example, a week or two at the end of which the borrower returns the principal and one hundred percent or fifty percent, respectively. To default on a loan in prison is not just economically inadvisable; it is often unhealthy as well. The inmate who cannot repay his loan at the end of the initial period is usually given an extension before he receives physical coercion. Men who owe others amounts they could not repay under the most relaxed conditions often request placement in segregation for protective custody. A storekeeper or loan shark in the penitentiary will hire enforcers to collect bad debts for him if his business is really professional. Experienced prison staff report that a sizeable proportion of the beatings quietly absorbed by inmates are caused by this system of usury. The following instance conveys the dangers attendant to purchasing beyond one's means. By providing information about a store, this inmate hopes his problem will be solved:

Dear Sir

I have borrow some cigarettes an other stuff from

Clayton Edwards, he lives in B Cellhouse and runs a store. Cookies he charges four or five pack [of cigarettes]. An coffy six pack. I did get this stuff an am willing to pay him for it but he tell me that I owes him double because I waited to long, that rates have gone up. And also said get out [inmate's name] before i put my knife in you. he has three books under his bed that he has peoples names an how much they owe him in them. You can pick them up right now. they are three little tablets like they used at the mill [industries]. Brown books them are. an you can see I don't owe him that much Sir. And I dont want to get hurt. He keep stuff in his locker (No. 7) and Billy Davis his home boy (No. 3) locker. an why cant everyone run a store if he can? You all have bust[ed] him in the Basement for running a store. they call him (skip) Clayton Edwards

(thank you sir, very very much sir). I am a white male. I live in B Cellhouse.[6]

If an inmate cannot or elects not to borrow money, there are numerous ways to earn it. Cigarettes are paid for a wide variety of services and for the supply of certain goods.[7] It will be informative to look at some of these in detail.

GAMBLING

Bets on the outcome of an event made between two inmates occur so often and are sufficiently innocuous that custodial staff take little notice. The troublesome forms of gambling which can produce serious incidents are large-scale bookmaking and betting in games of chance. A bookmaker at Atlanta makes up "pool tickets," which are sheets of paper listing the expected scores of impending sports events, and collects bets from interested speculators. He then holds his assets in a "bank" from which runners distribute payoffs to winners at the event's conclusion. Certain potential problems facing a banker can lead him to employ two kinds of personnel: "jiggers," who for a fee ensure that the book-

---

[4]Gresham M. Sykes and Sheldon Messinger, "The Inmate Social System," *Theoretical Studies in Social Organization of the Prison,* New York: Social Science Research Council, Pamphlet no. 15, 1960, p. 9.

[5]Predictably, "knocking lockers" is a gang activity which selects a locker used for a store and burglarizes it.

[6]Note dated December 30, 1969, U.S. Penitentiary, Atlanta.

[7]For an exhaustive description of these as they operate at the Rahway, New Jersey prison see Strange and McCrory, *op. cit.*, pp. 55–58.

making operation will avoid official notice, and enforcers, who ensure that the "bank" is secure even if the "banker" is placed in segregation or is hospitalized.

Prisoners, of course, are permitted to have decks of playing cards and these, in conjunction with "poker chips" made of cardboard by a silk-screen process (forms of nuisance contraband) are used in such games as poker, tonk and acey-deucy. The prudent gambler will hire a jigger whether he runs a card game, a dice game, or some other competition involving chance. Comparatively few prisoners are charged with misconduct for gambling, and it is rare for a gambler to be intimidated. Those who are compulsive gamblers often default on their financial responsibilities and suffer the usual retributions.

Gambling plays an important role for prisoners related to its function as a removal activity. Intelligent betting on a sporting event requires knowledge about the participants and their competition which is obtained from the outside world. A football fan who is the Washington Redskins' most unflappable cellblock spectator may spend several hours each week reading or debating about his team. In this way he derives many of the home world satisfactions which are otherwise denied him. Prison employees are not opposed to wagering among inmates for moral reasons; they are accustomed to the trouble, however, which often signals failure to collect a bad debt.

PORNOGRAPHY

Prison officials find it increasingly difficult to enforce regulations concerning erotic material because definitions of eroticism and pornography are highly subjective. In the absence of guidelines established by judicial authority, officers find themselves confiscating materials which *they* think are pornographic. The rule of thumb followed by most draws a distinction between "normal" heterosexual art, photography and literature as opposed to characterizations of

homosexuality, lesbianism, transvestism, flagellation, sodomy or autoeroticism. Nuisance contraband, then, would consist of items which pertain to these "perversions." Among the most frequently confiscated materials are three-ring notebooks which contain cut-out photographs of nude women pasted onto sheets, "pornographic" novels ("Blow the Man Down," "Campus Stud Lust"), and home-drawn cartoon books. The latter have two curiously consistent features. Although they usually depict heterosexual intercourse, some comment by one of the participants will often indicate that homosexual intercourse would have been better. For example, in one cartoon booklet about twenty pages are devoted to a male and female copulating while the former engages in a variety of weightlifts. On the last page, following an extended climax, he says to her, "Not bad, for a *woman*." The second unsual feature of cartoon books is a gross enlargement of male genitalia. If it can be assumed that imprisoned men had active sex lives before incarceration, the emphasis placed upon virility and potency in original drawings would seem to affirm those needs.

Cartoons, novels and three-ring notebooks are referred to as "fuck books" and are available to inmates on a rental basis. For instance, a notebook may be kept in one's cell overnight for two packs. The likelihood of an assault over debts incurred through rental of these materials is exceedingly rare. What operates to define "pornography" in the prison as contraband is an attempt by staff to discourage licentiousness. They operate not as agents of any tribunal or legal authority but as moral entrepreneurs.[8] Observations made at the Atlanta penitentiary revealed important differences between supervisors with respect to their feelings about "obscene" materials. During one quarter, erotic literature was readily available, and few if any "fuck books" were confiscated. The next quarter when job rotations produced a different set of

[8]For a discussion of this role, see Howard S. Becker, *Outsiders: Studies in the Sociology of Deviance*, New York: The Free Press of Glencoe, 1963, pp. 147–163.

Lieutenants who oversee the housing units, decorations, literature and booklets were seized in frequent raids. One of the hypocrisies of this system is that "good pornography" confiscated by officers usually made its way to the Lieutenant's office for "inspection" and eventually was recirculated back to the cellblock.

Many prison staff feel ambivalent about pornography in the institution. While they recognize that ostentatious display of nudes may offend some persons, particularly visitors and tour groups, and therefore may be in "bad taste," they assert that sexual fantasy is preferable to sexual expression in a monosexual environment.

*

"HOMEBREW" BEER AND DRUG TRAFFICKING

Although alcoholic beverages are technically central nervous system (CNS) depressants and, therefore, qualify as drugs, it is useful to discuss these two topics separately. Alcohol is legitimately consumed in the general society on such a wide scale that many drinking occasions have become institutionalized. Its use in the facilitation of social gatherings, in the reduction of anxiety and as a ritual (e.g., the "TGIF" party) is well known outside the prison. It would be reasonable to assume that alcohol consumption among imprisoned felons functions as a compensation for the deprivations they perceive.

Drinking in prison appears to take place on a small scale, principally for two reasons. First, commercial distilled spirits are almost unobtainable because someone would have to arrange for their passage through a security checkpoint. Even the smallest container, a half-pint, is bulky and requires destruction after it is consumed. Second, the availability of other drugs which are easily concealed and may have greater potency makes drinking less attractive. Nevertheless, the manufacture, distribution and consumption of "homebrew" beer is a thriving industry in many institutions, and it demands constant attention from correctional officers.

Homebrew is made by combining sugar, yeast, water and some kind of fruit, fruit peelings, or potato peelings and storing them in a warm place for a few days' fermentation ("working off"). Yeast is usually the critical component, since sugar can be "liberated" from the dining hall and the basic substance for fermentation is readily obtainable. Homebrew, often called "jack," "juice," "buck," "hootch," or just "brew," is made from milk, fruit cocktail, prunes ("pruno"), figs, raisins ("raisin-jack"), apples ("apple-jack"), potato peelings, or apricots. When working off, the solution emits a distinctive odor. The major problem confronted by a homebrew specialist, therefore, is to find a place which is preferably warm but also secure from discovery by officers. Large "stingers" (heating coils) which heat the mixture and thereby hasten fermentation are popular contraband. Specially-engineered stashes for homebrew,[9] as we saw earlier, are created by Atlanta inmates. Williams and Fish report similarly that Alabama state prisoners seal the mixture in plastic bags which they place between their legs in bed at night for warmth.[10] Drinking homebrew beer more often results in sickness than euphoria, but many prisoners feel that their efforts are worthwhile if they become mildly intoxicated.

Prison custodial staff confiscate homebrew stashes and collections of other drugs in large quantities just before weekends and prior to holidays. Note, for example, the frequency of shakedowns and disciplinary actions related to homebrew and drugs at Christmas and New Year's, 1968–1969:[11]

December 18   Ten pounds of sugar found in cell 5–9.

December 19   Mr. Curry found . . . a bottle of pills in A [cellhouse] basement. Mr. Disson took four capsules off Franklin 66091. Franklin was placed in segregation.

[9]Steel pans fabricated to exact dimensions are sometimes made to fit in the hollow space underneath cell lockers.

[10]Williams and Fish, *op. cit.*, p. 72.

[11]Derived from the Lieutenant's Log, U.S. Penitentiary, Atlanta, December 18, 1968 through January 1, 1969.

December 20 Approximately 4½ gallon of peach brandy (homemade) found in the storeroom of the kitchen. Stone 78275 placed in administrative segregation, drunk on pills. Three needles, two syringes, and one gallon brew found in B basement.

December 21 Twenty gallons of brew found in B cellhouse, cell 8–11. Approximately twenty gallon brew found in cell 9–11. Small amount of glue for "sniffing" found in cell 9–15.

December 22 Five gallon of brew found in cell 9–12. Thirty gallons of brew, a case of dried figs . . . found in shakedown of mattress factory.

December 24 Binns 49373 and Slatterly 74516 placed in administrative segregation for drinking. Approximately five gallons of "brew" found in cells 5–1 and 5–2.

December 25 Small amount of brew in 4–8. Real nice Xmas evening this watch. The inmates must have used up all their booze and pills.

December 26 A search of E cellhouse revealed two syringes and two hypo needles. A small portion of what might be marijuana was turned over to Mr. Follett for identification.

December 27 Some rumors that pills were received in the institution today. Unable to determine if they were received. Five pounds of sugar and one needle and syringe found in D-4 dormitory. McKinley 62219 and Robertson 81711 placed in administrative segregation (drunk). Trash baskets full of brew found in cells 5–6 and 6–8.

December 28 One gallon of brew found in cell 5–8.

December 29 Mr. Yeager found two inmates holding a five gallon bag of brew back of a ventilator in C cellhouse. Fifteen pounds of sugar and a hot water bottle full of brew found in B cellhouse. Six gallon jugs of brew found in vegetable room electric panel.

December 30 One gallon brew found in 8–4. Two large bags of brew picked up in A cellhouse made of raisins and raw bread dough.

January 1 Approximately nine gallons brew found in B cellhouse cut-off [utility corridor] in a special bag hanging with the utility pipes.

Correctional staff have a great deal of ambivalence toward homebrew. On the one hand, they may well appreciate the enjoyment which can be derived from a drinking occasion. This is reflected in comments made while dumping confiscated homebrew down the drain: "It's a shame we have to ruin this fellow's Christmas spirits"; "It don't smell like much, but if I was doing time I'd need a jolt every so often."[12] On the other hand, veteran officers recall the number of times they have had to confront an inmate who had been drinking, became progressively antagonistic, and finally assaulted someone in the vicinity. From a staff viewpoint, homebrew production and consumption are serious rule infractions because some inmates, not otherwise behavior problems, become assaultive when their inhibitions are reduced. Consider, for example, these episodes:

"A 222 call from F-ward in the hospital brought ten officers on the run. An inmate there named Goodlett was wrestling with two hospital employees and had partially torn their clothes. Goodlett was finally subdued by eight officers at which point he became incontinent. Other inmates in his work area stated that he had been drinking homebrew most of the morning."[13]

"Inmate Tyberson 27222 became inebriated and went beserk in B cellhouse on the evening shift. He was swinging at any inmate near him until restrained and held down by other prisoners. Then he was taken to the hospital and placed in restraints until he sobered up and calmed down."[14]

Since homebrew must be concocted in small quantities and is usually made for one's own enjoyment, it does not often exhibit the properties of a racket. An occasional "Homebrew King"

[12]Field notes, U.S. Penitentiary, Atlanta, December 23, 1969.
[13]Field notes, U.S. Penitentiary, Atlanta, January 7, 1970.
[14]Field notes, U.S. Penitentiary, Atlanta, December 12, 1969.

will appear in Atlanta's population, but hustling "brew" for profit is not very rewarding.

Some Atlanta officers and their supervisors believe that the appearance of homebrew is a healthy sign, since there is presumably an inverse relationship between homebrew production and drug trafficking in the institution. If searches for "brew" are unproductive, suspicion mounts that drugs are available in its place.

The prisoner who is determined to get "high" may select a number of solutions or substances for this purpose. He may seek access to lemon extract or nutmeg for a special effect, or he may "sniff" gasoline, ditto fluid, carbon tetrachloride (now prohibited in many prisons), lacquer thinner, or glue. For the drug user who is not squeamish, a solution made of concentrated coffee ("instant" or "freeze-dried") boiled down to a sludge and injected intravenously ("mainlined") is reported to induce a substantial "flash."[15]

Drug trafficking is considered a major form of misconduct in the penitentiary; drugs and their paraphernalia are classified as serious contraband. The demand for drugs makes it a profitable enterprise which in itself would explain the degree of staff attention given to it. But the fact that most drug supply systems involve *collusion* between those inside the walls with persons outside adds a special dimension to the problem. Aside from drugs stolen from the hospital (a comparatively rare event at Atlanta), most trafficking occurs when prisoners smuggle drugs supplied by a confederate past the security check points, arrange to have them concealed in shipments or on transportation vehicles traveling through the wall, have them brought into the visiting room, or conspire with an employee to bring them in. Few acts by a staff member are thought to be more reprehensible than supplying drugs to the inmates.

Several means have been devised for surreptitiously getting drugs into the prison. A "drop" is often made consisting of a package small enough to be picked up by a minimum custody prisoner working on the reservation. He then throws it over the wall at a prearranged spot, inserts it in a package or vehicle passing through the east gate, or conceals it on his body, anticipating that the officer routinely shaking him down as he reenters the institution will not discover it.

Another plan calls for a visitor to bring drugs to the prison in a very small plastic bag or tube-shaped receptacle.[16] In the course of his visit, the inmate takes the bag and swallows it, or takes the cylinder and inserts it in his rectum. A strip-search at the end of his visit usually proceeds uneventfully and the prisoner can then recover the package in his quarters. The occasional prisoner who is suspected of concealing drugs in this fashion may be removed to the hospital where fluoroscopic examination is made or a "finger-wave" (rectal inspection) performed to verify its presence.

Yet a third technique involves concealment of a package smuggled into the visiting room where it will be picked up by a member of the inmate cleanup crew later. A typical case here is:

"On March 24 information was received of an attempt to introduce contraband pills into the institution through the visiting room. The pills (one hundred 'black beauties') were found under the sandwich machine in the visiting room as we were informed. The package was placed back where it was found, minus the pills, in an unsuccessful effort to apprehend the pickup [man]."[17]

One of the reasons why drug hustles have their appeal is the comparative ease of conceal-

---

[15]Darvon was manufactured for some years in a capsule containing buffer powder and a tiny bead. Referred to by inmates as a "time bomb," this particle was put in solution and injected for extraordinary intoxication.

[16]Favorite containers are a standard "Benzedrex" nasal inhaler filled with drugs or a "finger-stall" made by cutting the finger from a rubber glove, filling it with tablets or capsules and closing the end with a rubber band. Either of these coated with a lubricant such as Vaseline can then be inserted in the rectum.

[17]Memorandum, U.S. Penitentiary, Atlanta, March 25, 1972.

ing and transporting them. Heroin, for example, can be brought into the institution in a small, flat packet and later be "cut" with a number of substances, placed in "papers" or "one-shots," and distributed to users. The advantage of packaging drugs in foil or paper packets, of course, is their ease of disposal, especially in the commode, if a shakedown is imminent. Most inmates, as this episode demonstrates, avoid carrying drugs on their persons:

"I received information from Lieutenant Willington this subject [Oliver 57893] had some form of narcotic in his possession. Officers Jones, Scranton, Phillips, Mumford and I went to D basement to search for this contraband. As Mr. Phillips and I approached Oliver's stall [cubicle], he stepped out. I stopped him and strip searched him there and found nothing on him. I went into his stall and searched a brown paper bag that was being used for a trash container. I found a Kent cigarette pack with an assortment of contraband pills and capsules and a white powder substance wrapped in gray cellophane. This package was found at approximately 2:50 p.m. this date. It was turned over to Lieutenants Willington and Burcham."[18]

An incredible array of drugs is found in prison settings. They range from those which induce mild intoxication or sedation to some which create psychological or physical dependency. A listing of some drugs[19] encountered at the Atlanta penitentiary in the last five years is found in Table I.

Drug trafficking in the prison receives about the same reaction by correctional staff as it is given in the outside community by law enforcement authorities. Correctional institutions experience violence from drug activity, e.g., homicides, overdose deaths, and drug-related suicides, which in the minds of staff is ample justification for its prohibition. The drug business and its profit potential are also likely to produce secondary problems, such as employee complicity, intimidation and favoritism. A closer look at drug distribution in the Atlanta penitentiary will show how this process operates.

Although no Atlanta inmates are likely to remain addicted to a drug after commitment by the court, it is theoretically possible to "score" intermittently over a relatively long period. For those who were intimately connected with the drug scene outside, the opiates are perhaps most sought after. "Drug busts" in the penitentiary reveal paraphernalia similar to that found outside, such as a spoon or bottle cap for cooking the solution, eyedroppers or disposable syringes and needles for injection, and material for a tourniquet. Paraphernalia associated with marijuana or hashish smoking are conventional pipes, water pipes, cigarette papers and "roach" (butt) holders. Heroin confiscated in Atlanta has been found to have twenty percent purity, but most "papers" contain three to five percent heroin.

Before the virtual disappearance of amphetamines from the pharmaceutical market, black beauties, footballs and L. A. turnarounds[20] were among the most frequently confiscated drugs at Atlanta. In recent years, these have been replaced by the barbiturates, while hallucinogenic and other drugs of experimentation are rarely found.

Most drugs are quite expensive even by street standards, and the "going price" varies with the supply. By way of illustration, at one time during the field research for this project, a single black beauty was worth a carton and a half of cigarettes. Heroin in large quantities is sometimes said to be worth "several human lives" if it falls into the wrong hands. Even by the most conservative estimates (authorities are prone to gross exaggeration when calculating the "street" value of confiscated drugs), correctional staff in

---

[18]Memorandum, U.S. Penitentiary, Atlanta, February 4, 1970.

[19]Excluded are alcohol and toxic vapors, which have already been discussed.

[20]These references are based in the first two cases upon physical appearance of the capsules. The third is a favorite of truck drivers who can hypothetically drive a tractor-trailer from the east coast to Los Angeles, turn around and drive back nonstop after ingesting one capsule.

Table I. Some Drugs Found at the Atlanta Penitentiary

Drug Type	Specimen Recovered	Pharmacology	Street and Prison Names
Opiates	Heroin "one-shots" or "papers"	Central Nervous System (CNS) Depressant	Smack, Shit, Dope, H, Junk
Cocaine	Cocaine "one-shots" or "papers"; vial of powder	Stimulant or Anesthetic	Coke, Snow
Marijuana/Hashish	Cigarettes; loose seeds, leaves, stems and flowering tops; foil packets of hashish in brown chunks	Intoxicant	Joints, Sticks, Reefers; Grass, Pot, Hash
Hallucinogens	LSD tablets, sugar cubes	Hallucinogen	Acid
	STP ("Serenity, Tranquility, Peace") liquid ampule	Hallucinogen	STP
Barbiturates	Sodium seconal capsules, Tuinal capsules, Pamine PB tablets, Nembudonna capsules, Nembutal capsules	CNS Depressant	Red Birds, Rainbows, Red Devils, Yellow Jackets, Blue Devils, Christmas Trees
Nonbarbiturate Sedative-Hypnotics and Minor Tranquilizers	Cortrax tablets, Darvon capsules	Tranquilizer without CNS depression	None
	Chloral hydrate liquid	Sedative for sleep	In combination with alcohol: "Mickey Finn" or knock-out drops
	Valium ampules	Anti-anxiety tranquilizer	None
Amphetamines	Methamphetamine powder, Dexedrine LA tablets, Obedrine LA (long-action) tablets, Dexamyl spansules, Biphetamine and Biphetamine-T (Tuazone) capsules	CNS Stimulant, mood elevator	Speed, Dexies, Hearts, Bennies, Black Beauties, Pep Pills, Footballs, L. A. Turnabouts, Co-Pilots, Uppers

Atlanta destroy thousands of dollars worth of drugs seized as contraband each year, usually by flushing them down the commode.

The characteristics of drug hustling or racketeering are intricate and not often clearly understood by staff. Sometimes all they know is that a prisoner dies from a homicidal attack and that snitches allege he failed to produce revenue for a shipment of drugs. Few cases of drug-related misconduct are prosecuted for lack of a suspect, witnesses, or even evidence. The drug dealer usually covers himself with protective layers of other personnel who maintain an outside source, arrange the means of importing supplies, create a distribution system, divert official surveillance, and collect debts indirectly. If drug trafficking in the institution flourishes, as it does sporadically at Atlanta, it almost certainly indicates financing ("bank-rolling") by sources beyond the walls. Arrangements for payments to outside participants in this network can be handled by visitors, by unscrupulous attorneys, or by a compromised employee.

PERSONALIZED SERVICES

The final hustle found in the penitentiary delivers personalized services to inmates. Many of these are innocuous and represent attempts to earn cigarette money. At an established rate of two packs, for example, one's clothes are given special attention in the laundry or one receives a custom haircut in the barber shop. Many prisoners ("runners") offer to deliver goods, ranging from weapons, escape equipment and drugs, to pornography, outdated newspapers or magazines, and sandwiches. For the risk he takes being caught en route with contraband (sometimes concealed in books with cut-out interiors) or being out-of-bounds, the runner collects a fee. In this same category are jiggers who maintain lookout for an officer or divert his attention for a fee.

More sophisticated hustles delivering personalized services operate within walls. There are "jailhouse lawyers" who, for modest retain-

ers (two "boxes" or more), will instruct a fellow prisoner in how to write a writ or will assist with his appeal. Inmate seers place their contraband advertisements in the cellblocks, offering to tell fortunes, remove curses, or confer a "hex" on enemies. Fortune-telling is popular because many things in a prisoner's life are problematic: whether he will make parole, when he will be released, whether his wife will await his return. Inmate prophets sometimes offer their services to staff, as in the case of a prisoner who devised his own "computerized" glimpse of the future. A "cop-out" bearing matrices of numbers and symbols (311 311 311 1–1–1 ∅∅∅) made this offer:

Lt. Ramey—

Please read [these symbols] computorially. And when you are alone.

If you wish to take a course from me I'll make you better than the Banker who I've robbed. Thank you, Lt.

E. Bledsoe 69871[21]

The "protection" racket is another means by which some inmates earn an income. Exploitation is most likely among new, "weak" prisoners, those who are disabled or afflicted, and those who are elderly. Most inmates who come to Atlanta know better than to divulge their financial holdings, but subtle means can be used to determine who can afford "services." Sometimes a prisoner will be told that he should "take out insurance" against "accidents" or for protection from "the psychopaths, killers, and perverts" in the population. Alternatively, he will be given to understand that a specific offender or a group of prisoners dislikes him and plans to take action. Extortion usually succeeds because most inmates will not seek assistance from the staff, but even if they do, protective custody or transfer is the only alternative. As one officer explained: "We can't do much for a convict who gets all 'jammed up.' Every third one of them's

[21] Inmate letter, U.S. Penitentiary, Atlanta, March 3, 1970.

got somebody after his ass and if we locked them all up for protection we'd need a segregation building big as this institution."[22]

Occasionally an ingenious hustle will surface, causing no small amount of conflict among staff. A good case in point is the following:

"Coming before the adjustment committee was a 'shot' on Howery 72448. Several officers present were surprised that Howery had gotten picked up on a contraband 'rap' since he reportedly dabbled in nothing less than narcotics.

The contraband in question was examined at great length. It consisted of a cigar box overflowing with magnifying glasses, sandpaper, pliers, screwdrivers, watch crystals, a container of banana oil, containers of shellac, aluminum foil, three spoons, and several ballpoint pen replacement cartridges.

Howery's explanation to the committee was that he had been given permission to repair watches. He produced a certificate authorizing his service and bearing the signatures of a Captain and an Associate Warden (both since transferred to other institutions). He was told the case would be taken under advisement.

In later discussion it was revealed that the present Captain had Howery's cell shaken down and personally wrote the 'shot.' Two Lieutenants then tried to 'lawyer' for Howery by arguing that he was going to hustle cigarettes one way or another and repairing watches was better than having him dealing drugs.

Howery was later given ninety days suspended segregation, his certificate was taken and his tool kit was destroyed."[23]

[22]Field notes, U.S. Penitentiary, Atlanta, January 22, 1970.

[23]Memoranda, Adjustment Committee transcript, and field notes, U.S. Penitentiary, Atlanta, October 27, 1969.

48. Women's Prison Families

VERGIL L. WILLIAMS
MARY FISH

THE WOMAN ENTERING PRISON FOR THE FIRST time faces a severe shock and then a period of painful adjustment. The newly incarcerated woman experiences a variety of feelings—anger, hate, deprivation, anxiety, futility, and loss of identity. Her experiences upon being convicted of a crime and imprisoned are a series of nightmares. Even the removal of the new inmate's personal possessions is an act carrying meaning beyond the simple process of taking away a quantity of commodities. It destroys some of the woman's self-identity or self-image. This removal of personal possessions is a deeply depriving act. A woman's clothes, her jewelry, her shoes, and especially her necessary purse are extensions of her personality. When these items are abruptly confiscated, a part of her is taken away.

The abruptness of this transition is described by Sarah Harris as she relates the experience of four women entering the former New York City House of Detention for Women. When their purses were abruptly taken away during the booking process, one of the women became quite disturbed and began to plead for some of the items in her purse. The matron refused to give her any of the cosmetics in the handbag, her prescription pills, or even her glasses. The prospect of getting along without her glasses was overwhelming to the woman because she

could not see anything without them. After some hysteria and a good deal of pleading, the woman was allowed to keep her glasses.[1]

The admission process becomes even more demoralizing for the woman as it proceeds. The procedures of admission into the prison include actions that humiliate, debase, and mortify the newly arrived. Harris, in describing the continuation of the admission procedures, describes the feelings of the four women as they are ordered to strip and shower before being subjected to a rectal search by another inmate. None of the four women had ever experienced such extensive invasions of their privacy.[2]

The woman newly arrived in prison spends time in an orientation section. After being told the rules and regulations of the institution, she is required to make some sort of adjustment to the fact that her freedom is gone and that the prison is to be her home. Separation from her family, her husband or lover, and her children will cause the most pain. But the absence of privacy,[3] the lack of a social life, and the complete removal of male companionship intensifies the impact of being locked away. Self-respect begins to disappear. She will be forced to live with women that she may dislike, but her feelings do not matter. For a short period of time, the shock

[1] Sara Harris, *Hellhole* (New York: E. P. Dutton, 1967), pp. 25–26.
[2] *Ibid.*, p. 26.
[3] Creighton Brown Burnham, *Born Innocent* (Englewood Cliffs, N.J.: Prentice-Hall, 1958), pp. 92–93.

▶SOURCE: *Convicts, Codes and Contraband. Cambridge, Mass.: Ballinger Publishing Co., 1974. Pp. 99–113. Reprinted by permission.*

of being in prison probably numbs the impact of prison life. However, unless her sentence is short or in the unlikely event that she can maintain close contact with her family and friends on the outside, the prison will soon become her world.

Incarcerated women adjust to their new lives in different ways. Esther Heffernan, in *Making It in Prison: The Square, The Cool, and The Life*, describes three basic reactions: (1) The square is a noncriminal who, perhaps in a moment of uncontrolled rage, murdered a husband who had been physically and mentally abusive for years. She strives to earn the respect of her sister inmates and officers by focusing on the code of her home town. She wants to be a "good Christian woman." (2) The recidivist prostitute, shoplifter, pusher and/or user of drugs epitomizes the life group, who represent over 50 percent of the inmate population. Prison life becomes important and meaningful to them.[4] To stand firm against prison authority and what it stands for, as the garment workers' local labor organizer speaks out against Butte Knitting Company, is regarded as meritorious. (3) The sophisticated, professional offender—the cool—is from the underground world of organized crime. With aloofness, she dispassionately manipulates her environment, but seldom truly participates in prison life because she is merely visiting for a time.[5] She has prestige, power, and wealth in prison. She "has it all together."

Prison life is not easily dissected. Women, as men, select different patterns of adjustment. Yet regardless of the role the new inmate will play, it rejects her and forgets her. Within a few weeks, the female offender adjusts to her new environment. She learns to accept the prison as home. She will begin to be a part of prison life—to make friends and a new life for herself. At first fearful of the guards and some of the inmates, she begins to slide into her new social world comprised of the sister inmates with whom she lives and works.[6]

PRISON FAMILIES

Organization and Roles

The social organization of correctional institutions where women are placed is centered around a family system. The array of family oriented roles is extensive. It includes father, mother, brothers and sisters, aunts and uncles, and grandmothers and grandchildren.[7] Because of different characteristics, different inmates will play specific roles; for example, the young first offender might be the baby sister in a family unit and elder long-timer could be the grandmother or grandfather. The extent to which the roles are internalized and acted out by each family member is impressive. In the New York House of Detention, one woman called "Granny" had a reputation for having a clean house. Her actions, described in detail by another prisoner clearly explain why this reputation was earned.[8]

"After she removed her furniture she would carry a pail of boiling water, reeking of disinfectant, and go down on her hands and knees with a brush and scrub every inch of the floor, a process similar to scrubbing the sidewalk. Next she would take a new pail of water and the odiferous antiseptic and sterilize her walls, plunge both hands and a big rag in the toilet bowl and scour that, and finally open the corridor windows and vigorously shake the ragged scraps of carpeting that served to cover a few inches of her floor. Every couple of weeks all her flopping shower curtains would be hauled down and others, stiffly starched, would take their place. This type of cleaning gave her a community reputation equivalent to that of a middle-class suburban matron who is active in church groups, entertains well, and is famous for her apple pies."

---

[4]Esther Heffernan, *Making It in Prison: The Square, The Cool, and The Life,* (New York: John Wiley, 1972), pp. 41 and 145.

[5]*Ibid.*, pp. 146 and 158–159.

[6]Joanna Kelley, *When the Gates Shut* (London: Longmans, Green, 1967), p. 31.

[7]James V. Bennet, *I Chose Prison* (New York: Alfred A. Knopf, 1970), pp. 138–139.

[8]Virginia McManus, *Not For Love* (New York: G. P. Putnam's Sons, 1960), p. 227.

Not all family members act out their roles with the unquestioned devotion and enthusiasm of Granny, but the roles are played and the members do interact as a family unit. A new inmate most likely will be asked to join a family group and will serve her sentence as a member of a family—a daughter, a sister, or, if she is serving a long term, she may eventually become a family mother or father. Centering most of her prison life activities around the family, she will eat with her family, watch television with them, and sit with them at special functions. If it can be arranged, the family will live together in the same cottage or dormitory, but the family structure is preserved even if the individual members are scattered throughout the institution. Of course, some prison families will be extremely close knit and others loosely structured.[9]

Prison families attempt to act as much like families on the outside as they can under the circumstances, which at best are constraining. In times of stress and crisis, it is the family structure that stands as a bulwark against threats posed by the rigors of prison life. The prison family also serves as the social unit through which the inmates find a relationship with other families and inmates. With the help of the family, the inmate orients to her incarceration, lives through prison marriages and divorces, goes about her daily work and acquires illicit goods and services. Due to their very nature, prison marriages are not lasting, but the structure of the family unit remains as a stable reference point in the social world of the women's prison. The female prisoner, through her participation in the social framework of the family unit, experiences relationships that the institution would otherwise not provide.

The daily activities of the family are framed by the family role perceptions that exist in the free society. Prison parents assume that one of the important tasks to be accomplished is the socialization of their siblings. Parents are assumed to be wiser than children and worthy of the children's respect. Children are taught how to live and survive in the prison; they are given advice about romance and marriage prospects; and they are told how to go about getting a parole. Rose Giallombardo provides some examples of this type of advice being given by parents to socialize their children.[10]

"Keep your nose clean and stay out of trouble. The officers are on one side and the inmates on the other and never the two shall meet. You say to them what you don't care that they know. They've got the keys. They've got a job to do. They lock doors and unlock them. They go home. They don't really care about us as people.". . .

"Don't put your business in the streets. Don't tell all the inmates your business, but act hep. You should be discreet about important matters.". . .

"Sandy comes to me for advice mostly about studs that kite her. She'll get a kite and she'll come to me and ask me, "Pop, should I write?" And I tell her, "Yes if the guy means what he says and isn't jivey." I tell her, it's not right to go whoring around. "Pick one guy and stick to him, but don't go whoring around."

The inmate can share her heartaches, frustrations, anger, sadnesses, and disappointments with the family members. But family members also argue and fight about the same problems that families on the outside quarrel about. For example, a kid brother may be perceived to be lazy and living off the generosity of the other family members. Siblings become jealous of one another. A daughter who misbehaves can humiliate the family.

Of course, a unisexual family cannot reproduce; even so, the family structure is continually changing because inmate-members are paroled and new inmates are accepted into the family. When a key figure like Granny is paroled, everyone pitches in to find a sterling replacement. While unisexual marriages and divorces occur, once the family roles are accepted, they become binding. The free world taboo against

[9]Rose Giallombardo, *Society of Women: A Study of a Women's Prison* (New York: John Wiley, 1966), p. 89, pp. 165–189.

[10]*Ibid.*, pp. 166–167.

incest is observed in the prison family. However, rules and taboos are broken on the inside as they are on the outside. An incestuous relationship may have to be overlooked occasionally.[11] The family roles do sometimes change: a couple who have divorced may assume a brother and sister relationship or an individual who has been playing a female role may switch to a male role.

Economic Organization of the Family

Although female inmates are allowed to spend $15 to $20 a month at the institution commissary for amenities of life, not all prisoners have access to such relatively large sums. Commissary items available for purchase generally include items like cookies, cigarettes, candy, shower caps, curlers, lipstick, face cream, nail polish, and shampoo.[12] In some prisons, inmates are allowed to receive money from the outside for commissary purchases; seldom are offenders allowed to receive packages or gifts other than money except at Christmas. Even at Christmas the types of presents that may be received are carefully specified. Yet poverty is necessarily a relative concept and the standard of living that the prisoners were accustomed to on the outside usually was not very grand. Chances are good that the offenders did not play golf at the Heritage Hill Country Club or engage Jerome of Exclusive Decor to refurbish their dining room and den every two years.

Still, goods and services available through legal channels in the prison are limited, leaving the inmates at least with the feeling that they are poverty-stricken.[13] In women's institutions inmates can steal institutional supplies, go into business for themselves or hustle other girls for commissary goods. Those inmates assigned desirable jobs, perhaps in the warden's office or in the kitchen, can pilfer state goods quite easily and can supply official information. And there

usually is a local tradesman or guard that can be bribed to bring in an order, which may include the most recent issue of *True Story*.[14]

Female and male prisoners are equally ingenious in exploiting the prison environment to better their standard of living. Drugs are stolen from the infirmary, food from the kitchen and dining room, and clothing and cleaning fluid from the laundry. As in prisons for men, services are performed·and manufacturing takes place. Florrie Fisher recalls the time they "made hooch in the supply closet."[15]

"We got the ingredients by stealing what we could, depending on where we worked. The kitchen help got potatoes, the ones in the hospital boosted alcohol, and the table setters got sugar.

"Back behind the closet door we could hear it going 'glug, glug, glug,' and it sounded great. We must have left it just an hour too long, though, for suddenly the whole thing blew up, spewing sour-smelling liquid and pieces of potato all over the walls and ceiling, the mops, brooms and buckets kept in the closet."

Not all prisoners are able to enjoy the benefits of illegal economic goods, other than a stale cookie from the dining room now and then or a nip from a rap buddy's (conversation partner) home brew on New Year's Day. Certain types of inmates are not allowed by the inmate community to participate in the illicit economy regardless of their financial condition. These are the low status inmates—snitchers, inmate cops, and occasional squares. By reason of the fact that these inmates disobey the code, they are pushed away when it is time to share the scarce illegal goods that circulate in the prison.[16] To carry on a flourishing illegal business requires a certain amount of secrecy and the social types of inmate cop, snitchers, and squares cannot be trusted.

The family is the primary economic unit in the female prison. The family unit cooperates in both the stealing and manufacturing of illicit

---

[11]*Ibid.*, pp. 172–173.

[12]*Ibid.*, pp. 119–120.

[13]F. E. Haynes, "The Sociological Study of the Prison Community," *The Journal of Criminal Law and Criminology* 39 (November–December 1948): 439, and Giallombardo, p. 97.

[14]Burnham, pp. 112–113.

[15]Florrie Fisher, *The Lonely Trip Back* (Garden City, N.Y.: Doubleday, 1971), p. 145.

[16]Giallombardo, pp. 106–117.

goods and in the consumption of such goods and services. The inmates frequently need commissary products that they have no money to buy and goods and services that cannot be manufactured or stolen without the cooperation of several inmates. The social fabric of the family provides the cooperative spirit and organization needed to procure goods and services. Each family member feels a responsibility to help provide economic benefits for all the other members of the family. A family shares both the legally obtained goods from the prison commissary and the illicit goods obtained through the sub rosa economic system. Family members have an implicit understanding that the members can borrow items of clothing and other objects from one another. Their spirit of generosity in these borrowing activities, of course, varies from time to time and with different individuals. Their behavior in this respect is not unlike the behavior of a family in the free world, wherein teenage sisters alternately argue over and lovingly share one another's clothes and cosmetics.

Punishment by the staff members—such as the removal of commissary privileges for a time—is softened by the family system or the homosexual dyad. If an inmate who is being punished is deprived of almost all economic goods, other inmates in the family group are expected to give her extra food, clothing, or information obtained from the kitchen, garden, or sewing room.[17]

Because of the reciprocal economic relationship that exists among family members, individual family members who play key economic roles in the subculture are of special importance. For example, the "connect" is an inmate who has a good job assignment in the institution which allows her to have access to information and prison supplies. She is in a position to act as middleman and distributor of goods and services.[18] A "booster" is an inmate who is not only especially successful in opportunistic stealing of institution provisions, but also operates an enterprising business.[19] The connect and the booster are able to fulfill important breadwinner roles in the family structure. If a family member has entrepreneurial talent or is placed in a strategic position where she has access to prison information or supplies, the other family members expect her to develop the skills of the connect or booster.

In the "togetherness" of family life, economic activities play an important role. For example, the lore of making alcoholic beverages may be passed along from mother to daughter or from father to son, with favorite recipes being kept as a family secret. Nor does the family neglect to provide technical training in the fine arts of boosting provisions from the prison kitchen or storeroom, although the classes are not exactly like those conducted in the local Allied City Technical School. The following example involves a family situation wherein Granny and Mary Helen, being expert thieves, had assumed the responsibility of instructing a new family member.[20]

"Now, look at me," Mary-Helen said, coming down the corridor. "Am I walkin' like I always does?" "Yes," the girl answered. "Now I wan' you to look." Mary-Helen reached up under her skirt and pulled out a foot-high can of orange juice from the kitchen. "Now look again," she instructed. She reached up and replaced the can and then lifted her skirts to show it held firmly above her knees. "Now watch." She walked down the corridor, turned and came back, without any indication that she held anything with her legs. "De elevator opirator stop 'bove de flo'," Granny laughed, "an she jest step up like nothin' wrong."

People first learning about homosexual families in women's prisons have varying reactions. The social scientist is apt to say, "Isn't that an interesting phenomenon?" The moral conscience in many is likely to trigger a comment

---

[17]Giallombardo, p. 121.
[18]Giallombardo, p. 120.

[19]*Ibid.*, pp. 120–121.
[20]McManus, p. 235.

something like, "They ought to be ashamed" or "That's unnatural and ungodly" or "We should clean up women's prisons." Nonetheless, the social structure is advantageous from the viewpoint of the incarcerated women. By building a family structure, the women are making an effort to overcome the fact that their world is comprised only of women; they are attempting to make their society as much like the outside world as possible.

Within the artificial society created, the offenders play roles which are much like the roles they play or want to play on the outside world. The family structure builds a matrix in which an identity that has meaning on the outside is preserved. Even in economic affairs, particularly with the less sophisticated offenders, their past experiences have been primarily in family unit arrangements. The identity so established in the prison setting is not irrelevant to the identity that a woman has on the outside. For rehabilitation goals, this structure has considerable merit because rehabilitation requires that the individual be able to function after leaving the institution.

In considering the reasons for the family type of social organization in women's prisons, there are no clear-cut answers.[21] A number of reasons have been suggested by researchers—all of which are probably partially valid and plausible. Inmates need a form of affection, a way of relating to people: the family is a way of belonging.[22] Certain types of protection and information are needed for survival in the prison and the family can provide those things. Material goods and services beyond those provided by the prison are not absolutely essential, but they are desired. The family is useful in obtaining both legal (from the prison commissary) and illegal goods and services. Another plausible explanation for the type of social structure found in women's

prisons is in terms of their preinstitution experiences. The family is the form of social organization that they have been a part of and so is the type that they feel comfortable with.

PRISON LOVE AND MARRIAGE

While the new inmate is being absorbed into a family, she may be experiencing another type of alliance. Experts on the subject do not agree, but most estimates are that between 50 to 70 percent of the inmates in women's prisons in the United States engage in some sort of homosexual activity. Furthermore, David A. Ward and Gene G. Kassebaum point out that even if only 50 percent are engaged in a homosexual alliance, the prison atmosphere is one of homosexual activity.[23] If we accept their statement and consider the range of the estimates on the extent of homosexual activity in women's prisons, it is obvious that homosexuality plays a central role in the daily life of women inmates. The extent of homosexual activity in girls' schools is thought to be even higher—in the vicinity of 70 percent.[24] The basic cause, of course, is the absence of the opportunity for heterosexual activity.[25] In the world of female inmates, the only men around are maintenance crews, ministers and priests, doctors, parole board members, possibly a male warden, and occasionally a husband, boyfriend, or brother vists. For some women, certainly not all, life pivots around her man or men or at least around a romantic relationship. Ward and Kassebaum, in *Women's Prison*, conclude that the homosexual relationship in female institutions fills this void; it provides an intimate, affectionate relationship with security and social status.[26] Homosexual relationships that develop among

[21]John H. Gagnon and William Simon, "The Social Meaning of Prison Homosexuality," *Federal Probation* 32 (March 1968): 28.

[22]Rose Giallombardo, "Social Roles in a Prison for Women," *Social Problems 13* (Winter 1966): 271–272.

[23]David A. Ward and Gene G. Kassebaum, *Women's Prison: Sex and Social Structure* (Chicago: Aldine, 1965), pp. 92–93.

[24]Seymour L. Halleck and Marvin Hersko. "Homosexual Behavior in A Correctional Institution for Adolescent Girls," *American Journal of Orthopsychiatry* 32 (October 1962): 913.

[25]Gagnon and Simon, 28.

[26]Ward and Kassebaum, p. 76.

female inmates are used to soften the impact of life in the penitentiary. The women strive to develop relationships that strengthen their ability to bear the emotional, social, and economic deprivations of institutional life.[27]

HOMOSEXUAL TYPES

There are basically two types of women who fall into the general category of homosexual. Those women who prefer homosexual activities to heterosexual activities in the free world are called true lesbians. Inmates frequently refer to these women as being sick or perverted. Investigators suspect that a large portion of these dedicated homosexuals are of the social types known as politicians and merchants in men's prisons. Ward and Kassebaum believe that they are like the experienced male convict who is not concerned with doing his time and winning an early release; rather he intends to make prison a way of life by getting a comfortable job and obtaining some material comforts.[28] For this type of female prisoner, prison life has advantages that outweigh the disadvantages.

The other general type that is involved in prison homosexuality is the penitentiary or jailhouse "turnout." This inmate engages in homosexual relations as a way of adjusting to prison life, but in the free world she prefers heterosexual activity. Factors that contribute to her decision to "turnout" include the sheer boredom of living a caged life and the pressure of being sought after by girls who consider her to be attractive. But more often than not a jailhouse turnout will accept a female lover for economic reasons. Harris illustrates how a new inmate learns about the economic advantages involved. The new inmate had noticed that Rusty, a prison butch, always wore nice sweaters. When the new inmate asked Rusty how she managed to obtain such clothes, Rusty intro-

duced her to a girl who worked in the clothing room. Within a few hours, novice Patrica returned to her cell to find a new sweater on her bed. Rusty had introduced the new girl as "good people"—implying that she was to be granted the special favors due to the cooperative.[29]

Should she decide to be half of a homosexual couple, the new inmate will choose to play the role of a man or a woman. If she plays the male role, she will be called a "stud broad," "daddy," "bulldyke," or "butch" and will try to act and look as masculine as possible. If she chooses to play the female role, she will be tagged as a "femme" or "mommy" and be courted by a stud broad.

Butches

"Drag butches," trying to be as manly as possible, cut their hair in a male fashion. They attempt to walk and sit like men. They even make an effort to hold and puff on cigarettes as men do. If institutional regulations allow it, they would prefer to wear slacks, ties, and shirts cut in a mannish style. Sometimes they will wear neckerchiefs as ties. At events where dresses or skirts are required, innumerable disguises are used to hide their feminine attire.[30] Butches prefer men's shorts and tee shirts, which can be easily made in the sewing department, to bras, girdles, and panties.

Not all stud broads dress in drag (men's clothes) or attempt to look and act like a man. Some sophisticated butches feel that such behavior is merely a facade—that clothes do not "make the man." Butches display the courtesies that men perform for women, such as opening doors, lighting cigarettes, and getting the refreshments. They play the aggressive role in the courtship and marriage relationships and act as the spokesman for the couple.

Researchers have attempted to determine if those prisoners who play the role of the butch are markedly different from prisoners who play

[27]A. J. W. Taylor, "The Significance of 'Darls' or 'Special Relationships' for Borstal Girls," *The British Journal of Criminology* 5 (October 1965): 417.

[28]Ward and Kassebaum, p. 118.

[29]Harris, p. 230.

[30]McManus, p. 237.

the role of a femme or those who do not participate in homosexual activities at all. The evidence is inconclusive; nonetheless, authorities do indicate that butches tend to be more homely than the general run of female prisoners. A young woman who is rather plain and dowdy may be told outright by a seasoned con that she would make a good butch—thus defining for her the role that she can play in the prison community. Yet there is no physiological characteristic that is statistically significantly different from that of the other prisoners. In a study done by Ward and Kassebaum, the butches had had less heterosexual experience than others before being imprisoned. In short, many of them have been less involved with men. Undoubtedly, butches are reacting to a number of factors both within and outside the prison.[31]

Economic need is a potential cause for becoming a butch. In the county jail, an old con might say, "Wow, if you don't have any money coming in, cut your hair and drop your belt and wear high socks and you've got it made,' and that's right. They do that and they come in—they've got all kinds of girls chasing them, buying them coffee, cigarettes, knitting them sweaters, and you name it, they've got it."[32] Prestige seems to be associated with playing the male role.[33] Once in a while a butch chooses to shift from the male to the female role, called "dropping the belt." This frowned upon act causes a loss of status to the one shifting. Since "on the reservation" there is a preponderance of femmes over butches, "dropping the belt" intensifies this supply shortage. Femmes may shift to the butch role, but that is not customary either.

Femmes

For a femme, physical attractiveness has much to do with her popularity. It is said that models, dancers, or strippers are in great demand. A high-priced call girl commands considerable re-

spect. The younger the woman, the more desirable. Although femmes are of higher status than those women who do not participate in homosexual relationships, they are of lesser status than butches.[34] There are exceptions in this type of prestige ranking—a few infamous inmates, notorious because of their exploits and impressive criminal records in organized crime, receive high status because of their reputation as well as their wealth and power.

The femme plays the stereotyped role of the woman: that is to say, she is submissive and does the housekeeping. She does the cleaning, the sewing, the bed making, and frequently the commissary shopping. She performs the functions of a nonliberated housewife. Should a femme be penniless, the stud broad will become a "commissary hustler" to provide goods for the wife if she is particularly fond of her.

COURTSHIP

A valuable source of information about the "going together" or courtship relationship between two inmates is their clandestine kites (letters) to each other. Most reformatories and prisons forbid the exchanging of notes—an official policy that does not appear to dampen enthusiasm for this activity. Possibly it adds the dimension of fear and excitement because the writer is in danger of getting caught. In this respect, two important research studies have been conducted, both describing the youthful female offender; the first, by Sidney Kosofsky and Albert Ellis, involved the analysis of 100 notes, randomly selected from several hundred illegal letters confiscated by the officers in a reformatory for female juvenile delinquents[35]; and the latest research by A. J. W. Taylor, which consists of a careful study of 46 notes passed between close friends in a New Zealand reformatory for

[31]Ward and Kassebaum, pp. 110–113.
[32]*Ibid.*, p. 144.
[33]Giallombardo, *Society of Women,* p. 124.

[34]Harris, pp. 232–234.
[35]Sidney Kosofsky and Albert Ellis, "Illegal Communication Among Institutionalized Female Delinquents," *The Journal of Social Psychology* 48 (August 1958): 155–160.

girls.[36] Kosofsky and Ellis reported that the notes were written on all sorts of scrounged paper, ranging from pages torn from books or magazines to bits and pieces of wrapping paper. Often they were folded into small triangular shapes—thus accounting for the term "kites"— so they could be tucked into a hiding place like a bra or shoe or cover of a book. Kites are passed between girls as they brush past one another going to and from the dining hall, their cottage or work. Sometimes a messenger will be used as an intermediary or the note will be hidden in a dead letter drop (a secret place where it can be recovered later).

The opening and closing sentences quoted from one of the notes confiscated by the researchers is an example of a young girl carefully using lines found in a novel or magazine article as her own: "While sitting here in the deepest of meditation, I thought I would take the greatest of pleasure in dropping you a few lines of love and devotion."[37] Because of their insecurity about themselves, their feelings, and their ability to write appropriate prose, the girls may copy the words of writers who they believe have said the proper and accepted things.[38] Often the notes were embellished with kiss signs (X marks) and other drawings, including pictures cut from magazines. Most of the notes were love letters dealing with the hundreds of intimacies that an infatuated couple share. Like those that pass between adolescent boys and girls, the love letters were less sexual than romantic.[39] The girls, with painstaking care (demonstrated by the many visible erasure marks often found on notes), compose and write down their feelings. A passage from one of these kites found in a library book, which serves as a common hiding place, demonstrates the emotional fervor often felt for each other by the young offenders:[40]

"My darling sweetheart!

Why don't you look at me no more? Why don't you smile at me no more? I cant sleep nights thinking maybe you dont love me no more please write me and dont tell me you love nobody else. Id die if you did. write the way you used to. say you love just me and if you dont Ill do something awful and youll feel bad. I dont love nobody but you."

The innocence depicted by the youthful offender is not necessarily present among the older female inmates. The femme/stud broad relationship characteristically seen in prisons for women probably has a less romantic and more sexual aura. With the passage of time, some of the romantic dreams of a teenager are gradually replaced by the realities of life. The orientation changes as the inmate gathers experience on the outside and the inside. The correspondence of women expresses threats, love, jealousy or even anger due to unfaithfulness. The following excerpt from an example of a kite in Ward and Kassebaum's *Women's Prison* illustrates that the tone of the notes between adult female prisoners can be quite different from that of the youthful offender.[41]

"My darling and My Secret Love, I miss you so much (no shit). Hey, like today is my day off plus no school this afternoon and where are we. Remember when we were talking about our periods I told you, oh, oh! That's bad. But I never said why. Well, I guess I am a little bit coo coo (smile). Superstitious maybe but it's strange how everything I believe in comes true. Yogi (smile) no, but at first our periods weren't together—but as soon as we start fucking and doing everything together, we did that too."

Love and Economics

The femme-stud broad relationship is reinforced if not motivated by economics. A femme often enters into a love relationship because the butch supplies the items she cannot get in any other way or, at least, the relationship offers a viable alternative source of goods. In some cases commissary goods (candy, cigarettes, and so on)

[36]Taylor, 406–418.
[37]Kosofsky and Ellis, 156.
[38]*Ibid.*, 159.
[39]Taylor, 411.
[40]Helen Bryan, *Inside* (Boston: Houghton Mifflin, 1953), pp. 279–280.

[41]Ward and Kassebaum, p. 157.

may be used to entice a femme to go with the stud broad or, once in awhile, the other way around. The new femme may be asked for a date, perhaps to go with a butch's crowd.[42] The nuances of this relationship bears closer inspection.

In the previous example where the new inmate learned how to obtain a sweater, the economic and sexual implications were clear.[43] Patricia experienced a series of frustrations in attempting to get items needed in the daily life of the prison. In each case, she was frustrated in her attempts to obtain the items through legitimate means. After obtaining the sweater with the help of her friend, Rusty, Patricia attempted to obtain bleach for doing her laundry. She knew that bleach was available within the institution because she smelled it when other inmates were doing their laundry. But when she tried to obtain bleach through legitimate channels, both staff members and inmates expressed surprise and denied that it was available.[44] She had the same type of disappointment when she attempted to obtain a douche bag. Patricia was never able to get either item via legal means, but influential butch Rusty had no difficulty in obtaining the necessary items for her in the illicit sub rosa system. Under such aggravating circumstances, Patricia quickly sensed that she needed a provider to survive in the prison setting.[45]

The economic dimensions of courting and sex are clearly demonstrated in a quotation in Ward and Kassebaum's *Women's Prison*. The initial part of an interesting prison game is illustrated. The inmate being quoted is telling the interviewer about some of her prison experiences, as follows:[46]

"They were all sort of trying to see who could get to me first. They gave me pajamas, and stuff to drink, they gave me pills to get loaded, weed and smokes and I had an offer for some *stuff* [heroin] that I used to use, but I don't anymore so I turned that down. But I took all the stuff [subject is not referring to heroin here] you know—I took it because I needed it, because I don't have anything . . . and I couldn't see those state nightgowns, so I took it, but I never gave anything in return. Some of the girls are pretty salty about it. The only time I did anything—I needed a sweater real bad. This is terrible, it sounds horrible, but I didn't have anything when I came in, they took everything away from me. And I needed a sweater—I was freezing to death. So this one girl I was with in county jail told me, 'Take me to bed and satisfy me and I'll give you a sweater.' And she had a wardrobe that was tremendous, even in here, because she'd been here since year one—she's one of the bigwigs. She's good to know anyway, so I took her to bed and I got my sweater. But I could never do anything like that again, I was loaded when I did it because I couldn't stand it—but I had to have something to wear."

Butches give presents when they are rushing new femmes; but once the devotion and affection of the femme is secure, the butch turns around and demands goods and services from the femmes in exchange for the butch's affirmation of fidelity—that she will not fool around with other femmes.[47] A butch, nonetheless, may demand commissary goods and cigarettes from several femmes at one time.[48] A butch exploits femmes for several reasons, one of which is squarely based on economic motivation. But butches want goods as status symbols as well as for consumption. As symbols of prestige, gifts show that they are beloved by their girls and are in command of the relationship.[49] Such provisions of goods on the part of the femmes is a form of tribute, which demonstrates their loyalty to the butch. The butch, or true lesbian for lack of a better term, does not like or trust the sometime lesbian or jailhouse turnout, knowing that she will revert

[42]*Ibid.*, p. 145.
[43]Haris, p. 230.
[44]*Ibid.*
[45]*Ibid.*, pp. 230–232.
[46]Ward and Kassebaum, p. 148.

[47]*Ibid.*, p. 178.
[48]Harris, pp. 232–234.
[49]Ward and Kassebaum, p. 192.

to heterosexual activity as soon as she leaves prison and returns to a bisexual society. Thus a butch may economically exploit the femme—using her but not trusting her.[50]

MARRIAGE

Within a short period of time after entering the prison, a new femme will usually marry a butch. The marriage relationship will be recognized by other inmates and the two will be referred to as a married couple. Acting as man and wife, they will do everything married couples do given the constraints placed upon them by nature and the need to avoid being caught and punished by the staff. Although the term has several meanings, the couple are said to be "making it." Ordinarily there is an element of romance in the marriage. A ceremony may be performed by Grandma or Daddy with the proper words as, "Do you take this woman?" or "Do you take this man?" Wedding rings may be exchanged and returned to a safe hiding place after the marriage ceremony.

Couples may walk arm in arm in halls and sit close together and hold hands in the movie or while watching television in the recreation room. Needless to say, opportunities for more serious expressions of affection are limited. In the prisons where the women live in cottage housing arrangements, the institution rules often forbid an inmate to close her door when she has a visitor in the room. Still the women can be alone in a room if they employ a pinner (lookout) to watch for staff members. Otherwise, lovers have some limited opportunities to be together during recreation, while in classes, and when moving from one part of the institution to another. The chapel is a favorite spot to rendezvous.

The fleeting moments that couples have to share is described rather pathetically by Helen Bryan in *Inside*. The inmates were returning from the school building at Alderson after listening to Christmas music on records: "I was

among the last to leave and as I walked down the steps, heavily shadowed by the pine trees and bushes on either side, I was surprised to bump into couples locked in each others arms."[51] Continuing, Bryan says, "But the embraces could not last long, for in another moment the officers would be coming down the hill. Furthermore, we were required to leave from and return to the cottage in a group, and girls not interested in amorous demonstrations would not wait too long for those who were." She concludes with this detail: "These girls would slowly walk on ahead and the girls involved would have to break away and run to catch up so that all would enter the cottage at the same time."[52]

Prison marriages are not without ups and downs: in other words, they are not all made in heaven. Most fights in women's institutions are rooted in a homosexual triangle. Problems caused by rivals, mistresses, and infidelity sometimes trigger stormy emotions that lead to physical violence complete with the use of weapons such as razor blades and scissors. The women rightfully fear that their faces will be permanently scarred or made ugly.[53] While an inmate at Bedford, Florrie Fisher taught the youthful offenders at Westfield located on the same campus. In pointing out how tough even a school for minor offenders is, she says:[54]

"When a mommy and a daddy had a fight at Westfield, the bull-dyker would stick a scissors in the girl's back, twist it and pull it out, then dare her to go to the clinic to have it treated. There were always deaths from blood poisoning or loss of blood because the kids who got stabbed with scissors or knives were afraid to tell the guards or go to the clinic. They knew they'd be killed when they got back."

Prison marriages last for about one year, sometimes a shorter or longer length of time. They obviously must end when the husband or wife is paroled and frequently end before this

[50]Harris, p. 235.

[51]Bryan, p. 281.
[52]*Ibid.*
[53]Giallombardo, "Social Roles," 274.
[54]Fisher, p. 145.

time because the butch finds herself a more desirable femme. A femme may obtain a more attractive husband, but this is an infrequent event because femmes are more plentiful than stud broads. If one of the parties to a marriage agreement is paroled and the other member is not, the usual conditions of parole will prohibit them from seeing one another. A woman newly released from prison has problems more pressing than seeing her old prison friends. But more to the point, the women want to begin new lives or go back to their old ones—to put aside the unpleasant memories of confinement.[55]

[55]Bryan, p. 277.

49. Social Types Among the Cons

LEO CARROLL

SOCIAL TYPES AMONG THE CONS

IMPRISONMENT PRESENTS THOSE CONFINED WITH a rather standard set of problems. Thus, it is not surprising that the crucial "axes of life" reflected in the social types identified by the white prisoners at Eastern Correctional Institution are quite similar to those identified previously by Sykes.[1] The focal concerns of the white prisoners at ECI include the following: relations to staff and the social world they represent, loss of freedom and autonomy, deprivation of material comforts including drugs, sex, and physical security. Inmates are typed in terms of which of these several concerns serves as the primary referent for their behavior. Labels with respect to one interest, however, carry implications for behavior in regard to other concerns as well. For example, a "stand-up guy" is defined primarily in terms of the staff-inmate axis, but the label also connotes a low interest in drugs because involvement in drugs makes a prisoner vulnerable to the power of the staff and is thus inconsistent with the behavior of a "stand-up guy." At ECI, then, inmates tend to play one role with respect to the entire prisoner population.[2]

▶SOURCE: *Hacks, Blacks and Cons. Lexington, Mass.: Lexington Books, 1974 Pp. 64–84. Reprinted by permission of the publisher.*

[1]Gresham M. Sykes, *The Society of Captives: A Study of a Maximum Security Prison* (Princeton, N.J.: Princeton University Press, 1958), Ch. 4.

[2]This is perhaps a function of the small size of the population. In large institutions, especially those with 3,000 or

Stand-up Guys and the Mafia

Stand-Up Guys. At ECI the "stand-up guy" is the counterpart to the "real men" described by Sykes. A "stand-up guy" is mentally and physically tough. He "takes his time" without complaint. To attempt to exploit or manipulate him in any way is to invite direct and personal retaliation. At the same time he is loyal. He does not abuse or exploit other inmates, nor will he betray another inmate, consciously or unconsciously. Were he to see two inmates fighting, for example, he would pass by rather than possibly draw the attention of an officer by stopping to watch or break it up. Most of all, a "stand-up guy" can be counted on "when anything is going down," when there is a collective disturbance. Disturbances, however, are not his preferred style. In his relations with the staff, the "stand-up guy" is cool and aloof. His behavior is artfully designed to display his personal integrity and autonomy without "bringing heat." Rather than refuse to stand for the count, he leans against the wall with his back to the cell door.

Of the 145 white inmates at ECI, no more than fifteen are recognized as "stand-up guys."[3]

more inmates, it would seem likely that few prisoners would be known by most others and that individuals may be able to segregate their behavior and thus be labeled differently by different audiences.

[3]My estimates of the number and characteristics of various types is based on two sources. In many informal conversations with inmates I asked them to define various types and to provide examples of each. Somewhat more precise identification was made with the aid of three informants from a list of all the white inmates present in Maximum

For the most part, the backgrounds of these individuals reflect an involvement in professionalized and organized crime. Five had been convicted of Armed Robbery and were serving sentences averaging eleven years. Five others were reputedly high-ranking members of an organized crime syndicate, having been convicted of Conspiracy to Murder and/or Murder and were serving sentences of close to twenty years on the average. For these individuals, their confinement represents "dead time," and their overriding interest is to do their time as quickly as possible. Speaking of his time, one of those convicted of Armed Robbery made the following comment:

"I been a thief all my life and I ain't about to change now. But if I flat out the bid I got (complete sentence without parole) I'll be too old for any big jobs. So I figure I gotta make parole so's I can make one more big score and retire."

The prison behavior of this particular individual, whom we shall call Sal, is fashioned by this interest in making early parole and is typical of most "stand-up guys." He has several acquaintances with whom he shares a particular interest—cards and dominoes—and spends much of his leisure time engaged in such activities or in his cell reading war novels. He works as a porter in one of the wings, a job with few duties and considerable freedom to move about the institution. Several evenings a week he works in the "Jay Cees" canteen. His presence there profits the "Jay Cees," as few inmates will attempt to "beat the stand"[4] while he is working. Through his work at the stand he is able to secure enough food to meet his own needs and to exchange for other commodities and services. So, for example, he has a "kid" with whom he occasionally engages in sexual activities. In return for this service, the "kid" is permitted to "beat the stand" when Sal is on duty.

He does not regard any of these acquaintances as friends, however, and is fond of saying, "If you want a friend you can trust, go to the cemetery." Other "stand-up guys" express similar attitudes toward friendship: "If you don't know a guy for fifteen or twenty years, you can't trust him 'cause you don't know who he is." A friend is someone whom the "stand-up guy" has known for a long period of time and who, by his actions, has proven he can be trusted and relied upon to "go all the way with you." Most inmates do not meet these criteria. They are "rats" and "punks," and the "stand-up guy" sees himself as above the petty and routine concerns that occupy them. For some "stand-up guys" the forced association with other inmates develops in them a sense of contamination.

"You got a low caliber of men in here. When I get out if anybody ever asks me if I was here I won't tell 'em. They might just know what this joint is like and then I'd be a 'rat' just 'cause I was here."

Among the "stand-up guys," then, there is little sense of any positive identification with the inmate body. In their behavior they remain nearly as aloof from the inmates as they do from the staff. Still, they personify the ideal of solidarity, are highly respected, and in the few inmate activities in which they become involved they are opinion leaders. One such activity was a committee established by the "Jay Cees" to improve the operation of the prison library. Murphy is a "stand-up guy" who, while not a member of the "Jay Cees," was asked to be on the committee because he had been a librarian at another institution. The following incident occurred during one of the meetings concerned with library policy.

"The problem arose as to what to do if inmates lost or refused to return books. After some discussion Lyons (Vice-President of the 'Jay Cees') made a motion to the effect that the administration be informed and the inmate be made to pay for the book out of his account. This seemed to reflect the majority view in

---

Security on March 19, 1971. A particular inmate was included in a category if all three agreed on the identification.

[4] "Beating the Stand" is a game by which inmates secure commodities from the stand without payment. This is done directly by looting or indirectly by charging the purchase to another inmate.

the preceding discussion. But Murphy got very angry. Standing up, he shouted, 'And what the hell are they gonna do? They'll start having shakedowns, that's what. I ain't gonna be part of nothing that brings heat on other guys. I say we just give him a notice and if he don't bring it back we talk to him. If he ain't got the book we rip up the card and forget it.' At first Lyons and the others objected, claiming that most inmates were treacherous and should be made to pay. But Murphy stood his ground, arguing that even if they were treacherous, they were still inmates and to betray them was to make oneself as treacherous as them. In the end a motion was passed that the 'Jay Cees' establish a special fund to pay for lost books."

In this incident we see the opinion forming influence of the "stand-up guy." Not an active member of the organization, Murphy nonetheless was able to effectively oppose the Vice-President of the organization by interpreting the decision within the framework of a code of solidarity. Murphy, and other "stand-up guys," however, are only infrequently involved in such activities, usually becoming involved only when the activity meets some interest of their own. This fact, and their aloofness from most inmates, limits their influence as opinion leaders.

The Mafia.   Both the ability of "stand-up guys" to exercise power and their limited use of it is most evident with respect to the five members of the organized crime group. Within the institution the individuals formed a cohesive clique variously termed "the mafia," the "purple gang," or the "untouchables." All inmates regard them with a mixture of respect, awe and fear.

"All the guys in here idolize 'em. All they have to do is suggest something and it'll be done right away."

"Everybody knows who they are and they respect 'em for it. Nobody would think of crossin' 'em 'cause they'd put the kiss of death on 'em."

"It ain't so much a power or influence thing. They got that all right. But the reason they got it is 'cause the other guys respect 'em. It's more respect than power, if ya know what I mean."

The deference shown to these individuals is evident in many small ways. Soon after they ar-

rived, for example, one of them let it be known that the noise after lights out was disturbing his sleep. Thereafter, there was little noise in his block after 10:30 p.m. On summer evenings most of the yard is cast in shadow except for a small area against the rear of the Industrial Building. This spot belongs to them and is seldom occupied by other inmates, even if the "mafia" are not in the yard at the time. At the periodic banquets sponsored by the "Jay Cees" and the *Beacon,* they are provided with a corner table complete with tablecloth, silverware, salt and pepper, and their food is brought to them and their guests while others, including the Warden, have to stand in line.

At one of these banquets, attended by some 100 prisoners and 200 guests, a popular inmate assaulted an officer who had apprehended him attempting to bring in a bottle of liquor. The inmate was removed from the dining hall to the Deputy Warden's office. Several of his friends then began to threaten a disturbance if any disciplinary action were taken against him. Faced with a difficult situation in which he would set a dangerous precedent were he to accede to the inmate demands, but would run the risk of a serious disturbance in which outsiders might be injured if he did not, the captain in charge requested the intervention of one of the "mafia." Through this intervention a compromise was reached. The captain permitted the offending inmate to return to the banquet in return for his assurance, guaranteed by the inmate mediator, that he would accept whatever disciplinary measures might be forthcoming. The banquet proceeded without further incident, and the next day the inmate and three of his friends were transferred to another institution.

On another occasion, the influx of drugs into the institution reached such a level that it began to cause considerable custodial concern. To avoid a general shakedown of the institution, the "mafia" and a group of their associates conducted their own shakedown and turned a large supply of drugs over to the custodians.

It is only in infrequent crisis situations such as

the above that the influence of the "mafia" is brought into the open. More commonly their influence is spread beneath the surface. None of them, for example, are members of the "Jay Cees" or other inmate organizations. But when the "Jay Cees" held their annual election, it was widely known whom the "mafia" wanted for President; he ran unopposed although he had been only a marginal member. They maintain rather close personal relations with another group of inmates, the "wise guys," and through them exert some control over the illicit activities within the institution.

It is not dominance of the inmate population nor control of illicit activities that concerns the "mafia." Their interests are in maintaining a degree of stability and order within the population so that they may do their time with comfort and ease. Their leadership role is one of mediation rather than control. Their identities as members of organized crime place them above the level of suspicion of betrayal of inmate interests. Their demonstrated lack of interest in and lack of dependence upon most illicit prison activities eliminates any question of ulterior motives. Because of "who they are" they are in a position to arbitrate disputes and conflicts both between staff and inmates and among inmates. By mediating such conflicts, they regulate the population to a degree sufficient to achieve their purposes.

Wise Guys and Politicians

In contrast to the "stand-up guys," there exists at ECI two loosely knit cliques that do attempt to dominate and control different aspects of inmate life. The "wise guys" are a loose confederation of some twelve or fifteen inmates whose major concern is personal aggrandizement through the use of force and the control of illicit activities. The "politicians" are those inmates who form the leadership of the "Jay Cees" and the *Beacon*.

Wise Guys.   In their background and prison behavior, the "wise guys" resemble closely the "young toughs" mentioned by McCleery[5] and the "state raised youth" described by Irwin.[6] Slightly younger than the white population as a whole (29.3 years vs. 29.7), they had twice as many prior convictions (3.4 vs. 1.7), and were serving sentences averaging some eighteen years.[7] In several cases their long sentences were the result of "parlaying their bids," convictions for crimes committed during imprisonment. "Wise guys," in the argot of the prison, are doing "life bids on the installment plan."

By several measures the "wise guys" are loyal and tough. Their hostility towards the staff is open and intense, they openly espouse the virtue and necessity of inmate unity, and they are likely to be in the forefront of any disturbance. In some ways, then, they resemble "stand-up guys." Like the "stand-up guy," they also see the majority of inmates as weaklings. But where this perception inclines the "stand-up guy" to avoidance, to the "wise guy" it is a license for exploitation. Prison, in their view, is the ultimate test of manhood. A man in prison is able to secure what he wants and protect what he has: "In here a man gets what he can," and, "Nobody can force a man to do something he don't want to," are key elements of their belief system. Any prisoner who does not meet these standards is not a man, "has no respect for himself," and is therefore not entitled to respect from others. Sharing such definitions, the "wise guys" work together in loose and shifting combinations and alliances to aggrandize themselves at the expense of those who prove themselves to be weak.

Several of them operate a betting pool on sports events. Bets are placed with cigarettes or

[5]Richard M. McCleery, *Policy Change in Prison Management* (East Lansing, Mich.: Governmental Research Bureau, Michigan State University, 1957), pp. 31–32. McCleery analyzes how a liberal revolution in the administration of Oahu prison undermined the position of the "old cons" resulting in a period of inmate violence led by "young toughs."

[6]John Irwin, *The Felon* (Englewood Cliffs, N.J.: Prentice Hall, 1970), pp.26–29.

[7]These figures are based on twelve inmates whom my informants agreed were in this clique.

order forms for various commodities at the inmate store, and winners are paid with the same. Losers who fail to make good on their bets are coerced into giving up a portion of their store orders for a considerable period of time or, failing this, are "piped."[8] When the "bank" runs low, i.e., the supply of cigarettes and store commodities controlled by the "wise guys," it is replenished by "shaking down" newly arrived inmates. None of the "wise guys" appear to have the necessary outside connections to provide a steady flow of drugs into the institution. Nonetheless, they are able to realize a profit from the available supply. For the most part, drugs are brought into the institution by individual inmates through their visits. An individual who has been able to "connect" in this manner may be hijacked. Other inmates having frequent visits may be pressured into requesting their visitors to bring in drugs. And the occasional prisoner with the necessary connections to secure a regular supply may have to buy the "protection" of the "wise guys" by providing them with a portion of his supply or profit.

The exploitation of white inmates by the "wise guys" extends into every facet of prison life. Prisoners are forced to provide them with coffee or sandwiches from the kitchen, to do their laundry, or to satisfy their sexual needs. Perhaps the most blatant form of exploitation in which they engage involves the "Jay Cees" snack bar. Each month inmates are allowed to purchase cards for use at the snack bar. These are kept at the stand, and as purchases are made the amount is deducted from the individual's card. "Wise guys," however, do not need cards. They enter the stand at will and take whatever they want. Often this is done in full view of 20 or 30 inmates waiting in line to be served.

"Wise guys" are hated and feared, but the average white inmate feels powerless to oppose them. Where the "wise guys" are aligned in a rather large clique, most white prisoners remain relatively isolated from each other and are unable to mobilize a significant counterforce to them. Nor, for several reasons, can they turn to the staff. First, many of the exploitive activities of the "wise guys" are not in direct violation of any regulation. Such is the case with the looting of the snack bar. As the custodians see it, the "Jay Cees" established and operate the snack bar, and it is a "Jay Cee" responsibility to protect its operation. Second, other of their activities involve the exploitation of inmates who themselves are engaged in some illicit activity such as drugs. To seek the assistance of the staff in such instances is to invite official sanctions against one's self. Third, to "rat" on a "wise guy" is to risk probable physical retaliation from other members of the clique. The only means of escaping this threat is to enter protective custody, which is highly punitive, necessitating nearly continual cell confinement.

All of this is not to say that the "wise guys" operate with complete impunity. They do not. Some inmates do "rat" and enter protective custody. Officers do occasionally come upon them in the commission of some act and report them. Moreover, there are prisoners, the "stand-up guys," who will retaliate, who are "men" and cannot be exploited. As noted above, when Sal is running the snack bar, the "wise guys" stay out. Nor are they likely to interfere with his sexual partner or other acquaintances. The existence, then, of some ten "stand-up guys," each with several acquaintances, excludes a portion of the population from direct, personal exploitation. It is the new inmate, the young and unaffiliated, those doing short time, who are the prime targets of the "wise guy's" tactics.

Another restraint upon the "wise guys" appears to be their close relation with the "mafia." Members of the "wise guys" and the "mafia" spend considerable time together playing cards, tripping the yard, and engaging in conversation on the steps of one of the cell blocks. The precise meaning of this relationship

[8]Assaulted with a lead pipe or some other heavy, blunt weapon.

is difficult to determine. Some staff and inmates believe that in fact the "mafia" control the rackets in the institution, and that the "wise guys" are their "leg men." What appears more likely, however, is that the relationship is one of co-optation. From their association with the "mafia," the "wise guys" derive considerable status, and there may also be the hope of some more secure future criminal employment. There are also more tangible rewards. Members of the "mafia" have been known to deposit money in the accounts of "wise guys," and on at least one occasion they have secured a job for a "wise guy" with a local union. Through their acceptance and favors the "mafia" are able to control the "wise guys" at critical points. Several such instances have been mentioned. The threatened disturbances at the banquet involved key figures in the "wise guy" clique. Despite the fact that "wise guys" profit from drugs, it was with their assistance that the drugs were collected to avoid a custodial shakedown. When the looting of the snack bar reached a point where the bar was operating at a loss, the leaders of the "Jay Cees" brought the matter to the "mafia," and the looting was promptly curtailed.

Such incidents are by no means conclusive evidence. But they do suggest that the close personal relations between the "mafia" and the "wise guys" are perhaps a means used by the "mafia" to control and restrain disruptive behavior in critical situations, whether the threat be from the "wise guys" themselves or some other element of the population.

Politicians.   From the viewpoint of those outside the institution and some staff as well, the leaders of the white prisoner population are those who occupy elected offices in the "Jay Cees" and on the *Beacon*. This group of some fifteen prisoners represents the inmate body to outside organizations and to the Warden and the staff. When the Warden was presented with a petition from another group to elect an inmate advisory council, he denied it on the grounds that he already had such a council in the elected leaders of the inmate organizations.

But, as the label "politician" implies, there is considerable alienation between this group of elected representatives and the majority of white inmates. While on the one hand they are accorded respect for their organizational abilities and accomplishments, on the other hand they are looked upon with considerable suspicion, envy, and jealousy. For one thing, despite their elected position, they are not representative of white inmates in terms of demographic characteristics. They are considerably older than the white population as a whole (32.4 years), have a far longer median sentence length (23.5 years), and slightly more than 50 percent of them are convicted of Murder.[9]

The ambivalence with which the "politicians" are regarded, however, stems more from a perspective implied in their activities than from the demographic differences between them and their constituents. Many of their activities are of direct benefit to the entire inmate population. As I have noted before, the organization sponsors a variety of banquets and parties, a family day, and a number of other functions that make time easier. Further, as I have also noted, they are actively engaged in prison reform. *The Beacon* is a vehicle to educate the public concerning abuses of the legal and penal systems. The "Jay Cees" sponsor an annual legislative forum by means of which they have been able to secure passage of some progressive legislation.

Throughout these legal activities, however, is a perspective that has been termed censoriousness.[10] The "politicians" attempt to achieve changes in the penal system by means of criticizing the administration for deviating from their own stated commitment to rehabilitation. In effect, this implies an acceptance of the label society has placed upon the inmate. By implication, it is a perspective admitting that inmates are criminals or are sick and require rehabilitation.

[9]These figures are based on fifteen inmates who held elected positions as officers or board members of the "Jay Cees," or were members of the editorial staff of *Beacon*.

[10]Thomas Matthiesen, *The Defences of the Weak* (London: Tavistock Publications, 1965), p. 12, 23.

The "politicians" do not "reject their rejectors." They accept this rejection, grant its legitimacy, and seek to use it as a weapon to achieve change within the system. Statements indicative of this perspective appear in every issue of *The Beacon*.

"The fact is that 80 percent of the men who are incarcerated in our prisons will eventually be free. Therefore, society must ask itself several basic questions such as: How do we want these men to return to the community? Do we want them to return the same way they went in, or do we want them to return as productive citizens?

The hardest lesson for over half the men incarcerated today is learning how to adjust to society's way of living. Odd as it may seem, a great majority of men in prison do not know how to act in the surroundings of people other than the environment of that in which they were brought up in. . . . Once taken out of that environment and introduced to a strange atmosphere of people who have lived on the right side of the street and learned how to conduct themselves, the first impulse is panic for fear that whatever he may say or do is not going to be up to the standards that good people abide by."

Many of the activities of the "politicians" seem to be an attempt to prove to society and themselves that they and other inmates are capable of rehabilitation. For instance, the general membership meetings of the "Jay Cees" take place in a room decorated with both the federal and state flags, Meetings are begun with a prayer by the chaplain, a pledge of allegiance to the flag, and a recitation of the "Jay Cee" creed:

"We believe that faith in God gives meaning and purpose to human life. That the brotherhood of man transcends the sovereignty of nations. That economic justice can best be won by free enterprise. That government should be of law rather than of men. That earth's great treasure lies in the human personality. And that service to humanity is the best work of life."

Of a total membership of some 60 inmates, no more than 20 attend a typical general membership meeting, and the discomfort of those attending in reciting this creed is overwhelming. Where the "politicians" stand and recite these incantations in a loud voice, the others bow their heads, scuffle their feet, look out the window, or engage in some action to place distance between themselves and the words they mutter.[11]

"Politicians" exhibit great concern about proper decorum in their meetings with outside guests. Most of these meetings occur in a room in which a table is set with a white cloth. Name cards are placed around the table, an agenda is prepared and distributed, and meetings are run in strict accordance with parliamentary procedure. To ensure proper appearances, only certain members, generally the "politicians" themselves, are admitted to these meetings. The majority of inmates probably could not care less about the content of the meetings, but the meetings often involve female visitors from surrounding colleges, and there is thus considerable resentment among the prisoners at their exclusion. After one such meeting an inmate commented angrily to another: "They musta had ten broads in there. The least they coulda done was send one or two out for us, them bastards."

The "politicians" are also resented because of the privileged positions they occupy. While they, like other inmates, have assigned jobs, they are able to schedule their organizational activities so that they seldom work. Because of their positions, they are granted considerable freedom of movement within the institution and are almost continually engaged in meetings with outside groups, the staff, or themselves. Thus, the "politicians" have a vested interest in protecting their position, and it is often apparent to other inmates that their actions are more self-serving than in the interests of the inmate population. An example of this occurred with respect to securing official permission for inmate representatives to attend monthly meetings of the Executive Board of the state "Jay Cees" and the Board of Directors meeting of Beacon House, a halfway house allied with *The Beacon*. The Warden agreed to permit representatives to attend these

---

[11]Goffman has conceptualized behavior of this sort as role distance. Erving Goffman, *Encounters* (New York: Bobbs Merrill, 1961), Ch. 2.

meetings and requested a list of the candidates from which he would select two. Over a six-month period, no inmate was selected because of the unwillingness of the "politicians" to submit names of inmates whom the Warden could approve. He would not approve any of the "politicians" because of the length of their sentences, and they refused to submit the names of any inmates who were not within their group.

Actions such as the above, their concern with appearances, and the perspective from which they view themselves and other inmates account for the ambivalence with which the prisoners regard the "politicians." Inmates are uncertain about what side the "politicians" are on. Their loyalty is always in question.

"I just don't trust them guys. If something was to go down tomorrow they might just be in here swinging clubs with the hacks."

The position of the "politicians" is thus quite vulnerable. Lacking a committed following, they do not themselves possess the necessary resources to maintain their position if opposition to their leadership were to arise. For this reason they are drawn into a cooperative relation with the "mafia." Many of the programs and activities of the "politicians' are in accordance with the interests of the "mafia." Legislative changes such as the bill to make "lifers" eligible for parole after ten years, administrative changes such as increased visiting privileges, and less stringent criteria for minimum custody and work release, and the yearly round of parties and banquets at which the "mafia" are honored guests have the potential for making time both shorter and more comfortable. The "mafia" recognize that there are few prisoners other than the "politicians" with the motivation and ability to achieve such changes and to sponsor such programs. Thus, the "mafia" use their influence to ensure the continued election of the "politicians" and at times to prevent opposition to some of their more controversial programs.

The informal social organization of the white prisoner population is depicted in Figure 1. As

can be seen there, leadership is vested in the "mafia," but their influence is exercised largely through the "wise guys" and the "politicians," the physical power of the "wise guys" being used to control other prisoners when necessary, and the organizational abilities of the "politicians" being used to achieve desired changes through negotiation and arbitration with the staff.

Administration Men and Hippies

Administration Men.   Some fourteen white inmates are known as "administration men." Where the loyalty of the "politicians" is suspect, that of the "administration men" is clear. They identify with the values of legitimate society. They see themselves as conventional people who, perhaps through being a victim of circumstances, are now forced to live among criminals. To the "administration men" the institution is "a vicious place," "a jungle," and "most of the guys in here are animals."To some extent the differences the "administration men" see between themselves and other inmates is borne out by their backgrounds. For twelve of the fourteen, their current confinement is their first. Eight have been convicted of Homicide, two of Mansiaughter, three of Assault, and one of Sodomy. Despite lack of prior criminal involvement, however, "administration men" are serving long sentences because of the seriousness of their offences. Their median sentence length is 35.5 years.

The prison behavior of the "administration men" is a self-conscious attempt to set themselves apart from the other inmates. One of their central concerns, and that which earns them the label of "administration men," is to develop a close relationship with the staff. This is most evident in the jobs they secure. Most have jobs that in some way place them in an intermediate position between the staff and other inmates. Two are proofreaders in the Print Shop, working in the supervisor's office correcting and often rejecting the work done by other prisoners. Two others work in the recreation office and, in the summer, officiate at in-

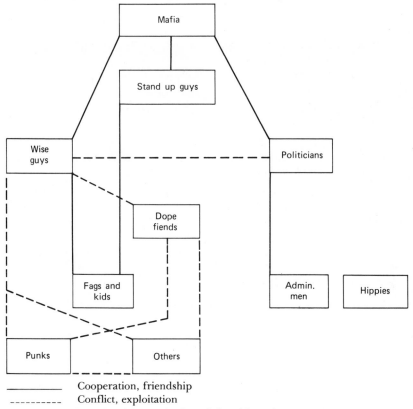

Figure 1.   Informal social organization of the white prisoners.

tramural sports activities. Another, over a long period of time, has established himself as the unofficial supervisor of the Plate Shop. Other positions occupied by "administration men" are those of first cook in the kitchen, inmate librarian, and "Rear Hall" porters, who are responsible for the maintenance of the administration offices.

With respect to other inmates, "administration men" are loners. They do not form close friendships either among themselves or with other prisoners. The focus of their non-job related activities is their case. Much of their time is spent in their cells studying law and preparing a variety of legal appeals. To some extent, this gives them a common interest with the "politicians," many of whom have similar backgrounds and with whom they occasionally share newly discovered legal information. But, unlike the

"politicians," "administration men" do not use their acquired legal knowledge to advance the interests of the inmate body as a whole. "Politicians" file class actions; "administration men" file personal appeals.

Apart from his case, the prison activity of the "administration man" is directed toward preparing himself for release. While they do not consider themselves criminals, most see in themselves some character flaw that must be overcome. The "administration men" form the core of those inmates involved in the few formally sponsored treatment programs such as Alcoholics Anonymous and group therapy. Others turn to religion, becoming near fanatics who spend large amounts of time in prayer and bible reading, and who surround themselves with religious objects.

The prison behavior of the "administration

men" earns them the contempt of other inmates, who see them as adjuncts to the custodial force. But the fact that most of the "administration men" have killed or violently assaulted another person is not lost on other inmates, and their contempt is tinged with fear. It leads to avoidance rather than dominance or exploitation. Murphy, a "stand-up guy," expressed this reaction clearly in recalling an incident involving Hank:

"I hate every one of them punks. I'd like to see every one of 'em dead. But to tell the honest truth there ain't too many I'd wanna tangle with myself. You know Hank? . . . Well him and me came into the joint about the same time and we worked in the laundry together for a while. I remember I used to think, how the hell could that ass kill two guys? Then one day I seen how. Some sheets he was doing got ripped up in the mangle. He went right outta his f—ing skull. He ripped up the mangle with his bare hands and then he started on the rest of the place. . . . It took ten or eleven hacks to stop him and you shoulda seen the damage he done there. . . . Guys that flip out like that, though, they're crazy. The best thing to do is just stay away from 'em."

Hippies.   Another group of white prisoners whose normative orientations lie beyond the prison are some eight inmates identified as "hippies." If, in some sense, "administration men" are the extreme right wing of the white population, the "hippies" are the extreme left. Their external identification is not with the values of legitimized authority but with the counter-culture. Like the "administration men," they also do not define themselves as criminals. They are political prisoners, victims of an inequitable and illegitimate politico-economic structure. From their perspective, it is not only they who are not criminals; no inmates are criminals except perhaps the "mafia." Committed to this perspective, they experience a curious mixture of solidarity with and alienation from other white inmates. On an ideological level, they feel a sense of unity as a result of their common oppression. On a personal level, however, they feel estranged due to what they perceive as the false consciousness, the lack of political awareness, and continued commitment to materialistic values of the average prisoner.

The "hippies" form a close-knit clique who remain detached from other inmates. Despite the definition of themselves as political prisoners, their prison behavior is devoid of any overt and immediate revolutionary direction. Most of their time is consumed in reading a diverse body of literature in philosophy and social science, and in extended "rap sessions" in these areas. In the summer of 1971, yoga became a way of life for the "hippies." They formed a Yoga Society and each evening gathered in a circle in one corner of the yard to perform their exercises and chants. To "stand-up guys" such as Sal and Murphy the "hippies" are "creeps."

Fags, Punks, and Kids

If one were to judge the intensity of the deprivations of incarceration by the frequency of topics that arise in inmate conversation, sexual deprivation would top the list. At ECI one cannot move about the yard or the wings for any length of time without coming upon a group of prisoners entertaining each other with stories of their sexual exploits. Generally these conversations are in the form of performances in which one inmate recounts, in explicit detail, glowing tales of the number of sexual conquests he has made, the particular acts at which each partner was most adroit, and of his own sexual endurance. The nature and content of these performances suggests that it is not merely the absence of heterosexual release that is frustrating for the prisoner, though this is undoubtedly true. Equally and perhaps more important seems to be the fact that the absence of heterosexual contact deprives the prisoner of a major means by which he may affirm his masculinity.[12] The in-

[12]For a fuller discussion of this aspect of prison homosexuality, see John H. Gagnon and William Simon, "The Social Meaning of Prison Homosexuality," *Federal Probation* 32 (March 1968), 23–29. It is also discussed by Sykes. See Sykes, pp. 71–72.

mates at ECI, like those in all prisons, are drawn predominantly from segments of the population in which dominance and conquest in heterosexual relations are of heightened significance in the assertion of claims to masculine status. Heterosexual deprivation, then, is frustrating for the prisoner not merely because of the absence of this form of sexual release, but also because its absence is experienced as a severe threat to masculinity.

This two-pronged nature of the sexual problem defines the form of sexual relations in the prison. A prisoner may find some measure of sexual release through masturbation. Activity of this sort resolves only one dimension of the problem, however, and may itself generate a threat to a prisoner's image of himself as a "man." Ritualized sexual conversations, as noted above, may partially resolve the problem of masculine identification. Beyond these outlets, however, there exists the opportunity for homosexual contact, which, accorded appropriate definitions, may resolve both problems. Within the culture of the prison, such a definition exists. The label homosexual is attached only to those prisoners who assume the passive role in a sexual act. A prisoner who assumes the active role, who does not reciprocate in the sex act, is not a homosexual. By acceptance of this definition, then, it is possible for prisoners to obtain some measure of sexual release in a non-solitary manner without threatening, and perhaps even enhancing, their claims to status as a male.

Fags.   At ECI, as elsewhere, two major types of homosexuals are identified, "fags" and "punks."[13] "Fags" are admitted homosexuals, prisoners who engaged in homosexual activity prior to their incarceration and for whom this is the preferred form of sexual relationship. Prior to his imprisonment, the "fag" may have played a "butch" or "fem" role, but in the prison he adopts only the passive role. A "queen" is a "fag" whose role-playing extends into every facet of his (her) behavior. "Queens" display exaggerated feminine mannerisms, wear tight pants, have long hair, a female name, and, in one case, simulated female breasts by silicone injection. Most "fags," however, confine their passive role to the sexual act itself.

"Fags" desire sexual contact within the prison and actively seek it. Their interests in these relationships, however, extend beyond the desire for sexual satisfaction and include needs for affection, intimacy, and security. Such interests complement many needs of prisoners with long sentences, and the typical relationship for a "fag" is a pseudo-marriage with an older long-term inmate. They may live in cells next to each other, work in the same shop, eat together, and engage in most activities in common. Such relationships are subject to enormous strain, however. One strain derives from the inability of the active partner to commit himself wholly to the role. To be engaged in a pseudo-marriage and at the same time to preserve his image of masculinity, he must at least publicly demonstrate some degree of disaffection from the relationship. Often this results in the active partner publicly degrading and demeaning the "fag." He may force his partner to engage in homosexual play activities as the butt of jokes for a group, or he may coerce the "fag" into providing sexual services for several of his friends. He may also exploit the "fag" for other interests. One "fag" described the breakup of a recent marriage in the following way:

"At first it was good, you know. We was having sex and that was good. But it was more than that. We were sharing everything and doing everything together. We was close and the best part was that he didn't have to keep that tough guy mask on. He told me things about himself that he wouldn't tell anybody else, and it made him feel good to have somebody to talk to. But them other guys he hangs with got into it,

[13]Most studies of prisons identify an active, aggressive role variously labeled a "wolf" or a "jocker." For example, Sykes, pp. 95–99. A comparable role at ECI was the "ripper." "Rippers," however, are black and thus not treated here. There were no labels applied to white inmates playing an active role, perhaps because the primary aggressors are seldom white.

and he started coming outta that tough guy bag. He began to treat me like dirt and he even tried to get me to put out for all them and beat the shit out of me when I wouldn't. One day he came into my cell. I had a diamond ring on the table. He grabbed it and put it on his finger and walked out. I think he was bullshitting me, he meant to give it back. But then he met Vic and Vic said, 'Why give it back? We could cop some dope with it,' and that's what they did. When that happened I said the hell with him and moved over to the side I'm on now."

Strain in the relationship also arises from the activities of the "fag." By prostituting himself, a "fag" may secure virtually any luxury available in the prison, and such covert activities are common. The common knowledge that "fags" are treacherous in this manner further crowds the relationship with mistrust and suspicion, adding to its instability. While "marriages" occur, then, they are usually of short duration, and within a year a "fag" may be involved in several of them.

Punks.   Of the 145 white inmates in the institution on March 19, 1971, only three were identified as "fags," and all three were involved in pseudo-marriages. The available supply of willing "passive" sex partners is, then, considerably less than the demand, and there is a constant tension to effect some balance between active and passive role players. This balance is effected by means of seduction, coercion, and threat. A "punk" is a young inmate who, at least initially, adopts the passive role as a result of force. Eleven white inmates were identified as "punks." The average age of the eleven was 21.3 years. Their average sentence length was 4.1 years, and only three of the eleven had a prior commitment. On the average, then, "punks" are young, serving short sentences, and are on their first sentence. Compared with other inmates, they also appear to be physically underdeveloped for their age, though this is only an impression.

The process by which a "punk" is made may begin prior to his arrival in the prison. Other inmates being transported to the prison with a potential "punk" may prepare him for his role.

"When I first came in I was scared. I'd never been in a jail before and I didn't know no one here. I didn't know what to expect. Coming up in the van all the others was pullin' and tuggin' at me, and laughing about what was gonna happen. They kept tellin' me how many lifers they got here and how they all like to have kids and what would happen if I didn't go along with 'em. I was scared, I didn't know what to do."

Soon after he arrived, this inmate was approached by two others carrying a jar containing some orange liquid. They told him the liquid was acid and threatened to throw it over him if he did not "come across" for them, which he immediately did, only to find out the liquid was orange juice. Thereafter he was repeatedly coerced into performing sexual services, and eventually placed himself in protective custody. After several months of continual confinement, however, he accommodated himself to his role and returned to the general population.

"Anything was better than that. I couldn't take being locked up 23 hours a day, never getting outta that wing, never being able to go to the movies or anything. So I decided if that's what they wanted, I'd give it to 'em. And after a while it got so I could tell who'd bang me in the head if I didn't come across and who wouldn't. So I just give it up to the 'wise guys' and them but if the others want it, they gotta pay in advance."

By thus accommodating himself to the role forced upon him, by developing an ability to discriminate between real and non-real threats, the "punk" is able to gain some measure of physical security as well as material reward.

Kids.   An occasional "punk" may be able to manage his sexual activities even further, confining them to a relatively small group. "Stand-up guys" shun entry into a pseudo-marriage as a sign of weakness. They may, however, offer protection and favors to a particularly attractive "punk" in return for his regular performance of sexual acts.The "punk" is then known as their "kid." Sal, the "stand-up guy" who works in the "Jay Cee" stand, was looking for a "kid":

"I gotta find me a kid, but it's hard, ya know. I don't want nothing to do with any of them 'punks' we got here now. But if some nice looking, clean punk comes in then I might just do something for him. . . . Well, like sorta take him under my wing and give him things from the stand. . . . It's just kinda nice to have a 'kid' around, ya know, one that you can count on and that's pretty much yours. I hate like hell to have to use one of them 'punks' that's 'catching lobs' [fellatio] from everybody else."

The relationship between "kids" and other inmates are distinct from both those of the "fag" and the typical "punk." Unlike the pseudo-marriages to the "fags," the "kid" relationship does not extend beyond the sex act itself, nor is it an exclusive relationship. It is a contractual exchange of sexual services for protection and material reward, and is devoid of emotion and intimacy. "Kids" do not necessarily live next to their sex partners, nor do they work, eat, or "hang out" together. Several inmates, usually known to each other, may share the same "kid." As long as the "kid" is able to fulfill his sexual obligations with respect to each one, there is no conflict. In contrast to most "punks," on the other hand, the "kid" is not coerced. "Kids" have already been "made" and are now offered assured compensation for their services. From a narrow point of view, then, they enter the relationship voluntarily and by means of it are protected from coercion or threat by others. As there is little emotional investment in the relationship, however, protection remains uncertain and "kids" in fact are often betrayed.

Dope Fiends and Others

Dope Fiends. Drugs have replaced liquor as the most desired illicit commodity at ECI. Even inmates who were not users prior to their imprisonment become occasional users in an effort to escape the realities of life within the walls. But inmates make a clear distinction between such occasional users and the "dope fiend." "Dope fiends" are inmates who were addicts prior to their incarceration and for whom "scoring drugs" and "getting high" remain their consummate interest while in prison. Despite this rather clear distinction, however, most "dope fiends" remain rather indistinguishable from the majority of the white population. My informants, for instance, were in general agreement that some 20 to 30 percent of the white inmates were "dope fiends," but they exhibited considerable disagreement over the identification of specific inmates as "dope fiends."

There are several reasons for this confusion. First, few inmates have been convicted of violations of narcotics laws. Most "dope fiends" have been convicted of Breaking and Entering, Larceny, or some similar property offense related to their addiction. Thus, most "dope fiends" are not labeled as such by the nature of their offense. Second, the offenses of "dope fiends" are usually of a minor nature, and they receive relatively short sentences. Being in maximum security for a relatively short period of time, they remain unknown to the majority of inmates. Third, not enough drugs enter the institution for the "dope fiend" to maintain his physical addiction. They are therefore distinguishable from the occasional users only by the degree of their desire for drugs and the effort they expend to obtain them. Finally, because of the risks involved and the high demand for drugs, "dope fiends" attempt to conceal their activities from inmates as well as from officers.

Despite their relative anonymity, "dope fiends" are deeply involved in the underlife of the institution. They stand at the center of a complex network of relationships that has arisen around the procurement, sale, and usage of drugs. Occasionally, a "dope fiend" may receive drugs as a gift from a visitor. More commonly, however, drugs must be purchased, whether from a visitor or another inmate, at highly inflated prices. A "nickel bag" ($5.00 worth) of heroin, for example, costs between $15.00 and $20.00 at ECI. And, unlike other transactions, drugs are sold only for cash. To secure drugs, then, "dope fiends" frequently form alliances with other inmates to raise the necessary cash. Even if they have the money, however, they may not have a set of "works," a hypodermic needle and syringe. Another inmate without money but with the "works" may then be brought into the combination. The effort to secure drugs thus drives "dope fiends" into symbiotic relationships with at least three or four other inmates.

An occasional "dope fiend" is able to maintain his street connections and thus secure a rather constant supply of drugs exceeding his immediate needs. He may then turn to "dealing" within the institution. By cutting a "nickel bag," purchased at $15.00 from a street connection, into rather minuscule portions sold for $5.00, the "dealer" can realize a considerable profit. "Dealing," however, is a risky business. Not only must the "dealer" protect himself from the staff, but if he is to realize a profit he must protect himself from inmate predators, such as the "wise guys," who will convert his profit into their own. To protect himself, the "dealer" may form a confederation with four or five other inmates. A non-user is given a portion of the profit in return for receiving the drugs from a visitor and "stashing" them. Two or three others, in return for a portion of the supply, act as "runners." They spread the word that drugs are available, collect the cash, and return it to the "dealer." The "dealer" secures the drugs from the "stash," who remains unknown to the "runners" and who turns the drugs over to the "runners" who distribute them.

It is a well-known fact that when it comes to narcotics, "dope fiends" have no friends. The relationships described, whether based on selling or consuming drugs, are not cohesive. They are symbiotic relations that hinge upon the common interest in "scoring" and "getting high." As such, the membership of the various combinations is constantly shifting, depending upon who has the necessary connections to secure drugs and who has the money to purchase them. Pervading these relationships is the fear of "getting beat." A "dope fiend" may be "beat" in various ways. The "dealer," for instance, is highly vulnerable. His operation may be, and often is, uncovered by the "wise guys," in which case he takes all the risks for little or no profit. Apart from that, his "stash" may use the supply

to begin "dealing" himself, or his "runners" may hijack his supply or profits. Users may likewise be "beat." One of the major confidence games within the institution is for "dope fiends" to present themselves as "runners" and then use the collected cash to make their own purchases. Or they may in fact be "runners," but fail to make the contracted delivery. In both cases, they may claim to have been "hijacked" by the "wise guys." A variant of this game is for a "dope fiend" to collect cash to make a purchase from a street connection, use the drugs himself, and then claim the connection failed to deliver.

Others. Confidence games and petty hijacking activities such as these are by no means the sole province of the "dope fiends." Nearly one-third of the white population are serving sentences of three years or less. Inmates at ECI are eligible for parole after completing one-third of their sentence, and it is a common practice to place prisoners in minimum security several months prior to parole. This makes for a high rate of population mobility among the white population. Close to one-third of them remain in maximum security for only three to six months. They exist only as nameless faces to the majority of whites and are not identified by any distinctive label. They are "others."

The steady flow of "others" through maximum security presents a difficult control problem for both the custodians and the long-term inmates. "Others" are generally an impoverished class and are not in the institution long enough to gain access to positions that would provide them with a "hustle," a means of engaging in informal exchange relations. Their very transiency and anonymity, however, afford them a measure of protection for a variety of disruptive activities. They form small cliques and hijack each other, and steal cigarettes, televisions, and other commodities from open cells. They use their anonymity to "beat the stand" by making purchases and charging them to another inmate's account. These and other exploitive activities serve to increase the level of suspicion with which the white inmates regard each other, and they contribute to the general absence of any sense of inmate solidarity.

Rats

Nowhere is the absence of white inmate solidarity more evident than in white views on "rats" and "rattings." A "rat" is an inmate who communicates information concerning inmate activities to the custodians. Among the white prisoners there is no clearly definable class of inmates termed "rats." With the exception of the "mafia"and "stand-up guys," any inmate not in the circle of one's immediate associates is an actual or potential "rat." From the standpoint of any particular inmate, then, nearly all others are "rats."

The norm against "ratting" remains an ideal but is not often realized in practice. Inmates do not expect another inmate to endure any pain or suffering without "ratting." Ideally, he should; realistically, few will. As one old-timer put it quite candidly: "The rule here is don't rat, but don't let your conscience kill ya." The norm against "ratting," then, is not seen as a moral absolute demanding unthinking and automatic compliance. It is relative and admits of many exceptions, one of which may be if another has "ratted" on you. The following conversation among three inmates occurred in my presence in the yard. Harry was dreading the fact that he was going to court in the morning and was seeking advice from Sam and Joe:

HARRY: They want me to testify against the guy that put me in here. I don't know what to do. I sure would like to get that bastard.

SAM: Wait 'till ya get out and then stick a shiv in him.

JOE: Don't be a fool, man. That'll just get ya more time. They got anything else on ya?

HARRY: Yeah, passing some paper.

JOE: Then, make a deal. You help them if they help you. That way you get the bastard now and get a break yourself. What you think, Sam?

SAM: It's one way of doing it, I guess.

In a solidary inmate group with a strong consensus on the norms against "ratting," the incidence of "ratting" may strengthen group solidarity. Strong group sanctions, including physical assault and death, imposed upon the "rat" may serve to unify the group against a common internal enemy. But, given the definition of "ratting" at ECI, sanctions against "rats" weaken the group further.[14] Accepting the norm as situationally specific, the inmates define "ratting" as a personal rather than a group concern. If one inmate "rats" on another, it is their "beef," to be settled by themselves.

"As long as he don't 'rat' on me why should I care? Why should I stick my neck out when the other guys don't give a shit and one of 'em might even 'rat' on me."

If we view the interest of third parties in punishing proscribed behavior as an indicator of the degree to which a norm is institutionalized, then this comment indicates that the norm proscribing "ratting" is not institutionalized at ECI. "Ratting" often is not penalized. Moreover, when it is penalized, the penalties are in the form of personal vendettas that, rather than unifying the group against a common enemy, fragment it into cliques in conflict with each other. This makes "ratting" even more likely. Anonymous "ratting" on the activities of another is another means of revenge, of evening the score. "Ratting," and the sanctioning of "rats," constitutes a vicious circle undermining and eroding the solidarity of the white population.

[14]Coser notes that renegades and heretics may serve to strengthen a solidary group, but disrupt one which is noncohesive. Lewis Coser, *The Functions of Social Conflict* (New York: The Free Press, 1956), pp. 69–71.

50. Social Types Among the Blacks

LEO CARROLL

BROTHERS AND PARTNERS

Brothers

FOR SOME BLACK INMATES A "BROTHER" MUST BE A black, but for most a "brother" is a member of any minority group who displays an awareness of white oppression and a rebellion against it. The following conversation between three black prisoners concerning the composition of a soccer team indicates the ambiguity surrounding the criteria by which one is judged to be a "brother":

"'I see they got one brother at least', Sam observed. 'Who's that?' Carl asked. 'Wally Hernandez.' Carl objected. 'He ain't no brother. He's Italian'. Sam replied, 'No, he's a brother. He came up to the meetings for a while. He's Spanish or Mexican or something.' Leroy, who had been quiet, agreed with Sam. 'That's right. He's a Mexican.' Carl sat up in his chair and concluded, 'He might be one of them Latins but that don't make him a brother does it?' Sam and Leroy looked uncomfortable but didn't answer."

In practice at Eastern Correctional Institution a black inmate becomes a "brother" through his membership in the Afro-American Society. The organization thus has something of the character of a family. The relationship between "brothers," however, need not be a deeply personal one. One need not know or even like another black inmate to consider him a "brother." One may even be suspicious and mistrustful of a "brother." Here is one of the perspectives of "soul," namely that life is a game and people often seek to corrupt contexts and relationships for personal profit. So, for example, one of the obligations of brotherhood is to acquaint a new "brother" with the institution. Unlike the whites who, as we have seen, avoid new inmates, the blacks seek them out both to "sound" on them and to "run it down" to them. But if one is "cool," he is careful in accepting such interpretations.

As soon as I got here, I didn't know none of these dudes, you know, but when I come in they started comin' around sounding on me to see where I was at. Then they hepped me to the different hacks, which ones was creeps and which ones was all right, you know, and all the things ya gotta know like how to get seconds in the dining hall or where ya can get coffee and toast, what the good jobs were, things like that. Same thing with the inmates. They be tellin' me who's a rat and who's okay. 'Course I didn't make no judgment right then. I keep all these things in my mind and I be careful, but I don't make no final judgment right then, not till I see for myself. Ya can't go by what ya hear 'cause ya don't know but what the dude that's running it down to ya might have some motive, ya know."

The essence of brotherhood, then, is not personal knowledge, liking or even trust. Brotherhood is based on the recognition of a shared fate

▶SOURCE: *Hacks, Blacks and Cons.* Lexington, Mass.: *Lexington Books, 1974 Pp. 98–113. Reprinted by permission of the publisher.*

at the hands of a common oppressor, and the essence of the relationship is mutual aid in the face of oppression. As in the above quote, "brothers" share information so as to protect each other and to make life easier. In the same vein they share material goods. Again, however, this is not an automatic or personal sharing of all that one possesses. If one has a radio, and a "brother" asks to use it, the owner is obliged to loan it. But the owner of a radio is not expected to offer it to a "brother" without one. Much of the sharing of material comforts is institutionalized in the Afro-American Society. Money collected from dues and fines is used to purchase records, books, and musical instruments for the use of all members. On several occasions, the membership voted to loan money to members for some purpose. Many inmates arrive without necessities such as toothbrushes, toothpaste, towels, and razors, and without the means to purchase these from the Inmate Store. Through an "Uptight Program" the Afro-American Society maintains a supply of such items for newly arrived black inmates in these circumstances.

Above and beyond all else, brotherhood implies an obligation of aid in the fact of conflict.

"As long as a man's a 'brother' you ain't gonna let nothing happen to him. If he's got a beef then it's your beef. If you got a beef, then it's his."

A "beef," from the standpoint of the "brother" is any conflict with a "non-brother." This may include staff, white inmates, or those black inmates defined as "Toms." In any conflict or crisis situation, a "brother" is obliged to "go down" with his "brothers." Again, in this context, however, there is the element of personal mistrust. A "beef" may in fact be a "game" in which a "brother" seeks to manipulate other "brothers" so as to utilize their collective power for his personal advantage. A "brother" may claim an officer took his radio, and demand that the organization secure its return. An investigation might reveal, however, that in fact the officer had only taken the radio after repeatedly

warning the inmate to turn it down as it was after 10:30 p.m. A "beef" of this sort is defined as a "bullshit beef" to which the obligations of brotherhood do not apply. The obligations of brotherhood apply only to "legitimate beefs" in which the "brother" has been wronged.

The brotherhood relation, then, is essentially a symbiotic relation pertaining to mutual aid in time of need. Grounded in the recognition of common oppression, it lacks any essential elements of personal knowledge and intimacy and is subject to several restrictions. Beneath this relationship, buttressing and supporting it, are the relations between "partners."

Partners

"Partners" are black inmates who are "up tight" with each other, who share common interests, who know each other well, who can "rap" easily with each other, and are thus intimate. The relationship between "partners" is diffuse and not subject to restriction. "Partners" automatically share whatever they have without being asked. A black inmate who receives an extra store order from a visit offers part of it to his "partner." Black inmates going to minimum security where they must live in a dormitory give to their "partners" televisions and other items not permitted in the dormitory setting. If a man's "partner" has a "beef," it is his "beef" as well, regardless of whether it is "legitimate" or "illegitimate," or with a "brother" or "non-brother." A "partner" is someone you go all the way with, no questions asked. "Partners" protect each other. They seek to live in cells near one another and to provide a buffer between their "partner" and the eyes of others be they staff inmates, or white researchers.

"Partners" are of different types and any one black inmate may have several. A basic distinction is made between "street partners" and "jail house partners." "Street partners" are inmates who were "up tight" with each other and "ran" together prior to confinement. Also included in this category are one's actual biological relations. "Jail house partners" are friends to whom one has become related during one's current sentence. "Jail house partners" form a clique or primary group that may or may not include "street partners." For example, several black inmates related by kinship tended not to have the same "jail house partners." But while one may not "hang" with his "street partner" during confinement, the obligations of "partnership" remain. One black inmate clearly explained this relation in an interview.

Q: But if you're "partners" like you say and you'd lay down your life for them, why don't you hang out together?

A: . . . Let's see. How can I explain that? . . . Me and another dude is 'street partners,' see, but he gets busted 'fore I do. When he comes in he's gonna get with some other dudes—'jail house partners,' you dig. Then I show, but he's already hooked up with three or four other dudes and they's swingin' out together. So I hook up with some others and swing out with them. That don't mean I ain't tight with him no more. We still be tight. I know he's there and he knows I'm over here. Then if he's got a beef I'm automatically involved and the three or four dudes I'm hanging with is involved too and the three or four dudes he be hanging with is involved.

From an adaptive and protective point of view then, it is a sound tactic not to hang with "street partners," but to develop a separate set of "jail house partners." As a result nearly the total black population is bound together by an interlocking structure of diffuse relationships that facilitates rapid mobilization in times of crisis and that provides most black inmates with aid and assistance of a routine nature. This structure of solidarity also serves to obscure a deep ideological division among "brothers" and "partners," a division reflecting the conflict between the perspectives of "soul" and the perspectives of revolutionary nationalism.

REVOLUTIONARIES AND HALF-STEPPERS[1]

It is probably no accident that revolutionary leaders such as Malcolm X, Eldridge Cleaver, and George Jackson developed in prison. The ideology of black revolution would appear to have immediate relevance for the black convict. Subjected to a series of pains, deprivations, and debasements that destroy their sense of self, all inmates face the problem of constructing a new identity. For many prisoners, black and white, the only alternative in the past has been that of "convict." From the perspective of the convict, inmates are able to preserve their self-esteem by "rejecting their rejectors" and on this basis to develop a form of negative solidarity by means of which other deprivations are neutralized or alleviated. Today, however, black revolutionary nationalism offers to black inmates a more inclusive and positive identity than that of the convict. By viewing themselves from the perspectives of nationalism, black prisoners are able to integrate their role as a prisoner with their role as a black man in a way which places them in the vanguard of a worldwide movement against colonial oppression.

With models such as Cleaver and Jackson, and through their interaction in the Afro-American Society, the black inmates at ECI have developed a collective definition of themselves as political prisoners. Regardless of the nature of their crime, by adopting a revolutionary perspective they are able to interpret it as a political act. Homicide, Robbery, Larceny, and Burglary involving white victims are justified as

[1]Unlike other labels I have used, the terms "revolutionary" and "half-stepper" are not consensual labels employed by the black prisoners themselves. Nonetheless they are indicative of distinct prison adaptive styles. As noted earlier the absence of consensual labels for this difference may be attributable to the character of the Afro-American Society, the need to maintain solidarity in the presence of white oppressors and to recruit and socialize new members. The term "half-stepping" is used by black prisoners to refer to verbal behavior in which one is not quite truthful.

acts of revolution or, at least, as a means of obtaining what is one's due. Few of their offenses are of this nature, however. In most cases the victims are black, and, in the case of drug offenses, themselves. But the revolutionary perspective is broad enough to include these as well. Such crimes, while not revolutionary acts, are the result of white racism. They are the means by which the white population maintains its dominance over the black. By pitting black against black, by supplying them drugs, whites inhibit the development of racial unity and revolutionary consciousness. As the following excerpt from an interview shows, even the rape of a black woman may be seen as the result of white racism:

Q: Do you feel guilty about anything you've done?

A: Guilty! For What? Them B & E's was 'cause I was on drugs. If I wasn't on drugs I wouldn't have done nothing, and I wouldn't be on drugs if you whites didn't put 'em in my community. You people put 'em there and keep 'em there. It's a round robin is what it is. It always comes back to white society. You're the ones that's guilty, not me.

Q: Is there any crime a black man might be guilty of?

A: What kind of crime?

Q: Say raping a black woman?

A: Ya can't tell, man. You read that book *Black Rage.* . . . Then you can see there ain't no telling why a black man's doing something. Even raping a black woman's probably 'cause of the brainwashing white society done on him.

Similar sentiments are expressed by nearly all the black inmates with whom I had contact. Except for a few, labeled "toms" by the majority, virtually all "talk the talk" of revolution. But "talking the talk" is quite distinct from "walking the walk." This is to say that while nearly all espoused revolution; and defined themselves as "revolutionaries," few fashion their prison behavior in terms of this perspective. The behavior of the majority reflects an orientation to the perspectives of "soul" rather than to the perspectives of revolution.

Revolutionaries

George Jackson provides a model of the committed black revolutionary doing time. He stated:

"I've trained myself not to be disorganized by any measure they take against me. I exercise in the yard, and pursue my studies. Since I know that I am the original man and will soon inherit this earth, I am content to just prepare myself and wait, nothing can stop me now."[2]

No more than six or seven black inmates acted in accord with such an orientation. For these few, whom we may identify as "revolutionaries," the significant reference group is not the black inmate population but revolutionary groups beyond the walls. Their orientation is not to the present but to the future. As they see it, it is the historic and obligatory duty of black prisoners, those who are surrounded by the ultimate symbols of white oppression, to utilize their time in preparation for the eventual revolution. Part of their preparation entails an effort to free themselves of attachments to material things, to purify themselves of any dependence upon the materialism of western white culture, and to steel themselves for the adversities to be encountered during the revolution. Their prison existence is stoic. Their cells remain unadorned and contain only necessities such as a bed, desk, typewriter, radio, and books concerned with revolution. Their clothing is, for the most part, only what the institution provides—khaki or green trousers, a khaki or

[2]George Jackson, *Soledad Brother: The Prison Letters of George Jackson* (New York: Bantam Books, 1970), p. 87.

white shirt, and a black wool jacket. They remain uninvolved in the exchange systems by which inmates seek to alleviate material deprivations. The desire for sandwiches or pies from the kitchen is seen as a sign of weakness. The most significant marks of weakness, however, are not pies and sandwiches but drugs and homosexual behavior.

"I seen what drugs done to the dudes down around 125th Street in New York. Drugs is genocide, man. It's the way the white system keeps the black man down. As long as his mind's frozen, he's defeated. The way I see it a man can't be black and be shooting drugs. You gotta be strong to be black and shooting drugs is weak. And I definitely can't see it in here. There ain't no reason to use it in here. There ain't enough of it in here for 'em to stay addicted but they keep going back for it.

. . .

"Any man who hits someone in the seat is weak as far as I'm concerned. He's a 'fag' just like the one he's hitting."

A second aspect of the prison style of the "revolutionary" is intense involvement in programs directed at self-improvement. To be a "revolutionary"one must rehabilitate oneself. He must rid himself of the "negative images" white society establishes for him. He must abandon any commitment to or identification with the life of the pimp, the hustler, or the dope fiend, as these are the most powerful and insidious weapons of white oppression. Attachment to these lifestyles must be extinguished, and can only be extinguished through "getting in touch with one's blackness" by intense involvement in the cultural and educational programs of the Afro-American Society. Beyond involvement in these programs, most of the "revolutionaries" are engaged in self-designed reading programs, the content of which ranges from Marx and Engels through Mao Tse-tung, Franz Fanon, and Che Guevara to peers such as Cleaver and Jackson. While remaining deeply suspicious of any programs offered by the prison administration, they are nonetheless quick to involve themselves in those in which they can perceive some

benefit. So, for example, all are active in the MDTA Vocational Training Program. Partly this is a gambit for earlier parole, partly an effort to prepare for a job after release, but it is also related to their desire to learn skills necessary in the event of the formation of a black state.

The almost complete immersion of the "revolutionary" in self-improvement activities leaves him little time for socializing or participation in recreational pursuits. They seldom go to movies on Friday nights, preferring to stay in their cells and read. Playing cards or pool, watching television, or, worse, just "hanging out" in the wings is "idling" and avoided. Most of their interpersonal relations are structured within the activities of the Afro-American Society, and they hold themselves aloof from the majority of the black population, whom they regard with some disdain.

"I don't consider most of the blacks in here to be 'brothers.' They must be jiving with all that loyalty and revolutionary rhetoric . . . if they was serious they'd be getting their heads together in them programs we got going."

Half-Steppers
For want of a better term we may identify the vast majority of the black inmates as "half-steppers." "Half-steppers" "talk the talk" of revolution, but do not "walk the walk." Their public behavior manifests an intense commitment to revolution. Their cells are decorated with portraits of revolutionary heroes and posters proclaiming "Power to the People," "The Revolution is Now," "Burn, Baby, Burn," and "Off the Pigs." Many wear buttons of a political nature—green buttons with a black outline of Africa, and others with slogans such as "Free Angela," "Free Huey," and "Dump Nixon." Their conversations in the yard and wings are frequently punctuated with loud comments denouncing the racist "pigs" and advocating revolution.

The very public and external nature of these affirmations, however, reveals them as self-conscious attempts to collectively claim and support an identity to which they in fact are not fully committed. The prison style of the "half-stepper," their actual behavior and private conversations, reflect an importation and enactment of the perspectives of "soul" within the prison. Where the orientation of the "revolutionary" is to the outside and the future, the orientation of the "half-stepper" is to the present and to opportunities for self-expression within the prison. As they see it, life in the prison is not so terribly different from life in the ghetto.

"I'm doing time all my life, man. Don't make much difference if I do it here or out there. It's still time."

Sharing this perspective, "half-steppers" support each other in efforts to collapse time to the immediate present. Even to mention one's case or to work on appeals, activities common among the whites and "revolutionaries," is cause for group sanctions in the form of "sounding," "signifying," or perhaps exclusion. One "half-stepper," for example, was denied parole solely because he had failed to clear up several minor additional charges in the court. To clear the charges would have meant an appearance in court, a guilty plea, and the probable acceptance of a sentence concurrent to the one he was serving. Having been notified several times to appear in court, he had requested continuances. After his parole was denied, I asked him why he had failed to appear in court. The only reasons he could offer were that there had been "too much going on" at the time, and that he had not realized his parole date was so close. A similar orientation was expressed by another black inmate in an interview:

"Do you think that black and white inmates might have a different outlook on their time?

"You got it there, man. Them white dudes be always looking ahead to the end of that ten or 25 and crying and complaining. I don't know any 'brothers' that even know how much time they got left. Take me. I don't think about my time. I know I'm getting short but if you was to ask me how many days I got left, I couldn't tell ya. I count the years, ya know, but not the days. All the 'brothers' take their time day by

day and involve themselves with the 'brothers' here. We be used to time so we be immune to it. . . . Because we been slaves for 400 years."

The final comment in this quote suggests the relation of the "half-steppers" view of time to the "soul" perspective. Through a history of oppression and suffering black people have developed a non-standardized and present-oriented sense of time that, in the prison or in the ghetto, enhances their capacity for "making it with dignity." Likewise, involvement with the "brothers," for the "half-stepper," means involvement in a variety of expressive activities. Unlike the "revolutionaries" or most white inmates, the "half-steppers" do not standardize or schedule the time not regulated by the formal system. I discovered this fact in trying to make contact with certain individuals during the study. I had no difficulty locating either whites or black "revolutionaries," as they tended to follow a standardized schedule I was able to learn and they were often engaged in solitary activities. This was not so with the majority of blacks. They tended to gravitate to wherever the action was at the moment, and to be continually involved in peer group activities that made my entrance awkward.

The content of such activities is extremely varied, but virtually all are expressive in nature. Most common is merely "hanging out" and "rapping" with six or seven others in the yard or wings. These conversations are loud, punctuated by peals of laughter, and involving much body movement and slapping of hands.

"At one point Bean stepped out from the group, cocked his head to the left, and opened his huge eyes to the fullest extent, and said in a falsetto voice, 'Little Boy, you ain't black! You be married!' The others responded with loud laughing and Bean held out both hands, palms up, and KP slapped on them. Little Boy remained quiet and soon left the group."

The above incident is a form of "signifying" or "sounding." Little Boy, a partner in a homosexual marriage was embarrassed and degraded by Bean in a manner to which he could not respond. Bean's status was enhanced by his ability to fashion an indirect verbal taunt, ("You be married," not a fag), and to express it with the appropriate body style and tone to make it effective. His reward was the highly stylized hand slap by KP, a leader of the clique, given only when one has made a significant point in a verbal exchange.

Verbal exchanges of this sort are a continual preoccupation of the "half-stepper,"and ability in such repartee is highly valued. But verbal exchanges are only one aspect of their expressive prison style. In direct contrast to the "revolutionary" who remains unconcerned with personal appearance, the "half-stepper" displays an intense concern with clothing. Hats particularly are one means by which they express their being in action. For the old institutional grey cap once required of all inmates, the "half-steppers" substitute a variety of multi-colored knit "bopper caps," Australian army campaign hats, and broad brimmed felt hats, usually brown or white. These are traded back and forth, an individual desiring one or another depending upon his mood or feeling at the moment. Sunglasses and brightly colored turtle neck shirts are used in the same manner and for the same purpose. On one occasion a "half-stepper" requested that I bring him a pair of "shades." He took great pains to draw me an exact sketch of the glasses he desired. Over the next week I brought him three pairs of glasses on separate occasions. He accepted the third pair, but only reluctantly: "They just ain't me, man."

The efforts of the "half-steppers" to express themselves in dress and action are validated by the individual identifications made by the group. Nicknames are uncommon among the whites, and the black "revolutionary" usually adopts an African name. But nearly all the "half-steppers" are identified by a nickname which, in some inexplicable way, summarizes essential qualities of his person. Names such as "Rump," "Cadillac," "Ticky," "Bean," "Little Boy," "Moose," "Harlem Nat," "Frankenstein," and "June Bug" could fit only those to whom they refer. And, tied as they are to the unique personal style of the individual, the frequent usage of these names reinforces the almost primary group cohesion of the "half-steppers."

This cohesion receives its strongest support through the commitment of the "half-steppers" to music. The Music Committee of the Afro-American Society is one of the most active. They maintain a record library of "soul" recordings that is replenished monthly. Members may borrow records for a weekend, and a frequent pastime of "half-steppers" is to gather at the cell of one who has an expensive stereo and "groove" on the latest hits. On Sundays, the organization utilizes the otherwise unused institutional radio station to produce its own "soul program" in which each member is accorded a turn at being the disc jockey. The committee also purchased several instruments for the use of members and the availability of these gives rise to constant jam sessions in the gym or yard.

"Half-steppers," then, have used the increased permeability of the institution and the greater freedom of interaction permitted inmates to elaborate an expressive prison style fashioned by the perspectives of "soul." The expressiveness of the "half-stepper" style is in decided contrast to the stoic existence of the revolutionary. Nowhere is the conflict between the two orientations more evident than their views concerning drugs, homosexuality, and the future. As we have seen, the "revolutionary" regards drugs as a form of genocide, and homosexual activity as a mark of weakness. From the perspective of the "half-stepper," drugs and homosexual behavior are necessities, and educational pursuits a waste of time that could more profitably be used in socializing with the "brothers" or engaging in a "hustle"to secure some desired commodity.

"Man, I got seven and a half years ahead of me and I'm gonna do my thing. I gotta escape from this here reality and I'm gonna score dope any time I can. . . .A lotta dudes think you can't be black and be a fag. I don't see that. There's a lotta black writers that's 'fags' and they're out there doing their black thing. I accept 'em for what they are. And in here they're a necessity. Ya need 'em."

"Half-steppers" involve themselves in the present and seldom talk of their future. But when they do, their comments indicate a continued commitment to the life of the pimp, the hustler, and the dope fiend rather than a commitment to revolution. The following conversation between two black inmates occurred in my presence in the yard:

J: I love that life, man. I don't like what it does to ya but I love the women, the hogs, and the fast money. What else is there for dudes like me? I was born to the life.

R: But what about all them commitments you made to the organization?

J: What about 'em? They wasn't real, man. I had to do it so's I could groove with my 'brothers.' I go along with what them dudes is saying but I'm too much into the life to change now. You be the same too, man. If I was to drop a bundle right now you'd break your neck fighting for it.

R: No I wouldn't.

J: You telling me you wouldn't touch it? You're jiving, man.

R: Hell, 'course I'd use it. But that don't mean I love it. I can take it or leave it.

This conversation continued for nearly an hour, during which time J. sought relentlessly to pierce R.'s pretension at non-commitment to the "life," an effort that was successful. It ended with both jokingly agreeing that as soon as they were released they would be "throwing rocks at the penitentiary," i.e., engaging in behavior that would result in future confinement.

Conflict

The disparity between the prison style of the "revolutionary" and the style of the "half-stepper," between the perspectives of "soul" and

those of nationalism, between future orientation and present orientation, between identification with external revolutionary groups and the black inmate population, made for strain and conflict within the Afro-American Society. The organization was established by the "revolutionaries." In their mind it was a vehicle by which they would be able to proselytize and convert the "half-steppers" to,—in the words of George Jackson—"transform the black criminal mentality into a revolutionary mentality."[3] They were able to secure two classrooms for the sole use of the organization, and they decorated these rooms with maps and flags of African states and posters of Angela Davis, Huey Newton, and Muhammed Ali. Every evening from 5 p.m. to 8:30 p.m. they scheduled a number of activities aimed at the goal of conversion. These activities ranged from courses in African cultures and history, through a high school equivalency program utilizing Afro-American materials, to frequent "rap sessions" dealing with problems surrounding the "brainwashing" perpetrated upon black people by white society.

The first President and Board of Directors were self-appointed and revolutionary in their orientation. The by-laws accorded them the power to make and enforce rules as they deemed necessary for the welfare of the organization and its members. Through a set of "Presidential Policies" they attempted to extend their control into the members' extra-organizational behavior. To be admitted to the organization, prospective members had to pledge that they would refrain from drug usage and homosexual activity. All members were required to attend classes. There was to be no "idling" in the wings, and no fighting or arguing outside of organizational meetings. Cells were to be thoroughly cleaned each day. There were to be no infractions of institutional rules. A committee was established to enforce these policies, and the President and Board of Directors sat weekly to dispose of infractions. Penalties imposed ranged

[3]Ibid., p. 21.

from fines of $.50 to $10.00 or more through suspension of membership for varying periods of time. Members were forbidden to communicate or interact in any way with suspended members, an infraction itself punishable by suspension.

Such programs and policies were completely at odds with the interests of most members. For the "half-steppers," the prime purpose of the organization was to make time easier. It was the social activities—the frequent jam sessions, the occasional banquets, the opportunities to meet girls from the street, to rap with each other free from the surveillance of the administration, and similar activities—that were their prime interest. Further, membership in the organization provided them with a sense of security. As one put it, "The main purpose behind the organization is to keep them whiteys off our backs."

As noted above, the obligations of brotherhood extend only to "legitimate beefs" in which a "brother" has been wronged. However, the legitimacy or illegitimacy of a grievance is often difficult to establish. One of the basic conflicts between "revolutionaries" and "half-steppers" was their viewpoint on this matter. Oriented to the outside and the future and placing a high priority on the cultural and educational aspects of the organization, the "revolutionaries" inclined toward a restrictive view and were reluctant to take any action on a grievance until a thorough investigation had been completed. "Half-steppers," with their greater orientation to the present and interest in the prison world itself, inclined toward a more diffuse view of the obligations of mutual aid. From their perspective, virtually any grievance was legitimate and demanding of supportive action.

The lack of consensus between "revolutionaries" and "half-steppers" on such matters as drugs and mutual aid in time of crisis generated considerable antagonism between them. Far from being seen as charismatic leaders, the "revolutionaries" came to be viewed as dictators. As one member put it, "It's like having two sets of hacks." After one meeting in which

22 of the 37 members present were fined for drug usage, one "half-stepper" gave expression to several of the disagreements between "revolutionaries" and "half-steppers," denying that "revolutionaries" were true "brothers":

"Ya know what I think. I think they ain't 'brothers' at all. They be weasels, sitting up there playin' them silly games in their rap sessions and classes and preachin' 'bout dope. There ain't but ten of 'em would go down on anything. If they be serious about revolution they be going down on every beef a 'brother' has 'stead giving him that jive that it ain't a legitimate beef. After all them whiteys done to us there ain't no beef that ain't legitimate."

Despite the rather sharp ideological conflict between the "revolutionaries" and "half-steppers," for several reasons the organization did not become dichotomized and dissolve. First, the revolutionary element saw themselves in the role of missionaries seeking to convert sinners. Deviations were to be expected, and while punished, they were forgiven. Second, the nature of the meetings and rap sessions were open and members were encouraged to express opposed viewpoints and vent their emotions. To some extent, then, the meetings served as a safety valve in which issues were dealt with as they arose.[4] Third, and perhaps most importantly, the "revolutionaries" composed only a small number of the membership and remained aloof from primary group relationships with the majority. As several of them were released, other members whose attitudes were more consistent with the majority were elected to their positions. Thus, the organization underwent a gradual change away from the perspectives of nationalism.

In August 1971, a "half-stepper," who had been a well-known pimp and drug dealer prior to his confinement, and who had been excluded

[4]Regardless of ideological conflict, the existence of such mechanisms would appear to be necessary for the stability of a group such as the Afro-American Society, in which there are close ties and a high degree of personal involvement. See Lewis Coser, *The Functions of Social Conflict* (New York: The Free Press, 1956), pp. 61–64.

from the organization for that reason, was admitted to membership and elected President on the next day. His rapid rise within the organization was due to his immersion in the network of partnerships. Immensely popular and a participant in several cliques, he was able to mobilize their support for his election. In his acceptance speech, he gave expression to a new and creative definition of the situation that neutralized the conflict between the opposed perspectives of nationalism and "soul":

"There's just a coupla things I wanna say about some things I been hearing. The first thing is dope. Now I ask you what's the answer to that? Most everybody in this room been into dope at one time or another. All the 'brothers' know how hard it is to stop using it. And how much we using anyway? Nobody here's strung out are they? I don't see nobody nodding. So what's the harm if a man scores a little dope in here now and then. He's still black ain't he? He can still be working for the revolution can't he? Everybody knows ya have to do things in jail you don't do on the street. You gonna tell a man that's got a life bid he can't use no pills once in a while. You can't do that. Every man's gotta get away from here once in a while. He can still think black, he can still act black, and he can still be there when the shit goes down. And that's what counts, 'brothers.' "

Thus, by conceptualizing the prison as an exceptional situation, by dissociating prison behavior from "street" behavior, and by restricting the definition of a revolutionary to one who can be counted upon in a crisis, the new President presented the membership with a definition of the situation that allowed them to retain an idealized image of themselves as revolutionaries while continuing to fashion their behavior according to the ghetto perspectives of "soul."

TOMS

Terms such as "stand-up guy," "wise guy," "administration man," "fag," and "rat," by which white inmates are labeled and identified are known and used by blacks as well. But among the blacks such labels are subordinate to the distinction between "brothers" and "toms." One might think the designation "tom" is an equivalent term for the pejorative roles identified by the whites. This is not the case. There is some overlapping, to be sure. One cannot be an "administration man" or "rat" and be a "brother." But many "brothers" are drug users or "dope fiends," and some are "fags." This lack of equivalence throws into relief the defining criterion of a "tom." A "tom" is any black inmate who displays accommodative behavior toward whites. Blacks who provide the staff with information or who accept a position of supervision over other inmates are not reproved because they are inmates violating an inmate code, but because they are blacks who reject the ideal of black unity. A "fag" may still be a "brother" if he confines his sexual activities to other blacks. But a "fag" who performs sexual services for whites is a "tom," as is the occasional black inmate who, while playing the active role in a homosexual relation, develops an emotional attachment for a white "fag" or "kid."

Of the approximately 46 black inmates, no more than eight were identified as "toms." Three of these were older "lifers" who had adopted the "administration man" role. One was a proof reader in the print shop, another the foreman of the upholstery shop, and the third was the institutional maintenance man. A fourth was a young "fag" who refused to change his behavior and entered freely into sexual liaisons with any inmate regardless of color. Three others were long-timers who played the active role in a homosexual marriage with white "kids." One other was a 51-year old man on a short sentence who openly engaged in fawning behavior with respect to the staff.

In no way are the "toms" a group or a clique. Except for the four engaged in homosexual activity, they are loners, scorned by the staff, excluded by the whites and hated by the "brothers." No class of individuals is more despised by a group than renegades, potential members who deny the values most affirmed by the group. "Toms" are renegades. Their behavior rejects and denies the very basis of black unity, and their existence is a constant threat to racial solidarity. Further, in the eyes of the "brothers," the behavior of the "tom" makes their time more difficult. As they see it, "toms" confirm the stereotypes held by the white officers concerning the proper role of a black man. The result is a definition of black behavior by the officers, behavior which in the eyes of the black prisoners is merely "being a man," as militant and threatening, and therefore more likely to be penalized. For all of these reasons the "toms" are regarded with utter hatred and disdain.

"Toms" are subject to continual harassment by the "brothers" ranging from verbal insults to occasional assaults. Again, however, such behavior is more typical of the "half-stepper" than the "revolutionary." The "revolutionary"opposes any conflict between blacks that is visible to whites. He avoids the "toms." But for the "half-stepper," caught as he is in a situation in which his behavior is at variance with an identity he claims for himself, verbal and physical aggression against "toms" is a means of proving to himself and others that he is in fact a black revolutionary. Thus, the existence of "toms" and their rejection of the value of racial unity reinforces that unity for a significant number of the black inmates.[5]

SUMMARY AND CONCLUSION

In this discussion we have seen that, unlike the white prisoners, the majority of black prisoners

[5]In Theodore Newcomb's terms, the "toms" function as a negative reference group for "half-steppers," as opposed to the positive reference group represented by the "revolutionaries." Unwilling or unable to attain the ideal standards of the "revolutionaries," "half-steppers" validate their identity claims more by reference to what they are not than by reference to what they should be. This process also occurs in their relation with the white staff. See Theodore M. Newcomb, *Social Psychology* (New York: Dryden Press, 1950), p. 227. From another perspective, Coser comments upon the functionality of a small group of renegades for the preservation of group solidarity (Coser, p. 71).

are united in a solidary group. The racial solidarity of the blacks is grounded in two ideological perspectives, "soul" and black nationalism, both of which have their origins in social movements outside the prison and are imported into the prison primarily through the Afro-American Society. While both "soul" and black nationalism provide bases for group solidarity, there is an inherent contradiction between them. "Soul" celebrates an historic black American culture; it affirms the value of perseverance and acceptance. Black nationalism, in contrast, celebrates past African glories, and presents visions of possible future greatness by means of a global revolution against the forces of racism, colonialism, and imperialism. This tension, along with the ideological perspectives which give rise to it, is imported into the prison and shapes the collective adaptations made by black prisoners.

Black prisoners recognize the argot labels used by the white inmates, but the focal concerns connoted by these terms are not the primary axes of life for the blacks. The primary axis of life for most black inmates is racial identification. They identify and act with respect to each other as "brothers," "partners"and "toms." Brotherhood is based upon the recognition of a shared fate at the hands of a common oppressor, and the essence of the relationship is mutual aid in the face of oppression. Underlying the relation between "brothers" and reinforcing it is the relation between "partners." Where the relation between "brothers" does not necessitate personal knowledge, liking, or even trust, these properties are at the heart of the relationship between "partners." The typical black inmate has one or more "jail house partners" and perhaps a "street partner." As a result, nearly the entire black population is bound together in an interlocking structure of diffuse relationships. Standing apart from this structure, and functioning as a negative reference group for the "brothers," is a small number of older "toms," so defined because they display what is regarded as accommodating behavior toward either the staff or white inmates.

From the perspective of an outsider, the majority of black prisoners seemingly are possessed of a single mind. There is, nonetheless, a deep ideological division within the Afro-American Society, a division that reflects the contradiction between "soul" and black nationalism. Black prisoners do not differentiate between prison adaptive styles embodying these perspectives by applying consensual labels to them, but I have labeled them "revolutionaries" and "half-steppers." "Revolutionaries" lead a stoic prison existence designed to prepare them for active participation in the black movement after release. In contrast, "half-steppers," while verbalizing revolutionary sentiments, retain an attachment to the life of the dope fiend or pimp and seek to make the most of their present existence by immersing themselves in the underlife of the institution. The contradiction between these orientations was apparent in disagreements concerning the goals and purposes of the Afro-American Society. The organization was established by the "revolutionaries" as a means of institutionalizing self-improvement programs and converting the "half-steppers." For the "half-steppers," the primary goals of the organization were social and protective. As a result of the restrictive policies of the "revolutionaries" concerning drugs, homosexuality, and relations with staff, they came to be seen as dictators and were displaced from the leadership of the organization near the end of the study period.

51. Stratification and Conflict Among Prison Inmates

JAMES B. JACOBS

PRISON STUDIES HAVE MOST OFTEN EMPHASIZED the inmate code, inmate distributive systems and the colorful argot roles which are said to be functional for the emergence and persistence of both normative and distributive systems. Little systematic attention has been paid to the significance of racial, political, and religious stratification or to formal inmate organizations. Yet, systems of stratification and formal organizations are the background against which primary groups, attitudes, and individual and group conflict develop. Inmate behavior cannot be understood without reference to these allegiances and commitments.

Donald Clemmer, the pioneer student of this subject, did offer some indication of the significance of intermediate level structures and allegiances among the confined when he spoke of the elite, middle, and hoosier classes.[1] These classes were rooted in pre-prison residency (urban versus rural) and criminal careers. There was a diffuse sense of class consciousness among the inmates in the penitentiary which Clemmer studied, and we may assume that primary group relations developed among individuals already linked by class ties. We may hypothesize that primary groups are formed among members of the same class, faction, or secondary group because of the emotional, and to a lesser degree,

material advantages of friendship cliques. Primary groups, however, do not necessarily reinforce the norms and values of the *inmate society*. Instead they may be said to reinforce the norms and values of those classes and secondary groups from which the primary groups are drawn.

What is at stake in focusing attention on inmate stratification systems and formal organizations is the viability of the background imagery which informs research on prison organization. The view of prisoners as isolated individuals who may or may not become socialized into an inclusive inmate culture through participation in primary groups is no longer useful in describing the contemporary prison. Issues of class and class conflict have been imported from the street into the prison so that inmate society is highly factionated at the intermediate or group level.

New analyses of prison organization must shake loose from the "total institution" model of imprisonment with its emphasis on individual and small group reaction to material and psychological deprivations. Perhaps a re-examination of the prisoner-of-war camp literature will yield a more fruitful perspective? Descriptions of prisons as diverse as Andersonville[2] and the camps of the Gulag Archipelego[3] have pointed to broad cleavages among inmates based upon pre-institutional allegiances to social classes, and upon participation in subcultures

▶SOURCE: *"Stratification and Conflict Among Prison Inmates," Journal of Criminal Law and Criminology* (1976) 66: 476–482. *Reprinted by permission.*

[1] D. Clemmer, *The Prison Community* (1958).

[2] J. McElroy, Andersonville: *A Story of Rebel Military Prisons* (1879).

[3] A. Solzhenitsyn, *The Gulag Archipelago* (1973).

and formal organizations. At Andersonville, the "N'Yaarkers" brought with them a solidarity based upon common cultural antecedents and an intact military formal organization. In the Gulag, the common criminals found a latent solidarity which served as a basis for collective action in their roots in a criminal subculture and exploited this solidarity in the brutalization of a weaker class—the politicals.

RACIAL STRATIFICATION

It is not surprising that in recent years of heightened racial consciousness throughout American society, racial identity within prison has become increasingly prominent.[4] Young prisoners today are supplanting their criminal identities with a racial-ethnic identity.[5] The development of race consciousness among blacks in recent years has been documented in the daily press and in a considerable black studies literature. Black awareness is not limited, however, to groups like Panthers and Muslims. It is the most significant referent even for those prisoners without formal and informal group ties.

At Illinois' Stateville Penitentiary, the racial lines are impregnable. It is unheard of for members of different races to cell together. Even under the ameliorative conditions of the minimum security facility at Vienna (as well as in Illinois' juvenile institutions), latinos, blacks, and caucasians constitute three separate and frequently conflicting societies. The following statement of a Soledad prisoner is indicative of the racial tension experienced in California.

"CTF-Central at Soledad, California is a prison under the control of the California Department of Corrections . . . However, by the 1960s the prison had earned the label in the system of "Gladiator School"; this was, primarily, because of the never-ending race wars and general personal violence which

destroyed any illusions about CTF-Central being an institution of rehabilitation . . . Two of the wings—O and X—are operated under maximum custody under the care of armed guards. There is no conflict between policy, intent and reality here: these are the specially segregated areas where murder, insanity and the destruction of men is accepted as a daily way of life. It is within the wings that the race wars become the most irrational; where the atmosphere of paranoia and loneliness congeal to create a day-to-day existence composed of terror."[6]

For most of American history, prisons were rigidly segregated societies. Even today, issues of segregation in prison are being debated in the courts.[7] As the movement toward racial equality gained momentum through the 1950's and 1960's minority groups increasingly came to see themselves as a solidary community. Beyond identifying with primary groups, minority group members began to form formal organizations and to identify with racial leaders.

Heightened racial awareness among whites for whom race was never before a particularly important identification is one consequence of continual racial tension. Whites outside of prison rarely have the experience of having been treated on the basis of their race per se but on the inside they soon realize that their racial identity has the greatest implications for their inmate career. During the turbulent years of 1970 and 1971, white inmates at Illinois' Stateville Penitentiary began passing messages and meeting secretly in order to organize a common defense against racial harassment by the black majority. More recently, they have begun to organize around neo-Nazi symbolism and ideology. In addition, white inmates appeal to racial solidarity when attempting to coalign with the mostly white custodial force. Tacit coalitions between white inmates and custodians in prison are not at all uncommon. White custodial officers at Stateville in 1972 identified with the

---

[4]Official Report of the New York State Special Commission on Attica 119 (1972) [hereinafter cited as Attica]. See L. Carroll, *Hacks, Blacks and Cons* (1974).

[5]J. Irwin, *The Felon* 80–82 (1970).

[6]Maguire, "Racism II," in *Inside Prison American Style* 84 (R. Minton ed. 1970).

[7]See e.g., *McClelland v. Sigler*, 327 F. Supp. 829 (D. Neb. 1971).

difficulties of the white minority and frequently tried to insulate them from vulnerability by finding for them safe "up front" jobs. In California prisons the rapid growth of the neo-Nazi Aryan Brotherhood can be explained as a movement in the direction of racial awareness and solidarity. The broad racial division in the inmate community is the background against which primary and secondary group behavior is to be understood.

The predominance of modern day "super-gangs" at Stateville Penitentiary and other Illinois prisons illuminates the way in which racial solidarity can generate formal organizations that make the prison look like a multi-national prisoner-of-war camp.[8] Four "super-gangs" (three black, one latino) with alleged memberships of thousands on Chicago streets have imported their organizational structure, leadership hierarchies, and activities into Illinois prisons. What proportion of the many hundreds of Stones, Disciples, Vicelords, and Latin Kings in Illinois prisons were members on the streets and how many were recruited in the County Jail or at the prison itself is not known, although gang leaders and independents estimate an even split. Dozens of interviews with gang leaders, old cons, and young blacks illuminate the difficulty for those wishing to remain unallied. One 28-year-old black who did manage to remain independent at Stateville for over a year had to fight every day against "recruiters" from the Stones and Disciples. In the morning he was awakened by taunts and sundry objects hurled by Stones who where out of their cells for work on the early shift. In the afternoon, he was regularly required to fight Disciples in the officers' dining room. An ugly scar on his neck evidences the seriousness of the dilemma. For an individual to remain "neutral" under such extreme conditions of group conflict may not be possible. If so, the situation is not substantially different from what has been said to occur within prisoner-of-

war camps where the apathetic are coerced into joining underground units.[9]

The gangs have attempted to operate in the prisons as they have on the streets. They have established formal chains of command in cell houses and on work assignments. They have forced independents out of the prison rackets and have themselves taken control. In addition, lower echelon members frequently are involved in the extortion and shakedown of independents, blacks and whites. Finally, the gang leadership, like the leadership of the Jehovah's Witnesses and Black Muslims before them, claim to be the spokesmen for their "people" and have attempted with varying success to have the administration accept their interventions in prisonwide matters as legitimate.

Since 1970 when the gangs rose to prominence in Illinois prisons, there have been regular outbursts of conflict *between* them. There were "gang wars" at Pontiac prison in August 1971 and December 1972 with several deaths and numerous serious injuries. The first major gang clash at Stateville occurred in April 1973 and resulted in a prison "lock-up" (prisoners confined to cells 24 hours per day) for more than six months. Fights on a lesser scale between the groups are a part of the prison's day-to-day life.

The point here is that the old picture of the prison as an inclusive normative and moral community toward which the individual had to take a stance is no longer accurate. The prison is now a conflict-ridden setting where the major battles are fought by intermediate level inmate groups rather than by staff and inmates or by inmates as unaligned individuals.

The situation of large scale gangs actively organizing and competing within the prisons for prestige, power, recruits, and control of illicit activities is not unique to Illinois. Similar situations have been reported in California and New York. In California, officials have identified

[8]Jacobs, "Street Gangs Behind Bars," 21 *Social Problems* 395 (1974).

[9]Walzer, "Prisoner of War: Does the Fight Go On After the Battle?," 63 *Am.Pol. Sci. Rev.* 781 (1969).

four gangs:[10] Mexican Mafia, Nuestra Familia, Black Guerilla Family, and the Aryan Brotherhood. During 1973, there were 146 stabbings and twenty deaths in California prisons and over the course of the past two years there have been 268 stabbings and fifty-six deaths. Most of these have been attributed to the four gangs and especially to the two Chicano gangs whose combined membership is estimated at 700. On December 14, 1973 the situation came to a head when a guard was stabbed to death and the entire California prison system was placed on "lock-up" (inmates confined to cells twenty-four hours per day).[11]

While the California gang situation appears to differ from the Illinois situation in its indigenous prison origins and, in some cases, in its greater politicization, the point remains that the inmate organization in these states is best characterized by latent and manifest conflict between well-organized secondary groups.

RELIGIOUS STRATIFICATION

Membership in traditional religious sects has not historically served as a basis for collective inmate behavior in prison. This may be explained by the fact that traditional Judeo-Christian values are offended by criminals and offer no radical redefinition of their situation upon which organized protest can be based. Unconventional religions, however, have achieved considerable success in providing an ideological shield to the assaults on self conception that attend imprisonment.

Perhaps the first instance of a large well-organized secondary group emerging within the prison is represented by the Jehovah's Witnesses.[12] During World War II, 3,992 Jehovah's Witnesses were incarcerated in federal prisons for refusing military service for reasons of conscientious objection. The highly knit, clannish, and well disciplined Jehovah's Witnesses posed a challenge to prison administrators that was never fully resolved.[13]

While the Jehovah's Witness were the first group to come to prison with the intention of serving "group time" rather than individual time, their impact was limited to the federal system and to a relatively short number of years. During that time they did engage in numerous work slowdowns, strikes, and other protests involving collective action. Their influence on American prisons is slight, however, in comparison to the sweeping organizational successes of

problems within Nazi concentration camps as well. See E. Kogon, *The Theory and Practice of Hell* (1958). "One cannot escape the impression that, psychologically speaking, the SS was never quite equal to the challenge offered them by the Jehovah's Witnesses." *Id.* at 43.

[13]Perhaps the most unconventional religion is the recently organized prison religion, the Church of the New Song, about which comparatively little is known at this time. See "Church of the New Song," 17 Christianity Today 73 (1973):

> "A two-year sect made up primarily of prison inmates is gaining considerable recognition throughout the United States, much to the consternation of corrections officials."

The Church of the New Song, founded by Maine born Harry W. Theriault, who is serving sentences for theft and escape (currently in a LaTuna, Texas prison), seems to focus its doctrines upon the rights of prisoners. Or at least that has been the source of its popularity. Wardens in several federal penitentiaries where the movement is strong have refused to accommodate these "rights," and the prisoners have taken the resulting disputes to courts. . . .

Theriault, 33, has made the most headway in litigation before Federal Judge Newell Edenfield of Atlanta. A year ago Edenfield ruled in effect that the Church of the New Song was a legitimate religious group as worthy of recognition by prison officials as a group of Protestants, Catholics, Jews, or Muslims would be. . . .

The New Song has a 600-page "bible drawn from an assortment of sources and using exotic terminology." Theriault, who calls New Song "the highest fulfillment of the Christian prophecy," has a ministerial license from the mail-order Universal Life Church in Modesto, California. (ULC also elevated a rapist at California's Folsom prison to "cardinal," causing a furor there).

See *Theriault v. Carlson*, 339 F. Supp. 375 (N. D. Ga. 1972).

---

[10]1963 *Law & Order* 63. For an account of the chicano organizations in California prisons during the late 1960's see T. Davidson, *Chicano Prisoners: The Key to San Quentin* (1974).

[11]Los Angeles Times, Dec. 14, 1973, at 3, col. 5.

[12]S. Mulford & A. Wordlaw, *Conscientious Objectors in Prison* 1940–1945 (1945). It should also be pointed out that the Jehovah's Witnesses presented significant management

the Black Muslims in prisons across the country.

The Black Muslims are undoubtedly the largest and most organized group ever to reside in American prisons. Their impact upon the field of corrections, particularly on prisoners' rights litigation, has yet to be adequately assessed.[14] Under the direction of Elija Muhammad, the Black Muslims throughout the 1950's and 1960's strove to become a broad based mass movement. Prisoners were not excluded from the movement. On the contrary, they were from the beginning, seen as a potentially important source of recruitment. In fact, when Lincoln wrote his history of the Black Muslims in 1961 there were three temples behind prison walls.[15] For convicted men the Black Muslims offered a redefinition of their situation which replaced individual guilt for criminal behavior with an explanation placing blame on white racism and oppression. This allows the individual a rationale by which he can "reject his rejectors."[16] The active proselyzation of prisoners into the Muslim religion is alluded to in the writings of both Malcolm X[17] and Eldridge Cleaver.[18] That this Muslim activity within the jails and prisons consisted of more than the self-aggrandizing exploits of a few hard core members is nicely brought out by Claude Brown in his autobiographical account of life in Harlem in the late 1950's.[19]

"It seemed to me that everybody who was coming out of jail was a Black Muslim. While he was raving, I was thinking about this. I said, 'Damn, Alley, what the hell is going on in the jails here? It seems that everybody who comes out is a Muslim.'"

It is scarcely possible at this time to even estimate the numbers of Muslims who have passed through American prisons since World War II. In a survey of a "random sample" of seventy-one wardens and superintendents of federal and state penal institutions across the country in 1967, Caldwell found that 31 per cent claimed substantial Muslim activities while 21 per cent acknowledged some or limited Muslim activities.[20] Those administrators who reported no Muslim activities "came from states with relatively small Negro populations and small percentages of Negroes in prison."[21] How many Black Muslims there were in each prison was not asked but Caldwell cites a correspondence with California prison officials indicating 400 to 500 inmates in California's thirteen major correctional institutions who can be identified as Black Muslims.[22]

At Attica the organizational discipline of the Black Muslims in protecting the D-yard hostages and in contributing to the negotiation process during the 1971 turmoil has been extensively reported.[23] The Black Muslims at Attica had a lengthy history of organizing, recruiting, and waging legal battles. By 1960, the Muslim activity had spread rapidly through the whole New York prison system. An Attica inmate testifying before the House Committee on Internal Security in the aftermath of the Attica riot estimated Muslim membership at Attica at 230 to 300.[24] This does not seem an extravagant figure in light of the New York State Special Commission's statement that in March 1971 thirty Orthodox Muslims and 200 members of the Nation of Islam attended the first Muslim service in the

---

[14]For some suggestion as to the role of the Black Muslims in stimulating litigation on prisoners' rights see Rothman, "Decarcerating Prisoners and Patients," *Civ. Lib. Rev.* 1 (1973). It is actually remarkable that this movement in the prisons has stimulated hardly a single scholarly article.

[15]C. Lincoln, *The Black Muslims in America* (1961).

[16]Korn & McKorkle, "Resocialization Within Walls," 93 *Annals* 88 (1954).

[17]*Autobiography of Malcolm X* (1964).

[18]E. Cleaver, *Soul on Ice* (1968).

[19]C. Brown, *Manchild in the Promised Land* 336 (1965).

[20]Caldwell, "A Survey of Attitudes Toward Black Muslims in Prison," 16 *J. Hum. Rel.* 220 (1968).

[21]*Id.* at 222.

[22]*Id.* at 224.

[23]Attica, *supra* note 4, at 123.

[24]*Hearings on Revolutionary Activities Directed Toward the Administration of Penal or Correctional Systems Before the House Comm. on Internal Security,* 93d Cong., 1st Sess., pt. 1, at 113 (1973) (testimony of Thomas Henry Hughes) [hereinafter cited as *Hearings*].

history of Attica.[25] In any case, the Black Muslims clearly represented a sizeable faction of an inmate population numbering 2,243.

What is significant for our purposes is the contrast this poses to the traditional description of the prison community as composed of primary groups and solitary men. Today, to ask inmates at Attica, Stateville, or San Quentin whether they have two or more close friends (a popular question in studies of prison societies) would not contribute information relevant to understanding the social organization of prison inmates.

POLITICAL STRATIFICATION

The allegiance of incarcerated men to political groups is something new in this country. At least until recently, the political parties did not evince much concern with prisons or convicts. Since the prisoners have been disenfranchised in all states either by law or by inability to get to the polls, they were never seen as the basis of a political constituency.

Radical groups however, have seen in prisoners not merely bodies to swell their membership, but a revolutionary force that needs only to be mobilized. The prison is at the center of radical politics. Revolutionary politics have become a part of prison society through the efforts of prisoners like George Jackson,[26] Eldridge Cleaver,[27] and Huey Newton.[28]

The two most significant radical political groups to emerge to date are the Black Panther Party and the Young Lords Party, although there also appears to have been a small group of Weathermen and other radicals at Attica.[29] Both the Panthers and the Young Lords figured

prominently in the events leading up to the Attica riot and representatives of both groups were among those in the negotiating party of neutral observers brought to Attica in the hopes of finding a peaceful settlement. Before the House Committee on Internal Security, witnesses estimated the number of Black Panthers at Attica before the riot at 300[30] and 200.[31] An official of the California Department of Corrections has estimated the membership of the Black Panthers at San Quentin at its height under the leadership of George Jackson to have been 200 to 300.[32]

The Black Panthers have described themselves as a Marxist-Leninist revolutionary party, although in recent years some members have turned toward working within the system. During the late 1960's and early 1970's radical leaders of the Panthers saw prisoners as a disgruntled, embittered, and potentially revolutionary force. Offering them a redefinition of their situation as "political prisoners," the Panthers sought to earn the commitment of former apolitical individuals. The Panthers linked the prison and its authorities to "repressive" organizations within American society and attempted to generate symbols with appeal for all inmates. This appears to be the contribution of both political and religious organizers within organizations. Their appeal attempts to bridge local cleavages and to subordinate other ties and interests to a more inclusive ideology. Thus, the Panthers argued against racism, for example, urging that white prisoners were also oppressed victims of reactionary political forces. Huey Newton explained from his cell in Los Padres, California:

"The black prisoners as well as many of the white prisoners identify with the program of the Panthers. Of course by the very nature of their being prisoners

[25]Attica, *supra* note 4, at 73.

[26]G. Jackson, *Blood in My Eye* (1972); G. Jackson, *Soledad Brothers—The Prison Letters of George Jackson* (1970).

[27]E. Cleaver, *Soul on Ice* (1968).

[28]See Newton, "Prison, Where is Thy Victory?," in *The Black Panthers Speak* 75 (P. Foner ed. 1970).

[29]Attica, *supra* note 4, at 118. See also S. Melville, *Letters from Attica* (1972).

[30]*Hearings, supra* note 24, at 109.

[31]*Hearings, supra* note 24, at 169 (testimony of John Stratten).

[32]*Hearings, supra* note 24, at 1184 (testimony of William E. Harkins).

they can see the oppression and they've suffered at the hands of the Gestapo. They have reacted to it. The black prisoners have all joined the Panthers, about 95% of them. Now the jail is all Panther and the police are very worried about this. The white prisoners can identify with us because they realize that they are not in control. They realize there's someone controlling them and the rest of the world with guns. They want some control over their lives also. The Panthers in jail have been educating them and so we are going along with the revolution inside of the jail."[33]

The Young Lords Party, composed of Puerto Ricans, began as a Chicago street gang and moved to New York in 1969. Like the Panthers, it describes itself as a revolutionary, anti-imperialist organization guided by Marxist-Leninist principles. At the time of the Attica riot, their membership is estimated to have been twenty-five to seventy-five. Most interesting is their role in carrying out a truce between the Black Muslims and the Black Panthers.

"In mid-August, shortly after the transfer of the Muslim leader, officers in one of the exercise yards observed a ceremony that seemed to confirm their worst fears. Standing in a line along one side of the yard, arms folded across their chests, was a group of inmates recognized as Muslims. Facing them was another group, similarly stationed, and recognized as Panthers. Seated and standing around a table between them were leaders of both groups and a number of Young Lords, apparently serving as intermediaries. The officers' apprehensions soared at the prospects of an inmate population unified in its hostility, and capable of speaking with a single voice."[34]

The implications of radical political organization in prison are profound. The prison experience becomes defined as a period for the development of political consciousness and revolutionary organization. Under such circumstances, the "program" of the prison ad-

ministrator interested in rehabilitation is interpreted as irrelevant, and counter-revolutionary. Political radicals do not want to be adjusted to the system.

This stance toward the formal organization should be distinguished from the position of other groups. The Illinois gangs and the Black Muslims are interested in prison programs. They desire to have their members educated and trained. The gangs might aptly be described as "illegitimate capitalists" as Newton had neatly rephrased Merton's "innovative deviants." The Black Muslims might best be characterized as legitimate capitalists who urge a program of economic self-sufficiency based upon notions of Black Capitalism. The Chicago gangs have never been cordial to the Panthers, on the streets or in prison. For their part, the Panthers view both gangs and religious groups like Muslims as counter-revolutionary.

CONCLUSION

We have attempted to emphasize two main points. First, the individual, primary group and inmate group are not the only relevant units in the social organization of the prison. Indeed, the primary group has been eclipsed as the most important constituent of prison society. We have identified criss-crossing secondary groups active within prison competing for the loyalties of prisoners. No longer can the individual without a primary group be thought of as unintegrated within the prison society. His identity with and participation in various organizations makes him very much *of* the prison.

The model of the lone inmate struggling against the pangs of imprisonment through assimilation into an integrated normative community and through participation in a functional inmate distributive system needs reexamination. The inmate system, at least in some of our larger states, finds inmates committed to racial, political, and religious symbols and to organizations characterized by large size, charismatic leadership, varying degrees of

---

[33]Newton, "Huey Newton Talks to the Movement About the Black Panther Party, Cultural Nationalism, SNCC, Liberals and White Revolutionaries," in *The Black Panthers Speak* 65 (P. Foner ed. 1970).

[34]Attica, *supra* note 4, at 139.

bureaucratic organization, and close contact with sympathetic outside groups.

Perhaps the prison community is more fruitfully viewed as an arena where competing groups seek at each other's expense larger memberships and greater power. In such a struggle the administration may become irrelevant except as it serves as a symbol around which political leaders can unite all dissident factions. The secondary groups described above are rooted in the wider society. Within the prison, conflicts have consequences which may resound beyond the prison walls. Prison should thus be understood as an arena in which solidary groups may emerge, recruit membership, organize for the future, and promote their ideologies.

A revised imagery of the prison community might well have important implications for penal policy at the legislative, judicial and administrative levels. It must become clear to decision makers, particularly to those outside the prison world, that "reforms" do not always benefit a solidary and unified inmate community in their struggle to limit the exercise of administration authority. Where the prison community is characterized by organized groups locked in conflict with one another, reforms may have the effect of benefiting one group at the expense of another or even at the expense of the equilibrium of the social system as a whole. This is not to say, of course, that reforms should not be implemented. Quite the contrary; reforms should be designed, implemented, and evaluated in light of concrete empirical situations rather than according to an historical imagery which no longer accurately describes the situation.

52. The Pains of Imprisonment

GRESHAM SYKES

THE DEPRIVATION OF LIBERTY

OF ALL THE PAINFUL CONDITIONS IMPOSED ON THE inmates of the New Jersey State Prison, none is more immediately obvious than the loss of liberty. The prisoner must live in a world shrunk to thirteen and a half acres and within this restricted area his freedom of movement is further confined by a strict system of passes, the military formations in moving from one point within the institution to another, and the demand that he remain in his cell until given permission to do otherwise. In short, the prisoner's loss of liberty is a double one—first, by confinement to the institution and second, by confinement within the institution.

The mere fact that the individual's movements are restricted, however, is far less serious than the fact that imprisonment means that the inmate is cut off from family, relatives, and friends, not in the self-isolation of the hermit or the misanthrope, but in the involuntary seclusion of the outlaw. It is true that visiting and mailing privileges partially relieve the prisoner's isolation—if he can find someone to visit him or write to him and who will be approved as a visitor or correspondent by the prison officials. Many inmates, however, have found their links with persons in the free community weakening as the months and years pass by. This may explain in part the fact that an examination of the visiting records of a random sample of the inmate population, covering approximately a one-year period, indicated that 41 percent of the prisoners in the New Jersey State Prison have received no visits from the outside world.

It is not difficult to see this isolation as painfully depriving or frustrating in terms of lost emotional relationships, of loneliness and boredom. But what makes this pain of imprisonment bite most deeply is the fact that the confinement of the criminal represents a deliberate, moral rejection of the criminal by the free community. Indeed, as Reckless has pointed out, it is the moral condemnation of the criminal—however it may be symbolized—that converts hurt into punishment, i.e. the just consequence of committing an offense, and it is this condemnation that confronts the inmate by the fact of his seclusion.

Now it is sometimes claimed that many criminals are so alienated from conforming society and so identified with a criminal subculture that the moral condemnation, rejection, or disapproval of legitimate society does not touch them; they are, it is said, indifferent to the penal sanctions of the free community, at least as far as the moral stigma of being defined as a criminal is concerned. Possibly this is true for a small number of offenders such as the professional thief described by Sutherland[1] or the

▶SOURCE: *The Society of Captives. Princeton: Princeton University Press, 1958. Pp. 65–78. Copyright 1958 by Princeton University Press; Princeton Paperback, (1971). Reprinted by permission.*

[1]Cf. Edwin H. Sutherland, *The Professional Thief,* Chicago: The University of Chicago Press, 1937.

psychopathic personality delineated by William and Joan McCord.[2] For the great majority of criminals in prison, however, the evidence suggests that neither alienation from the ranks of the law-abiding nor involvement in a system of criminal value is sufficient to eliminate the threat to the prisoner's ego posed by society's rejection.[3] The signs pointing to the prisoner's degradation are many—the anonymity of a uniform and a number rather than a name, the shaven head,[4] the insistence on gestures of respect and subordination when addressing officials, and so on. The prisoner is never allowed to forget that, by committing a crime, he has foregone his claim to the status of a full-fledged, *trusted* member of society. The status lost by the prisoner is, in fact, similar to what Marshall has called the status of citizenship—that basic acceptance of the individual as a functioning member of the society in which he lives.[5] It is true that in the past the imprisoned criminal literally suffered civil death and that although the doctrines of attainder and corruption of blood were largely abandoned in the 18th and 19th Centuries, the inmate is still stripped of many of his civil rights such as the right to vote, to hold office, to sue in court, and so on.[6] But as important as the loss of these civil rights may be, the loss of that more diffuse status which defines the individual as someone to be trusted or as morally acceptable is the loss which hurts most.

In short, the wall which seals off the criminal, the contaminated man, is a constant threat to the prisoner's self-conception and the threat is continually repeated in the many daily reminders that he must be kept apart from "decent" men. Somehow this rejection or degradation by the free community must be warded off, turned aside, rendered harmless. Somehow the imprisoned criminal must find a device for rejecting his rejectors, if he is to endure psychologically.[7]

THE DEPRIVATION OF GOODS AND SERVICES

There are admittedly many problems in attempting to compare the standard of living existing in the free community and the standard of living which is supposed to be the lot of the inmate in prison. How, for example, do we interpret the fact that a covering for the floor of a cell usually consists of a scrap from a discarded blanket and that even this possession is forbidden by the prison authorities? What meaning do we attach to the fact that no inmate owns a common piece of furniture, such as a chair, but only a homemade stool? What is the value of a suit of clothing which is also a convict's uniform with a stripe and a stencilled number? The answers are far from simple although there are a number of prison officials who will argue that some inmates are better off in prison, in strictly material terms, than they could ever hope to be in the rough-and-tumble economic life of the free community. Possibly this is so, but at least it has never been claimed by the inmates that the goods and services provided the prisoner are equal to or better than the goods and services which the prisoner could obtain if he were left to his own devices outside the walls. The average

[2]Cf. William and Joan McCord, *Psychopathy and Delinquency,* New York:Grune and Stratton, 1956.

[3]For an excellent discussion of the symbolic overtones of imprisonment, see Walter C. Reckless, *The Crime Problem,* New York: Appleton-Century-Crofts, Inc., 1955, pp. 428–429.

[4]Western culture has long placed a peculiar emphasis on shaving the head as a symbol of degradation, ranging from the enraged treatment of collaborators in occupied Europe to the more measured barbering of recruits in the Armed Forces. In the latter case, as in the prison, the nominal purpose has been cleanliness and neatness, but for the person who is shaved the meaning is somewhat different. In the New Jersey State Prison, the prisoner is clipped to the skull on arrival but not thereafter.

[5]See T. H. Marshall, *Citizenship and Social Class,* Cambridge, England: The Cambridge University Press, 1950.

[6]Paul W. Tappan, "The Legal Rights of Prisoners," *The Annals of the American Academy of Political and Social Science,* Vol. 293, May 1954, pp. 99–111.

[7]See Lloyd W. McCorkle and Richard R. Korn, "Resocialization Within Walls." *Ibid.,* pp. 88–98.

inmate finds himself in a harshly Spartan environment which he defines as painfully depriving.

Now it is true that the prisoner's basic material needs are met—in the sense that he does not go hungry, cold, or wet. He receives adequate medical care and he has the opportunity for exercise. But a standard of living constructed in terms of so many calories per day, so many hours of recreation, so many cubic yards of space per individual, and so on, misses the central point when we are discussing the individual's feeling of deprivation, however useful it may be in setting minimum levels of consumption for the maintenance of health. A standard of living can be hopelessly inadequate, from the individual's viewpoint, because it bores him to death or fails to provide those subtle symbolic overtones which we invest in the world of possessions. And this is the core of the prisoner's problem in the area of goods and services. He wants—or needs, if you will—not just the so-called necessities of life but also the amenities: cigarettes and liquor as well as calories, interesting foods as well as sheer bulk, individual clothing as well as adequate clothing, individual furnishings for his living quarters as well as shelter, privacy as well as space. The "rightfulness" of the prisoner's feeling of deprivation can be questioned. And the objective reality of the prisoner's deprivation—in the sense that he has actually suffered a fall from his economic position in the free community—can be viewed with skepticism, as we have indicated above. But these criticisms are irrelevant to the significant issue, namely that legitimately or illegitimately, rationally or irrationally, the inmate population defines its present material impoverishment as a painful loss.

Now in modern Western culture, material possessions are so large a part of the individual's conception of himself that to be stripped of them is to be attacked at the deepest layers of personality. This is particularly true when poverty cannot be excused as a blind stroke of fate or a universal calamity. Poverty due to one's own mistakes or misdeeds represents an indictment against one's basic value or personal worth and there are few men who can philosophically bear the want caused by their own actions. It is true some prisoners in the New Jersey State Prison attempt to interpret their low position in the scale of goods and services as an effort by the State to exploit them economically. Thus, in the eyes of some inmates, the prisoner is poor not because of an offense which he has committed in the past but because the State is a tyrant which uses its captive criminals as slave labor under the hypocritical guise of reformation. Penology, it is said, is a racket. Their poverty, then, is not punishment as we have used the word before, i.e. the just consequence of criminal behavior; rather, it is an unjust hurt or pain inflicted without legitimate cause. This attitude, however, does not appear to be particularly widespread in the inmate population and the great majority of prisoners must face their privation without the aid of the wronged man's sense of injustice. Furthermore, more prisoners are unable to fortify themselves in their low level of material existence by seeing it as a means to some high or worthy end. They are unable to attach any significant meaning to their need to make it more bearable, such as present pleasures foregone for pleasures in the future, self-sacrifice in the interests of the community, or material asceticism for the purpose of spiritual salvation.

The inmate, then, sees himself as having been made poor by reason of his own acts and without the rationale of compensating benefits. The failure is *his* failure in a world where control and possession of the material environment are commonly taken as sure indicators of a man's worth. It is true that our society, as materialistic as it may be, does not rely exclusively on goods and services as a criterion of an individual's value; and, as we shall see shortly, the inmate population defends itself by stressing alternative or supplementary measures of merit. But impoverishment remains as one of the most bitter attacks on the individual's self-image that our society has to offer and the prisoner cannot ignore the implications of his straitened circumstances.[8] Whatever the discomforts and irritations of the prisoner's Spartan existence may be, he must carry the additional burden of social definitions which equate his material deprivation with personal inadequacy.

THE DEPRIVATION OF HETEROSEXUAL RELATIONSHIPS

Unlike the prisoner in many Latin-American countries, the inmate of the maximum security prison in New Jersey does not enjoy the privilege of so-called conjugal visits. And in those brief times when the prisoner is allowed to see his wife, mistress, or "female friend," the woman must sit on one side of a plate glass window and the prisoner on the other, communicating by means of a phone under the scrutiny of a guard. If the inmate, then, is rejected and impoverished by the facts of his imprisonment, he is also figuratively castrated by his involuntary celibacy.

Now a number of writers have suggested that men in prison undergo a reduction of the sexual drive and that the sexual frustrations of prisoners are therefore less than they might appear to be at first glance. The reports of reduced sexual interest have, however, been largely confined to accounts of men imprisoned in concentration camps or similar extreme situations where starvation, torture, and physical exhaustion have reduced life to a simple struggle for survival or left the captive sunk in apathy. But in the American prison these factors are not at work to any significant extent and Lindner has noted that the prisoner's access to mass media, por-

nography circulated among inmates, and similar stimuli serve to keep alive the prisoner's sexual impulses.[9] The same thought is expressed more crudely by the inmates of the New Jersey State Prison in a variety of obscene expressions and it is clear that the lack of heterosexual intercourse is a frustrating experience for the imprisoned criminal and that it is a frustration which weighs heavily and painfully on his mind during his prolonged confinement. There are, of course, some "habitual" homosexuals in the prison— men who were homosexuals before their arrival and who continue their particular form of deviant behavior within the all-male society of the custodial institution. For these inmates, perhaps, the deprivation of heterosexual intercourse cannot be counted as one of the pains of imprisonment. They are few in number, however, and are only too apt to be victimized or raped by aggressive prisoners who have turned to homosexuality as a temporary means of relieving their frustration.

Yet as important as frustration in the sexual sphere may be in physiological terms, the psychological problems created by the lack of heterosexual relationships can be even more serious. A society composed exclusively of men tends to generate anxieties in its members concerning their masculinity regardless of whether or not they are coerced, bribed, or seduced into an overt homosexual liaison. Latent homosexual tendencies may be activated in the individual without being translated into open behavior and yet still arouse strong guilt feelings at either the conscious or unconscious level. In the tense atmosphere of the prison with its known perversions, its importunities of admitted homosexuals, and its constant references to the problems of sexual frustration by guards and inmates alike, there are few prisoners who can escape the fact that an essential component of a man's self conception—his status of male—is called into question. And if an inmate has in fact en-

---

[8] Komarovsky's discussion of the psychological implications of unemployment is particularly apposite here, despite the markedly different context, for she notes that economic failure provokes acute anxiety as humiliation cuts away at the individual's conception of his manhood. He feels useless, undeserving of respect, disorganized, adrift in a society where economic status is a major anchoring point. Cf. Mirra Komarovsky, *The Unemployed Man and His Family*, New York: The Dryden Press, 1940, pp. 74–77.

[9] See Robert M. Lindner, "Sex in Prison," *Complex*, Vol. 6, Fall 1951, pp. 5–20.

gaged in homosexual behavior within the walls, not as a continuation of an habitual pattern but as a rare act of sexual deviance under the intolerable pressure of mounting physical desire, the psychological onslaughts on his ego image will be particularly acute.[10]

In addition to these problems stemming from sexual frustration per se, the deprivation of heterosexual relationships carries with it another threat to the prisoner's image of himself—more diffuse, perhaps, and more difficult to state precisely and yet no less disturbing. The inmate is shut off from the world of women which by its very polarity gives the male world much of its meaning. Like most men, the inmate must search for his identity not simply within himself but also in the picture of himself which he finds reflected in the eyes of others; and since a significant half of his audience is denied him, the inmate's self image is in danger of becoming half complete, fractured, a monochrome without the hues of reality. The prisoner's looking-glass self, in short—to use Cooley's fine phrase—is only that portion of the prisoner's personality which is recognized or appreciated by men and this partial identity is made hazy by the lack of contrast.

[10]Estimates of the proportion of inmates who engage in homosexuality during their confinement in the prison are apt to vary. In the New Jersey State Prison, however, Wing Guards and Shop Guards examined a random sample of inmates who were well known to them from prolonged observation and identified 35 per cent of the men as individuals believed to have engaged in homosexual acts. The judgments of these officials were substantially in agreement with the judgments of a prisoner who possessed an apparently well-founded reputation as an aggressive homosexual deeply involved in patterns of sexual deviance within the institution and who had been convicted of sodomy. But the validity of these judgments remains largely unknown and we present the following conclusions, based on a variety of sources, as provisional at best: First, a fairly large proportion of prisoners engage in homosexual behavior during their period of confinement. Second, for many of those prisoners who do engage in homosexual behavior, their sexual deviance is rare or sporadic rather than chronic. And third, as we have indicated before, much of the homosexuality which does occur in prison is not part of a life pattern existing before and after confinement; rather, it is a response to the peculiar rigors of imprisonment.

THE DEPRIVATION OF AUTONOMY

We have noted before that the inmate suffers from what we have called a loss of autonomy in that he is subjected to a vast body of rules and commands which are designed to control his behavior in minute detail. To the casual observer, however, it might seem that the many areas of life in which self-determination is withheld, such as the language used in a letter, the hours of sleeping and eating, or the route to work, are relatively unimportant. Perhaps it might be argued, as in the case of material deprivation, that the inmate in prison is not much worse off than the individual in the free community who is regulated in a great many aspects of his life by the iron fist of custom. It could even be argued, as some writers have done, that for a number of imprisoned criminals the extensive control of the custodians provides a welcome escape from freedom and that the prison officials thus supply an external Super-Ego which serves to reduce the anxieties arising from an awareness of deviant impulses. But from the viewpoint of the inmate population, it is precisely the triviality of much of the officials' control which often proves to be most galling. Regulation by a bureaucratic staff is felt far differently than regulation by custom. And even though a few prisoners do welcome the strict regime of the custodians as a means of checking their own aberrant behavior which they would like to curb but cannot, most prisoners look on the matter in a different light. Most prisoners, in fact, express an intense hostility against their far-reaching dependence on the decisions of their captors and the restricted ability to make choices must be included among the pains of imprisonment along with restrictions of physical liberty, the possession of goods and services, and heterosexual relationships.

Now the loss of autonomy experienced by the

THE PAINS OF IMPRISONMENT

inmates of the prison does not represent a grant of power freely given by the ruled to the rulers for a limited and specific end. Rather, it is total and it is imposed—and for these reasons it is less endurable. The nominal objectives of the custodians are not, in general, the objectives of the prisoners.[11] Yet regardless of whether or not the inmate population shares some aims with the custodial bureaucracy, the many regulations and orders of the New Jersey State Prison's official regime often arouse the prisoner's hostility because they don't "make sense" from the prisoner's point of view. Indeed, the incomprehensible order or rule is a basic feature of life in prison. Inmates, for example, are forbidden to take food from the messhall to their cells. Some prisoners see this as a move designed to promote cleanliness; others are convinced that the regulation is for the purpose of preventing inmates from obtaining anything that might be used in the *sub rosa* system of barter. Most, however, simply see the measure as another irritating, pointless gesture of authoritarianism. Similarly, prisoners are denied parole but are left in ignorance of the reasons for the decision. Prisoners are informed that the delivery of mail will be delayed—but they are not told why.

Now some of the inmate population's ignorance might be described as "accidental"; it arises from what we can call the principle of bureaucratic indifference, i.e. events which seem important or vital to those at the bottom of the heap are viewed with an increasing lack of concern

with each step upward. The rules, the commands, the decisions which flow down to those who are controlled are not accompanied by explanations on the grounds that it is "impractical" or "too much trouble." Some of the inmate population's ignorance, however, is deliberately fostered by the prison officials in that explanations are often withheld as a matter of calculated policy. Providing explanations carries an implication that those who are ruled have a right to know—and this in turn suggests that if the explanations are not satisfactory, the rule or order will be changed. But this is in direct contradiction to the theoretical power relationship of the inmates and the prison officials. Imprisoned criminals are individuals who are being punished by society and they must be brought to their knees. If the inmate population maintains the right to argue with its captors, it takes on the appearance of an enemy nation with its own sovereignty; and in so doing it raises disturbing questions about the nature of the offender's deviance. The criminal is no longer simply a man who has broken the law; he has become a part of a group with an alternative viewpoint and thus attacks the validity of the law itself. The custodians' refusal to give reasons for many aspects of their regime can be seen in part as an attempt to avoid such an intolerable situation.

The indignation aroused by the "bargaining inmate" or the necessity of justifying the custodial regime is particularly evident during a riot when prisoners have the "impudence" to present a list of demands. In discussing the disturbances at the New Jersey State Prison in the Spring of 1952, for example, a newspaper editorial angrily noted that "the storm, like a nightmarish April Fool's dream, has passed, leaving in its wake a partially wrecked State Prison as a debasing monument to the ignominious rage of desperate men."

The important point, however, is that the frustration of the prisoner's ability to make choices and the frequent refusals to provide an explanation for the regulations and commands

[11]The nominal objectives of the officials tend to be compromised as they are translated into the actual routines of day-to-day life. The modus vivendi reached by guards and their prisoners is oriented toward certain goals which are in fact shared by captors and captives. In this limited sense, the control of the prison officials is partly concurred in by the inmates as well as imposed on them from above. In discussing the pains of imprisonment our attention is focused on the frustrations or threats posed by confinement rather than the devices which meet these frustrations or threats and render them tolerable. Our interest here is in the vectors of the prison's social system—if we may use an analogy from the physical sciences—rather than the resultant.

descending from the bureaucratic staff involve a profound threat to the prisoner's self image because they reduce the prisoner to the weak, helpless, dependent status of childhood. As Bettelheim has tellingly noted in his comments on the concentration camp, men under guard stand in constant danger of losing their identification with the normal definition of an adult and the imprisoned criminal finds his picture of himself as a self-determining individual being destroyed by the regime of the custodians.[12] It is possible that this psychological attack is particularly painful in American culture because of the deep-lying insecurities produced by the delays, the conditionality and the uneven progress so often observed in the granting of adulthood. It is also possible that the criminal is frequently an individual who has experienced great difficulty in adjusting himself to figures of authority and who finds the many restraints of prison life particularly threatening in so far as earlier struggles over the establishment of self are reactivated in a more virulent form. But without asserting that Americans in general or criminals in particular are notably ill-equipped to deal with the problems posed by the deprivation of autonomy, the helpless or dependent status of the prisoner clearly represents a serious threat to the prisoner's self image as a fully accredited member of adult society. And of the many threats which may confront the individual, either in or out of prison, there are few better calculated to arouse acute anxieties than the attempt to reimpose the subservience of youth. Public humiliation, enforced respect and deference, the finality of authoritarian decisions, the demands for a specified course of conduct because, in the judgment of another, it is in the individual's best interest—all are features of childhood's helplessness in the face of a superior adult world. Such things may be both irksome and disturbing for a child, especially if the child envisions himself as having outgrown such servitude. But for the adult who has escaped such helplessness with the passage of years, to be thrust back into childhood's helplessness is even more painful, and the inmate of the prison must somehow find a means of coping with the issue.

THE DEPRIVATION OF SECURITY

However strange it may appear that society has chosen to reduce the criminality of the offender by forcing him to associate with more than a thousand other criminals for years on end, there is one meaning of this involuntary union which is obvious—the individual prisoner is thrown into prolonged intimacy with other men who in many cases have a long history of violent, aggressive behavior. It is a situation which can prove to be anxiety-provoking even for the hardened recidivist and it is in this light that we can understand the comment of an inmate of the New Jersey State Prison who said, "The worst thing about prison is you have to live with other prisoners."

The fact that the imprisoned criminal sometimes views his fellow prisoners as "vicious" or "dangerous" may seem a trifle unreasonable. Other inmates, after all, are men like himself, bearing the legal stigma of conviction. But even if the individual prisoner believes that he himself is not the sort of person who is likely to attack or exploit weaker and less resourceful fellow captives, he is apt to view others with more suspicion. And if he himself is prepared to commit crimes while in prison, he is likely to feel that many others will be at least equally ready. . . . Regardless of the patterns of mutual aid and support which may flourish in the inmate population, there are a sufficient number of outlaws within this group of outlaws to deprive the average prisoner of that sense of security which comes from living among men who can be reasonably expected to abide by the rules of society. While it is true that every prisoner does not live in the constant fear of being robbed or beaten, the constant companionship of

[12]Cf. Bruno Bettelheim, "Individual and Mass Behavior in Extreme Situations," in *Readings in Social Psychology*, edited by T. M. Newcomb and E. L. Hartley, New York: Henry Holt and Company, 1947.

thieves, rapists, murderers, and aggressive homosexuals is far from reassuring.

An important aspect of this disturbingly problematical world is the fact that the inmate is acutely aware that sooner or later he will be "tested"—that someone will "push" him to see how far they can go and that he must be prepared to fight for the safety of his person and his possessions. If he should fail, he will thereafter be an object of contempt, constantly in danger of being attacked by other inmates who view him as an obvious victim, as a man who cannot or will not defend his rights. And yet if he succeeds, he may well become a target for the prisoner who wishes to prove himself, who seeks to enhance his own prestige by defeating the man with a reputation for toughness. Thus both success and failure in defending one's self against the aggressions of fellow captives may serve to provoke fresh attacks and no man stands assured of the future.[13]

[13]As the Warden of the New Jersey State Prison has pointed out, the arrival of an obviously tough professional hoodlum creates a serious problem for the recognized "bad man" in a cellblock who is expected to challenge the newcomer immediately.

The prisoner's loss of security arouses acute anxiety, in short, not just because violent acts of aggression and exploitation occur but also because behavior constantly calls into question the individual's ability to cope with it, in terms of his own inner resources, his courage, his "nerve." Can he stand up and take it? Will he prove to be tough enough? These uncertainties constitute an ego threat for the individual forced to live in prolonged intimacy with criminals, regardless of the nature or extent of his own criminality; and we can catch a glimpse of this tense and fearful existence in the comment of one prisoner who said, "It takes a pretty good man to be able to stand on an equal plane with a guy that's in for rape, with a guy that's in for murder, with a man who's well respected in the institution because he's a real tough cookie. . . ." His expectations concerning the conforming behavior of others destroyed, unable and unwilling to rely on the officials for protection, uncertain of whether or not today's joke will be tomorrow's bitter insult, the prison inmate can never feel safe. And at a deeper level lies the anxiety about his reactions to this unstable world, for then his manhood will be evaluated in the public view.

53. The Impact of Confinement

ANTHONY GUENTHER

"THERE ARE NO EXITS FOR THE INMATE IN THE SENSE of a device or series of devices which can completely eliminate the pains of imprisonment. *But if the rigors of confinement cannot be completely removed, they can at least be mitigated by the patterns of social interaction established among the inmates themselves.* In this apparently simple fact lies the key to our understanding of the prisoner's world."[1]

Gresham Sykes' well known essay on the "pains of imprisonment" suggests that inmates develop fairly standardized means for coping with their existence. Prisons are just a special case, then, of organizations whose distinctive feature is that they process *people* rather than inanimate materials. Expressed differently, the greatest challenge faced by people-processing organizations is the reactivity of their clients.

The concept of confinement subsumes in reality a set of psychologically debilitating events. In retaliation for lawlessness and as a consequence of aggregating large numbers of prisoners over extensive time periods, correctional institutions bestow a series of deprivations upon offenders. As Sykes has noted, these involve the deprivation of goods and services, the denial of heterosexual relationships, loss of autonomy,

►SOURCE: *The Social Dimensions of a Penitentiary. Report to the National Institute of Law Enforcement and Criminal Justice (1975), unpublished mimeo. 5:23–39. Reprinted by permission of the author.*

[1]Gresham M. Sykes, *The Society of Captives*, Princeton, New Jersey: Princeton University Press, 1958, p. 82 (emphasis in the original).

compromised security and a feeling of well-being, and suspended liberty.[2]

It will be the purpose of this selection to show how some properties of confinement affect the lives of men in prison settings and to note some of their responses. Our focus will be upon routinization; debasement, mortification and dehumanization; contact with the home world; time; and making the best of adversity.

ROUTINIZATION

One of the most durable stereotypes of the prison is based upon its regimen. The goal of such order and patterned regularity is, of course, the efficient handling of aggregated men. A secondary objective of routine activities is uniform treatment of inmates, thereby eliminating the need for specialized facilities and discretionary judgments. But prisons never quite achieve a total regimentation, for there are those who cannot, or will not be cared for in that manner. For example, special dietary provisions must be made for Black Muslims who require pork-free meals, and men with physical disabilities are given bottom-tier, lower bunk quarters in the cellhouses. Furthermore, adjustments must be made to work assignments for men who are convalescing from surgery, who are released for an appearance in court, or who are taken to the segregation unit.

Every prison must develop a mechanism for

[2]*Ibid.*, pp. 65–78.

the routine handling of events comprising its schedule. The clearest indicator of its attention to these matters is an intricate system of memoranda, forms, routing slips and passes.[3] From admission to release, applications and releases are required for nearly every activity in which an inmate engages. For example, a newly-arrived prisoner signs a form verifying an accounting of his personal property. If he wants an appointment with a staff member he uses another form called a "cop-out," and if he wants a Christmas photograph taken for his family still another form is required. When he is released from prison he must verify that fact by written acknowledgment.

Inmates usually understand why the routinization of conduct is necessary, for they realize that 2,200 sets of individualized needs cannot be accommodated. What they object to is the mind-numbing tedium that accompanies a nearly flawless schedule. In part this means that the ponderous routine of awakening, eating, working, engaging in recreation, and retiring is punctuated only by the incessant reminders of surveillance: being counted, reporting in, and reporting out. But they are also denied access to the possessions and privileges that would make their days correspond more to those of the normal world.[4] Although clinical documentation would be difficult, many prisoners become "stir-crazy" or "cell-simple" from the monotony of doing time.

---

[3]As recently as ten years ago prisoners in federal institutions were permitted to move from one location to another only if they had passes. A correctional officer signed his initials and noted the time on it when the inmate left point A and another officer did the same at point B. The same process was followed in returning to A. Two predictable outcomes finally caused the demise of this system: first, disciplinary court (the "Adjustment Committee") had to process many misconduct reports on prisoners who consumed too much time enroute or who were caught out-of-bounds; second, widespread counterfeiting or theft and forgery of blank passes occurred. The only passes now used are for inmates who have work assignments outside the wall.

[4]Minute privileges taken for granted in the

DEBASEMENT, MORTIFICATION, AND DEHUMANIZATION

Whatsoever is brought upon thee, take cheerfully,
And be patient when thou art changed to a low estate,
For gold is tried in fire
And acceptable men in the furnace of adversity.

This pronouncement appears in the dining hall of the U.S. Penitentiary, Terre Haute, Indiana. The letters carved into stone are so megalithic that the inscription covers three walls. Some three decades have passed since the Terre Haute prison was built, but the philosophy underlying this inscription has changed little. What has become vividly clear in recent correctional history is the severe deprivation which accompanies imprisonment under the most humane and progressive circumstances.

Goffman's[5] analysis of the processes by which ties to the stable arrangements of a home world are abrogated is instructive here, for total institutions appear to mortify the self in similar ways. At first there are admission procedures designed to make inmates or patients uniform[6] and capable of programming. Their commitment papers, in the case of prisoners, are legal evidence that they have been deemed unsuited and too untrustworthy to remain in the community. Once admitted, attempts to create a standard and pliable inmate are relegated to the admission and orientation program. Thereafter publication is usually made of the standards

---

community—ordering a cup of coffee at the local diner, meeting friends for lunch, or window-shopping downtown—assume much greater importance for the man in confinement.

[5]Erving Goffman in Donald R. Cressey (ed.), *The Prison: Studies in Institutional Organization and Change,* New York: Holt, Rinehart & Winston, Inc., 1961, pp. 23–48.

[6]Striped uniforms were phased out at Atlanta's penitentiary in 1912 and close-clipped hair was no longer required after 1914. The apparel worn by inmates, however, is almost invariably ill-fitting, drab, and crudely laundered. Consisting mostly of military surplus blues or khakis, clothing is inconspicuously stamped with the prisoner's number. For two packs of cigarettes [the form of currency in most prisons] per week, "special handling" of clothing can be obtained.

against which conduct and life style are to be compared. In the Atlanta penitentiary, the policy on "Housekeeping and Personal Conduct Regulations for Inmates"[7] makes these explicit with respect to the following topics:

Bed-making
Lockers
Sanitation
Clothing and personal appearance
Dining room
Radio earphones
Combination locks
Contraband
Gambling
Personal conduct
Commissary
Magazines, newspapers and books
Legal papers and books
Medication
Musical instruments
Photographs and personal letters
Handicraft items
Visiting between quarters

Further discussion by Goffman points out the ways in which dispossession of property, personal defacement and disfigurement, verbal and gestural indignities, assignment of an alien and usually nonessential role, and mental and physical exposure are debasing. Few would deny that a shakedown of one's personal property, wearing a uniform set of clothes, and just being confined are humiliating events, yet they probably have less impact than the subtle processes in penitentiary life which degrade and stigmatize prisoners in the ways that Goffman suggests. Three of these deserve special mention.

First, prison staff employ traditional stereotypes in referring to inmates both publicly and privately. Designations such as "thugs," "hoods," "thieves," and "convicts" are generally applied, but there are specialized references as well. Most are based upon alleged homosexual behavior ("daddy," "flaming faggot," "punk," "pussy," "Miss Julie"), racist beliefs ("hoodoo," "stud," "buck-nigger"), presumed drug use ("junkie," "hop-head," "wino," "lush"), type of criminal ("bank robber," "moonshiner," "car thief," "agitator," "slingshot bandit,"[8] "draft dodger"), or state of emotional disorder ("psycho,""dingbat"). Inmates retaliate in this context of mutual insult with references to correctional officers as "screws," "hacks," "cops," "turnkeys," "policemen," "bulls," and "the man." There is no doubt some contempt expressed in using these terms but a few officers can use them in ways that are inoffensive. For instance an officer whose rapport with inmates is exceptional and whose general style is devoid of contempt may introduce a prisoner to someone as "just an old counterfeiter," or "our number one dingbat." The vast majority of employees, however, do not feel comfortable in such circumstances.

A second source of debasement with which inmates have to contend is the involuntary assumption of a work role which is incompatible with their previous experience. Of course, there are prisoners who have never held gainful employment in their entire lives but they are a minority. Since everyone in the inmate population is expected to work, those who held meaningful and rewarding jobs outside often find prison employment demeaning. For reasons of fiscal limitations some inmates hold jobs which would ordinarily be filled by civilian workers, and these can be challenging. Many of them, such as inmate nurse, industries payroll clerk, or classification and parole clerk, require intelligence, initiative and exceptional responsibility. Most jobs, however, are menial, require at most two or three hours per day, and have been performed more or less in the same manner for decades. "Goldbricking" becomes a virtual in-

[7]United States Penitentiary, *Policy Statement A-7300.36*, Atlanta, Georgia, March 2, 1970.

[8]A bad-check artist, petty thief or other offender whose career consists alternately of short excursions into crime followed by "bits" in prison.

dustry in itself, for few staff are assigned to supervise prisoners at work. Employees frequently encourage make-work, fearing that "idle hands do mischief make." In Atlanta the best single index of worker dissatisfaction is found at the hospital, where staff regularly confront malingerers requesting "idle slips" (excused absenteeism for illness).

Third, the exposure which prisoners experience is so encompassing that correctional institutions are often said to be dehumanizing. On the one hand, the term refers to disclosure of highly personalized events, for the prison dossier includes much that is discrediting.[9] On the other hand, dehumanization is akin to Goffman's observation that total institutions violate boundaries between private (*my* thoughts, *my* possessions) and public (*their* environment) spheres. Thus collective sleeping arrangements, open toilet facilities, "inspected" mail, and mass dining diffuse information about oneself to an unselected audience. I suspect that this feature of institutional living is most abrasive to inmates, for they regularly object to their enforced interaction with other inmates. Responses given by prisoners to a question about annoying aspects of doing time focus upon personal indignities and lack of respect ("someone shaking down my personal possessions"; "not being treated like a man"), routinization and constraint ("the funny and childish rules"; "being locked up like a dog"), but most substantially, *other inmates to contend with* ("living with niggers"; "living with honkies"; "hearing other convicts tell of the things they've gotten away with"; "associating with 'teachers of crime' ").

The psychological compression which results from living at close quarters with hundreds of others is, of course, made less tolerable by the fact that the proximity of inmates is endured twenty-four hours a day. If the conditions of existence become unacceptable, whether through intimidation, personal repulsion or default, it is not ordinarily possible to "resign" or even withdraw to a private sphere. The reaction of prisoners to each other then follows their having seen interpersonal conflict poorly resolved. In the words of an inmate who has spent most of his adult years in prison:

"One afternoon, a lifelong thief, Richard Ohlmsted, and I were walking the yard here at Atlanta. Suddenly Rick stopped and said, 'Look at these bastards we have to live with, Pat. It makes me think that we have been on the wrong side all our lives.' Rick expressed great truth.[10]

CONTACT WITH THE HOME WORLD

Removal from the free community to confinement in prison is disruptive in ways that few men can anticipate. On most occasions the offender finds himself ill-prepared to arrange his personal affairs, and the period of pre-trial custody is generally one of incapacitation. After conviction and sentencing the defendant is usually conveyed to prison so quickly that his first attempt to reconstruct months of disarray is from there. The sources available for him to use[11] are limited to (a) restricted numbers of telephone calls; (b) correspondence; and (c) visits with approved persons (usually close relatives) and attorneys.

The use of telephones by inmates is a relatively new phenomenon. In the Atlanta penitentiary calls for special purposes can be placed by prisoners to outside persons if satisfactory billing is arranged. Nominal supervision is pro-

---

[9]For a discussion of secrets and the extent to which they are threats to one's social self, see Erving Goffman, *The Presentation of Self in Everyday Life*, Garden City, New York: Doubleday, 1959. A more concentrated work on discreditation and its management is Erving Goffman, *Stigma*, Englewood Cliffs, New Jersey: Prentice-Hall, 1963.

[10]Personal communication, December 23, 1973.

[11]Two other ways of handling the problem are: (1) to escape, and (2) to give instructions to an inmate who is due for release. There are unquestionably many escapes from prison each year which are motivated by crises, real or imaginary, in the home community. With respect to the second means, it is clear that prisoners returning to the community are in a good position to take messages, perform services, and have communication directed back to their imprisoned friends.

vided by caseworkers, thus removing some of the personal, intimate contact between the caller and say, family members. Inmates usually find themselves poorly situated to assist with family problems in the community, but telephone communication may help relieve the acute distress which accompanies illness or other crises.

Although there are many inmates who never receive correspondence (or visits for that matter) during their entire prison terms, the foremost means for retaining ties with the outside world is the mail. In a penitentiary the size of Atlanta, the mail room processes thousands of letters, packages, magazines, and newspapers weekly. As a practical matter outgoing mail is at best "spot-checked,"[12] but incoming mail is inspected at adult penitentiaries for money, drugs or other contraband. A few inmates may have their correspondence restricted or closely watched, particularly if they are labeled major security risks, significant participants in organized criminal activities, or if they are notorious or highly-publicized offenders.[13]

The distribution of mail in Atlanta's institution is carefully organized, for the importance of prompt and faultless delivery is appreciated by both staff and inmates. The system occasionally goes awry, of course, and someone's mail gets misplaced or even lost. To the man in prison, a mistake of this type may deny him a letter from his attorney, one pertaining to litigation, or a package from his family.

Correspondence in an institutional setting, like that in the home world, brings news that is sometimes good, sometimes bad. Considering the strain placed upon those with whom a prisoner was once associated on the outside, many letters reflect pessimism or disillusionment. It is not difficult to imagine the impact of the following letters[14] independently received by two inmates:

Daddy

I am happy you are in prison. When you get out you can't live with use [sic]. I hope you never get out. I think that you are a rotten father. I wanta father that [does] things with me and take me fishing. You are a lier [sic] because you said [you] where going to give me five dollars. I wanta father that can teach me how to swim. My mother is nicer than you.

Carl

Daddy

I hope you never get out of there. When you get out stay 15 miles away from us.

I want a father that can stay out of Jail. You never gave me 22 dollars from working on the truck and I'm going to get it. Like it or not.

I want a father that can teach me how to be a good man and show me the right way to do things.

I think I can do better than you are in staying out of trouble.

Your a lousy father I never like you.

I don't work for nothing you know. I hope you like our letters. HA HA HA. You better answer all the letters.

Nicky

HA HA HA

Visits at Atlanta's prison are limited by the space allocated for their conduct, the number of supervisory personnel available, and the need to maintain other institutional activity. Visitors are required to arrange trips in advance, and upon their arrival the inmate is summoned to the visiting room where he is discretely shaken down.

[12]All inmates may address letters which are neither opened nor inspected to the President, Vice-President, and Attorney General of the United States; the Director, Bureau of Prisons; members of the United States Board of Parole; the Pardon Attorney; the Surgeon General, United States Public Health Service; the Secretary of the Army, Navy and Air Force; United States Courts; members of the United States Senate and House of Representatives; and representatives, specified by name or title, of the news media. (See United States Bureau of Prisons, "Prisoner's Mail Box," *Policy Statement 7300.2B*, Washington, D.C., August 7, 1972.

[13]"Flagging" the mail of such persons is the procedure used in Atlanta, where there is suspicion that a prisoner is trying to conduct a business, discuss criminal activities, make threats, transmit information on escape plots, etc.

[14]The second of these was originally discussed in Anthony L. Guenther and Mary Quinn Guenther, "Screws vs. Thugs," *Society*, 11 (July/August, 1974), pp. 42–50.

An informal atmosphere not unlike that of a cafeteria is provided, with tables for use by visitors and inmates. Vending machines dispensing drinks and rest rooms for guests complete the facility.

The visiting facility in Atlanta is one of those places in the institution whose potential for fostering constructive, rewarding interchange between inmates and the home world is diminished by the antics and abuses of a few. On a busy day the room will be filled with children, tears of joy are present on many faces, and the meeting of personal needs is readily apparent. Yet the stance assumed by correctional officers is in clear opposition to the ostensibly open, free, unmonitored climate in which visits occur. There prevail suspicions that contraband will be passed, that notes are smuggled in or out, that prisoners will be visited by persons falsely identified (e.g., girl friends posing as wives), or that sexual "hanky-pank" will take place. Thus custodial routine surrounds every visit: guests are told that firearms, cameras, drugs, and other contraband are prohibited in the institution and are reminded of federal penalties for noncompliance; the inmate is "pat-searched" before entering the room and is strip-searched upon departure;[15] a brief embrace and kiss are permitted at the beginning and conclusion; visitors must sign in and out; and a record of approved visitors and their appearances is maintained.

Special visits are arranged with inmates and their attorneys or for law enforcement personnel in connection with official business. Inmates are given access to their attorneys on an unlimited basis. In the case of law enforcement officers, two small interview rooms (also used for strip-searching the inmate following his visit) are maintained for their purposes.

[15]Pat-searching involves an officer running his hands along the limbs and trunk of a fully-clothed inmate who has emptied his pockets of contents for inspection. In strip-searching the prisoner fully disrobes, steps away from his clothing piled on a table or the floor, and submits to a visual check of his body. The latter takes place in complete separation from visitors, but several inmates may be searched in each other's presence.

Every prisoner, except a very few who have reportedly abused their privileges, can receive visitors. This rule includes those who are hospitalized (unless, of course, it is medically inadvisable) and those who are in segregation. Since advance notice is given of a visit, the inmate who is confined in segregation can be given a shower, permitted to shave, and have a normal issue of clothing. On occasion, prior notice is not given and the visitors may be delayed for as much as two hours while the prisoner is made ready. Hospital visits are more rare and security is greater. Visitors for a hospital patient are escorted to and from a closed room, constant visual supervision is maintained, and the room is searched immediately after the visit is terminated.

In theory the length of time a visit may continue and the frequency with which an inmate may receive visits is regulated. Although officers in the visiting facility are given wide discretion in this matter, the general practice is to let a man be with his guests only if others are not being denied their turn. For visitors who have come a great distance or who can schedule a trip only irregularly, an almost indefinite period is permitted the inmate.

There is a certain paradox in the visiting program, for it is at once a source of enormous satisfaction and a source of great cruelty. Visiting room officers are not infrequently the recipients of profuse thanks and even "fan letters":

Thank you all for your courtesy and understanding when I have been there to see my son Robert Rodriguez. You are all been very nice and hope you have a wonderful year full of Health and happiness.

Thank you,
Mr. Manuel Rodriguez
740 E. 45th Street
Miami, Florida[16]

But visits are reminders of fractured lives, and their termination symbolizes the return of an inmate to his enforced dependency. Departing

[16]Source: Christmas card, "To Officers in Visiting Room, Box PMB, Atlanta, Georgia 30315," December 23, 1969.

visitors often find that the experience was emotionally draining; there are always reservations about having discussed certain topics or asked too many questions.

There is a certain unanticipated consequence of visits by women to the prison related to the fact that many girl friends and wives are extraordinarily handsome. In the Atlanta penitentiary "girl-watching" begins from the moment a woman arrives. Inmates in the front cellblocks watch visitors entering and then position themselves along entrances to the main corridor for a closer look. The visiting room often assumes the climate of a fashion bazaar and is permeated by perfumes and colognes. Men who are denied heterosexual encounters for months and even years find that their capacity for sexual arousal is not attenuated, and they may be acutely anxious over their visits with desirable women.

A wife who is provocative, albeit unconsciously, can generate two kinds of problems when she visits a prisoner. First, her presence may cause him to question for the first time how "the government" can deny him sexual access to his spouse. He knows, of course, that conjugal visits in the federal penitentiary are not possible, but he is desirous of them nonetheless. Second, when other inmates notice her, the inmate whom she visited may be the recipient of comments about "Jody." One of the most durable stories in prison folklore concerns the lonely wife who consorts with Jody when her husband goes to prison.[17] It is plausible, as anyone who has admired someone else's wife can attest, and becomes verified by the actual experiences of prisoners.

TIME

Contrasted with the home world where time is a scarce commodity, the inhabitants of penitentiaries find time in abundance. Prisoners are known to each other as much for the lengths of their sentences as for their crimes, and initial impressions have these two bases.

The time a man is given when sentence is pronounced is deceptive, for almost no one ever serves his full term. Under federal law, a specified amount of "statutory good time" is automatically calculated and applied in accordance with a schedule. An inmate with a three-year sentence, for example, earns seven days of good time per month. Unless he "loses" part or all of his good time through misconduct, he will be released after about two years and three months. Another inmate serving ten years will be released after about six years and eight months (termed his "mandatory release date"), for he receives ten good time days per month.[18] Extra good time is also available to those who are assigned to a prison camp, work in industries, or have earned a meritorious service award.

Another mechanism for truncating a sentence is through parole. Federal law regarding parole is fairly complex, but in general offenders are eligible for parole after serving one-third of their full terms. Under some sentencing procedures, prisoners are eligible at any time. From the viewpoint of inmates, parole is a mixed blessing: early release is obtained but supervision on the outside is required for the remainder of one's sentence. Inmates who are close to the end of their prison terms will often decline a parole hearing because they would rather not have to report to outside authorities.[19]

When a prisoner is committed to Atlanta with a very lengthy sentence, say, sixty years, or when his multiple sentences are "stacked" (consecutive), he is sometimes said to "have more time

---

[17]In the Atlanta version of this story she concludes her visit with him at the institution, then walks to the main lobby where she uses the public telephone ("Jody phone") to call her lover.

[18]A judge can take advantage of good time provisions in the case of a worthy offender by pronouncing sentence of one year and one day instead of one year. The former earns good time at the rate of six days per month, while it is five per month for the latter. The beneficiary of such a sentence alternative would obtain release eleven days earlier.

[19]In the parlance of inmates this is doing time "flat out."

than he can ever do," or it is claimed that "he'll never see daylight." A long sentence distinguishes a man in the eyes of correctional staff, and he consequently can expect much closer supervision. In terms of the social stratification among inmates, a man with "lots of time" is initially given high ranking. Nonetheless he proceeds arduously on his sentence, for in the vernacular of prisoners, one "pulls" or "builds" time.

Persons outside the prison world are accustomed to measuring progress at any given moment as the ratio of time expended to time available. Prisoners adhere to this mechanism too, for in a sense they are making progress toward release. But that proportion can also symbolize regress as well, for during the weeks, months and years behind bars, undesirable changes may occur. In the outside community, wives succumb to loneliness, and former employers change their manpower needs. And inside there is the insidiousness and malevolence associated with men who do their time by victimizing others.

During a prison career there are periods of "hard time" and periods of "easy time." Hard time occurs when you are under intimidation, when you are worried about a problem whose solution is unavailable, or when you dwell excessively on the years before release. Most men do hard time on weekends when the regular working schedule does not help time pass quickly. Perhaps the most depressing period of hard time in prison is during holidays. As one inmate put it:

"Just walk around the [cell]block tonight and look at the long faces. We've all been watching T.V. with the Christmas ads, programs showing families around the tree, and shots of a winter wonderland we aren't going to see. Then everybody gets to thinking what sorry sons-of-bitches we are to be in the can at Christmas."[20]

For prisoners, then, time is not to be conserved; it is to be expended in large batches and without regard to what was accomplished during its passage. Almost no one wants to make reference, once released, to his attainments in confinement. As Goffman has observed:

"[A]mong inmates in many total institutions there is a strong feeling that time spent in the establishment is time wasted or destroyed or taken from one's life; it is time that must be written off; it is something that must be 'done' or 'marked' or 'put in' or 'pulled.' In prisons . . . a general statement of how well one is adapting to the institution may be phrased in terms of how one is doing time, whether easily or hard. This time is something its doers have bracketed off for constant conscious consideration in a way not quite found on the outside. As a result, the inmate tends to feel that for the duration of his required stay—his sentence—he has been totally exiled from living."[21]

[20]Field notes, U.S. Penitentiary, Atlanta, December 25, 1969.

[21]Goffman, *Asylums,* New York: Doubleday & Co., 1961, pp. 67–68.

54. Escapes and Escape Attempts

ANTHONY GUENTHER

AN ESCAPE IS THE INCIDENT WHICH PRISON STAFF fear most and ironically invest the greatest amount of time and energy in devising protective tactics.[1] The total effort made to ensure that no one departs from the institution prior to his authorized date—in the form of performing counts, operating locking devices, and checking rosters—is enormous. Therefore, an escape threatens the very philosophical basis of a penitentiary, which is not founded upon penitence but rather upon *custody*.

▶SOURCE: *The Social Dimensions of the Penitentiary. Report to the National Institute of Law Enforcement and Criminal Justice. (1975), unpublished mimeo. 7: 118–133. Reprinted by permission of the author.*

[1]The literature on escapes is impoverished and what exists is often focused upon runaways at youth institutions. A sampling of work in this area is Donald Clemmer, *The Prison Community*, New York: Rinehart, 1958 (originally published 1940), pp. 199–203; Nelson N. Cochrane, "Escapes and Their Control: A Brief Study of Escape Data," *Prison World*, 10 (May/June, 1948), pp. 28–29; W.S. Loving, F.E. Stockwell, and D.A. Dobbins, "Factors Associated With Escape Behavior of Prison Inmates," *Federal Probation*, 23 (September, 1959), pp. 49–51; David I. Morgan, "Individual and Situational Factors Related to Prison Escape," *American Journal of Correction,* 29 (March/April, 1967), pp. 30–32; Richard J. Hildebrand, "The Anatomy of Escape," *Federal Probation*,33 (March, 1969), pp. 58–66; Norman Holt and Rudy A. Renteria, "The Anatomy of an Escape,"*American Journal of Correction,* 33 (January/February, 1971), pp. 10–15; Charles A.Bender, *The Effects of Early Adjustment Upon Escape from Seagoville Federal Correctional Institution, Texas,* unpublished M.A. thesis (Institute of Contemporary Corrections and the Behavioral Sciences), Sam Houston State University, 1972; Helene Enid Cavior and Robert Beyer, "Escapes from the Robert F. Kennedy Youth Center: 1969 to 1973," unpublished manuscript, March, 1974, 75 pp.

There are several ways in which an escape may have dramatic and often tragic consequences. First, in its commission inmates and staff may suffer injury or even death.[2] Prisoners at Atlanta have been fired upon and struck by tower officers, they have injured themselves using makeshift ladders and ropes while scaling the wall, and have nearly died of suffocation or claustrophobic terror in tunnels and sewage lines. Employees have been injured or otherwise incapacitated by prisoners in the course of escaping, when apprehending them inside the walls, or on manhunts. Second, prisoners who successfully escape often commit other crimes in the process, including automobile theft, assault, robbery, burglary and kidnapping. Public apprehension following news of an "escaped convict" precisely reflects the fear that in his desperation the escapee will harm them or forcibly take their property. Third, if the attempt to escape is unsuccessful and there is any feeling that an informer or a conspirator was to blame, retaliation may be taken against those believed responsible. And fourth, in the political climates of some correctional systems, an escape may cause job insecurity among top administrators. Often a "reform warden" who has just taken control of a badly disorganized and racket-ridden prison has an escape occur early in his administration. Requests for his resignation may

[2]A remote possibility is that gunfire from the towers will reach beyond the penitentiary grounds. This happened during a 1969 escape at Atlanta when two .30 caliber rifle bullets struck an occupied dwelling across from the prison.

604

be demanded before any changes can have taken effect.

There are actually three types of "escapes" possible from a correctional institution. One is by forcibly penetrating or breaching the security perimeter, usually a wall or fence. A second requires concealment aboard a vehicle leaving the institution or creating a disguise by means of which passage through established exits can be made. Third, escapes from outside details and authorized trips are a frequent occurrence. Examination of these in more detail will occupy our attention for the remainder of this selection.

In the final analysis, it is the wall which symbolizes isolation from the free community. Since the wall is probably impenetrable, the alternatives are to scale it with a ladder, or with a hook and length of rope, or to tunnel underneath it. These are the classic escapes depicted in myriad novels and motion pictures. From the incomplete records on escapes at Atlanta, it appears that a successful tunnel has never been dug, but there is ample evidence that they are partially constructed every few years. There are so many obstacles to this escape route, seen in the following case, that little can be said in its favor:

"At 3:00 p.m. a meeting was held in the Associate Warden's office following a report by Mr. Edwards and Mr. Tarber that they had detected an unusual amount of muddy water in one of the sewer lines running South from the institution. Evidently the muddy water was caused by a tunnel being dug inside the institution. Mr. Tarber and Mr. Edwards had traced the water flow into the area of the vegetable room.

"When the 4:00 p.m. count was being taken Lieutenant Willington and four officers were assigned to search the area. At 4:15 p.m. Mr. Beason discovered the entrance to a tunnel in the ice cream room, which is a section of the main vegetable room. This hole was covered by a table and other equipment placed over a section of tile about four feet square which had been removed, fastened on a piece of plywood and replaced easily without detection.

"Photographs were made of the tunnel entrance after which Mr. Beason entered the tunnel and re-

moved a number of contraband tools and other equipment. The tunnel was about five feet deep and about five feet in length. The area was sealed off and a search of the surroundings was unproductive."[3]

Attempts to scale the wall, by comparison, are made frequently although usually without success. Prisoners seen pacing off the distance between towers or throwing tennis or softballs up against the wall are suspected of planning escape. Equipment, including ladders made of wood, pipe and rope, have been constructed in Atlanta. They are usually a compromise between construction which will support the weight of a man yet will be small enough to conceal and simple enough to assemble and place in position quickly. There are important obstacles to this means of escape as well:

"On December 16, Mr. Earl, the machine shop foreman observed two inmates acting suspicious. Although having other duties to perform, he investigated and observed several lengths of pipe in their possession . . . [whereupon] he defined the situation as an escape attempt in progress.

"Mr. Earl was handicapped by not having a telephone or other communication in the immediate area. He called to another employee in another area and had the alarm sounded for an emergency.

"Further investigation resulted in the recovery of the pipe which had been fashioned into a ladder with a hook on the end. The pipes were threaded on each end with sleeves to join them together to scale the wall."[4]

Escape attempts through concealment inside the institution have taken many forms. Prisoners have dressed in civilian clothes, joined a large group of visitors at the end of their tour, and tried to accompany them through the sallyport. They have hidden in the trash compactor, hoping to be removed together with its contents. A few fabricate counterfeit release papers or contrive passes to work outside the wall. The

[3]Combined memoranda, U.S. Penitentiary, Atlanta, May 18–29, 1970.

[4]Memorandum, U.S. Penitentiary, Atlanta December 16, 1970.

escape-minded prisoner often gives close attention to construction projects going on inside the
wall since they usually require heavy machinery
or trucks in the vicinity. Institutions with fences
have experienced escapes in which a truck
commandeered by inmates is driven into or
through the fence, often under heavy gunfire.
When the top section of each tower was being
replaced in Atlanta, information was received
that an inmate planned to conceal himself inside
the hollow roof just before it was lifted into
place on the wall and was later to break his way
out. Another plan was to remove the interior
components of a large, heavy-duty transformer
being replaced by the utility company. Since the
transformer core was large enough to contain a
man, the only remaining problem was to
reinstall the top with false bolts to have the original appearance when a truck came to remove it.
As before, the attempt was thwarted by an informer.

The third method of escape differs from
others because it originates outside the walls.
The man who works on a minimum-custody
farm, on a landscape crew, or at the powerhouse
is designated an escapee if he takes unauthorized leave, just as if he had scaled the wall.
Representative cases of escaping during an authorized trip would be inmates who are sent to
the community treatment center (a pre-release
facility) and never arrive at their destination,
who go on an unescorted funeral trip or a bedside visit and fail to return, or who escape from
U.S. Deputy Marshals while en route to court
for an appearance. This final type of escape is
particularly interesting because prisoners who
spend a significant proportion of their time
planning an escape have increasingly shown a
preference for it in recent years. An episode
which is fictitious but resembles many actual occurrences will show what basic steps are involved:

Matish and Nittoli are serving twenty and twelve
years, respectively, for bank robbery. Both were
transferred to Atlanta from Terre Haute, another
federal institution, for control purposes.

In surveying the prospects for escape, they rule out
'hitting the wall.' The lighting system is prohibitively
bright at night, the inmate population is full of
snitches, and there are two Lieutenants who know
them and their intentions so that officers watch them
almost constantly. Moreover, the necessary equipment is costly, almost impossible to conceal, and at
least their cellmates plus the supplier must know their
plans.

Matish and Nittoli hear through the 'grapevine'
that their friend, Roselli, still in Terre Haute, was
recently involved in a serious assault on three officers,
one of whom was nearly killed. Roselli is to be prosecuted for attempted murder. Matish and Nittoli get
word to him that they want to appear as character
witnesses in his case. Roselli's attorney obtains an
order for their appearance in federal court in Indianapolis, Indiana.

With prior knowledge of their journey to court in
custody of U.S. Deputy Marshals, the two inmates
purchase homemade handcuff keys[5] which they conceal under the stitching of their waistbands. While
being driven to Indiana, they free themselves of restraining equipment, seize the Marshal's firearm in the
ensuing struggle, and escape.

This type of event actually occurs so often that a
special form has been executed in federal
penitentiaries to alert Marshals to the fact that
a dangerous offender or escape risk is being
placed in their custody. Some observers feel that
much of the litigation initiated by prisoners is a
long-range attempt to make court trips, and if
opportunity arises, to escape. Their evidence for
this is the inordinate number of trips taken by
really dangerous, escape-motivated prisoners
with lengthy sentences.

In Atlanta's history escape attempts greatly
outnumber successes. An "attempt" may be
defined by the staff as anything from being in
possession of a length of rope to scaling a ladder
placed against the wall. Similarly, an inmate who
"hides out" through a count and thus causes a

---

[5]These are constructed from a short length of ballpoint
pen cartridge to which a small drop of solder is attached at
one end and filed to shape. A handcuff key like this can be as
small as one inch.

search of the institution may be charged with attempted escape.

Unscheduled departures from the Atlanta penitentiary began in 1902, the year it opened, and have continued to the present. According to an historical account[6] there were three escapes in that first year. One prisoner made good his flight and was at large for four months. Another climbed between the iron window guards and the granite sill in a cellhouse, but was recaptured after only eleven hours. A third escaped by departing through a ventilator of the ice plant and was located two days later. Vignettes from Atlanta's escape history, by no means even a good sampling, will illustrate the ingenuity of confined men whose most abundant commodity is time:[7]

In 1923 a "master thief" sentenced to twenty-five years for a multi-million dollar mail truck robbery, scaled the wall with another inmate just as the floodlights illuminating it were mysteriously extinguished. He escaped from custody two more times while still at large from Atlanta.

In 1948 a twenty-four year old prisoner serving a thirty month sentence for automobile theft escaped by concealing himself aboard a truck which departed through the east gate.

In 1953 two inmates concealed themselves in the movie projection room for seventeen hours while prison staff, Atlanta police, the state police, and the F.B.I. sought them outside. One of the men had a record of hideouts at each of three federal prisons before his confinement at Atlanta.

In 1954 two convicted bank robbers, pushing bar-cutting or spreading equipment ahead of them, crawled several hundred yards through a storm sewer made of fifteen inch pipe. Two other inmates followed the same route, which had not been discovered

by officers, two days later. All were recaptured within five days.

Three prisoners in 1956 attempted to escape by concealing themselves in a boxcar loaded with mattresses. They had cut a hole in the boxcar bottom and after crawling inside, covered it with a piece of sheet-metal.

A twenty-four year old prisoner in 1958 climbed over the roof of cellblocks at the front of the institution, attached sheets to a bar and lowered himself to the ground. He was seen by a tower officer just as he crossed the main street in front of the prison.

In 1969 a prisoner with a twenty-five year sentence sawed through the bars of his cell, swung over to an abandoned catwalk in the cellblock and from there sawed through a set of bars leading to a stairwell. He cut one more set of bars in a window, dropped a long rope to the ground and escaped in a fog. He was at large for forty-three minutes.

Two prisoners assigned to an outside work detail walked away in 1969. One of them had just been awarded ten days 'good time' on the recommendation of an Associate Warden so he could be released before Christmas. He escaped nineteen days prior to his release date.

A young black prisoner planned to escape in 1970 by riding a homemade balloon off the top of the Industries Building and across the east wall. When caught getting his equipment together, he was dressed in 'crash gear'; his gondola, balloon, gas for inflating it, and other equipment were found on top of the building. A full set of engineering plans and formulae was also recovered.[8]

Two inmates working on the night shift at the powerhouse outside the walls walked away in 1970 and vanished into the darkness.

---

[6]See H. Park Tucker, *A History of the Atlanta Federal Penitentiary, 1901–1956*, unpublished manuscript, 670 pp., n.d.

[7]These events are documented in an inmate-maintained scrapbook of newspaper clippings, press releases, and incident files maintained at the penitentiary. A complete history of escapes probably does not exist.

[8]Comments by staff were unanimous that, aerodynamically, this escape plan was entirely feasible. The inmate had checked prevailing wind directions and found that he needed to "float" (since his point of departure was higher than the wall) only about 160 feet before descending. For the flight he had fashioned a crude helmet, taped thick pads of foam rubber to the bottoms of his feet, and tied socks filled with pepper to the insides of his legs. His plan was to spread the pepper around the spot where he landed to disable a team of bloodhounds.

In 1973 ten prisoners, several of whom were listed in the "Hot Book,"attempted to escape by concealing themselves in a railway boxcar.

In the absence of systematic research, no one knows what motives prisoners have for taking the extraordinary risks incurred through a forcible departure. On the one hand, these risks are physically dangerous: being shot with a carbine, shotgun, or revolver; falling thirty or forty feet from the wall; being crushed by faulty apparatus; or suffocating. There is, on the other hand, a psychological impairment which can follow an unsuccessful escape attempt. For the prisoner in this circumstance may find himself both envied for his pluck and derided for foolhardiness. From the staff he receives at least temporarily increased surveillance and a loss of trust, if not privilege. He is often impelled to try again, but his attempt will have to be more sophisticated and in any event will occur under different ground rules than before.

Informal discussions with prison staff and inmates suggest that many of the reasons convicted offenders escape from custody are the same reasons any of us would resist restrictive circumstances.[9] Inmates hope to resolve personal problems or family crises, or to alleviate the anxiety produced by confinement and denial. Some undoubtedly feel that there is little to lose, especially if their present sentences are substantial or if they have detainers for serious crimes elsewhere. Others are willing to risk possible injury or even death in exchange for a chance to enjoy the amenities of the outside community. On occasion a man will escape simply because he is becoming too institutionalized and fears that he will be destined to spend his life in prison if he does not act immediately.

[9]In a study of mental hospital patients who departed without medical permission, R. Wayne Kernodle found that the reasons most frequently accounting for escapes revolved around family relationships and responsibilities. He makes a case for nonmedical departures as therapeutic, arguing that such patients refuse assimilation of a "hospital patient" identity and that their objectives in leaving are usually quite rational. See his "Nonmedical Leaves from a Mental Hospital," *Psychiatry*, 29 (February, 1966), pp. 25–41.

Under federal law the maximum sentence that can be imposed for an escape is five years. To an Atlanta prisoner that sanction is not a very strong deterrent, particularly since most sentences following a successful prosecution are on the order of fifteen months.[10] A federal judge often makes the sentence for escape concurrent with the sentence being served at that time, thus imposing little additional criminal sanction.

Escape plans formulated by inmates, if they are to have any prospect of success, require attention to several matters.[11] First, there is security. A general guideline is to share your plans only with those who are essential parties. These might include other inmates who are knowledgeable about weak points in the institution's perimeter, who have access to places along the escape route for which reconnaissance is needed, or who own or will fabricate escape equipment. A second consideration is timing. In part this could mean waiting a period of months, possibly years, before an increase in privileges can be obtained which would permit working outside the wall. But timing also refers to a season of the year, a day of the week, and a choice between daylight and darkness. Third, the prudent inmate will make an assessment of the staff assigned to each shift and the distribution of Lieutenants in supervisory positions. Some officers are more expert in shakedowns, for example, and certain tower officers are known to be inattentive to surveillance. Similarly, it might be worthwhile to wait until a Lieutenant whose "string of rats" is legion has gone on leave or is assigned to a training course. Fourth, prisoners will normally construct a mental history of past escapes and attempts. This must be done with the utmost caution since suspicions will be aroused if inquiry about these

[10]*Federal Offender Datagraphs*, Washington, D.C.: Administrative Office of the United States Courts, May, 1972, p. A-14.

[11]Escapes from youth institutions or reformatories are much less likely to be carefully planned. Many are impulsive, spontaneous attempts which succeed only because they are a complete surprise to staff and because informers obviously know nothing about them.

matters is not casual. Fifth, prospects for assistance must be weighed. This might take the form of outside transportation at the moment of escape, a weapon or change of clothes concealed on the grounds beyond the wall, or a diversion (for example, a large fire) staged inside simultaneously with the escape attempt. Sixth, an escape plan involves the acquisition of equipment and arrangement for its storage. The prisoner who purchases equipment which is used unsuccessfully in an escape attempt may find himself financially encumbered. For instance, in the 1969 escape from Atlanta in which three sets of bars were cut, the following purchases were made: (1) two hacksaw blades at a cost of five boxes each; (2) a "hot wire" and instructions for its use in stealing a car; (3) a knife; (4) a length of rope; and (5) two twenty dollar bills and two one dollar bills.[12] Additionally problematic, of course, is the assumption that these were acquired from sources who honor the confidential nature of such transactions.

From the perspective of staff, contraband associated with an impending escape attempt merits the highest degree of attention. A systematic listing of escape contraband would include bar spreaders and cutters; keys, lockpicks, drills and punches, excavating and wall-penetrating equipment; ladders and scaling hardware; and escape plans and other aids.

There are two ways of passing through the bars that enclose cells, contain cellblocks, form door grilles, cover windows, and block tunnels or sewers. The traditional method calls for sawing bars with a file or a hacksaw blade held in a homemade frame.[13] A more sophisticated blade now available is a thin rod of carbon steel which reportedly cuts bars far more quickly than blades. Still more advanced is a "diamond strand" which resembles dental floss but consists of diamond dust affixed to a thin, strong piece of wire or synthetic fiber. Sawing bars is noisy, fatiguing work and is being rendered obsolete by alternatives which cut or spread bars. One cutting device is a Stillson wrench, having teeth which grip the metal clamped in its "jaws" increasingly tighter as the wrench is rotated. Eventually metal fatigue will cause the bar to part. Another such tool is a clamp-type cutter with commercial-grade discs for cutting a groove in the bar. Bolts holding it together are tightened as the cutting wheels rotate around the bar. But the second and more ingenious contrivance is a bar spreader. Operating on the screw principle, it is portable, relatively quiet, and easy to operate. Bars only have to be spread a width sufficient to pass the head in most cases.[14] Examples of their construction would be a four-piece concentric pipe with holes for a rod to expand the pieces; a simple threaded rod with pipe extensions, turned by a wrench; and a clamp-type "crusher" which pulls adjacent bars together, thus creating an opening. The compression placed upon the threads of a bar spreader is appreciable; correctional officers report that the quality of threads limits their effectiveness.

Passage through doors and grilles can be accomplished with greater subtlety by using fabricated keys or lockpicks to move the tumblers in the heavy locks that are found in prison construction. Keys are made of materials which appear to be flimsy, but it must be remembered that they are only expected to operate once. Lockpicks, on the other hand, range from a commercial type with movable "fingers" and ad-

---

[12]Interview, U.S. Penitentiary, Atlanta, November 3, 1969.

[13]The length of time needed to saw through a bar varies with its diameter, the type of steel, the energy applied, and the quality of the blade. Prisoners who "saw out" of confinement are ordinarily surprised how long it takes to make the four cuttings (two places in each of two bars) usually required. A tool-resistant bar, defined as "[O]ne which is not severed within a working period of six hours by using six hacksaw blades..." presents the ultimate challenge. See United States Bureau of Prisons, *Correctional Institution De-*

sign and Construction, Leavenworth, Kansas: United States Penitentiary, 1949, p. 229.

[14]A celebrated case of escape at the Federal Reformatory, Chillicothe, Ohio, in the mid-1960s involved a prisoner who starved himself from 160 to 135 pounds and squeezed between a window sill and a set of bars exactly 6¼ inches apart.

justments for spring tension, to small U-shaped rods of simple design. Alternatively, locks can be punched or drilled, but these methods are noisy and often fail because locks are constructed more durably than was anticipated.

Excavation for tunnels requires, of course, implements that function as picks and shovels. Prisoners who gain access to utility tunnels use drills, flycutters, cold chisels, crowbars and heavy hammers to break through steel plate or masonry walls.

Ladders to scale the wall are constructed from pieces which may be kept in separate places and assembled quickly for use. Wooden two-by-fours, pipe or tubing are the usual materials, with rungs made of clamps or long bolts. Two other components are needed: a hook for the top of the wall and a piece of strand or rope ladder for climbing down the outside facing. Concealment of a ladder is challenging, but a considerable length of rope can be wound around an inmate's body, then covered with clothing. To reiterate an earlier point, escape attempts involving ladders have their best prospects, as officers well know, during a heavy rainstorm, fog or snowstorm.

A last category of escape paraphernalia includes plans, maps, blueprints, identification, dummies, civilian clothing, and money. Among the many items of this nature found at Atlanta have been a plat plan of the institution (to scale), a diagram of the tunnel system, maps of the Atlanta area, a listing of gun store locations, blank identification cards for presentation as an employee of such firms as General Electric and the National Geographic Society, a plaster-of-Paris face for use as a dummy in bed, and counterfeit twenty-dollar bills.

Attempts to escape are such an expected event in the penitentiary that certain preventive measures are taken. The most systematic of these is the count taken several times each day. Shakedowns are conducted in hopes that equipment will be found or evidence of escape intentions will be discovered. Thus grilles, locks, bars, windows, and other security barriers are frequently examined for tampering. The cells of "hot," i.e., escape-minded prisoners, are searched irregularly, and these men are accounted for by officers even between formal counts. Informers play an important role in the anticipation of escapes; their provision of information on an escape "caper" is comparable to the value of information on impending assaults in the eyes of staff. Furthermore, special custodial procedures to increase surveillance are enacted when visibility is impaired between the towers. The best illustrations of these are "fog line" procedures, which restrict all except the most essential inmate work details to their housing units, and place extra personnel along fog lines between towers both inside and outside the wall. Under these conditions, inmates moving anywhere inside the walls must be taken under escort by an employee. Fog conditions, then, force a slowdown of the entire institution and place very heavy demands upon the custodial staff.

Institutional Treatment and
Its Effectiveness

THE "TREATMENT" OF CONVICTED CRIMINALS HAS, UNTIL THE LAST FEW YEARS, BEEN largely a myth, an empty phrase trotted out for speeches, conventions, and interviews with the press. Professional personnel in prison were few in number, powerless, and usually preoccupied with administrative duties which made meaningful work with prisoners impossible. Rehabilitative programs that did exist, usually academic or vocational instruction, were almost never rigorously evaluated to see if they worked. Administrators and professional clinicians alike usually assumed that the key to successful rehabilitation was more personnel and larger budgets. Faced with the increasingly obvious failure of this state of affairs, the 1960s and 1970s saw large-scale application of a new variety of theraputic and correctional techniques within prisons and a number of careful studies to test the effects of such programs on subsequent criminal behavior. "Corrections" was beginning to take its new title more seriously.

This section is devoted to descriptive accounts of these techniques, some from the viewpoint of the therapist and some by outside researchers who have tried to capture the inmates' views. We have also included, when available, studies that attempt to evaluate the outcomes of such programs.

The increased use of rigorous research methods to evaluate various corrective treatment regimens in prison has raised a series of ethical issues that are not easily dismissed. Although it can be pointed out that the use of incarceration itself may be considered an arbitrary experiment imposed on convicts, the newer techniques and the intentional separation of prisoners into treated and untreated control groups for purposes of research, adds a certain specificity and poignancy to the ethical issues. In addition, the need for knowledge concerning the effectiveness and side-effects of some newly developed drugs and the cheap availability of prisoners has led to strongly conflicting opinions about drug research in prison, separating, on the one hand, prison administrators, drug company officials, and prisoners themselves, and on the other, some professionals and civil libertarian groups. Geis's article details some of these conflicts and points out some of the hazards that can arise from such practices.

Careful evaluative research on correctional techniques became an integral part of the administrative policy of the California prison system during the 1960s. Early results were discouraging, and, partly in response to this, attempts were made to develop various typologies of offenders so that inmates could be matched with appropriate correctional techniques, following the medical model that treats different illnesses differently. One of the most enduring of these typologies has been "I-Levels." Austin, in an article written for this volume, describes the use of these in the rehabilitation of juvenile offenders. This technique involves placing inmates in one of seven "levels of maturity" based on perceptual and interpersonal capabilities. He further attempts to evaluate three I-Level rehabilitation projects.

Although prison labor and vocational training were among the earliest efforts at rehabilitation, studies of the effectiveness of such programs have been rare. Perhaps because the public generally supports and feels that they understand such measures, we have developed untested assumptions about their value. McKee's paper on the cost benefit values of such training reports that the postrelease income of vocationally trained releasees was significantly higher than the income of prisoners who did not receive similar training.

One of the "pains of imprisonment" has been the uncertainty surrounding the criteria used in determining release and the actual time of release itself. Mutual Agreement Programming (M.A.P.) is based on the idea that all inmates need a firm parole date and clearly specified, contractually defined criteria for parole in which correctional administrators *and* prisoners agree openly. Such a program, it is argued by Rosenfeld in an American Correctional Association sponsored study, would improve the inmate performance through his participation in the decision concerning his own release.

Because individual psychotherapy for large numbers of inmates is not economically feasible, various forms of group therapy and group counselling have been increasingly adopted in prison settings. The most thorough study of group counselling, carried out by Kassebaum and his associates in a California institution, compared a number of different treatment groups with carefully matched controls who received no treatment. In the group sessions inmates were free to discuss emotions and attitudes under the unobtrusive leadership of a trained professional. After a three-year follow-up, no significant differences were found.

One of the most controversial correctional facilities in the country is the Patuxent Institution in Maryland. It is designed for repeated offenders who are committed under a special law which makes release contingent upon psychiatric judgments by institutional staff. Maryland officials continue to make claims of considerable success for this program. Wilkins, reanalyzing their own data, successfully demolishes these claims of a low recidivism rate and questions the arbitrary exercise of power under the guise of the "medical model."

Rehabilitative efforts are usually initiated by behavior specialists or by educators. An unusual program of plastic surgery was carried out on New York

City offenders. It was set up in such a way as to compare subsequent criminality among those prisoners who received surgery and social services, those who received one but not the other, and controls who received no form of treatment. For nonaddicts, the surgery—on deformities of face or hands usually—seems to be effective in reducing criminality. Surgery on addicts, which customarily involved eradication of needle marks, was not as successful as social casework alone.

Without question, the issue in corrections which arouses strong passions and equally strong fears is the various forms of what has come to be known as "behavior modification." The first selection dealing with "behavior mod" is by Stolz, tracing the roots in psychological theory and experimentation, detailing the various forms of both positive and negative reinforcement, and discussing some of the ethical and legal implications. Although practitioners often disavow negative or aversive conditioning—the sort made famous by the novel and motion picture *A Clockwork Orange,* its use has not been uncommon in mental hospitals and correctional institutions. A particularly severe form of aversion therapy, discussed by Mattocks and Jew, involves the use of Anectine, a drug that produces temporary muscular paralysis and respiratory arrest, but which "works" for some offenders.

Critics of the use of behavior modification in prisons claim that its primary purpose is to "manage" the inmate and make it easier to run the institution and, further, that prisoners are being changed against their will. Supporters of this technique suggest that because behavior modification is much more effective than any other known measure, inmates are spared the indignities of prison life for long periods because they can be released when cured after a relatively short period of time. Russell, in a detailed review of the evidence, claims that the short-range apparent success of this form of therapy is due to such factors as the "Placebo Effect," well known to medical experimenters, and that the long-range effect is so negligible that opposition to such programs may be unjustified. In the final selection on behavior modification, Friedman, a lawyer, looks at some of the court cases that have set legal limits on such issues as the competency of an inmate of an institution to give consent to such treatment.

Although the public is interested in humanitarian treatment of criminals, there is an increasingly strong sentiment that we have gone too far in a "permissive"society. Those who hold this view believe that prisoners should not be let out too soon, and a greater proportion of convicted offenders should get prison terms rather than "get off the hook" by one means or another. Does time served in prison affect postrelease criminality? Beck and Hoffman's study of Connecticut prisoners followed for two years subsequent to release generally finds no substantial relationship between time served and recidivism. On the same problem, Hopkins examines much current research that shows prisoners do less well than those noninstitutionalized offenders who remained in the community. He finds these research projects to be questionable because of serious methodological flaws. With his own improved design he found that imprisonment is indeed less effective than noninstitutional alternatives in preventing further crime. Kitchner and his colleagues tackle the issue of how to measure success of penal treatment in terms of number of successful years after release. In an 18-year follow-up of federal prisoners they found that the rate of those returning to prison rises sharply in the second and third year in the community and by five years, two-thirds of all who will be reinstitutionalized for criminal activity will have been returned to prison.

General pessimism concerning corrections generally is evinced by Robison and Smith who found no significant differences between those incarcerated and those receiving probation; those who served long sentences and those who served short ones; those receiving group counselling and those who do not; or releasees supervised by a parole officer with a large case load compared with those supervised by an officer with a small case load. This view is sustained in the most important evaluation and critique of prisons and prison treatment of our time—what has come to be known as the Martinson Report. A summary in this volume examines education, vocational training, individual and group counselling, the effect of sentencing, noninstitutional treatment methods, and differing degrees of supervision. The results are almost uniformly bleak and one might well ask, with Martinson, "What works?" Palmer sharply takes Martinson to task for alleged inconsistencies in his well-known summary of the larger report (by Lipton, Martinson, and Wilks, *The Effectiveness of Correctional Treatment*), of selecting the more pessimistic outcomes, and working with an ambiguous and unsatisfactory concept of "success." Palmer concludes that a correct interpretation of the larger study shows that some methods of treatment do work.

55. Ethics of Prisoner Experimentation

GILBERT GEIS

THE PROBLEMS INVOLVED IN RESEARCH WITH AND upon human beings are ironic, vicious, and often intensely paradoxical. The subject itself is pervaded with a good deal of piety and self-righteousness, and with two sets of antipodal values, neither of them inherently superordinate, which clash fiercely at times. Adherents who press for experimentation in the face of hesitation by others are apt to proclaim proudly that they are "scientists"and that their antagonists are "anti-intellectual" and "fuzzy intuitionists." Their opponents often find the experimenters lacking in compassion and human feeling, without sound comprehension of the legal elements basic to a democratic society. They believe that the experimenters sometimes use the scientific ethos as a camouflage for the infliction of gross indignity and deprivation upon helpless and uninformed people.

The irony lies, of course, in the exigencies of everyday existence, in which all sorts of injustice prevail as the consequence not of scientific experimentation but of happenstance. For most of us, it would be unthinkable that a sample of armed robbers be divided into two groups on the basis of random assignment—one group to spend 10 years in prison, the second to receive a sentence of 2 years on probation. Nonetheless, at a recent federal judicial conference, after examining an elaborate presentence report concerning a bank robber, 17 judges said they would have imprisoned the man, while 10 indicated they favored probation. Those voting for imprisonment set sentences ranging from 6 months to 15 years.[1] From the offender's viewpoint, the vagaries of random assignment for experimental purposes might seem preferable to the lottery of exposure to the considered judgment of a member of the judiciary.

COMPETING VALUES

The difficulty involved in attempts to gain consensus on working principles for correctional experimentation with offender populations stems in part from the fact that both major competing values have almost total support. Few persons are opposed to verified, accurate information; and few persons are opposed to the idea of human decency and justice. The dispute centers about the point at which one value is to be given priority, and it is also involved in judgments regarding the true character of the experimental intervention, the statistical likelihood of different outcomes, and the general importance of the findings, measured in terms of their cost.

The dilemma of correctional research, therefore, arises with great intensity not in the extreme cases but in those where both sides of the value equation are almost equally matched. Few persons, for instance, would be apt to say that

▶SOURCE: *"Ethical and Legal Issues in Experimentation with Offender Populations," in Joint Commission on Correctional Manpower and Training, Research in Correctional Rehabilitation. Washington, D.C. 1967. Pp. 34–41.*

[1]"Test Presentence and Summary of Ballot," 27 Federal Rules Decisions 383 (1961).

the cause of science is sufficient to support an experiment in which, without exception, persons convicted of first-degree murder during a given year are executed in order to determine whether capital punishment does in fact have a deterrent impact when categorically applied. Probably just as few persons would maintain that it is unjust to allow a convicted offender to choose between probation in the jurisdiction where he committed his offense and probation in one a thousand miles away, because an investigator wants to determine whether there is a deterrent factor in voluntary removal from the eliciting scene of criminal circumstances.

A HYPOTHETICAL ILLUSTRATION

But how do we judge a situation[2] in which a foundation grant permits attorneys to be supplied for all cases being heard by a juvenile court where attorneys have previously appeared only in rare instances? A fundamental study hypothesis may be that the presence of an attorney tends to result in a more favorable disposition for the client. This idea may be tested by comparing dispositions prior to the beginning of the experiment with those ensuing subsequently, though it would be more satisfactory to supply attorneys to a sample of the cases and withhold them from the remainder, in order to calculate in a more experimentally uncontaminated manner the differences between the outcomes in the two situations.

The matter takes on additional complexity if the researchers desire to determine what particular attorney role is the most efficacious in the juvenile court. They may suspect that an attorney who acts as a friend of the court, knowingly taking its viewpoint as *parens patriae* and attempting to interpret the court's interests to his client, will produce more desirable results than one who doggedly challenges the courtroom

procedure and the judge's interpretation of fact, picks at the probation report, raises constant objections, and fights for his client as he would in a criminal court. But what results are "more desirable"? Perhaps the argumentative approach will win dispositions more in the client's immediate interest, but the cooperative approach might in the long run better serve society and the client too by decreasing recidivism and by contributing to such measurable items as employment and earnings, marital stability, and general social adjustment.

Persons favoring the experimental use of divergent attorney roles—such roles can readily be inculcated in the attorneys by standard training techniques—might stress that, without the project and its foundation funds, no juvenile would be apt to have an attorney and thus any kind of representation is an improvement over normal conditions. They might also insist that the attorneys' views of their clients' best interest represent little more than a combination of myth and supposition, particularly in so uncharted an area as that of the juvenile court. In the long run, they could argue, will juveniles stand to benefit from this empirical determination of the consequences of diverse attorneys' roles.

Opponents of the experimental program, relying first on what they regard as an immutable professional obligation of the attorney, would be apt to suggest that it is unconscionable to deprive a single person of the effort that an attorney regards as his best in the interest of an experimental design. Failure to appeal a case to a higher court when the attorney suspects that an appeal is in order but the research blueprint does not call for intensive pursuit of technical legal points in stipulated cases, may result in commitment of a juvenile who otherwise would have been set free. That the deprivation of liberty may be in the juvenile's best interests, the opponents of the experiment would probably say, is the kind of pious cant that underlay the Inquisition and that provides paving for that well-traveled historical highway to perdition.

[2]This hypothetical situation owes its genesis to discussions of the advisory committee for a study conducted by the National Council of Juvenile Court Judges, when that committee met in Washington, D.C. in 1966.

The dialogue could be carried farther to convey the subtle nature of the issues involved in the manipulation of a situation suffused with ethical and legal considerations, in order to obtain empirical data. It might be suggested, for instance, that the appeal of a case would result in the freedom of a given juvenile but such a tactic could so antagonize the judge that he would handle all subsequent cases with greater harshness. Perhaps this view could be countered with one suggesting that to soar far beyond the given situation moves the debate into realms so remote that they are beyond speculative redemption. Perhaps it might be said that each juvenile must be allowed to determine for himself his own best interest and that, if attorneys are available, they must be available for all who desire them.

But suppose that there are only enough attorneys to handle half of the cases, the experimenter says. Then why cannot a random assignment schedule be employed to determine which cases they will handle? No, it is countered, a fairer method would be to decide which cases can most benefit from the services of an attorney and to see that these are given representation. Would anyone object, the experimenter counters, if the foundation grant had allowed for the hiring of ten attorneys and all ten were assigned to one court, while in a neighboring jurisdiction no lawyers were assigned, and then comparing the results between the two sites? If this seems reasonable, then certainly it must be reasonable to use other arbitrary techniques of denying representation for the greater good of science and the acquisition of experimental knowledge.

In such matters, the delicate ethical problems of correctional research become evident. Perhaps the only resolution lies in a series of loose dicta. The unjust vagaries of human existence are one thing. The matter at hand is that an experimenter is under the obligation to inflict no further injury or deprivation upon his subjects than necessary, and that the ends of science are irrelevant if they contribute to unreasonable human hurt. Presumably, it must be given to the intelligence and to the conscience of the individual researcher to fill in the teasingly non-specific components of his ethical obligations.

NECESSITY FOR INFORMED CONSENT

Informed consent by an offender who participates in a correctional experiment vitiates to some extent the allegations that his captive condition is being exploited for scientific ends, that he is being manipulated as an object rather than treated as a human being. Informed consent means consent given by subject who has been provided with adequate information regarding the nature of the experiment, who is fully aware of the possible outcome, and who is free to choose alternative courses without incurring the risk of added disabilities.

There are major difficulties involved in the matter of informed consent in correctional experimentation. For one thing, it often appears self-defeating to convey to the subject the nature of the experimental undertaking, because such information is apt to distort the outcome. As Campbell has indicated:

"In any of the experimental designs, the respondents can become aware that they are participating in an experiment, and this awareness can have an interactive effect, in creating reactions to X which would not occur had X been encountered without this 'I'm a guinea pig' attitude.... Such effects limit generalization to respondents having this awareness and preclude generalizations to the population encountering X with non-experimental attitudes. The direction of the effect may be one of negativism, such as an unwillingness to admit to any persuasion or change."[3]

In addition, there are correctional experiments in which the deliberate aim is to hide from the subject what is being done to him in order to arouse anxiety and thus, it is hoped, to impel him toward what is believed to be a more

[3]Donald T. Campbell, "Factors Related to the Validity of Experiments in Social Settings," *Psychological Bulletin*, LIV (1967), 304.

mature and enabling confrontation of the necessity for him to resolve his own difficulties, rather than to depend upon previous self-defeating modes of adaptation.[4] Presumably, under such conditions, informed consent could extend only to acceptance of the rather vague outline of the program, not to its underlying camouflaged elements. Since the outcome is apt to be quite uncharted, little could be told the subject regarding the possible benefit or harm of participation. It is arguable whether such an experiment meets minimum requirements of ethical acceptability, but it seems clear that the subject would have to be accorded the option of leaving the experiment at any time, with no penalty attached to such departure.

In addition, of course, restriction of subjects to volunteers, particularly in correctional research, may undercut the usefulness of the experimental findings. A stricture consistently leveled against Synanon, the facility in California run by former narcotic addicts for addicts, is that its subjects are highly motivated toward success; in fact, that the screening process deliberately excludes persons who do not appear to possess adequate desire to remain drug-free. Under such conditions, claims by Synanon that various elements of its program are productive of success and that its program has general utility for the treatment of addiction, are susceptible to the charge that its work has demonstrated only that persons who desire strongly enough to cease use of narcotics are able to do so, to an unknown extent (for Synanon is inordinately vague about its success and failure rate). Corrections is more apt to want to know whether a given arrangement can benefit all of its clientele or stipulated segments of it—not merely whether it is advantageous for volunteers—because corrections is obligated not only to aid the individual but also to protect society from harm and from unnecessary expense.

[4]See La Mar Empey and Jerome Rabow, "The Provo Experiment in Delinquency Rehabilitation," *American Sociological Review*, XXVI (1961), 679, and the subsequent exchange of letters in XXVII (1962), 256.

Informed consent also implies that there be no coercion involved in an experimental subject's participation. Direct coercion is, of course, rather readily recognized, but the particularly vulnerable status of correctional subjects makes them notably susceptible to subtler forms of persuasion. It is clearly established in the law that confessions induced by hints of leniency cannot be regarded as voluntary statements, though the translation of this fundamental principle to correctional research poses difficult issues.

Perhaps the point might be illustrated by the use of prisoners in medical experimentation, for it is in the area of medicine that the subject of ethical behavior has received its most intense scrutiny and soul-searching examination. In the United States, the first use of correctional subjects for medical experiments took place at the Mississippi state prison in 1914, when researchers attempted to discover the relationship between diet and pellagra.[5] The Governor of Mississippi promised pardons to persons volunteering for the experiment. The situation may be contrasted to a more recent experiment in New York in which eight prisoners were inoculated with a venereal infection in order to test possible cures. For their voluntary participation, the subjects in their own words "got syphilis and a carton of cigarettes."[6]

It is difficult to draw a hard line at the point where the hope of reward moves from the realm of the reasonable into that of the unreasonable. All human behavior includes self-serving elements. The suspect who confesses may do so to relieve feelings of guilt, to avoid further questioning, to gain attention or to obtain the quixotic satisfaction involved in pleasing one's accus-

[5]Joseph Goldberger, "Pellagra: Causation and a Method of Prevention," *Journal of the American Medical Association*, LXVI (1916), 471; Goldberger and G. A. Wheeler, "Experimental Pellagra in White Male Convicts," *Archives of Internal Medicine*, XXV (1920), 451. Cf. the account by Ralph L. Smith, "Research behind Bars," *New York Times Magazine*, Dec. 4, 1960.

[6]Quoted by Howard A. Rusk in "Medical Research and Prisoners," *New York Times*, Nov. 15, 1962.

ers. As Justice Holmes suggested: "Nature makes self-love an instrument of altruism and martyrdom, but the self-lover is not required to know it, although he is more intelligent if he does."[7]

The hope of favorable parole action may seem quite acceptable motivation for voluntary participation in an experimental undertaking, both to the prisoner and to the experimenter. Ivy has suggested as a working rule the following proposition:

"An excessive reduction which would exercise influence in obtaining the consent of prisoners to serve as subjects would be inconsistent with the principle of voluntary participation."[8]

Presumably such words as "excessive" and "undue" have to undergo meticulous examination in terms of the nature of the experiment and its risks, as well as in terms of the correctional status of the volunteer. It is probably sufficient for the moment to reiterate a principle often overlooked in correctional research that, for a desperate man, hope of reward is apt to undercut his freedom of choice and the requirement of voluntary participation necessary as an ethical stipulation for correctional research.

Lessons from medicine provide corollary guidelines for correctional research. The experiments on human subjects, many of them convicted criminals, which were conducted during the Hitler regime by medical doctors, will always serve as a reminder of the potential abuse inherent in power given to the state over captive groups.[9] Standing beside these gruesome episodes in medical annals are stirring examples of research designed for human betterment that were conducted with rigid ethical etiquette. Suffice it to mention, as a suggestion for correctional researchers, the example of Walter Reed, who participated as a subject in his own experiments on yellow fever because he could ask no subject to undergo anything that he himself was not willing to suffer.

FOR THE BENEFIT OF THE SUBJECT

In the absence of voluntary consent—either because it is unavailable or because the nature of the experiment precludes its being sought—no correctional subject should be required to participate in an experimental program that does not redound to his advantage, both as he and as impartial persons would be apt to see that advantage. In corrections, this principle demands that no added restraints be placed upon persons for experimental purposes. A new condition of parole, designed to test its efficacy, could not be imposed upon a random sample of parolees, nor could sentences arbitrarily be increased to 15 instead of 9 months in order to measure deterrent impact. The requirement demands that careful attention be paid to the relative advantages of correctional dispositions and particularly to the subjects' convictions concerning these advantages.

There is, of course, something of a dilemma implicit even in so straightforward a principle because it neglects the relative disadvantage falling upon persons unfortunate enough not to fall within the experimental group. It is possible to suggest that such persons are suffering no consequences which ordinarily would not have come their way; perhaps, for example, they had been sentenced to a 15-month prison term. If so, they should have anticipated serving the usual amount of time involved in their sentence. That their confreres, drawn by random lot, are

---

[7]Quoted by Mark DeWolfe Howe in *Justice Oliver Wendell Holmes* (Cambridge, Mass: Harvard, 1963) II, p. 49.

[8]A. C. Ivy, "History and Ethics of the Use of Human Subjects in Medical Research," *Science*, CVIII (July 2, 1948), 5. Dr. Ivy was responsible for drawing up the provisions of the Nuremberg Code on this subject, which were based on his experiences at the Nuremberg war crimes trials. See also Irving Ladimer and Roger W. Newman, eds., *Clinical Investigation in Medicine: Legal, Ethical, and Moral Aspects* (Boston: Law-Medicine Institute, Boston University, 1963); Henry K. Beecher, "Ethics and Clinical Research," *New England Journal of Medicine*, CCLXXIV (1966), 1354; and Note, "Legal Implications of Psychological Research with Human Subjects," *Duke Law Journal* (1960), 265.

[9]See Fredric Wertham, "The Geranium in the Window" in *A Sign for Cain* (New York: Macmillan, 1966).

being released much earlier is not their ill fortune but rather the others' good fortune. So the matter would appear in logic. To the unchosen inmate, however, it may seem quite different and, interestingly enough, such perception might provide another of those experimental situations where the design itself conditions the results of the experiment. Persons released early may perform in superior fashion only as they perceive such beneficence as a matter of luck; those left behind may do less well only so long as they view their misfortune as a testament of the cold-blooded random-number mentality of the system.

Fewer ethical issues are presented when eased conditions—or even harsher conditions—are imposed upon *all* persons falling into the categories effected. Constitutional requirements of equal protection are usually met when correctional conditions, imposed as part of administrative discretion, bear some reasonable relationship to the end being sought. In practice, most correctional change encompasses all relevant subjects uniformly, with common sense—that is, the view that "it certainly sounds like a good idea"—or work done elsewhere, such as in mental hygiene, providing the impetus for rearrangements. Evaluative work, of necessity, depends upon measurement of subsequent outcomes in comparison to those prevalent prior to the inauguration of the new program. The difficulty, of course, is that extrinsic circumstances rather than program ingredients may have conspired to produce the results.

Such possibilities pressure the researcher into demands for experimental-control research designs, despite anguished cries by service personnel that it is despicable to deprive claimants of services which are obviously—or, at least, almost obviously—of merit. Experimenters may recall the early days of work with the Salk vaccine when only first-graders were inoculated as part of the task of determining the value of the new drug, because only a limited amount of the vaccine was available. Purists in the ranks of science might insist that only a random sample of first-

graders should have been included in the experiment. Parents of children below school age and of children in other grades who that year contracted infantile paralysis are not likely to gain solace from lectures regarding the value of pure research or the requirements of controlled experimentation. For correctional researchers, the polio experience may provide grim support for the thesis that verified knowledge is sometimes dependent upon rigid adherence to an adequate research undertaking. But, researchers should also keep in mind, sound ethics requires that experimental-control designs be undertaken only when alternative evaluative methods clearly fall short of requirements. If adequate alternatives are possible, experimental-control designs should be used only when limited resources are all that are available.

SUMMARY AND CONCLUSIONS

There are few legal restraints upon experimentation with prisoners, probationers and parolees, and juveniles largely because there exist few sophisticated court considerations of the due process implications of these statutes.[10] Tort law suggests that persons may be treated in diverse ways, within limits, so long as their treatment is related to some reasonable therapeutic theory.[11] Untoward consequences generally will not result in liability if the authorities were acting satisfactorily in terms of their delegated responsibility. Thus, when a prisoner escaped from a minimum security farm and procured a weapon with which he threatened a civilian, who died of a brain

[10]Cf. Sanford F. Kadish, "The Advocate and the Expert Counsel in the Correctional Process," *Minnesota Law Review*, XLV (1961), 803. See generally Norval Morris and Colin Howard, "Penal Sanctions and Human Rights" in *Studies in Criminal Law* (New York: Oxford, 1964); Paul A. Freund, "Is the Law Ready for Human Experimentation?" *Annals of Psychology*, XXII (1967), 394; Oscar M. Ruebhausen and Orville G. Brim, "Privacy and Behavioral Research," *Columbia Law Review*, LXV (1965), 1184.

[11]See *Jackson v. Burnham*, 20 Colo. 532, 39 Pac. 557 (1895), and Note, "Legal Implications of Psychological Research with Human Subjects," *Duke Law Journal* (1960), 265.

hemorrhage possibly brought on by fright, the court dismissed the claim for damages from the state for its alleged negligence. It would be against public policy, the judgment stated, to "dissuade the wardens and principal keepers of our prison system from continuing experimentation with 'minimum security' work details which provide means for encouraging better-risk prisoners to . . . prepare themselves for their eventual return to society."[12]

Nonetheless, administrative discretion is no excuse for the neglect of ethical considerations in correctional research. For one thing, it is evident that the courts are beginning to look much more intensely at those areas of criminal justice heretofore peripheral to appellate scrutiny, and that due process protections will inevitably be extended into the prisons and parole in the manner that they recently have been catapulted into the juvenile court.[13] Clearly the days are numbered, for instance, for such administrative judgments as that in a recent case in a western state. In this case, which is probably not atypical, a twice-convicted burglar, sentenced for a period of three to fourteen years, was accused by prison authorities of sodomy. He was tried in the county court and acquitted. Though burglars normally are released in three or four years, the prisoner was retained for the maximum period of his sentence, with the justification that it would be a disservice to society to permit a known aggressive homosexual to be set loose.

The ethical difficulties involved in correctional research lie predominantly in the nature of corrections as a social enterprise. Corrections has recourse to diverse forms of suasion, such as reward and argumentation, but, most persuasively, it uses force and deprivation to achieve its aims. Its goal is fairly clear: to protect the society by deterring convicted persons and others from engaging in illegal conduct. Ethical difficulties emerge most pointedly when the aim becomes

so insistent that it blurs judgment of the means by which it is being achieved or may acceptably be achieved.

In the United States, the most pressing ethical concern of corrections appears to involve the utilization of programs upon involuntary subjects who do not adequately comprehend them. Presumably no correctional program employing suasion beyond that point at which it can be demonstrated that such suasion produces a desirable result should be allowed to continue. Programs must be examined in terms of whether they achieve things which would not occur were they absent. Unless it is clear that persons choosing to avoid group therapy and educational programs, for instance, represent more serious threats to the society without having such experiences than they do with them, it would appear indefensible to require these activities on an involuntary basis. Obviously there is an amount of coercion necessary for the maintenance of any operation, and it is reasonable to expect that individuals do certain things or do without other things. But this is not the same as deprivation of free choice based on unsubstantiated claims of social advantage.

There are a number of concluding observations which may set the subject into clearer perspective. They insist upon the importance of research, but upon research tied to ethical responsibility. They warn us that well-meaning attempts to aid individuals against their will may be a form of tyranny and, if so, should be zealously resisted. Finally, they suggest that, however vital and important a goal scientific exactitude and experimentation may be, there are dangers inherent in uncritical adherence to its values, as there are in uncritical adherence to any dogma.[14]

[12]*Williams v. State*, 308 N.Y. 548, 127 N.E. 2d 545 (1955).

[13]*In re Gault*, 387 U.S. 1 (1966). See also Comment, "Rights of Prisoners while Incarcerated," *Buffalo Law Review*, XV (1965), 397.

[14]See further Richard A. Brymer and Buford Farris, "Ethical and Political Dilemmas in the Investigation of Deviance: A Study of Juvenile Delinquency" in Gideon Sjoberg, ed., *Ethics, Politics, and Social Research* (Boston: Schenkman, 1967), 297–318; and Solomon Kobrin, "Legal and Ethical Problems of Street Gang Work," *Crime and Delinquency*, X (1964), 152.

Justice Holmes, among many others, has pointed out the pressing need for experimentation in the area of criminal justice: "What have we better than a blind guess to show that the criminal law in its present form does more good than harm?" Holmes asked. "Do we deal with criminals on proper principles? Is it idle to talk of deterring the criminal by the classical method of imprisonment?"[15]

George Santayana, approaching the matter from another side, entered further reservation about programs without specified and monitored purpose. "Fanatics," Santayana said, "are those who redouble their effort when they have forgotten their goal."[16] What can happen under such circumstances was indicated by Holmes' colleague, Louis D. Brandeis.

"Experience should teach us to be most on our guard to protect liberty when the Government's purposes are beneficent. Men born to freedom are naturally alert to repel invasion of their liberty by evil-minded rulers. The greatest dangers to liberty lurk in insidious encroachment by men of zeal, well-meaning but without understanding."[17]

[15]Oliver Wendell Holmes, Jr., *Collected Legal Papers* (New York: Harcourt Brace, 1921), pp. 188–89.

[16]Quoted in Walter Gellhorn, *American Rights* (New York: Macmillan, 1960), p. 94.

[17]*Olmstead v. U.S.*, 277 U.S. 479 (1927).

56. I-Level and Rehabilitation of Delinquents

ROY L. AUSTIN

MOST DISCUSSIONS OF THE REHABILITATION OF delinquents implicitly or explicitly assume that different strategies are needed for optimum success because delinquents are different; and over the years a number of programs have suggested that proper matching of treatment and delinquent (differential treatment) might alter the perennial record of failure associated with rehabilitation programs. The Camp Elliot Study (Grant and Grant, 1959) is one supporting this approach, the highest success rates being reported for high maturity nonconformists under mature and flexible supervisors. Other combinations of supervisors and nonconformists yielded lower success rates that were not different from one another. The Fricot Ranch Study (Jesness, 1965) is also supportive of differential treatment, neurotic subjects gaining more from an intensive "internally-oriented program functioning in a smaller group-living unit" than in an "externally-oriented program functioning in a larger 50-boy living unit." Other types of subjects showed no differential effects. However, the Community Treatment Project (CTP) in California is larger, more costly, and has received more national attention[1]

▶SOURCE: *Paper written especially for this volume.*

[1]According to Lerman (1975), between 1961 and 1969, the National Institute of Mental Health spent over one million dollars on CTP and the State of California about four million dollars. Funding from these sources continued until 1975. Lerman also observes that the project was recommended as a community treatment prototype by the President's Commission on Law Enforcement and Administration of Justice and by the National Commission on the

than any other systematic program of differential treatment. The typology employed in CTP as well as at Camp Elliot is based on Interpersonal Maturity Level theory (I-Level theory; Sullivan et al., 1957); and its success in the rehabilitation of delinquents is the subject of this study.

I shall first state some of the key propositions in I-Level theory and the typology derived from it, then proceed to an investigation of the relationship between the theory and earlier studies claimed to be supportive of it. Next, three rehabilitation projects that utilized I-Levels are evaluated; and this is followed by an examination of some research problems that might explain limited success in I-Level projects. Finally, there is a summary that includes additional considerations for policy makers.

MAJOR PROPOSITIONS IN I-LEVEL

I-level theory proposes that fixation at one of seven levels of maturity determines a person's perceptual and interpersonal capacities. Fixation occurs at a level at which emotional security is restored after tension occasioned by exposure to disconcerting stimuli. For example, an extremely threatening situation might cause a child to fear new situations and restrict further emotional-social development. The distinctive

Causes and Prevention of Violence. In addition, by 1970, corrections personnel from ten states and two Canadian provinces had been trained in differential diagnosis and differential treatment at the Center for Training in Differential Treatment which was directed by Marguerite Warren, then principal investigator in CTP (Palmer, 1969).

set of attitudes and expectations associated with each level is displayed especially under conditions of stress.

The original description of the seven maturity levels (Sullivan et al., 1957) mentioned some subtypes; but to facilitate treatment of delinquents, Grant (1961; 1966) clearly distinguished nine subtypes within levels 2 through 4, Sullivan et al. (1957) having indicated that delinquency was likely at the lower levels. Whereas the types reflect ways of perceiving the world, the subtypes represent modal responses. The following summary of type and subtype characteristics for the three levels most frequently studied[2] are taken from Sullivan et al. (1957) and Grant (1966):

Maturity Level 2 (I_2)

At level 1, rules are contravened because the person's only system of reference lies within himself. At level 2, self is distinguished from other, there is extreme dependence on others, and demands that they meet the actor's needs. There is little understanding of the reactions of others, rules are regarded as deriving from individual whims, and denial results in impulsive assault or withdrawal. This person interprets institutionalization as further denial and is a constant escape risk in correctional institutions.

Subtypes   (1) *Aa* (Unsocialized, Aggressive) and (2) *Ap* (Unsocialized, Passive). These two subtypes had earlier (Grant, 1961) been distinguished primarily by their use of active, crude attempts to obtain satisfaction of their desires or by the use of passive withdrawal. Later (Grant, 1966), this distinction was regarded as insufficiently complex and a revision expected.

Maturity Level 3 (I_3)

Rules are now seen as governing relationships and the person recognizes that his own behavior influences the satisfaction of desires. However, immediate gratification is still sought and others

are regarded as means to ends. Manipulation of others takes the form of sophisticated swindles or overconformity aimed at obtaining concessions by granting other persons their desires. There is no guilt over breaking rules although expressions of guilt may occur.

Subtypes   (3) *Cfm* (Immature Conformist). The need for social approval forces compliance with the wishes of the power holder in any situation. (4) *Cfc* (Cultural Conformist). The need for approval forces compliance especially with the wishes of the delinquent peer group although any power holder is likely to obtain similar compliance when this is unavoidable. (5) *Mp* (Manipulator). Attempts to create an image of having full control over his own behavior and the behavior of others.

Maturity Level 4 (I_4)

This person perceives the influence of others and their expectations of him. Identification with powerful figures leads to guilt when the person fails to satisfy internalized standards. Neurotic symptoms may emerge because of conflict over the incompatible goals of self-expression and complete identification with others. Sometimes, identification with delinquent role models or attempts to gain respect from friends encourages antisocial behavior.

Subtypes   (6) *Na* (Neurotic, Acting-out). Delinquency may result from the acting-out of internal conflicts due to internalization of parental values or values of other authorities (7) *Nx* (Neurotic, Anxious). Similar to Na but shows more motivation to understand and resolve difficulties. (8) *Se* (Situational-Emotional Reaction). Delinquency results from emotional conflict over immediate personal or family situations. (9) *Ci* (Cultural Identifier). Respect for delinquent friends or internalization of deviant beliefs leads to delinquency.

THEORETICAL AND EMPIRICAL BASES OF I-LEVEL THEORY

The adequacy of I-level theory will be enhanced if it agrees in important respects with other

---

[2]Grant (1966) claims that maturity levels in delinquent populations range from level 2 through level 5 with level 5 being so infrequent that it may be ignored.

theories and with empirical findings. Sullivan et al. (1957) refer to the works of Erik Erikson, George Herbert Mead, Theodore Sarbin, and Jean Piaget as support for various aspects of the theory while Grant and Grant (1959) cite the investigation of Croft and Grygier (1956) and Gough and Peterson (1952) as favorable to I-levels. In addition, Warren[3] (1966) shows the similarities between I-levels and 16 other offender typologies. However, a comparison of I-levels with some of the theories mentioned showed significant differences that leave the adequacy of I-levels in doubt. Likewise, examination of the empirical studies reveal no clear support for I-level claims. Examples of some of these problems follow.

The idea of immature fixation and the drawing of inferences from childhood development to understand adolescent and later behavior are crucial to I-level theory; but comparison of I-levels with Piaget's stages questions the inferences drawn from the fixation assumption. For example, I-levels and Piaget agree that during one stage of development the child accords exceptional importance to rules even while violating them. However, Piaget regards violation as the result of the rules being imposed on the child and claims that the child at this stage makes *no effort to gain control* over others. On the other hand, the comparable I-level 3 person is portrayed as concerned with manipulating rules to satisfy the *strong desire to control* others, the confidence man being an example of an adult operating at this level. If Piaget's observations and interpretation are accurate, some aspect of the I-level description does not conform with reality.

The claim by Grant and Grant (1959) that the investigation of Croft and Grygier (1956) and Gough and Peterson (1952) are favorable to I-levels is also problematic. The study by Croft and Grygier shows that more deviant boys have fewer friends, more rejections, and less general acceptance than less deviant boys. This finding

<hr>

[3]M. Grant and M. Warren are the names used by the same person at different times.

agrees with the I-level assumption that delinquents are less capable of sustaining meaningful social relationships than other youths; but if it is the known delinquency of the boys that reduced the number of schoolmates willing to have them as friends, the causal ordering of the variables implied in I-level theory is reversed. It is conceivable that the attachments of a deviant label to a boy for minor violations may have as much influence on his interaction patterns as social immaturity.

A problem in interpreting results also limits the extent to which Gough and Peterson's study may be regarded as offering empirical support for any I-level proposition. The emphasis in the study on the inability of the delinquent "to visualize himself in the role of another person" (Grant and Grant, 1959: 27) is regarded as favorable to the I-level concern with interpersonal relationships. However, the findings of the researchers do not clearly support their emphasis. While their De Scale reliably differentiated between delinquents and nondelinquents, the part played by the scale items derived from role-theory is not clearly indicated.

The above examples of problems in relating I-level theory to supposedly supportive earlier studies suggest that I-levels may not have benefited as much from previous studies as the authors claim. Further, Beker and Heyman (1972: 19) are correct in stating that the theory "is not rooted in previously existing theories of personality development, although elements of the thinking of . . . G. H. Mead, Piaget . . . and others are apparent." Therefore, the adequacy of I-level theory must be judged mainly by studies not mentioned by its authors, particularly studies that have appeared subsequent to its formulation.

I-LEVEL REHABILITATION PROJECTS AND RESULTS

The Camp Elliot Study

Four variables were manipulated in this study, maturity level, predicted supervisor effectiveness, duration of supervision, and order of supervision. While the findings, some of which were mentioned earlier, support the use of I-level in differential treatment, the discussion by Grant and Grant (1959) obscures important results. For instance, the authors claim that the evidence "does not support a closed Living Group Program for low maturity inmates" (p. 134); but the data presented (Grant and Grant, 1959: Table 1) show that a low maturity group under the most immature and inflexible supervisors had the highest success rate for unmixed groups. Also, the authors claim that the high maturity subjects benefit only when supervisors are mature and flexible; but the data show that type of supervision makes no difference for the success rates of nine-week high maturity groups.

The most serious problem with the erroneous interpretation is that it may have contributed to poor matching of subjects and treatments in CTP. For example, while low maturity trainees at Camp Elliot were most successful under the strictest, least socially mature supervisors, the level 2 treater in CTP is expected to be "tolerant, supportive, protective . . . personally secure" (Warren, 1966: 10).

California's Community Treatment Project (CTP)

The following description of CTP was given by Palmer (1969: 11), then principal investigator for the project:

"The Community Treatment Project is a combined experimental and demonstration research project originally designed to study the feasibility of substituting an intensive program in the community for the traditional state training-school program in the case of California's Youth Authority wards undergoing their first commitment from the Juvenile Court. . . . Jointly financed by the NIMH and the California Department of the Youth Authority, Phase I of the Project began operation in 1961 in the urban areas of Sacramento and Stockton. Phase II, proposed as a five year study, included San Francisco as well and began in October 1964. As of September 1967, the city of Modesto was added to the former study area. In all, four separate experimental units

are involved, with each unit handling 80–85 cases at full build-up."

A third phase of CTP, lasting from 1969 until 1974, investigated the feasibility of a residential treatment setting for boys who had failed in the traditional institution. Further discussion is focused mainly on the first two phases.

In all phases of CTP, I-level classification and differential treatment were utilized. During Phases I and II, youths in the experimental program were matched[4] with a parole officer with a case load not usually exceeding 12 youths and received "intensive treatment" for two to three years while on parole in the community (Palmer, 1973). Youths in the control group underwent traditional institutionalization for eight to ten months and were then placed in a regular parole program with no special treatment and the usual large case load.

It is claimed that by 1964 CTP had established the superiority of community treatment over traditional programs or certain kinds of youth offenders (Warren, 1966: 1; Warren 1970: 420). Likewise, Palmer and Werner (1972: 1) refer to the CTP approach as having "been applied with considerable success."

The CTP measures of program effectiveness were of two kinds: psychological measures of adjustment and indicators of performance on parole. Pretest to post-test change scores on the Jesness Inventory and the California Psychological Inventory give a slight edge to community treatment (Warren et al., 1966: X), but were given little weight in the investigator's conclusions. Of greater significance were data on 235 Experimentals (community treated) and 217 Controls (traditional institution) who after 15 months on parole showed a failure[5] rate of 30

---

[4] To aid proper matching of worker and delinquent, CTP parole agents undergo an interview lasting 1½ to 2 hours which allows rating on a 105-item checklist. Palmer (1973) reports significant differences in parole revocation and court recommitment that favor boys who were closely matched with workers over those not closely matched.

[5] Failure refers to violation of parole (revocation or recommitment) and unfavorable discharge from the Youth Authority.

percent for Experimentals (32% boys, 22% girls) and 51% for Controls (51% boys, 51% girls). The statewide failure rate for a comparable population over the same parole period is given as 45% (48% boys, 33% girls). Data for a 24 month parole period based on 176 Experimentals and 186 Controls showed failure rates of 40% (43% boys, 25% girls) and 61% (63% boys, 50% girls), respectively (Palmer and Warren, 1967).

Although these data suggest a better parole performance for the group treated in the community, Lerman (1968) used other reported data to show that for every offense category (low, medium, or high seriousness) the Control youths were more likely to have their parole revoked than the Experimentals. Only for the most serious offenses was the difference negligible. Experimentals had also apparently engaged in more delinquency as indicated by an average parole suspension of 2.8 versus 1.6 for Controls. He therefore concluded that the delinquent behavior of both groups after parole may be quite similar and that differences in favor of community treatment may reflect only a differential response on the part of parole agents. CTP agents may be less inclined to revoke parole.

Warren (1970: 426–427) agrees that the success/failure rate may suffer some distortion because experimental cases are more often restored to parole after an offense than are control cases. However, she feels that any advantage thereby gained by Experimentals is offset by more "hidden delinquency" among Controls since their parole officers provide less zealous supervision than CTP parole agents.

Palmer (1974) has more recently reported data on failure four years after favorable discharge[6] from the California Youth Authority.

For boys, these data show that the community program is more beneficial for certain, subtypes while other subtypes benefit more from traditional institutionalization.[7] More specifically, among the Neurotics (Na's and Nx's) there was an average of 1.88 convictions for Controls versus 1.58 for Experimentals. Among the Power Oriented (Cfc's and Mp's), Controls averaged 1.47 convictions versus 2.55 for Experimentals. Among Immature Conformists (Cfm's), Controls averaged 1.44 convictions versus 1.80 for Experimentals. For Neurotic and for Power Oriented boys, arrest rates for Controls and Experimentals ran in the same direction as conviction averages; but for the Immature Conformists arrest rates were the reverse of the conviction averages. Thus, traditional institutionalization was more successful with the Power Oriented while the community program was more successful with the Neurotics; and assuming conviction to be a more valid measure of serious delinquent involvement than arrest, the traditional program was apparently also more successful with Immature Conformists.

Significantly, conviction rates are unlikely to suffer the biases noted by Lerman for parole violation while offenders were under CYA jurisdiction. There is also some consistency in the better performance of Experimental Na's. This was the only subtype for which Experimentals showed significantly lower failure rates than Controls after 15 and 24 months of parole (Palmer and Warren, 1967). Further, the results are favorable to I-levels and differential treatment, although apparently not meeting the expectations of CTP investigators. In CTP, systematic differential treatment strategies are applied only between experimental subtypes. However, there is also differential treatment between Experimentals and Controls; and the differences between the community program for Experimentals and traditional institutionalization for Controls may exceed differences within

---

[6]Termination of the California Youth Authority's jurisdiction over their delinquent charges is classified either as a favorable or unfavorable discharge. This disposition as well as revocation of parole and recommitment to the Youth Authority usually results from arrest by the police and subsequent conviction. One-half of the Experimentals and the same proportion of Controls who were unfavorably dis-

charged were immediately sent to a state or federal prison with a relatively long maximum sentence (Palmer, 1974).

[7]The CTP data on *favorable discharges* show no evidence that I-level treatment is effective for girls (Palmer, 1974: 6)

the experimental group. The finding of interaction between program and subtype for favorable dischargees may be an unintended consequence of this differential treatment.

In Phase III, offenders were classified as requiring initial residential treatment then intensive community treatment or suitable for direct release to the intensive community program. For each group, random placement into the appropriate program or the one deemed inappropriate then took place. Offenders for whom initial residential treatment was prescribed showed a substantially lower parole violation average when appropriately placed than when immediately placed in the community. There was no difference in parole violation for offenders diagnosed as suitable for immediate community placement whether they were appropriately placed or given initial residential placement. Once again differential treatment appears to have been effective; but the role of I-levels in this phase of CTP is unclear. Palmer's (1974: 9) statement that Neurotic subtypes account for the difference between comparison groups explains little.

The Preston Study

This research project attempted to use I-levels and differential treatment to rehabilitate some of the California Youth Authority's more serious offenders (45% had previously been institutionalized) in an institution (Jesness, 1971). As in CTP, there was an experimental unit in which homogeneous maturity groups received different treatments, and a control group exposed to traditional institutional procedures that took no account of maturity level. In addition, there was a psychiatric treatment unit for which boys likely to benefit from psychotherapy were selected, and a special control unit consisting of boys whose characteristics made them good risks for farm work, maintenance, and other outside assignments.

Parole violation rates after 15 and 24 months showed no significant difference between the experimental and control groups or between experimental and control *subtype* groups. The

Psychiatric unit showed a substantially lower violation rate (46% and 55%) than the Experimentals (54% and 64%) and Controls (54% and 65%) after 15 months as well as after 24 months. Jesness (1971: 48) reports that when parole risk status was controlled the better performance of the Psychiatric unit was no longer apparent. However, his Table 3 shows that within the poorest parole risk group, the parole violation rate of the Psychiatric unit (58% and 63%) remains substantially below that of the Experimentals (67% and 78%) and Controls (66% and 77%). Also, both expert ratings and the subjects' responses to a questionnaire show the treatment program in the psychiatric unit to be better developed than the programs in the experimental and control units. Therefore, the absence of a difference between Experimentals and Controls may be due to the failure to develop a workable treatment program in the Experimental unit; and the data from these two groups may be unsuitable for evaluating I-levels.

The results of the three I-level projects that have been reviewed leave some uncertainty about the value of I-levels in rehabilitating delinquents. However, the high frequency of negative findings for delinquency control programs (Robison and Smith, 1971) and the importance given to the development of such programs give added significance to every positive result; and all three projects yielded some encouraging findings. Therefore, the reasons for the relatively poor performance of I-level treatment, especially in CTP, merits further investigation.

TESTING THE I-LEVEL INTERACTION HYPOTHESIS

The basis of differential treatment with I-levels is the assumption of interaction between treatment and maturity level; that is, the treatment program effective for offenders of a certain maturity level is not expected to be similarly effective for other maturity levels. However, of the three I-level projects discussed, only the Camp Elliot project had a design suitable for a direct test of the interaction hypothesis; and erroneous interpretation of the Camp Elliot results may have reduced the value of the interaction test for subsequent studies.

An interaction analysis of the Preston data by Austin (1973) yielded findings for the psychiatric unit with important similarities to the correctly interpreted Camp Elliot findings. In particular, Preston level 3 subjects benefited most from the authoritarian environment most successful with lower level Camp Elliot subjects that included I-3's. Likewise, favorably discharged Cfc's and Mp's (two of three level 3 subtypes) from CTP apparently gained more from the authoritarian environment in the traditional institution than from the community program. In addition, Austin's analysis shows that a relatively permissive environment is best for level 4 subjects, a finding in agreement with the Camp Elliot study and the better performance of CTP's level 4 subjects in the community. This consistency in the results of the three studies recommends a more favorable evaluation for I-levels than the criticisms of Gibbons (1970), Lerman (1968), and Beker and Heyman (1972) suggest.

INTENSIVE TREATMENT IN I-LEVEL PROJECTS

Data reported by Warren and Palmer were used by Lerman (1975: 34) to estimate "intensive treatment" in CTP as consisting of two hours a week in "direct service to each ward and family when his caseload has a median of ten cases." The results of the Preston study suggest that the lower parole violation rates in the Psychiatric unit could be related to the better development of the treatment program in this unit. Therefore, there is some basis for speculating that the results of CTP might be more favorable should the intensity of treatment be increased.

CONSTRUCT VALIDITY OF I-LEVEL CLASSIFICATION

Many studies, using data from different sources, have shown a relatively strong relationship between intelligence and I-level (Cross and Tracy, 1971; Zaidel, 1973; Werner, 1975; Austin, 1975). Further, Austin (1975) shows that intelligence makes a greater contribution to I-level classification than do social maturity (measured by the Jesness immaturity scale) and personal relationships (indicated by relationship with family members). However, social maturity and personal relationships are given as key variables in determining I-level while intelligence receives no mention. The findings on intelligence therefore suggest that modification of the classification procedures and/or revision of treatment strategies with some attention to intelligence might improve I-level rehabilitation results.

CONCLUDING REMARKS

Valid questions may be raised about the extent to which I-level theory benefited from earlier studies; but the three I-level rehabilitation projects discussed in this study provide evidence favorable to the important hypothesis of interaction between I-level and treatment environment. However, the apparent expectation of greater rehabilitation success for all Experimentals has not encouraged enthusiasm for the CTP results in which only Neurotics show clear benefit from differential treatment *in the community*. Nor has the relatively successful post-institutionalization record of Power Oriented Controls been recognized as a finding favorable to I-levels. In addition, Jesness' report of no difference in parole outcome between Preston Experimentals and Controls justifies increased skepticism over the efficacy of I-levels; but apparently inadequate levels of treatment make the data on these Preston groups unsuitable for this judgment.

There is some evidence that better matching of treatment and offender than presently used in CTP is possible. Therefore, the positive findings for CTP matching procedures should not encourage complacency about this aspect of the project. In addition to improved matching, more intensive treatment and informed use of offenders' intelligence in classification and treatment are the conspicuous revisions warranted by the findings in the I-level projects examined.

The reliability of the classification system has so far been ignored; but a weakness in this area increases the probability of misleading rehabilitation results because of the greater likelihood that offenders will be wrongly classified. Inter-rater agreements of 62% for subtype and 81% for I-level have been reported for CTP data (Palmer and Werner, 1972: 44). However, Beker and Heyman's (1972) concern over a possible lack of independence between CTP raters remains a problem.

There can be greater confidence in the reliability estimates of the classification of 30 subjects at Preston using a shortened form of the CTP interview. Two geographically separated interviewers who did not communicate before classifying the subjects obtained agreements of 57% for subtype and 63% for I-level (Jesness, 1969: 36). Such low levels of agreement are not assuring but the reduced length of the classification instrument might partly explain the lower reliability than in CTP. Further, while low reliability estimates constitute a negative finding in one respect, improved classification procedures will reduce classification errors, thereby reducing matching errors, and perhaps yield rehabilitation results more favorable to I-level; that is, present empirical evidence might underestimate the value of I-levels.

Another matter deserving some attention is a comparison of I-level program costs with the cost of traditional programs. Estimates of the average cost of sending a youth through each program show that for the early, middle, and recent periods of CTP, cost ratios were, respectively, 0.80 to 1, 0.88 to 1, and 0.98 to 1 in favor of the traditional program (Palmer, 1975). Palmer states that costs increased more during the 1961–1969 period in the traditional program than in CTP. With the expectation that increases continued to favor the CTP program, Palmer therefore argues that by the mid-1970s the traditional program might be more expensive; and this conclusion is more likely to be correct if capital outlay costs are included.

Comparative cost estimates of I-levels and a traditional program for the future or for other areas of the country must consider the amount of time that will be spent in the most expensive portions of each program. Lerman (1975: 68) shows that in 1964–1965 eight months in a California institution cost $3,000 per youth versus a cost of $1,424 for eight months of intensive treatment in CTP. On the other hand, 24 months of regular parole cost $600 per youth versus $4,272 for 24 months of continued intensive treatment in CTP. Certainly, reduced time in any part of a program might increase the likelihood of recidivism and therefore increase the total cost.

The current interest in diversion of offenders from the criminal justice system (Carter and Klein, 1976) suggests that the development and testing of offender typologies is a critical need for the immediate future. Presently, most decisions on who should be diverted appear to be made without the benefit of any scientifically tested classification instrument. I-levels might be an appropriate instrument when "intensive treatment" can be used for those offenders that I-levels research indicates as likely to benefit from treatment in the community. I-levels research is silent on the question of whether no treatment in the community might be a useful strategy for some offenders.

REFERENCES

Austin, R. (1973) Interpersonal Maturity Level Theory: An Evaluation. Ph.D dissertation, University of Washington, Seattle.

Austin, R. (1975) "Construct validity of I-level classification." *Criminal Justice and Behavior*, 2, 2 (June): 113–129.

Beker, J. and D. Heyman (1972) "A critical appraisal of the California differential treatment typology of adolescent offenders." *Criminology*, 10,1 (May): 3–58.

Carter, R. and M. Klein (1976) *Back on the Street: The*

Diversion of Juvenile Offenders. Englewood Cliffs, N.J.: Prentice-Hall.

Croft, I. and T. Grygier (1956) "Social relationships of truants and juvenile delinquents." *Human Relations*, 9, 4: 439–465.

Cross, H. and J. Tracy (1971) "Personality factors in delinquent boys: differences between blacks and whites." *Journal of Research in Crime and Delinquency*, 8, 1(January): 10–22.

Gibbons, D. (1970) "Differential treatment of delinquents and interpersonal maturity level theory." *Social Service Review*, 44, 1 (March): 22–33.

Gough, H. and D. Peterson (1952) "Predispositional factors in crime and delinquency." *Journal of Consulting Psychology*, 16, 3 (June): 207–212.

Grant, J. and M. Grant (1959) "A group dynamics approach to the treatment of non-conformists in the navy." *The Annals of the American Academy of Political and Social Science*, 322 (March): 126–135.

Grant, M. (1961, 1966) Interpersonal Maturity Level Classification: Juvenile Diagnosis and Treatment of Low, Middle and High Maturity Delinquents. California: Department of the Youth Authority, Division of Research.

Jesness, C. (1965) The Fricot Ranch Study. Research Report No. 47. California Youth Authority.

Jesness, C. (1969) The Preston Typology Study Final Report. California Youth Authority.

Jesness, C. (1971) "The Preston typology study: An experiment with differential treatment in an institution." *Journal of Research in Crime and Delinquency*, 8,1 (January).

Lerman, P. (1968) "Evaluative studies of institutions for delinquents: Implications for research and social policy." *Social Work*, 13, 3 (July): 55–65.

Lerman, P. (1975) *Community Treatment and Social Control*. Chicago: The University of Chicago Press.

Palmer, T. (1969) California's Community Treatment Project in 1969: An Assessment of Its Relevance and Utility to the Field of Corrections. Prepared for the U.S. Joint Commission on Correctional Manpower and Training.

Palmer, T. (1969) Stages of Psycho-Social Development as Reflected in Two New Levels of Interpersonal Maturity. Community Treatment Project Report Series, No. 5 (Fall).

Palmer, T. amd E. Werner (1972) The Phase III Experiment: Progress to Date. California's Community Treatment Project Research Report No. 12.

Palmer, T. (1973) "Matching worker and clients in corrections." *Social Work*,18, 2 (March): 95–103.

Palmer, T. (1974) The youth authority's community treatment project. *Federal Probation* (March): 3–14.

Robison, J. and G. Smith (1971) "The effectiveness of correctional programs." *Crime and Delinquency*, 17, 1 (January): 67–80.

Sullivan, J. D. Grant, and M. Grant (1957) "The development of interpersonal maturity: applications to delinquency." *Psychiatry*, 20, 4: 373–385.

Warren, M. (1966) Classification of Offenders as an Aid to Efficient Management and Effective Treatment. Prepared for the President's Commission on Law Enforcement and Administration of Justice: Task Force on Corrections.

Warren, M., V. Neto, T. Palmer, and J. Turner (1966) An Evaluation of Community Treatment for Delinquents. Community Treatment Project Research Report No. 7 (August).

Warren, M. (1970) "The Case for Differential Treatment of Delinquents." Pp. 419–430 in Harwin Voss (ed.), *Society, Delinquency and Delinquent Behavior*. Boston: Little, Brown and Company.

Werner, E. (1975) "Psychological and ethnic correlates of interpersonal maturity among delinquents." *The British Journal of Criminology*, 15, 1 (January):51–68.

Zaidel, S. (1973) "Intelligence and affect awareness in classifying delinquents." *Journal of Research in Crime and Delinquency*, 10, 1 (January): 47–58.

57. Cost Effectiveness and Vocational Training

GILBERT J. McKEE

INTRODUCTION

THE ECONOMIC THEORY OF CRIME PRESUPPOSES that the offender chooses a criminal career on some rational basis. This theory is nothing more than a special case of the theory of economic choice. Criminals find it impossible to move to equilibrium by offering their productive services because they lack or cannot market their job skills. An alternative is to acquire goods illegally, that is, to adopt the occupation of criminal. Obviously not all crimes are the action of rational choice, however, if we limit consideration to crimes of enrichment as opposed to victimizing crimes then a case can be made for such a theory. The emphasis on the economic function of criminal activity is not meant to ignore the social function such crimes may serve. As Glaser points out, noncriminal satisfaction can more easily be substituted for such crimes of enrichment than for crimes of emotion and, furthermore, the "non-criminal satisfaction of economic needs may be prerequisite for non-criminal satisfaction of social needs. . . ."[1]

The apparent solution to a large part of the problem of crime is to train potential offenders so that they can compete successfully for jobs in the labor market. Until this is done, the second-best solution is to retrain the offenders so that they do not continue their criminal careers.

Cost-Benefit Analysis

Cost-benefit analysis is an evaluative technique used to judge the efficiency of governmental programs. The technique is best applied to programs that have explicitly stated economic efficiency goals. The technique has been successfully applied to the manpower training programs of the 1960s where the objectives were increased productivity and more efficient utilization of labor resources. The returns were measured as the increased output that resulted from the improved skill level of trainees. Returns are measured by the changes in real output effected by these programs.

The question arises as to whether the expenditures on training programs are justified in terms of their returns relative to the return from equal expenditures on alternative programs. The government is confronted with the problem of optimizing the allocation of scarce resources within a given program and is also faced with the need to determine the factors influencing costs and returns.

Limited resources in the private sector are allocated by the pricing mechanism. The very nature of government operations precludes reliance on such a mechanism. Certain wants provided by the government could be satisfied by

►SOURCE: *Paper written especially for this volume.*

[1] Daniel Glaser, Research and Potential Application of Research in Probation, Parole and Delinquency Prediction. "Parole Follow-up Studies in the Federal Correctional System." Citizens Committee for the Children of New York City, Inc., Research Center, New York School of Social Work, Columbia University, 1968.

the private sector but have been assumed by the government because of the divergence of private from social costs and benefits. Retraining programs are an example of such an instance where the employer may not be able to accrue the benefits of expenditures on training. What remains to be determined is whether the provision of certain social wants by the government are carried on efficiently, consistent with the objectives for which it has assumed the responsibility. Cost-benefit analysis attempts to establish the equivalent of a set of market principles for the governmental sector.

Human Capital

The application of cost-benefit analysis to the evaluation of vocational training presupposes that we can treat retraining as just another form of investment. The concept of human capital was first advanced by Theodore Schultz:

> "Although it is obvious that people acquire useful skills and knowledge, it is not obvious that these skills and knowledge are a form of capital, that this capital is in a substantial part a product of deliberate investment, that it has grown in Western societies at a much faster rate than conventional (nonhuman) capital, and that its growth may well be the most distinctive feature of the economic system."[2]

Definition of Costs and Benefits

The social product gains (benefits) from retraining may be categorized as either primary or secondary. Primary gains consist of the increase in aggregate output (income) attributable to the increased productivity of the trainees and ignores the multiplier effects on the total economy of government expenditures supporting the program. Secondary gains would include the reduction of assistance payments to parolees' families, reduction in the level of unemployment, reduction in the rate of recidivism and commitments of new crimes, and the increase in

the general living standards of the parolee population.

The costs of retraining may be broken down into distinct categories. The first category includes costs not directly related to the programs such as subsistence costs. These custodial costs will become the basis for quantifying the secondary benefits of successful retraining as measured by a lower rate of recidivism. These costs do not enter directly into the costs of vocational training as the inmate would continue to be institutionalized in the absence of the program. The second type of costs relate to the "investment" phase of the program. These include: (1) the direct cost of instructor's salaries, (2) overhead costs such as administrative overhead, and (3) opportunity costs, which attempt to measure the output foregone during the training period.

The Employment Prospects of the Parolee

The released offender has, in most instances, secured employment as a precondition of parole. The consequence of this requirement is that a premium is placed on employment per se. More often than not, the employment is temporary in the sense that it is offered by friends or relatives or is unsatisfactory to the parolee. The employment prospects of parolees are poor not just because they are criminals but because of their lack of education, skill, and preconfinement employment histories.

Parolees do not have many of the resources available to other job seekers. In particular, since they often come from a culturally deprived and impoverished area, the likelihood that they obtain "good" jobs through friends or relatives is very much reduced. Sullivan characterizes the release procedure as "legal re-insertion" instead of "restoration to society."[3] He takes issue with the labeling of the criminal as unemployable.

[2]Theodore W. Schultz, "Investment in Human Capital: A Theoretical Analysis," *American Economic Review*, 51, 1 (March, 1961), 12–20.

[3]Clyde E. Sullivan, "Job Development and Placement of the Ex-offender," *Manpower Development and Training in Correctional Programs*, M.D.T.A. Experimental and Demonstration Findings no. 3 (Washington, D.C.: U.S. Department of Labor Manpower Administration, 1968).

The problem is rather that the jobs available to released offenders are low-paying and short-term. While most workers accept entry-level jobs as a ladder to better jobs, these particular jobs more often than not lead nowhere. Unfortunately, even if the possibility for advancement is present, narrow time horizons prevent parolees from perceiving this. The problem is further complicated in that unemployment is a technical violation of the terms of parole, a fact that greatly reduces the mobility of parolees. The mere fact that parolees are steadily employed and thus have less time to engage in criminal activities is not enough to counter the low pay, low prestige, and lack of future. Steady employment at marginal jobs merely confirms the parolee's self-image and probably contributes to recidivism.

The California Survey

The sample was composed of 1,581 of the 5,284 parolees released between July 1, 1967 and June 30, 1968, for whom income data were available. The income data were obtained from the California State Employment Service. The data were available only for those parolees whose social security numbers were recorded in their files. If the parolee was known to have been returned to prison his reported income for the study was zero. The incomes of parolees working at jobs not covered by social security was also reported as zero. The sample was classified into five categories: forestry comparison group (479); clerical comparison group (144); skilled maintenance (113); vocational trainees (666); and correctional industries (179). The vocational trainee's group consists of inmates with hours of training ranging from 200 to 7,595.

The results of the survey indicate that the expenditures on the vocational training program represent a highly attractive form of investment in human capital. The average annual earnings for the respective groups for the 18 month period, January 1, 1968 through June 30, 1969, are given in Table I. The average earnings are the arithmetic mean income earned and includes parolees' incomes of those who were returned to finish terms, were unemployed or in county jails, as well as those parolees who had reported incomes.

The Social Product Gains Attributable to Vocational Training

The social product gain should measure directly the effect of vocational training on the earnings of the parolees. Unfortunately, income data on the preconfinement earnings of the parolees were not available. The problem then is to select a comparison group who have comparable characteristics, exclusive of the training, and to compare their earnings over the same period.

There is the further methodological issue of deciding who has had vocational training. Inmates enter the training program for a number of reasons. Some wish to improve their job skills, some wish to create a favorable impression with the Adult Authority, while still others enroll at the direction of the Adult Authority. Unfortunately it is not possible to identify the motivation of the inmate trainees.

John Hacker's survey of vocational training indicates some institutional problems.[4] Inmates are removed from class for transfer to other institutions (primarily to fill camp quotas) and are not assimilated into other classes. This is particularly true for the younger inmates who are especially in need of training. Furthermore, if inmates are removed from a course for lack of interest, limited ability, or at their own request, they are not permitted to enroll in a different course.

The average number of hours required to complete the training programs varies from institution to institution for the same course as well as between the courses themselves. The problem is to select a minimum number of hours for which the inmate could be considered to have gained a measurable increase in skills.

---

[4]John Hacker, *Report on the Special Study of Vocational Training Programs*. Sacramento, California: Department of Corrections, 1967.

The figure 1,000 hours was selected as the breaking point with the 321 inmates receiving less than 1,000 hours considered as receiving only partial training and the 345 inmates receiving 1,000 or more hours of training as completing training. The reason for selecting so large a number of hours of training is that for the Training Group total the average number of months between training termination and parole is 9.24 months. The investment in human capital, like physical capital, is subject to depreciation and deterioration. For the group that had 1,000 or more hours of training, the average months was 6.97 so that inmates needed to have acquired a fairly high level of proficiency to retain their skills. The problem is further complicated by the production quotas assigned to some courses where a part of the class time is used up by a few highly trained inmates meeting the production requirements while the remaining members of the class furnish essentially unskilled labor. For most classes 1,512 hours of training are necessary for a certificate of completion. Some inmates, however, remain in the classes to fulfill the production requirements so that a large number of hours of vocational training is not necessarily indicative of a commensurate increase in skills. What a large number of hours does is to shorten the time elapsed between training termination and parole and gives an indication of the effect of timing training termination and parole or providing adequate refresher courses prior to parole.

Selection of a Comparison Group

The problem of selecting a control group for comparison with the vocationally trained parolees is to select a group that is alike in every respect save training. The various alternatives in defining the control group are to divide the trainee group into two categories based on the accummulated number of hours of training or to establish a control group composed of parolees who had different institutional assignments.

If we choose as the comparison group those trainees who have completed less than 1,000 hours of training and compare this group's earnings with the group that completed 1,000 or more hours of training, i.e., the dichotomy completed-training and partial-completes, we can control for selectivity of trainees. The trainee retention process and the potential motivational problems of this group of trainees, however, rule out such a direct comparison.

The correctional industries group has a relatively low proportion of commitments for economic crimes. Correctional industries are concentrated in the medium and heavy security institutions so that the institutional experiences of the correctional and trainee group are quite different. Educational levels and ethnic proportions also rule out this group for comparison purposes.

The skilled maintenance group is inappropriate since these men possessed marketable skills prior to incarceration. The relatively low percentage of convictions for economic crimes supports this conclusion. The ethnic composition of this group also differs greatly from the trainee group.

The conservation camp study group consists of men who are paroled with essentially the same skills possessed as when they entered the institution. The relatively higher proportion of narcotics convictions and relatively low educational level and age rule out use of this group.

The clerical group has the highest educational attainment and the highest percentage of convictions for economic crimes. This group is better adjusted socially than the average trainee and over the short run should fare better in the job market than would the average vocational trainee. The ethnic proportions and low percentage of convictions for narcotic offenses would predict a better than average chance of success on parole.

Since none of the institutional study groups individually meets the requirements for a matched group, the group for this study will consist of those inmates whose institutional assignments were clerical, conservation camps, and skilled maintenance. The training group has such a diversity of pretraining acquired skills that this approach is necessary. Inmates who have existing job skills are not precluded from requesting and receiving vocational training in the institution to either maintain proficiency or upgrade job skills. The postrelease experience of the skilled maintenance group will provide the basis for computing the benefits of retraining for this segment of the trainee group. The conservation camp group will provide the basis for calculation of the benefits for the segment who lacked marketable job skills prior to commitment. The minimum educational requirements that qualify the inmate for vocational training are controlled for by including the clerical study group in the control group.

Primary Benefits

Average estimated annual earnings for the study and control groups based on reported incomes for the 18 month period, January 1, 1968, through June 30, 1969, are given in Table I. The average earnings are the arithmetic mean income earned and includes parolees (at zero income) who were returned to finish terms, were unemployed or in county jails (shown as zero incomes for some of the quarters) as well as those parolees who had reported incomes for each of the quarters.

Secondary Benefits

Research has indicated that the "quality of employment" may be as important to the parolee as the employment per se. The parolee must perceive the benefits of training if the training is to be successful. Furthermore, since the trainee group represents substantially better parole risks, the question arises as to whether the difference in average incomes is accounted for only by differences in recidivism rates. The problem of shifting the incidence of unemployment from the vocationally trained parolee to the untrained parolee is equally as important when social benefits are to be measured. The average of the nonzero incomes are compared for the trainee and control group to provide a partial answer to these questions (Table II). While income is admittedly an imperfect measure of the quality of employment it should reflect this attribute of employment.

The vocational training program generates additional secondary benefits when the trainee who is successful in the job market satisfactorily completes parole and abandons his criminal career. The differences in recidivism rates using a definition of recidivism as reimprisonment, presented in Table III, provide a basis for quantifying these secondary benefits.

The average yearly cost of incarcerating a felon is $3,000, based on the cost for the year 1970. The differential in the recidivism rates would account for an average reduction of $108 per year per trainee in custodial costs. This re-

Table I. Average Annual Earnings for Parolees

Study Group		Average Annual Earnings
Training group total (200–7,595 hours)		$2,749
Training Partial (200–999)	$2,372	
Training (1,000–7,595 hours)	3,100	
Training (1,000–1,999 hours)	2,961	
Comparison groups		2,534
Conservation camp	2,511	
Skilled maintenance	2,423	
Clerical	2,691	
Correctional industries	2,282	

Table II. Nonzero Incomes by Group

Study Group		Average Nonzero Income
Trainee group total (200–7,595 hours)		$4,201
Training partial (200–999 hours)	$3,808	
Training (1,000–7,595 hours)	4,580	
Training (1,000-1,999 hours)	4,517	
Comparison groups		4,184
Conservation camp	4,100	
Skilled maintenance	4,178	
Clerical	4,384	
Correctional industries	3,655	

Table III. Recidivism Rates by Type of Study Group

Study Group		Recidivism Rate
Trainee group total		· 14.4%
Training partial (200–999 hours)	16.5%	
Training (1,000–7,595)	12.4	
Comparison groups		17.9
Conservation camp	19.1	
Clerical	16.9	
Skilled maintenance	14.9	
Correctional industries	16.2	
Based on recidivism rates Region II (L.A. District parole office)		

turn is exclusive of the other secondary benefits, which unclude the reduced assistance payments to the families of parolees who successfully complete parole and the reduced unemployment payments to parolees who remain steadily employed.

Costs of the Vocational Training Program

The social economic cost of the vocational training program is measured as the output foregone by society through the diversion of resources into retraining. The opportunity costs of production (institutional) foregone because of retraining does not enter into the costs of retraining for this particular program. The nature of the prison economy is such that the marginal product of an inmate shifted from vocational education to prison industries would probably be zero over a wide range. Furthermore, since the vocational education program is productive in terms of products turned out for state use, the true social costs are overstated.

Table IV indicates estimates of the costs by trade of vocational training. The hourly costs are based on data for the programs at C.I.M. for fiscal year 1967–1968. The weighted mean cost per hour of training was $.495.

The true social costs are understated as no depreciation is recorded for machine and equipment. The capital assets are used until they become unrepairable or greatly obsolete. The objective of vocational training as practiced in the institutions is to give the inmate a basic knowledge of the skills in a trade and not the

Table IV. Estimated Hourly Costs of Vocational Training for Selected Trades

1. Shoe repair	$ .671
2. Sheet metal	.643
3. Machine shop	.570
4. Masonry	.570
5. Welding	.525
6. Offset printing	.514
7. Office machine repair	.491
8. Landscape gardening	.485
9. Bakery	.465
10. Auto mechanics	.404
11. Electronics	.395
12. Auto body and fender	.389

operation of the most modern machinery. This aspect is left for on-the-job training. John Hacker found much of the equipment to be outdated so that the omission of depreciation charges probably does not result in appreciable understatement of the costs. The program is not burdened with excessive maintenance costs since the institution employs inmates to effect the necessary repairs to equipment.

Evaluation of the Program—Cost-Benefit Analysis

Table V indicates the costs of retraining for the various vocational groups. The large number of hours invested per trainee is an indication that the type of training given in the prisons is not merely "vestibule training" which is only intended to give the trainee scant familiarity with a trade but represents a substantial investment in human capital.

Table V shows the income gains of trainee groups based on the data in Table I. As indicated in the table the payback period that recovers the investment in training is less than three years for parolees who received any training whatsoever. If we exclude both partially trained and those trained and retained in classes to meet production requirements, we see that for the training (1,000–1,999) costs are recovered in 15 months. This quick recovery of costs without relying on the secondary benefits of reduced re-

cidivism and the probable greater future income gains makes this investment very attractive to the state.

Analysis by Trade

Table VI indicates the average incomes and hours of training for the productive trades.

It is important to draw the distinction between "specific" and "general" training, first made by Becker.[5] The term "general training" is broader in the sense that it applies to the type of program that increases the marginal product of the trainee in many other fields as well as the particular trade. Assuming that the potential employers recognize the generality of the training they should be more inclined to hire the vocational trainee. Completely specific training can be defined as training that has no effect on the productivity of trainees that would be useful in other occupations.

If we examine Table VI, the top five trades (highest incomes) represent trades which are characterized as general in terms of the acquisition of skills applicable to a number of occupations. The bottom five trades represent the most specific trades in terms of transferability of job skills. This lack of transferability at least partially explains the income differentials.

The special trades: sewing machine repair, office machine repair, offset printing, and silk screen achieved high placement percentages through special placement efforts. What is interesting is that the more general trades achieved a better showing. This seems to verify the hypothesis that the type of training, general versus specific, is a determinant of success in the labor market. The experience with the "special trades" indicates that if special placement efforts had been made for these other trades a higher pay-off would have been observed.

Table VII, based on multiple regression analysis indicates which variables are significant

[5]Gary S. Becker, "Investment in Human Capital: A Theoretical Analysis," *Journal of Political Economy*, 70. (1962 Supplement), 9–49.

Table V. Average Hours of Training, Estimated Expenditure and Income Gain per Trainee for Three Study Groups

Study Group	Hours	Cost	Annual Income Gain
Training group total (200–7,595 hours)	1,255	$627	$215
Training (1,000–7,595 hours)	1,923	967	427
Training (1,000–1,999 hours)	1,388	694	566

Table VI. Average Annual Income and Hours of Training by Trade

Trade	Sample Size	Average Income	Average Hours of Training
1. Machine shop	35	$4,117	1,677
2. Welding	76	3,344	925
3. Sheet metal	32	3,214	1,427
4. Auto mechanics	83	3,177	1,898
5. Body and fender	35	3,140	1,353
6. Electronics	49	3,077	1,244
7. Sewing machine repair	6	2,954	1,499
8. Office machine repair	20	2,941	2,113
9. Offset printing	33	2,787	1,293
10. Silk screen	13	2,768	1,364
11. Baking	45	2,542	1,520
12. Meat cutting	26	2,516	1,414
13. General shop	28	2,444	713
14. Culinary	59	2,416	778
15. Hill and cabinet	39	2,318	1,154
16. Landscaping	40	2,203	1,111
17. Refrigeration and air conditioning	15	2,132	569
18. Masonry	37	1,924	1,237
19. Dry cleaning	20	1,895	1,027
20. Shoe repair	20	828	1,975

predictors of the level of income for the various trades. What is significant is that for six out of the top ten trades hours of training was a significant predictor of the level of income. If we look at Table VIII, we can compare the additional income attributable to an hour's training (a comparison that is valid about the mean number of hours). This gives us an indication of the benefit and cost on a per hour basis. Reference to Table VII indicates that an hour of welding training costs $.525 and is worth $.819 in increased income. For auto mechanics the cost is $.525 while income increases by $.765.

For the machine shop and baking trades, the longer the time between training termination and parole the lower the income. For welding, auto mechanics, office machine repair, and offset printing the same relationship was observed, however this relationship was not statistically significant at the .05 level. Training skills, like capital investment, are subject to depreciation, especially when the skills are not reinforced through practice for long periods. The strong relationship between hours of training and income reflects in part the reduced depreciation when training termination more closely coin-

Table VII. Variables That Are Significant Predictors of the Level of Income for Various Trades

Trades	More Recent Training	More Training Hours	Overall Adjustment	Higher Training Grades	Prior Periodic Employment	Prior Generally Unemployed
Machine shop	X					
Welding		X				
Sheet metal					X	X
Auto mechanics		X	X			
Body and fender		X				
Electronics		X				
Office machine repair		X				
Silk screen		X				
Baking	X					
Meat cutting				X		
General shop		X				
Refrigeration and air conditioning			X			
Shoe repair		X			X	

Table VIII. Value of an Hour of Training in Income Gain

1. Body and fender	$ .633
2. Auto mechanics	.765
3. Welding	.819
4. Electronics	1.07
5. Office machine repair	1.18
6. Silk screen	1.48
7. General shop	2.97

cides with release dates. For the welding trade, income fell by $119 for each month between training termination and parole. The average number of months between training termination and parole was 9.10 for welding trainees. For the baking trade income fell $91 per month for the 9.93 months on average between completion and release.

The variables associated with preconfinement employment histories are significant for the sheet metal, body and fender, electronics, and shoe repair trades. The fact that these variables are not significant predictors of incomes for all but these four trades indicates that the training may have helped to break the cycle of long-term unemployment and underemployment. The shoe repair trade is the epitome of the type of job that should be avoided by parolees (Sullivan). The relationship between hours and income was negative and significant. This appears to indicate that those inmates who attempt to follow that career have reduced incomes. The high number of hours associated with this trade, (1975) and high hourly cost ($.671) indicate that this is probably a production course and not a training course designed to impart marketable skills. The benefits would be reflected in the state use of the output and not in the parolee's incomes. The relatively low number of hours (569 average) for the refrigeration and air conditioning trades indicates that few if any marketable skills have been taught, since this is an area where the minimum job requirements are usually two years experience and the hours indicate only 15 weeks of training. The low average hours for culinary and general shop probably explains the relatively low performance of these two trades—performance again measured in terms of income.

CONCLUSIONS

The social product gain attributable to vocational training was measured by means of comparison groups. The low mobility and entry level positions secured by trainees would lead us to suspect that the income differential between trainees and nontrainees would become greater with the passage of time. The measured differential is probably understated because all parolees must have secured employment prior to release and remain employed until parole is completed. The lack of placement effort for vocational trainees, length of time between training and release, and pressure to secure any type of job works to the detriment of the program.

What is remarkable is that the vocational training program has such high apparent benefits in spite of all the limitations imposed on the program. The gains to society from this program warrant further investment and some reallocation of present investment to strengthen and extend the program. Such investment promises immediate and high returns which are measurable and probably large secondary benefits in terms of reduced costs of criminal careers.

58. Mutual Agreement Programming

ANNE H. ROSENFELD

PROGRAM ORIGINS

MUTUAL AGREEMENT PROGRAMMING WAS DE-veloped in response to several problems endemic to prisoner training programs and parole review. Due to lack of communication and coordination between prison and parole authorities, training programs were not well synchronized with the timing of release, and prisoner participation in those programs was not being considered in release decisions. Underlying these problems was the frequent arbitrariness of Parole Boards in deciding release readiness. Criteria for release, often subjective and rarely explicit, were not known to prisoners or prison personnel and release times were uncertain, subject to the private decisions of Parole Boards; release could be denied arbitrarily, with little or no accountability for such decisions.

Ideally, the completion of training should be coordinated with release and job placement so that newly acquired skills could be put to best use. In practice, prisoners often had to wait an indefinite period before release, and could not plan effectively for outside employment as long as their release date was unknown. The U.S. Department of Labor, sponsor of many prisoner training programs, concluded that these conditions interfered with the efficacy of its rehabilitative efforts.

It became plausible that for the inmate programs to be fruitful and financially justifiable, some means was needed which would establish a firm parole date and criteria for parole and would allow a man or woman to be released on completion of training and placed in a training-related occupation.

The Parole-Corrections Project was therefore funded in 1971 by the Office of Manpower Research and Development, Manpower Administration of the Department of Labor, to design and implement a method to overcome some of these problems. Basic guidelines for what was to become Mutual Agreement Programming were developed by parole and correctional administrators themselves in cooperation with Project staff.[1] The MAP concept developed from what was first a "prescriptive" solution, whereby the Parole Board prescribes programs for an inmate and promises to consider him for parole release upon program completion. This notion was extended subsequently to include prisoner participation and responsibility as a vital program element on both humanistic and rehabilitative grounds.

As the program evolved, it included the following main elements *within a legal contract:*

1.   Establishment of a certain release date;

▶SOURCE: *An Evaluative Summary of Research. MAP Program Outcomes in the Initial Demonstration States.* American Correctional Association Document No. 7. College Park, Md.: A.C.A., 1975. Pp. 3–7, 44–55, 57–59. *Reprinted by permission.*

[1]See *Proceedings: The National Workshop of Corrections and Parole Administration,* February 1972, New Orleans, Louisiana, Resource Document #2, American Correctional Association, Washington, D.C.

2. Explicit, objective conditions for release;

3. Explicit statement of responsibility for prisoners, parole authorities, and institutional personnel;

4. Prisoner participation in decision-making and responsibility for carrying out contract terms;

5. Prisoner choice of individualized rehabilitative programs.

Each element of the program could be viewed as contributing to a number of desired results—both short-term and long-term.

RATIONALE

Short-Term Outcomes

Considering the short-term outcomes, it was expected that *establishing a certain release date* would reduce prisoner anxiety and uncertainty about release and would help both inmates and institutional personnel coordinate training plans with post-release work placement. It would also potentially help prison personnel plan for better allocation of training services. In addition, inmates would be in a better position to negotiate for a job while still in prison.

Allowing prisoners to choose their own rehabilitative programs and giving them an opportunity to earn release through their participation would presumably increase their motivation to work in programs they viewed as relevant to their own needs and to avoid behavior that would jeopardize their chances of release at the stated date. Prisoners would also be less likely to be involved in disciplinary infractions.

By consulting with prisoners about what they perceived their rehabilitative needs to be, prison personnel could learn about the relevance of their services to prisoners and could have an information base from which to modify or augment currently available programs.

If contract terms were objective and explicit and if there were a clear definition of responsibility among the three parties, Parole Boards would have less grounds for arbitrariness and delay in release decisions; parole and prison authorities as well as prisoners would be held to a "lawful" standard of accountability. If prisoners were not released because they violated their contracts, the causes of parole delay would be clearer to all parties than they are in current parole practice. Prisoners would perhaps less readily blame prison or parole personnel for their further confinement than they do at present. Prisoners would also have a clearer notion of what behavior would be expected of them in order to obtain release and would be more likely to exert effort toward the contract objectives.

By requiring Parole Boards to decide upon and set definite parole dates and explicit conditions for parole, there would be pressure to consider parole readiness on more rational grounds with fewer opportunities for last-minute revocations and delays. This could be expected to advance the actual release time closer to the minimum eligibility date and thus could shorten the average time of imprisonment. For prisoners, shorter stays would be an obvious bonus; and for prison administrators and taxpayers, reduced cost without increased criminality would be a significant gain.

The program's expected *short-term results* would, therefore, be of several types:

1. *From the perspective of social justice and human rights*, prisoners would be treated as responsible individuals, capable of judging their needs and bargaining within a legal system to satisfy them. Prisoners would participate in a system which is lawful, in which all three contracting parties are held accountable for their actions. Release decisions would be made more fairly, on more explicit, objective grounds, with less room for arbitrariness and inequity. Prisoners would know what was expected of them to earn release and would be spared the uncertainty of not knowing their release date.

2. *From the perspective of prisoner rehabilitation,*

prisoners would be more motivated to use prison time and rehabilitative resources more constructively because they would be rewarded for doing so and would participate in programs of their own choosing. Participation in a more lawful and equitable system and the achievement of planned objectives through industrious, constructive behavior might be expected to contribute to better attitudes toward the social system and greater self-esteem. Having a definite release date, prisoners would have less anxiety and uncertainty about release and could better integrate prison training in their post-release plans.

3. *From the perspective of prison administration*, better prisoner motivation would mean smoother program operation and fewer disciplinary problems. The presence of a certain release date and access to prisoner feedback would mean more efficient and effective allocation and planning of prison services. Shortened stays could reduce costs. Clarification of the administrative role vis-à-vis parole criteria could free prison personnel from prisoner criticism stemming from poor morale and unrealistic expectations.

4. *From the Parole Board perspective*, objective release criteria could simplify the decision-making process and provide a common ground for decision-making. A clear definition of Parole Board responsibilities, combined with greater accountability, could free them from charges of arbitrariness and unfairness.

The likelihood of these hypothetical, short-term outcomes actually materializing obviously varies depending on the degree to which they are within the program's control, and the way the program is actually implemented. Some of these short-term effects may be generally considered to be "structural" and highly likely, being inherent in the program. Others, such as reduced prison stay and better allocation of prison services depend on many other factors beyond the project's control, such as willingness of the

Parole Board to use the minimum eligibility time or the availability of human and financial resources to improve prison services. One might call such program outcomes "contingent." It should be noted that these particular projects were implemented under the assumption that no augmentation of prison services would be undertaken (or if they were, they would be equally available to the experimental and control groups). MAP personnel would attempt to use whatever resources were available and put them to better use.

Long-Term Outcomes

A primary concern of those within and without the prison system is its ultimate impact on prisoner behavior after release. If prisoners are released to the community, will they behave as law-abiding citizens in the future? Although there is disagreement among experts in penology, many believe that employment is a critical key to reducing recidivism. Looking at the program's elements, there are several aspects that seem likely to contribute to more adaptive attitudes and improved employability of prisoners. If these can occur, then these may contribute to lowering recidivism rates as well. The general rationale runs as follows: If prisoners are given a choice of services and an opportunity to assume responsibility for obtaining release at a certain date through their own actions, they are likely to utilize prison training and therapeutic services more constructively and gain better work preparation as a result. If, because of a certain release date, their post-release work placement can be better arranged and follows immediately upon training completion, their chances of obtaining and keeping a job should be improved. Ex-offenders with good, well-paying jobs are less likely to be rearrested.

It is obvious, however, that the chances of an ex-offender's obtaining and keeping a well-paying job for which he is trained depend on many factors beyond the program's structural control. At best, prisoners may receive relevant training under high motivational levels, with improved coordination in release placement. But these conditions obviously are not sufficient, given the weight of other factors, such as the actual quality of job preparation, the availability of jobs, and the marketplace for ex-offenders within the larger job market. Thus, the program's long-term benefits for prisoner employment must be regarded as contingent. They are possible, but are not as likely as many of the program's expected short-range outcomes.

Some believe that the post-release behavior of prisoners depends more on their own attitudes and motivation than on external circumstances, economic or otherwise. If this is true then there is reason to believe that participation in an individually tailored rehabilitative program that fosters responsibility and realistic planning and involves experience with a system that operates fairly and legally may, for some individuals, alter attitudes sufficiently to encourage responsible, legal behavior after release. However, given the complexity of human behavior and motivation and the limited state of knowledge about the psychological underpinnings of criminal behavior, these effects must be regarded as unpredictable.

*

QUESTIONS AND CAVEATS

The early experiments in Arizona, Wisconsin, and California have demonstrated MAP's feasibility and have given us some insight into the reactions of prisoners and prison personnel. However, there are still a number of unanswered questions about how and whether MAP fulfills the objectives set forth in the first section. The following section will be addressed to considering some of these major questions, and, in the light of greater experience, suggesting some directions in which answers may be found. While the initial MAP experimentals have yielded little conclusive evidence that might bear on future MAP projects, they have produced both greater awareness of the likely variables involved, and greater appreciation of

the limits of our knowledge and assumptions. This section is not intended to be an exhaustive examination of the state of knowledge concerning MAP; rather, it is meant to illustrate, through the examination of a few important issues, the kind of inquiry still needed. It will focus on some of the program's main areas of anticipated short-term benefit, and examine how the program might be structured and implemented to achieve them more effectively.

Inmate Attitudes and Motivation: Can MAP Result in Improved Attitudes Toward Self and Increased Effort?

Many of the goals of MAP directly or indirectly assume a change in attitudes and/or effort by inmates which should contribute to better performance in prison, and possibly following release. Beyond the possible positive response of prisoners to more fair and humane treatment (if they perceive it that way), the program's psychological impact is expected to stem primarily from (1) involvement in decision making, with inmates' assumption of responsibility for their own behavior, and (2) the contingency of release at a specific date based upon the inmate's fulfillment of objectives stated in the contract. Psychological theory, based on substantial empirical evidence, supports both of these major assumptions. However, psychological studies also indicate that changes in motivation through promised rewards and participation in decision-making depend on a number of factors, as yet only partially delineated. In the case of MAP, we do not know whether it results in greater inmate involvement and effort, nor do we know whether as a result of MAP participation inmates have more favorable attitudes toward themselves and life. There are a number of factors which might be expected to affect these outcomes, among which might be:

1. The freedom with which the choice of individual activities is made;

2. The quality and relevance of available resources for prisoners to choose from;

3. Individual capability of prisoners to identify meaningful goals, maintain effort to reach them, and believe that they are worth reaching;

4. Prisoners belief that the rewards are valuable;

5. Belief that they must adhere to contract terms and achieve a given amount by a specific time in order to gain their reward;

6. Belief that the reward will indeed follow if the effort is made.

We do not know to what extent any or all of these conditions must be fulfilled in order to elicit appreciable effort by inmates. It appears, however, that in Arizona and Wisconsin many of these conditions may have been only partially met. How free were inmates to choose their own activities, and how much were they coerced by "guidance" by others (even intended in the inmate's own best interests)? Given limited contract time and rehabilitative resources, what alternatives were realistically available to them? To what extent could prisoners assess their own goals and work to reach them?

We have some evidence that the goal of release certainty was a meaningful one for many inmates, but its effects were confounded by the expectation that early release would also result. How does the possibility of early release color the choice of rehabilitative programs? Does the reward conflict with the goal of more appropriate programs? Are there other rewards that might be more effective for given individuals? Should the rewards, as well as the means to them be individualized? Can the reward of release certainty provide motivation for improved behavior after release? Would a succession of rewards, extending into the release period be more effective? Do those with MAP contracts have greater feelings of self-worth, dignity, optimism, or responsibility for their actions as a result of their participation? If not, why? Could positive feelings elicited by MAP improve their behavior while in prison? Might they endure,

and affect long-term behavior after release? At present we do not know. Answers to such questions require a type of attitudinal research which was not undertaken in the studies reported here.[2]

We are unsure how contract experimentals viewed the conditions of their contracts. Did they know explicitly what they had to do, and how well? Did they believe they could just go through the motions of participation and obtain release? To what extent did they expect the Parole Board to behave arbitrarily, despite the presence of a contract?

If inmates are to feel that they must try hard, their contracts must be relatively specific, explicitly stating the level of achievement expected of them. And contract standards must be enforced rigorously, so that all who perform satisfactorily are released, but only those. In Arizona and Wisconsin were contracts specific enough? Did the fact that no contracts were revoked for inadequate performance (except on disciplinary grounds) reflect excessive vagueness of contract terms, leading to laxity? How could contract terms be expressed more specifically without risking excessive rigidity and perhaps unrealistic standards? (How many professional staff members are qualified to predict accurately what a given individual should be able to accomplish within a given amount of time?)

[2]While attitudinal information might provide greater insight into how and why MAP does or does not affect prisoner attitudes both before and after release, there are those, including Robison, who believe that the risks of obtaining such information outweigh any possible benefits that might result. For these individuals, there is a risk that attitudinal change, rather than overt performance in rehabilitative programs might be used as a release criterion, returning the parole process to the types of psychological criteria which have heretofore resulted in delayed and arbitrary parole decisions. There is a further, related issue: the extent to which individual psychological privacy of prisoners can and should be invaded, even ostensibly for their own good.

Those who implement other MAP projects with a research component will clearly have to decide for themselves whether the knowledge gained by attitudinal investigation is worth the risk of its possible abuse.

As MAP is now designed, with contracts up to two years, usually signed at the beginning of incarceration, will inmates be better able to assess and ascertain their goals and design better programs to meet them? Will the graduated rewards of a decompression model sustain motivation? Once there has been more experience with MAP, and inmates know how many contract experimentals actually are released and why, will this information affect the quality of their participation?

Given the program's structure, the Project Coordinator's role will always be a crucial one in eliciting inmate participation and enthusiasm, in representing and enforcing the fairness of the prison system, in advising (but not coercing) inmates as they choose their rehabilitative activities, negotiate with the Parole Board, and carry out their commitments. The role obviously requires great skill and tact. How well can the Project Coordinator maintain credibility as an inmate advisor and advocate, while accommodating prisoner expectations to the realistic constraints of finite rehabilitative resources and particular Parole Board demands and requirements? We have had no thorough assessment of the Project Coordinator's functions in Arizona, Wisconsin, and California, (although evidence from one study of MAP[3] suggests that they were highly sympathetic to the prisoners' point of view) nor do we know how they affected prisoner participation. Clearly, in any future MAP projects, the choice of Project Coordinator, and definition of the role will be important.

In summary, although MAP offers a foundation for inmate participation and choice, there is no guarantee that the program can make inmates actually feel that they are participating fully, or that it can elicit better effort on their part. Given the fact that MAP is administered within a highly authoritarian system, we do not know whether it is ever possible to achieve these

---

[3]See doctoral dissertation by Ellen Dunbar, University of Southern California, Los Angeles, "Politics of Policy Change," 1975, Department of Sociology and Urban Studies.

goals. We do know that if MAP is to achieve its full motivational potential, it requires careful attention to the way it is implemented, and great skill on the part of those who carry it out.

Social Justice
Can MAP Reduce Parole Board Arbitrariness?
MAP is designed to reduce Parole Board arbitrariness by requiring that a definite parole date be set, by basing release decisions on relatively objective and explicit grounds, and by holding all parties to the contract accountable for their actions. In its initial trials in Arizona and Wisconsin, it appears that in adherence to parole date commitments and acceptance of contract terms based on performance criteria, the Parole Boards in those states indeed bahaved less arbitrarily (even in Arizona, where changes in contract wording might have permitted certain abuses of power).

However, there may still be some areas for arbitrariness which deserve further examination. On the preceding pages we have already alluded to the problems of contract wording. If contract terms are too vague, there is room for arbitrariness in assessing contract satisfaction; excessive leniency or harshness in interpretation may result. If terms are too rigidly defined, unrealistic demands may jeopardize contract fulfillment. In either case, the program would not be fair.

While MAP can affect release date certainty (assuming that contract terms are adequately specified), we do not know whether it can affect the way release dates are set. Parole Boards may set release dates as they wish, within the bounds of custom and law, for whatever reasons. Does the presence of the Program Coordinator and the bargaining process that is inherent in MAP influence the way release time decisions are made? Are they now on a less arbitrary basis than before? Does MAP invite shorter sentences or longer by focusing on individual needs? What would be fair and non-arbitrary standards for sentence length? Is it reasonable to expect that MAP's rehabilitative goals could be met if all inmates were released at the minimum eligibility date? (Would MAP, as currently structured, be necessary?) Would the presence of an outside arbitrator bring about greater accountability for Parole Board members concerning their release decisions and criteria?

An additional area in which Parole Board arbitrariness may still exist concerns their approval of inmates for contracts. Although inmates may meet the program's general eligibility standards (which have tended in the initial projects to be extremely broad), the Parole Board may then impose its own unstated standards and reject those individuals they consider unsuitable. In the Arizona and Wisconsin projects, individuals were rejected ostensibly on the grounds that there would have been insufficient time to complete their contracts within the project's time boundaries. However, a comparison of background characteristics of those accepted or rejected for MAP suggests that other criteria may have been operating, such as the level of education or training achieved prior to the project. While the presence of such criteria may be valid, there is obviously room for abuse, unless they are shared. Did inmates in Arizona and Wisconsin who were rejected for MAP feel fairly treated? Did the absence of complaints indicate satisfaction, or the lack of an adequate outside arbitration mechanism? It seems that if there is to be less arbitrariness, there should be more arbitration.

Does MAP Have an Adverse Effect for Those Without Contracts?   MAP attempts to introduce greater justice and humanity into the criminal justice system. Ideally, if it improves the fairness with which prisoners are treated, it should be accessible to all. Because MAP was new and untried, it was introduced in Arizona and Wisconsin on a limited basis, with only a relatively small group of experimentals permitted to participate. What were the program's effects on those not allowed to participate? According to the Wisconsin staff survey, about one-third of the staff thought MAP experimentals were resented by other prisoners. What

were the grounds for this resentment? Did they disagree with the fairness of lottery selection? Were they simply jealous that they did not have access to what they believed would be earlier release? Did they feel that they had less access to desired activities because MAP contractees used up the available slots? Did they feel that those under contract were treated more leniently, or more supportively? There are suggestions from the Arizona and Wisconsin studies that in some ways they may have benefited somewhat from MAP, through expansion of rehabilitative resources (especially in Arizona), and perhaps from a tendency for the Parole Board to grant earlier release to both controls and experimentals. Did they perceive these as benefits? At present, we do not know how the program's presence affected them.

As long as MAP is offered to less than the full inmate population, and as long as there are insufficient rehabilitative resources to accommodate all who wish to use them, there will be questions concerning MAP's fairness to prisoners as a whole.

Administrative Effects

Does MAP Result in Easier Inmate Management and Discipline?   The MAP concept assumes that if inmates are treated with fairness, are held accountable for their actions, are allowed to participate in activities they consider relevant, and are rewarded for their effort, they will be better behaved in prison, and easier to work with. While ideally better behavior could come about through a genuine sense of responsibility and involvement, it might also arise through the simple realization that one at least needs to "keep one's nose clean" if the contract terms are to be satisfied.

In Arizona and Wisconsin, there is no objective evidence available by which to judge the program's effects. While there were disciplinary infractions (some of which were sufficiently serious to jeopardize contracts), they appeared to be considered as infrequent, and the Project Coordinators believed that inmates were better behaved under MAP. (We do not know the rate of disciplinary infractions for the control group.) In Wisconsin, the impression that inmates were better behaved apparently was influential in the program's adoption on a state-wide basis.

In attempting to assess MAP's effects on inmate behavior, it is difficult to obtain objective evidence, since the judgment of disciplinary infractions rests with staff. Overreporting, or abuse of power is obviously possible with MAP, as is underreporting. (There are indications from one staff member in Wisconsin that staff members there tended to be lenient, to avoid jeopardizing inmates' chances of contract completion.) There are at present no safeguards to assure that reporting will be fair, other than attempts to share the program's procedures and goals with staff members, and to invite their honest participation.

In the absence of objective information, we must regard the question of inmate discipline as unresolved. It seems likely, that even in the absence of deep motivational and attitudinal changes, many inmates would attempt to stay within disciplinary bounds, if only to achieve the program's rewards. If the program can achieve deeper motivational impact, the chances of improved behavior are in all likelihood increased. But this, too, is an unanswered question.

Does MAP Result in Reduced Total Time Served and Reduced Costs to the State?   There are many aspects of MAP which in principle should lead to a reduction in time served. The presence of a certain release date, set in advance, contingent on satisfaction of relatively objective criteria is likely to reduce arbitrary delays and parole denials. In addition, there is the possibility that contract negotiations will result in shortened stays in exchange for additional contractual requirements, particularly if the Project Coordinator is effective.

However, as mentioned earlier, whatever pressure MAP may exert on Parole Boards, ultimately release time decisions remain their prerogative. Essentially under MAP all that can re-

liably be controlled are delays in the parole review process itself, or parole rejections for arbitrary reasons.

It was not possible to demonstrate statistically a time savings in Arizona or Wisconsin, despite a prevailing impression among prisoners, staff, and Project Coordinators that it occurred. We do not know what would happen in other settings. If, as was suggested earlier, the presence of MAP resulted in shorter stays for both experimentals and controls, there would obviously be a significant savings in time and money. At present, it cannot be demonstrated.

Could MAP result in reduced costs other than through reduced stay? Because MAP provides a basis for knowing in advance when prisoners will be released (assuming that most complete their contracts), it presumably could aid in more rational planning and allocation of prison services and personnel, since both prison input (calculable from known court loads and sentencing practices) and output could be better estimated. In addition, since it encourages advanced program planning, future demands on prison resources could be known. If MAP indeed can result in more effective use of services by highly motivated inmates, it also can offer benefits in greater payoff for money invested, particularly if its intended long-term benefits of improved employment and reduced recidivism can be realized. Any of these effects might lead to reduced costs to the state. However, it appears, on the basis of the initial MAP experiments, that they cannot be achieved without greater expense in staff and services. While an economic analysis of MAP's costs and benefits cannot be undertaken here, it is obvious that if the program were undertaken on an institution-wide or state-wide basis (as it would have to be to achieve its planning benefits), it would require extensive augmentation of staffing and services to accommodate MAP contract requirements. It would also require a rather sophisticated information system to match inmate requests for services with available resources, both within and without the prison.

In all probability, placement services for post-release employment would also have to be expanded. Whether these expenses would be offset by eventual savings through greater efficiency in internal operation, and perhaps savings through better inmate employment or less returns to prison cannot be determined at present. It should be noted that in Arizona and California, the program was not implemented state-wide partly in recognition of the immediately increased costs such changes would require. In Wisconsin, however, and in a number of other states, the program has been adopted on a state-wide basis, apparently on the assumption that the program's eventual benefits will justify or offset the initial cost.

Does MAP Result in a Rehabilitative Program More in Keeping with Rehabilitative Need?
Because the MAP program is individualized and based upon inmate participation and choice, it appears to offer an opportunity for an appropriate match between inmate needs and rehabilitative services. The program deliberately requires inmate participation rather than Parole Board prescription, on the assumption that inmates can assess their own needs in the areas of job training, coursework, skill training, therapy, etc. (with guidance from staff and the Project Coordinator).

The success of this aspect of MAP probably depends upon:

1. The inmates' knowledge of theirselves, their needs, and the demands and opportunities of the society to which they will return;

2. The breadth and quality of services available;[4]

[4]In these initial MAP projects, it was assumed that, as Robison expressed it, ". . . the nature of MAP programming concerns not so much the availability of enhanced program resources as it does the nature of the formal relationship between the prisoner and whatever resources happen to be currently available." Therefore, minimal research attention was given to examining how background characteristics, contract terms and services were related to one another, and to outcomes. Similarly, there was no extensive investigation

3. The quality of information available to the Project Coordinator concerning the inmate and the rehabilitative resources that might be used;

4. The diagnostic and vocational guidance skills of those who help inmates prepare their contract proposals;

5. The time available for inmate consultation and service coordination;

6. The willingness and ability of staff and Parole Board members to strike a balance between overly manipulative bargaining with inmates (even for desirable rehabilitative ends) and unduly permissive indulgence of inmate wishes which may sometimes be unrealistic or require too little effort;

7. The duration of contracts and their relation to release date considerations.

In the pilot MAP projects in Arizona and Wisconsin, inmate initiative and choice was apparently encouraged, but in a context of existing staffing and services. Since contracts were of short duration, and implemented late in most inmate's period of incarceration, we do not know to what extent the specific contract terms for individuals represented a compromise between what was actually wanted and needed, and what was (a) available, (b) feasible within the project's time constraints and existing training cycles, (c) acceptable to the Parole Board, and (d) reasonable in the light of whatever rehabilitative activities inmates had participated in prior to the project. Nor do we know the information base upon which these decisions were made.

Clearly, the Project Coordinator's role is pivotal in guiding inmates to assess their life of ways in which the services received by MAP experimentals may have differed from those received before the program, or by controls. However, since according to Daniel Glaser (*Journal of Research on Crime and Delinquency*, July 1974), there is a relation between the quality of the prison learning experience and later recidivism, these variables deserve further examination.

goals and shape an appropriate program. As mentioned earlier, we do not know what skills were brought to this very difficult role. In all probability, even if Project Coordinators and inmates were able to devise an optimally appropriate rehabilitative program, it could not have been carried out within the constraints of the pilot projects.

The Parole Board's role is also of great importance. Since they too have input into the contract terms, their suggestions must be appropriate to actual inmate needs. In Arizona, where contract negotiations tended to be formalized and participation in therapy or counseling routinely required of all contract experimentals, it is doubtful whether contracts always reflected the wishes of those who signed them. (In one case, in Arizona, an inmate refused to sign once he realized that therapy would be required).

Because the experiments in Arizona and Wisconsin were subject to special constraints which probably would not be present in other projects, it would be difficult to predict how well rehabilitative programs might be designed under MAP in other settings. As indicated earlier, counseling individuals about their life goals, and providing appropriate services to help individuals meet them requires great skill, time, information, and probably money. Even assuming the presence of skilled staff and a wide variety of available services (as with a voucher system), there are still questions remaining about the ability of prisoners to assess and articulate their occupational and therapeutic objectives and determine which resources best suit their needs.

Does MAP Result in Improved Coordination of Training and Release?

One of the primary reasons for MAP's development was to improve the coordination of training and release. It was assumed that once a release date was known, it would be easier to plan training schedules so that training termination coincided with release.

There is evidence from the pilot MAP studies that despite the presence of a certain release date, and efforts to coordinate training and release, there was nonetheless a lag between the two for many prisoners. For example, in Arizona, the skill training condition was often on the verge of completion (and sometimes already completed) at the point of contract entry, and yet the contractual release date was usually set some months away, in violation of the MAP tenet that release should coincide with completion of training.

Greater attention to the administrative workings of MAP, particularly the intermeshing of training and release plans and facilities may reveal better ways of accomplishing the program's ends. Clearly, while MAP can provide a facilitative mechanism for smoother, more efficient administration, considerable effort is required to see that these effects actually occur. We do not know whether, beyond the initial negotiations required to implement MAP in a particular locale, the program resulted in continued closer planning and coordination between the Parole Board and corrections personnel in Arizona and Wisconsin. If it did occur, what forms did it take, and how could it have helped inmates and/or the system? Obviously, the coordination of training and release can be accomplished in two major ways: by adjusting training program choices and times to fit with release times, and by setting release times which are concordant with training time requirements to reach a given success level. Fragmentary evidence from the programs reported here suggests that the first method was used in these two projects, partially because of their time limitations. Further study is needed to determine the optimal procedure for assuring maximal benefit from prison programs without necessarily delaying release.

It is important to remember that although coordination may be desirable, it does not of itself necessarily produce enhanced prisoner performance before or after release (unless the quality of post-release performance is critically dependent upon the recency of training).

Is a MAP Contract Legally Valid?

A major unknown administrative area regarding MAP is the legal status of the contracts themselves. Despite legal research suggesting that the contracts are valid, unless or until they are challenged in court, there is no way to know their status in the eyes of the law. To date, no contract violation suits have been brought by inmates.

According to a memo by one legal consultant to the MAP project staff,[5] there are a number of legal questions as yet unanswered. In his opinion:

"Perhaps the most basic legal question presented by the MAP concept deals with the right of an incarcerated individual to enter into a binding contract and the secondary question as to his right to enforce the conditions of a contract.

"Case law has progressed from the concept presented in the early 1900's that an inmate was a ward of the state and possessed only those rights as the state, in its humanity, granted to the inmate, to the series of cases developed since 1940 which led to the position that an inmate retains all the rights of a free person except those taken from him, specifically, by statute or are taken as implied by the fact of incarceration. The vast difference between the two legal concepts and the wide grey area inbetween have enormous implications for the MAP contract. . . ."

Among the legal questions posed in this memo are:

1. Is a contract made by an inmate and a governmental agency enforceable? By the inmate? What is the correct remedy for a breach by the Board of Parole or the Department of Corrections?

2. What is the implied obligation of the Department of Corrections in providing services?

3. Does the MAP contract give rise to any obligation by the state to provide the type of training that would be acceptable in the community?

4. If a contracted service becomes unavailable in the middle of a training program, is the

inmate required to renegotiate a contract or has he or she fulfilled the obligation?

5. To what extent must MAP be offered to the entire prison population? In the event the criteria for selertion are vague, would an inmate not on MAP be able to force the Board of Parole or the institution to offer a MAP contract?

6. Can someone be refused MAP because of the length of his sentence, type of crime, age, prior record, etc.? What criteria could be used?

The tenor of these questions suggests that what might at first appear to be social justice issues may indeed be legal issues. Clearly, considerable thought and legal research are required in designing and implementing MAP contracts and programs within the current "grey area" of the law.

*

CONCLUSIONS

Mutual Agreement Programming, first tried on an experimental basis in Wisconsin, Arizona, and California is an approach to prison and parole reform whose potentially far-reaching effects are still largely unknown.

As designed, the program is intended to provide the relatively immediate benefits of release date certainty (and possibly shorter prison stays), less Parole Board arbitrariness, greater inmate participation and choice in rehabilitative activities (with greater effort and self-esteem resulting), easier inmate management, rehabilitative programs more in accord with rehabilitative needs, better coordination of training programs with release, and more rational allocation of prison resources and personnel. These effects are expected to contribute to the long-range outcomes of improved inmate employment and reduced recidivism.

On the basis of the two early pilot projects in which research was primarily focused on long-range program effects on recidivism and employment, it appears that prisoner rehabilita-

[5]Milton Gordon, Esq., Internal memo, May, 1975. UCLA—Law School, Los Angeles, Proposal for Legal Resource Document, June, 1975.

tion is not MAP's major area of benefit. Using either outcome measure, experimentals did not perform significantly better than controls. At present we do not know why. However, given these findings, it is unlikely that the program can or will be justified by its long-term rehabilitative effects (unless other studies, in other settings provide more definitive demonstrations of its efficacy).

There are suggestions from this study and from data in the hands of project staff that MAP can and does yield benefits of a more immediate sort, both humanistic and administrative. The pioneering projects have shown MAP to be a feasible method of assuring release date certainty, acceptable to prison administrators, inmates, and Parole Board members alike. The presence of a known release date can facilitate (although not necessarily guarantee) other benefits, such as reduced inmate anxiety and more realistic post-release employment planning, improved coordination of training programs with release, and more rational and efficient administrative planning.

MAP appears to reduce Parole Board arbitrariness (although not entirely), and to place release decisions on a more objective, explicit and rational basis than formerly. Despite MAP's effects on release date certainty and release criteria, the program has not yet provided demonstrable time savings in prison terms.

Whether the program can improve inmate management is still an unresolved issue, although impressionistic data suggest that it can. (Contract experimentals are not free of disciplinary problems, however.)

As yet there is little information about MAP's impact on inmate motivation and attitudes. While we do know that almost all of those with contracts in Arizona and Wisconsin were motivated to complete them, and performed satisfactorily in the eyes of the institutional staff and Parole Board members, we do not know their level of effort or the psychological benefits they may have gained.

The program appears to have facilitated the coordination of training programs and release for many inmates, but not all.

We do not know, for the initial MAP projects, whether rehabilitative programs were more in accord with inmate needs. While their may have been some gains, due to greater inmate participation and initiative, constraints unique to these projects limited inmate options, resulting in continuation, for many inmates, in activities undertaken prior to project entry.

It is still unknown whether more rational planning and allocation of prison services resulted from the initial MAP projects, since these effects are likely to have occured after the research study ended. (Subsequent developments in Wisconsin, where the program has been adopted on a state-wide basis suggest that these effects can occur if adequate resources are allocated.)

Given the novel and limited nature of the pilot MAP studies, it is difficult to predict the program's effects in other settings over longer time periods. The intelligence and sensitivity with which MAP is implemented is likely to affect its outcomes, particularly regarding the quality of inmate participation opportunities. In additon, the quality of counseling in contract term selection, and the types and quality of services offered appear to be critical variables.

MAP potentially has a catalytic effect on the correctional system, stimulating numerous changes which may affect the efficacy and humanity of prisons. It is not yet known how long it takes for the program's full impact to be felt. It is assumed that program effects will be largely confined to improved behavior and motivation of inmates before release, to more just and fair treatment of inmates, and to administrative benefits. It is of course possible that the program may also yield improved prisoner outcomes after release, but we have no grounds at present for such expectations. Obviously, many questions remain concerning MAP's full impact on inmates and the correctional system.

While the program's total impact has not been assessed, there has been sufficient evidence of its more immediate effects to stimulate its actual or potential adoption in over 15 states. The MAP concept is still under development. Current MAP programs reflect changes suggested by these initial trials. It is expected that with further implementation and study the program can be refined to better yield its intended benefits for inmates and the system of which they are involuntarily a part.

59. Assessing Group Counselling Effects

GENE KASSEBAUM
DAVID WARD
DANIEL WILNER

GROUP COUNSELING: ITS DEFINITION AND AIMS

What Is Group Counseling?

IN ONE SENSE OUR TASK OF EVALUATING GROUP counseling is less problematic than that of evaluating psychotherapy because in the California Department of Corrections (CDC) it is primarily based on the precepts and procedures articulated by one man, Dr. Norman Fenton. Fenton introduced group counseling into the department at San Quentin's Reception-Diagnostic Center in 1944, and his book is the department's training manual for group counselors.[1] For these reasons, conflicting definitions and techniques have plagued our research less than they have plagued the research efforts described by Eysenck. Nonetheless, Fenton's description of the interactional processes of the sessions (what goes on between group members and between group members and the leader) is couched in very general terms, and the theoreti-

cal bases on which group counseling is built are not clearly spelled out. The aims of group counseling are not easily operationalized, nor is it described in terms that lend themselves to the precise analysis of group structure or process.

Essentially, we are told that a therapeutic technique called group counseling, involving periodic meetings of staff and inmates to talk over matters of concern, has certain consequences for the participants—consequences that have rehabilitative effects. But we are not sure just what it is about the group sessions that promote changes in attitudes and behavior. This limitation in conceptional precision, however, does not prevent us from studying the *effects* of group counseling participation when an appropriate research design is employed.

Operationally, group counseling means that ten or twelve inmates meet one or two hours a week under the guidance of a lay group leader. Some leaders are administrative personnel, caseworkers, teachers, guards, or clerical and technical staff workers; others are therapeutic specialists (physicians, social workers, and psychologists). Nonprofessional personnel in group leader roles, to some extent, are trained and supervised by the group counseling supervisor in each prison. In most cases, these supervisors hold B.A. degrees and have received graduate training in social work. Participation in group counseling is normally voluntary for inmates.

▶SOURCE: *Prison Treatment and Parole Survival: An Empirical Assessment.* New York: John Wiley and Sons, 1971. Pp. 58–63, 207, 213–217, 229–242. *(Editorial Adaptations.) Reprinted by permission.*

[1]The following material is abstracted from Norman Fenton, *Group Counseling: A Preface to Its Use in Correctional and Welfare Agencies,* Sacramento; I.S.C.D., 1961, pp. 7–12. See also, Norman Fenton, "Mental Health Applications in the California Correctional System," paper presented at the conference on "Mental Health Aspects of Corrections," Chatham Bars Inn, Massachusetts, June 4, 1960.

The key proposition underlying the operation of these groups is the assertion that a given group can affect a member's attitudes and behavior.[2] Fenton states that if a group is to positively influence a group member's behavior, two basic requirements must be met.

The first requirement is the *development of the group setting necessary for clients to feel free to discuss with security their own and each other's feelings and attitudes toward the situation in which they find themselves.* The group members must perceive the leader as someone who accepts them as persons in whom he has a sincere interest and about whose welfare he is genuinely concerned. Members will then "... feel free to say what is on their minds or in their hearts" and the group will be able to offer to its members "... a kind of sanctuary or refuge from the callous environment of the prison yard."[3]

The second requirement for effective group counseling is a *condition of mutual acceptance among those in the group.* The atmosphere of the group must be supportive if members are to help each other and be helped by the leader. "This is especially true in the treatment of those in conflict with the law, because rejection, the poisonous opposite of acceptance, so often seems to have played a significant role in the explanation of the origin of the symptoms of criminality."

Fenton asserts that in the early life of the criminal, rejection by other people, notably parents or others in authority, has been a significant factor in arousing and establishing feelings of hostility or resentment. These feelings are expressed later in life in theft, robbery, or assaultive behavior.[4]

These two requirements work to promote a "mutually trustful understanding between the group leader and the client." Fenton refers to statements by Carl Rogers that the procedures and techniques used in counseling are of secondary importance to warm and accepting attitudes and to the freedom of the client to make choices and to respond spontaneously in the treatment situation.[5]

When the above requirements are met, the goals of group counseling may be successfully pursued.[6] They are:

1. To help prisoners adjust to the frustrations that are an unalterable part of life in an institution and in society.

2. To enable the clients to recognize the significance of emotional conflicts as underlying criminality.

3. To provide the opportunity for the client to learn from his peers about the social aspects of his personality.

4. To make possible a better understanding of make-believe, of phantasy, and of how costly may be behavioral responses to the antisocial content of daydreams.

5. [To improve] the emotional climate of the institution.

Group counseling, as defined by Fenton, thus involves the use of techniques with which the leader can counsel a group of individuals and can direct or facilitate constructive interpersonal relationships. The leader seeks to promote a situation in which the interaction of the group members themselves have favorable effects on those in attendance.[7]

This group program seems to be based essentially on certain tenets of Freudian psychology, Roger's nondirective counseling, group psychotherapy, social casework practice, and sociological studies of the social organization of the inmate community.[8] Group counseling is

---

[2]Ibid., p. 46.
[3]Ibid., p. 46.
[4]Ibid., p. 49.

[5]Ibid., pp. 49–50.
[6]Ibid., pp. 51–55.
[7]Ibid., p. 101.
[8]A comparison of Fenton's group counseling with Eysenck's "middle-of-the-road" definition of psychotherapy indicates considerable similarity:

viewed as a therapeutic device that attempts to provide the warm, supportive relationship with authority figures that inmates were denied as youngsters and that underlies their criminality. The group leader is to regard outbursts against the prison, its officials, or himself as evidence of the immaturity of clients who are really reacting to father figures. An atmosphere of interest and support by the leader and other group members will help the inmate mature (resolve his emotional problems). His relationships with others will improve, and the likelihood of his returning to patterns of criminal behavior will be reduced. Although the group leader should be as nondirective as possible, it should be remembered that the techniques for conducting the session are of lesser importance than the general atmosphere that prevails in the group.

Fenton's perspective can be observed in the descriptions of the purposes of the group counseling program that were expressed to us in numerous interviews and conversations with

1. There is an interpersonal relationship of a prolonged kind between two or more people.
2. One of the participants has had special experience and/or has received special training in the handling of human relationships.
3. One or more of the participants have entered the relationship because of a felt dissatisfaction with their emotional and/or interpersonal adjustment.
4. The methods used are of a psychological nature, that is, involve such mechanisms as explanation, suggestion, persuasion and so forth.
5. The procedure of the therapist is based upon some formal theory regarding mental disorder in general, and the specific disorder of the patient in particular.
6. The aim of the process is the amelioration of the difficulties which cause the patient to seek the help of the therapist.

Hans J. Eysenck, "The Effects of Psychotherapy," *International Journal of Psychiatry,* vol. 1, no. 1, 1965, p. 103. The major differences between individual psychotherapy and group counseling are: (1) the lesser degree to which "felt dissatisfaction" motivates some inmates to join groups, (2) the lesser degree to which group leaders have received professional training in the theory and method of treatment, and (3) the degree of importance attached to the group as a factor in modifying attitudes and behavior. Group therapy combines the elements of both approaches.

CDC employees. A general agreement existed that group counseling was supposed to provide an opportunity for the following.

1. The psychological ventilation through the expression of feelings toward society, the judicial system, the prison, and prison personnel.

2. A self-understanding on the part of inmates, derived from guided group discussion, from witnessing the expression of feelings by other inmates, and from the interpretation of these feelings by other inmates, and by the group leader.

3. A ventilation and self-understanding on the part of the group leaders.

The latter point is an extension of Fenton's approach and is based on the feeling of many group leaders that they have developed a better understanding of individual inmates, of inmate perspectives, and of inmate life through their group sessions. In fact, when discussing group counseling, the most frequently used word by staff and inmates is "understanding."

One other program development should be mentioned at this point because it has evolved out of group counseling and embodies many of its features. That program is called "community living"; it combines group counseling with some of the features of the therapeutic community programs developed by Maxwell Jones and Harry Wilmer.[9] The California Department of Corrections carries out this somewhat more complex form of treatment by housing inmates in organized groups of 50 to 100 men, with many routine prison activities centered on the housing unit. The community living unit holds daily general assemblies of all its members under the leadership of the treatment, custodial, and administrative personnel who are responsible for the men in the unit. At Men's Col

[9]Maxwell Jones, *The Therapeutic Community,* N.Y.: Basic Books, Inc. 1953. See also, Fenton's paper, op. cit.

ony these units consisted of 50 inmates and three staff members, generally, including a caseworker, a correctional officer, and a treatment or custodial staff administrator.

It is not really accurate to call community living the CDC's version of the therapeutic community because the theory and practices of Jones and Wilmer are not employed. Instead, community living is to be regarded as an extension of group counseling, but with bigger groups and more frequent meetings. The leaders of community living groups receive the same training and instructional materials as the ones given to the regular group counseling leaders.[10] The content and character of the discussions in the community living sessions are identical to those of the smaller groups.

In this study we do not attempt to discuss the validity of all of Fenton's contentions about the etiology of criminal behavior nor do we discuss some of his specific statements, for instance, the assertion that group counseling sessions are "a haven" for the inmate. Whether this is true, or whether, as some inmates have implied, the yard is the only haven from nosy and interfering treatment staff members, is not a major issue. Other issues—such as whether an inmate's group discussions with a staff member and other inmates, in fact, can be free and unlimited; whether staff members will regard inmate criticism of them as childish outbursts; whether the probability of future criminal behavior can be modified by a warm relationship with an authority figure once or twice a week; whether, in fact, warm supportive relationships prevail in prison group sessions; whether inmate attitudes and behavior change for the better as a result of group treatment—are closely related to the purpose of this study. But our

[10]Group counseling and community living units throughout the California Department of Corrections are directed by a "Group Counseling Supervisor," whose headquarters are at Sacramento. During the course of our study this position was held by Robert M. Harrison, a psychiatric social worker.

main purpose is to evaluate the effects of the counseling program.

In the pages that follow, it thus should be kept in mind that this program was not developed by the writers or by the administrators of the prison studied. It is one application of a program used throughout the California Department of Corrections.

*

MEASUREMENT OF OUTCOME

Does a program of group counseling conducted in prison have an effect on postrelease behavior that is *different* from the effect of imprisonment itself? This was the major research question of our study. Issues about the impact of imprisonment per se or about group counseling in a noninstitutional setting were not central to our purposes. Our data only incidentally show the extent to which being in prison changes the likelihood of committing another crime. For this, we would have needed a control group of comparable offenders who were not imprisoned. Recidivism rates cited in this study apply to prison inmates only.

*

Parole Outcome: Operationalizing the Concept
The Research Division of the California Department of Corrections has established a well-ordered operation to record the status of all releasees. This system brings together information sent by police departments to the California Criminal Identification and Intelligence Division, information submitted by parole agents and reports of actions taken by the Adult Authority. Hence, by providing the Research Division with a list of names and departmental identification numbers, we were able to obtain parole status information for all members of the sample at 6-, 12-, 24-, and 36-month intervals from date of release.

Most serious disposition known and whether the parolee had been *returned to prison* were the two items used to determine parole status (outcome) for our cohort. These designations were taken from the Research Division's 12-point scale for recording parole status. The items comprising the scale are as follows.

Minor Disposition

1.   Returned to Narcotic Treatment Control Unit (both suspended or not suspended).

2.   Arrest on technical charges only.

3.   Parolee at Large with no known violation (PAL).

4.   Arrest and release.

5.   Trial and release.

6.   Conviction with misdemeanor probation, with fine or bail forfeited, or with jail under 90 days.

Major Disposition

7.   Parolee at large with a felony warrant (PVAL). Arrest on felony charge and release (guilt admitted and restitution provided) or arrest on felony charge and dismissed (guilt admitted in written statement and would be released if Adult Authority did not revoke parole in cooperation with District Attorney's wishes).

Awaiting trial or sentence on felony charge.

Death in commission of a crime or from drug overdose.

8.   Ninety days to six months in jail.

9.   Six months to nine months in jail.

10.   Nine months or more in jail. Federal probation and/or suspended prison sentence.

11.   Return to prison *in lieu of* new commitment, that is, arrest on felony charge more serious than in No. 7 above and would be prosecuted if Adult Authority did not revoke parole.

12.   Return to prison anywhere with new commitment (WNT).

Since this category coded revocations, based only on new felony convictions (that is, it excluded technical revocations), it was necessary for us to check the second item—*return to prison*—to locate parolees recommitted for reasons *other* than a new crime. For example, a subject whose most serious disposition was drunkenness would be coded by the CDC (California Department of Corrections) as having received a minor disposition, *even though he might have been returned to prison* for excessive drinking. To obtain this latter information, it was necessary to combine the disposition code with the item "return to prison."

In sum, our classification was made as follows: parolees for whom no disposition was recorded were placed in the *No Problems* category; those who received a minor disposition (Nos. 1 to 6) or a major disposition (Nos. 7 to 11) but were not returned to prison were placed in the *Minor Problems and Major Problems* categories, respectively; men returned to prison either to finish term or with a new commitment were placed in the *Return to Prison Category. No Problem* and *Minor Problem* subjects were regarded as "successes"; *Major Problem* cases and men *Returned to Prison* were considered "failures." Figure 1 diagrams this classification scheme.

We feel reasonably confident that our measure of parole outcome is a valid summary of the parolee's legal status with police and parole authorities at various times during his parole. There is very little chance that a return to prison would go unrecorded, since that determination is made by the Department of Corrections. There were 273 men who successfully completed their paroles in periods of less than 36 months after release and, hence, they were discharged from parole supervision. Our data reflects the best information available to the Criminal Investigation Division concerning any involvement with California law enforcement

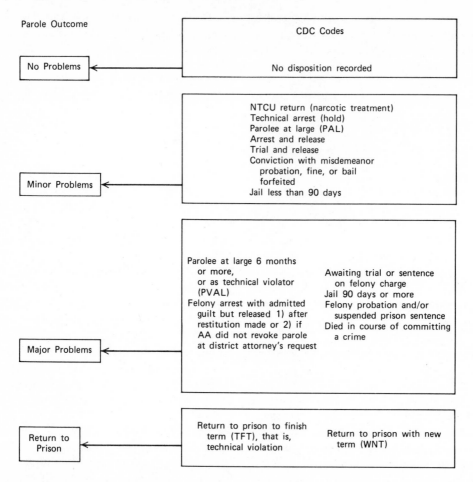

Figure 1.   Parole outcome classification, based on California Department of Corrections parole follow-up data.

agencies for these 273 men *subsequent* to their discharge, up to the 36-month cut off point for our sample. It was possible, therefore, to specify a 36-month outcome for every man in the sample regardless of whether he was in custody, still on parole, or discharged from parole.[11]

[11]The State Criminal Identification and Investigation Division notifies the FBI of California parolees who are "at large" and receives information from them as to arrests and dispositions, which have been reported to the FBI, of California parolees in other states. Hence, arrests made outside of California for parolees in our study are included in the determination of parole status.

Two points concerning our outcome categories must be kept in mind. First, discrimination between adjacent categories—minor, major, and return to prison—is difficult, since placement may be, in part, a vagary of time and thus not entirely a characteristic of the inmate's behavior. That is, minor arrests, in sufficient numbers, can lead to parole revocation, and major arrests often are the prelude to court conviction or parole revocation. During one in-

Data on *post-parole criminal behavior* that occurred *outside of California* may be lacking.

terval a parolee may be classified in the latest parole records as a major arrest, but his recommitment may be, in fact, already decided. If the return takes place after that interval, it will appear as a return to prison in the next interval; recommitments occurring more than 36 months after release were not reflected in our figures.

Second, the Research Division's method of recording parole status categorizes the parolee according to the most serious disposition that applies to him in the time period covered. In most cases this represents a realistic indication of his legal status, but for some men it undoubtedly masks improvement over time. For example, if a parolee was arrested on a drunk-and-disorderly charge in the first week of parole, but thereafter conducted his drinking with more prudence and discretion for thirty-five and three-quarter months, he would be carried in the *Minor Problems* category. The same outcome designation would apply to the man who after many arrest-free months was arrested several times on drunk-and-disorderly conduct charges. The difficulties and expense of creating a separate record-keeping operation of our own to get independent monthly or quarterly ratings for each parolee outweighed the advantage of such profiles; hence, we have used the CDC classification system. The best we have been able to do in taking the time factor into account in recording parole experience is to note the length of time served on parole prior to revocation. Since the status of each parolee is recorded during the first, second, and third years of release, it is possible to make comparisons between study subjects who were returned to prison soon after release and men who stayed on parole longer.

*

TREATMENT AND PAROLE PERFORMANCE

In this section we compare the treatment and control groups in terms of the problems each experienced on parole—problems including unemployment, financial dependence, alcohol and drug use, the number and seriousness of arrests, the length of confinement, and the type of parole offense—as well as parole outcome. These data are primarily based on analyses of parole file records representing a subsample ($N = 647$). The analyses of parole offenses and outcome make use of parole disposition data and thus involve the entire study sample.

Employment and Financial Dependence

Considering the subsample for whom parole agent reports were available, approximately one in five of the men in each treatment category was unemployed within one month of release; over one half were working in some unskilled or semiskilled job; and between 10 and 20 percent had skilled white collar jobs. By eight months, about one in four men from each treatment and control group was in jail or prison. Mandatory controls were the least likely to have been unemployed during the time period covered in the parole narrative. Men from mandatory large groups and voluntary controls had the highest proportions of subjects unemployed. Differences were not significant, however. Men changed jobs to some extent within eight months, but fewer than one third of each treatment category had had more than three; about the same proportion of each group had one job only (see Table I).

Again, based on subsample data, men from treatment groups were neither more nor less likely to have money available to them on release other than the funds provided by the Department of Corrections. They did not depend on others for financial support anymore than did the controls. Support tended to come from families instead of from official sources for about two thirds of the parolees considered "partially dependent"[12] (see Table II).

[12]Sources of support were familial rather than official for about two thirds of the "partially dependent" men. Financial independence was significantly related to 12-month outcome. Twice as many men receiving aid from nonfamilial (that is, official) sources as men considered self-reliant were

Table Ia. Employment at One Month and at Eight Months on Parole by Treatment Status (in Percent)

	One Month from Release[a]					Eight Months from Release[b]				
					Employment					
	Mandatory Controls	Voluntary Controls	Mandatory Large Group Counseling	Mandatory Small Group Counseling	Voluntary Small Group Counseling	Mandatory Controls	Voluntary Controls	Mandatory Large Group Counseling	Mandatory Small Group Counseling	Voluntary Small Group Counseling
Employed Unskilled, Semi-skilled	61	64	51	62	56	39	43	43	36	40
Skilled or White collar	18	10	21	14	21	18	9	14	15	16
Unemployed	18	19	25	19	20	22	24	7	24	18
In custody	3	7	5	5	3	21	24	36	25	26
Total	100	100	100	100	100	100	100	100	100	100
N	(150)	(131)	(44)	(114)	(170)	(130)	(120)	(28)	(97)	(141)

[a]Parole Subsample
  Table $N = 609$
  No information = 38
  $\chi^2 = 19.54$; df = 16
  Not significant

[b]Parole Subsample
  Table $N = 516$
  No information or not on parole eight months at the time the data was collected = 131
  $\chi^2 = 18.34$; df = 16
  Not significant

Table Ib. Employment History on Parole for Men from Each Treatment Category (in Percent)

Treatment Category	Parole Employment			
	Employed All of the Time Since Release	Employed Some of the Time	Unemployed All or Most of the Time	Total (N)
Mandatory controls	40	51	9	100 (151)
Voluntary controls	38	45	17	100 (127)
Mandatory large group counseling	46	34	20	100 (41)
Mandatory small group counseling	46	41	13	100 (112)
Voluntary small group counseling	44	44	12	100 (170)

Parole Subsample
Table N = 601
No information = 46
χ^2 = 8.64
Degrees of freedom = 8
Not significant

Table II. Financial Independence and Dependence on Parole as Proportion of Each Treatment Category (in Percent)

Treatment Category	Financial Experience		
	Self-Supporting	Dependent	Total (N)
Mandatory controls	66	34	100 (149)
Voluntary controls	59	41	100 (126)
Mandatory large group counseling	73	27	100 (44)
Mandatory small group counseling	65	35	100 (111)
Voluntary small group counseling	72	28	100 (169)

Parole Subsample
Table N = 599
No information = 49
χ^2 = 6.28
Degrees of freedom = 4
Not significant

Drugs and Alcohol

A history of the use of drugs or the excessive use of alcohol had several implications for post-release behavior.[13] As we have stated, a drug history that included the use of heroin required periodic nalline tests to prove nonuse; this had the effect of intensifying supervision. Rather than impose a special condition of abstinence for inmates who had had drinking problems (a condition whose violation could result in revocation), more commonly the agent was alerted that closer supervision might be required in these instances. Prison files revealed that about one out of three of our sample was classified as either a problem drinker or as an alcoholic, and a like proportion had a history of narcotics use. Parole subsample data indicates that the proportion was smaller than one in three: one in five had trouble associated with liquor; one in six had trouble associated with drugs.

Apparently, participation in group counseling did not reduce the likelihood of being cited for these problems. Differences between categories were not statistically significant (see Table III).

Arrests and Jail Confinement

There were also no treatment or control group differences on the number of misdemeanor or felony arrests recorded in the parole records, no differences in total number of weeks spent in jail, and no differences in the most serious disposition received within three years after release. Notice that although differences were not significant, mandatory controls were less frequently arrested, especially for felony offenses, and less often confined in jail than men from any treatment category.

Parole Outcome at 36 Months

The outcome index described earlier is a more systematic measure of parole outcome for the Men's Colony—East study sample. It distinguishes between men returned to prison, jailed for major trouble, jailed for minor trouble and, finally, those with no recorded arrests. The measure of outcome at 36 months for treatment and control groups are presented in Tables VI to IX. Data on the year of return to prison and on the seriousness of revocation also are given. All versions tell essentially the same story: *treatment and controls do not have significantly different outcomes.* That is, mandatory and voluntary control groups do about the same as their treatment counterparts. The exception was mandatory large group counseling that had the smallest proportion of no problem cases and the largest proportion of men returned to prison (15 percent and 59 percent, respectively).

This conclusion was unchanged when we used the dichotomy employed by the California Department of Corrections, in which success equals no dispositions and only arrests or jail terms of less than 90 days, and failure refers to jail terms exceeding 90 days, federal probation or return to prison. A one-way analysis of variance (also using a dichotomized outcome) shows nearly identical means for the five categories of treatment status. F ratio of between group variance versus within group variance is not significant. (Notice the homogeneity between categories.)

Tables IXa and IXb compare treatment status on expanded versions of the outcome variable. One version distinguishes between repeats of trouble occurring on parole or following discharge; the other version indicates when revocation occurred. First, regarding successful completion of parole, although differences were not significant, mandatory controls had the highest percentage of men discharged by the end of the three-year follow-up period; mandatory large group counseling had the lowest percentage. With the exception of this latter category, nearly 1 in 5 of the men in each of the other treatment categories had had no recorded arrests while on parole, had been discharged from parole supervision, and had had no subsequent contact with law enforcement agencies up to 36 months following their release from CMC—E.

Table IXa distinguishes between technical re-

---

returned to prison within 12 months (36 percent versus 18 percent). Twenty-six percent of the men aided by their families were returned to prison within a year. p < .01.

[13] A preprison history of excessive use of alcohol was not related to outcome at 24 months; preprison history of drug use was significant at the .001 level.

Table III. Problems on Parole with Alcohol or Drugs by Treatment Status (in Percent)

| Treatment Categories | Alcohol[a] | | | Drugs[b] | | |
	Percent Arrested on Parole for Drunkenness or Regarded as Problem Drinker	No Alcohol Problem	Total	Percent Known or Alleged to Use Drugs on Parole	No Drug Problem	Total
Mandatory controls (N = 163)	19	81	100	18	82	100
Voluntary controls (N = 138)	21	79	100	13	87	100
Mandatory large group counseling (N = 47)	17	83	100	17	83	100
Mandatory small group counseling (N = 120)	18	82	100	15	85	100
Voluntary small group counseling (N = 179)	20	80	100	18	82	100

[a]*Parole Subsample*
Table $N = 647$
$\chi^2 = .56$
Degrees of freedom = 4
Not significant

[b]*Parole Subsample*
Table $N = 647$
$\chi^2 = 2.09$
Degrees of freedom = 4
Not significant

vocations and those that reflect new convictions.[14] Mandatory large group counseling had a higher proportion of men convicted of new crimes than other groups, but the number of cases in this category is small. Revocations to finish term (technical violations) accounted for about two thirds of all returns within 36 months, and insofar as we could ascertain, once discharged from parole supervision, a man was rarely returned to prison during the follow-up period.

Table IXb considers only cases returned to prison. This analysis allows for the possibility that participation in group treatment might, at

[14]Theoretically, a return with a new term (WNT) refers to a more serious violation than recommitment to finish term (TFT), which implies unsatisfactory parole performance but "cooperation" with police and judicial agencies makes this distinction, in practice, an unreliable indicator of the severity of behavior leading to revocation.

least, have delayed revocation. But, again, treatment and control cases had about the same experiences. The bulk of returns to prison occurred early in the follow-up period regardless of treatment status: 29, 28, and 26 percent of the three forms of group counseling, and 26 and 31 percent of the two control groups were revoked during the first year.

Group Treatment and Parole Success: The Null Hypothesis Is Supported
Before proceeding further, the findings and analyses presented thus far should be summarized. The total sample of men released from prison during our study included some who were randomly assigned to living units where counseling was mandatory (one group was large, the others small) or to a quadrangle in which group counseling was not available (mandatory controls). The remainder of the sample

Table IV. Number of Misdemeanor and Felony Arrests by Treatment Status (in Percent)

Number of Arrests	Mandatory Controls	Voluntary Controls	Mandatory Large Group Counseling	Mandatory Small Group Counseling	Voluntary Small Group Counseling
Misdemeanors [a]					
None	62	57	60	62	62
One	28	28	26	22	27
Two or more	11	15	15	17	12
Total	100	100	100	100	100
N	(163)	(138)	(47)	(120)	(179)
Felony [b]					
None	81	72	79	75	77
One or more	19	28	21	25	24
Total	100	100	100	100	100
N	(163)	(138)	(47)	(120)	(179)

[a] *Parole Subsample*
Table $N = 647$
$\chi^2 = 4.63$
Degrees of freedom = 8
Not significant

[b] *Parole Subsample*
Table $N = 647$
$\chi^2 = 3.84$
Degrees of freedom = 4
Not significant

Table V. Time Spent in Jail During Parole Period by Treatment Status (in Percent)

Time Spent in Jail During Parole	Mandatory Controls	Voluntary Controls	Mandatory Large Group Counseling	Mandatory Small Group Counseling	Voluntary Small Group Counseling
Not confined	53	42	45	43	47
Confined					
less than 1 week	6	10	9	8	9
1 to 2 weeks	5	10	2	5	9
3 to 4 weeks	6	5	13	15	9
5 to 8 weeks	8	12	13	13	6
9 to 16 weeks	17	18	18	16	17
17 to 52 weeks	4	3	—	1	3
Total	100	100	100	100	100
N	(157)	(136)	(45)	(120)	(177)

Parole Subsample
Table $N = 635$
No information = 12
$\chi^2 = 28.28$
Degrees of freedom = 24
Not significant

Table VI. Most Serious Parole Disposition at Thirty-Six Months by Treatment Status[a] (in Percent)

Parole Disposition[b]	Mandatory Controls	Voluntary Controls	Mandatory Large Group Counseling	Mandatory Small Group Counseling	Voluntary Small Group Counseling
			Treatment Category		
Robbery	3	5	7	2	3
Burglary	6	7	10	5	6
Forgery	3	5	9	5	4
Theft	10	13	7	12	10
Assaultive and sex	4	4	2	3	2
Narcotic	5	5	9	5	6
Marijuana	2	4	2	4	3
Other felonies	11	7	12	5	9
Misdemeanor or technical	29	24	25	33	31
No disposition	27	26	17	26	25
Total	100	100	100	100	100
N	(270)	(175)	(69)	(173)	(276)

Table N = 963
No information = 5
χ^2 = 35.07
Degrees of freedom = 36
Not significant

[a]Unlike the regular outcome data, this source of disposition has not been updated to include actions taken against a man after discharge from parole, that is, completion of sentence.
[b]CDC classifications.

contained men who were assigned to living units in which group counseling was available but where the inmates had the option to join (voluntary small groups) or not to join (voluntary controls).

The comparison on a variety of preparole items indicated that no one treatment-control category was favored in terms of having attended preparole classes, whether release was as scheduled or whether employment had been arranged prior to release. Each of the five categories were equally likely to be comprised of men paroled with special conditions, and men with criminal records in the communities to which they were released. Each category contained, to about the same degree, the four inmate types. An analysis of variance established no significant difference in parole prognosis between treatment and control groups.

In addition to parole outcome at 36 months, experience of the study groups were compared for a subsample of parolees in terms of several additional indicators of problematic parole performance—unemployment, drug and alcohol use, jail terms, financial dependence, and the like. Although some small percentage differences were found (usually in favor of the voluntary control group), they were not of sufficient magnitude to allow us to reject the null hypothesis.

In short, parole performance, as measured by the specific criteria described above, was no different for the participants in group counseling than it was for nonparticipants. These findings were consistent at each follow-up interval. That is, there were no differences in parole outcome by treatment status measured at 6, 12, 24, and 36 months after release.

Table VII. Parole Outcome at Thirty-Six Months by Treatment Status (in Percent)

Parole Outcome at Thirty-Six Months	Mandatory Controls (N = 269)	Voluntary Controls (N = 173)	Mandatory Large Group Counseling (N = 68)	Mandatory Small Group Counseling (N = 171)	Voluntary Small Group Counseling (N = 274)	Total[a] (N = 955)
Dichotomized *						
Success	42	34	30	43	40	39
Failure	58	66	70	57	60	61
Total	100	100	100	100	100	100
Four-Way **						
No problems	24	23	15	22	21	22
Minor problems	18	11	15	21	19	17
Major problems	10	10	11	7	10	10
Return to prison	48	56	59	50	50	51
Total	100	100	100	100	100	100

*χ^2 = 6.62
Degrees of freedom = 4
Not significant

**χ^2 = 11.68
Degrees of freedom = 12
Not significant

[a]By 36 months, 8 men of the 968 were dead, and information was incomplete on 5 others.

Table VIII. Analysis of Variance of Parole Outcome and Treatment Status

	Mandatory Controls	Voluntary Controls	Mandatory Large Group Counseling	Mandatory Small Group Counseling	Voluntary Small Group Counseling
Number of cases	269	173	68	171	274
Means of outcome	1.41	1.33	1.29	1.42	1.40
Standard deviation	.49	.47	.46	.50	.49

	Sum Squares	Degrees of Freedom	Mean Squares	F Ratio
Between groups	1.53	4	.382	1.44
Within groups	225.79	950	.238	
Total	227.32	954		Not significant

Table IXa. Postrelease Status at Thirty-Six Months by Treatment Status (in Percent)

	Mandatory Controls	Voluntary Controls	Mandatory Large Group Counseling	Mandatory Small Group Counseling	Voluntary Small Group Counseling
Returned to Prison					
With new term	16	18	27	19	15
To finish term	31	37	29	31	35
After discharge from parole	1	1	3	—	—
Major Problems					
During parole	5	3	10	5	6
After discharge from parole	4	7	1	1	4
Minor Problems					
During parole	7	3	7	8	9
After discharge from parole	11	8	7	13	10
No Problems					
Still on parole	4	5	3	4	4
Discharged from parole	21	18	12	19	17
Total	100	100	100	100	100
N	(269)	(173)	(68)	(171)	(274)

Table N = 955
Dead = 8, incomplete information = 5
χ^2 = 36.19
Degrees of freedom = 32
Not significant

Table IXb. Revocations by Treatment Status: First, Second, and Third Year from Prison Release (in Percent)

Returned to Prison	Mandatory Controls	Voluntary Controls	Mandatory Large Group Counseling	Mandatory Small Group Counseling	Voluntary Small Group Counseling	Total
During first year	26	31	29	28	26	28
During second year	16	15	20	13	16	15
During third year	6	10	10	9	8	8
Total	48	56	59	50	50	51
N	(130)	(97)	(40)	(86)	(137)	(490)

^{2} = 3.78
Degrees of freedom = 8
Not significant

60. "Treatment" on Trial: The Case of Patuxent

LESLIE WILKINS

SINCE RECORDED HISTORY AND DOUBTLESS BE-
fore, various persons in authority have been
punishing other members of their societies for
varieties of acts. There has not, however, been
much consistency with regard to the definition
of the acts conceived to be punishable—or of the
punishments considered appropriate. From
time to time there has been some consideration
of utility in the kinds of punishments
awarded—slavery, galleys, work camps, and the
like. At times there was consideration of sym-
metry between offense and punishment—an eye
for an eye, bludgeoning of an architect if the
building he constructed collapses (Hammurabi's
Code), and so on. Punishment was frequently a
matter of public display, which doubtless contained an element of deterrence to others but
also provided a form of entertainment for the
masses or an elite. (Crime retains a large entertainment value today, although we do not provide many public spectacles. News reports of actual crimes, of police work to detect criminals, of
court proceedings, only add to fictional representations in the mass media to make up a
large portion of our entertainment fare.) In any
case, until recently there was relatively little regard paid to the probable effect of the punishment on the future life styles of the offenders.

The idea of using punishment as a way of reducing the probability of further crimes on the part
of the individual punished has gained its present prominence only in recent times. One expression of this idea is the widespread use of the
term "treatment" for what happens to prisoners,
carrying the suggestion that behavior control
techniques, usually conceived within a medical
or semi-medical framework, offer the proper
approach to dealing with criminal offenders.

Let us begin, therefore, with a consideration
of "treatment," the meaning of the term in the
context of criminal justice and the evidence for
its effectiveness. Within that context, we will
examine closely the claims made for one of the
most far-reaching examples of the clinical approach to treatment of offenders—the Patuxent
Institution for "defective delinquents" in Jessup,
Maryland. We will go on to examine some of the
moral implications of using a "medical model"
for the disposition of offenders, especially in the
light of our current rudimentary ability to identify potentially violent individuals. Finally, we
will consider some alternative ways of thinking
about and coping with violence in our society.

I. EFFECTIVENESS OF TREATMENT OF OFFENDERS

Within the last decade or so new questions have
come to be asked with regard to the ways in
which offenders are disposed of by the courts.
Among these new kinds of questions two dis-

▶SOURCE: *"Putting 'Treatment' on Trial"*, The Hastings Center
Report (February, 1975), No. 5: 35–36, 39–48. Copyright Institute
of Society, Ethics and the Life Sciences, 360 Broadway, Hastings-
on-Hudson, New York 10706. Reprinted by permission.

tinctly different classes of questions may be noted. One set of questions relates to the idea of "efficiency" (e.g. cost-effectiveness), while the other set is concerned with moral issues (e.g. equity and prisoners' rights).

There is, of course, no question of the effectiveness of one kind of punishment (and it cannot be called "treatment"), namely, the punishment of death. Certainly, no recidivism rate can be quoted, and the cost, or at least the money cost, of putting the punishment into effect is not large. But it is self-evident that this assessment of efficiency leaves much to be desired in terms of the contemporary concerns of society. Even the question of "efficiency" quickly begins to break down into a series of other questions, in which elements of moral values are intermingled. For example, since the death penalty is completely effective in preventing recidivism, the emphasis turns, in this case, to the issue of general deterrence. We ask whether the fact of the death penalty reduces the probability that others will commit a capital crime in the first instance. That is a question of efficiency, but one involving the assumption that deciding the fate of one man on the basis of predicted behavior by *others* is morally justified.

At least for purposes of analysis, then, we can discriminate three classes of issues—the effectiveness/efficiency questions in direct terms; the simple, direct moral/value issues; and issues which concern both morality and efficiency. In the main our discussion will be concerned with the last-mentioned category because in all practical operations of the criminal justice machinery it is not possible to separate considerations of efficiency from considerations of moral constraints. Despite this real life interaction, it is sometimes important to think about these categories as though they were separate. For example, it is important to question whether a treatment which can be described as "efficient" or "effective" is, by that token alone, also morally acceptable. If the answer is no, then it is necessary to examine the nature of

the constraints imposed on moral grounds. Can any of the aspects of this conflict be resolved by a redefinition of "efficiency," or is it necessary to see the moral considerations as orthogonal to those of efficiency? If the latter is the case, perhaps the resolution of some questions may be approached by stating them in the form of "trade-off" problems.

Questions with regard to the "effectiveness" of the "treatment" of offenders are not only difficult questions, they are non-specific questions and as such cannot be answered in specific terms. Not only are "treatment" and efficacy multi-dimensional concepts, but the moral referent can differ with regard to the dimensions which may be selected for discussion, e.g., a "treatment" of doubtful "efficacy" may be morally acceptable if it is assessed to be pleasant or unintrusive. We will turn to some of the more direct issues first and examine some practical cases.

Implications of the Idea of Treatment

The term "treatment of offenders" is often taken to be no more than a euphemism for the "punishment of offenders." The term "treatment" can mean no more than "what is done" to the person—he may be "treated" badly or well; he may be treated kindly or unkindly: indeed we even use the term in the phrase "treated to a drink"! The use of the word "treatment" in the field of criminal justice is often as varied as are its many uses among laymen. Nonetheless, underlying the loose use of this term is some strong suggestion of a clinical medical analogy. Offenders are seen as having much in common with sick persons; hence, if they can be made well, they will be "rehabilitated" and will fit in with society. The use of a clinical medical analogy in relation to the "treatment" of offenders has many ramifications. We may note particularly that the relationship between considerations of efficiency and morals as criteria for action vary, and they vary according to the nature of the model we use for our description and analysis.

There may also be variations within any model which utilizes probability assessments.

What Is "Treatment"?

In most prisons, and especially in the institutions for "defective delinquents" (such as Patuxent), the language of the medical analogy goes so far that, at least *in the terminology*, it is hardly possible to disguish the institution from a hospital. The appearance of the buildings is usually very different from that of hospitals, but the "warden" is called a "medical superintendent" and often addressed, by staff and inmates ("patients"), as "doctor." If, then, in considering what these institutions do, we use a quite strict analogy with medical practice, this could hardly be thought unfair. It is not our analogy: it is theirs.

How then is it possible to distinguish punishment from "treatment"?

A person from another environment than ours, observing for the first time many procedures which are clearly accepted as normal "treatment" of patients in a conventional hospital, might be confused. Needles are being stuck into people. When a substance is given by mouth, there is often a response which he would associate with unpleasantness. In another part of the establishment, people are being cut up in various ways. There is plenty of blood shed. Previously he might have observed (in some obviously remote part of our world) similar things being done, which he correctly interpreted as torture to extract information from captured soldiers. He might ask how he should distinguish "treatment" from torture, since to his eyes many of the actions and reactions are similar in both cases. He might be told that he should not consider the superficial acts as he sees them but rather consider the consequences for the patient. He must refer to both theoretical knowledge and to past experience with the procedures being used. More specifically he may be given an explanation in terms of the intent of the action; if he wished to know whether what he observed was "treatment" or "punishment," he should ask those doing it what are their intentions. If he was told that what was done was for the benefit of the patient, then he should conclude that it was "treatment," or so it might be argued.

But is the intent of the actor an adequate basis for determining the classification of the act and hence for the kind of model we select? I do not think so. It seems necessary to add some element of prognosis before we may call any set of operations a "treatment." Until it can be established that the operations concerned have the probable consequence of reducing the probability of death or increasing the well-being of the patient, it would seem inappropriate to call them "treatments." Moreover, there should be more than a *belief* on the part of the actors that the actions will decrease the probability of death or increase well-being; there should be some form of evidence. If the treatment is new, it should be built upon theoretical constructs and trials with animals. The *probability* of pay-off (decreased risk of death or increased welfare); the *probability* of failure (regret value) and other considerations are relevant to the moral issues.

If we wish to use the medical analogue in relation to the treatment of offenders, it would seem only reasonable that we should use the same definition of treatment as would suffice in the medical field. We would, then, require that there be *some evidence* that the outcome of whatever was done to the offender was a change in the probabilities of his future behavior, a change which is seen as beneficial to the individual and society. Rising from this definition of treatment is the suggestion that an essential element involves the *assessment of probability*. Treatment is forward-looking, punishment looks backwards; treatment is not concerned with what the individual did, but rather with what he may be expected to do; for the treatment perspective, the past is to be used only as a guide to estimation of the future.

In the treatment of offenders this may sound attractive, but there is a price to be paid; the price is equity. What the individual did—the seriousness of his crime—is not significant for treatment determinations such as the length of time in custody; the person is to be held until he is "cured." The events in the past record of the offender are not seen as "events" but rather as symptoms of a "state"; and in some cases as representing a "state of dangerousness."

Events and States

Clearly it is not possible to provide *treatment* for events, particularly when these have passed. If an offender is to be "treated" he must be seen as having a *present condition* (i.e. "state") which exists during the period of his treatment. When the condition has passed, there is no need for further "treatment." When does a person who has stolen cease to be in the "state" of being a "thief"? If we assume a state (being a thief), we must make some determination as to when the "state" has ceased to exist. We may, of course, assume that it lasts for life. If we make the latter assumption, there would seem to be no point in attempting treatment (the "state" remains no matter what we do), nor any criterion whereby we could assess whether any action might be termed "treatment." If we cannot determine when the "state" has changed, and even make some measurements of that change—whether towards recovery or relapse—then again there is no rational basis for the use of any medical analogy.

There is a further difficulty. The phenomenon of spontaneous remission is well-known in the medical field, and before we can accept a treatment as being effective, it is necessary to show that it has benefits which *exceed* the spontaneous remission rate. Thieves and other offenders may cease offending—there may be a spontaneous remission rate—but we will never know about it because as soon as a person is found guilty of a crime something is done about it. The results of any penal treatment may be of less value than the spontaneous remission rate for similar offenders who might go "untreated." Some treatments or the essential concomitants of the treatments may encourage crime or recidivism. Perhaps the best we can do is the least

that social pressures will let us get away with doing to the offender. As we will note later, this does not mean condoning crime, and it does not assert that *punishment* is irrelevant. As for treatment, however, there is no way of knowing whether any penal measures could ever qualify as "treatment" in terms of the strict medical analogy. At some future date it may be possible to carry out experiments to determine whether no action is better or worse than some action with regard to certain kinds of crime and certain kinds of offenders. In the interval we can refer only to the results of studies which have attempted to correct for (i.e. "partial out") factors which obscure the associations between variables so as to assess the differential impact of different kinds of dispositions of offenders.

Very few such studies have made claims to identify any differences in outcome related either to the duration or type of treatment/punishment given. Those carried out by persons not involved with the treatment programs have normally shown no association between outcomes and kinds of treatments, although there has been a tendency to note somewhat better results for those treatments which are, from the perspective of the offender, the least intrusive. In other words:

1.   The less that has been done to reform the offender, the better the outcome has tended to be!

2.   Where studies have been carried out by persons involved in a specific treatment program, there have been more claims to effectiveness and better outcomes than for other kinds of treatments. However, one study obtained blind rating of the rigor of the experiments or research designs and then correlated these with claims to success; not unexpectedly, the result was a strong negative correlation between rigor and claims of positive results.

It seems safe to conclude that it is extremely doubtful whether any variants of present methods of treatment/punishment of offenders make any difference to the reconviction rate. In other words, there is no demonstration that a "treatment" exists among all the techniques currently known and applied by correctional or probation agencies. It seems clear that the clinical medical model is inadequate and inaccurate as a basis for any theory or practice of the treatment of offenders on two different counts. First, it is not possible to treat either a "probability" or a past event; hence a postulated present state (which can be treated) must be described before the idea of treatment or diagnosis can hold. Such descriptions are not generally forthcoming in respect of cases where we use the criminal justice procedures. Indeed it would seem that when such a state can be adequately described, the individual is not appropriately considered within the ambit of the criminal justice process. Secondly, there has been no demonstration that any activity which has been termed "treatment" possesses the necessary characteristics to justify the use of that term. Treatment, to be "treatment" in clinical practice must be shown to be advantageous to the treated person by means of its impact upon the dysfunction which is "treated." Among the many different forms of "treatment" (institutional and community-based) there is no evidence of any differential reduction in the probability of the commission of further crime in respect of persons of the same initial risk ategory. Indeed, there is no evidence as to whether the initial probability is decreased or increased by what is done, although there are strident claims in either direction.

II. THE CASE OF PATUXENT

At this point, however, we should backtrack just a bit. One reaction to evidence that "treatment" has not yet been proven to have its intended effect, is to maintain that genuine "treatment" has not been tried; what is needed, in other words, is more, not less. Indeed this is the implicit claim of one effort which has not been included in the studies cited so far. Patuxent

Institution in Jessup, Maryland, a penal institution operating since 1955, is a thorough-going application of the medical-model treatment approach. It combines the functions of a mental hospital and a prison. Its inmates, called "patients," are "committed" for an indeterminate period—that is, until they get "well." Its director is a psychiatrist, its staff includes numerous psychiatrists, psychologists, and psychiatric social workers. It is organized on a graded-tier system meant to reward socially acceptable behavior and penalize the unacceptable; extensive efforts at diagnosis and group therapy are carried out. Release is by stages and, except when courts so order against staff recommendations, it depends on the vote of the Institution's Board of Review.

Patuxent Institution seems to recognize "efficiency" as at least a minimal criterion of its performance: necessary if not sufficient. Everyone agrees that the Institution is expensive to run. Everyone also agrees that inmates are often detained longer than would be the case if they had gone to prison and had served the full length of their sentence. Since Patuxent's procedures and expense are justified in terms of the protection of society and the reform of the offender, there should be some evidence that these ends are, in fact, attained.

Society is provided with some "protection" if the offender is "reformed," such that when he is released, he represents a much reduced or zero risk. Clearly, if society is separated from an offender, a claim to "protection" is justified only if the offender represents some real *risk*. But the *labelling* of the isolated person as a "dangerous offender" does not, of itself, justify the claim to be providing society with protection.

Patuxent claims to provide protection in two ways: (a) the offender is detained while he is dangerous, and (b) when released he is no longer dangerous. As we will discuss in more detail, there are severe problems in estimating the probability of an offender committing another crime, whether trivial or "dangerous." At present, simply recall that while a person remains in Patuxent, he cannot commit crimes against free civilians other than those who work in proximity to him. We may *believe* that while he is in such safe custody he remains dangerous, but unless there is *some* opportunity for at least *some* incarcerated offenders to commit *some* crimes, we shall not know whether it was the lack of opportunity or the lack of tendency which was responsible for the "success."

Measuring Success

It is necessary, therefore, to seek estimates of the probabilities of further crimes and to assess the success or failure of the treatment by examining information relating to those persons who have, for whatever reason, left the close custody of the Institution. There may, of course, be cases where it is believed that the offender could never be released. As the Patuxent's 1973 *Progress Report* states (quoting Maryland Defective Delinquent Statute, under which Patuxent was established), "The treatment may, and in many cases would, involve incarceration for life . . . not because of guilt, but to protect the defective from himself and society." Indeed another quotation makes this more specific. "The *primary* purpose" the *Report* quotes, adding the emphasis, "of such legislation is to protect society from this segment of the criminal population who probably will again commit crimes if released on the expiration of a fixed sentence. . . ."[1]

Ordinary prisons, it seems to be argued in these and like statements, are in a less privileged position than institutions like Patuxent since they have less discretion and must release at a time determined by others and not when those concerned with the treatment of the offenders believe him to be "cured." We may take "cured" to mean that the *probability* of a further offense being committed by the person after release, is minimal. It is, of course, not clear what actual probability (in numerical terms) would meet the criterion of "minimal," but it is important that the test is recognized to be one of *relative* (rather than absolute) *probabilities*.

It might be expected that the probability of further convictions (i.e. recidivism) in respect of persons released from institutions such as Patuxent should be somewhat lower than that of other institutions such as prisons. The former class of institution can detain those cases which they regard as representing "a risk" without reference to the length of time served or the sentence of the court or the nature of the committal offense. If, in fact, the institutions like Patuxent are successful in their mission, they should show extremely low recidivism rates. The "failure" in such situations is not the "failure" (reconviction) of the offender, but the failure of the institution to identify the kinds of cases in which they claim expertise. Indeed, the rationale for the establishment of such institutions as Patuxent is that the staff *will* be able to recognize potentially dangerous offenders and to hold them until they are safe to be released. If no such special skill is demonstrated by the staff, then the institutions are, by that single, simple fact, shown to be ineffective.

Patuxent holds a privileged position, in that it may determine which of its cases would represent a risk if released, and may detain them until it judges the risk minimized. The justification for that special status of Patuxent (and other institutions like it) is that it can perform a special function—yield a lower recidivism rate, a less delinquent population. For Patuxent merely to show results neither worse nor better than other institutions—for instance, than ordinary prisons without those special discretionary powers—would be to destroy its philosophical foundations. It would also raise a moral difficulty; for it is by right of those special skills and functions that discretionary powers are granted which touch on inmates' equity.

According to its *Report*, Patuxent is far more successful with those cases it releases than are other institutions, but the direct comparison is not valid. It is necessary to attempt to sort out from the figures given in the Patuxent *Report* a category of cases compared to which a similar group of offenders can be identified who were dealt with in a different manner. Further, as we shall see, categories of time for confinement and for limited release (parole, out-patient treatment, and so on) are not similar. By such criteria of comparison, Patuxent's recidivism rate does not differ substantially from that of other kinds of detention facilities.

The Patuxent "Recidivism Rate"

The report notes that "the most frequently quoted [recidivism rate] for adult offenders" is 65 percent.* The reader is invited to compare this rate with that of Patuxent, namely, 7 percent.

Before we may assess the significance of the quoted 7 percent recidivism rate or the later breakdown of this rate into figures for the 1955–1959 cohort of offenders (13 percent) and for the 1960–1964 cohort (3 percent), we must note especially that this group is described as being "released at the recommendation of staff and Institutional Board of Review, with in-house and continued treatment for three years on parole," and that they were then not reconvicted within three years. (This applies only to the cohort data—the other figures seem to relate to varying and unspecified periods of follow-up.) The total number of cases in this category was 145 (both cohorts), of whom ten were shown in the "committed new offenses" category. The exact definition of this "failure" category is not clear, but it seems to relate to the commission of another offense followed by a "conviction." While the conviction rate may be a reasonable measure for most kinds of cases, it leaves in doubt a number of possible categories of disposition of persons who had previously been detained in an institution for defectives. However, it is not necessary to press this point since, despite first impressions to the contrary, it will be seen that the "failure" rate of one in fourteen quoted (ten out of 145) for the cohort data is approximately that which may be expected of a

*This is not an unreasonable claim; without precise definition it is not possible to dispute it.

similar group where the base "failure" rate was 65 percent—if we accept the claim that this is a fair comparison. Some proofs of this will be attempted in a moment.

Recidivism Rates

Meanwhile, we ought to examine certain general qualities of "recidivism rates." First, it has been a universal finding in all countries of the Western world as well as within the United States, that violent offenders as a total class reveal a lower recidivism rate than do other offenders. On this ground alone, it might be expected that Patuxent, specializing in violent offenders, would show a somewhat lower recidivism rate, and that the base comparison should be less than the 65 percent suggested. Perhaps a more reasonable comparison is that given in Tables IV and V of Patuxent's *Report*, where it is stated that 47 percent and 42 percent recidivism was experienced for the 1955–1959 and the 1960–1964 cohorts respectively where the offenders "were released at rehearing against staff advice, in-house treatment only."

Second, a striking general characteristic of recidivism rates is their tendency to peak abruptly and then to decline rapidly after the release of the offender. (See Chart 1.) The most probable time for an offender to be reconvicted is about three months after his release from an institution. The rate of reconviction (recidivism) has not, with any degree of consistency, been shown to be influenced by supervision while on parole after release. Follow-up studies and experimental designs have, in general, concluded that there was no significant difference between "spontaneous recovery" and "treatment" effects due to aftercare of supervision.[2] These negative results are supported also by data of a very different kind. Mathematical curves fitted to the trend in reconviction rates do not show any "kink" at the point when the offenders are released from supervision but rather a smooth function with time from release.* Rates of re-

*Recidivism rates are often quoted on a fixed base (i.e., the

Chart 1.   Survivor based reconviction — a typical curve
showing—rates of reconviction by months to risk.
(Based on Borstal Training data base rate = 55% failure.)

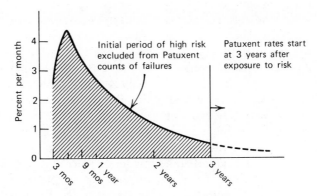

conviction can be compared only when the base is known and where the time of exposure to risk is comparable, both in respect of duration and in terms of time from release; that is to say, *high risk periods may not be included in one set of figures and excluded from the other.*

The criterion, therefore, to which we must refer for purposes of comparison with the Patuxent recidivism rate is that which applies at three years after release, where the treatment given has been that of a prison or similar establishment lacking the special privileged position of Patuxent. It would be necessary to show that the generally expected rate of recidivism at three years (and for a similar period of follow-up to that given to the Patuxent cases) was greater than that of Patuxent in order to justify any belief that there was any superiority in the latter's method of treatment.*

number released or treated). It must, however, be remembered that as offenders who make up the initial released cohort begin to "fail," the sample of those *remaining at risk* is diminished accordingly. Thus, in the form often quoted, say 1000 are released and 500 fail in the first year (*50 percent failure rate*) and 250 fail in the next year (*25 percent of sample*) and 125 fail in the second year (*12.5 percent of sample*) the rate of conviction is apparently diminishing. It is, of course, constant at 50 percent throughout the period, 500 out of 1000 = 50 percent: 250 out of 500 = 50 percent and 125 out of 250 = 50 percent.

*It is unfortunate that there are very small numbers of

It is difficult to find any adequate test of the "success rate" for Patuxent because the time of "exposure to risk" which is used as the basis for the recidivism rate of the fully "treated" case is not available from data from other institutions. However, we might obtain some indication of the possible comparative success rates for treatment forms which vary from that of Patuxent if we could either (a) find a very similar treatment, but one for which the indeterminacy which characterizes this case did not apply and data were available in a similar form, or (b) identify a general "law" relating to the regularity with which reconvictions take place with time, that is, after discharge from institutions and after it becomes possible for ex-inmates to offend again in the community, whether or not they are under supervision. It is possible to carry out some analyses along the lines of both of these procedures. Let us consider the latter, the general case, first.

Patterns of Reconviction

As already mentioned, all studies which have followed up offenders after release, no matter from what kind of institution and irrespective of

cases in the category for which Patuxent provides cohort data, and that the proportion of "failures" is quite different in the two periods: 12 percent and 3 percent respectively (n = 8 and n = 2), giving the mean of about 7 percent.

the form of supervision or surveillance in the community, consistently report one general result. The probability of the ex-inmate to be reconvicted for another crime quickly reaches a peak, and then falls rapidly. By the end of the third year during which the offender/patient has had any opportunity to commit another crime, often about 80 percent of those who will ever do so will already have been reconvicted. Gottfredson reports an eight year follow-up of 1,810 California parolees. Of 729 failures, only 119 were noted in the second half of the period of follow-up.[3] In England, Hammond studied a very different sample of offenders, namely those committed to "preventive detention" (i.e. very serious cases where an additional penalty was imposed beyond that which the instant offense might attract—somewhat similar in this regard to Patuxent committals). A general failure rate over a period of three years of between 60–70 percent was noted, but with these groups the percentages of all failures which occurred in the third year varied from 8.6 percent as the highest to 6.5 percent as the lowest observed ratio. In each case the rate in the third year was considerably less than half of the rate for the preceeding year, which in turn was about half of that for the year before.[4] The *log-linear* time base was noted also for the California data by Gottfredson. General belief (and much data) hold that younger offenders are worse risks. It is interesting then to note some results with offenders in the age range 17–21 (males). Data are available in respect of youths given borstal training in England and Wales. Of a total of 362 "failures" in a follow-up of three and one-half years, only 47 cases occurred *after the end* of the second year.[5] Again a log-linear time base fitting was noted. Thus, it is clear that the success rate for those Patuxent offenders who were "released at recommendation of staff and Institutional Board of Review, in-house and continued treatment for *three years on parole*" (emphasis added), cannot be compared with those other offenders who became at risk to further crime and classification as "failures" immediately upon release. The "recommended" group had had

three years "trial" under supervision and presumably could be recalled if they did not seem to be likely to avoid further convictions. The relevant rate with which to compare the Patuxent "success" rate would be Hammond's fourth, fifth, and sixth year from release: thus a figure in the range of 8–11 percent might be expected. This is remarkably close to the figure given in the Patuxent case. This is not an unexpected result; it fits the general nature of follow-up study results to date in all countries of the Western world. However, it is not a strong piece of evidence since it relies upon different kinds of offenders in a different country.

The most that can be done with the data provided by Patuxent Institution in terms of general mathematical curve fitting is to show that the claims to success are exaggerated; indeed, it is possible and even probable that the Patuxent success rate does not exceed those for comparable groups who have served time in ordinary prisons or jails under determinate sentences or who were subject to normal parole procedures.

A Similar Treatment

Reference has already been made to borstal training in England and Wales. This treatment is one which approximates to many of the elements of the treatment at Patuxent—and thus provides a basis for our other line of analysis—but it is also one which has some interesting differences. A young offender (17–21 years) may be sentenced to borstal training for three years. Training consists of from six to twenty-four months (minimum and maximum) in an institution; the remaining period, up to three years, is spent on "after-care." At the end of three years, the ex-inmate is discharged. (Violent offenders are, however, seldom or never sentenced to borstal training.) The conviction record of borstal inmates tends to be heavy (4.3 average convictions) and is somewhat similar to that of the inmates at Patuxent. The borstal data provide some indication of the order of magnitude of the expected Patuxent recidivism rates, but little more. The published data do not provide a similar period of time at risk; however, it may be noted that the failure rate was 12 percent where borstal training had been continued in the community for two years (the corresponding period at Patuxent is three years). However, among the differences (in addition to the fact that the data refer to a different country), are some which would lead us to expect a higher figure, and others a lower figure. Tending to make the borstal rate *high* for comparative purposes we may note: (a) the inmates were younger males; (b) they were not violent or sex offenders; (c) the rate relates to *two years* treatment after discharge from the institution and not three. On the other hand, tending to make the borstal rate *low* for comparative purposes, (d) the period of follow-up was shorter. All things considered, it seems fair to suggest that the borstal training "treatment" has similarities to that of Patuxent and that the 12 percent borstal rate provides some estimate of the order of magnitude of the expected recidivism rate for Patuxent Institution.

It is also possible to reanalyze Gottfredson's data on California parolees in terms of "survival rates" and again to compare the results with a similar time of "exposure to risk." It seems that a three-year exposure to risk after three years on parole, for California parolees, gives a "failure" rate of almost 20 percent, but this includes "technical violations." The reconviction rate (that is, excluding technical violations) might be as high as 17 percent in the same period. But it should be noted that by the end of the sixth year only about a third of the original sample had a "clear" record. By the end of the follow-up of eight years, only 29.7 percent were without a record of violation of some kind. This is a failure rate of 70 percent; a figure considerably higher than the 47 or 42 percent which represent the "released at rehearing" for the Patuxent cohort, and higher also than the 65 percent suggested as comparable in the Patuxent report.

Patuxent "Success"—Conclusion

No manipulation of figures can provide a sound basis for assessing the success of the treatment of Patuxent Institution. The figures given in the Institution's report are not comparable. Comparisons are possible only where the offenders/patients have been "exposed to" comparable risks for comparable times. Sundry data have been examined and it can be firmly stated that Patuxent Institution is not as successful as it claims, nor are other penal institutions by comparison as bad as the Institution's report suggests. In the absence of any data to the contrary, and with many indications in favor of the hypothesis, we may assume that there is no difference in the outcome of cases "treated" by the Patuxent method from those of any other currently available treatment in the penologists' repertoire. (See Table I for summary of data.)

Thus, with the possible exception of a very small percentage of those presently processed through the criminal justice system, the term "treatment" should be dropped as a dishonest description of what is done to offenders. We should use words which honestly describe the several activities occurring. For example, the public is *protected* when offenders are isolated; we should acknowledge that and assess its value. Offenders are *punished* for their crimes; we should use this word with care and note the use of this concept in the disposition of offenders by the courts and throughout the criminal justice processes.

III. MODELS AND MORAL CONSIDERATIONS

I once asked a judge whether he had ever made any errors in his disposition of offenders. His reply was interesting. No, he said, every decision he had made was quite correct at the time he made it! Most people would admit, however, that they do make errors in their decisions and that what happens afterwards indicates this. They might claim that at the time they did their best, but they would not claim that this was sufficient as a criterion of correctness.

It is in regard to consideration of possible errors that moral issues become most clearly evident. It is extremely important to note that the clinical medical model for the disposition and

Table I. Summary of Estimates of Recidivism Rates

	General Recidivism Rate (for three years dating from release from the institution).	Recidivism rate estimated to apply to the sample noted in column 1 but where the rate is that which applies after three years on parole.
Patuxent "approved" releases (given full treatment)	Not estimated or revealed in Report	12% for one cohort 3% for a second cohort 7% average
Patuxent releases without (complete?) treatment	42-47%	None given
Borstal training group	55%	About 12%
Group studied by Hammond and Chayen	60-70%	About 12%
California group studied by Gottfredson	70%	Less than 20%

This tabulation is meant to facilitate an appreciation of the various calculations and estimates. No strictly comparable rates are available, however.

treatment of offenders raises quite different questions in relation to possible errors from those raised by the "equity" model, because the nature of the errors in the decisions are of a different order. If we are concerned with *past events* and neither make any projections as to the future nor infer *present states*, then what is known is fairly surely known; the moral decisions relate in this case only to considerations of the *past*. The past cannot, by definition, be changed, although it may be perceived differently at different times. Present moral standards are brought face to face with the perception of the past *event(s)* and a decision is made accordingly. At a future time a different decision might be reached on moral grounds because the event(s) were seen as implying different moral significance, but in each case the questions are, as it were, two-dimensional—the moral standard and the event(s) as ascertained. There is neither consideration of probability nor other matters of inference in this kind of determination.

The clinical medical analogue (treatment of offenders) presents a very different structure for the moral determinations. In the "treatment" model the *past event(s)* are not directly considered since they cannot be "treated," rather the past is used to make inferences about either a present state or probable future outcomes which might be *changed* by our actions; that is to say, might be *"treated."* The nature of the "treatment" is determined with regard to the inferences about a state or about a probability (prognosis) and not solely in terms of the past. The intervention of the procedures of inference with regard to the future make a considerable difference in the ways in which we must consider the moral questions. Involved are issues of technology (efficacy of treatment) and logical sophistication (inference) as well as ethics. Of course, incorrect decisions may be made with either the clinical model or the equity (past events) model; but, the nature of the incorrectness, it must be stressed, is not the same. If we consider only past events, then clearly our action

has to be justified in terms of those events. This is not a very technical matter and depends far less upon our state of knowledge than upon our beliefs about what is a suitable punishment or our other reactions to the past.

The past events model may not be a simple one involving wholly, or mainly, issues of equity. It is possible to add some considerations of general deterrence ("example," or learning model). The offender may be dealt with (not "treated") fairly in relation to what he did (not with regard to what he might do), but the justification is then made in terms of the impact of the action upon others. Society learns what is just by observing what is done to those who depart from the moral or social requirements of their society. Essentially the general deterrence model is similar to the equity model in that the offender's past provides the informational base for the moral decision.

General deterrence must be distinguished from special deterrence—the term by which is expressed the belief that what is done to the offender will modify *his* behavior in the future. This model invokes not so much a clinical medical analogy as a teaching analogy. There is, of course, little difference between this model and the "treatment" model; indeed conditioning is often one of the techniques of choice for those who advocate a medical model for treatment of offenders. The one is a more sophisticated form of the other, and the nature of the justification must be similar, since both refer to the *future*.

Under conditions of a "treatment" model there are two ways in which any decision may be incorrect. Our prognosis may be that the offender will "succeed" (or "learn"), and he does not do so, or alternatively we may predict failure in cases where the individual will succeed. These errors are known, reasonably enough, as "errors of the first and second kind." We may reject a hypothesis when it is true, and we may accept it when it is false: these two kinds of error may have quite different consequences. Indeed in matters of industrial quality control one is the "producer risk" and the other the "consume risk." It may be remarked in passing that there are producers and consumers of the products of criminal justice machinery!

There is no treatment for offenders which has a *certainty* of success: not even the claims of Patuxent Institution go that far. There is no *certain* way in which potentially dangerous offenders or potential recidivists can be identified. Since we cannot claim certainty in respect of either case there will be errors in the dispositions we may make. There is, then, the question of how large these errors may be expected to be. If the errors of either kind are small and the consequences of an incorrect decision for the persons involved are also small, we may assess the "trade-off" in these terms—where by "trade-off" is meant the balance of the two kinds of error affecting the risk to society and the risk of dealing inappropriately with the suspected persons.

A recent study provides some measure of the power of presently available techniques for identification of "potentially violent persons." Wenk and Emrich carried out exhaustive research utilizing many psychological tests and case data and subjecting their data to very complex analysis. They showed that when 50 percent of the potentially violent persons were successfully identified by their tests, they also identified nine persons incorrectly for every one correctly classified.[6] The 9:1 ratio is known as the "false positive" rate, since these persons (i.e. false positives) reveal the same profiles as those who are subsequently found guilty of violent offenses. If more than 50 percent of the potential violent population is to be isolated, then the false positive rate will increase sharply, and conversely, if we reduce the false positive rate, the proportion of the population correctly identified drops sharply.

The moral question now can be stated in terms of the "trade-off" thus: Is it reasonable to classify falsely as "potentially violent offenders" nine persons in order correctly to treat one, where such a procedure would still involve in treatment only half of those "needing" such treatment? If we cannot accept a 9:1 ratio at the 50 percent cutoff point, then what ratio might we find morally acceptable? If not 9:1, then what of 5:1? Even if the latter ratio is acceptable, it is unlikely to be possible to achieve this degree of power without very costly research and after some few years of work. Clearly the false positive ratio is not the only moral consideration. Much may depend upon how expensive or intrusive is the treatment proposed, and we would do well to assess and consider the efficiency of such treatment. In this regard there is one further difficulty. If we have to subject to treatment nine false positives for every one "true" positive since these cannot be distinguished from each other (by definition), then this fact will need to be considered in our evaluation of the treatments. If we select from a given population those persons who are "violence prone" according to the best predictive information, then 90 percent will *not* recidivate to violent crime—these are the "false positives" again! On the assumption that treatment did no harm in terms of increasing the probability of violent crime,* any treatment with a 90 percent success rate seems an attractive proposition; and of course, better success rates might be obtained with an even higher proportion of false positives! And again, persons incarcerated for violent crimes may be reconvicted, but not necessarily for another violent crime; indeed the repetition of violent crimes is a rare event.

IV. A MODIFIED IDENTIFICATION AND PREVENTIVE MODEL

Whether we concern ourselves with the concept of treatment or of reform, of preventive detention for the protection of society, or indeed with any concept of a procedure which deals with the projection of future behaviors, we are involved

---

*It must be stressed, the prediction tables which give the 50 percent cutoff point at a cost of 9:1 false positives *included* the fact that some among the sample of offenders had already committed a violent crime—indeed this was the most predictive item of evidence relating to further such crime.

in questions of moral trade-off assessments. We can assure ourselves of absolute protection from future criminal or socially dysfunctional acts only by incarcerating *all* persons, since there is some small risk that *any* person may engage in such behavior: there is nobody for whom the probability of committing a crime (or another crime) is absolutely zero. As soon as we invoke the idea of future acts, or as soon as we make inferences about a "state of mind" (whatever we may mean by "mind"), dispositions, or physical conditions, we must attend to the problems of decision errors of two kinds and with the consequent false positives which will result from any action.* The balance between errors of the first and second kind is recognized in legal philosophy with respect to the finding of guilt, where it is acknowledged that some guilty persons may go free because of the safeguards against conviction of the innocent. The balance of error is not seen as equal, and indeed in this particular case, moral issues are debated in probabilistic terms. But we are not now concerned with the finding of guilt but with dispositions of the convicted. In the disposition of offenders we are faced with two alternative structures: (a) we may deal with the person in terms of what he has done—the past events which we have designated criminal and the restricted factors surrounding those behaviors, or (b) we must reckon with the moral trade-offs implicit in making any predictions with regard to future behaviors. The past is known more certainly and in a different form and quality from the future. Furthermore, the techniques for reducing our uncertainties about the past are substantially

*A critical problem is that of inference with regard to states or conditions—concepts central to the treatment approach. We can presume to treat a condition or state but it is not possible to treat a probability! The soundness of any inference which may be made with respect to any kind of state (e.g. state of dangerousness, state of mind, physical condition) must depend upon factors other than that of the crime (event) itself, since no crime is specific to a particular state or condition. It is, of course, questionable whether the legal process is suited for making inferences with regard to "states," but this can not be pursued here.

different from those we use to test our inferences about the future. Nonetheless, it seems that we desire to make decisions with respect to probable futures by taking preventive action. There is some rational attraction about this approach despite its difficulties.

What level of protection against incorrect inference should the average citizen expect as his right in a moral society? Clearly it cannot be absolute and all-embracing (or nobody could be incarcerated). Perhaps we might argue the moral basis for a model which suggested that a person who had once (in the past) committed a violent act (or perhaps some other crime which we regard as significant) *by that very token* forfeited some part of his right to be protected from false positive classifications. He might not claim the same level of trade-off as a person who had not been found guilty in the past. We might even argue for a progressive rate of decline in the false positive probabilities as the number or seriousness (or both) of prior acts increased. Such a loss of "rights" would be in addition to the fact that the predictive power of any methods of inference regarding future probability of violent crimes is itself increased by knowledge of the criminal record. Thus we might object to a false positive ratio of 9:1 for persons who had no previous record of violent crime, while for persons who had already committed three such crimes we could accept this risk of incorrect decision; indeed there would be few persons in the 9:1 category who had a prior record of such proportions. This model seems capable of investigation in terms of the necessary statistics, and it seems possible that it could provide the necessary focus for the assessment of moral trade-offs through the medium of some sound data. Assessments would be facilitated mainly because the model would require a number of separate moral assessments which could be combined into the model—a clearer if not simpler task than attempting to deal with the whole gestalt at the same time. It would be necessary to rank "preferences" in something like the form of Table II; the left-hand list of

Table II

Category of past acts:	Required level for trade-off probabilities:
No proved offenses	Minimal level of false positive risk
One prior, non-violent crime	Some slight increase in risk
One prior violent crime	Greater risk than above
Two prior non-violent crimes	(?)

increasing criminality" corresponds with the right-hand "loss of rights."

Some of the difficulties which at the same time are possibly useful elaborations of the issues become immediately obvious. Do we treat two non-violent crimes as more serious (and hence to be penalized more heavily in terms of assurances against false positive decisions) than one violent crime? Clearly this depends upon the nature of the crime as assessed in terms of its "seriousness." But if we can agree that we can match the "seriousness" scale to a function of "loss of rights" in terms of the risk of incorrect treatment/insulation from society, we have developed an important transformation of the problem. Decisions with regard to the seriousness of crimes are continuously being made in many sectors of the political and justice system. If we can accept the principle that as the seriousness of the criminal career increased (past events) the right to protection (in terms of probabilities) from classification as a false positive decreased, it would be possible to fill out the model to "map" a much higher degree of complexity. The courts might have some difficulties in interpreting probability estimates calculated in the necessary form, but they already deal with concepts of "probable cause" and "sufficient cause."

If this model has any attraction, it is perhaps mainly in that it reveals in some detail the complexity of the issues. It will be obvious that expressing the two dimensions (seriousness and probability of recidivism) as some function of

each other does not provide a model covering all that we can now specify of the problem. This model accommodates neither the variations in the proposed treatment—its intrusiveness, painfulness or other qualities—nor does it accommodate variations in the impact upon the persons who would be concerned. Development of further scales would, however, be possible. It should, for example, be possible to scale the "seriousness" of any *penalty* of detention or supervision or enforced treatment. Offenders may be assumed to have preferences and these preferences could provide some basis for our consideration of moral constraints.

A Substitute Model

The more we explore the individual treatment model where the criteria for treatment are personal characteristics and past actions of the offender, the greater become the moral difficulties in any philosophy of enforced treatment. One alternative approach is to invoke the concept of voluntarism with respect to treatment and to separate the idea of community protection and punishment from the treatment methods which would be voluntarily submitted to. The concept of voluntarism is, however, another thorny area of moral constraints. No one is completely free; we are all constrained by economic, situational, and personal factors. Within any system which deals with anti-social behavior, the problems of freedom of choice are exacerbated. How many alternatives must be available before we can discuss the idea of choice? It may be possible to relate the constraints normally present in the "free" world to those available to individuals involved with the criminal justice processes. Clearly there is considerable variation between persons both in their available information and in their ability to utilize it in making a "free" choice. There may be some value in exploring issues along these lines once we have reasonable support for our beliefs that any systems of treatment can be effective. Where there is more evidence of the effectiveness of behavior modification techniques, the methods seem to be more intrusive and more damaging to our moral belief in the autonomy of the individual. It may be suggested that to be a volunteer a person must be informed both of the impact of the treatment (pain, risks, uncertainty of side-effects, etc.) and also provided with some assessment of the probability of the treatment being successful with respect to his "sickness" or "problem." If a person is not informed, he cannot make rational choices, and hence it is difficult to regard him as a volunteer. Here, again, we face the issue of the probability of the outcome of treatment, and until this is solved there seems little point in wrestling with the concepts of the relative freedoms of volunteers for behavior modification.*

A different approach which may be examined briefly is that of providing training in violence de-escalation techniques and in methods for reducing the probability of violent reaction to events by seeking to modify the qualities of the trigger events. If violent behavior can be learned, and if it is role-related as it seems, at least in part, to be, then it may be that role-related non-violent behavior can also be learned.

Many would like to believe that:

(a)   criminal violence is not related to violence in society;

(b)   the offender is either sick or wicked and must, therefore, be isolated as dangerous;

(c)   to be able to control violence we must identify personal violence-potential profiles for individuals.

If we take this viewpoint, there are certain observations which are expected to follow. If "personality" is the clue, then considerable levels of

association are to be expected between frequencies of observed violent behavior and test measures which are known to discriminate personality differences and traits. In fact, correlations of this kind are found to be extremely small, explaining little more than a few percentage points of the variance between persons who have and who have not committed violent crimes.* It is particularly interesting to note that while it is possible to predict "*crime* potential" (in terms of the probability of recidivism) for property offenders with reasonably high correlations (values between $r = 0.3$ and 0.4 are common), it has proved impossible *by the use of exactly similar methods*, or even of alternative methods, to predict *violent* crime with better than a quarter of that power. That is to say, the violent offender is more like everybody else (in terms of personality tests and case history) than is the non-violent property offender. Yet contrary to this empirical evidence, it is usually the property offenders who are considered to be more "normal," while the violent offender is the more likely to be considered abnormal—and sent to an institution like Patuxent!

These findings are consistent with the suggestion that the important factor in the likelihood of violent behavior is that of role. It would seem desirable to take these kinds of evidence into account in our decisions about violence control. Possibly we could gain more control of violent behavior if we were to work upon *situations* and role skills, developing *de-escalating techniques* for those who perform high risk tasks, or who are expected, in other ways, to become involved in violent situations.

It may prove possible to classify "trigger" events or "gambits" in various role behaviors which have a high probability of escalating into violence. If "cues" can be identified and classified, then we may be able to find ways in which *situations* could be modified by *procedural revi-*

*There may be little logical point in such discussion. But since behavior modification is being used in prisons (where the situation, apart from anything else, casts doubt on the meaning of the term "voluntary") it may be necessary to assert moral claims based on intuitive humanitarian principles.

*Certainly there are some violent criminals who are "odd," disturbed, or whatever; but there are also odd, disturbed, and most peculiar people who are not violent.

sions or by training persons involved in such situations in violence de-escalation measures. Many difficult ethical questions can be avoided if we concentrate upon roles and procedures or situations in our attempts to deal with violence, rather than by seeking remedial action in regard to individual persons.* In addition to the special risk situations and role-required behavior, there may be general principles of violence de-escalation which can be discovered, and these principles could then form the basis for training in schools. In any case, we must not reduce the problem of violence to the problem of the *violent individual*. Moreover, as we break away from the concept of violence as an individual problem, we can offer some new means for dealing with the social and personal elements of violent events.

Hans Toch observed that the models we have used in the past to think about human violence are unsatisfactory.[7] He noted that we have assumed that "all men are reservoirs of bloody destructiveness" and "maintained that civilization equips most persons with the means of discharging their hatreds judiciously and selectively—although there are instances in which this effort fails. Some persons are presumed to remain unchecked in their aggressiveness, so that they become promiscuously violent upon slight provocation." In *A Clockwork Orange*, Anthony Burgess imagines an individual who is conditioned against violence and who, for this reason, finds life impossible.[8] The conditioning is unselective—affecting the whole person—rather than specific to narrowly defined categories of events. It is, however, reasonably certain that, as Burgess suggests, a person who was totally non-violent could not survive in contemporary society. Certainly, many problems of social organization are brought to light by violent acts, and these problems are not solved merely by allocating blame to an "offender."

*That is not to say that there are no serious or difficult moral questions with regard to situation modification, but such questions seem more manageable than those involving personality modification—at least they are different, and herein lies some hope.

Every offender is, by his act, commenting not only upon himself, but to a greater or lesser extent upon society.

Conclusion

In the light of recent research, it is impossible to retain any belief in the notion that the problem of violence is "all in the mind."[9] Nor can we affirm that all violent offenders are sick. Research results are consistent with the belief that violent behavior is learned role behavior for some part, and possibly failure to learn for another. It may be "normal" to be violent—the abnormality resides mainly in the time and place, or perhaps in terms of the nature and medium of the manifestation of that violence. A sense of time and place which is supposed to be specific to the use of force against others (violent behavior) is presumably neither to be discovered by personality analysis nor modified effectively by the treatment of the individual personality. Something different must be tried if we are to seek to control behaviors involving the use of force by man upon other men. Control must be *role-restricted* (the "Clockwork Orange" problem) and *situation-modified*; otherwise our present socio-political system will not continue to function. A completely violence-free society does not seem to be a feasible ideal at this time. It does not follow, however, as some have suggested, that violent crime is the price we must pay for the kind of social structure we now have. There are some actions which can be taken now on the basis of information we already have, and many more which could be discovered to reduce the problem of violence to more manageable proportions.

What we now do to those we define as offenders is the product of much history, and many of the historical features have residues that influence the social consciousness in highly complex ways. The relationship between law and religion, between religion and political power, and the influence of symbolic behavior in each of these areas, cannot be ignored when we seek explanations of current practice and examine alternatives for the disposition of offenders which seem more reasonable than those of the past or present. Nonetheless, a strategy might be sought for both research and action derived from very different constructs than those now fashionable. The need to study violent behavior in all its manifestations and to seek ways to control human destructiveness is greater now than ever. The need to modify the violence potential of situations, role behaviors, and political systems applies whether the destructiveness is individual or collective.

REFERENCE

1. Patuxent Institution, *Maryland's Defective Delinquent Statute: A Progress Report* (State of Maryland Department of Public Safety and Correctional Services, January 9, 1973). This document is apparently intended to be an authoritative statement of the work of the Institution, addressed to the Governor of Maryland. References throughout the paper to the "report" are references to this publication.

2. R. Martinson, "What Works? Questions and Answers about Prison Reform," *The Public Interest*, no. 35 (Spring 1974): 22–54; and Leslie T. Wilkins, *Evaluation of Penal Measures* (New York: Random House, 1969).

3. D. Gottfredson et al., *Four Thousand Lifetimes: A Study of Time Served and Parole Outcomes* (Davis, California: N.C.C.D. Research Center, 1973).

4. W. H. Hammond and E. Chayen, *Persistent Offenders* (London: Her Majesty's Stationery Office, 1963).

5. H. Mannheim and Leslie T. Wilkins, *Prediction Methods in Relation to Borstal Training* (London: Her Majesty's Stationery Office, 1955).

6. E. A. Wenk and R. L. Emrich, "Assaultive Youth," *Journal of Research in Crime and Delinquency* 9 [2] (1972): 171–96.

7. Hans Toch, *Violent Men: An Inquiry into the Psychology of Violence* (Chicago: Aldine, 1969).

8. Anthony Burgess, *A Clockwork Orange* (New York: W. W. Norton, 1962).

9. For example, Wenk and Emrich, "Assaultive Youth."

61. Plastic Surgery on Offenders

RICHARD L. KURTZBERG
WALLACE MANDELL
MICHAEL LEWIN
DOUGLAS S. LIPTON
MARVIN SHUSTER

THE SSR EXPERIMENT

THE CONCEPT OF PLASTIC SURGERY WAS A DISTANT one to most inmates at Rikers Island, who, as members of disadvantaged groups, had no experience with costly elective surgery. Some inmates were surprised to discover that protruding ears or broken noses could be corrected. Despite their lack of familiarity with plastic surgery, 1,424 inmates responded to the prison publicity and orientation about the project. Figure 1. presents an outline of the procedures.

Screening the Candidate
Interested candidates underwent an examination by the project plastic surgeon to determine whether their disfigurements were reparable. Disfigurements were classified into four degrees of severity: (1) minimal, (2) moderate, (3) marked, and (4) gross. In addition, the surgeon made a prognosis as to the surgical outcome which was also ranked on a four-point scale from poor (1) to excellent (4). The surgeon's

▶SOURCE: *Surgical and Social Rehabilitation of Adult Offenders. Volume I. New York: Montefiore Hospital and Medical Center with Staten Island Mental Health Society and New York Department of Corrections (1968). Pp. 35–42, 44–45, 47, 49–52, 57–61, 63–67, 70–73, 75. (Editorial adaptations.)*

decision to accept or not accept a candidate was based on degree of both severity and prognosis. Candidates with minimal disfigurements or minimal reparability were eliminated to maximize the possibility of achieving a noticeable physical change, and thus provide a fair test of the hypothesis. This reduced the number of candidates from 1,424 to 663 (47%).

Those subjects who were accepted then underwent psychological screening. The psychological screening served two purposes. One was to collect data for later pre-post treatment comparisons. The screening was also used in an attempt to predict the psychological reactions of the subject to surgical changes. Four tests were used: the Minnesota Multiphasic Personality Inventory (MMPI), the Tennessee Self-Concept Scale, the Sacks Sentence Completion Test, and the Draw-A-Person Test. In addition, an individual interview was conducted. When a candidate's acceptance could not be determined as a result of the routine psychological screening, additional individual testing sessions and psychiatric interviews were scheduled. Rorschach and thematic techniques were administered.

The New York City male prison population has a higher incidence of psychopathology than

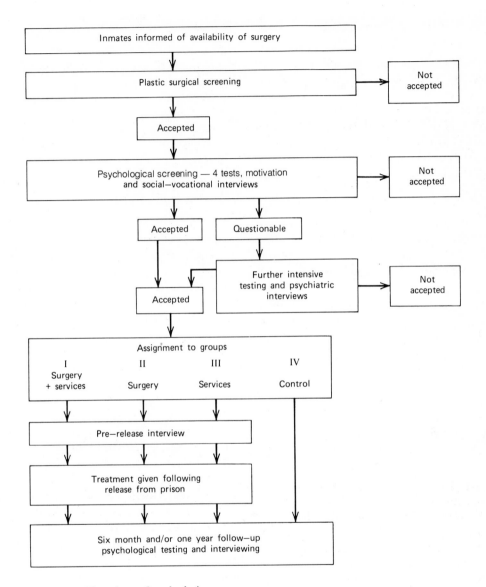

Figure 1. Flow chart of study design.

the general population and those inmates requesting elective surgery evidenced even more psychopathology. Since it is obvious that psychopathology increases the likelihood of irrational post-operative reactions, a sensitive screening technique was particularly important with our study population. If it appeared likely that the subject's reactions would be dangerous to himself or to others, he was eliminated.

One of the primary contra-indications to cosmetic surgery was irrational overemphasis on the disfigurement, which we have called "focusing." This focusing was almost exclusive to candidates with developmental disfigurements, and was most common among rhinoplasty candidates. Of all rhinoplasty candidates, 12% were eliminated because of excessive focusing and an additional 39% overemphasized the role of their disfigurement. Less than one percent of all other disfigurement groups were rejected due to focusing. It is noteworthy that developmentally disfigured groups also showed higher psychopathology than all other disfigurement groups.

*

A candidate's request for a cosmetic operation as a magical solution for all problems must be viewed with utmost caution. The focusing individual attributes all or most of his problems to one factor, such as a physical deformity, using it as a "crutch" to relieve his own sense of failure. The sudden withdrawal of this crutch may leave him without defenses against his feelings of inadequacy and may plunge him into a deep depression. A focusing patient, despite excellent cosmetic results after the operation, may continue to be preoccupied with his appearance. The possibility of suicide in extreme cases of this type cannot be overlooked.

*

The screening and interviewing procedure was often tedious and time consuming. Many subjects who had expressed initial interest in the project were unwilling to sit through the two or three sessions required. Other subjects felt threatened by the tests or did not have sufficient motivation for surgery. This resulted in a loss of 213 surgically approved subjects which considerably reduced the sample sizes.

*

Assignment to Group and Pre-Release Interview

Subjects who had satisfactorily completed the psychological screening (425) were assigned to one of four treatment groups:

Group I—surgery *and* social-vocational services

Group II—surgery

Group III—no surgery but social-vocational services

Group IV—no treatment (Control)

Groups I and II were the major experimental groups of the project, both receiving plastic surgery. Group I, in addition to receiving surgery, also received certain social and vocational services. Thus, Group I was used to determine the combined effects of surgery and services. Group II was used to determine the effects of plastic surgery without additional social and vocational services. Groups III and IV did not receive plastic surgery. Group III received only social and vocational services and was included in the study design to determine the effects of services administered without plastic surgery. Group IV received no treatment and served as the control group.

Initially, subjects were assigned to a treatment group on a rotation basis, regardless of ethnicity, addiction status or disfigurement. Since ethnicity and addiction status were found to be important factors influencing recidivism and vocational success, the groups were compared for distribution of these variables midway through the project. Since the groups were found to be disproportionate, subsequent assignment to groups was based on ethnicity and addiction status and the rotation was carried out separately for each category.

All experimental subjects (Groups I, II & III) were interviewed immediately prior to their release from custody. At this time arrangements were made with each subject for receiving plastic surgery and/or social-vocational services.

Plastic Surgery

Pre-surgery Following release from prison, 104 Group I subjects and 95 Group II subjects were scheduled for admission to the hospital for surgery. An attempt was made to admit these subjects as quickly as possible. Due to lack of space in the hospital, however, many subjects had to wait anywhere from several days to a month for admission.

Often a waiting period of even a few days was enough of a discouragement to the subject to deter him from his original desire. The offender who felt he had been disappointed by treatment agencies in the past began to feel that he was being let down again. He was unable to understand why, after making his decision to have surgery and reporting to the hospital, he was then told he must wait. As a result of this discouragement it was often difficult to locate the subject when admission was finally possible. Even when arrangements for admission were finally made the subject would often fail to appear at the hospital, saying later he had forgotten or been busy at that time.

In an attempt to alleviate some of the problems related to the admission procedure, it was decided to have an SSR staff member escort the subject to the hospital. Many subjects were escorted directly from Rikers Island to the hospital on the day of their release from custody. Others were escorted from their homes or from the SSR Manhattan office at a later date. Since the majority of our subjects were addicts, and SSR follow-up data showed that 25% of addicts return to drugs the first day after release, it was thought that escorting subjects directly from prison would tend to alleviate the attrition of addict subjects from our study. In spite of these efforts, 39 Group I subjects and 54 Group II subjects were never admitted to the hospital. A total of 65 subjects in Group I and 41 in Group II were admitted.

In a research program involving voluntary participation on the part of the subjects, there is a possibility that those who initially accept the offer of treatment but later drop out, are different in personality or background characteristics from those who actually remained in the project long enough to receive treatment. With this in mind comparisons on 9 major variables were made between the 100 Group I and II subjects who received surgery and the 93 subjects who refused surgery.

There were few differences between those accepting and those rejecting surgery. The higher the educational level of the subject, the more likely he was to refuse surgery. This may reflect the more cautious attitude toward new experimental programs of those with more education.

It was also found that subjects who had facial disfigurements showed significantly fewer refusals of surgery than subjects with needle tracks or tattoos. This may be explained by the stronger level of motivation for surgery shown by those with facial disfigurements during the screening.

*

Surgery A total of 100[1] subjects were operated on by plastic surgery residents under the supervision of attending physicians. Wherever possible, procedures were completed in one surgical session, since it was felt that many subjects would not return for subsequent procedures. As anticipated a number of subjects (19) for whom multiple procedures were necessary, did not return for the second procedure. Eight of these subjects were addicts who had needle tracks on both arms. These subjects had procedures performed on one arm and never returned for the procedure on the other arm. Although the most conspicuous tracks were removed first and the subjects may have been satisfied, the repairs were considered incomplete.

---

[1]6 subjects were dropped for medical reasons.

Since the main purpose of the study was to evaluate the effects of plastic surgery as a rehabilitative device, those for whom plastic surgery procedures were incomplete were eliminated from the basic surgery groups and their data were analyzed separately. Although this separation was necessary, it reduced the surgery sample size even further.[2]

It is essential to obtain the cooperation of the subject during the healing period for obtaining optimal surgical results. For a number of reasons, SSR subjects were often uncooperative during this period. Many SSR subjects had unrealistic expectations of the surgical results. They expected fulfillment of their hopes immediately after the operation, and did not anticipate discomfort or imperfect results. Their disappointment with the immediate result at times led to embitterment and a refusal to cooperate in further medical treatment.

Another difficulty arose from lack of effective communication between the subject and the surgeon. Although detailed instructions were given for post-operative care, some subjects were unable to comprehend what was required of them. For example, a subject thought that changing bandages meant unwrapping and rewrapping the same bandage.

Post-Hospital Care Both Montefiore and Morisania Hospitals have plastic surgery outpatient clinics which are held once a week. The number of clinic visits required for a subject depended upon the type of surgical procedure and the rate of healing.

The rate of attendance at the clinic was found to be generally poor and sporadic. Although 90% of SSR subjects made at least one clinic visit, many subjects failed to appear when they were scheduled. This often meant that they did not receive necessary care and instructions at the time when these were most important.

Among the reasons for this lack of cooperation were: dissatisfaction with early surgical results, inability to understand the need for clinic visits, return to crime or drugs, and impatience with clinic procedures.

Social and Vocational Services

Following release from prison, 104 subjects in group I and 77 subjects in Group III were offered a variety of social and vocational services. A total of 65 subjects in Group I and 47 in Group III accepted the offer of services. It is noteworthy that the rate of refusal of the group receiving services was similar to the rate of the groups receiving surgery. The drop-out rate is similar to that found in other offender treatment programs. Although some direct counseling and placement were provided, the services offered Group I and III subjects consisted generally of referrals to agencies in the following areas:

a.   Drug rehabilitation and detoxification.

b.   Liaison with New York City Department of Welfare.

c.   Vocational services.

d.   Other services.

In addition, Group I and II subjects were provided services directly related to surgery. These consisted of referrals to welfare for financial support prior to surgery, referral to legal aid service, liaison with parole (many subjects could not work since they were awaiting admission to the hospital), and counseling of subjects while in the hospital.

Drug Rehabilitation and Detoxification Since 66% of Group I and 71% of Group III subjects were heroin addicts, a major portion of the services performed for these individuals related to their addiction. SSR social service staff members established liaison with community drug rehabilitation and detoxification centers and referrals were made to these agencies when re-

[2]The procedures of 12 subjects were judged incomplete in Group I, leaving a sample of 49, and 7 subjects in Group II had incomplete surgery, leaving a sample of 32.

quested by the subject. Detoxification referrals were for the immediate problems associated with helping the individual break his physiological addiction to heroin. Rehabilitation referrals involved a specific program seeking to aid addicts who are trying to stop or stay away from drugs.

*

Welfare Services   A large percentage of inmates released from Rikers Island are in need of public assistance since they have no family or friends with whom to live nor can they find employment quickly. Referrals to the New York City Department of Welfare were made for Group III by Rikers Island social service. Those subjects scheduled for plastic surgery (Groups I and II) who were in need of welfare services were referred by the SSR staff prior to surgery.

When SSR subjects attempted to obtain welfare services, some difficulties were encountered. Many welfare personnel seemed to regard offender-clients, particularly addicts, as individuals highly likely to misuse funds. SSR clients were received, at times, with suspicion and hostility. Less experienced welfare workers were more cooperative in their dealings with SSR clients than their older colleagues, who had more negative experiences with this population.

When SSR clients were not well received at the Welfare interview, they reacted in one of two ways. Some clients were passive and did not attempt to convince the welfare worker of their needs. They were less likely to receive the services to which they were entitled. Some subjects became offensive and demanding. These outbursts, though infrequent, had a strong negative effect on the welfare worker which was generalized to all offenders.

A number of SSR clients who did receive welfare assistance lost their eligibility for services fairly quickly by not following welfare regulations. For example, an addict who used any of his welfare funds for drugs is misusing public funds, and thus his case will be closed as soon as this is discovered.

Vocational Services   SSR vocational services consisted generally of referrals to community agencies which offered programs for training to improve skills, to learn a particular vocation, or to continue academic education. In addition, referrals were made to the Correctional Vocational Rehabilitation Service (CVRS) of the New York State Employment Service, a special division designed to handle ex-offenders in need of jobs.

*

The legal and addiction history of SSR clients often made acceptance into vocational programs difficult. For example, in one program, (BEST) Better Essential Skills Training Program, sponsored by the New York City Department of Labor and Department of Welfare, the reading and educational level of subjects qualified them only for heavy vehicle driver training courses. Their legal histories, however, presented difficulties in obtaining New York State Chauffeurs' licenses, necessary for operating these vehicles.

Another problem faced by SSR clients in seeking vocational training was that most vocational training programs in New York City limit eligibility to those aged 16–21. The state vocational rehabilitation agency (DVR) Division of Vocational Rehabilitation which offers training to adults based on disability was available for only three clients who were eligible due to serious hand or arm deformities.

Other Services   Several additional services were offered to subjects. These included legal aid, court appearances on behalf of subjects, liaison with parole, and referrals for medical or dental care.

Follow-Up

Follow-up interviews and tests using the original test battery were conducted six months and one year after hospital discharge for Groups I and II and after prison release for Groups III and IV. In attempting to carry out the follow-up interviews, it was often difficult or impossible to locate subjects. This was especially true for Group IV subjects who had not been contacted since they were originally accepted into the project. Similar difficulties have been encountered in other research attempts to follow-up released offenders.

To facilitate follow-up, it was decided to offer ten dollars to each subject as an incentive. This, coupled with intensive location efforts, proved highly successful. Follow-up interviews were conducted with 174 of the 212 experimental subjects.[3]

Although it was planned to interview subjects both six months and one year following their release, it was not possible to interview all subjects on schedule. It was decided, therefore, to use the latest available interview for data analysis. Three-fourths of the subjects were interviewed after a period of at least nine months.

While follow-up of treatment subjects averaged 89%, the rate of follow-up of control subjects was 69%. One of the major assumptions of a treatment study conducted with randomly assigned groups of subjects is that, prior to treatment, there are no significant differences among experimental and control groups on important variables associated with the possible outcome. To test this assumption, pre-treatment data on SSR subjects on nine major variables[4] were analyzed for such differences.

The results indicate that with the exception of deformity, the major variables checked were randomly distributed among the four treatment groups. With regard to deformity, there were relatively more subjects with tattoos and tracks in Groups III and IV than there were in Groups I and II. This can be explained by the high

proportion of Group I and II subjects with tattoos and tracks refusing surgery. As noted previously, the motivation for plastic surgery among inmates requesting correction of tattoos and needle tracks is low.

THE FINDINGS

Analysis of Recidivism Data

In analyzing recidivism data for this project, two main questions needed investigation:

1. Do the treatments differentially reduce the proportion of inmates in the various groups returning to prison within the follow-up period?

2. Do the treatments delay return to prison?

To determine the proportion of subjects recidivating within the follow-up period, an index of *incidence of recidivism* was obtained by establishing whether or not an individual was convicted of a new crime or returned to prison during the period in which he was followed. Comparisons were then made of the number and proportion of individuals in each treatment group who recidivated. Chi-square and Fisher's Exact Tests were performed to test for the statistical significance of differences between groups.

To investigate delay in return to prison *the proportion of recidivism-free months* was computed. Here the time between the individual's release from prison (or from the hospital, for surgical subjects) and his recidivism is summed over a base of 12 months (the follow-up period) for recidivists. For non-recidivists the time from release to the date of follow-up is computed. Thus, the index for a recidivist might be as follows:

$$\frac{\text{Months from release to recidivism}}{\text{Months from release to follow-up}} = \frac{6}{12} = 50\%$$

and for a non-recidivist interviewed at 10 months:

---

[3]Seventeen of the 174 followed up were subjects with incomplete surgery. This left 157 subjects for whom we could evaluate the effects of surgery and services. An additional eleven subjects for whom we had corroborated information from governmental sources were used in the analysis of recidivism bringing the total sample for the recidivism analysis to 168.

[4]These variables were: addiction status, ethnicity, disfigurement, prior arrests, prior convictions, education, age, marital status and parole status.

$$\frac{\text{Months from release to follow-up}}{\text{Months from release to follow-up}} = \frac{10}{10} = 100\%$$

The ratio was, therefore, 100% for all non-recidivists. These ratios were then summed for all individuals in each treatment group yielding the average proportion of recidivism-free months in each group.

Z tests for differences between proportions were then conducted to test for the statistically significant differences among groups.

The employment of these two analyses provided both a measure of overall recidivism and a more detailed determination of the association between treatment and the length of time individuals in each treatment group remained recidivism-free.

Effects of Treatments on Addicts

Table I presents incidence of recidivism data for addict subjects. Among addicts there was no statistically significant reduction in recidivism as a function of plastic surgery (Groups I and II compared with Groups III and IV). Of the addicts receiving services alone, however, (Group III), only 48% recidivated as compared with 79% of the addicts in the control group. This represented a statistically significant 31% reduction in recidivism (Chi-square, p.<.05). Those addicts receiving both surgery and services

(Group I) also showed a significant reduction in recidivism when compared with the No Treatment Group (Chi-square, p.<.05). The difference in incidence of recidivism between addicts receiving surgery, but not extra services (Group II) and control subjects (Group IV), was not significant. . . .

The disfigured addict is handicapped by many problems. He is a criminal, socially ostracized, he has difficulty finding employment, feels dependent on drugs and on other individuals, and has a physical disfigurement. It appears that the plastic surgery treatment alone was insufficient to affect the wide array of problems faced by disfigured addict subjects.

Disfigurement and Treatment for Addicts

These findings were examined more intensively by comparing treatment groups for each of the following five disfigurement categories separately:

1. Developmental facial disfigurements

2. Traumatic facial disfigurements

3. Hand deformities

4. Tattoos

5. Needle tracks

Table II presents incidence of recidivism as a function of treatment for the five addict disfigurement groups.

The direction of the differences between traumatic and developmental facially disfigured addicts, although not statistically significant because of small cell size, suggest that addicts with traumatic facial disfigurements recidivated less after services and more after surgery, while developmentally disfigured addicts recidivated more following services. This is interesting in the light of earlier findings that developmentally disfigured addicts showed greater psychological disturbance as compared with non-disfigured addicts. Addicts with facial disfigurements re-

Table I. Incidence of Recidivism as a Function of Treatment for Addicts

Group	Total	Recidivists	
		No.	%
I–Surgery and Services	28	14	50
II–Surgery	21	14	67
III–Services	31	15	48
IV–No treatment	38	30	79
Total	118	73	62
Surgery I and II	49	28	57
No surgery III and IV	69	45	65
Chi-Square	Not significant		

Table II. Incidence of Recidivism as a Function of Disfigurement and Treatment for Addicts (N = 118)

Group	Developmental Facial			Traumatic Facial			Hand			Tattoos			Needle Tracks		
	Total	Recid. No.	%	Total	Recid. No.	%	Total	Recid. No.	%	Total	Recid. No.	%	Total	Recid. No.	%
I—Surgery and services	8	6	75	11	5	45	2	1	50	3	2	67	4	1	25
II—Surgery	2	1	50	11	9	82	1	0	—	7	4	57	0	0	—
III—Services	3	3	100	12	5	42	0	0	—	8	3	38	8	4	50
IV—No treatment	5	5	100	17	10	60	2	2	100	7	6	86	7	7	100
Totals	18	15	83	51	29	57	5	3	60	25	15	60	19	12	63
I and II Surgery	10	7	70	22	14	64	3	1	33	10	6	60	4	1	25
III and IV No surgery	8	8	100	29	15	52	2	2	100	15	9	60	15	11	73
Chi-Square or Fisher's extract	NS			NS			—	—		NS			$P < .10$		

sulting from trauma, on the other hand, were comparatively better adjusted.

[Earlier research] suggested that an addicted individual may benefit from the psychological after-effects of a traumatic injury, so that removal of the disfigurement without additional services may not be desirable. Eighty-two percent of the addicts with traumatic facial disfigurements receiving surgery without additional services recidivated within one year as compared with 60% of the controls and 42% of those receiving services but not surgery. Further investigation of this issue with larger samples is needed. Those screening addicts for plastic surgery programs should consider the positive as well as negative psychological and social effects associated with traumatic disfigurements or tattoos.

Tattoos are common in jail and prison populations. There was no benefit demonstrated as a result of surgery or any combination of treatments for individuals who had requested removal of tattoos. As noted previously, only a small proportion of individuals with tattoos volunteered for surgery and of these, most dropped out before surgery. Unfortunately, all of the tattooed subjects who received surgery were addicts. Their addiction may have been the factor which mediated against positive effects of the surgery. Surgery for the removal of tattoos is followed by a long period during which the results are not aesthetically pleasing. This may have been frustrating and thus may have presented a problem to subjects who, despite careful preparation, expected a much shorter healing period.

*

Addicts who had surgery to revise needle tracks showed a tendency to recidivate less than controls. (Fisher's Exact Test, $p < .10$). Whereas only one of four addicts operated upon for needle tracks recidivated within the one-year period, eleven of fifteen controls (73%) recidivated during the same period. These surgical subjects remained out of prison 81% of the time

measured, as compared with 49% of the time measured for control subjects with needle tracks. This difference, while not statistically significant, is encouraging since it was obtained on a small addict sample and indicates a possibility that addicts concerned with removing needle tracks can be aided. Several addicts reported that the surgical result was excellent since they were no longer recognized as addicts because of the lack of identifying stigma. For the first time since they began using heroin, they no longer felt like addicts.

*

A number of positive findings have been obtained with addict subjects in this study. The mechanism through which plastic surgery aids the addict's rehabilitation is not clear. The positive trend suggests a need for further intensive investigation of this issue with a larger sample. The administration of services to addicts in the present study yielded clear reductions in recidivism. It should be emphasized that these services continued for the duration of the follow-up period. It is possible that these addicts formed a dependent relationship with the service staff and that this relationship led to the lower incidence of recidivism. The termination of this relationship may increase recidivism rates for this group. Psychological test data indicated that addicts who received services became more passive, dependent, and female oriented than those who did not. This possibility could only be determined by a follow-up investigation continuing beyond the termination of services.

*

Effects of Treatment on Non-Addicts

Table III presents incidence of recidivism data as a function of treatment for non-addict subjects. Those non-addict groups receiving plastic surgery recidivated significantly less (32%) during the follow-up period than disfigured non-addicts not receiving surgery (68%) (Chi-square, $p < .025$). This represents a *36% difference in incidence of recidivism*. Similarly, non-addicts receiv-

Table III. Incidence of Recidivism as a Function of Treatment for Non-Addicts

		Recidivists	
Group	Total	No.	%
I–Surgery and services	15	5	33
II–Surgery	10	3	30
III–Services	9	8	89
IV–No treatment	16	9	56
Total	50	25	50
Surgery I and II	25	8	32
No Surgery III and IV	25	17	68
Chi-Square	5.1*		

*$p < .025$, one-tailed

ing surgery remained out of prison, on the average, 30% longer than non-addict disfigured controls (Z test, $p < .01$).

*

Non-Addict Subjects and Social Services

While the administration of social and vocational services appeared to have positive effects in significantly reducing the incidence of recidivism among addict subjects, services were associated with an *increase* in the incidence of recidivism among non-addict subjects.

A greater proportion of non-addict subjects receiving services only (Group III) recidivated (89%) as compared with non-addicts receiving surgery (30%), surgery and services (33%) or no treatment (56%). Thus, non-addicts receiving services but not surgery showed the highest incidence of recidivism in the study—even higher than control subjects.

These findings are similar to those reported recently which indicate that traditional counseling and placement techniques often have null or even negative effects when applied to problem populations.

One explanation of the findings in the present study may lie in the higher proportion of non-addict subjects in the services group receiving sentences which involved parole upon termination of imprisonment. These subjects were different in the eyes of the courts before being sent to jail. They may have been poorer rehabilitation risks to begin with, or may have been subject to pull in different directions from the parole and SSR counselors. These factors may be related to the high incidence of recidivism in this group. If parole status is not the determining factor, then a more serious examination must be made of the counseling process. Such an explanation centers on the demands made by the service worker on the client. The major demand of treatment agencies on a client is that he cooperate in treatment. Most service agencies require that the client express this willingness by maintaining contact and by following directions or a mutually agreed upon plan. Often, especially with offenders, the client is not motivated because he feels that the agency may not be able to help him because of his past. Unless the agency can solve his problems immediately, the client's doubts about the agency are reinforced.

*

Disfigurement and Treatment for Non-Addicts

To analyze the effects of the experimental treatments upon non-addict subjects with different disfigurements, data from four separate categories of disfigurement were compared.

1. Developmental facial disfigurements

2. Traumatic facial disfigurements

3. Hand deformities

4. Tattoos

The results of these comparisons may be found in Table IV. As can be seen, non-addicts with traumatic facial disfigurements who received surgery showed a significantly lower incidence of recidivism (33%) when compared with non-addict controls with traumatic facial disfigurements (Chi-square, $p < .025$).

*

To summarize, the non-addict group showed

Table IV. Incidence of Recidivism as a Function of Disfigurement and Treatment for Non-Addicts (N = 50)

Group	Developmental Facial			Traumatic Facial			Hand			Tattoos		
	Total	Recid. No.	Recid. %	Total	Recid. No.	Recid. %	Total	Recid. No.	Recid. %	Total	Recid. No.	Recid. %
I—Surgery and services	5	1	20	10	4	40	0	0	—	0	0	—
II—Surgery	0	0	—	8	2	25	1	0	—	1	1	100
III—Services	2	1	50	4	4	100	0	0	—	3	3	100
IV—No treatment	1	0	—	10	7	70	2	1	50	3	1	33
Totals	8	2	25	32	17	53	3	1	33	7	5	71
I and II Surgery	5	1	20	18	6	33	1	0	—	1	1	100
III and IV—No surgery	3	1	33	14	11	79	2	1	50	6	4	67
Chi-square or Fisher's Exact	NS[a]			4.78*			— —			NS[a]		

[a]Not significant.
*p < .025

clear gains following surgery. These gains were most pronounced in the group operated on to correct traumatic facial disfigurements. The administration of social and vocational services to non-addicts had negative effects on both psychological adjustment and incidence of recidivism. Thus, the results for non-addicts are almost the opposite as those for addicts, who seemed to benefit more from services than from surgery. This emphasizes the need for careful evaluation of each individual to tailor a rehabilitation program suited to his needs. In this light, the SSR study results represent one step toward a differential diagnosis approach to offender rehabilitation. To be most effective, attempts to rehabilitate a disfigured individual must take into consideration crucial differences such as type of disfigurement and addiction status.

62. Behavior Modification

STEPHANIE B. STOLZ
LOUIS A. WIENCKOWSKI
BERTRAM S. BROWN

IN THE HISTORY OF CIVILIZATION, PEOPLE HAVE continuously tried to control their environment and find ways of teaching themselves and their children better means of acquiring new skills and capabilities. Commonsense notions of the ways in which reward and punishment can change behavior have existed since time immemorial. Thus, elements of what is now referred to as *behavior modification* were used long before psychologists and other behavioral scientists developed systematic principles of learning.

As behavior modification procedures are used ever more widely, many different concerns are being expressed. On the one hand, the public and mental health professionals are concerned about whether behavior modification procedures have been sufficiently well demonstrated through research to be generally recommended and widely disseminated. On the other hand, behavior modification has acted as a conceptual "lightning rod" in the midst of stormy controversies over ethical problems associated with attempts at social influence, drawing to it such highly charged issues as fear of "mind control" or concerns about the treatment of persons institutionalized against their will. Apparent or actual infringements of rights, as

▶SOURCE: *"Behavior Modification: A Perspective on Critical Issues," American Psychologist (November, 1975), 30(11): 1027–1034, 1039–1044, 1047–1048. Copyright 1975 by the American Psychological Association. Reprinted by permission.*

well as some abuses of behavioral procedures, have led to litigation and calls for curbs on the use of behavior modification.

All of us try continually to influence our own and others' behavior, so that individuals using behavior modification procedures are distinctive only in that they attempt to influence behavior more systematically. Commenting on this issue, one attorney said that to be opposed to behavior modification is to be opposed to the law of gravity. Rather, the key issue is what sort of care, caution, and control should be exercised when behavioral principles are applied precisely and systematically.

This article is intended to provide an objective overview of the current methods of behavior modification and to review some critical issues in an effort to aid the reader in differentiating warranted from unwarranted concerns. We also make some suggestions regarding ethical standards and practices.

To understand behavior modification, it is helpful first to clarify its relationship to a broader concept, behavior influence.

Behavior influence occurs whenever one person exerts some degree of control over another. This occurs constantly in such diverse situations as formal school education, advertising, child rearing, political campaigning, and other normal interpersonal interactions.

Behavior modification is a special form of behavior influence that involves primarily the application of principles derived from research in experimental psychology to alleviate human suffering and enhance human functioning. Behavior modification emphasizes systematic monitoring and evaluation of the effectiveness of these applications. The techniques of behavior modification are generally intended to facilitate improved self-control by expanding individuals' skills, abilities, and independence.

Most behavior modification procedures are based on the general principle that people are influenced by the consequences of their behavior. Behavior modification assumes that the current environment is more relevant in affecting an individual's behavior than most early life experiences, enduring intrapsychic conflicts, or personality structure. Insofar as possible, the behaviorally oriented mental health worker limits the conceptualization of the problem to observable behavior and its environmental context.

In the professional use of behavior modification, a contractual agreement may be negotiated, specifying mutually agreeable goals and procedures. When the clients are adults who have sought therapy, such a contract is made between them and the mental health worker. When the behavior modification program is to benefit a mentally disadvantaged group, such as the retarded, senile, or psychotic, the contract is often made between the individuals' guardians or other responsible persons and the mental health worker. Parents, who usually make decisions affecting their young children, generally are consulted by the mental health worker regarding treatment for their children. Who the appropriate person is to make the contractual agreement for a prisoner is a complex and unsettled issue taken up later in this article in our discussion of the use of behavior modification procedures with prisoners.

Behavior therapy is a term that is sometimes used synonymously with behavior modification. In general, behavior modification is considered to be the broader term, while behavior therapy refers mainly to clinical interventions, usually applied in a one-to-one therapist–patient relationship. That is, behavior therapy is a special form of behavior modification.

In behavior modification, attempts to influence behavior are typically made by changing the environment and the way people interact, rather than by intervening directly through medical procedures (such as drugs) or surgical procedures (such as psychosurgery). Thus, behavior modification methods can be used in a broad range of situations, including the child-rearing efforts of parents and the instructional activities of teachers, as well as the therapeutic efforts of mental health workers in treating more serious psychological and behavioral problems. The effects of behavior modification, unlike the results of most surgical procedures, are relatively changeable and impermanent.

Behavior modification procedures require that the problem behavior be clearly specified. That is, the mental health worker must be able to define objectively the response that the service recipient wants to learn or to have reduced. Thus, certain kinds of problems treated by dynamic psychotherapy appear to be inappropriate candidates for behavior modification. In particular, the patient who seeks therapy primarily because of an existential crisis—"Who am I? Where am I going?"—is probably not an appropriate candidate for behavior modification. This quasi-philosophical problem does not lend itself to an approach dealing with specific identifiable behavior in particular environmental contexts. It is possible that a patient who describes his problem in this way actually has some specific behavioral deficits that may underlie his existential difficulties or occur alongside them. Whether a careful behavioral analysis of the patient's difficulties would reveal such deficits is not now known, however.

Although it is alleged that secret, powerful psychotechnological tools are being or could be used to control the masses, researchers in behavior modification point out that they have encouraged the dissemination of information about behavior processes. In fact, workers in this area believe that increased knowledge of behavior modification will help people understand social-influence processes in general and will actually enable them to counteract many attempts at control, should such attempts occur. Many persons using behavior modification methods not only evaluate the effectiveness of their procedures but also measure the consumers' satisfaction with the behavior modification program used.

IS BEHAVIOR MODIFICATION MERELY COMMON SENSE?

Many persons who learn about the general procedures of behavior modification say that they seem to be nothing more than common sense. To some considerable extent, this is true. For example, parents use behavior modification techniques whenever they praise their children for good report cards in the hope of encouraging continued interest and application. In employment, promotions and incentive awards are universally accepted ways to encourage job performance. The very structure of our laws, which specifies fines and penalties for infractions, is intended to modify behavior through aversive control.

Behavior modification, however, like other scientific approaches, imposes an organization on its subject matter. While common sense often includes contradictory advice (both "out of sight, out of mind," and "absence makes the heart grow fonder"), the principles of behavior modification codify and organize common sense, showing under what conditions and in what circumstances each aspect of "common sense" should be applied. The parents and grandparents who use what can be described as behavior modification procedures may often do so inconsistently and then wonder why they fail.

WHAT BEHAVIOR MODIFICATION IS NOT

As more publicity has been given to behavior modification, the term has come to be used loosely and imprecisely in the public media, often with a negative connotation. Thus, behavior modification has sometimes been said to include psychosurgery, electroconvulsive therapy, and the noncontingent administration of drugs, that is, the administration of drugs independent of any specific behavior by the person receiving the medication. However, even though procedures such as these do modify behavior, that does not make them *behavior modification techniques* in the sense in which most professionals in the field use the term. In this article, the use of the term *behavior modification* will be consistent with its professional use; that is, *behavior modification* will be used to refer to procedures based on the explicit and systematic application of principles and technology derived from research in experimental psychology, procedures that involve some change in the social or environmental context of a person's behavior. This use of the term specifically excludes psychosurgery, electroconvulsive therapy, and the administration of drugs independent of any specific behavior by the person receiving the medication.

CURRENT PRACTICE OF BEHAVIOR MODIFICATION

Behavior modification is a family of techniques. The diverse methods included under the general label have in common the goal of enhancing persons' lives by altering specific aspects of their behavior. Ideally, the mental health worker and the service recipient should decide together on a mutually agreeable set of treatment goals and on the means for attaining these goals. The service recipient or his representative should be kept fully informed of the results of the treatment as it progresses and also participate in any modification of goals or techniques.

Initial analysis of the person's problem should typically begin with a detailed description of the behavior causing distress or interfering with optimal functioning of the individual in familial, social, vocational, or other important spheres of activity. The behavioral goals should be viewed in the context of everything the person is able to do and also in terms of what kinds of support his usual environment is capable of providing over the long term.

This description, whenever possible, should be based on observations of the individual in the setting in which he reports distress. These observations may be careful quantitative records, or they may be statements about the relative frequency of various behaviors. The person making the observations may be the therapist or his agent, a peer of the individual receiving the service, or the individual himself. For example, a parent might be trained to tally the frequency with which a child stutters; a teacher or hospital aide might keep a record of a child's aggressive outbursts; and a well-motivated individual could count the frequency of occurrence of an unacceptable habit such as nail biting.

In addition to obtaining this description of what the individual does and does not do, the behavioral mental health worker should try to find how the individual's behavior relates to various events and places in his current and past experiences. Events relevant to behavior modification are those that immediately precede and immediately follow the problem behavior. The goal should be to determine the circumstances under which the behavior seems to occur and the environmental consequences that might be maintaining it.

Behavior modification, then, involves the systematic variation of behavioral and environmental factors thought to be associated with an individual's difficulties, with the primary goal of modifying his behavior in the direction that, ideally, he himself (or his agent) has chosen.

Transition to the Nontreatment Setting
The goal of all treatment is the maintenance of improvement after the termination of therapy. An ideal behavior modification program includes a specification of the environment in which the individual normally lives and a provision for establishing and strengthening behavior desired or useful in that environment. Generali-

zation to the natural environment is helped if the behavior modification program includes a planned transition between the therapeutic program and the natural environment. The following example illustrates this principle.

O. Ivar Lovaas (University of California, Los Angeles) has been studying autistic children for a number of years. He has found that when parents have been trained to carry on with a behavior modification program, children continue to improve after they have left his special treatment ward. On the other hand, the children regress if they are returned to institutions after leaving the ward and no longer participate in a special training program.

Examples of Behavior Modification Methods
This section briefly describes some of the most common behavior modification methods. This is a young field, and other techniques are continually being developed and evaluated by clinical researchers. Thus, the methods included here should not be considered an exhaustive list.

Methods Using Positive Reinforcement. Positive reinforcement is a technical term roughly synonymous with *reward*. A positive reinforcer is defined as any event following a given response that increases the chances of that response recurring. Typical positive reinforcers include tangible items, such as money or food; social events, such as praise or attention; and activities, such as the opportunity to engage in recreation or to watch television. However, what is reinforcing or motivating for some people—what they will work for—is not necessarily reinforcing for others. As a result, when using behavior modification procedures with any individual, the mental health worker needs to determine what particular items and activities will reinforce that person's behavior at that time.

Methods that use positive reinforcement form the major class of methods among behavior modification techniques. In general, positive reinforcement is used to develop and maintain new behavior, and the removal of positive reinforcement is used to decrease the frequency of undesired behavior. Positive reinforcement is used in teaching social behavior, in improving classroom management, in motivating better and faster learning of academic materials, in maintaining necessary weight loss, and in teaching new skills of all sorts.

In one research project, positive reinforcement is being used to help disruptive, underachieving children. Among a variety of procedures being used, teachers praise the children for appropriate behavior and send home daily reports. The children's parents reward them for good daily reports. The researcher, K. Daniel O'Leary (State University of New York at Stony Brook), reports that the children's disruptive behavior is reduced as a result of this program.

Although some positive reinforcers are much more effective if a person has been temporarily deprived of them, others continue to be reinforcing virtually regardless of how often an individual is exposed to them. Thus, by carefully selecting reinforcers, it should not be necessary to deprive an individual beyond the natural deprivations that occur in daily life, to be able to reinforce him positively.

One increasingly common use of positive reinforcement is in the group-management procedure called *token economy* (Ayllon & Azrin, 1968).[1] In a successful token economy program, the participants receive tokens when they engage in appropriate behavior and, at some later time, exchange the tokens for any of a variety of positively reinforcing items and activities, just as money is used in society at large. Thus, the token economy is basically a work-payment incentive system. As such, it can be used with institutionalized persons to strengthen behavior compatible with that needed in the society at large, such as regular performance on a job, self-care, maintenance of one's living quarters, and exchange of currency for desired items.

[1]Because the report on which this article was based was prepared for the general public, we have not attempted a thorough or scholarly review of the literature. Rather, we have selected current and pertinent examples of articles and books to support our points.

One advantage of the token economy, given the limitation in professional manpower, is that nonprofessional personnel are typically the actual agents of therapeutic change. If therapeutic procedures are to be extended to the many persons who require help, professional personnel must make increased use of those in direct contact with the persons requiring service. Those persons who can administer a token economy without special advanced training include nurses, aides, correctional officers, and friends and family members of the individual receiving the service. Such persons should, of course, receive appropriate professional supervision.

The early development of the token economy system took place almost exclusively in closed psychiatric wards. Token economies were found quite useful in preventing or overcoming the deterioration of normal social behavior, or what Gruenberg (1967) has called the "social breakdown syndrome," that accompanies prolonged custodial hospitalization, whatever the initial diagnosis. The token economy method is now being extended to acute psychiatric programs, to public school classrooms, and to classrooms for disadvantaged, hyperactive, retarded, and emotionally disturbed children (Anderson, 1967; O'Leary & Drabman, 1971). Such programs are also used with persons described as delinquents or as having character disorders, to enhance their educational achievement and to improve their adjustment to military or civilian environments (Cohen & Filipczak, 1971; Colman, 1971). Tokens are also used to increase children's attention spans and to improve self-help skills in retardates (e.g., Minge & Ball, 1967).

In the behavior modification technique of *shaping*, a desired behavior is broken down into successive steps that are taught one by one. Each of the steps is reinforced until it is mastered, and then the individual moves on to the next step. In this way, the new behavior is learned gradually as the individual comes closer and closer to an approximation of the behavioral goal.

New behavior can also be taught by means of

modeling. In this method, a person who already knows how to engage in some desired behavior demonstrates it for the individual who is learning. For example, if a client was learning socially appropriate ways to greet members of the opposite sex, another person would demonstrate them for him or her.

The model demonstrating the appropriate behavior can be an actual one or an imaginary one. Alan E. Kazdin (Pennsylvania State University) is conducting a study of some facets of imaginary, or covert, modeling. Persons who have problems with assertiveness are taught to imagine one or several other persons engaging in the sort of assertive behavior they hope to learn themselves; then they are tested to see how much their own assertiveness has increased.

In *contingency contracting*, the mental health worker and the client decide together on the behavioral goals and on the reinforcement the client will receive when the goals are achieved. For example, a parent and child might agree that it would be desirable if the home were neater, specifically, if the child's playthings were appropriately stored after a certain time in the evening. The child might request that the parent agree to take him to a favorite activity after he had put away his playthings for a specified number of days. A contract often involves an exchange; that is, each person entering into the contract agrees both to change his own behavior and to provide reinforcement for the changes the other person makes. Such a mutual contract is frequently used in marriage counseling.

The methods of contingency contracting are being studied by Henry M. Boudin (University of Florida) to see how they can be made effective for dealing with the special behavior problems characteristic of drug abusers. The goal of this project is to reduce drug dependence in addicts being treated in an outpatient setting.

Aversive Control.   Some types of inappropriate behavior, such as addictions and certain sexual behaviors, appear to be maintained because their immediate consequences are naturally reinforcing for the individual. In such cases, aversive control techniques are sometimes used to combat long-term consequences that may be much more detrimental to the individual than the aversive methods themselves. Aversive methods are also used for behaviors that are life-threatening, such as severe self-mutilation.

In general, an aversive stimulus, that is, something unpleasant to the person, is used to help the person reduce his desire to carry out the inappropriate behavior (Rachman & Teasdale, 1969). After aversive therapy, for example, a man who formerly became sexually excited only when thinking of women's shoes might report that he had lost interest in the shoes. In the aversive control technique, the individual can avoid the aversive stimulus, that is, it will not occur, as long as he does not perform the behavior that he and the mental health worker have agreed is undesirable. When aversive therapy is appropriately conducted, it is accompanied by positive reinforcement of normal behavior. No explanations of how aversive therapy works or why it is effective only under some conditions are generally accepted yet.

Perhaps the most commonly used aversive stimulus in behavior modification is a brief, low-level electric shock. This type of aversive stimulus has been highly effective in ameliorating severe behavioral problems such as self-injurious behavior (e.g., see Bucher, 1969). When properly used, the shocks are very brief. Shock used this way causes no lingering pain or tissue damage and can be administered with precise control (Baer, 1970). The use of shock as an aversive control procedure is entirely different from its use in electroconvulsive therapy, a procedure completely outside the scope of behavior modification.

A different method of aversive control uses the removal of positive reinforcement, such as privileges, following a given undesirable behavior. This is a technique commonly used by American parents (Sears, Maccoby, & Levin, 1957). One technique involving the removal of positive reinforcement is the *time-out* procedure, in which inappropriate behavior is followed by a period of brief social isolation.

The time-out procedure is one of a number of behavior modification techniques being used in a study of preschool children with poor social, language, and cognitive skills. The goal of the investigator, Donald M. Baer (University of Kansas), is to reduce the children's hyperactive and rebellious behavior. When a child engages in disruptive behavior, he is placed for a brief period in a small room adjoining the classroom. This aversive control for disruptive behavior is combined with a wide variety of positive reinforcing procedures for appropriate behavior.

Fines are another example of aversive control; fines require the individual to give up some positive reinforcement following an instance of inappropriate behavior.

Aversive stimuli are commonly used in attempts to reduce excessive drinking by associating the drinking experience with an aversive stimulus. For example, recent research on alcoholism has employed electric shock as an aversive stimulus to teach the alcoholic patient to avoid continued drinking beyond a criterion blood alcohol level. This has reportedly been successful in helping problem drinkers learn to limit their intake to moderate levels typical of social drinking (Lovibond, 1970).

In research being conducted by Roger E. Vogler (Patton State Hospital and Pacific State Hospital, California), alcoholic persons receiving treatment either in the hospital or as outpatients receive electric shock if they drink too much alcohol in a barlike setting in the hospital. Shock is also used to train the patients to drink slowly and to discriminate when their blood alcohol concentration exceeds a specific level.

Drugs such as Anectine and Antabuse have also been used as aversive treatment for alcoholic persons.

Another relatively common use of aversive stimuli is in the control of self-injurious and self-destructive behavior such as head banging or tongue biting. Such behavior can apparently be eliminated by brief application of a strong aversive stimulus immediately after the response (Bucher & Lovaas, 1968; Risley, 1968).

Occasionally, infants, young children, and some mentally retarded persons "ruminate," that is, they apparently voluntarily eject food from their stomachs into their mouths where it is either reswallowed or further ejected from their mouths. When this problem is severe, it can be life-threatening and may have serious detrimental effects on the physical, emotional, and social development of the child. Thomas Sajwaj (University of Mississippi) has developed a procedure using lemon juice as a mild aversive stimulus to control the ruminative behavior: When the infant or child regurgitates, a small amount of lemon juice is immediately squirted into his mouth by an attendant. Preliminary results with a few children suggest that this aversive therapy eliminates the rumination and that no other maladaptive behavior appears.

A consistent finding from research on aversive control is that the effects of the therapeutic use of aversive stimuli seem to be restricted to the particular behavior that is associated with the aversive stimulus, in that particular situation, with that particular therapist. That is, the effects of aversive stimuli do not seem to generalize very much (Bucher & Lovaas, 1968; Risley, 1968).

In contrast to the somewhat limited effects of aversive stimuli in controlling the specific undesirable behaviors, the positive side effects of this treatment seem to be rather widespread. For example, it is commonly reported that once the use of aversive stimuli has eliminated patients' self-injurious behavior, they avoid people less and are more responsive to other therapy aimed at teaching them adaptive responses.

Although the effects of aversive stimuli may, in many cases, be only temporary, the individuals will not respond with the undesirable behavior for at least some period of time. During that time, they are more amenable to learning new, appropriate responses. On the whole, research suggests that the most effective way of eliminating inappropriate behavior is to follow it with aversive stimuli, at the same time positively reinforcing desired behavior. If the environment then continues to support the new, desired responses, the inappropriate behavior will soon cease to occur. Then, because the aversive stimuli are used only following inappropriate behavior, they need no longer be administered. The effects of the initial aversive control will, however, be lasting, because the individual will now have learned to make appropriate responses.

It is important to note, however, that in the absence of rewarded alternatives, a response suppressed by an aversive technique is likely to recur. To ensure that it does not, the individuals being treated should be taught behavior maintainable by rewards occurring naturally in their environment.

In some instances, simply stopping the undesirable behavior enables the individual to obtain natural rewards. For the "ruminating" child, for example, stopping the ejection of food, in itself, allows proper digestion of food, greater comfort, and normal eating, growing, and developing. In addition, the infant is then more receptive to normal learning experiences.

Overcorrection. Overcorrection is a behavior modification method combining positive reinforcement and aversive control, and is used to discourage inappropriate or disruptive behavior. In this procedure, the person who has engaged in the inappropriate behavior not only remedies the situation he has caused, but also "overcorrects" it. That is, he is required to restore the disrupted situation to a better state than existed before the disruption. For example, a violent patient in a mental institution who overturns a bed in a dormitory might be required not only to right that bed and make it up again, but also to straighten the bedclothes on all the other beds in that dormitory. Making up the bed that was overturned corrects the situation

that the violent behavior disrupted; making up all the other beds is the "overcorrection."

Often, an inappropriate or disruptive behavior receives some sort of reinforcement. For example, stealing results in the thief acquiring goods he desires; turning over a bed might get a patient attention and concern from an otherwise busy ward staff. Thus, one function of the overcorrection procedure is to terminate any such reinforcement associated with the inappropriate behavior: The thief must return the stolen goods, for example.

Moreover, overcorrection is an aversive stimulus, because it requires effort to complete the overcorrection and because the person cannot engage in other behavior while he completes the overcorrection task. In addition, the overcorrection procedure itself may often be educative, in that the process of restoring the original situation generally requires the individual to engage in appropriate behavior.

Overcorrection has been a particularly effective technique in eliminating aggressive and disruptive behavior in institutionalized patients (Foxx & Azrin, 1972; Webster & Azrin, 1973). One of the advantages of overcorrection over other methods for dealing with these problems is that severe aversive stimuli may not be involved in overcorrection.

Systematic Desensitization. Gradual, progressive exposure to feared situations has long been advocated as a means of eliminating or reducing maladaptive anxiety or avoidance behavior. In systematic desensitization, the exposure is preplanned in graduated steps. In general, this procedure involves teaching the patient to relax and then having him imagine or actually encounter increasingly disturbing situations. The patient usually does not move on to a more disturbing item until he can remain deeply relaxed with a less disturbing one. Recent research, however, has suggested that some degree of forced exposure can also be effective in reducing fears.

If a patient is afraid of heights, for example,

the therapist works together with the patient to develop a list of increasingly fearful situations. For example, the patient might say he is very afraid of looking out from the top of the Empire State Building, but hardly afraid at all of climbing a small ladder. He then is trained to relax, and the therapist asks him to imagine each of the series of situations, starting with the one he is least afraid of, the one arousing little or no tension or fear. Over a series of therapy sessions, the patient is then exposed systematically to the whole list of fearful situations and, at the end of treatment, is able to maintain his relaxed state even while imagining scenes that were initially extremely fearful. Patients are usually encouraged to try out their newly learned ability to relax in the face of the formerly fearful situation outside of the therapy setting. Generalization of the effects of systematic desensitization from the treatment setting to real life is typically found, especially when the patient has done the "homework" of gradually facing what used to be fearful.

Systematic desensitization is used clinically by behavior therapists to treat unreasonable fears, frigidity, insomnia, interpersonal anxiety, and other clinical problems in which anxiety is a core problem.

Thomas L. Creer (Children's Asthma Research Institute and Hospital, Denver) demonstrated the effectiveness of systematic desensitization in the treatment of children's asthma. As a result of the treatment, the children learned to be less afraid of having asthma attacks and used significantly less medication.

Assertive Training. When a person fails to stand up for his rights in an appropriately firm manner, he may not have acquired appropriate assertive behavior, or he may not be engaging in behavior that he actually knows how to do. Similarly, persons who do not express positive feelings in appropriate situations also may lack appropriate assertive skills or an appreciation of the situations in which those skills should normally be used.

Assertive training is taught by a combination of methods, including modeling of appropriate behavior by the therapist or some other person and reinforced practice by the patient. The overall goal of this type of behavior therapy is the alteration of the patients' interpersonal interactions.

Methods Using Drugs. On the whole, behavior modification procedures emphasize environmental manipulation. However, drugs are occasionally used as an integral part of a behavioral treatment, either following a particular behavior or as an adjunct to a behavioral program.

A few case studies in the literature report the use of drugs as aversive stimuli when the therapist was attempting to reduce some inappropriate behavior. For example, succinylcholine chloride (Anectine) was given to one individual with a severe dependency on sniffing various substances such as airplane glue. In the treatment, the patient sniffed one of these substances and was immediately injected with Anectine, which produces an extremely unpleasant sensation of drowning and suffocating. The treatment was conducted under the supervision of an anesthesiologist. After this treatment, the patient refrained from sniffing the substance associated with the Anectine (Blanchard, Libet, & Young, 1973).

Anectine and emetic drugs such as Antabuse are also used as aversive treatment for alcoholic persons, although the evidence suggests that the treatments are not strongly effective.

When drugs are used as part of an aversive control program in behavior modification, they must take effect immediately after the occurrence of a specific inappropriate behavior. This temporal relationship between the behavior and the aversive action of the drug is considered to be an essential aspect of the therapy. As noted later in this article, giving aversive drugs independently of a person's behavior is not behavior modification in the sense in which we are using that term.

Drugs are also sometimes used to facilitate the

progress of a behavioral program. Brevital is a drug that enhances relaxation. Some practitioners who use systematic desensitization give their patients small doses of Brevital if the patients are otherwise having trouble learning to relax in the therapy sessions (Brady, 1966). Usually, the dosage level of the drug is gradually adjusted so that the patient soon relaxes without the assistance of the drug.

*

Behavior Modification in Prisons

Behavior modification has become an increasingly controversial yet important law enforcement tool. Many people feel that the use of behavior modification in prisons conflicts with the values of individual privacy and dignity.

Persons using behavior modification procedures are being particularly criticized for their attempts to deal with the rebellious and nonconformist behavior of inmates in penal institutions. Because the behavioral professional is often in the position of assisting in the management of prisoners whose rebelliousness and antagonism to authority are catalysts for conflict within the institution, the distinctions among his multiple functions as therapist, manager, and rehabilitator can become blurred and his allegiance confused. Although the professional may quite accurately perceive his role as benefiting the individual, he may at the same time appear to have the institution, rather than the prisoner, as his primary client.

Frequently, the goal of effective behavior modification in penal institutions is the preservation of the institution's authoritarian control. Although some prison behavior modification programs are designed to educate the prisoners and benefit them in other ways, other programs are directed toward making the prisoners less troublesome and easier to handle, thus adjusting the inmates to the needs of the institution.

A related problem is that in prisons, as elsewhere, the term *behavior modification* is often misused as a label for any procedure that aims to alter behavior, including excessive isolation,

sensory deprivation, and severe physical punishment. Behavior modification then becomes simply a new name for old and offensive techniques.

The question of voluntary consent is an especially difficult problem when those participating in a program are prison inmates (Shapiro, 1974). It is not clear whether there can ever be a real "volunteer" in a prison, because inmates generally believe they will improve their chances for early parole if they cooperate with prison officials' requests to participate in a special program. There are other pressures as well; for example, participation in a novel program may be a welcome relief from the monotony of prison life.

The use of behavior modification in the prisons came to national attention recently when the Law Enforcement Assistance Administration (LEAA) withdrew its support from some behavior modification programs. According to a spokesman for LEAA, this was done because the agency staff did not have the technical and professional skills to screen, evaluate, or monitor such programs. The termination of the programs was criticized by the American Psychological Association (APA) as an injustice to the public and to prison inmates. An APA news release said that the LEAA decision would tend "to stifle the development of humane forms of treatment that provide the offender the opportunity to fully realize his or her potential as a contributing member of society."

A similar point of view was expressed by Norman A. Carlson, Director of the Federal Bureau of Prisons (U.S. Congress, 1974), in discussing the difficulty of determining which programs should be described as behavior modification programs:

"In its broadest sense, virtually every program in the Bureau of Prisons is designed to change or modify behavior. Presumably, the Federal courts commit offenders to custody because their serious criminal behavior is unacceptable to society. The assumption is that during the period of incareeration, individuals will change their patterns of behavior so that after release, they will not become involved in further criminal activity."

In general, when behavior modification programs are introduced in federal prisons, it is important that they be consistent with this philosophy.

A Perspective on the Use of Behavior Modification in Prisons. A major problem in using behavior modification in prisons is that positive programs begun with the best of intentions may become subverted to punitive ones by the oppressive prison atmosphere. Generally, behavior modification programs are intended to give prisoners the opportunity to learn behavior that will give them a chance to lead more successful lives in the world to which they will return, to enjoy some sense of achievement, and to understand and control their own behavior better. Unfortunately, in actual practice, the programs sometimes teach submission to authority instead.

Critical questions in the use of behavior modification in prisons are thus: How are the goals to be chosen for the program? How is continued adherence to those goals to be monitored? Behavior modification should not be used in an attempt to facilitate institutionalization of the inmate or to make him adjust to inhumane living conditions. Furthermore, no therapist should accept requests for treatment that take the form "make him *behave*," when the intent of the request is to make the person conform to oppressive conditions.

Currently, a common position is that of recommending the elimination of behavior modification programs in prisons, on the grounds that such therapy must be coercive since consent cannot be truly voluntary. However, before this drastic step is taken, careful consideration should be given to the consequences. If constructive programs are eliminated, it would deny the opportunity of improvement for those inmates who genuinely want to participate and who might benefit from the programs. It seems far better to build in safeguards than to discard all attempts at rehabilitation of prison inmates, whether behavior modification or any other rehabilitative method is involved.

Suggested Procedures. The appropriate way to conduct treatment programs in prisons and, in fact, whether such programs should even be offered are matters by no means settled. Because of the custodial and potentially coercive nature of the prison setting and the pervasive problem of power imbalance, special procedures are needed to protect the rights and dignity of inmates when they engage in any program, not only behavior modification. Some procedures are suggested here in an attempt to add to the dialogue about ways to give prisoners the option of participating in programs and yet not coerce them into doing so.

A review committee should be constituted to review both the methods and goals of proposed treatment programs and to monitor the programs once they are in effect. The committee should be kept continually informed of the results of the programs, including short- and long-term evaluations, and of any changes in goals or procedures. A meaningful proportion of the members of this committee should be prisoner representatives, and the committee should also include persons with appropriate legal backgrounds. The person conducting the behavior modification program should be accountable to this committee and, ultimately, to all the individuals participating in the program.

As is always the case with such review panels, conflicting philosophies and differing loyalties may make it difficult for the panel members to agree unanimously on decisions. Such a panel would, however, provide a regular opportunity for conflicting points of view to be expressed, an opportunity generally not otherwise available. Thus, the group's discussions could, at a minimum, sensitize program administrators and prison officials to the critical issues.

When this committee, including both prisoners and staff members, has chosen the goals and methods of the program, each potential participant should have a realistic right to decline participation. If a prisoner refuses to cooperate, he should neither lose privileges he already has, nor receive additional punishment, for so declining. Presentation of the program to the prisoner should include a description of the potential benefits of participation both in the institution and later outside of it. Ideally, the prisoner should be offered a choice among several different kinds of programs, rather than the single alternative of a behavior modification program or nothing.

Implications for Behavior Modification of Emerging Legal Rulings

In the last few years, the courts have begun to make rulings on the rights of institutionalized persons, including the mentally ill. The emerging law may have a major impact on behavior modification programs, in particular, because the recent rulings extend rights that are considered basic and presumably available to all persons. Although even the major decisions apply legally only in the jurisdiction where they are announced (unless they are ratified by the U.S. Supreme Court), often other areas adopt rules or pass legislation consistent with them, so that such decisions often have impact far beyond a circumscribed geographic area.

The recent decisions are an important step forward in more clearly defining the rights of patients. In particular, the identification of specific items and activities to which patients are entitled under all circumstances seems to be a major advance. Even though these legal rulings in effect require the behavioral worker to be far more ingenious in selecting reinforcers for use in institutions (as explained below), this professional inconvenience is far outweighed by the gain in human rights for patients. No therapeutic program should have to depend for its existence on the continuation of a dehumanizing environment.

Judicial rulings are not necessary to emphasize that aversive techniques are neither legally nor ethically acceptable when used solely for oppressive purposes or without the consent of the person on whom they are used, or his guardian. The recent legal reinterpretations relating to human welfare are concerned mainly with limiting possible abuses of positive reinforcement.

For example, one of the most common ways for mental hospital patients to earn money or tokens for token economy programs is by working in on-and off-ward jobs. Such employment is justified by mental health professionals on the grounds that it has an educational purpose: It teaches the patients skills needed in the outside world. The decision in *Wyatt v. Stickney*[2] seems to restrict the use of hospital work as a means of earning money or tokens. In that decision, the court barred all involuntary work by mentally handicapped patients on hospital operations and maintenance and specifically stated that privileges should not be contingent on the patients' work on such jobs. A similar ruling was made in *Jobson v. Henne*.[3]

Usually when patients work on hospital jobs, they are compensated at a level far below the prevailing wage or even below the minimum legal wage. This practice of employing institutionalized persons to perform productive labor associated with the maintenance of the institution without normal compensation has been called "institutional peonage" (Bartlett, 1964). The *Wyatt* decision specified jobs that may be performed by mentally handicapped patients and held that the patients must be compensated for that work at the prevailing minimum wage. Another recent case, *Souder v. Brennan*,[4] extended the principle of minimum wage compensation to all institutionalized persons in non-federal facilities for the mentally ill and mentally retarded. Although the minimum wage requirement may seem reasonable on the

---

[2]325 F.Supp. 781 (M.D.Ala.1971), 334 F.Supp. 1341 (M.D.Ala.1971), 344 F.Supp. 373 (M.D.Ala.1972), and 344 F.Supp. 387 (M.D.Ala.1972). This case, known as *Wyatt v. Aderholt* on appeal, was affirmed in part and modified in part, 503 F.2d 1305 (5 Cir., 1974).

[3]335 F.2d 129 (2d Cir., 1966).

[4]367 F.Supp. 808(D.D.C.1973).

face of it, it could be a problem for many mental institutions and institutions for the retarded that cannot afford even the minimum wage. Under *Wyatt*, apparently the only types of work exempt from minimum wage coverage are therapeutic work unrelated to hospital functioning and tasks of a personal house-keeping nature (Wexler, 1973).

Among the reinforcers used in some token economies are such basic necessities of life as food, mattresses, grounds privileges, and privacy. That is, in these programs, the patients have been able to have these items or engage in these activities only if they were able to purchase the item or activity with their tokens. According to recent legal developments, such as the *Wyatt v. Stickney* case, patients have a constitutional right to a residence unit with screens or curtains to insure privacy, a comfortable bed, a closet or locker for personal belongings, a chair, a bedside table, nutritionally adequate meals, visitors, attendance at religious services, their own clothes or a selection of suitable clothing, regular physical exercise including access to the outdoors, interaction with members of the opposite sex, and a television set in the day room. In other cases (*Inmates of Boys' Training School v. Affleck*[5] and *Morales v. Turman*[6]), similar kinds of activities and amenities were ordered to be available for juveniles in residential facilities. Thus, these legal rulings appear to have defined as basic rights many of the items and activities that have until now been employed as reinforcers in token economies.

The *Wyatt* decision was upheld on appeal by the U.S. Court of Appeals for the Fifth Circuit.[7] Even before that action, the ruling was already influential. However, because of inconsistencies among rulings, it is not clear at the moment just how much these rulings entitle the members of various institutionalized populations to have and what sorts of items and activities can be restricted to those persons with sufficient tokens to purchase them (Wexler, 1973).

Furthermore, the new rulings do not totally prevent the inclusion in a token economy of the various items and activities named in the rulings. Rather, the result of the rulings is to permit the restriction in availability of these items and activities only with the consent of the patients or representatives of the patients. That is, these constitutional rights, like other constitutional rights, can be waived in suitable circumstances by the individuals involved. For example, a patient may consent to having his access to television restricted so that television programs are available to him only following changes in his behavior that he desires to make.

Mental health workers who want to use the token economy procedure are now beginning to search for new types of reinforcers or new methods of reinforcement delivery that will not require special waivers of constitutional rights by the patients. Suitable reinforcers would be those beyond which any patient would ordinarily be entitled or to which he would normally have access. Many professionals believe that such new types of reinforcers can be developed, that behavior change can be produced without depriving patients of basic necessities or asking them to waive their constitutional rights, and that this entire legal development is a significant step forward. The rulings, however, are recent one, and extensive changes in practice have yet to occur.

Recent legal rulings have implications for behavior modification procedures other than the token economy. For example, the *Wyatt* decision specified in detail the conditions under which electric shock devices could be used with mentally retarded residents. That ruling and also the ruling in *New York State Association for Retarded Children v. Rockefeller*[8] set limits on the use of seclusion in treating mentally retarded and mentally ill patients.

Other legal rulings (e.g., *Rouse v. Cameron*[9]

---

[5] 346 F.Supp. 1354 (D.R.I.1972).

[6] 364 F.Supp. 166 (E.D.Tex.1973), Memorandum Opinion, 383 F.Supp. 53 (E.D.Tex., Aug. 30, 1974).

[7] *Wyatt. v. Aderholt*, 503 F.2d 1305 (5 Cir., 1974).

[8] 357 F.Supp. 752 (E.D.N.Y.1973).

[9] 373 F.2d 451 (D.C.Cir., 1966).

and *Donaldson v. O'Connor*[10]) have held that patients have a right to treatment. A possible implication of this might be an extension of patients' rights with concomitant restrictions on the use of some behavior modification techniques. At the same time, a right to effective treatment might result in a requirement that all therapies include the sort of continual monitoring of effectiveness that is generally standard practice in behavior modification. Judicial rulings in this area have been inconsistent, however, some supporting a right to treatment (e.g., *Rouse v. Cameron* and *Wyatt v. Stickney*) and some holding that there is no legal obligation to provide treatment (e.g., *Burnham v. Department of Public Health of the State of Georgia*[11] and *New York State Association for Retarded Children v. Rockefeller*). In the 1974 appellate court decision upholding *Wyatt* (see Footnote 7), the court also overruled the lower court decision in the *Burnham* case. Thus, the Fifth Circuit Court has ruled, for that jurisdiction, that mental patients as a class have a federal constitutional right to adequate treatment when committed against their will to state institutions. Inconsistencies remain, however, especially in decisions regarding voluntary hospitalization (Budd & Baer, in press). It is still too early, also, to draw clear implications for behavior modification from the appellate court decisions on right to adequate treatment.

ETHICS IN BEHAVIOR MODIFICATION

Recently, many people have expressed increasing concern that those conducting behavior modification programs should take special care that their methods are ethical and that the individuals undergoing behavior change are protected. Although, on the whole, researchers and therapists using behavior modification methods exercise normal caution, some aspects of the

problem do not always receive the attention they deserve.

One difficulty in establishing ethical standards for behavior modification is that the issues and problems are different for different populations in different settings. Informed consent, for example, is clearly meaningful when a normal adult voluntarily goes to an outpatient clinic to obtain guidance in altering a specific behavior that he wants to change. However, when prisoners are offered the opportunity of participating in behavior modification, it is by no means clear that they can give truly voluntary consent.

A further difficulty in this area is that the appropriate person to determine the means and goals of treatment is different for different populations in different settings. The mental health professional must decide in each instance who his client is, that is, who the person or group is with whom he should negotiate regarding the choice of means and goals for a behavior modification program. It is often both obvious and correct that the ostensible client is the actual one. For example, a neurotic patient comes to a clinic to be relieved of his fear of flying in planes: The patient, determining for himself the goal of therapy, is the true client. Or, when a husband and wife are referred to a mental health worker to learn contingency contracting as a method of improving their marriage, it is generally clear that both partners have chosen the goal of improvement of their interpersonal relations. The mental health worker's responsibility is to assist them in achieving this goal.

On the other hand, when a behavioral consultant is asked to help a teacher keep pupils in their seats working quietly at all times, the ethical situation is less clear. Are these the optimum classroom conditions for learning, and are the children's best interests served by teaching them to be still, quiet, and docile (O'Leary, 1972; Winett & Winkler, 1972)? The mental health professional may want to suggest alternative goals or work together with the class and the teacher in developing appropriate goals.

Similarly, when an administrator of an in-

---

[10]493 F.2d 507 (5 Cir., 1974), 95 S.Ct. 171 (1974).

[11]349 F.Supp. 1335 (N.D.Ga.1972), appeal docketed, No. 72–3110, 5 Cir., Oct. 4, 1972. This case was consolidated for argument on appeal with *Wyatt* (see Footnote 2).

stitution for the retarded asks a behavioral professional to establish a token economy to motivate the inmates to work on jobs for the hospital, the professional may want to work together with an advisory committee to determine the relative value of that work activity for the hospital and for the retardates. When he is asked to have the hospital as his client, he needs also to consider the rights of the patients, the potential benefits to them of the activity, and any risks that may be involved. The professional may decide, for example, that such hospital jobs have minimal benefit for the patients and thus may feel the institution's goal is an inappropriate one. Identifying the true client is also a critical problem when behavior modification programs are used in prisons.

*

REFERENCES

Anderson, R. C. Educational psychology. *Annual Review of Psychology,* 1967, *18,* 129–164.

Ayllon, T., & Azrin, N. H. *The token economy.* New York: Appleton-Century-Crofts, 1968.

Baer, D. M. A case for the selective reinforcement of punishment. In C. Neuringer & J. L. Michael (Eds.), *Behavior modification in clinical psychology.* New York: Appleton-Century-Crofts, 1970.

Bartlett, F. L. Institutional peonage: Our exploitation of mental patients. *Atlantic Monthly,* 1964, *214*(1), 116–119.

Blanchard, E. B., Libet, J. M., & Young, L. D. Apneic aversion and covert sensitization in the treatment of a hydrocarbon inhalation addiction: A case study. *Journal of Behavior Therapy and Experimental Psychiatry,* 1973, *4,* 383–387.

Brady, J. P. Brevital-relaxation treatment of frigidity. *Behaviour Research and Therapy,* 1966, *4,* 71–77.

Bucher, B. Some ethical issues in the therapeutic use of punishment. In R. D. Rubin & C. M. Franks (Eds.), *Advances in behavior therapy, 1968.* New York: Academic Press, 1969.

Bucher, B., & Lovaas, O. I. Use of aversive stimulation in behavior modification. In M. R. Jones (Ed.), *Miami symposium on the prediction of behavior, 1967.* Coral Gables, Fla.: University of Miami Press, 1968.

Budd, K., & Baer, D. M. Behavior modification and the law: Implications of recent judicial decisions. *Journal of Applied Behavior Analysis,* in press.

Cohen, H. L., & Filipczak, J. *A new learning environment.* San Francisco, Calif.: Jossey-Bass, 1971.

Colman, A. D. *Planned environment in psychiatric treatment.* Springfield, Ill.: Charles C. Thomas, 1971.

Foxx, R. M., & Azrin, N. H. Restitution: A method of eliminating aggressive-disruptive behavior of retarded and brain damaged patients. *Behaviour Research and Therapy,* 1972, *10,* 15–27.

Gruenberg, E. M. The social breakdown syndrome—Some origins. *American Journal of Psychiatry,* 1967, *123,* 12–20.

Lovibond, S. H. Aversive control of behavior. *Behavior Therapy,* 1970, *1,* 80–91.

Minge, M. R., & Ball, T. S. Teaching of self-help skills to profoundly retarded patients. *American Journal of Mental Deficiency,* 1967, *71,* 864–868.

O'Leary, K. D. Behavior modification in the classroom: A rejoinder to Winett and Winkler. *Journal of Applied Behavior Analysis,* 1972, *5,* 505–511.

O'Leary, K. D., & Drabman, R. Token reinforcement programs in the classroom: A review. *Psychological Bulletin,* 1971, *75,* 379–398.

Rachman, S., & Teasdale, J. *Aversion therapy and behaviour disorders.* Coral Gables, Fla.: University of Miami Press, 1969.

Risley, T. R. The effects and side effects of punishing the autistic behaviors of a deviant child. *Journal of Applied Behavior Analysis,* 1968, *1,* 21–34.

Sears, R. R., Maccoby, E., & Levin, H. *Patterns of childrearing.* Evanston, Ill.: Row, Peterson, 1957.

Shapiro, M. H. Legislating the control of behavior control: Autonomy and the coercive use of organic therapies. *Southern California Law Review,* 1974, *47,* 237–356.

U.S. Congress, House, Committee on the Judiciary, Subcommittee on Courts, Civil Liberties, and the Administration of Justice. *Oversight hearing: Behavior modification programs in the Federal Bureau of Prisons,*

93rd Cong., 2nd sess., 27 February 1974 (Serial No. 26). Washington, D.C.: U.S. Government Printing Office, 1974.

Webster, D. R., & Azrin, N. H. Required relaxation: A method of inhibiting agitative-disruptive behavior of retardates. *Behaviour Research and Therapy*, 1973, *11*, 67–78.

Wexler, D. B. Token and taboo: Behavior modification, token economies, and the law. *California Law Review*, 1973, *61*, 81–109.

Winett, R. A., & Winkler, R. C. Current behavior modification in the classroom: Be still, be quiet, be docile *Journal of Applied Behavior Analysis*, 1972, *5*, 499–504.

63. Aversive Behavior Modification with Drugs

ARTHUR L. MATTOCKS
CHARLES C. JEW

THE DRUG SUCCINYLCHOLINE (ANECTINE) HAS been widely used during recent years by medical practitioners as a muscle relaxant in proper dosages. Succinylcholine, when injected intravenously, results in a brief muscle paralysis and respiratory arrest. Administered in sufficient dosage, the patient goes through a sensation of suffocation similar to drowning although he remains fully conscious of the experience (temporary paralysis and apnea). This experience, to some, can be a highly frightening experience which psychologists would term "aversive."

*

Concerned with the inability to prevent self-destructive and/or assaultive behavior among extreme acting-out patients despite psychotherapy, phenothiozine tranquilizers, anti-depressant drugs, therapeutic milieu, electro-shock therapy and other resources, a program of Anectine treatment as a last resort was initiated at the California Medical Facility [CMF] in January, 1967. The first case was a patient who had continued inexorably to mutilate himself and imperil his life by swallowing six- to nine-inch sharpened metal wires which required multiple laparotomies. He then persistently reopened his laparotomy wounds and shoved pieces of wood and metal under his skin.

▶SOURCE: *"Assessment of an Aversive 'Contract' Program with Extreme Acting–Out Criminal Offenders,"* in Jay Katz (Ed.) *Experimentation with Human Beings.* (New York: Russell Sage Foundation, 1972. Pp. 1016–1018. Reprinted by permission.*

The use of Anectine treatment prevented the patient from harming himself for many weeks which led to the continuation of the program to handle similar patients who posed a constant serious threat to themselves (self-mutilation, suicidal attempts) or to others (assaults on other inmates or staff) for whom all available treatments within the institution have been exhausted and failed to alter their behavior. The conceptual scheme was to develop a strong association between any violent or dangerous acting-out behavior and the drug Anectine (and its frightful consequences) such that it would be an effective suppressant to further contemplation or commission of these acts.

The Anectine program was begun in January, 1967 and continued until April, 1968. During that time, sixty-four inmates participated by signing a treatment contract with the institution's Special Treatment Board.[1] The aversive

[1] . . . On five patients, consent was not received from the patient himself, but was granted by the institution's Special Treatment Board. Thus, these five patients were included in the treatment program against their will.

*

It is interesting to note that although only five of those interviewed in the present study were signed up involuntarily for the aversive treatment program, eighteen indicated they involuntarily signed the treatment contract indicating that they felt some implied pressure to do so in the doctor's request. Related to this is the fact that a sizable number of the patients perceived the motive of the doctor as one of punishing them even though the medical staff exerted efforts to assure the patients that this was not to punish but to

cues of the drug were described by the medical staff as each individual become involved in the program. The contract emphasized that he would receive an Anectine injection *if, and only if,* he indulged in behavioral acts such as (1) violently attacking others, (2) serious self-mutilation, or (3) suicidal attempts, but he would receive no injection if he did not commit such acts. It was therefore up to him whether he ultimately would receive an injection since this was determined by his own behavior.

As it will be seen later in the study, only a small portion of the patients involved in the program actually had violated their contracts and received Anectine injections. The actual administration followed closely the patients' acting-out behavior. Because the administering procedure is also a crucial part of the aversive program, it is outlined here as it was described by one of the medical staff administering the program:

"Our technique is simply to administer 20 to 40 mg. of succinylcholine intravenously with oxygen and an airway available, and to counsel the patient while he is under the influence of the drug that his behavior is dangerous to others or to himself, that it is desirable that he stop the behavior in question, and that sub-

sequent behavior of a nature which may be dangerous to others or to himself will be treated with similar aversive treatments. During the entire time, oxygen is administered so that there is no danger of anoxia and . . . there is no pain accompanying the procedure, only cessation of respiration for a period of approximately two minutes duration. We have been very careful to explain to all individuals involved that they will suffer no permanent ill effects, that the treatment is safe as long as it is given by competent medical personnel, that it will not cause pain, and that at all times they will be supervised closely so that they need not worry about ill effects of the treatment."

Most of the sixty-four patients in the program were housed in the acute treatment area due to their recurring pattern of extreme and potentially dangerous behavior both to themselves and others. Nearly all could be characterized as angry young men who directed their anger impulsively outwards in attacks on others, or inwardly towards themselves, or exhibited both types of behaviors at various times. The average age of the subjects was twenty-five years and the mean time at the institution was fifteen months. The frequency and repetition with which they engaged in these dangerous behaviors cannot be overstated. Examples of violent behavior of two of the patients read as follows:

---

help the patient control his own behavior. While the staff was successful in convincing a majority of the subjects interviewed of their helpful intentions, it is clear that in the environmental context, and with the experiential background of the subjects in the type of population used in this study, such efforts are not apt to meet with total success.

How severe is the Anectine experience from the point of view of the patient? Sixteen likened the experience to dying. Three of these compared it to actual experiences in the past in which they had almost drowned. The majority described it as a terrible, scary, experience. Nearly all of these subjects based their descriptions not only upon what the doctor had told them, but either on personal experience or the firsthand description from patients who had had an Anectine injection. Again, two patients denied the experience bothered them at all, and two were noncommittal. It would seem therefore that the perception of the aversive consequence by the patients was of sufficient severity to warrant consideration of this factor as a possible explanation for the inhibition of agressive behavior. [From an earlier draft of the same paper.]

"He was a twenty-four-year-old committed to prison for murder 2nd originally, who, while he was in the county jail, hanged his cell partner. On being sent to the California Department of Corrections he was placed in an adjustment center where he engaged in self-mutilative efforts which gained him admission to the institution hospital. While there he murdered another time (a defenseless psychotic prisoner) and was sent forthwith to us for psychiatric observation while he was waiting to stand trial. His stay at our institution was without self-mutilation or assault under the promise of Anectine treatment and he received no treatments.

"Another patient under the treatment program was considered by institution officials as very dangerous. He had killed one man and assaulted another with a bayonet (commitment offense). During his stay in the institution he accumulated twenty-three violations of rules necessitating thirteen placements in administrative segregation and/or isolation. He had threatened officers and recently 'stabbed' another inmate a few days ago."

Three months prior to the termination of the program, an evaluation strategy was developed by the CMF Research Unit to assess the impact of the Anectine program. The evaluation goals were to determine: (1) whether Anectine had an impact in inhibiting the continued repetition of suicidal, homicidal, and self-mutilative behavior(s), (2) whether a generalization effect will occur leading to the overall reduction of undesirable behavior, including those not specified within the treatment contract, and (3) whether the response to Anectine differs according to the type of commitment offense of the patient.

At the time of the data collection most of the patients had been under the Anectine "contract" for at least three months. Considering the frequent repetition of aggressive behavior among this population, the results shown tend to suggest Anectine is highly effective in inhibiting the commission of "contract" behavior in that only twenty-eight percent (18) of the population had received one or more injection of Anectine. Seventy-two percent (46) had not committed any of the specified acts and did not receive an injection of Anectine. This constitutes an improvement in that they fulfilled the treatment contract. While there is no way in which one can accurately estimate the number of assaults, stabbings, self-mutilations, and suicidal attempts inhibited through the use of the Anectine program, a fact not to be ignored is that fifty-seven percent of the patients were able to be assigned later to a psychiatric program or sufficiently stabilized for transfer to other prisons for programming.

Indeed, at the time of the evaluation, sixteen of the participants had been transferred to other penal institutions for programming. The remaining thirty-five were interviewed and their disciplinary records reviewed. . . .

*

A most unexpected result from the Anectine program data is the differential effect it has upon different types of criminal offenders, which came to light through comparing increases and decreases in disciplinary infractions among offense types. Patients who committed "crimes against persons" (i.e., robberies, homicides, assault, sex, rapes) responded entirely differently to the Anectine program than patients who committed crimes against property (fraud, theft, tax evasion, etc.) The former offense types tended to decrease while the latter tended to increase the overall number of disciplinary infractions as a result of the Anectine "contract."

*

This type of program seems to be particularly useful in institutions where the concern is to inhibit highly dangerous behavior through the temporary application of an aversive stimulus in which more effective alternatives are not to be found. However, extreme caution needs to be exercised in the use of Anectine because more knowledge is certainly needed to understand the subsequent anxiety and the side effects derived from its usage, especially the "paradoxical" effects of punishment in which the use of aversive stimuli may increase the rate of the punished behavior when the aversive stimulus is removed. In addition, not everyone in the program had considered the Anectine program "aversive." In subsequent interviews with some of the patients who received Anectine injections several indicated that they enjoyed undergoing the Anectine experience. In a similar vein, nine persons not only did not decrease but had actually exhibited an increase in their overall number of disciplinary infractions. Thus, careful selection as to who may be included in programs of this nature seems mandatory because the application of aversive stimuli to inhibit one or a series of behaviors may be highly effective to some patients, ineffective for some, and for still others may stimulate an increase in behaviors which the aversive stimuli were intended to inhibit.

64. Limitations of Behavior Control Techniques

ELBERT W. RUSSELL

ONE AREA OF CONTROL TO WHICH BEHAVIORISTIC methods have been applied is the area of coercive control. In this area operant methods, such as token economies, predominate since they have generally been applied in involuntary institutional settings. A coercive situation is defined here as any authoritarian program where participation by the S is involuntary. In these situations, the control of all aspects of the environment is placed in the hands of the behavior modifier by persons who are already in authority over the S prior to the assumption of control by the behaviorist. This effectively removes all but the most drastic countercontrol methods from the S. Although London[25] would probably prefer to class token economies under "informational control," he includes prisons and other involuntary institutions in his chapter on coercive controls. Thus, token economies and many other operant control measures properly belonged under his definition of coercive control.

In regard to the problem of the power of behavior controls, operant control situations, like token economies, demonstrate the effectiveness of behavior control methods when the therapist or E has been given extensive control over environmental conditions *prior* to the application of behavior methods. Since the more traditional coercive control methods found in involuntary

SOURCE: *"The Power of Behavior Control: A Critique of Behavior Modification Methods,"* Journal of Clinical Psychology (Special Monograph Supplement) (April, 1974), 30:125–132. Reprinted by permission.

institutions are already quite powerful, the problem is to identify the amount and areas in which operant methods increase this power to determine whether such group operant methods as the token economy can be applied with any power to a society which does not use coercive methods. If behavior methods do not increase the effectiveness of traditional coercive methods, they would hardly be effective in a free situation. Skinner's[32] Utopia, of course, is just exactly the application of such operant methods to a non-coercive situation.

So far, the literature does not reveal any major use of such operant methods in a non-coercive situation. Operant group methods have been applied to situations that are not institutional[29]. Nevertheless, in these situations the Ss usually have been children and coercive authority rested with their parents or teachers.

Among the behavioristic methods that have been studied, the most prominent have been token economies and "brain washing," and for reasons of space only these will be used as examples of behavior methods applied in a coercive situation.

TOKEN ECONOMIES

Before dealing with the effectiveness of operant methods, it should be noted that contrary to operant literature and Skinner's concepts, token economies, as usually operated, are constructed on an aversive foundation. They are far from being pure reward situations. In some cases, such as Burchard's[9] work, both reward and punishment are directly utilized. However, in most cases when reward alone is used, to make the rewards effective, the inmates must be deprived of certain basic needs, including food, either by placing them in a closed ward or by using an institutional facility which has previously deprived inmates of certain basic needs, due to a lack of, or unwillingness to spend, funds. In fact, all operant token programs require some method of preventing Ss from acquiring tokens or money from non-experimental sources. Thus, patients are deprived of alternative sources to satisfy their needs. While behaviorists may not consider this to be aversive, inmates do. They resent it and this increases the interpersonal distance between inmates and ward personnel. This type of information about S resentment is not obtained or published in normal research reports. However, an inside eyewitness to a token economy, Lachenmeyer,[22] describes this effect. The inmates, delinquent boys, in a token economy felt that "they had to work to obtain what boys in other units already had . . ."[22] (p. 55). This reinforced their feeling of "us against the authorities." Thus, in spite of obtaining much of the specific behaviors required by the program, total effect of the program may have been antitherapeutic.

Token economies also involve other problems stated by Lachenmeyer[22] but only briefly mentioned here. (These may not apply to all token economies but they are chronic with token economies in many institutional settings.) In the situation described by Lachenmeyer[22], the inmates had methods of controlling the attendants, countercontrols, so they could avoid some control. The attendant occasionally used tokens to reinforce inappropriate behavior for selfish reasons. In situations which lack extensive supervision, abuse of the operant system is easy and incidents of such abuse in other institutions are already known to most people close to this field. (This may be one reason that the behaviorists are so concerned with ethics[21].) Aides

were not sufficiently well paid, nor was sufficient time taken to train and supervise them. Many delinquent behaviors were not directly controlled by either reward or punishment using tokens, so they continued. The institutional administration did not adequately support the unit, but used it to "control" the worst troublemakers.

To Lachenmeyer's[22] suggestions as to how these problems could be cured, the author[9] of the original article on this token economy answered, "Instead, his 'easy solutions' provide few realistic suggestions for any program which hasn't access to unlimited funds and unlimited sources of skilled or highly educated personnel. This, then, excludes most institutional settings. Even given adequate funds and skilled personnel to carry out the proposed solutions, social behaviors remain subject to a wide spectrum of interpretation, are difficult to define objectively, and often serve to elicit or cue inappropriate staff behavior despite sophistication in behavioral management"[10] (p. 260). This comment could also have been written by a traditional insight therapist 20 years ago or today with almost no change in wording.

These problems and aversive elements might be expected to produce a certain amount of resistance and lack of cooperation, which is contrary to Skinner's theory[33]. According to that theory, if the experimenter has total control over all environmental contingencies, he can control any and all behavior.

The first reports[2,3] concerning token economies indicated that they were extremely effective in modifying the behavior of patients in mental hospitals. However, even in this early research, the ability to control institutionalized people was not complete. Atthowe and Krasner[2] report that 10% of the patients did not cooperate. It should be pointed out to people unfamiliar with institutionalized mental patients that with any kind of mild pressure most patients are cooperative to some extent (see Allen and Magaro's[1] study below).

However, resistance to a token economy does

occur. Cotter[12] described a situation labeled improperly as operant conditioning, although it was behavioristic aversive conditioning in conception. This situation utilized extreme negative reinforcements such as ECT or complete deprivation of food to force mental patients in Vietnam to work in fields where they might be shot at by the Viet Cong. Less severe methods had not been effective so that the severe reinforcements had to be instituted. Aside from the ethical misuse of behavior methods involved, this study demonstrated that unless backed by severe traditional coercive methods, group behavioristic methods are of limited power, when there is real resistance on the part of the patients. Another form that resistance may take is demonstrated in a study by Colter, Applegate, King and Kristal[11], which described a token reward system applied to disturbed adolescents in a state hospital, designed to increase their productivity in doing classwork. It was found that while the quantity of problems completed increased, the quality of work (number of problems done correctly) actually deteriorated.

The question of the general effectiveness of behavior methods is the primary concern here and recent studies of token economies have not demonstrated as high a level of effectiveness as was reported in the early studies. Lloyd and Garlington[24] published a study which used an ABAB design with 13 chronic schizphrenic women. Concerning their results they say, "The absolute magnitude of the changes between the different experimental conditions was not great, but was consistent both within and between patients." Ayllon and Azrin[4] reported changes of much greater magnitude but not of greater consistency. In a study by Allen and Magaro[1] designed to examine the effect of tokens on different types of patients' attendance at OT, they found that 18 (group 0 and 2) of 39 patients went to OT without receiving tokens; only 5 more (group 3) began going to receive tokens; but 16 (group 4) of 39 did not begin attending even to obtain tokens. The patients who did not care for OT simply did not respond to tokens.

Their main finding, consequently, was that by far the largest proportion of the total group rate of attendance was contributed by patients who would have gone to OT even if they were not given tokens. The group that began to attend OT only when paid tokens contributed little to the total group rate. Thus, the rates for token economies may be quite greatly inflated by patients who would have engaged in the required activities in any case. The need for control wards and patients is obvious.

In a rather ingenious study, Lloyd and Abel[23] set up three types of wards for 52 schizophrenics, ranked according to the amount of privileges and freedom granted in each ward. The "best" ward was provided the most freedom and privileges. The total program was designed to help patients leave the hospital. Patients moved to "better" or "worse" wards according to the amounts of tokens earned. At the end of 27 months, 63% of males and 71% of females had moved up, while 37% of males and 29% of females had moved down. However, most of the movement was only between the bottom two groups. Of the 52 patients, only 7 had been discharged and 5 were on visits at the end of the 27 months. 9 had been removed for illness or severe emotional disturbances. As might be expected, the patients who were discharged tended to be the least chronic—under 1.5 years of hospitalization. It should also be noted that the patients were pre-selected by the staff as those expected to do well on a token economy. These results cannot be called highly successful. There was no control ward, so a comparison could not be made with non-treated patients. In addition, the discharge rate appears to be approximately the same as that expected from hospitalized patients who received the usual treatment or lack of treatment.

Other studies, such as those by Burchard[9], Marks, Sonoda and Schalock[26], Meichenbaum, Bowers and Ross[28], Gripp and Magaro[15], and Richard and Saunders[31], were not designed to measure absolute effectiveness, but all apparently produced moderate increases in the specific behaviors rewarded. However, none appear to have equalled the results of the earlier studies. The recent studies indicate that, although perhaps not as successful as earlier studies, token economies are able to control certain specific behaviors, as have all coercive systems. Moreover, the operant methods appear to be somewhat more effective in dealing with a fairly wide range of specific behaviors than traditional methods, but they also appear to require additional effort and cost in terms of increased or at least specially selected personnel[15, 26].

Since it is impossible to isolate every type of behavior, much less control every item of behavior[10], a further question in the evaluation of effectiveness is, will these methods control behavior that is not specifically rewarded? Eyewitness accounts indicate that this often does not occur[13, 22]. On the other hand, several authors[2, 3, 5, 15, 26] have reported or documented that there is a general improvement in behavior of the wards with token economies. Atthowe and Krasner[2] raised the possibility that this might be due to a Hawthorne effect, but dismissed it.

THE HAWTHORNE EFFECT

The Hawthorne effect is an improvement in general behavior of a group due to a non-specific source, produced by *any* form of treatment which gives attention and encouragement to people. The improvement is undoubtedly due to suggestion. There have been at least two experiments that are partially related to this problem, though an adequately controlled study of this effect does not yet appear to have been published.

The study by Gripp and Magaro[15] was specifically designed to test the generalization effect of a token economy on such tests as the Psychiatric Reaction Profile and the Elgrin Behavior Rating Scale. They set up one token economy ward and compared the results against three control wards in which the treatment was not changed. However, the morale on the control wards, as measured by the Ward Atmos-

phere Scale, deteriorated at the time that the morale on the token treatment ward improved. Evidently, the personnel felt slighted. This attitude could be reflected in patient treatment. Groups of patients were transferred from one ward to another before the 6 month treatment began, to produce equivalent wards. As expected, the patients in the token economy ward improved to a statistical degree on many of the scales used, although in absolute terms the improvement was only moderate. A Hawthorne effect might be expected since the aides and graduate students used on the token economy ward were specially selected to be enthusiastic and the general morale on that ward did increase, while it became worse on control wards. One piece of information strongly indicates a Hawthorne effect: ". . . patients transferred from D$_2$ (token economy ward) to other wards prior to treatment improved in as many areas (5) as did those transferred to D$_2$ prior to treatment"[15] (p. 148). This improvement could be due to attention paid to the patients who were selected to be moved.

Another test of both this effect and of insight treatment was made by Marks, Sonoda and Schalock[26]. They compared token program treatment with relationship therapy using 22 (11 matched pairs) schizpohrenics. Patients in the reinforcement group were included in the planning of treatment and received some personal encouragement of a relationship variety; thus, there was the basis for a Hawthorne effect in the reinforcement group. The matched patients received relationship therapy for an equal length of time. Both groups demonstrated improvement of about equal amounts as measured on a group of 11 tests, including the Hospital Adjustment Scale. This does not fully answer the question about the Hawthorne effect; but it does indicate that relationships are a major element in treatment effects and may have as powerful effects as the operant elements of a token economy.

When all treatments are equally effective, the operation of a non-specific Hawthorne effect is highly suspect. Since the non-specific placebo effect is evidently the major source of effectiveness in individual therapy, the similar non-specific Hawthorne effect may be expected to account for much of the generalized effect of group operant procedures. Although no studies have been sufficiently controlled to determine the strength of the Hawthorne effect, the studies which do give some "measure" of this effect appear to indicate its presence quite strongly.

GENERALIZATION

If there is no specific generalization due to operant techniques, one may expect no therapeutic or behavior control that lasts beyond the specific operant procedures. This lack of generalization is exactly what appears to be happening. In most situations such a lack is found in verbal conditioning[17] and in operant methods applied to children[29]. In the area of coercive operant methodology with children, very few studies have demonstrated any generalization. One study, Walker, Mattson and Baston[36], indicated some generalization. 6 children in a token classroom were transferred to a regular school and 3 months after the end of the program 4 of the children still showed study efficiency 25% above previous work prior to token classroom treatment. However, since the teacher in the public school had been trained to maintain a reinforcement program, this was still not a full test of generalization. Blanchard and Johnson[7], using 5 children in the 8th grade, reported that the effect of concrete rewards and punishment did generalize from one classroom to another, while attitudinal rewards did not. In a recent review, Krasner[21] pointed out this lack of generalization as a major problem for behavior methods, but gave no data. Gruber[16] discussed some of the problems related to generalization, including the high relapse rate of patients who have undergone behavior therapy.

In regard to token economies in mental institutions, Lloyd and Abel[23] indicated that the effect of the token economy did not generalize enough to produce many hospital discharges and those who were discharged could have been affected by the Hawthorne effect that is general in nature. Thus, it is fairly evident that while affecting specific behaviors, token economies, and probably most other behavioristic techniques, have little power to produce a generalized effect not accounted for by suggestion or non-specific effects.

"BRAIN WASHING"

In regard to coercive behavioristic methods, there is one other area that needs to be examined. This is the power of behavior methods to affect people in severely coercive conditions. Here the effect of "brain washing" during the Korean war is an outstanding example. During the frenzy of the war, the American people believed that new, powerful behavior methods had been developed, and popular articles, books, and even movies were made based on the supposed power of such new behavior methods. Even in professional psychology, Jerome Frank's book, *Persuasion and Healing*[14], assumed that brain washing techniques were extremely powerful.

After the war was over, men[6] who were the most familiar with the material in this area became disillusioned with the "power" of these methods. Bradbury's[8] study of the Chinese POWs demonstrated very thoroughly the strengths and weaknesses of such group social behavioristic methods as the Chinese Communists used on their own soldiers. These methods could maintain control over individuals as long as the authoritarian system remained intact; however, when that system disintegrated, only those Chinese soldiers who were converted to the system prior to the application of the behavioristic methods remained loyal. Also, "the data clearly indicate that in Communist China, as in other totalitarian states, the amount of manipulation and coercion utilized to silence opposition and secure protestations of loyalty is an important cause of permanent alienation from the authority system"[8] (p. 81). The methods produce overt compliance, but covert resistance. The entire situation, in regard to Korean "brain washing," is well summarized by Radloff[30]: "As everyone knows, the Korean War marked the decline and fall of the West . . . Americans who had the misfortune to be captured either gave up and died or were enslaved by a terrifying mind-altering process called brain washing. Wholesale collaboration, including confessions of germ warfare attacks, was easily elicited; some captives succumbed completely and stayed in China; others, released back to the U.S., were human time bombs; ready to radiate irresistible Marxian madness throughout the helpless body politic whenever some sinister Sino-Svengali pushed the button. The never-say-die Communist automatons continued their fanatical activism even in captivity with riotous rebellions against camp authorities."

So much for fiction, now let's try a few facts. Out of 4,450 U.S. captives who survived internment, 22 (about 0.5%) chose to remain with the Communists. Countless hundreds of U.S. prisoners resisted the crude terror and torture influence techniques employed by their captors, many unto death. On the other hand, 14,325 of the 21,014 Chinese captives (over 67%) refused to return home. Furthermore, most of the prison camp riots were internal stuggles, pro-repatriation Communists fighting anti-repatriation anti-Communists"[30] (p. 106–107). So much for brain washing; the facts are clear, it did not work.

The conclusion from this examination of behavioristic methods used in a coercive situation is that, when backed by traditional coercive authority, behavioristic methods are somewhat more effective in controlling detailed behavior (probably at a greater expense) than traditional methods; but the effect does not generalize beyond that which can be accounted for by a Hawthorne effect. Generalization fails to occur to non-rewarded behaviors during the treatment and to all behavior outside or after treatment. Here is a clear indication that while behavioristic methods affect performance, they do not produce learning in the sense of generalization beyond the specific situation.

This is exactly the kind of result that would be predicted from Hull's[19] final formulation of behavior theory. Hilgard[18] in his description of Hull's final system, says "The distinction between performance and learning, so long insisted upon by Tolman, was formally accepted in the 1943 postulates, but by now has greatly reduced the quantitative influence of reinforcement upon associative learning"[18] (p. 132). In Tolman and Hull's terms, behavioral, especially operant, methods affect performance but not learning. In more common language terms, in an operant behavior modification situation, the S is aware of the contingencies. To satisfy his own needs and the behaviorist's demands, he temporarily changes his behavior, but there is no effect on his basic, pre-existing motivations and personality, nor is there learning beyond that required to adapt to the existing situation.

Thus, it can be said that the power of operant behavior methods is limited to performance and does not apply to learning or to permanent change in the person's behavior. This situation has been true throughout the history of coercive methods. Consequently, nothing essentially new has been added by operant methods except to apply coercive control a little more closely to specific behaviors. The greater part of the power of operant methods is produced by the traditional coercive situation in which the operant procedures are applied. In a free, non-coercive situation they provide no new source of power at all.

CONCLUSION

This examination of the major areas in behavior modification now provides an answer to the central question of this study: How much power to control behavior do the behavior modification methods really have? At present, several areas of psychological or behavioristic concern presuppose such power. Traditional therapy and diagnostic methods would be of questionable value and validity, if behavioristic methods demonstrated sufficient power to support the learning theory model of behavior pathology put forth by Ullman and Krasner[35]. More central to the purpose of this paper, however, is the concern that if behavior methodology proves to be of great effectiveness in controlling people's actions, a powerful tool would be placed in the hands of psychology which could be a threat to man as well as a benefit to him. This possibility has engendered a concern with the ethics of control among behaviorists. Finally, the existence of powerful behavior control methods would strongly support Skinner's[33, 34] condemnation of mentalistic terms and make the establishment of his Utopia described in *Walden Two*, with all its subtle totalitarian controls, a feasible, or even an inevitable, occurrence.

Summary of Results

This investigation of the power of behavioristic methods began by examining behavior therapy methods with an emphasis on systematic desensitization, since there is extensive experimental literature on this method. In these studies, the power of behavior methods could be examined when applied to behavior that the individual himself wanted changed; consequently, the cooperation of the S would be maximal. If specific behavior methods were not powerful here, they would probably not be so under less propitious situations. This examination first concluded that over a short period of time, when applied to specific behaviors, systematic desensitization, and probably most behavior methods, are superior to traditional therapy methods which in themselves are not particularly powerful methods.

We then attempted to determine the source of the power in behavior therapy. An examination of recent literature pointed rather definitely to non-specific suggestion or a placebo effect as the major source of this therapy's

power. Evidently, the "power" of behavior therapy does not come from sources based on existing behavior theory but from such mentalistic phenomena as "suggestion," "hope," "faith," "expectation" and "attention." Thus, while the power of specific behavior methods in therapy has not been fully determined, it does not appear to be very great according to this recent research. The power of suggestion is ancient, limited and controllable, so it ultimately poses no great threat as a source of control over human behavior.

The second area examined was that in which the S was neither seeking behavior change nor was he being coerced. Verbal conditioning was used as the major example due to the extensiveness of studies in this area. The exploration of verbal conditioning indicated that awareness of the S was necessary for such conditioning to occur; that the S had to discover what the E required, using the cues that the E emitted. Consequently, verbal conditioning is, in fact, a rather inadequate method of communicating information. Finally, the cooperation of the S was essential to conditioning. It was concluded that psychology now does not possess any great power to change behavior without people being aware of the process. The attempted control is not possible without the knowledge and voluntary compliance of the S. As such, the ultimate control lies in the hands of the S, not the behaviorist. It is even questionable whether the manipulations of the E should be designated as "control" under these circumstances and it is certainly true that the "counter-control" by Ss is quite strong enough to nullify or strongly modify all control by the behaviorist in a voluntary situation. It is therefore evident that behavior methods have little power to control people in a non-coercive situation.

The final section investigated the amount of control that behavior methods can exercise in coercive situations, where the behaviorist is delegated coercive authority over all environmental reinforcements *prior* to the utilization of behavior methods. Traditional coercive methods themselves, of course, have rather great power; so the question here is how much *more* power do behavioristic methods add? Examination of the literature, especially that related to token economies, indicates that behavior methods may increase control over certain specific behaviors in a coercive situation, though it is probably accomplished only at some cost. In any case, there appears to be little, if any, generalization, that behavior can be controlled outside and beyond the specific coercive situation. It was demonstrated that the power of "brain washing" is considerably exaggerated and its controlling effect will not last beyond the situation of coercion. Certainly the "brain" is not "washed" so that thinking is changed. Thus, even in a coercive situation, behaviorists can add little but refinements to traditional coercive control.

The Potential Power of Behavior Methodology
The sole remaining question is whether behaviorists have a potential for developing the powerful methods that they do not now possess. Certainly Skinner[34], London[25], Krasner[20], and Ullman and Krasner[35] have been rather careful not to say specifically that behavior methods are powerful at this time. Rather, they imply the existence of power and refer to the potential in behavior theory for producing such powerful methods in the near future. The statement by Ullman and Krasner[35] is typical, "Research during the last quarter of a century has provided improved methods of behavior change. In the light of these results and the expectation of an increasingly effective technology of behavior influence, it is now imperative to face the question of the direction in which behavior should be changed"[35] (p. 596).

The question is whether the basis for such expectation or potential actually exists. It is possible that such an "expectation" may have no basis beyond behavioristic theory, which certainly implies that such control is theoretically possible. However, behavior learning theory may not be related to behavior technology[25], and the lack of existing power, which has been

demonstrated in this paper, does not lend strong support to behavior theory. The behavioristic theories have, of course, been criticized strongly on other grounds[27].

A major indication of potential power would be the existence of fairly powerful behavioristic techniques at this time. Again, this review does not support the existence of such powerful techniques. A second, and perhaps stronger, indication of potential power would be the existence of a fairly rapid increase in the power of behavior technology. This increase should be obvious now after 20 years and the vast amount of research that has occurred. However, the reverse is obvious. Behavior methods are increasingly found to be less powerful year by year. The claimed cure rates have continued to drop from 90% to 80% to 70% to 60% to even 50% for some areas. And the existing "power" in these therapeutic methods has been increasingly demonstrated to be provided by non-specific suggestion effects, rather than by the specific behavior technology directly derived from behavior theory. The decrease in "power" accompanying increasing research sophistication was found in this paper to be characteristic of every major area and method of behavior modification that was examined. Under these circumstances, the only possible conclusion is that the potential power of behavior technology exists only as a faith for those who believe in this "ideology"[25] and not as a scientifically based prediction.

The Power of Behavior Methodology: Conclusion
These results lead to the final conclusion of this study: behaviorism as a theory or method contains no new power over mankind. Behavioristic methods appear to have almost no greater ability to change behavior than other methods previously developed. The press, advertisers, and politicians are probably at least as effective. After 20 years of research, there is no reliable evidence that behavior technologies are much more effective than time-honored methods of

control. They work, with some cost, in a coercive environment; they work well enough with patients desiring change to be recommended for certain limited psychopathological conditions; but there is no evidence that they work at all in an open society with people who do not wish to have their behavior changed.

In regard to the possibility of a behavioristic Utopia, Skinner states that "The fundamental question in all utopias is, 'would it really work?"[34] (p. 154). The answer now is clearly that it would not. Behavior control methods are too weak and the normal "counter-controls" are too strong. In fact, it is ironical that the very things that may be most reinforcing to man in the long run are those things that Skinner[34] tried to rule out of existence: freedom, dignity and self-actualization. Thus, behaviorists have not changed the accepted conception that "... so far as the real world is concerned, the word utopian means unworkable"[34] (p. 155).

In regard to the urgent need to discuss the ethics of behavior control, London pointed out that "There are no meaningful ethics of impotence; that is, there can be no meaningful debate about the ethics of methods that do not work"[25] (p. 30). Thus, from the evidence at hand, it might be thought that a discussion of the ethics involved in psychological control is now rather academic.

REFERENCES

1.   Allen, G. J. and Magaro, P. A. Measures of change in a token economy program. *Behav. Res. Ther.*, 1971, *9*, 311–318.

2.   Atthowe, J. M. and Krasner, L. Preliminary report on the application of contingent reinforcement procedures (token economy) on a "chronic" psychiatric ward. *J. abn. Psychol.*, 1968, *73*, 37–43.

3.   Ayllon, T. and Azrin, N. H. Reinforcement and instructions with mental patients. *J. exper. Anal. Behav.*, 1964, *7*, 327–331.

4.   Ayllon, T. and Azrin, N. H. The measurement and reinforcement of behavior of psychotics. *J. exper. Anal. Behav.*, 1965, *8*, 357–383.

5.   Ayllon, T. and Azrin, N. H. *The Token Economy: A Motivational System for Therapy and Rehabilitation*. New York: Appleton-Century-Crofts, 1968.

6.   Biderman, A. D. The image of brainwashing. *Pub. Opin. Quart.*, 1962, *26*, 547–563.

7.   Blanchard, E. B. and Johnson, R. A. Generalization of operant classroom control procedures. *Behav. Ther.*, 1973, *4*, 219–229.

8.   Bradbury, C., Meyers, S. M. and Biderman, A. D. (Eds.) *Mass Behavior in Battle and Captivity: The Communist Soldier in the Korean War*. Chicago: University of Chicago Press, 1968.

9.   Burchard, J. D. Systematic Socialization: A programmed environment for the rehabilitation of anti-social retardates. *Psychol. Rec.*, 1967, *17*, 461–476.

10.   Burchard, J. D. Residential behavior modification programs and the problem of uncontrolled contingencies: A reply to Lachenmeyer. *Psychol. Rec.*, 1969, *19*, 259–261.

11.   Cotler, S. B., Applegate, G., King, L. W. and Kristal, S. Establishing a token economy program in a state hospital classroom: A lesson in training student and teacher. *Behav. Ther.*, 1972, *3*, 209–222.

12.   Cotter, L. H. Operant conditioning in a Vietnamese mental hospital. *Amer. J. Psychiat.*, 1967, *124*, 23–28.

13.   Davison, G. C. Appraisal of behavior modification techniques with adults in institutional settings. In Franks, C. M. (Ed.) *Behavior Therapy: Appraisal and Status*. New York: McGraw-Hill, 1969, pp. 220–278.

14.   Frank, J. D. *Persuasion and Healing*. Baltimore: Johns Hopkins Press, 1961.

15.   Gripp, R. F. and Magaro, P. A. A token economy program evaluation with untreated control ward comparisons. *Behav. Res. Ther.*, 1971, *9*, 137–149.

16.   Gruber, R. P. Behavior therapy: Problems in generalization. *Behav. Ther.*, 1971, *2*, 361–368.

17.   Heller, K. and Marlatt, G. A. Verbal conditioning, behavior therapy and behavior change: Some problems in extrapolation. In Franks, C. M. (Ed.) *Behavior Therapy: Appraisal and Status*. New York: McGraw-Hill, 1969, pp. 569–588.

18.   Hilgard, E. R. *Theories of Learning* (2nd Ed.). New York: Appleton-Century-Crofts, 1956.

19. Hull, C. L. *Essentials of Experimental Psychology*. New Haven: Yale University Press, 1951.

20. Krasner, L. Behavior control and social responsibility. *Amer. Psychol.*, 1962, *17*, 199–204.

21. Krasner, L. The operant approach in behavior therapy. In Bergin, A. E. and Garfield, S. L. (Eds.) *Handbook of Psychotherapy and Behavior Change: An Empirical Analysis*. New York: Wiley, 1971, pp. 612–652b.

22. Lachenmeyer, C. W. Systematic socialization; Observations on a programmed environment for the rehabilitation of antisocial retardates, *Psychol. Rec.*, 1969, *19*, 247–257.

23. Lloyd, K. E. and Abel, L. Performance on a token economy psychiatric ward: A two year summary. *Behav. Res. Ther.*, 1970, *8*, 1–9.

24. Lloyd, K. E. and Garlington, W. K. Weekly variations in performance on a token economy psychiatric ward. *Behav. Res. Ther.*, 1968, *6*, 407–410.

25. London, P. *Behavior Control*. New York: Harper, 1969.

26. Marks, J., Sonoda, B. and Schalock, R. Reinforcement versus relationship therapy for schizophrenics. *J. abn. Psychol.*, 1968, *73*, 397–402.

27. McCall, R. J. Beyond reason and evidence: The metapsychology of Professor B. F. Skinner. *J. Clin. Psychol.*, 1972, *28*, 126–139.

28. Meichenbaum, D. H., Bowers, K. S. and Ross, R. R. Modification of classroom behavior of institutionalized female adolescent offenders. *Behav. Res. Ther.*, 1968, *6*, 343–353.

29. Patterson, G. R. Behavioral intervention procedures in the classroom and in the home. In Bergins, A. E. and Garfield, S. L. (Eds.) *Handbook of Psychotherapy and Behavior Change: An Empirical Analysis*. New York: Wiley, 1971, pp. 751–775.

30. Radloff, R. The dilemmas of prisoners. *Contemp. Psychol.*, 1970, *15*, 106–107.

31. Rickard, H. C. and Saunders, T. R. Control of "clean-up" behavior in a summer camp. *Behav. Ther.*, 1971, *2*, 340–344.

32. Skinner, B. F. *Walden Two*. New York: Macmillan, 1948.

33. Skinner, B. F. *Science and Human Behavior*. New York: Macmillan, 1953.

34. Skinner, B. F. *Beyond Freedom and Dignity*. New York: Knopf, 1971.

35. Ullmann. L. P. and Krasner, L. *A Psychological Approach to Abnormal Behavior*. Englewood Cliffs, N.J.: Prentice-Hall. 1969.

36. Walker, H. M., Mattson, R. H. and Baston, P. Teaching parents and others principles of behavior control for modifying behavior in children. In Benson, F. A. M. (Ed.) *Modifying Deviant Social Behaviors in Various Classroom Settings*. Eugene, Ore.: University of Oregon, 1969, No. 1.

65. Legal Regulation of Behavior Modification

PAUL R. FRIEDMAN

DETERMINING COMPETENCY

MOST PRISONERS, EXCEPT POSSIBLY THOSE WHO are psychotic or severely retarded, are competent to make decisions about their treatment or rehabilitation. Moreover, it is now generally recognized that persons who are mentally handicapped may have impaired functioning in some areas but be perfectly functional and competent in others.[1] For example, the Second Circuit has noted:

"[T]he law is quite clear in New York that a finding of "mental illness" even by a judge or jury, and commitment to a hospital, does not raise even a presumption that the patient is "incompetent" or unable adequately to manage his own affairs. Absent a specific finding of incompetence, the mental patient retains the right to sue or defend in his own name, to sell or dispose of his property, to marry, draft a will, and, in general to manage his own affairs."[2]

Nevertheless, because the very nature of a total institution impairs a patient's capacity to make important decisions concerning his life, the issue of whether a prisoner or mental patient is competent to give consent is always a difficult one.

▶SOURCE: *"Legal Regulation of Behavior Modification,"* *Arizona Law Review (1975), 17(1): 75–94 (Editorial adaptations.) Copyright 1975 by Arizona Board of Regents. Reprinted by permission.*

[1]*See Winters v. Miller*, 446 F.2d 65, 68 (2d Cir.), *cert. denied*, 404 U.S. 985 (1971); *Henry v. Ciccone*, 315 F. Supp. 889 (W.D. Mo. 1970).

[2]*Winters v. Miller*, 446 F.2d 65, 68 (2d Cir.), *cert. denied*, 404 U.S. 985 (1971).

For example, while recognizing that involuntarily-detained mental patients may have sufficient IQ's to intellectually comprehend their circumstances, the *Kaimowitz* court noted with concern that "the very nature of [a confined mental patient's] incarceration diminishes his capacity to consent. . . . He is particularly vulnerable as a result of his mental condition, his involuntarily [*sic*] confinement, and the effects of 'institutionalization.'"[3]

Defining capacity to consent is, along with defining voluntariness, one of the thorniest of all issues involved in the regulation of applied behavior analysis. As a general proposition, it may only be stated that capacity, like voluntariness, "is a requirement of variable demands."[4] Greater care must be taken when the proposed procedure is experimental, dangerous, or intrusive than when it is routine.

The goal in choosing a standard of competency is, on the one hand, to enhance self-

[3]*Kaimowitz v. Michigan Dep't of Mental Health*, 42 U.S.L.W. 2063, 2064 (C.A. 73–19434–AW, Cir. Ct. Wayne County, Mich., July 10, 1973). As the court explained the problem:
"The fact of institutional confinement has special force in undermining the capacity of the mental patient to make a competent decision on this issue, even though he is intellectually competent to do so. . . . Institutionalization tends to strip the individual of the support which permits him to maintain his sense of self worth and the value of his own physical and mental integrity. An involuntarily confined mental patient clearly has diminished capacity for making a decision . . . ."
Id. (material not reported in U.S.L.W.).
[4]42 U.S.L.W. at 2063.

autonomy and guard against paternalism and, on the other, to provide for vicarious judgment in the best interest of patients when necessary. As with so many of the difficult issues in mental health law, there may be no ideal approach. Under too lax a standard of competency, persons will be allowed to act in ways which may be viewed as being contrary to their best interests. Under too strict a standard, the opportunity for self-determination may be undermined and personal integrity denigrated by the paternalism of the state. Horror story hypotheticals can be formulated to expose potential weaknesses in any standard of competency that has been proposed. The real question is under which standard will undesirable results be most effectively minimized. Unfortunately, very little attention has been devoted to this problem to date, and it is, therefore, possible only to identify some of the different standards of competency which have been used and to briefly discuss the likely effects of choosing one standard over another.

Competency Defined as Reaching a Reasonable Result

One approach to determining competency requires the reviewer to decide whether the result of the client's decision is one which a "reasonably competent man might have made."[5] Thus, "[p]ersons who, because of mental illness, would be likely to make decisions about their own interests which would result in substantial damage to their own mental or physical well-being," should be deemed incompetent.[6] This approach

has been criticized as being extremely paternalistic and drawing a probably unsupportable distinction between the decision-making freedom of persons with physical illnesses and mental disabilities.[7] Under this standard, a mentally ill person who decides to forego a treatment despite a substantial risk to his mental well being might be labelled incompetent and thus denied his basic right to self-determination. Any determination of the reasonableness of a result is based on the balancing of complex factors and is likely to be subjective. Thus, adoption of this standard may result in a Catch-22 logic—any decision with which the reviewer of competency disagreed would provide a basis for labelling the client incompetent and for substituting the reviewer's opinion as to the best result for the client.

Competency Defined as the Capacity to Reach a Decision Based on Rational Reasons

Under this standard, competency is defined as the capacity to understand the nature of the behavioral procedure, to weigh the risks and benefits, and to reach a decision for rational reasons. This standard is most commonly advanced in scholarly writing.[8] While it is an improvement on the first proposed standard, it has its own difficulties. To be sure, this standard tends to protect against the paternalistic tendency to substitute the reviewer's decision for the client's by focusing on the client's overall patterns of thought rather than on the result of

that the authorities are concerned only with the capacity of the individual. The issue is "whether he is *capable* of making a responsible, not necessarily a wise, decision . . . ." *Id.* at 469.

[7]*See* Dix, "Hospitalization of the Mentally Ill in Wisconsin: A Need for a Reexamination," 51 *Marq. L. Rev.* 1, 26–27 & n.79 (1967); Shapiro, "Legislating the Control of Behavior Control: Autonomy and the Coercive Use of Organic Therapies," 47 *S. Cal. L. Rev.* at 288 (1974).

[8]*See*, e.g., Dix, *supra* note 7, at 26; Postel, "Civil Commitment: A Functional Analysis," 38 *Brooklyn L. Rev.* 1 (1971); Siegel, "The Justifications for Medical Commitment—Real or Illusory," 6 *Wake Forest L. Rev.* 21, 32–33 (1969), "Developments in the Law—Civil Commitment of the Mentally Ill," 87 *Harv. L. Rev.* 1217 (1974).

[5]Green, "Proof of Mental Incompetency and the Unexpressed Major Premise," 53 *Yale L. J.* 271, 306–07 (1944); Note, "Civil Commitment of the Mentally Ill: Theories and Procedures," 79 *Harv. L. Rev.* 1288 (1966).

[6]Note, *supra* note 5, at 1295. *See also* Nat'l Institute of Mental Health, Draft Act Governing Hospitalization of the Mentally Ill § 9(g)(2) (1952), *found in Am. Bar Foundation, The Mentally Disabled and the Law* 39 (S. Brakel and R. Rock, eds. 1971), at 457, 459. This section proposes involuntary commitment of patients who lack "sufficient insight or capacity to make responsible decisions with respect to hospitalization." The commentary to this section, however, indicates

a particular decision.[9] Thus, the patient's total decisionmaking process is evaluated to determine if there is evidence of incoherent reasoning or eccentricities of emotion. The insolvable problem of any rationality test, however, is that it may express a value preference for a particular kind of thinking, the results of which have not been proved to be less valid than other modes of reasoning. As is commonly observed, the line between genius and madness is a thin one, and many sound decisions have been made on the basis of unconscious or preconscious thought or on the basis of what might be characterized as irrational or intuitive reasons. Arguably, any attempt to assess the quality of reasoning, as distinguished from the ability to decide at all, carries with it the danger that the reviewer of competency will substitute his own manner of thinking and value preferences for those of the client.

Competency Defined as the Capacity to Make a Decision

A minority of courts and scholarly commentators have suggested an approach to defining competency which would avoid the difficulties inherent in evaluating whether a person's thought processes are rational or irrational but which also would preclude the apparent consent of persons clearly out of touch with reality. Under this approach, so long as the client has a sufficient understanding of the nature of the procedure, its risks and benefits, and the possible alternatives, his decision, provided there is a decision, will be honored.[10] Of course, here again, the question of what constitutes sufficient understanding is highly subjective.

In re Yetter,[11] a decision by a Pennsylvania lower court, provides a good illustration of the

application of this approach. Maida Yetter had been committed to Allentown State Hospital in 1971, and her diagnosis at that time was chronic undifferentiated schizophrenia. Subsequently, because Mrs. Yetter was discovered to have a breast discharge, the doctors recommended a surgical biopsy and any additional necessary corrective surgery. Mrs. Yetter refused the surgery because she was afraid of that type of operation, which she claimed had resulted in the death of her aunt. The caseworker indicated that at the time of the refusal, Mrs. Yetter was "lucid, rational, and appeared to understand that the possible consequences of her refusal included death."[12] The court described Mrs. Yetter's refusal as "informed" and "conscious of the consequences," and stated:

"The ordinary person's refusal to accept medical advice based upon fear is commonly known and while the refusal may be irrational and foolish to an outside observer, it cannot be said to be incompetent in order to permit the State to override the decision.

. . . .

". . . Upon reflection, balancing the risk involved in our refusal to act in favor of compulsory treatment against giving the greatest possible protection to the individual in furtherance of his own desires, we are unwilling now to overrule Mrs. Yetter's original irrational but competent decision."[13]

While the *Yetter* standard of competency would appear to be more objective and less likely to provoke disagreement in its application than a rationality standard, it is not without its own problems. There was, for example, evidence in the *Yetter* case that Mrs. Yetter's decision to forego corrective surgery was based not only on irrational reasons but also on fundamental misperceptions of reality. Mrs. Yetter justified her objections to surgery on the basis that her aunt had died following surgery for cancer. In fact, the aunt's death was unrelated to her cancer operation and occurred some 15

---

[9]Shapiro, *supra* note 7, at 311–13.

[10]*See, e.g., In Re Yetter*, 62 D. & C. 2d 619 (C.P. Northampton County, Pa. 1973); *Grannum v. Berard*, 70 Wash. 2d 304, 422 P.2d 812 (1967); Note, "Informed Consent and the Dying Patient, 83 *Yale L. J.* 1366 (1974).

[11]62 D. & C. 2d 619 (C.P. Northampton County, Pa. 1973).

[12]*Id.* at 621.

[13]*Id.* at 624.

years after that operation.[14] Other evidence that Mrs. Yetter's reasoning had a delusional component came from her responses to questions by the court and counsel; she indicated that the proposed operation would interfere with her genital system, affect her ability to have children, and would prohibit a movie career.[15] At the time of these questions, Mrs. Yetter was 60 years of age. It might, therefore, have been decided that Mrs. Yetter was not competent even under this standard because she lacked sufficient understanding of the nature of the procedure, the risks and benefits, and the alternatives involved.

Clearly, if a client is psychotic or hallucinating and cannot assimilate information about a proposed procedure at all, he is incompetent to make a decision one way or the other. More difficult situations are presented where the client cannot accurately "hear" and weigh the pertinent information for delusional reasons. Consider, for example, the difference between the decision of a child molester to reject proposed aversive conditioning on the ground that the pain of the proposed procedure is not, in his opinion, worth the possibility of a change in his behavior and the decision of a similarly situated person to refuse aversive conditioning based on a paranoid belief that all behavior modifiers are conspiring in a plot to kill him or that he has a little man inside him who is his true self and who would be fried by any electricity. What this and similar hypothetical comparisons point up is that we are dealing with a question which involves the balancing of complex factors and the delicate evaluation of personal preferences.[16]

The task of framing an ideal standard for competency and studying its operational effectiveness is beyond the scope of this article.

*

DETERMINING WHETHER CONSENT IN THE INSTITUTIONAL CONTEXT IS TRULY VOLUNTARY AND COMPETENT

After noting that a crucial element of informed consent is voluntariness, the *Kaimowitz*[17] court also gave an informative description of the great difficulty of eliciting a truly voluntary consent in an institutional setting:

"It is impossible for an involuntarily detained mental patient to be free of ulterior forms of restraint or coercion when his very release from the institution may depend upon his cooperating with the institutional authorities and giving consent to experimental surgery. The privileges of an involuntarily detained patient and the rights he exercises in the institution are within the control of the institutional authorities. As was pointed out in the testimony of John Doe, such minor things as the right to have a lamp in his room, or the right to have ground privileges to go for a picnic with his family assumed major proportions. For 17 years he lived completely under the control of the hospital. Nearly every important aspect of his life was decided without any opportunity on his part to participate in the decisionmaking process.

. . .

"Involuntarily confined mental patients live in an inherently coercive institutional environment. Indirect and subtle psychological coercion has profound effects upon the patient population. . . . They are not

---

[14]*Id.* at 622.

[15]*Id.*

[16]An approach to defining competency which would obviate these problems would be to forego any inquiry into understanding at all, provided a client is able to hear the question of whether he is willing to consent to a particular therapy and to answer either yes or no. Barring some additional requirement of a causal connection, the response of a client who automatically said, "no, no, no," to any and all questions which he was asked would be a competent refusal.

Even with a causal connection requirement, this standard would require the response of a client who could hear the information given, but whose hallucinations caused serious distortions in his thinking, to be honored. This very low standard for competency was adopted by the federal district court in *Wyatt v. Aderholt*, 368 F. Supp. 1383 (M.D. Ala. 1974), with regard to consent by the mentally retarded to sterilization. The court's order provided that even legally incompetent residents may not be sterilized unless they have "formed . . . a genuine desire to be sterilized." *Id.* at 1385.

[17]42 U.S.L.W. 2063 (C.A. 73–19434–AW, Cir. Ct. Wayne County, Mich., July 10, 1973). For a discussion of *Kaimowitz*, see text and notes 94–99 *supra*.

able to voluntarily give informed consent because of the inherent inequality in their positions."[18]

If the *Kaimowitz* court's analysis is read to mean that no involuntarily-confined patient may ever be subjected to any treatment since he can never give legally adequate consent, the thrust of normalization theory and the attempts of advocates of the mentally handicapped to restore to them the fullest possible degree of personal autonomy would be seriously undercut. Such a reading, however, would suggest a very unsophisticated understanding of the underlying issues of voluntariness, and a failure by the court to recognize that degrees voluntariness exist in all situations, even those outside the confines of institutions. Read this way, the *Kaimowitz* decision would appear to assume that persons in the community always act with unimpaired voluntariness. Perhaps, they do in a very general sense; however, the husband or wife seeking private psychotherapy under pressure from a spouse who has threatened separation or divorce may actually act less voluntarily than a mental patient or prisoner agreeing to undertake psychotherapy. Clearly, involuntary

confinement is only one of many variables, albeit a very important one, which can and do limit the voluntariness of a person's acts.

Fortunately, the *Kaimowitz* court does not appear to have intended to suggest that confined persons may never give a valid consent. As the court itself commented:

"We do not agree that a truly informed consent cannot be given for a regular surgical procedure by a patient, institutionalized or not. The law has long recognized that such valid consent can be given. But we do hold that informed consent cannot be given by an involuntarily detained mental patient for experimental psychosurgery. . . ."[19]

The analytical framework employed by the court does not regard consent as an all or nothing concept. In deciding whether there has been voluntary consent in a particular factual setting, a number of factors must be balanced. Consent must be more carefully scrutinized if the right to be waived is constitutionally protected, if the procedure to be employed is dangerous, or if the nature of the setting in which consent is to be given undermines capacity and voluntariness.[20]

---

[18]*Kaimowitz v. Michigan Dep't of Mental Health*, 42 U.S.L.W. 2063 (C.A. 73–19434–AW, Cir. Ct. Wayne County, Mich., July 10, 1973) (material not reported in U.S.L.W.). The appropriateness of the court's observations about the difficulty of assuring the voluntariness of a decision made by an involuntarily-confined person was nicely illustrated by subsequent events in this very case. While he was confined in Ionia State Hospital, the patient involved in the case staunchly maintained that he genuinely and voluntarily desired to participate in the psychosurgery experiment. Two review committees pressed him on whether his decision was the result of coercion, and he convinced them that he genuinely desired to participate, even if he were released from Ionia. Nevertheless, after he was released from the institution and after the sexual psychopath statute justifying his commitment was held to be unconstitutional, he suddenly saw things very differently and withdrew all consent for the performance of the proposed experiment. *Id.* (material not reported in U.S.L.W.). Moreover, whether or not the hope of early freedom or improved conditions destroys decisionmaking capacity or constitutes duress, an explicit or implicit offer of such benefits by the state may amount to an unconstitutional condition for freedom or privileges. Shapiro, *supra* note 7, at 318.

[19]*Kaimowitz v. Michigan Dep't of Mental Health*, 42 U.S.L.W. 2063 (C.A. 73–19434–AW, Cir. Ct. Wayne County, Mich., July 10, 1973) (material not reported in U.S.L.W.).

[20]As the *Kaimowitz* court stated:
"Informed consent is a requirement of variable demands. Being certain that a patient has consented adequately to an operation, for example, is much more important when doctors are going to undertake an experimental, ddangeoous, and intrusive procedure than, for example, when they are going to remove an appendix. When a procedure is experimental, dangerous, and intrusive, special safeguards are necessary. The risk-benefit ratio must be carefully considered, and the question of consent thoroughly explored."
Id. at 2063–64. The result reached in *Kaimowitz* is probably correct, but the opinion is very unclear on the issue of informed consent and probably confused the understanding of this important concept. As noted above, to the extent that it suggests that mental patients or prisoners may not be able to give consent to at least some procedures, it has potential for undermining their integrity and autonomy. What the *Kaimowitz* court was actually doing was making a basic social policy judgment that the potential harms of psychosurgery were so great and the potential benefits so small that

This is the approach which has been adopted by several federal courts which have scrutinized ostensibly voluntary decisions by mental patients to undergo sterilization,[21] aversive conditioning,[22] or to labor without compensation in an institutional setting.[23] In such circumstances, and in acknowledgement of the inherently coercive pressures of an institution, the courts have scrutinized consent with special care, but have permitted residents to consent to procedures after ascertaining that reasonable efforts have been undertaken to ensure capacity and voluntariness.[24] These courts recognized the fallibility

involuntarily-confined mental patients, subject to especially strong coercion, should not be allowed to give consent to such a procedure. But to say that patients or prisoners should not be allowed, as a matter of social policy, to consent to certain procedures, or, to put it another way, to erect a ban on certain procedures in certain settings for social policy reasons is significantly different from saying that patients lack the ability to give a legally valid consent. Unfortunately, informed consent was the legal handle which the court utilized to accomplish an arguably worthy result at the cost of conceptual clarity and at the risk of undermining developing public notions that mental patients and prisoners are able to exercise autonomy and should be allowed to exercise autonomy to the fullest possible extent.

[21]See Wyatt v. Aderholt, 368 F. Supp. 1383 (M.D. Ala. 1974); cf. Relf v. Weinberger, 372 F. Supp. 1196 (D.D.C. 1974).

[22]See Knecht v. Gillman, 488 F.2d 1136 (8th Cir. 1973).

[23]See Henry v. Ciccone, 315 F. Supp. 889 (W.D. Mo. 1970); Parks v. Ciccone, 281 F. Supp. 805 (W.D. Mo. 1968). In Henry v. Ciccone, the court denied an involuntary servitude claim only after it found that the patient knowingly and freely signed a form which "fully informed him of his right not to work . . . ." 315 F. Supp. at 891. The court further found that "inmates who do not sign the waiver are permitted all normal privileges and no punitive action is taken against them . . . and that the work agreement form is not binding . . . ." Id.

[24]For example, in Knecht v. Gillman, 488 F.2d 1136 (8th Cir. 1973), the Eighth Circuit laid down specific safeguards designed to ensure that consent to an aversive conditioning program for inmates with behavioral problems was truly voluntary. The action was brought by two residents of the Iowa Security Medical Facility who sought to enjoin the use of apomorphine on nonconsenting residents. For a further discussion of Knecht, see text & notes 115–23 supra. The court ordered that all treatment using apomorphine be enjoined unless a written consent was obtained from the inmate specifying the nature, purpose, and risks of the treat-

of consent in a total institutional setting. They also recognized, however, that to assume that institutionalized populations are incompetent to make any decisions affecting their lives would have serious consequences; it would erode the notion of personal autonomy and might well lead to a situation in which the state would invoke alleged incapacity to consent as justification for substituting its own judgment on a whole range of issues personally involving a patient or prisoner. Such a situation would not only involve bad therapy or rehabilitation fostering dependency and loss of self-control but also might involve an unconstitutional abridgment of the first, fifth, or fourteenth amendment rights of prisoners and mental patients. Sound public policy requires that courts and legislators formulate standards for consent which balance the threat of coercion against the equally serious threat of paternalism.[25]

ment; advising the inmate of his right to revoke his consent at any time; and, certifying by a physician that the inmate had read and understood the terms of the consent and that the inmate was mentally competent to understand the consent. While a step in the right direction, these standard procedures to ensure informed consent could certainly be improved. See App. I, infra at 97–99.

[25]One of the most interesting and difficult issues relating to voluntariness arises in the context of contingency contracting procedures. Simply explained these procedures are used for clients who express a wish to change certain deep-rooted behavior, such as excessive eating, drinking, or smoking or a sexual fetish, but who lack the "self control" to do so by themselves. In such procedures, various reinforcements are set forth in advance for participation in therapy. In the behavioral treatment of obesity, for example, applied behavior analysts have eliminated the notorious tendency of obese clients to drop out of on-going therapy programs by making a refundable deposit contingent upon attendance at group sessions. See, e.g., Romanczyk, Tracey, Wilson & Thorpe, "Behavioral Techniques in the Treatment of Obesity: A Comparative Analysis," in Behavior Research & Therapy 629–40 (1973). In another variation on the same theme, applied behavior analysts often contract with clients to have post-dated checks sent off to the client's most disliked organization if therapeutic directives which have been mutually agreed upon are not followed. Boudin, "Contingency Contracting as a Therapeutic Tool in the Deceleration of Amphetamine Use," 3 Behavior Therapy 604, 604–08 (1972).

Applied behavior analysts argue with much persuasion

that once clients have voluntarily agreed to enter into such a contract they should be legally required to see the behavioral procedure through, even if at a subsequent time the clients express the desire to dispense with the procedure in question. Such a requirement would appear to be most necessary in connection with procedures involving aversive stimuli. A client may very desperately wish to rid himself of an alcohol addiction or a sexual fetish and may therefore agree to a program involving aversive stimuli, but when it is time for the aversive stimulus—electric shock or a nausea-inducing drug, for example—to be applied, the client may suddenly see the matter in a very different perspective and vigorously attempt to withdraw his consent.

The essential dilemma here is that the time in the presence of the aversive stimuli which will ultimately make it possible to stop drinking or having perverse sexual fantasies is the very time at which the value of being able to stop seems lowest to the client. As soon as the aversive stimuli are removed, the value of not drinking or the wish to be free of the sexual fetish assumes its usual high place. The commitment to accept the consequences in this situation must be offered and accepted at a time when the value of not smoking or not drinking is high. The effect of the commitment is to reduce the client's choice—to *compel* him to give up his addiction. Rachlin, *supra* note 8, at 100–04. Perhaps the classic expression of this commitment strategy is Homer's recounting of how Odysseus arranged to have himself bound to the mast of his ship ahead of time so that when he sailed by the island of the Sirens, he could not be tempted by their dangerous enticements.

Seen from this perspective, the attempt of the court in *Knecht v. Gillman*, 488 F.2d 1136 (8th Cir. 1973), to set forth specific safeguards to assure the voluntariness of resident consent to behavioral programs involving aversive stimuli is very important and controversial. In *Knecht*, the Eighth Circuit held as a matter of constitutional law that in order to ensure informed consent, an inmate must have "the right to terminate his consent at any time." Applied behavior analysis would argue that this approach might frustrate well-meaning attempts to utilize contingency contracting procedures involving aversive stimuli and would make it legally impossible for clients with self-control problems to adopt an effective "commitment" strategy. With regard to such procedures, applied behavior analysts also argue a contractual theory that once a client makes a valid "contract" to undergo such a procedure, and the applied behavior analyst goes to the trouble of designing an individualized program, they should have a right to compel the client to perform this part of the contract or at least to pay the designated forfeits.

This analysis grows out of discussion with Professor David B. Wexler and Dr. G. Terence Wilson. The problems associated with a rule of revocability have, for the past few years, been of particular interest to Professor Wexler. *See* Wexler, "Foreword: Mental Health Law and the Movement Toward Voluntary Treatment," 62 *Calif. L. Rev.* 671, 688–91

The problem of securing a valid informed consent from institutionalized populations has been recognized by behaviorists as well as the courts,[26] and the meaning of informed consent has been considered in the context of behavior therapy. One approach relies on the individuals' ability to learn behavioral principles and understand how environmental events can control their own behavior.[27] The hope is that as be-

(1974); Wexler, "Of Rights and Reinforcers," 11 *San Diego L. Rev.* 957, 970–71; Wexler, "Reflections on the Legal Regulation of Behavior Modification in Institutional Settings," 17 *Ariz. L. Rev.* 132, 138–40 (1975); Wexler, "Therapeutic Justice," 57 *Minn. L. Rev.* 289, 330–31 (1972); Wexler, Token and Taboo: Behavior Modification, Token Economies and the Law, *Calif. L. Rev.* 81, 108 n.151 (1973).

[26]Some exponents of applied behavior analysis challenge the applicability of the concept of informed consent to the treatment of institutionalized mental patients and prisoners. *See* R. K. Schwitzgebel, A Contractual Model for the Protection of the Rights of Institutionalized Patients, 1975 (unpublished paper). They argue that informed consent is a notion derived from the medical model of treatment. While it may be appropriate to a decision concerning therapy, it is not a relevant concept under a learning theory model of behavior change. The more appropriate model, it is argued, would be a contractual model in which the client and the therapist agree upon explicit goals and the means by which these goals will be achieved, each undertaking specified responsibilities in this regard. Adoption of the contractual model, however, would give only illusory relief to the therapist who believes that under this model the nagging problem of informed consent disappears. In the first place, courts have traditionally exercised their power to review and, on occasion, declare contracts void when the bargaining was not between parties of equal status or power or where one side was able to effectively coerce or influence the other into signing. A. Corbin, *Contracts* § 228 (1952). Courts have also held contracts which are based on fraud on inaccurate information to be voidable, *id.* §§ 6, 146, 228, and contracts made by minors or incompetents are voidable as a matter of public policy. *Id.* §§ 6, 146, 227. Thus, the issues of knowledge, competency, and voluntariness will be just as relevant under a contractual model of behavioral therapy as under a medical model. Finally, if the Constitution protects mentation and privacy against coercive intrusion by the state in at least some situations, then a necessary condition for use of such therapies by the state is the informed consent of the subject. Shapiro, *supra* note 7, at 307.

[27]Stolz, Ethical Issues in Research on Behavior Therapy, Mar. 28, 1974 (unpublished paper presented at the First Drake Conference on Professional Issues in Behavior

havioral principles are more widely disseminated and understood by the public, the client population will become increasingly sophisticated about issues of control and will resist controls with which they are not in sympathy. It is recognized, however, that "until behavioral understanding is more widespread than it is at present, experimenters should be particularly sensitive to the manner in which they describe research and ask for the subject's cooperation. [Behaviorists] should help [their] subjects by making them aware of variables that may affect their decision."[28]

A third behaviorist would, however, go even further. Noting that possible remedies for exploitative use of psychological techniques are usually discussed in terms of individual safeguards and that increased knowledge about modes of influence is prescribed as the best defense to manipulation, he observes that awareness alone is insufficient.

"If protection against exploitation relies solely upon individual safeguards, people would continually be subjected to coercive pressures. Accordingly, they create institutional sanctions which set limits on the control of human behavior. The integrity of individuals is largely secured by societal safeguards that

place restraints upon improper means and foster reciprocity through balancing of interests."[29]

One behaviorist has offered the following helpful definition of uncoerced consent in behavioral terms:

We may now define contingencies of consent. The behaviors of the subject are on the left and the consequences provided are on the right. Aversive confinement is in parentheses because it may not be involved in non-penal institutions:

1. Ongoing program participation →Standard custodial consequences (and standard aversive confinement).

2. Program participation absent →Standard custodial consequences (and standard aversive confinement).

AND

3. Ongoing program participation →Program-specific consequences.

4. Program participation absent →No program-specific consequences.

Stated otherwise, the institution provides or eliminates no custodial (or confinement) consequences contingent on participation or nonparticipation in the program. What maintains participation is the delivery and nondelivery of consequences which derive from the program itself. The presence of this set of options defines a *noncoercive* situation.

. . . .

This method not only defines the options as noncoercive, but as involving full consent.[30]

Analysis, Mar. 28–29, 1974, Des Moines, Iowa), on file in the *Arizona Law Review* office; *see* Davidson, "Countercontrol in Behavior Modification," in *Behavior Change: Methodology, Concepts, and Practice* 153 (L. Hammerlynck, L. Handy & E. Mash eds. 1973) (arguing that "nearly everything we do in behavior modification requires the active cooperation of the client. This is especially true when the therapist cannot be present whenever the problematic behavior may occur, and/or when the therapist's presence cannot insure the forcing out of a particular response at any given time."). *See also* Freund, "Some Problems in the Treatment of Homosexuality," in *Behavior Therapy and the Neuroses* (H. Eysenck ed. 1960). Freund's study found that markedly fewer homosexuals referred for therapy by the courts or coerced by relatives achieved changes in sexual orientation than patients who seemed to have come of their own accord.

[28]Stoltz, *supra* note 27, at 12–13. *See also* Nat'l Prison Project, Comments on DHEW-NIH Draft and Regulations: Prisoners (undated) (comments by Holland); Ulrich, "Behavior Control and Public Concern," 17 *Psychological Record* 229–34 (1967).

[29]Bandura, Behavior Theory and the Models of Man, 29 *Am. Psychologist,* 868 (1974). It is the discussion of just such institutional sanctions and restraints, of course, which is the purpose of the conference for which this article is written.

[30]Goldiamond, "Toward a Constructional Approach to

The approach taken to formulating the protective standards later set forth in this article* is in harmony with that of the cases and commentators cited above. Informed consent is not treated as a unitary concept. The model invoked recognizes that coercive influences[31] and diminished capacity will depend upon the setting in which consent takes place and the nature of the procedure for which consent is requested. Just as a person may be competent for some purposes but not for others, the same person may be competent to consent to some procedures and not to others. The more coercive the

---

Social Problems: Ethical and Constitutional Issues Raised by Applied Behavior Analysis," 2 *Behaviorism* 1–84 (1974).

Other behaviorists offer a proposal for securing consent which involves a hierarchy of protections responsive to the level of benefit to the client; level of risk; the validational status of the procedure to be used; and the extent to which the client can freely render informed consent. G. Davison & R. Stuart, *supra* note 12, at 15–16. This proposal can be diagramed as follows: [See table following page]

*Not included in this selection.

[31]The danger of abuse of prisoners' rights is obvious. Most glaring is the possibility that the degrading and depressing aspects of prison life, combined with the lure of parole, will make a truly voluntary consent impossible. Given this inherent coercion, critics have called for a temporary or permanent ban on the use of prisoners for research. *See* Capron, "Medical Research in Prisons," 1973 *Hastings Center Rep. 4*.

While admitting the possibility of coercion, other critics have refused to call for an outright ban on such prison research and instead have urged greater supervision and control over the consent process. Among those proposing means for greater control are: Alberts & DeRiemer, "Connecticut "Watchdogs" Human Research Experiments," 1973 *Am. J. of Correction* 40; Hodges & Bean, "The Use of Prisoners for Medical Research," 202 *J. Am. Medical Ass'n* 177 1967. Rules promulgated by HEW on May 30, 1974 adopt such a regulatory position. *See* 39 Fed. Reg. 18914 (1974). On August 23, 1974, HEW proposed additional regulations providing more safeguards for vulnerable groups, such as prisoners and the mentally disabled. *See* 39 Fed. Reg. 30647 (1974).

A Commission for the Protection of Human Patients has been recently established by Congress and charged with identifying the basic ethical principles which should underlie research, developing guidelines accordingly, and making recommendations to the Secretary of HEW concerning administrative action. *See generally* "Human Experimentation Regulations: Too Little or Too Much?," 3 *Federation of Am. Scientists* Professional Bull., Feb. 1975.

pressures to which a person is subjected and the more potentially harmful, intrusive, or experimental are the procedures for which consent is requested, the stricter and more numerous must be the safeguards erected to protect the person from an unwarranted intrusion. Although none of the generally accepted applied behavior techniques appear to be so offensive as to require an absolute protective ban, some are potentially abusive and require the strictest control.

DETERMINING BEST INTEREST

The functional equivalent of consent by a competent patient is the notion that the treatment of an incompetent patient must be in his best interest. The idea that a procedure is in the client's best interest would require, at a minimum, that the benefits of the contemplated procedure clearly outweigh both the known harms and the possible risks or side effects. Ideally, there should be assurance that the proposed procedure is in fact efficacious; and that where the procedure is either intrusive or hazardous, less intrusive or less hazardous procedures have first been exhausted.

Since a best interest determination requires a balancing, it must be the outcome of a decision-making process and cannot be objectively described. The numerous variables, such as intrusiveness, risk, potential harm, or side effects, the degree to which the procedure is established or experimental, and the efficacy of the treatment, cannot be fully quantified. For example, a relatively safe procedure may not be in a person's best interest if there are even safer and more efficacious procedures available to effect the same behavioral change; conversely, a highly risky or intrusive procedure may be in a client's best interest if the available alternatives are even more risky, more intrusive, or less effective.

Procedures which would normally be considered intolerable may be acceptable if they are successful in eliminating even less desirable conditions:

Level of Potential Benefit to Subject	High Potential Benefit to Subject		Low Potential Benefit to Subject/High Potential Benefit to Society	
Novelty of Procedure	Established	Experimental	Established	Experimental
Level of Risk — Likelihood of free Consent				
Low Risk — Great freedom	1	3	2	4
Low Risk — Some Coercion	4	5	7	8
High Risk — Great freedom	2	4	5	10
High Risk — Some coercion	6	7	9	N/A

The above graph ranks the degree of consent which is required in relation to the variable factors. The number 1 signifies that the consent can be simply verbal. The number 10 signifies consent that must be witnessed and approved by an outside review panel.

"It can be argued . . . that elimination of severe self-abusive behavior warrants the use of painful stimuli, since the damage to the subject is relatively milder and of much shorter duration. Again, these questions are ethical rather than empirical in nature and value judgments must be made in reaching decisions. The making of value judgments is inescapable in such cases, since deciding not to use aversive conditioning is itself a decision based on value considerations which can have major consequences for the subject. For example, without recourse to aversive conditioning, prevention of self-injury or possibly death may require indefinite use of restraint which can effectively totally curtail the individual's development and freedom of action."[32]

Consequently, one must carefully balance a wide variety of factors in determining whether a particular procedure is in the best interests of an incompetent patient.

THE VALIDITY OF VICARIOUS PARENTAL CONSENT FOR CHILDREN

Traditionally, minors have been presumed to be incompetent, and parents have given vicarious consent on their behalf for various therapies and even for civil commitment. Recently, however, the assumption that parents always effectively represent the best interests of their children when giving such consent has been called into question.[33] With regard to civil commitment, for example, a New York federal court held that:

"There may be a fundamental conflict of interest between a parent who is ready to avoid the responsibility for caring for an abnormal child, and the best interests of the child. . . . A "voluntary admission" on the petition of the parents may quite properly be treated in the same category as an "involuntary admission," in the absence of evidence the child's interests have been fully considered."[34]

One commentator has observed that factors motivating parents to seek institutionalization of their children include the interest of other children in the family, the mental and physical frustration of the parents, economic strain resulting from caring for the child at home, the stigma of retardation, hostility resulting from the burdens of caring for the child, and the parents' success-oriented expectations of the child.[35]

[32]Roos, "Human Rights and Behavior Modification," 12 *Mental Retardation*, June 1974, 3. An interesting issue relating to best interest determinations is whether prior competent indications of a desire to undertake or refuse specific procedures by a now incompetent client should be honored. The theoretical issue underlying this question is whether the purpose of substitute judgment for incompetent clients is to make the decision which they themselves would have made were they competent or whether it is to make the decision that a reasonable man would make under all the circumstances known. Those commentators who have addressed this issue seem to agree that where the essential facts remain the same and where the prior decision was competent, it should be honored even though the client is now incompetent and others may feel that a reasonable man would have made a different decision. *See. e.g.*, Cantor, "A Patient's Decision to Decline Life-Saving Medical Treatment: Bodily Integrity vs. The Preservation of Life," 26 *Rutgers L. Rev.* 228 (1973); "Developments—Civil Commitment," *supra* note at 1218 n.95; Note, "An Adult's Right to Resist Blood Transfusions: A View Through *John F. Kennedy Memorial Hospital v. Heston*," 47 *Notre Dame Law.* 571 (1972). This issue is by no means academic since many mental disorders have the effect of intermittently causing their victims to become disoriented while leaving them completely lucid otherwise. *See Developments—Civil Commitment, supra* note 8, at 1217 n.91.

[33]*See generally* J. Goldstein, A. Freud & A. Solnit, *Beyond the Best Interests of the Child* (1973); Ellis, "Volunteering Children: Parental Commitment of Minors to Mental Institutions," 62 *Calif. L. Rev.* 840 (1974).

[34]New York State Ass'n for Retarded Children v. Rockefeller, 357 F. Supp. 752, 762 (E.D.N.Y. 1973) (citations omitted); *accord,* Saville v. Treadway, Civ. No. 6969 (M.D. Tenn., Mar. 8, 1974) ("possible conflicts of interest between a mentally retarded child and even a parent" render apparently "voluntary" commitments of mentally retarded children under the Tennessee statute constitutionally inadequate); *see* Heryford v. Parker, 369 F.2d 393, 396 (10th Cir. 1968); Horacek v. Exon, 357 F. Supp. 71 (D. Neb. 1973) (preliminary relief); Frazier v. Levi, 440 S.W.2d 393 (Tex. Civ. App. 1969); *cf.* Strunk v. Strunk, 445 S.W.2d 145 (Ky. Ct. App. 1969). *See generally* Ellis, *supra* note 217, at 844–50; Herr, "Retarded Children and the Law: Enforcing the Constitutional Rights of the Mentally Retarded," 23 *Syracuse L. Rev.* 995 (1972); Murdock, "Civil Rights of the Mentally Retarded: Some Critical Issues," 48 *Notre Dame Law.* 133, 139–43 (1972).

[35]Murdock, *supra* note 34, at 139–43.

At least one federal court has extended the questionability of parental consent from the civil commitment process to the intrusive surgical procedure of sterilization. In *Relf v. Weinberger*,[36] plaintiffs challenged the statutory authorization and constitutionality of regulations of the Department of Health, Education, and Welfare governing sterilizations under the programs funded by the Department of Public Health Services. The *Relf* court found uncontroverted evidence in the record that minors and other incompetents had been sterilized in a family planning program which Congress had intended to function on a purely voluntary basis. In order to ensure that sterilizations under the program were voluntary in the full sense of the term, the court found it necessary to enjoin or revise substantial portions of the regulations which had allowed the "voluntary" participation of minors and other incompetents.

An analysis of the revisions suggests that an institution utilizing constitutionally intrusive behavioral procedures on children would be advised to seek consent directly from the child as well as the parent.[37] Review of proposed procedures by a committee which would not have the possible conflict of interest problems of a parent would help protect against biased decisions. Some procedures, like sterilization, however, may be so intrusive and irreversible that they call for a per se rule enjoining their use until such time as a child becomes an adult and is capable of giving a legally valid consent.

DETERMINING INTRUSIVENESS

Not every behavioral procedure is sufficiently intrusive to require either waiver by competent patients or a best interest determination for incompetent patients. Where such a determination is required, however, there exists a need for criteria determining intrusiveness and a consensus about a hierarchy of alternative behavioral procedures based upon their intrusiveness.

Without criteria for intrusiveness, for example, it is difficult to determine whether, in any given situation, psychoanalysis is more or less intrusive than aversive conditioning by electric shock.

One commentator has suggested the following six criteria for intrusiveness:

"(i) the extent to which the effects of the therapy upon mentation are reversible; (ii) the extent to which the resulting psychic state is "foreign," "abnormal" or "unnatural" for the person in question, rather than simply a restoration of his prior psychic state (this is closely related to the "magnitude" or "intensity" of the change); (iii) the rapidity with which the effects occur; (iv) the scope of the change in the total "ecology" of the mind's functions; (v) the extent to which one can resist acting in ways impelled by the psychic effects of the therapy; and (vi) the duration of the change."[38]

Even guided by these criteria of intrusiveness, deciding which treatments are more restrictive is largely a matter of subjective opinion and theoretical disposition. But the idea that some techniques may be viewed as more onerous than others and that they may be categorized may contribute to making the search for the least restrictive alternative less difficult.[39]

It is beyond the scope of this discussion to improve upon the important initial efforts made by these commentators. Ultimately, in order to make judgments about the client's right to re-

[36]372 F. Supp. 1196 (D.D.C. 1974).
[37]*Id.* at 1204–05.

[38]Shapiro *supra* note 7, at 262.
[39]Another commentator has formulated a "coerciveness continuum" for various therapeutic techniques, ranking coerciveness according to three criteria: (1) the nature, extent, and duration of the primary and side effects of the technique; (2) the extent to which an "uncooperative" patient can avoid the effects of the technique; and (3) the extent of the physical intrusion. Note, "Conditioning and Other Technologies Used to 'Treat?' 'Rehabilitate?' 'Demolish?' Prisoners and Mental Patients", 45 *S. Cal. L. Rev.* 3, at 619 (1972). This resulted in the following ranking of therapies from the least to the most intrusive: milieu therapy, psychotherapy, drug therapy, behavior modification, aversion therapy, electroconvulsive therapy, electronic stimulation of the brain, lobotomy, and stereotactic psychosurgery. *Id.* at 619–33. It might be questioned, however, whether behavior modification is amenable to such a ranking since it covers a small universe of different procedures, all of which have varying degrees of intrusiveness. . . .

fuse and determinations of best interest, the exponents of applied behavior analysis and other concerned individuals must systematically establish the range of specific behaviors which are presently sought to be promoted or extinguished. Then, for each specific behavior, they must list all the various techniques which are thought to promote or extinguish that behavior and must indicate for each procedure: (1) both its short and long-term effectiveness; (2) its intrusiveness upon the personal autonomy of the patient; (3) the harms and the probability of such harms resulting from its use; (4) how experimental, from a medical view, the use of the technique to promote or extinguish the specific behavior is; and (5) how the alternative procedures available to modify each specific behavior compare in terms of the above categories.

PROCEDURAL LIMITATIONS ON IMPOSING TREATMENT—DUE PROCESS REVISITED

The primary focus of this article has been the right to refuse treatment. Accordingly, primary emphasis has been placed on developing and analyzing the possible bases for the applied behavior analyst's duty to refrain from utilizing hazardous or intrusive behavioral procedures except under special circumstances. A discussion of applied behavior analysis in mental institutions and prisons would not be complete, however, without a brief discussion of procedural due process and the limitations which it may impose on the utilization of behavioral procedures.

Procedural due process requires that persons be given adequate notice, an opportunity to be heard, and other procedural protections where impending state action will deprive them of a significant property or liberty interest.[40] The fundamental question in each case is whether a

deprivation without notice and an opportunity to be heard violates traditional notions of fairness.[41] A determination that liberty or property interests protected by due process are being invaded, however, is only the beginning of the inquiry. The nature and extent of the procedural protections required will depend on the importance of the liberty or property interest involved and the nature of the proceedings.[42]

The due process rights of prisoners and mental patients have been the subject of acute controversy. In the past, courts have ordered hearings before patients were transferred to sections of a hospital with greater security and fewer privileges[43] or were returned to prison after receiving hospital treatment.[44] Courts also have accorded prisoners the right to a hearing before allowing changes in the conditions of confinement.[45]

Of particular interest in the behavior modification area is *Clonce v. Richardson*,[46] a recent right-to-refuse rehabilitation case resting on procedural due process grounds. The challenged program, Special Treatment and Rehabilitative Training [START], was developed at the Medical Center for Federal Prisoners at Springfield, Missouri, in September 1972. START was an involuntary program. Prisoners who were selected for placement in START

---

[40]*See*, e.g., *Wolff v. McDonnel*, 418 U.S. 539 (1974); *Fuentes v. Shevin*, 407 U.S. 67 (1972); *Goldberg v. Kelley*, 397 U.S. 254 (1970).

[41]*See*, e.g., *Duncan v. Louisiana*, 391 U.S. 145 (1968); *Gideon v. Wainwright*, 372 U.S. 335 (1963); *Palko v. Connecticut*, 302 U.S. 319 (1937).

[42]*See*, e.g., *Fuentes v. Shevin*, 407 U.S. 67 (1972); *Cafeteria & Restaurant Workers Local 473 v. McElroy*, 367 U.S. 886 (1961); *Hannah v. Larche*, 363 U.S. 420 (1960).

[43]*Jones v. Robinson*, 440 F.2d 249 (D.C. Cir. 1971).

[44]*Burchett v. Bower*, 355 F. Supp. 1278 (D. Ariz. 1973).

[45]*Wolff v. McDonnell*, 418 U.S. 539 (1974) (placement in punitive segregation); *Schumate v. People*, 373 F. Supp. 1166 (S.D.N.Y. 1974) (termination of work-release privileges); *Cousins v. Oliver*, 369 F. Supp. 553 (E.D. Va. 1974) (reclassification leading to reduced privileges); *White v. Gillman*, 360 F. Supp. 64 (S.D. Ia. 1973) (transfer to an institution of increased security); *Park v. Thompson*, 356 F. Supp. 783 (D. Hawaii 1973) (transfer to an out-of-state prison).

[46]379 F. Supp. 338 (W.D. Mo. 1974).

were not notified that they were being considered for the program, nor were they granted an opportunity for a hearing at the time of their selection.

The stated purpose of START was to teach participants to adjust to the requirements demanded in a prison environment, rather than to make them better adapted to life in the community after release from prison. No prisoner was permitted to leave the START unit for the purpose of attending religious services, and Muslim petitioners were not provided with any opportunity to consult with or to seek guidance from a Muslim spiritual leader. START prisoners in the "orientation" phase, the lowest level of the program, were prohibited from possessing, reading, or otherwise using political and educational literature, religious materials, and political publications. They were denied the opportunity to view television and possess or utilize a radio. Their actions, including communications with others in the START program, were under continual surveillance for the purpose of determining the inmates' rate of progress.

The START program had several ingredients of a behavior modification system, including deprivation state, reinforcement arrangement, and a graded progression of criteria for reinforcement. The program operated as a form of a token economy designed to teach prisoners to live according to the rules of a penal institution by taking away all privileges and rights, and then offering to restore them in graduated steps as the prisoner "progressed."

On the merits, the court held that "a prisoner transferred into START or into a behavior modification program like START, which . . . involves a major change in the conditions of confinement is entitled, at a minimum, to the type of hearing required by the Supreme Court's opinion in Wolff v. McDonnell."[47] The Wolff Court had required prison officials to provide a hearing, written notice to a prisoner of his alleged violation, a written statement of findings

[47]Id. at 348.

of fact, and a right to call witnesses, all prior to the imposition of solitary confinement or the deprivation of good-time credits.[48]

Undoubtedly, Clonce foreshadows the application of procedural due process protections to prisoners and mental patients participating in other behavior modification programs. The limitations of the case's impact, however, should be noted. The START program involved extensive deprivations for lengthy periods and major changes in the conditions of confinement. Thus, it is unclear to what extent the requirements of Wolff would apply to most behavior modification programs. Further case law development will be necessary to define the scope of procedural protections required for various behavior modification programs. In this regard, a major concern of the standards proposed in this Article* is the assurance of adequate procedural safeguards

---

[48]The Clonce court declined to answer, on grounds of mootness, the questions whether a prisoner selected to participate in START had a right to freely withdraw without penalty and whether the START program, as designed and applied, violated protected constitutional rights such as freedom of religion, freedom of speech and association, the right to be free from unwarranted search and seizure, the right of privacy, and the prohibition against cruel and unusual punishment. The court's opinion, however, implicitly recognizes the nonfrivolity of these constitutional claims. Serious constitutional issues were clearly raised since

[f]orced participation in S.T.A.R.T. was obviously designed to accomplish a modification of the participant's behavior and his general motivation. He was forced to submit to procedures designed to change his mental attitudes, reactions and processes. A prisoner may not have a constitutional right to prevent such experimentation but procedures specifically designed and implemented to change a man's mind and therefore his behavior in a manner substantially different from the conditions to which a prisoner is subjected in segregation reflects a major change in the conditions of confinement."

F. Supp. at 350. In context, the meaning of this somewhat ambiguous statement appears to be that the court did not have to reach the issue whether other constitutional rights were denied by the START program in order to hold that due process is violated if prisoners are transferred without a notice and hearing.

*Not included in this selection.

for mental patients prior to the imposition of behavioral treatments.

CONCLUSION

It is difficult at present to give precise advice to applied behavior analysts or other therapists as to the legal limitations on the use of behavioral or other procedures. The greater volume of legal precedent suggests an overly deferential respect by courts for the discretionary judgments of administrators and staff of mental institutions and prisons. Nevertheless, one senses that newer and stricter notions of accountability are gaining acceptance. Cases such as *Kaimowitz, Knecht, Mackey,* and *Wyatt* suggest a new and more activist judicial scrutiny of enforced therapy.

66. Time Served and Release Performance

JAMES L. BECK
PETER B. HOFFMAN

THERE IS PRESENTLY CONSIDERABLE THEORET-ical support for the position that prison experience is criminogenic in nature: that prisons breed crime.[1] The argument that long prison terms will deter offenders from future criminal behavior appears to have fallen into disfavor. Recent assessments of the effectiveness of institutional treatment programs have reported extremely disappointing results.[2] It is now frequently argued that any prison experience is dysfunctional for rehabilitation and that longer periods of incarceration will be associated with higher rates of recidivism.[3]

Empirical investigations, however, have not demonstrated any strong association between time served and release performance. One recent study was able to utilize an experimental design in which release dates for a randomly assigned group of prisoners were arbitrarily advanced. No difference in release performance between this group and a group released under the normal procedure was observed, although the generalizability of this finding is somewhat limited because the differences in time served between members of the two groups were small (on the order of six months).[4] The more usual method has been to compare groups serving different amounts of time while attempting to exercise control statistically for the effects of offense or background variables known or assumed to be related to release outcome (e.g., by matching on offense, age, prior record and/or experience table score). In general, these studies have concluded that length of time served either has no association or has a slightly negative association with favorable release performance.[5]

▶SOURCE: *"Time Served and Release Performance: A Research Note," Journal of Research in Crime and Delinquency,"* (July, 1976), *13(2): 127–132. Reprinted with permission of the National Council on Crime and Delinquency.*

[1]See, for example, J. Robison and G. Smith, "The Effectiveness of Correctional Programs," *Crime and Delinquency,* 17 (1971), pp. 67–80; J. Irwin, "The Prison Experience: The Convict World," in R. Carter, D. Glaser, and L. Wilkins, eds., *Correctional Institutions* (New York: J. B. Lippincott Co., 1972), pp. 173–192; President's Commission on Law Enforcement and Administration of Justice, *The Challenge of Crime in a Free Society,* Chapter VI, (Washington, D.C.: United States Government Printing Office, 1967), pp. 159–185.

[2]D. Lipton, R. Martinson, and J. Wilks, *The Effectiveness of Correctional Treatment: A Survey of Treatment Evaluation Studies* (New York: Praeger Publishers, 1975); G. Kassebaum, D. Ward, and D. Wilner, *Prison Treatment and Parole Survival* (New York: John Wiley & Sons, Inc., 1971); W. Bailey, "Correctional Outcome: An Evaluation of 100 Reports" (Los Angeles: School of Social Welfare, University of California, 1961).

[3]See, for example, J. Robison and G. Smith, *supra* note 1.

[4]J. Berecochea, D. Jaman, and W. Jones, "Time Served in Prison and Parole Outcome: An Experimental Study" (Sacramento: Research Division, California Department of Corrections, 1973).

[5]See D. Jaman, "Parole Outcome and Time Served for First Releases" (Sacramento: Research Division, California Department of Corrections, 1968); D. Jaman and R. Dickover, "A Study of Parole Outcome as a Function of Time Served" (Sacramento: Research Division, California Department of Corrections, 1969); D. Babst, M. Koval, and M. Neithercutt, "Relationship of Time Served to Parole Out-

The present research involves an empirical attempt to examine the association between time served and release performance for a sample of adult male federal offenders. As in the second of the two types of research design cited above, statistical rather than experimental control for factors known to be associated with release performance was utilized.

RESEARCH METHOD

One thousand five hundred and forty six (1546) adult male prisoners released from the federal system to the community for the first time on their sentences during 1970 by all forms of release (parole-mandatory release-expiration of sentence) comprised the sample for this study. Coded as part of a larger project,[6] the sample contained case information for all releasees whose prison register (identification) numbers ended in selected digits. As register numbers are assigned sequentially, this method may be assumed to approximate random selection.

Two year followup from date of release was coded for each individual to determine release performance. If the subject was released with supervision, followup information was obtained from the parole file. If the subject was released without supervision or if supervision was terminated prior to the end of the followup period, additional information was obtained from the subject's "rap sheet" record provided through

the cooperation of the Federal Bureau of Investigation. A favorable release outcome was defined as no new conviction resulting in a sentence of sixty days or more, no return to prison for administrative violation, no absconder warrant outstanding, and not deceased as a result of a criminal act.[7]

An actuarial device termed a "salient factor score" was used to classify the sample subjects according to expected probability of favorable release performance. The salient factor score, presently in use in actual case decision-making by the United States Board of Parole as a risk assessment aid,[8] contains nine items (Table I) producing a score from zero to eleven (0–11) points: the higher the number of points, the more favorable the expected prognosis.

It is to be noted that no attempt was made to exercise control for any type of institutional treatment or program experience. In light of the recent research evidence concerning the lack of institutional program effectiveness,[9] the assumption that institutional programming is not significantly related to release outcome was deemed warranted.

Table II displays the percent favorable outcome observed for each score group. Adjacent score categories with similar outcome rates were collapsed to form five risk categories with the following scores: (1–2/3–4/5–6/7–9/10–11). Subjects in each risk category were then divided into three approximately equal groups: the third serving the least amount of time (Group A); the third serving a middle amount of time (Group B); and the third serving the greatest amount of time (Group C).[10] For each of the five risk

---

come for Different Classifications of Burglars Based on Males Paroled in Fifty Jurisdictions in 1968 and 1969," *Journal of Research in Crime and Delinquency,* 9 (1972) pp. 99–116; D. Jaman, R. Dickover, and A. Bennett, "Parole Outcome as a Function of Time Served," *The British Journal of Criminology,* 12 (1972) pp. 5–34; D. Gottfredson, M. Neithercutt, J. Nuffield, and V. O'Leary, "Four Thousand Lifetimes: A Study of Time Served and Parole Outcomes" (Davis, California: National Council on Crime and Delinquency, 1973).

[6]D. Gottfredson, L. Wilkins, P. Hoffman, and S. Singer, "The Utilization of Experience in Parole Decision-Making: A Progress Report" (Davis, California: National Council on Crime and Delinquency, 1973).

[7]For cases having arrest(s) without disposition(s) during the two year followup period, the arresting agency was contacted to obtain the missing disposition(s). Disposition(s) outstanding as of November, 1973, were coded as favorable outcome.

[8]P. Hoffman and J. Beck, "Parole Decision-Making: A Salient Factor Score," *Journal of Criminal Justice,* 2 (1974), pp. 195–206.

[9]*Supra* note 2.

[10]Cases in each risk category were divided as closely as

Table I. Salient Factor Score

Item A	☐

No prior convictions (adult or juvenile) = 2
One or two prior convictions = 1
Three or more prior convictions = 0

Item B	☐

No prior incarcerations (adult or juvenile) = 2
One or two prior incarcerations = 1
Three or more prior incarcerations = 0

Item C	☐

Age at first commitment (adult or juvenile) 18 years or older = 1
Otherwise = 0

Item D	☐

Commitment offense did not involve auto theft = 1
Otherwise = 0

Item E	☐

Never had parole revoked or been committed for a new offense while
on parole = 1
Otherwise = 0

Item F	☐

No history of heroin, cocaine, or barbiturate dependence = 1
Otherwise = 0

Item G	☐

Has completed 12th grade or received GED = 1
Otherwise = 0

Item H	☐

Verified employment (or full-time school attendance) for a total of at least
6 months during the last 2 years in the community = 1
Otherwise = 0

Item I	☐

Release plan to live with spouse and/or children = 1
Otherwise = 0

Total Score	☐☐

categories, the percentage of cases with favorable release outcome in each of the three time served groups could now be observed.

possible into three equal time served groups without subdividing on cases serving exactly the same number of months.

FINDINGS

Figure I displays the results for each risk category/time served group. In general, the percentage of cases with favorable release outcome tends to decrease as one moves within a risk category from the group serving the least

Table II. Percent Favorable Outcome for Each Salient Factor Score

Salient Factor Score	Percent Favorable Outcome	Number of Cases	Salient Factor Score	Percent Favorable Outcome	Number of Cases
0	—	0	6	77.7%	175
1	42.2%	45	7	83.1%	148
2	48.0%	127	8	87.1%	140
3	61.4%	207	9	87.6%	97
4	67.6%	225	10	94.6%	112
5	72.0%	214	11	100.0%	56

Point biserial (r) = .318.   Mean Cost Rating (M.C.R.) = .42.

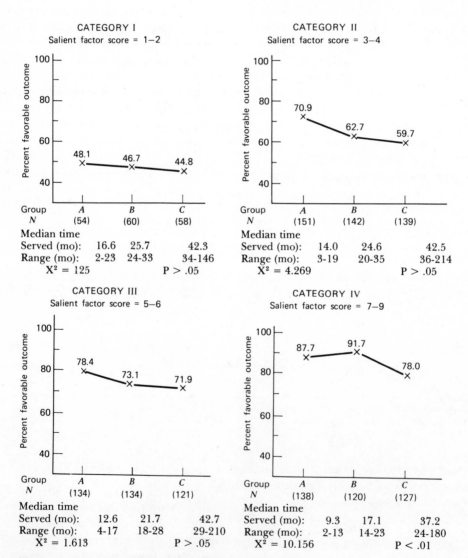

Figure 1. Percent favorable outcome by time served group.

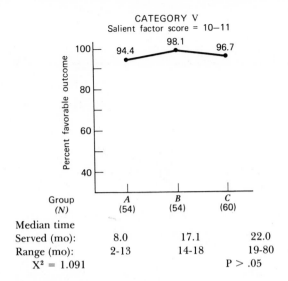

CATEGORY V
Salient factor score = 10–11

Group (N):	A (54)	B (54)	C (60)
Median time Served (mo):	8.0	17.1	22.0
Range (mo):	2-13	14-18	19-80
$X^2 = 1.091$			P > .05

Figure 1. (Cont.)

amount of time to the group serving the most amount of time.[11] However, these results are not uniform or consistent. The difference in release outcome across the three time served groups is statistically significant (P<.01) only for Category IV, but even this category contains a

slight inversion. Comparisons of only the extreme time served groups (those serving the least and most amount of time) reveal differences of five percentage points or more in only three of the five risk categories with only one of these differences exceeding ten percentage points (Category II). None of these individual differences reaches statistical significance at the .05 level (chi square).

These results are consistent with the findings in the previous studies cited.[12] That is, there appears to be slight, if any, association between time served and release outcome when selected background factors are controlled. This would seem to argue against the theory that longer prison terms will enhance individual (special) deterrence or rehabilitation, although this study does not presume to address the effects of longer prison terms upon goals of general deterrence, incapacitation,[13] or community condemnation (prevention of anomie). On the other hand, the theory that longer prison terms will result in dramatically higher recidivism rates upon release also is not supported by this data.

[11]Also, as one moves from Category I (low salient factor scores) to Category V (high salient factor scores), median time served (for the Category as a whole) tends to decrease. This would appear to reflect the impact of the "variables" that make up this score on judicial/parole board behavior.

[12]*Supra* notes 4 and 5.

[13]Obviously, with extremely long prison terms age at release, itself, may become a significant factor. However, the vast majority of the subjects in this study served less than five years.

67. Imprisonment and Recidivism

ANDREW HOPKINS

ONE OF THE PURPOSES OF IMPRISONMENT IS TO prevent offenders from returning to crime. But whether the prison experience actually has this effect has not been adequately established. Figures indicate that between one third and one half of those released from prison are returned either for new felonies or for parole violation (Glaser, 1964), and such findings are frequently taken as demonstrating the failure of the prison system and the need for alternative approaches to the correction of offenders. Yet according to Glaser, the figures show that "imprisonment and parole, as procedures for dealing with felons, are far from complete failures" (1964: 31). This discrepancy in interpretation of the data stems from the fact that recidivism rates of those released from prison can have little meaning in themselves. Only when imprisonment is compared with some alternative and its *relative* effectiveness assessed can meaningful conclusions be drawn. The present study is concerned with the effectiveness of incarceration *vis-a-vis* its standard non-institutional alternatives (probation and suspended sentencing).

There are substantial methodological problems involved in making adequate comparisons. It is not sufficient, for example, to compare the raw recidivism rates of those sentenced to prison with those in the same jurisdiction sentenced to probation, since the former are usually imprisoned because they are more serious or more persistent offenders and thus more likely to recidivate, regardless of the treatment employed. Useful comparisons can be made only if the groups compared are similar in all respects save for the method of treatment; only then can differences in recidivism rates be attributed unequivocally to differences in treatment.

The optimal research design in this context involves the *random allocation* of convicted offenders to groups which are treated differently: one sentenced to prison and the other, say, to probation. The two groups can then be compared for number of reconvictions at some point in time after the expiration of the sentences.

The optimal technique, random allocation, has been little used in correctional research for two reasons. First, many judges feel that offenders have a right to equal treatment under law and that deliberately to allow procedures of chance to determine otherwise is an injustice (Morris, 1972; Geis, 1972). Second, because of the need to allow for a reasonable follow-up period such experiments usually take years to complete.

One area in which this kind of experimental research *has* proved practicable is in the evaluation of specially devised treatments as alternatives to regular incarceration for juvenile offenders (Empey, 1971; Warren, 1971). But to my knowledge, it has not been used to compare the effectiveness of *standard* treatments. Instead, researchers have relied on a variety of retrospective techniques. These techniques all make use

▶SOURCE: *"Imprisonment and Recidivism: A Quasi-Experimental Study," Journal of Research in Crime and Delinquency, (January, 1976), 13:13–32.* Reprinted with permission of the National Council on Crime and Delinquency.

of data gathered from official records and involve the *ex post facto* construction of groups of offenders comparable in terms of background factors but having undergone different treatments.

One way in which such comparable groups can be constructed is by matching; that is, by including an individual in one group if and only if another individual with similar characteristics is included in the other. This method was used by Wilkins in a small-scale study of probation in which 50 offenders convicted in a court which made extensive use of probation were matched in respect of age, current offence, and number of previous convictions with 50 offenders convicted at another court which used probation much less frequently. The matching was done without regard to treatment, so each group contained cases given institutional sentences and cases given probation. Of course the group dealt with by the "lenient" judge contained a much higher proportion of probationers than the other. Comparing the subsequent recidivism rates of the two groups, Wilkins concluded that "the use of probation as treatment for a large proportion of cases which many courts would have sent to prison does not result in a greater proportion of reconvictions" (1958: 207).

An important problem with Wilkins' work is that he matched his cases on only three background factors. (In any matching procedure the number of matched characteristics will inevitably be small.) The difficulty is that there may be other characteristics related to recidivism which remain uncontrolled. For example, in Wilkins' case, the two courts operated in different parts of London and, although he argues that the court districts were similar, there may well have been a social class difference between the two groups of offenders. Since class is known to be related to delinquent behavior, it is quite possible that had this variable been controlled for, a relationship between treatment and recidivism might have been revealed.

A second, and more widely used, retrospective technique attempts to control for background factors related to recidivism by sub-dividing offenders into groups, each of which consists of individuals with a common set of pretreatment characteristics. Offenders in each such group will have been sentenced to a variety of treatments and by comparing their subsequent reconviction rates the researcher can assess the effectiveness of those treatments.

One such study, by the U.K. Home Office research unit, controlled for age and number of previous convictions, and showed that for 1316 offenders convicted in London in 1957, reconviction rates of probationers were similar to those of offenders given institutional treatment, while fines and discharges were much more effective than incarceration. A second study, dealing with offenders who came before the superior courts of California's 13 largest counties, and using a follow-up period of one year, showed that 34% of probationers recidivated as compared with 51% of incarcerees. The differences persisted when the following factors were individually controlled for: county, sex, age, race, prior record, offense; and when the following factors were controlled simultaneously: offense and age, offense and race, offense and prior record (Levin, 1971: 25; Beattie and Bridges, 1970). Yet another study of this type (Babst and Mannering, 1965) found that in some control categories probationers were more likely than parolees to recidivate while in others the reverse was true.

The studies just mentioned compare recidivism rates of incarcerees and probationers within each control category. When the number of control categories is at all large such comparisons become unwieldy and the technique of regression analysis with its associated prediction table methodology can be used to summarize the information (Manheim and Wilkins, 1955). In recent years prediction tables have been widely used in penological research, but there appear to be no published reports which make use of the technique to compare institutional with standard non-institutional treatment.

The major problem with all studies which seek to control for relevant background factors is similar to the problem involved in individual matching: since the number of control variables which can be used is limited, it is always possible, even probable, that uncontrolled variables are confounding the relationship between treatment and recidivism. Glaser puts the matter well as follows:

"Even when we compare only prison with probation cases that are matched by every index considered relevant (number of previous arrests, age, employment record, marital status and so forth), it is possible that within each category of classification by those variables the judges have differentially selected the worse risk cases for prison and the better risk cases for probation, employing some subjective indices or weights not taken into account by the researcher's categories" (1971: 185).

Under these circumstances, differences in outcome after treatment may be functions of prior recidivism probabilities rather than of the treatment processes themselves.

This difficulty undermines all the research which has so far been done in the area. Prima facie, the general conclusion of most of this work is that whether you incarcerate the convicted offender or place him on probation makes little differences to his chances of recidivating. However, the bias I have pointed to is such as to underestimate the effectiveness of imprisonment in preventing recidivism. It is possible, therefore, that were research to be carried out using truly comparable groups of offenders, imprisonment might be found to be *more* effective than probation. The principal aim of this study is to develop and apply a rather different research strategy in order to present data which is not subject to the bias just discussed.

A QUASI-EXPERIMENTAL METHOD

Retrospective data are not always subject to the imperfections of the previous studies. In some circumstances they can have the quality of a planned, controlled experiment. The classic case of this is the study of sets of identical and fraternal twins where, at least in theory, comparisons can be used to settle questions about whether certain kinds of behavior are environmentally or genetically determined. (Admittedly, most of the twin studies done to date are not above criticism—see Sutherland and Cressey, 1970: 115–7).

Zeisel has pointed out that "sometimes administrative routine will present the investigator with a natural experiment, that is, with an experimental and control group that were not purposely designed by him" (1967: 85). He provides the following illustration. To discover whether judges' personalities affect their sentencing, we may take advantage of the fact that many courts assign cases at random to the different judges who sit there. Since these cases are drawn from the same court district, the groups of offenders coming before the various judges will be comparable, and so, if one group receives harsher treatment than another, this will be attributable to the idiosyncracies of the judges rather than to differences in the cases coming before them.

In his discussion, Zeisel is concerned to show how the natural random allocation of cases to judges in the same court can be used to demonstrate the existence of sentencing disparities. Although he does not mention it, such a natural experimental situation can also be used to study the effectiveness of punishment, in particular imprisonment, in preventing recidivism. *If disparities occur in the sentencing practices of judges sitting in the same court and dealing with comparable groups of offenders, then differences in the subsequent recidivism rates of these groups can be attributed to the differential treatment they received.* This observation provides the basis for the quasi-experimental method to be developed shortly.

It should be stressed that the validity of this particular natural experiment does not require all of those coming before one judge to be given one kind of treatment and all of those coming before another to be given a different treatment. It is enough that the proportion of offenders treated in a particular way differ from group to group.

It should also be made clear that the concept

of treatment used here does not distinguish between the treatment itself and the offender's perception of it. Thus, for example, no attempt is made to identify the effects of incarceration as distinct from the effects of the sense of injustice which an offender might feel at being incarcerated. It is the total experience which is the subject of comparison.

A comparison with Wilkins' earlier mentioned study is appropriate at this point. Wilkins, too, compared the recidivism rate of groups subjected to differential sentencing. However, in this case the judges were sitting in different parts of London. Thus, the cases coming before them were not comparable and Wilkins had to resort to matching in an effort to control for distortions introduced by the non-comparability of his two groups. But with natural random allocation, there should be no need to identify and control for background factors related to recidivism.

It will be evident that within any one jurisdiction, variation in judicial sentencing practice must be limited: many, if not most, of those incarcerated by a harsh judge would fare no differently with a lenient judge. There may be a relatively small number of offenders who would be incarcerated by one judge but not the other. Yet it is this group which will make the difference (if any) in overall recidivism rates. In the following paragraphs we will develop a method of analysis which isolates the offenders who are actually subject to this discrepant sentencing and which enables us to compute their recidivism rate after incarceration and after non-institutional treatment.

Consider two groups of offenders, one coming before a harsh judge and the other before a lenient judge. Let us *assume for the time being only* that the groups are of the same size.

We *assume* further that a process of random allocation has yielded perfectly comparable groups of offenders. This will mean that the groups contain the same number of offenders with any given set of background characteristics. For example they will contain an identical number of offenders in the category: under 25,

previously incarcerated and currently charged with robbery. The more variables we use in defining such categories the fewer will be the number of offenders in any one category (case attenuation). Obviously, the categories can be drawn so finely that there is at most one person per category. Thus, the ultimate implication of the assumed equivalence of the two groups of offenders is that there is a perfect 1:1 matching of offenders with respect to any number of background characteristics. This assumption underlies all experimental-control group comparisons. However, it is clearly impossibly stringent and in practice can be replaced by a weaker one; namely, that any departures from perfect matching are of such a nature that they do not significantly affect the experimental outcome. Although the following analysis logically requires only the weaker assumption, in order to facilitate discussion, I shall proceed on the basis of the stronger.

Let H and L be the sets of offenders coming before the harsh and lenient judges respectively (see Figure 1). Let X_L be the subset of offenders in L who are sentenced to prison. By the assumption discussed above these individuals can be matched in terms of background characteristics with individuals in H. Let X_H be this set of matched offenders in H.

Let us now *assume* that the harsh judge sentences all the offenders in X_H to prison. Because he is the harsh judge, he will also sentence some additional set Y_H to prison. The assumption that all individuals in X_H are sentenced to imprisonment is critical. It is equivalent to assuming that for every category of offenders the harsh judge will sentence a higher proportion to prison than the lenient; in short, the assumption is that the harsh judge is consistently harsher than the lenient.

Now let Z_H be the subset of H not imprisoned and Z_L its duplicate subset in L. Further, Let Y_L be the duplicate of Y_H. These last two are sets of offenders matched in terms of all background characteristics but subject to different treatment; individuals in Y_H are all imprisoned while those in Y_L are not. Such offenders are "border-

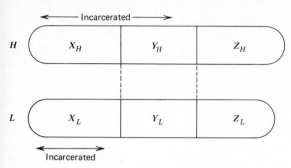

Figure 1.   Set diagram of offenders sentenced by a harsh and a lenient judge.

line" in the sense that one judge would sentence them to prison and the other would not.

We have, then, six subsets of offenders. A certain proportion of offenders in each subset recidivate and this proportion can be treated as the probability that any one individual in that subset will recidivate. There is thus a particular recidivism probabilty associated with each subset. Probability of recidivism is a function of background characteristics and treatment, and since individuals in X_H and X_L are matched in terms of background characteristics (by previous assumption) and subject to the same treatment (also by previous assumption) it follows logically that they have the same probability of recidivism. We can denote this probability by p_X. Similarly we define p_Z as the common re-

cidivism probability of individuals in Z_L and Z_H. However, although individuals in Y_L and Y_H are matched in terms of background characteristics, they are treated differently and so their recidivism probabilities may be different. We can denote these different probabilities by p_{YL} and p_{YH} respectively. Our analysis will be designed to determine the value of these last two probabilities.

It is appropriate here to reiterate the importance of the recidivism probabilities of borderline offenders. The difference in the overall recidivism rates of the two groups L and H must be entirely due to the differing recidivism rates of Y_L and Y_H. As already suggested, harsh and lenient judges may not differ very greatly in their sentencing practices, and so there may be a relatively small group of borderline cases. Given this circumstance, even though the recidivism rates of Y_L and Y_H differed markedly, the overall recidivism rates of L and H would differ only slightly. So, by concentrating on those offenders actually subject to discrepant sentencing, the consequence of the discrepancy will be more apparent.

Unfortunately, the calculation pf p_{YL} and p_{YH} is not straightforward because Y_H cannot be distinguished empirically from X_H, and Y_L cannot be distinguished empirically from Z_L. However, we can proceed as follows.

Let

    n   be the number of offenders in H and therefore in L

    n_X be the number of offenders in X_H and therefore in X_L

    n_Y be the number of offenders in Y_H and therefore in Y_L

    n_Z be the number of offenders in Z_H and therefore in Z_L

    r_H be the number of offenders in H who subsequently recidivate

    r_L be the number of offenders in L who subsequently recidivate

We therefore have the following equations:

$$n_X p_X + n_Y p_{YH} + n_Z p_Z = r_H \text{ for offenders dealt with by the harsh judge}$$

$$n_X p_X + n_Y p_{YL} + n_Z p_Z = r_L \text{ for offenders dealt with by the lenient judge}$$

Now Z_H is an empirically identifiable group of offenders; therefore n_Z and p_Z are known. Further, X_L is an empirically identifiable group of offenders; therefore n_X and p_X are known. r_L and r_H are also known. Finally, $n_Y = n - n_X - n_Z$. So, the only unknowns in the above two equations are p_{YL} and p_{YH} which can thus be calculated. (It should be stressed that these equations are soluble only because our assumptions enabled us to define a single recidivism probability for individuals in X_L and X_H, and another single probability for individuals in Z_L and Z_H).

So far, in order to facilitate exposition, it has been assumed that the numbers of offenders in H and L are identical. However, in general, this will not be the case. We must therefore relax this assumption and carry out the analysis using a necessarily more complex notation. H and L are assumed to remain perfectly comparable sets in the sense of containing the same proportions of offenders of any given type, but the absolute numbers of such offenders may now differ.

Let n_{XL}, n_{XH}, n_{YL}, n_{YH}, n_{ZL}, n_{ZH}, n_L, n_H be the numbers of offenders in X_L, X_H, Y_L, Y_H, Z_L, Z_H, L and H respectively.

The equations now become

$$n_{XH}\, p_X + n_{YH}\, p_{YH} + n_{ZH}\, p_Z = r_H$$

$$n_{XL}\, p_X + n_{YL}\, p_{YL} + n_{ZL}\, p_Z = r_L$$

Here, n_{XL} and n_{ZH} are known; n_{XH}, n_{ZL}, n_{YH}, n_{ZL}, n_{YH} and n_{YL}, are not known. However because of the equivalence of H and L, we have

$$\frac{n_{XH}}{n_H} = \frac{n_{XL}}{n_L}; \quad \frac{n_{ZH}}{n_H} = \frac{n_{ZL}}{n_L}$$

Moreover,

$$n_{YH} = n_H - n_{XH} - n_{ZH}$$

$$n_{YL} = n_L - n_{XL} - n_{ZL}$$

These relationships allow us to solve all the un-

known n's. Since p_X, p_Z, r_L and r_H are known as before, we can again solve for p_{YL} and p_{YH}.

Specifically, manipulating the above equations gives us:

$$p_{YH} = \frac{r_H\, n_L - n_{ZH}\, n_L\, p_Z - n_{XL}\, n_H\, p_X}{n_H\, n_L - n_{XL}\, n_H - n_{ZH}\, n_L}$$

$$p_{YL} = \frac{r_L\, n_H - p_X\, n_{XL}\, n_H - n_{ZH}\, n_L\, p_Z}{n_H\, n_L - n_{XL}\, n_H - n_{ZH}\, n_L}$$

THE DATA SOURCE

In order to apply the technique developed above, a study was made of all offenders disposed of in the Hartford (Connecticut) superior court between July 1962 and March 1964—some 882 usable cases. At least one and sometimes three judges are assigned to the court at any one time but one alone is designated the "presiding" judge for the session (a period of about three months). The great bulk of defendants, including all those who plead guilty, are sentenced by the presiding judge. If additional judges are appointed for the session they handle the relatively few but time-consuming jury trials. Five presiding judges rotated through the Hartford court during the period under consideration. The data were collected without any prior knowledge of the sentencing practices of these men and it was simply assumed on the basis of other sentencing studies (e.g., Schrag, 1971: 180; Glueck, 1958: 463) that disparities amongst them would be sufficient to yield usable results.

Consideration of the way in which cases came before the presiding judges indicated that there was nothing in formal court procedures to destroy the comparability of the groups of offenders. Moreover, it was assumed that there was no consistent seasonal variation in the type of offender coming before the court. (This assumption was subsequently borne out by the data.)

One other possible source of interference with the comparability of the offender groups was also considered. If a defense attorney were aware of differences in judicial severity, it is conceivable that he might attempt to postpone the time of his client's appearance from one three month session to the next, in order to secure more favorable treatment for his client. If all defense attorneys were equally inclined to use these tactics there would be no problem as far as the research design is concerned. However, there is a possibility that a certain group of lawyers with a distinctive clientele might be more prone to this than others. More than half the defendants appearing in the superior court are represented by public defenders who are assigned in cases where the defendant is too poor to be able to afford a private attorney. By contrast, the private attorneys tend to represent a wealthier class of offenders. Such offenders will have less economic incentive to recidivate, and even if they do engage in further criminal activity, they are better placed to avoid detection and arrest. In short, this group is likely to have a lower than average rate of recidivism. Furthermore, it has been argued that the private attorney will be more committed to the welfare of his client than the public defender is to his. He will thus be more likely than the public defender to exploit the possibility of a lenient sentence by delaying his client's appearance. If this happens, the lower subsequent recidivism rates of those appearing before a lenient judge could be attributed to the characteristics of the defendants coming before him rather than, as intended by the research design, to the leniency of the sentence.

However, a private attorney, a public defender, and a public prosecutor I spoke with all denied that such manipulation was taking place in the Hartford court. The opinion of the public defender is particularly significant for he would surely have been sensitive to any delaying tactics on the part of private attorneys which won for their clients more lenient treatment than his own received. It thus seems most unlikely that any systematic distortion of the research design could have arisen in this way.

One further topic must be dealt with at this point: the definition of recidivism. For the purpose of this study an offender was deemed a recidivist if, during a five-year period at risk subsequent to the original offense he was either convicted of a felony in a lower court or bound over on a serious felony charge to a superior court, in either case, in the state of Connecticut. A full discussion of this index of recidivism is provided in the appendix.

DATA ANALYSIS

Table I presents the basic data on recidivism and incarceration rates, measured for groups coming before the five presiding judges. The "average" column includes, in addition to those five groups, the few offenders coming before other judges sitting in the court in the same period. The time sequence in which the presiding judges sat is A, B, C, D, and E. For ease of interpretation, they are arranged in the table in descending order of severity (as measured by the percentage of offenders they incarcerated). The data are also presented visually in the scatterplot (Figure 2). It is apparent that judges A and C incarcerated a substantially smaller proportion of offenders than did judges, B, E, and D. Correspondingly, the recidivism rates for offenders dealt with by judges A and C are much lower.

At first sight, these figures suggest that incarceration is a criminogenic experience. Moreover, it would seem that, for the calculation of borderline probabilities we should choose either A or C as the lenient judge and B, E, or D as the harsh. However, before drawing any conclusions from these data we must investigate the two crucial assumptions on which the method depends.

The Assumption of Judicial Consistency
Let us first consider the assumption that the judges are consistently harsh (or lenient) from

Table I. Recidivism and Incarceration Rates by Judge

	Judge					
	B	E	D	A	C	Average
% incarcerated	79	76	75	60	58	68
	(108)	(118)	(139)	(206)	(149)	(743)
% recidivating	39	40	39	30	32	35
	(105)	(116)	(137)	(200)	(146)	(727)

Note: In this and all subsequent tables, bracketed figures are the numbers on which the percentages are based. The 'average' columns in these tables include the few offenders who came before judges other than A, B, C, D or E.

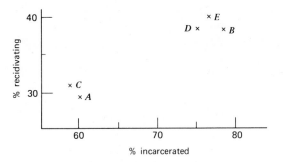

Figure 2. Scatterplot of comparison groups, arrayed by incarceration and recidivism rates.

one category of offenders to another. Table II presents some relevant data. The bottom line of the table represents the overall harshness of the judges. The second panel of the table reveals a rather striking degree of consistency. The two generally lenient judges, A and C, are to be found in the 3rd, 4th, or 5th columns of the panel for every offense category: for no offense is A or C the harshest or the second harshest judge. For two categories D is actually the most lenient judge, but since in terms of overall sentencing he is the "median" judge, this does not represent a gross distortion of the general pattern. In the case of burglary, the generally harshest judge, B, is actually the most lenient. However, the first panel shows that he is not much more lenient than A, C, or E and since he sentenced only 15 burglars it seems likely that his apparent lenience in this case is a matter of

chance rather than of any real bias in favor of burglars, especially since, true to form, he is harsher than any other judge on both robbers and thieves and he could hardly have reason to separate burglars out from this group for special treatment.

In short, judges who are generally lenient tend to be lenient with each offense category, while those who are generally harsh are similarly consistent. From this point of view, then, the assumption of judicial consistency would be approximately satisfied regardless of which pair of harsh and lenient judges was chosen for the calculation of borderline recidivism probabilities. It may still be, of course, that judges are inconsistent on some other dimension, but lacking adequate data to test this, it must remain an assumption that they are not.

Equivalence of Comparison Groups
We must now deal with the assumed comparability of the groups coming before the five judges. Table III shows these groups broken down by offense. Scrutinizing most lines in the upper section of the table reveals no obvious differences among the groups, with two exceptions: judges D and E seem to have rather more burglars than other judges do and rather fewer minor offenders. The significance of this is apparent if we look at the last column of the table: burglars are more likely than most to return to crime, while those convicted of minor crimes are among the least likely to recidivate. Thus, it is

Table II. Severity of Judges by Offence

	Panel I Percent Incarcerated Judge						Panel II Order of Severity (Most to Least)				
	A	B	C	D	E	Average					
Assorted violence*	79 (14)	91 (11)	80 (10)	100 (5)	86 (7)	85 (48)	D	B	E	C	A
Robbery	75 (8)	100 (9)	91 (11)	88 (16)	92 (12)	90 (57)	B	E	C	D	A
Burglary	74 (31)	67 (15)	71 (24)	94 (35)	74 (43)	79 (159)	D	E	A	C	B
Theft	76 (21)	90 (10)	39 (13)	83 (18)	83 (6)	73 (70)	B	D	E	A	C
OMFP	54 (24)	83 (12)	78 (9)	56 (9)	81 (16)	70 (74)	B	E	C	D	A
Sex Offences	54 (24)	86 (7)	62 (21)	89 (18)	73 (15)	69 (85)	D	B	E	C	A
Drug Offences	70 (10)	88 (8)	47 (15)	42 (12)	83 (6)	58 (53)	B	E	A	C	D
Other major	60 (20)	73 (11)	75 (12)	86 (7)	100 (20)	71 (52)	E	D	C	B	A
Other minor	43 (54)	64 (25)	32 (34)	26 (19)	46 (11)	41 (145)	B	E	A	C	D
Overall	60 (206)	79 (108)	58 (149)	75 (139)	76 (118)	68 (743)	B	E	D	A	C

*Assorted violence consists of aggravated assault, assault with intent to murder, manslaughter, murder, negligent homicide. Burglary includes receiving stolen goods. OMFP (obtaining money by false pretenses) includes forgery, embezzlement and check offences. Other major crimes are felonies such as abortion, arson, jail-breaking etc. Other minor crimes are misdemeanors such as gambling, lascivious carriage, etc.

possible that the high recidivism rates of offenders who came before judges D and E reflect the nature of their crimes rather than the higher rates of incarceration experienced by these two groups.

To highlight the problem, let us observe that the offense categories fall into two natural groupings with respect to likelihood of subsequent recidivism: property crimes and drug offenses, all relatively likely to be followed by further crime, and other crimes, all of which are associated with much lower rates of recidivism.

The lower section of Table III shows that judges D and E dealt with more than their fair share of the highly recidivism-prone offenders. So it is all the more clear that there is at least some degree of spuriousness in the apparent relationship between incarceration and recidivism.

Further analysis of offender groups in terms of age, previous record, and type of legal representation in court—all variables which are related to likelihood of subsequent recidivism—confirmed that judges D and E had disproportionately many recidivism-prone offenders

Table III. Comparison Groups by Offence and Recidivism by Offence

	Comparison (Judicial) Groups						Percent Subsequently Recidivating
	A	B	C	D	E	Average	
Assorted Violence	6	9	6	4	7	6	23
Robbery	4	9	7	12	9	7	48
Burglary	15	17	16	24	36	21	44
Theft	9	8	9	12	4	9	48
OMFP	12	10	7	8	13	10	42
Sex Offences	12	7	15	13	12	12	16
Drug Offences	5	9	12	8	7	8	42
Other Major	8	8	8	7	2	7	29
Other Minor	28	23	20	13	9	19	28
Total*	101%	100%	100%	101%	101%	99%	
(N)	(239)	(138)	(177)	(157)	(140)	(875)	
Property and Drug Crime	45	54	51	63	69	56	44
Other Crime	55	46	49	37	31	44	24
Total	100%	100%	100%	100%	100%	100%	
(N)	(239)	(138)	(177)	(157)	(140)	(875)	

*Not exactly 100% because of rounding errors.

while judges A and C had disproportionately few. In other words, in terms of likelihood of recidivism, the groups coming before the various judges were not strictly comparable.

The reason for the distortion of the equivalence of offender groups is not clear. It should be mentioned, though, that analysis of the data supported neither the hypothesis of seasonal variation nor that of interference by private attorneys with the process of random allocation of offenders to the various judges. But whatever the explanation, it is really of peripheral concern here; the important thing is to recognize that this distortion renders problematic any simple comparison of lenient and harsh judges.

Fortunately, if we modify the research design slightly, we can avoid this difficulty. Instead of seeking to compare judges who are identified as either harsh or lenient, let us simply compare the harshest judge, B, against the average. This comparison is chosen because the groups involved are as nearly as possible equivalent in terms of background characteristics. For example, the bottom half of Table III shows that B had slightly fewer than average property and drug offenders; that is, from this point of view his offenders were better than average risks. Moreover, analysis of other background variables known to be related to likelihood of recidivism confirmed that in terms of pretreatment recidivism probabilities there was no reason to expect B's group to recidivate more often than average. The fact is though that they do. In so far as this is not simply a matter of chance variation, the explanation must be the disproportionate use of incarceration made by judge B.

Having established that B's offenders are "average" in terms of background characteristics and that B is fairly consistently harsher than average, the two critical assumptions of our method are satisfied, and we may proceed to calculate borderline recidivism probabilities using B as the harsh judge and a composite judge constructed by averaging all the available data, for the lenient.

The data necessary for the calculations are presented in Table IV and the results in Figure 3. The values of PYL and PYH are .32 and .70, respectively. What this means is that for the small number of borderline individuals who are incarcerated by judge B and who would not have been by the "composite" judge, the subsequent recidivism rate was 70 per cent; the equivalent group for the "composite" judge had a recidivism rate of 32 per cent. Apparently, therefore, for individuals subject to discrepant sentencing in this context, incarceration rendered them more than twice as likely to recidivate. Put another way, the findings suggest that for offenders about whom judges disagree as to the appropriate treatment, non-institutional sentences are considerably more effective than incarceration in preventing their return to crime.

Of course, this conclusion must be advanced with caution since it is obvious that with only 11 borderline offenders dealt with by judge B the calculated probabilities will be highly unstable. Indeed, we would expect the recidivism rates of the borderline groups to lie between those of the two extreme groups. For non-incarcerated borderlines, the figure *is* intermediate, but for the incarcerated borderlines, it is not. Had judge B been much harsher than average, the group of offenders coming before him who are defined as borderline in this analysis would have been somewhat larger. The calculated recidivism

probability for this group might then have been more reliable and, presumably, a lot lower.

It is worth observing here that the relatively slight variation in incarceration rates encountered in this study is in part a consequence of the institution of plea bargaining which operates in the Hartford superior court. In return for guilty pleas from defendants, prosecutors make certain sentencing recommendations to judges who feel constrained not to exceed the recommended sentences, although they do feel free to be more lenient. Since sentencing recommendations do not vary much from one three month session to the next, this system tends to standardize the sentences handed down by the various presiding judges. Future research using this method will need to take account of this problem. Possibly there are jurisdictions in the United States where replication might be fruitful, but since plea bargaining is so widespread in the U.S., it seems likely that the full potential of the method might best be realized in jurisdictions in other countries where plea bargaining and other court procedures do not interfere with the freedom of the judge to impose sentence.

AN ALTERNATIVE METHOD OF ANALYSIS

The preceding findings demonstrate the potential of the method of analysis developed in this paper. However, the computed probabilities are obviously highly unstable. Furthermore, the calculations do not make full use of the variation in

Table IV. Data for Calculation of "Borderline" Recidivism Probabilities

	Percent Recidivating			Number Recidivating
	Incarcerated	Not Incarcerated	Average	
Judge B— Harsh		9 (23)	39 (105)	41
Composite— Lenient	44 (493)		35 (727)	255

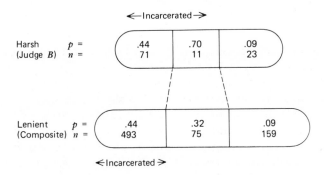

Figure 3. Set diagram of the offender groups actually used in the computation of borderline recidivism probabilities.

incarceration and recidivism rates present in the data collected. The need to reduce the data to two comparison groups was a function of our interest in borderline cases and the loss of information involved in this process can be avoided if, instead of seeking to calculate borderline recidivism probabilities, we simply compare the overall recidivism rates of all five offender groups. Scrutinizing the scatterplot (Figure 2) suggests that we treat "percent recidivating" and "percent incarcerated" as variables measured on five units of analysis—the five offender groups. We can then calculate the product-moment correlation coefficient of these two variables, obtaining a value of r = .96. Such a high correlation suggests a remarkably strong relationship but it should be remembered that with an N of 5 the correlation coefficient will be very unstable. Some indication of this instability is provided by the fact that even using a one-tailed testing procedure a value of r = .82 is necessary to reach the .05 level of significance. Nevertheless, the result does suggest that the higher the incarceration rate the higher will be the recidivism rate. Unfortunately, however, this result cannot be taken at face value since, as we already know, the offender groups are not strictly comparable and the apparent relationship between the two variables is thus, at least in part, spurious. Attempts were made to allow for this by controlling for a number of background variables and

examining the relationship between the two variables of interest within each category of the control variables. However, while the correlations remained positive, analysis revealed that even within control categories offender groups were not strictly comparable. Thus the possibility remained that the relationship between incarceration and recidivism revealed by this particular method of analysis was a consequence of the non-equivalence of the comparison groups rather than of the causal impact of incarceration on recidivism.

SUMMARY

Most previous research concerned with the relative effectiveness of imprisonment has simply compared the recidivism rates of those incarcerated with those not, controlling for one, two or three variables at a time. However, this procedure is in principle inadequate since it is probable that within each control category, judges sentence the worst risks to prison and place those with the best prognosis on probation. Consequently, despite the controls, the possibility remains that differences in outcome are due to differences in the pre-treatment recidivism probabilities of the groups compared.

The research strategy adopted here was designed to overcome this difficulty by identifying truly comparable groups of offenders who were nevertheless subject to differential treatment. The idea was that if cases are allocated at random to judges sitting in the same court, and if some judges are harsher than others, incarcerating a higher proportion of those who come before them, then differences in the subsequent recidivism rates of the groups coming before the various judges can be attributed to differences in the incarceration rates. To facilitate comparisons, a technique was developed for calculating recidivism probabilities for offenders who would be incarcerated by a harsh judge but not by a lenient.

Data for the study were collected for five Hartford superior court judges to whom it appeared that cases were allocated in an essentially random manner. Unfortunately the offender groups coming before these judges were found to be somewhat dissimilar. However, it proved possible to construct a "composite" judge whose group of offenders was comparable with the group coming before one of the harsher judges. Computations based on this comparison revealed that the recidivism probability of borderline offenders (those who would be incarcerated by the harsh judge but not by the lenient) was considerably higher after incarceration than after non-institutional treatment. This conclusion was qualified by the fact that relatively slight variation in incarceration rates made the computed values quite unstable.

An alternative method of analysis, designed to make greater use of the variation actually present in the data collected, tended to confirm the finding that non-institutional treatment was, if anything, preferable to incarceration, although this conclusion, too, was qualified by the

fact that it had not been possible to control adequately for background factors affecting the relationship between incarceration and recidivism.

This study provides further evidence for the proposition generated in previous studies that incarceration is no better than non-institutional treatment at preventing recidivism and may actually be worse. It is appropriate to stress again the need for this apparently redundant research. Previous findings were based upon imperfect research designs. The present research, too, can be criticized on methodological grounds. Nevertheless, the methodological weaknesses of the present work are not those of the previous studies. The importance of this observation is brought out by Zimring and Hawkins (1973: 252).

"While the single application of any particular nonexperimental method in deterrence research may mean little, the cumulative import of many different imperfect approaches to the same question may be of critical significance . . . A series of imperfect exercises can sometimes produce reliable conclusions because each different but imperfect method may remove an element of doubt left by its predecessor."

In the light of this, Zimring and Hawkins make the following recommendation (1973: 253).

"It is our belief that research in deterrence should be both purposefully repetitive in topic and selective method. If a single question cannot be investigated through a perfect controlled experiment (which it seldom can), than this shortcoming must be compensated for by adopting a variety of approaches rather than a single method."

The present study may be viewed as a response to this imperative.

APPENDIX

OPERATIONALIZING RECIDIVISM

Operationalizing the concept of recidivism is a task fraught with difficulties. Conventionally, it is assumed that offenders can be divided into successes and failures—those who do not return to crime and those who do. Yet, as Glaser points out, it is more realistic to distinguish four different outcomes; complete or marginal success and complete or marginal failure.

"The fully reformed pursue legitimate occupations and avoid fraternization with delinquents or criminals; the marginally reformed do not violate the conditions of their release, but neither do they settle into acceptable jobs nor shun dubious companions. Those who fail are marginal if they commit misdemeanors but not felonies following release, and are truly recidivist if they return to careers of felonious behavior" (1969: 31–2).

Glaser observes that even this fourfold classification is inadequate since releasees will often move from one category to another. It may simply be circumstance which determines whether a man is a marginal failure or a marginal success, and circumstances can change. Indeed, the offender may live in both the criminal and the noncriminal world and walk a zigzag path between them before eventually making a clear turn toward one or the other (Glaser, 1969: 31).

Despite these complexities, for statistical research purposes we must classify offenders as either successes or failures. Even so, two further questions arise immediately, the first of which concerns how serious a violation must be before it is interpreted as evidence of recidivism. The Californian results cited earlier related to serious (largely felony) violations only, while the English studies were both concerned with any offense which led to a court conviction. Babst and Mannering defined recidivism as any violation which led to the revocation of parole and probation. However, this last definition is hardly adequate since parole and probation violation may be very marginal forms of failure. Parolees can be declared in violation for changing jobs or marrying without permission and for failure to make regular reports to their parole officers. Such behavior is non-criminal and hardly deserves to be classified as recidivism. In the light of the innocuous nature of marginal failure, be it parole or probation violation or misdemeanor crime, this study is concerned with felony recidivism only. (There are two exceptions: all theft is counted as recidivism although theft is a felony only when the value of the goods stolen exceeds a certain amount, and all gambling is excluded, although gambling in Connecticut is felonious under certain circumstances.)

The second issue which then arises is whether to use rearrest or reconviction as the indicator of return to crime. The FBI Careers in Crime study uses rearrest as the indicator of recidivism. Moreover, a Task Force Report of the President's Commission on Law Enforcement and Administration of Justice justifies this practice on the grounds that it "reduces the error in ignoring people freed for legal or technical reasons, even though they did commit the crime" (1967: 60). On the other hand, as the Task Force Report also admits, such a definition of recidivism may encompass people who are not guilty. Paul Ward has analyzed the FBI statistics and shown that only half of those arrested are subsequently convicted. It doesn't follow, of course, that the other half were innocent, but these findings led Ward, at least, to conclude that to treat persons arrested as recidivists "prejudges their guilt and is grossly misleading" (1970: 209).

It should be noted that both measures are subject to the difficulty that a large volume of crime is unreported and unsolved (President's Commission on Law Enforcement and Administration of Justice, 1968: 99). However, in the context of a comparative study this is not a problem. Provided that the measures of recidivism after incarceration and after non-institutional treatment suffer the same limitations, valid comparative conclusions are still possible.

Neither indicator appears, then, to be clearly superior to the other. However, reconviction is used in most previous comparative studies. Moreover, it is, in logic, closer to the concept of recidivism than is rearrest. On the basis of these somewhat arbitrary considerations, the decision was made to use reconviction as the indicator of recidivism in this study.

An important problem has been glossed over in the preceding discussion: is it true that the reconviction rates of those incarcerated and those given non-institutional treatment are similarly flawed? It is possible that parolees are more closely watched and more likely to be suspected, arrested and convicted than probationers. Were this the case, it would account at least partially for any positive relationship between incarceration and recidivism which the data revealed. I know of no research dealing with this point and there was unfortunately no systematic way of checking whether such a bias existed in the present data.

The only practicable way of following up the subsequent criminal histories of my cohort of offenders was through the files of the Connecticut state police department where records are maintained of every arrest made in the state. The police also maintain records on the outcome of all circuit court but not superior court cases. Thus, the best available way of operationalizing the concept of recidivism was to define an offender as a recidivist if subsequent to the original offense, he was either convicted of a felony in a circuit court (minor felonies fall within the circuit court jurisdiction) or bound over on a serious felony charge to a superior court. A finding of probable cause in the circuit court is apparently a good indication of guilt since nearly all cases which come before the superior court either result in a conviction,

or they are dropped not for lack of evidence but because a more serious charge is being pressed or because the offender is already behind bars in another state. Since a bindover is tantamount to a determination of guilt, the indicator constructed here yields a measure of recidivism which is akin to a reconviction rather than a rearrest rate.

The police files available to me contained reliable records of arrests and convictions in the state of Connecticut only. Thus, if offenders in my cohort recidivated in other states I would have no way of knowing. However, since the study is concerned with comparative, not absolute recidivism rates this would present a problem only if there were differential migration out of the state; that is, if former prisoners, say, were more likely than former probationers to leave the state and be rearrested elsewhere. It might well be argued that former prisoners will be more likely than former probationers to feel themselves "marked men" in the district from which they come and therefore to migrate to new areas where they will not be personally known to the police. It also seems likely that periods of imprisonment will weaken whatever ties a man has with his family and local community thereby reducing further his incentive to stay put.

FBI statistics reveal that such differential migration does indeed take place (UCR, 1967: 38). Moreover, the resulting bias yields an under-estimate of recidivism rates of parolees relative to the recidivism rates of those given non-institutional sentences. Consequently the recidivism rates of those sentenced by the harsh judges may be a little on the low side. However, since the data in this study yield higher recidivism rates for those sentenced by the harsher judges, the bias is a conservative one: the differences in experimental outcome occur in spite of the bias, not because of it. In short, in the absence of differential out-of-state migration, the discovered differences in recidivism rates would have been more pronounced than they were.

A final problem in connection with the

operationalization of the concept of recidivism concerns the follow-up period to be used. FBI figures indicate that "rearrest, if it happens, occurs within five years after release in about 99 per cent of the cases and within two years in over 60 per cent of the cases" (President's Commission Task Force Report 1967: 60). The Home Office study reported earlier used a five-year follow-up period, but the other studies used periods of from one to three years. They thus underestimated considerably the full extent of recidivism. Again, in the context of comparative research, this is not a problem, but for present purposes a full five-year follow-up period was chosen in order to give as complete an indication as possible of recidivism.

Deciding for each criminal just when his five-year period began and ended was a complex procedure. It was not sufficient simply to allow five years from time of sentence since many offenders spent part or all of that period behind bars and were thus not in a position to recidivate. To ensure that each offender was given a full five years at risk required a careful analysis of the possibilities of incarceration subsequent to sentencing. This resulted in the definition of a "follow-up date" for each offender; that is, a date to which his record would be scanned for subsequent felony violations. The cases fell into a number of categories with respect to experience of incarceration subsequent to conviction and I shall go through these in turn.

If an offender was sent to prison or reformatory, his release date was ascertained from corrections department records and, if he was not subsequently return for parole violation, his follow-up date was simply taken as five years from the time of release. If, some time after release, he was returned for a parole violation, his follow-up date was set equal to the date of first release plus five years plus the additional time served as a result of the parole violation. In this way the offender was allowed a full five-year period at risk. Offenders whose prison sentences were so long that they had not had five years of freedom at the time when the data were

gathered in early 1973 were excluded from the study, unless they had already recidivated. Probably no more than half a dozen were excluded in this way.

If the offender was sent to jail, where the maximum time which can be served is one year, an arbitrary period of six months behind bars was assumed and the follow-up date set at five years and six months from the time of original sentence. This arbitrariness may need some justification. In the first place, it would have been difficult if not impossible to gain access to jail records. Secondly, the procedure used means that calculated follow-up dates can be off by at most six months. However, since 60 per cent of all recidivism occurs within two years and 90 per cent within three years, whether the actual follow-up period used here is 4½ or 5½ years can make little difference to measured rates of recidivism.

If the offender was given a non-institutional sentence, which almost invariably consisted of a period of probation whatever else it involved, and if he was not subsequently incarcerated for a violation of probation, his follow-up date was simply five years from the date of sentence. If he was given a non-institutional sentence and was subsequently incarcerated as a result of a felony violation of probation, his follow-up date was again set at five years from the date of original sentence and he was, of course, counted as a recidivist after non-institutional treatment.

The thorniest problem arose in the case of the relatively few offenders given non-institutional sentences who were subsequently incarcerated as a result of a non-felony violation of probation. The experience of these offenders was certainly not non-institutional, but neither was it a simple experience of incarceration. It represents a third category of disposition. However, to introduce a third disposition category would greatly complicate the analysis, and since there were so few cases involved (4.5 per cent of all offenders), it was decided to simply exclude them. This did not affect one judge's group of offenders more than another and so cannot bias the results.

REFERENCES

Babst, D.V. and J.W. Mannering
1965   "Probation vs. Imprisonment for Similar Types of Offenders." J. of Research in Crime and Delinquency 2.

Beattie, R.H. and C.K. Bridges
1970   Superior Court Probation and/or Jail Sample. Sacramento: Bureau of Criminal Statistics, Department of Justice.

Carter, R.M., D. Glaser and L. Wilkins (eds.)
1972   Correctional Institutions. New York: Lippincott.

Empey, L.T.
1971   "The Provo Experiment: Research and Findings." Pp. 272–83 in Radzinowicz and Wolfgang.

Geis, G.
1972   "Ethical and Legal Issues in Experimenting with Offender Populations." Pp. 488–98 in Carter, Glaser and Wilkins.

Glaser, D.
1964   The Effectiveness of a Prison and Parole System. New York: Bobbs-Merrill.
1969   The Effectiveness of a Prison and Parole System—Abridged Edition. New York: Bobbs-Merrill.
1971   "Correctional Research: An Elusive Paradise." Pp. 182–7 in Radzinowicz and Wolfgang.

Glueck, S.
1958   "Predictive Devices and the Individualization of Justice." Law and Contemporary Problems 23:461–76.

Home Office (U.K.)
1964   The Sentence of the Court. London: H.M.S.O. Reprinted in Radzinowicz and Wolfgang, pp. 260–5.

Hopkins, A.
1973   Return to Crime: A Quasi-Experimental Study of the Effects of Imprisonment and Its Alternatives. Unpublished Ph.D. dissertation. University of Connecticut

Levin, M.A.
1971   "Policy Evaluation and Recidivism." Law and Society Review 6: 17–46.

Manheim, H. and L. Wilkins
1955   Prediction Methods in Relation to Borstal Training. London: H.M.S.O.

Morris, N.
1966   "Impediments to Penal Reform." University of Chicago Law Review 33. Reprinted in Carter et al. 1972.

President's Commission on Law Enforcement and the Administration of Justice Task Force
1966   Science and Technology, Washington: U.S. Printing Office.

President's Commission on Law Enforcement and Administration of Justice
1968   The Challenge of Crime in a Free Society. New York: Avon.

Radzinowicz, L. and M. Wolfgang (eds.)
1971   The Criminal in Confinement, vol. 3 of Crime and Justice. New York: Basic Books.

Schrag, C.
1971   Crime and Justice: American Style. Washington: N.I.M.H.

Sutherland, E. and D. Cressey
1970   Criminology. New York: Lippincott.

Uniform Crime Reports
1967   Crime in the United States. Washington: Department of Justice.

Ward, P.
1970   "Careers in Crime: The FBI Story." Journal of Research in Crime and Delinquency 7:207–18.

Warren, M.Q.
1971   "The Community Treatment Project: History and Prospects." Pp. 296–312 in Radzinowicz and Wolfgang.

Wilkins, L.
1958   "A Small Comparative Study of the Results of Probation." British Journal of Delinquency 8:201–9.

Zeisel, H.
1967   "The Law." Ch. 4 in P.F. Lazarsfeld, W. Sewell and H. Wilensky (eds.), The Uses of Sociology. New York: Basic Books.

Zimring, F.
1971   Perspective on Deterrence. Washington: N.I.M.H.

Zimring, F. and G. Hawkins
1973   Deterrence: The Legal Threat in Crime Control. Chicago: University Press.

68. How Frequent Is Post-Prison Success?

HOWARD KITCHENER
ANNESLEY K. SCHMIDT
DANIEL GLASER

WE OFTEN WISH TO KNOW THE POST-RELEASE crime rates of prisoners, but wonder how long we must wait to find out what they are. If we learn what happens to releasees in their first 6 months out, how confident can we be that this foretells their status 2 years later? Or 5 or 10 years? Or longer?

Until recently it was hard to ascertain the post-release criminal history of groups of prisoners unless they were under parole supervision, and then only until their discharge from parole. In many juridictions this knowledge still is not procured easily. Yet an increasing number of state criminal identification agencies and the F.B.I. today can supply to appropriate research offices the current records of groups of past releasees. These are essential if statistics on recidivism are to be tabulated so that we may assess the benefits or costs from pretrial diversion, sentencing, or correctional policies.

THE FEDERAL EFFECTIVENESS STUDY

In 1958, as part of a Ford Foundation funded study of the Federal correctional system, Glaser procured a 10 percent systematic sample of the approximately 10,000 male Federal prisoners released in 1956. The post-release criminality of those in the sample was determined in 1959–

▶SOURCE: *"How Persistent is Post-Prison Success?"* Federal Probation (March, 1977), 41(1): 9–15. Reprinted by permission.

1960 by: (1) checking files to determine the record of those under parole supervision during the followup period and if any not under supervision received new Federal sentences; (2) simultaneously checking the files of those not on parole for correspondence indicating that they were later sentenced for state offenses; (3) procuring, through the Bureau of Prisons, current "rap sheets" from the F.B.I. on some of the sample; (4) for the remainder on whom there was no post-release information, sending letters to Federal probation offices at the sentencing court to determine if any local criminal record was acquired by these individuals since release in 1956.

Computerization of files, mainly in the past decade, has greatly facilitated retrieval of criminal record information on past offenders. In 1970 the F.B.I. began computerization of criminal history files and the Federal Bureau of Prisons established a direct computer link with the F.B.I. In 1974 the Bureau procured from Glaser the list of his 1956 sample, with the data that his staff had coded on each case from prison classification reports. The current criminal records of 903 of these 1,015 subjects were located—some with the F.B.I. computer and the remainder from F.B.I. Identification Division current rap sheets. Forty-six individuals were removed from the sample because they had been deported (16 after new offenses). Additional inquiry is in progress on the remaining 66 cases. Thus F.B.I. followup data were procured for 93.2 percent of the nondeported cases, and the following conclusions apply to these 903 F.B.I.-traced releasees.

FINDINGS

A "failure" was operationally defined in Glaser's original study as someone returned to prison as a parole violator or receiving any new sentence (including jail or probation) for a felony or felony-like offense. Felony-like offenses are those that are not exclusively misdemeanors. Some, such as petty larceny, can be adjudicated a felony on second offense, if not on first offense (poor luck in finding little loot or good luck in plea bargaining were presumed to have saved such offenders from new felony terms). Possession of weapons by an ex-prisoner was also assumed to indicate a felony orientation even when it resulted in a misdemeanor sentence.

In Glaser's original study, in a followup period of under 4 years, 31 percent were reimprisoned while an additional 4 percent were convicted for a felony-like misdemeanor, yielding 35 percent who were designated "failures."[1] In the current 18-year followup of the same cases, more complete information was available from the F.B.I. The findings were, cumulatively: 15 percent failure by 1 year after release; 34 percent failure by 2 years after release; 51 percent failure by 5 years after release; 59 percent failure by 10 years after release; 63 percent failure by 18 years after release.

The percent of releasees who failed rose sharply for the first 2 years after they left prison. For the next 3 years—up to 5 years after release—the cumulative growth in failure rate each year diminished somewhat, and it slowed further between 5 and 8 years. Thereafter the annual increment of failures was very slight.

The crucial period for failure seemed to be between 1 and 2 years after release: 20 percent of all failures in 18 years occurred between 12 and 16 months after release. The first 2 years accounted for over half of the total failures.

After the first 2 years the failure rate declined. By the end of 3 years after release, two-thirds of those who would fail during 18 years had already done so, after 4 years three-quarters of the failures had occurred, and after 5 years four-fifths of the failures in 18 years already had happened. At 10 years it was 94 percent and at 15 years 98 percent. If the study were extended, another failure probably would occur from time to time, but from 10 years after release through the 18th year, less than 1 percent of the failures occurred each year.

Therefore, it seems reasonable to assume that in a longer followup the incidence of failure and its effect on the overall success rate would be minimal.

One may also ask how these conclusions would be affected if "failure" were defined differently, except for parole revocation which is always considered a failure. Tabulations were made with three additional definitions of postrelease failure: (1) any sentence of 60 days or more, including probation, regardless of the offense; (2) any reimprisonment for 60 days or more; or, (3) any reimprisonment for a felony or felony-like offense. The agreement among pairs of these four definitions of failure was 98 to 99 percent at the end of 1 year and 92 to 98 percent at the end of 5 years. Thus, neither a longer followup period nor a different definition of failure would have a pronounced effect on the conclusions.

The practical implications of these findings on the concentration of failures in the first few years are twofold. From a service standpoint, it would appear that any post-release assistance which reduces failure rates, as economic aid demonstrably does for many who would otherwise be poor risks,[2] should be available when

[1]Daniel Glaser, *The Effectiveness of a Prison and Parole System.* Indianapolis: Bobbs-Merrill, 1964, pp. 19–21.

[2]*See*: Craig Reinarman and Donald Miller, *Direct Financial Assistance to Parolees: A Promising Alternative in Correctional*

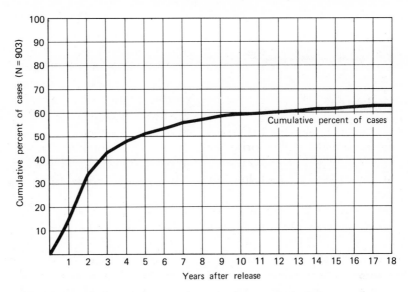

Figure 1.   How many fail within eighteen (18) years after release.

needed for at least 2 years and preferably for 5 years. Secondly, from a research standpoint, longer followup studies seem desirable, rather than the 2 years heretofore considered acceptable. But what of the relative failure rates for different groups of releasees? Can they be assessed at the end of 2 years?

OUTCOME FACTORS RELATED TO TIME OF FAILURE

This 1956 sample of Federal prison releasees can be divided into four outcome groups according to the period in which their failure, if any, occurred:

Early Failures: those who failed within 2 years after release—33.9 percent of the sample.

Midterm Failures: those who failed 2 to 5 years after release—17.2 percent of the sample.

Programming. Sacramento: California Department of Corrections, Research Report No. 55, May 1975. Kenneth J. Lenihan, *Theft Among Ex-Prisoners: Is it Economically Motivated? An Experimental Study of Financial Aid and Job Placement for Ex-Prisoners.* Washington, D.C.: Bureau of Social Science Research, Inc.: March, 1974.

Late Failures: those who failed over 5 years after release—11.8 percent of the sample.

Successes: those for whom no failure record could be found 18 years after release—37.0 percent of the sample.

The following background factors had the relationships indicated to outcome groups:

Offense

Auto thieves had both the highest failure rate at the end of 18 years—75 percent—and the highest proportion of failures in the first two years—69 percent. This high early failure rate presumably reflects the fact that they were the youngest category of Federal prisoners and the flightiest—most were confined for interstate transportation of a stolen vehicle. The 51 percent failure in 18 years for "moonshiners"—the Federal liquor law violators—was the lowest of any large offense category and was closest to being evenly divided between early, midterm and late violators. These offenders are from well-institutionalized businesses in rural areas, in which customers are not complainants, so they apparently have continuing opportunities

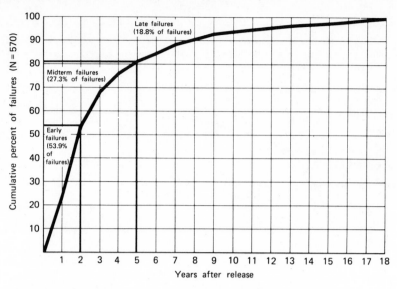

Figure 2.   When failure occurs within eighteen (18) years after release.

to drift back into this trade, and perhaps are not quickly caught.

Age at First Arrest
The younger an offender was at first arrest, the greater his probability of failure at any later age.[3] For the 18-year followup period, total failure rates declined from 78 percent for those first arrested when less than 14 years old to only 19 percent for those first arrested when 35 years of age or older. Similarly, the proportion of the failures that were early—in the first 2 years after release—declined from 62 percent for those who were under 14 years of age when first arrested, to 38 percent for those first arrested when 28 years or older. Prior experience at a law-abiding life appears to be the strongest insulation against reverting to crime after release from prison, but early involvement in crime apparently is the promptest precipitant of further offenses. Special efforts to provide youth with gratifying early experiences at alternatives to crime, such as rewarding jobs, therefore seem to

be especially warranted, as other findings also suggest.

Prior Employment
The longer releasees were previously employed at a single job in the community, the less were their failure rates and the smaller the proportion of their failures that occurred soon after release. Also, those employed three-quarters or more of their last 2 years in the free community had a 47 percent failure rate, as compared with a 70 percent failure rate for those employed less than three-fourths of their last 2 years in freedom. The less their fraction of this period employed, the sooner their post-release failure was likely to occur.

Anticipated Home at Release
Those who expected to live with their wives at release had 53 percent failures in 18 years, the lowest proportion of any group classified by this factor, and only one-third of their failures were early. This record contrasted with that of the group for whom a home at release was not indi-

[3]*See:* Glaser, *op. cit.,* p. 474.

cated in the last classification progress report; they had a 77 percent failure rate at the end of 18 years and almost two-thirds of their failures were early.

Race

At the end of the 18-year study period, 60 percent of whites and 71 percent of nonwhites were failures. Of the whites who failed, however, 57 percent were early failures, as compared with 47 percent of the nonwhites. It appears that long-run concern with post-release assistance would affect outcome rates more for nonwhites than for whites, perhaps because our society gives whites more persistent legitimate employment opportunities than it provides for nonwhites.

CONFIGURATION OF FACTORS

In the original study, Glaser investigated the possibility of improving the differentiation of groups of cases by outcome rate through classifying them by combinations of factors. The optimum system developed for this purpose was a configuration table based on 10 variables in a sequence of cross-classifications producing 12 categories. These ranged in success rate from a high of 93 percent for the group characterized by "no prior institutional commitment, and 36 years old or older at release" to a low of 34 percent for the group characterized by "one or more prior institutional commitments, an unsatisfactory institution adjustment on first current classification report, employed less than 26 percent of the time and not a student or unemployable 75 percent of time or more in last two years of civilian life." These extreme categories each had 7 percent of the sample's cases; the remaining 86 percent were in 10 other groups intermediate between these two groups in outcome.[4]

In the current longer followup by the Bureau of Prisons, the releasees were again sorted into the categories of Glaser's configuration table and the outcome rates for each group were determined for 2, 5, 10, and 15 years after their 1956 release (Figure 3). These categories proved dramatically stable in relative success rate, but the contrast in outcome between the highest and the lowest success groups—hence the predictive value of the table—increased over time. The most favorable always was the same highest category (defined above), with a success rate of 97 percent 1 year after release that declined only to 83 percent after 15 years. The lowest cases (as defined above) were least successful at 1 year out, when they had a 73 percent success rate, and also after 15 years, when only 13 percent were successful. They had the lowest success rate at every checked time except 2 years after release, when a slightly lower success rate was found for the category with "one or more prior institutional commitments, satisfactory prison adjustment, longest job less than four years, violated a prior parole and age 18 or under at first arrest." This group, 8 percent of the sample, had a 27 percent success rate at the end of 15 years. By 15 years the second worst category was one which differed from the last category described above only in being 19 or over in age at first arrest; this group comprised only 5 percent of the sample and only 14 percent were successful in this long followup span. All other categories were intermediate between these two lowest groups and the highest success rate category at the end of the followup period, and remarkably stable in relative outcome rates when checked earlier.[5]

---

[4]Glaser, *op. cit.*, p. 296. For a discussion of the construction of such tables and their advantages, see: Daniel Glaser, *Routinizing Evaluation: Getting Feedback on Effectiveness of Crime and Delinquency Programs*, NIMH Crime & Delinquency Issues Monograph Series, DHEW Publication No. (HSM) 73–9123 Washington: U.S. Government Printing Office, 1973, chapter 9.

[5]When the 12 categories were ranked from highest to lowest in success rate at each of the years after release when outcome rates were determined, the coefficient of rank correlation between the ranks of the categories 1 year after release and 15 years after release was 0.88, that between their rank at 2 years out and 15 years out was 0.90 and that

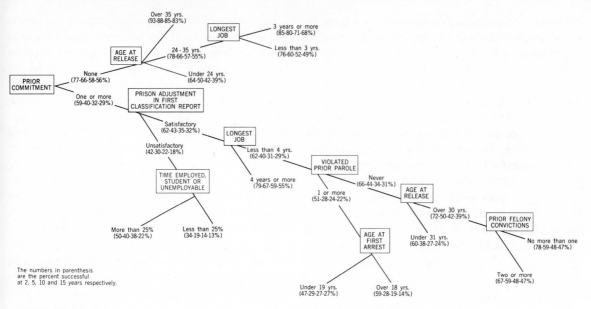

Figure 3. Percent successful at four time intervals for groups with characteristics as presented in Glaser's original configuration table.

OTHER FOLLOWUP STUDIES

The 1956 releasees on whom the above conclusions are based were imprisoned more than 20 years ago. How applicable are findings from that period today, when probation is used much more and drug addiction is more prevalent, so that prison inmates now are poorer risks for success than those released two decades ago? To check on the relevance of the long-run followup data, newer studies are desirable, but of course, an equally long followup is not possible on offenders released more recently.

A 2-year followup of Federal prisoners released in 1970 revealed that they had a failure

rate of 33 percent, defining failure as parole revocation or any new sentence of 60 days or more, including probation.[6] Charges still were pending on about 5 percent, so these rates may increase, but they are remarkably similar to those presented here for the 1956 releasees when 2 years out of prison. The 1970 releasees, however, were significantly greater failure risks than the 1956 releasees, whether both groups are compared by the Parole Guidelines Severity Scale derived from experience in the 1970's[7] or

[6]*Success and Failure of Federal Offenders Released in 1970.* Washington, D.C.: U.S. Bureau of Prisons, Office of Research, January 1974 (mimeographed).

[7]Don M. Gottfredson, Leslie T. Wilkins, Peter B. Hoffman, and Susan M. Singer, *The Utilization of Experience in Parole Decision-Making: Summary Report,* Washington, D.C.: Law Enforcement Assistance Administration, November 1974. Peter B. Hoffman and Lucille DeGostin, "Parole Decision-Making: Structuring Discretion," *Federal Probation,* December 1974. By this six-point scale, the average rating for the 1956 releasees was 2.59 and the average rating for the 1970 cases was 2.89, a difference statistically significant at the .01 level.

between their rank 3 years after release and 15 years out was 0.95. This indicates that the relative ranks of the 12 categories in success rates 15 years after release can be predicted quite accurately before the prisoners are out many years. Mean Cost Rating increased from .36 for the configuration table based on outcomes 1 year after release to .45 for that based on success rates 15 years out. See: James A. Inciardi, et al., "Computing Mean Cost Ratings (MCR)," *Journal of Research in Crime and Delinquency,* January 1973.

by the configuration table cited above, based on factors differentiating groups by success rates in the 1956 sample.

Since the 1970 Federal releasees were worse risks than the 1956 releasees but had no worse failure rates, it appears that correctional services for Federal prisoners in the 1970's are more effective in countering recidivism than were the correctional services fourteen years earlier.[8] An appreciable proportion now have work release, and preparole Community Treatment Center (halfway house) assignments, not available in 1956, in addition to procuring more financial aid at release now than was provided in the 1950's. Separate followups of Federal prisoners released through Community Treatment Centers in fiscal years 1969 and 1970 revealed lower failure rates for those employed than for those unemployed while in these centers, as well as lower failure rates for those who received "help in strengthening family ties" and "service mainly provided by a community resource," than for those residents of these centers who received no such aid. While these findings are not based on comparison of randomly differentiated treatment and control groups, they suggest that such centers, initiated in the 1960's, have made the prospects of many released prisoners achieving a law-abiding life greater than they would be with the abrupt and unaided transition from prison to parole that prevailed in 1956.

In the "Provo Experiment," LaMar T. Empey procured cooperation of a Utah judge in randomly dividing youth sentenced to probation into an experimental group required to participate in a daily guided group interaction and work program, and a control group of probationers without this requirement. The judge also was to select randomly half those he sent to a training school and grant them probation with the condition that they participate in the experimental program, but he soon changed all training school commitments to this type of probation. Most of the prospective training school cases from Provo, therefore, were experimentally not sent there, and for evaluation they had to be compared with similar youth sent to the training school from other counties.

Empey and Erickson compared the delinquency and crime records of all experimental and control or comparison groups for 4 years after release to the community with their records in the 4 years preceding their adjudication. For those originally ordered on probation, there was significantly greater decline in offenses in the experimental than in the control group during the first year after adjudication, but the difference in the records of these two groups diminished thereafter and was no longer statistically significant. The experimental group diverted from training school to the special probation program, however, had little contrast in offense rate change with the incarcerated comparison group during the first year after their release, but differences between these two groups in volume and seriousness of offenses increased as the years elapsed, with the incarcerated group steadily more and more involved in crime than the experimental group. This study dramatically demonstrated the desirability of long-run followup research in evaluating the consequences of markedly different correctional experiences for high risk young offenders, as well as the criminalizing effects of early incarceration in traditional juvenile correctional institutions.[9]

---

[8]Question may be raised as to whether any changes in parole revocation policy could account for the apparent "improvement" in recidivism rates between the 1959 and 1970 releases. The number of failure cases which were parole revocations for technical violations is not available. However, the extent to which such policy changes could affect these recidivism rates would be minimal because less than 10 percent of the failures (48 cases) were for parole or conditional release violation. Also, these failures include cases where there was a new criminal offense, but prosecution deferred to parole revocation. It is not possible to determine the number of such occurrences.

[9]LaMar T. Empey and Maynard L. Erickson, *The Provo Experiment: Evaluating Community Control of Delinquency.* Lexington, Massachusetts: D. C. Heath, 1972, chapter 10.

In sharp contrast to our data are findings in California that 70 percent of parolees during the early 1970's were arrested in their first year out of prison, but that this outcome increased only to 73 percent at 2 years out. Similarly, data on 1968–1970 parolees from almost all states and territories of the United States except California revealed that about 50 percent had "serious difficulty" (defined as return to prison for any reason) during their first year on parole, but only about 56 percent had such difficulty at the end of 2 years and 58 percent by the end of their third year under supervision.[10]

The proportion of releasees covered and the criteria of outcome differed in these two state studies, since California has a higher proportion of its prisoners released by parole than most states. Both also differed in these respects from our Federal studies, yet it is nevertheless difficult to explain why the ratio of first to second year outcomes in our 1956 study was so different from theirs. In our 1956 sample, 38 percent were discharged from their sentence at release, as they had completed its term (less up to 180 days time off for good behavior or for special assignments). The remaining 62 percent of our sample were released under further supervision, as though on parole; slightly over half of this residual were on parole and just under half were on "conditional release" (now called "mandatory release"), which meant that they had been denied parole but were under supervision as though on parole for all of the "good time" off their sentence in excess of 180 days. The failure rate, for the 18-year followup period, was 66 percent for expiration of sentence releasees, 50 percent for parolees and 74 percent for conditional releasees. Sixty percent of the conditional releasee failures were "early failures" (in the first 2 years out); 55 percent of

expiration case failures and 46 percent of parolee failures were early failures.

SUMMARY AND CONCLUSION

An 18-year followup of 1956 Federal prison releasees indicates that their rate of return to prison increased markedly in their second year out, and also rose significantly for 3 years thereafter. By the end of 5 years, however, two-thirds of those who would fail during the 18-year period had already done so. Most offenders in the highest failure rate categories—particularly auto thieves, those first arrested in their early teens, those with little prior employment, and those not indicating with whom they would live at release—were also the quickest to become reincarcerated. However, while a larger proportion of nonwhites than of whites became post-release failures, the whites who failed were more likely to fail soon after release than were the nonwhites who failed.

A configuration table developed by Glaser from his earlier followup data on these cases also was applied in our current followup. Its classification of the releasees by 10 variables into the 12 categories that most differentiated them by outcome proved extremely stable, in that the ranking of the 12 categories from highest to lowest in success rate was quite similar at 1 year as at 2, 3, 5, 10, and 15 years after release. The contrast in success rate between the better and the worse outcome groups progressively increased, however, as the years elapsed.

Followup studies of more recent Federal prison releasees suggest that Federal community correctional services since 1956 have enabled the system to reduce recidivism more effectively than it did 20 years ago. All these research findings and others are interpreted as indicating a need for more extensive and prolonged post-release aid to prisoners, and for more long-run followups in evaluating these services.

The contrasting findings for different correctional systems and diverse historic periods suggest the need first, for consistency in the way

[10]Letter from Lawrence A. Bennett, chief of research, California Department of Corrections, December 30, 1975. See also: Lawrence A. Bennett and Max Ziegler, "Early Discharge: A Suggested Approach to Increased Efficiency in Parole," Federal Probation, September 1975.

outcome is measured, and secondly, for comparisons based on theoretically distinct types of offenders rather than on a cross-section of a correctional agency's clients. With such sampling, conclusions would be on failure rates of particular types of criminal, for example, young recidivist auto thieves, narcotic addicted property offenders, etc. Findings on recidivism rates for such types should be more consistent and stable than findings on all of each agency's clientele, since the proportions of each type may vary greatly for the different agencies compared or for different periods in the history of any agency.

69. The Irrelevance of Correctional Programs

JAMES ROBISON
GERALD SMITH

THE INTRODUCTION OF REFORM MEASURES in correctional programs in the latter part of the nineteenth century was largely the result of a desire for humane treatment of offenders. The offender was no longer regarded as an evil person who "freely chose" to engage in criminal activities; rather, he was viewed as having been "socially determined" to take deviant roles and now in need of "treatment" to "reform" or "rehabilitate" him into a socially adequate individual. His change in status from an "evil" person to one who is "sick" was paralleled by the growth of a "correctional" system to handle the "patients." The retributive slogan, "Let the punishment fit the crime," was displaced by a new principle, "Let the treatment fit the needs of the offender," which called for educational training, psychotherapy (primarily group counseling), and community treatment (usually some variation of probation or parole).

These new correctional programs focused primarily on the offender; however, recent efforts have also been directed toward the community.[1] How effective any of these various reform measures has been in rehabilitating offenders (i.e., in reducing the probability of recidivism) was not studied very rigorously until recently because of numerous problems of evaluation.

Assessment of the relative effectiveness of various correctional programs is difficult because adequate measures of performance have not been authoritatively established. Very often the attempt to measure the behavior of the system's clients is confounded by the reporting procedures of the system. The results of such research yield insights about the personnel of the system but tell us little about its clients.[2]

Research into the correctional system has been concerned with answering these five basic questions about the behavior of convicted persons subjected to alternative procedures:

1. Will they act differently if we lock them up rather than place them on probation?

2. Will they recidivate less if we keep them locked up longer?

3. Do educating and "treating" in prison reduce recidivism?

4. Does supervising them more closely in smaller parole caseloads reduce recidivism?

5. What difference does it make whether we discharge prisoners outright or supervise them on parole?

▶SOURCE: *"The Effectiveness of Correctional Programs,"* *Crime and Delinquency,* *(January, 1971) 17(1): 67–80.* Reprinted with permission of the National Council on Crime and Delinquency.

[1]President's Commission on Law Enforcement and Administration of Justice, *The Challenge of Crime in a Free Society* (Washington, D.C.: U.S. Government Printing Office, 1967).

[2]J. Robison and P. Takagi, "Case Decisions in a State Parole System," California Department of Corrections, Research Division, Administrative Abstract, Research Report No. 31, 1968.

The answers to these questions are not easy to obtain because of all the influences that act on the measuring instruments. Nevertheless, a review of current research will illustrate the problems of evaluation of correctional effectiveness and will yield insights into the probable effects of various penal measures.

1. LOCK THEM UP?

Deciding whether to place an offender on probation or to imprison him is not determined by the relative rehabilitative efficacy of the two approaches. The courts place only their "best risks" on probation; the persons who are imprisoned differ in many ways from those given probation. Hence a simple analysis of the difference in recidivism rates between prison and probation cases will not answer questions about their relative effectiveness. Exploring this difference requires control for case differences.

One possible way to control for case differences is to make random assignment of cases to either probation or prison, as in, for example, the California Youth Authority's Community Treatment Project (CTP), which has been in operation since 1961 and has been widely acclaimed for its promise. After commitment to the Reception Center, wards were randomly assigned either to (1) a "control" group, confined in an institution and then given regular parole, or to (2) an "experimental" group, released immediately to small special caseloads in the community (9.5 parolees per agent, compared with 55 per agent under regular supervision).[3] A cohort follow-up has demonstrated statistically significant differences favoring community treatment. At the fifteen-months period, 30 per cent of male experimentals had "violated parole or had been unfavorably discharged," compared with 51 per cent of male controls (and 45 per cent of regular statewide Youth Authority

releasees). At the 24-months period, these outcomes were 43 per cent and 63 per cent, respectively, again favoring the experimental group. If we take these findings at face value, we are forced to conclude that probation has been proven to be a more effective correctional program than imprisonment for reducing recidivism. But has it?

Within certain boundaries, the recidivism rate can be influenced by the decision-making authorities.[4] The technical violation rate has been shown to vary between parole agents handling similar cases and has markedly influenced the recidivism rates of their wards.[5] In the CTP study, the recidivism rates were managed in such a way as to make the experimentals appear favorable. "The bulk of control failures (68%) was accounted for by the category of Parole Agent Casework Decision (i.e., agent's recommendation to the Youth Authority Board that a given ward's parole be revoked), although this same category accounted for no more than 29% of the Experimental failures."[6] In reexamination of the data, Lerman found that "the chance that an Experimental boy's offense will be handled in a 'revoking' manner is lower if the offense is low or moderate in severity. Experimentals are judged similarly to the Controls only when the offenses are of high severity."[7] The experimentals were no less delinquent in their behavior than the controls; in fact, they committed more "known" delinquent offenses than the controls (2.81 per experimental boy;

[3]California Legislature, "Analysis of the Budget Bill of the State of California for the Fiscal Year July 1, 1968, to June 30, 1969," 1969.

[4]Robison and Takagi, *supra* note 2, and J. Robison, M. Gagerstrom, G. Smith, and R. Kingsnorth, "2943 PC Follow-up: Review of the First Year of Adjustment Subsequent to Consideration of Parole Termination," California Department of Corrections, Bay Area Research Unit, 1967.

[5]J. Robison and P. Takagi, "The Parole Violator as an Organization Reject," University of California, School of Criminology, 1968.

[6]R. Warren, T. Palmer, et al., "An Evaluation of Community Treatment for Delinquents," California Youth Authority, Community Treatment Project Research Report No. 7, 1966.

[7]P. Lerman, "Evaluating the Outcome of Institutions for Delinquents," *Social Work*, July 1968.

1.61 per control boy).[8] This is probably an effect of increased supervision—i.e., if the controls had been watched as carefully, there would have been no differences between the two. The important point, however, is that an ideological belief in the effectiveness of community treatment apparently altered the experimental results.

In the light of these facts CTP gives little support to the thesis that probation is superior to institutionalization for reducing the recidivism rate. There appears to be no difference between the two approaches. One might, however, still argue in favor of "community treatment" on humanitarian and economic grounds.

Another relevant project that attempted to test the relative effectiveness of community treatment was conducted by the Northern California Service League; it involved adult offenders given professional casework service in lieu of a jail or prison term.

"It provided for the treatment of any adult offender referred by the Superior or Municipal Courts of San Francisco who had been found guilty of an offense other than one relating to drunkenness and whose sentence would ordinarily be a county jail or prison term, were the offender not referred to the project for treatment. . . . The second condition, namely that the offender would ordinarily receive a jail or prison term were it not for referral to the project, was to insure that the group treated by the project would be the group that would ordinarily be going to jail or prison and would not include those who would ordinarily be given probation."[9]

Assignment was, thus, not random. Checks upon whether referrals were representative of those being confined revealed that project cases tended to be somewhat younger and included fewer minority ethnic group members, a disproportionately low number of narcotic offenders, and a disproportionately high number of property offenders (e.g., crimes against property, 67 per cent vs. 48 per cent for those jailed

and imprisoned in the same year; assaultive crimes, 15 per cent vs. 16 per cent; sexual abuse, 4 per cent vs. 5 per cent; narcotics indulgence or abuse, 12 per cent vs. 25 per cent). The attempt to evaluate outcome matched project cases with jail releasees on age, sex, race, type of offense, and time of release. By the criterion chosen (no arrests or only one or two arrests but no convictions), project cases (N = 95) appeared to do better than jail releasees: 80 per cent favorable, compared with 70 per cent; however, the project sponsors consider the findings tentative and comment that the evaluative techniques are faulty.[10] Nevertheless, it would be safe to conclude that project cases did just as well as those confined. The study does not support any claim that institutional confinement is more effective than community supervision.

2. KEEP THEM LOCKED UP LONGER?

The phrase "optimum time for release" suggests that the releasing authority knows when that point in time has been reached and is ready to act on that knowledge. Implicit in it is the notion that there is a relationship between the amount of time served and the probability of recidivism. But is there?

The findings of the California Department of Corrections study of Advanced Release to Parole for the 1954–57 release years are shown in Table I. The performance difference of 4 per cent in favor of early releases after six months is attributable to their being low risk cases. When base-expectancy controls are introduced for quality of case, early release makes no difference. "All differences appear to be accounted for by base expectancies or length of parole term variability."[11] This was found true when follow-up comparisons were extended to analysis of one-, two-, and three-year exposure

[8]Ibid.

[9]E. Conbrose, "Final Report of the San Francisco Rehabilitation Project for Offenders," Northern California Service League, 1966.

[10]Ibid.

[11]P. Mueller, "Advanced Releases to Parole." California Department of Corrections, Research Division, Research Report No. 20, 1965.

periods, and regardless of the size of the parole caseload to which men were released.[12]

On the other hand, there is some evidence that the practice of keeping men in prison longer in itself increases the probability of recidivism. Jaman[13] recently compared parole performances, since 1957, of California first prison releases of persons originally committed for Robbery 1st or 2nd. (On June 30, 1968, 41.6 per cent of the adult felon prison population consisted of men in these offense categories.[14]) They were compared according to whether they had served less or more than the median time in prison for the offense in the particular release year. Cohort follow-up for six-, twelve-, and 24-month periods consistently shows, by almost every criterion (percentage "favorable," percentage returned with new commitment, percentage returned to finish term), a performance advantage favoring those released earlier. To counter the argument that such findings proved merely that the poorer risks were retained longer, Jaman extended the analysis to include control matching on age, ethnic group, base-expectancy level, parole region of release, and type of parole supervision received ("work unit" or "conventional" caseload) and applied it to prisoners released in 1965.

"For all offense categories and in all follow-up periods, the percent of favorable outcome among the men who served less than the median time was greater than among those who served more than the median months. Almost half of the testable comparisons showed statistically significant differences. In fact, in the matched samples of men who had been committed for Robbery 1st, those who served less than the median months had a much higher percent of favorable outcome in all three follow-up periods."[15]

It is difficult to escape the conclusion that the act of incarcerating a person at all will impair whatever potential he has for crime-free future adjustment and that, regardless of which "treatments" are administered while he is in prison, the longer he is kept there the more will he deteriorate and the more likely is it that he will recidivate. In any event, it seems almost certain that releasing men from prison earlier than is now customary in California would not increase recidivism.

The likelihood of recidivism, however, may play relatively little part in the decision to retain many prisoners beyond their legal minimum term.

Sheldon Messinger points to another "hardly surprising" consideration—order within the prisons:

"The felt need to maintain control over inmates moves prison officials to seek discretion over sentencing.... Prison officials are charged with the management of prisons; whatever the ultimate ends of imprisonment, from the officials' point of view a first requisite is effective influence over inmate conduct. So long as inmates desire freedom, restrictions of freedom—threatened and actual—will provide a possible strategy for control, for effective influence; and the correctional establishment as a whole is premised on the desire of inmates for freedom."[16]

Thus, just as prison overcrowding creates a pressure for either shorter average terms or increased capital outlay, the need for inmate control creates a pressure for lengthened confinement to maintain, by example, incentives for cooperative conduct.

3. DO SOMETHING WITH THEM INSIDE?

Group counseling had been one of the most widely applied and recommended prison treat-

[12]*Ibid.*

[13]D. Jaman, "Parole Outcome and Time Served by First Releases Committed for Robbery and Burglary, 1965 Releases," California Department of Corrections, Measurement Unit, 1968.

[14]California Department of Corrections, "California Prisoners, 1964–66." Research Division, Administrative Statistics Section, 1968.

[15]D. Jaman, "Parole Outcome for First Releases for Selected Commitment Offenses by Time Served before First Release." California Department of Corrections, Research Division, Measurement Unit, 1968.

[16]S. Messinger, "Strategies of Control," University of California, Center for the Study of Law and Society, 1968.

Table I. Percentage of Completely Clean Parole Records Within Six Months after Release to Parole in 1954-57 by SIPU assignment and Types of Parole Release

Type of Parole Release	All Assignments (1954-1957)		Type of Assignment (1954-1957)		
	No. Released	Per cent "Clean"	Small or Medium Caseloads	SIPU Large Caseloads	Non-SIPU Large Caseloads
Regular	7,884	68%	70%	68%	69%
Advanced	3,116	73%	74%	72%	72%
Difference	—	—	4%	4%	3%

ment techniques. Elements of this treatment (e.g., ventilation of feelings and help toward self-understanding) were presumed to advance "rehabilitation" and, secondarily, to support institutional order by helping prisoners "adjust to the frustrations" and "improve the emotional climate of the institution."[17] To assess its effect on the primary goal of rehabilitation (operationally defined as the reduction of recidivism or the probability of recidivism), it is necessary to design an experimental situation utilizing rigorous controls. Only infrequently are treatment programs subject to the types of experimental testing necessary for valid evaluation.[18] Much of the published research on group counseling in a prison setting deals with simple descriptions of the program,[19] theoretical justifications,[20] or shoddy "evaluations" without an adequate control group and random assignment of cases.

A recent study conducted to test the effect of group counseling in prison on postrelease behavior used a randomized assignment procedure and an adequate control group.[21] It is a true cohort follow-up (N = 968), with 36-months outcome obtained for each subject regardless of whether he was in custody, still on parole, or discharged from parole. All the subjects were from the prison, "a medium-security institution with its population an almost perfect representation of modal departmental prisoner characteristics"[22]; hence, there was no control group of nonimprisoned felons. While in prison the men were randomly assigned to (1) small counseling groups (Research Group Counseling, N = 171), (2) large groups (Community Living, N = 68), and (3) a control group (C-Quad, N = 269) where no counseling was given; the remainder of the men in the sample chose either to join group counseling (Regular Group Counseling, N = 274) or to not participate at all (Voluntary Nonparticipation, N = 173). The study sample was limited to those who had at least six months' exposure to programming; the average number of group counseling sessions was forty. The results of the study are shown in Table II.

"There were no differences in parole outcome by treatment status measured at 6, 12, 24, and 36 months after release, ... no treatment or control group differences on the number of misdemeanor or felony arrests recorded in the parole records, no differences in total number of weeks spent in jail, and no differences in most serious disposition received within three years after release."[23]

[17]A. Fenton, "Group Counseling—A Preface to Its Use in Correctional and Welfare Agencies," Sacramento, Calif., Institute for the Study of Crime and Delinquency, 1961.

[18]L. T. Wilkins, *Evaluation of Penal Measures* (New York: Random House, 1969).

[19]G. Sykes, *The Society of Captives* (New York: Atheneum, 1966).

[20]R. R. Korn and L. W. McCorkle, *Criminology and Penology* (New York: Holt, Rinehart, and Winston, 1966), ch. 20.

[21]G. Kassebaum, D. Ward, and D. Wilner, *Prison Treatment and Its Outcome* (to be published by John Wiley).

[22]The parole performance of the sample after thirty-six months was nearly identical with that in a earlier study of all men (N = 1,810) released to California parole in 1956.

[23]Kassebaum *et al.*, *op. cit. supra* note 21.

Table II. Postrelease Status at 36 Months by Treatment Status (in Percentage)

Returned to Prison	"C" Quad	Voluntary Non-partici- pation	Community Living	Research Counseling	Regular Counseling
			Treatment Category		
With New Term	16%	18%	27%	20%	15%
To Finish Term	31	37	29	31	34
After Discharge from Parole	1	1	3	—	—
Major Problems					
During Parole	5	3	10	5	6
After Discharge from Parole	4	7	1	1	4
Minor Problems					
During Parole	7	3	7	8	9
After Discharge from Parole	11	8	7	13	10
No Problems					
Still on Parole	4	5	3	4	4
Discharged from Parole	21	18	12	18	18
Total[a]	100%	100%	100%	100%	100%
N = 955[b]	(269)	(173)	(68)	(171)	(274)

[a]Percentage totals are rounded.

[b]Not including: Dead = 8, Incomplete Information = 5.

The researchers concluded:

"Thousands of inmates and hundreds of staff members were participating in this program at a substantial cost to the Department of Corrections in time, effort, and money. . . . Contrary to the expectations of the treatment theory, there were no significant differences in outcome for those in the various treatment programs or between the treatment groups and the control group.

"Furthermore, contrary to sociological expectations, participation in group counseling and community living did not lessen even the limited endorsement of the inmate code, nor did it result in a demonstrable decrease in frequency of prison discipline problems. . . .

"It would seem that in order for the Department of Corrections to continue to justify the widespread use of group counseling some new arguments must be advanced, such as 'participation in group counseling gives custodial officers a real part in the treatment program and seems to improve their morale' or 'group sessions add a little variety to inmate life and take up time.'"[24]

Nevertheless, the advocates of "treatment" programs can still argue that if group counseling improved in overall quality, it would indeed have an impact on recidivism.

The correctional treatment program just discussed is not atypical; it is unusual only in that it was subjected to a rigorous evaluation. Walter

[24]D. Ward, "Evaluation of Correctional Treatment: Some Implications of Negative Findings," *Proceedings of the First National Symposium on Law Enforcement Science and Technology* (Washington, D.C.: Thompson Book Co., 1967).

Bailey evaluated one hundred reports on correctional programs and outcome and found no solid indications of treatment efficacy[25]; Robert Martinson completed a similar study for the New York Governor's Special Committee on Criminal Offenders.[26] Despite the continuing popularization of various treatment programs and the increased attention devoted to more rigorous designs for their evaluation, *there are still no treatment techniques which have unequivocally demonstrated themselves capable of reducing recidivism.*

One of the major proposed efforts of the California Department of Corrections in institutional treatment is "medical-psychiatric" programing despite the absence of any evidence that its current model for such operations, the California Medical Facility, is superior in rehabilitative efficacy to routine prison programing.[27] Professionalization and upgrading of treatment services are defensible on the grounds of important secondary objectives—special client needs and benefits—but it is doubtful that these services are useful for reducing recidivism.

Processing an offender as ill (and he may, in fact, be ill) is hardly an advance over processing him as evil (and he may also, in fact, be evil). Neither formulation has much relevance in prison, since the inmate's primary status is that of a warehoused object. The California Department of Corrections plans to confer openly the patient status of "medical-psychiatric" bed upon many who are now looked upon as only inmates ("general purpose" beds). The change in nomenclature may enhance the Department's image and will certainly spiral its costs, but any measurable improvement in performance is unlikely.

Just as, historically, the number of witches rose as a consequence of an increase in the number of witch hunters and then declined, not in response to the hunters' rehabilitative efforts but rather as a consequence of corrective excesses that thinned the ranks of the witch hunters,[28] correction may be approaching a turning point. Yet even today, we find passages such as the following, freshly in print:

"Society's perception of criminals is changing. Criminals now can be seen as bad or sick. If they are bad, they require custody; if they are sick, they require treatment. The treatment-versus-custody controversy has raged in the Corrections field for several decades, but today the treatment advocates appear to be winning."[29]

Since nothing much is won if either side wins, maybe it's time to call off the game.

The narcotic addict has recently been transferred from the ranks of the bad to those of the sick, through little more than a change in the procedural labels: civil rather than criminal commitment; outpatient rather than parole supervision. Opposition to commitment for a treatment not proven effective has been voiced on the grounds that it is cruel and unusual punishment, that it denies to a person "accused" of illness the stringent legal protections afforded a person accused of crime, and that it is hardly different from imprisonment.[30]

In this movement to civil commitment, California was, as usual, in the forefront, having established in 1961 a model that was recently copied in New York. The program, the California Rehabilitation Center (CRC), has recently been evaluated. Findings from a three-year

---

[25]W. Bailey, "Correctional Outcome: An Evaluation of 100 Reports," University of California, Los Angeles, School of Social Welfare.

[26]R. Martinson, Department of Sociology and Anthropology, City College of New York (personal communication).

[27]Similarly, there has been no evidence that the Department's Outpatient Psychiatric Clinics have any effect on recidivism.

[28]"With the rise of rationalism, and the disbelief in a personal God, came a corresponding disbelief in his opposite, the Devil. . . . A decline in the acceptance of miracles meant a decline in the acceptance of spells." P. Hughes, *Witchcraft* (Baltimore: Penguin Books, 1965), p. 42.

[29]M. Mathews, "Correctional Rehabilitation: Boom or Bust?" Federal Offenders Rehabilitation Program, Fourth Annual Conference, San Antonio, 1968.

[30]J. Kramer, J. Berecoches, and R. Bass, "Civil Commitment for Addicts," *American Journal of Psychiatry,* December 1968.

cohort follow-up on CRC program performance of 1,209 first releasees to outpatient status indicated:

"1. Seventeen per cent received a discharge from the program after completing three continuous years on outpatient status.

"2. Sixty-seven per cent were returned to the CRC.

"3. Thirty-three per cent received a new criminal conviction during their first release (22 per cent misdemeanors and 11 per cent felonies).

"4. Seventy-one per cent were detected as having used drugs illegally (63 per cent opiates and 8 per cent other dangerous drugs of marijuana).

"5. Characteristics most strongly related to completing the three-year period successfully were: being white; staying at CRC a short time; living with one's spouse; living outside of Los Angeles, Orange, San Francisco, or Sacramento counties; and working 75–100 per cent of the time."[31]

The findings, applicable only to first releasees, speak for themselves. Those returned to the center perform even more poorly, of course, upon subsequent release. For example, of all men released in 1966, 50 per cent were returned before a single year in the community had elapsed; the rates were 48 per cent for first releasees, 54 per cent for second releasees, and 61 per cent for third releasees.[32] Note also (see item 3 above) that one out of three shuttled from the ranks of the sick to the ranks of the bad—"new criminal conviction"—though relatively few to the extent of a felony.

When such results are interpreted as "a modest degree of success,"[33] the emphasis certainly belongs on "modest," and one must also ask, "results more successful than what?" That a treatment of this caliber continues to expand

and obtain funding makes it obvious that demonstration of effectiveness is a token promise rather than a consequential issue in determining where public investment will be placed. There are now two "habits" to support—the ailment and the costly treatment.

While group counseling has been the most popular special treatment in prison programming, reduced caseload size represents the major approach in parole and probation to the problem of curbing recidivism. Findings on the efficacy of this approach will be reviewed next.

4. WATCH THEM MORE CLOSELY AFTERWARD?

The question of caseload size has been more exhaustively studied than any of the others, and hopes attached to caseload reduction have served to justify numerous demonstration projects. These projects typically ask complicated questions about the nature as well as the "intensity" of the supervision technique and explore offender-variable questions as well.

California has led the field in experimentation with caseload size in parole; for the past fifteen years, the Department of Corrections has been involved in manipulation of caseload size. The Special Intensive Parole Unit (SIPU), conducted from 1953 to 1964 in four phases, provides interesting information about the effects of variation in caseload size on recidivism. Following is a summary of the results of each phase of this project:

"Phase One (SIPU I)—Provided for random assessment of cases released from the Department of Corrections to special fifteen-man caseloads (experimental) or the regular ninety-man caseloads. Cases remained in an experimental caseload for three months (believed to be the most vulnerable months for failure) and were then transferred to a regular caseload. An evaluation of Phase One revealed that the reduced caseloads had no measurable effect on parole outcome.

"Phase Two (SIPU II)—The experimental caseloads were increased to thirty men, and the length of stay was increased to six months before

[31]J. Berecoches, California Department of Corrections, Research Division, 1968 (personal communication).

[32]J. Berecoches, R. Bass, and G. Sing, "Analysis of First-Year Experience of All Released from California Rehabilitation Center to Outpatient Status in 1966," California Rehabilitation Center, Narcotic Addict Outpatient Program Report No. 8, 1968.

[33]Kramer et al., supra note 30.

transfer to a regular caseload. Again, no evidence of the superiority of the reduced caseload was demonstrated.

"Phase Three (SIPU III)—The experimental caseloads were increased to thirty-five men, and the length of stay was increased to one year before transfer to a regular caseload. A two-year follow-up revealed that reduced caseload parolees did slightly better than those on regular caseloads and that the improvement was attributable to medium-risk parolees.

"Phase Four (SIPU IV)—Attempts were made to explore the effects of parolee and officer types on case outcome. Caseload size was reduced to thirty and fifteen, and officers and parolees were matched on characteristics thought to be favorable to parole outcome. The results of the study indicated that these characteristics did not measurably affect parole outcome and that the only variable which mattered was the amount of time an officer had to devote to supervision. The fifteen-man caseload did no better than the thirty-man caseload."[34]

Phase Four of the study has been criticized for lack of precision.[35] There is also evidence that SIPU agents were responding to violations by their parolees in the same fashion as the Youth Authority's Community Treatment Project agents.[36] Thus, it is not known whether significant findings occurred because parolees were behaving differently or because parole agents were reacting differently to violations.

Despite the absence of good evidence supporting reduced caseloads, the California legislature in 1964 gave approval to the Work Unit program in parole. The result was that half the adult male parolees in the state were placed under reduced-caseload supervision, which required the hiring of many parole agents. The assignment of cases to the Work Unit program (average caseloads of about thirty-five based on

an elaborate grading system whereby each case is assigned points according to the seriousness of the offense and other factors) was left to the regional classification representative. Thus, Work Unit cases are different from Conventional Unit cases (i.e., regular supervision caseloads averaging about seventy cases), and a comparison of performance for the two has to take this difference into account. In 1965, its first year of operation, there were 2,948 prison releases to Work Unit parole supervision, and 4,353 to Conventional supervision. The performance figures for the two types of supervision, based on a one-year cohort exposure period, are presented in Table III.[37]

The difference in performance between the two types of supervision appears slight; nevertheless, the 3.2 per cent advantage in favorable outcome of Work Unit over Conventional is statistically significant. In interpreting these data, however, we must remember that the two populations are not directly comparable. For example, all persons classified as having a high potential for violence were assigned to the Work Unit program, which was found to be composed of better-risk parolees as measured by an actuarial prediction device (California Base Expectancy 61A). *When controls for parolee risk level were introduced, the difference in favorable outcome between the Work Unit and the Conventional Unit was erased, and conventional supervision was found to have a significantly lower rate of technical prison return.*[38]

In 1964 the federal probation system inaugurated the San Francisco Project, experimenting with caseloads of four sizes and andom assignment. Like the Work Unit program, the project experienced an increase in the technical violation rates accompanying reduction in caseload size:

"The minimum supervision caseload has a violation rate of 24.3%; and the 'intensive' caseload, a violation rate of 37.5%. . . . In the "ideal" caseloads some five

[34]See S. Adams, "Some Findings from Correctional Caseload Research," *Federal Probation*, December 1967.
[35]*Ibid.*
[36]See text *supra* at notes 4–8; also J. Robison, Progress Notes toward the Proposed Study of Parole Operations, California Department of Corrections, Bay Area Research Unit, 1965.

[37]Robison and Takagi, *supra* note 2.
[38]*Ibid.*

Table III. Actual Parole Performance by Caseload Size

| | | Outcome | |
| | | | Technical |
Type of Parole Supervision	No. Released	Favorable	Return
Work Unit Supervision	2,948	65.8%	15.7%
Conventional Supervision	4,353	62.6%	14.4%
Total	7,301	63.9%	15.0%

or six times as much attention, as measured by direct contact with the offender and with others about him, did not produce a reduction in violations; and in the 'intensive' caseloads, despite fourteen times as much attention as provided the minimum supervision cases, the violation rate not only failed to decline significantly, but increased with respect to technical violations. . . ."[39]

The researchers concluded that the technical violation rate was a function of the amount of supervision—i.e., the intensified supervision enabled agents to discover a greater number of minor technical violations. Caseload groupings did not differ in regard to nontechnical violations.[40] Thus the small caseload was not demonstrated to be more effective in reducing recidivism.

5. CUT THEM LOOSE OFFICIALLY?

California prides itself on its extensive use of aftercare; about 90 per cent of male felons released from prison in recent years were released to parole supervision. Relatively little attention has been given to comparing men officially discharged from prison with men released on parole.

From 1960 through 1966, 4,854 male felons were discharged from prison at expiration of sentence.[41] Of these, 47 per cent were first re-

leases, and it seems reasonable to assume that many of these men were kept the full time because of problems in their prison adjustment or concerns about releasing them. More than half the prison discharges had been previously returned from parole as violators—10 per cent with a new commitment and 43 per cent to finish their original term. One out of every five men who are returned to prison as technical violators is subsequently discharged from prison and the remainder are reparoled, compared to one out of ten who are returned with new commitment and one out of twelve leaving on first prison release.[42]

In general, then, one would expect men discharged from prison to be poorer risks than those placed on parole. While cohort follow-up is routinely available only for parolees, some return-to-prison data are available from the California Department of Corrections. Examination of these data indicate that discharged men have fewer return-to-prison dispositions than men released to parole supervision. This does not mean that men discharged from prison are better risks. The difference can most likely be accounted for by the circumstance that men in discharged status are not subject to administrative returns as are technical violators of parole.

In a more detailed study of men discharged or paroled from prison in California (781 discharged vs. 2,858 paroled), Mueller found that, during the first two years, discharged cases had a more favorable postinstitutional outcome (i.e.,

[39]J. Lohman, A. Wahl, R. Carter, and S. Lewis, "The Intensive Supervision Caseload: A Preliminary Evaluation," University of California, School of Criminology, San Francisco Project No. 11, 1967.

[40]*Ibid.*

[41]California Department of Corrections, *supra* note 14.

[42]These proportions vary slightly from year to year.

no trouble or no disposition with a sentence over 89 days) than cases released to parole.[43] However, after three years there was no difference between the two groups in postinstitutional dispositions. The parolees' less favorable dispositions during the first two years were probably attributable to their "return to finish term," a disposition not possible for discharged men.[44]

The threshold of criminal or antisocial behavior that may result in return to prison is obviously higher for the ex-prisoner who is no longer officially under commitment to a correctional system. Does the convenience offered by administrative return to confinement offer sufficient protection to warrant its expense? Are we paying more for protection than it is worth?

CONCLUSION

In the opening section of this essay we noted that reform movements have been generated primarily by humanitarian rather than pragmatic considerations. "Treatment," the presumed antithesis of "punishment," becomes the banner under which such a movement takes shape, and the slogan "Let the treatment fit the offender" replaces "Let the punishment fit the crime." Punishment and treatment, however, are not opposites; the opposite of punishment is reward, and the "law of effect" posits the utility of both in shaping future behavior. Since punishment may be a rehabilitative tool, to talk of punishment *versus* rehabilitation is foolish. But to speak of reward vis-à-vis offenders becomes awkward, since it plays havoc with the concept of deterrence: openly rewarding persons to stop being criminals would seemingly impel others to commit criminal acts in order to secure the benefits offered for retirement from crime. Consequently, it becomes politically more convenient or less embarrassing to introduce the concept of treatment to counterbalance punishment. Punishment is manifestly unpleasant and

may or may not "work," whereas treatment, while not intrinsically pleasant, escapes the definitely unpleasant connotations of punishment; furthermore, it is impliedly effective: treatment; almost by definition, is that which results in improvement of a condition. Thus, treatment gains an aura of being both nicer (more humane) and better (more effective).

In correctional practice, treatment and punishment generally coexist and cannot appropriately be viewed as mutually exclusive. Correctional activities (treatments) are undertaken in settings established as places of punishment. Restriction of freedom is a punishment, no matter whether it is imposed by physical confinement (jail or prison) or by surveillance of movement in the community (probation or parole). The punitive conditions are viewed as necessary for the administration of treatment, and the treatments are believed to account for whatever favorable results occur.

The real choice in correction, then, is not between treatment on one hand and punishment on the other but between one treatment-punishment alternative and another.

Analysis of findings in a review of the major California correctional programs that permit relatively rigorous evaluation strongly suggests the following conclusion: *There is no evidence to support any program's claim of superior rehabilitative efficacy.*

The single answer, then, to each of the five questions originally posed—"Will the clients act differently if we lock them up, or keep them locked up longer, or do something with them inside, or watch them more closely afterward, or cut them loose officially?"—is: *"Probably not."*

Examination of correctional programs in states other than California would probably yield essentially similar results and the conclusion may generally apply. There is considerable evidence that different types of offenders have markedly different likelihoods of recidivating, and there can be little doubt that the different available correctional program options have markedly different degrees of unpleasantness

---

[43]Mueller, *supra* note 11.
[44]*Ibid.*

associated with them. Since the more unpleasant or punishing alternatives are more likely to be invoked for those offenders with serious present offenses or multiple past offenses, it is natural that different success rates and *apparently* different degrees of effectiveness will attach to some alternatives, though these differences of effectiveness are illusory. Since the more unpleasant or punishing alternatives tend also to be the more expensive, the choice of appropriate disposition for offenders should be determined by the amount of punishment we want to impose and the amount of money we are prepared to spend in imposing it; it should not be obscured by illusions of differential rehabilitative efficacy.[45] If the choice is, in fact, merely between greater and lesser punishments, then the rational justification for choosing the greater must, for now, be sought in concepts other than rehabilitation and be tested against criteria other than recidivism.

[45]J. Robison, "It's Time to Stop Counting," Special Report to California Legislature Ways and Means Committee, Select Committee on Criminal Justice, 1969.

70. What Works? "The Martinson Report"

ROBERT MARTINSON

IN THE PAST SEVERAL YEARS, AMERICAN PRISONS have gone through one of their recurrent periods of strikes, riots, and other disturbances. Simultaneously, and in consequence, the articulate public has entered another one of its sporadic fits of attentiveness to the condition of our prisons and to the perennial questions they pose about the nature of crime and the uses of punishment. The result has been a widespread call for "prison reform," i.e., for "reformed" prisons which will produce "reformed" convicts. Such calls are a familiar feature of American prison history. American prisons, perhaps more than those of any other country, have stood or fallen in public esteem according to their ability to fulfill their promise of rehabilitation.

One of the problems in the constant debate over "prison reform" is that we have been able to draw very little on any systematic empirical knowledge about the success or failure that we have met when we *have* tried to rehabilitate offenders, with various treatments and in various institutional and non-institutional settings. The field of penology has produced a voluminous research literature on this subject, but until recently there has been no comprehensive review of this literature and no attempt to bring its findings to bear, in a useful way, on the general question of "What works?." My purpose in this essay is to sketch an answer to that question.

▶SOURCE: *"What Works? Questions and Answers about Prison Reform,"* The Public Interest *(1974), 35: 22–54. Reprinted by permission.*

THE TRAVAILS OF A STUDY

In 1966, the New York State Governor's Special Committee on Criminal Offenders recognized their need for such an answer. The Committee was organized on the premise that prisons could rehabilitate, that the prisons of New York were not in fact making a serious effort at rehabilitation, and that New York's prisons should be converted from their existing custodial basis to a new rehabilitative one. The problem for the Committee was that there was no available guidance on the question of what had been shown to be the most effective means of rehabilitation. My colleagues and I were hired by the committee to remedy this defect in our knowledge; our job was to undertake a comprehensive survey of what was known about rehabilitation.

In 1968, in order to qualify for federal funds under the Omnibus Crime Control and Safe Streets Act, the state established a planning organization, which acquired from the Governor's Committee the responsibility for our report. But by 1970, when the project was formally completed, the state had changed its mind about the worth and proper use of the information we had gathered. The Governor's Committee had begun by thinking that such information was a necessary basis for any reforms that might be undertaken; the state planning agency ended by viewing the study as a document whose disturbing conclusions posed a serious threat to the programs which, in the meantime, they had determined to carry forward. By the spring of

1972—fully a year after I had re-edited the study for final publication—the state had not only failed to publish it, but had also refused to give me permission to publish it on my own. The document itself would still not be available to me or to the public today had not Joseph Alan Kaplon, an attorney, subpoenaed it from the state for use as evidence in a case before the Bronx Supreme Court.[1]

During the time of my efforts to get the study released, reports of it began to be widely circulated, and it acquired something of an underground reputation. But this article is the first published account, albeit a brief one, of the findings contained in that 1,400-page manuscript.

What we set out to do in this study was fairly simple, though it turned into a massive task. First we undertook a six-month search of the literature for any available reports published in the English language on attempts at rehabilitation that had been made in our corrections systems and those of other countries from 1945 through 1967. We then picked from that literature all those studies whose findings were interpretable—that is, whose design and execution met the conventional standards of social science research. Our criteria were rigorous but hardly esoteric: A study had to be an evaluation of a treatment method, it had to employ an independent measure of the improvement secured by that method, and it had to use some control group, some untreated individuals with whom the treated ones could be compared. We excluded studies only for methodological reasons: They presented insufficient data, they were only preliminary, they presented only a summary of findings and did not allow a reader to evaluate those findings, their results were confounded by extraneous factors, they used unreliable measures, one could not understand

[1]Following this case, the state finally did give its permission to have the work published. [Eds.: the book *The Effectiveness of Correctional Treatment* by Douglas Lipton, Robert Martinson and Judith Wilks was published by Praeger in 1975].

their descriptions of the treatment in question, they drew spurious conclusions from their data, their samples were undescribed or too small or provided no true comparability between treated and untreated groups, or they had used inappropriate statistical tests and did not provide enough information for the reader to recompute the data. Using these standards, we drew from the total number of studies 231 acceptable ones, which we not only analyzed ourselves but summarized in detail so that a reader of our analysis would be able to compare it with his independent conclusions.

These treatment studies use various measures of offender improvement: recidivism rates (that is, the rates at which offenders return to crime), adjustment to prison life, vocational success, educational achievement, personality and attitude change, and general adjustment to the outside community. We included all of these in our study; but in these pages I will deal only with the effects of rehabilitative treatment on recidivism, the phenomenon which reflects most directly how well our present treatment programs are performing the task of rehabilitation. The use of even this one measure brings with it enough methodological complications to make a clear reporting of the findings most difficult. The groups that are studied, for instance, are exceedingly disparate, so that it is hard to tell whether what "works" for one kind of offender also works for others. In addition, there has been little attempt to replicate studies; therefore one cannot be certain how stable and reliable the various findings are. Just as important, when the various studies use the term "recidivism rate," they may in fact be talking about somewhat different measures of offender behavior—i.e., "failure" measures such as arrest rates or parole violation rates, or "success" measures such as favorable discharge from parole or probation. And not all of these measures correlate very highly with one another. These difficulties will become apparent again and again in the course of this discussion.

With these caveats, it is possible to give a

rather bald summary of our findings: *With few and isolated exceptions, the rehabilitative efforts that have been reported so far have had no appreciable effect on recidivism.* Studies that have been done since our survey was completed do not present any major grounds for altering that original conclusion. What follows is an attempt to answer the questions and challenges that might be posed to such an unqualified statement.

EDUCATION AND VOCATIONAL TRAINING

1. *Isn't it true that a correctional facility running a truly rehabilitative program—one that prepares inmates for life on the outside through education and vocational training—will turn out more successful individuals than will a prison which merely leaves its inmates to rot?*

If this *is* true, the fact remains that there is very little empirical evidence to support it. Skill development and education programs are in fact quite common in correctional facilities, and one might begin by examining their effects on young males, those who might be thought most amenable to such efforts. A study by New York State (1964)[2] found that for young males as a whole, the degree of success achieved in the regular prison academic education program, as measured by changes in grade achievement levels, made no significant difference in recidivism rates. The only exception was the relative improvement, compared with the sample as a whole, that greater progress made in the top seven per cent of the participating population—those who had high I.Q.'s, had made good records in previous schooling, and who also made good records of academic progress in the institution. And a study by Glaser (1964) found that while it was true that, when one controlled for sentence length, more attendance in regular prison academic programs slightly decreased the subsequent chances of

parole violation, this improvement was not large enough to outweigh the associated disadvantage for the "long-attenders": Those who attended prison school the longest also turned out to be those who were in prison the longest. Presumably, those getting the most education were also the worst parole risks in the first place.[3]

Studies of special education programs aimed at vocational or social skill development, as opposed to conventional academic education programs, report similarly discouraging results and reveal additional problems in the field of correctional research. Jacobson (1965) studied a program of "skill re-education" for institutionalized young males, consisting of 10 weeks of daily discussions aimed at developing problem-solving skills. The discussions were led by an adult who was thought capable of serving as a role model for the boys, and they were encouraged to follow the example that he set. Jacobson found that over all, the program produced no improvement in recidivism rates. There was only one special subgroup which provided an exception to this pessimistic finding: If boys in the experimental program decided afterwards to go on to take three or more regular prison courses, they did better upon release than "control" boys who had done the same. (Of course, it also seems likely that experimental boys who did *not* take these extra courses did *worse* than their controls.)

Zivan (1966) also reported negative results from a much more ambitious vocational training program at the Children's Village in Dobbs Ferry, New York. Boys in his special program were prepared for their return to the community in a wide variety of ways. First of all, they were given, in sequence, three types of vocational guidance: "assessment counseling," "development counseling," and "preplacement counseling." In addition, they participated in an

---

[2]All studies cited in the text are referenced in the bibliography which appears at the conclusion of this article.

[3]The net result was that those who received *less* prison education—because their sentences were shorter or because they were probably better risks—ended up having better parole chances than those who received more prison education.

"occupational orientation," consisting of role-playing, presentations via audio-visual aids, field trips, and talks by practitioners in various fields of work. Furthermore, the boys were prepared for work by participating in the Auxiliary Maintenance Corps, which performed various chores in the institution; a boy might be promoted from the Corps to the Work Activity Program, which "hired" him, for a small fee, to perform various artisans' tasks. And finally, after release from Children's Village, a boy in the special program received supportive after-care and job placement aid.

None of this made any difference in recidivism rates. Nevertheless, one must add that it is impossible to tell whether this failure lay in the program itself or in the conditions under which it was administered. For one thing, the education department of the institution itself was hostile to the program; they believed instead in the efficacy of academic education. This staff therefore tended to place in the pool from which experimental subjects were randomly selected mainly "multi-problem" boys. This by itself would not have invalidated the experiment as a test of vocational training for this particular type of youth, but staff hostility did not end there; it exerted subtle pressures of disapproval throughout the life of the program. Moreover, the program's "after-care" phase also ran into difficulties; boys who were sent back to school before getting a job often received advice that conflicted with the program's counseling, and boys actually looking for jobs met with the frustrating fact that the program's personnel, despite concerted efforts, simply could not get businesses to hire the boys.

We do not know whether these constraints, so often found in penal institutions, were responsible for the program's failure; it might have failed anyway. All one can say is that this research failed to show the effectiveness of special vocational training for young males.

The only clearly positive report in this area comes from a study by Sullivan (1967) of a program that combined academic education with special training in the use of IBM equipment. Recidivism rates after one year were only 48 per cent for experimentals, as compared with 66 per cent for controls. But when one examines the data, it appears that this difference emerged only between the controls and those who had successfully *completed* the training. When one compares the control group with all those who had been *enrolled* in the program, the difference disappears. Moreover, during this study the random assignment procedure between experimental and control groups seems to have broken down, so that towards the end, better risks had a greater chance of being assigned to the special program.

In sum, many of these studies of young males are extremely hard to interpret because of flaws in research design. But it can safely be said that they provide us with no clear evidence that education or skill development programs have been successful.

TRAINING ADULT INMATES

When one turns to adult male inmates, as opposed to young ones, the results are even more discouraging. There have been six studies of this type; three of them report that their programs, which ranged from academic to prison work experience, produced no significant differences in recidivism rates, and one—by Glaser (1964)—is almost impossible to interpret because of the risk differentials of the prisoners participating in the various programs.

Two studies—by Schnur (1948) and by Saden (1962)—*do* report a positive difference from skill development programs. In one of them, the Saden study, it is questionable whether the experimental and control groups were truly comparable. But what is more interesting is that both these "positive" studies dealt with inmates incarcerated prior to or during World War II. Perhaps the rise in our educational standards as a whole since then has lessened the differences that prison education or training can make. The only other interesting possibility emerges from a study by Gearhart (1967). His study was one of those that reported vocational education to be non-significant in affecting recidivism rates. He did note, however, that when a trainee succeeded in finding a job related to his area of training, he had a slightly higher chance of becoming a successful parolee. It is possible, then, that skill development programs fail because what they teach bears so little relationship to an offender's subsequent life outside the prison.

One other study of adults, this one with fairly clear implications, has been performed with women rather than men. An experimental group of institutionalized women in Milwaukee was given an extremely comprehensive special education program, accompanied by group counseling. Their training was both academic and practical; it included reading, writing, spelling, business filing, child care, and grooming. Kettering (1965) found that the program made no difference in the women's rates of recidivism.

Two things should be noted about these studies. One is the difficulty of interpreting them as a whole. The disparity in the programs that were tried, in the populations that were affected, and in the institutional settings that surrounded these projects make it hard to be sure that one is observing the same category of treatment in each case. But the second point is that despite this difficulty, one can be reasonably sure that, so far, educational and vocational programs have not worked. We don't know why they have failed. We don't know whether the programs themselves are flawed, or whether they are incapable of overcoming the effects of prison life in general. The difficulty may be that they lack applicability to the world the inmate will face outside of prison. Or perhaps the type of educational and skill improvement they produce simply doesn't have very much to do with an individual's propensity to commit a crime. What we do know is that, to date, education and skill development have not reduced recidivism by rehabilitating criminals.

THE EFFECTS OF INDIVIDUAL COUNSELING

2. *But when we speak of a rehabilitative prison, aren't we referring to more than education and skill development alone? Isn't what's needed some way of counseling inmates, or helping them with the deeper problems that have caused their maladjustment?*

This, too, is a reasonable hypothesis; but when one examines the programs of this type that have been tried, it's hard to find any more grounds for enthusiasm than we found with skill development and education. One method that's been tried—though so far, there have been acceptable reports only of its application to young offenders—has been individual psychotherapy. For young males, we found seven such reported studies. One study, by Guttman (1963) at the Nelles School, found such treatment to be ineffective in reducing recidivism rates; another, by Rudoff (1960), found it unrelated to *institutional* violation rates, which were themselves related to parole success. It must be pointed out that Rudoff used only this indirect measure of association, and the study therefore cannot rule out the possibility of a treatment effect. A third, also by Guttman (1963) but at another institution, found that such treatment was actually related to a slightly *higher* parole violation rate; and a study by Adams (1959b and 1961b) also found a lack of improvement in parole revocation and first suspension rates.

There were two studies at variance with this pattern. One by Persons (1967) said that if a boy was judged to be "successfully" treated—as opposed to simply being subjected to the treatment experience—he did tend to do better. And there was one finding both hopeful and cautionary: At the Deuel School (Adams, 1961a), the experimental boys were first divided into two groups, those rated as "amenable" to treatment and those rated "non-amenable." Amenable boys who got the treatment did better than non-treated boys. On the other hand, "non-amenable" boys who were treated actually did *worse* than they would have done if they had received no treatment at all. It must be pointed out that Guttman (1963), dealing with younger boys in his Nelles School study, did not find such an "amenability" effect, either to the detriment of the non-amenables who were treated *or* to the benefit of the amenables who were treated. But the Deuel School study (Adams, 1961a) suggests both that there is something to be hoped for in treating properly selected amenable subjects and that if these subjects are *not* properly selected, one may not only wind up doing no good but may actually produce harm.

There have been two studies of the effects of individual psychotherapy on young incarcerated *female* offenders, and both of them (Adams 1959a, Adams 1961b) report no significant effects from the therapy. But one of the Adams studies (1959a) does contain a suggestive, although not clearly interpretable, finding: If this individual therapy was administered by a psychiatrist or a psychologist, the resulting parole suspension rate was almost two-and-a-half times *higher* than if it was administered by a social worker without this specialized training.

There has also been a much smaller number of studies of two other types of individual therapy: counseling, which is directed towards a prisoner's gaining new insight into his own problems, and casework, which aims at helping a prisoner cope with his more pragmatic immediate needs. These types of therapy both rely heavily on the empathetic relationship that is to be developed between the professional and the client. It was noted above that the Adams study (1961b) of therapy administered to girls, referred to in the discussion of individual psychotherapy, found that social workers seemed better at the job than psychologists or psychiatrists. This difference seems to suggest a favorable outlook for these alternative forms of individual therapy. But other studies of such therapy have produced ambiguous results.

Bernsten (1961) reported a Danish experiment that showed that socio-psychological counseling combined with comprehensive welfare measures—job and residence placement, clothing, union and health insurance membership, and financial aid—produced an improvement among some short-term male offenders, though not those in either the highest-risk or the lowest-risk categories. On the other hand, Hood, in Britain (1966), reported generally non-significant results with a program of counseling for young males. (Interestingly enough, this experiment *did* point to a mechanism capable of changing recidivism rates. When boys were released from institutional care and entered the army directly, "poor risk" boys among both experimentals *and* controls did better than expected. "Good risks" did worse.)

So these foreign data are sparse and not in agreement; the American data are just as sparse. The only American study which provides a direct measure of the effects of individual counseling—a study of California's Intensive Treatment Program (California, 1958a), which was "psychodynamically" oriented—found no improvement in recidivism rates.

It was this finding of the failure of the Intensive Treatment Program which contributed to the decision in California to de-emphasize individual counseling in its penal system in favor of group methods. And indeed one might suspect that the preceding reports reveal not the inadequacy of counseling as a whole but only the failure of one *type* of counseling, the individual type. *Group* counseling methods, in which offenders are permitted to aid and compare experiences with one another, might be thought to have a better chance of success. So it is important to ask what results these alternative methods have actually produced.

GROUP COUNSELING

Group counseling has indeed been tried in correctional institutions, both with and without a specifically psychotherapeutic orientation. There has been one study of "pragmatic," problem-oriented counseling on *young* institutionalized males, by Seckel (1965). This type of counseling had no significant effect. For adult males, there have been three such studies of the "pragmatic" and "insight" methods. Two (Kassebaum, 1971; Harrison, 1964) report no long-lasting significant effects. (One of these two did report a real but short-term effect that wore off as the program became institutionalized and as offenders were at liberty longer.) The third study of adults, by Shelley (1961), dealt with a "pragmatic" casework program, directed towards the educational and vocational needs of institutionalized young adult males in a Michigan prison camp. The treatment lasted for six months and at the end of that time Shelley found an improvement in attitudes; the possession of "good" attitudes was independently found by Shelley to correlate with parole success. Unfortunately, though, Shelley was not able to measure the *direct* impact of the counseling on recidivism rates. His two separate correlations are suggestive, but they fall short of being able to tell us that it really is the counseling that has a direct effect on recidivism.

With regard to more professional group *psychotherapy*, the reports are also conflicting. We have two studies of group psychotherapy on young males. One, by Persons (1966), says that this treatment did in fact reduce recidivism. The improved recidivism rate stems from the improved performance only of those who were clinically judged to have been "successfully" treated; still, the overall result of the treatment was to improve recidivism rates for the experimental group as a whole. On the other hand, a study by Craft (1964) of young males designated "psychopaths," comparing "self-government" group psychotherapy with "authoritarian" individual counseling, found that the "group therapy" boys afterwards committed *twice* as many new offenses as the individually treated ones. Perhaps some forms of group

psychotherapy work for some types of offenders but not others; a reader must draw his own conclusions, on the basis of sparse evidence.

With regard to young females, the results are just as equivocal. Adams, in his study of females (1959a), found that there was no improvement to be gained from treating girls by group rather than individual methods. A study by Taylor of borstal (reformatory) girls in New Zealand (1967) found a similar lack of any great improvement for group therapy as opposed to individual therapy or even to no therapy at all. But the Taylor study does offer one real, positive finding: When the "group therapy" girls *did* commit new offenses, these offenses were less serious than the ones for which they had originally been incarcerated.

There is a third study that does report an overall positive finding as opposed to a partial one. Truax (1966) found that girls subjected to group psychotherapy and then released were likely to spend less time reincarcerated in the future. But what is most interesting about this improvement is the very special and important circumstance under which it occurred. The therapists chosen for this program did not merely have to have the proper analytic training; they were specially chosen for their "empathy" and "non-possessive warmth." In other words, it may well have been the therapists' special personal gifts rather than the fact of treatment itself which produced the favorable result. This possibility will emerge again when we examine the effects of other types of rehabilitative treatment later in this article.

As with the question of skill development, it is hard to summarize these results. The programs administered were various; the groups to which they were administered varied not only by sex but by age as well; there were also variations in the length of time for which the programs were carried on, the frequency of contact during that time, and the period for which the subjects were followed up. Still, one must say that the burden of the evidence is not encouraging. These programs seem to work best when they are new, when their subjects are amenable to treatment in the first place, and when the counselors are not only trained people but "good" people as well. Such findings, which would not be much of a surprise to a student of organization or personality, are hardly encouraging for a policy planner, who must adopt measures that are generally applicable, that are capable of being successfully institutionalized, and that must rely for personnel on something other than the exceptional individual.

TRANSFORMING THE INSTITUTIONAL ENVIRONMENT

3. *But maybe the reason these counseling programs don't seem to work is not that they are ineffective per se, but that the institutional environment outside the program is unwholesome enough to undo any good work that the counseling does. Isn't a truly successful rehabilitative institution the one where the inmate's whole environment is directed towards true correction rather than towards custody or punishment?*

This argument has not only been made, it has been embodied in several institutional programs that go by the name of "milieu therapy." They are designed to make every element of the inmate's environment a part of his treatment, to reduce the distinctions between the custodial staff and the treatment staff, to create a supportive, non-authoritarian, and non-regimented atmosphere, and to enlist peer influence in the formation of constructive values. These programs are especially hard to summarize because of their variety; they differ, for example, in how "supportive" or "permissive" they are designed to be, in the extent to which they are combined with other treatment methods such as individual therapy, group counseling, or skill development, and in how completely the program is able to control all the relevant aspects of the institutional environment.

One might well begin with two studies that have been done of institutionalized adults, in regular prisons, who have been subjected to such treatment; this is the category whose results are the most clearly discouraging. One study of such a program, by Robison (1967), found that the therapy did seem to reduce recidivism after one year. After two years, however, this effect disappeared, and the treated convicts did no better than the untreated. Another study by Kassebaum, Ward, and Wilner (1971), dealt with a program which had been able to effect an exceptionally extensive and experimentally rigorous transformation of the institutional environment. This sophisticated study had a follow-up period of 36 months, and it found that the program had no significant effect on parole failure or success rates.

The results of the studies of youth are more equivocal. As for young females, one study by Adams (1966) of such a program found that it had no significant effect on recidivism; another study, by Goldberg and Adams (1964), found that such a program *did* have a positive effect. This effect declined when the program began to deal with girls who were judged beforehand to be worse risks.

As for young males, the studies may conveniently be divided into those dealing with juveniles (under 16) and those dealing with youths. There have been five studies of milieu therapy administered to juveniles. Two of them—by Laulicht (1962) and by Jesness (1965)—report clearly that the program in question either had no significant effect or had a short-term effect that wore off with passing time. Jesness does report that when his experimental juveniles did commit new offenses, the offenses were less serious than those committed by controls. A third study of juveniles, by McCord (1953) at the Wiltwyck School, reports mixed results. Using two measures of performance, a "success" rate and a "failure" rate, McCord found that his experimental group achieved both less failure *and* less success than the controls did. There have been two positive reports on milieu therapy programs for male juveniles; both of them have come out of the Highfields program, the milieu therapy experiment which has become the most famous and widely quoted example of "success" via this method. A group of boys was confined for a relatively short time to the unrestrictive, supportive environment of Highfields; and at a follow-up of six months, Freeman (1956) found that the group did indeed show a lower recidivism rate (as measured by parole revocation) than a similar group spending a longer time in the regular reformatory. McCorkle (1958) also reported positive findings from Highfields. But in fact, the McCorkle data show, this improvement was not so clear: The Highfields boys had lower recidivism rates at 12 and 36 months in the follow-up period, but not at 24 and 60 months. The length of follow-up, these data remind us, may have large implications for a study's conclusions. But more important were other flaws in the Highfields experiment: The populations were not fully comparable (they differed according to risk level and time of admission); different organizations—the probation agency for the Highfield boys, the parole agency for the others—were making the revocation decisions for each group; more of the Highfields boys were discharged early from supervision, and thus removed from any risk of revocation. In short, not even from the celebrated Highfields case may we take clear assurance that milieu therapy works.

In the case of male youths, as opposed to male juveniles, the findings are just as equivocal, and hardly more encouraging. One such study by Empey (1966) in a residential context did not produce significant results. A study by Seckel (1967) described California's Fremont Program, in which institutionalized youths participated in a combination of therapy, work projects, field trips, and community meetings. Seckel found that the youths subjected to this treatment committed *more* violations of law than did their non-treated counterparts. This difference could have occurred by chance; still, there was certainly no evidence of relative improvement. Another study, by Levinson 1964), also found a lack of improvement in recidivism rates—but Levinson noted the encouraging fact that the treated group spent somewhat more time in the community before recidivating, and committed less serious offenses. And a study by the State of California (1967) also shows a partially positive finding. This was a study of the Marshall Program, similar to California's Fremont Program but different in several ways. The Marshall Program was shorter and more tightly organized than its Fremont counterpart. In the Marshall Program, as opposed to the Fremont Program, a youth could be ejected from the group and sent back to regular institutions before the completion of the program. Also, the Marshall Program offered some additional benefits: the teaching of "social survival skills" (i.e., getting and holding a job), group counseling of parents, and an occasional opportunity for boys to visit home. When youthful offenders were released to the Marshall Program, either directly or after spending some time in a regular institution, they did no better than a comparable regularly institutionalized population, though both Marshall youth and youth in regular institutions did better than those who were directly released by the court and given no special treatment.

So the youth in these milieu therapy programs at least do no worse than their counterparts in regular institutions and the special programs may cost less. One may therefore be encouraged—not on grounds of rehabilitation but on grounds of cost-effectiveness.

WHAT ABOUT MEDICAL TREATMENT?

4. *Isn't there anything you can do in an institutional setting that will reduce recidivism, for instance, through strictly medical treatment?*

A number of studies deal with the results of

efforts to change the behavior of offenders through drugs and surgery. As for surgery, the one experimental study of a plastic surgery program—by Mandell (1967)—had negative results. For non-addicts who received plastic surgery, Mandell purported to find improvement in performance on parole; but when one reanalyzes his data, it appears that surgery alone did not in fact make a significant difference.

One type of surgery does seem to be highly successful in reducing recidivism. A twenty-year Danish study of sex offenders, by Stuerup (1960), found that while those who had been treated with hormones and therapy continued to commit both sex crimes (29.6 per cent of them did so) and non-sex crimes (21.0 per cent), those who had been castrated had rates of only 3.5 per cent (not, interestingly enough, a rate of zero; where there's a will, apparently there's a way) and 9.2 per cent. One hopes that the policy implications of this study will be found to be distinctly limited.

As for drugs, the major report on such a program—involving tranquilization—was made by Adams (1961b). The tranquilizers were administered to male and female institutionalized youths. With boys, there was only a slight improvement in their subsequent behavior; this improvement disappeared within a year. With girls, the tranquilization produced worse results than when the girls were given no treatment at all.

THE EFFECTS OF SENTENCING

5. *Well, at least it may be possible to manipulate certain gross features of the existing, conventional prison system—such as length of sentence and degree of security—in order to affect these recidivism rates. Isn't this the case?*

At this point, it's still impossible to say that this is the case. As for the degree of security in an institution, Glaser's (1964) work reported that, for both youth and adults, a less restrictive "custody grading" in American federal prisons

was related to success on parole; but this is hardly surprising, since those assigned to more restrictive custody are likely to be worse risks in the first place. More to the point, an American study by Fox (1950) discovered that for "older youths" who were deemed to be good risks for the future, a minimum security institution produced better results than a maximum security one. On the other hand, the data we have on youths under 16—from a study by McClintock (1961), done in Great Britain—indicate that so-called Borstals, in which boys are totally confined, are more effective than a less restrictive regime of partial physical custody. In short, we know very little about the recidivism effects of various degrees of security in existing institutions; and our problems in finding out will be compounded by the probability that these effects will vary widely according to the particular *type* of offender that we're dealing with.

The same problems of mixed results and lack of comparable populations have plagued attempts to study the effects of sentence length. A number of studies—by Narloch (1959), by Bernsten (1965), and by the State of California (1956)—suggest that those who are released earlier from institutions than their scheduled parole date, or those who serve short sentences of under three months rather than longer sentences of eight months or more, either do better on parole or at least do no worse.[4] The implication here is quite clear and important: Even if early releases and short sentences produce no improvement in recidivism rates, one could at least maintain the same rates while lowering the cost of maintaining the offender and lessening his own burden of imprisonment. Of course, this implication carries with it its concommitant

[4] A similar phenomenon has been measured indirectly by studies that have dealt with the effect of various parole policies on recidivism rates. Where parole decisions have been liberalized so that an offender could be released with only the "reasonable assurance" of a job rather than with a definite job already developed by a parole officer (Stanton, 1963), this liberal release policy has produced no worsening of recidivism rates.

danger: the danger that though shorter sentences cause no worsening of the recidivism rate, they may increase the total amount of crime in the community by increasing the absolute number of potential recidivists at large.

On the other hand, Glaser's (1964) data show not a consistent linear relationship between the shortness of the sentence and the rate of parole success, but a curvilinear one. Of his subjects, those who served less than a year had a 73 per cent success rate, those who served up to two years were only 65 per cent successful, and those who served up to three years fell to a rate of 56 per cent. But among those who served sentences of *more* than three years, the success rate rose again—to 60 per cent. These findings should be viewed with some caution since Glaser did not control for the pre-existing degree of risk associated with each of his categories of offenders. But the data do suggest that the relationship between sentence length and recidivism may not be a simple linear one.

More important, the effect of sentence length seems to vary widely according to type of offender. In a British study (1963), for instance, Hammond found that for a group of "hard-core recidivists," shortening the sentence caused no improvement in the recidivism rate. In Denmark, Bernsten (1965) discovered a similar phenomenon: That the beneficial effect of three-month sentences as against eight-month ones disappeared in the case of these "hard-core recidivists." Garrity found another such distinction in his 1956 study. He divided his offenders into three categories: "pro-social," "anti-social," and "manipulative." "Pro-social" offenders he found to have low recidivism rates regardless of the length of their sentence; "anti-social" offenders did better with short sentences; the "manipulative" did better with long ones. Two studies from Britain made yet another division of the offender population, and found yet other variations. One (Great Britain, 1964) found that previous offenders—but not first offenders—did better with *longer* sentences, while the other

(Cambridge, 1952) found the *reverse* to be true with juveniles.

To add to the problem of interpretation, these studies deal not only with different types and categorizations of offenders but with different types of institutions as well. No more than in the case of institution type can we say that length of sentence has a clear relationship to recidivism.

DECARCERATING THE CONVICT

6. *All of this seems to suggest that there's not much we know how to do to rehabilitate an offender when he's in an institution. Doesn't this lead to the clear possibility that the way to rehabilitate offenders is to deal with them outside an institutional setting?*

This is indeed an important possibility, and it is suggested by other pieces of information as well. For instance, Miner (1967) reported on a milieu therapy program in Massachusetts called Outward Bound. It took youths 15½ and over; it was oriented toward the development of skills in the out-of-doors and conducted in a wilderness atmosphere very different from that of most existing institutions. The culmination of the 26-day program was a final 24 hours in which each youth had to survive alone in the wilderness. And Miner found that the program did indeed work in reducing recidivism rates.

But by and large, when one takes the programs that have been administered in institutions and applies them in a non-institutional setting, the results do not grow to encouraging proportions. With casework and individual counseling in the community, for instance, there have been three studies; they dealt with counseling methods from psycho-social and vocational counseling to "operant conditioning," in which an offender was rewarded first simply for coming to counseling sessions and then, gradually, for performing other types of approved acts. Two of them report that the community-counseled offenders did no better than their institutional controls, while the third notes that although community counseling produced fewer arrests per person, it did not ultimately reduce the offender's chance of returning to a reformatory.

The one study of a non-institutional skill development program, by Kovacs (1967), described the New Start Program in Denver, in which offenders participated in vocational training, role playing, programmed instruction, group counseling, college class attendance, and trips to art galleries and museums. After all this, Kovacs found no significant improvement over incarceration.

There have also been studies of milieu therapy programs conducted with youthful male probationers not in actual physical custody. One of them found no significant improvement at all. One, by Empey (1966), did say that after a follow-up of six months, a boy who was judged to have "successfully" completed the milieu program was less likely to recidivate afterwards than was a "successful" regular probationer. Empey's "successes" came out of an extraordinary program in Provo, Utah, which aimed to rehabilitate by subjecting offenders to a non-supportive milieu. The staff of this program operated on the principle that they were *not* to go out of their way to interact and be empathetic with the boys. Indeed, a boy who misbehaved was to be met with "role dispossession": He was to be excluded from meetings of his peer group, and he was not to be given answers to his questions as to why he had been excluded or what his ultimate fate might be. This peer group and its meetings were designed to be the major force for reform at Provo; they were intended to develop, and indeed did develop, strong and controlling norms for the behavior of individual members. For one thing, group members were not to associate with delinquent boys outside the program; for another, individuals were to submit to a group review of all their actions and problems; and they were to be completely honest and open with the group about their attitudes, their states of mind, their personal failings. The group was granted quite a few sanctions with which to enforce these norms: They could practice derision or temporary ostracism, or they could lock up an aberrant member for a weekend, refuse to release him from the program, or send him away to the regular reformatory.

One might be tempted to forgive these methods because of the success that Empey reports, except for one thing. If one judges the program not only by its "successful" boys but by all the boys who were subjected to it—those who succeeded and those who, not surprisingly, failed—the totals show *no* significant improvement in recidivism rates compared with boys on regular probation. Empey did find that both the Provo boys and those on regular probation did better than those in regular reformatories—in contradiction, it may be recalled, to the finding from the residential Marshall Program, in which the direct releases given no special treatment did *worse* than boys in regular institutions.

The third such study of non-residential milieu therapy, by McCravey (1967), found not only that there was no significant improvement, but that the longer a boy participated in the treatment, the *worse* was likely to do afterwards.

PSYCHOTHERAPY IN COMMUNITY SETTINGS

There is some indication that individual psychotherapy may "work" in a community setting. Massimo (1963) reported on one such program, using what might be termed a "pragmatic" psychotherapeutic approach, including "insight" therapy and a focus on vocational problems. The program was marked by its small size and by its use of therapists who were personally enthusiastic about the project; Massimo found that there was indeed a decline in recidivism rates. Adamson (1956), on the other hand, found no significant difference produced by another program of individual therapy (though he did note that arrest rates among the experimental boys declined with what he called "intensity of treatment"). And Schwitzgebel (1963, 1964), studying other, different kinds of therapy programs, found that the programs *did* produce improvements in the attitudes of his boys—but, unfortunately, not in their rates of recidivism.

And with *group* therapy administered in the community, we find yet another set of equivocal results. The results from studies of pragmatic group counseling are only mildly optimistic. Adams (1965) did report that a form of group therapy, "guided group interaction," when administered to juvenile gangs, did somewhat reduce the percentage that were to be found in custody six years later. On the other hand, in a study of juveniles, Adams (1964) found that while such a program did reduce the number of contacts that an experimental youth had with police, it made no ultimate difference in the detention rate. And the attitudes of the counseled youth showed no improvement. Finally, when O'Brien (1961) examined a community-based program of group psychotherapy, he found not only that the program produced no improvement in the recidivism rate, but that the experimental boys actually did worse than their controls on a series of psychological tests.

PROBATION OR PAROLE VERSUS PRISON

But by far the most extensive and important work that has been done on the effect of community-based treatments has been done in the areas of probation and parole. This work sets out to answer the question of whether it makes any difference how you supervise and treat an offender once he has been released from prison or has come under state surveillance in lieu of prison. This is the work that has provided the main basis to date for the claim that we do indeed have the means at our disposal for rehabilitating the offender or at least decarcerating him safely.

One group of these studies has compared the use of probation with other dispositions for offenders; these provide some slight evidence that, at least under some circumstances, probation may make an offender's future chances better than if he had been sent to prison. Or, at least, probation may not worsen those chances.[5] A British study, by Wilkins (1958), reported that when probation was granted more frequently, recidivism rates among probationers did not increase significantly. And another such study by the state of Michigan in 1963 reported that an expansion in the use of probation actually improved recidivism rates—though there are serious problems of comparability in the groups and systems that were studied.

One experiment—by Babst (1965)—compared a group of parolees, drawn from adult male felony offenders in Wisconsin, and excluding murderers and sex criminals, with a similar group that had been put on probation; it found that the probationers committed fewer violations if they had been first offenders, and did no worse if they were recidivists. The problem in interpreting this experiment, though, is that the behavior of those groups was being measured by separate organizations, by probation officers for the probationers, and by parole officers for the parolees; it is not clear that the definition of "violation" was the same in each case, or that other types of uniform standards were being applied. Also, it is not clear what the results would have been if subjects had been released directly to the parole organization without having experienced prison first. Another such study, done in Israel by Shoham (1964), must be interpreted cautiously because his experimental and control groups had slightly different characteristics. But Shoham found that when one compared a suspended sentence plus

---

[5]It will be recalled that Empey's report on the Provo program made such a finding.

probation for first offenders with a one-year prison sentence, only first offenders under 20 years of age did better on probation; those from 21 to 45 actually did *worse*. And Shoham's findings also differ from Babst's in another way. Babst had found that parole rather than prison brought no improvement for recidivists, but Shoham reported that for recidivists with four or more prior offenses, a suspended sentence was actually *better*—though the improvement was much less when the recidivist had committed a crime of violence.

But both the Babst and the Shoham studies, even while they suggest the possible value of suspended sentences, probation, or parole for some offenders (though they contradict each other in telling us *which* offenders), also indicate a pessimistic general conclusion concerning the limits of the effectiveness of treatment programs. For they found that the personal characteristics of offenders—first-offender status, or age, or type of offense—were more important than the form of treatment in determining future recidivism. An offender with a "favorable" prognosis will do better than one without, it seems, no matter how you distribute "good" or "bad," "enlightened" or "regressive" treatments among them.

Quite a large group of studies deals not with probation as compared to other dispositions, but instead with the type of treatment that an offender receives once he is *on* probation or parole. These are the studies that have provided the most encouraging reports on rehabilitative treatment and that have also raised the most serious questions about the nature of the research that has been going on in the corrections field.

Five of these studies have dealt with youthful probationers from 13 to 18 who were assigned to probation officers with small caseloads or provided with other ways of receiving more intensive supervision (Adams, 1966—two reports; Feistman, 1966; Kawaguchi, 1967; Pilnick, 1967). These studies report that, by and large,

intensive supervision does work—that the specially treated youngsters do better according to some measure of recidivism. Yet these studies left some important questions unanswered. For instance, was this improved performance a function merely of the number of contacts a youngster had with his probation officer? Did it also depend on the length of time in treatment? Or was it the quality of supervision that was making the difference, rather than the quantity?

INTENSIVE SUPERVISION: THE WARREN STUDIES

The widely-reported Warren studies (1966a, 1966b, 1967) in California constitute an extremely ambitious attempt to answer these questions. In this project, a control group of youths, drawn from a pool of candidates ready for first admission to a California Youth Authority institution, was assigned to regular detention, usually for eight to nine months, and then released to regular supervision. The experimental group received considerably more elaborate treatment. They were released directly to probation status and assigned to 12-man caseloads. To decide what special treatment was appropriate within these caseloads, the youths were divided according to their "interpersonal maturity level classification," by use of a scale developed by Grant and Grant. And each level dictated its own special type of therapy. For instance, a youth might be judged to occupy the lowest maturity level; this would be a youth, according to the scale, primarily concerned with "demands that the world take care of him. . . . He behaves impulsively, unaware of anything except the grossest effects of his behavior on others." A youth like this would be placed in a supportive environment such as a foster home; the goals of his therapy would be to meet his dependency needs and help him gain more accurate perceptions about his relationship to others. At the other end of the three-tier classification, a youth might exhibit high maturity. This would be a youth who had internalized "a set of standards by which he judges his and others' behavior. . . . He shows some ability to understand reasons for behavior, some ability to relate to people emotionally and on a long-term basis." These high-maturity youths could come in several varieties—a "neurotic acting out," for instance, a "neurotic anxious," a "situational emotional reactor," or a "cultural identifier." But the appropriate treatment for these youths was individual psychotherapy, or family or group therapy for the purpose of reducing internal conflicts and increasing the youths' awareness of personal and family dynamics.

"Success" in this experiment was defined as favorable discharge by the Youth Authority; "failure" was unfavorable discharge, revocation, or recommitment by a court. Warren reported an encouraging·finding: Among all but one of the "subtypes," the experimentals had a significantly lower failure rate than the controls. The experiment did have certain problems: The experimentals might have been performing better because of the enthusiasm of the staff and the attention lavished on them; none of the controls had been *directly* released to their regular supervision programs instead of being detained first; and it was impossible to separate the effects of the experimentals' small caseloads from their specially designed treatments, since no experimental youths had been assigned to a small caseload with "inappropriate" treatment, or with no treatment at all. Still, none of these problems were serious enough to vitiate the encouraging prospect that this finding presented for successful treatment of probationers.

This encouraging finding was, however, accompanied by a rather more disturbing clue. As has been mentioned before, the experimental subjects, when measured, had a lower *failure* rate than the controls. But the experimentals also had a lower *success* rate. That is, fewer of the experimentals as compared with the controls had been judged to have successfully completed their program of supervision and to be suitable for favorable release. When my colleagues and I

undertook a rather laborious reanalysis of the Warren data, it became clear why this discrepancy had appeared. It turned out that fewer experimentals were "successful" because the experimentals were actually committing more offenses than their controls. The reason that the experimentals' relatively large number of offenses was not being reflected in their failure rates was simply that the experimentals' probation officers were using a more lenient revocation policy. In other words, the controls had a higher failure rate because the controls were being revoked for less serious offenses.

So it seems that what Warren was reporting in her "failure" rates was not merely the treatment effect of her small caseloads and special programs. Instead, what Warren was finding was not so much a change in the behavior of the experimental youths as a change in the behavior of the experimental *probation officers*, who knew the "special" status of their charges and who had evidently decided to revoke probation status at a lower than normal rate. The experimentals continued to commit offenses; what was different was that when they committed these offenses, they were permitted to remain on probation.

The experimenters claimed that this low revocation policy, and the greater number of offenses committed by the special treatment youth, were *not* an indication that these youth were behaving specially badly and that policy makers were simply letting them get away with it. Instead, it was claimed, the higher reported offense rate was primarily an artifact of the more intense surveillance that the experimental youth received. But the data show that this is not a sufficient explanation of the low failure rate among experimental youth; the difference in "tolerance" of offenses between experimental officials and control officials was much greater than the difference in the rates at which these two systems detected youths committing new offenses. Needless to say, this reinterpretation of the data presents a much bleaker picture of the possibilities of intensive supervision with special treatment.

"TREATMENT EFFECTS" VS. "POLICY EFFECTS"

This same problem of experimenter bias may also be present in the predecessors of the Warren study, the ones which had also found positive results from intensive supervision on probation; indeed, this disturbing question can be raised about many of the previously discussed reports of positive "treatment effects."

This possibility of a "policy effect" rather than a "treatment effect" applies, for instance, to the previously discussed studies of the effects of intensive supervision on juvenile and youthful probationers. These were the studies, it will be recalled, which found lower recidivism rates for the intensively supervised.[6]

One opportunity to make a further check on the effects of this problem is provided, in a slightly different context, by Johnson (1962a). Johnson was measuring the effects of intensive supervision on youthful *parolees* (as distinct from probationers). There have been several such studies of the effects on youths of intensive parole supervision plus special counseling, and their findings are on the whole less encouraging than the probation studies; they are difficult to interpret because of experimental problems, but studies by Boston University in 1966, and by Van Couvering in 1966, report no significant effects and possibly some bad effects from such special programs. But Johnson's studies were unique for the chance they provide to measure both treatment effects and the effect of agency policy.

Johnson, like Warren, assigned experimental subjects to small caseloads and his experiment had the virtue of being performed with two separate populations and at two different times. But in contrast with the Warren case, the Johnson experiment did not engage in a large continuing attempt to choose the experimental

counselors specially, to train them specially, and to keep them informed about the progress and importance of the experiment. The first time the experiment was performed, the experimental youths had a slightly lower revocation rate than the controls at six months. But the second time, the experimentals did *not* do better than their controls; indeed, they did slightly worse. And with the experimentals from the first group—those who *had* shown an improvement after six months—this effect wore off at 18 months. In the Johnson study, my colleagues and I found, "intensive" supervision did *not* increase the experimental youths' risk of detection. Instead, what was happening in the Johnson experiment was that the first time it had been performed—just as in the Warren study—the experimentals were simply revoked less often per number of offenses committed, and they were revoked for offenses more serious than those which prompted revocation among the controls. The second time around, this "policy" discrepancy disappeared; and when it did, the "improved" performance of the experimentals disappeared as well. The enthusiasm guiding the project had simply worn off in the absence of reinforcement.

One must conclude that the "benefits" of intensive supervision for youthful offenders may stem not so much from a "treatment" effect as from a "policy" effect—that such supervision, so far as we now know, results not in rehabilitation but in a decision to look the other way when an offense is committed. But there is one major modification to be added to this conclusion. Johnson performed a further measurement (1962b) in his parole experiment: He rated all the supervising agents according to the "adequacy" of the supervision they gave. And he found that an "adequate" agent, whether he was working in a small *or* a large caseload, produced a relative improvement in his charges. The converse was not true: An *in*adequate agent was more likely to produce youthful "failures" when he was given a *small* caseload to supervise. One can't much help a "good" agent, it seems, by

---

[6]But one of these reports, by Kawaguchi (1967), also found that an intensively supervised juvenile, by the time he finally "failed," had had more previous *detentions* while under supervision than a control juvenile had experienced.

reducing his caseload size; such reduction can only do further harm to those youths who fall into the hands of "bad" agents.

So with youthful offenders, Johnson found, intensive supervision does not seem to provide the rehabilitative benefits claimed for it; the only such benefits may flow not from intensive supervision itself but from contact with one of the "good people" who are frequently in such short supply.

INTENSIVE SUPERVISION OF ADULTS

The results are similarly ambiguous when one applies this intensive supervision to adult offenders. There have been several studies of the effects of intensive supervision on adult parolees. Some of these are hard to interpret because of problems of comparability between experimental and control groups (general risk ratings, for instance, or distribution of narcotics offenders, or policy changes that took place between various phases of the experiments), but two of them (California, 1966; Stanton, 1964) do not seem to give evidence of the benefits of intensive supervision. By far the most extensive work, though, on the effects of intensive supervision of adult parolees has been a series of studies of California's Special Intensive Parole Unit (SIPU), a 10-year-long experiment designed to test the treatment possibilities of various special parole programs. Three of the four "phases" of this experiment produced "negative results." The first phase tested the effect of a reduced caseload size; no lasting effect was found. The second phase slightly increased the size of the small caseloads and provided for a longer time in treatment; again there was no evidence of a treatment effect. In the fourth phase, caseload sizes and time in treatment were again varied, and treatments were simultaneously varied in a sophisticated way according to personality characteristics of the parolees; once again, significant results did not appear.

The only phase of this experiment for which positive results were reported was Phase Three. Here, it was indeed found that a smaller caseload improved one's chances of parole success. There is, however, an important caveat that attaches to this finding: When my colleagues and I divided the whole population of subjects into two groups—those receiving supervision in the North of the state and those in the South—we found that the "improvement" of the experimentals' success rates was taking place primarily in the North. The North differed from the South in one important aspect: Its agents practiced a policy of returning both "experimental" and "control" violators to prison at relatively high rates. And it was the North that produced the higher success rate among its experimentals. So this improvement in experimentals' performance was taking place only when accompanied by a "realistic threat" of severe sanctions. It is interesting to compare this situation with that of the Warren studies. In the Warren studies, experimental subjects were being revoked at a relatively *low* rate. These experimentals "failed" less, but they also committed more new offenses than their controls. By contrast, in the Northern region of the SIPU experiment, there was a policy of *high* rate of return to prison for experimentals; and here, the special program *did* seem to produce a real improvement in the behavior of offenders. What this suggests is that when intensive supervision *does* produce an improvement in offenders' behavior, it does so not through the mechanism of "treatment" or "rehabilitation," but instead through a mechanism that our studies have almost totally ignored—the mechanism of *deterrence*. And a similar mechanism is suggested by Lohman's study (1967) of intensive supervision of probationers. In this study intensive supervision led to higher total violation rates. But one also notes that intensive supervision combined the highest rate of technical violations with the lowest rate for *new* offenses.

THE EFFECTS OF COMMUNITY TREATMENT

In sum, even in the case of treatment programs administered outside penal institutions, we simply cannot say that this treatment in itself has an appreciable effect on offender behavior. On the other hand, there is one encouraging set of findings that emerges from these studies. For from many of them there flows the strong suggestion that even if we can't "treat" offenders so as to make them do better, a great many of the programs designed to rehabilitate them at least did not make them do *worse*. And if these programs did not show the advantages of actually rehabilitating, some of them did have the advantage of being less onerous to the offender himself without seeming to pose increased danger to the community. And some of these programs—especially those involving less restrictive custody, minimal supervision, and early release—simply cost fewer dollars to administer. The information on the dollar costs of these programs is just beginning to be developed but the implication is clear: *that if we can't do more for (and to) offenders, at least we can safely do less.*

There is, however, one important caveat even to this note of optimism: In order to calculate the true costs of these programs, one must in each case include not only their administrative cost but also the cost of maintaining in the community an offender population increased in size. This population might well not be committing new offenses at any greater rate; but the offender population might, under some of these plans, be larger in absolute *numbers*. So the total number of offenses committed might rise, and our chances of victimization might therefore rise too. We need to be able to make a judgment about the size and probable duration of this effect; as of now, we simply do not know.

DOES NOTHING WORK?

7. *Do all of these studies lead us irrevocably to the conclusion that nothing works, that we haven't the faintest clue about how to rehabilitate offenders and reduce recidivism? And if so, what shall we do?*

We tried to exclude from our survey those studies which were so poorly done that they simply could not be interpreted. But despite our efforts, a pattern has run through much of this discussion—of studies which "found" effects without making any truly rigorous attempt to exclude competing hypotheses, of extraneous factors permitted to intrude upon the measurements, of recidivism measures which are not all measuring the same thing, of "follow-up" periods which vary enormously and rarely extend beyond the period of legal supervision, of experiments never replicated, of "system effects" not taken into account, of categories drawn up without any theory to guide the enterprise. It is just possible that some of our treatment programs *are* working to some extent, but that our research is so bad that it is incapable of telling.

Having entered this very serious caveat, I am bound to say that these data, involving over two hundred studies and hundreds of thousands o individuals as they do, are the best available and give us very little reason to hope that we have in fact found a sure way of reducing recidivism through rehabilitation. This is not to say that we found no instances of success or partial success; it is only to say that these instances have been isolated, producing no clear pattern to indicate the efficacy of any particular method of treatment. And neither is this to say that factors *outside* the realm of rehabilitation may not be working to reduce recidivism—factors such as the tendency for recidivism to be lower in offenders over the age of 30; it is only to say that such factors seem to have little connection with any of the treatment methods now at our disposal.

From this probability, one may draw any of several conclusions. It may be simply that our programs aren't yet good enough—that the education we provide to inmates is still poor education, that the therapy we administer is not administered skillfully enough, that our intensive supervision and counseling do not yet provide enough personal support for the offenders who are subjected to them. If one wishes to believe this, then what our correctional system needs is simply a more full-hearted commitment to the strategy of treatment.

It may be, on the other hand, that there is a more radical flaw in our present strategies—that education at its best, or that psychotherapy at its best, cannot overcome, or even appreciably reduce, the powerful tendency for offenders to continue in criminal behavior. Our present treatment programs are based on a theory of crime as a "disease"—that is to say, as something foreign and abnormal in the individual which can presumably be cured. This theory may well be flawed, in that it overlooks—indeed, denies—both the normality of crime in society and the personal normality of a very large proportion of offenders, criminals who are merely responding to the facts and conditions of our society.

This opposing theory of "crime as a social phenomenon" directs our attention away from a "rehabilitative" strategy, away from the notion that we may best insure public safety through a series of "treatments" to be imposed forcibly on convicted offenders. These treatments have on occasion become, and have the potential for becoming, so draconian as to offend the moral order of a democratic society; and the theory of crime as a social phenomenon suggests that such treatments may be not only offensive but ineffective as well. This theory points, instead, to decarceration for low-risk offenders—and, presumably, to keeping high-risk offenders in prisons which are nothing more (and aim to be nothing more) than custodial institutions.

But this approach has its own problems. To begin with, there is the moral dimension of crime and punishment. Many low-risk offenders have committed serious crimes (murder, sometimes) and even if one is reasonably sure they will never commit another crime, it violates our sense of justice that they should experience no significant retribution for their actions. A middle-class banker who kills his adulterous wife in a moment of passion is a "low-risk" criminal; a juvenile delinquent in the ghetto who commits armed robbery has, statistically, a much higher probability of committing another crime.

Are we going to put the first on probation and sentence the latter to a long-term in prison?

Besides, one cannot ignore the fact that the punishment of offenders is the major means we have for *deterring* incipient offenders. We know almost nothing about the "deterrent effect," largely because "treatment" theories have so dominated our research, and "deterrence" theories have been relegated to the status of a historical curiosity. Since we have almost no idea of the deterrent functions that our present system performs or that future strategies might be made to perform, it is possible that there is indeed something that works—that to some extent is working right now in front of our noses, and that might be made to work better—something that deters rather than cures, something that does not so much reform convicted offenders as prevent criminal behavior in the first place. But whether that is the case and, if it is, what strategies will be found to make our deterrence system work better than it does now, are questions we will not be able to answer with data until a new family of studies has been brought into existence. As we begin to learn the facts, we will be in a better position than we are now to judge to what degree the prison has become an anachronism and can be replaced by more effective means of social control.

BIBLIOGRAPHY OF STUDIES REFERRED TO BY NAME

Adams, Stuart. "Effectiveness of the Youth Authority Special Treatment Program: First Interim Report." Research Report No. 5. California Youth Authority, March 6, 1959. (Mimeographed.)

Adams, Stuart. "Assessment of the Psychiatric Treatment Program: Second Interim Report." Research Report No. 15. California Youth Authority, December 13, 1959. (Mimeographed.)

Adams, Stuart. "Effectiveness of Interview Therapy with Older Youth Authority Wards: An Interim Evaluation of the PICO Project." Research Report

No. 20. California Youth Authority, January 20, 1961. (Mimeographed.)

Adams, Stuart. "Assessment of the Psychiatric Treatment Program, Phase I: Third Interim Report." Research Report No. 21. California Youth Authority, January 31, 1961. (Mimeographed.)

Adams, Stuart. "An Experimental Assessment of Group Counseling with Juvenile Probationers." Paper presented at the 18th Convention of the California State Psychological Association, Los Angeles, December 12, 1964. (Mimeographed.)

Adams, Stuart, Rice, Rogert E., and Olive, Borden. "A Cost Analysis of the Effectiveness of the Group Guidance Program." Research Memorandum 65-3. Los Angeles County Probation Department, January 1965. (Mimeographed.)

Adams, Stuart. "Development of a Program Research Service in Probation." Research Report No. 27 (Final Report, NIMH Project MH007 18.) Los Angeles County Probation Department, January 1966. (Processed.)

Adamson, LeMay, and Dunham, H. Warren. "Clinical Treatment Of Male Delinquents. A Case Study in Effort and Result," *American Sociological Review,* XXI, 3 (1956), 312–320.

Babst, Dean V., and Mannering, John W. "Probation versus Imprisonment for Similar Types of Offenders: A Comparision by Subsequent Violations," *Journal of Research in Crime and Delinquency,* II, 2 (1965), 60–71.

Bernsten, Karen, and Christiansen, Karl O. "A Resocialization Experiment with Short-term Offenders," *Scandinavian Studies in Criminology,* I (1965), 35–54.

California, Adult Authority, Division of Adult Paroles. "Special Intensive Parole Unit, Phase I: Fifteen Man Caseload Study." Prepared by Walter I. Stone. Sacramento, Calif., November 1956. (Mimeographed.)

California, Department of Corrections. "Intensive Treatment Program: Second Annual Report." Prepared by Harold B. Bradley and Jack D. Williams. Sacramento, Calif., December 1, 1958. (Mimeographed.)

California, Department of Corrections. "Special Intensive Parole Unit, Phase II: Thirty Man Caseload Study." Prepared by Ernest Reimer and Martin Warren. Sacramento, Calif., December 1958. (Mimeographed.)

California, Department of Corrections. "Parole Work Unit Program: An Evaluative Report." A memorandum to the California Joint Legislative Budget Committee, December 30, 1966. (Mimeographed.)

California, Department of the Youth Authority. "James Marshall Treatment Program: Progress Report." January 1967. (Processed.)

Cambridge University, Department of Criminal Science. *Detention in Remand Homes.* London: Macmillan, 1952.

Craft, Michael, Stephenson, Geoffrey, and Granger, Clive. "A Controlled Trial of Authoritarian and Self-Governing Regimes with Adolescent Psychopaths," *American Journal of Orthopsychiatry,* XXXIV, 3 (1964), 543–554.

Empey, LeMar T. "The Provo Experiment: A Brief Review." Los Angeles: Youth Studies Center, University of Southern California. 1966. (Processed.)

Feistman, Eugene G. "Comparative Analysis of the Willow-Brook-Harbor Intensive Services Program, March 1, 1965 through February 28, 1966." Research Report No. 28. Los Angeles County Probation Department, June 1966. (Processed.)

Forman, B. "The Effects of Differential Treatment on Attitudes, Personality Traits, and Behavior of Adult Parolees." Unpublished Ph.D. dissertation, University of Southern California, 1960.

Fox, Vernon. "Michigan's Experiment in Minimum Security Penology," *Journal of Criminal Law, Criminology, and Police Science,* XLI, 2 (1950), 150–166.

Freeman, Howard E., and Weeks, H. Ashley. "Analysis of a Program of Treatment of Delinquent Boys," *American Journal of Sociology,* LXII, 1 (1956), 56–61.

Garrity, Donald Lee. "The Effects of Length of Incarceration upon Parole Adjustment and Estimation of Optimum Sentence: Washington State Correctional Institutions." Unpublished Ph.D. dissertation, University of Washington, 1956.

Gearhart, J. Walter, Keith, Harold L., and Clemmons, Gloria. "An Analysis of the Vocational Training Program in the Washington State Adult Correctional Institutions." Research Review No. 23. State of Washington, Department of Institutions, May 1967. (Processed.)

Glaser, Daniel. *The Effectiveness of a Prison and Parole System.* New York: Bobbs-Merrill, 1964.

Goldberg, Lisbeth, and Adams, Stuart. "An Experimental Evaluation of the Lathrop Hall Program." Los Angeles County Probation Department, December 1964. (Summarized in: Adams, Stuart. "Development of a Program Research Service in Probation," pp. 19–22.)

Great Britain. Home Office. *The Sentence of the Court: A Handbook for Courts on the Treatment of Offenders.* London: Her Majesty's Stationery Office, 1964.

Guttman, Evelyn S. "Effects of Short-Term Psychiatric Treatment on Boys in Two California Youth Authority Institutions." Research Report No. 36. California Youth Authority, December 1963. (Processed.)

Hammond, W. H., and Chayen, E. *Persistent Criminals: A Home Office Research Unit Report.* London: Her Majesty's Stationery Office, 1963.

Harrison, Robert M., and Mueller, Paul F. C. "Clue Hunting About Group Counseling and Parole Outcome." Research Report No. 11. California Department of Corrections, May 1964. (Mimeographed.)

Havel, Joan, and Sulka, Elaine. "Special Intensive Parole Unit: Phase Three." Research Report No. 3. California Department of Corrections, March 1962. (Processed.)

Havel, Joan. "A Synopsis of Research Report No. 10, SIPU Phase IV—The High Base Expectancy Study." Administrative Abstract No. 10. California Department of Corrections, June 1963. (Processed.)

Havel, Joan. "Special Intensive Parole Unit—Phase Four: 'The Parole Outcome Study.'" Research Report No. 13. California Department of Corrections, September 1965. (Processed.)

Hood, Roger. Homeless Borstal Boys: *A Study of Their After-Care and After-Conduct.* Occasional Papers on Social Administration No. 18. London: G. Bell & Sons, 1966.

Jacobson, Frank, and McGee, Eugene. "Englewood Project: Re-education: A Radical Correction of In-

carcerated Delinquents." Englewood, Colo.: July 1965. (Mimeographed.)

Jesness, Carl F. "The Fricot Ranch Study: Outcomes with Small versus Large Living Groups in the Rehabilitation of Delinquents." Research Report No. 47. California Youth Authority, October 1, 1965. (Processed.)

Johnson, Bertram. "Parole Performance of the First Year's Releases, Parole Research Project: Evaluation of Reduced Caseloads." Research Report No. 27. California Youth Authority, January 31, 1962. (Mimeographed.)

Johnson, Bertram. "An Analysis of Predictions of Parole Performance and of Judgments of Supervision in the Parole Research Project," Research Report No. 32. California Youth Authority, December 31, 1962. (Mimeographed.)

Kassebaum, Gene, Ward, David, and Wilnet, Daniel. *Prison Treatment and Parole Survival: An Empirical Assessment.* New York: Wiley, 1971.

Kawaguchi, Ray M., and Siff, Leon, M. "An Analysis of Intensive Probation Services—Phase II." Research Report No. 29. Los Angeles County Probation Department, April 1967. (Processed.)

Kettering, Marvin E. "Rehabilitation of Women in the Milwaukee County Jail: An Exploration Experiment." Unpublished Master's Thesis, Colorado State College, 1965.

Kovacs, Frank W. "Evaluation and Final Report of the New Start Demonstration Project." Colorado Department of Employment, October 1967. (Processed.)

Lavlicht, Jerome, et al., in *Berkshire Farms Monographs,* I, 1 (1962), 11–48.

Levinson, Robert B., and Kitchenet, Howard L. "Demonstration Counseling Project." 2 vols. Washington, D.C.: National Training School for Boys, 1962–1964. (Mimeographed.)

Lohman, Joseph D., et al., "The Intensive Supervision Caseloads: A Preliminary Evaluation." The San Francisco Project: A Study of Federal Probation and Parole. Research Report No. 11. School of Criminology, University of California, March 1967. (Processed.)

McClintock, F. H. *Attendance Centres.* London. Macmillan, 1961.

McCord, William and Joan. "Two Approaches to the Cure of Delinquents," *Journal of Criminal Law, Criminology, and Police Science*, XLIV, 4 (1953), 442–467.

McCorkle, Lloyd W., Elias, Albert, and Bixby, F. Lovell. *The Highfields Story: An Experimental Treatment Project for Youthful Offenders.* New York: Holt, 1958.

McCravy, Newton, Jr., and Delehanty, Dolores S. "Community Rehabilitation of the Younger Delinquent Boy, Parkland Non-Residential Group Center." Final Report, Kentucky Child Welfare Research Foundation, Inc., September 1, 1967. (Mimeographed.)

Mandell, Wallace, *et al.* "Surgical and Social Rehabilitation of Adult Offenders." Final Report. Montefiore Hospital and Medical Center, With Staten Island Mental Health Society. New York City Department of Correction, 1967. (Processed.)

Massimo, Joseph L., and Shore, Milton F. "The Effectiveness of a Comprehensive Vocationally Oriented Psychotherapeutic Program for Adolescent Delinquent Boys," *American Journal of Orthopsychiatry*, XXXIII, 4 (1963), 634–642.

Minet, Joshua, III, Kelly, Francis J., and Hatch, M. Charles. "Outward Bound Inc.: Juvenile Delinquency Demonstration Project, Year End Report." Massachusetts Division of Youth Service, May 31, 1967.

Narloch, R. P., Adams, Stuart, and Jenkins, Kendall J. "Characteristics and Parole Performance of California Youth Authority Early Releases." Research Report No. 7. California Youth Authority, June 22, 1959. (Mimeographed.)

New York State, Division of Parole, Department of Correction. "Parole Adjustment and Prior Educational Achievement of Male Adolescent Offenders, June 1957-June 1961." September 1964. (Mimeographed.)

O'Brien, William J. "Personality Assessment as a Measure of Change Resulting from Group Psychotherapy with Male Juvenile Delinquents." The Institute for the Study of Crime and Delinquency, and the California Youth Authority, December 1961. (Processed.)

Persons, Roy W. "Psychological and Behavioral Change in Delinquents Following Psychotherapy,"

Journal of Clinical Psychology, XXII, 3 (1966), 337–340.

Persons, Roy W. "Relationship Between Psychotherapy with Institutionalized Boys and Subsequent Community Adjustment," *Journal of Consulting Psychology*, XXXI, 2 (1967), 137N141.

Pilnick, Saul, *et al.* "Collegefields: From Delinquency to Freedom." A Report . . . on Collegefields Group Educational Center. Laboratory for Applied Behavioral Science, Newark State College, February 1967. (Processed.)

Robison, James, and Kevotkian, Marinette. "Intensive Treatment Project: Phase II. Parole Outcome: Interim Report." Research Report No. 27. California Department of Corrections, Youth and Adult Correctional Agency, January 1967. (Mimeographed.)

Rudoff, Alvin. "The Effect of Treatment on Incarcerated Young Adult Delinquents as Measured by Disciplinary History." Unpublished Master's thesis, University of Southern California, 1960.

Saden, S. J. "Correctional Research at Jackson Prison," *Journal of Correctional Education*, XV (October 1962), 22–26.

Schnur, Alfred C. "The Educational Treatment of Prisoners and Recidivism," *American Journal of Sociology*, LIV, 2 (1948), 142–147.

Schwitzgebel, Robert and Ralph. "Therapeutic Research: A Procedure for the Reduction of Adolescent Crime." Paper presented at meetings of the American Psychological Association, Philadelphia, Pa., August 1963.

Schwitzgebel, Robert and Kolb, D. A. "Inducing Behavior Change in Adolescent Delinquents," *Behavior Research Therapy*, I (1964), 297–304.

Seckel, Joachim P. "Experiments in Group Counseling at Two Youth Authority Institutions." Research Report No. 46. California Youth Authority, September 1965. (Processed.)

Seckel, Joachim P. "The Fremont Experiment, Assessment of Residential Treatment at a Youth Authority Reception Center." Research Report No. 50. California Youth Authority, January 1967. (Mimeographed.)

Shelley, Ernest L. V., and Johnson, Walter F., Jr. "Evaluating an Organized Counseling Service for Youthful Offenders," *Journal of Counseling Psychology*, VIII, 4 (1961), 351–354.

Shoham, Shlomo, and Sandberg, Moshe. "Suspended Sentences in Israel: An Evaluation of the Preventive Efficacy of Prospective Imprisonment," *Crime and Delinquency*, X, 1 (1964), 74–83.

Stanton, John M. "Delinquencies and Types of Parole Programs to Which Inmates are Released." New York State Division of Parole, May 15, 1963. (Mimeographed.)

Stanton, John M. "Board Directed Extensive Supervision." New York State Division of Parole, August 3, 1964. (Mimeographed.)

Stuerup, Georg K. "The Treatment of Sexual Offenders," *Bulletin de la societe internationale de criminologie* (1960), pp. 320–329.

Sullivan, Clyde E., Mandell, Wallace. "Restoration of Youth Through Training: A Final Report." Staten Island, New York: Wakoff Research Center, April 1967. (Processed.)

Taylor, A. J. W. "An Evaluation of Group Psychotherapy in a Girls' Borstal," *International Journal of Group Psychotherapy*, XVII, 2 (1967), 168–177.

Truax, Charles B., Wargo, Donald G., and Silber, Leon D. "Effects of Group Psychotherapy with High Adequate Empathy and Nonpossessive Warmth upon Female Institutionalized Delinquents," *Journal of Abnormal Psychology*, LXXI, 4 (1966), 267–274.

Warren, Marguerite. "The Community Treatment Project after Five Years." California Youth Authority, 1966. (Processed.)

Warren, Marguerite, *et al.* "Community Treatment Project, an Evaluation of Community Treatment for Delinquents: a Fifth Progress Report." C.T.P. Research Report No. 7. California Youth Authority, August 1966. (Processed.)

Warren, Marguerite, *et al.* "Community Treatment Project, an Evaluation of Community Treatment for Delinquents: Sixth Progress Report." C.T.P. Research Report No. 8. California Youth Authority, September 1967. (Processed.)

Wilkins, Leslie T. "A Small Comparative Study of the Results of Probation," *British Journal of Criminology*, VIII, 3 (1958), 201–209.

Zivan, Morton. "Youth in Trouble: A Vocational Approach." Final Report of a Research and Demonstration Project, May 31, 1961-August 31, 1966. Dobbs Ferry, N.Y., Children's Village, 1966. (Processed.)

71. A Critique of Martinson

TED PALMER

IN RECENT MONTHS MANY PRACTITIONERS AND administrators have expressed the thought that a recent article by Robert Martinson. "What Works?—Questions and Answers about Prison Reform," may have sounded the death knell for the field of correctional intervention, commonly known as "treatment." (1) It therefore seems timely to ask: *Does* a careful reading of this challenging and influential article really warrant the pessimistic forecast which has been made, especially by individuals who have drawn upon it to support their suspicions regarding the futility of intervention in general?

To answer this question, we will begin by taking a second, or perhaps closer, look at what Dr. Martinson has in fact said. This "second look" may help us focus not only upon the actual presence but also upon the significance of certain *positive* findings and relatively optimistic observations which were an integral part of Martinson's presentation. This, in turn, may lead us to reassess the appropriateness—i.e., the consistency and representativeness—of the following, rather sweeping *conclusion* which was offered in "What Works? . . . ," a conclusion which has since triggered such widespread pessimism within corrections:

"It is possible to give a rather bald summary of our findings: *With few and isolated exceptions, the rehabilitative efforts that have been reported so far have had no appreciable effect on recidivism.*" (1, p. 25)

▶SOURCE: *"Martinson Revisited," Journal of Research in Crime and Delinquency (July, 1975), 12(2): 133–152. Reprinted by permission.*

To see whether this conclusion actually takes account of the facts that were presented, we will now turn to the description and commentary which Martinson himself has provided in relation to a number of research studies. (In the selections which follow, each such study will appear in connection with the section heading that was used in "What Works?. . . ." Again, all quotes are directly from Martinson.)

STUDIES FROM MARTINSON

(A) From the section titled, "The effects of individual counseling:

1. A study by Adams (2) of adolescent and young adult inmates:

"Amenable boys who got the treatment did better than non-treated boys. On the other hand, 'non-amenable' boys who were treated actually did *worse* than they would have done if they had received no treatment at all. [This study suggests] there is something to be hoped for in treating properly selected amenable subjects. . . ." (1, p. 29)

2. A study by Adams (3) of therapy with adolescent female inmates:

"[Adams] found that social workers seemed better at the job than psychologists or psychiatrists. This difference seems to suggest a favorable outlook for these alternative forms [viz., 'counseling' and 'casework'] of individual therapy." (1, p. 30)

3. A study by Bernsten and Christiansen (4) of male offenders in Denmark:

"Bernsten (1961) reported ... that socio-psychological counseling combined with comprehensive welfare measures—job and residence placement, clothing, union and health insurance membership, and financial aid—produced an improvement among some short-term male offenders, though not those in either the highest-risk or the lowest-risk categories." (1, p. 30)

4. A study by Persons (5) of adolescent males:

"If a boy was judged to be "successfully" treated—as opposed to simply being subjected to the treatment experience—he did tend to do better." (1, p. 29)

In relation to two of the above studies it may be noted that Martinson makes direct or indirect reference to "treatment amenable" and "middle-risk offenders." Similar groups, and related factors, may be noted in connection with other studies and evaluative remarks which he presents.

(B) From the section titled, "Group counseling":

1. A study by Persons (6) of young adult males:

"[Results were] that this treatment did in fact reduce recidivism. The improved recidivism rate stems from the improved performance only of those who were clinically judged [prior to follow-up] to have been "successfully" treated; still, the overall result of the treatment was to improve recidivism rates for the experimental group as a whole." (1, p. 31)

2. A study by Craft et al. (7) of young adult males:

"[This study of] males designated "psychopaths," comparing "self-government" group psychotherapy with "authoritarian" individual counseling, found that the "group therapy" boys afterwards committed *twice* as many new offenses as the individually treated ones. Perhaps some forms of group psychotherapy work for some types of offenders but not others. . . ." (1, pp. 31–32)

3. A study by Truax (8) of young female inmates:

"Girls subjected to group psychotherapy and then released were likely to spend less time reincarcerated in the future. But what is most interesting about this improvement is the very special and important circumstance under which it occurred. The therapists chosen for this program did not merely have to have the proper analytic training: they were specially chosen for their "empathy" and "non-possessive warmth." In other words, it may well have been the therapists special personal gifts rather than the fact of treatment itself which produced the favorable result. This possibility will emerge again when we examine the effects of other rehabilitative treatment later in this article. . . . These programs seem to work best when they are new, when their subjects are amenable to treatment in the first place, and when the counselors are not only trained people but "good" people as well." (1, p. 32)

The reader will note that, in the above, Dr. Martinson has in fact stated that "these programs seem to *work*," albeit under specified conditions. (Emphasis added.)

4. A study by Shelley and Johnson (9) of adult male inmates:

"[This study] dealt with a "pragmatic" casework program, directed towards the educational and vocational needs. . . . Shelley found an improvement in attitudes; the possession of "good" attitudes was independently found by Shelley to correlate with parole success. Unfortunately, though, Shelley was not able to measure the *direct* impact of the counseling on recidivism rates. His two separate correlations are [nevertheless] suggestive. . . ." (1, p. 31)

(C) From the section on "Transforming the institutional environment" ("milieu therapy"):

1. Two studies (10, 11) of adolescent male inmates:

"[Levinson found] a lack of improvement in recidivism rates—but [he] noted the encouraging fact that the treated group spent somewhat more time in the community before recidivating, and committed less serious offenses. And a study by the State of California (1967) also shows a partially positive finding. This was a study of the Marshall Program. . . ." (1, p. 35)

2. A study by Goldberg and Adams (12) of adolescent female probationers:

"[This study of milieu therapy] found that such a program *did* have a positive effect. This effect declined when the program began to deal with girls who were judged beforehand to be worse risks." (1, p. 33)

(D) From the section on "The effects of sentencing":

1. A study by Fox (13) of adolescent males in differing residential settings and a second study by McClintock (14) of British Borstal boys:

"For "older youths" who were deemed to be good risks for the future, a minimum security institution produced better results than a maximum security one. On the other hand, the data we have on youths under 16 . . . indicate that so-called Borstals, in which boys are totally confined, are more effective than a less restrictive regime of partial physical custody. In short, we know very little about the recidivism effects of various degrees of security in existing institutions; and our problems in finding out will be compounded by the probability that these effects will vary widely according to the particular *type* of offender that we're dealing with." (1, p. 36)

2. A study by Garrity (15) of adult male parolees:

"The effect of sentence length seems to vary widely according to type of offender. . . . [Garrity] divided his offenders into three categories: "pro-social," "anti-social," and "manipulative." "Pro-social" offenders he found to have low recidivism rates regardless of the length of their sentence; "anti-social" offenders did better with short sentences; the "manipulative" did better with long ones." (1, p. 37)

Once again Dr. Martinson has made note of an apparent relationship between *type of offender,* on the one hand, and level of treatment effectiveness on the other. This is apart from his particular focus, in the present section, upon the differential outcomes that are associated with given *types of setting* and, possibly, various lengths of sentence.

(E) From the section on "Decarcerating the convict":

1. A study by Miner et al. (16) of an Outward Bound program for adolescent male offenders:

"Miner found that the program did indeed work in reducing recidivism rates." (1, p. 38)

2. A study by Empey (17) of adolescent male probationers and parolees:

"[A Provo youth] who was judged to have "successfully" completed the milieu program [i.e., Guided Group Interaction] was less likely to recidivate afterwards than was a "successful" regular probationer. . . . If one judges the program not only by its "successful" boys but by all the boys who were subjected to it . . . the totals show *no* significant improvement in recidivism rates compared with boys on regular probation. [Nevertheless] Empey did find that both the Provo boys and those on regular probation did better than those in regular reformatories. . . ." (1, p. 39)

(F) From the section on "Psychotherapy in community settings":

1. Two studies (18, 19) of adolescent male offenders:

"There is some indication that individual psychotherapy may "work" in a community setting. Massimo (1963) reported on one such program, using what might be termed a "pragmatic" psychotherapeutic approach, including "insight" therapy and a focus on vocational problems. The program was marked by its small size and by its use of therapists who were personally enthusiastic about the project; Massimo found that there was indeed a decline in recidivism rates. Adamson (1956), on the other hand, found no significant difference produced by another program of individual therapy (though he did note that arrest rates among the experimental boys declined with what he called "intensity of treatment")." (1, p. 40)

Here, in addition to stating that "individual psychotherapy may "work" under specified conditions, Martinson is suggesting the possibility of a direct link between treatment effectiveness and type of therapist, or, at least level of therapist motivation. The factor of "therapist skill" is referred to in more definitive and equally positive terms in his review of the investigations by Truax (above) and Johnson (below).

(G) From the section on "Probation or parole versus prison":

1. A group of studies (20, 21, 22, 23), with adolescent male probationers:

"Quite a large group of studies deals not with probation as compared to other dispositions, but instead with the type of treatment that an offender receives once he is *on* probation or parole. These are the studies that have provided the most encouraging reports on rehabilitative treatment and that have also raised the most serious questions about the nature of the research that has been going on in the corrections field.

Five of these studies have dealt with youthful probationers from 13 to 18 who were assigned to probation officers with small caseloads or provided with other ways of receiving more intensive supervision (Adams, 1966—two reports; Feistman, 1966; Kawaguchi, 1967; Pilnick, 1967). These studies report that, by and large, intensive supervision does work—that the specially treated youngsters do better according to some measure of recidivism. Yet these studies left some important questions unanswered. For instance, was this improved performance a function merely of the number of contacts a youngster had with his probation officer? Did it also depend on the length of time in treatment? Or was it the quality of supervision that was making the difference, rather than the quantity?" (1, p. 42)

Here, Martinson expresses full acceptance of a set of findings to the effect that some forms of intensive supervision do work. The validity of the investigations in question and the significance of Dr. Martinson's acceptance of their findings are not diminished by the fact that some important questions may have remained unanswered as to *why*, not whether, the specific programs had been effective.

2. A study by Johnson (24) of male Youth Authority parolees[1]:

"[Johnson] rated all the supervising agents according to the "adequacy" of the supervision they gave. And he found that an "adequate agent, whether he was working in a small *or* a large caseload, produced a relative improvement in his charges. . . . An *in*adequate agent was more likely to produce youthful "failures" when he was given a *small* caseload to supervise. [Thus the benefits that were observed] may

[1]Within the original article this study appeared in the section titled "'Treatment effects' vs. 'policy effects'"; however, for present purposes it can be reported together with other studies of intensive supervision.

flow not from the intensive supervision itself but from contact with one of the "good people" who are frequently in such short supply." (1, p. 46)

MARTINSON REVISITED

As part of his review, Martinson thus concurred with several findings regarding the beneficial effects of intensive supervision and individual psychotherapy, for at least "some types of offenders." Specified were individuals prejudged to be "middle-risk" on base expectancy, "treatment amenable," and/or "pro-social." Martinson did not characterize such offenders as being rare or in other respects exceptional. In accounting for these positive results he suggested such possible variables as level of therapist skill and, to a lesser extent, nature of the treatment setting.

Later, in his principal summary statement, Martinson specifically acknowledged that a number of programs had produced beneficial effects:

"[Taken together, the studies that were reviewed] give us very little reason to hope that we have in fact found a sure way of reducing recidivism through rehabilitation. This is not to say that we found no instances of success or partial success; it is only to say that these instances have been isolated, producing no clear pattern to indicate the efficacy of any particular method of treatment." (1, p. 49)

His main concern in this statement did not lie with specific programs which, as indicated, had achieved some degree of success. Nor was reference made to the clues which these programs may have provided; e.g., in relation to the goal of matching up certain types of treatment with certain kinds of offenders. Instead, his emphasis was upon the indisputable fact that *no sure way* of reducing recidivism—or, presumably, no fairly sure way—had been found in connection with *any category of treatment* under consideration; e.g., group counseling or milieu therapy. (The fact that the programs in question were not "isolated" exceptions will be discussed later.)

It would be useful to further examine Martinson's rather important summary statement by first considering the issue of "patterns." It will be recalled that one or two patterns—i.e., trends which emerged on the basis of various studies—*had* previously been suggested by Martinson. For example, "These programs seem to work best when they are new, when their subjects are amenable to treatment in the first place, and when the counselors are not only trained people but 'good' people as well." (1, p. 32) Similarly, "There is some indication that individual psychotherapy may 'work' in a community setting."[2] (1, p. 40) As seen in their original context, these trends were portrayed as something meaningful; i.e., of relevance to the field. How might one account for their omission from the summary statement in question? In part, the answer is that Martinson was not especially concerned with the subject of individual variables (e.g., age, offense history, "amenability") in the first place, and with the specific tendencies with which they were associated. Throughout his review, he was much more interested in assessing the efficacy of each given *treatment method as a whole*, on the basis of its relationship to *all* the variables that had been studied, collectively. As indicated below, his focus was on the field of penology at a broad, social-policy level. This level of concern was expressed in the question of whether there existed any treatment methods that could be recommended on an across-the-board basis—i.e., for the offender population as a whole.

As compared with the above omissions, it might seem somewhat harder to account for the inconsistency which is found between the given summary statement (in effect: "no treatment method seems to really work"), on the one hand, and Martinson's earlier, somewhat *optimistic* assessment of intensive supervision, on the other[3]: As quoted before, "These are the studies that have provided the most encouraging reports on rehabilitative treatment. . . . [They suggest that], by and large, intensive supervision does work— that the specially treated youngsters do better according to some measure of recidivism." (1, p. 42) However, it is quite possible to account for these omissions, *and* for the inconsistency as well, by assuming that Martinson's summary statement does in fact reflect a strong emphasis upon the search for treatment methods that might, literally, have turned out to be successful in almost every context that had been examined. When viewed within the framework of such an objective, also a rather exacting standard, the discrepancy entirely disappears and the omissions acquire a plausible explanation. Thus, when judged by this criterion even intensive supervision had failed to make the grade. That is to say, it, too, could understandably be classified as unsuccessful in light of its association with at least *some* negative or inconclusive research findings.

At this point it would be useful to review more specifically the context, and sense, in which this absence of any "sure way" was apparently of major significance to Martinson; the main limitations which are related to this exacting criterion will also be outlined. It will then be possible to highlight a number of crucial issues more effectively.

We may recall that in the introductory section of his article Martinson described his objective as follows:

"The field of penology has produced a voluminous

[2]Martinson may have regarded "some indication" of effectiveness as being quite different, and amounting to far less, than a "clear pattern" of effectiveness. If so, the former information or situation may not have been considered entirely worthy of mention within the context of his major, concluding statement. On the other hand, information which related to "treatment amenability," to "higher quality treatment personnel," etc., *did*, in context, seem to have been characterized by Martinson in a manner that would be consistent with the concept of a "clear pattern." However, this latter information was not reflected in the given summary remarks.

[3]It seems safe to assume that Martinson considered "intensive supervision" to be more or less on a par with other modes of treatment which, while also fairly broad in scope, had nevertheless been presented as distinctive approaches to rehabilitation.

research literature on this subject [of rehabilitation], but until recently there has been no comprehensive review of this literature and no attempt to bring its findings to bear, in a useful way, on the general question of "What works?" My purpose in this essay is to sketch an answer to that question." (1, pp. 22–23)

To achieve this broad-ranging objective, Martinson examined, one by one, approximately twelve distinguishable modes and levels of intervention—e.g., individual counseling, group counseling, milieu therapy, and medical treatment. His systematic review enabled him to establish, beyond any doubt, that *not one* of these rather general approaches had "produced" positive results on every, or nearly every, occasion in which it had been implemented and researched. In fact, almost every method turned out to be associated with some combination of positive results, mixed or partially positive results, inconclusive or ambiguous results, and negative results (i.e., no significant difference between experimentals, E's, and controls, C's). For instance, within the area of individual counseling for male offenders in residence, Martinson reported three instances of positive or partially positive outcome and six instances of no E/C difference; and within the area of group counseling for males and females in residence, he noted four instances of positive outcome and four of no E/C difference. ("Within-area" results which were positive in the case of some studies and inconclusive or negative in others were referred to as "conflicted" or "contradictory.") These, then, were the types of individual findings and apparent, inter-study contradictions that allowed Martinson to answer his original question ("What works?") with a straightforward assertion to the effect that not one method had been found which could be recommended as a *sure* way of reducing recidivism.[4] One by one, each method had failed

to satisfy this exacting standard of success; no one "serum" had even approached being universally applicable. Later we shall see why a strict application of this criterion made it very difficult for "success" to be achieved by any given method.

By keeping in mind the *combined* operation of the above-mentioned features—first, a frame of reference which placed highest value upon "across-the-board-issues," and second, an exacting standard of success—it is possible to account for inconsistencies such as the following:

"These [counseling] programs *seem to work best* when they are new . . . and when the counselors are not only trained people but "good" people as well. Such findings, which would not be much of a surprise to a student of organization or personality, are hardly encouraging for a policy planner. . . . But maybe the reason these counseling programs *don't seem to work* is not that they are ineffective per se, but that the institutional environment outside the program is unwholesome enough to . . . [etc.]." (1, pp. 32–33; emphases added)

(These inconsistent statements were separated by no more than a single sentence, and section heading, in the original article.) In the final sentence of this quote, Martinson had shifted his frame of reference in order to reflect his principal level of concern—namely, issues of an across-the-board nature. As he did this, he applied his stringent standard of success to the treatment modality (counseling) *as a whole*—i.e., he applied it across all offender populations and/or all organizational settings. It was a similar shift in frame of reference which allowed him to express virtually unqualified rejection of given treatment methods in the closing sections of his article, after having presented reasons for at least qualified optimism during his earlier review of those same methods.

Let us turn to Martinson's index of success. Specifically, what condition would have to be met by any given treatment method—e.g.,

---

[4]This situation generally applied at the level of major physical and organizational settings/environments as well—e.g., community-based efforts, incarceration per se, standard probation or parole. It would presumably have applied to various *combinations* of intervention strategies as well; however, the subject of treatment-combinations was never discussed.

group counseling—in order for that method to qualify, even figuratively, as "a sure way" of reducing recidivism? Basically, it would be necessary for all studies of that method, at least those studies which were considered valid, to yield almost exclusively positive results, accompanied perhaps by a scattering of mixed or partly positive results. For example, if, out of ten studies, three or four were associated with negative outcomes, then the findings for *group counseling as a whole* would be considered conflicting or contradictory, even though all remaining studies may have produced clear positive results. Whether or not any specific patterns of success had been observed—e.g., in connection with older adolescent girls (say that every study of this offender group, four in all, yielded positive results)—it would still be the case that the method of group counseling, when viewed as a totality, would have failed to satisfy the criterion in question: Since *group counseling* was not associated with positive results in connection with all or nearly all remaining categories of offenders that had been the focus of other studies— e.g., studies of younger adolescent males—it could not validly be recommended on a really widespread or across-the-board basis. In this sense, or context, it did not "work."

Many of the treatment methods which Martinson reviewed had been researched in relation to a fairly wide range of "background characteristics." Among others, these included early teen-agers and older adolescents, younger and older adults, first/second time offenders and multiple offenders, misdemeanants and felons, males as well as females. As indicated by Martinson in his review of group counseling, "there were also variations in the length of time for which the programs were carried on, the frequency of contact during that time, and the period for which the subjects were followed up." (1, p. 32) Similar variations were common in areas other than group counseling, as well.[5] In

short, each new and different "experimental condition" or "background characteristic" that was added to any total set of studies—e.g., studies of group counseling—further increased the chances of obtaining contradictory results when various studies were compared with one another.[6]

Even if the above conditions and background characteristics were to be held fairly constant across any two or more studies, there would remain at least two major sources of difficulty:

(A) Given two hypothetical group counseling studies, say that study #1 mostly contained offenders of "personality type A" while #2 primarily included those of "type B."[7] If the counseling turned out to work with personality type A but not with B,[8] the studies would of course be classified as contradictory. In effect, the results of study #2 would have detracted from the assessed value of group counseling as a whole, while those of study #1 would in no way have added to it. This type of situation, the product of major variations in "modal personality" of offenders within differing study samples, was almost certain to have been present across many of the studies that were reviewed.

(B) Take two other studies that each deal with essentially the same type of youth, types A, B, and C (and no others), though in somewhat differing proportions. The first, study #3, may have analyzed each type *separately*—reporting, for experimentals as versus their corresponding controls, better performance for A, no difference for B, and worse performance for C. It may also have reported that the experimentals as a whole—i.e., all three groups combined—

---

[5] In addition, studies which had been conducted within highly secure and/or rigidly structured residential settings were sometimes compared with those carried out in partially "open" or generally "looser" residential settings.

[6] In general, the larger the number of individual items or variables that are being compared with one another, the greater is the chance that differences or conflicts will be observed. The same principle would apply with respect to the absolute number of studies or programs that are being compared.

[7] The same considerations could be applied to risk level as well.

[8] In relation to appropriate control groups.

performed somewhat better than the controls; this could happen if type A had comprised the largest single group, numerically. Study #4, on the other and, may never have attempted to make a separate analysis of what might be termed its three "unidentified offender types." Let us assume that if such an analysis had been made, the results would have been the same as those in study #3, for types A, B, and C *individually*. Under the circumstances, however, study #4 may only be able to report that its *total* group of experimentals had performed, say, somewhat *worse* than the controls. This could easily have happened if type *C* had comprised its largest single group. In short, the overall results from study #4 would be negative while those from study #3 would be positive. As before, the results (in combination) would have detracted from the overall value of group counseling even though, in the present case, the basic problem was chiefly a product of the differing proportions of certain offenders with whom group counseling had been *effective*—differentially effective. As noted, both studies may have done relatively well with type *A* offenders, the only individuals with whom the treatment had actually paid off. This type of difficulty was probably not uncommon among the studies that were reviewed; by itself, it could have accounted for numerous "inter-study contradictions."

Taken together, the various factors and conditions that have been described made it very difficult for any one treatment method to avoid being associated with a number of conflicting results. Given these practical and methodological "realities," only an unusually powerful and flexible mode of intervention would have been able to satisfy, even figuratively, Dr. Martinson's criterion of success for methods of treatment as a whole. This situation is of particular relevance in light of the fact that his major summary assessment was itself addressed to the subject of treatment methods *as a whole*. This, in turn, is independent of the fact that his earlier—i.e., original evaluative—statement had given greater, possibly even primary emphasis to each

study *individually:* "With few and isolated exceptions, the rehabilitative efforts that have been reported so far have had no appreciable effect on recidivism." (1, p. 25)

As seen in this statement, and in the summary assessment as well, Martinson had indicated that only a sprinkling of studies had produced favorable results. To verify this we tabulated the results[9] for each of 82 individual studies (90% of all studies) that were mentioned or discussed in "What Works . . .?"[10] The findings, which may be somewhat surprising, are shown in Table I.

Table I indicates that Martinson originally referred to 39 studies—48% of the total—as having yielded positive or partly positive results.[11] In light of this, it was surely amiss to have elsewhere characterized these same studies as being "few and isolated exceptions." This inaccuracy would continue to exist even if his characterization had been in reference to all 231 technically adequate studies which had been located, and not simply those (from among the 231) which were presented in "What Works . . .?"[12]

---

[9]That is, the evaluative statements regarding program impact which were made by, or accepted by, Martinson.

[10]In all, Martinson had described the results of over 90 studies. In our final tabulations, we excluded only those studies which had appeared in the section entitled. "The effects of sentencing." This was because the specific context (when combined with the research design) made it unlikely that anything other than *"partially positive"* results could possibly have been obtained. Results of this type were, in fact, observed in almost all studies reported.

[11]In the case of partially positive results, some 70% of the studies had reported positive impact for (a) one or more specific offender groupings within the total study sample, or, to a much lesser extent, for (b) a given portion of the total sample (e.g., youths who completed the particular program). Among the remaining studies, three had used two different measures of recidivism, and had reported positive results on one; in a different study, positive results were reported on two of the three measures that were used.

[12]All studies which Martinson included had measured "the rates at which offenders return to crime"—in other words, "the effects of rehabilitative treatment on *recidivism . . .*" (1, p. 24; emphasis added). While considered valid from a technical point of view, the 140 studies which Martinson had excluded were apparently lacking in a mea-

Table I. Number of Specified Outcomes for 82 Studies Reported by Martinson

Setting and Sample	Outcome			
	Positive	Partly Positive	Ambiguous	Negative
1. Residential, Juv. boys	1	11	0	12
2. Residential, Adult males	3	3	1	9
3. Residential, All males	4	14	1	21
4. Community, Juv. boys	6	6	1	8
5. Community, Adult males	2	3	1	5
6. Community, All males	8	9	2	13
7. Resid. + Commun., All males	12	23	3	34
8. Resid. + Commun., All females[13]	2	2	0	6

This issue, one which relates to the proportion of *individual studies* that yielded favorable or differentially favorable results, is quite different from that of "inter-study contradictions." It also differs from that which relates to the exacting criterion of success which Martinson used when evaluating each *method of treatment,* viewed as a whole. With respect to individual studies, favorable/partly favorable results were somewhat more likely to be found in the case of community versus residential programs (55% vs. 43%), and among juveniles versus adults (52% vs. 39%).[14] Similarly, a larger number of favorable than unfavorable/ambiguous results were noted in relation to the use of (a) probation rather than prison and (b) small caseloads and intensive supervision. The numbers were about equal in the case of (c) group counseling within residential settings and (d) psychotherapy within the community.

Within some of these latter areas, a generally

comparable proportion of favorable outcomes has been noted by reviewers other than Martinson, particularly in relation to juvenile offenders. The following, e.g., was reported by Adams:

"Speer (1972) examined 21 controlled experimental studies of psychotherapy in corrections and identified 11 studies that included followup data on community performance after treatment. Of the 11 studies, 6 (or 55 percent) indicated a reduction in subsequent arrests and amount of time spent in jail. The most definitive finding was that out of 8 studies of juvenile treatment, 6 showed significant improvement; of the 3 involving adults, none showed significant improvement. . . . Adams (1967) reviewed 22 experimental studies of the effectiveness of reduced probation and parole caseloads in California. Thirteen (59 percent) of these experiments showed either significant reduction in recidivism or a benefit/cost ratio higher than unity." (25)

Judging from all available information, the percentage of favorable outcomes appears to be neither very small nor very large. While Martinson's data have made it clear that success is not to be expected on an across-the-board basis for each of the presently known methods of treatment,[15] they have, at the same time, supported the view that it would not be justified to *abandon* these methods completely; e.g., simply because

sure of recidivism per se. Their evaluation had instead been focused upon educational achievement, personality and attitude change, general adjustment to the outside community, etc.

[13] The breakdown for females was as follows (nearly all studies were of juveniles): *Residential programs:* positive, 2; partly positive, 1; ambiguous, 0; negative, 6. *Community programs:* positive, 0; partly positive, 1; ambiguous, 0; negative, 0.

[14] For males only, the corresponding figures were 53% vs. 45%, and 53% vs. 41%.

[15] This would probably apply irrespective of the earlier-mentioned, practical and methodological difficulties.

of their obvious limitations.[16] Thus, several of the positive and differentially positive results which were reported have given direct support to the view that the use of certain methods— e.g., individual counseling—would in fact be quite *appropriate*, at least under certain conditions. Support of this type usually comes from investigations which have thrown some light on the relationships between level of program effectiveness, on the one hand, and such factors as (1) "type" of offender, (2) type of treatment setting, and (3) type of worker or "change agent," on the other.

We will now briefly expand on these three classes of data, using information which was generally not covered by Martinson. This may further illustrate the fact that a number of promising leads do indeed exist within the field of correctional intervention. It might also suggest that if we are to be serious about increasing our overall rate of progress, research efforts will have to be considerably more sophisticated and differentiated than they have ordinarily been to date.

OFFENDER CHARACTERISTICS

In a review of several reduced caseload programs for juvenile offenders, and of a county work unit program in particular, Schrag made a number of general observations:

"Instead of relying primarily on supervision as a means of control, more attention was focused [in the work unit program] on treatment—casework, group counseling, halfway houses, family assistance, forest camps, and the like—and on the delivery of social services. Again there was a reduction in the amount of time probationers spent in detention or other forms of supervision, along with a considerable increase in the speed and efficiency with which law violations and rule infractions were handled. There was also some indication that certain types of offenders performed best under intensive interaction with their agents, while others were more successful when con-

tacts were minimal. Although this finding is reported in numerous studies, there is yet no clear identification of the relevant characteristics of the offender types." (26)

Glaser has focused more specifically upon various offender characteristics:

"[It appears that] those correctional clientele who can communicate fairly well, who have not previously had predominantly positive reinforcement from delinquent or criminal pursuits, and who have also not had predominantly negative reinforcement from legitimate alternatives to delinquency or crime, will have their recidivism rates reduced by correctional staff that are oriented to developing personal rapport with their clients, and to providing individual counseling and assistance. Such offenders were called the "high maturity" type in a controlled experiment with Navy prisoners by the Grants (1959) at Camp Elliot; they were called "amenable" by Adams (1961) in the PICO—Pilot Intensive Counseling—project; and, they were called "I4 Neurotic" by Warren and Palmer in the Community Treatment Project (CTP). I shall call them the *conflicted* type here: . . .

"[Thus, at CTP], for the youths classified as neurotic the contrast between experimentals and controls stands up for every criterion, especially the most rigorous.[17] The experimentally treated neurotic cases had more completion of Youth Authority supervision without felony convictions and . . . also had fewer new convictions than neurotics in the control group after complete discharge from Youth Authority supervision—after they left the project. Also, those consistently assigned to the prescribed type of staff for the neurotic type were more successful, by all criteria, than those for whom staff turnover prevented consistent assignment of the prescribed staff supervisor. . . .

"In Massachusetts . . . psychotherapy in prison was

---

[16]This is apart from the question of "What might be their substitute"?

[17]The "rigorous" criterion to which Glaser refers is *monthly rate of offending (r.o.o.)*, as derived from Department of Justice rapsheets. This is a measure of actual youthbehavior. All such behavior takes place prior to, and can therefore not be influenced by, the "discretionary decisions" of Youth Authority staff—i.e., decisions to either revoke or not revoke parole, as a consequence of the behavior in question. The use of r.o.o. obviates the legitimate concerns which have been expressed, by Lerman and others, relative to the factor of "differential decision-making."

found to be associated with less recidivism, but only for those penitentiary inmates who participated in the psychotherapy for 25 weeks or longer, had five or fewer prior arrests, or, regardless of prior arrests, were over 33 years old (Carney). Apparently, sufficient contact with a psychotherapist to build up a personal relationship was effective in reducing crime, but only for those inmates least fully committed to crime. . . .

"The SIPU—Special Intensive Parole Unit—experiment with reduced adult parole caseloads finally showed some difference in recidivism between experimentals and controls in its Phase III, but only for parolees in middle Base Expectancy risk categories who were long in small caseloads with the same parole agent (Havel and Sulka, 1962). . . . It seems reasonable to infer that the middle-risk categories are those who are most conflicted between being clearly criminal and clearly legitimate in their orientations, hence most closely approximating the conflicted types in the cited experiments. . . .

"An interesting parallel with the one positive SIPU finding is that an extensive inquiry into the effectiveness of group counseling in California prisons found it associated with somewhat lower parole violation rates only for one category of participant, those in the middle-risk Base Expectancy groups who were long-term participants in counseling groups that had no turnover in staff (Harrison and Meuller, 1964). Apparently it was again only an appreciable personal involvement with staff that diminished recidivism rates somewhat, and then only for the middle-risk cases." (27)

In his account of the earlier-mentioned Marshall program, Knight observed the following:

"Marshall boys of a certain kind were conspicuous for their successful performance both during the program and after release. This differentially successful Marshall group was comprised of the older, apparently more sociable boys (sociability here referring to the tendency to participate in group activities—other than pair behavior—with a minimum of conflict). . . . The in-program failures (transfers) were over-represented not only by boys with more extensive delinquent backgrounds, but also by lone offenders and younger boys. As a group . . . they were more likely than graduates to be alienated from peers, staff, and program." (28)

In a review of differential intervention Warren reported the following:

"A study of Project Outward Bound (survival training in primitive areas) in Massachusetts showed that program to be effective with those delinquents who were "reacting to an adolescent growth crisis" and not to be effective with the more immature, emotionally disturbed, or characterologically deficient boys. . . .

"A number of guided group interaction studies within the California Youth Authority have indicated a more positive impact of the program on those offenders who were comfortable with confrontive interactions. Data collected in the guided group interaction study conducted within the Community Treatment Project supported this finding. . . .

"Less is known about how to bring about change in the Power Oriented group[18] than in other I-level groups. Data on delinquent careers show this group (compared to other subtypes) to have the highest rate of assaultive behavior and felony-type offenses. As a result, incarceration is typically called for." (29)

In view of Martinson's lengthy discussion of, and emphasis upon, California's Community Treatment Project (1, pp. 42–44), it might be useful to clarify a point or two before proceeding. Drawing upon CTP's 7th and 8th Research Reports (1966–67), Martinson noted that (1) "the experimentals' probation [i.e., parole] officers were using a more lenient revocation policy" than the controls', and (2) "experimentals were actually committing more offenses than their controls." While the former statement is indeed a reasonable inference from the data in question, the latter holds up only if one has included, in the overall analysis, offenses which are of a minor nature—more specifically, technical violations, status offenses, and various infractions; e.g., "uncooperative attitude toward program," "missed group meeting," poor home or school adjustment, curfew, truancy and non-injury/non-felony traffic citations. A larger number of these minor offenses had been "credited" to the E's essentially because of (1) the

[18]E.g., habitual manipulators.

closer supervision that existed within the CTP program, (2) the specific CTP program requirements—e.g., attendance at group meetings, and, of course, (3) the correspondingly greater awareness of, and subsequent recording of, the given infractions and violations in CTP field folders and also in the form of official CTP reports to CYA Board Members—the individuals who, alone, had the actual legal authority to either revoke or not revoke any given youth.

These factors notwithstanding, even when minor violations/infractions—i.e., "severity levels 1 and 2"—were eliminated, the monthly rate of arrests was nevertheless found to be *equal* among E's and C's; i.e., equal in connection with all *remaining* offenses (severity levels 3–10). This finding still lent support to Martinson's point regarding differential revocation decisions on the part of the respective staffs. However, the literature survey which formed the substantive base for "What Works . . . ?" unfortunately did not extend beyond 1967. Thus, when one does take into account the entire phase 1 and 2 CTP sample (intake continued to mid-1969) and, accordingly, increases the followup period as well (through 1973)—thereby greatly increasing the earlier sample-size and parole followup period—E's are then found to have committed offenses at a significantly lower rate than their C's:

"Based on CI & I rap sheets [which control for the factors of differential staff awareness and reporting], the arrest rate [for level 3–10 offenses] was found to be .065 among controls and .040 among experimentals, for each month on parole. This 63 percent difference in favor of the intensive, CTP program cannot be explained in terms of "chance." (A similar nonchance difference was found when offenses of minor severity were included.) In practical terms, this would amount to at least 750 fewer arrests per CYA career, for every 1,000 experimentals as vs. 1,000 controls." (32)

The E/C difference in delinquent behavior was even greater in the case of "conflicted" youths. (32, p. 5) These findings held up in relation to *convictions* as well. They also held up at every level of severity, including the most severe (levels 6–10); e.g., assault and battery, first degree burglary, sale of narcotics, ADW, robbery, and rape. Thus, the monthly rates of arrest and conviction were as follows (here, figures are updated through 1974; conviction rates are shown in parentheses):

Monthly Rates of Arrest and Conviction

Levels of Severity	1–10	3–10	6–10
Controls	.095	.076	.028
	(.059)	(.048)	(.017)
Experimentals	.053	.042	.017
	(.036)	(.028)	(.011)

As before, E/C differences were even greater in the case of "conflicted" individuals. (37) (Space limitations preclude further detailing and discussion of this point.) Quite apart from this, it would seem that the differential *revocation* rates to which Martinson referred should no longer be explained simply as a function of differential *policies* or discretionary *decision-making* on the part of CYA staff. Instead, they may now be viewed, at least to a large extent, as an outgrowth of actual E/C differences in relation to rate of arrest and conviction, per se; this applies irrespective of offense-severity, as well. Revocation policies aside, perhaps the most fundamental or significant finding is simply that CTP's experimentals did, in the first place, engage in considerably less *illegal behavior* than the controls.

INTERACTION WITH TREATMENT SETTING

As seen above, research into offender characteristics has provided some meaningful direction. However, this in itself does not make for smooth sailing; in fact, the problem of sorting out "what works" seems to be more complex than might originally have been expected. For one thing, there is considerable evidence of a major interaction between characteristics of offenders, on the one hand, and "optimal type of treatment setting" on the other. Fortunately, there is at least some consistency among the various results. Some of these studies have been recapped by Warren:

"The Borstal studies and Weeks's study of Highfields [both conducted in the 1950's] are examples of research showing a relationship between kind of inmate and kind of correctional setting. Both studies show the main advantage of open institutions over closed institutions to be for the better risk inmates. A study by Reiss suggests that all delinquents with relatively strong personal controls should be assigned to home and community placement; whereas, assignments to short terms in institutions or to community placement contingent on case progress should be made for delinquents with relatively weak personal controls; and assignment to closed institutions should be made for those with marked social deterioration or very immature personalities. . . .

"[Meuller found that] conforming and over-inhibited boys had higher parole success rates when assigned to non-institutional or open institutional programs. Assigning aggressive or insecure delinquents to any program did not lead to greater success. Subjects least like socialized delinquents and most like emotionally disturbed delinquents were more successful on direct parole, almost as successful in and following camp assignment, and more inclined to fail than succeed in and following a training school experience." (30)

In a more recent study of Borstal boys, Sealy and Banks observed that:

"In terms of reconviction rates . . . the difference in success rate between open and closed institutions is greatest for boys of the lowest levels of maturity [l_2 & l_3] and is negligible for boys of higher maturity." (31)

Reporting on phase 3 (1969–74) of California's Community Treatment Project (CTP), Palmer noted the following:

"Status 1 youths [individuals who were pre-judged to be unusually troubled or vulnerable[19]] who were

---

[19]Individuals who were seen as needing an initial period of institutionalization were referred to as "Status 1"; those seen as *not* needing this type of initial setting were termed "Status 2."

inappropriately placed are performing *considerably* worse than those who were appropriately placed; however, in the case of Status 2 youths [individuals seen as not very troubled, etc.] *no substantial differences* are observed between individuals who were inappropriately placed and those who were appropriately placed. . . . [Together with other findings this suggests that] appropriate placement may perhaps help to offset or moderate certain pre-existing differences in level of coping ability, on the part of Status 1 vs. Status 2 youths. On the other hand, *inappropriate* or less-than-optimal placement may be more likely to accentuate or activate various differences which relate to their personal or interpersonal liabilities. (32)

At the close of this experiment the results were the same as those reported above.

MATCHING OF WORKER AND YOUTH

Martinson has suggested that successful workers may simply be unusually talented individuals whose interpersonal skills allow them to "get through to" a very high proportion of the offender population. This is an intriguing possibility; and while evidence to this effect has been reported, it is relatively rare and generally impressionistic. Somewhat independent of this, other data have suggested that *most* change agents (workers) are likely to be successful with only a delimited portion of the offender population, and that it is their specific professional orientation and personality characteristics which help determine the particular kinds of offenders with whom they will be most, and least, successful. This at least seems to be the case with most change agents who are selected to work with offenders on a relatively intensive and/or extensive basis; however, it has been reported in relation to standard-sized caseloads as well. These data suggest that, as with methods of treatment themselves, most change agents are not likely to be either successful or unsuccessful on an across-the-board basis. It seems, instead, as if we are dealing with yet another *interaction,* this one between type of offender and type of change agent. Along these lines, three studies will briefly be mentioned.

In a study of military offenders Grant and Grant observed that:

"The interaction between the maturity level of the subjects and the supervisor characteristics significantly affected later success rate of subjects. Not only were the treatment methods of some supervisory teams (internally oriented) effective in increasing the success rates of some kinds of offenders (high maturity), but they were markedly detrimental to the success chances of other kinds of offenders (low maturity). Furthermore, the externally oriented supervisory team had the reverse effect on high and low maturity subjects, although this particular finding did not reach the .05 level of significance." (33)

In a study of juvenile probationers on standard-sized caseloads, Palmer reported that:

" 'Relationship/Self-expression' officers [change agents] achieved their best results with youths who were Communicative-alert, Impulsive-anxious, or Verbally hostile-defensive; they did less well with those who were Dependent-anxious. 'Surveillance/Self-control' officers had their greatest difficulties with individuals who were Verbally hostile-defensive or Defiant-indifferent; they did considerably better with those who were Dependent-anxious. 'Surveillance/Self-expression' officers seemed uniquely matched with probationers who Wanted to be helped and liked." (34)

The differential effects of matching upon various groups of youth may be seen in relation to phases 1 and 2 of California's Community Treatment Project:

"Among "conflicted" youths, those described as "neurotic, acting-out" (with little felt-anxiety) performed better when assigned to matched parole agents than to all remaining agents, combined; however, this was not the case with individuals described as "neurotic, anxious."[20] Similarly, among "power oriented" youths, those described as "manipulators" performed better with matched agents while those who were called "subcultural conformists" did not. These findings have reference to law enforcement arrests and convictions, i.e., to actual *youth-behavior*, and not to Youth Authority staff decisions in response to that same behavior."[21] (37)

SELECTED TRENDS

These and other studies of offender characteristics, treatment-control setting, and matching have moved us a few steps closer to realistically focusing in on "what works"? In this connection the following are among the trends that have emerged thus far, on the basis of converging evidence:

(1) Various methods of intervention—e.g., individual or group counseling—are more likely to be associated with positive behavioral outcome (i.e., less "recidivism") in relation to some offenders as compared with others. The former, more successful individuals have been described as "higher maturity," "more sociable," "prosocial," "neurotic," "middle risk on base expectancy," and/or (in the case of adolescents) "older as vs. younger." The less successful individuals are briefly described in the paragraph below. (In all probability neither the former nor the latter "set" of offenders represents a *homogeneous* grouping of individuals.) This trend has been observed in relation to institutional and community settings alike. Within the former setting, positive outcome for "middle-risk" or "higher maturity" individuals is associated with offender-staff or offender-offender interactions which seem to be of a relatively "stabilized," "extensive," and possibly "intensive" nature—e.g., less staff turnover and greater total number of contacts. With regard to community settings it is generally associated with smaller-sized caseloads or relatively comprehensive, pragmatically oriented utilization of resources—e.g., "job and residence placement" and "delivery of social services." It has been associated with offender-staff matching as well.

---

[20]"Neurotics"—i.e., Glaser's "conflicted" youths—comprised 53% of the total sample of E + C males.

[21]The present study dealt with male, Youth Authority parolees (multiple-offenders) within two medium-sized urban settings. The efficacy of matching has also been noted with respect to female probationers within a large-sized urban setting, also in California. (36)

(2) Once again using positive behavioral outcome, it is these same "middle risk" offenders, and/or those who have "relatively strong personal controls," who appear to be better suited than remaining *offenders* (see below) when it comes to placement on probation or on parole in lieu of institutionalization. This also applies to their placement within institutional settings that are usually described as "open" or "minimum security." To perhaps a lesser extent, the concept of "better suited" also applies to the placement of middle-risk offenders into open or minimum security *settings* as compared, e.g., to their placement within those which are of a highly secure/long-term nature. The "remaining" offenders, mentioned above, are those who seem to respond more favorably to closed or higher security settings than to open or minimum security settings. These individuals are often described as "lower or middle maturity," "power oriented," "having extensive delinquent backgrounds," "aggressive" (whether as lone offenders or as members of a gang), and/or "younger as vs. older" (among adolescents). They are also the ones who seem less likely to respond positively to earlier-mentioned modes of intervention such as individual counseling, etc.

OVERVIEW AND CONCLUSIONS

Martinson's review strongly suggested that no known methods of treatment contain the "answer" for all offenders. Together with other data, it also indicated that some methods are nevertheless of value to at least *some* offenders. However, this latter suggestion did not appear in his oft-quoted concluding remarks. These remarks were focused on the question of whether any methods of treatment are of value, not for particular types of offenders, but for all or nearly all offenders. In effect, his conclusion was that (1) there are no sure ways of reducing recidivism for offenders as a whole and that (2) in this particular sense our available methods do not "work." Having given this general answer to

his original question, Martinson let the matter rest. He did not return to the level of specific data, a level which had contained several promising leads.

As indicated, Martinson never focused upon the subjects of "differential value" and "*degree* of effectiveness." This was partly a by-product of the particular criterion that he used when assessing the success-claims which existed, implicitly or explicitly, relative to each method of treatment: Martinson evaluated these claims specifically in terms of the presence or absence of substantial differences, or inconsistencies, among the results of the several studies that had been reported for any given method. However, because of the heterogeneous nature of these studies it was probable, from the start, that a certain percent of all results would turn out to be mutually inconsistent, as, in fact, they did. Because the criterion of "inconsistency" was then applied in a fairly rigorous manner, the related concept of "success" barely seemed to admit of degrees. As a result, methods of treatment which had been of value to only *some* offenders were of necessity classified as unsuccessful. This was entirely aside from Martinson's rather inaccurate description of *individual studies,* whose results had been favorable or partially favorable, as being "few and isolated exceptions."

A few closing remarks. Rather than ask "What works—for offenders as a whole?" we must increasingly ask "Which methods work best for *which* types of offenders, and under *what* conditions or in what types of setting?" As shown above, there does exist the start of an answer to this latter, unfortunately more complex question. However, lest we think that a complete answer lies just around the corner, the following "reminder" may not be entirely amiss: The history of science teaches that all-encompassing solutions are seldom to be found and that neither "break-throughs" nor "comprehensive approaches" emerge without careful preparation. As corrections comes to accept its place among the experienced empirical sciences, it will perhaps recognize that it, too, must live with these rather general and sobering facts of life. Despite its understandable pressures and frustrations, corrections will have to cultivate not just imagination but, above all, patience and precision. With this, Martinson would doubtlessly agree.

In view of the long road ahead, it is fortunate that correctional researchers can offer at least some meaningful clues to policy-makers who seek a basis for immediate action and constructive change. Because of this, the shortcomings which have been brought to light by Martinson need not serve as a signal for practitioners and reformers to polarize the "past" and the "present" and to then overlook or uniformly reject whatever has been learned thus far concerning intervention. However, one last caution. Few things are known to stimulate policy-makers *less* than such concepts as "complexity" and "steady scientific progress." This undoubtedly adds to the fact that the search for rapid or glamorous solutions, and for methods that will work with everyone, is sure to die very hard, if at all. Given this reality we might be wise to at least keep in mind that it is precisely this type of search, the search for the impossible, which has ended in so much disillusionment thus far.

REFERENCES

1. Martinson, R. "What works?—questions and answers about prison reform," *The Public Interest*, Spring, 1974, 22–54.

2. Adams, S. "Effectiveness of interview therapy with older Youth Authority wards: An interim evaluation of the PICO Project." Res. Rept. No. 20. California Youth Authority, 1961. (Mimeo)

3. Adams, S. "Assessment of the Psychiatric Treatment Program, Phase 1: Third Interim Report." Res. Rept. No. 21. California Youth Authority, 1961. (Mimeo)

4. Bernsten, K. and Christiansen, K. "A resocialization experiment with short-term offenders," *Scandinav. Stud. in Criminol., I* (1965), 35–54.

5. Persons, R. "Relationship between psychotherapy with institutionalized boys and subsequent community adjustment," *J. of Consult. Psychol., 31*, 2 (1967), 137–141.

6. Persons, R. "Psychological and behavioral change in delinquents following psychotherapy," *J. of Clin. Psychol., 22*, 3 (1966), 337–340.

7. Craft, M., Stephenson, G. and Granger, C. "A controlled trial of authoritarian and self-governing regimes with adolescent psychopaths," *Amer. J. of Orthopsych., 34*, 3 (1964), 543–554.

8. Truax, C., Wargo, D. and Silber, L. "Effects of group psychotherapy with high adequate empathy and nonpossessive warmth upon female institutionalized delinquents," *J. of Abnorm. Psychol., 71*, 4 (1966), 267–274.

9. Shelley, E. and Johnson, W. "Evaluating an organized counseling service for youthful offenders," *J. of Counsel. Psychol., 8*, 4 (1961), 351–354.

10. Levinson, R. and Kitchener, H. "Demonstration Counseling Project." 2 vols. Washington, D.C.: National Training School for Boys, 1962–1964. (Mimeo)

11. California, Department of the Youth Authority. "James Marshall Treatment Program: Progress report." 1967. (Mimeo)

12. Goldberg, L. and Adams, S. "An experimental evaluation of the Lathrop Hall Program." Los Angeles County Probation Department, 1964. (Summarized in: Adams, S. "Development of a program research service in probation," pp. 19–22.)

13. Fox, V. "Michigan's experiment in minimum security penology," *J. of Crim. Law, Criminol. and Police Sci., 41*, 2 (1950), 150–166.

14. McClintock, F. *Attendance Centres*, London. Macmillan, 1961.

15. Garrity, D. "The effects of length of incarceration upon parole adjustment and estimation of optimum sentence: Washington State Correctional Institutions." Unpublished Ph.D. dissertation, Univ. of Washington, 1956.

16. Miner, J., Kelly, F. and Hatch, M. "Outward Bound Inc.: Juvenile Delinquency Demonstration Project. Year end report." Massachusetts Division of Youth Service, 1967.

17. Empey, L. "The Provo Experiment: A brief review." Los Angeles: Youth Studies Center, University of Southern California. 1966. (Mimeo)

18. Massimo, J. and Shore, M. "The effectiveness of a comprehensive vocationally oriented psychotherapeutic program for adolescent delinquent boys," *Amer. J. of Orthopsych., 33,* 4 (1963), 634–642.

19. Adamson, L. and Dunham, H. "Clinical treatment of male delinquents. A case study in effort and result," *Amer. Sociol. Rev., 21,* 3 (1956), 312–320.

20. Adams, S. "Development of a program research service in probation." Res. Rept. No. 27 (Final Report, NIMH Project MH007-18.) Los Angeles County Probation Department, 1966. (Mimeo)

21. Feistman, E. "Comparative analysis of the Willowbrook-Harbor Intensive Services Program, March 1, 1965 through February 28, 1966." Res. Rept. No. 28. Los Angeles County Probation Department, 1966. (Mimeo)

22. Kawaguchi, R. and Siff, L. "An analysis of intensive probation services—phase II." Res. Rept. No. 29. Los Angeles County Probation Department, 1967. (Mimeo)

23. Pilnick, S., et al. "Collegefields: From delinquency to freedom." A Report . . . on Collegefields Group Educational Center. Laboratory for Applied Behavioral Science, Newark State College, 1967. (Mimeo)

24. Johnson, B. "An analysis of predictions of parole performance and of judgments of supervision in the Parole Research Project," Res. Rept. No. 32. California Youth Authority, 1962. (Mimeo)

25. Adams, S. "Evaluative research in corrections: status and prospects." *Fed. Probation, 38,* 1 (1974), 14–21.

26. Schrag, C. "Crime and justice: American style." NIMH Crime and Delinquency Issues, 1971.

27. Glaser, D. "The State of the art of criminal justice evaluation." Keynote speech presented to the Assoc. for Criminal Justice Research (Calif.). Los Angeles, Calif., Nov. 9, 1973. (Mimeo)

28. Knight, D. "The Marshall program: assessment of a short-term institutional treatment program." Sacramento: Dept. of the Youth Authority. Res. Rept. No. 56, 1969. (Mimeo)

29. Warren, M. Q. "Differential intervention with juvenile delinquents." Paper delivered at: Juvenile Justice Standards Conference, American Bar Association. Berkeley, Calif., Oct. 13–15, 1974.

30. Warren, M. Q. "Classification as an aid to efficient management and effective treatment." *J. of Crim. Law, Criminol., and Pol. Sci., 62,* 2 (1971), 239–258.

31. Sealy, A. and Banks, C. "Social maturity, training, experience and recidivism amongst British borstal boys." *Brit. J. Criminol., 11,* 3 (1971), 245–264.

32. Palmer, T. "The Youth Authority's Community Treatment Project." *Fed. Probation, 38,* 1 (1974), 3–14.

33. Grant, J. and Grant, M. Q. "A group dynamics approach to the treatment of nonconformists in the Navy." *Ann. of Amer. Acad. of Political and Soc. Sci., 322,* (1959), 126–135.

34. Palmer, T. "Types of treaters and types of juvenile offenders." *Youth Authority Quart., 18,* (1965), 14–23.

35. Palmer, T. "Reply to Lerman's 'Methodological Note on CT' " California Youth Authority, Community Treatment Project Report Series: 1974, No. 1.

36. Adams, S. and Hopkinson, C. "An evaluation of the Intensive Supervision Caseload Project," Los Angeles County Probation Dept., Res. Rept. No. 12, 1964. (Mimeo)

37. Palmer, T. "Final report of the California Community Treatment Project." Sacramento: Calif. Youth Authority, 1976. (In press)

Noninstitutional Treatment

THIS FINAL SECTION DEALS WITH ATTEMPTS TO WORK WITH CONVICTED CRIMINALS outside prison and with strategies to discourage crime in the community. The use of probation (supervision in the community in lieu of incarceration) and parole (supervision following incarceration) are two of the earliest forms of so-called "community treatment." In spite of its widespread use, especially with juveniles, probation has rarely been adequately evaluated as to its effectiveness. Scarpitti and Stephenson deal with probation effectiveness for young male delinquents compared with a control group and find some evidence of success.

Parole, the subject of the next four items, has come under increasing criticism from many quarters. Whereas a few years ago professionals were asking for better prediction devices and more parole supervisors, serious proposals for the complete elimination of parole are increasingly put forth. In the first selection Dawson presents a realistic portrait of the criteria used by parole boards in their deliberations. Stanley describes with remarkable accuracy what actually happens in a parole hearing in exchanges between parole board members and prisoners. The crucial matter of how the parole decision is made and how this is relayed to the prisoner is also indicated. The question of how to predict behavior on parole was the basis of a major three year study done by Gottfredson and his associates. The selection describes the items of information selected and developed into an experience table and suggests how best to use such tables.

Once released on parole or discharged, the inmate who has been impatiently anticipating release discovers that the transition from an authoritarian, regimented, and cloistered existence to the risks and choices of the free community requires some painful adjustments. This "settling down" is perceptively described by John Irwin with an insider's view.

The Community Treatment Project, first started in Sacramento, California, has become a prototype for community treatment of juveniles. Convicted youths continue to live in their communities but come to the C.T.P. facility for essentially the same range of treatment techniques that they would have been exposed to in an institution, and they are supervised by probation officers with small case loads.

A vast literature exists on measures used in schools, by government and private agencies working with delinquents and gangs, job placement services, volunteers, and other strategies intended to reduce or prevent delinquency in the community. Wright and Dixon review 96 studies of community prevention and treatment, all of which contain sufficient empirical data to be analyzed and judged for validity and policy implications. Generally the studies were found to be "low" in validity and policy utility. There were also methodological problems, including unclear and varying definitions of such basic terms as "prevention," "delinquency," and "treatment." The picture is not unlike the recent careful surveys of rehabilitative measures within correctional institutions considered in the last section: the more rigorous the evaluation, the less likely the particular project or technique being tested will turn out to be successful.

Social workers, police, and behavioral scientists are not the only professionals interested in crime prevention. In response to the very high incidence of crime in public housing projects, Oscar Newman, an architect and planner, has developed the concept of "defensible space." In the selection reprinted here Newman examines two different architectural layouts of two housing projects in New York City, and indicates the architectural features that have resulted in relatively low crime rates in one and high rates in the other. He suggests implications for planners and architects.

Behavior modification, alias *A Clockwork Orange,* is not the only contemporary development in the treatment of criminals with a futuristic—and to some, sinister—aura to it. Current developments in electronics and space technology have produced telemetry, the monitoring of bodily functions. Medical advances now make it possible to implant devices in the brain with such accuracy that through electrical stimulation some kinds of behavior can be inhibited. In the selection by Ingraham and Smith, the authors consider the potential of these technological developments for the monitoring of possible criminal behavior by law enforcement officials; the neutralizing of such behavior by computer-assisted remote control; and some of the ethical objections to such systems in terms of an invasion of privacy and the potential for misuse.

The final item in this volume, by John Conrad, deals with corrections as it is presently practiced and future developments such as the rejection of the rehabilitation model and the increased impact of science on corrections.

72. A Study of Probation Effectiveness

FRANK R. SCARPITTI
RICHARD M. STEPHENSON

OF THE TWENTY-TWO RECOMMENDATIONS MADE by the President's Commission on Law Enforcement and Administration of Justice in the area of corrections, eight call for the expansion of community based treatment programs.[1] Prominent among the Commission's recommendations is a call for the expanded use of probation services for both juvenile and adult offenders. Citing the detrimental effects of institutionalization, especially on the young, the Commission's report concludes that placing an offender on probation allays these effects as well as increases his chances for a successful adjustment.[2] The negative consequences of institutionalization are well documented,[3] and ob-

viously, keeping one out of the reformatory or prison will prevent his experiencing their debilitating effects. However, the effectiveness of probation as a rehabilitating program is not as well documented, and its crime or delinquency reducing impact upon offenders continues to be subject to many sceptical questions.

Conclusions regarding the effectiveness of probation are generally based upon the number of probationers who complete their supervision without revocation or the amount of post-release recidivism occurring among those who complete supervision. It can be seen that these are actually two different measures of success. In the former instance, many unknown and uncontrollable variables may influence the outcome of the probation experience: the philosophy of the probation department in revocation, the intensity of the officer's contacts with the probationer, the unknown offenses committed by the probationer while on probation, and the philosophy of the court in continuing or extending probation for known offenses. Nevertheless, England's review of eleven probation studies indicates that from 60 to 90 per cent succeed on probation.[4] A 1944 study of juvenile

▶SOURCE: *"A Study of Probation Effectiveness," Journal of Criminal Law and Criminology (September, 1968), 59(3): 361–369. Reprinted by permission.*

[1]*The Challenge of Crime in a Free Society*, a Report by the President's Commission on Law Enforcement and Administration of Justice, United States Government Printing Office, Washington, D.C., Chap. 6 (1967).

[2]*Ibid.*, 165–171.

[3]Of the many studies that have attested to the anti-rehabilitation effects of total institutions such as prisons and reformatories, see, for example: Sykes, *The Society of Captives* (1958); Clemmer, *The Prison Community* (1948); Cloward, "Social Control in Prison," Chap. 2, Cloward, et al., *Theoretical Studies in Social Organization of the Prison* (1960); Garrity, "The Prison as a Rehabilitation Agency," Chap. 9, and Glaser and Stratton, "Measuring Inmate Change in Prison," Chap. 10, Cressey, Ed., *The Prison: Studies in Institutional Organization and Change* (1961); Goffman, *Asylums* (1961); Ward and Kassebaum, *Women's Prison* (1965); Street, "The Inmate Group in Custodial and Treatment Settings," 30

Amer. Soc. Rev. 40–45 (1965); Berk, "Organizational Goals and Inmate Organization," 71 *Amer. J. Soc.* 522–534 (1966); and Giallombardo, *Society of Women: A Study of a Women's Prison* (1966).

[4]England, Jr., "What is Responsible for Satisfactory Probation and Post-Probation Outcome?," 47 *J. Crim. L. & C.*, 674 (1957).

probationers showed that 35 per cent failed,[5] and a later study of 11,638 adult probationers revealed that only 29 per cent had their probation revoked.[6]

These success-failure rates are based upon official probation records and of course suffer from the deficiencies listed above. As such, they present a most favorable picture of probation success. Using more stringent, but perhaps unfair and unrealistic criteria of failure, the Gluecks have reported probation failure rates of 57.9 per cent for youthful offenders and 92.4 per cent for adult male offenders.[7]

Perhaps the second method of determining probation effectiveness, recidivism, is a better indicator of the true success or failure of probation as a rehabilitation mechanism. Again, England reports that of the eleven studies reviewed, eight fall within the 70 to 90 per cent range in terms of post-probation success. These include Diana's study of juvenile probationers (84 per cent success), and England's study of adult Federal probationers (82.3 per cent success).[8] In addition, other studies of post-release recidivism among both adult and juvenile offenders show success or non-recidivism rates of 72, 79, 88 and 83 per cent.[9] These rates compare favorably with those reported for in-program success and appear to substantiate the call for increased probation usage.

Nevertheless, the high rates of probation and post-probation success are puzzling to those who are aware of the difficulties of resocialization and rehabilitation. Probation supervision and guidance has traditionally been only superficial, generally involving infrequent and ritualistic contacts between officer and offender.[10] At the same time, few if any special programs of more intensive treatment and worker-client contacts can approximate the probation success rates.[11] Such contradictory evidence causes one to ask questions that have not yet been or have only partially been answered. Are probationers the least likely of the offender population to become recidivists? Are probationers different from other adjudicated offenders? What differentiates the in-program successes from the failures? How does recidivism among ex-probationers compare with that of other offenders who have experienced alternative methods of treatment? This paper will attempt to answer these and other questions pertaining to the effectiveness of probation as a treatment method.

THE PRESENT STUDY

Data presented in this paper were collected as part of a larger comparative study of delinquency treatment facilities. From January, 1962 to January, 1965 some 1210 adjudicated male delinquents between the ages of 16 and 18 from Essex County (Newark), New Jersey were admitted into the study.[12] Of these, 943 were committed to county probationary supervision, 100 to a non-residential guided group interaction center in the county, 67 to residential guided group interaction centers in the state, and 100 were sent to the State Reformatory at Annandale. All boys were followed up for recidivism until June, 1966.

The special admission criteria used by the court in committing boys to the group centers were also used to select participants in this

[5]Reiss, Jr., "Delinquency as the Failure of Personal and Social Control," 16 *Amer. Soc. Rev.* 196–207 (1951).

[6]*The Challenge of Crime in a Free Society, op. cit.,* p. 166.

[7]Glueck, S. and E., *Juvenile Delinquents Grown Up,* 153, (1940) and *Criminal Careers in Retrospect,* 151 (1943).

[8]England, *op. cit., supra* note 4, at pp. 667, 674.

[9]Reported in Sutherland and Cressey, *Principles of Criminology* 497 (7th ed. 1966).

[10]England, *op. cit. supra* note 4; Diana, "Is Casework in Probation Necessary?," 34 *Focus* 1–8 (1955).

[11]See, for example, any or all of the following: Weeks, *Youthful Offenders at Highfields* (1958); *The Community Treatment Project After 5 Years,* California Youth Authority, no date; Empey and Erickson, *The Provo Experiment in Delinquency Rehabilitation,* Annual Progress Report for 1964, unpublished report to the Ford Foundation, 1965; Stephenson and Scarpitti, *The Rehabilitation of Delinquent Boys,* report to the Ford Foundation (mimeographed), 1967.

[12]During this period nearly 15,000 children appeared before the Essex County Juvenile Court. Some 4761 of these youths were boys sixteen or seventeen years of age.

study. Hence, all delinquents in this sample were male, 16 or 17 years of age, had no evidence of psychosis, severe neurosis or serious mental retardation, and had no prior commitment to a correctional institution. Assurance of reasonable comparability among cases, with respect to such differentiating factors as social background, psychological profiles, and delinquency history, presents a major problem in any comparative study. Ideally, it would be desirable to have boys assigned by the court to treatment facilities on a basis that would assure such comparability or, at least, on a random basis. In this study, as in others, this was not possible. However, it was felt that it would be possible to match boys across facilities on pertinent variables so as to control to some extent differences that might be found among the groups.

In order to obtain data upon which to match boys by treatment programs and to see how such data are releated to progress in treatment and recidivism after release, the following information was obtained for each boy: first, social background data consisting of the usual demographic items relating to the boy and his family; second, delinquency history data consisting of the boy's entire court record (this information was up-dated during the post-treatment follow-up period); and third, a psychological profile determined by responses to questions on the Minnesota Multiphasic Personality Inventory.[13] The personality inventory was given whenever possible to each boy after his court

appearance and before entrance into one of the treatment programs. Because of the large number of probationers relative to the other treatment groups, the MMPI was not administered to members of this group after January, 1964. In order to test for change during treatment, the study subjects were again given the inventory at the time of their release.[14]

Hence, it was not only possible to test the impact of the probation experience as measured by program completion, psychological change, and recidivism, but also to compare the results of probation with those of other programs available to the committing judge. The programs used for such comparison can be thought of as more "intense" and confining than probation. The non-residential group center (Essexfields) program included a regimen of work and group interaction for approximately four months while the boys continued to live at home. The Group Centers program entailed the same elements for the same length of time, but boys resided in the Centers. At Annandale, the state reformatory, the program was restricted and irregular, and commitments averaged about nine months.

CHARACTERISTICS OF THE GROUPS

As Table I indicates, the social background characteristics of each group are roughly associated with assignment to their treatment facility. Although the association is not always marked or consistent, Annandale tends to have a greater proportion of boys who are negro, in the lower range of the socio-economic continuum, and more likely to terminate their education before high school graduation. Probationers, on the other hand, are equally divided

[13]Of the several psychological instruments available, the MMPI appeared to be most feasible for this purpose. Resources would not permit an exploration in depth, nor was it possible to design, test, validate and complete an instrument more suitable for this particular study. On the other hand, the MMPI has been widely used, is readily administered, and gives a reasonably broad psychological profile. Moreover, a number of studies have used the MMPI on both delinquent and non-delinquent populations. See: Hathaway and Monachesi, *Analyzing and Predicting Juvenile Delinquency with the MMPI* (1952); *Adolescent Personality and Behavior* (1963); Dahistrom and Welsh, *An MMPI Handbook* (1960); Welsh, *Basic Readings on the MMPI in Psychology and Education* (1956).

[14]Since some of the boys were non-readers or failed to cooperate, it was impossible to test all in both pre- and post-treatment situations. Further attrition of cases was occasioned by changes in institutional personnel administering the tests, in-program failures, and a variety of administrative circumstances. When the inventories were scored and examined for validity, further losses were experienced. In all, there were 491 valid pre-treatment and 325 valid post-treatment MMPI inventories available.

Table I. Percentage Distribution of Social Factors by Treatment Programs

Background Factor	Probation	Essexfields	Group Centers	Annandale
Race:	(N = 943)	(N = 100)	(N = 67)	(N = 100)
White	50	41	55	29
Negro	50	59	45	71
Family Income:	(N = 938)	(N = 100)	(N = 67)	(N = 95)
Welfare	15	18	12	26
Less than $2,000	2	6	3	1
$2,000-4,000	20	19	25	25
$4,001-6,000	28	33	28	24
$6,001-8,000	19	15	21	12
$8,001-10,000	9	4	8	8
$10,000 or more	8	5	3	3
Occupation of Breadwinner:	(N = 737)	(N = 76)	(N = 52)	(N = 67)
Unskilled	21	35	25	33
Semi-skilled	44	41	27	39
Skilled	14	12	19	8
Clerical	12	7	14	8
Owner-Manager	5	3	8	13
Professional & Semi-Professional	4	3	8	—
Education of Breadwinner:	(N = 891)	(N = 99)	(N = 61)	(N = 56)
Grammar school grad. or less	16	15	5	27
Some high school	59	65	66	54
High school grad	19	17	21	11
Some college	3	3	5	7
College graduate	3	—	3	2
Parents' Marital Status:	(N = 943)	(N = 100)	(N = 67)	(N = 100)
Unknown	1	—	—	2
Never married	2	2	2	5
Married	49	47	46	40
Separated	20	22	13	27
Divorced	10	12	13	6
One or both dead	18	17	25	20
Boy Lives With:	(N = 943)	(N = 100)	(N = 67)	(N = 100)
Both parents	49	45	45	39
Parent and step-parent	11	13	15	10
Mother only	30	33	28	31
Father only	4	4	6	3
Relatives, foster home, or institution	6	5	6	17
Boys' School Status:	(N = 943)	(N = 100)	(N = 67)	(N = 100)
In school	48	68	48	28
Expelled	4	2	—	14
Quit	39	20	39	51
Excluded	7	9	13	7
Graduated	2	1	—	—

racially and generally tend to be more positive on the socio-economic, family organization, and education variables. Between the extremes of Annandale and Probation are the other two treatment groups.

In addition, 37 per cent of the Probation group had completed the tenth grade or more compared with 24 per cent in the Group Centers, 18 per cent in Essexfields, and 14 per cent in Annandale. More of the Probation group also had some employment experience prior to their treatment assignment.

A fairly clear pattern of progression with respect to the association between delinquency history and treatment program is also evident. This pattern indicates that the extent of delinquency tends to increase from Probation through Essexfields and Group Centers to Annandale. This progression is most clearly indicated by the number of past court appearances. Nearly half of the Probationers had no prior court appearance, while only seven per cent or less of the other boys fall into this category. Twenty per cent of the boys at Annandale, 15 per cent at Group Centers, 6 per cent at Essexfields, and 3 per cent on Probation had five or more appearances. Only 40 per cent of the Probationers, but over 90 per cent of the boys in the other groups had one or more prior petitions sustained by the court. Forty-one per cent of the Annandale boys had three or more petitions sustained, but only 5 per cent of the Probationers. Eighty per cent of the Probationers but only 19 per cent of the Annandale boys had never been on probation before. As a group, Probationers were older and Annandale boys younger at the time of the first court appearance. Almost two-thirds of the Probationers were 16 or 17 years of age at their first court appearance; less than a third of the boys in any other group were that old. Insofar as previous court history and age of first court appearance are associated with continued delinquency, the Probationers appear to be the best risks and Annandale boys the worst.

When the psychological characteristics of the four groups are examined, rather distinct differences can also be seen.[15] As with many of the social background and delinquency history characteristics, the Probation and Annandale groups are the most different, with the Essexfields and Group Centers groups falling between these two extremes. These results suggest that the Probation boys as a group are somewhat less anti-social, less delinquent (although exhibiting a distinctively delinquent personality pattern), and better emotionally adjusted than the boys in the other groups. They are also less anxious and less hostile, exhibit a slightly better attitude toward themselves, have a better work attitude, and score higher on the social responsibility dimension of the inventory.

From all indications, it would appear that Probation received the less delinquent and better socially and psychologically adjusted juvenile offender. In this sense, it becomes responsible for what might be termed "easier" cases, or boys for whom the probability of success is greater. The relationship between pre-treatment probability of success and actual success can be seen in terms of (1) program completion, (2) change during the program, and (3) post-treatment recidivism.

IN-PROGRAM SUCCESS AND FAILURE

"In-program failure" is used to refer to any boy who was sent back to the court during the course of the treatment program and who was not returned by the court to the same program. It refers to those boys returned to the court for committing a new delinquent offense, being incorrigible or unmanageable while in the program, or, in the case of Essexfields and Group

[15] In addition to the regular fourteen basic clinical and validity scales, fifteen other measures selected from Dahlstrom and Walsh (*op. cit.*) and other sources were used in the analysis of the MMPI's. For a detailed discussion, see Stephenson and Scarpitti, *The Rehabilitation of Delinquent Boys*, report to the Ford Foundation (1967) (mimeographed). The authors gratefully acknowledge the contribution of Dr. Richard Lanyon, Department of Psychology, Rutgers, The State University, in the analysis of these data.

Centers, being socially or emotionally unsuitable for the program. In essence, the in-program failures were those boys upon whom the various rehabilitation programs had the least immediate effect, not even providing them with an opportunity to experience the entire treatment process.

Aside from Annandale, a custodial institution where program completion is not a question, the in-program success and failure rates for the other facilities were strikingly similar. Although the failure rate for Probation, 28 per cent of the committed boys, is higher than that for Essexfields, 23 per cent, and the Group Centers, 27 per cent, these differences are not statistically significant. These rates do indicate, however, that the over-whelming majority of the boys in non-custodial programs complete their treatment experiences without becoming involved in further difficulty. Using only this criterion of success, probation fares no better than some others, and theoretically more meaningful, programs of treatment. In addition, some 219 Probationers appeared in court for a new offense during their probationary period, but were given dispositions of "Probation Extended" or "Probation Continued." Hence, they were not counted as in-program failures.

Examination of pertinent background, delinquency and personality variables shows interesting differences between Probation successes and failures. In Probation, whites have a lower failure rate and a higher success rate than negroes. Failure is also more likely to occur for those boys who were out of school at the time of their admission. The same is true for those boys with a negative educational status score, a composite index which includes present school status, number of grades completed, and number of years retarded in school. The delinquency history score, another composite index consisting of age first known to court, number of delinquent offenses, and types of delinquent offenses, presents further evidence that the less delinquent and less delinquency-prone do better on probation than the more seriously delin-

quent. All of these differences are statistically significant at the .05 level or better. The same relationship, however, is not necessarily found between failures and successes in the other groups. Generally speaking, failures in the other groups are similar to Probation failures, but do not differ as markedly from the successes in their groups.

The MMPI data corroborate these findings. Again, the greatest differences are found between the Probation successes and failures. Nineteen of the 29 scales used in this study differentiate these two groups at the .05 level of significance or better. Among those tests which distinguish between the groups are the psychopathic deviancy, hypomania, schizophrenia, and F (indicating an attempt by the respondent to show himself in a bad light), as well as the delinquency, escapism, and social responsibility scales. As with the other tests which differentiate, the Probation successes score more positively than do the failures. The failures clearly have a more delinquent personality pattern, conforming closely to the classic pattern for delinquents.

All of the scores for the Probation successes indicate that they are not very disturbed and are fairly well adjusted. Probation failures, as indicated, are less so, but are similar to both the failures and successes in Essexfields and Group Centers. In these groups, there are practically no significant differences between program successes and failures as determined by the MMPI tests. Failures in both programs, however, generally score more negatively than do successes on most scales. Although many of the success-failure differences in the Essexfields and Group Centers programs are in the same direction as those found in Probation, they are milder and less able to distinguish between the criterion groups.

These data seem to indicate that the Probation successes are less delinquent and better adjusted than all other boys in this study, successes or failures. In Essexfields and Group Centers the successes and failures are more similar to each other, as well as to the Probation failure group.

CHANGES DURING TREATMENT

The pre- to post-treatment MMPI changes made by boys while on Probation were relatively minimal. Of the basic MMPI scales, the significant changes were an increase on the depression and defensiveness scales, and a decrease on the paranoia and social introversion scales. While this pattern of change is not readily meaningful, it becomes clearer upon examination of the remaining scales. Decreases occurred on the anxiety and neuroticism scales, although these changes tend to be inconsistent with the increase in depression. Other changes were an improvement in attitude toward others, in attitude toward self, in work attitude, in intelligence and in dominance.

These scores suggest that a definite though slight change did take place in the boys during their probationary term. However, the changes were not in the scores characteristic of delinquency (psychopathic deviancy, hypomania, and schizophrenia), but in a variety of other areas. Overall, the boys became a little less anxious, and more outgoing, secure, and intellectually efficient. Also, there was improvement in attitudes toward themselves, others, and work. The slight decrease in paranoia seems to have little meaning, since larger decreases were shown by all other groups.

Changes shown by the Essexfields and Group Centers boys were somewhat more marked than those shown in the Probation sample. Although the changes were not necessarily the type associated with delinquency reduction, they reflected general improvement in attitudes and ego-strength and a reduction of anxiety. Annandale boys, however, did not exhibit any of these positive changes and showed a greater tendency for change in a negative direction. Most noteworthy, perhaps, was an increase in the hostility score over the period of institutional confinement.

These findings indicate that the greatest positive changes, as measured by the MMPI, occurred in the group programs. Changes for the Probation group were slight, but in a positive direction. To account for Probation's more favorable initial group profile, groups within the four programs were matched on clinical scales regarded as predictive of delinquency. The changes for these matched groups were very similar to those of the unmatched groups. We might conclude then that Probation's effect in this respect is slight but positive. It is not as effective as either the non-residential or residential group programs, but much more beneficial than the reformatory experience.

RECIDIVISM

Perhaps the most crucial indicator of probation effectiveness is whether or not boys who complete the program continue to experience difficulty with the law. Objections to the use of recidivism as a criterion of "successful" treatment may be raised on several grounds. Recidivism indicates only one aspect of the effectiveness of a program of rehabilitation. Improvement in work habits, educational orientation, family adjustment, or personality characteristics are not necessarily indicated by the fact that a new offense is or is not committed. In addition, a person may commit numerous infractions of the law without arrest or conviction and still be regarded as a "success." Nevertheless, an avowed goal of corrections is to inhibit a return to crime and delinquency. Short of daily surveillance of individual cases or reliable community sources of informal information concerning them, the available evidence for estimating effectiveness in reaching this goal is the official record of court appearances and dispositions. This evaluation therefore seeks to answer one major question: to what extent do those released from a program of treatment become involved in delinquency or crime as indicated by court action?

Boys who completed treatment and had no court appearances from their date of release to June of 1966 are clearly non-recidivists. Those who had one or more court appearances after release are not so readily disposed of since a court appearance is not sufficient to regard a case as a recidivist. A wide range of alternative dispositions are available to the court that may indicate a minor offense or even none at all. Therefore, the following court dispositions were used as the basis for determining recidivism: fine, jail, probation, Essexfields, Group Centers, reformatory, and prison. A court appearance resulting in any other disposition[16] was regarded as non-recidivism, since the court obviously did not view the case as demanding intensive correctional treatment or punitive action.

Setting aside for the moment the fact that boys in different programs differ in social background and delinquency history, it can be seen from Table II that Annandale boys have

the highest recidivism rate (55 per cent) and Probationers the lowest (15 per cent). Essexfields and Group Centers fall between these extremes, although recidivism is somewhat lower for Group Centers boys (41 per cent) than for Essexfields boys (48 per cent) and terminates earlier than that of any other program. It also is apparent that this general pattern is repeated when recidivism is calculated for each six month post-release period. The differences in rates of recidivism between Probation and each of the other three programs are statistically significant at a level greater than .001.

Among all recidivists, the highest percentage of recidivism was within the first six months, and nearly 75 per cent of the recidivism took place within a year after release. Probation recidivists appear to have the highest rate of recidivism within the first year and decrease strikingly thereafter. Noting the early termination of recidivism among Group Centers boys, the other three programs appear to spread out recidivism over a longer time span.

Since boys in the four programs of treatment were found to differ with respect to social background and delinquency history, an attempt was made to match cases across programs. With the exception of Probation, the total

[16]Court dispositions not regarded as recidivism included dismissal, petition withdrawn, private placement, hospital placement, restitution ordered, counseled, adjustment to be reviewed, referred to parole (no further action taken), probation extended or continued (for Essexfields and Group Centers releasees), probation vacated, bench warrant issued and case pending.

Table II. Number of Recidivists, Cumulative Recidivists and Cumulative Per Cent of Releases Who Are Recidivists by Six Month Periods

Months	Probation (N = 671)			Essexfields (N = 77)			Group Centers (N = 49)			Annandale (N = 97)		
	#R	CR	C%	#R	CR	C%	#R	CR	C%	#R	CR	C%
6	50	50	7	12	12	16	8	8	16	20	20	21
12	37	87	13	9	21	27	5	13	27	16	36	38
18	9	96	14	8	29	38	5	18	37	9	45	46
24	5	101	15	6	35	45	2	20	41	6	51	53
30	1	102	15	1	36	47	—	—	—	1	52	54
36	—	—	—	1	37	48	—	—	—	1	53	55

N—Number of releasees (completed treatment).
#R—Number of recidivists.
CR—Cumulative recidivists.
C%—Cumulative percentage of releases.

number of boys in each program was relatively small. This meant that to match on more than two or three variables was not feasible. At the same time it was desirable to include as many of the relevant factors as possible. One way to handle this problem was to combine several related variables into one index. Three factors were selected for matching purposes: socioeconomic status (index comprised of family income, education and occupation of family breadwinner), delinquency history (index described earlier), and race.

It was possible to match only 44 boys across all four programs on the three matching factors. After elimination of in-program failures, the following rates of recidivism were observed: Probation (N = 34), 21 per cent; Essexfields (N = 35), 49 per cent; Group Centers (N = 31), 45 per cent; and Annandale (N = 41), 56 per cent. The differences in rates between Probation and each of the other three programs are statistically significant at a level greater than .01. Probationers were then matched separately with Essexfields boys since these two programs were most similar. Ninety-nine boys were matched in each group and, after eliminating the in-program failures, recidivism rates of 19 per cent for Probation (N = 69) and 48 per cent for Essexfields (N = 76) were found. As these results from matched groups indicate, the relative proportion of recidivists for each program does not change greatly even when seemingly significant variables are controlled.

It appears that Probation is highly successful as a treatment device when compared with alternative methods of dealing with delinquent boys. Probationers who complete their treatment have lower rates of recidivism than those who complete other types of programs, even when matched on background and delinquency factors. A great difference can be observed, however, between the recidivism rates of Probationers who complete and those who fail to complete the program. This is a significant consideration because recidivism rates of in-program failures may bear upon the finding

concerning recidivism among boys who successfully completed treatment.

The data suggest that boys who fail during treatment and are reassigned to another program are poor risks for rehabilitation. Although this is true for all programs in which in-program failure was possible, it is especially true for Probation. Not only do Probation failures have a much higher rate of recidivism than failures in other programs, but they also have a significantly higher (p > .001) rate than those who complete treatment. When program successes and failures are combined, that is, all boys originally assigned to Probation by the court, the recidivism rate for Probation more than doubles, although it still remains lower than that of the other programs.

DISCUSSION

This paper has presented data on the effectiveness of probation as a treatment program for 16 and 17 year old delinquent boys. Boys assigned to probationary supervision were compared with delinquents committed to group treatment programs and to the state reformatory. Pertinent data were collected for each group at the time of program assignment, during the programs, and after release from treatment.

As a group, boys assigned to Probation appear to be "better" or "easier" cases than those assigned to other treatment facilities. They appear to come from more stable family backgrounds, are less deprived, and have a more positive educational history. Their delinquency careers are shorter and involve fewer past offenses and official court actions. The MMPI scores suggest that Probation boys are less delinquent, less anti-social and better adjusted than boys in the other groups. Of the more than 1200 delinquent boys selected for this study, it is clearly evident that the best "risks" were assigned to Probation. As others have indicated,[17] the bulk of Probationers are

[17]Diana, op. cit. supra note 10; and England, op. cit. supra note 4.

not seriously delinquent and probably not in need of intensive rehabilitative efforts.

Once assigned to Probation, some 72 per cent of the group completes the program and are successfully discharged. This is comparable to the percentage completing the group programs. More significantly, however, are the differences observed between the Probation successes and failures. On practically every count, the in-program failures are worse off than the successes. These differences are not seen between successes and failures in the other programs. Probation failures conform more to the profiles of all boys in the other groups than they do to the successes in Probation. Hence, it would appear that Probation rids itself during the course of treatment of those boys who are most delinquent and hardest to resocialize.

For those who complete probation, little change is reflected on the psychological and attitudinal dimensions of the MMPI. This is not surprising since the pre-tests did not indicate gross abnormalities among these youths and since the most disturbed, who had the greatest margin for improvement, were eliminated as in-program failures. It seems significant then that even modest positive changes were found in attitude, ego-strength and anxiety. Although not as great as the changes made by boys in the group-oriented programs, they are certainly more favorable than those of the reformatory group.

In the last analysis, the crucial test of program effectiveness is recidivism, despite its many short-comings. Again, boys assigned to Probation do much better in staying out of legal difficulty after release than their counterparts in other treatment programs. The Probation recidivism rate of 15 per cent is substantially below that of other programs. Although this low rate may result from Probationers' having the most favorable social backgrounds and delinquency histories, when boys were matched across programs, the relative rates of recidivism remained substantially unchanged.

The low rate of recidivism of the Probationers who complete treatment may partially be accounted for by the high rate of recidivism of in-program failures, on the grounds that Probation rids itself of high recidivism risks. By returning high risk boys to the court for further disposition, Probation may increase its chances of non-recidivism among boys who complete treatment. This is possible to a much lesser extent at Essexfields and Group Centers, and practically impossible at Annandale. This possibility must be considered as a strong conditioning factor in assessing the very low 15 per cent recidivism among Probationers who completed treatment.

On the basis of the criteria used in this study, Probation does appear to be an effective treatment agent, at least for certain types of boys. Those who are less delinquent and come from fairly stable backgrounds complete their treatment program and remain free of delinquency involvement. More severe cases, similar to those assigned to intensive or punitive programs, do not do as well on Probation.

These findings lead us to a note of caution. It would appear that the good performance of probation is often misunderstood and thought to mean that all offenders can benefit from being placed under probationary supervision. This is clearly not the case. If probation is extended greatly, failure and recidivism rates will grow markedly, unless, of course, there is some monumental change in treatment techniques. barring such change, a backlash effect is possible, with the public's reacting against probation, which they will assume to be ineffectual, and demanding more incarceration. The use of probation should be expanded, but its direction must be carefully guided and those assigned to it must be chosen with rigor.

73. The Decision to Grant Parole

ROBERT O. DAWSON

PAROLE CRITERIA IN PRACTICE

IN PRACTICE, THE PAROLE DECISION IS BASED UPON numerous considerations, only some of which are reflected in the statutes which provide the legal criteria for the decision. It is useful to group these considerations into three categories, although, admittedly, this introduces an element of artificiality into the analysis. In one category are the factors which a parole board considers for the purpose of determining the probability of recidivism by the inmate if released on parole. A parole board is vitally concerned with the probability of recidivism. That is viewed as the index of the extent to which the inmate has been rehabilitated; it is also some measure of the risk to society which his release would entail.

Recidivism probability is by no means the sole concern of a parole board. A second category of factors consists of those which, in the view of a parole board, justify granting parole despite serious reservations about whether the inmate will recidivate. Indeed, in some instances, a parole board may believe an inmate is very likely to commit a criminal offense if released but, for other reasons, may feel compelled to grant parole. A third category, the converse of the second, consists of those factors which, in the view of a parole board, justify a parole denial despite its own judgment that if released the inmate would be very unlikely to recidivate.

A. The Probability of Recidivism as a Consideration in the Parole Decision

A basic consideration in the decision to grant or deny parole is the probability that the inmate will violate the criminal law if he is released. If for no other reason, parole boards are concerned with the probability of recidivism because of the public criticism which often accrues to them when a person they have released violates his parole, especially by committing a serious offense.[1] But they also regard the parole decision as an integral part of the rehabilitation process and consider the probability of recidivism to be an index of the extent to which the inmate is rehabilitated.

Parole boards do not use a fixed or uniform standard of recidivism probability to determine whether an inmate should be paroled. A parole board may demand a low probability of recidivism in some cases while it may be satisfied with a mery high probability in others.

It is clear from the field study* that in no case does a parole board require anything approaching a certainty of non-recidivism. Considering

---

[1] A parole board is likely to think of the probability of recidivism in terms of the probability of parole success. A parolee who completes his parole period without revocation of his parole is a success; one who has his parole revoked—in most cases for conviction of or commission of a new offense—is a failure.

*[Ed: parole decisions in Kansas, Michigan and Wisconsin].

▶SOURCE: *"The Decision to Grant or Deny Parole: A Study of Parole Criteria in Law and Practice," Washington University Law Quarterly. Volume 1966, Pp. 248–285 (June, 1966). Reprinted by permission.*

the nature of the judgment involved, that would be an unreasonably high standard. It is also clear that in all cases the parole board requires at least some evidence that the inmate may make his parole; it is difficult to imagine a parole following a statement by an inmate that he will immediately commit a new offense, no matter how minor. The standard varies, then, from great doubt as to parole success to great confidence that the inmate will make it through his parole period and beyond without a mishap.

The standard varies depending upon a number of factors. It varies according to the seriousness of the offense which the parole board anticipates the inmate will commit if he violates his parole. If a parole board believes an inmate has assaultive tendencies and that if he violates parole he will do so by committing a physical assault, perhaps homicide, it will demand a great deal of proof that he will not recidivate before it releases him. If an inmate has limited his offenses to forgery, however, and it seems unlikely he will do anything more serious than violate parole by becoming drunk and forging a check, the board may use a considerably lower standard of likelihood of parole success. There are a number of other factors which raise or lower the standard.

While the probability of success required varies from case to case, the factors to which the board looks to determine the probability remain relatively constant. Obviously not all of them are present in every case. A number recur with sufficient frequency to permit isolation and discussion.

1. Psychological Change

Illustration No. 1: The inmate, age twenty-three, had originally received a two to five-year sentence for auto theft. He was paroled and was returned to the institution within four months for parole violation. About three months after his return, he and two other inmates escaped from within the walls. He was apprehended quickly and was given a three to six-year sentence for the escape. Two and one-half years after the escape he was given a parole hearing. Despite his escape record, he was recommended for parole by the institution screening committee. The

psychologist's report showed that he received frequent counseling and had apparently benefited from it. A parole board member asked him the usual questions concerning any altered viewpoint on his part or any change that had taken place within himself. The inmate was able to explain that he had begun to understand himself better after many talks with the psychologist and felt that his past behavior would not be repeated since he now understood how senseless it had been. The psychologist's report indicated the inmate had actually gained much insight into his motivation. The board unanimously decided to grant parole.

The indication of parole success most frequently searched for at parole hearings in Michigan and Wisconsin is evidence of a change in the inmate's attitudes toward himself and his offense. This is commonly referred to as an inmate's gaining "insight" into the problem which caused his incarceration. This criterion is based on the assumption the offense was the result of a personal problem, and unless some gains are made in solving that problem the likelihood of recidivism is high. Rehabilitation, then, becomes a matter of changing the problem aspects of the inmate's personality.[2] There are some cases in which the parole board apparently feels the offense was truly situational—that is, the result of a peculiar combination of circumstances external to the inmate which are unlikely to recur.[3] These are rare, however, and it is an unusual case in which a parole board becomes convinced of reformation without some basic personality change. Paroles are often granted without evidence of psychological change, but it is clear the parole board considers it the best indication of successful adjustment on parole.[4]

[2] Probably the most dramatic examples of psychological change occur in the plastic surgery cases. In one case in Michigan, the parole board gave as the major reason for the parole of a long-time recidivist the fact that plastic surgery on his disfigured nose gave him an entirely different attitude toward life. For a description of the plastic surgery program at the Connecticut State Prison at Somers see National Council on Crime and Delinquency News, Jan.–Feb. 1965, p. 3.

[3] See pp. 264–65 *infra*.

[4] The emphasis placed by parole boards on psychological

In Kansas, evidence of psychological change is usually not a factor in the parole decision. This is not necessarily because the parole board considers it to be irrelevant. Rather, it seems to be based on the fact that at the time of the field survey the parole board had very little social and psychological data on parole applicants. There were also no programs in the institutions for aiding in changing attitudes, and the time spent in parole hearings was inadequate to permit questioning beyond cursory inquiry into disciplinary infractions and the parole plan.

The factor of psychological change is frequently expressed in terms of when the inmate has reached his peak in psychological development. The problem of parole selection becomes one of retaining the inmate until he has reached his peak and then releasing him; incarceration after this point is regarded as detrimental to adjustment on parole.[5] Often the institutional summary and recommendation, prepared specially for the parole board, will indicate that further incarceration will not help the inmate— that the institution has done as much for him as it can. Conversely, when an inmate is receiving counseling or therapy and it is reported that he has made some gains in insight but more can be done, the parole board is likely to take the position that the inmate has not reached his peak and will deny parole to permit further treatment. Alcoholics and narcotic addicts seem unique in that the parole board apparently takes the position that the longer the incarceration the better the chances of rehabilitation. These inmates will sometimes be denied parole at the initial hearing for this reason despite other favorable factors.

Parole board members recognize that it is often very difficult to apply the criterion of psychological change. A member of the Michigan parole board stated: "A parole board's most difficult task is to determine if any worthwhile change has taken place in an individual in order that he might take his place in society." In Michigan, the parole board frequently questions the inmate about his offense in order to determine whether he freely admits his guilt and has feelings of remorse for his conduct. These are regarded as favorable signs that an inmate has taken full responsibility for his offense and has begun the process of rehabilitation. Denial of guilt or lack of remorse does not preclude parole, because criteria other than probable success are considered, but it is an extremely unfavorable factor.

The difficulty which parole board members experience in attempting to determine whether there has been a change in the inmate's attitudes finds expression in a universal fear of being "conned."[6] The parole board shows considerable concern about the inmate who is too glib, who seems to have everything down pat and is so smooth that every detail of his story fits neatly into place. The board members resent inmates who seem to be trying to "con" them or to "take them in." One parole board member in Michigan showed considerable concern in particular over the difficulty which "psychopaths" cause a parole board which looks for signs of psychological change in inmates:

"I believe the psychopath is especially adept at similating rehabilitation and reformation and gives parole boards as much trouble as he does psychiatrists. I believe that they can be characterized only through a careful case history of their actions and that any standard description of them lacks a sharp focus unless it relates to their past behavior extended over many years."

change creates problems when dealing with mentally defective inmates because of the extreme difficulty of effecting change with present prison resources.

[5] Often when the parole board releases an inmate who has served a long sentence, it will refer to psychological change in the inmate in terms of maturation. Some parole board members have remarked that for certain types of offenders the only hope of rehabilitation lies in the slow processes of maturation.

[6] This fear prevailed even among members of the Kansas parole board, which puts little emphasis upon psychological change in making its decisions. In one case, the inmate seemed to the parole board to be too glib, so it quickly dismissed him and denied parole on the ground he was a "con man."

Board members especially suspect simulation in the claims of inmates who report remarkable insight and gains from therapy. For this reason, they frequently question such an inmate on whether he found it difficult at first to talk about his problems in therapy. They are much more favorably disposed toward the inmate who found insight hard to gain at first, rather than one who claims he found it easy to understand himself and to profit quickly from counseling or psychotherapy.

Illustration No. 2: The screening committee of the institution recommended granting parole in this case. The inmate had received intensive psychotherapy, four months in group therapy and ten months individual therapy. The committee felt it should concur with the psychiatrist who recommended parole because of the progress made in therapy. The parole board granted parole.

Difficulty discovering whether an inmate has made progress in understanding himself accounts in large part for the great reliance which parole board members place on the recommendations of the counselors and psychiatrists who treat inmates. The Michigan parole board pays close attention to psychological and psychiatric reports, when available. Because of personnel shortages, many inmates are not diagnosed or treated by psychologists, psychiatrists, or social workers. However, examinations are made on repeated offenders, those with case histories involving assaultive criminal acts, and those who exhibit some apparent psychological disturbance. The parole board very often follows the recommendation of the counselors or psychiatrists treating the inmate. In Wisconsin, both the institutional committees, which make recommendations to the parole board, and the parole board place considerable emphasis upon the recommendations of psychiatrists who have observed or treated particular inmates. If an inmate received therapy and the prognosis is hopeful, it weighs heavily in favor of parole, although this fact alone may not be sufficient reason to persuade the board to grant it. How-

ever, if an inmate makes no effort to obtain therapy, or worse, refuses it, he is almost certain to be denied parole unless other very important positive factors are present. A negative recommendation from a psychiatrist treating an inmate almost invariably results in denial of parole.[7]

2. *Participation in Institutional Programs*

Illustration No. 3: The inmate, sentenced for forgery, had been a valuable asset to the institution because he was an experienced electrician. The institutional recommendation was for parole denial, characterizing him as a "chronic offender." The social services supervisor noted that no one had observed any change in him and he had not requested psychotherapy. When he was called into the parole hearing room, the first question was whether he had a job plan if released. The prisoner indicated that he wanted to look for work as a refrigeration mechanic. A parole board member then noted the inmate's drinking problem and its possible effect in the future. The prisoner indicated he felt he could make it. The parole board member then asked the inmate if he had done anything about his alcohol problem while confined. The inmate indicated he could not do anything about it because he was working seven days a week in the institution. The parole board member asked which was more important, working at the institution or seeking psychiatric help concerning the very problem that would bring him back to the institution. He told him if he really wanted psychotherapy he could have received it despite the seven-day work schedule at the institution. The inmate was asked what in his present situation had changed that would make him a good parole risk. To this the prisoner replied that he would have to make it or give up. He claimed that if he works steadily he has no problems, and that as long as he has work on the outside he feels he can adjust on parole. A parole board member then noted to him that working was not the problem because he always had a good work record and was considered a very skilled person. He was told that this type of case was the most difficult to

---

[7]In one Wisconsin case, the screening committee recommendation was as follows: "Paranoid psychosis. Thinks wife maneuvered him into murdering her. Psychiatrist reports too dangerous for release. Deny." The parole board quickly denied parole on the basis of the psychiatric recommendation.

decide, principally because of the alcohol problem involved. After the hearing, the board unanimously denied parole.

In many institutions there are a number of programs and activities designed to assist the inmate in changing his attitudes and eliminating the problems thought to be causative of his criminal conduct. Examples of these are group and individual therapy, alcoholics anonymous, self improvement (Dale Carnegie) courses, academic education and vocational training, and opportunity for religious training and worship. One of the indications of probable parole success used by the board is the extent to which the inmate has availed himself of these programs. This is viewed as indicating that the inmate is making a serious attempt to rehabilitate himself. The inmate who participates in these programs is regarded as a better risk even if no noticeable personality change is effected than is the inmate who is just "serving his time" with no genuine effort at change.

If an inmate appears before the parole board with a problem which might be alleviated by participation in any of these programs, he may be urged to participate if parole is denied. He may in fact be told that in his case, participation is the surest way to be paroled.[8]

One of the difficult problems in applying this criterion is the availability of institutional programs,[9] particularly psychotherapy. This is a

problem of particular concern to the Michigan parole board because at the state prison the average caseload per counselor is 325. One parole board member stated:

"What good does it do to select a good risk for a parole camp, thinking that fresh air and sunshine will automatically rehabilitate him, and not provide him with anyone to discuss his personal problems with over a period of three or four years? I have asked dozens of inmates if they have ever had an opportunity to discuss personal problems with anyone during a period of many years' imprisonment and most of them have said that they have not. I believe that psychological treatment, counseling, and guidance must begin with the inmate's entrance into an institution and should be a continuing process leading up to parole. I do not believe that custodial care alone ever led to any spontaneous rehabilitation of an inmate."

Concern over lack of adequate personnel for bringing about change in imprisoned offenders is illustrated by the statement of another board member: "It would almost be better not to have any counseling or psychotherapy available than to have a negligible amount and claim we have sufficient to cause any change for the better in an inmate."

The availability of programs in an important factor in the weight given to participation or failure to participate in programs. At the time of the field survey, Kansas had virtually no counseling or similar programs in its adult penal institutions. As a result, the parole board was unable to use this factor in its decisions. In Wisconsin's new medium security institution, however, many programs are available. At that institution, the parole board gives even more attention to participation in programs than it does at other Wisconsin institutions.

There is evidence that in some cases in which parole is denied, the parole board may be concerned about the effects on the other inmates of a parole grant to one who has not availed himself of any of the institutional programs. One

---

[8]Prison personnel may also foster the notion that participation in institutional programs is important for parole, as the following statement concerning prison academic and vocational education indicates: "Other kinds of corruption in prison schooling are stimulated by the fact that most correctional systems, appropriately, let their inmates know that participation in prison school will be rewarded. The main reward, an uncertain one, is that schooling may impress the parole board favorably. Although the validity of this belief varies, it usually is cultivated assiduously by prison staff." Glaser, "The Effectiveness of Correctional Education," *American J. Correction*, March–April 1966, p. 4, 8.

[9]A Michigan parole board member criticized the institutions for not taking advantage of awakening religious interests in inmates who have shown a desire for religious counseling and instruction. He said this is partially due to the

"determinist" training of those on the institutional staffs with training in the social sciences.

parole board member in Wisconsin said that if an inmate appeared for parole and all prognosticating factors were in his favor for adjustment under supervision, and even if he, the parole board member, thought the individual would successfully complete parole, he still would vote to deny parole if the inmate had made no effort at all to change himself by participation in institutional programs. Thus conceived, the parole decision becomes a means of encouraging participation in the institution's programs, much as it may be used to encourage compliance with the institution's rules of discipline.

3. Institutional Adjustment

Illustration No. 4: The inmate had received concurrent sentences totaling three to fifteen years for assault with intent to rob, assault and armed robbery, and larceny. He had served four years at the time of the hearing. Parole had been denied at two previous hearings. The inmate had maintained he was innocent. Institutional reports characterized him as a guardhouse lawyer who was always critical of other inmates, had a quick temper, and was difficult to get along with. His adjustment in his work assignment in the laundry was satisfactory, although he was always finding fault with the institution. The institutional committee recommended denial of parole because of the inmate's hostility to authority. At the hearing, the inmate still asserted his innocence. In denying parole, the board listed the following reasons: "resents institutional authority, jail house lawyer, denies offense, has a bad temper, has a generally poor institutional adjustment."

One factor in the parole decision is the way in which the inmate has adjusted to the daily life of the institution. In Michigan and Wisconsin, records of conformity to institutional disciplinary rules, of work progress and adjustment, and of other contacts by institutional personnel bearing on adjustment are contained in the case file. In Kansas, information on the inmate's institutional adjustment is limited to a record of disciplinary infractions. The parole board in each of the states apparently regards the inmate's ability to conform to the institution's rules and to get along with other inmates, custodial personnel,

and supervisors as some indication of his probable adjustment under parole supervision. Most inmates appearing for parole have a record of fairly good institutional adjustment. The fact that for many of them parole is denied indicates that good adjustment itself is not sufficient for a parole grant. It is likely that good adjustment is a minimum requirement for parole, one which must be met in order to qualify an inmate for favorable parole consideration but which is itself not sufficient for a favorable decision. In Kansas, where parole information is scanty, the fact that the board has a record of disciplinary infractions probably gives the factor of institutional adjustment greater weight than in the other two states. Also, both members of the Kansas parole board were former wardens, persons who would be expected to give more weight to institutional adjustment.

In all three states, poor adjustment can be a negative factor in the parole decision, sufficient in itself for a parole denial. For example, if an inmate with a record of assaultive behavior continues this pattern within the institution, it is regarded as evidence that there has been no personality change. It is often difficult to determine whether the board is interested in the inmate's disciplinary record as an indication of his probable adjustment on parole or whether it is concerned about the effect which parole of an inmate with a bad institutional record would have on the efforts of the institutional administrator to maintain discipline. In many cases it seems likely that the board is interested in both.

4. Criminal Record

Illustration No. 5: The inmate was a fifty-three year old man serving two concurrent terms of three to five years for forging and uttering. He was an eleventh offender. He had served almost two years of the present sentence and was appearing for his first parole hearing. He had made a good institutional adjustment, but the screening committee of the institution recommended a denial of parole because of his criminal record. His record began in 1927 and involved convictions and prison sentences for abduction, rape, larceny, and forgery. The interview did not last longer than two or three minutes, only long enough for the inmate to smoke a cigarette. He was asked if he had a final comment to make and, after he left the hearing room, the board briefly discussed his prospects if released. No parole plan had been developed. The board members unanimously denied parole without further discussion.

Most inmates appearing for parole hearing have had at least one criminal conviction prior to the one for which they were sentenced. The extent and nature of the criminal record is a factor of considerable importance in the parole decision.[10] The inmate's criminal record is regarded as evidence of his potentiality for "going straight" if released on parole. Other factors being equal, it will take more evidence of change in attitude to convince the parole board that an inmate with a long record has reformed than one without.

Statutes in some states exclude the possibility of parole or greatly postpone the parole eligibility of inmates with prior convictions.[11] A Kansas statute provided that inmates who have served two prior terms in a penitentiary are ineligible for parole.[12] Even in a jurisdiction with liberal parole eligibility laws, an extensive prior criminal record may result in a routine denial of parole at the first hearing.[13] In the illustration case, the inmate received his first parole hearing

[10]In a study of parole criteria used by the Wisconsin parole board, the inmate's prior criminal and juvenile record was the factor mentioned by the board most frequently as a strong reason for denial of parole. Hendrickson and Schultz, A Study of the Criteria Influencing the Decision to Grant or Deny Parole to Adult Offenders in Wisconsin Correctional Institutions 36–37, 1964 (unpublished thesis in University of Wisconsin School of Social Work).

[11]For a collection of these statutes see Model Penal Code § 305.10, comment (Tent. Draft No. 5, 1956).

[12]Kan. Laws 1903, ch. 375, § 9, repealed by Kan. Laws 1957, ch. 331, § 37.

[13]The supervisor of the Social Service Department at the Wisconsin State Reformatory and a member of the Wisconsin parole board agreed that although all inmates are given their initial parole hearings after serving nine months at the Reformatory, offenders with a long criminal record will not be released at the initial hearing unless there is a remarkable improvement in attitude.

under Wisconsin law[14] after two years. Although there would normally be a strong expectation that a forger would be released at the end of two years in Wisconsin, parole was routinely denied because of the long criminal record. It could theoretically be asserted that routine parole denials because of prior record would be less likely to occur in a jurisdiction, like Michigan, where parole eligibility depends upon a judicially set minimum sentence, because the trial judge could be expected to increase the minimum as a result of the prior criminal conduct. The Michigan parole board has frequently complained, however, that inmates sentenced from Detroit with long records are often given minimum sentences which are so short that they compel routine denial at the first hearing. This can be explained largely by the necessity for keeping minimum sentences low in Detroit in order not to interfere with guilty plea bargaining.[15]

Although routine denials at the initial hearing because of prior record are common in Michigan, the parole board has consciously refrained from using a rule of thumb excluding parole consideration for serious recidivists. One member of the board said that he does not believe in any rule of thumb such as four-time losers cannot be rehabilitated, but believes that the process of maturation comes late with many persons and that rehabilitation can take place within the personality of a multiple offender as well as a first offender.

In many cases it seems clear the board is more concerned with whether an inmate has had prior penitentiary experience than with the criminal record itself. Indeed, an inmate with

[14]Wis. Stat. Ann. § 57.06 (Supp. 1965).

[15]The pressures to reward a guilty plea with leniency in sentencing appear to be greatest in the urban areas, apparently because that is where the problems of court congestion are most severe. It would be expected, therefore, that one would find shorter sentences from the urban areas of a state than from the rural. This expectation seems substantiated in all three states, although no systematic exploration of this thesis was made.

only a juvenile record, an adult arrest record, or adult conviction resulting only in probation will be regarded by the institution and the parole board as a "first" offender. Parole may be granted rather early despite prior failure under community supervision on the theory that the inmate's first adult institutional experience may have had a shock value.

The parole board also considers offenses the inmate has admitted committing but for which he has not been convicted. In both Michigan and Wisconsin, an offender who has confessed to a number of offenses is normally charged only with the one or two most serious ones. The uncharged offenses are described in the presentence report for consideration by the trial judge in sentencing. The presentence report describing the uncharged offenses is normally included in the parole board case file. Doubtless, the uncharged offenses influence the board in its decision. Members of the Michigan parole board stated they consider the presentence report to be particularly valuable in determining the extent and nature of the uncharged offenses.

A member of the Wisconsin parole board said uncharged offenses are not, without more, an important factor in the board's estimation of probable parole success.[16] As an example, he cited a case of a young man who for the first time in his life went on a drinking spree and committed ten burglaries. The mere fact that he committed ten burglaries probably would not influence the parole board in its decision to grant parole. The parole board member added, however, he did not intend to say that if the numerous offenses committed by an inmate, whether charged or not, indicated a pattern of serious behavior and a seriously disturbed personality, they would not be taken into consideration. He concluded that what the offenses represent in terms of the individual's entire personality and the risk to the community is considered, rather than the isolated fact that he committed a certain number of offenses.

5. Prior Experience Under Community Supervision

Illustration No. 6: The inmate was serving a one to four-year sentence for larceny. He was sentenced in December 1953, paroled in July 1955, and violated his parole in November 1955. The violation consisted of drinking and absconding. This was his first parole hearing since his return as a violator nine months ago. Prior to the sentence for this offense he had been on probation for a different offense and had violated probation. The Board unanimously denied parole. One member, in dictating his comments on the case, said the inmate had been back in the institution only nine months and while his institutional adjustment was good, he was a previous probation and parole violator, had an alcohol problem, and was not interested in treatment.

The inmate's experience under community supervision is an important consideration in the parole decision. Many of the inmates appearing for parole hearings have had probation, which they may or may not have violated, and some of them are serving a sentence imposed because they violated probation.[17] Many inmates with long criminal records have had experience on parole as well as probation; this is regarded as an especially important indication of what behavior can be expected of them if they are paroled.[18]

---

[16]As an aside he added that whether sentences are imposed consecutively or concurrently has no influence on the parole decision if the inmate is legally eligible for parole.

[17]There is an indication that inmates committed to the Wisconsin State Reformatory for probation violation are routinely denied parole at their initial hearing, held after nine months in the institution. It is clear the nature of the probation violation is as important as the fact of violation. In one case at the Reformatory, an inmate who was appearing for his initial hearing on a probation violation commitment was denied parole. He had been placed on probation on a conviction for armed robbery. He violated probation by carrying a gun and the probation was revoked. He admitted to the parole board that he had intended to use the gun in a hold-up to get money to abscond from the state.

[18]Again, it is clear that the nature of the violation is as important as the fact of violation, particularly whether the violation and the original offense form a pattern which seems to indicate a personality trait and whether there is any evidence of a change in the problem aspects of the inmate's

The extent the parole board should rely on the inmate's parole experience is a problem which inevitably arises when, as in the illustration case, an inmate who has been returned to the institution as a parole violator appears before the board in a hearing for re-parole. More evidence of a change in outlook is required to convince the board to parole him than when he originally was given parole. Parole boards in the states studied do not have a flat rule with regard to re-paroles. Many inmates are given second paroles and some even third paroles, although the board may warn them that this is their "last chance," and that a violation of this parole will result in service of the maximum sentence.[19]

Illustration No. 7: The inmate was sentenced to two and one-half to five years for larceny by conversion. He had already served twenty months. He had a long criminal record and had previously been in three other prisons in various states on charges of breaking and entering. All of his prior sentences were "flat" sentences and he had never spent time on parole. The inmate demonstrated some signs of beginning to understand his problem. His case was continued for ten months, an indication that he probably would be paroled at his next hearing.

The absence of experience on parole may be a favorable factor. In the illustration case, one of the parole board members said they were in effect promising a parole grant because although the inmate had a long prior record, he had never had a parole from any institution and it was not actually known what he could do under supervision. The board is understandably unwilling to assume that recidivism without parole is a clear indication of a high probability of recidivism with parole.

6. Parole Plan

Illustration No. 8: The inmate, a youth, had no family to which he could return upon release. He indicated a desire to work as a machinist and live at the YMCA in a particular small city. The pre-parole report pointed out that it was probably impossible for a seventeen year old boy to secure employment as a machinist and, in any event, such positions in that particular small city were practically non-existent. The parole agent conducting the pre-parole investigation reviewed the inmate's long juvenile record and concluded that placement in a YMCA was unrealistic because he needed considerably more supervision. The agent felt the youth was not a proper subject for a group home because he had leadership qualities which might lead other boys into trouble. He was too old for a foster home and probably would not adjust in that setting. Therefore, the agent felt the only alternative available was to place the inmate on a farm until he reached an age when he could support himself fully without control and discipline. The board paroled the inmate to a farm placement.

The inmate's parole plan—his employment and residence arrangements—is considered in some cases an important factor in determining the probability of parole success. It is considered a favorable sign if an inmate has made a serious attempt to develop a suitable parole plan because it indicates he is thinking about his future. Even when a parole plan has been developed and its feasibility verified by the pre-parole investigation, it is still necessary to determine whether it will help or hinder the inmate's adjustment on parole.[20]

personality. However, the supervisor of the Social Service Department at the Wisconsin State Prison stated that he believed that normally parole violated by a new offense is much more of a negative factor than is a technical violation.

[19]Some of the re-paroles probably occur because the mandatory release date is approaching and the board prefers to give the inmate some community supervision even though he has shown a tendency not to profit from it in the past.

In Michigan, the parole board, with the consent of the sentencing judge, can parole an inmate prior to his legal eligibility under a statutory procedure called "special consideration." Mich. Stat. Ann. § 28.2303 (1954). There is an indication that a violation of such a "special parole" weighs particularly heavily against re-parole because the parole board has, in a measure, vouched for the inmate by securing special parole in the first place.

[20]The pre-parole report in Kansas simply verifies home and job arrangements, if any. No attempt is made to evaluate community sentiment or the suitability of the placement plan. Parole board members in Kansas complained frequently about the scanty information they received from the field.

When an inmate's parole plan seems inadequate, the parole board may deny parole or defer it for a short time. If the original plan seems inadequate but an alternative has been developed by the field agent conducting the pre-parole investigation, or is otherwise available, the parole board may immediately grant parole on the condition that the inmate accept the new plan. Unlike other factors relating to probable parole success, then, the parole plan can be manipulated in order to increase the probability of success. In the illustration case, the job plan was not feasible and the residence plan was considered inadequate. A new job and residence plan was developed and parole was granted on the basis of it.

In Wisconsin, the Special Review Board, the release authority for persons incarcerated under the Sex Crimes Law,[21] makes extensive use of special parole plans for certain types of offenders. The Board's experience has been that the best solution in incest cases is to parole the inmate to a place other than that where the relative with whom he was having incestuous relations lives. Similarly, the Board has developed "protective placements" in rural areas of the state for higher risk indecent liberties cases.

The unavailability of employment for parolees and its general inadequacy causes problems. Statutes in some states require the inmate to have a job before he can be released on parole.[22] Parole boards and field agents find it difficult to comply with these statutes and often must be satisfied with only a vague promise of a temporary, unsubstantial job, or even with no job offer but only an expectation that some job can be found shortly after release. If the parole board feels unemployment may seriously jeopardize adjustment on parole, it may deny parole until the employment picture brightens. With many unskilled workers, this necessitates a denial of parole in the winter in the expectation that the possibility of securing unskilled employment will be greater in the summer and the inmate can be paroled then.[23] Normally, the parole board must be satisfied if the inmate has only a possibility of an unsubstantial job. In cases in which prior involvement with the law has repeatedly occurred during periods of unemployment, however, the board may refuse to parole the inmate unless he has a firm offer of substantial employment.[24]

Normally, the inmate's residence plan is investigated to verify that he will be accepted in the home or institution and to determine what the physical conditions are and who the inmate's associates will be. The parole board usually attempts to persuade the inmate to return to his family, if he has one and they are willing to take him back, especially if he is young.[25]

[23]Often, the lack of immediate available employment is adverted to, almost as an afterthought, as one of several reasons for denial of parole. For example, one institutional recommendation for denial read: "Repeater. He has done nothing toward self-improvement. His type of work is available in the spring." In another case, one reason given by a board member for denial of parole was that the inmate should be paroled in the summer because employment suitable to his defective mental ability would be easier to secure then.

[24]In one case, the information before the parole board revealed that the inmate had a very unstable employment history and that all of his offenses, including the present burglary, were committed during periods of unemployment. One of the parole board members said he would not parole the inmate to another car washer, barber shop porter, or other tenuous and unsubstantial job. It was agreed that parole should be granted on the conditions of no drinking and a substantial and firm job offer before release.

[25]In one case, the inmate, upon questioning as to his parole plan, responded that although he had a mother and two brothers living in another state he would like to be paroled in this state. One board member asked him if he didn't think it would be best for him to go back with his family. The inmate replied, "It makes me feel pretty bad to think of the way I've lived and I don't want to go back around them." The board member pointed out that the inmate would have a better chance if he had relatives to help him make his initial adjustment on parole. He explained that the parole board usually prefers to parole an individual where he has family ties because it finds the chances for success on parole are greater. The other board member in-

[21]Wis. Stat. Ann. § 959.15 (1958).

[22]See, e.g., Kan. Laws 1903, ch. 375, § 5, repealed by Kan. Laws 1957, ch. 331, § 37.

The attitude of the community in which the inmate wishes to reside and work is sometimes considered an important factor in adjustment on parole. This is especially likely if the inmate plans to go to a small community, where the attitudes of a number of citizens may make a substantial difference. If the inmate plans to work and live in a large city, a negative attitude by some of its citizens may make less difference.[26]

7. Circumstances of the Offense

Illustration No. 9: The inmate was convicted of armed robbery and was sentenced to two to fifteen years, of which he had served eighteen months at the time of the hearing. He had no previous convictions and only a few arrests for misdemeanors. The inmate's account of the offense was that he held up a bus and was arrested almost immediately. His file showed he had been destitute at the time of the offense, was unemployed, and had been sleeping in parks. The file also showed a good work record when he was employed. He had a letter to show the parole board verifying the fact that if there were an opening he could get his old job back. He was granted parole subject to home and employment placement.

The basic indication of probable recidivism used by the Michigan and Wisconsin parole

tervened to say, "I'll go for parole but not if he stays in this state where he got into trouble due to drinking and bad associates." It was decided to parole the inmate to his family out of state, subject to approval of home conditions and employment plans.

In another case, the inmate, thirty-six years of age, had been convicted several times of check forgery. On most of these occasions, he had been placed on probation because his mother made restitution. The inmate's plan called for parole to the city where his mother lived. A parole board member asked the inmate if he felt he should return to the city in which his mother lived. The inmate replied that he would not let his mother interfere with his life this time. The other board member noted that perhaps such a long pattern of dependency on his mother would be hard to break and it would probably be best to consider placement elsewhere. It was decided to continue the case to investigate the possibility of placement with some of the inmate's other relatives.

[26]The concern of the parole board with the attitude of the community toward the inmate goes beyond its effect on parole adjustment and reflects, in part at least, the board's desire to remain free of public criticism of its decisions.

boards is evidence of personality change during the period of institutionalization. There are cases, however, in which the parole board may regard the offense as situational in nature and not necessarily the result of a personality defect. If the parole board has some assurance that the situational factors have changed during the period of incarceration, it may be willing to grant parole despite lack of evidence of personality change. In the illustration case, the offense seemed the result of the inmate's prolonged unemployment, and the parole board became convinced that the probability of success on parole would be high if the inmate were employed.

The number of cases in which the boards seem to regard the situational factors as predominating is small. Certainly, in comparison with the number of cases in which inmates explain their criminal conduct in situational terms—bad associates, drinking, unemployment, family disputes—the number of cases is small. It is difficult to determine whether the situational factors in the offense go exclusively to the probability of parole success or also to a judgment of the moral blame which the inmate should bear for his conduct. In the illustration case, one member of the board concluded that although there was no excuse for the offense, the inmate's circumstances did appear to be desperate at the time he committed it, implying that the offense was "understandable."

B. The Decision To Grant Parole for Reasons Other Than the Probability of Recidivism

In practice, inmates are paroled who would not be released if the probability of recidivism were the sole criterion for the decision. Often, inmates are paroled despite the board's judgment that they are likely to commit new criminal offenses. That a parole board sometimes feels compelled to parole inmates who are not rehabilitated may in part reflect deficiencies in institutional treatment programs. It is clear, however, that even great advances in that area would not entirely eliminate the necessity for making decisions of this kind.

1. Seriousness of the Anticipated Violation

Illustration No. 10: The inmate, a fifty year old man, had served two years on concurrent sentences of one to five and one to seven years for forgery. No parole plan had been developed. He was a seventh felony offender. His record for forgery extended back to 1933. He had served two previous prison terms. The institution made the following parole recommendation: "Seventh offender. Chronic offender. Social adjustment in institution was good. Psychiatrist seemed to think superficial progress was being made, however, never accepted alcoholism as a problem. Deny." A parole board member began discussing with the inmate the necessity for accepting alcoholism as a problem and told him he knew he would be back as a parole violator if he did not stop drinking. He suggested the inmate join Alcoholics Anonymous after release. The board voted to grant parole.

Parole board interest in predicting behavior on parole does not end when the probability of the inmate's violating the law becomes apparent. The board is also deeply concerned with the type of violation likely to occur if the inmate does in fact violate. The board is willing to parole on less evidence of probable success when it is apparent that a violation, if it occurs, is not likely to be serious. In the illustration case, one of the parole board members said he was voting for parole because the inmate was the type of individual who just wrote small checks when drunk and who did not constitute a serious threat to the community. Another board member said he was voting to grant parole and added that "all were granting with tongue in cheek."[27]

The potential benefit from further institutional treatment is also a factor in these decisions. Thus, although one inmate was clearly al-

---

[27]In another case, the board paroled a twenty-four year old man convicted of check forgery. He had one prior conviction for the same offense on which he had been given probation. There had been other forgeries but he was not convicted of them because he had made restitution. When he was paroled one of the institutional personnel remarked that the inmate looked like a good parole risk. To this a member of the parole board replied, "Nonsense. Statistics show that 70% of all forgers are repeaters."

coholic and had a long record of arrests for public intoxication, he was paroled at his initial hearing. The parole board concluded he was a harmless person. It could see little point in keeping him in the institution any longer because he had shown little indication of having enough strength to quit using alcohol. The board concluded, therefore, not only had the institution been unable to do much for the inmate, but it was extremely unlikely he would ever be able to make significant gains in solving his problem.

Finally, the board is concerned in these cases about the effect of parole on the inmate's family. If the inmate is retained in the institution there is little opportunity for him to make significant contributions to the support of his dependents. If he is paroled, however, he at least has the opportunity to support his family. In Wisconsin, nonsupport offenders normally are paroled as soon as they are eligible. The parole board states there are three reasons for this policy: they are unlikely to commit a serious violation of the criminal law, the institutional program is of little aid in their rehabilitation beyond the first several months, and parole may provide financial support for the family for a time as well as the benefits which may accrue from having a father in the family again.

2. Mandatory Release Date Near

Illustration No. 11: The inmate was a nineteen year old girl serving a sentence of six months to one year for larceny. Her prior record consisted of one conviction for drunkenness, for which she successfully completed a one-year probation period. At the time of the hearing she had served eight months on the sentence. Her conditional release date would be reached in another three months. If parole were denied, she would be released then and, after one month under supervision, would receive an absolute discharge. The board decided to parole her.

Parole boards sometimes find themselves in the position of choosing between a need to retain the inmate in prison and a need for supervision and control over him after he is released. This occurs when at the time of the parole hearing the inmate has only a short period to serve until he must be released from the institution. These are all cases in which the maximum sentence, whether set by statute or by the trial judge, is, in the view of the parole board, too short under the circumstances. The parole board frequently paroles an inmate despite its estimate of a high probability of recidivism, if, in its view, parole supervision is needed more than continued institutionalization.

In Kansas and Michigan, the inmate must be released unconditionally when he has served his maximum sentence, less allowances for good time.[28] No period of parole supervision follows release. When the inmate has only a short period to serve until his maximum, less good time, the parole board frequently feels it is forced to parole him to provide supervision and control over him when he is released. In Michigan,[29] the inmate must be discharged from parole supervision when he has served his maximum sentence, less good time earned in the institution and on parole, and in Kansas,[30] when he has served his maximum, less good time earned while incarcerated.

In Wisconsin, the inmate must be released from the institution when he has served his maximum sentence, less good time, but the release is conditional and a mandatory period of parole supervision follows during which the releasee is subject to the same conditions and possibilities of revocation which apply to parolees released by act of the parole board. He must be discharged from parole when he has served his maximum sentence without allowances for good time.[31] When, as in the illustration case, the maximum sentence is short, the period of mandatory parole supervision following release at the maximum, less good time, is, of necessity, quite short. In the illustration case, the period of supervision would have been one month had the inmate been kept until her mandatory release date. Nevertheless, the parole board felt that further incarceration would be useful in her case. Thus, it was forced to choose between what it regarded as an inadequate period of institutionalization and an inadequate period of post-incarceration supervision. It chose to lengthen the period of supervision at the expense of the institutionalization.

The position might be taken that this is one factor to consider in determining whether the maximum sentence should be fixed by the trial judge or set by statute. Thus, it could be argued that paroles based on the approach of the mandatory release date would be less frequent when the maximum is set by statute than when set by the trial judge. One would expect to find, therefore, that this is more of a problem in Wisconsin than in Kansas and Michigan.[32] This does not seem to be the case. There may be any number of reasons for this, including, perhaps, the fact that the Wisconsin parole board may be more liberal in granting paroles than the boards in Michigan and Kansas. Another reason may be that in Wisconsin the mandatory release is followed by a mandatory period of supervision. Unlike the boards in the other two states, the parole board in Wisconsin must simply determine whether the period of supervision permitted by the good time awarded the prisoner is adequate.[33] It is only when the maximum sen-

---

[28]Kan. Stat. Ann. § 76–2421 (1964); Mich. Stat. Ann. § 28.1403 (1954); Kan. Laws 1913, ch. 219, § 4, repealed by Kan. Laws 1957, ch. 331, § 37; Kan. Laws 1903, ch. 375, § 1, repealed by Kan. Laws 1957, ch. 331, § 37.

[29]Mich. Stat. Ann. § 28.2312 (Supp. 1965). Mich. Stat. Ann. § 28.2308 (1954) provides in part: "A parole granted a prisoner shall be construed simply as a permit to such prisoner to go without the enclosure of the prison, and not as a release, and while so at large he shall be deemed to be still serving out the sentence imposed upon him by the court, and shall be entitled to good time the same as if he were confined in prison."

[30]The Kansas good time laws apply only to prisoners confined in correctional institutions. Kan. Laws 1905, ch. 317, § 1, as amended, Kan. Laws 1957, ch. 472, § 30.

[31]Wis. Stat. Ann. § 53.11(7) (1958). This provision is commonly referred to as the conditional release law.

[32]In Wisconsin, the maximum sentence is selected by the trial judge, while in Kansas and Michigan it is usually fixed by statute.

[33]In Wisconsin, juvenile boys transferred from the training school to the reformatory are subject to the release juris-

tence is quite short that there is any need for a parole to increase the length of the period of supervision. In Wisconsin, one finds such paroles when the maximum is short, while in Kansas and Michigan, one finds such paroles when the inmate has been denied parole in the past or has been paroled and returned for a violation.[34]

3. Length of Time Served

Illustration No. 12: The inmate had received a sentence of three to twenty years for armed robbery, auto theft, and forgery. He was paroled after three years but shortly thereafter violated his parole and received a new sentence for operating a con game. He served three years since his last parole. His criminal career began twenty years previously and involved numerous convictions. The psychiatric report was that the inmate was "instinctively vicious. Any rehabilitative program will be futile." The institutional recommendation was that the inmate "has adjusted in excellent manner in institution. Has served lengthy sentence. Should be tried. Grant." The parole board decided to grant parole.

Every decision to grant parole reflects the opinion of the parole board that the inmate has served enough time, but there are some cases in which the length of time served is itself the most significant factor in the case. This typically occurs when an inmate has received a relatively long sentence, but fails to respond to the rehabilitative programs at the institution. In addi-

tion, he may have been tried on parole once or twice and had his parole revoked. The parole board may then be faced with the choice of denying parole when it is evident that further institutionalization will not increase the probability of success on parole or of granting parole ho an inmate who presents some risk of violation.

In the illustration case, one of the parole board members commented that "just maybe" the inmate will make parole after so long an institutionalization. He felt that in such cases institutionalization reaches a point when it serves no purpose in terms of rehabilitation. The only question remaining is that of protection of the community, he continued. In this case, the board members all felt they would have to try the inmate on parole sooner or later, but none expressed any confidence in his capacity for success.

A factor mentioned in many cases of this type is maturation. When a relatively young man receives a long sentence and serves a fairly long term before parole, the board may comment that despite the absence of any apparent effect of the institution's program, he may have matured enough to enable him to live a lawful life in the community.

4. Parole to a Detainer

Illustration No. 13: A twenty-seven year old man serving a one to five-year sentence for larceny appeared before the parole board for a hearing. He had a long criminal and juvenile record. While on parole in Ohio, he came to Wisconsin and committed the offense for which he was serving time. An institutional psychologist said the inmate had admitted using narcotics and drugs; he stated that the prognosis was poor. The institutional committee recommended parole to a detainer, partly because only about seven months remained until conditional release would be required; he had served approximately three years of a one to five-year sentence, and it was thought he might as well start on his Ohio sentence. The final decision of the board was to grant parole to the Ohio detainer. The chairman commented that he did not think Ohio would come after the inmate, in which event he would be detained at the prison until his conditional release date. None of

diction of the adult parole board. Because they are still juveniles, however, the conditional release law does not apply to them. When they reach the age of twenty-one they must be released unconditionally. It is a common practice for the parole board to grant paroles to juveniles who are approaching age twenty-one simply to give them a period of supervision in the community, which would be denied them under release by operation of law.

[34]The problem was particularly acute in Michigan due to an administrative directive which prohibited the parole board from forfeiting good time earned in the institution when an inmate violated parole. This resulted in a number of returned violators having only a short time remaining until their mandatory, unconditional release date. In some of these situations, the parole board felt it was forced to grant parole in order to provide the inmate with some community supervision.

the board members felt the inmate could possibly adjust on parole. The board rationale in this case was dictated by the chairman: "Claims he owes Ohio five years. He has been locked up for the past sixteen years except for twenty-nine months. Gullible, ambitionless, and no insight. Has used heroin. Practically hopeless."

The parole decision may be influenced by the fact that a detainer has been filed against the inmate. The prisoner against whom a detainer is filed may be charged with a crime for which he has not yet been tried, may be a probation or parole violator from another state, may be wanted for completion of a prison term which was interrupted by an escape, or may have been ordered deported by a court or administrative agency.

The effect of a detainer on the parole decision varies from state to state. In some states, a detainer automatically precludes the inmate from the possibility of parole.[35] Sometimes this position is based on the view that parole implies community supervision—that a "parole to a detainer" is not really a parole and, hence, not within the authority of the parole board. In the three states, the parole boards do parole to detainers, although this is specifically authorized by statute in only one of them.[36] However, the circumstances under which they parole to a detainer vary.

The problem of whether an inmate should be paroled to a detainer normally arises only when prior attempts to secure removal of the detainer have failed. Sometimes the trial judge may be successful in obtaining removal of a detainer at the sentencing stage. If a defendant whom the judge has sentenced to prison is wanted in other counties of the state, he may order that the defendant be taken to those counties and tried for the offenses before being transported to the correctional institution. If a defendant is wanted in another state or by federal authorities, the judge may arrange to increase the sentence in exchange for an agreement to drop the detainer, or he may grant the defendant probation or a suspended sentence and turn him over to the requesting authority.

In some correctional institutions, officials contact authorities which have lodged detainers against inmates in an attempt to discover their intentions. Effort is made to persuade the requesting authority to drop the detainer or at least to specify the circumstances, such as the number of years the inmate must serve, under which they would drop it.[37]

There are some circumstances under which an inmate of a correctional institution may demand disposition of a detainer against him as a matter of right. If the detainer represents an untried charge, the inmate may be able to require that he be taken from the institution and tried, or that the state be barred from ever trying him on that charge, on the ground that he is enforcing his right to a speedy trial.[38] In some states, statutes give an inmate this right.[39] Even in a state which contains full provision for mandatory removal of detainers, the problem of parole to a detainer remains with respect to detainers for revocation of probation or parole and deportation detainers. Unless institutional authorities are successful in negotiating their removal, the problem comes before the parole board.

In Kansas, the parole board grants parole to inmates who have detainers filed against them as soon as they are eligible. The board apparently does not distinguish between in-state, out-of-state, and deportation detainers, nor between detainers based on charges yet to be proved and detainers for revocation of probation or parole. During one day's hearings, seven inmates were paroled to detainers. In many of these cases, it

---

[35]Tappan, Crime, Justice and Correction 724 (1960): "In some states any prisoner who is wanted under a detainer for further court action or imprisonment is automatically rejected [for parole] unless or until the writ is lifted."

[36]Mich. Stat. Ann. § 28.2303(c) (1954).

[37]See Tappan, *op. cit. supra* note 35, at 724 n.32.

[38]E.g., State *ex rel.* Fredenberg v. Byrne, 20 Wis. 2d 504, 123 N.W.2d 305 (1963).

[39]E.g., Mich. Stat. Ann. §§ 4.147, 28.969 (Supp. 1965); Wis. Stat. Ann. § 955.22 (Supp. 1966).

was apparent that the inmate would not have been paroled had there not been a detainer lodged against him. In each instance, the board explained to the inmate that it could do nothing but parole him to the detainer. Apparently, no effort is made during the inmate's confinement to determine whether the requesting authority is willing to drop its detainer. When an inmate has been paroled to a detainer and the requesting authority fails to take custody of him at the institution, the detainer is dropped and the inmate is scheduled for the next parole hearing to be held at his institution to determine whether he should be paroled to community supervision.[40]

The Wisconsin parole board's policy on paroles to detainers was detailed in a booklet published shortly after the field survey was conducted, but reflected practices in effect at the time of the survey:

Persons eligible for parole under Wisconsin Statute but against whom detainers have been filed by Federal, Immigration, Out-of-State or local authorities may be granted parole to the detainer. Normally, parole is not granted to a detainer unless the usual criteria for parole selection can be met.

Institutions will be responsible for correspondence on parole planning with authorities who file detainers except when the detainer has been filed by a paroling authority.[41] In such

cases the Parole Board will be responsible for the necessary correspondence. (Institutions should refer cases of this type to the Parole Board.)

Detainers from other states placed against persons serving sentences in Wisconsin Correctional Institutions normally fall within three groups:

1.   Those cases in which the individual was under field supervision at the time he was received.

2.   Those in which the individual had been previously convicted in another state and it is expected that he will, upon release from a Wisconsin Institution, go to an institution in the other state to serve his unexpired term. As a matter of practice, parole is usually not granted to this type of detainer until such time as the applicant has less time remaining to serve in Wisconsin than he will have to serve in the other state.

3.   Those in which the individual has been charged with an offense in another state but has not yet been tried. In this situation, it is expected that the individual will be taken to court in the other state to face prosecution when paroled in Wisconsin.[42]

In Michigan, paroles to detainers are specifically authorized. The statute provides:

---

[40]The Kansas parole board's practice of paroling inmates with detainers at the first hearing has caused some discipline problems at the institutions because inmates with detainers are certain they will be paroled to the detainer no matter what their behavior. Occasionally, the parole board has declined to parole a troublesome inmate to his detainer in order to enforce the institution's disciplinary code. See notes 51–53 infra and accompanying text.

[41]An official in the Wisconsin Division of Corrections explained that the Social Service Departments of the various institutions have responsibility for requesting the other jurisdictions to remove detainers and do all the negotiating. The time when the Social Service Departments contact requesting authorities is in their discretion. Usually, they pre-

fer to let the inmate serve long enough on the Wisconsin sentence so that the other state will be willing to release the detainer, particularly in cases of detainers for prosecution. Negotiation occurs because usually no plan can be developed for release and no effective program can be formulated for a prisoner who is not sure where he is going to be, or is not particularly motivated toward the prospect of a new sentence in another jurisdiction. All of these are administrative practices and are not a matter of statute. The same official indicated that with in-state detainers for prosecution, the Wisconsin institutions are successful in obtaining removal in about seventy-five per cent of the cases. Frequently, these detainers involve bad check charges, in which removal is easily effected by making arrangement for payment of restitution.

[42]Wis. Department of Public Welfare, Parole Board Procedures and Practices 11 (Feb. 1959).

"Paroles-in-custody to answer warrants filed by local, out-of-state agencies or immigration officials are permissible, provided an accredited agent of the agency filing the warrant shall call for the prisoner so paroled in custody."[43] The effect of the detainer on the parole decision differs depending upon the type of detainer involved.

Detainers filed by agencies within the state of Michigan are usually for the purpose of having the inmate answer an untried felony charge. If an inmate who has such a detainer filed against him is not regarded as parolable at the time of his initial hearing, a "custody parole" is almost always given to allow disposition of the untried charges. If the local requesting authority upon notice of the parole does not take custody of the inmate at the institution, the detainer is considered dropped. If the requesting authority takes custody, the inmate is not permitted to make bond while waiting trial or disposition, and, regardless of the outcome of the proceedings, he is returned to the institution after their completion. If a new prison term is imposed, he will become eligible for parole again when he serves the new minimum sentence, less good time. If no new prison sentence is imposed, he will be reconsidered for parole in the usual manner.[44]

In acting on a detainer filed by another state to bring an inmate to trial in that state, the parole board decides whether the inmate should be paroled to the community. When an inmate is released on such a detainer it is with the intent that if he is found not guilty, or if the charges are dropped, he will be placed on parole supervision in the other state. Commenting on this type of parole to a detainer, one parole board member stated, "We must handle such cases with the expectation that the inmate may be released entirely from custody, and cannot afford to take the long risk if the person is deemed not a proper subject for return to society." The board apparently works on the assumption in this type of case that the inmate will be set free in the other state, although he may be convicted and sentenced to prison. Therefore, the board apparently requires that the inmate be parolable under the usual criteria.

If the detainer issued by another state is for the return of the inmate as a probation or parole violator or an escaped prisoner, the board has more indication of what treatment is to be accorded the prisoner by the requesting jurisdiction. Because the risk of the inmate's being freed is considerably less than when the detainer is based on untried charges, the parole board is likely to be considerably more liberal in its attitude toward parole. The board learns the length of the sentence remaining for the prisoner to serve and the character of the parole supervision in the state. If, for example, the parole board considers the inmate a menace to society and learns that the period of time remaining to be served in the requesting state is limited, it would decide against honoring the detainer. If the parole board believes the inmate is ready for community supervision, it may suggest to the requesting state that the inmate be released to that state for dual parole supervision.

The effect on the parole decision of a detainer filed for deportation of an inmate varies depending on the country to which the inmate is to be deported. In considering deportation to Canada or Mexico, the board, aware of the ease with which the parolee can return to michigan, tends to be somewhat cautious in granting parole. Nevertheless, even in these cases, the board is sometimes willing to grant parole when otherwise it would not. One parole board member noted:

"In some quarters of this state, and particularly among some members of the judiciary, there is present a philosophy that we should not clutter up our institutions with persons who are deportable, and that

---

[43]Mich. Stat. Ann. § 28.2303(c) (1954).

[44]The 1957 legislation providing for mandatory disposition of in-state detainers on untried offenses was designed to replace the practice of custody paroles. See note 39 *supra*.

we should, as a matter of fact, pursue a very liberal policy in such cases. I do not think that the board subscribes to this philosophy, nor does it operate under it to the extent that some would desire."

A greater degree of liberality is evident in considering paroles to detainers for deportation to countries overseas.

5. Reward for Informant Services

Illustration No. 14: The inmate had been convicted of assault with intent to rob, for which he was placed on probation. After one year on probation, he violated and received a prison sentence of one to ten years. This was his initial parole hearing. The sentencing judge and the prosecuting attorney both recommended a parole denial. He had a prior record of assault. His I.Q. was recorded as sixty-three. Shortly before his hearing, the inmate had learned of an escape plot involving four inmates who were hiding in a tunnel. He tipped off a guard and the inmates were apprehended. The board decided to grant parole.

In current administration, the services of informants are sought and rewarded by enforcement officials. Typically, the informant has engaged in criminal behavior himself. The most persuasive inducement and reward for information is lenient treatment of the informant. The leniency may take the form of failure to arrest for minor offenses,[45] refusing to charge an informant despite sufficient evidence, convicting him of a less serious offense, or probation or a lighter sentence.

Occasionally, the parole decision may be used as a reward for informant services, especially for information about the activities of inmates in the correctional institution. In the illustration case, the inmate would not have been paroled on the basis of his rehabilitation. His informant services were not discussed during the parole hearing, but the board was told of them before the hearing and discussed them after the inmate left the hearing room.

In many states, statutes authorize the granting of special good time to inmates who perform extra work or other meritorious duties, includ-

ing giving information to prison officials.[46] It is not certain how often these provisions are used to reward inmate informant services and, if they are used, whether they are effective in eliminating the need to use the parole decision for the same purpose.[47]

The chairman of the Michigan parole board indicated in a speech the difficulty which the informant causes the board in reaching a decision:

"Parole was designed to serve society as a means of assisting the individual to make the transition from prison confinement to existence in the free community. There are times, however, when offenders render great assistance to law enforcement or perform some valorous or meritorious act. Testifying against dangerous criminal offenders and thereby placing their own lives in jeopardy, saving the life of an officer or helping him in a serious situation, and giving information preventing a serious escape threat of dangerous persons are acts which seem to warrant special consideration. As valuable as these acts may be, they must be interpreted as to the intent of the individual in performing them. It is said that "virtue is its own reward," but sometimes people expect something more tangible—say, a parole! The motivation of the individual and the circumstances in which his valor was evidenced are as important here as they are in the crime for which he was sentenced. They may be sincere expressions of a better set of social values, or they may be selfish efforts to gain personal advantage even if it means taking a personal risk. Such acts can be a spectacular evidence of deep significance or only an exhibition of self-aggrandizement."[48]

In some situations there may be a need, which parole can meet, for the removal of the in-

---

[45]See generally LaFave, *Arrest* 132–37 (1965).

[46]The Kansas statute provided: "The board of administration is hereby empowered to adopt a rule whereby prisoners . . . may be granted additional good time for . . . giving valuable information to prison officials. . . ." Kan. Laws 1935, ch. 292, § 1.

[47]For example, it is probably true in Michigan that the great majority of prison inmates are routinely awarded the maximum possible good time and special good time.

[48]Address by R. H. Nelson, Chairman, Michigan Parole Board, at a meeting of Michigan prosecutors, July, 1957.

forming inmate from the institution for his own safety. It is not clear whether this is an important consideration in the decision to grant parole to the informant and, if so, whether a transfer of the informant to another institution would be a satisfactory alternative.

C. The Decision To Deny Parole for Reasons Other Than the Probability of Recidivism

Parole is often denied to inmates for reasons other than perceived probability of recidivism. Often this decision is made despite the board's own estimate that the inmate would very likely complete his parole period successfully if he were released. That this should occur is surprising in view of the chronic crowded conditions of most prisons. Ironically, however, in some situations prison overpopulation may be a factor contributing to a decision to deny parole despite a high probability of parole success. It might be argued, for example, that when a parole board denies parole to a good risk because it is enforcing prison discipline, a major reason it feels compelled to do so lies in the strain on prison discipline created by overcrowding.

It has been contended that parole boards tend to be too "conservative" in their release practices. In part this contention goes to the point that parole boards may require too high a probability of parole success before granting parole, but it also may go to policy considerations upon which parole denials are based in cases in which the board's own requirements of probable parole success have clearly been met. This may be the situation, for example, with regard to denials because the inmate has assaultive tendencies or because a parole grant would subject the correctional system to severe public criticism.

1. Cases Involving Assaultive Behavior

Illustration No. 15: The inmate, thirty-one years of age, was convicted of carrying a concealed weapon and sentenced to one to five years. When he was arrested on the present offense, he was believed to be trying to draw a gun on the arresting officer. His prior record consisted of convictions for "shooting another" and for felonious assault. He had been denied parole at a previous hearing because of several misconduct reports from the institution, one of which consisted of possession of a knife. Since his last hearing, however, he had received no misconduct reports. When the questioning of one of the board members revealed he was thinking of a parole grant, the other member interrupted him with: "I want a discussion on this." The first member replied that the record showed the inmate had greatly improved his attitude since the last hearing. Nevertheless, the inmate was told his case would have to be discussed with other members of the parole board and he would hear their decision in about a month.

Parole boards tend to be more conservative in their release practices when the inmate has demonstrated he is capable of assaultive behavior. Sometimes this consideration is regarded as sufficiently important to justify a denial of parole to an inmate who would otherwise be regarded as having a sufficiently high probability of parole success to justify release. The rationale is, of course, that the parole board has an obligation to protect the public from possible assaultive behavior which overrides its obligation to release inmates at the optimum point in their rehabilitative progress.[49]

The Michigan parole board has a practice of refusing to grant parole to an inmate with a demonstrated capacity for assaultive behavior until the case has been discussed by the full five-man membership of the board in executive session. In the illustration case, one of the two parole board hearing members said after the inmate left the room that he did not believe parole was appropriate because of the inmate's history of assaultive conduct. He said he believed a further psychiatric evaluation would be necessary since on at least three occasions the inmate had pro-

---

[49]The board is especially unlikely to release inmates who appear to be directing aggression against particular persons. In one case, for example, an inmate was continually denied parole because he persisted in sending threatening letters to his wife.

ved himself capable of serious assaultive behavior.

Shortly after the field survey was conducted, the Wisconsin parole board adopted the policy of requiring a discussion in executive session before an inmate with a history of assault may be paroled. In these cases, the two members of the board conducting the parole hearing tell the inmate a discussion with a third member is necessary before a decision can be made. The director of the Social Service Department of one of the institutions noted that both institutional authorities and the parole board are more cautious in cases involving assault, particularly in cases of murder, because although the probability of recidivism may be low, the probable seriousness of the new offense, if one is committed, is great.

Normally, the board determines whether the inmate is capable of assaultive behavior on the basis of his prior record and the offense for which he is serving time. The board may also have the benefit of a psychiatric evaluation. In such cases, the latter is given great weight. An evaluation which concludes that the inmate is still capable of assaultive behavior or is still too dangerous for release will almost automatically result in a denial of parole.[50]

2. Supporting Institutional Discipline

Illustration No. 16: The inmate, twenty-six years of age, was convicted of larceny in a building and received a sentence of one and one-half to four years. This was his first parole hearing. A parole board member questioned the inmate about his institutional record, which showed he had three institutional reports, two for being "lazy" and refusing to work and one for having dice in his possession. He had several misdemeanor arrests and at one time had been arrested on a narcotics investigation charge. An immediate parole was not granted but the case was continued for office review in six months. It was explained to the inmate that his institutional record had been poor and that if he corrected this and tried to obtain some help from his counselor, he would be given consideration again in six months.

Maintaining discipline among inmates is a major concern of all prison administrators. Although there are wide variations among penal institutions as to the degree to which the details of daily living are regulated by the administration, even in relatively permissive institutions there are disciplinary rules and sanctions for their infraction. Infractions of prison discipline are often interpeted by the parole board as signs of what the offender is likely to do when he is released on parole. They suggest an inability of the offender to adjust to his position and to respect authority. Quite a different consideration is primary, however, when the board denies parole because of the effect its decision may have on prison discipline. The major interest shifts from a concern with the future adjustment of the offender to a concern with order and control in the penal institution. Parole becomes an incentive for good behavior and a sanction against undisciplined conduct by inmates.[51]

It is frequently not easy to distinguish between actions of the board which are designed to have an impact on the discipline of the institution and those which relate to the offender's future adjustment. It is likely that even the parole board members are unable to articulate clearly their reasons for reacting as they do to inmates with disciplinary problems. In Kansas, a parole board member may sometimes say, "How can you expect to be paroled when you can't even behave in the institution?" which might be interpreted by the inmate to indicate the board feels he lacks sufficient control. On the other

[50]For example, an institutional recommendation such as the following is virtually certain to result in a parole denial: "Paranoid psychosis. Thinks wife maneuvered him into murdering her. Psychiatrist reports too dangerous for release. Deny."

[51]Mich. Admin. Code ch. II, rule 6, p. 191 (1944): "No prisoner shall be released on parole . . . merely as a reward for good conduct or efficient performance of duty during his incarceration, but only when the board feels that it is reasonably certain that the parole will not be violated, and that as a parolee he will not become a menace to society or to the public safety."

hand, the board member will sometimes say, "I can't parole anyone who has become involved in so serious a breach of prison discipline," which might more readily be interpreted as supportive of prison discipline. Treating misbehavior during confinement as an unfavorable sign for future parole success leads in most cases to the same decision which would be made if the order of the institution were the sole consideration.

Parole is only one of many sanctions which are used to maintain discipline in penal institutions. Violations of disciplinary rules may result in denial of certain privileges or in solitary confinement. Repeated disciplinary violations may result in a transfer of the inmate to a less desirable institution. In most states, good time laws permit reduction of the maximum or minimum sentences, or both, as a reward for infraction-free conduct, and permit revocation of reductions already given for disciplinary violations.[52] In some states, parole eligibility may be specifically contingent on the existence of no recent disciplinary infractions.

That parole is used to support institutional discipline may reflect the failure of these other devices to provide the necessary controls. This may be particularly true of the good time laws. In some institutions, it seems clear that good time laws have degenerated into automatic reductions of sentence, possibly as a result of the heavy release pressures of prison overpopulation, and thus have little, if any, effect on the conduct of inmates. A member of the Michigan parole board indicated that in practice the good time system has broken down and that it is an exception for an inmate to appear before the parole board who has not earned all possible regular and special good time. The board member indicated that in order to be denied good time, an inmate would have to "spit in the warden's eye."

It is difficult to determine whether it is possible, assuming for the moment it is desirable, to strengthen other control devices enough to enable the parole decision to remain free of the necessity for its use as a disciplinary device. It is probably true that, assuming administration of the good time laws has resulted in their uniform application without regard to conduct, the parole decision is currently a necessary device for control within the institution. Certainly the Model Penal Code regards it as a proper use of parole because it authorizes a denial of parole when the inmate's "release would have a substantially adverse effect on institutional discipline."[53] It is impossible to know whether this reflects a judgment that parole must inevitably be used as a control device, or whether, given current conditions, it must be so used. It would be possible to devise a system whereby the institution did preliminary screening of parole applicants and had the power to postpone parole hearings several months on the basis of institutional misconduct. This would have the effect of retaining the parole decision as a sanction for nonconformance to the institution's code, while at the same time relieving the parole board from the necessity of taking prison discipline into account when it makes parole decisions.

3. Minimum Amount of Time

Illustration No. 17: The inmate, age twenty-two, had been convicted of unlawfully driving away an auto, for which he received two years' probation. After he had served twenty-one months on probation, it was revoked for failure to report, failure to pay costs and restitution, and involvement in an auto accident. The judge imposed a prison term of six months to five years, stating to the inmate that he would probably be back home in about four and one-half months. He spent two months at the main prison and was then transferred to the prison camp where he had served almost a month by the time of his parole hearing. The camp recommended a short continuance of the case on the ground little was known about the inmate. Most of the hearing was consumed by the parole board attempting to explain to the inmate that he had been in the institution "too short a time for the of-

---

[52]See Model Penal Code § 305.9, comment (Tent. Draft No. 5, 1956).

[53]Model Penal Code § 305.9(1)(c) (Proposed Official Draft 1962)

fense" and, further, that the institution knew little about him. The board explained it could not conscientiously recommend parole for him in light of its lack of knowledge of his case. The case was continued for discussion in executive session.

A problem which some parole boards must frequently face occurs when an inmate appears for his initial parole hearing after he has served only a short length of time, normally under six months. Whatever the reasons, the parole board is likely to be quite reluctant to give serious consideration to the case until the inmate has served more time. The normal disposition when such a case appears is to schedule a rehearing, or sometimes only a conference in executive session, in several months, at which time the decision to grant or deny parole will be given usual consideration.

Because of its sentencing structure, the problem is particularly noticeable in Michigan. There, the maximum sentence for most offenses is fixed by statute but the judge has discretion to set any minimum sentence he wishes.[54] Regular and special good time are deducted from the judicially set minimum to determine parole eligibility,[55] and the inmate normally receives his first parole hearing one or two months before he becomes eligible for parole. As a result, when the judge sets a minimum sentence of six months, the inmate is eligible for parole after he has served about four months and appears for his first parole hearing after he has served only three months. The typical disposition of such cases is a continuance for six months or a year, at which time he will be given usual parole consideration.

It is possible, of course, to have a judicial minimum system which does not as readily lead to the difficulties experienced in Michigan. Under the judicial minimum system proposed in the Model Penal Code, the judge may not set the minimum sentence at less than one year.[56]

With the necessary allowances for deducting good time and scheduling the hearing a month in advance of parole eligibility, this would normally result in an inmate's not receiving his first parole hearing before he has served nine months.

A potential problem of the same type was handled by parole board policy in Kansas and Wisconsin. There, inmates of the reformatories and women's prisons are by statute eligible for parole as soon as they arrive at the institution.[57] In each state, the inmate, although statutorily eligible for parole immediately, does not normally receive his first parole hearing until he has served nine months of his sentence. This doubtless reflects a judgment that about that much time is necessary before it makes sense to consider the question of parole.

While there seems to be a consensus that a minimum time, probably between nine months and one year, is necessary before serious consideration should be given to parole, there is lack of agreement as to why this is true. One reason given is that the institution is incapable of having any rehabilitative effect on the inmate in less time. The assumption is that all persons sentenced to prison are in need of rehabilitation, which takes time, or at least that it takes time to determine whether they are in need of rehabilitation.[58] A related reason sometimes given is that the parole system and institution are incapable of formulating sound post-release programs for inmates in less ime. Further, parole boards sometimes contend that adequate infor-

---

[54]Mich. Stat. Ann. §§ 28.1080, .1081 (1954).

[55]Mich. Stat. Ann. § 28.2304 (1954).

[56]Model Penal Code § 6.06 (Tent. Draft No. 2, 1954).

[57]Wis. Stat. Ann. § 57.07 (1958); Kan. Laws 1949, ch. 461, § 1, as amended, Kan. Laws 1957, ch. 331, § 37; Kan. Laws 1901, ch. 355, § 17, as amended, Kan. Laws 1957, ch. 472, § 12. Although inmates committed under the Wisconsin Sex Crimes Act are immediately eligible for parole, Wis. Stat. Ann. § 959.15 (10) (1958), in practice release is not considered until they have served one year.

[58]In one case, the parole board denied parole to an inmate who had served only three months, commenting: "He has only been in the institution for three months and I believe this is too short a time to expect a change in him if it is possible for any change to occur in such an individual."

mation on the inmate cannot be obtained in less time and, therefore, a short continuance is necessary in order to obtain information.[59] At other times, however, parole boards have indicated a certain minimum time is necessary in order to justify the risk entailed by every decision to grant parole. The assumption in such cases is that the inmate has served such a short length of time that the parole board can afford to be more conservative in its release decision. Also implicit is the fear that if an inmate were granted parole after serving only four or six months and violated parole in a spectacular fashion, the parole board would be subject to more than the usual amount of criticism.[60]

4. To Benefit the Inmate

Illustration No. 18: The inmate, a young man who appeared to be in his late teens, had come from what many would describe as a "good home." He had two brothers, both of whom were ordained ministers, and his parents were respected members of the community. The inmate's father constantly demanded more of the inmate than the latter thought he had the ability to accomplish and continually compared him unfavorably with his older brothers. This comparison was also made by the inmate's school teachers because the inmate, although of high average intelligence, did rather poorly in school. Nevertheless, he had completed all but part of his senior year in high school by the time he had been sentenced to the reformatory. In its pre-parole summary, the classification committee of the institution recommended that the inmate be permitted to complete his high school education, on the ground that it would aid him in the achievements of which he was capable. Some members of the parole board believed that if the inmate finished high school,

he might go to college. The parole board decided to defer the case for five months to permit the inmate to complete his high school education prior to his release.

Cases sometimes arise in which it may appear to the parole board that a denial of parole would bring a benefit to the inmate which would be unobtainable if parole were granted. It is arguable, of course, that whenever the board denies parole because it believes the inmate has not reached the optimum time for release in terms of rehabilitation, this is, in reality, a benefit to the inmate. But there are other cases in which the benefit obtainable only through a parole denial may be at least as real, but may have no direct connection with the inmate's rehabilitation. Perhaps the clearest examples are those in which the inmate is suffering from a physical illness which is correctable in the prison but which release to the community would aggravate, or those in which the inmate would benefit from devices, such as dental plates or a hearing aid, which could be provided at no cost to him if he remains an inmate but which may not be as readily obtainable on the outside.[61] The illustration case is one in which the benefit accruing to the inmate by remaining in the institution is related both to his rehabilitation and to his more general welfare. The parole board may sometimes be faced with the dilemma of having an inmate who in terms of its rehabilitation standard might best be released, but who in terms of the interest of the institution in the inmate's

---

[59] A similar basis exists for the provision that female misdemeanants may be committed to the Wisconsin Home for Women instead of local jails, but only if the sentence is six months or longer. Wis. Stat. Ann. § 959.045(4) (Supp. 1966). An official in the Wisconsin Division of Corrections said that the six months requirement exists because the board of parole and the institution could not develop enough information to formulate a program for them in less time.

[60] In denying parole to an inmate who had served only four months before the hearing, a parole board member commented: "There has not been a sufficient period of time to warrant the parole risk in this case."

[61] The Model Penal Code authorizes denial of parole to obtain a benefit for the inmate which is related to his rehabilitation. Model Penal Code § 305.9(1) (Proposed Official Draft 1962) provides in part:

Whenever the Board of Parole considers the first release of a prisoner who is eligible for release on parole, it shall be the policy of the Board to order his release, unless the Board is of the opinion that his release should be deferred because:

. . . .

(d) his continued correctional treatment, medical care or vocational or other training in the institution will substantially enhance his capacity to lead a law-abiding life when released at a later date.

total welfare ought to be retained to receive a special benefit which the institution can provide.

5. To Avoid Criticism of the Parole System

Illustration No. 19: The inmate had been convicted of embezzling $25,000 from a veterans' service group. He had absolutely no prior criminal record. Before the offense he had been a prominent member of the community and was well liked. This was his initial parole hearing. When the parole board learned that as a result of the offense the attitude of the community was very much against the inmate, it voted to deny parole.

There is a feeling shared among many parole board members that the success of the parole system depends in part on whether it achieves public approval and confidence. In some states the parole board publishes literature on the parole system for the public, and members make speeches or give demonstrations of parole hearings to civic and social groups. The parole board may also invite community leaders to be present at parole hearings and observe how the board functions.

While a desire to be free of public criticism and to gain the confidence of the public is a characteristic probably common to all criminal justice agencies, the parole board seems particularly sensitive. Whatever the reasons for this concern, it is sometimes reflected in the parole decision. Parole boards are often reluctant to release assaultive offenders despite their own estimate of the high probability of parole success. One reason for this is the board's concern for the safety of the community—that while the probability of recidivism may be low, the seriousness of the violation, if it occurs, is likely to be quite great. But another reason for the board's reluctance to release assaultive offenders is its concern about adverse public reaction if the offender violates parole in a spectacular manner.[62]

The concern about public criticism is even more clearly an important factor in the trust violation cases. The parole board normally views public or private officials who have embezzled funds as good parole risks in terms of the likelihood of parole success. One parole member even said that he thought these persons should not be sent to prison since, because of the usual publicity surrounding their apprehension and conviction, they are very unlikely to repeat the same or a similar offense. Nevertheless, the question whether they should be paroled raises the difficult problem of determining what weight the parole board should give to community attitudes. If the attitude of the community toward the inmate is good, he is likely to be paroled as soon as he is eligible. When the community attitude is negative, parole is likely to be denied. One reason may be that a negative community attitude is likely to seriously hamper the inmate's efforts to adjust. Another reason, and probably the more important one, is that parole of such an inmate would expose the board and the parole system to public criticism. One parole board member expressed his attitude toward the trust violation cases in terms of a dilemma, stating that to some extent a parole board must defer to certain community attitudes but that no parole board member can go beyond a certain point without violating his own conscience.

The board's concern with public criticism of the parole system also affects the parole decision in cases in which the inmate or a member of his family has attempted to put unusual pressure on the parole board for his release. This normally occurs in cases in which the inmate has received a long sentence, often a life sentence. The inmate may write letters to influential persons in state government or to anyone else whom he thinks might be able to influence the board.

---

[62]One member of a parole board indicated that although parole prediction studies have shown that murderers, sex offenders, and men who have committed assaults are among the best parole risks, the fact remains that if one is paroled and repeats the same type of crime, the unfavorable publicity is many times that when a sixth forgery offender is paroled and again forges checks.

Sometimes, the inmate or his family may hire attorneys whom they think have unusual influence with the board. The attitude of the parole board in such cases toward the release of the inmate is likely to be extremely negative. In one case, a member of the board said that if a lifer who wrote great numbers of letters trying to get someone to influence the board would cease writing for six months, he would be released, but so long as he persisted in his present behavior the board member was determined that he "do it all."[63] If the board were to grant parole to such an inmate on the merits of the case, it would expose itself to the accusation that the parole grant was the result of special influence. The board prefers to keep the inmate in prison rather than incur that risk.

[63]One parole board uses a special investigator attached to the corrections department to investigate suspected attempts to secure parole through unethical pressure.

74. The Parole Board Hearing

DAVID T. STANLEY

"WE HAVE THIS TERRIBLE POWER; WE SIT UP HERE playing God," said the chairman of the U.S. Board of Parole after a day's hearings that were reported in detail in a magazine article.[1] The power may seem godlike, but the premises and proceedings are on a decidedly lower level. The typical parole hearing takes place in a small, plain room inside the prison. In a hall outside half a dozen prisoners wait their turn under the eye of a guard. Inside the room the panel of two or three board members or hearing examiners[2] sits behind a table holding a stack of files and a tape recorder. Sitting nearby is a prison caseworker who maintains the docket, calls prisoners in to be heard, and records the decisions.

The Dialogue

When the prisoner enters, often visibly tense or sullen, he is greeted by the member who will question him. It is customary to take turns interviewing and for one to talk to the prisoner while the others review files of prisoners scheduled next and pay partial attention to the hearing.

Normally the questioner gives the others a chance to ask a question when he is finished. About half of the time they do, generally only a single question or piece of advice. Wisconsin board members, however, all of whom are educated as social workers, were more likely to participate in hearings they do not conduct themselves, and at much greater length, than members in the other governments studied.

The prisoner is greeted by name—usually his first name—and an effort is made to put him at ease. The tone adopted is normally friendly, but in a majority of hearings observed in the present study it became patronizing and sometimes demeaning: "Well, John, have you been behaving yourself lately?" "What can we do with you now, Bill?" (In fairness to parole board members it must be acknowledged that the stakes in this proceeding are very high, that the situation is tense, and that anything the member says can be objected to by a rubbed-raw prisoner or a critical observer.) The conversation usually centers on one or more of three subjects: the inmate's prison record, his parole plans, and the circumstances of his crime. Whatever the topic, the members are watching for indications of the inmate's willingness to face his problems, both past and future.

Prison Record. Referring to the inmate's file, the board member moves quickly to discussion of disciplinary infractions, assigned duties, and training. Talking about discipline is usually not productive. The prisoner caught fighting, talking back to a correctional officer, or possessing weapons, drugs, or excess food has already been dealt with by a prison disciplinary board. He may simply acknowledge his offense to the

▶SOURCE: *Prisoners Among Us: The Problem of Parole.* Washington: The Brookings Institutions, 1976. Pp. 34–46. Reprinted by permission.

[1]Robert Wool, "The New Parole and the Case of Mr. Simms," *New York Times Magazine* (July 29, 1973), pp. 14–16, 18–20, 24–25, 30.

[2]Those who conduct the hearing will be called "members" whether they are actually board members or employees.

parole board and say he will do better in the future. Sometimes he will claim that he was unfairly treated or argue about the specifics ("I was just carrying those pills to Robinson; he had forgotten them," or "I didn't do it; they wrote up the wrong man"). Infrequently there is an outburst, as when one hearing examiner kept criticizing the prisoner for disciplinary failures recorded in the file and the inmate angrily said, "When I come to the Board you never talk to me. You talk to my jacket [file]. That's not me. You should tell me how much progress I must make."

Board members whom we observed usually did tell prisoners what they expected of them in terms of improved behavior or participation in therapy or training. There was occasional resistance: "If I learn a trade I won't use it." "That group therapy—man, all they do is hassle you." Normally, however, prisoners try to sound cooperative: "Yeah, I been going to AA [Alcoholics Anonymous]." "Expect to get my high school certificate." Humor may appear:

PAROLE BOARD MEMBER: "Why did you have that knife, Jim?"

INMATE (in very impressive manner): "Why *did* I have that knife, Mr. J——? Well, you might say it was for social purposes."

Parole Plans.   This is another natural topic. Even though the board member has studied a report showing what the inmate expects to do when he gets out, he asks the prisoner to tell him about his job prospects and living arrangements. In the governments studied here the prisoner was not pressed for a specific job with a specific employer if his prospects seemed reasonable considering his qualifications ("I'll work with graders and bulldozers in the Tampa area").

A recent survey of fifty parole boards showed that thirty-eight of them require that an offender have a job or "satisfactory other resources, which could include a place to stay where the person would be taken care of until he could find a job, a social security check, personal financial resources, a training slot, and the like" before he can be released on parole.[3]

The inmate is also questioned about whom he will live with, what his relationship with that person has been, and whether he will have problems with transportation to work. Parole boards naturally object to a prospective parolee's living with someone who seems to have led him or driven him to crime in the past (though autocratic parents seem to be an exception to this). If he plans to go to school he will be asked about his expected income and residence.

This sort of questioning can be constructive. The board gets an understanding of how realistically and sensibly the inmate is facing the future (if he is being candid). The inmate, in turn, may benefit from the board members' reactions. The discussion will also be useful in cases where the board has conflicting recommendations in the file. It is not unusual, for example, for the prison staff to endorse the prisoner's wish to be paroled to San Diego, but for a parole officer in that area to recommend against it. In some cases, the board may defer decision until a satisfactory parole plan is agreed upon. In others, they may grant parole anyway, feeling that the prisoner is "ready," even if he has no job lined up and is headed for an unwholesome neighborhood.

The constructive tone was shattered in some hearings when the member abruptly and harshly asked something like "How do we know you can stay out of trouble there?" "What makes you think you can stay on the wagon?" Such questions are hard on a scared inmate, who feels that anything he replies will seem wrong. The more confident, experienced convicts handled them easily: "I've learned my lesson, sir. Nothing like that will ever happen again, sir."

"Retrying the Case."   The board member has

[3]William Parker, *Parole: Origins, Development, Current Practices and Statutes,* American Correctional Association, Parole Corrections Project Resource Document no. 1 (College Park, Md., 1975), p. 217.

"played God" in both of the above types of questioning. He does so also when he questions the prisoner about his crime. He "plays prosecutor," too. The prisoner may be interrogated in some detail about the facts of the crime: "What got you started on this?" "Who drove the car? How did you break in?" "Why didn't you go home sooner?" If the prisoner's answers do not match the reports in the file he is cross-examined. Some prisoners respond openly and penitently, others become defensive or evasive. We heard numerous arguments about locations, times, actions. The manner of the board member may be firm and objective, or sternly prosecutorial, or even morbidly interested. Some board members keep after inmates about sex crimes, others on drug-related cases. Their interests differ, and their motives are not always apparent. What appears to be pointless harassment may be an effort to get the inmate to face up to his responsibility for the crime. The effort is not always successful, as in the case of one convicted rapist who just kept saying that he had been drunk and the victim was willing.

Many of the offenders who come before parole boards have been imprisoned after plea bargaining. In the cases we observed the board's questioning clearly assumed guilt of the major crime: armed robbery instead of possession of a dangerous weapon, burglary instead of possession of burglar's tools, murder instead of neglect resulting in death of a child. Such a course of questioning is defended by parole board members on the grounds that they are trying to find out more about the inmate—how dangerous a person is he? The opposing argument is that it is unfair to the prisoner to grill him about a crime other than the one for which he is in prison. It would be interesting to know (if one could find out) how frequently prosecutors accept plea bargains knowing that the parole board will take into account the greater crime and may therefore decide to deny parole for a few more months, or even longer.

Such retrials in general are pointless. They may contribute something to the board's under-standing of the inmate by testing his attitude toward his crime and his intentions for the future. But how much does it mean for an inmate to look the board in the eye and say something contrite? It is not hard for a prisoner to be sincere when he tells the board that he regrets the crime that brought him to prison.

Counseling Efforts.   In all the jurisdictions we visited, particularly Colorado and Wisconsin, the hearings were used for counseling as well as inquisition. Inmates were advised to "get their heads together," that is, to make up their minds to stay out of trouble. More specifically they were told to quit fighting, to attend alcohol or drug therapy sessions, to work for their high school equivalency certificates, or to learn a trade. Inmates usually respond cooperatively but sometimes explain why it is difficult to take part: they can't leave their work; there are no vacancies in the class; even "the therapist turns me off."

Some counseling efforts are decidedly inexpert and unhelpful, like these observations from members of one board:

> "You are small in stature. Do you feel inadequate?"
> "You have a fear syndrome."
> "You have made a career of avoidance and under-achieving."
> "Tony, when are you going to stop acting like a juvenile delinquent?"
> "It's just a matter of time before you are a rumdum again, walking down the street with a stolen eight-dollar ratio under your arm."

To the convict the hearing is a big moment—which is about how long it seems. He has only a few minutes to present his case for a crucial decision. Jessica Mitford writes that the California Adult Authority averages a little less than seventeen minutes per prisoner, but she was told by one prisoner, "In my experience, five to seven minutes is more like it."[4] Both statements are probably right.

The average numbers of hearings per day

---

[4]Jessica Mitford, "Kind and Usual Punishment in California," *Atlantic Monthly*, vol. 227 (March 1971), p. 49.

conducted by parole boards in fifty-one jurisdictions, according to the National Council on
Crime and Delinquency survey, are as follows:[5]

Average number of cases per day	Number of jurisdictions
1–19	11
20–29	15
30–39	14
40 and over	11

The national median based on these figures is
twenty-nine cases a day. Field observations for
this study show a far lower number: board
members and hearing examiners thought they
were doing "well" if they got through more than
fourteen or fifteen cases in a day.

First of all, a board panel probably spends
only six hours a day in actual sessions, hearing
and deciding cases. Why not eight hours? Because they use some time in the morning
traveling to the institution, then conducting
necessary business with the warden or members
of his staff. An hour must be subtracted for
lunch, coffee breaks, other discussions with
prison staff, and rest periods. And they cannot
run late in the afternoon because prisoners may
have a 4:30 P.M. "count" in their cells or a 5:00
P.M. evening meal. Of the six hours left in the
day our field observations suggest that two
thirds is spent hearing cases and one-third deciding them and dictating or noting the decision. So four hours are available for hearing
prisoners.

This means that at ten cases a day, each prisoner gets twenty-four minutes; at fifteen cases a
day, fifteen minutes; at twenty cases, twelve minutes; at twenty-six cases, nine minutes; at
thirty-five cases, seven minutes; at forty cases,
six minutes. Fifteen cases a day was our own
observation; twenty is the maximum recommended by the National Advisory Commission

on Criminal Justice Standards and Goals;[6] and
twenty-nine is the median of the boards surveyed by NCCD.[7] Six minutes was the average
time per prisoner in New York State hearings,
"including the time for reading the inmate's file
and deliberation," according to the commission
that investigated the Attica prison disaster.[8] A
later New York study showed a range of four to
twenty-five minutes, with the majority between
six and twelve.[9]

Prisoners are plainly right when they say, in
effect, that any of these periods is a short time to
get acquainted with a man and size him up for a
decision that will affect his liberty for months or
years. Parole boards would reply that the hearing is only a part of what they base their decision
on. They have test results, prison caseworkers'
reports, recommendations of psychologists,
comments on the parole plan, and other data to
consider. They could add that prisoners are
bitterly and understandably critical of any process that does not result in their prompt release.

Attorneys, Witnesses, Records

Brief as the hearings are, informal as they are,
there must still be some procedural protections
of the parolees' rights. Due process in the usual
legal meaning of that term does not as yet apply
to parole release hearings,[10] but some states
have taken modest steps in that direction. The
NCCD survey in 1972 showed that twenty-one
out of fifty-one boards allowed inmates to have
counsel present but that the prisoners rarely did
so because they were unable to pay for attor-

[5]O'Leary and Nuffield, *Organization of Parole Systems in the United States* (Hackensack, N.J.: N.C.C.D., 1972), p. xxx. Data exclude Georgia, Hawaii, and Texas, where no hearings were conducted at the time.

[6]National Advisory Commission on Criminal Justice Standards and Goals, *Corrections* (GPO, 1973), p. 422.

[7]O'Leary and Nuffield, *Organization of Parole Systems*, p. xxx.

[8]New York State Special Commission on Attica, *Attica* (Bantam Books, 1972), p. 96.

[9]Citizens' Inquiry on Parole and Criminal Justice, *Prison without Walls: Report on New York Parole* (Praeger, 1975), p. 49.

[10]For a brief general discussion of due process in parole release decisions see David Gilman, "Developments in Correctional Law," *Crime and Delinquency*, vol. 21 (April 1975), pp. 163, 167–68.

neys.[11] Seventeen boards permitted the inmate to present witnesses, "but in no instance are witnesses permitted when counsel is not."[12]

The prisoner may need a lawyer in a parole hearing, but not in the same way that he needs one in a court trial. Parole is not an adversary proceeding, and courtroom rules of evidence are not applicable. Nevertheless the typical prisoner needs a better advocate than himself. Some inmates are indeed articulate, forceful "jailhouse lawyers," but most have limited analytical powers and verbal facility; they do not have the skill to "sell" their readiness for parole. Nor are the witnesses they call—wives, other relatives, former employers—likely to be better. Any reasonably competent attorney (or for that matter law student or even lay volunteer) could help them present themselves more effectively, by putting adverse material in perspective and by emphasizing the inmate's progress in gaining responsibility and skills. But the inmate rarely has an advocate of any kind to assist him.

Hearings were recorded verbatim in twenty of the fifty-one boards surveyed by the NCCD[13] and in oour of the six covered in the present study. The normal practice is not to transcribe the proceedings but to save the tapes, disks, or belts for replay if there are later inquiries or challenges. In some cases this can be helpful to the prisoner (or the board) if the record shows that certain factors were or were not considered in the hearing.

The Prison Caseworker's Role

The prison caseworker (variously called social worker, counselor, classification and parole officer, or by some other title) present at the hearings does more than hand records to the board and make sure its decisions are recorded. He may be called upon to solve a problem about eligibility dates, clarify some discussion of a training assignment or a disciplinary problem, or supply other information needed by the board. He may even help an inarticulate prisoner make a point to the board.

Caseworkers sometimes feel they can offer their own judgments about inmates' readiness for release: "If there are grounds for parole, sir, there are community-based psychiatric program [sic] in his home state. He needs very intensive individual psychotherapy. He won't recover in a state institution. He *might* in a community-based program."[14] Another example comes from the present study. We heard one caseworker turn to the board member after the prisoner had left the room and say, "That son of a bitch will never make it on parole." Another one said after another hearing, "I think he can probably make it this time." Such comments may or may not be valid, but two points should be made about them. First, they amplify the influence that information from prison authorities already has on the presumably independent parole board. Second, as a matter of fairness in this important proceeding, adverse comments should be made in the presence of the inmate or his attorney. (One board we observed prohibited such "late shots" from prison personnel.)

APPRAISING THE HEARINGS

Members of parole boards interviewed for this study do not question the need for hearings; they take it for granted that a prisoner must be heard before a decision is made. Board members differ in their confidence in their own ability to appraise prisoners, but most of them believe they can tell when the inmate is trying to con them, whether his attitude toward crime has changed, and whether he has violent propensities. Sometimes they predict well, sometimes poorly. Mainly, however, board members wanted to talk to us about the rigors of their

[11]O'Leary and Nuffield, *Organization of Parole Systems,* p. xxxiv.

[12]*Ibid.,* pp. xxxiv, xxxvi.

[13]*Ibid.,* p. xxxiv.

[14]Wool, "The New Parole," pp. 15–16.

hearing work—days away from home, hours spent in automobiles, excessive caseloads of inmates to see, and the tensions involved in making wise, safe decisions under the hostile scrutiny of inmates, prison officers, judges, and the press.

The Prisoner's View

The hearing is a highly traumatic experience for the inmate, according to board members, prison officials, and the prisoners themselves. A statement by a prisoner in one of the states we studied is particularly vivid. He describes on tape what it is like to anticipate and take part in a hearing.

"Sat down by myself and started thinking really heavy on what the parole board was going to say to me and what I was going to say to them. God, I really caught a drag.

"I was sort of expecting the parole board to be loud and more or less belligerent and tell me where I messed up at and get on my case over bad things I had done and I spent all that night up thinking about what I was going to say and what I was going to do. I did sleep that night for about two hours but woke up when the doors opened and I was bright-eyed, I was ready to go and meet that parole board.

"I went to breakfast, came back and thought a little more about what I was going to say—their questions, my answers—and they called me that afternoon, it wasn't till afternoon and they called me down about 2:15, I think it was, and I sat down to wait for the parole board and I started thinking and thinking hard. I started pacing back and forth and then I walked back to my house [cell] and got sick, vomited. It was just something. All of a sudden my mind was a blur. I couldn't think, I couldn't talk or nothing. Then they came to the door and told me to come in and I walked to the door and sort of stood there for a second or so and looked the room over. The man in the middle was the guy that really struck me. I felt as though he knew what he was talking about just by looking at him. The other two I didn't think too highly of. They looked like second-rate people types. I walked over, I sat down and said my hellos more or less and I was still feeling upset over being sick and

my mind really wasn't working at all. The first question that guy asked me took me a long time to answer. The first big question. He asked me what I was trying to prove to the world and all the questions that ran through my mind the night before and all that day that wasn't one of them that I thought about. That question I just didn't have an answer for and I just couldn't rap to this guy and I couldn't tell him what it was. I couldn't speak right. I was nervous and shaky and my hands were twitching.

"I wanted to look around the room and see who else was there. You know, I just couldn't move my head. I couldn't take my eyes off this guy because I was afraid he was going to throw something under the table. You know a question under the table I wasn't ready for and I wanted to be ready for it. I waited for the other two guys to start firing you know saying you should have done this or you shouldn't have done that or why didn't you do that and they never said a word, not once. I got uptight because nobody yelled at me. No one yelled and no one said you should have done this or you should have done that. Nobody got on my case. It upset me."[15]

This reaction is typical of prisoners' feelings about parole hearings, though milder perhaps than some in the literature.[16]

The Value of Hearings

Parole hearings need to be evaluated both in themselves and as part of the criminal justice decision-making process. To begin with the most important point, they are of little use in finding out whether the inmate is likely to succeed on parole. The authors of a large-scale research project on parole point out that "evidence that interviews are useful in parole prediction . . . has been preponderantly negative; repeatedly, comparisons have shown that statistical prediction devices are more valid. . . . Interviewer judgments disagree notoriously with

[15]Remarks of a state reformatory inmate taped by a parole officer; tape loaned to the author.

[16]See Robert J. Minton, Jr., ed., *Inside: Prison American Style* (Random House, 1971), pp. 176–93.

one another and have little to do with parole outcome."[17]

A strong case can be made for abolishing hearings on commonsense grounds alone. In cases where the information in the file and the board's own precedents plainly show that parole must surely be granted or denied, the hearing is a charade. In cases where the outcome is not so obvious it is a proceeding in which the inmate is at a great disadvantage and in which he has reason to say anything that will help his chances for parole. The atmosphere at such a hearing is full of tension and latent hostility. Under these circumstances the hearing is an ineffective way to elicit information, evaluate character traits, and give advice, all of which parole boards try to do. Hearings entail expense for travel, recording equipment, and paperwork that would otherwise be unnecessary. Prison routine is disrupted; inmates must be excused from classes or tasks; guards and caseworkers must be diverted from other duties. Board members are fatigued and strained; prisoners are upset. So why have hearings at all?

Given the present parole system, hearings are necessary as an expression of our national tradition and culture. A man has his day in court before he is convicted and sentenced. In all sorts of situations we feel outraged if a person is not even confronted with the evidence before something adverse is done to him. In the hearing the prisoner is at least given a chance to state his case, correct erroneous statements, and impress the board with his determination (real or alleged) to reform. Board members feel that they have at least a chance to learn more about the prisoner. His

"employment history, relations with his family, feelings about authority, his disappointments and his expectations, all are frequent topics. The interview may reveal something of his abilities and interests, his sexual attitudes or defenses against anxiety, his values,

and his plans. . . . [It] may suggest a further treatment plan (on parole or in prison), particular areas of weakness to be guarded against, and special potentials to favorable adjustment in certain situations."[18]

Nice work if the board members can get all this out of an overpowered and resentful individual in nine, eleven, or even fifteen minutes!

Nevertheless, as a matter of apparent fairness and decency the prisoner has to be interviewed, and the information gained is believed by the board to be useful. The prisoners themselves believe they must be heard, although they denounce any hearing with an adverse outcome. Board members feel frustrated and guilty if they make decisions about a person who is only a name, a number, and a collection of data in a file. Hearings are called for by the standards recommended by the American Correctional Association[19] and by the National Advisory Commission on Criminal Justice Standards and Goals.[20] So as long as there are parole decisions there will be hearings.

MAKING THE DECISION AND NOTIFYING THE PRISONER

As soon as the inmate leaves the hearing room the parole board or panel makes its decision.[21] These are complex and difficult problems, but the board usually decides quickly. The member who led the questioning of the prisoner generally states his view, which may be phrased in figures, initials, or abbreviations unintelligible to an uninitiated observer, or even conveyed by a wink or a gesture. Examples of the most common decisions are:

To grant parole effective in six months and

[17]Don M. Gottfredson, Leslie T. Wilkins, and Peter B. Hoffman, *Summarizing Experience for Parole Decision-Making*, National Council on Crime and Delinquency, Research Center, Report no. 5 (Davis, Calif.: 1972), p. 8.

[18]*Ibid.*, pp. 8–9.

[19]American Correctional Association, *Manual of Correctional Standards* (1965), p. 116.

[20]National Advisory Commission, *Corrections*, p. 422.

[21]Although this statement is a fair generalization it is oversimple. The boards that hold hearings differ widely in number of members, use of panels, delegation to nonmember examiners, and voting procedure. See O'Leary and Nuffield, *Organization of Parole Systems*, pp. xix–xxxi, xxxii–xxxiii, and, in much greater detail, 1–167.

recommend a work-release assignment (to prepare for parole) as soon as possible.

To continue in prison and reconsider parole at a future time, such as in three, six, twelve, eighteen, or twenty-four months (some state laws require reconsideration every year).

To continue imprisonment until expiration of the prisoner's maximum term.

The other one or two members present agreed with the decision in most cases observed. In a few there was discussion of a condition of parole, such as the need for drug therapy or an injunction to stay away from certain people or places. Strong disagreement over whether or when to parole the man was rare. In a three-person board or panel this is resolved by a vote. When two are present one gives way, probably the member with the milder personality.

There may be no decision, only a recommendation at this stage. A panel may refer its recommendation for later decision by the full board, as in some cases of famous or notorious persons, or a panel may have a disagreement that needs to be resolved by the full board. When hearings are held by examiners or representatives without power to parole they also record their recommendations at this time. The usual practice in the hearings observed was for the member who led the discussion with the prisoner to dictate or write the decision, giving reasons for the decision in those systems that followed this practice (only eleven of the fifty-one boards in the NCCD survey recorded reasons).[22]

The prisoner, tense and anxious after his ordeal and, indeed, about his whole future, may get his answer right away or may have to wait weeks for it. The typical inmate can predict whether his parole will be granted or denied from the way the board has questioned him. The members do not conceal their reactions to the inmate's progress, behavior, and attitude.

[22]Ibid., p. xxxiv.

They may state, or hint, their conclusions as to whether he has been punished enough or whether he can safely be returned to the community. In any event he wants to know, and know soon, what the decision is.

In twenty-two of the fifty-one governments where hearings are held, the prisoner gets the news at once in person from whoever conducted the hearing.[23] In the others, as in those that do not hold hearings, the inmate is notified by mail or by prison staff (usually his caseworker) after the prison receives the board's decision. Getting the word in writing varies from "immediately" (Maine) and "same day" (Kentucky) to "4–6 weeks" (South Carolina).[24] For news of such importance a short time is a long time, and a long time unbearable. The intensity of a prisoner's feeling when parole is deferred, even when the wait for notification is brief, is suggested by more of the taped observations of the inmate quoted earlier.[25] (In this case he did not predict the board's decision correctly.)

"It was about 1:00. I just came back from lunch and they shut my door. I heard them call work lines out and I knew they weren't going to open my door because you know I was going to find out if I was going home or find out if I got a set-back. Everybody left and on the way they stopped and said what did you get. I told them I hadn't got it yet and about five minutes later it was really quiet. It was nice and easy, no disturbance, my radio was off and I heard the footsteps coming up from the house. I knew who was coming down. I sat down on my bed. He sort of knocked on my door and gave me a big smile and he said "here you go," and he slipped it under the door. I just brooded. I sat there for a minute or so and I flashed back on the parole board before I picked it up. You know, I flashed on them not yelling at me. I flashed on them just talking about my home town, my wife and so on and how they had talked real good to me. I thought there was a good possibility I'll go home and I stood up and the paper was face down, the writing was down, and reached over and picked it up. I didn't look at it right away. I walked over to my desk

[23]Ibid., p. xxxi.
[24]Ibid., pp. 1–167 passim.
[25]See n. 15 above.

and sat down. I flipped the paper up and started reading from the top. It had my name and the date and started running it down. I got to the bottom where it said I had been deferred parole by a unanimous vote and that part really didn't bother me because I was really sort of expecting that but it said I would meet the board again in July. When I seen the July part I counted the months on my fingers and just said well fuck it. That's a fucking six and dropped the paper down and sort of leaned back and started thinking well let's see, let's make sure. That's February, March, April, May, June, July. God damn, that's a fucking six. They just gave it to me just like that. Well shit! I got up and paced around and walked back over to my desk and put the paper in my hand and looked at it and set it back down and made sure the name was mine on there. Walked over to my door and sort of knocked on it and asked them to let me out. I was getting upset and I didn't want to be in my house. I walked back and sat down on my bed. I was feeling like I was going to be sick for a minute so I took the cover off my shitter and was getting already

in case I did get sick. Then I flashed back on the parole board again and thought what a bunch of bastards. Those guys are really fucking pricks. To slap a six on me the way they did and talk to me the way they did, as good as they did. It was a trip."

This prisoner was told the board's decision fairly soon, but the message was impersonal and gave no reasons.

Prompt personal notification by the board is obviously most desirable: the anxious period is shortened, and the inmate hears just what they have decided and why, in some of the states. Mail notification has the advantage of official clarity, but it is a chilling way to convey bad news. When the prisoner is notified by prison staff there is an opportunity for discussion and for ventilation of feelings. The caseworker or other staff member may be able to explain the board's policy or to make some constructive suggestions.

75. Prediction of Parole Behavior

DON M. GOTTFREDSON
LESLIE T. WILKINS
PETER B. HOFFMAN
SUSAN M. SINGER

GENERAL OBJECTIVES OF THE STUDY

THE GENERAL AIM OF THE PROJECT WAS TO DE-velop, test, and demonstrate programs of improved information for parole decision-making. Thus, the general goals were to provide objective, relevant information for individual case decisions; to summarize experience with parole, as an aid to improved policy decisions; and to aid paroling authorities in more rational decision-making for increased effectiveness of prison release procedures.

Two general classes of decisions are made by paroling authorities: they make decisions on individual persons (case decisions); and they make "decisions about their decisions," i.e., paroling policy decisions. The project included the study of each of these types. The general problems in each case, of course, included the identification and definition of decision objectives, of information elements demonstrably relevant to the decision (i.e., to the decision outcomes) of the available decision alternatives, and of the consequences of those alternatives.

The information provided paroling authorities, if it is to be useful in decision-making, must meet the usual tests of reliability and validity. In this context, however, the issue of val-idity hinges upon definitions of the objectives of the decision. The explicit definition of the objectives of individual parole decisions (or of policy decisions) is not nearly the straightforward task that it might appear to the uninitiated observer. The parole decisions are complex; even in a context of general agreement as to aims, considerable disagreement concerning specific objectives may be expected; and various measurement problems will be encountered in seeking the clear, consensually validated definitions that would serve as anchoring points for the program.

On the assumption that a further requirement should be that the information for decision-making must—if it is to be useful—be immediately available at the time of decision, an on-line computerized system for retrieval and analysis of information for decisions was developed and its use explored.

A series of meetings was held with staff and members of the U.S. Board of Parole, and with other paroling authorities and representatives, to seek assistance in defining decision objectives, the available alternatives and constraints, the information presumed to be relevant to these decisions, and the decision consequences (i.e., the outcome criteria), which ought to be included within the scope of the study.

Further original objectives included the following:

▶SOURCE: *The Utilization of Experience in Parole Decision-Making. Summary Report. U.S. Department of Justice, Law Enforcement Assistance Administration (November, 1974), Pp. 5–19.*

1. To develop a data base (appropriate for continuation by the Board at the close of the project) containing information on the offenders, the paroling decisions, and the outcomes to parole, mandatory release, and discharge, permitting measures of the relations among offender attributes, decision outcomes, and decision consequences. The data base should lend itself to (but not be limited to) the development and validation of "experience tables." It should permit the study of all methods of prison release, rather than only of parole, in order to enable examination of the major decision alternatives which are discretionary to the board (parole, continue) and of the consequences to the major forms of prison release (parole, mandatory release and discharge).

2. To develop and demonstrate procedures for rapid retrieval of both numerical data and case history abstract information pertinent to individual case decisions. The provision of such a system for retrieval of this information for all parole decisions in the Federal system was considered beyond the scope of the project; the project aimed, rather, to develop and demonstrate models for procedures which might be employed usefully.

3. To develop monitoring or "policy control" procedures to advise the board periodically and on short notice concerning general trends in their decision-making, significant deviations in trends, deviations from established policy, and on simulated consequences to policy modifications which might be considered by the board.

4. To conduct a series of seminars with staff of the U.S. Board of Parole for development and demonstration of these procedures, and conduct similar seminars with other paroling authorities in the nation.

In short, the original objectives of the project were to define parole objectives and information needs, to describe parole decisions, to test rela-

tions between information available for parole decisions and the outcomes to those decisions (whether persons are paroled, mandatorily released, or discharged), to present relevant information quickly when needed for decisions, to develop procedures for policy control, to evaluate the utility of any new procedures developed, and to disseminate the results to parole systems of the United States.

COLLABORATING AGENCIES

During the first year of the project, 17 state parole systems (Arizona, Florida, Idaho, Illinois, Maryland, Minnesota, Missouri, Montana, Nevada, New Mexico, Ohio, Oklahoma, Oregon, Pennsylvania, Vermont, Virginia, and Wisconsin), the District of Columbia Board of Parole, and the National Parole Board of Canada volunteered to participate as "observers" of the project. These 19 agencies contributed data on a "parole opinion survey" aimed at providing information on perceived objectives and information needs of the paroling decision.

The number of "observer states" increased, however, with a national meeting held in Washington, D.C., in June of 1971. Representatives of 40 paroling agencies from Hawaii to the eastern seaboard states participated with the U.S. Board of Parole in that meeting. A second, similar meeting was conducted in 1972 in Denver, Colorado, and a third meeting, attended by 69 persons representing 48 agencies was held in New Orleans, Louisiana, in April 1973, when some results of the project were presented and discussed.

These programs served the dual purpose of explanation to participants of the project objectives and methods and their enlistment as active contributors to the research effort. Thus, following presentation of an overview of the project that described its history, objective, and methods, small group sessions were conducted in order to provide further orientation to the project methods and to obtain assistance in further elaboration of the procedures. These sessions included, for example, a demonstration of use of the on-line retrieval system using the computer terminal; a simulation of terminal use for case decisions; a group task to clarify issues concerning information selection in parole decision-making; a discussion based upon the questionnaire regarding parole board goals and information needs; an exercise in parole decision-making from short case abstracts which examined the role of base expectancy measures in parole decision-making; a discussion concerning constraints in parole decision-making; discussions of the role, utility, and limitations of parole prediction methods; and the presentation and critique of the policy control procedures developed. Generally, criticisms of the project were obtained from participating agency representatives from a questionnaire interview concerning the project and from the meetings outlined above.

The collaborative nature of the project was thought to be especially important to the development of useful procedures for providing information. Similarly, it was believed to be especially important to the possible utilization, later, of any such procedures. Information, if it is to be used, should have a degree of acceptance in the field as relevant and practically useful. That is, if utilization is to be increased, the information must be perceived as useful by the decision-makers. It may be argued that valid information, demonstrably related to the decision-makers' goals, will be ignored in the decision process unless the person responsible for the decision perceives the information as relevant and useful. Thus, three approaches aimed at increasing the likelihood of utilization of project results were taken: (1) development of the information in concert with the decision-makers themselves; (2) seminars conducted for the decision-makers in order to bring additional, possible relevant information to their attention; and (3) the preparation of a film

report to supplement written reports of project results.

SOME PROBLEMS, METHODS, AND PRELIMINARY RESULTS

Dialogue with Decision-Makers

A variety of methods were employed in seeking to attain the objectives indicated above. Some of these methods are commonly used and straightforward; others were invented in response to specific needs of the project.

It has been emphasized above that an important part of the approach taken in this study was a continuing dialogue among the project staff, the members and representatives of the U.S. Board of Parole and representatives of the funding agency, i.e., the National Institute of Law Enforcement and Criminal Justice. An interesting feature of the program has been the convergence of objectives among persons of quite different orientations. Generally, the detailed planning of the study stemmed from meetings of representatives of the above groups with the Scientific Advisory Committee.

During the 3 years of this study, the U.S. Board of Parole was the target of unprecedented criticism from various individuals, the press, and Members of the Congress of the United States. Charges of secrecy, arbitrariness, capriciousness, susceptibility to Executive pressure, defensive self-protectiveness, lack of research staff, failure to specify reasons for parole denial, and working at cross-purposes to rehabilitation were among the complaints.[1]

At the same time, the Board was seeking to deal with the issues of secrecy, arbitrariness, delay and appropriate notification of reasons

---

[1] See, for example, *The Washington Post*, March 29, 1971, and February 26, 1972; *Harper's Magazine*, November 1971.

Se also H.R. 13118, the "Parole Improvement and Procedures Act of 1972," introduced by Congressman Kastenmeier in February 1972, and S. 3993, the "Parole Commission Act of 1972," introduced by Senator Burdick.

after hearings, and the development of explicit policy. They were seeking to establish a continuing research unit as a continuation of the project reported here, which they had requested. These issues, and particularly the issue of general policy, were related to plans for a proposed regionalization of the Board's functions. Given an explicit statement of general policy, some decision-making functions might be delegated—a necessary concomitant to regionalization.

The Nature of the Decision Problems

It was mentioned above that two kinds of decisions are made by paroling authorities, and both of these general classes of their actions were studied. Corresponding to the different types of decisions are different (but overlapping) sets of information relevant to the decision problems. Paroling authorities make individual *case* decisions. They also make paroling *policy* decisions which set a broad framework within which the individual case decisions are made. The major problems of both individual decisions and general policy decisions involve the identification and definition (1) of objectives; (2) of information items demonstrably relevant to the decision (i.e., to the decision outcomes); (3) of the available decision alternatives; and (4) of the consequences of the decision alternatives (in terms of the objectives).

Also mentioned above was the point that the issue of validity (of the information used) hinges upon the definitions of the objectives of the decision. The nonuse of experience tables, in the several jurisdictions where these have been developed, emphasizes the need for clear and adequate identification of objectives. Research experience in this area is extensive enough that it is a straightforward task to develop adequately reliable and reasonably valid experience tables with respect to a single, somewhat crude dichotomous criterion of "success" or "failure" on parole. Only the quite unsophisticated would argue, however, that the measurement of parole risk in these terms is the only (or even the over-

riding) issue in parole decision-making. Other concerns relate to sanctioning, to due process, to system-regulatory, and to citizen representation objectives. Generally, throughout the correctional process, a more rigorous and thorough attention to decision objectives is needed; and then the question of validity of information for decisions must be addressed for each of the major objectives of the decision-makers.

Perceived Goals and Information Needs for Individual Decision-Making

A survey of perceived goals and factors considered in parole selection was completed early in the project. Questionnaires were sent to state and Federal parole board members asking them to rate 26 goals and 101 factors considered in granting parole. The ratings were requested on a scale ranging from "very unimportant" to "very important." Fifty-seven state and twelve Federal parole board representatives responded.

Federal and state paroling authorities agreed in rating three suggested goals as most important: (1) protection of the public; (2) the release of inmates at the optimal time for most probable success on parole; and (3) the improvement of inmate adjustment in the community after release. These general statements of goals obviously require more precise definition in operational terms for adequate measurement; nevertheless, they provide a general framework of consensus from which such work can proceed.

Other goals rated as important by Federal parole board members were the encouragement of inmate program participation and the release of persons on the basis of individual response and progress within the prison. In general, the ratings appeared to reflect the view that a major function of the board is the protection of the public and that the public may be best protected by release of offenders at the optimal time for most likely success on parole. Generally, there was considerable agreement in the ranking of goals by the Federal parole board members and their counterparts in state paroling authorities.

The kinds of information thought to be important by representatives of the Federal parole board in making individual case decisions are of interest, particularly as many of them may be considered to represent hypotheses which may be tested. Examples of information items rated as very important are the adequacy of the parole plan, presence of a past record of assaultive offense, the offender's present family situation, the attitude of the inmate's family toward him, or the use of weapons in the offense.

Since one focus of the study was upon the possible utility of experience tables, it was noteworthy that these were not generally thought to be of much importance. Of the 101 items, an item "statistical prediction of likelihood of parole violation (base expectancy)" ranked 68th in importance by the Federal parole board representatives and it was 70th in rank according to ratings by the representatives of state parole systems.

Developing a Data Base

A variety of data collection procedures were developed in order to provide an information collection system which would meet the project objectives and which could be instituted as an ongoing system by the U.S. Board of Parole. The resulting data base includes information abstracted from records of the Federal Bureau of Prisons, the U.S. Board of Parole, the Administrative Office of the U.S. Courts, and the Federal Bureau of Investigation.[2]

The major source of information regarding offenders, the paroling decisions, and outcomes during supervision for persons who are paroled is the case files used by the U.S. Board of Parole. Unfortunately, these files are not uniformly complete, frequently including conflicting in-

[2]Singer, S. M. and Gottfredson, D. M., *Development of a Data Base for Parole Decision-Making*, Report Number One, and *Parole Decision-Making Coding Manual*, Report Number Two, Davis, California: Parole Decision-Making Project, National Council on Crime and Delinquency Research Center, June 1973.

formation, and thus set limits upon the quality of information which may be extracted reliably from them. This source of data is augmented by information available from the additional Federal agencies as mentioned above.

Drawing upon the available sources of information, three basic sets of information have been accumulated. These include a large sample of offenders appearing for parole consideration ($N > 4,000$), a large sample of offenders released from prison with 2-year follow-up ($N > 1,800$), and several smaller samples of persons released on parole with follow-up.

1. *Information on Cases Appearing for Parole Consideration.*—Beginning in August, 1970, various samples of offenders being considered for parole were taken. This set included a 50 percent sample of all persons considered for parole between November, 1970, and November, 1971 (a full year), and a 30 percent sample for the period between November, 1971, and mid-June, 1972. This sample provided material for describing paroling policies and, when follow-up becomes available, may be used to validate and update experience table devices.

2. *Information on Offenders Assumed to be Representative of Persons Released from Prison on Parole.*—(a) A 10 percent sample of persons paroled in fiscal year 1968 ($N = 430$) with a 2-year follow-up study; (b) A 10 percent sample of persons paroled in fiscal year 1966 ($N = 270$) with a 3-year follow-up study; and (c) A 20 percent sample of persons sentenced under the Youth Corrections Act and paroled in fiscal year 1969 ($N = 230$) with 2-year follow-up.

These samples provided the basis for preliminary experience table development.

3. *Information on Offenders Assumed to be Representative of Persons Released from Prison with or without Supervision.*—One project objective was to compare outcomes for subjects released from prison with, and those released without, parole supervision. This retrospective sample

(50 percent of releases, January, 1970, through June, 1970) includes persons released on parole, persons mandatorily released with supervision, and persons released at expiration of sentence without supervision. A 2-year follow-up study is included.

This sample provided the major data base necessary for the development and testing of experience tables. It also provides the data needed for a comparison of various decision outcomes with their later consequences in terms of offender performance after release from prison. The information on cases appearing for parole permits description of the persons granted parole and those who are not. It also allows the development of procedures permitting the parole board to assess its trends in decisions over time. This data base enables development of a systematic program for periodic assessment and revision of experience-table-type information and of information relating to paroling policy.

A major resource which provided a stepping-stone for developing a data collection system for Federal offenders is the Uniform Parole Reports Project. The Uniform Parole Reports data base includes information on more than 130,000 offenders paroled since 1965, by the various paroling authorities of the states and other jurisdictions.[3]

Discussion of sampling techniques, the coding forms used, data collection procedures, items coded, and definitions of terms are included in the reports cited above.

Developing Experience Tables

Studies of the validity of some existing experience table methods when applied to Federal of-

fenders were completed, and one prediction method was developed on the basis of the adult Federal offender retrospective samples. This work has called into question the usefulness and applicability of the more "sophisticated" statistical manipulations commonly applied, given the quality of data available for parole decision-making for Federal offenders.

Discussion of the relevance of experience tables to individual parole decisions, of prior studies of parole prediction, and of the results of the preliminary studies were given in a separate draft report submitted to the National Institute.[4] The results support the following conclusions:

1.   Examples of offender attributes which discriminate between favorable and unfavorable parole outcomes are the commitment offense, the admission type (new case or parole violator), the history of probation or parole violations, time free in the community without commitment, prior records of commitment, sentences and incarcerations, prior juvenile delinquency convictions, the employment history, the prison custody classification, the punishment record and escape history, a prior history of mental hospital confinement, and aspects of the parole plan. Most of these examples confirm the results of earlier studies.

2.   Two forms of a base expectancy measure developed from study of California adult parolee samples were found to be valid with respect to adult Federal offenders (with validity equivalent to that for California adult parolees), but not valid for use with Federal youth samples.

3.   A classification method based upon Uniform Parole Reports data was found to have

[3]Gottfredson, D. M., et al., *A National Uniform Parole Reporting System,* Davis, California: National Council on Crime and Delinquency Research Center, December, 1970; and Gottfredson, D. M., Neithercutt, M. G., and Wenk, E. A., *Parole in the United States: A Reporting System,* Davis, California: National Council on Crime and Delinquency Research Center, October 1972.

[4]Gottfredson, D. M., Wilkins, L. T., and Hoffman, P. B., *Summarizing Experience for Parole Decision-Making,* Report Number Five, Davis, California: Parole Decision-Making Project, National Council on Crime and Delinquency Research Center, February 1972 (draft).

some validity as an experience table for Federal parolees.

4. A modification of a Bureau of Prisons' configuration table (experience table) for Youth Corrections Act releasees provides a valid prediction method for these cases.

5. A 20-item "Burgess"-type experience table has some predictive validity as well, sufficient to support its experimental use by the U.S. Board of Parole.

The same report lists a number of specific steps suggested toward the improvement of experience tables, discusses some technical problems arising from the use of relatively unreliable data, and includes a comparison of the consequences of use of several experience table methods under two hypothetical release policies. These efforts toward improvement of experience tables can continue by means of the data base discussed above, especially with implementation of its continuation by the Board.

The Problem of Overlap in Experience Table Construction

Statisticians have devised a variety of procedures for combining information (such as items concerning offenders taken from case files) in order to use them *efficiently* in predicting later behavior or administrative action (such as parole violation). The concept of efficiency can take a variety of meanings, but one meaning relates to the question of whether or not all the information is needed or contributes usefully to the accuracy or validity of the prediction.

Many items "overlap" with one another; that is, they are correlated among themselves. For example, auto thieves tend to be younger than offenders in general; persons with more prior convictions tend to have more prior arrests and sentences; and those with prior parole violations necessarily have had prior prison terms. Statisticians, therefore, have invented procedures which take such overlapping into account. When this is done it typically is found that only a

few items, appropriately weighted, may be expected to do the work—in prediction—of a much larger number.

From various studies in correctional systems, however, it now appears that less sophisticated methods of combining the information—such as simply adding favorable items together without weighting—may end up, in practice, as better than the more sophisticated techniques. This curious result suggests not that the statistical theory is wrong, but that the nature of the data does not satisfy the assumptions which are made in statistical theory.

An implication—thought to be extremely important for both research and practice—is that major advances in both must await the development of better quality data. This topic is discussed in a supplementary report.[5]

Do Experience Tables Matter?

At one of the national conferences on parole decision-making, an experiment was conducted to elicit participant attitudes toward use of base expectancy devices as aids in individual case decision-making and to examine the effect of base expectancy scores on their decisions. Participants were randomly allocated to six groups and asked to make decisions about a set of hypothetical case summaries, some with and some without a base expectancy score item. Unknown to the participants, different groups received the same cases with different base expectancy scores.

Although the statements of the participants suggested that even a reliable and valid base expectancy measure would be of marginal utility, the results of the experiment indicated otherwise. While the presentation of base expectancy scores did not appear to reduce the variations in the decisions within the various experimental groups, the presentation of *different* base ex-

[5]Wilkins, Leslie T., *The Problem of Overlap in Experience Table Construction,* Report Number Three, Davis, California: Parole Decision-Making Project, National Council on Crime and Delinquency Research Center, June 1973.

pectancy scores for the *same case* did appear to shift the average time held before release. A full report of the study is given in a supplementary report.[6]

Information Selection and Use in Parole Decision-Making

A series of experiments was conducted in order to further identify ways in which information is selected and used in parole decision-making; in part, they may be seen as "simulating" operations performed by means of computer assistance.[7] A first study employed an "information board" previously used; the second extended this procedure to the use of a random access slide projector for a computer retrieval simulation.

Different decision-makers go about their task in different ways. Decisions are made with reference to information about offenders, and decision-makers have preferences for *kinds* of information and for *methods* of presentation. Decision outcomes may be associated with the methods of presentation as well as with the qualities of the information itself. Further, the decision outcomes may be associated with the ways in which the information is "processed" by decision-makers.

Decision-makers may be of several "types"; and possibly differences among them, as they relate to information search strategies, are of importance in relation to the planning of computer-assisted decision analysis.

From these experiments several general results can be derived. Persons paroling, compared with persons not paroling, sought different information. Different items of information were generally considered important for different cases. The same decision often was made on entirely different bases; that is, different information was used by different people to arrive at the same conclusion. Information may *reduce* confidence in the decision as well as increase it. There is no unanimity among decision-makers as to the relative importance of information available to the decision, and procedures for improvement of information as aids to the decision may have to be based upon an improved understanding of differing "styles" of decision-making.

Use of an Information Retrieval System for Parole Decision-Making

The development of an on-line system for retrieval of information from the data base described above was described elsewhere.[8] The DIALOG system, which is in wide use in the National Aeronautics and Space Administration, the Office of Education, the Atomic Energy Commission, and the European Space Research Organization, was used. By means of a terminal at the offices of the U.S. Parole Board, data could be retrieved instantly, and a variety of analyses were conducted from the data loaded in a computer at the Lockheed Missiles and Space Company's Information Science Laboratory in Palo Alto, California. The terminal consists of a video screen with key boards and a teletype for printed output. A manual describing how to use the terminal and the retrieval system was prepared, and it was included, with examples of requests and analyses initiated by the parole board, in a separate report submitted to the National Institute.[9]

[6]Hoffman, Peter B. and Goldstein, Harvey M., *Do Experience Tables Matter?*, Report Number Four, Davis, California: Parole Decision-Making Project, National Council on Crime and Delinquency Research Center, June 1973.

[7]Wilkins, L. T., Gottfredson, D. M., Robison, J. O., and Sadowsky, C. A., *Information Selection and Use in Parole Decision-Making*, Report Number Five, Davis, California: Parole Decision-Making Project, National Council on Crime and Delinquency Research Center, June 1973.

[8]Wenk, E. A., Gottfredson, D. M., Summit, R. K., and Radwin, M. S., "Progress in Combining a National Data Base with DIALOG, a General Purpose On-line Retrieval System for Computer Assisted Parole Decision-Making," in *Proceedings of the National Symposium on Criminal Justice Information and Statistics Systems*, Buck, G. A., ed., Sacramento, California: California Crime Technological Research Foundation, 1970, pp. 171–181.

[9]Zeigler, M., Singer, S. M., and Hoffman, P. B., *Use of an*

Inefficient Statistics

As a research project nears its end, the investigators will usually wish to review the status of their work. What more might have been done? What contribution was made, and was this the most appropriate contribution? What factors militated against doing more? What considerations should be taken into account by those who may carry out research in the area at a later date? This questioning will involve speculation and self-criticism. A separate supplemental report attempts to deal with some of these questions.[10]

Is the development of prediction methods as important as it has been thought to be? Our answer on this issue is a qualified one: prediction methods are useful, but mainly as a research tool. In assisting in the decision-making processes of parole discretion, prediction is one element only, and its relevance involves a value judgment. Can prediction methods be improved? Our answer is that we are confident that improvements could be made and we make several suggestions as to how this might be achieved. A different form of prediction, which might be loosely termed "individual prediction," is considered and thought to be possible if and when different kinds of data become available. Some possible values and dangers of this approach are noted.

A distinction is noted between research aimed at the production of instruments for operational use and research investigations. It seems that fundamental research cannot be divorced from operational research, and vice versa. There are now noted problems arising out of operational research requiring a kind of research approach which would normally be considered as "fun-

Information Retrieval System for Parole Decision-Making, Report Number Ten, Davis, California: Parole Decision-Making Project, National Council on Crime and Delinquency Research Center, February 1972 (draft).

[10]Wilkins, Leslie, T., Inefficient Statistics, Report Number Six, Davis, California: Parole Decision-Making Project, National Council on Crime and Delinquency Research Center, June 1973.

damental research," before more progress is probable. One important area is that of investigation of the processes of decision-making. The information search strategies of decision-makers (as well as the goals they seek) are important, but little understood at the present time. There is clearly a relationship between "degrees of belief" and "probability," and there are very important issues of moral values which impinge upon research methods.

It is thought that the present methods whereby research funds become available may not be such that an optimal research strategy is to be developed. It is considered that the relevance of research to social problems is not related to whether the research is at a high or low level of abstraction. High levels of abstraction may also be highly relevant; the difficulty arises in demonstrating this.

The Operational Use of an Experience Table

Since one objective of the Parole Decision-Making project was the development of experience tables for operational use by the U.S. Board of Parole to aid in individual case decision-making, a supplementary report describes the interaction of parole board members and project staff in the development of an experience table acceptable to the parole board for operational use.[11]

The results of this experiment indicated that the provision of an experience table:

1. influenced the parole board members' clinical risk estimates (primarily in cases in which the statistical score was lower than expected);

2. increased the relationship between statistical score and decision (in terms of time held). A similar result was produced merely by focus-

[11]Hoffman, P. B., Gottfredson, D. M., Wilkins, L. T., and Pasela, G. E., The Operational Use of an Experience Table, Report Number Seven, Davis, California: Parole Decision-Making Project, National Council on Crime and Delinquency Research Center, June 1973.

ing the parole board members' attention upon the parole risk issue by having them complete clinical risk estimates;

3. increased, rather than decreased, the average time held for all but the best risk cases, although the experience table scores were generally higher (more favorable) than the parole board members' clinical estimates;

4. increased the agreement of clinical risk estimates between pairs of parole board members considering the same case, but did not reduce the proportion of decision disagreements (split votes);

5. did not affect the subjective ease-difficulty rating given the decision.

Paroling Policy Feedback
Paroling policy decisions set the framework within which individual decisions are made. The former generally are not explicitly stated, and the lack of clearly articulated policy guidelines has resulted in considerable criticism of parole board decision-making practices.

A study of policy conducted in collaboration with members of the Youth Correction Division of the U.S. Board of Parole is reported in a supplementary report.[12] Its aim was to provide a feedback device capable of making more explicit the presently implicit policies used in making case decisions. A feedback device of this type may enable parole board members to: compare actual policies with those desired, and take corrective action if indicated; reduce disparity in individual case decision-making by noting decisions which appear to vary substantially from usual practice; and reduce the criticism leveled against the parole board as having unfettered discretion.

The relations between decision-makers' evaluations of four specific case factors (severity of the offense, institutional program participation, institutional discipline, and chances of favorable parole outcome) and paroling decisions were studied. From these relations a method of describing and articulating implicit paroling policy was demonstrated and the relative weights given to the above factors in practice were described.

Paroling Policy Guidelines: A Matter of Equity
In the appendix to this report* the Chairman of the U.S. Board of Parole discusses the need for more explicit definition of factors used in parole selection and the problem of determining how various factors should be weighted; and he points out that *implicit* policy may be made *explicit* through an analysis of present practice. The major task of the parole board is to set standards and explicit policies; in order to further these objectives, a Federal Pilot Regionalization Project makes use of decision guidelines which do not remove discretion, but enable its exercise in a fair and rational manner. They are designed to structure and control discretion and to provide an explicit, uniform policy contributing to the issues of fairness and equity.[13]

Justice and Fairness. The concept of fairness is not exactly the same as the concept of justice. There is, however, seldom any clear distinction made in the use of the two terms in law. Some dictionaries define "fairness" as lack of injustice, but the absence of injustice is not the same as the presence of justice—thus "justice" is not defined as fairness, but rather as "an accord with truth." That is to say, there seems to be reasonable agreement among authorities of English usage that nothing can be just which is unfair; but

---

*[not included in this selection].

[13]This appendix is included as a Preface in Hoffman, P. B. and Gottfredson, D. M., *Paroling Policy Guidelines: A Matter of Equity*, Report Number Nine, Davis, California: Parole Decision-Making Project, National Council on Crime and Delinquency Research Center, June 1973, which describes and discusses the development and use of the decision guidelines in more detail.

[12]Hoffman, Peter B., *Paroling Policy Feedback*, Report Number Eight, Davis, California: Parole Decision-Making Project, National Council on Crime and Delinquency Research Center, June 1973.

fairness is not necessarily justice; or justice includes fairness, but is more demanding. It may be that we could claim that this is because fairness is a relative term, but justice implies absolute values. This is a convenient distinction and accordingly, since words have uses rather than meanings, we propose to use the words in this way. In order to make clear the nature of the use we intend, the diagram below may suffice:

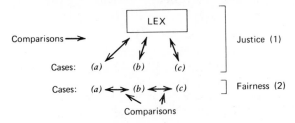

That is to say (or indicate) if a, b, c, . . . , n are each compared in an appropriate manner, and adjusted with respect to LEX (Equation [1]), then they will be adjusted with respect to each other. Ensuring "justice" (accord with truth/law) also ensures fairness. In the first case (justice), there is an external criterion. In the second case (fairness) (Equation [2]), the elements can be in adjustment with each other, but are not necessarily in accord with respect to an external criterion. By "fairness" we mean that *similar* persons are dealt with in *similar* ways in *similar* situations. Thus, the idea of fairness implies the idea of similarity and of comparisons; it cannot relate to the unique individual since, obviously, if every person is unique, there are not grounds for comparisons and, hence, no ways in which it is possible to discuss fairness. Will an individual, then, see his treatment as "fair" if he sees himself as (in all significant ways) similar to another person who received exactly similar treatment? Not quite, since it would seem to require more than one other person—it would not be unreasonable to claim that both were treated unfairly. However, as the sample of "similar" persons increases, so the idea of similar treatments among that sample becomes more likely to be regarded as "fair."

The moral, or at least metaphysical, idea of "fairness," thus, becomes closely related to statistical concepts of similarity (or variance) and sample size. Any claim on the part of a citizen or another who asserts that the parole board is "unfair" is implicitly stating that, according to his beliefs (knowledge?), similar persons involved in similar crimes are receiving different treatments. The factors which are taken into consideration in the reference set sample of persons and characteristics may vary in some degree from on critic to another; some will look with particular care at race (unfairness which is related to racial characteristics is defined as "racism" because "race" is not seen as a reasonable or morally acceptable factor to justify differences in treatment); some will look with particular care at the type of offense; and some at both types of offenses and racial factors. However, the scale and scope of comparison upon which critics may rely are not likely to be wider than the scale and scope of factors which the board might consider. By the use of a model which is built upon these common elements of comparison (fairness criteria), the board could respond with precision to criticisms. If the board sustains a balance with respect to probability of reconviction, crime seriousness and behavior in the institutional setting, and ignores race, it will be unlikely to be accused of racial bias.

If the board were to have before it, in each case in which a decision is to be made, a chart which indicated the balance between the three or four most obvious factors which arise in any discussion of "fairness," the decision-makers could always depart from the calculated figure; but, in doing so, they would be making a value judgment of further factors not included in the model. If these further factors were made explicit in the decision (this may seem similar to the recent requirement of the courts for boards to "state reasons"), a sound case for each decision would seem to be made. However, the general policy of the board would not be defended by such a model; but, clearly, the decisions *within* the model would be "fair." The question of justice is one of beliefs; but we can, by the use of research methods and the preparation of models, address the question of fairness. If attention were diverted from individual cases (". . . his case was not fairly determined . . .") to questions of general principles of parole, the understanding and control of the system would, it seems, be increased in great measure. Human attention could then be more thoroughly devoted to humanitarian considerations because the routine comparative work (even although highly complex) could be delegated to "models" of "fairness."

In addition to and moderating the idea of fairness is the idea of effectiveness. We may also see the idea of effectiveness as modulated by "fairness." This interaction is presently without specification of intensity or direction. Estimates of the probability of reconviction would, of course, be included in the "model"; and the expectation of reconviction would have to be reasonably equal among offenders (who were also otherwise similar) for the treatment to be expected to be equal. This would not hold, of course, if the idea of probability of reconviction were ruled as outside the consideration of parole on policy, moral, or other grounds. The effect upon the pattern of decisions, which would be probable under changed emphasis upon the probability of reconviction or seriousness of crime, could be examined. Thus, if the board were known to be taking into account the seriousness of the offense and the courts determined that this was inappropriate, the effect of removing this variable could be plotted. Again, if the behavior of the offender in the institution were thought to be given too little attention relative to other factors, the model could be changed. If the model takes a factor or factors into account, it is possible to show what the expected results would be if any of those factors were changed or eliminated.

The study of criteria used in making paroling decisions (as distinguished from criteria used in predicting parole outcome), cited above, in which board members completed a set of sub-

jective rating scales for a sample of actual decisions, indicated that three factors or focal concerns (severity, parole prognosis, and institutional behavior) were primary.[14] Youth Corrections Act cases (which have no minimum sentence and are seen generally within three months of reception) were studied. Using the variable—time to be served before review—as the criterion at the initial decision, it was found that parole board decisions could be predicted fairly accurately by knowledge of their severity and prognosis ratings. Similarly, at review considerations, parole board decisions (parole or continue) were strongly related to ratings of institutional discipline.

From this knowledge, the development of an explicit indicant of parole selection policy was possible. Concerning initial decisions, a chart with one axis reflecting the concern of offense severity and another the concern of parole prognosis (risk) was developed. At each intersection of these axes, the expected decision given (in months to be served before review hearing) is shown.

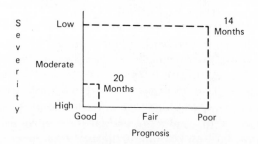

In the example above, for high severity-good prognosis cases (such as armed robbery-first offender), the expected decision is 20 months to be served before review consideration. For low severity-poor prognosis cases it is 14 months. At review considerations, cases with adequate-very good institutional adjustment (discipline and program progress ratings were highly correlated) were generally released; those with below

[14]Hoffman, *op. cit., supra* note 12.

average-poor ratings were likely to be continued for another hearing.

As an aid in actual case decision-making, this type of chart could be used in the following manner. After scoring the case on the concerns of severity and prognosis, the parole board member or hearing examiner would check the table to see the expected decision. In practice, a range (e.g., 20 to 24 months) would be appropriate to allow for some variation within broad severity or risk categories. Should the board member or examiner wish to make a decision outside of the expected range, he would be obligated to specify the factors which make that particular case unique (such as unusually good or poor institutional adjustment, credit for time spent on a sentence of another jurisdiction, etc.). At review hearings, the decision to parole or continue would be based primarily on institutional performance. That is (with a few specific exceptions[15]), cases with satisfactory institutional performance could expect release at this time.

Actual Use.   In October, 1972, a pilot project was launched by the U.S. Board of Parole to test the feasibility of regionalization of its operations. This pilot project, comprised of five institutions in the Northeast (which contain about one-fifth of the total board workload), contained a number of innovative features, including panels of two examiners to conduct institutional hearings, the opportunity for inmates to be represented by nonlawyer advocates, speedier decisions, written reasons for parole denial, a two-stage appeal process, and the *use of decision guidelines.*

For all initial hearings, the hearing panels were instructed to complete an evaluation form which included a severity rating scale and a "prognosis" score (experience table score, called on the form "salient factors"). Should they make a recommendation outside of the guideline

[15]Such as long-term sentence cases involving serious offenses in which the initial continuance (limited to 3 years by board policy) is deemed insufficient.

table, they were instructed to specify the factors in the case which resulted in this decision. The hearing format summary was designed so that the last section begins with a standard paragraph:

"The hearing panel considers this to be a *moderate* offense severity case with a salient factor score of 9. The subject has been in custody for a total of 2 months.

"A decision to *continue for 10 months* is recommended. (Indicate reasons if outside guidelines.)"

For review hearings, completion of the evaluation form was required before any continuance (for reasons other than institutional discipline or failure to complete specific institutional programs) was recommended. If a parole grant was recommended, form completion was not necessary. This was designed so that the guidelines would not be exceeded by arbitrary continuances at review hearings. One exception is that, if the previous continuance was 30 months or more, the evaluation form and guideline table must be completed. This was necessary to deal with the highest offense severity levels where the guidelines might indicate a time to be served longer than possible at the initial hearing (by board policy, continuances are limited to 3 years at one time). At early review hearings (if an inmate shows exceptional institutional progress, he may be recommended by the institution for earlier review consideration), the guidelines are consulted also to see whether the exceptional progress justifies the advanced parole date recommended.

Reports from parole board staff have been extremely favorable concerning both the guidelines and the other regionalization project features. The need for greater consistency in decision-making had long been acknowledged, and the use of the decision guidelines appears to be accepted as serving this need.

Guidelines Modifications.   As the danger of rigidity exists with guideline use as much as the danger of disparity exists without them, procedures for the updating and modification of the guidelines were developed. First, the board may at any time vote affirmatively to change parole selection policy by modifying any guideline category or combination of categories. Second, at 6-month intervals, feedback from the decision-making of the previous 6 months will be given to the board.

Implications and Limitations. The use of explicit decision guidelines for parole selection attunes to a much stressed need for parole boards to formulate a consistent general policy. By articulating the weights given to the major criteria under consideration, it can allow interested publics to assess the rationality and appropriateness of the policy set by their representatives (the parole board). It acknowledges that parole selection is actually a deferred sentencing decision (particularly in the case of low [or no] minimum sentences, as is the general trend), which determines the time to be served before release, rather than a dichotomous yes/no decision. For individual case decision-making, it provides a method of structuring and controlling discretion without eliminating it and holds considerable promise for decision improvement with respect to the issue of fairness or equity. Furthermore, as the factors of severity and risk will be considered at the initial hearing, subsequent hearings, if any, primarily will consider institutional behavior. This procedure should substantially reduce the present uncertainty felt by inmates under indeterminate sentences as to when they will be actually released (and as to what they must accomplish to obtain this release).

The decision guidelines method has implications not only for original parole selection decisions, but also for decisions about parole violation and reparole consideration as well. The method appears equally applicable to (judicial) sentencing decisions where similar problems of disparity arise.

It is important to stress that much work *ought* to be done in refining the guidelines concept, the scales used, the procedures for applying them in individual cases, and the procedures to

be used in their modification. At present, these are admittedly crude. Nevertheless, they appear to be seen as useful. The U.S. Board of Parole has taken the step of attempting to formulate an explicit policy and is facing the knotty issues of discretionary control.

Parole Selection: A Balance of Two Types of Error

In making parole selection decisions, a parole board runs the risk of making two types of error: the first concerns the premature release of individuals who will commit new offenses or parole violations; the second involves not releasing individuals who, if released, would have completed parole without violation. A supplemental report focuses upon a method of assessing the incidence of both error types and describing the balance between them.[16] A feedback device to provide information concerning the potential consequences of changes in parole selection policy upon this balance, and the resultant "social costs," is then discussed.

Information Overload: Peace or War with the Computer

Decision research may be considered as developing along two independent lines of inquiry, namely:

1.   the axiomatic approach based upon the work of statisticians and game theorists (this method focuses upon what kinds of decisions ought to be made under specified conditions); and

2.   the observational or empirical approach (the major thrust in this area has been in the study of small group performance of decision tasks or individual preferences in gaming).

The implications for fundamental research in

[16]Hoffman, Peter B., *Parole Selection: A Balance of Two Types of Error*, Report Number Ten, Davis, California: Parole Decision-Making Project, National Council on Crime and Delinquency Research Center, June 1973.

decision theory and the practice of many of the issues which came into focus during the Federal Parole Decision-Making Project are discussed in a supplemental report.[17] It may be that the strategy for research should now direct more effort toward advancing understanding of the relations between memory and decision-making, and between the axiomatic and the empirical approaches. There are also important moral and philosophical questions which come into the picture through the coincidence between probability and degrees of belief.

This report was originally prepared for publication in the *Journal of Criminal Law and Criminology,* with the aim of directing the attention of legal and criminological research workers to some of the fundamental research issues and findings which were an important byproduct of the Decision-Making Project. No new materials are included in the report but, rather, an attempt has been made to consider the possible impact of the materials reported elsewhere in a more general setting. There are implications for decision-making in almost all fields of endeavor and, particularly, in all those areas of the criminal justice system where discretion is exercised.

The Reliability of Information in the Parole Decision-Making Study

The collection of information on approximately 6,000 cases and the use of such data for prediction or risk tables requires that some measure of the reliability of that data be made. Although the validity of the information found in Federal prison inmates' files could not be determined, procedures for uniform interpretation and coding of that information were defined. Collection of a reliability sample provided a measure of the degree of agreement among coding staff. The procedure also uncovered areas of coding difficulty and served as a training device for new staff. These issues, with results from two separate reliability studies, are discussed in a supplementary report.[18]

It was noted above that various studies suggest that less sophisticated methods of combining information—for example, the development of prediction methods—may end up in practice as better than the more sophisticated techniques. It was asserted also that this curious result suggests not that the statistical theory is wrong, but that the nature of the data does not satisfy the assumptions which are made in statistical theory.

An implication—thought to be extremely important for both research and practice—is that major advances in both must await the development of better quality data.

Doubtless some persons concerned with the correctional management system will regard this finding as a blinding glimpse of the obvious. Everybody, it may be claimed, who is closely connected with the processing of offenders knows that the recording of information is not treated with any great respect; and that, in some establishments, the offenders themselves have some responsibility for some of the recording procedures. To arrive at this result, the research workers, as usual, have gone the long way around and have introduced plenty of inconsequential theory! Perhaps the poor quality of the basic data is obvious to some persons, but those persons presumably use the information recorded, or some of it, to make their decisions regarding disposition of offenders, provisioning, or transportation and other questions. It has, it must be assumed, generally been regarded that the quality of the information was "good enough" for its purpose and that any investment of money to increase the quality of

---

[17]Wilkins, Leslie T., *Information Overload: Peace or War with the Computer,* Report Number Eleven, Davis, California: Parole Decision-Making Project, National Council on Crime and Delinquency Research Center, June 1973.

[18]Beck, James L. and Singer, Susan M., *The Reliability of Information in the Parole Decision-Making Study,* Report Number Twelve, Davis, California: Parole Decision-Making Project, National Council on Crime and Delinquency Research Center, June 1973.

data was unjustified. This is now clearly shown not to be the case. As a temporary measure to accommodate poor quality data, we may apply less sophisticated methods to the utilization of it because this strategy provides a better result than that which we can obtain by the use of higher grade methods. There is some analogy with extraction of minerals: high quality ore is needed if powerful methods of extraction are to be used; poor quality ore can be used in rougher methods of extraction. But data are not natural products over which we have no control; data about offenders are generated within the criminal justice system. The criminal justice system is the "consumer" of that data, and the same system is concerned (or should be) with the quality of the product. The products generated out of data are decisions. Decisions cannot be better than the data upon which they are based, no matter what techniques of handling the data may be employed. The conflict of statistical theory with experience in the practical world of decision-making in criminal justice has revealed a fundamental problem of the quality of the raw material, and it has shown beyond all reasonable doubt that the quality of the basic information is not inconsequential.

The Practical Application of a Severity Scale
Since prior study had shown the importance of the concept "offense severity" for parole decision-making, two exercises were conducted with decision-makers in order to develop procedures for more consistent offense severity judgments. Hearing examiners and board members of the U.S. Board of Parole ranked offense descriptions from least to most severe. The results are presented in a supplementary report.[19]

[19]Hoffman, Peter B., Beck, James L., and DeGostin,

Agreement on severity ratings, among both examiners and members, was quite high. Differences between members' and examiners' ratings were examined and discussed; but there was a high correlation between average ratings of the two groups.

The categorization of offenses according to judged severity resulting from these exercises was incorporated in guidelines for parole decision-making developed in order to provide a consistent paroling policy. Since these guidelines are presently in use in a pilot project of actual decision-making, the results found immediate application in a policy revision.

The Balance of Time
Since one major result of the study of parole decision-making reported here was the development and operational use of paroling policy guidelines, it was thought especially important to communicate this aspect of the study to other parole systems. Although those matters were described in the supplemental report cited above,[20] it was believed that a film report could be more effective and better focus the discussion at the third national meeting on parole decision-making. The film briefly describes the decision problems of the U.S. Board of Parole, the objectives of the parole decision-making study, and the development and use of the guidelines, emphasizing the need for policy control procedures and their potential contribution through increased equity.[21]

Lucille K., *The Practical Application of a Severity Scale*, Report Number Thirteen, Davis, California: Parole Decision-Making Project, National Council on Crime and Delinquency Research Center, June 1973.

[20]Hoffman and Gottfredson, *op. cit., supra* note 13.

[21]*The Balance of Time*, written and directed by Lew Shaw, 23 minutes, black and white, 16 mm.; produced through the generous cooperation of the State University of New York, Albany, New York.

76. Getting Settled Down

JOHN IRWIN

TWO IMPORTANT AND RELATED THEMES APPEARED in interviews of convicts about to be released on parole. First there was considerable optimism in their plans and expectations, and most revealed the belief that their chances were average or better to live outside without being brought back. It seems that at this point in their prison career, at its termination, they had acquired considerable real or feigned optimism. Most of them expressed the belief that making it is up to the individual, and now that they had decided to try to make it their chances were very good. Most who come back, they believed, don't want to make it. Only four of the sample expressed doubts about their chances of making it.[1]

The second theme was a widely expressed concern for "getting out and getting settled down." Whatever their long-range plans, the great majority indicated an immediate desire to "get their feet on the ground," to "get into a groove of some kind." Most indicated an awareness that they would be starting from scratch, from the bottom, that "the streets" would be strange at first and that before they could begin real progress toward any goals there would be a period during which they must familiarize

▶SOURCE: *The Felon. Englewood Cliffs, N.J.: Prentice-Hall, 1970. Pp. 112–119. Reprinted by permission of Prentice-Hall, Inc., Englewood Cliffs, N.J.*

[1]In a recent study of parolees undertaken by social welfare students, this prerelease optimism was also detected. See Lanny Berry, et al., "Social Experiences of Newly Released Parolees" (unpublished master's thesis, University of California, 1966), p. 68.

themselves with the outside world, meet a lot of immediate exigencies, and build up a stock of material necessities—clothes, toiletries, furnishings, etc.:

"I am going to move very slowly at first. I'm going to look twice to see if the light is green before crossing the street. I'm not going to look for a job right away. After this 7½ years I just want to get my feet into the earth again. I have a friend who is giving me a place to stay. He has some kids and some animals. I just want to relax and learn about these things again. Then I am going to get a job, any job, a dishwashing job. I don't care what work I do, because it is going to be the leisure time that counts. I'm going to find out what I want to do with my leisure time." (Taped interview, San Quentin, June 1966)

"I wanna get out and get to work. Then I wanna see my kids. As soon as I sees the parole officer I'm goin'a see my kids. I'm goin'a get a little room at first and then in a coupl'a weeks I'm goin'a look for an apartment with some extra rooms. Then I'm goin'a take it easy for awhile, get my hair fixed. I ain't goin'a look for no woman for awhile. I'm goin'a have to see about my driver's license and I wanna look around for a little car. I'm goin'a need a car to visit my kids, some of them are over in Oakland. I like the job I got, but I would like a little more money. I need some rent money, some furniture and some money for a car." (Taped interview, Soledad Prison, July 1966)

"First I just want to get a forty hour a week job. I don't care what it pays, if I just have a check coming in every week. Then I can plan on something. I can start working towards something. If I don't have no job, or if I just work one or two hours here and a couple of hours there, like last time, then I can't look ahead to nothing and I probably won't make it." (Taped interview, Soledad Prison, July 1966)

The ex-convict's attempts to settle down and to get his feet on the ground are, however, often thwarted by a barrage of disorganizing events which occur in the first days or weeks on the outside. In spite of his optimism, preparedness, and awareness of the experiences in store for him, the disorganizing impact on the personality of moving from one meaning world into another, the desperation that emerges when he is faced with untold demands for which he is ill prepared, and the extreme loneliness that he is likely to feel often prevent him from ever achieving equilibrium or direction on the outside. Often a sincere plan to "make it" in a relatively conventional style is never actualized because of the reentry impact. Many parolees careen and ricochet through the first weeks and finally in desperation jump parole, commit acts which will return them to prison, or retreat into their former deviant world. Many others, though they do not have their plans destroyed and do not immediately fail on parole because of the experiences which accompany their return to the outside community, have their plans, their perspectives, and their views of self altered. At the very least, reentry involves strains which are painful and which deserve attention.

In exploring this phase of the reentry phenomenon, the ex-convict as an individual or a type will not be considered. Identities and modes of adaptation to the prison milieu will be suspended for the time being and reentry will be examined as a general phenomenon experienced by all parolees. Other instances of reentry or similar phenomena will also be examined in order to produce wider understanding of this transitional experience.

WITHSTANDING THE INITIAL IMPACT

The ex-convict moves from a state of incarceration where the pace is slow and routinized, the events are monotonous but familiar, into a cha-

otic and foreign outside world. The cars, buses, people, buildings, roads, stores, lights, noises, and animals are things he hasn't experienced at firsthand for quite some time. The most ordinary transactions of the civilian have dropped from his repertoire of automatic maneuvers. Getting on a streetcar, ordering something at a hot dog stand, entering a theater are strange. Talking to people whose accent, style of speech, gestures, and vocabulary are slightly different is difficult. The entire stimulus world—the sights, sounds, and smells—is strange.

Because of this strangeness, the initial confrontation with the "streets" is apt to be painful and certainly is accompanied by some disappointment, anxiety, and depression.

"I don't know, man, I was just depressed the first few days. It was nothing that I could put my finger on." (Field notes, San Francisco, September 1966)

"The thing I remember was how lonely I was out there the first few weeks." (Interview, San Quentin, January 1967)

"I mean, I was shook, baby. Things were moving too fast, everybody rushing somewhere. And they all seemed so cold, they had this up tight look." (Interview, San Quentin, July 1967)

"My dad picked me up at the prison and we spent the day driving up to San Francisco. It was night by the time we got to the city, 'cause we stopped and ate and looked at the ocean on the way. Well he dropped me off at my brother's where I was going to stay and left. My dad and my brother don't particularly dig each other. It was late and my brother was in bed. He had this couch set up for me. It was right under a window and this apartment was up about five stories or so. Well, it was one of these drippy nights in San Francisco. The bay was pretty close and a fog horn was blasting out every minute or so. I laid down and tried to go to sleep. Man, it was weird. I was thinking, so this is the big day that I had waited so long for. Man, I was depressed and nervous. The whole thing was unreal." (Interview, San Francisco, June 1968)

These experiences are not unique to the return of the felon or unique to the reentry phenomenon. Travelers to foreign places usually experience similar feelings.[2] Often when one returns home after a short absence, there is an immediate reaction of disappointment, self-doubt, and meaninglessness.[3] The reports of other returnees reveal similar experiences.

Three Components of the Initial Impact

The released felon, as is the case with other persons who suddenly find themselves in a strange world, is disoriented by the new physical surroundings and social settings in different ways. First, the strangeness of the sensory experience unsettles him in a very subtle manner. He is usually proceeding to an urban center upon release, and the intensity and the quality of the new stimulus world can be overpowering. There is more noise and different types of noise. There are many more lights and colors, and there is a great deal more rapid motion:

"The first thing I noticed was how fast everything moves outside. In prison everybody even walks slow. Outside everyone's in a hurry." (Field notes, San Francisco, September 1966)

"The lights at night kind of got me." (Interview, San Quentin, January 1967)

"The first time I started across the street, I remember, I was watching a car coming and I couldn't judge his speed very good. I couldn't tell if he was going to hit me or not. It was weird." (Interview, San Francisco, June 1968)

"Riding in the car was like riding in a boat. It was rolling back and forth. I got sick right away." (Interview, San Francisco, June 1968)

Usually the discomfort and the resultant disorientation is not explicitly identified and traced to its sources. The returnee often feels an uneasiness which he can't identify or he feels a sense of "unrealness"; that is, a feeling that he is not really experiencing this but is witnessing it as an observer or he is dreaming it.

Second, he is disorganized because of his lack of interpretive knowledge of the everyday, taken-for-granted outside world. Alfred Schutz in discussing the situation of the stranger approaching a foreign social world describes a type of knowledge of everyday activity that strangers do not possess:

"Any member born or reared within the group accepts the ready-made standardized scheme of the cultural pattern handed down to him by ancestors, teachers and authorities as an unquestioned and unquestionable guide in all the situations which normally occur within the social world. This knowledge correlated to the cultural pattern carries its evidence in itself—or, rather, it is taken for granted in the absence of evidence to the contrary. It is a knowledge of trustworthy *recipes* for interpreting the social world. . . ."[4]

The ex-convict to some extent reenters the outside world as a stranger. He has been away and has forgotten many of the cultural patterns, and in the passage of time changes in these patterns have occurred. He too finds that immediate interpretive recipes which smooth social functioning (and without which every encounter becomes a strained, embarrassing, and difficult trial) have been lost to him and will have to be learned again:

"They were talking different and doing different things. I felt like a fool." (Interview, San Francisco, July 1966)

"The clerk asked me what I wanted and for a minute I couldn't answer her. It was like I didn't understand her." (Interview, San Francisco, June 1968)

Third, he is ill-prepared to function smoothly in interaction with outsiders in the outside world because he has lost the vast repertoire of taken-for-granted, automatic responses and actions. These are what Schutz calls "recipes for handl-

[2]For a literate description by a traveler of this experience see H. M. Tomlinson, *The Face of the Earth* (New York: Dell Publishing Co., 1960), p. 34.

[3]A character in Thomas Wolfe's *The Web and the Rock* (New York: Dell Publishing Co., 1960) gives us a good example of this situation (p. 350).

[4]"The Stranger: An Essay in Social Psychology," *American Journal of Sociology* (May 1944), p. 501.

ing things and men in order to obtain the best results in every situation with a minimum of effort by avoiding undesirable consequences."[5] Here again the ex-convict is like the stranger. He has lost the ability to perform many ordinary civilian skills which have no use in the prison world and, therefore, are not practiced. For instance, he has not made change, boarded streetcars and buses, paid fares, or bought movie tickets or items across a store counter. He had done these things before prison, but during the prison experience he lost his ability to perform these actions in the unthinking, spontaneous manner in which citizens perform them and expect others to perform them:

"On about the second day I'm out I get on this trolley and start fumbling in my pocket for money. There're a lot a people behind me trying to get on, but I can't figure out how much to put in the box. You know what, man, I don't know how to find out how much to put in the box. The driver's getting salty and I don't want to ask him cause I'm embarrassed, so you know what I do? I back off the fucking thing and walk fifteen blocks." (Interview, San Francisco, July 1966)

There is a process of escalation in actual interactional settings when it is discovered that one does not have these interpretative and behavior recipes. As soon as others who automatically assume that the stranger possesses the taken-for-granted knowledge and responses discover that he doesn't, they too become self-conscious, move from the level of taken-for-granted interpretations and responses, and start doubting the reliability of their own recipes and patterns.[6] The doubt and self-consciousness is fed back and forth, further disorganizing each member of the setting, especially the stranger

who is aware that he is responsible for getting this confrontation off its firm foundation of the taken-for-granted social patterns. During several hours spent with a parolee on his first day outside, I witnessed the difficulty the simple act of purchasing a coke at a hot dog stand can present the unprepared "stranger." He went to the window and a young waitress brusquely asked him for his order. He was not able to reply immediately and when he did, his voice was not sure, his pronunciation not clear. The waitress, who appeared unsettled, didn't understand the order even though I did with ease. The second time she understood it and went to fill his order. When she returned, handed it to him and quoted the price, he was still unsettled. He did not have the money ready. After a brief hesitation, during which the waitress waited quietly but nervously, he started searching his pockets for money. He was especially slow at getting the money out of his pocket and could not rapidly pick either the right change or a larger sum to cover it which most people would do in this situation. He seemed to have to carefully consider these somewhat strange objects, cogitate on their relative value, weigh this against the price quoted, and then find some combination of them which would be equal to or more than that price. He admitted afterwards that he had been very unnerved by this experience and had been having similar difficult experiences since his release.

Impact on the Self

How do these disorganizing experiences which all releasees seem to experience lead to the feelings of self-doubt, self-estrangement, and meaninglessness which they report? We must take a hard look at the relationship between these disorganizing experiences and the nature of self-conceptions and perspective to understand the reactions. Our conceptions of self—the definitions, values, beliefs, and meanings which constitute the design we recognize and act upon as our "self"—are interwoven into a fabric of a total world perspective—our meaning

[5]*Ibid.*, p. 501.

[6]Harold Garfinkel has conducted experiments in which students purposely encountered unprepared persons and refused to take for granted that which normally is. The unprepared persons usually indicated some disorganization, and the interaction could not be continued while the student persisted in doubting the taken-for-granted basis of the interaction. ("Studies of the Routine Grounds of Everyday Activities," *Social Problems* (Winter 1964), pp. 225–50.)

world. The patterns and designs of this world exist only in the interweavings of all the component strains; the self as a cohesive design exists only in the interweavings of meanings pertaining directly to the self and meanings of the world in general. But the fabric is never completed. Like Penelope's tapestry, it is constantly being unraveled and then rewoven daily in ongoing interactional settings. Our meanings of self and the world are being tested, supported, or reshaped within a situation in interaction with others who are engaged in the same process. In order for there to be a continuity of design in the fabric of perspective, there has to be some degree of continuity of familiarity in the setting. A radical change, a shift in setting, where the objects and meanings of the new setting are unfamiliar, interrupts the weaving—the maintenance of the patterns and designs. Not only does the world seem strange; the self loses its distinctiveness. Not only does the person find the new setting strange and unpredictable, and not only does he experience anxiety and disappointment from his inability to function normally in this strange setting, but he loses a grip on his profounder meanings, his values, goals, conceptions of himself.

In this situation, planned, purposeful action becomes extremely difficult. Such action requires a definite sense of self, a relatively clear idea of one's relation to other things, and some sense of one's direction or goals. All of these tend to become unraveled in a radical shift of settings.

Variations in the Initial Impact

Although all released felons experience this facet of the reentry problem to some degree, most endure it and reorient themselves and continue to act with some continuity and stability relative to their former definitions, conceptions, and plans. The intensity of this shock varies from ex-convict to ex-convict. For instance, returning to a familiar setting helps to reduce the duration of the initial impact. I interviewed one parolee after he had been out for one week, who said that he had been slightly "shook up," but was over it now. His appearance and behavior supported this claim. This parolee had moved back into his parents' home, into his old room. The clothes he left were waiting for him; they only needed some minor alterations. His wife and child, although they had not gone back together, were visiting him and the family almost nightly. He had succeeded in securing a desirable job. The familiarity of the setting, coupled with the removal of other obstacles, helped this person to quickly reestablish some continuity with a familiar world. For him the initial reentry impact was minimal. For others, especially those who are coming to a strange city where they have no friends, possibly no secure job, the disjointed experience is tremendous. I spent several hours on several occasions in the first week of another parolee. This person was born and raised in Colorado and lived in San Jose when he was sent to prison. This was his first stay in San Francisco, and he had no job upon release. During the prerelease interview he had impressed me as a person with exceptional control over his actions. He had definite plans and stated that he was determined not to do anything which would deter him from following them. On the outside, however, he admitted that he was extremely "shook." For the first four or five days he couldn't eat a meal; he tried several times but after several bites found he could not force any more food down his throat. When he finished his daily routine of job hunting, he couldn't stay in his room, so he walked the city for hours, sometimes late into the night. He reported having a great deal of trouble talking to people, even though he had fancied himself as outgoing and glib. He felt foolish when he tried to buy something in a store because he seemed to have difficulty taking the money out of his pocket and finding the correct amount of change. During these transactions he reports that "the saleslady was looking at me like I was some kind of idiot." This individual, in spite of the intensity of his reactions, maintained his self-control. He went through this period with detachment and amusement. He seemed to be operating on two levels. On one level he had lost grip of himself, of his reactions, his body and his feelings; but on the other level he was witnessing himself reacting in this abnormal fashion.[7] He said that he knew that he would eventually settle down "once I get a job and get a routine."

Others do not take this experience with such aloofness. One parolee with a long background of alcoholism told me in a prerelease interview that he had found a solution to his alcohol problem and would not be troubled with it this time on the outside. He further disclosed relatively specific immediate plans. A man in his forties who had finally overcome his "inferiority complex," he was going to report immediately to the union where there was a job waiting for him, join an Alcoholics Anonymous group and participate religiously, join one or two social clubs so that he might meet a woman his age whom he would marry and then begin "living a normal life." He was released by an oversight of the parole agent on July 3, a Sunday before the Fourth of July. It would be two days before he could report to the union or the parole agent. He wandered the streets of San Francisco feeling "nervous," "depressed," "scared," and "lonely." He walked into a Market Street bar and plunged into a two-day "drunk." He so-

bered up enough on Tuesday to report to the parole agent, fearful that he would be locked up immediately for violating the conditions of his parole by drinking. The parole agent was not too severe with him and after a "bawling out" directed him to report to the union. The parolee, in somewhat better spirits, but still hung over, left the parole office, cashed the check the agent had given him—the remainder of his $60—and launched another "drunk." He made his way to skid row, a milieu he was well acquainted with from his former years of drinking. A week passed and his funds were depleted. He sobered up and contacted his parole agent, who placed him in city jail for four days to "dry out." The agent picked him up from the jail and after a conference with the district parole supervisor took him to the union where he secured a job. He had no money for rent and the agent would not advance him any, but he found a room in a Salvation Army hotel for derelict seamen. He lasted two more weeks, during which time he worked and remained sober. But then he quit his job and absconded. Although alcohol seems to be an important factor in this man's failure, the initial shock of reentry certainly was instrumental in preventing him from reestablishing some self-organization so that he might start executing the plans he had made in prison. When I reminded him of these plans on four different occasions during his chaotic first month, he variously shrugged them off, desperately assured me that he was going to begin following them, or didn't respond.

---

[7]Bruno Bettelheim describes a similar type of detachment from himself in his adjustment to a concentration camp in "Individual and Mass Behavior," *Journal of Abnormal Psychology* (October 1943), p. 431.

77. The Community Treatment Project

TED PALMER

FROM 1961 TO THE PRESENT, THE CALIFORNIA Youth Authority (CYA) has been conducting a large-scale, two-part experiment known as the Community Treatment Project (CTP). Part 1 was completed in 1969. Its basic goal was to find out if certain kinds of juvenile offenders could be allowed to remain right in their home communities, if given rather intensive supervision and treatment within a small-sized parole caseload. Here, the main question was: Could CYA parole agents work effectively with some of these individuals *without first locking them up for several months* in a large-sized, State institution? The 1961–1969 phase of the Youth Authority's experiment was carried out mainly in Sacramento and Stockton, with San Francisco being added in 1965. Within each of these cities all areas or regions were included. We will now describe part 1 of the experiment. After that, we shall turn to part 2 (1969–1974).

WHO PARTICIPATED?

Eight hundred and two boys and 212 girls participated in the 1961–1969 effort. All economic levels and racial backgrounds were included; and in this respect the CTP "sample" proved to be typical of the Youth Authority's population within the State as a whole. Most of the participants were between 13 and 19 years of age when

▶SOURCE: *"Youth Authority's Community Treatment Project," Federal Probation (March, 1974), 38(1): 3–14.* Reprinted by permission.

first sent to the CYA and placed into the experiment. Typically, these individuals had been in trouble with the law on 5.8 occasions at the time they were sent to the Youth Authority by the local juvenile court. Their "troubles" had usually begun several years prior to the burglary, auto theft, etc., which typically preceded their CYA commitment.

Certain youths were not allowed to participate in the experiment. For example, it was necessary to exclude everyone who had been sent to the CYA for offenses such as armed robbery, assault with a deadly weapon, or forcible rape. (These nonparticipants were called "ineligibles"; participants were known as "eligibles.") Despite such restrictions, it was still possible to *include* a total of 65 percent of all boys and 83 percent of all girls who had been sent to the CYA for the first time, from the Sacramento, Stockton, and San Francisco Juvenile Courts. Along this line, it should be kept in mind that the presence of such things as the following did not, in themselves, prevent any youths from participating in the 1961–1969 experiment: Marked drug involvement, homosexuality, chronic or severe neurosis, occasional psychotic episodes, apparent suicidal tendencies.

THE PROGRAM

Part 1 of the CYA experiment was conducted in a careful, scientific manner: A "control" group was set up from the start. This made it possible to compare the performance of (1) youths who were placed directly into the intensive CTP program, without any prior institutionalization, against that of (2) "controls"—i.e., youths who were sent to an institution for several months prior to being returned to their home communities and then being given routine supervision within standard-sized parole caseloads which were operated by a different (non-CTP) group of parole agents.[1] Thus, all eligible youths were randomly assigned to either the *experimental (CTP)* or the *control (traditional)* program—both of which were operated entirely by the Youth Authority. Six hundred and eighty-six experimentals and 328 controls eventually became part of the 1961–1969 experiment, and all research costs were picked up by the National Institute of Mental Health (NIMH).

All CYA youths, or "wards," who were assigned to the *experimental* (CTP) part of the program were placed on a caseload which contained no more than 12 youths for each parole agent. Based upon (1) detailed initial interviews, (2) a careful review of written background material, and (3) a joint conference by responsible CTP staff, a "treatment plan" was developed for each experimental youth shortly after his assignment to the program. This plan tried to take into account each youth's major strengths, weaknesses, and interests, together with his overall "level of maturity," and various circumstances of his personal, family life, and social situation. Since the resulting plan could vary a great deal from one youth (or type of youth) to the next, the particular approach used in CTP was referred to as

"differential treatment." This feature was separate and apart from that of *community-based treatment* per se.

The caseload of each CTP parole officer was limited to only certain "types" of youth or particular "levels of maturity." That is to say, it included only those youths who exhibited a particular *range* of personality characteristics, or who usually displayed certain distinguishing patterns of behavior. In order to make best use of the CTP parole agent's particular skills and interests, each such agent was selected to work primarily with only *certain types* of youth, or "personality patterns." In this sense, they were paired, or "matched," with all youths who were placed on their caseload; and as a result, they were not expected to be all things to *all kinds* of Youth Authority wards.

Certain principles, strategies, and techniques were followed in connection with all youths who were assigned to Community Treatment Project caseloads. Included were: (1) A determination on the parole agent's part to work with individual youths for a number of years if necessary; (2) careful placement planning (e.g., Exactly *where* is this youth going to live, and with *whom?*), especially during early phases of each ward's parole program; (3) parole agent contact on behalf of youths, with any of several community or volunteer agencies (e.g., probation, employment, school); (4) ready access to the parole agent, by the youths, if and when a need or emergency would arise on the youths' part; (5) flexible agent-youth contacts (office or streets; formal or informal), and on a daily basis if necessary; (6) extensive surveillance by the parole agent (e.g., during evenings or weekends) with respect to the youths' community activities, if and as needed.

The following were among the major program elements which could be made available, depending upon the youth's needs and life-situation at the time: (1) Individual and/or group-centered treatment; (2) group homes, individual foster homes, and other out-of-home placements; (3) an accredited school program

---

[1] It should be mentioned that experimental and control youths both spent an average of 4 to 6 weeks at the Youth Authority's Northern Reception Center and Clinic (NRCC), immediately after having been committed to the Youth Authority. This period of "routine processing" consisted of necessary medical and dental work, standard diagnostic workups and related achievement testing, appearance before the Youth Authority Board, etc. Upon release from NRCC, youths were either sent to a CYA institution for a period which averaged several months or else they were returned directly to their home community, on parole status.

which was located within the CTP "community center" building, and which included tutoring as well as arts and crafts; (4) recreational opportunities and socializing experiences (e.g., outings and cultural activities) both within and outside the community center.

The next section will contain the main results of the 1961–1969 effort. To help state these findings in a succinct yet meaningful way it will be necessary to: (1) Focus upon the Sacramento-Stockton area alone;[2] (2) talk about boys only—although, later on, the main results for girls will be mentioned as well; and (3) refer to three separate groups, or "types," of youth.

A few words must be said about the three groups of youth: *"Passive Conformist," "Power Oriented,"* and *"Neurotic."* These groups have long been recognized by perhaps the majority of practitioners and theorists. They are usually referred to by names which are similar to the ones which are used in this report. Each group is briefly reviewed in Section A of the Appendix. As to quantities, these groups accounted for *14 percent, 21 percent,* and *53 percent* of the 1961–1969 sample of boys, respectively. (Incidentally, the Passive Conformist group seems to account for a considerably larger proportion of the typical California *probation*—i.e., local city and county—population, when compared with that observed within the CYA.[3]) Thus, taken together, the three groups accounted for 7 of every 8—i.e., 88 percent—of the eligible boys.[4] The remaining 12 percent were made up of four rather rare groups of youth, and will be referred to later on.

[2]In part, this is because the necessary, detailed analyses have not been completed relative to San Francisco youths. Nevertheless, relevant analyses which have been completed suggest that the overall results may be fairly comparable to those which appear in the present report, for the Sacramento-Stockton location alone.

Of the 1,014 eligibles, 72 percent of the boys and 58 percent of the girls were from the Sacramento-Stockton area.

[3]For example, an estimated 25 percent of the overall probation population—in contrast to the 14 percent which was observed during the CYA's 1961–1969 effort.

[4]They accounted for 94 percent of the eligible girls.

For readers who are familiar with "I-level" theory,[5] it should be mentioned that many practitioners and theorists would refer to the Passive Conformists as "immature conformists" (Cfm's). Similarly, one may think of the Power Oriented group as being made up of "cultural conformists" (Cfc's) and "manipulators" (Mp's), whereas the Neurotic group would be comprised of individuals who are often referred to as "neurotic acting-out" (Na's) and "neurotic anxious" (Nx's).

MAIN RESULTS OF THE 1961–1969 EXPERIMENT

A.—First we will talk about the group which was by far the largest—*Neurotics.* These individuals appeared to perform much better within the intensive CTP program than within the traditional program (i.e., institution plus standard parole). For example, Criminal Identification and Investigation (CI&I) "rap sheets,"[6] which covered each ward's entire Youth Authority "career,"[7] showed that the controls were arrested 2.7 times more often than experimentals. (Offenses of minor severity were excluded.[8]) More specifically, the rates of arrest in connection with

[5]See: Warren, M. Q. et al., "Interpersonal Maturity Level Classification: Juvenile. Diagnosis and Treatment of Low, Middle, and High Maturity Delinquents." (Sacramento: California Youth Authority, 1966), pp. 1–52 (mimeo.).

[6]These documents are compiled by the State of California, Department of Justice (D.J.). They are based on reports which are routinely, and directly, received by D.J. from police, probation, and sheriffs' departments throughout California. Among other things, the documents may include listings of antisocial activities which had not been mentioned in the (a) formal suspension reports, and (b) "special incident reports," of Youth Authority parole agents who participated in the 1961–1969 effort. (For a variety of reasons, omissions of this nature occurred significantly more often relative to the traditional program, as compared with the CTP program.)

[7]The figures which will next be given refer to all youths who received either a favorable or an unfavorable discharge from the CYA by the close of the 1961–1969 experiment, or shortly thereafter.

[8]Arrests of "minor severity" are those which relate to traffic (noninjuries/nonfelonies), runaway, incorrigibility, etc.

each month "at risk"—i.e., for *each month on parole, in the community*—were .080 for controls and .030 for experimentals. This amounted to a difference of about 1.4 arrests per youth, per CYA *career*. In practical terms, this would mean 1,400 fewer arrests per career, for every 1,000 "Neurotic" youths in the CTP program as compared with an equal number of these youths within the traditional program.

When offenses of minor severity were included, the arrest rates per month-at-risk were .101 for controls (C's) and .044 for experimentals (E's)—a difference of 130 percent in favor of the latter. Statistically speaking, neither of the C vs. E differences which have been mentioned could be explained on the basis of chance alone.

Additional information and findings are given in Section C of the Appendix. The present set of results, which of course apply to the Neurotic group alone, are probably of greater relevance today than they were during much of the 1961–1969 period. This is because the Neurotic group currently appears to make up an even larger proportion (perhaps 70–75 percent) of the Youth Authority's entire population of males, and of females as well. This increase seems to have been an indirect and rather complicated byproduct of the continually increasing average age of CYA first commitments and, of course, recommitments.

B.—*Power Oriented* youths who participated in the intensive CTP program performed substantially *worse* than those within the traditional program, particularly in connection with followup periods of relatively long duration. This was in spite of their better showing on a 24-month "recidivism index." See the Appendix, for details.

C.—On balance, *Passive Conformists* who participated in CTP performed somewhat better than those in the traditional program, at least while under Youth Authority jurisdiction. However, the subsample of experimentals who received a *favorable discharge* from the CYA performed somewhat worse than their controls in terms of convictions (but somewhat better in

terms of arrests), when one looked at the 4-year period immediately following the termination of that jurisdiction. (See the Appendix.)

D.—*The Relatively Rare Types of Youth:* What about the four groups of youth who, when taken together, accounted for the remaining 12 percent of the sample? Basically, too few cases were present within each of these groups to allow for really firm or definite conclusions. Yet, it makes some sense to briefly state the findings which we do have, on at least a tentative or provisional basis, in contrast to reporting nothing at all about these individuals.

In the case of one particular group, however, there happened to be a complete absence of cases within the Sacramento-Stockton, experimental sample; as a result, nothing can be said about them. In I-level terms, these youths are referred to as *"asocialized aggressives"* (Aa's). (I-level terminology will also be used in referring to the three remaining personality types: "Ap's, Se's, and Ci's" (see below). Aa's, Ap's, Se's and ci's accounted for *1 percent, 4 percent, 2 percent, and 5 percent* of the present sample of E + C boys, respectively.

(1) All things considered, the *"asocialized passive"* group (Ap's) seemed to perform somewhat better within the intensive CTP program than in the traditional Youth Authority program. (2) No substantial E vs. C differences were observed in relation to the *"situational emotional reaction"* group (Se's). Youths of this type appeared to perform consistently well, regardless of which particular program they were in. (3) The *"cultural identifier"* group (Ci's)[9] appeared to perform somewhat better in the traditional program than in CTP.

E.—*The Total Group of Boys (Viewed Collectively).* In this section, the results for *all* Sacramento-Stockton boys are reviewed. This includes the 12 percent which had earlier been set aside.

Based on CI&I rap sheets, the arrest rate was found to be .065 among controls and .040

---

[9]More recently referred to as higher maturity "delinquent identifiers" (Di's).

among experimentals, for each month on parole. This 63 percent difference in favor of the intensive, CTP program cannot be explained in terms of "chance." (A similar nonchance difference was found when offenses of minor severity were included.) In practical terms, this would amount to at least 750 fewer arrests per CYA career, for every 1,000 experimentals as vs. 1,000 controls.

On 24-months-parole followup, experimental boys performed significantly better than control boys in terms of recidivism rate: 44 percent vs. 63 percent. (Recidivism is defined in Section C of the Appendix.) Other results are: Fifty percent of the controls, as vs. 69 percent of the experimentals, received a *favorable* discharge from the CYA within 60 months of their first release to the community. Twenty-three percent of the controls, as vs. 16 percent of the experimentals, received an *unfavorable* discharge within 60 months.

It seems clear from the above that boys who participated in the CTP program performed substantially better than those in the traditional program at least during the 2-to-4-year, typical duration of their Youth Authority jurisdiction.

What happened *after* some of these youths left the Youth Authority? If one looks at the subsample of individuals who received a *favorable* discharge from the CYA, control boys were found to have chalked up an average of 1.42 convictions within 48 months after they had left the CYA. The figure for experimentals was 1.67. (Focusing on arrests alone, the figures were 1.72 and 1.94—a difference of 13 percent. As before, nonsevere offenses were excluded.)[10]

It should be mentioned that this 18 percent difference, one which favored the traditional program, seemed to largely reflect the comparatively good performance which was chalked up by what amounted to a relatively large number of *Power Oriented* individuals among the "favorable-dischargee control-subsample,"

[10]As indicated in footnote 31, we have not completed the analysis of post-CYA offense behavior on the part of individuals who had received an *unfavorable* discharge.

when compared with the performance of the relatively smaller number of control *Neurotics* who had also received a favorable discharge. (As seen in Section C of the Appendix, Neurotic *experimental* boys, taken by themselves, performed better than their controls, after having left the CYA on the basis of a favorable discharge. Very much the opposite was found in the case of Power Oriented experimentals.) In short, the Power Oriented individuals contributed enough "points" to have tipped the postdischarge balance in favor of the control group—i.e., when all youths were counted at the same time and when the performance of the Power Oriented youths was weighted according to the number of such individuals who were present in this subsample of favorable dischargees.

F.—Girls. The following relates to the total sample of girls: On balance, these individuals seemed to perform equally well in the traditional program and in CTP. We say "on balance" because control girls appeared to perform better when one focused on certain measures of effectiveness only, whereas results of an opposite nature were noted when still *other* measures were used. Even when these individuals were analyzed separately with regard to each of the three major personality groupings—Passive Conformist, Power Oriented and Neurotic—no really substantial, overall E vs. C differences were observed.

WHAT ABOUT COSTS?

What was the average cost of sending a youth through the traditional program, as compared with that of CTP? In addressing this question, the first thing we found was that costs for *both* programs rose a great deal from 1961 through 1969. This was mainly due to "normal" increases in salaries and wages, price-of-living, etc. Secondly, costs increased more within the *traditional* program than within CTP; moreover, this trend continued into the 1970's. (See below.)

This "differential rise in costs" was largely related to the greater relative, and total, amount of time which the control youths were spending within the

CYA's increasingly expensive-to-operate institutions, beginning in the middle and later 1960's. In other words, it was mainly a reflection of the amount of institutional time which was being accumulated by controls (particularly those whose parole had been revoked on one or more occasions[11]) as compared with that of experimentals. (Experimentals had been revoked and institutionalized less often than controls, on the average.)

The costs which appear below relate to all Sacramento-Stockton boys who had entered either CTP or the traditional program during 1961–1969, and who received either a favorable or an unfavorable discharge as of March 1, 1973. All reception center (NRCC), institution, camp, and parole costs were included. Separate analyses were made on these 162 C's and 192 E's, depending upon the year in which each individual had first entered the program (i.e., the experiment):

For youths who entered during the experiment's early years, or *"early period,"* 1963 prices were used. For those entering during the *"middle period,"* 1966–67 prices were used. For youths who entered during the later years—the *"recent period"*—1971–72 prices were used.[12]

The average CYA career costs per ward were as follows:

Early period: C—$ 5,734; E—$ 7,180
Middle period: C—   8,679; E—   9,911
Recent period: C— 14,327; E— 14,580

Thus, in earlier years the traditional program was noticeably less expensive than CTP. How-

ever, the C vs. E "cost-ratio" underwent a definite change as time went by. This was seen in relation to the early, middle, and more recent cost-ratios, respectively: 0.80 to 1;[13] 0.88 to 1; and 0.98 to 1. As a result, the earlier advantage which was observed for the traditional program had largely faded away by the early 1970's. Stated directly, the actual C vs. E cost difference per youth amounted to *$1,446* during the early period, *$1,232* during the middle period, and *$253* during the more recent period. When one looks at the 1971–72 data in relation to the duration of the average youth's CYA career, the figure of $253 is found to involve a control/experimental difference of $66 per year, or 18 cents a day.

In light of price increases which have been experienced since the early 1970's, it is possible that the cost-balance has by now tipped in "favor" of the CTP program. Aside from this possibility, one which centers around the above figures alone, it should be pointed out that the 1971–72 "per ward costs" would be at least a few hundred dollars higher for the traditional program than for CTP if *capital outlay costs* were added to the picture. These costs, which were not included in the figures shown above, would relate to the construction of new institutions. They are estimated as being close to $10,000,000 for each "up-to-date," physically secure, 400-bed facility. Finally, the above figures do not take into account the fairly substantial, *non-CYA correctional costs* which were accounted for by unfavorable dischargees who had been sent directly to a State or Federal prison. In this connection, it will be recalled that a greater percentage of controls than experimentals had received a discharge of this type. (Also see footnote 31.)

It appears, then, that current costs for the community program would in no event be substantially greater than those for the traditional program. To all indications they would, in fact, be a little less. This would be highlighted if one

[11]The periods of incarceration which resulted from these revocations are over and beyond the *initial* period of incarceration which was experienced by the controls, but not by the experimentals, shortly after their original commitment to the Youth Authority.

[12]In connection with the "recent period" the primary question was: What would the program costs look like on the basis of early 1970 prices—yet in relation to the performance of an actual sample of experimentals and controls who had entered the CYA during the later part of the 1961–1969 effort?

[13]Thus, 5,734 divided by 7,180 yields a ratio of 0.80 to 1.

focused upon the "Neurotic" youths alone, regardless of whether any post-CYA "career costs" were brought into the picture.

THE PRESENT EXPERIMENT (1969–1974)

Despite the early promise shown by CTP with various groups of youth, it was quite clear by 1965 that there was much room for improvement with regard to still other groups. By 1967–1968, it was the consensus of CTP operations staff, and on-site researchers, that the difficulties and delinquent orientation of 25 to 35 percent of the eligible boys were hardly being influenced by the intensive CTP program. In fact, it had been found that at least one-third of these individuals were again involved in delinquency within a few weeks or months after having entered the program. Much the same was observed with similar types of individuals who had been assigned to the traditional program— i.e., with youths (control subjects) who had spent some 8 or 10 months in a regular CYA institution (or camp) prior to being parolled. These, then, were the type of experiences, findings and impressions which led to the present experiment—part 2 of the Youth Authority's Community Treatment Project.

"Part 2" has several objectives; however, its main thrust relates to the following question: Would many of the above-mentioned youths become less delinquently oriented if they began their CYA career within a certain kind of residential setting (described below), and *not within the community itself*? Thus the title of this 1969–1974 effort: "Settings for the Differential Treatment of Delinquents."[14]

To be sure, the idea of using a residential facility, on a fairly long-term basis if necessary, involved a definite departure from the philosophy which was behind the 1961–1969 effort. Under that philosophy, or set of hypotheses, the treatment-and-control of *all* eligible youths could just as well have begun within the

community itself.[15] (Basically, only the research requirement that there be a control group prevented this from actually occurring.) Furthermore, during 1961–1969 the residential setting—in this case NRCC—was to be used (a) only *after* the youths' intensive community program had gotten underway, and (b) on a short-term "temporary detention" basis alone, if at all.

The "Settings" experiment obtains its sample of youths from the greater Sacramento area. This consists entirely of males who (a) may be 13 to 21 years old at intake, and (b) are no longer restricted to being juvenile court commitments. The *key* "ineligibility criteria"—i.e., bases for exclusion—relate to the youths' commitment offense and offense history, as before. However the present set of offense-criteria allow for the inclusion, within the experiment, of a *broader range* of individuals than was possible in 1961–1969. (See below for details.)

PROCEDURES AND OPERATIONS (1969–1974)

The following question is asked by project staff in connection with each newly committed youth who—in accordance with the above criteria— seems likely to later be judged eligible by the Youth Authority Board:[16] "Within which type of setting would it probably be best to initiate the treatment-and-control of this individual"? The choice is between: (1) Initial assignment to an intensive, CTP-staffed-and-operated residential program—later to be followed by release to the intensive CTP community program (staffed-

---

[14]As before, the research costs are picked up by NIMH.

[15]At any rate, there seemed to be little if any scientific evidence to suggest that it would be *inappropriate or impractical* to begin the treatment-and-control of eligible wards outside of a traditional institutional setting.

[16]As in 1961–1969, the Youth Authority Board gives the final, legal approval in regard to eligibility. (In the event that the youth is declared eligible, a "random drawing" will alone determine exactly *where* he is to begin his treatment-and-control. See the text.) Prior to the time that a ward is officially declared eligible, he would be referred to as a "pre-eligible."

and-operated as in 1961–1969); (2) direct release to the intensive CTP community program (again as per the 1961–1969 pattern).

The project staffing team approaches the above question by first making a careful study of the individual's interests, limitations, immediate pressures and underlying motivations. The main object is to figure out what the most appropriate, yet practical, short-range and long-range goals might be. The resulting "close look" allows staff to next "check the youth out" in terms of written guidelines which are designed to further focus their attention on the question of *where* the given treatment-and-control plan might best be started. The guidelines relate to certain categories of youth who, as mentioned earlier, were found to be unusually difficult to "reach" during 1961–1969.

In these guidelines, a number of distinguishing characteristics are spelled out with regard to five groups of individuals. (According to the hypotheses of this experiment, youths who appear to "fit" any one or more of these descriptions "should" begin their CYA career within the above-mentioned residential setting.) More specifically, the guidelines contain short descriptions of (a) certain patterns of interacting with others, (b) outstanding personality characteristics, (c) underlying motivations, and/or (d) immediate pressures and life-circumstances.[17] The guidelines are outlined in Section D of the Appendix.

Individuals who are seen as needing an initial period of institutionalization are referred to as "Status 1"; those seen as *not* needing this type of initial setting are termed "Status 2." When the staffing team completes its evaluation of an individual and finalizes his "status," a random drawing is then made to determine whether his initial *placement* is to be within the CTP residential component (i.e., program) or else within its community-based component.[18] All CTP parole

agents serve both parts of CTP. (Prior to the youth's actual placement into either one or the other of these CTP settings/components, the Youth Authority Board must declare him eligible for CTP per se. It makes this decision without having learned the outcome of the random drawing.)

This random assignment procedure results in the establishment of four separate youth-groups—two "residential" and two "community-based," with each of the two containing a subgroup of Status 1 and, in addition, Status 2 individuals. The research team later compares each one of these four youth-groups with each of the remaining three, in terms of community adjustment.[19] With certain planned exceptions, parole agents who participate in the experiment can have caseloads which contain individuals from all four youth-groups.

The parole agent who is assigned to work with a given youth, and who has therefore been part of the staffing team, remains assigned to that youth regardless of whether the latter's placement happens to be within the residential or the community section of CTP at any particular point in time. This helps promote continuity within and across settings, with respect to long-term treatment-and-control efforts.[20]

Before presenting the results to date, a few

youth may have to begin within the residential facility. (These "less-than-optimal," initial placements serve an essential function in terms of the research design.) When this type of initial placement is called for, the Operations section of the staffing team prepares what is called a "modified treatment-and-control" plan. This differs in several respects from the "optimal . . . plan" which they had prepared just prior to the drawing. The main object of the modified plan is to (a) develop goals which are appropriate to the less-than-optimal setting in which the youth's program is to be initiated, yet which will remain relevant to the individual's needs, and (b) develop strategies which will allow for and at the same time encourage a maximum sse of the resources which are available within the particular setting.

[17]Since 1969, these descriptions have been found to be largely, though ot entirely, mutually exclusive.

[18]As a result of the random drawing, it not infrequently happens that a Status 1 youth will have to begin his program within the community setting. By the same token, a Status 2

[19]The groups which are being compared thus serve as "controls" for one another.

[20]In many cases, individuals whose parole is revoked while they are in the community can be placed into, or returned to, the CTP residential facility. This allows them to remain part of the overall program.

words should be added about the CTP residential unit. This unit ("Dorm 3") is located at NRCC and is a 5- or 10-minute drive from CTP's community center in Sacramento. Dorm 3 normally houses 23 to 25 youths at any one time—CTP youths (males) exclusively—although the number has ranged from 15 to 32. It is staffed by carefully selected "youth counselors" and "group supervisors," and is readily as well as continuously accessible to all remaining CTP personnel. Some parole agents have their office on the dorm. All dorm staff are individually, and officially, paired up with one or two agents. This makes for better dorm-agent as well as dorm-dorm coordination of efforts with respect to implementing stated goals and strategies for residence-located youths who are on the caseload of the given agents.

Two additional points. (1) *Expanding CTP's Applicability.* Part of the 1969–1974 effort centers around the following question: Can the CTP approach[21] be applied to a *broader range and variety* of offenders than that which was available in connection with the 1961–1969 experiment? This question is dealt with at two levels: First, the "ineligibility criteria" which were used during 1961–1969 have been trimmed back in order to allow for the inclusion of many individuals who would otherwise be *excluded* on the basis of (a) commitment offenses relating to armed robbery, forcible rape, etc., or (b) offense histories of a particularly disturbed or aggressive-appearing nature.[22] However, the Board will declare these particular youths eligible for CTP only with the understanding that their program is to be initiated within Dorm 3. (For research purposes, all such individuals are therefore analyzed as a separate group. They are called "Category B" youths.[23]) Secondly, and

aside from the matter of offenses, all first commitments to the CYA from the Sacramento County Superior Court have been made available for inclusion within CTP. This is the first time that adult court commitments have become part of the CTP studies. No restrictions are applied as to *where* these particular individuals may begin their program; etc. (2) *Terminology.* The following should facilitate the presentation of findings:

RR = Status 1 youths who were *appropriately placed:* These individuals were diagnosed as needing to begin their program within a residential setting. Their program *did* begin within a residential setting (i.e., Dorm 3).

RC = Status 1 youths who were *inappropriately placed:* Diagnosed as needing to begin in a residential setting; however, their program was initiated within a community setting, as in 1961–1969.

CR = Status 2 youths who were *inappropriately placed:* Diagnosed as being able to begin their program within a community setting; however, their program was initiated within a residential setting (i.e., Dorm 3).

CC = Status 2 youths who were *appropriately placed:* Diagnosed as being able to begin their program within a community setting. Their program *did* begin within a community setting, as in 1961–1969.

MAIN FINDINGS TO DATE (1969–1974 EXPERIMENT)[24]

Status 1 youths who were inappropriately placed are performing considerably worse than those who were appropriately placed: 94 percent of

---

[21]In the present case this includes the "differential treatment" feature in addition to the community-based aspect per se.

[22]That is, regardless of the possible lack of severity of the *commitment* offense itself.

[23]All other youths are referred to as "Category A."

[24](a) These results relate to the first 106 eligible "Category A" males who were paroled as of December 15, 1972. (See footnote 23.) When "Category B" cases are included, the results hardly change. (b) Neurotic, Power Oriented, Passive Conformist, and "rare types" are combined into a single group—74 percent of which is comprised of the Neurotic

the RC's (inappropriately placed) as vs. 58 percent of the RR's (appropriately placed) have chalked up one or more offenses during their first year-and-a-half on parole.[25] The number of offenses per youth is 1.56 among RC's and 0.96 among RR's. For each month at risk the mean rate of offending is .140 among RC's as vs. .066 among RR's—in other words, one offense for every 7.1 months in the case of RC's, and on per 15.2 months among RR's.[26] This 112 percent difference in rate of offending cannot be explained in terms of "chance."[27]

These findings suggest that the delinquent behavior of the Youth Authority's more troubled, troublesome and/or resistive wards may be substantially reduced—provided that they are first worked with in a setting such as is represented by Dorm 3, as distinct from one which is community-based in the usual sense of the term. The scope, and the potential importance,

of any such "reductions" should not be thought of as slight: Status 1 youths represent 46 percent of the total CTP sample.[28] It is likely that they comprise a sizable portion of the Youth Authority's total population, as well.[29]

What about the remaining 54 percent—i.e., the *Status 2* youths? (These youths, it will be recalled, are the less troubled, troublesome and/or resistive individuals.) On balance the present findings suggest that there is little if anything to be gained, with regard to parole performance, by initially placing Status 2 youths into a residential facility,[30] even of the type represented by Dorm 3: The average monthly rates of offending are .086 for CR's (inappropriately placed) and .068 for CC's (appropriately placed)—a difference of 26 percent. On the surface, these rates might suggest that an "inappropriate" (in this case, residential) placement would be slightly *detrimental* to the Status 2 youths, at least when compared with the more appropriate, alternate placement. However, this particular difference in rates of offending may be accounted for by "chance" alone. Together with results from three other measures of performance, the overall picture is one of few substantial and consistent CR vs. CC differences.

Inappropriately placed youths (RC's + CR's) are performing worse than appropriately placed youths (RR's + CC's): For each month spent within the community, the mean rate of offending is .107 among "inappropriates" (INP's) and .067 among "appropriates" (APR's). This amounts to one offense for every 9.3 months on

category alone. (The findings which are reported—more specifically, the differences between comparison groups—are very largely accounted for by the latter individuals. They receive little if any support in relation to the remaining 26 percent of the sample, when the latter are viewed as a single, separate entity.) This population-distribution probably reflects a broader trend within the CYA as a whole. (c) The present results take into account offenses of all severity levels; however, they are virtually unchanged when those of minor severity are excluded. The latter account for 7 percent of the present, 120 offenses. (d) "Offense" is defined as any delinquent act which results in any one or more of the following, official actions: Revocation of parole; court recommitment; adjudicated court referral to CTP; unfavorable transfer from CTP; suspension of parole. (During the coming year an analysis of CI&I rap sheets will be undertaken for the first time, relative to the 1969–1974 sample.)

[25]As before, "months on parole" is used synonymously with "months in the community" and "months at risk."

[26]By using a closely related yet possibly more refined statistical approach, an even larger difference was obtained between RC's and RR's with respect to the average (mean) monthly rate of offending. When the *median* rather than the *mean* was used in relation to this alternate approach, the monthly rate of offending was .180 for RC's and .060 for RR's.

[27]Nor can various background factors account for this difference. These factors include age, IQ, socioeconomic status, race, I-level, "subtype," and level of parole risk ("base expectancy").

[28]With "Category B" youths included, the figure is 49 percent.

[29]In 1968, research staff estimated that 39 percent of all eligible youths would receive a Status 1 diagnosis during the present experiment. Wards who were received by the CYA during the past few years appear to be more involved with delinquency than those received during the 1960's. For example, the present sample of eligible Category A subjects had accumulated an average of 7.1 delinquent contacts by the time of their commitment to the CYA. The figure for 1961–1969 eligibles was 5.8.

[30]This is generally consistent with the main results of the 1961–1969 experiment.

parole in the case of INP's, and one per 14.9 months among APR's. This 60 percent difference cannot be accounted for by "chance." Results from the remaining performance-indicators are consistent with this basic finding, although not as clear-cut.

The various findings which have been presented might seem to suggest the obvious: Delinquent behavior can probably be reduced in connection with community and residential programs *alike,* by means of careful diagnosis and subsequent placement of individuals into appropriate rather than inappropriate or less-than-optimal settings and programs. In short, it might be said that it matters *which* youths (or types of youth) are placed into *which* type of setting, and that careful selection may lead to higher rates of success for residential and community-based programs alike. Yet, it is recognized that such a viewpoint or conclusion would by no means be universally accepted as being "obvious," within corrections. For one thing, many people feel that nothing really has much effect on delinquent behavior; others believe that one single approach, and perhaps one particular setting, may well contain "the answer" for all but a tiny portion of the population. At any rate, the present findings will hopefully add new information to a long-standing placement issue which many practitioners do regard as being less than entirely obvious in the majority, if not large majority, of cases: Which youths would best be placed into which types of setting, or program?

Two final points in this connection. (1) The difference in rate of offending which is found *between* the Status 1 groups (RC's *vs.* RR's) is considerably larger than that found between the Status 2 groups (CR's *vs.* CC's). More specifically, Status 1 youths who were inappropriately placed are performing *considerably* worse than those who were appropriately placed; however, in the case of Status 2 youths *no substantial differences* are observed between individuals who were inappropriately placed and those who were appropriately placed. This raises the possibility that an initial placement within an inappropriate or less-than-optimal setting might make more of a difference to Status 1 youths than to those diagnosed as Status 2. It may be that the latter, presumably "stronger" individuals are in a better position to compensate for, or otherwise cope with and make the best of, an environment of this nature. (2) The significance, or possible differential significance, of the initial treatment-and-control setting is also suggested by the following: Appropriately placed youths (RR's *and* CC's) are performing about equally well on parole—i.e., regardless of status. However, *inappropriately* placed *Status 1* youths (RC's) are performing substantially worse than inappropriately placed *Status 2* youths (CR's). In other words, appropriate placement may perhaps help to offset or moderate certain pre-existing differences in level of coping ability, on the part of Status 1 vs. Status 2 youths. On the other hand, *inappropriate* or less-than-optimal placement may be more likely to accentuate or activate various differences which relate to their personal or interpersonal liabilities.

Thus far, the CTP approach does seem applicable to categories of offenders other than those which were studied in 1961–1969: Briefly, *Adult Court* commitments have presented few if any special operational problems, or, for that matter, diagnostic problems. Their treatment-and-control requirements differ only slightly from those of Juvenile Court commitments who fall within the 16-and-older age range. In addition, *Category B* youths have presented few unusual or serious operational and diagnostic problems. However, partly because of Board restrictions which are frequently placed upon these individuals with regard to day passes, furloughs or minimum length of residential stay, it has sometimes been difficult to develop treatment-and-control plans which closely resemble those observed in the case of many other residence-located youths. Operations staff nevertheless feel able to engage in productive interactions with most such youths. The parole performance of these individuals has yet to be evaluated in detail.

OVERVIEW AND CONCLUDING REMARKS

Within and outside of corrections, many concerned individuals are currently engaged in an ideological battle over whether to "keep almost all offenders on the streets," or else "lock up nearly all offenders, except for first-timers." This, of course, may be exaggerating the situation to a certain degree; yet at the same time, it may be accurate in its reflection of certain feelings which are often involved. Feelings aside, the facts which have emerged from California's 12-year experiment thus far suggest that both of the above positions may be too extreme, and that a more differentiated or flexible approach may be appropriate. (These considerations would at least apply to the type of individuals who have been studied thus far—youths who have had numerous contacts with the law.) A brief review may illustrate this point.

When an NIMH-funded research team combined several hundred Youth Authority males into a single study group (one which included the full range of CYA "personality types"), it found that (a) "experimentals" who participated in the intensive, 1961–1969 *community-based program (CTP)* had produced substantially less delinquent behavior than (b) "controls" who had participated in the traditional CYA program. (The experimentals and controls had been well-matched on such characteristics as age, IQ, socioeconomic status, race, etc.) However, the researchers also found that much of this difference in favor of the CTP—i.e., noninstitutional—program was accounted for by youths who were referred to as "Neurotics." During the 1960's, these individuals accounted for half of the CYA's population; they currently account for considerably more. By way of contrast, the *traditional CYA program* was found to have a greater influence than CTP in the case of individuals described as "Power Oriented." This

particular group now comprises about one-tenth of the CYA population; it previously accounted for twice that amount.

Quite aside from these particular findings and developments, it was observed, prior to 1969, that roughly one-third of the *total* sample were responding somewhat indifferently, and often quite unfavorably, to the community-based and traditional programs alike. Included within this broad, "difficult-to-reach" category were some individuals from nearly all personality groupings. However, it was the difficult-to-reach Neurotics who accounted for the largest total number. (This was possible despite the relatively positive performance by the Neurotic group as a whole.) Since 1969, the distinguishing characteristics of difficult-to-reach "Neurotics" have been largely singled-out. In many cases (perhaps half) operations staff have helped them to engage in less by way of delinquent behavior while in the community. But before this could occur, it was necessary for these individuals to *begin* their Youth Authority program, (a) not within the community per se, (b) not inside a standard CYA institution, but rather (c) within a *medium-sized, CTP-staffed residential facility*—one which was operated in accordance with the 1961–1969 "differential treatment" philosophy. As to the difficult-to-reach "Power Oriented" youths, this same "residence-first" (CTP facility) approach seems to be resulting in relatively little overall improvement in terms of parole performance. Thus, the *traditional* program may still represent the Youth Authority's best alternative for the majority of these particular individuals—especially the sub-group known as "Cfc's." Finally, during 1961–1969 the "Passive Conformists" (now one-tenth of the population) performed somewhat, though not a great deal better in CTP than within the traditional CYA program. Nevertheless, their response to CTP's residential facility (1969-present) has been unfavorable. Thus, in this particular instance the 1961–1969 type of community-based approach would seem to be the treatment of choice.

CTP's originally stated ideal—that of changing delinquents into lifelong nondelinquents—is not being achieved in the large majority of cases. Obviously, the CTP program does not contain a "special potion" which, after having been taken, is capable of eliminating all traces of delinquency, and of fortifying the youths against every form of stress. Nevertheless, the "differential treatments" and "differential settings" which have been utilized in this program do seem capable of *reducing* the total volume of delinquent behavior on the part of many, but by no means all, eligible males. This holds true during the period of their CYA jurisdiction and, to a lesser extent, subsequent to the termination of that jurisdiction. In order to bring about this "reduction," it has very often seemed unnecessary to initially place these individuals within a residential setting (traditional or otherwise); in many other cases, it has seemed quite necessary. As suggested above, it is what goes on *within* the given setting that seems to count, and not just the setting itself. This, of course, may also vary from one type of youth to another.

Nothing in our experience suggests that it is an easy matter to operate a program such as CTP. Implementation and maintenance of a community-based, intensive differential treatment-and-control program involves critical issues, and requires steadfast commitments, with respect to personnel selection, quality of supervision, administrative support, etc. In one form or another, issues of this nature will also be encountered outside the context of large-sized, State agencies such as the CYA. Although challenges of this type have been adequately met in certain instances, it might be well to recognize the fact that any thoroughgoing implementation of CTP—even of the 1961–1969 approach alone—is, at the present time, probably beyond the reach of most probation and parole departments within the USA on anything other than a limited scale. Even so, worthwhile modifications and adaptations of the California program do seem to be well within the realm of possibility; in several instances, they are already in existence.

Whatever the immediate future may hold for programs such as CTP, the research information which has been gathered since 1961 may continue to be of interest to practitioners, administrators and social scientists who still place value upon the concept of actively and directly intervening in the life of personally troubled, developmentally lacking and/or disturbing-aggressive youths and young adults. This should apply in relation to community-based and residential-centered programs alike.

APPENDIX

SECTION A

The three groups of youth which were first mentioned on page 899 may be briefly described as follows:

(1) *Passive Conformist:* This type of youth usually fears, and responds with strong compliance to, peers and adults who he thinks have the "upper hand" at the moment, or who seem more adequate and assertive than himself. He considers himself to be lacking in social "know-how," and usually expects to be rejected by others in spite of his efforts to please them.

(2) *Power Oriented:* This group is actually made up of two somewhat different kinds of individuals, who, nevertheless, share several important features with one another. The first likes to think of himself as delinquent and tough. He is often more than willing to "go along" with others, or with a gang, in order to earn a certain degree of status and acceptance, and to later maintain his "reputation." The second type, or "subtype," often attempts to undermine or circumvent the efforts and directions of authority figures. Typically, he does not wish to conform to peers or adults; and not infrequently, he will attempt to assume a leading "power role" for himself.

Passive Conformist and Power Oriented youths are usually thought of as having reached a "middle maturity" level of interpersonal development. The group which is described next is said to have reached a "higher maturity" level. The "level of interpersonal maturity" concept is briefly explained in Section B of this Appendix.

(3) *Neurotic:* Here again, we find two separate personality types which share certain important characteristics with one another. The first type often attempts to deny—to himself and others—his conscious feelings of inadequacy, rejection, or self-condemnation. Not infrequently, he does this by verbally attacking *others* and/or by the use of boisterous distractions plus a variety of "games." The second type often shows various symptoms of emotional disturbance—e.g., chronic or intense depression, or psychosomatic complaints. His tensions and conscious fears usually result from conflicts produced by feelings of failure, inadequacy, or underlying guilt.

SECTION B

The following are brief definitions of the three main levels of interpersonal maturity which are observed within the CYA:

Maturity Level Two (1^2): An individual whose overall development has reached this level, but has not gone beyond it, views events and objects mainly as sources of short-term pleasure, or else frustration. He distinguishes among individuals largely in terms of their being either "givers" or "withholders," and seems to have few ideas of interpersonal refinement beyond this. He has a very low level of frustration-tolerance; moreover, he has a poor capacity for understanding many of the basic reasons for the behavior or attitudes of others, toward him.

Maturity Level Three (1^3): More than the 1^2, an individual at this level recognizes that certain aspects of his own behavior have a good deal to do with whether or not he will get what he wants from others. Such an individual interacts mainly in terms of oversimplified rules and formulas rather than from a set of relatively firm, and generally more complex, internalized standards or ideals. He understands few of the feelings and motives of individuals whose personalities are rather different than his own. More often than the 1^4 (see below), he assumes that peers and adults operate mostly on a rule-oriented or intimidation/manipulation basis.

Maturity Level Four (1^4): More than the 1^3, an individual at this level has internalized one or more "sets" of standards which he frequently uses as a basis for either accepting or rejecting the behavior and attitudes of himself as well as others. (These standards are not always mutually consistent, or consistently applied.) He recognizes interpersonal interactions in which individuals attempt to influence one another by means other than compliance, manipulation, promises of hedonistic or monetary reward, etc. He has a fair ability to understand underlying reasons for behavior, and displays some ability to respond, on a fairly long-term basis, to certain moderately complex expectations on the part of various peers and adults.

SECTION C

For the *Neurotic* group, the additional information and findings are as follows:

(1) Despite its known shortcomings, "rate of recidivism" has long been one of corrections' most widely used measures of parole *failure.* As used in this report, recidivism reflects the occurrence of any one or more of the following events: (a) Revocation of the youth's parole by the Youth Authority Board; (b) recommitment of the youth to the CYA, by either a Juvenile or an Adult Court; (c) unfavorable discharge of the youth by the Youth Authority Board, from the CYA itself. Any one of these events is usually the result of some type of police arrest and subsequent conviction. Events (a) and (b), above, are usually followed by a period of incarceration for several months, within one or another of the Youth Authority's large-sized institutions. (See below, regarding (c).) Thus, the higher the recidivism rate, the greater is the amount of "failure" in one sense of the term. Now then, on 24-months parole followup the recidivism rate was 66 percent for controls and 45 percent for experimentals.

(2) Within 60 months from the time of their first release to the community (literally, their date of initial parole), 40 percent of the C's as vs. 77 percent of the E's had been officially released by the Youth Authority Board from the CYA's jurisdiction—on the basis of a *favorable discharge.* Also within a period of 60 months, 40 percent of the C's as vs. 17 percent of the E's were released on the basis of an unfavorable discharge. (It should be noted that depending upon an indi-

vidual's behavior subsequent to one or more prior parole revocations which he may have received, the individual will still be able to eventually obtain *either* a favorable *or* an unfavorable discharge from the CYA.)[31]

(3) What happened *after* the CYA's jurisdiction had ended, in the case of Neurotic youths and young adults who had been given a *favorable discharge* (see (2), above)? At least this much is known: Many of these individuals did not entirely relinquish their delinquent tendencies—despite their experiences within the CYA. Be this as it may, those who had gone through the traditional CYA program seemed, on the average, to have remained somewhat *more* delinquent than those who had completed CTP: Within 48 months after having left the Youth Authority, controls chalked up an average of 1.88 convictions; the figure for experimentals was 1.58. (A somewhat larger C vs. E difference was obtained when one looked at *arrests,* and not simply convictions. As before, arrests of minor severity were not counted.) In practical terms, this would amount to a difference of about 300 convictions for every 1,000 experimental as well as control "favorable-dischargees," over a 4-year span of time. (The reader may note that this analysis of *post-CYA,* CI&I data has been completed on "arrests" and, also, on the "convictions" which related to those arrests. However, because the earlier-mentioned *parole (CYA-time)* CI&I data were first analyzed during 1973, only the "arrest" information has been looked at thus far, with regard to *parole* time. Judging from the "post-CYA" findings on arrests vs. convictions, the "parole time" results for these same two levels of analysis should be very similar to one

---

[31]Taking into account all "groups" of boys—i.e., all nine "subtypes"—50 percent of the experimentals and 50 percent of the controls who received an unfavorable discharge from the Youth Authority were sent to a State or Federal prison immediately upon receipt of their discharge. Their Court sentence commonly specified a maximum of several years' incarceration. Partly because of this, followup (i.e., post-CYA, postprison) analyses have not been completed for the unfavorable dischargee sample.

another.) Using a 10-point scale, the penalties received for each conviction were somewhat more severe among controls than among experimentals—5.75 as vs. 4.25, on the average.

The following results relate to *Power Oriented* youths:

(1) CI&I rap sheets showed an arrest rate of .060 for controls and .071 for experimentals, with regard to each month spent within the community. This difference favored the traditional program by 18 percent. (Again, offenses of minor severity were excluded, although the picture hardly changed when they were included.) (2) On 24-months' parole followup, the recidivism rate was 66 percent for controls and 40 percent for experimentals. (3) Despite the better showing by experimentals on the 24-month recidivism index, it was found that 53 percent of the controls as vs. 43 percent of the experimentals received a favorable discharge from the Youth Authority within *60* months of their first release to parole. Similarly, 15 percent of the C's as vs. 23 percent of the E's received an unfavorable discharge. (4) Within 48 months after being released from the CYA's jurisdiction, the Power Oriented, control *"favorable-dischargees"* had chalked up an average of 1.47 convictions; the figure for experimentals was 2.55. (The C vs. E difference was even larger when one focused upon arrests alone, rather than convictions alone.) This was a 73 percent difference in favor of Power Oriented youths who had successfully completed the Youth Authority's traditional program.

The following relates to *Passive Conformist* youths:

(1) CI&I rap sheets showed an arrest rate of .066 for controls and .037 for experimentals, for each month within the community. This difference favored the CTP program by 78 percent. (2) On 24-months' parole followup, the recidivism rate was 59 percent for controls and 51 percent for experimentals. (3) 54 percent of the C's as vs. 78 percent of the E's received a favorable discharge from the Youth Authority within 60 months of their first release to the commun-

ity. Similarly, 14 percent of the C's as vs. 6 percent of the E's received an unfavorable discharge. (4) Within 48 months after termination of their CYA jurisdiction, the Passive Conformist, control "favorable-dischargees" had chalked up an average of 1.44 convictions; the figure for experimentals was 1.80. This was a 25 percent difference in favor of the traditional program.

SECTION D

Basic to the 1969–1974 experiment is the hypothesis that certain youths (five groups in all) would probably derive greater benefit from a course of treatment-and-control which would begin within a residential setting, in contrast to a community setting. Briefly, the groups are:

(1) Youths who are quite disturbed and openly disorganized relative to overall, everyday functioning, and who at times become highly agitated or even delusional when under the pressure of everyday life. (Mostly found among Nx's, Ap's and Aa's.)

(2) Youths who have an intensive drive to prevent other persons from exerting controls upon them, or from substantially influencing the direction of their lives. They are prepared to use virtually "everything" in their power—including runaway, physical resistance, etc.—to avoid the ongoing confrontation of concerned authority figures, and to avoid involvement in nonexploitive relationships with adults in general. (Mostly found among Mp's and Cfc's—the "Power Oriented" group.)

(3) Youths who are unable to recognize, or who vigorously attempt to deny, the existence and influence of the unusually destructive relationships and loyalty-binds in which they are involved, at home and within the community. Were these youths released directly to the community setting, conditions such as these would undermine the youth/parole agent relationship at a time when this relationship would still be in its formative stage, and would operate so as to lead the youth into delinquent acting-out of a

| Criterion Measure | | | Treatment | | | Funding[g] | | | | Mos. in Operation |
Variables	Out-come[e]	Follow-up	Amt. D.[f] H M L	Duration	F	S	L	O	
Court records	—	1 yr.	X		X		X	X	
Court records	0	6 mos.	X	5 mos./ subject	X	X			18 mos.
Court records	+	3 yrs.	X		X		X	X	36 mos.
In-program failures	0								
Personality	0								
Court records	0	2 yrs.	X	4 hrs./wk. for 6 wks.		X			6 mos.
Number of petitions filed	+								
Weeks on probation	+								
Court records	+		X	Weekly for 6 wks.	X				12 mos.
Release from probation	+		X						12 mos.
Court records	0								
Personality	+		X	Weekly for 8 mos.					8 mos.

Table II. Programs Employing Volunteers and Indigenous Nonprofessionals

Reference, Project Type, Location	Subject Referral Source	Sample Size[a]		Race[b]			Sex		Age	Group Assign.[c]			Stat. Anal.[d]	
		E(n)	C(n)	C	N	O	M	F		R	M	O	Y	N
Fo & O'Donnell (1973) (Buddies) Honolulu, Hawaii	Multiple agencies	35	7	X		X	X	X	11-17			X	X	
Forward et al. (1973) (Partners) Denver, Colo.	Police	26	22	X	X	X	X	X	11-17	X				X
Community Council Board (1973) Big Brothers Phoenix, Ariz.	Police	100		X	X	X	X		7-17		X			X
Morris (1970) (Volunteers) Royal Oak, Mich.	Court	500	250				X		17-25		X			X
Rosenbaum et al. (1969) (Volunteers) Royal Oak, Mich.	Court	92	82				X		17-25		X		X	
Carter et al. (1974) (VISA) Orange Co., Calif.	School	156							6-12		X			X
Elliott & LeBouef (1973) (Y-Pais) Lincoln, Neb.	Multiple Agencies	112					X	X	6-15		X			X
Pines & Ridgley (1974) (Youth Advocate Project) Baltimore, Md.	Court & School	142	396	X	X	X	X	X	11-17		X			X
Howell (1972) (Volunteers vs. Probation Officers) Adams County, Colo.	Court	40	40	X		X	X		15-17	X				X

NOTE: For legend see footnote to Table I.

Criterion Measure / Variables	Outcome[e]	Follow-up	Treatment Amt. D.[f] H	M	L	Duration	Funding[g] F	S	L	O	Mos. in Operation
Truancy	+		X				X	X			12 mos.
Self-reported delinquency	+	8 mos.	X			3 hrs./wk.	X	X			12 mos.
Court records	+										
Self-concept	0										
Social attitudes	0										
Expectations	0										
Alcohol & Drug Use	−										
Attitudes toward police	−										
Police records	+			X			X	X			18 mos.
Type of offense	0										
Court records	+	5-18 mos.	X				X	X			48 mos.
Employment	+										
School dropout	−										
Personality	+										
Court records	+	18 mos.		X			X	X			
Personality	+										
Area police rates	+		X				X	X			30 mos.
Attitude of parents, teachers, staff	+										
Police records	+			X		7.4 mos./ subject		X	X		24 mos.
Court records	+	22 wks.	X			6 mos./ subject	X	X			18 mos.
Court records	0				X	8 mos./ subject	X	X	X		15 mos.
Police records	0										
Counselor & teacher rating	0										
Personality	0										
Interpersonal Relationships	+										

Table III. Individual and Group Counseling

Reference, Project Type, Location	Subject Referral Source	Sample Size[a] E(n)	C(n)	Race[b] C	N	O	Sex M	F	Age	Group Assign.[c] R	M	O	Stat. Anal.[d] Y	N
Powers & Witmer (1951) (Individual) Boston, Mass.	Court	325	325	X	X		X		13-32		X		X	
McCord et al. (1959) (Individual) Boston, Mass.	Court	253	128	X	X		X		13-22		X		X	
Thomas (1968) (Individual) Location unlisted	School	25	25							X			X	
Pooley (1971) (Graduate student counselors) Carbondale, Ill.	School	24	13.	X	X		X	X				X	X	
Wallace (1969) (Intensive counseling) Tulsa, Okla.	Court	75	84	X	X	X	X	X	13-21		X		X	
Szymanski & Fleming (1971) (Individual) Boston, Mass.	Court	8					X		14-16			X		X
Holliman (1970) (Individual vs. Group) Location unlisted	Court	24	24				X	X	14-17			X	X	
Cole et al. (1969) (Group) Cheyenne, Wyo.	Multiple agencies	14	8					X	13-17			X	X	
Ostrom et al (1971) (Group) Columbus, Ohio	Court	19	19	X	X		X		15-16		X		X	
Daane et al. (1969) (Group) Albuquerque, N. M. & Phoenix, Ariz.	Neighborhood Youth Corps	160	64				X	X				X	X	

NOTE: For legend see footnote to Table I.

Criterion Measure Variables	Outcome[e]	Follow-up	Amt. D.[f] H	M	L	Duration	Funding[g] F	S	L	O	Mos. in Operation
Court records	0		X							X	120 mos.
Personality	+										
Adjustment rating	—										
Court records	0		X							X	120 mos.
Police records	0				X	Weekly-1 yr.					12 mos.
Court records	+										
School record	+										
Personality	+										
Teacher ratings	+										
Personality	+		X					X			36 mos.
School offenses	0		X			1 hr./day	X	X			36 mos.
Court records	0										
Court records	0	1 yr.		X		4-5 meetings					12 mos.
Behavior factors	0				X						
Personality	+			X		10 weeks	X		X		3 mos.
Police record	0	10 mos.	X			7 meetings	X		X		2 mos.
School record	0										
Personality	+										
Court records	+		X			Twice weekly-8 weeks	X				
Job absenteeism	0										
School record	0										
Attitudes	+										
Personality	0										

Table IV. Social Casework

Reference Project Type, Location	Subject Referral Source	Sample Size[a] E(n)	C(n)	Race[b] C	N	O	Sex M	F	Age	Group Assign.[c] R	M	O	Stat. Anal.[d] Y	N
Craig & Furst (1965) (Child Guidance Clinic) New York, N. Y.	1st grade	29	29	X	X	X	X		5-6		X			X
Tait & Hodges (1962, 1971) (Social Casework) Washington, D.C.	School	98	49	X	X	X	X	X	5-14			X	X	
Meyer et al. (1965) (Social Casework) New York, N.Y.	School	189	192	X	X	X		X	14-17	X				X
Braxton (1966) (Family Casework) Detroit, Mich.	Police	71			X		X		10-16		X			X
Baron et al. (1973) (Family Crisis Therapy) Sacramento, Calif.	Police, Schools, Parents	803	558				X	X			X			X
Berleman & Steinburn (1967) Ikeda (1969) Berleman et al. (1972) (Social Services) Seattle, Wash.	Court & School	52	50	X	X		X		12-14	X			X	

NOTE: For legend see footnote to Table I.

Criterion Measure Variables	Outcome[e]	Follow-up	Amt. D.[f] H	M	L	Duration	Funding[g] F	S	L	O	Mos. in Operation
Court records	0	10 yrs.	X			50 mos.			X		60 mos.
Teacher reports	0										
Court records	0	14 yrs.		X							36 mos.
School record	0		X							X	48 mos.
Truancy	+										
Pregnancy	0										
Police record	+		X			1-8 Interview				X	12 mos.
Court records	+	7 mos.	X			1-5 sessions			X		9 mos.
Petitions filed	+										
Detention	+										
School discipline records		18 mos.	X			1-2 yrs.	X	X	X		72 mos.
records	—										
Police records	—										
Commitments to training schools	0										
Parent ratings	+										

Table V. Street-Corner Workers

Reference, Project Type, Location	Subject Referral Source	Sample Size[a]		Race[b]			Sex		Age	Group Assign.[c]			Stat. Anal.[d]	
		E(n)	C(n)	C	N	O	M	F		R	M	O	Y	N
Gandy (1959) (Street-club work) Chicago, Ill	Gang membership	326		X	X		X	S				X		X
Miller (1959, 1962) (Gang work) Boston, Mass.	Gang membership	205	195	X	X	X	X	X	12-21			X	X	
Adams (1967) (Group-Guidance) Los Angeles, Calif.	Gang membership	43	57		X	X	X		13-14			X		X
Caplan (1968) (Street-gang work) Chicago, Ill.	Gang membership	109		X	X		X		13-18			X	X	
Klein (1969) (Group-guidance) Los Angeles, Calif.	Gang membership	798			X		X	X	13-20			X	X	
Klein (1971) (Gang-disruption) Los Angeles, Calif.	Gang membership	118				X	X	X	10-18			X	X	

NOTE: For legend see footnote to Table I.

Variables	Out-come[e]	Follow-up	Amt. D.[f] H	M	L	Duration	Funding[g] F	S	L	O	Mos. in Operation
Index of anti-social behavior	0			X		6-18 mos.				X	36 mos.
Court records	0	18 mos.	X			1-2-1/2 yrs.					36 mos.
Illegal behavior	0										
Disapproved behavior	0										
Under supervision		6 yrs.		X		3 yrs.				X	72 mos.
	+										
Cost effectiveness	+										
Effect on siblings	+										
Adjustment scale	+	1 yr.		X						X	
Court records	−		X					X		X	48 mos.
Court records	+	6 mos.	X				X	X		X	18 mos.
Area arrest rate	0										
Reduce gang recruitment	+										

927

strategy that should be tested further and carefully evaluated.

Area and Youth Service Projects (Table VI).   Area projects have a long history, over 30 years, beginning with the work of Clifford Shaw and the Chicago Area Projects. The area approach assumes that delinquency in slum areas stems from a lack of neighborhood cohesiveness and a lack of residents' concern about the welfare of their children. Area projects, therefore, attempted to involve people in changing the character of their neighborhood and thereby making it a better place for children to grow up. Witmer and Tufts (1954) found very few reports on area projects. No recent evaluation reports were discovered.

The area approach seems to have evolved into the youth services approach (Youth Projects, Youth Service Systems, Youth Service Bureaus, Youth Resource Centers, Youth Development, Youth Diversion). Youth Service Bureaus were included in the suggestions of the 1967 President's Commission on Law Enforcement and the Administration of Justice (Task Force Report: Juvenile Delinquency and Youth Crime, 1967). Youth service systems represent a variety of efforts centered around coordinating existing services, stimulating others to fill service gaps, providing for nonexistent but needed services when necessary, and diverting youth from further involvement with the criminal justice system.

Few of the projects in Table VI have performed adequate evaluations. Of the 12 reports, ten described relatively positive outcomes. However, some common threats to the validity of this finding are the lack of comparison groups, the lack of follow-up information, and a heavy reliance on subjective opinion.

Educational Programs (Table VII).   Educational programs for delinquency prevention represent a varied collection of strategies. These include teaching law, counseling by police, graduate students and public agency personnel, providing special courses and classes for the "delinquent-prone," and coordination of public services. Few of the programs reviewed in Table VII used delinquent behavior as a criterion for evaluation purposes.

It is interesting to note that many projects which incorporate the goal of delinquency prevention and reduction often fail to include, for evaluation purposes, the criterion which justifies their finding. Instead, process measures such as number of youth contacted or public opinions about the project are offered as proof of effectiveness. These are poor substitutes. Without outcome measures as reduction in police contacts or court appearances or self-reported delinquency, nothing can be learned about the goals of delinquency prevention or reduction. But a word of caution must be heeded. It may be inappropriate to tie the objective of delinquency reduction to programs which have legitimate objectives in their own right, such as improving educational levels. Venezia (1975) has argued that tieing more limited goals, like delinquency prevention, with broader social goals, such as eliminating poverty, has the effect of both subverting the broader program and diluting the focus of the more limited program. Therefore, policy-makers should give careful consideration to establishing realistic goals.

Vocational Programs (Table VIII).   Work-study projects generally take the form of providing a half-day in school and a half-day of supervised work experience. The work experience is seen as the experimental variable, that is, the treatment. There is some indication that youth in work-study programs react negatively to being selected for those programs, especially when their work experiences keep them on the school grounds in public view (Ahlstrom & Havighurst, 1971). It may be that these students are sensitive to peer comments about being placed on "work gangs."

Those programs which have focused more on job training and manpower services than on educational remediation seem to have proven more successful. However, there may be some differential effects due to the different age ranges of participants in these programs or subject selection procedures. There are also problems associated with providing work experiences to youth who are still legally "committed" to school—the 15- to 16-year-old group. The provision of job training, once a youth is legally old enough to leave the school system, may be a much more cost-efficient strategy for both the youth and the community than is the provision of such services to younger age groups, especially where a job and school activities are combined.

Community Treatment Programs (Table IX). The services provided by community projects included differential parole treatment, guided group interaction counseling techniques, foster-home care, group-homes, and residential youth centers. Community treatment may best be considered "prevention after-the-fact" since the referral source is almost always the juvenile court and these projects are often viewed as alternatives to incarceration.

The community treatment approach is a relatively new one in delinquency prevention. Of the 22 recommendations made by the President's Commission on Law Enforcement and the Administration of Justice (1967) in the area of corrections, eight called for community-based programs. Evaluation reports of the community treatment approach are not consistent in their findings, but one conclusion has not been contested: ". . . even if one remains cautious in his interpretation of the evidence, the indication is always that *community intervention is at least as effective as incarceration*. This is a matter not to be taken lightly" (Empey & Erickson 1972, p. 200). Furthermore, the costs of community treatment have been reported to be as little as one-fourth the cost of institutional treatment.

One issue to be addressed by community treatment programs is the threat that participants represent to the community which would not be present if they were incarcerated (Koshel, 1973). Empey and Lubeck (1971) and Empey and Erickson (1972) reported that, after one- and four-year follow-ups, those youths who had been incarcerated committed more serious crimes when they were returned to their communities than did the youths who had been in the community treatment program. These reports should not be interpreted, however, as an unqualified vote for community programs. The findings did more to document that incarceration clearly has an undesirable impact than to indicate that community treatment was a success.

Miscellaneous Programs (Table X). A number of reports which did not fit into the preceding categories are presented in Table X. The most recent of these reported an unusual project using mini-bikes as a tool to establish rapport between youth and project staff which is currently being funded by the YMCA and private business. The objectives of this program were to reduce recidivism, reduce delinquency, improve attitudes, and improve self-regard. It was estimated that over 14,000 youths have been involved in the National Youth Project Using Mini-bikes (NYPUM) since its inception. The initial report indicated that the project was successful in reducing recidivism. Given the level of funding and the number of projects that are in operation (449 cities), it is unfortunate that the evaluation did not control for subject selection bias and depended so heavily upon subjective opinion.

Validity and Utility

Less than half of these 96 reports came from published sources. There were 11 books, four chapters in books, and 32 journal articles. Fourteen of the reports were obtained from repositories such as the National Technical Information Service and Education Resources Information Center and two of the reports were found in *Dissertation Abstracts*. The remaining 33 reports were unpublished and were obtained from a variety of sources.

The definition of "delinquency" was seldom made explicit in these 96 reports. Delinquency may be defined as either "delinquent behavior," behavior which violates social norms, or "officially perceived delinquency," behavior which is

Table VI. Area and Youth Service Projects

Reference, Project Type, Location	Subject Referral Source	Sample Size[a] E(n)	C(n)	Race[b] C	N	O	Sex M	F	Age	Group Assign.[c] R	M	O	Stat. Anal.[d] Y	N
Brewer et al. (1968) (Lane County Youth Project) Eugene, Ore.	Multiple agencies	114	114				X	X	12-21			X		X
Jones & Fishman (1967) (Cardoza Area Program) Washington, D.C.	Ghetto residence	525			X		X	X	14-17			X	X	
Reuthebuck (1971) (Kentucky's Y.S.B.'s) Kentucky (4 communities)	Multiple agencies	153		X	X		X	X	12-18			X		X
Community Services for Children (1972) Olympia, Wash.	Multiple agencies	273							10-18			X		X
City of Chicago (1972) (Joint Youth Development Program) Chicago, Ill.	Police	412					X	X	9-18			X		X
Elliott & LeBouef (1973) (Youth Service System) Lincoln, Neb.	Court, Schools, Police	137		X	X		X	X	6-20			X		X
Carter & Gilbert (1973) (Alternate Routes Project) Orange County, Calif.	Court, Police, Schools	99		X		X	X	X	M=14.7			X		X
Community Council (1973) (Youth Service Bureau) Phoenix, Ariz.	Multiple agencies	100					X	X	10-18			X		X
Duxbury (1973) (California Y.S.B.'s) California (statewide)	Multiple agencies	1340		X	X	X	X	X	10-18			X		X
ABT Associates (1974) (Neighborhood Youth Resources Center) Philadelphia, Pa.	Multiple agencies	2 districts			X	X	X	X	10-17			X		X

Variables	Outcome[e]	Follow-up	Amt. D.[f] H	M	L	Duration	Funding[g] F	S	L	O	Mos. in Operation
Court records	+		X				X		X	X	24 mos.
School record	+										
Attitude-school	−										
Court records	+		X				X				24 mos.
Area arrest rates	+			X			X	X			12 mos.
Police record	+	6 mos.		X			X	X			12 mos.
Court records	+										
Increase in services	+										
Parent & staff ratings	+										
Recidivism to center	+		X				X		X		24 mos.
Court records	+			X				X	X	X	24 mos.
Youth attitudes	+			X			X		X		24 mos.
Community attitudes	+										
Cost reduction	+										
Court records	+		X						X		36 mos.
Court records	+	6 mos.	X				X	X	X		24 mos.
Area arrest rates	+										
Area arrest rates	+			X			X		X		18 mos.
Truancy	+										
Penetration	+										
PINS referrals	+										

Table VI. Area and Youth Service Projects *(con't)*

Reference, Project Type, Location	Subject Referral Source	Sample Size [a]		Race [b]			Sex			Group Assign. [c]			Stat. Anal. [d]	
		E(n)	C(n)	C	N	O	M	F	Age	R	M	O	Y	N
Baker (1974) (Youth Development Corporation) Lansing, Mich.	Court, Police	90	90	X	X	X	X	X	13-20		X		X	
Liedtke et al. (1974) (Youth Diversion) Portland, Ore.	Court	57	40	X	X	X	X	X	10-18	X				X

NOTE: For legend see footnote to Table I.

acted on by community control agencies. Most of the projects provided services to youths who had been charged with adult crimes or juvenile status offenses. The next largest group of youth were perceived by school and community welfare agencies as being in need of services. A relatively small percentage of youths came into the programs either as a result of familial or personal difficulties or as a result of referral by friends or self. Seventy-nine percent of the projects used police or court records as a criterion of effectiveness. Only two of the 96 reports contained measures of self-reported delinquency.

As might have been expected, no definitional consensus for the term "prevention" was found. A definition was seldom made explicit and the distinction between "prevention" and "treatment" was equally ambiguous. If prevention is defined as action taken before a criminal or delinquent act has occurred, and treatment is defined as action taken after such an act has occurred (Harlow, 1969), then 66% of the projects which provided services to youths referred by the police and courts were "treatment" rather than "prevention" projects. At best such efforts can only be classified as tertiary prevention (Kahn, 1969).

Even within a particular prevention or treat-

ment strategy, there was a great deal of variation. For example, the counseling projects (Table III) utilized a range of techniques which included weekly counseling sessions conducted by school personnel, personalized social work by "big brothers," lessons in personal attractiveness conducted by women's club volunteers, and discussions between delinquent youth and convicted adult prisoners. The only common feature of these projects seemed to be the term "counseling" itself.[2]

Lack of adequate description was a characteristic of most of the reports. Only 33% contained an acceptable degree of description of their intervention strategies and only 40% contained any indication of treatment intensity. Less than 10% of the reports explicitly used theory to generate intervention methods of research questions.

These reports indicate a low degree of sophistication in research design. Only 50% of these studies used some form of comparison group, and 53% of these (28% of the total) used

[2]The authors wish to thank M. A Kemp and R. Lee for raising this point about the variation of treatment strategy within the broad categories of this paper. Martha Kemp and Robert Lee are the research associate and project director of Project CREST, a professional counseling project for juvenile offenders in Gainesville, Fla.

Variables	Criterion Measure		Treatment					
	Out-come [e]	Follow-up	Amt. D.[f] H M L	Duration	Funding[g] F S L O	Mos. in Operation
Police record	0		X		X X	15 mos.
Court record	0					
School suspension	+					
Client & staff ques-tionnaire	+					
Court record	0	3 mos.	X		X	6 mos.

a randomized or matched subjects design. Fifty-six percent of the evaluations were based on multiple outcome measures, 42% contained inferential analyses of their data, and 45% gathered follow-up data at least six months after the subjects had left the program.

Only nine of the 96 studies used random assignment of subjects, inferential analyses of their data, an outcome measure of delinquent behavior (self-reported, police records, court records), and at least six months follow-up after the subjects had left the project. Of those nine, three reported positive outcomes, three reported differential effectiveness, two reported nonsignificant outcomes, and one reported negative outcomes. The three projects which reported positive outcomes had the three smallest sample sizes among the nine reports.

The primary criteria that decision-makers use to judge programs are feasibility, efficiency and practicality, and program suitability to their own particular situation. Specifically, they are concerned about funding, funding sources, resources needed to implement a project, the project's cost effectiveness, and its success relative to institutional programs. Policy makers at the management and sponsoring agency level are less interested in attributing delinquency rates to their project efforts than they are in meeting the demands of service delivery, public opinion, and agency survival. Their concerns are centered around the problems associated with successfully operating juvenile delinquency prevention and treatment projects.

This review of the juvenile delinquency prevention literature indicates a pervasive lack of that kind of policy utility information. Only 28% of the reports even contained either total project costs or average cost per subject.

Summary

The 96 empirical (broadly defined) studies confirm that an extremely small percentage of delinquency prevention efforts are ever evaluated, even minimally. Furthermore, even when adequate evaluation is performed, few studies show significant results. Finally, information which policy makers most frequently request is virtually nonexistent.

"No responsible business concern would operate with as little information regarding its success or failure as do nearly all of our delinquency-prevention and control programs. It is almost possible to count on one hand the number of true experiments in which alternative techniques are compared; the number of systematic, though nonexperimental, evaluations is not a great deal larger. We spend millions of dollars a year in preventive and corrective

Table VII. Educational Programs

Reference, Project Type, Location	Subject Referral Source	Sample Size[a] E(n)	C(n)	Race[b] C	N	O	Sex M	F	Age	Group Assign.[c] R	M	O	Stat. Anal.[d] Y	N
Seagraves (1973) (Teaching Law) Redwood City, Calif.	Grades 7 & 8	1079	745	X	X	X	X	X		X			X	
Bouma & Williams (1970) (Police-counselor program) Bridgeport, Mich.	Grades 6–12	2 schools	1 school	X	X		X	X			X			X
Dailey (1967) (Anti delinquency school programs) Washington, D.C.	School	1634		X	X		X	X	M=17			X	X	
Demsch & Garth (1968) (Truancy prevention) Chicago, Ill.	School	48					X		7-13			X		X
Bartlett & Newberger (1973) (Court-centered school) Sioux Falls, S.D.	Court	60										X		X
Reckless & Dinitz (1972) (Special classes) Columbus, Ohio	Teacher nominated	632	462	X	X		X		M=13.2	X			X	
Radabaugh & Kirby (1973) (Project CARE) Charleston, W.Va.	School	4 schools							1-12 grade			X		X
Rader (1972) (Service coordination) Oklahoma (4 cities)	School	4 schools		X	X	X	X	X	K-4 grade			X	X	
School Board of Leon County (1974) (Youth Service Agency) Tallahassee, Fla.	School	1 county							Elem.-high school					X

NOTE: For legend see Table I.

Criterion Measure			Treatment								
			Amt. D.[f]				Funding [g]				
Variables	Outcome[e]	Follow-up	H	M	L	Duration	F	S	L	O	Mos. in Operation
Attitude toward law	+		X			10 hrs.				X	12 mos.
Knowledge of law	+										
Attitude toward police	+		X				X	X			12 mos.
Reading	+			X			X				12 mos.
Truancy	+	4 yrs.		X		10 mos.			X		60 mos.
Return to public school	+			X			X	X			9 mos.
Educators' ratings	+										
Parents' ratings	+										
Students' ratings	+										
Police records	0	1 yr.	X			9 mos.	X	X			60 mos.
Self-reported delinquency	0										
School dropout	0										
School grades	0										
Attitudes	0										
Reading ability	+										
School dropout	+			X			X	X			12 mos.
Absenteeism	+										
Referrals to court	+										
Education ratings	+										
Teacher rating of delinquency potential	+	1 yr.	X				X	X			24 mos.
Teachers' rating	+										
Parents' ratings	+										
Attendance rate	+			X			X		X		6 mos.
Suspension rate	+										

Table VIII. Vocational Programs

Reference, Project Type, Location	Subject Referral Source	Sample Size[a] E(n)	Sample Size[a] C(n)	Race[b] C	Race[b] N	Race[b] O	Sex M	Sex F	Age	Group Assign.[c] R	Group Assign.[c] M	Group Assign.[c] O	Stat. Anal.[d] Y	Stat. Anal.[d] N
Womack & Wiener (1968) (Work study program) Houston, Tex.	Court	303		X	X	X	X	X	15-21			X		X
Jeffrey & Jeffrey (1969) (Work Study program) Washington, D.C.	School	167			X		X	X	16-21			X		X
Ahlstrom & Havighurst (1971) (Work study program) Kansas City, Mo.	School	200	200	X	X		X		13-14			X		X
Kent Co. (1973) (Work-study) Grand Rapids, Mich.	Court	54					X		14-16			X		X
Hackler (1966) & Hackler & Linden (1970) (Work program) Seattle, Wash.	Housing project	160	80	X	X		X		13-15	X			X	
Walther & Magnusson (1967) (Neighborhood Youth Corps) Cincinnati, Durham, N.C., E. St. Louis, St. Louis	Multiple sources	325	135	X	X		X	X	16-20			X		X
Goodwill Industries (1967) (Job Training) Springfield, Mass.	Court	48	19	X	X		X		14-23			X	X	
National Committee for Children and Youth (1971) (Manpower services) Washington, D.C.	Court	123		X	X	X	X	X	15-18			X	X	

Criterion Measure			Treatment								
			Amt. D.[f]				Funding[g]				
Variables	Outcome[e]	Follow-up	H	M	L	Duration	F	S	L	O	Mos. in Operation
Police records	0		X				X				12 mos.
Commitments to training school	+										
Passing G E D	0			X			X				36 mos.
Project dropout	0										
Reduction of delinquent acts	0										
Police records	0	5 yrs.	X						X	X	72 mos.
High School graduation	0										
Work experience	0										
School attitudes	0										
Court records	+		X			13 wks.	X				48 mos.
Program graduate	+										
Police record	0			X					X	X	12 mos.
Self-perceptions	0										
Alienation	0										
Public support	+										
Police records— females	+	1 yr.	X			8 mos.	X				24 mos.
Police records—males	0										
Unemployment— females	+										
Unemployment— males	0										
Supplemental education	+										
Occupational aspirations	0										
Police record	+		X				X		X		18 mos.
Employment	+										
Job stability	+										
Police record	0	1 yr.	X				X				36 mos.

Table VIII. Vocational Programs *(con't)*

Reference, Project Type, Location	Subject Referral Source	Sample Size [a] E(n)	C(n)	Race [b] C	N	O	Sex M	F	Age	Group Assign. [c] R	M	O	Stat. Anal. [d] Y	N
New York State (1973) (Job training) New York, N.Y.	Court									X				X
Shore & Massimo (1966, 1969) (Vocational psychotherapy) Boston, Mass.	School	10	10				X		15-17	X			X	

NOTE: For legend see Table I.

efforts, with little other than guess work to tell us whether we are getting the desired effects." (Wheeler, Cottrell, & Romasco, 1970, p. 440)

DISCUSSION

Research findings in other areas have shown that techniques and procedures such as social work, psychotherapy, counseling, and corrections which attempt to effect social problems such as alcohol and drug abuse and adult criminality also have not produced consistently positive results.

Mullen and Dumpson (1972) reviewed the field of social work and found that there were either no significant differences between experimental and control groups, or very limited and questionable gains. They concluded that there is no evidence that professional social work and intervention (including social work plus counseling and psychotherapy) is effective. Likewise, positive benefits from psychotherapy as a means of dealing with neurotic children and the emotional problems of adults have not been established. Meltzoff and Kornreich (1970) reported some positive chages in those who have undergone psychotherapy, but Eysenck (1952, 1960, 1965) and Levitt (1957) did not. The same

is true for counseling. Truax and Carkhuff (1967) came to the conclusion that, in general, social problems are not effected by the current counseling techniques.

Mann (1972) reviewed the evaluative research literature of four content areas: psychotherapy, counseling, human-relations training, and education. She concluded that there is little difference in the results of evaluate studies conducted in different content areas.

In the area of health and welfare, Elinson (1972) reviewed 10 papers on social action programs. His conclusion was ". . . none of the ten programs of social intervention achieved striking positive results (p. 299)." Ward and Kassebaum (1972) reviewed the literature and several unpublished reports on corrections and arrived at the conclusion that corrections has not demonstrated an ability to increase inmate docility or decrease recidivism. Vinter and Janowitz (1959) found that despite some efforts, juvenile correctional institutions have not made significant advances beyond mere custody. Bailey (1966) reported that correctional outcomes are slight, inconsistent, and of questionable reliability.

These reviews offer concurrent validity for the results of this paper. There is a consensus of

Variables	Criterion Measure Outcome e	Follow-up	Treatment Amt. D. f H M L	Duration	Funding g F S L O	Mos. in Operation
Police record	0		X		X	
Attitudes	+					
Police record	+	3 yrs.	X		X X X	10 mos.
Employment record	+					
Academic achievement	+					
Personality	+					

opinion that changing human behavior is no simple task. Evaluating the effectiveness of "people changing" strategies is no easy task either. In searching for an interpretation of the fact that we found relatively few studies which could lead us to recommend specific prevention or treatment strategies, we perceived three general categories of problems, political, methodological, and theoretical, which may have contributed to this state of affairs.

Political Considerations

The primary purpose of this review was to determine if particular methods of prevention have been shown to be causally related to changes in delinquency rates. We therefore undertook a review of evaluation studies. But "evaluation" differs conceptually from "research" in that its fundamental purpose is to provide useful information for decision-making rather than knowledge in general (Stufflebeam et al., 1971; Weiss, 1972). As such, evaluation is a political activity: ". . . evaluating social action programs is only secondarily a scientific enterprise. First and foremost it is an effort to gain politically significant information on the consequences of political acts" (Cohen, 1970, pp. 236–237). This does not mean that scientists are

necessarily more rational than politicians, just that they operate with different sets of values. These differences may lead to some discomfort for researchers. Empey and Erickson (1972) provided a poignant description of an ideological and political conflict during the demise of a community treatment project (Chapter 8—The Struggle for Survival).

The concept of evaluation as a tool for political decision-making rather than knowledge generation does not mean that research has no utility for decision-making. Being able to attribute outcomes to activities should be an important consideration in deciding whether or not to continue that set of activities. Smith (1975) has written that the greatest political pressures will be for this kind of "outcome research" or product evaluation. But generating this kind of knowledge requires certain constraints on program activities. This kind of evaluation requires, at the very least, that a project is operating in some systematic and stable manner—an unlikely state of most social action programs. The lack of positive findings for delinquency prevention strategies may be due, in part, to both an inappropriate use of and unwillingness to live within the constraints of outcome research strategies.

Most of the reports that were reviewed in this

Table IX. Community Treatment Programs

Reference, Project Type, Location	Subject Referral Source	Sample Size[a] E(n)	C(n)	Race[b] C	N	O	Sex M	F	Age	Group Assign.[c] R	M	O	Stat. Anal.[d] Y	N
McCord et al. (1968) (Foster-home) Boston, Mass.	Court	19	19				X		9-17	X			X	
Wilgosh (1973) (Group-homes) Toronto, Can.	Court	21					X	X	12-16		X			X
Palmer (1972) (Group-homes) Sacramento & Stockton, Calif.	Court	12	84	X	X	X	X		M=17		X		X	
Wolf et al. (1971) (Achievement Place) Lawrence, Kan.	Court	16	18				X		12-16		X			X
City of Chicago (1972) (Youth Service Homes) Chicago, Ill.	Court	26					X	X	13-16		X			X
New York State (1973) (Short-term Aid to Youth) New York, N.Y.	Multiple Agencies	1065		X	X	X	X		15-18		X		X	
Pilnick et al. (1968) (Collegefields) Essex Co., N.J.	Court	25					X		14-15		X		X	
Stephenson & Scarpitti (1969) (Essexfields) Essex Co., N.J.	Court	100	1100	X		X	X		16-17		X			X
Weeks (1970) (Highfields) Highfields, N.J.	Court	233	122	X	X		X		16-17		X			X
Palmer (1971) (Community Treatment Project) California, (4 Comm.)	Court	686	328	X	X	X	X	X	13-19	X			X	

Variables	Outcome[e]	Follow-up	Amt. D.[f] H	Amt. D.[f] M	Amt. D.[f] L	Duration	Funding[g] F	Funding[g] S	Funding[g] L	Funding[g] O	Mos. in Operation
Rate of deviance	–	12 yrs.			X		X			X	96 mos.
Court records	0	2 yrs.			X					X	
Subsequent placements	0										
Returned home	–										
Parole failure	0	2 yrs.	X			10 mos.	X	X			36 mos.
Community acceptance	+										
Police records	+	2 yrs.	X			M=10 mos.	X		X		36 mos.
Court records	+										
School attendance	+										
Grades	+										
Court records	0			X		M=8 mos.	X		X		15 mos.
Completion of probation	–										
Arrest record	0	2 yrs		X		M=3 mos.		X			72 mos.
Court record	+	6 mos.	X			10 hr./day		X			16 mos.
Court record	+	3 yrs.			X	4-5 mos.	X			X	60 mos.
Program graduate	+										
Personality	+										
Institutional recidivism	+	1 yr.	X					X	X		96 mos.
Attitude change	0										
Personality change	0										
Parole suspensions	–	5 yrs.	X					X	X		60 mos.
Recidivism	+										
Favorable discharge	0										
Unfavorable discharge	+										
Psychological tests	+										
Post-discharge arrests	0										

Table IX. Community Treatment Programs *(con't)*

Reference, Project Type, Location	Subject Referral Source	Sample Size [a]		Race [b]			Sex		Age	Group Assign. [c]			Stat. Anal. [d]	
		E(n)	C(n)	C	N	O	M	F		R	M	O	Y	N
City of Chicago (1973) (Y.M.C.A. Residential Program) Chicago, Ill.	Court	45			X		X		16-18			X		X
Hussey et al. (1970) & Steinman & Fernald (1968) (Residential Youth Center) Portland, Me.	Multiple Agencies	67						X	14-18			X	X	
Goldenberg (1971) & Boys Residential Youth Center (1968) New Haven, Conn.	Multiple Agencies	20	20	X	X	X	X		15-22	X			X	
Empey & Erickson (1972) (Provo Experiment) Provo, Utah	Court	115	211	X			X		14-18	X			X	
Empey & Lubeck (1971) (Silverlake Experiment) Los Angeles, Calif.	Court	140	121	X	X	X	X		15-18	X			X	

NOTE: For legend see Table I.

Variables	Outcome [e]	Follow-up	Amt. D. [f] H	M	L	Duration	Funding [g] F	S	L	O	Mos. in Operation
Police records	0	8 mos.	X			M=6 mos.	X	X			24 mos.
Successful termination	−										
Client ratings	+										
Time lag to finding a job	−		X				X	X			24 mos.
Hours worked	−										
Staff ratings	−										
School performance	−										
Publicity	+										
Self-concept	0										
Police records	+	6 mos.	X				X				24 mos.
Days in jail	+										
Weekly wages	+										
Attitudes	+										
Program dropouts	0	4 yrs.	X			4-7 mos.			X	X	60 mos.
Arrests during program	+										
Tech. efficiency rating	0										
Arrests—probation group	0										
Arrests—committed group	+										
Confinements—probation group	+										
Confinements—committed group	+										
Arrests rates	+	1 yr.	X				X	X	X		36 mos.
Program graduates	−										
Reduction of offenses	0										
Degree of seriousness	+										

Table X. Miscellaneous Programs

Reference, Project Type, Location	Subject Referral Source	Sample Size[a] E(n)	C(n)	Race[b] C	N	O	Sex M	F	Age	Group Assign.[c] R	M	O	Stat. Anal.[d] Y	N
Bomberger (1970) (Youth Police Reserves) Sheridan, Ore.	Self						X	X	14-21		X			X
Elliott & LeBouef (1973) (Temporary shelter) Lincoln, Neb.	Multiple sources	160					X	X	12-18	X				X
Schwitzgebel & Kolb (1964) & Schwitzgebel (1964) (Tape-recorded interviews) Boston, Mass.	Project solicited	20	20				X		15-21		X	X		
Olson & Carpenter (1971) (Nationwide School Vandalism Survey)		248 schools										X		
Brown & Dodson (1968) (Boys' Club) Louisville, Ky.		1 club					X							X
YMCA (1973) (Mini-bikes Project) 296 projects in 45 states	Multiple sources	7370					X		15-21					X

NOTE: For legend see Table I.

Criterion Measure			Treatment								
			Amt. D.[f]				Funding[g]				
Variables	Outcome[e]	Follow-up	H	M	L	Duration	F	S	L	O	Mos. in Operation
Vandalism	+	2 yrs.			X				X		60 mos.
Possession of alcohol	+										
Police record	+				X	M=7 days	X			X	24 mos.
Number of arrests	+	3 yrs.	X			2-3 hrs./wk.				X	10 mos.
Mos. incarcerated	+										
Prison recidivism	0										
School size	—						X				
Type of facilities	0										
School value	—		X								
Amount of glass	+										
Surveillance	0										
Extra curricular operations	—										
Area police arrest rates	+	8 yrs.			X				X	X	96 mos.
Recidivism	+				X		X		X	X	24 mos.
Community attitudes	+										

paper did not contain a description of treatment intensity or consistency. Only one of the 96 papers was strictly process oriented. Caplan (1968; Table 5) reported a process analysis of treatment intervention by gathering repeated measures on the same individuals through time. He consistently found that the boys would progress satisfactorily toward treatment goals only to "fail" at the time the treatment goals moved toward final objectives. Such repeated failures seemed to involve both the "treater" and the "treated." "In fact, because of the services and favors preferred, there may be considerably more advantages in being 'Reached' repeatedly than in being changed" (p. 83). The mutually dependent client-practitioner interactions were viewed as being more accommodative than functional from the standpoint of preventing delinquency. Thus, it would seem inappropriate to judge this project by its "products." Rather, the evaluation generated information about the program's process about which judgements could be made.

There are also political processes which lead us to expect a higher degree of success for experimental programs than is warranted. We allocate resources to efforts which political arguments deem most likely to provide answers to social problems, and these arguments often promise that social interventions are going to have large effects. This is an unrealistic belief for at least two reasons. First, decision-making rules of inferential analyses are conservative. Second, research in the natural sciences, with their greater capacity for experimental control, also have a relatively high failure rate (Adams, 1975, p. 10). We have not yet reached the level of the "experimenting society" dreamed of by Campbell (Tavris, 1975). Consequently:

"Politicians, bureaucrats, indeed society at large, expect final solutions, not small increments of information or negative findings. The practical solutions it (field experimentation) can provide are usually so small that administrators are inevitably disappointed and usually angry. It is their inclination, therefore, to quote the old saying: 'The program was a flop, but the

research was a success. I'll never do that again.' " (Empey & Lubeck, 1971, pp. 333–334)

Most of the 96 reports surveyed in this review were of low validity by scientific criteria and of low utility for decision-makers. As such, few of them should have seen the light of day. Successful product or outcome evaluation requires consistent design, adequate measurement, and appropriate analyses as well as a stable program, administrative support, and adequate resources. "Summative evaluation should be done rather rarely, when the political context is right for it to be taken seriously; and it should be done very well if at all" (Smith, 1975, p. 297). We concur.

Methodological Considerations
Undoubtedly, much of the outcome variance in any summary paper is due to the variable definitions of delinquency, prevention, and success. The question of whether delinquency is the behavior of an individual, or the behavior of various levels of the socio-legal systems which detects and interprets the behavior of individuals is not resolved. More than one report showed different outcomes when data were gathered at the police stations and at the courts, e.g., no reduction in police records but a positive effect on court records. A similar problem occurs in defining prevention. More than half of these projects were "treating" adjudicated delinquents rather than preventing nonadjudicated youth from becoming wards of the court.

Even within a particular treatment strategy, there was a dearth of information describing the variation of treatment effort and treatment staff. Not one report described, before the intervention occurred, the minimum level of intervention which would have been expected to yield positive outcomes. Consequently, none of the projects reported whether or not a minimal level of treatment or prevention was provided. But there are some indications that outcomes may be related to the quality and intensity of treatment. Among these 96 reports, Empey and Erickson (1972) reported: "When length of exposure is controlled, the findings suggest that intensity of supervision is a vital force in delinquency control, and that to the degree this intensity is diminished, in-program arrest rates will increase" (p. 84). Shore and Massimo (1966, 1969) reported positive treatment results after three years follow-up. Their treatment group of ten males received ten months of intensive, individualized psychotherapy, remedial education, and job counseling and employment. Goldenberg (1971) reported positive results for a group of 20 males after an average of 5.2 months of treatment in a residential center, i.e., virtually 24 hour per day treatment.

Other areas of correctional research tend to confirm these findings. Jesness and his colleagues have shown that treatment effectiveness, in part, is attributable to the quality of service provided, irrespective of the setting or treatment strategy (Jesness, De Risi, McCormick, & Wedge, 1972; Jesness, Allison, McCormick, Wedge & Young, 1975). In a review of correctional research, Glaser (1974) found four separate studies in which positive outcomes were related to low rates of staff turnover and longer periods of exposure to treatment conditions.

Neglect of Theory

One reason for the lack of treatment data among these reports may be due to the paucity of theory. It is possible that many of these projects did not know what they wanted to do before they began and they did not know why they expected their efforts at "preventing" delinquency to succeed. Therefore, when faced with "no significant differences," do you interpret a failure to reject the null hypothesis as a failure to adequately implement your experimental manipulations or as a failure of the theory from which you deduced the treatment?

"If a program is unsuccessful, it may be because the program failed to 'operationalize' the theory, or because the theory itself was deficient . . . Furthermore, in a very few cases do action or service programs directly attack the ultimate objective. Rather they attempt to change the intermediate process which is 'causally' related to the ultimate objective. Thus, there are two possible sources of failure (1) the inability of the program to influence the "causal" variable, or (2) the invalidity of the theory linking the "causal" variable to the desired objectives." (Suchman, 1969, p. 16)

Perhaps the best reported use of theory to guide intervention principles and reformulate theory among the 96 reports surveyed here is the report by Empey & Lubeck (1971). The Silverlake Experiment was an attempt to develop a *Field Experiment Model* in which both research and implementation could coexist. There were four basic elements to the model: (1) a specific theory of delinquency; (2) an intervention strategy related to the theory; (3) a research strategy which reflected on both the adequacy of treatment and of theory; and (4) an assessment of the findings for both theory and correctional intervention. The authors suggested that the major significance of the field experiment was that it provided a framework for simultaneously examining basic theoretical postulates, day-to-day program operations, and field research problems.

The lack of theoretical specification could lead to confounding results in yet another way. It is logically absurd to assume that any one intervention which would have been expected to yield positive outcomes. Consequently, none of the entire population of youth, youth at risk, or even delinquent youth. As mentioned above, among the nine reports with relatively high degree of internal validity, three reported positive results. These projects also had the smallest experimental samples of 10, 20, and 26 subjects. It is possible that these projects had selected relatively homogeneous samples for treatment. Three of the four projects with the largest experimental sample sizes, 632, 115, 140, 686, reported differential outcomes for various client subgroups. Empey and Erickson (1972) reported different effects by treatment groups; the Provo experiment was superior to institutionalization but not to regular probation. Empey and Lubeck (1971) found differential impacts of both the institutional (control) and community (experimental) programs. When they examined recidivism data, they found that background variables, such as family disorganization, were predictive of recidivism for experimental subjects, and peer identification variables were predictive for control subjects. Between program differences were also found. For the experimental program, personality was predictive of recidivism for the successful graduates while previous offense history was predictive for the program failures and runaways. Just the opposite was found for the institutional program; previous offense history waspredictive of successful graduates and personality was predictive of failures and runaways. But overall, there was no difference in recidivism rates between the two groups.

Only one project began with a differential treatment strategy. The Community Treatment Project (Palmer, 1971) randomly assigned 686 youths to a small caseload, community-based parole program, and 328 youths to institutional programs. Each of the youths was classified by a typology of "interpersonal maturity levels" and an attempt was made to match the experimental youth with parole agents who would apply "differential" treatment based on the interpersonal maturity level of the youth. When arrest and recidivism data were viewed by type of youth, it was found that the "neurotic" group (which comprised 53 percent of the wards) performed substantially better in the intensive CTP program, the "Power Oriented" group (21 percent of the youth) performed substantially better in the traditional institutional program, and the "Passive Conformist" group (14 percent of the youth) performed somewhat better in the CTP. For females, the personality groupings did not show this same advantage of community-based, differential treatment over institutional treatment. "Some 36 percent of the sample perform better within CTP than in the traditional program, while 10 percent do better within the traditional program. Close to 25 percent do rather poorly within both types of program" (p. 91).

Differential outcomes have been found in other correctional evaluations. Kelley and Baer (1971) found that some, but not all, delinquents responded to a program of physical challenge such as Outward Bound. During Part 2 of the Community Treatment Project (Palmer, 1974),[3] youths were classified as "Status 1," or those youths who were seen as needing an initial period of institutionalization, and "Status 2," those seen as not needing this type of setting. The results showed that Status 1 youth who had been inappropriately placed, i.e., in the community, were doing substantially worse (more offenses during their first 18 months on parole) than the status 1 youth who had been appropriately placed. No differences were observed between the status 2 youth who began their treatment in the community and status 2 youth who began in the institution. Jesness (1971) compared the effectiveness of 20-bed institutional living units with 50-bed institutional units by type of youth. Analyses of probation outcomes showed that the "neurotic" boys gained the most from the small units and that "non-neurotic" boys did equally well in either unit. Glaser (1974) also supported this notion of differential treatment effects. His review indicated that the "conflicted" offender (high maturity, amenable, or neurotic) responded more to "personal counseling and rapport-oriented assistance" than to traditional institutional programs while the "committed" offender (power-oriented, low-maturity, or nonamenables) evidenced less recidivism from the traditional programs than from the personal assistance programs.

In short, delinquency prevention and treatment strategies which deal with individuals or any other target for change and which choose a univariate theoretical base or a singular intervention strategy should expect only limited successes, and their evaluation designs should reflect that expectation. "When different or-

---

[3]This report was not included in the original sample and therefore is not included in Table IX because it was published after January 1, 1974.

ganizations are involved, the differential interaction of personal and organizational characteristics are likely to create conditions that will alter significantly the capacity of any input factors to be universally, predictable" (Empey & Lubeck, 1971, p. 272).

Conclusion

The purpose of this review was first, to determine if particular methods of prevention have been shown to be causally related to changes in delinquency rates, and, second, to determine if the evaluation literature contained other information, such as cost-effectiveness comparisons, that policy-makers might find useful.

The results showed that the evaluation literature is low in both scientific validity and policy utility, and that no delinquency prevention strategies can be definitively recommended. We conclude that changing or preventing certain kinds of behavior is a difficult task, that positive results are probably related to quality and quantity of intervention, that any one intervention strategy is probably going to be differentially effective given a heterogeneous population, that theory-based strategies are going to be in a better position to profit from evaluations than are atheoretical strategies, and that sound research design is needed if we wish to be able to attribute changes in delinquency rates to prevention efforts.

REFERENCES

Adams, S. *Evaluative research in corrections: A practical guide* (U.S. Department of Justice, Law Enforcement Assistance Administration, National Institute of Law Enforcement and Criminal Justice). Washington, D.C.: U.S. Government Printing Office, 1975.

Amos, W. E., Manella, R., & Southwell, M. A. *Action programs for delinquency prevention.* Springfield, Ill.: Charles C. Thomas, 1965.

Bailey, W. C. Correctional outcome: An evaluation of 100 reports. *The Journal of Criminal Law, Criminology and Police Science,* 1966, 57, 153–160.

Beck, B. M., & Beck, D. B. Does recreation prevent delinquency? In J. R. Stratton & R. M. Terry (Eds.),

Prevention of delinquency: Problems and programs. New York: Macmillan, 1968. Pp. 271–273.

Berleman, W. C., & Steinburn, T. W. The value and validity of delinquency prevention experiments. *Crime and Delinquency,* 1969, 15, 471–478.

Burns, V. M., & Stern, L. W. The prevention of juvenile delinquency. In the President's Commission on Law Enforcement and Administration of Justice. *Task Force Report: Juvenile delinquency and youth crime.* Washington, D.C.: U.S. Government Printing Office, 1967, Pp. 353–408.

Cohen, D. K. Politics and research: Evaluation of social action programs in education. *Review of Educational Research,* 1970, 40, 213–238.

Elinson, J. Effectiveness of social action programs in health and welfare. In C. H. Weiss (Ed.), *Evaluating action programs.* Boston: Allyn & Bacon, 1972. Pp. 294–299.

Eysenck, H. J. The effects of psychotherapy: An evaluation. *Journal of Consulting Psychology,* 1952, 16, 319–324.

Eysenck, H. J. The effects of psychotherapy. In H. J. Eysenck (Ed.), *Handbook of abnormal psychology.* London: Pitman, 1960.

Eysenck, H. J. The effects of psychotherapy. *International Journal of Psychiatry,* 1965, 1, 99–142.

Glaser, D. Remedies for the key deficiency in criminal justice evaluation research. *Journal of Research in Crime and Delinquency,* 1974, 11, 144–154.

Glueck, S., & Glueck, E. *One thousand juvenile delinquents.* Cambridge, Mass.: Harvard University Press, 1934.

Glueck, S., & Glueck, E. *Unraveling juvenile delinquency.* Cambridge, Mass.: Harvard University Press, 1950.

Harlow, E. Prevention of crime and delinquency. A review of the literature. *Information Review on Crime and Delinquency,* 1969, 1(6), 1–43.

Jesness, C. F. Comparative effectiveness of two institutional treatment programs for delinquents. *Child Care Quarterly,* 1971, 1, 119–130.

Jesness, C. F., DeRisi, W. J., McCormick, P., & Wedge, R. F. *The Youth Center Research Project.* Sacramento, CA.: California Youth Authority, 1972.

Jesness, C. F., Allison, T. S., McCormick, P. M.,

Wedge, R. F., & Young, M. L. *The Cooperative Behavior Demonstration Project.* Sacramento, CA.: California Youth Authority, 1975.

Kahn, A. J. *Studies in social policies and planning.* New York: Russell Sage Foundation, 1969.

Kelley, F. J., & Baer, D. J. Physical challenge as a treatment for delinquency. *Crime and Delinquency,* 1971, *17,* 437–445.

Koshel, J. *Deinstitutionalization: Delinquent children.* Washington, D.C.: The Urban Institute, December 1973.

Lemert, E. M. *Instead of court: Diversion in juvenile justice.* Washington, D.C.: U.S. Government Printing Office, 1971.

Levitt, E. G. The results of psychotherapy with children: An evaluation. *Journal of Consulting Psychology,* 1957, *21,* 189–196.

Logan, C. H. Evaluation research in crime and delinquency: A reappraisal. *Journal of Criminal Law, Criminology and Police Science,* 1972, *63,* 378–387.

Mann, J. The outcome of evaluative research. In C. H. Weiss (Ed.), *Evaluating action programs.* Boston: Allyn & Bacon, 1972. Pp. 267–282.

Meltzoff, J., & Kornreich, M. *Research in psychotherapy.* New York: Atherton Press, 1970.

Mullen, E. J., & Dumpson, J. R. (Eds.) *Evaluation of social intervention.* San Francisco: Jossey-Bass, 1972.

Palmer, T. The Youth Authority's Community Treatment Project. *Federal Probation,* 1974, *38,* 3–14.

The President's Commission on Law Enforcement and Administration of Justice. *Task Force Report: Juvenile delinquency and youth crime.* Washington, D.C.: U.S. Government Printing Office, 1967.

Schreiber, P. *Juvenile delinquency facts-facets No. 9: How effective are services for the treatment of delinquents.* Washington, D.C.: U.S. Government Printing Office, 1960.

Smith, M. B. Beyond journalistic scouting: Evaluation for better programs. *Journal of Applied Behavioral Science,* 1975, *11,* 290–297.

Stufflebeam, D. L., Foley, W. J., Gephart, W. J., Guba, E. G., Hammond, R. L., Merriman, H. O., & Provus, M. M., *Educational evaluation and decision-making.* Itasca, Ill.: F. E. Peacock, 1971.

Suchman, E. A. Evaluating educational programs: A symposium. *The Urban Review,* 1969, *3*(4), 15–17.

Sullivan, C. E., & Bash, C. S. Current programs for delinquency prevention. In W. E. Amos & C. F. Wellford (Eds.), *Delinquency prevention: Theory and practice.* Englewood Cliffs, N.J.: Prentice-Hall, 1967. Pp. 51–72.

Tavris, C. The experimenting society: A conversation with Donald T. Campbell. *Psychology Today,* 1975, *9*(4), 47–56.

Truax, C. G., & Carkhuff, R. R. *Toward effective counseling and psychotherapy.* Chicago: Aldine, 1967.

U.S. Interdepartmental Council to Coordinate All Federal Juvenile Delinquency Programs. *Report.* Washington, D.C.: U.S. Government Printing Office, 1972.

Venezia, P. S. Erroneous notions of delinquency prevention. Davis, CA.: Research Center, National Council on Crime and Delinquency. Unpublished manuscript, 1975.

Vinter, R., & Janowitz, M. Effective institutions for juvenile delinquents: A research statement. *Social Service Review,* 1959, *33,* 118–130.

Ward, D. A., & Kassebaum, C. G. On biting the hand that feeds: Some implications of sociological evaluations of correctional effectiveness. In C. H. Weiss (Ed.), *Evaluating action programs.* Boston: Allyn & Bacon, 1972. Pp. 300–310.

Weiss, C. H. *Evaluation research: Methods for assessing program effectiveness.* Englewood Cliffs, N.J.: Prentice-Hall, 1972.

Wheeler, S., Cottrell, L. S. Jr., & Romasco, A. Juvenile delinquency: Its prevention and control. In The President's Commission on Law Enforcement and Administration of Justice, *Task Force Report: Juvenile delinquency and youth crime.* Washington, D.C.: U.S. Government Printing Office, 1967. Pp. 409–428.

Wheeler, S., Cottrell, L. S. Jr., & Romasco, A. Juvenile delinquency—its prevention and control. In P. Lerman (Ed.), *Delinquency and social policy.* New York: Praeger, 1970. Pp. 428–443.

Witmer, H. L., & Tufts, E. *The effectiveness of delinquency prevention programs.* Washington, D.C.: U.S. Children's Bureau Publication No. 350, 1954.

Yaryan, R. B. Federal efforts to coordinate juvenile

delinquency and related youth development programs. *Journal of Abnormal Child Psychology*, 1973, *1*, 308–316.

REFERENCES IN TABLES I–X

ABT Associates, Inc. Exemplary project validation report: Neighborhood Youth Resources Center, Philadelphia, Pa. Cambridge, Mass.: ABT Associates, March 1974.

Adams, S. A cost approach to the assessment of gang rehabilitation techniques. *Journal of Research in Crime and Delinquency*, 1967, *4*(1), 166–182.

Ahlstrom, W. M., & Havighurst, R. J. *Four hundred losers: Delinquent boys in high school*. San Francisco: Jossey-Bass, Inc., 1971.

Austin, K. M., & Speidel, F. R. Thunder: An alternative to juvenile court appearance. *Youth Authority Quarterly*, 1971, *24*(4), 13–16.

Baker, A. A. Youth Development Corporation evaluation. Lansing, Mich.: Program Information & Resource Development Division of the Lansing City Demonstration Agency, March 1974.

Baron, R., Feeney, F., & Thornton, W. Preventing delinquency through diversion: The Sacramento County 601 Diversion Project. *Federal Probation*, 1973, *37*(1), 13–18.

Bartlett, M. K., & Newberger, J. M. Educational Life Enrichment Program. Kids receiving academic motivation and socialization (KRAMS). Fourth District County Court, Sioux Falls, S.D. Independent School District #1, July 1973.

Berleman, W. C., Seaberg, J. R., & Steinburn, T. W. The delinquency prevention experiment of the Seattle Atlantic Street Center: A final evaluation. *Social Service Review (Chicago)*, 1972, *46*(3), 323–346.

Berleman, W. C., & Steinburn, T. W. The execution and evaluation of a delinquency prevention program. *Social Problems*, 1967, *14*(4), 413–423.

Bomberger, A. E. Project Youth: Sheridan Youth Police Reserves. Sheridan, Oregon Police Department, 1970.

Bouma, D. H., & Williams, D. G. An evaluation of a police-school liaison program as a factor in changing student attitudes toward police and law enforcement.

Michigan Department of State Police, September 1970.

Boys Residential Youth Center. Effect of innovative, supportive services in changing attitudes of high risk youth. Final report. Springfield, Va.: National Technal Information Service, U.S. Department of Commerce, 1968.

Braxton, D. Family casework and juvenile first offenders. *Social Casework*, 1966(Feb), 87–92.

Brewer, E. W., et al. Lane County Youth Project. Final report. *Research in Education*, 1968. (ERIC Reproduction Service No. ED 014 352)

Brown, R. C. Jr., & Dodson, D. W. The effectiveness of a boys' club in reducing delinquency. In J. R. Stratton & R. M. Terry (Eds.), *Prevention of delinquency: Problems and programs*. New York: Macmillan Company, 1968, Pp. 265–270.

Caplan, N. Treatment intervention and reciprocal interaction effects. *Journal of Social Issues*, 1968, *24*(1), 63–88.

Carter, G. W., & Gilberg, G. R. An evaluation progress report of the Alternate Routes Project—following nineteen months of development and demonstration. Orange County Probation Department, Orange County, California. Los Angeles: Regional Research Institute in Social Welfare, University of Southern California, June 1973.

Carter, G. W., Gilbert, G. R., & Reinow, F. D. An analysis of student achievement through a volunteer program: An evaluation research report of the VISA Project, Orange County Probation Department, Orange County, California. Los Angeles: Regional Research Institute in Social Welfare, University of Southern California, February 1974.

City of Chicago. Evaluation report: Rehabilitation program for juvenile delinquents. Chicago: Department of Human Resources Research Division, September 1973.

City of Chicago. Evaluation report: Youth Service Homes—4186. Chicago: Department of Human Resources Research Division, December 1972.

City of Chicago. Prevention and control of juvenile delinquency: Joint Youth Development Program. Chicago: Department of Human Resources Research Division, November 1972.

Cole, C. W., Oetting, E. R., & Miskimins, R. W. Self-concept therapy for adolescent females. *Journal of Abnormal Psychology*, 1969, *74*, 642–645.

Community Council. Evaluation of Maricopa County Youth Service Bureau. Phoenix, Ariz.: Community Council, December 1973.

Community Council Board. Evaluation of the Valley Big Brothers Juvenile Court Project. Third and final report. Phoenix, Ariz.: Community Council Board, September 1973.

Community Services for Children. Comprehensive juvenile delinquency prevention and control. Final progress report to Law & Justice Planning Office, Community Affairs Agency, Office of the Governor, Olympia, Washington, November 1, 1972 to December 31, 1972.

Craig, M. M., & Furst, P. W. What happens after treatment: A study of potentially delinquent boys. *Social Service Review*, 1965, *39*(2), 165–171.

Daane, C., Gold, R., McGreevy, P., Maes, W., & Kenoyer, D. Developing group counseling models for the Neighborhood Youth Corps. Springfield, Va.: National Technical Information Service, U.S. Department of Commerce, January 1969.

Dailey, J. T. Evaluation of the contribution of special programs in the Washington, D.C. schools to the prediction and prevention of delinquency. *Research in Education*, 1967. (ERIC Document Reproduction Service No. ED 010 431)

Demsch, B., & Garth, J. Truancy prevention: A first step in curtailing delinquency proneness. *Federal Probation*, 1968, *32*(4), 31–37.

Douglas, E. D., Fike, D., & Wierzbinski, E. J. Effects of group counseling: An experiment evaluated by objective tests. *Crime and Delinquency*, 1965, *11*, 360–365.

Duxbury, E. Evaluation of youth service bureaus. State of California: Department of Youth Authority, 1973.

Elliott, D. S., & LeBouef, R. Final report: Lincoln Youth Services System evaluation, Lincoln, Nebraska. Boulder, Colo.: Behavioral Research and Evaluation Corporation, September 11, 1973.

Empey, L. T., & Erickson, M. L. *The Provo Experiment: Evaluating community control of delinquency.* Lexington, Mass.: Lexington Books, 1972.

Empey, L. T., & Lubeck, S. G. *The Silverlake Experiment: Testing delinquency theory and community intervention.* Chicago: Aldine, 1971.

Faust, F. L. Group counseling with juveniles: By staff without professional training in groupwork. *Crime and delinquency* 1965, *11*, 349–354.

Fo, W. S. O., & O'Donnell, C. R. The Buddy System Model: Community-based delinquency prevention utilizing indigenous nonprofessionals as behavior change agents. *Research in Education*, 1973. (ERIC Document Reproduction Service No. ED 074 394)

Forward, J. R., Kirby, M., Mendoza, M., & Wilson K. Research and evaluation of Partners, INC.: A volunteer intervention program for court-referred youths in Denver, Colorado (Court-to-Partners Diversion Project). Report prepared for Partners, Inc., Denver, Colorado, December 1973.

Gandy, J. M. Preventive work with street-corner groups: Hyde Park Youth Project, Chicago. *Annals of the American Academy of Political and Social Science,* 1959, *322*, 107–116.

Goldenberg, I. I. *Build me a mountain: Youth, poverty, and the creation of new settings.* Cambridge, Mass.: MIT Press, 1971.

Goodwill Industries Vocational Service. The vocational rehabilitation of the youthful offender. Final report. Springfield, Va.: National Technical Information Service, U.S. Department of Commerce, March, 1967.

Hackler, J. C. Boys, blisters, and behavior. *Journal of Research in Crime and Delinquency*, 1966, *2*, 155–164.

Hackler, J. C., & Linden, E. The response of adults to delinquency prevention programs: The race factor. *Journal of Research in Crime and Delinquency*, 1970, *7*, 31–45.

Holliman, E. E., A differential analysis of the comparative effectiveness of group counseling and individual counseling processes in producing behavior changes of juvenile delinquents using direct behavioral referents as measures of change. *Dissertation Abstracts International*, 1970 (Oct.), *31*(4-A), 1511.

Howell, J. C. A comparison of probation officers and volunteers. Springfield, Va.: National Technical Information Service, U.S. Department of Commerce, April 1972.

Hussey, F. A., Talbot, J. H., Garroway, M., & Davis,

V. An experiment in change. Phase II. Final report and evaluation, Girls Residential Youth Center, Portland, Maine. Springfield, Va.: National Technical Information Service, U.S. Department of Commerce, March 1970.

Ikeda, T. Project follow-up summary: Effectiveness of social work with acting-out youth. Seattle, Wash.: Seattle Atlantic Street Center, 1969.

Jeffrey, C. R., & Jeffrey, I. A. Dropouts and delinquents: An experimental program in behavior change. *Education and Urban Society*, 1969, *1*, 325–336.

Jones, R. J., & Fishman, J. R. The impact of the UPO Demonstration Program on a selected group of Cardoza area youth—A study of juvenile delinquency prevention. Second year report, 1965–66. *Research in Education*, 1967. (ERIC Document Reproduction Service No. ED 012 294)

Kent County Juvenile Court. Kentfields rehabilitation program. Grand Rapids, Mich.: Kent County Juvenile Court, 1973.

Klein, M. W. Gang cohesiveness, delinquency, and a street work program. *Journal of Research in Crime and Delinquency*, 1969, *6*, 135–166.

Klein, M. W. *Street gangs and streetworkers.* Englewood Cliff, N.J.: Prentice-Hall, 1971.

Liedtke, K., Malbin, N., & Mech, E. V. Portland Youth Diversion Project. City of Portland, Maine, Office of Youth Diversion Services, March 1974.

McCord, J., McCord, W., & Thurber, E. The effects of foster home placement in the prevention of adult antisocial behavior. In J. R. Stratton & R. M. Terry (Eds.), *Prevention of delinquency: Problems and programs.* New York: Macmillan Company, 1968. Pp. 178–183.

McCord, W., McCord, J., & Zola, I. K. *Origins of crime.* New York: Columbia University Press, 1959.

McEachern, A. W., Taylor, E. M., Newman, J. R., & Ashford, A. E. The juvenile probation system simulation for research and decision-making. *American Behavioral Scientist*, 1968, *11*(3), 1–45.

Meyer, H. J., Borgatta, E. F., & Jones, W. C. *Girls at vocational high: An experiment in social work intervention.* New York: Russell Sage Foundation, 1965.

Miller, W. B. Preventive work with street-corner groups: Boston Delinquency Project. *Annals of the American Academy of Political and Social Science*, 1959, *322*, 97–106.

Miller, W. B. The impact of a 'total community' delinquency control project. *Social Problems*, 1962, *10*(2), 168–191.

Morris, J. A. *First offender: A volunteer program for youth in trouble with the law.* New York: Funk & Wagnalls, 1970.

National Committee for Children and Youth. Project Crossroads: Pre-trial intervention with first offenders. Springfield, Va.: National Technical Information Service, U.S. Department of Commerce, March 1971.

New York State. Characteristics of delinquent youths at various stages of the treatment process: A study of youths referred to treatment centers of the New York State Division of Youth. New York: Division of Youth Research Department, August 1970-October 1973.

Olson, H. C., & Carpenter, J. B. A survey of techniques used to reduce vandalism and delinquency in schools. McLean, Va.: Research Analysis Corp., January 1971.

Ostrom, T. M., Steele, C. M., Rosenblood, L. T., & Mirels, H. L. Modification of delinquent behavior. *Journal of Applied Social Psychology*, 1971, *1*(2), 118–136.

Palmer, T. B. California's Community Treatment Program for delinquent adolescents. *Journal of Research in Crime and Delinquency*, 1971, *8*, 74–92.

Palmer, T. B. Differential placement of delinquents in group homes. Final report. Sacramento: California Youth Authority, Spring 1972.

Pilnick, S. et al. From delinquency to freedom. *Research in Education*, 1968. (ERIC Document Reproduction Services No. ED 016 244)

Pines, M. W., & Ridgley, D. Baltimore Youth Advocate Project. Final Report. Baltimore, Md.: Mayor's Office of Manpower Resources, March 1974.

Pooley, R. An experiment in delinquency prevention and control. Carbondale, Ill.: Southern Illinois University Center for the Study of Crime, Delinquency and Corrections, August 1969-August 1971.

Powers, E., & Witmer, H. *An experiment in the prevention of delinquency: The Cambridge-Somerville Youth Study.* New York: Columbia University Press, 1951.

Radabaugh, F., & Kirby, J. H. Project Care: Final report. Charleston, W. Va.: Kanawha County Schools, July 1, 1972-December 1973.

Rader, L. E. Community services coordination in elementary schools. A final report. Oklahoma City, Okla.: Oklahoma Department of Public Welfare, December, 1972.

Reckless, W. C., & Dinitz, S. *The prevention of juvenile delinquency: An experiment.* Columbus, Ohio: Ohio State University Press, 1972.

Reuthebuck, G. Evaluation of Kentucky's Youth Service Bureaus. Kentucky Department of Child Welfare: Division of Administrative Services Research Section, October 29, 1971.

Rosenbaum, G., Grisell, J. L., Koschtial, T., Knox, R., & Leenhouts, K. J. Community participation in probation: A tale of two cities. *Proceedings of the 77th Annual Convention of the American Psychological Association,* 1969, *4*, 863–864.

San Diego County Probation Department. Research and evaluation of the first year of operations of the San Diego County Juvenile Narcotics Project (California Council on Criminal Justice, Project No. 0215). San Diego, Ca.: San Diego County Probation Department, 1970.

Scarpitti, F. R., & Stephenson, R. M. A study of probation effectiveness. *Journal of Criminal Law, Criminology and Police Science,* 1968, *59*(3), 361–369.

School Board of Leon County. Supplementary Assistance Center Manual. Tallahassee, Fla.: Leon County Delinquency Prevention Youth Services System, 1974.

Schwitzgebel, R. *Street-corner research: An experimental approach to the juvenile delinquent.* Cambridge, Mass.: Harvard University Press, 1964.

Schwitzgebel, R., & Kolb, D. A. Inducing behavior change in adolescent delinquents. *Behavior Research and Therapy,* 1964, *1*, 297–304.

Seagraves, R. W. Research results of teaching law by the case study method in the Redwood City, California, schools. Menlo Park, Ca.: Foundation of Research in Education, 1973.

Shore, M. F., & Massimo, J. L. Comprehensive vocationally oriented psychotherapy for adolescent delinquent boys: A follow-up study. *American Journal of Orthopsychiatry,* 1966, *36*(4), 609–615.

Shore, M. F., & Massimo, J. L. The alienated adolescent: A challenge to the mental health professional. *Adolescence,* 1969, *4*(13), 19–34.

Steinman, R., & Fernald, B. Phase I final report: The Residential Youth Center of Downeast WICS, Inc., Portland, Maine. Springfield, Va.: National Technical Information Service, U.S. Department of Commerce, October 1968.

Stephenson, R. M., & Scarpitti, F. R. Essexfields: A non-residential experiment in group centered rehabilitation of delinquents. *American Journal of Correction,* 1969, *31*(5), 12–18.

Szymanski, L., & Fleming, A. Juvenile delinquent and an adult prisoner. A therapeutic encounter? *Journal of the American Academy of Child Psychiatry,* 1971, *10*(2), 308–320.

Tait, C. D. Jr., & Hodges, E. F. Jr. Maximum Benefits Project: A Washington study of delinquency. In C. D. Tait & E. F. Hodges (Eds.), *Delinquents, their families and the community.* Springfield, Ill.: Charles C. Thomas, 1962. Pp. 5–76.

Tait, C. D. Jr., & Hodges, E. F. Jr. Follow-up study of predicted delinquents. *Crime and Delinquency* 1971, *17*(2), 202–212.

Thomas, E. S. Effects of experimental school counseling of delinquency-prone adolescents. *Dissertation Abstracts,* 1968, *28*(7-A), 2572.

Venezia, P. S. Unofficial probation: An evaluation of its effectiveness. *Journal of Research in Crime and Delinquency,* 1972, *9*, 149–170.

Wallace, G. K. A cooperative program for the alleviation of juvenile behavior problems. Final report. *Research in Education,* 1969. (ERIC Document Reproduction Service No. ED 029 341)

Walther, R. H., & Magnusson, M. L. A retrospective study of the effectiveness of out-of-school Neighborhood Youth Corps programs in four urban sites. Springfield, Va.: National Technical Information Service, U.S. Department of Commerce, November 1967.

Weeks, H. A. The Highfields Project. In J. Teele (Ed.), *Juvenile delinquency: A Reader.* Itasca, Ill.: F. E. Peacock, 1970. Pp. 380–391.

Wilgosh, L. Study of group home placements as a possible correction of delinquent behavior. *Canadian Journal of Criminology and Corrections,* 1973, *15*(1), 100–108.

Wolf, M. M., Phillips, E. G., & Fixsen, D. L. Achievement Place: Behavior modification with pre-delinquents. Final report. National Institute for Mental Health, Center for Studies of Crime and Delinquency, January, 1, 1969 through April 30, 1971.

Womack, M., & Wiener, F. A work-study program for socio-economically deprived delinquent youth. Final report. Springfield, Va.: National Technical Information Service, U.S. Department of Commerce, October 1968.

YMCA. National Youth Project Using Mini-bikes. Final report. Los Angeles: National Board of YMCA, September 2, 1972—November 15, 1973.

79. Architectural Planning to Discourage Crime

OSCAR NEWMAN

THE CRIME PROBLEMS FACING URBAN AMERICA will not be answered through increased police force or firepower. We are witnessing a breakdown of the social mechanisms that once kept crime in check and gave direction and support to police activity. The small-town environments, rural or urban, which once framed and enforced their own moral codes, have virtually disappeared. We have become strangers sharing the largest collective habitats in human history. Because of the size and density of our newly evolving urban megalopoli, we have become more dependent on each other and more vulnerable to aberrant behavior than we have ever been before.

In our society there are few instances of shared beliefs or values among physical neighbors. Although this heterogeneity may be intellectually desirable, it has crippled our ability to agree on the action required to maintain the social framework necessary to our continued survival. The very winds of liberation that have brought us this far may also have carried with them the seeds of our demise. It is clear to almost all researchers in crime prevention that the issue hinges on the inability of communities to come together in joint action. The physical environments we have been building in our cities for the past twenty-five years actually prevent such amity and discourage the natural pursuit of a collective action.

The anonymous cities we have built, for maximum freedom and multiple choice, may have inadvertently succeeded in severely curtailing many of our previous options. Collective community action, once easy, is now cumbersome. But even in the absence of a community of minds, joint action has become essential to the survival of urban life in America. Police forces operating without community consent, direction, and control are a wasted effort—more irritant than deterrent. Means must be found for bringing neighbors together, if only for the limited purpose of ensuring survival of their collective milieu. Where the physical design of the living environment can be used for this purpose, it must be so exploited.

Over the past fifteen years, the crime problem in our urban metropolitan areas has become severe enough to prompt a major exodus of middle-income families to the suburbs. However, the results of 1971 crime survey statistics indicate that the crime problem is shifting to the outer reaches of the city. The horizons of escape promised by suburbia and the barricaded inner city towers seem to be narrowing. The only recourse now appears to be total lockup and self-restriction of movement: a self-imposed curfew and police state.

*

Over the past three years, the New York University Project for Security Design in Urban Residential Areas has been studying the nature, pattern, and location of crime in urban residential areas across the country. Our conclusion is

▶SOURCE: *Defensible Space. New York: Macmillan, 1972. Pp. 1–4, 39–49. Reprinted by permission.*

that the new physical form of the urban environment is possibly the most cogent ally the criminal has in his victimization of society. The concentration of population in large metropolitan areas has produced an urban form that makes hapless victims of its occupants.

The time has come to go back to first principles, to reexamine human habitat as it has evolved, to become attuned again to all the subtle devices invented over time and forgotten in our need and haste to house the many. For even within the widespread chaos of our cities, it is still possible to find isolated examples of working living environments which are crime-free, although at times located in the highest crime precincts of cities. Architectural design can make evident by the physical layout that an area is the shared extension of the private realms of a group of individuals. For one group to be able to set the norms of behavior and the nature of activity possible within a particular place, it is necessary that it have clear, unquestionable control over what can occur there. Design can make it possible for both inhabitant and stranger to perceive that an area is under the undisputed influence of a particular group, that they dictate the activity taking place within it, and who its users are to be. This can be made so clearly evident that residents will not only feel confident, but that it is incumbent upon them to question the comings and goings of people to ensure the continued safety of the defined areas. Any intruder will be made to anticipate that his presence will be under question and open to challenge; so much so that a criminal can be deterred from even contemplating entry.

Defensible space is a model for residential environments which inhibits crime by creating the physical expression of a social fabric that defends itself. All the different elements which combine to make a defensible space have a common goal—an environment in which latent territoriality and sense of community in the inhabitants can be translated into responsibility for ensuring a safe, productive, and well-maintained living space. The potential criminal perceives such a space as controlled by its residents, leaving him an intruder easily recognized and dealt with. On the one hand this is target hardening—the traditional aim of security design as provided by locksmiths. But it must also be seen in another light. In middle-class neighborhoods, the responsibility for maintaining security has largely been relegated to the police. Upper-income neighborhoods—particularly those including high-rise apartment buildings—have supplemented police with doormen, a luxury not possible in other neighborhoods. There is serious self-deception in this posture. When people begin to protect themselves as individuals and not as a community, the battle against crime is effectively lost. The indifferent crowd witnessing a violent crime is by now an American cliché. The move of middle- and upper-class population into protective high-rises and other structures of isolation—as well guarded and as carefully differentiated from the surrounding human landscape as a military post—is just as clearly a retreat into indifference. The form of buildings and their arrangement can either discourage or encourage people to take an active part in policing while they go about their daily business. "Policing" is not intended to evoke a paranoid vision but refers to the oldest concept in the Western political tradition: the responsibility of each citizen to ensure the functioning of the *polis*.

"Defensible space" is a surrogate term for the range of mechanisms—real and symbolic barriers, strongly defined areas of influence, and improved opportunities for surveillance—that combine to bring an environment under the control of its residents. A *defensible space* is a living residential environment which can be employed by inhabitants for the enhancement of their lives, while providing security for their families, neighbors, and friends. The public areas of a multi-family residential environment devoid of defensible space can make the act of going from street to apartment equivalent to running the gauntlet. The fear and uncertainty generated by living in such an environment can slowly eat away and eventually destroy the security and sanctity of the apartment unit itself. On the other hand, by grouping dwelling units to reinforce associations of mutual benefit; by delineating paths of movement; by defining areas of activity for particular users through their juxtaposition with internal living areas; and by providing for natural opportunities for visual surveillance, architects can create a clear understanding of the function of a space, and who its users are and ought to be. This, in turn, can lead residents of all income levels to adopt extremely potent territorial attitudes and policing measures, which act as strong deterrents to potential criminals.

*

A TALE OF TWO PROJECTS

Brownsville and Van Dyke are strikingly different in physical design, while housing comparatively identical populations in size and social characteristics. The high-rise towers at Van Dyke are almost totally devoid of defensible space qualities, while the buildings at Brownsville are comparatively well-endowed with such qualities. It should be mentioned, even before beginning the comparison, the Brownsville, the better of the two projects, is still far away from answering all defensible space design directives.

Review of the objective data on the physical characteristics of the two projects reveals many striking parallels. The projects are almost identical in size, each housing approximately 6,000 persons, and are designed at exactly the same density: 288 persons per acre. Major differences arise in the composition of buildings and the percentage of ground-level space they occupy. Brownsville buildings cover 23 percent of the available land, whereas Van Dyke buildings cover only 16.6 percent of the total land area—including nine, three-story buildings which occupy a large percentage of space but house only 24 percent of the total project

population. In addition, the two projects differ in design (see Figure 1) in that Brownsville is comprised of low, walk-up and elevator buildings, three to six stories, while the latter is comprised of a mix of three-story buildings and fourteen-story high-rise slabs (87 percent of the apartment units at Van Dyke are located in the high-rise slabs). The two projects are located across the street from one another and share the same Housing Authority police and New York City police services.

Differences in physical design of the Brownsville and Van Dyke projects are apparent even to the casual observer. Van Dyke Houses has the appearance of a large, monolithic project. The most dominant buildings are the thirteen, fourteen-story slabs. In less evidence are the nine, three-story structures. Each of the buildings at Van Dyke sits independently on the site, with large open spaces separating it from its neighbors. At the center of the project is a single, large open area, used for a Parks Department playground and for automobile parking. By means of its design, this large open area has been distinctly separated from and is unrelated to the surrounding buildings.

None of the buildings at Van Dyke may be entered directly from the public street. Entrance requires that tenants leave the public street and walk onto project paths that wind into internal project areas, blind to street surveillance. The only areas of the project grounds which relate somewhat to buildings are the small seating areas in the channel of space between the double row of buildings. The functional entrance to the high-rise buildings is a small door shared by 112 to 136 families. This door is located directly off the project paths, with no gradation or distinction indicated by the design of the grounds in front of the building lobby.

Two low-speed elevators carry families to their living floors in each of the high-rise buildings. Elevators are placed directly opposite the building entrances, as mandated by the Housing

Figure 1. Site plan of Brownsville and Van Dyke Houses.

Authority, to improve surveillance from the outside. Full benefit is not derived from this arrangement, however, since entrances face the interior of the project rather than the street.

The housing floors of the high-rise buildings are each occupied by eight families. The elevator stops in the middle of the corridor, and the apartment units are reached by walking left or right down a dead-end corridor with apartments positioned on both sides (a double-loaded corridor. See plan Fig. 2).

In contrast, Brownsville Houses presents the appearance of being a smaller project, due to the disposition of units in smaller and more diverse clusters of buildings. It might be said that the buildings and the way in which they were placed on the site has been used to divide the project into smaller, more manageable zones. The ground areas have been humanized through their relationship with the individual residential buildings. Activities that take place in small project spaces adjoining buildings have become the business of the neighboring residents, who assume a leading role in monitoring them. (See Figure 3).

All residents and police who have been interviewed at Brownsville perceive the project as smaller and more stable than Van Dyke. All intruders, including police and interviewers, feel more cautious about invading the privacy of residents at Brownsville. By contrast, their attitude toward the invasion of the interior corridors at Van Dyke is callous and indifferent.

This emphasis on space division carries over into the design of the building interiors of Brownsville Houses. Individual buildings are three- and six-story structures with six families sharing a floor. The floor is further divided, by an unlocked swinging door, into two vestibules shared by three families each. In the six-story buildings there is an elevator which stops at odd floors, requiring residents of upper stories to walk up or down one flight, using an open stairwell around which apartment doors are clustered. Vertical communication among families is assured by this relationship of elevators to apartments, and also by the presence of open stairwells connecting the floors.

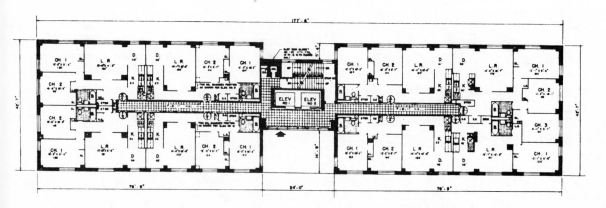

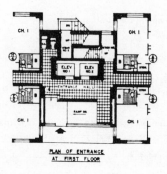

Figure 2.   Floor plan of Van Dyke Houses.

At the ground level, the building lobby leads up a short flight of stairs to several apartments that maintain surveillance over activity in this small entryway. On all floors, tenants have been found to maintain auditory surveillance over activity taking place in the halls by the device of keeping their doors slightly ajar. These features of the building have allowed occupants to extend their territorial prerogatives into building corridors, hallways, and stairs. Those mothers of young children at Brownsville who allow their children the freedom to play on landings and up and down the stairwells monitor their play from within the apartment. A mere interruption in the din of children at play was found to bring mothers to their doors as surely as a loud scream.

By contrast, most young children at Van Dyke are not allowed to play in the corridors outside their apartments. The halls of Van Dyke and other high-rise buildings are designed solely for their corridor function and are inhospitable to the fantasy-play of children. In addition, too many families utilize a typical high-rise hall for a mother to comfortably leave her child there unsupervised. For the same reason, mothers are reluctant to leave their door ajar for surveillance—too many people, including strangers and guests of neighbors, wander through the Van Dyke halls unchecked and unquestioned. Finally, to give children real freedom in the use of the building would require their using the elevator or fire stairs to gain access to other floors. But both these areas are frightening and would take the children out of the surveillance zone of the mother and other tenants. The elevator cab is sealed by a heavy metal door that cannot be opened manually. The fire stairwells are designed to seal floors in the event of a fire. A by-product of their fireproofing is that noises within the stairwells cannot be heard in the corridors outside. Criminals often force their victims into these areas because the soundproofing feature and low frequency of use make the detection of a crime in progress almost impossible.

The sense of propriety which is apparent in the way tenants of Brownsville Houses use their halls to monitor and maintain surveillance over children and strangers appears to have carried over to the grounds adjacent to building entrances. Because of the unique construction of the buildings, there are areas on the ground level

Figure 3. Brownsville Houses from Street. The buildings dispositions at Brownsville create triangular buffer areas which are used for play, sitting, and parking. These areas are easily observed from the street and from apartment windows. Entry to buildings is typically from the street through these buffer zones. Residents regard these areas as an extension of their own buildings and maintain active surveillance over them.

just outside the front door of the building where parents can allow their children to play, while maintaining contact with them through their kitchen windows. Interviews have revealed that the range of spaces into which young children are permitted to roam is greater in Brownsville than in Van Dyke.

Finally, where entries to Van Dyke high-rise buildings serve 130 families, Brownsville buildings are entered through different doors, each serving a small number of families (nine to thirteen). The ground area adjacent to these entries has been developed for use by adults, and for play by young children. Parents feel confident about allowing their children to play in these clearly circumscribed zones. Frequently, these entry areas are located just off the public street, and serve to set off the building from the street itself by acting as an intervening buffer area. The placement of entrances just off the street avoids the dangers created at Van Dyke: forcing tenants to walk along blind interior project paths to get to their buildings.

Inspection of Tables I and II, reveals that the tenants of Brownsville and Van Dyke are rated similarly on overall indexes of socio-economic status, family stability, and ethnic, racial, and family composition. It is also clear that these

rough similarities are consistent from year to year. Comparison of demographic data over the period 1962 to 1969 reveals few exceptions to this overall pattern of identity between the projects.

It was a widely held belief that many so-called "problem families," displaced by the Model Cities renewal programs, were among recent move-ins to Van Dyke. Many people drew an immediate correlation between the higher crime rate at Van Dyke and this change in population. Information was therefore obtained on a representative sample of families who have moved into the two projects over the past three years. Sample data on one of every five move-ins reveal no striking differences in the social characteristics of residents in both projects.

The total number of move-ins in the past three years in any case constituted fewer than 5 percent of the project population in both Van Dyke and Brownsville. To blame problems of the Van Dyke project on a small number of "bad seeds" is clearly gratuitous. However, to insure that these mean figures were not misleading, frequency distributions were plotted for each variable which permitted such treatment. For example, the frequency of each family size varying from one to fifteen was plotted separately

Table I. Tenant Statistics

Characteristic	Van Dyke	Brownsville
Total population	6,420	5,390
Average family size	4.0	4.0
Number of minors	3,618 (57.5%)	3,047 (57.8%)
Percent families black	79.1%	85.0%
Percent families white	5.6%	2.6%
Percent families Puerto Rican	15.3%	12.4%
Average gross income	$4,997	$5,056
Percent on welfare	28.8%	29.7%
Percent broken families	29.5%	31.7%
Average number of years in project	8.5	9.0
Percent of families with two wage earners	12.2%	11.0%
Number of children in grades 1–6	839	904

Source: New York City Housing Authority Records, 1968.

Table II. A Comparison of Physical Design and Population Density

Physical Measure	Van Dyke	Brownsville
Total size	22.35 acres	19.16 acres
Number of buildings	23	27
Building height	13–14 story	6-story with some
	9–3 story	3-story wings
Coverage	16.6	23.0
Floor area ratio	1.49	1.39
Average number of rooms	4.62	4.69
Avper apartment		
Density	288 persons/acre	287 persons/acre
Year completed	1955 (one building added in 1964)	1947

Source: New York City Housing Authority Project Physical Design Statistics.

for Brownsville and Van Dyke and reveals no apparent reason to doubt the representativeness of these summary statistics.

Crime and vandalism are major problems at both Van Dyke and Brownsville Houses. The problem has become serious over the past ten years, with the decline of the old Brooklyn community and the failure to create renewal opportunities. The area surrounding both projects is severely blighted; store owners conduct business in plexiglass booths to protect themselves from addicts. The local library requires two armed guards on duty at all times. The local hospital claims it records fifteen teen-age deaths per month due to overdoses of drugs.

Table III presents data on major categories of crime expressed in terms of rate per thousand population. Data are also presented on specific crimes, including robbery, possession of drugs, and loitering. A comparison of 1969 crime incident rates (see Table III) and maintenance rates (see Table IV) for the two projects was quite revealing. In summary, Van Dyke Homes was found to have 66 percent more total crime incidents, with over two and one-half times as many robberies (264 percent), and 60 percent more felonies, misdemeanors, and offenses than Brownsville. Another measure of security can be understood from examination of the rate of de-

cline of facilities. Even though Brownsville Houses is an older project, beginning to suffer from natural decay, Van Dyke annually required a total of 72 percent more maintenance work. It is interesting to note that the average outlay of time and funds for upkeep of Van Dyke is significantly higher than that of Brownsville. Not only is there less need of repair at Brownsville, but tenants themselves play a greater role in seeing to the cleanliness of buildings either through insistence on the upkeep of janitorial services or by individual effort.

One of the most striking differences between the two projects concerns elevator breakdowns. The far greater number of breakdowns at Van Dyke is primarily a function of more intensive use. However, more breakdowns are due to vandalism at Van Dyke than at Brownsville. This form of vandalism is especially diagnostic, showing that adolescents who tamper with Van Dyke elevators do not have a sense of identity with the people they inconvenience.

As a measure of tenant satisfaction, Brownsville Houses, with smaller room sizes in similarly designated apartment units, has a lower rate of move-outs than Van Dyke Houses. To avoid historical accident and subsequently limited conclusion, results were tabulated annu-

Table III. Comparison of Crime Incidents

Crime Incidents	Van Dyke	Brownsville
Total incidents	1,189	790
Total felonies, misdemeanors, and offenses	432	264
Number of robberies	92	24
Number of malicious mischief	52	28

Source: New York City Housing Authority Police Records, 1968.

Table IV. Comparison of Maintenance

Maintenance	Van Dyke (constructed 1955)	Brownsville (constructed 1947)
Number of maintenance jobs of any sort (work tickets) 4/70	3,301	2,376
Number of maintenance jobs, excluding glass repair	2,643	1,651
Number of nonglass jobs per unit	1.47	1.16
Number of full-time maintenance staff	9	7
Number of elevator breakdowns per month	280	110

Source: New York City Housing Authority Project Managers' bookkeeping records.

ally over an eight-year period, including sampling of move-ins to the two projects. These data have provided additional confirmation of the differences in crime and vandalism between the projects that cannot be assigned to differences in their tenant populations.

It is unwarranted to conclude that this data provide final and definitive proof of the influence of physical design variables on crime and vandalism. It is equally misleading to assume, as management officials initially did, that the differences can be explained away by variations in tenant characteristics in the two projects. The project manager assumed that Van Dyke Houses had a larger number of broken families and that these families had a larger number of children than those at Brownsville. The statistics do not bear out this assumption, but the image described by the manager and other public offi-

cials suggests the extent of the problem and may in turn contribute to it.

There are some elementary differences in the physical construct of the projects which may contribute to the disparity of image held by officials. Police officers revealed that they found Van Dyke Houses far more difficult to patrol. To monitor activity in the enclosed fire stairs requires that a patrolman take the elevator to the upper floor and then walk down to the ground level, alternating at each floor between the two independent fire-stair columns.

Police express pessimism about their value at Van Dyke Houses. About Brownsville they are much more optimistic and, in subtle ways, respond to complaints with more vigor and concern. All these factors produce a significant positive effect in Brownsville. At Van Dyke the negative factors of anonymity, police pessimism,

pessimism about police, and tenant feelings of ambiguity about strangers (caused by large numbers of families sharing one entrance) conspire to progressively erode any residual faith in the effectiveness of community or official response to crime.

In summary, it seems unmistakable that physical design plays a very significant role in crime rate. It should also be kept in mind that the defensible space qualities inherent in the Brownsville design are there, for the most part, by accident. From a critical, defensible space viewpoint, Brownsville is far from perfect. The comparison of the crime and vandalism rates in the two projects was made using gross crime data on both projects. Twenty-three percent of the apartments at Van Dyke consist of three-story walk-up buildings serving a small number of families. It is likely that comparative data on crime rates in the low buildings versus the towers at Van Dyke would reveal significant differences. This would make the comparison of crime rates between Van Dyke and Brownsville even more startling.

80. Electronic Surveillance and Control of Behavior

BARTON L. INGRAHAM
GERALD W. SMITH

IN THE VERY NEAR FUTURE, A COMPUTER technology will make possible alternatives to imprisonment. The development of systems for telemetering information from sensors implanted in or on the body will soon make possible the observation and control of human behavior without actual physical contact. Through such telemetric devices, it will be possible to maintain twenty-four hour-a-day surveillance over the subject and to intervene electronically or physically to influence and control selected behavior. It will thus be possible to exercise control over human behavior and from a distance without physical contact. The possible implications for criminology and corrections of such telemetric systems is tremendously significant.

The purpose of this paper is: (1) to describe developments during the last decade in the field of telemetry and electrophysiology as they relate to the control of human behavior; (2) to dispel, if possible, some of the exaggerated notions prevalent amongst legal and philosophical Cassandras as to the extent of the power and range of these techniques in controlling human behavior and thought; (3) to discuss some applications of these techniques to problem areas in penology and to show how they can make a useful contribution, with a net gain, to the values of individual freedom and privacy; and (4) to

▶SOURCE: *"The Use of Electronics in the Observation and Control of Human Behavior and Its Possible Use in Rehabilitation and Parole," Issues in Criminology (Fall, 1972) 7(2): 35–53. Reprinted by permission.*

examine critically "ethical reservations" which might impede both valuable research in these areas and the application of their results to solving the problem of crime control.

ELECTRONIC TECHNIQUES FOR OBSERVING AND CONTROLLING BEHAVIOR IN HUMANS

A telemetric system consists of small electronic devices attached to a subject that transmit via radio waves information regarding the location and physiological state of the wearer. A telemetry system provides a method whereby phenomena may be measured or controlled at a distance from where they occur—i.e., remotely (Grisamore, 1965). The great benefit derived from the use of such systems in studying animals (including man) lies in the ability to get data from a heretofore inaccessible environment, thus avoiding the experimental artifacts which arise in a laboratory setting (Slater, 1965; Schwitzgebel, 1967b). It also provides long-range, day-to-day, continuous observation and control of the monitored subject, since the data can be fed into a computer which can act as both an observer and a controller (Konecci, 1965a).

Telemetry has been put to many and diverse uses. In aerospace biology, both man and animal have been telemetered for respiration, body temperature, blood pressure, heart rate (ECG's), brain waves (EEG's) and other physiological data (Konecci, 1965b; Slater,

1965; Barr, 1960). Telemetric devices have been placed on and in birds, animals and fish of all kinds to learn about such things as migration patterns, hibernation and spawning locations, respiration rates, brain wave activity, body temperatures, etc. (Slater, 1965; Lord, 1962; Sperry, 1961; Mackay, 1961; Young, 1964; Epstein, 1968). Telemetry has also been used in medicine to obtain the EEG patterns of epileptics during seizures, and to monitor heart rhythms and respiration rates in humans, for purposes of diagnosis and rescue in times of emergency (Slater, 1965; Caceres, 1965). The technology has proceeded so far that one expert in the field remarked (Mackay, 1965):

"It appears that almost any signal for which there is a sensor can be transmitted from almost any species. Problems of size, life, and accuracy have been overcome in most cases. Thus, the future possibilities are limited only by the imagination."

Telemetric systems can be classified into two types of devices—"external devices" and "internal devices."

External Devices

For the past several years, Schwitzgebel (1967a, b; Note: *Harvard Law Review*, 1966) at Harvard has been experimenting with a small, portable transmitter, called a Behavior Transmitter-Reinforcer (BT-R), which is small enough to be carried on a belt and which permits tracking of the wearer's location, transmitting information about his activities and communicating with him (by tone signals). The tracking device consists of two containers, each about the size of a thick paperback book, one of which contains batteries and the other, a transmitter that automatically emits radio signals, coded differently for each transmitter so that many of them may be used on one frequency band. With a transmitting range of approximately a quarter of a mile under adverse city conditions and a receiving range of two miles, the BT-R signals are picked up by receivers at a laboratory base station and fed into a modified missile-tracking device

which graphs the wearer's location and displays it on a screen. The device can also be connected with a sensor resembling a wristwatch which transmits the wearer's pulse rate. In addition, the wearer can send signals to the receiving station by pressing a button, and the receiver can send a return signal to the wearer.

At present, the primary purpose of the device is to facilitate medical and therapeutic aid to patients, i.e., to effectuate the quick location and rescue of persons subject to emergency medical conditions that preclude their calling for help, such as cases of acute cardiac infarction, epilepsy or diabetes (Schwitzgebel, 1967a). Also, so far, the use of the device has been limited to volunteers, and they are free to remove the device whenever they wish (Schwitzgebel, 1967b). Schwitzgebel has expressed an interest in applying his device to monitoring and rehabilitating chronic recidivists on parole.

At the University of California, Los Angeles, Ralph Schwitzgebel's brother, Robert Schwitzgebel, has perfected a somewhat similar device in which a miniature two-way radio unit, encased in a wide leather belt containing its own antenna and rechargeable batteries, is worn by volunteer experimental subjects (R. Schwitzgebel, 1969). Non-voice communication is maintained between a central communications station and the wearer by means of a radio signal which, when sent, activates a small coil in the wearer's receiver unit that makes itself felt as a tap in the abdominal region, accompanied by a barely audible tone and a small light. Information is conveyed to the subject by a coded sequence of taps. In turn, the wearer can send simple coded signal messages back to the central station, indicating his receipt of the signal, his general state of well being, or the lack of it, and many other matters as well. So far, this device and its use depend entirely upon a relationship of cooperation and trust between experimenter and subject.

Another use of radiotelemetry on humans which has reached a high level of sophistication is the long-distance monitoring of ECG (electro-cardiogram) waves by Caceres (1965) and his associates (Cooper, 1965; Hagan, 1965). They have developed a telemetry system by which an ambulatory heart patient can be monitored continuously by a central computer in another city. The patient has the usual electrocardiograph leads taped to his chest, which are connected to a small battery powered FM radio transmitter on the patient's belt. The ECG waves are transmitted, as modulated radio frequencies, to a transceiver in the vicinity which relays them via an ordinary telephone (encased in an automated dialing device called a Dataphone). The encoded signals of the ECG can then be transmitted to any place in the world which can be reached by telephone. On the receiving end, there is an automatic answering device that accepts the call and turns on the appropriate receiving equipment. In the usual case this will be an analog-to-digital converter, which quantizes the electrical waves and changes them to a series of numbers, representing amplitudes at certain precise times. The computer than analyzes the numerical amplitude values and, when an abnormal pattern appears, it not only warns the patient's physician (with a bell or light) but will produce, on request, some or all of the previous readings it has stored. The computer can monitor hundreds of patients simultaneously by sharing computer time among hundreds of input signals, and produce an "analysis" of ECG activity for each in as little as 2.5 minutes—the time required for the signal to get into the computer's analytical circuits. Although this "analysis" does not yet amount to a diagnosis of heart disease or the onset of an attack, there is no reason why computers could not be taught to read ECG patterns as well as any heart specialist, and with their ability to make stochastic analyses, in time they should become better at it than most doctors.

The third area where external telemetry has been used to advantage is also in the medical field. For several years, Vreeland and Yeager (1965) have been using a subminiature radiotelemeter for taking EEG's of epileptic children. The device is glued to the child's scalp with a special preparation and electrodes extend from it to various places on the child's scalp. A receiver is positioned in an adjoining room of the hospital and sound motion pictures record the child's behavior, his voice and his EEG on the same film. Some of the benefits derived from the use of this equipment are: (1) that it permits readings to be taken of an epileptic seizure as it occurs; and (2) it allows studies to be made of EEG patterns of disturbed children without encumbering them in trailing wires. At present however, the device is "external" in the sense that the electrodes do not penetrate into the brain, and only surface cortical brain wave patterns are picked up by the transmitter. It is believed, however, that many epileptic seizures originate in areas deep in the subcortical regions of the brain (Walker, 1961), and to obtain EEG readings for these areas, it would be necessary to implant the electrodes in these areas stereotaxically. The significance of such a modification would be that if the transmitter were transformed into a transceiver (a minor modification), it would then be possible to stimulate the same subcortical areas telemetrically. This would, then, convert the telemetry system into an "internal" device, such as the ones we are now about to describe.

Internal Devices

One of the leaders in the field of internal radiotelemetry devices is Mackay (1961). He has developed devices which he calls "endoradiosondes." These are tiny transmitters that can be swallowed or implanted internally in man or animal. They have been designed in order to measure and transmit such physiological variables as gastrointestinal pressure, blood pressure, body temperature, bioelectrical potentials (voltage accompanying the functioning of the brain, the heart and other muscles), oxygen levels, acidity and radiation intensity (Mackay, 1965). In fact, in many cases for the purposes of biomedical and physiological research, internal telemetry is the only way of obtaining the desired data. In the case where the body functions do not emit electrical energy (as the brain, heart and other neuromuscular structures do), these devices have been ingeniously modified in order to measure changes in pressure, acidity, etc., and to transmit electrical signals reflecting these changes to receivers outside the body. In this case the transmitters are called "transducers." Both "active" and "passive" transmitters have been developed, "active" transmitters containing a battery powering an oscillator, and "passive" transmitters not containing an internal power source, but having instead tuned circuits modulated from an outside power source. Although "passive" systems enjoy the advantage of not being concerned with power failure or battery replacement, they do not put out as good a signal as an "active" system. Both transmitter systems, at present, have ranges of a few feet to a dozen—just enough to bring out the signal from inside the body (Mackay, 1965). Thus, it is generally necessary for the subject to carry a small booster transmitter in order to receive the weak signal from inside the body and increase its strength for rebroadcasting to a remote laboratory or data collection point. However, with the development of integrated circuits, both transmitters and boosters can be miniaturized to a fantastic degree.

Electrical Stimulation of the Brain

The technique employed in electrophysiology in studying the brain of animals and man by stimulating its different areas electrically is nothing new. This technique was being used by two European physiologists, Fritsch and Hitzig, on dogs in the latter half of the 19th Century (Sheer, 1961; Krech, 1966). In fact, much of the early work in experimental psychology was devoted to physiological studies of the human nervous system. During the last twenty years, however—perhaps as a result of equipment which allows the implantation of electrodes deep in the subcortical regions of the brain and the brain stem by stereotaxic instruments—the science of electrophysiology has received new impetus, and our understanding of neural activity within the brain and its behavioral and experiential correlates has been greatly expanded.

The electrical stimulation of various areas of the brain has produced a wide range of phenomena in animals and humans. An examination of published research in electrical stimulation of the brain suggests two crude methods of controlling human behavior: (1) by "blocking" of the response, through the production of fear, anxiety, disorientation, loss of memory and purpose, and even, if need be, by loss of consciousness; and (2) through conditioning behavior by the manipulation of rewarding and aversive stimuli (Jones, 1965). In this regard, the experiments of James Olds (1962; 1967) on animals and Robert G. Heath (1960) and his associates at Tulane on humans are particularly interesting. Both have shown the existence in animals and humans of brain areas of or near the hypothalamus which have what may be very loosely described as "rewarding" and "aversive" effects. The interesting thing about their experiments is that both animals and man will self-stimulate themselves at a tremendous rate in order to receive stimulation "rewards" regardless of, and sometimes in spite of, the existence of drives such as hunger and thirst. Moreover, their experiments have put a serious dent in the "drive-reduction" theory of operant conditioning under which a response eliciting a reward ceases or declines when a point of satiation is reached, since in their experiments no satiation point seems ever to be reached (the subject losing consciousness from physical exhaustion unless the stimulus is terminated beforehand by the experimenter). Thus their experiments indicate that there may be "pleasure centers" in the brain which are capable of producing hedonistic responses which are independent of drive reduction. In humans, however, the results of hypothalamus stimulation have not always been as clear as those with animals, and some experimenters have produced confusing and inconsistent results (King, 1961; Sem-Jacobsen, 1960).

Current research in the field of electrophysiology seems to hold out the possibility of exerting a limited amount of external control over the emotions, consciousness, memory and behavior of man by electrical stimulation of the brain. Krech (1966) quotes a leading electrophysiologist, Delgado of the Yale School of Medicine, as stating that current researches "support the distasteful conclusion that motion, emotion and behavior can be directed by electrical forces and that humans can be controlled like robots by push buttons." Although the authors have the greatest respect for Delgado's expertise in his field, they believe he overstates the case in this instance. None of the research indicates that man's every action can be directed by a puppeteer at an electrical keyboard; none indicates that thoughts can be placed into the heads of men electrically; none indicates that man can be directed like a mechanical robot. *At most,* they indicate that some of man's activities can possibly be deterred by such methods, that certain emotional states might be induced (with very uncertain consequences in different individuals), and that man might be conditioned along certain approved paths by "rewards" and "punishments" carefully administered at appropriate times. Techniques of direct brain stimulation developed in electrophysiology thus hold out the possibility of influencing and controlling selected human behavior within limited parameters.

The use, then, of telemetric systems as a method of monitoring man, of obtaining physiological data from his body and nervous system, and of stimulating his brain electrically from a distance, seems in the light of present research entirely feasible and possible as a method of control. There is, however, a gap in our knowledge which must be filled before telemetry and electrical stimulation of the brain could be applied to any control system. This gap is in the area of interpretation of incoming data. Before crime can be prevented, the monitor must know what the subject is doing or is about

to do. It would not be practical to attach microphones to the monitored subjects, nor to have them in visual communication by television, and it would probably be illegal (Note: *Harvard Law Review,* 1966). Moreover, since the incoming data will eventually be fed into a computer,[1] it will be necessary to confine the information transmitted to the computer to such non-verbal, non-visual data as location, EEG patterns, ECG patterns and other physiological data. At the present time, EEG's tell us very little about what a person is doing or even about his emotional state (Konecci, 1965a). ECG's tell us little more than heart rhythms. Certain other physiological data, however, such as respiration, muscle tension, the presence of adrenalin in the blood stream, combined with knowledge of the subject's location, may be particularly revealing— e.g., a parolee with a past record of burglaries is tracked to a downtown shopping district (in fact, is exactly placed in a store known to be locked up for the night) and the physiological data reveals an increased respiration rate, a tension in the musculature and an increased flow of adrenalin. It would be a safe guess, certainly, that he was up to no good. The computer in this case, *weighing the probabilities,* would come to a decision and alert the police or parole officer so that they could hasten to the scene; or, if the subject were equipped with an implanted radiotelemeter, it could transmit an electrical signal which could block further action by the subject by causing him to forget or abandon his project. However, before computers can be designed to perform such functions, a greater knowledge derived from experience in the use of these devices on human subjects, as to the correlates between the data received from them and their actual behavior, must be acquired.

---

[1]Obviously, no system monitoring thousands of parolees would be practical if there had to be a human monitor for every monitored subject on a 24 hour-a-day, seven-day-a-week basis. Therefore, computers would be absolutely necessary.

CONDITIONS UNDER WHICH TELEMETRY TECHNIQUES MIGHT INITIALLY BE APPLIED IN CORRECTIONAL PROGRAMING

The development of sophisticated techniques of electronic surveillance and control could radically alter the conventional wisdom regarding the merits of imprisonment. It has been the opinion of many thoughtful penologists for sometime that prison life is not particularly conducive to rehabilitation (Sutherland, 1966; Sykes, 1966; Vold, 1954; Morris, 1963). Some correctional authorities, such as the Youth and Adult Corrections Agency of the State of California, have been exploring the possibilities of alternatives to incarceration, believing that the offender can best be taught "to deal lawfully with the given elements of the society while he functions, at least partially, in that society and not when he is withdrawn from it" (Geis, 1964). Parole is one way of accomplishing that objective, but parole is denied to many inmates of the prison system, not always for reasons to do with their ability to be reformed or the risk of allowing them release on parole. The development telemetric control systems could help increase the number of offenders who could safely and effectively be supervised within the community.

Schwitzgebel suggests (1967b) that it would be safe to allow the release of many poor-risk or nonparolable convicts into the community provided that their activities were continuously monitored by some sort of telemetric device. He states:

"A parolee thus released would probably be less likely than usual to commit offenses if a record of his location were kept at the base station. If two-way tone communication were included in this system, a therapeutic relationship might be established in which the parolee could be rewarded, warned, or otherwise signalled in accordance with the plan for therapy."

He also states:

"Security equipment has been designed, but not constructed that could insure the wearing of the transmitting equipment or indicate attempts to compromise or disable the system."

He further states that it has been the consistent opinion of inmates and parolees interviewed about the matter that they would rather put up with the constraints, inconveniences and annoyances of an electronic monitoring system, while enjoying the freedom outside an institution, than to suffer the much greater loss of privacy, restrictions on freedom, annoyance and inconveniences of prison life.

The envisioned system of telemetric control while offering many possible advantages to offenders over present penal measures also has several possible benefits for society. Society, through such systems, exercises control over behavior it defines as deviant, thus insuring its own protection. The offender, by returning to the community, can help support his dependents and share in the overall tax burden. The offender is also in a better position to make meaningful restitution. Because the control system works on conditioning principles, the offender is habituated into non-deviant behavior patterns—thus perhaps decreasing the probability of recidivism and, once the initial cost of development is absorbed, a telemetric control system might provide substantial economic advantage compared to rather costly correctional programs. All in all, the development of such a system could prove tremendously beneficial for society.

The adequate development of telemetric control systems is in part dependent upon their possible application. In order to ensure the beneficial use of such a system, certain minimal conditions ought to be imposed in order to forestall possible ethical and legal objections:

1.   The consent of the inmate should be obtained, after a full explanation is given to him of the nature of the equipment, the limitations involved in its usage, the risks and constraints that will be placed upon his freedom, and the option

he has of returning to prison if its use becomes too burdensome.

2. The equipment should not be used for purposes of gathering evidence for the prosecution of crimes, but rather should be employed as a crime prevention device. A law should be passed giving the users of this equipment an absolute privilege of keeping confidential all information obtained therefrom regardless of to whom it pertains, and all data should be declared as in-admissible in court. The parole authorities, if they be the users of this equipment, should have the discretionary power to revoke parole whenever they see fit without the burden of furnishing an explanation, thus relieving them of the necessity of using data obtained in this fashion as justification for their actions. The data should be destroyed after a certain period of time, and, if the system is hooked up with a computer, the computer should be programmed to erase its tapes after a similar period of time.

By employing the above safeguards, the use of a telemetric system should be entirely satisfactory to the community and to the convicts who choose to take advantage of it. Nevertheless there are a number of ethical objections which are bound to arise when such a system is initially employed that deserve special discussion.

ETHICAL OBJECTIONS

The two principal objections raised against the use of modern technology for surveillance and control of persons deemed to be deviant in their behavior in such a degree as to warrant close supervision revolve around two issues: privacy and freedom (Note: *Harvard Law Review,* 1966; King, 1964; Miller, 1964; Fried, 1968; Ruebhausen, 1965).

Privacy

It has often been said that privacy, in essence, consists of the "right to be let alone" (Warren,

1890; Ernst, 1962). This is a difficult right to apply to criminals because it is precisely their inability to leave their fellow members of society alone that justifies not leaving them alone. This statement, however, might be interpreted to mean that there is a certain limited area where each man should be free from the scrutiny of his neighbors or his government and from interference in his affairs. While most people would accept this as a general proposition, in point of fact it is not recognized in prison administration, where surveillance and control are well-nigh absolute and total (Sykes, 1966; Clemmer, 1958). Therefore, it is difficult to see how the convict would lose in the enjoyment of whatever rights of privacy he has by electronic surveillance in the open community. If the watcher was a computer, this would be truer still, as most people do not object to being "watched" by electric eyes that open doors for them. It is the scrutiny of humans by humans that causes embarrassment—the knowledge that one is being judged by a fellow human.

Another definition of privacy is given by Ruebhausen (1965).

"The essence of privacy is no more, and certainly no less, than the freedom of the individual to pick and choose for himself the time and the circumstances under which, and most importantly, the extent to which, his attitudes, beliefs, behavior and opinions are to be shared with or withheld from others."

To this statement the preliminary question might be raised as to the extent to which we honor this value when we are dealing with convicts undergoing rehabilitation, mental patients undergoing psychiatric treatment, or even minors in our schools. Certainly it is not a statement that can be generally applied, especially in those cases where every society deems itself to have the right to shape and change the attitudes, beliefs, behavior and opinions of others when they are seriously out of step with the rest of society. But a more fundamental objection can be raised, in that the statement has little or no relevance to what we propose. Not only does the envisioned equipment lack the power to affect or modify directly the "attitudes," "beliefs" and "opinions" of the subject, but it definitely does not force him to share those mental processes with others. The subject is only limited in selected areas of his behavior—i.e., those areas in which society has a genuine interest in control. The subject is consequently "free" to hold any set of attitudes he desires. Of course, on the basis of behavioral psychology, one would expect attitudes, beliefs and opinions to change to conform with the subject's present behavior (Smith, 1968).

Still a third definition of privacy has been proposed by Fried (1968) in a recent article in the Yale Law Journal, an article which specifically discusses Schwitzgebel's device. He advances the argument that privacy is a necessary context for the existence of love, friendship and trust between people, and that the parolee under telemetric supervision who never feels himself loved or trusted will never be rehabilitated. While this argument might have some validity where the device is used as a therapeutic tool—a point that Schwitzgebel (1967b) recognizes since he would use it partly for that purpose—it is not particularly relevant where no personal relationship is established between the monitors and the subject and where the emphasis is placed upon the device's ability to control and deter behavior, rather than to "rehabilitate." Rehabilitation, hopefully, will follow once law-abiding behavior becomes habitual.

As far as privacy is concerned, most of the arguments are squarely met by the conditions and safeguards previously proposed. However, when one begins to implant endoradiosondes subcutaneously or to control actions through electrical stimulation of the brain, one runs into a particularly troublesome objection, which is often included within the scope of "privacy," although perhaps it should be separately named as the "human dignity" or "sacred vessel of the spirit" argument. This is the argument that was raised when compulsory vaccination was proposed, and which is still being raised as to such things as birth control, heart transplants, and proposals for the improvement of man through eugenics. The argument seems to stem from an ancient, well-entrenched belief that man, in whatever condition he finds himself, even in a state of decrepitude, is as Nature or God intended him to be and inviolable. Even when a man consents to have his physical organism changed, some people feel uneasy at the prospect, and raise objections.

Perhaps the only way to answer such an argument is to rudely disabuse people of the notion that there is any dignity involved in being a sick person, or a mentally disturbed person, or a criminal person whose acts constantly bring him into the degrading circumstances, which the very persons praising human dignity so willingly inflict upon him. Perhaps the only way to explode the notion of man as a perfect, or perfectible, being, made in God's image (the Bible), a little lower than the angels (Disraeli), or as naturally good but corrupted by civilization (Rousseau), is to review the unedifying career of man down through the ages and to point to some rather interesting facets of his biological make-up, animal-like-behavior, and evolutionary career which have been observed by leading biologists and zoologists (Lorenz, 1966; Morris, 1967; Rostand, 1959). Unfortunately, there is not time here to perform such a task or to rip away the veil of human vanity that so enshrouds these arguments.

Freedom

The first thing that should be said with regard to the issue of human freedom is that there is none to be found in most of our prisons. As Sykes (1966) remarks:

". . . the maximum security prison represents a social system in which an attempt is made to create and maintain total or almost total social control."

This point is so well recognized that it need not be belabored, but it does serve to highlight the irrelevancy of the freedom objection as far as the prison inmate is concerned. Any system which allows him the freedom of the open community, which maintains an unobtrusive surveillance and which intervenes only rarely to block or frustrate his activities can surely appear to him only as a vast improvement in his situation.

Most discussions of freedom discuss it as if man were the inhabitant of a natural world, rather than a social world. They fail to take into account the high degree of subtle regulation which social life necessarily entails. As Hebb (1961) put very well:

"What I am saying implies that civilization depends on an all-pervasive thought control established in infancy, which both maintains and is maintained by the social environment, consisting of the behavior of the members of society. . . . What we are really talking about in this symposium is mind in an accustomed social environment, and more particularly a social environment that we consider to be the normal one. It is easy to forget this, and the means by which it is achieved. The thought control that we object to, the 'tyranny over the mind of man' to which Jefferson swore 'eternal hostility,' is only the one that is imposed by some autocratic agency, and does not include the rigorous and doctrinaire control that society itself exercises, by common consent, in moral and political values. I do not suggest that this is undesirable. Quite the contrary, I argue that a sound society must have such a control, but let us at least see what we are doing. We do not bring up our children with open minds and then, when they can reason, let them reason and make up their minds as they will concerning the acceptability of incest, the value of courtesy in social relations, or the desirability of democratic government. Instead we tell them what's what, and to the extent that we are successful as parents and teachers, we see that they take it and make it part of their mental processes, with no further need of policing."

"The problem of thought control, or control of the mind, then, is not how to avoid it, considering it only as a malign influence exerted over the innocent by foreigners, Communists, and other evil fellows. We all exert it; only, on the whole, we are more efficient at it. From this point of view the course of a developing civilization is, on the one hand, an increasing uniformity of aims and values, and thus also of social

behavior, or on the other, an increasing emotional tolerance of the stranger, the one who differs from me in looks, beliefs, or action—a tolerance, however, that still has narrow limits."

Discussions of freedom that one customarily finds in law journals also fail to take into account the distinction between objective and subjective freedom. Objective freedom for each man is a product of power, wealth or authority, since it is only through the achievement of one or more of these that one can control so as not to be controlled—i.e., it is only through these that one can, on one hand, guard against the abuses, infringements, and overreaching of one's fellow man which limit one, and, on the other hand, commit those very offenses against one's neighbor and, by doing so, obtain all one's heart desires. This is not to neglect the role of the law in preventing a war of all against all, in providing the freedom that goes with peace, and with ensuring that all share to a certain extent in the protections and benefits of a well-ordered society. But laws are themselves limitations imposed upon objective freedom. Radical objective freedom is inconsistent with social life, since in order for some to have it, others must be denied it. Such a radical freedom may also be intolerable psychologically; one may actually feel "constrained" by an excess of options (Fromm, 1963).

Subjective freedom, on the other hand, is a sense of not being pressed by the demands of authority and nagged by unfulfilled desires. It is totally dependent on *awareness*. Such a concept of freedom is easily realizable within the context of an ordered society, whereas radical objective freedom is not. Since society cannot allow men too much objective freedom, the least it can do (and the wise thing to do) is to so order its affairs that men are not aware or concerned about any lack of it. The technique of telemetric control of human beings offers the possibility of regulating behavior with precision on a subconscious level, and avoiding the cruelty of depriving man of his subjective sense of freedom.

CONCLUSION

Two noted psychologists, C. R. Rogers and B. F. Skinner, carried on a debate in the pages of *Science* magazine (1956) over the issue of the moral responsibility of behavioral scientists in view of the everwidening techniques of behavior control. Skinner said:

"The dangers inherent in the control of human behavior are very real. The possibility of misuse of scientific knowledge must always be faced. We cannot escape by denying the power of a science of behavior or arresting its development. It is no help to cling to familiar philosophies of human behavior simply because they are more reassuring. As I have pointed out elsewhere, the new techniques emerging from a science of behavior must be subject to the explicit counter control which has already been applied to earlier and cruder forms."

Skinner's point was that the scientific age had arrived; there was no hope of halting its advance; and that scientists could better spend their time in explaining the nature of their discoveries so that proper controls might be applied (not to stop the advance, but to direct it into the proper channels), rather than in establishing their own set of goals and their own *ne plus ultra* to "proper research." This is a valid point. Victor Hugo once said: "Nothing is as powerful as an idea whose time has arrived." The same holds true for a technology whose time is upon us. Those countries whose social life advances to keep pace with their advancing technology will survive in the world of tomorrow; those that look backward and cling to long-outmoded values will fall into the same state of degradation that China suffered in the 19th and early 20th Centuries because she cherished too much the past. These are not inappropriate remarks to make here, because the nations that can so control behavior as to control the crime problem will enjoy an immense advantage over those that do not. Whether we like it or not, changes in technology require changes in political and social life and in values most adaptable to those changes. It would be ironic indeed

if science, which was granted, and is granted, the freedom to invent weapons of total destruction, were not granted a similar freedom to invent methods of controlling the humans who wield them.

Rogers agreed with Skinner that human control of humans is practiced everywhere in social and political life, but framed the issues differently. He said (1956):

". . . They can be stated very briefly: Who will be controlled? Who will exercise control? What type of control will be exercised? Most important of all, toward what end or what purpose, in pursuit of what values, will control be exercised?"

These are very basic questions. They need to be answered, and they should be answered.

Jean Rostand (1959), a contemporary French biologist of note, asks: can man be modified? He points to the fact that, since the emergence of *homo sapiens* over 100,000 years ago, man has not evolved physically in the slightest degree. He has the same brain now that he had then, except that now it is filled up with the accumulated knowledge of 5,000 years of civilization—knowledge that has not seemed to be adequate to the task of erasing certain primitive humanoid traits, such as intraspecific aggression, which is a disgusting trait not even common to most animals. Seeing that man now possesses the capabilities of effecting certain changes in his biological structure, he asks whether it isn't a reasonable proposal for man to hasten evolution along by modifying himself into something better than what he has been for the last 100,000 years. We believe that this is a reasonable proposal, and ask: What better place to start than with those individuals most in need of a change for the better?

REFERENCES

Barr, N. L.
1960 "Telemetering Physiological Response During Experimental Flight." *American Journal of Cardiology* 6:54.

Caceres, C. A. and James K. Cooper
1965 "Radiotelemetry: A Clinical Perspective." *Biomedical Telemetry*. Edited by C. A. Caceres. New York: Academic Press.

Clemmer, Donald
1958 *The Prison Community*. New York: Holt, Rinehart and Winston.

Cooper, James K. and C. A. Caceres
1965 "Telemetry by Telephone." *Biomedical Telemetry*. Edited by C. A. Caceres. New York: Academic Press.

Ernst, Morris L. and Alan U. Schwartz
1962 *Privacy: The Right to Be Let Alone*. New York: Macmillan.

Epstein, R. J., J. R. Haumann and R. B. Keener
V1968 "An Implantable Telemetry Unit for Accurate Body Temperature Measurements." *Journal of Applied Physiology* 24(3):439.

Fried, Charles
1968 "Privacy." *Yale Law Journal* 77:475.

Fromm, Erich
1963 *Escape From Freedom*. New York: Holt, Rinehart and Winston.

Geis, Gilbert
1964 "The Community-Centered Correctional Residence." Correction in the Community: Alternatives to Incarceration. Sacramento, California: Youth and Adult Corrections Agency, State of California.

Grisamore, N. T., James K. Cooper and C. A. Caceres
1965 "Evaluating Telemetry." *Biomedical Telemetry*. Edited by C. A. Caceres. New York: Academic Press.

Hagan, William K.
1965 "Telephone Applications." *Biomedical Telemetry*. Edited by C. A. Caceres. New York: Academic Press.

Heath, R. G. and W. A. Mickle
1960 "Evaluation of Seven Years' Experience with Depth Electrode Studies in Human Patients." *Electrical Studies of the Unanesthetized Brain*. Edited by E. R. Ramey and D. S. O'Doherty. New York: Paul B. Hoeber, Inc.

Hebb, D. O.
1961 "The Role of Experience." *Man and Civiliza-*

tion: Control of the Mind; A Symposium. Edited by Seymour M. Farber and R. H. L. Wilson. New York: McGraw-Hill.

Jones, H. G., Michael Gelder and H. M. Holden
1965 "Behavior and Aversion Therapy in the Treatment of Delinquency." *British Journal of Criminology* 5(4):355–387.

King, D. B.
1964 "Electronic Surveillance and Constitutional Rights: Some Current Developments and Observations." *George Washington Law Review* 33:240.

King, H. E.
1961 "Psychological Effects of Excitation in the Limbic System." *Electrical Stimulation of the Brain*. Edited by Daniel E. Sheer. Austin: University of Texas Press.

Konecci, E. B. and A. James Shiner
1965a "The Developing Challenge of Biosensor and Bioinstrumentation Research." *Biomedical Telemetry*. Edited by C. A. Caceres. New York: Academic Press.
1965b "Uses of Telemetry in Space." *Biomedical Telemetry*. Edited by C. A. Caceres. New York: Academic Press.

Krech, David
1966 "Controlling the Mind-Controllers." *Think* 32(July-August):2.

Lord, R. D., F. C. Bellrose and W. W. Cochran
1962 "Radiotelemetry of the Respiration of a Flying Duck." *Science* 137:39.

Lorenz, Konrad
1966 *On Aggression*. New York: Harcourt, Brace and World, Inc.

Mackay, R. S.
1961 "Radiotelemetering from Within the Body." *Science* 134:1196.
1965 "Telemetry from Within the Body of Animals and Man: Endoradiosondes." *Biomedical Telemetry*. Edited by C. A. Caceres. New York: Academic Press.

Miller, A. S.
1964 "Technology, Social Change and the Constitution." *George Washington Law Review* 33:17.

Morris, Desmond
1967 *The Naked Ape*. New York: McGraw-Hill.

Morris, Terrence and Paulene Morris
1963 *Pentonville: A Sociological Study of an English Prison*. London: Routledge and Kegan Paul.

Note
1966 "Anthropotelemetry: Dr. Schwitzgebel's Machine." *Harvard Law Review* 80:403.

Olds, James
1962 "Hypothalamic Substrates of Reward." *Physiological Reviews* 42:554.
1967 "Emotional Centers in the Brain." *Science Journal* 3(5):87.

Reubhausen, O. M. and O. G. Brim
1965 "Privacy and Behavior Research." *Columbia Law Review* 65:1184.

Rogers, C. R. and B. F. Skinner
1956 "Some Issues Concerning the Control of Human Behavior." *Science* 124:1057.

Rostand, Jean
1959 *Can Man Be Modified?*. London: Secker and Warburg.

Schwitzgebel, Ralph, Robert Schwitzgebel, W. N. Pahnke and W. S. Hurd
1964 "A Program of Research in Behavioral Electronics." *Behavioral Science* 9:233.

Schwitzgebel, Ralph
1967a "Electronic Innovation in the Behavioral Sciences: A Call to Responsibility." *American Psychologist* 22(5):364.
1967b "Issues in the Use of an Electronic Rehabilitation System with Chronic Recidivists." (unpublished paper).

Schwitzgebel, Robert L.
1969 "A Belt from Big Brother." *Psychology Today* 2(11):45–47, 65.

Sem-Jacobsen, C. W. and Arne Torkildsen
1960 "Depth Recording and Electrical Stimulation in the Human Brain." *Electrical Studies of the Unanesthetized Brain*. Edited by E. R. Ramey and D. S. O'Doherty. New York: Paul B. Hoeber, Inc.

Sheer, Daniel
1961 "Brain and Behavior: The Background of Interdisciplinary Research." *Electrical Stimulation of the Brain*. Edited by Daniel Sheer. Austin: University of Texas Press.

Slater, Lloyd E.
1965 "A Broad-Brush Survey of Biomedical Telemetric Progress." *Biomedical Telemetry*. Edited by C. A. Caceres. New York: Academic Press.

Smith, Gerald W.
1968 "Electronic Rehabilitation and Control: An Alternative to Prison." Paper read at the American Correctional Association Meeting, San Francisco.

Sperry, C. J., C. P. Gadsden, C. Rodriguez and L. N. N. Bach
1961 "Miniature Subcutaneous Frequency-Modulated Transmitter for Brain Potentials." *Science* 134:1423.

Sutherland, Edwin and Donald R. Cressey
1966 *Principles of Criminology*. Seventh Edition. Philadelphia: Lippincott.

Sykes, Gresham
1966 *The Society of Captives*. New York: Atheneum.

Vold, George B.
1954 "Does Prison Reform?" *Annals of the American Academy of Political and Social Science* 293:42–50.

Vreeland, Robert and C. L. Yeager
1965 "Application of Subminiature Radio Telemetry Equipment to EEG Analysis from Active Subjects." Paper delivered at Sixth International Congress of Electroencephalography and Clinical Neurophysiology, Vienna.

Walker, A. E. and Curtis Marshall
1961 "Stimulation and Depth Recording in Man." *Electrical Stimulation of the Brain*. Edited by Daniel Sheer. Austin: University of Texas Press.

Warren, Samuel D. and Louis D. Brandeis
1890 "The Right to Privacy." *Harvard Law Review* 4:193.

Young, I. J. and W. S. Naylor
1964 "Implanted Two-Way Telemetry in Laboratory Animals." *American Journal of Medical Electronics* 3:28.

81. The Future of Corrections

JOHN CONRAD

"JUSTICE IS THE FIRST VIRTUE OF SOCIAL INSTITU-tions, as truth is of systems of thought. A theory how-ever elegant and economical must be rejected or re-vised if it is untrue; likewise laws and institutions no matter how efficient and well-arranged must be re-formed or abolished if they are unjust. Each person possesses an inviolability founded on justice that even the welfare of society as a whole cannot over-ride. . . . The only thing that permits us to acquiesce in an er-roneous theory is the lack of a better one; analog-ously, an injustice is tolerable only when it is necessary to avoid an even greater injustice. Being first virtues of human activities, truth and justice are uncom-promising."[1]

JOHN RAWLS
A Theory of Justice

Until very recently, thoughtful and humane scholars, administrators, and clinicians generally held that it was the business of the prison and other incarcerating facilities to rehabilitate of-fenders. In addition to a rhetoric of rehabilita-tion appropriate for the influence of public opinion, this conviction was substantively ex-pressed in the organization of services for of-fenders. Educators, psychologists and social workers were added to the permanent staff in the contemporary prison.

In the last few years, however, the weight of informed opinion in the United States about correctional rehabilitation has shifted to the negative. Rehabilitation, while still recognized as a meritorious goal, is no longer seen as a practi-cal possibility within our correctional structure by the empirical observer. Nevertheless, the ideology of people-changing permeates correc-tions. Modern prisons remain committed to treatment; echelons of personnel to carry it out are established on every table of organization. The belief that a prisoner should be a better man as a result of his confinement guides judges in fixing terms and parole boards in reducing them. Rehabilitation continues to be an objective in good standing.

The dissonances produced by this conflict be-tween opinion and practice are numerous, pro-found, and destructive of confidence in the criminal justice system. Whether these disso-nances can be settled remains to be seen, but, clearly, understanding is critically important to improvement of the situation. In this article I shall explain the change in rehabilitative thought and consider the significance of that change. I shall then review some of the more striking examples of policy departures grounded on rejection of the concept of re-habilitation and conclude with a new concep-tualization of the place of corrections in criminal justice. My analysis and conclusions are in-tended to contribute to the vigorous dialogue which is necessary for the understanding and resolution of any public problem in a democra-tic society. In the case of corrections, the prob-lem is the attainment of simple justice, a goal which must be achieved if civilized order is to continue.

▶SOURCE: *"Corrections and Simple Justice," Journal of Crimi-nal Law and Criminology* (1973) 64(2): 208–217. Reprinted by *permission.*

[1]J. Rawls, *A Theory of Justice* 3–4 (1971).

THE DEVELOPMENT AND REJECTION OF THE REHABILITATIVE NOTION

The idea of rehabilitation is not rooted in antiquity. Until the eighteenth century, charity was the most that any deviant could hope for and much more than most deviants—especially criminals—received. Any history of punishment before that time is an account of grisly and stomach-turning horrors administered by the law to wrong-doers.[2] Our forebears behaved so ferociously for reasons which we can only reconstruct with diffidence. The insecurity of life and property must have played an important part in the evolution of sanctions so disproportionate to harm or the threat of harm, but there was certainly another source of our ancestors' furious response to the criminal: The war they waged against crime was partly a war against Satan. They believed that crime could be ascribed to original sin, that Satan roamed the world seeking the destruction of souls, and that his handiwork could be seen in the will to do wrong. The salvation of the innocent depended on the extirpation of the wicked. It is only in light of belief systems of this kind, varying in detail from culture to culture, that we can explain the Inquisition, the persecution of witches, and the torturing, hanging, drawing, and quartering of common criminals.

The Enlightenment changed all that. If pre-Enlightenment man teetered fearfully on the brink of Hell, desperately condemning sin and sinners in the interest of his own salvation, the *philosophes* conferred an entirely new hope on him. Rousseau's wonderful vision of man as naturally good relied partly on an interpretation of primitive society which we now dismiss as naive, but the world has never been the same since he offered his alternative.[3] Once relieved of a supernatural burden of evil, man's destiny can be shaped, at least partly, by reason.

Reason created the obligation to change the transgressor instead of damning him or removing him by execution or transportation. The history of corrections, as we now know it, can be interpreted as a series of poorly controlled experiments to see what could be done about changing offenders. It started with incarceration to remove offenders from evil influences which moved them to the commission of crime, a reasonable proposition, given what was known about the conditions which created crime.[4] It is noteworthy that the theoretical basis for expecting benefits from incarceration depended on the perception that the causes of crime might be found in the community rather than in the criminal.

This theory did not survive for long. The actual benefits of incarceration were difficult to identify in support of the expectations of the early American idealists responsible for the original notion. Incarceration was now seen as a satisfactory punishment to administer to the criminal, and if a rationale was needed for it, Jeremy Bentham and the Utilitarians provided it.[5] Punishment would rehabilitate if administered by the "felicific calculus," according to which the proper amount of pain could be administered to discourage the transgressor from continuing his transgressions.

Nineteenth century Americans were finicky about human misery, and they did not like to see it administered intentionally. They responded to the rhetoric of rehabilitation as expressed, for example, in the famous 1870 Declaration of Principles of the American Prison Association.[6] This time, reason provided a new objective, and a new logic to justify it. The prison's purpose was no longer simply to punish the offender,

[4]See D. Rothman, *The Discovery of the Asylum* (1972), in which the author traces the origins of this hypothesis, its consequences, and the influences it has exerted long since it was disconfirmed.

[5]See J. Bentham, *An Introduction to the Principles of Morals and Legislation* (rev. ed. 1823).

[6]See Transactions of the National Congress on Penitentiary and Reformatory Discipline, Prison Association of New York, 26th Annual Report (1870).

[2]See, e.g., H. Barnes, *The Story of Punishment* (1930); G. Ives, *A History of Penal Methods* (1970).

[3]See J. Rousseau, *An Inquiry into the Nature of the Social Contract* (1791).

but the prisoner was to be cured of his propensity to crime by religious exhortation, psychological counseling, remedial education, vocational training, or even medical treatment. The Declaration of Principles maintained that some of the causes of crime are to be found in the community. However, while incarcerated, the offender was to be changed for the better lest he be released to offend again. No one seriously advocated that felons should be confined until there was a certainty of their abiding by the law; it was impractical to carry this logic that far.

Gradually, empiricism took control of correctional thought. Its triumph was hastened by the peculiarly available data on recidivism, which was easily obtained and obviously related to questions of program success or failure. Correctional rehabilitation was empirically studied in details ever more refined. In a 1961 paper, Walter Bailey reviewed the evidence available in a hundred studies of correctional treatment and found it wanting in support for the belief that prison programs are related to parole success.[7] A much more massive review, by Lipton, Martinson, and Wilks, was completed in 1969 and reaches the same conclusion.[8] In their impeccably rigorous evaluation of group counseling, Kassebaum, Ward, and Wilner fully substantiate the negative conclusion of their predecessors.[9] In the absence of any strong evidence in favor of the success of rehabilitative programs, it is not possible to continue the justification of policy decisions in corrections on the supposition that such programs achieve rehabilitative objectives.

Paralleling the last twenty years of evaluative research has been much empirically based theoretical work. The classic study of the prison community by Clemmer[10] imposes a structure

on observation which, in turn, leads to the theoretical contributions of such writers as Schrag,[11] Sykes,[12] Goffman,[13] and Irwin.[14] Each of these workers brought a different perspective to his analysis, and the methodologies vary fundamentally. However, the picture of the prison which emerges clearly accounts for the unsatisfactory results of all those evaluative studies. The prison is an institution which forces inmates and staff alike to adjust to its requirements. These accommodations are inconsistent with rehabilitation. They are directed toward the present adjustment of the individual to the austerely unnatural conditions in which he finds himself. In some prisons survival becomes a transfixing concern. In any prison, regardless of the hazards to personal safety, the discomforts and irritations of the present occupy the attention of everyone. Inmates are obsessed with their places in an unfamiliar but constricted world and their hopes for release from it. Staff members are required to give most of their attention to the "here and now" problems of life in custody, whose relationship to rehabilitation is strained at best.

Under these conditions, relationships and attitudes in even the most enlightened prison are determined by group responses to official coercion. The ostensible program objectives of rehabilitation may be a high school diploma, a new trade, or increased psychological maturity, but the prevailing attitudes towards programs will be determined by group opinions about their value in obtaining favorable consideration for release. Whatever his motivations, man may learn a lot by engaging in a vocational training program. However, the statistical success of such programs in increasing the employability of released inmates is imperceptible. The reasons for this situation are still subject to speculation, but the inference is that few of

[7]Bailey, "An Evaluation of 100 Studies of Correctional Outcomes" in *The Sociology of Punishment and Correction* 733 (2d ed. N. Johnston, L. Savitz & M. Wolfgang, eds. 1970).

[8]D. Lipton, R. Martinson & J. Wilks, *The Effectiveness of Correctional Treatment* (1975).

[9]G. Kassebaum, D. Ward and D. Wilner, *Prison Treatment and Parole Survival* (1971).

[10]D. Clemmer, *The Prison Community* (1958).

[11]Schrag, "Leadership Among Prison Inmates," 19 *Am. Sociol. Rev.* 37 (1954).

[12]G. Sykes, *The Society of Captives* (1958).

[13]E. Goffman, *Ayslums* (1961).

[14]J. Irwin, *The Felon* (1970).

those involved take the program seriously. The learning process passes the time which must be served and qualifies the individual for the favorable consideration which he desperately seeks. But expectation of a career in a learned vocation does not influence the learner.

The data are not as exhaustive as one would like. Perhaps Glaser's study of the effectiveness of the federal prison system[15] provides the most conclusive picture of the bleak situation. The motivation to enroll in various self-improvement activities for release qualifications is conceded by the author. Neither in Glaser's own study of federal prisoners nor in the studies by others reported by him is there any strong evidence that educational and vocational training are related to post-release success. To this day, we have only anecdotal evidence that any inmate graduates of vocational training programs are successfully placed in careers for which they were trained.

The final word on coercion in the administration of rehabilitation programs may have been pronounced by Etzioni,[16] whose analysis of compliance structures uses the prison as a paradigm of coercion. In Etzioni's formulation, the response to coercion is alienation. He holds that alienation from authority is at its highest when authority uses force to obtain compliance. As force is explicit and to be encountered continuously in the prison, it is obvious that alienation will be universal, although it will take many forms, both active and passive. Indeed, Etzioni hypothesizes that when a prison administration attempts to obtain compliance by other means than coercion it loses stability. Yet it is the very alienation of the prisoner which severely restricts his will to accept the goals of the staff. To choose to be committed to any activity is one of the few choices which cannot be denied the

prisoner. For the inmate to accord the staff his volition is an act of enlightened self-interest which exceeds the perspective of most prisoners.

Rehabilitation has been deflated as a goal of correctional custody by empiricism and by sociological theory. Its claims, however, have not been refuted by these forces alone. The findings of research have been paralleled by staff disappointment, scepticism in the media, and administrative policy changes.

It is not possible to document so subjective a change as the loss of confidence in rehabilitation by correctional staff. Indeed, there are still many who continue with program development in the prisons and hope for the best. The establishment in 1969 of the Kennedy Youth Center in Morgantown, West Virginia, represents the persisting faith of the staff and consultants of the Federal Bureau of Prisons. It seems that the Bureau's faith is indomitable. For example, an experimental prison will be built in Butner, North Carolina, to study further the potentiality of treatment in custodial conditions. However, it would be difficult to find a comparable professional investment in institutional treatment. The fervid hopes engendered by the group counseling movement of the late fifties and early sixties have faded into routines and motions.

The part played by journalists in the change of correctional ideology is also hard to evaluate. The contributions of observers so diverse as Jessica Mitford,[17] Ben Bagdikian,[18] Ronald Goldfarb,[19] and Eddie Bunker,[20] have vividly documented the futility of the prison as a rehabilitative agency. The extent to which they

[15]See D. Glaser, The Effectiveness of a Prison and Parole System 260–84 (1964).

[16]See A. Etzioni, The Active Society 370–75 (1968). See also A. Etzioni, A Comparative Analysis of Complex Organizations 12–22 (1961).

[17]Mitford, "Kind and Usual Punishment in California," The Atlantic Monthly, March, 1971, at 45, in B. Atkins and H. Glick, Prisons, Protest and Politics 151 (1972).

[18]B. Bagdikian and L. Dade, The Shame of the Prisons (1972).

[19]Goldfarb and Singer, "Redressing Prisoners' Grievances," 39 Geo. Wash. L. Rev. 175 (1970).

[20]Bunker, "War Behind Walls," Harper's Magazine, February, 1972, at 39. See also E. Bunker, No Beast So Fierce (1972).

have changed public opinion is open to some question, in the absence of a recent poll, but there is a consistent theme in their writing which runs counter to the assumptions of rehabilitation. This theme flourishes without evident response to the contrary.

Administrative policy change has been easy to document. The California Probation Subsidy Act of 1965,[21] a landmark piece of legislation, states that as many offenders as possible should be channeled into probation, limiting the use of incarceration to cases where the protection of the public requires it. The program has been described in detail elsewhere,[22] but it is firmly based on the proposition that correctional rehabilitation cannot be effectively carried out in conditions of captivity. Whether it can be carried out in the community remains to be seen. As Hood and Sparks have remarked, the research which shows that probation is at least as effective as incarceration "cannot be interpreted as showing that probation is especially effective as a method of treatment."[23]

Nevertheless, the California act has been emulated in several states.[24] It represents a gradual shift which has already emptied some prisons and training schools. The shift has taken a much more abrupt form in Massachusetts, where in March, 1972, all juvenile correctional facilities were closed. The commissioner then responsible, Jerome Miller, acted on the conviction that such facilities do much more harm than good—if they can be said to do any good at all. The attention which the Massachusetts program has drawn because of its almost melodramatic timing has evoked singularly little debate. The local response in Massachusetts has been a fierce controversy, which the program has so far survived, but there has been at least a tacit acceptance throughout the country that the juvenile correctional facility is an institutional arrangement which can and should be terminated.

These academic and public developments portend the collapse of correctional rehabilitation as we have known it for the past twenty-five years. They confront the nation with a continuing need for the prison and no way to make it presentable. The apparatus of education, social casework, and psychiatry at least serve to disguise the oppressive processes required to hold men, women, and children in custody. To rehabilitate is a noble calling; to lock and unlock cages has never been highly regarded. The issue is apparent to many observers, but it is not surprising that we lack a consensus on its resolution.

IMPACT OF EMPIRICISM ON CORRECTIONS POLICY

The Report of the Corrections Task Force of the President's Commission on Law Enforcement and the Administration of Justice in 1967 initiated a series of public considerations of the problems of corrections. Its opening adjuration in the chapter of summary recommendations begins:

"It is clear that the correctional programs of the United States cannot perform their assigned work by mere tinkering with faulty machinery. A substantial upgrading of services and a new orientation of the total enterprise toward integration of offenders into the main stream of community life is needed."[25]

[21]Cal. Welf. 9 inst. Code § 1820 et seq. (West 1972).

[22]See R. Smith, A Quiet Revolution (1972). See also Keldgord et al., Coordinated California Corrections: The System (1971) (known as The Keldgord Report). See also L. Kuehn, Probation Subsidy and the Toleration of Crime, August, 1972 (paper presented at the Criminology Session of the Annual Meeting of the American Sociological Association, New Orleans, Louisiana).

[23]R. Hood and R. Sparks, Key Issues in Criminology 187–88 (1970).

[24]See, e.g., Nev. Rev. Stat. § 213.220 et seq. (1971); Wash. Rev. Code Ann. § 13.06.010 et seq. (1962). The state of Ohio has legislation under study which would approach the California model. At the time of this writing, the California model is the most advanced in concept and implementation.

[25]President's Commission on Law Enforcement and Administration of Justice, Task Force Report: Corrections 105 (1967).

With this blessing a profusion of community-based correctional programs ensued. Furloughs, work-release units, and half-way houses are now common rather than experimental. The use of volunteers is seen as natural and necessary rather than an administrative inconvenience suffered in the interests of public relations. The improvement of the old programs of probation and parole is slow and, in some states, imperceptible, but the Corrections Task Force started a movement which has gained momentum. The growing confidence in corrections in the community is reflected in the decelerated growth of prison populations at a time when crime rates are increasing as never before. In some states, especially California, the numbers of felons in state prisons has dramatically declined. In many others, including Ohio, Minnesota, and Illinois, the decline in actual institutional populations has been more modest, but that they have declined at all is significant in view of the rise in both populations and rates of crime and delinquency.

These events reflect hundreds of decisions by judges and parole board members. Policy is changing before our eyes. We can see from the data where it seems to be going. We can also see from current official studies that there is much concern about corrections at high executive levels. There is a continuing agreement that something must be done about its apparent ineffectiveness, its wastefulness, and the danger to society presented by the processes of incarceration.

The most prominent of these studies is the massive report of the Corrections Task Force of the National Commission on Criminal Justice Standards and Goals.[26] The Commission's recommendations are exhaustive, but some of

them are particularly significant of the great shift which has taken place. Perhaps the greatest achievement of the Commission is its forthright recognition of the community at large as both a breeder of criminal activity and the most logical correctional base. The reasons behind this conclusion include findings that traditional penal institutions tend to compound rather than alleviate the problems they are designed to correct, that most offenders are treated disproportionately to their potential violence and danger, and that imprisonment has a negative rather than positive effect on the offender's ability to reassimilate into the community upon release. On the other hand, the Commission concluded that community-based programs seem to be capable of providing community protection and by their very nature do not create the environmental problems inherent in the traditional penal institutions. "The move toward community corrections implies that communities must assume responsibility for the problems they generate."[27]

The results of the study find practical expression in recommendations which are stunningly direct. The Commission prescribed that no new juvenile institutions be built and that existing institutions be replaced by local facilities and programs. The suggestions concerning adult corrections were somewhat more cautious: absent a clear finding that no alternative is possible, no new adult institutions should be built either. The point is that the Commission has no confidence in the value of the prison for any purposes other than punishment and incapacitation. The logic carries the Commission to the conclusion that the country has more prisons than it needs and that it should entirely discontinue the incarceration of juvenile offenders.

Obviously, if the Commission's plan is to be carried out, the correctional continuum must heavily stress alternatives to incarceration. Such a continuum must call for communities to in-

[26]The Report of the Corrections Task Force is in press at the time of this writing. Necessarily, its citation at this point cannot be specific. The reader is particularly referred, however, to the introductory Chapter 1, a summary of the findings, and the final Chapter 18, Priorities and Implementation.

[27]*National Advisory Commission on Criminal Justice Standards and Goals, Working Papers C-3* (1973).

crease social service resources to provide for diversion of offenders from criminal justice processing to the greatest extent possible. It must call for a sentencing policy which relies much more explicitly on suspended sentences, fines, court continuances, and various forms of probation in which emphasis is given to the provision of services. Prisons must be reserved for offenders guilty of crimes of violence, and perhaps for other offenders whose crimes are so egregious as to require this level of severity to satisfy the community's desire for retributive justice.

The Commission is not alone in its outspoken demand for change. Compared to the final report of the Wisconsin Citizens' Study Committee on Offender Rehabilitation,[28] the recommendations of the National Advisory Commission are conservative. The Wisconsin report, issued in July, 1972, begins by establishing as "its most fundamental priority the replacement of Wisconsin's existing institutionalized corrections system with a community-based, non-institutional system." The reasons for this admittedly radical proposal are unequivocal. First, "current Wisconsin institutions cannot rehabilitate." Second, "de-institutionalization of Wisconsin's correctional system would, in the long run, save considerable tax dollars." The Committee considered action to "de-institutionalize" the correctional system so urgent that its accomplishment before mid-1975 was recommended. Although the Governor to whom this recommendation was addressed has not adopted it, the significance of such a recommendation from a committee composed of persons drawn from the informed and established professional and business communities is not to be dismissed as an exercise in flighty liberalism. The Wisconsin correctional apparatus has long been admired as an adequately funded, professionally staffed, and rationally organized system, second to none in these respects. If prisons

could rehabilitate, some sign of their capabilities to do so should have emerged in that state. This committee looked carefully for such a sign and could find none.

The alternative system recommended for Wisconsin begins with a call for pre-trial diversion of some offenders on the decision of the District Attorney, the use of restitution as an alternative to the full criminal process, and decriminalization of

"fornication, adultery, sexual perversion, lewd behavior, indecent matter and performances, noncommercial gambling, fraud on inn or restaurant keepers, issuance of worthless checks, fraudulent use of credit cards, non-support, the possession, sale and distribution of marijuana, and public drunkenness."[29]

The confirmed addict and the chronic alcoholic are recognized as helplessly infirm persons. The Task Force urged a policy of treatment rather than prosecution, and a program of services rather than incarceration. The recommendations call for the establishment of services which do not now exist in Wisconsin. There is a realistic confrontation with the probable outcome of most services for these gravely handicapped persons: "[T]he committee feels that flexible programming and expectation of failure must be a part of any development of drug treatment programs."[30]

Nevertheless, it is the clear responsibility of the state to provide treatment within a framework in which at least some success can be rationally expected. Even some custodial care will be required for addicts and alcoholics who can be treated in no other way. It is noteworthy, however, that the possibility of providing such custodial care in prison settings is considered only for those addicts who have been guilty of ordinary felonies, and even then such persons are to have the option of treatment in facilities designed for addicts. No consideration was

[28]*Wisconsin Council on Criminal Justice, Final Report to the Governor of the Citizen's Study Committee on Offender Rehabilitation* (1972).

[29]*Id.* at 50.
[30]*Id.* at 77.

given to the use of correctional facilities for standard treatment for addicts of any kind.

The Wisconsin Task Force saw that their recommendations went several steps beyond the current public consensus. Nobody knows for sure what the limits of public tolerance for change in corrections may be, but even the forthright writers of this report knew that there is a wide gap between a rationally achieved position in these matters and its acceptance by the electorate. This is especially true in the field of narcotics addiction, where lack of accurate information and a plethora of well-meant misinformation, have done so much to distort public opinion. We are so thoroughly committed to the use of the criminal process for the control of social deviance that alternatives are difficult to design with confidence, notwithstanding our knowledge that the criminal justice system is demonstrably ineffective for many kinds of social control. Recognition of the irrationality of this situation does not provide us with obvious remedies. The weakness of this excellent report is that its recommendations can be readily dismissed by the administrator as impractical, even though the present system is itself shown to be thoroughly impractical on the basis of its results.

The Wisconsin study of corrections provides a startling example of the disatisfaction evoked by an apparently advanced correctional program when dispassionately studied by citizens concerned with the claims of justice and rationality. In Ohio, another Citizens' Task Force on Corrections reported to the governor on the state of the corrections system, but in this case, the Task Force was confronted by one of the most decrepit correctional programs in the country. Generations of pound-foolish fiscal maladministration had produced a situation in which underpaid, poorly supervised staff worked in slovenly, malodorous prisons filled to the bursting point with idle prisoners. The atmosphere thus created had exploded more than once, convincing even the most fiscally conservative persons that something had to be done. The response was the construction of a large new prison in the most remote area in the state. It was obsolete at the time of its design and will probably be a burden to distort the criminal justice system of Ohio for centuries to come.

The *Report of the Ohio Citizens' Task Force on Corrections*[31] was written in the context of a perceived need for "de-institutionalization." Concerned with bringing about some organizational coherence in an agency which conspicuously lacked this basic element, it devotes much time and space to recommendations for the creation of an effective management structure, an equitable personnel policy, a Training Academy, and a Division of Planning and Research. However, the Task Force stresses at the outset of its report that even if all its recommendations were to be immediately implemented, "the public would not be protected one iota more."[32] The report emphatically asserts:

"We must cease depending on institutionalization as an adequate response to the law offender and protection of the public. Instead, we *must* develop a system of community-based alternatives to institutionalization. . . . The emphasis of the future must be on alternatives to incarceration. The rule, duty, and obligation of this Task Force is to communicate this vital conclusion to the public."[33]

Since the publication of this report in December, 1971, the Division of Correction has been transformed into an adequately staffed Department of Rehabilitation and Correction. An administrative group is at work on the development of an adaptation of the California Probation Subsidy Act as the most likely strategy for the creation of a sufficient range of community-based alternatives to incarceration. The new penitentiary at Lucasville has been opened. In spite of its preposterous location far from the cities from which its inmates come, it at least has made possible a decision to demolish the infamous old prison at Columbus. The Ohio

[31]*Ohio Citizens' Task Force on Corrections, Final Report to Governor John J. Gilligan* (1971).
[32]*Id.* at A-8.
[33]*Id.* at A-8, A-9 (emphasis in original).

Youth Commission, charged with the maintenance of a correctional program as well, has reorganized to make its preventive program more than nominal. The de-institutionalization of Ohio corrections has not been accomplished, nor will it be accomplished soon, but a structure of administrative planning, research, and evaluative management has been created on the basis of which rational change can be expected. Already the state's confined population has declined by ten percent, in spite of a steadily increasing rate of commitments. Drift and expediency were the villainous influences identified by the Citizens' Task Force; they have been replaced by policies which require rational decision-making. The transformation is not fool-proof, but it will at least discourage fools from rushing in.

Faced with a rapid expansion of its population and the unique problems brought about by its isolation from the rest of the country, Hawaii has drawn on the resources of the National Clearinghouse for Criminal Justice Planning and Architecture to Develop a Correctional Master Plan.[34] The plan explicitly credits the state with a more adequate delivery of correctional services than is available in many states. However, it does not go far enough. It retains a significant emphasis on traditional institutionalization which "is probably the most expensive response and also the least effective that a criminal justice system can make in dealing with criminal behavior."[35] Cited as support for the ineffectiveness of such institutionalization are the increased crime rate and high recidivism.

The approach adopted by the Hawaii planners borrows from the concept of the National Clearinghouse and represents the best current example of a fully developed correctional program based on the Clearinghouse guidelines. To summarize the work of the Clearinghouse in an article such as this is a daunting task; the published *Guidelines*[36] constitute a weighty volume addressed to the whole span of correctional issues. However, the core ideas are simple and identifiable. First, the planning of correctional systems will eliminate the costly waste incurred by needless building of security housing. Second, community-based alternatives to incarceration can afford both protection for the community and effective reinstatement services for the vast majority of offenders. Third, the safe assignment of offenders to correctional services requires a process of differential classification, preferably in an "Intake Service Center." Fourth, for the control of dangerous offenders a "Community Correctional Center" should be incorporated in the system with full provision for maximum custody. Throughout the conceptual development of the Clearinghouse *Guidelines* there is the tacit assumption that environmental influences are the most accessible points of intervention as to any offender and the diagnostic task is to identify those influences which can be brought to bear on his resocialization. Most social science students of criminal justice issues will recognize these assumptions as hypothetical at best, but their humane and rational intent is obvious. Clearly, an urgent task for research is the evaluation of the consequences of their implementation under such circumstances of full acceptance as the state of Hawaii has accorded.

The momentum of the traditional correctional policies will not be suddenly halted. Regardless of the enjoinders of the Law Enforcement Assistance Administration and of the recommendations of Citizens' Commissions across the country, more jails will be built, and many offenders will occupy their cells who might just as well be enrolled in an appropriate community program. Neither the staff, the agencies, nor the

---

[34]See *State Law Enforcement and Juvenile Delinquency Planning Agency, Correctional Master Plan* 26 (1973).
[35]*Id.*

[36]F. Moyer, E. Flynn, F. Powers and M. Plautz, *Guidelines for the Planning and Design of Regional and Community Correctional Centers for Adults* (1971). See particularly Section D, Planning Concepts.

sentencing policies are fully enough developed to allow for an immediate implementation of the enlightened recommendations of the Task Force Reports. In a world in which the costs of incarceration have reached annual per capita costs which far exceed average citizen incomes, the future of incarceration must be constrained by a policy of rigorous selectivity. The informed opinion that coerced rehabilitation is an impractical objective is equally welcome to humane liberals and fiscal conservatives. The task of research is to collect the information which will support the strategy of change.

THE DEMOBILIZATION OF CORRECTIONS

Where will the momentum of change in corrections lead the criminal justice system? In so emotionally charged a set of issues as surrounds the disposition of convicted offenders, it is futile to predict the probable course of events. Criminologists have known for a long time that the execution of murderers cannot be shown to deter murder, but the retributive motive still permeates our culture, and it is not at all certain that the abolition of capital punishment is permanent. Hatred of the criminal and fear of his actions have nothing to do with reasoned plans to protect ourselves from him or to change his behavior. In a period in which crime has assumed the quality of obsessive concern in our society, the wonder is that so many are able to accept the dispassionate view of the offender which characterizes the recommendations of the numerous study commissions working on the renovation of the correctional system. The threat of an irrationally repressive policy is still a real one. The recent demand by Governor Rockefeller for draconian laws to imprison for life the vendor of narcotics will at least serve as a reminder how tenuous may be our hold on rational correctional concepts. Nevertheless, this portent and others like it can be offset by the widespread belief that rational change is possible and desirable. Some encouragement how-

ever, may be taken in the support of this position by a broad spectrum of political opinion. The concern for correctional change is not confined to the various liberal shades.

We should specify the structural changes in the criminal justice system which the new correctional ideology implies. Much of the rhetoric of skepticism challenges us to justify the retention of any part of the present correctional system. We are told that the criminal justice system is nothing more than an instrument for the regulation of the poor, and that therefore the interests of justice would be best served by its abolition. This kind of effervescence serves to discredit the motives and good sense of the correctional reform movement, which draws on the evidence of social research to reach conclusions which both establish the obsolescence of the present system and indicate fruitful directions for its renovation. It is time that we considered where these directions will take us.

First, although we do not know how the prison can be converted into a rehabilitative institution, it will have to be retained for the protection of society from some violent and dangerous offenders from whom no alternative means of protection exist. These prisons must be small. They must provide for the long-term prisoner in ways which support psychological stability and his integrity as a person. These objectives require that he should have latitude for choice, that he should have a sense of society's concern for his welfare, and that his life should be restricted as little as possible given the purposes to be achieved in restricting him at all.

The retention of the prison for the containment of the dangerous offender assumes that he can be identified. This assumption is open to attack. The inference that all offenders who have been guilty of major violence will present continuing hazards to the public is refuted by the consistently low rates of recidivism of released murderers. Therefore, we are reduced to predicting a hazard of future danger from the determination of a pattern of repetitive violence. Many authorities on criminal justice will be dissatisfied with the potential for abuse in this kind of prediction.[37] Acknowledging the validity of this criticism, I can only respond that the confidence which a changing system of social control must maintain will rapidly erode if dangerous and predatory offenders are released from prison to resume the behavior for which they were confined in the first place. Until a more satisfactory basis for their identification can be found, we shall have to tolerate some injustice in order to avoid the greater injustices of needlessly confining the obviously harmless. Social science must persist in the improvement of our power to identify the dangerous offender. The quality of justice is heavily dependent on the increase of knowledge in this age when vengeance is being replaced with reconciliation.

The remainder of the correctional panoply is a dubious asset to justice. We have established probation and parole, halfway houses, work-release programs, group homes, and community correctional centers in an effort to create alternatives to incarceration. The effort has largely succeeded; informed observers have been convinced, and policy has changed sufficiently to reduce the rate of commitment to prison in most of the jurisdictions of the country. As humanitarian reforms, these alternatives were essential. They still are. But, there is little evidence to show that these programs are really more effective than the prisons they replace. They are certainly no worse.

But the point is to *improve* the effectiveness of the criminal justice system. It must be made possible for the offender to choose a lawabiding life and to act on that choice. Offenders must be seen as people with personal problems of great difficulty. They are now provided with second-rate services, if they receive services at all. It is incumbent upon a society which creates much of its crime burden from persistence in social injustice to make available services which can extricate criminals from criminal careers. In most communities these services exist. The Massachusetts experiment of last year in large part consisted of an effort to bring to the offender the regular community services which are available to ordinary citizens, rather than select the offender for special correctional versions of these services. The latter do not assure effective assistance. Instead, they assure that the help offenders receive will have some stigma attached, and that treatment will be affected by the persistence of the myth that criminality itself is a condition to be treated.

Courts, as the administrators of justice, should induce service agencies of all kinds to make their services accessible. The court thus becomes a referral agency, opening doors by its authority, perhaps even by the purchase of services, but not by coercion or the implication that the freedom of the offender depends on his obtaining benefits from services rendered. This is a model of service delivery which will be difficult to learn and even more difficult to live with. There will always be an inclination to draw an invidious conclusion from the offender's inability to persevere in a program intended for his benefit, but it is an important step in itself to make it possible for offenders to choose the services. Those who can choose but reject them anyway will not benefit from compulsion.

If services can be made more effective by projecting offenders into the mainstream of community activity instead of keeping them in a correctional backwater, the surveillance of these services can also be improved by transferring that responsibility to the police. No one is served by the pretense that probation and parole officers possess qualifications for the discharge of this function. Law enforcement duties should be performed by the police, who are trained for the task and organized to do it. To expect that probation and parole officers can accomplish anything in this respect that could not be better done by the police is to compound confusion with unreality.[38]

[37]See, e.g., von Hirsch, "Prediction of Criminal Conduct and Preventive Confinement of Convicted Persons," 21 *Buff. L. Rev.* 717 (1972).

[38]See E. Studt, *Surveillance and Service in Parole: A Report of the Parole Action Study* 70–96 (1972).

There are two functions now discharged by probation and parole officers which cannot be easily transferred. The decisions related to the sentence, its imposition, its terms, its completion and revocation cannot be made without essential information systematically collected. The reports which probation officers make to the court and the parole officers make to the parole boards are services to the court which should be carried out by officials under the control of the court.

The information collected by this officer of the court (his functions are so much more specific than those of the present probation officer that we might accurately designate him the Information Officer) will be essential for the service referrals which the court should make. In small courts, information and referral could well be carried out by the same officer; there may be advantages in differentiating the functions in large courts. These residual responsibilities must be maintained, but their discharge will hardly call for the large and many-layered staffs which are to be found in present day probation and parole departments.

There remains the question of sanctions to be imposed on offenders. Less severity but more certainty in punishment will better serve the public protection. The victims of crime should receive restitution from the offender to the limit that restitution is practical. The graduated use of fines, relating them to the offender's resources, has been successfully used in Sweden. An English study, reported by Hood and Sparks,[39] indicates that for property crimes, at least, the fine may well be the most effective sanction. Suspended sentences have not been definitively evaluated as to their effect on recidivism. The tolerance of the system for probation and parole services in which contact does not take place after adjudication suggests that we can safely rely on the suspended sentence for a substantial proportion of offenders. Where

there is reason to believe that surveillance is necessary, provision for regular police contacts could be made to assure that reliable control is maintained.

Such a system would limit the use of incarceration to pre-trial detention of some exceptional defendants, and post-trial detention of only the most dangerous offenders. It would provide protection where it is needed, service where it is desired by the offender himself, and control in the measure that the circumstances of the community and the offender require it. The victim would no longer have to comfort himself with the knowledge that the law had taken its course toward retribution; he would now receive restitution from the offender or compensation from the public funds as the situation might require.

The system would be adjustable by feedback. Increased control would be obtained by increased use of the more severe sanctions where the data on crime rates called for it. This system would be retributive, but the nature of the retribution would be the minimum required by measured experience rather than the ancient demands made by hatred and custom. Where reconciliation can be achieved, it will be eased, and where control is required it will be exercised, but the claims of simple justice will be essential elements of policy.

Justice can only be approached, never fully achieved. However, unless it is indeed the first virtue of the public institutions which administer it, none of the other virtues these institutions may possess will matter. The claims of simple justice are not satisfied merely by the administration of due process, but by the operation of the whole system by methods which restrict liberty only to the degree necessary for public purposes, but nevertheless assure that these restrictions are effective. We are far from such a system now. The removal of the assumptions which the belief in rehabilitation has engendered will make possible a system which will be more modest in aims, more rational in its means and more just in its disposition.

---

[39]Hood and Sparks, note 23 *supra*, at 188–89.